THE SHAPING

OF THE

AMERICAN

TRADITION

VOLUME I

THE SHAPING
OF THE
AMERICAN
TRADITION

Text by LOUIS M. HACKER
Documents edited by LOUIS M. HACKER
and HELENE S. ZAHLER

VOLUME I

1947 COLUMBIA UNIVERSITY PRESS *New York*

11680

TO MY CHILDREN, ANDREW AND BETSY

CONTENTS

VOLUME I

Part One: Leaving Europe and Settling America

INTRODUCTION   3
1. The European World from Which the Americans Came, 3; 2. The English
Background, 8; 3. The Early Settlers of America, 14; 4. Early Economic Activities,
19; 5. Colonial Agriculture, 24

THE ENGLISH BACKGROUND   29
English Society, 29; Harrison, *The Description of England*, 30; The Authoritarian
State, 35; Laud, Two Sermons, 37; Monopolies, 40; James I, *Proclamation Touch-
ing Grievances*, 40; Colepeper, *Speeches Relating to Grievances*, 42; Enclosures,
43; Winstanley, *Declaration . . .*, 45; The Moral Rejection of the Poor, 49;
Defoe, *Giving Alms No Charity*, 50

THE ENGLISH HERITAGE   56
Toleration, 56; Locke, *A Letter Concerning Toleration*, 57; Civil Rights, 65;
Locke, *Of Civil Government*, 66

THE SETTLEMENT OF AMERICA   79
Virginia, 79; Smith, *Description of Virginia*, 79; Pennsylvania, 85; Thomas, *An
Account of Pensilvania*, 86; The Scotch-Irish, 94; *Letters . . . by Hugh
Boulter . . .*, 95; The Plight of Indentured Servants, 97; Personal Narratives, 102

AMERICAN VALUES   107
Religious Liberties, 107; Williams, *Bloudy Tenant of Persecution*, 108; The
Land of Opportunity, 110; Franklin, *Observations Concerning the Increase of
Mankind*, 110; The Duty to Rebel, 113; Mayhew, *A Discourse Concerning Un-
limited Submission*, 114

Part Two: The First American Revolution

INTRODUCTION   123
1. The Colonial Scene, 123; 2. The Colonial under Mercantilism, 124; 3. Colonial
Commerce, 127; 4. Colonial Currency, 130; 5. Colonial Business Depressions, 133;
6. The Tightening of the Mercantilist System, 134; 7. Background of the American Revolution, 136; 8. Winning the Revolution, 138

THE AMERICAN MIND   145
Jonathan Edwards, 145; Edwards, *The Personal Narrative*, 147; Benjamin Franklin, 153; Franklin, *Autobiography*, 154

THE AMERICAN SCENE   160
J. Hector St. John de Crèvecoeur, 160; Crèvecoeur, *Letters from an American
Farmer*, 161

AMERICAN PROBLEMS   171
English Colonial Administration, 171; The Appointment and Removal of a Royal
Governor, 172; The Disallowance of a Colonial Statute, 174; The Refusal of the
Cape Breton Concession, 175; The Navigation Acts, 176; Smith, *The Wealth of
Nations*, 178; Tucker, *Tracts*, 184; The Stamp Act, 196; *Examination of Dr.
Franklin*, 196; The American Revolution, 202; Paine, Appendix to *Common Sense*,
203; Paine, *The Crisis*, 206; Some Results of the American Revolution, 210; The
Articles of Confederation, 210; Madison, *Views of the Political System . . .* , 212;
The Charter of the Bank of North America, 215; The Virginia Statute of Re-
ligious Liberty, 217; Jefferson, *The Virginia Statute . . .* , 217; The Land Ordi-
nances of 1785 and 1787, 218

THE UNITED STATES AND THE WORLD   226
Two Foreign Views of the American Revolution, 226; Turgot, *The American
Revolution*, 226; Price, *Observations on the Importance of the American Revolu-
tion*, 228

Part Three: Establishing the New Republic

INTRODUCTION   233
1. The Critical Period, 233; 2. Framing the Constitution, 236; 3. The Hamiltonian
Program, 238; 4. The Defeat of the Federalists, 245; 5. The American Scene at the
Century's Turn, 248

THE AMERICAN MIND   253
Elihu Palmer, 253; Palmer, *Principles of Nature*, 254; Timothy Dwight, 257;
Dwight, *Travels in New England . . .* , 258

THE AMERICAN SCENE   264
Virginia, 264; Jefferson, *Notes on Virginia*, 264

AMERICAN PROBLEMS   271
The Constitutional Convention, 271; Randolph, *The Virginia Plan*, 272; Patterson, *The New Jersey Plan*, 273; Alexander Hamilton's Plan, 275; The Debate over
the Constitution, 281; *The Federalist*, 282; Richard Henry Lee, 288; Lee, *Letters*

of a Federal Farmer, 289; The Bank of the United States, 292; Jefferson, *Opinion against . . . a National Bank*, 292; Hamilton, *On the Constitutionality of a National Bank*, 295; Manufactures, 299; Hamilton, *Report on . . . Manufactures*, 300; Tench Coxe, 305; Coxe, *A View of the United States*, 305; The End of an Era, 309; Jefferson, *The First Inaugural*, 310

THE UNITED STATES AND THE WORLD   312
The Louisiana Purchase, 312; *Correspondence of Thomas Jefferson*, 314; *Correspondence of James Madison*, 316; Jefferson, *Message to Congress, 1803*, 320; The War of 1812, 322; Randolph, The House Debate . . . on . . . War, 323; Johnson, Rejoinder, 326

Part Four: Jacksonian Democracy

INTRODUCTION   331
1. The Growth of America, 331; 2. The Mercantile Economy of America, 333; 3. Leveling Tendencies, 337; 4. Problems of the Eighteen Thirties, 340; 5. American Expansion, 345

THE AMERICAN MIND   348
Ralph Waldo Emerson, 348; Emerson, *Nature*, 348; Henry C. Carey, 354; Carey, *Principles of Political Economy*, 356; George Bancroft, 364; Bancroft, *The Office of the People*, 366

THE AMERICAN SCENE   369
Alexis de Tocqueville, 369; Tocqueville, *Democracy in America*, 370

AMERICAN PROBLEMS   379
Business Enterprise, 379; Hunt, *Lives of American Merchants*, 380; Labor and Immigration, 387; Luther, *Address to the Working Men of New England*, 388; Morse, *Imminent Dangers to the Free Institutions . . .* , 391; Internal Improvements, 395; Clay, *Speech on Internal Improvement*, 395; List, *Early Railroads in America*, 400; Nullification, 403; Webster, *The Second Speech on the Foote Resolution*, 405; *South Carolina Ordinance of Nullification*, 410; The Second Bank of the United States, 413; Benton, Speech on the Bank . . . , 416; *The Correspondence of Nicholas Biddle*, 424; The Depression of 1837–43, 426; *Specie Circular of 1836*, 428; Biddle, *Letters to John Quincy Adams*, 429; Smith, *Letters on American Debts*, 431

THE UNITED STATES AND THE WORLD   434
Genesis of the Monroe Doctrine, 434; Correspondence of Canning and Rush, 437; *Memoirs of John Quincy Adams*, 441; Texas, 445; Wharton, *Address . . .* , 446

Part Five: The Impending Conflict

INTRODUCTION   455
1. Continued Expansion, 455; 2. Economic Growth, 458; 3. The World of the Workers, 460; 4. The Cotton South, 462; 5. The Struggle over the Territories, 467; 6. Overseas Interests, 470

THE AMERICAN MIND   472
Albert Brisbane, 472; Brisbane, *The Social Destiny of Man*, 473; Henry D. Thoreau, 478; Thoreau, *Civil Disobedience*, 479; John C. Calhoun, 482; Calhoun, *A Disquisition on Government*, 484; Richard Hildreth, 489; Hildreth, *Theory of Politics*, 490

THE AMERICAN SCENE   493
Charles Dickens, 493; Dickens, *American Notes . . .* , 493; Bayard Taylor, 498; Taylor, *Eldorado*, 499

AMERICAN PROBLEMS   505
Building the Railroads, 505; *The Illinois Central Railroad*, 507; Business Enterprise, 514; *New York State Constitutional Convention of 1846*, 515; The South, the West, and New York, 524; Articles from *De Bow's Review*, 526; Condition of the Working Class, 534; *The Way to Wealth*, 536; The Sociology and Economics of Slavery, 541; Fitzhugh, *Cannibals All!*, 543; Helper, *The Impending Crisis of the South*, 546; Abolitionism, 553; The Weld-Grimké Letters, 555; Still, *The Underground Railroad*, 559

THE UNITED STATES AND THE WORLD   563
Manifest Destiny, 563; O'Sullivan, *Annexation*, 563; The Opening of Japan, 568; Perry, *Correspondence Relative to the Naval Expedition to Japan*, 569

VOLUME II

Part Six: The Second American Revolution

INTRODUCTION   579
1. The Election of 1860, 579; 2. Southern Secession, 580; 3. Lincoln and the Radicals, 583; 4. Fighting the War, 584; 5. The Military Aspects of the War, 586; 6. The Triumph of Industrial Capitalism, 590; 7. The Failure of Reconstruction, 593

PRELIMINARIES   597
The Party Platforms of 1860, 597; The Constitutional Union Platform, 598; The Democratic Platform, 598; The Democratic (Breckinridge Faction) Platform, 598; The Republican Platform, 599; The South Carolina Convention, 600; *Declaration of the . . . Causes . . .* [of] *Secession*, 601

THE REPUBLICAN PROGRAM   605
Charles F. Dunbar, 605; Dunbar, *The Establishment of the National Banking System*, 606

SLAVERY AND EMANCIPATION   614
Greeley-Lincoln Correspondence, 614; Greeley, *The Prayer of Twenty Millions*, 615; Lincoln's Reply . . . , 616; Lincoln, *The Preliminary Emancipation Proclamation*, 617; Lincoln and the Radicals, 618; Julian, *Radicalism and Conservatism*, 620

RECONSTRUCTION   628
The South Carolina Freedmen's Code, 628; The South Carolina Constitution of 1868, 637; Joint Select Committee, 644; Minority Report, 645; Travelers in the South, 653; Andrews, *The South since the War*, 654; King, *The Great South*, 658

THE UNITED STATES AND THE WORLD   665
European Intervention and the Civil War, 665; Slidell's First Audience with Napoleon, 666; Slidell's Second Audience . . . , 669; Roebuck's Audience with Napoleon, 670; Napoleon and Mexico, 672; Seward, *Diplomatic Correspondence*, 673

Part Seven: Growing Pains in the Post-Civil War Decades

INTRODUCTION   681
1. Party Government, 681; 2. Settling the Country, 684; 3. Industrial Capitalism's Victories, 688; 4. Farmers and Workers, 694; 5. Isolationist America, 698

THE AMERICAN MIND   703
Walt Whitman, 703; Whitman, *Democratic Vistas*, 704; Henry George, 710; George, *Progress and Poverty*, 711; William Graham Sumner, 717; Sumner, *What Social Classes Owe to Each Other*, 718

THE AMERICAN SCENE   725
David A. Wells, 725; Wells, Report of the Special Commissioner of the Revenue, 726

AMERICAN PROBLEMS   735
Settling the Northwest, 735; *Minnesota* . . . , 735; Agrarian Discontents, 741; Godkin, Editorials from the *Nation*, 742; Munn v. Illinois, 747; Labor, 753; Powderly, *Thirty Years of Labor*, 753; Panic and Depression, 758; Cairnes, *Some Leading Principles of Political Economy*, 759; The Crises of 1837 and 1873, 764; The New York Clearing House Association Report, 768

THE UNITED STATES AND THE WORLD   772
Josiah Strong, 772; Strong, *Our Country*, 772; James G. Blaine, 776; Blaine, *Two Addresses* . . . , 777

Part Eight: Unrest and Expansion in the Nineties

INTRODUCTION 781
1. The First Steps toward Government Intervention, 781; 2. The Populist Rising, 784; 3. 1896, 788; 4. The Gilded Age, 790; 5. Expansion Overseas, 793

THE AMERICAN MIND 799
William James, 799; James, *Philosophical Conceptions and Practical Results*, 800; Andrew Carnegie, 806; Carnegie, *Wealth and Its Uses*, 807

THE AMERICAN SCENE 811
James Bryce, 811; Bryce, *The American Commonwealth*, 812

AMERICAN PROBLEMS 819
Discontented America, 819; William A. Peffer, 819; Peffer, *The Farmer's Side*, 820; Charles H. Otken, 824; Otken, *The Ills of the South*, 825; Henry Demarest Lloyd, 828; Lloyd, *Wealth against Commonwealth*, 829; Ignatius Donnelly, 834; Donnelly, *People's Party Platform of 1892*, 835; Benjamin R. Tillman, 838; *Journal of the Proceedings of the South Carolina Constitutional Convention*, 839; Henry Cabot Lodge, 842; Lodge, *Immigration Restriction*, 843; Justice Brewer, 847; Brewer, Opinion of the Court *in re* Debs, 848; Expanding America, 851; Carroll D. Wright, 851; Wright, First Annual Report of the Commissioner of Labor, 852; Wright, *Industrial Evolution of the United States*, 854; The Crisis of 1893, 860; John DeWitt Warner, 860; Warner, *The Currency Famine of 1893*, 861; The Money Debate, 867; Donnelly, *The People's Money*, 868; Laughlin, *Facts about Money*, 872

THE UNITED STATES AND THE WORLD 877
Expansion, 877; Mahan, *The Lessons of the War with Spain*, 878; The Open Door, 882; Beresford, *The Break-up of China*, 884; Basis of the "Open Door" Notes, 885; The Hippisley Memorandum, 885; The Rockhill Memorandum, 886

Part Nine: The New Freedom

INTRODUCTION 893
1. The Political Scene, 893; 2. Big Business and Finance Capital, 896; 3. Other Influences on the Reform Movement, 898; 4. The Workers, 899; 5. The New Freedom, 901; 6. Foreign Affairs under Roosevelt, Taft, and Wilson, 904; 7. World War I, 907; 8. Winning the War and Losing the Peace, 910

THE AMERICAN MIND 914
Thorstein Veblen, 914; Veblen, *The Limitations of Marginal Utility*, 915; John Dewey, 920; Dewey, *The Development of American Pragmatism*, 921

THE AMERICAN SCENE   927

The Muckrakers, 927; Steffens, *The Shame of the Cities*, 927; Wealth and Income, 930; Hunter, *Poverty*, 931; Streightoff, *The Standard of Living*, 934; King, *Wealth and Income*, 936

AMERICAN PROBLEMS   942

Corporate and Finance Capitalism in America, 942; Commissioner of Corporations, 942; *Report on the United States Steel Corporation*, 943; The Pujo Committee, 948; *Report on Concentration of Control of Money and Credit*, 949; Labor in America, 955; Oliver Wendell Holmes, 955; Holmes, Dissenting Opinion in *Lochner* v. *New York*, 956; Samuel Gompers, 957; Gompers, Two Editorials, 958; Eugene V. Debs, 961; Debs, Two Speeches, 961; Vincent St. John, 966; St. John, Testimony Concerning the I.W.W., 967; The New Freedom, 972; Woodrow Wilson, 972; Wilson, *The New Freedom*, 973; The National Monetary Commission, 976; Defects of the National Banking System, 977; Carter Glass, 979; Glass, Speech on the Federal Reserve Act, 979; Robert J. Bulkley, 983; Bulkley, *The Federal Farm-Loan Act*, 984

THE UNITED STATES AND THE WORLD   988

Sir George Paish, 988; Paish, *Trade Balance of the United States*, 988; Theodore Roosevelt, 992; Roosevelt, *The Panama Canal*, 993; Corollary to the Monroe Doctrine, 998; Roosevelt, *Corollary to the Monroe Doctrine*, 1000; Roosevelt, Message to the Senate on the Dominican Treaty, 1003; Woodrow Wilson, 1004; Wilson, Two Addresses to Congress, 1004; Henry Cabot Lodge, 1011; Lodge, *The Senate and the League of Nations*, 1012

Part Ten: The Golden Nineteen Twenties

INTRODUCTION   1019

1. Work and Wealth, 1019; 2. Politics in the Twenties, 1023; 3. Some Questions of the Hour, 1025; 4. Dark Corners in the United States, 1028; 5. The Course of Business, 1030; 6. Foreign Relations of the Twenties, 1032

THE AMERICAN MIND   1039

Wesley C. Mitchell, 1039; Mitchell, *Business Cycles*, 1039

THE AMERICAN SCENE   1047

Edwin F. Gay, 1047; Gay, *Recent Economic Changes*, 1048; Robert S. Lynd and Helen M. Lynd, 1054; R. S. and H. M. Lynd, *Middletown*, 1055; André Siegfried, 1059; Siegfried, *America Comes of Age*, 1060

AMERICAN PROBLEMS   1066

The Workers of America, 1066; Robert W. Dunn, 1066; Dunn, *The Industrial Welfare Offensive*, 1066; Sterling D. Spero and Abram L. Harris, 1071; Spero and Harris, *The Black Worker*, 1072; The Farmer, 1076; Chase, *Prosperity, Fact or Myth*, 1077; The Boom, 1081; Seligman, *Economics of Installment Selling*, 1082; Pecora, *Wall Street under Oath*, 1086; Allen, *Only Yesterday*, 1089

THE UNITED STATES AND THE WORLD   1094
    International Economic Relations, 1094; Klein, *Frontiers of Trade*, 1095; Mann, *Foreign Reactions to the American Tariff Act*, 1099; Two Failures in Foreign Policy, 1104; Ichihashi, *The Washington Conference and After*, 1106; Kellogg, *The Settlement of International Controversies by Pacific Means*, 1110; Two Successes in Foreign Policy, 1113; Morrow, On Mexico, 1114; Stimson, The United States and the Other American Republics, 1117

Part Eleven: The Third American Revolution

INTRODUCTION   1125
    1. The Election of Franklin Delano Roosevelt, 1125; 2. Theory and Tactics of the New Deal, 1126; 3. The New Deal Agencies, 1130; 4. The Progress of Recovery, 1134; 5. The Cost of the New Deal, 1135; 6. Labor under the New Deal, 1136, 7. The New Deal Continues in Power, 1138; 8. The Third-Term Election, 1140; 9. The New Deal and the Problem of Bureaucracy, 1141; 10. International Relations under the New Deal, 1142

THE AMERICAN MIND   1147
    Franklin D. Roosevelt, 1147; Roosevelt, Commonwealth Club Address, 1149; Alvin H. Hansen, 1154; Hansen, *Fiscal Policy and Business Cycles*, 1154; John Dewey, 1160; Dewey, *Democracy*, 1161

THE AMERICAN SCENE   1165
    The Bonus Army, 1165; Jackson, *Unknown Soldiers*, 1165; Anderson, *Tear-Gas, Bayonets, and Votes*, 1167; Three Demagogues, 1169; Robinson, *Fantastic Interim*, 1170; Income, Wages, and Productivity, 1172; *Consumer Incomes in the United States*, 1174; Bell, *Productivity, Wages, and National Income*, 1177; Clark, *The Conditions of Economic Progress*, 1180

AMERICAN PROBLEMS   1185
    NRA and AAA, 1185; Means, *Industrial Prices and Their Relative Inflexibility*, 1185; TVA, 1189; Lilienthal, *TVA—Democracy on the March*, 1191; Banking and Public Finance, 1195; Eccles, Two Addresses, 1197; Williams, *Deficit Spending*, 1205

THE UNITED STATES AND THE WORLD   1212
    Foreign Trade, 1212; Buell, *The Hull Trade Program and the American System*, 1213; Continentalism versus Internationalism, 1218; Beard, *A Foreign Policy for America*, 1220; Roosevelt, The Four Freedoms Address, 1222; Lend-Lease, 1225; Stettinius, *Lend-Lease: Weapon for Victory*, 1226; World War II, 1231; Roosevelt, Two Addresses, 1232; One World, 1235; Willkie, *One World*, 1236

INDEX OF DOCUMENTS   1241
    Index of Authors, 1241; Index of Titles, 1244

GENERAL INTRODUCTION

American Uniqueness. Americans have always been convinced of the unique qualities of their civilization—not in a narrowly chauvinistic sense and rarely because of a missionary zeal. They have not sought to persuade other peoples to abandon their own ways of life; nor have they been too clamorous about the superiority of their own. But they have felt its differences. To express these differences concretely, however, has not always been easy.

One of the explanations for uniqueness which Americans have advanced has been their frontier experiences. This explanation is usually associated with the name of the historian Frederick J. Turner, although as far back as the 1820s we find the German philosopher Hegel speaking largely in the same terms. The frontier theory runs as follows: The United States has been isolated from the main currents of European development by three thousand miles of ocean and, because of this, for the first three centuries of its history, the country has been preoccupied with its own internal problems. These have centered in the conquest of a movable frontier of wild lands where the soil has been arable and also rich in timber and mineral resources. In the fusing fires of this process there has developed an American civilization.

The American, as a type, became an individualist, a democrat, an equalitarian, and a utilitarian. He came to look upon government only as an effective device for assuring his happiness and for curbing the oppressive tactics of privilege-hunters. And all because the frontier served as a safety valve. In the wild zones of the West, where land was easily accessible, the American could find both haven and opportunity. Because he conquered the wilderness with his own hands and carved out a freehold for himself and his family, because he erected governments by free association, because he started with his compeers from the same bottom level—for these reasons the attitudes and institutions of his way of life were profoundly conditioned to individualism, democracy, equality, and utilitarianism.

To a certain extent, all this is true. Nevertheless, important reservations must be noted. All the underprivileged and all the little men did not go West; indeed, could not. For the physical act of transference was a capital operation. Funds were needed for the purchase and improvement of the wild lands, for transportation costs, for maintaining families while they waited to harvest their first crop, for stocking farms and acquiring implements. Also, democratic institutions were as much a part of the settled East as they were of the pioneering West. The traditional American attitude toward government was as familiar to the older New Yorker and Virginian as it was to the newer citizen of Michigan and Wyoming.

One notable effect of the frontier, however, should be emphasized. The very fact that there was a West made possible the maintenance of higher wage scales and superior standards of living, and hence made for the traditional American values. For, if driven to it by necessity—as the farmers of New England were, for example—the American could migrate and start life over again in new surroundings. In other words, if industrial workers in America did not migrate westward in great numbers to become free farmers, certainly *potential* industrial workers did. The small farmers and the rural laborers of New England, New York, the British Isles, Germany, Scandinavia, who began to fill up first the Old Northwest and then the prairie states, would have been converted easily into an industrial proletariat (as were those from the same classes in England,

Germany, and Scandinavia who remained behind), if they had not had the opportunity to continue farming under more satisfactory conditions. Such opportunity was to be found in the American West, and to this extent the West as a safety valve was a reality.

Even so, the frontier theory is only a partial explanation of the traditional American way of life. This is of richer stuff, and it is well to examine, at this point, the other contributory factors that have had their effects.

Religious Freedom. Freedom of religious worship and freedom from church authority are important cornerstones of the American tradition. In the colonial period, efforts were made—and successfully—to restrict religious toleration and to create established churches. But during the American Revolution many of the new states moved in the direction of religious freedom, and also disestablished churches. The First Amendment of the Constitution for all time fixed the American attitude: it forbade the "establishment of religion" by Congress and guaranteed freedom of worship. By the end of the second decade of the nineteenth century, state established churches were gone.

Freedom from an established church not only meant freedom from a single ecclesiastical and educational authority; it also meant a fuller measure of political freedom. For, it is important to observe, established churches have always acted to support the traditional, or conservative, institutions of the societies in which they have functioned. They have a life of their own; they are largely selfperpetuating; they are great property owners; they frequently interpret educational policy in terms of their own needs rather than of those of the whole society. The absence of such a powerful force in the United States made possible the existence of a freer climate for social experimentation, particularly in the educational and political realms.

Freedom of Enterprise. Freedom of enterprise is another important cornerstone of the American tradition. Unlike Europeans, Americans never found themselves in a climate of precapitalistic influences; that is, feudalism and its relics have been entirely absent from the American scene. To generalize about feudalism is not easy and qualifications are frequently necessary, but certain observations may be made in order to emphasize the differences between the European and American experiences.

While the struggle against feudalism in Europe began quite early—in some regions as far back as the eleventh century—the battle was not easily won. It took western Europe a long time—in many areas almost five hundred years—to shake off feudalism's grip. And even then there continued to survive traces of feudal authoritarianism.

Feudalism possessed distinctive qualities as opposed to those associated with free enterprise, or capitalism. Feudalism, for example, supported what was essentially a society of status, where people were irrevocably fixed in their stations, except as they took refuge in the bosom of the medieval Church. Again, in the feudal age economic production was largely on a nonexchange and nonprofit basis; in fact, most production was simply for local use whether it was carried on in the manorial estates or under the supervision of the craft guilds. Also, much of this production was communal. On the land, the customs of the manor governed not only the distribution of the small strips of arable land to the individual peasant but also the planting programs which occupied his whole life. The use of the common lands, which were a part of each village community, was likewise controlled by communal custom, not by individual choice or enterprise. A similar sort of communal regulation controlled the operations of the medieval craft guilds, or associations of craftsmen—tailors, carriage makers, ironmongers—whose authority as regards quality of ware, prices, the training of apprentices, and the accumulation of capital was rarely challenged.

Even when the feudal land system began to disintegrate in Europe, starting in the fourteenth century, and when tenants at will began to replace manorial serfs, the break with communal agriculture was painfully slow. The consolidation of strips into family farms went on over a long time; and the same was true of the gradual termination of the rights in the common lands.

This is a significant fact. When Europeans, in the seventeenth, eighteenth, even nineteenth centuries were migrating across the seas to take up their homes in the New World and establish themselves as free and independent farmers, they were leaving behind them relatives and friends who were still living under the village agricultural system and within the restrictions of feudal landlordism. Strip cultivation, rights in the common, village organization, the dues and obligations that the landlord still possessed, these continued to exist in Europe. Not so in the United States; the American farmer started out by being a free enterpriser from the very beginning. And he became a freeholder.

Similar important differences existed in industry and trade. The guild controls were monopolistic restraints upon free enterprise. And even when the local guilds began to lose their power, monopoly, as an instrument of regulation and control, was not abandoned. The emerging national states used monopoly devices tellingly and in every sector of enterprise. And they employed their monopoly powers to control wages and apprenticeship. The influence of the guilds as state agencies of regulation did not begin to diminish in significance in England until the eighteenth century. Monopolies in industry and trade, with state charters, were not entirely gone until the nineteenth century. In France and Germany, these institutions lingered on even later. By contrast, the European immigrant to America found neither guilds nor state-supported monopolies. Like the farmer, the enterpriser in industry or trade in America functioned freely; he was not restrained by the remnants of an ancient feudalism.

The American suspicion of monopoly is deep-seated. The classic struggle against the chartering of the First Bank of the United States, led by Thomas Jefferson in 1791, is a case in point. Even industrial corporations were regarded in America with hostility for a long time, and it was not until after the 1850s that the states were ready to pass general enabling acts for their creation. The American was fearful of the anonymous character of corporate power.

Many early industrialists have shown this typical distaste for institutionalized business. Andrew Carnegie in an earlier generation, Henry Ford in our own, are examples. Both looked on their businesses as personal creations. They were much more concerned with the processes of expansion than with individual profits. The result of this attitude was that undistributed earnings plowed back into new capital plant made possible the building of the great steel and automobile industries in America. Another interesting parallel between Carnegie and Ford is to be noted: both got rid of partners—Carnegie buying out Frick, and Ford buying out the Dodges—because their partners resented a business policy based on low productive costs rather than on high profits.

The Weak State. The weak state is a third cornerstone of the American tradition. The early settlers came to America from European countries which were dominated by the theories of Mercantilism, that is to say, by a conception of state power which was not unlike the present-day theory of totalitarianism. The political and economic well-being of the state was the key to individual and social activity. Many of the colonists had fled in protest against authority, whether in religious or economic realms, and their allegiance to Mercantilism was correspondingly weakened because it was associated with the authority of the state.

The American Revolution cut the connection completely. The American Revolution was as much a revolt against the limitations and penalties that hindered free enterprise under colonial relations with England as it was a struggle for political independence. It was only natural that Americans, emerging from that conflict with the mother country, should regard the state with suspicion and seek to limit its powers. They struck the first blow for freedom in the new state constitutions that were written during the period of the American Revolution. They would not ratify the Constitution until a Bill of Rights had been promised as a part of it. They carried the fight, under Jefferson and Jackson, into the federal sphere and also into the states. The theory and practices of the weak, or laissez-faire, state have been as old as American political experiences themselves.

If one looks at the histories of England, France, and Germany, one realizes how far the United States moved from the Old World view. It was not until the 1840s that the props of English state control—the Acts of Trade and Navigation and the Corn Laws—were finally removed. Also, legal recognition of trade unions did not come until the 1870s. In France, despite the extraordinary achievements of the French Revolution, the French middle class was compelled to struggle against a long line of usurpers seeking to reestablish the principle of absolute monarchy, or state power. It was not until the 1880s that the French state was made responsive to the rights of the individual. And as for Germany, the incubus of state authority was never really shaken off. When it comes to an unbroken history of respect by the state for the individual's natural rights—his rights to life, liberty, and the pursuit of happiness—that of the United States has been the longest, and this despite the lateness with which the United States entered the company of nations.

Equality of Opportunity. A fourth cornerstone of the American tradition is the ideal of equality of economic and social opportunity. The American people are a middle-class people, and they believe that through the cultivation of the virtues of hard work and thrift they can in time achieve economic independence and social equality. There can be no question that the belief is solidly founded in reality:

that for a long time and for sizable portions of the population such opportunities to achieve measurable independences flourished. Nor can there be question that the hope of their achievement—if not by members of the present generation, at least by their children—still remains an important part of the American credo.

This confidence has supported the vast educational structure of America. Education is not so much education for leadership; it is education for citizenship and education to equalize opportunities. It is inevitable that a people still "on the make" should place greater store in practical values in education than in the conservative and conserving values of settled and privileged societies.

What made possible equality of opportunity in the United States? The first and most important influence has already been referred to, that is, accessibility to a vast public domain on which the prior rights of landlords did not have to be respected. There were other factors of which mention should be made briefly.

Equality of opportunity also existed in connection with industrial production, for there were no privileged and entrenched interests to check the little man in his upward climb. The contrast with England is illuminating. Thanks to the mercantilist system imposed by England upon the American colonies, opportunities for industrial production, except in limited fields (shipbuilding, iron manufacture), were closed to Americans during the seventeenth and eighteenth centuries. In England, on the other hand, industrial production had had the direct support of the state—with bounties, tax remissions, the establishment of monopolies, crown subscriptions to joint-stock companies. As a result, large-scale industrial enterprise was flourishing there as early as the sixteenth and seventeenth centuries, in mining and in the manufacture of ironware, chemicals, glass, textiles, and the like. Production was not yet by machinery, of course; but the organization of production was so far advanced that all the characteristics of modern capitalism were already common, that is, division of labor, unified workshops, the wage system, and large capitalizations.

When the industrial revolution came in England in the third quarter of the eighteenth century, when machine techniques increasingly came to supplant hand processes, there existed therefore an enterpriser class which, while small, was schooled in the methods of large-scale industry. This class had already amassed a sizable capital fund. With its managerial skills and its capital, the English middle class was able to move easily into the widening field of industrial capitalism where so many opportunities appeared with the invention of the automatic spindle, the power loom, and the steam engine. Furthermore, transfer from mercantile pursuits to industrial pursuits took place in England. In the United States this was not so; all the industrial capitalists started virtually from scratch. Alexander Hamilton's program to encourage manufactures not only by protection but also by subsidy was never carried out. In the United States, consequently, no established wealth and no especially favored groups checked the young, the daring, and the enterprising.

We do not always realize to what an extent the typical early industrial enterpriser came from the small towns and the countryside of America. His equipment for his extraordinary achievements often consisted entirely of his youthful training in hard labor, a religious education which stressed frugality and application to his calling, and a confidence in his own capacities and the opportunities which his country afforded. Andrew Carnegie, John D. Rockefeller, Cyrus H. McCormick, the Big Four who built the Central Pacific and the Southern Pacific railroads, the great meat-packers of Chicago, Henry Ford—in all cases the story was much the same. In no case did there exist a family inheritance or any kind of special privilege.

Equality of opportunity also existed in the United States in the exploitation of its mineral resources. Thanks to the presence of the great public domain and to a generous land policy, it was possible for a lucky prospector and a small capitalist to make a lucky strike and to hit and work rich coal, iron, lead, copper, or oil deposits. Many early mining fortunes, in no way connected with special advantage, grew up in pre-Civil War America out of modest beginnings. Exactly the reverse was the case in Europe. In England and Germany, for example, the land had already been preempted by landlords, and monopolies in coal production had been flourishing long before industrialism matured. Mining in Europe has always been a favored area of privilege; in the United States it was one of the regions in which free enterprise was able to flourish for a considerable length of time.

Equality of opportunity in the United States was also due to the fact that America did not become an economic and financial dependency of Europe. Capital accumulations began to appear in Europe on a large scale in the nineteenth century. Some of these were retained at home to be used for railroad and industrial-plant construction. A considerable part, however, flowed overseas for the development of plantations and mines and for the building of railroads and factories. This process was linked with what we have come to call "economic imperialism." Only a small part of such investable funds, however, moved into the United States, and for a simple reason: neither the Federal government nor the state governments would furnish political guarantees that such foreign loans would be serviced or paid back.

European capital, it is true, had helped in the original financing of public improvements (including railroads) in the United States as far back as the 1830s. This was due to the fact that many of the securities floated in the London and Amsterdam money markets were state-government issues. The depression of 1837–1843 threw many of these securities into default; in some cases actual repudiation occurred; and the foreign investor discovered that he was without legal remedy in the federal courts because the state governments were sovereign bodies. Investment, in America, in other words, was attended by measurable risks.

The program of economic imperialism, on the other hand, had real advantages. Either by outright conquest or by the creation of spheres of influence or by the extraction of governmental guarantees or by extraterritoriality, European governments in the nineteenth century began to expand their areas of political domination. And the businessmen and their bankers, who followed in the wake of missionaries, traders, and soldiers and who sank large sums in mines, plantations, railroads, and factories, knew they were risking little. For economic and military sanctions could always be imposed on the subject peoples. At the very time, therefore, that the United States offered golden opportunities for capitalist development, notably in the post-Civil War decades, the English, French, Germans, Belgians, and Dutch were turning their attention to Africa, India, China, and Eastern Europe.

The Strength of the American Middle Class. This economic penetration by European capital and enterprise had an interesting and significant consequence: it stunted the growth of a native middle class in the regions where it took place. Industries were dominated by foreign capital, and the profits flowed outward. The workers were "proletarianized" and labored, quite literally, under the whips of overseers; while the thin middle layer of managers and functionaries was made up either of foreigners themselves or of educated natives whose loyalties were overseas. The classic example of such foreign exploitation was Ireland under English landlordism; Russia became another example toward the end of the nineteenth century.

Not so in the United States; here the role of foreign capital was slight (except in the case of railroading and even there the foreign investors were usually bondholders and not shareholders). The upshot was that after the close of the American Civil War it took a full generation before large-scale capitalist activities appeared in industrial production. And this was the period in which the small enterpriser

emerged. If he were diligent, abstemious, and shrewd, he could increase a small stake into a respectable and frequently an immense fortune. The annals of American enterprise, particularly the annals of industrial and smelting fortunes, are filled with the histories of hundreds of young fellows who, starting obscurely, made money, plowed profits back into capital plant or bought out competitors, and ended by becoming rich.

Contrast this situation in the United States with that in Ireland or Russia or India or China during the same period, and the greater stability of the American middle class is startlingly revealed. In the United States, a home-grown, home-rooted middle class nursed its profits carefully, expanded its capital plant out of its own surpluses, maintained owner-management, rewarded the top layer of salaried employees by admitting them into its own ranks, and at the same time was able to pay out high wages. In short, it presented tangible proofs on every side of the reality of the American dream that equality of economic opportunity existed. For the middle class in the United States, life was rich with promise. In all those countries under the sway of foreign or imperialist capitalism, by contrast, society was sharply polarized, with a small upper class having a foreign and not a native allegiance. When economic and political shocks came—as they did in Russia, for example—there were no middle layers to cushion the blows.

One is to note, finally, the recurrent strain of equalitarianism in our political thinking and party history. Leveling ideas here have always been linked to property rights; the property rights of land and kine and small workshops, however, and not rights of privilege and monopoly. The political ideas and leadership of Jefferson, Jackson, the Radical Republicans, the Populists, La Follette, the New Dealers—these have had as profound influences in shaping the middle-class ideas and ideals of America as have any other set of beliefs.

Americans have fought, again and again, for liberty and equality. The First American Revolution (the War of Independence) sought to free the American people from the domination of an oversea authority and to establish equality of opportunity for all men in the economic sphere. The Second American Revolution (the Civil War), in the hands of the Radical Republicans, was an instrument with which to achieve the freedom of the Negroes and to create equality of opportunity for blacks and whites in the South and for enterprisers everywhere. The Third American Revolution (the New Deal)—happily carried out peacefully—had a powerful equalitarian strain in its composition; through the intervention of the state, the little men of America were to be made secure in their possessions and opportunities to rise were to be reestablished.

It is false to assume that the concept of equality of opportunity is only a wistful and nostalgic hankering after an earlier and simpler world. True, our ways of living have become institutionalized; we move among Big Corporations, Big Trade Unions, and the Big State. But we are not powerless: as long as the rights of free discussion and free association are preserved.

The Democratic Institutions of the United States. American political institutions reflect the attitudes here outlined, in both the establishment and protection of personal rights and the limitations imposed upon government. We like to call our government a democracy, although in the literal meaning of the term—direct government by all the people—it is not really that. It is a republic and, in fact, the Founding Fathers referred to themselves as republicans and not democrats. Charles A. Beard calls attention to the fact that in the eighteenth century the word "republic" was employed broadly, that is to say, not in an institutional sense but in a moral one. In short, the representatives of the people, acting through government, sought to create welfare and assure the happiness of the greatest number.

As the instruments of government came increasingly under popular control, more and more the limitations upon government which characterize the American system began to make themselves felt. It is one of the most significant characteristics of the American political scheme that it is based upon limited powers. The limitations upon government are imposed in a variety of ways:

1. Ours is a government of laws and not of men. Highest of all is the natural law which Jefferson, obtaining the notion from John Locke, embodied in the Declaration of Independence. "We hold these truths to be self-evident, that all men . . . are endowed by their Creator with certain unalienable rights . . . life, liberty, and the pursuit of happiness." To defend these natural rights of the individual against usurpation at the hands of government the Bill of Rights was added to the Constitution. The individual is specifically protected against an established church; he is assured freedom of worship, speech, assembly, and the press; he is safeguarded against a too zealous police authority and tyrannical courts. His property rights are defended by the famous "due process" clause of the Fifth and Fourteenth Amendments. Interestingly enough, this appeal to natural law (or a "higher law") was also used by the Abolitionists in their attacks on Negro slavery.

In addition to the Lockian natural law, we have the protection of the common law, constitutional law, and statute law. In each case, the law is interpreted by the judiciary, but it is a mistake to assume—as is sometimes too easily done—that this procedure results in judge-made law. It is true that at times, particularly in the processes of judicial review at the hands of the Supreme Court, the courts have violated the intention of the legislative branch, whether in the states or in Congress. But not for too long; sooner or later the judges come to understand that the popular will is supreme in the American scheme of things. They did so in the 1870s; they have come to do so again in the 1930s.

Henry Steele Commager has expressed this thought in the following words: "The state is an organic, not a static, thing, and constitutions are designed to permit growth, adaptation, and experimentation . . . The police power is not narrowly restricted to emergency legislation but covers all great public needs. The great value of the federal system is that it permits experiments in forty-eight political laboratories and such experiments are to be encouraged. There must be play for the joints of political machinery if it is to work, and restrictions should be limited to jurisdiction, not to political power or administrative activities. Majorities have a right to make mistakes, and there is nothing in the Constitution which prevents them from committing errors or follies."

2. The separation of powers—the division of functions into the executive, the legislative, and the judicial—is another means by which governmental power is limited. Congress, notably, has always been jealous of its authority, and it has used its rights again and again to cut down Executive pretensions. It has been able to do this especially through its control over the purse strings (as a result of which it can eliminate executive agencies at will) and through the Senate's participation in foreign affairs. The executive, on its part, has the important right of veto and in this way can impose limitations on legislative conduct. The judiciary operates in its own sphere. In general, the separation-of-powers theory has worked out well, and there is no question of the fact that the American people are devoted to their system. Substitution for the three independent branches of government of a single authority—as has been true of totalitarian states—is not likely to meet with much support in America.

3. The division of functions between the central government and the states—between Nationalism and Federalism—is a third means by which the power of government is limited. By the Constitution the Federal government is granted specific functions: the rights to make war and peace, to maintain a uniform currency, to raise money, to regulate commerce among the states, and the like. All unspecified rights are reserved to the states, and in their sphere

they have sovereign powers. The struggle between central authority and state rights has been recurrent in American political annals, and the pendulum has swung persistently from one position to the other. The original Federalists believed in a powerful central union, particularly for the purposes of creating a sound credit system in the new republic and of holding in check the leveling tendencies in the states themselves. The Jeffersonians (later Democrats) moved to the opposite extreme: they sought to narrow down as far as possible the functions of the Federal government and to make the states completely expressive of the popular will. The Republican party, from 1860 to 1932, again looked to the national government, first to abolish slavery and then to defend property rights. Under the New Deal, curiously enough, the two positions were reversed. The Democrats came to regard the central government as the only possible agency for the protection of human rights and the promotion of the public welfare. The Republicans, more and more, began to speak of decentralization and of the necessity for buttressing the sovereignty of the separate states.

True, in recent years, because of governmental interventionism, operating in the interests of welfare, liberty has appeared to be in danger at the hands of an overzealous and excessive state authority. Frequently, it has been. The pendulum, in a free society, does swing over a wide arc. From the 1860s through the 1920s, the state was too passive; during the 1930s and 1940s, it has been too active. Just as—once and for all—we have rejected laissez faire, so we must always be suspicious of statism.

American institutions and attitudes furnish us with the weapons: the balancing of the legislative power against the executive power, decentralization of authority, responsibility in office, grass-roots democracy—these are ways and means. Again, an alert people has the power to defend its rights.

Parties and Pressure Groups. Against this general background of personal rights and governmental limitations, the American political institutions operate. They are made up, as has been said, of the executive and its agencies, the legislature, and the courts. The popular will is exerted chiefly in two ways: through the party system and through pressure groups. Americans go to the polls to vote not for individuals but for party candidates. The party itself is controlled by the membership through the district clubs and the direct primaries. The party, in its turn, is significant for the crystallization of public issues, for its ability to discipline office holders, and for its willingness to scrutinize constantly, as an opposition, the acts of the party in power.

At times in our history, it is evident, the American two-party system has caused the confusion rather than the clarification of important questions. But at critical periods in our history, the parties have become rallying centers and have not hesitated to act boldly. This was true in the struggles over slavery, free silver, and the League of Nations, to take a few examples. Also, at critical periods, the parties have represented clear-cut class alignments. In the free-silver debate, for instance, the Democratic party was the spokesman for labor and the lower-middle classes; it has been, too, under the New Deal. And this significant functioning of the parties takes place despite the fact that they often appear to be mere local groups and leaders who band together every four years only to participate in national elections.

Pressure groups also make possible a greater responsiveness on the part of the executive and the legislature to the popular will. At first blush this is difficult to believe, since pressure groups have usually been assumed to be sinister agencies operating secretly. In the beginning this was unquestionably so, and there can be no doubt that the earliest pressure groups used their power to force concessions from government to powerful property interests. Early tariff-making is justly associated with the lobbying activities of so-called wool institutes, iron and steel associations, and the like. In recent years, however, pressure groups have func-

tioned more and more in the open, so that the agencies of government have the means of judging their strength and of balancing the articulate forces in the nation. Today it is no longer possible to say that the secret government of Big Business runs public affairs. For side by side with the representatives of business at Washington are to be found the equally capable representatives of the organized farmers and the organized trade unionists. All these groups are very strong, and the result is that government in the United States is government by compromise. This, in the long run, is the most stable kind of government.

Equipped, then, with certain traditional beliefs regarding the foundations of their common life and having remarkable opportunities to work out these beliefs in practice, Americans have developed the resources of their land, growing from a small community to one of the great Powers in the world. They have also demonstrated that democracy is a working system.

It is the intention of this book—by the use of examples—to show how American ideas and institutions have been developed. Its materials fall into two parts: text and contemporary documents. The text, in effect a book in American history, serves as a series of introductions to the documents. These are fitted into a pattern which has been followed faithfully in nine of the eleven parts into which the book is divided. In each of the parts, in other words, four divisions have been set up: the American Mind, the American Scene, American Problems, and the United States and the World. It is hoped that, by these devices, the reader will be able to catch the body and the spirit, the enduring values and the transitory—albeit pressing—problems of the world in which Americans lived as they marched ahead to create a civilization.

I have sought to do other things as well. I have tried to make the documents representative—not only of the strains in the American tradition that are still alive but of the best thinking in and about America. Thus, in the field of philosophy, there has been included selections from the writings of Williams, Edwards, Franklin, Palmer, Emerson, Thoreau, Whitman, James, and Dewey. In the field of economic thought, there are selections from Franklin, Hamilton, Carey, George, Wells, Godkin, Sumner, Wright, Veblen, Mitchell, and Hansen. In the field of political thought, there are selections from Mayhew, Jefferson, Madison, Hamilton, Lee, Bancroft, Webster, Calhoun, Hildreth, Wilson, and Franklin D. Roosevelt. There have been included pieces from the works of distinguished foreigners who have written about America—Adam Smith, Josiah Tucker, Hector St. John Crevècoeur, Robert Turgot, Richard Price, Alexis de Tocqueville, Charles Dickens, J. E. Cairnes, James Bryce, André Siegfried, Colin Clark. Also, through documents, an effort has been made to point up the staples of American foreign policy—the Monroe Doctrine, the Open Door, the Defense of the Panama Canal, the Good Neighbor, International Collaboration.

The greater part of the text has been written as an original work, although, of course, it leans heavily on other writings by myself. In a few places it repeats word for word things I have said elsewhere. I wish to acknowledge my thanks to my other publishers for permission to reprint passages or condensations from other writings of mine: to F. S. Crofts and Company for materials from *The United States Since 1865* (New York, 1932); to Simon and Schuster for materials from *The Triumph of American Capitalism* (New York, 1940); and to D. C. Heath and Company for materials from *The United States and Its Place in World Affairs, 1918–1943*, edited by Allan Nevins and Louis M. Hacker (Boston, 1943).

This book has grown out of the requirements of the Contemporary Civilization course at Columbia College, and more particularly its work in the second year. I am deeply grateful to my colleagues for the aid and encouragement I have received. I have discussed my outlines with them fully and at many points have been saved from errors of omission and commission. Notably, I wish to acknowledge my debt here to Dean Harry J. Carman and to Professors Dwight C. Miner and Horace Taylor. In another sense, this book is peculiarly a Columbia product. It was prepared at the Nicholas Murray Butler Library, and I am under great obligations to the staff of the library for the facilities that were placed at my disposal. And it is being published by the Columbia University Press, which handled with skill and imagination the mechanical problems involved in getting out a book of these great proportions. I acknowledge my thanks here to Charles G. Proffitt, Henry H. Wiggins, Matilda L. Berg, and Eugenia Porter. Helene S. Zahler worked with me on this from the beginning—sifting the documents, writing many of the forewords, and reading the proof. I am grateful to her for her very capable assistance. My wife, Lillian L. Hacker, helped me with her encouragement and understanding: to her my deep thanks.

Louis M. Hacker

Columbia University
New York, August 1, 1946

Part One

LEAVING EUROPE AND SETTLING AMERICA

INTRODUCTION

1. THE EUROPEAN WORLD FROM WHICH THE AMERICANS CAME

ALL MANNER OF FOLK left Europe to come to America in the seventeenth and eighteenth centuries. They came from many lands and various stations of life; they came willingly and unwillingly. Some left Europe behind forever —not only physically but emotionally and intellectually as well—and America was both an asylum and a new beginning. Others brought Europe along with them. In one sense, of course, they were the products of a Western civilization that had been centuries in process of developing; in another, they were the children of the Western World. All of which is to say, they became Americans.

The original settlers were in the main English men and women. But by the eighteenth century there were to be found among them Scotch-Irish and Germans in large numbers as well as a sprinkling of Dutch, Welsh, Swedes, and Frenchmen. For the most part, they came from the small villages and towns of the country, although urban dwellers (from London, Bristol, Plymouth, Nantes, Amsterdam) were in their company. Nearly always, they were humble men and women, of little means and simple education, who had been farm workers and tenants—and only occasionally small freeholders. Some had been skilled artisans and mechanics; some had been sailors and fishermen. There were, it is true, among them, a small proportion of the well-born: younger sons of country squires, here and there a merchant or a professional soldier, occasionally—but quite rarely— a man of sizable possessions. But none of Europe's great came to America. At the other pole, there were the completely underprivileged: dispossessed small agricultural tenants, the recipients of parish poor relief, the wid-

owed and orphaned, those who were unwanted for religious reasons. And—in the eighteenth century—there were the Negro slaves.

The Transforming European World. The European economic and social world from which the original Americans came had been in process of transformation for at least half a millennium. By the seventeenth century—at least as far as England, France, and Holland were concerned—the feudal society of Thomas Aquinas and Dante and the Knights Templar was finished. It had been a society based upon a caste system and it had revolved about agricultural production with the individual's position in it firmly fixed through a complicated program of rights and obligations. It had also been, thanks to the ethical system created by the medieval Catholic Church, a society in which the market relation had been clearly subordinated. But that feudal polity and economy had not been wiped out with a single bold and clean stroke; the processes of change had left behind many vestigial traces.

The world out of which the American settlers came was no longer the tight, local, self-contained feudal world. It was a world into which the free air of enterprise had already entered. The caste system of feudalism was being dissolved. The individual was beginning to claim and establish certain rights to the liberty of his person. Above all, he was extending the sphere of operations of his property rights. He could buy and sell in a market; he could hire himself out and hire the labor of others; he could save money capital and transform it into wealth, in the economic sense. It must not be assumed that he possessed that full liberty with which we associate private and property rights today; but, certainly, he had moved far down that road which mankind in the West had blazed since the thirteenth century—and which had resulted in the loosening of the bonds that tied the individual to authority.

For the authorities of the Catholic Church, the manor, and the guilds—all of which had rejected the profit motive and man's ability to improve his station in life as the bases for personal action and social organization—the men of the fifteenth and sixteenth centuries, therefore, were substituting free enterprise. Their loyalties, notably in western and northern Europe, were shifting from a lower to a higher plane in another area as well. And that was the political. The feudal world had been a particularistic one. A man was associated with a village, if a rural dweller, or with a commune, if an urban one. The great outside beat upon his gates only occasionally, in the person of a begging friar or in the awful passage of an armed troop. The villagers lived and married and died within the narrow sphere of their own stripped fields and commons; the townsmen clung to the shelter of the great walls they helped erect around their communes.

But in the fourteenth and fifteenth centuries, these confining horizons were being pushed out. Wayfarers—itinerant merchants, wandering students, soldiers, sailors, runaway serfs—had appeared increasingly on natural highways. Merchants had taken to pitching their tents and bazaars outside walled cities, thus extending the areas of urban settlement. Feudal lords, in the great valleys of western Europe, had accorded these itinerants protection as they moved from fair town to fair town. Powerful overlords, by conquest and agreement, were expanding the spheres of their own influence. These last, in time, were destined to become the national and absolute monarchs of early modern Europe. By the fourteenth and fifteenth centuries—in Portugal, Spain, France, England, Denmark, Sweden—such monarchies had emerged. They were mighty centralizing and pacifying influences; and, as a result, the loyalty of the individual was shifting from his

locality and his local lord to those of the national monarch and the state.

The National Monarchies. How had these monarchies emerged? Largely because of successful wars against the feudal lords, the independent communes, and the Church, wars which the new merchant princes were aiding by making loans to the kings so that mercenary soldiers could be hired, supplied and provisioned, and siege equipment acquired. The muskets and the cannon of the national monarchs blew the armored knights and the walled towns out of the history of Europe. Churches were nationalized, and Church properties, either by seizure or through royal appointment to ecclesiastical office, came under the control of the kings. National monarchs, merchants, even the little men of Europe profited in a hundred and one different ways.

The national monarchs expanded the territorial areas of the state; established their absolute sway; created great courts in which they reduced the turbulent barons to docile and even humanist courtiers; fostered new and superior tastes in manners, clothes, and house furnishings; and completely controlled the public revenues. Private enterprise also grew in stature. For the monarchs pacified the land and reduced the corporate privileges of the communes. Here was a widening national market, protected by the king's soldiers and the king's judges, into which business could move. Roads and bridges were built; weights and measures were regularized; for varying periods, the coinage was stabilized; provincial and local barriers to the free movement of goods were leveled—partially in some countries, entirely in England. In the nations that broke with the Catholic Church, in the sixteenth century, properties were taken over by the national monarchs to enrich their personal estates and to build up a new court nobility.

The Rising Middle Class. Businessmen gained directly and indirectly. Indirectly, because the market was expanded. Directly, because they received from the kings certain concessions and monopolies—to work mines, to manufacture capital goods, to form regulated and joint-stock companies for oversea trade and the planting of colonies. The little men of Europe profited as well. The more enterprising and ambitious now had wider fields in which to range. They could move out of the villages and incorporated towns—where opportunity was restrained and thwarted by local custom and guild privileges—into a freer climate. They could enter the king's service or take to the sea or engage in manufactures. Nothing is more interesting than the emergence of the little man —the petit bourgeois, the interloper, the parvenu—in times of great social change. Many of the later great merchant families of the sixteenth and seventeenth centuries stemmed from obscure forebears who boldly followed the main chance. The same was true of the great railroading and industrial families of the nineteenth and twentieth centuries. When human affairs take a sudden leap forward, the innovators are not the scions of ancient privilege, but unknowns, whose strength is to be found in their courage and their ability to endure privations—and, frequently, in their lack of scruples.

Out of such a world, the American settlers emerged; a world of royal and dynastic absolutism but, at the same time, a larger and freer world in the economic sense. There was still a third profoundly conditioning force which released the energies and the minds of men from their loyalties to an old authority; this was Protestantism.

The Protestant Reformation. Protestantism cut the individual loose from the penitential system of the Catholic Church. The achievement of grace was to be no longer an unending preoccupation with good works through the constant ministrations of the clergy. Now, salvation was to be won by faith: by the individual's own and direct approach to God, upon whose mercies he threw himself, through his free conscience. The Catholic Church had taught that man was born and lived in sin; and that it was his pride (the greatest of human failings) that prompted him to improve his

worldly station. A too close devotion to the creation of wealth, out of which individual profit might be derived—so had held the Church's great fathers from Augustine to Aquinas—was equally unchristian. The ideal medieval man was the ascetic of the monastery who eschewed all this world's goods and who prayed for his fellow Christians.

Protestantism, on the other hand, was individualistic, classless, anti-authoritarian and productive in the economic sense. It created a climate where the guides to conduct and action were many and varied: working and saving; the hustle and bustle of the market place; individual striving and personal choices rather than group sanctions were parts of the new social morality. Notably from John Calvin did Protestantism derive its ethical justification of work and thrift. The English, Scottish, Scotch-Irish, French, Dutch, and German followers of the Calvinist and reformed Lutheran creeds —the Puritans, Quakers, Presbyterians, Huguenots, Dutch Reformed, and Pietists who played such a large part in the settlement of America and the creation of its individualistic psychology—were impatient with the notions of humility and poverty just as they rejected the whole program of medieval other-worldly asceticism.

The Calvinist doctrine of predestination—that there was a small company of God's elect alone chosen for salvation—instead of turning Protestants from the world threw them fully into it. Regardless of their birth, they were picked to rule. Faith, therefore, came first; and it produced works. Faith, too, was linked with application to an everyday "calling." The asceticism of work—of the daily application to one's job—was more significant for the Christian life than the asceticism of contemplation. Thus by labor, diligence, sobriety, and thrift, by production and by saving, the good Christian was destined to achieve grace in both this world and the next.

The English historian, R. G. Tawney, in these words has described the world-view of the seventeenth century English Puritan and Scottish Presbyterian:

Convinced that character is all and circumstance nothing, he sees in the poverty of those who fall by the way not a misfortune to be pitied and relieved, but a moral failing to be condemned, and in riches not an object of suspicion . . . but the blessing which rewards the triumph of energy and will. Tempered by self-examination, self-discipline, self-control, he is the practical ascetic whose victories are won not in the cloister, but on the battlefield, in the counting house, and in the market.[1]

The American publicist, William Allen White, has shown how these values have been carried over into America:

Men sought heaven for their immortal souls through the acceptance of salvation. . . . Moreover, they have set up reason as the final arbiter in the relations of men. Out of this establishment of government and the social order upon reason rather than force, men have come into democracy. . . . Men in the pioneer West have had to be hardworking to clear off the wilderness. They have had to be thrifty if they survived the economic rigors of pioneering. They have had to be punctual if they got on with their busy neighbors. They have had to be debt-payers or fail. They have had to cultivate a rather strict sense of social duty. In other words, the western Protestantism carried over the Puritan virtues into the continental West. All those hard virtues, all those social ideals, all those yearnings for the establishment of justice after debate and under reason, erected a social order wherein each individual came to rely with easy confidence upon the guidance of his conscience.[2]

Geographical Expansion. There was a fourth influence operating on the old world, that of the discoveries and geographical expansion. The heart of medieval Europe had been the Mediterranean lands. Here Rome had been established, here were the Holy Places associated with the nativity and passion of Christ; here had worked Paul, Augustine, and other great Church Fathers. The Crusades had reopened a portion of these lands to direct physical contact on the part of western Christendom. The Italian merchants and traders occasionally had

penetrated personally into the farther regions of Asia. They had brought back tales of the fabulous lands of Cathay (China) and Zingu (Japan): of rich and populous cities, of great navigable rivers, and of incalculable wealth in precious stones, metals, and fine fabrics. Europe knew of these distant places of Asia as it knew of a dark continent to the south. But Europeans did not go there, for they were compelled, in their little boats, to keep constantly in sight of land lest the vast uncharted seas engulf them.

But by the fifteenth century Europeans had become bold seafarers. The revival of learning —and the greater knowledge of geography and astronomy—that had come about in the Moorish universities in the twelfth century, had been a significant influence. Men had learned to know once more that the earth was a sphere; they had come to believe that the continent of Africa could be rounded and the Far East reached by southern—and perhaps, too, by northern and western—all-water routes. The science of navigation had matured. The compass and the astrolabe made it possible for navigators to strike out into the great seas; larger and safer ships were built; portolan charts were now drawn up. The invention of printing helped to advance the easy and cheap circulation of geographical knowledge. Theoretical and technical aids thus existed to make adventuring possible.

The adventurers, by the fifteenth century, were in existence. They operated under the new monarchies of western Europe. Not the Italian or North German city-states fitted out navigators and explorers but the kings and princes of Portugal, Spain, France, England, and Holland. In a sense, these journeys of discovery and exploration were linked with the ambitions of dynastic monarchy; for the expansion of territories and rulership over distant places added to the glory of the royal crown. Missionary zeal played its part. A desire to find precious metals for decoration and coinage— for European supplies of gold and silver were limited—contributed to the impulses to dis-

[1] R. G. Tawney, *Religion and the Rise of Capitalism* (New York, 1926), p. 230.
[2] W. A. White, *The Changing West* (New York, 1939), pp. 29–30.

covery and exploration. Of equal importance was the desire to be freed of the dominance of the Italian and German traders who monopolized the trade with the Near East in spices and textiles.

There was still a further consideration: and this had to do with the dislocations in the Near East as a result of the appearance of the Turks. The Turks, when they took Constantinople in 1453 and Egypt in 1517, did not shut off the trade with these lands and close the avenues into Middle Asia; but they burdened business with heavy impositions. That is to say, the Italians were permitted to operate as before; except now they were required to pay registration fees, tolls, tariffs, and similar charges. All these exactions—as well as the monopoly prices of the Italians and the fact that land-borne traffic is dearer than water-borne—kept the prices of Eastern wares high.

Portugal was the first nation to seek escape from the iron ring of the Mediterranean. Under the leadership of Prince Henry, son of the first Portuguese national monarch, navigators moved out into the Atlantic and began the circuit around Africa. They reached the Canary Islands, Madeira, and the Azores. They moved south, feeling their way around the African coast as Prince Henry carried on a war against the Moors. The Moorish power collapsed; and the Portuguese found on the African coast gold and slaves and ivory tusks. All this whetted their appetites. They discovered the Congo in 1482; reached the Cape of Good Hope in 1487; and in 1497 they sailed out into the Indian Ocean and in the following year put foot on Indian soil. In another fifty years, from their own concessions and factories in India, Portuguese merchants and sailors were penetrating into all the archipelagos of the Spice Islands and reaching even into China and Japan. The all-water link between East and West had been established.

Spain followed the example of Portugal. Christopher Columbus, the Genoese sailor, struck due west—whether in search of the East or simply a group of new islands beyond the Azores is unimportant. In any case, he brought back gold from his first voyage; and in subsequent ones he explored parts of the coasts of Central and South America. As Portugal had laid out claims to an empire in the Indian Ocean, so Spain did similarly in the West —calling its new possessions the Spanish Indies.

Before the sixteenth century was half over, English, French, and Spanish captains and explorers had penetrated deep into the New World. John Cabot, an Italian sailing for the English king Henry VII, discovered Newfoundland in 1497. Another Italian, John Verrazano, sailing for the French king Francis I, reached the Canadian coast proper a quarter of a century later. The St. Lawrence River was opened up to the white man. The northern coast of South America was explored. Mexico and Peru were penetrated, conquered, and despoiled. When Ferdinand Magellan's ships, during 1519–22, rounded the globe, Europe knew that a great land mass lay between the eastern Atlantic and the China Sea. By 1550, it had learned that great riches were to be obtained from the slave traffic with Africa, from direct trade relations with the East, and from the operation of the silver mines of the Spanish Indies.

Spanish Treasure. The appearance of the Spanish treasure in Europe was one of the most momentous occurrences in early modern European history. From 1530 to the end of the century, in a seemingly unending flood, silver and (to a lesser extent) gold poured from the great Mexican and Peruvian mines. From 1600 on, the supply began to taper off; by 1660, it had largely ceased. In this hundred and thirty years, something like 18,000 tons of silver and 200 tons of gold had been officially recorded in the Spanish assay offices. Only a part of this precious stream remained in Spain. A goodly part of it went out to the Orient and thus made possible a great increase in the trade with the Far East. Another goodly part moved into the commercial life of western Europe generally, so that in time France, Holland, and England also profited from the Spanish discoveries.

Thanks to the revitalized trade with the East and the treasure that tumbled into Europe from the Spanish Indies, the settlement of America by English colonists took place in an age characterized by great economic changes and advances.

2. THE ENGLISH BACKGROUND

The English homeland of most of the original settlers was also undergoing a transforming process, and because this was so, many dislocations were occurring. On the one hand, while feudalism was gone, part of its authoritarian patterns remained. On the other hand, the new England that was emerging—an England of commercialized agriculture, mercantile expansion, industrialization, all under the authority of a powerful and centralized state apparatus—was producing its own disequilibriums. Some of the settlers left in flight from the old England; some left to escape from the new; others were rejected by England altogether, and were virtually deported. It was no wonder that so many of England's institutions were left behind when the settlers came to create a new civilization in the Western World.

The Enclosure Movement. In sixteenth century England, the attack on one of the most important of the feudal hangovers began to take place—that of the village organization of agriculture. Since the fourteenth century, the great majority of the rural dwellers had been freed from serfdom; but the living and the techniques of the manorial system had continued to exist. Country folk dwelt in compact villages and functioned not in terms of family farms but in those of the open-field system. Freeholders were few and have always remained few in England. Most of the agricultural workers were either copyholders—hereditary tenants whose rents were fixed at least for one life—or laborers, who worked for wages. Whether freeholders, copyholders, or laborers —as under feudalism—the countryman possessed rights in a large number of scattered strips lying in open fields. These he cultivated in terms of the planting program of the whole village, which was generally a three-crop rotation (wheat, oats or barley, and fallow). In addition to these controls, there was a second characteristic of the village system: the countryman had rights in the common lands, which belonged to the village and were communally managed. In these commons (made up usually of meadow, waste, and wood lot), the countryman cut hay for winter forage for his livestock and turf and timber for his fuel and buildings. In England, the squire or landlord was also an operating farmer and along with the freeholders and copyholders he cultivated his strips all over the open fields of the village. The laborers worked for him but supplemented their meager livelihoods from their rights in the commons.

It was this scheme of things that was increasingly falling under attack in the sixteenth century. It came to be called the enclosure movement, largely because enterprising landlords were seeking to eliminate the commons and enclose them. But another and equally important part of the program had to do with combination of field strips into unified farming properties. And still a third part was directed against the traditional rights of the copyholders. That is to say, landlords sought to raise rents in violation of the customary arrangement; or they raised the alienation fine (the charge that had to be paid when the copyhold passed from father to son); or they evicted the copyholders altogether.

This enclosure movement—which was usually carried out illegally—began to shake the foundations of the old England. The consolidation of fields and the elimination of the commons led to the squeezing out of the small operators and the laborers, or cottagers. Agricultural properties were therefore becoming increasingly concentrated and copyholders were being turned into tenants at will, or leaseholders in our modern sense. Second, the countryside was becoming overpopulated. This was partially due to the fact that the large landlords, on their consolidated holdings, were more efficient than had been the many small cultivators. But even more important was the fact that arable was being converted into pasture and instead of the small grains being grown exclusively, Englishmen more and more were turning to the breeding of sheep. And sheep husbandry required fewer human hands than did the old system. The roads of England were being filled with dispossessed and unwanted countrymen—the vagabonds and beggars about whom the English penal code was so savage. It was about the sad lot of these unfortunates that Thomas More cried out in that memorable passage in his *Utopia:* Sheep "that were wont to be so myke and tame, and so smal eaters, now, as I heare saie, be become so great devowerers, and so wylde, that they eat up and swallow down the very men themselfes."

The Woolen Industry. This commercialized agriculture, with its unhappy social consequences, turned England more and more to the development of a mercantile economy. The expanding European market—in the Low Countries, the north German communities, Italy—clamored for wool and for white (or undressed and undyed) woolen cloths. England at once became the leading source for the raw-material and semimanufactured supplies of the European woolen textile centers. Thanks to the aggressiveness of a regulated company of individual English merchants, the so-called Merchants Adventurers, by the sixteenth century, English white woolens were dominating the northern European markets; and in the seventeenth century, these white woolens as well as finished cloths were to be found in the Levantine centers. The profits from this trade did much to help English business enterprise to mature.

The Price Revolution. Its greater participation in foreign trade brought sizable portions of Europe's augmented money stocks into England. Prices moved up—at first slowly and then very rapidly. Businessmen made profits—in fact great profits, so that here existed a capital fund for the launching of new mercantile and also industrial adventures. While prices sharply rose in England (from 1501 to 1650, they increased something like 250 percent) significantly enough, wages lagged behind. By 1700, *real* wages were only 50 percent of what they had been in 1500. As a result, this great price revolution was accompanied by a profit inflation in view of the fact that at least half of the costs of production at the time was represented by wage payments.[3]

The First Industrial Revolution. England was able to expand her Far Eastern trade; and the profit inflation contributed mightily to the appearance of her first industrial revolution and the start of her heavy industries in the sixteenth and seventeenth centuries. A new ebullience filled the land. Agricultural productivity was being stepped up. Oversea commerce was growing by leaps and bounds. Towns were pushing out into the countryside. And heavy industry—in coal, iron, lead mining, the metallurgical trades, salt and glass manufacture, soap and alum making, building-material fabrication—was beginning to utilize large capital funds for factories, machinery, and the hire of tens of thousands of wage workers. In the middle of the seventeenth century the smoke from coal furnaces hung like a pall over London.

The industrial use of coal, according to another American scholar, played as large a role as the profit inflation—if not greater—in England's transformation. According to John U. Nef, the increasing exhaustion of England's timber resources necessitated the employment of coal and the technological changes that went with its use. Says Nef:

[3] An American scholar was the first to point out the significant relations that developed between the price revolution and wage payments. Cf. E. J. Hamilton, "American Treasure and the Rise of Capitalism," *Economica,* XXVII (1929), 338-57, and his *American Treasure and the Price Revolution in Spain* (Cambridge, Mass., 1934). Lord Keynes, the English economist, following Hamilton, described in detail the nature of the English profit inflation. Cf. J. M. Keynes, *A Treatise on Money* (2 vols., New York, 1930).

The opening for profits arose mainly because costs of production were reduced by the widespread adoption of better machinery and improved kilns and furnaces, by the increase in the scale of industrial enterprise, and by the discovery and use of new supplies of raw materials such as calamine, alum, stone, and above all, coal.[4]

Foreign Trade. Oversea trade grew, helped and protected by the English crown. Two types of organization were employed in the exploitation of foreign commerce—the regulated company and the joint-stock company. The regulated company—an earlier form—consisted of a fellowship of merchants each of whom used his own capital but functioned in terms of the common rules imposed by the group; the fellowship supported joint services like docks, warehouses, and courts, and restricted membership on the basis of apprenticeship. As in modern-day cartels, each member's share of the market was prorated. The joint-stock company was more like our contemporary corporation, for the capital fund was raised from a general subscription and management was in the hands of a governor, treasurer, and board of assistants (or directors). The only difference between the original joint-stocks and our modern corporations is the fact that limited liability did not become a safeguard for investors until the nineteenth century. In another and even more important sense, these companies were unlike modern-day firms: for whether a regulated or a joint-stock company, each had the exclusive right to trade in the particular geographical region to which it had been assigned by the crown. Outstanding regulated companies were the Merchant Adventurers (with monopoly trading privileges in the North Sea countries), the Eastland Company (with monopoly trading privileges in the Baltic lands), the Russia

Company, and the Levant Company. Outstanding joint-stock companies were the East India Company, the African Company, and the Hudson's Bay Company. One may observe that these exclusive trading privileges continued right into the early nineteenth century.

Frequently, joint-stocks were created to finance a single voyage or a particular piece of promotion. One of the most successful ventures of this type was Francis Drake's second voyage in the *Golden Hind*, in which he circumnavigated the globe. Financed by a group of court nobles (with Queen Elizabeth a secret participant), Drake set out on a piratical and trading journey in 1577, during the course of which he harassed the Spanish communities along the South American coast and hunted down the Spanish treasure ships. He finally returned to England in 1580 with a valuable cargo of pepper from the Spice Islands and with profits of £600,000 on an investment of £5,000. The greatest company of all was the East India Company, first chartered in 1600 as a limited joint-stock to develop the vast area lying between the Cape of Good Hope and the China Sea. The company underwent various vicissitudes but by the last quarter of the seventeenth century was on a permanent footing. It was able, as a result, to establish its own factories, enter into treaty arrangements with native rulers, support armies, and maintain a constant vigilance against interloping traders. At times, its profits were enormous. Its trading monopolies continued in India until 1813 and in China until 1833.

The same company device was employed to launch colonization projects. In 1583, Humphrey Gilbert, seeking to plant a colony in Newfoundland, was acting for such a company. So was Walter Raleigh, when he made three unsuccessful attempts, during 1584–87, to establish English settlements in Virginia. Indeed the first successful ventures in English colonization in America were the work of a joint-stock enterprise; for in 1606 the Virginia Company was organized to send out settlers. The voyage of the Pilgrims was financed by a

---

[4] See among others, these articles: J. U. Nef, "A Comparison of Industrial Growth in France and England from 1540 to 1640," *Journal of Political Economy*, XLIV (1936), 289–317, 505–33, 643–66; "Prices and Industrial Capitalism in France and England, 1540–1640," *Economic History Review*, VII (1937), 155–185; "Industry and Government in France and England, 1540–1640," *Memoirs of the American Philosophical Society*, XV (1940), 1–162.

group of Plymouth and London merchants, who put up £7,000 to outfit the ships and the colonists. Massachusetts Bay Colony, the seat of the Puritans, was founded by a similar company in which many of the settlers themselves held stock. Manhattan Island and the shores of the Hudson River, in New York, were opened to trade by the Dutch West India Company. A Swedish company was responsible for the planting of the first settlement on the Delaware River.

Population and Wealth. As England rose in mercantile stature, her population and wealth also increased. Customs figures for the period are inadequate and must be taken for what they are worth, but they show an extraordinary development. At the beginning of the seventeenth century, the total value of imports and exports came to £5,600,000; at the beginning of the eighteenth century, to £12,400,000; in the middle of the eighteenth century, to £25,500,-000. In 1700, when all exports were valued at £6,500,000, those of woolens alone were worth £3,000,000. The beginning of the seventeenth century saw the English population consisting of 4,000,000 souls; in a century, they numbered 8,000,000; and by 1750, 10,000,000. The national wealth stood at £17,000,000 in 1600 and at £88,000,000 in 1688.

The effects of these various processes on the social map of England were profound. A new middle class was appearing and expanding, with one foot firmly planted in the country and the other in the towns. In it were to be found the improving landlords, the mine owners, the new industrialists, the monopolists. These were the enterprisers in foreign trade, the private bankers and the leaders in the domestic wholesale business. In this last connection, the new middle class entered into and gained control over many of the guilds, some of which simply became organizations specializing in the wholesale trades, while others became closely dominated corporate monopolies in the skilled crafts. Again, the gulf between the new middle class and the humble countrymen, artisans, and common laborers was widening. A large laboring

force was springing up—because of enclosures, sheep raising, guild exclusionism—and its members were becoming wage earners in industry and sailors and fishermen in the growing merchant marine. In the seventeenth and eighteenth centuries, from these urban and rural folk, were coming the tens of thousands of men, women, and children—out of England, Scotland, Ulster —who sought the hazard of new fortunes in America.

The Theory of Mercantilism. The political-economic and moral climate out of which the settlers of America came was profoundly influenced by the nature and requirements of the absolute state. Political authoritarianism and royal absolutism were two sides of the same shield. The royal monarch was supreme; and the state apparatus he erected and maintained—through a nationalized church, a court nobility, a mercenary army, a great corps of functionaries and bureaucrats—had as its purpose the perpetuation of dynastic power. This dynastic state-power was linked with the concept of national self-sufficiency. According to the men of the sixteenth, seventeenth, and eighteenth centuries, the wealth of the world was fixed; if England was to prosper, Holland or Spain or France (or all three together) had to be compelled to surrender their possessions. The wars of the period were therefore both dynastic and commercial struggles: so that trading areas could be expanded and the limits of the area of self-sufficiency pushed out.

Not only was the wealth of the world fixed; the wealth of each nation was derived from its foreign trade. Colonies therefore had to be safeguarded against foreign encroachments and permitted to develop only as their economies complemented those of the mother country. In the second place, a nation's foreign trade could expand—at the expense of its rivals—only as it kept its costs of production at home at low levels. The wealth of the nation was to be found in its labor supply engaged in the production of goods and services for export; and the size, docility, and poverty of its workers (the period referred to them collectively as "The Poor") made possible the riches of the whole body politic.

The Morality of Mercantilism. Out of this conception flowed extraordinary moral and social consequences. The poor were needed and they were assured the right to work—by apprenticeship laws, labor contracts, guild restrictions; but they also had the duty to labor. Public authority used persuasion and discipline; in the last resort—through the institution of the workhouse, established in England at the end of the seventeenth century—it used coercion and punishment. Work was demanded; but the worker was held in contempt. He was kept badly fed, ill clad, and wretchedly housed, while lay and ecclesiastical moralists constantly called attention to his improvidence and his want of industry. Arthur Young, toward the end of the eighteenth century, summed up the traditional attitude toward the English poor in these words: "Every one but an idiot knows that the lower classes must be kept poor or they will never be industrious." And a contemporary of his, William Temple, in order to achieve this result, advocated a fully rounded program which included workhouses, the reduction of real wages, and positive encouragement to population growth.[5]

These programs and attitudes of the absolutist and authoritarian state of the sixteenth, seventeenth and eighteenth centuries we call today the Mercantilist System. The state sought to achieve them through a variety of policies.

Mercantilist Unification. One of these was through national unification. The crown waged an unceasing war against the particularism of the towns and the feudal landlords. It brought the guilds under national control—as in England, through the Statute of Artificers—or used

them as agencies of regulation, as in France. It broke down the internal barriers to trade and established a royal system of justice.

Mercantilist Protectionism. Another of these was through protectionism. The crown sought to encourage the development of a favorable trade balance by stimulating the export industries, preventing the appearance of foreign finished goods in the domestic markets, and giving the country's merchant marine special advantages. At home, in the domestic industries, there was set up a ramified scheme of public regulation, intervention, and participation. The crown imported artisans; it granted bounties; and it created elaborate codes for the supervision of those industries whose wares moved into foreign trade.[6]

Mercantilist Bullionism. Another of these was through bullionism. The increase of the money stocks of the nation was to be encouraged; the chief method for obtaining precious metals was through a favorable balance of trade. Soldiers and adventurers stripped conquered peoples of their gold and silver and forced them to buy the goods of the mother country instead of manufacturing their own. While, it is true that in eighteenth century England monetary theory became somewhat more subtle—so that the outflow of specie to the Far East was permitted under limitations, and

[5] For a full exposition of these concepts of the rights and duties of the poor, see E. S. Furniss, *Position of the Laborer in a System of Nationalism* (Boston, 1920). The rights of the poor, in England, were set forth in the great Statute of Artificers, passed in Elizabeth's reign in 1563. The medieval apprenticeship period of 7 years was extended to most of the highly skilled industries; labor contracts were to run for at least a year; and the local justices of the peace were given the power to fix minimum (and also maximum) wages.

[6] These regulations assured the quality of English wares in the foreign markets, but they also protected privileged producers at home. The statutes affecting the woolen industry prescribed the length, breadth, and weight of the various kinds of textiles; provided for governmental inspection and governmental seals; prohibited the use of new machines; and, in order to curb the growth of enterprise and check competition, forbade fullers and finishers to employ weavers in their establishments. The same attitude prevailed toward other industries. To quote Nef: "An attempt was made to fix the size of bricks, statutes were passed regulating the quality of the malt and the hops used in brewing. . . . The authority of the crown was being used to fix the number of producers, as well as to fix the prices of their products and to prescribe their methods of production. Restrictions on the number of enterprises were imposed in industries such as printing, brewing, iron-ore smelting, sugar-refining, brick and tile making . . . a well as in . . . the manufacture of alum, glass, and gunpowder. . . ." ("Industry and Government in France and England, 1540–1640," *op. cit.*, pp. 29–30.)

greater emphasis was placed upon the circulation of money rather than its physical quantity—nevertheless trade and employment continued to be linked with the idea of an adequate money supply.

Mercantilist Monopoly. Another of these was through monopoly. Starting under Elizabeth, the refinements of monopoly operations under James I and Charles I became increasingly subtle. Initially, the crown charged fixed annual rents for the monopoly privileges it granted. Then it imposed a royalty fee on each item of sale. Monopolies were also disposed of to the highest bidders. In time, they came to cover virtually every aspect of economic enterprise. There were monopolies in the export trade, in the import trade, in the domestic trade, and in many fields of manufacture. In this last, the monopolies were particularly oppressive because they, unlike the monopolies of the corporate guilds, were established on a national scale. To uphold the crown, the Court of Star Chamber was permitted to take jurisdiction over patents and monopolies on the ground that infringement constituted a contempt of the royal prerogative.

Mercantilist Colonialism. Still another was through colonialism. The crown chartered trading companies and gave them the right to found colonies; it also sent armies overseas to pacify native populations. Elaborate regulations were drawn up to compel the colonial peoples to produce raw materials required by the mother country and to absorb the finished goods the mother country turned out in surplus. Here, too, balances were to be paid in specie, even if colonies were stripped of their coin and forced to suffer deflation and ensuing hard times.

The Heritage of the Settlers. Out of such a background, the settlers of the New World emerged; part of Europe's tradition and institutions they left behind, part they carried along with them as a living heritage. They were escaping from the tyranny of an authoritarian state and an authoritarian church: the separation of Church and State was one of America's important contributions to the concept of liberty.[7] They were escaping from the tyranny of the village and the restrictions of the guild system. They were escaping from engrossing landlords and mercantile and industrial monopolists. They were escaping from a morality which debased the common man and made him the victim of a theory of political-economic power that linked the wealth of the nation with his own poverty. The European villages, guilds, copyhold tenures, and monopolies were not carried across the seas.

Yet the settlers, notably the English, came with a heavy intellectual and institutional baggage, even if their purses and packs were light. They brought Protestantism, which invested with dignity the individual and his rationality and made his personal striving the basis of a Christian life. They brought the Rule of Law, to defend men and their minds from the oppression of a royal prerogative and the awful authority of star chamber and inquisitional courts. Judiciaries were to be free bodies engaged in protecting the rights and liberties of the citizens. They brought the doctrine of the higher law—that the law of God and of nature was superior to those emanating from human authority—and later, they were to write this principle into the Declaration of Independence. They brought a constitutional theory based on popular sovereignty and the supremacy of the legislature. The English Constitution, representative government, trial by jury, free speech, a free press, religious toleration and freedom, local self-government, the sanctity and freedom of private property; these were some of the ideas and ideologies that did cross the ocean to take firm root in America.[8]

[7] For the first time in modern history, church and state were separated in the four colonies of Rhode Island, Delaware, New Jersey, and Pennsylvania. One of the great achievements of the American Revolution was the extension of the idea, which was incorporated into the First Amendment of the Constitution. By the end of the first quarter of the nineteenth century, there were no state-supported churches anywhere in the United States.

[8] F. A. Hayek, *The Road to Serfdom* (Chicago, 1944), p. 72: "Nothing distinguishes more clearly conditions

What they brought was largely, although not entirely, derived from the English cultural pattern. A passion for the land and a close identification with it was northern European rather than English in origin. The idea of group loyalty came with the Irish and the Scotch-

in a free country from those in a country under arbitrary government than the observance in the former of the great principles known as the Rule of Law. Stripped of all technicalities, this means that government in all its actions is bound by rules fixed and announced beforehand—rules which make it possible to foresee with fair certainty how the authority will use its coercive powers in given circumstances and to plan one's individual affairs on the basis of this knowledge." Hayek quotes A. V. Dicey's classical exposition (*The Law of the Constitution*, 8th ed., p. 198): The Rule of Law "means, in the first place, the absolute supremacy or predominance of regular law as opposed to the influence of arbitrary power, and excludes the existence of arbitrariness, of prerogative, or even of wide discretionary authority on the part of government." See also L. M. Hacker, *The Triumph of American Capitalism* (New York, 1940), pp. 79–81, for the results of the Puritan Revolution.

Irish. Dutch, Swedish, and German architecture, household furnishings, cookery, and words were also transplanted in America. But for the most part the forms of living and acting together were English in origin. Why was this? Most important, of course, was the fact that the English-speaking groups made up the great majority of the settlers in the seventeenth century. In the eighteenth century, the Germans, who emigrated in such large numbers, came from a disunited land in which there were no common experiences of nation or people; and they came as the victims of persecution, war, and starvation. In the second place, particularly in the eighteenth century as a result of the tightening of the Mercantilist system, economic —and also, intellectual and social—intercourse was with the United Kingdom exclusively. English thinking, English books, English manners and habits therefore continued as living forces.

3. *THE EARLY SETTLERS OF AMERICA*

The American Physical Scene. The original voyagers and adventurers to America expected to find a populous land and treasure troves. Instead, they encountered a vast and silent continent clothed in an unbroken forest that was entered through the valleys of short rivers. The climate was vitalizing; the succession of the four seasons made possible the planning and growing of food crops; rainfall was adequate; in many sections bog deposits of iron abounded. Not immediate luxury was their portion, but hard work; and from their unremitting physical toil they created a greater wealth than had the Portuguese in the eastern islands or the Spaniards in Mexico and Peru.

Nature showered its riches on the pioneers of America. With their first implements of conquest—the axe, gun, fishing tackle—they were able to sustain life. The axe cut a clearing in the dense forests and supplied wood for fuel and for dwellings, fences, ships, tools, and household utensils. In the clearings they planted

corn, beans, squash, and sweet potatoes—all acquired from the Indians. Later, the small grains brought over from Europe were sown. In the south they planted tobacco. Their guns kept marauding Indians at a distance and shot down the deer, bear, turkeys, and other wild life of the forest. In this way the settlers obtained meat, hides, and furs. From the eastern end of Long Island out into the Atlantic as far as the Great Bank of Newfoundland was to be found one of the world's great fishing grounds. Here the mighty cod was caught as well as mackerel, herring, bass, halibut, and sturgeon.

The Indians. The original settlers were fortunate in still another sense. The American continent was populated by Indians, but so sparsely that white colonization and advancing settlement could not be retarded. In 1630, it has been estimated, the Indians north of Mexico did not number more than 1,000,000. In the east, particularly, those encountered by the English were broken up into many tribes, which were divided by language differences and long-standing feuds over hunting grounds. These Indians were already fairly well advanced as far as agriculture was concerned, although foodstuffs were supplemented by and clothing was dependent upon hunting and trapping. Living in villages, the Indians had succeeded in domesticating corn, squash, and beans; but they had no domesticated animals.

Initially friendly to the white man (Indians helped the early Jamestown and Plymouth settlements survive), the American aborigines were turned into enemies as a result of ceaseless pressure on their lands. The Spaniards, to the south, had brought the more numerous tribesmen under control through conquest, missionary effort, and intermarriage. In the Spanish, and also in the French, possessions, there was a greater intermingling of cultures. Not so in the case of the English. Because they were settlers, requiring land, they carried on a steady and ruthless attack on the Indians. Trade goods—cloth, guns and ammunition, ironware, trinkets—originally was the basis of the fur traffic, as a result of which the settlers obtained the pelts the Indians had hunted and trapped. It soon was discovered that the Indians had a weakness for strong liquor, and rum became an important device in breaking down their resistance. They were tricked into signing away their tribal lands; frequently, too, under the influence of rum, they challenged the white men—only to be defeated in the long run with many deaths on both sides.

Thus the Indians were conquered. But they left their impress on the young civilization growing in the wilderness. Because the Indians were so few, the settlers' insatiable appetite for freeholds of land could be satisfied. The settlers also learned to cultivate the corn-beans-squash cycle. From the Indians they got tobacco. The Indians opened up the back country with their trails and their light canoes made the utilization of the inland waters easy. The fur traders followed the Indians into the interior and the pioneering farmers were not far behind the traders. Thus the process continued, until

the end of the nineteenth century saw the frontier gone, a good part of the available free lands preempted, and the Indians rounded up in reservations where they remained the wards of the Federal government.

Companies and Proprietors. Into the wilderness of America came capital and men—the results of individual and private enterprise. True, the English colonies were regarded as the possessions of the crown, and crown charters and patents made their settlement possible. The only English colony on the mainland to have been initiated directly through the royal power was Georgia; certain others were obtained through conquest—Jamaica, New York, Nova Scotia, ultimately the whole of Canada. But most of them were planted because individuals, alone or in companies, sought to enrich themselves by the exploitation of the new domain overseas or because they were looking for religious and civil liberties. Of the latter type were the settlements established by the Pilgrims at Plymouth, by Roger Williams and Anne Hutchinson in Rhode Island, by John Wheelwright and John Underhill in New Hampshire, by Thomas Hooker in the Connecticut Valley, by the German Pietists in Pennsylvania, and by the Huguenots and Jews in Maryland and the Carolinas.

In the hunt for private gain, two agencies were employed. One was the chartered company—used in the founding and settlement of Virginia, Plymouth, and Massachusetts Bay by the English, New Amsterdam by the Dutch, and New Sweden along the Delaware by the Swedes. The other was the proprietorship—used in the establishment of Maryland, Pennsylvania, the Carolinas, and New Jersey.

The promoters of the Virginia settlement had been associated with earlier joint-stocks, when, in 1606, a company made up of some two hundred persons received a charter from the crown to develop the trade of and colonize a portion of America.[9] Between 1609 and 1619, the com-

[9] Actually, the Virginia Company's charter called for the functioning of two groups, known as the London and Plymouth companies. To the "adventurers" of

pany sent out about 1,500 settlers. Failing in its original hope of discovering and working precious metal deposits, the Virginia Company turned to the creation of "plantations."

Under this scheme, the colonists—as company employees—were to be expected to labor for seven years on company enterprises, the profits to go to the stockholders. They were, in other words, to produce pitch, tar, soap ashes, hemp, iron, steel, and glass, as well as their own food. These industrial activities proved unsuccessful and the "plantations" turned to the cultivation of tobacco. But in an agricultural economy it was hard to withstand the demand for freeholds; the "plantation" device therefore was soon abandoned. The company's lands were distributed: among its shareholders, among the servants who had signed up for the seven-year terms, and among such new "adventurers" as were ready to bring capital and laborers of their own into the colony. The company itself found it impossible to survive and in 1624 its charter was withdrawn. It had invested almost £90,000 in the promotion; the only profits its stockholders received were land grants. But it had founded a great colony and it had firmly established the idea of private property in land, and the culture of the tobacco plant.

The humble Pilgrims were Separatists who had cut themselves off from the Church of England. They were settled at Plymouth because a joint-stock, subscribed to by 70 London merchants, had raised £7,000 to finance their voyage. A "plantation" here, too, was set up; it was also unsuccessful. In 1627, the London merchants relinquished their claims on the colony for £1,800; the obligation to pay this sum was assumed by the leaders of the colony, and in fifteen years the debt was discharged through the sale of furs, forest products, and fish. These colonists also became freeholders.

London were given the rights to trade and colonize between the 34th and 41st parallels; to the "adventurers" of Bristol, Exeter, and Plymouth were given similar rights in the region between the 38th and 45th parallels. The area between the 38th and 41st parallels was open to both, under certain conditions. In 1609, the London and Plymouth companies were separated.

The settlers of Massachusetts received a charter from the crown but the company's capital was largely raised from among the colonists themselves. Because, in considerable part, these Puritans originated from the yeomanry of England, they were able to bring livestock, agricultural implements, and housefurnishings along with them. The company management, too, was transplanted overseas. No "plantation" system was established here; nor were trading and land operations conducted on a joint-stock basis. It has been estimated that the immediate expenses incurred in the establishment of Massachusetts Bay came to about £200,000. Here, too, the colonists became freeholders; and they became interested in fish and furs almost at once.

The proprietary colonies sprang from the desire of their owners—the recipients of the crown grants—to build up fortunes from the establishment of private estates (to be worked by tenants and laborers) and from the sale of land. Although, to a certain extent, the feudal land-relationship was preserved in the payment of quitrents, the proprietors were given the right to alienate, hypothecate, devise, or convey in trust the whole or parts of the territories given to them. Property, as the legal phrase is, was allodial instead of feudal. Therefore, the Calverts of Maryland, the Penns of Pennsylvania, Ashley and his associates in the Carolinas, and Carteret and Berkeley in New Jersey, were landlords, land jobbers, and capitalist promoters, and not feudal lords. To the Calverts and the Penns, the proprietaries undoubtedly were profitable. Their own investments encouraged others with money to migrate to and develop properties in their colonies. Both families also obtained sizable sums from the quitrents, which became a kind of general property tax.

These English colonies, both on the mainland and on the islands, in time turned out to be very successful, notably from the mercantilist point of view. The forests of the New World furnished masts and naval stores, releasing England from its dependence upon Russia and the Baltic States for these products. The island colonies grew coffee, oranges, lemons, pepper and ginger; and the Eastern trade, with its drain of the precious metals, no longer became all-important. These island colonies also supplied England with cabinet woods. The mainland colonies produced whale products (oil and fins), fish, furs and skins, and potashes, pearl ashes, and saltpeter. Some iron was exported and much rice and indigo. Even more important than these commodities were the great surpluses of sugar (the product of the island colonies) and tobacco (the product of Maryland and Virginia), which were carried to England for either home consumption or reexport. Back to the colonies moved a steady stream of manufactured goods—iron ware, textiles, notions, chinaware, housefurnishings, paper, and books. The handling of this two-way commerce employed the capital and the energies of a great number of English shipowners, brokers, commission men, financiers, processers, and manufacturers. When the Revolution broke out, the English colonies in America were consuming one third of all the English goods entering into foreign trade.

The Settlers. Who came to America? The hard times that characterized the English economy of the 1620s and 1630s and the uncertainties and instabilities that flowed from the absolutist and authoritarian rule of the early Stuart kings, prompted many solid burghers and country squires to seek escape in emigration. These middle classes had their representatives in Massachusetts Bay and Connecticut, and also in Maryland, Virginia, and the Carolinas. The same classes made up a sizable part of the Dutch settlers in New York and of the Huguenots in the Carolinas, the Jews in Rhode Island, and the English Quakers in Pennsylvania.

In particular, America offered a haven to the members of the lower middle classes—those who were finding themselves the victims of disordered economic and civil processes. The enclosure movement and the cruel vagabondage laws had many victims in the rural countryside. The guilds more and more were shutting their doors to the humble. The Thirty Years' War in the seventeenth century had ravaged a good part of central Europe and left it a smoking ruin. On a smaller scale, the story was repeated a century later when Louis XIV's armies laid waste the German Palatinate. Religious intolerance forced the Huguenots out of France and the Pietists out of Germany. Mercantilist proscriptions against the manufacture of woolens, the decline of their linen industry, the ancient and oppressive land laws, and church tithes drove the Presbyterian Scotch-Irish out of Ulster in Ireland. Lower middle-class Englishmen streamed out of England in the seventeenth century: between 1607 and 1640, from 50,000 to 70,000 persons moved overseas. Their fellow Germans and Scotch-Irish—as many as 75,000 Germans and 150,000 Scotch-Irish, perhaps—quit their native and adopted lands for America in the fifty years between 1720 and 1770. Moreover, largely in the eighteenth century, about 250,000 Negro slaves were brought to mainland America.

The exodus of a significant proportion of these emigrants was assisted or forced. How large this proportion was, it is impossible to say. One estimate has it that by 1770 fully one half of the original immigrants came as unfree laborers, these being divided equally between white indentured servants and Negro slaves.

Indentured Servants. An indentured servant was a man or woman—sometimes, even a child—who could not pay his own ocean passage and who therefore bound himself to a contractor (often the ship's captain acting in his own right or as an agent) for a term of years, in order to work off his transportation costs. An indenture, or contract, was usually entered into by both parties and fixed the length of unremunerated service. The period ran from three to seven years for adults; for children it ran until they attained their majority. Upon arrival, the captain sold the contracts to persons requiring laborers: in the seventeenth century, usually to the tobacco planters of Virginia and Maryland; in the eighteenth century, to the farmers of Pennsylvania. The purchaser of the contract—in the seventeenth century—also received a headright, that is to say, a grant of 50 acres for each servant he was responsible for bringing into the colony. In the late seventeenth and the eighteenth century, and more particularly among the German immigrants, the servant simply arranged with the shipmaster that he was to be sold to the highest bidder from an auction block. Such servants were called redemptioners.

When the servants and redemptioners completed their labor terms—for which, of course, they were not paid, receiving only food, clothing and shelter—they were free men. They received "freedom dues"—a small tract of land (this was so in the seventeenth century at any rate), some agricultural implements, a bag of seed, perhaps a cow and a new suit of clothes; and, as a rule, they set themselves up as farmers. By and large, they became absorbed into the numerous lower middle classes of the period— the general farmers, small traders and skilled workers of colonial America.

Not a few of these white servants were forced out of England. The so-called vagabonds and women and children on local parish relief were virtually deported. Up to the 1670s, kidnapping was winked at and tens of thousands of servants were obtained in this fashion. Also, because of the cruelty of the penal code in seventeenth-century England, jails were thronged and therefore had to be emptied out periodically. During the first three quarters of this century as many as 50,000 men, women, and children (whose crimes were largely minor ones) were taken from the jails and transported overseas. Also transported, notably in the Cromwellian period, were Irish and Scotch political prisoners and prisoners of war. From about 1680 on, assisted immigration came less from England itself, and more from Ulster and Germany. The Germans went to Pennsylvania; the Scotch-Irish to Pennsylvania, Maryland, and New Jersey. But soon, a second generation of the Scotch-Irish was to move west into that great interior valley of Eastern America which lies between the Blue Ridge Mountains and the Appalachians and which stretches southward from Pennsylvania clear into Georgia. By

the end of the seventeenth century—except in the case of Pennsylvania—the flow of white indentured servants was tapering off.

Negro Slaves. This decline came about not because the planters of Virginia and Maryland required fewer field hands, but simply because, from about 1675 on, they began to use Negro slaves in sizable quantities. Negro slaves, of course, offered many advantages over white servants: they were property and not a laboring force; they could not escape very easily; their women could be worked in the fields along with the men. Moreover, the movement of Negroes to the New World was regularized as a result of the appearance of the Royal African Company in 1672 and the South Sea Company in 1710.

Native African chieftains became integral parts of the slavery system, selling their prisoners of war and sometimes their own tribesmen to the white traders. Originally the merchants of Bristol and Liverpool dominated the traffic, and the trade goods were textiles and ironware. But when American slavers entered the scene in the eighteenth century, the trade goods became largely bar iron and rum. Thus there developed that extraordinary triangular trade that linked the northern mainland colonies, the West India sugar islands, and the African Guinea coast in a single chain. To the West Indies went Connecticut Valley and Long Island flour, packed meats, fish, barrel staves, and live animals. Back to the distilleries of Massachusetts and Rhode Island went sugar and molasses to be made into rum. Over the sea went the rum and bar iron to Africa. And from Africa across the Middle Passage to the Caribbean sailed the slavers—little vessels of 100 to 200 tons burden—packed with their human cargo.

The growing of sugar in the West Indies and that of tobacco, rice, and indigo in the Southern mainland colonies expanded greatly in the eighteenth century; and, as the market grew, prices for Negro slaves advanced. In the 1690s, the price for a prime field hand—a male between the ages of 18 and 30—was £18 to £25;

in 1770, it was £50 to £80. Negro slavery was not inefficient; under the gang-labor system, as it was practiced in sugar and rice cultivation, it turned out to be a highly profitable means of production. And as for tobacco—a soil-depleting crop—the presence of large quantities of virgin land made possible the postponement of diminishing returns from slave labor for a long time. In fact, it was not until after the Revolutionary War was over that, in Virginia and Maryland, tobacco began to give way to general farming. It should also be remembered that the Negroes were capital—and this accounts for the continuance of slavery long after the use of slaves on the land was no longer worth while economically; through the breeding of young Negroes, the planter's capital fund was being added to regularly. In Pennsylvania, many Negroes were employed on the so-called iron plantations, which were located in the country because charcoal was so important as the basic fuel. In Rhode Island, plantations growing cereals and cattle used slave labor extensively. Otherwise, in the northern colonies, the Negroes were primarily house servants and unskilled workers. In the middle of the eighteenth century, there were about 500,000 Negro slaves in the mainland colonies, of whom about 116,000 were in Virginia and 104,000 in Maryland and the Carolinas.

4. EARLY ECONOMIC ACTIVITIES

Coming from rural backgrounds as they did, and being made up of the rural dispossessed in such great numbers, it was natural that most of the immigrants should seek land. Right through the colonial period the American economy was largely an agricultural one; in fact, at the time of the Revolution, nine out of every ten of its people lived in the country. Various systems of land settlement and land tenure were established, usually following regional patterns. In New England, settlements were by communities—the so-called towns—although the village did not play the same institutional role that it did in England and on the Continent. Freehold tenure was also established. In the Southern and Middle colonies, settlement was on a family-farm basis. While, however, land was held as a freehold or a leasehold, quitrents had to be paid to the proprietors (or to the crown, wherever it succeeded them). In the Hudson Valley of New York, the original Dutch grantees, called patroons, set up large estates on which a tenure approximating the copyhold (hereditary leases, fixed rents, and alienation fines upon transfer) was installed. The English tried to continue copyhold tenure here—and it was the only colony where this was done significantly—when they replaced the Dutch.

Land Tenure and Land Laws. In the seventeenth century, particularly, there was a good deal of conflict over the land. Land monopolists tried to appear in all the regions and little men had to fight for their rights. In New England, the original town fathers tried to preempt for themselves the undistributed lands of the towns and there were many disputes over these so-called commons. In New York, where the patroonships had been established, six great manors in Westchester county took in one half of the whole region. In Pennsylvania, William Penn, in order to attract immigrants from lands outside England, sold farms at low prices and also granted headrights for the transportation of laborers. But his heirs raised the prices, so that, at the time of the Revolution, at least two thirds of the inhabitants of the colony were squatters. In the Southern colonies great estates were created; and in order to maintain these properties intact, some of the English land institutions were brought over. Here, entail (under which the heirs received only a life interest in the family properties) and primogeniture (by which the inheritance of real property went entirely to the first-born) were introduced.

Thus, a gentry made its appearance, copying the attitudes of the English country gentle-man, and a great middle-class yeomanry also emerged. There were no peasants in America. Land companies quickly appeared to sell free-holds at low prices in the back country; squat-ters on crown and proprietary lands defied—usually with success—law officers to evict them; tenancy was of the ladder variety, as we have come to call it in the United States. In other words, it was a temporary rung in the climb upward from farm laborer to freeholder. Dif-fusion of land ownership and freehold tenure were the two significant characteristics of land settlement in America; and nothing more dis-tinctively set America apart from Europe than these facts.

Before we examine the nature of the agri-cultural economy, it would be well to look briefly at the extractive industries that sprang up.

In a new country, it is inevitable that the first preoccupation of enterprise should be with the exploitation of natural resources. Not only is agriculture originally exploitative—because of the dearth of capital and the dearness of labor—but the same is true of the working of other raw materials. But the new land of America had great natural wealth among its resources; so that depletion was a long, although, it is true, a cumulative process. We are to see the workers in the fur, lumbering, shipbuilding, ironmaking, fishing, and milling industries—those that one would naturally expect to exist in the Ameri-can environment—originally as farmers who also labored in the forest and on the sea. Their functioning in these pursuits was occasional and sporadic. And then, as settlements filled up, markets developed, and resources became more difficult to work, specialization set in. The iron-masters, shipwrights, lumbermen, and millers—investing capital in plants, hiring workers, em-ploying credit—became full-time businessmen. If they were successful, they ploughed profits back into plant expansion, so that their busi-nesses grew and concentration began to appear. If unsuccessful, they reverted to agriculture or became wage workers.

The Fur Trade. Colonial America was rich in wild life; and in Europe there was a steady demand for furs and skins. In the Northern colonies, the principal fur-bearing animals were the beaver, otter, bear, raccoon, fox, and mink; in the Southern colonies, they were the rac-coon, fox, and beaver; but in the South, the deer was more important than these three named. As a result, in the North the leading article of trade became the beaver pelt, which was sent to Europe to be made up into hats; and in the South, deerskins, which were made up into leather. In the beginning, it was a simple matter for the pioneering farmer, using his gun and traps, to be his own fur trader. But as farm lands replaced forests and the tide of civiliza-tion pushed inland, the collecting of furs and skins became a more complicated procedure. Increasingly, the Indians became the center of the fur trade. In some regions, they were in-vited to bring their furs to the mansions, or forts, maintained by the fur dealers; in others, dealers sent out their agents into the Indian country to collect the pelts and hides. The Dutch at New Amsterdam (later New York) and Fort Orange (later Albany) used the former method, as did the English colonials in the North generally. The French used the latter, and so did the English colonials in the South. In exchange for their wares the Indians received rum and trade goods. As the years passed, a smaller and smaller company of wealthy men, who were also landlords and mer-chants, came to monopolize the fur business.

The fur trade played an important part in in-ternational and imperial relations. The struggle over it involved England and France in a long series of colonial wars in America. The chief bones of contention were the Iroquois country (central New York) and the northern lands watered by the tributaries of the Ohio (the so-called Wabash and Illinois countries). Further-more, the desire to continue to participate in the fur trade was one of the reasons for colo-nial interest in the wild lands beyond the crest of the Appalachians. With the successful ter-mination of the Seven Years' War in 1763, the

English got rid of their French rivals. But efforts to close the newly gained lands of the West to colonial land promoters and fur dealers brought about suspicion and recriminations; and also helped to precipitate the break between the mother country and the colonies.

Lumbering. It was to be expected that lumbering should engage the attention of the colonists from the start. Everywhere forests abounded; in the Northern colonies they came right down to the sea's edge. In the North, the softwood white pine, cedar and spruce, as well as the hardwood oak stands, were important; in the South, the yellow pine was outstanding. Wood products were at the basis of a settled life. From the forests came the logs and clapboards for dwellings and farm buildings; the posts and poles for fences; the handles for farm implements and tools. Household utensils were made of wood. Trees were burned down into charcoal for use in the iron industry. From the ashes of the hardwoods came the potash and pearl ash which were needed in making soap and treating cloth. The softwoods yielded tar, resin, and pitch—the famous naval stores; and they were also cut up into planks and converted into barrels, staves, hoops, and heads. The shipbuilding industry was based upon the forest resources of the country.

As in the case of the fur industry, the original lumbermen were farmers who worked in their own wood lots and in the ungranted lands. But the forests kept on retreating; increasingly, therefore, the operators became millowners who erected their plants near fall-river lines, used water power, and installed power-driven saws. Lumbering became localized in the northern New England coast region from Boston to the Kennebec River in Maine, and also in New Hampshire, the Hudson Valley of New York, Pennsylvania, and North Carolina. South Carolina became the chief center for the production of naval stores.

Shipbuilding. Colonial shipbuilding became a significant industry. Shipyards sprang up along the New England coast—from Massachusetts to Maine—and were also to be found in New York and Philadelphia. In the seventeenth century, Boston and Salem were the leading building centers, and, as far as smaller vessels were concerned, continued to hold their preeminence into the eighteenth century. In the decades before the Revolution, Philadelphia became more important for the construction of larger ships.

A variety of reasons account for the importance of shipbuilding in America's early economy. The fishing industry depended upon it. Shipping did not become an independent business until the nineteenth century; the earlier merchants had to own their own ships. Wrecks and losses from brigandage were high because piracy continued to flourish on the Spanish Main (Caribbean Sea) until the seventeenth century and in the Mediterranean and Red Seas throughout the eighteenth century. Ships were very small: having limited capital, the owners had to diversify their risks among a number of vessels; the art of port improvement was in its infancy; and, as interior roads were few, transatlantic ships must be small enough to go right up the Connecticut River to Hartford, for example. Boats in the fishing industry were not more than 10 tons; those in the West India trade ran from 24 to 60 tons; and those in the transatlantic trade averaged about 125 tons.

Colonial shipyards were encouraged by the mother country because of its own failing timber supply. Skilled shipwrights were permitted to emigrate; bounties were offered for the making of yards and masts in 1705 and 1709; and in the 1720s England refused to yield before the clamor of its own shipbuilders that the importation of American vessels be stopped. Consequently, at the outbreak of the Revolution, at least 75 percent of the colonial foreign trade moved in American bottoms; and at least 30 percent of the whole English merchant marine had been constructed in American yards.

Fishing and Whaling. The colonials—the New Englanders particularly—became fishermen from the very beginning. Their soil was inhospitable and the raising of meat products was therefore difficult. Moreover, many had been trained in the fishing fleets of the English West Country. They fished to eat and they fished to sell. They fished mackerel, bass, herring, halibut, sturgeon and, above all, the mighty cod. Boston, Gloucester, and Salem were the leading fishing centers in the seventeenth century; Ipswich, Yarmouth, Chatham and notably Marblehead joined their company in the eighteenth century.

At first, operations were on a small scale and seamen shared in the catches with owners. Before the first half of the seventeenth century was over, West Country rivals had been driven out of the New England home waters; and, as the market expanded, New Englanders themselves ventured out to the Newfoundland Banks, the Nova Scotia coast, and the St. Lawrence Gulf. Ships became larger; and outfitting and provisioning them for long journeys required fairly large capital funds. Therefore, Boston and Salem merchants bought shares in the ships and began to handle the trade at both ends. They sent up cargoes of salt, tackle, packed meats, lumber, and rum to the Newfoundland fisherman (who were English, French, and Colonial); and they moved the packed and salted fish into foreign trade. The better grades of fish (so-called merchantable) were sold to the Catholic countries of Spain, Portugal, Italy, and Ireland and to the Madeira and Canary Islands. The poorer grades (so-called refuse) went to the West Indies as the basic food of the Negro slaves working on the sugar plantations. By the end of the seventeenth century, New England's exports of fish exceeded those of the mother country. In the decade before the Revolution, there were 665 vessels in New England fishing fleets and another 350 vessels that carried the fish into foreign commerce.

The hunting of whales was another enterprise linked with the fisheries. Whales were common off the New England coast and in the beginning they were harpooned and towed to shore, where their oil was extracted. This oil was the chief source of illuminants and lubricants up to the appearance of petroleum products in the 1850s. The whalebone (called fins) was largely exported to be made into buttons, supports for stays, and the like. Plymouth, Salem, the eastern Long Island towns and, most important of all, Nantucket, became the center of the industry. Beginning with the second quarter of the eighteenth century, as the whaling grounds spread out as far as the eastern South American coast and even into the Arctic, the whalers became larger. Before the revolution, at least 360 vessels were employed in the industry; and something like 4,000 tons of whale oil was being shipped annually to England.

The Milling Industries. Flour milling became an industry early in colonial times. Mills were to be found on the many small streams existing all over the colonies. In the beginning, the miller was also a farmer. He ground the grain for his neighbors for a proportion of the meal, receiving in New England about one twelfth of the meal and in the South, about one sixth. Soon, however, grains began to be produced in surplus, and a large foreign market developed for flour. The Connecticut Valley produced small surpluses for the West India trade; notably New York and Pennsylvania became great granaries from which grains and flour moved into commerce. Milling operations therefore expanded and the miller became a full-fledged businessman. He increased the size of his plant; he erected a bolting plant (to remove the impurities from the meal); he put up a cooperage works (to pack his own flour); and sometimes he added bake ovens. And because he was paid in meal and flour, the next step was to become a shipper in his own right. In the Connecticut Valley, on Long Island, and in Philadelphia, particularly, the functions of these businessmen began to multiply. They ground malt and made paper out of linen rags. They handled local grain on commission and sold bolted flour in the domestic and West India markets. They operated retail stores (sometimes in a chain), where they traded foreign wares for country produce. And they became local private bankers, advancing store credit to their customers on notes and farm credit on mortgages.

The Iron Industry. Iron production was a significant industry in colonial America but it turned out for the most part heavy iron. Hardware as we understand it—cutlery, finer tools (as well as wire and pins)—was not manufactured here; in fact, it ranked next to textiles as the outstanding import from England. The existence of bog-iron deposits everywhere and of surface outcroppings of ore veins in Virginia, Maryland, and Pennsylvania quickly attracted attention to the possibilities of iron exploitation. Early experiments with ironworks—in Virginia in 1622 and in Massachusetts in 1641—were failures. By the eighteenth century, however, there were many forges and furnaces in Virginia, Maryland, New York, New Jersey, and Massachusetts.

It was Pennsylvania, however, that became the great iron center of colonial America. The industry was organized around the so-called plantation. The ironmaster, that is to say, lived and worked in the country, and he was also, therefore, a miller, an orchardist, a grain grower, and a sheepherder. Why was he a country man? Small ironworks were erected near ore veins and limestone beds; when these were exhausted superficially—for shaft-mining did not become common until the nineteenth century—the furnaces and forges were abandoned. Furthermore, the basic fuel mixed with the ore and limestone was charcoal, made from the burning of wood. It was important, therefore, that ironmaking take place in heavily forested regions. The industry was never adequately capitalized, and the problem of obtaining working capital was particularly vexatious. As a result, the ironmaster was compelled to domicile his workers and pay them wages in truck out of his own store—in meal and flour, cloth, shoes, rum, bacon, molasses, and notions.

A Pennsylvania plantation ran to several thousands of acres of land. Here were the mines, the charcoal houses, the homes of the workers, the store and office of the master, the farm buildings, the gristmill and sawmill—and the furnace and the forge. The blast furnace produced pig iron and out of this was cast hollow ware—that is to say, pots, pans, stove plates, and firebacks. The forge was used to refine and hammer the pig iron into blooms, or bars, and these were sold to blacksmiths—as so-called merchant iron—to be made into axes, hoes, shovels, chains, and scythes. For finer purposes, bar iron was sold to various kinds of mills located in the towns. Slitting mills made nails. Plating mills hammered bar iron into sheet iron. Steel furnaces fabricated small amounts of blister steel for the manufacture of tools. But the wrought-iron industry was a small one in colonial America.

The capital for the Pennsylvania industry came usually from slow accumulations or from the profits of commerce. Philadelphia merchants bought partnerships in ironworks or built their own plants to be run by managers. Properties were frequently very large. In the 1770s, for example, the Durham Iron Works sold for £12,000. Because England needed heavy iron badly, mercantilist policy did not frown on the investment of overseas capital in American ironworks. Two spectacular ventures were embarked on in the middle of the eighteenth century—one by Peter Hasenclever in New York and New Jersey and the other by William Henry Stiegel in Pennsylvania—but both failed. One was successful: the Principio Company of Maryland, launched in 1724 with English capital and in which George Washington's father was interested. In time it acquired 30,000 acres of ore lands and owned many furnaces and forges; at the outbreak of the Revolution its properties were worth £100,000.

After the 1720s, the American iron industry began to attract English attention but, because of the struggle between the English ironmongers and the English ironmasters, thirty years were to elapse before a policy was devised. The ironmongers sought the encouragement of colonial ironworks so that they might get their pigs, bars, and blooms cheaply in America; the ironmasters sought to eliminate this competition and demanded that insurmountable barriers be erected. While the Parliament debated, colonials—during the 1740s—began to build rolling and slitting mills and plating forges of their own. England took alarm, and in 1750 the Iron Act was passed in the interests of her ironmongers: American pigs were placed on the free list and bars could enter the port of London duty free; also, the erection of new slitting and rolling mills, plating forges, and steel furnaces was forbidden. Exports, to England, however, failed to expand.

5. COLONIAL AGRICULTURE

In addition to growing crops to feed themselves and their livestock, the colonial farmers soon began to produce surpluses for local and distant markets. That is, the great colonial staple producers—the tobacco planters of Maryland and Virginia, the rice growers of South Carolina, the wheat farmers of New York and Pennsylvania—were also general farmers. They raised corn, beans, and peas, as well as cattle, hogs, and poultry, and they also engaged in orcharding. They entered the market for the purchase of foods and feeds to a much lesser extent than is true today.

With these qualifications, we may, nevertheless, say that specialization existed in colonial agriculture. From 1612 on, when the first tobacco harvest was brought in, tobacco was the great money crop of American agriculture. Its cultivation spread through the whole of Virginia and Maryland and into a part of North Carolina. This tobacco was sold to London and, later, too, to outport merchants (Bristol, Liverpool, Plymouth and Glasgow). From England and Scotland as much as 90 percent of it was reexported to the European continent. The second great money crop was wheat, and here, too, there was specialization functionally and regionally. In the seventeenth century, a good deal of surplus wheat was raised in New England's Connecticut Valley. In the eighteenth century, however, the Middle colonies of New York, New Jersey, and Pennsylvania became colonial America's rich granary. A third money crop was rice, produced in South Carolina, Georgia, and a stretch of the North Carolina coastal plain. With it—for the growing seasons complemented each other—on the same plantations appeared indigo. Both of these were developments of the eighteenth century and were ideal mercantilist crops, rice going to the mother country and also to southern Europe, and indigo going to the mother country to serve the requirements of the important cloth-making industry.

New England Farming. Diversified agriculture, in a commercial sense, appeared everywhere. By the eighteenth century, even in New England with its stubborn soil, cash crops were being produced. Beef cattle, hogs, and work animals were being raised. Dairying and sheepherding, on a small scale, were engaging farmers. And country produce—cheeses, dried fruits, flaxseed, honey—was being collected by the retail storekeepers of the Connecticut Valley for sale in New York and Boston. In addition to wheat specialization, the farmers of the Middle colonies produced beef and pork and work animals—and these products, too, were being sent into local and foreign markets.

Of the three regions, as far as agricultural developments was concerned, it was New England that lagged behind. This was not simply due to a difficult terrain; nor was it caused by ignorance of scientific agriculture. New Englanders knew of the work of the great English innovators Tull, Bakewell, Coke and Townshend, who, in the mother country in the seventeenth and eighteenth centuries, had been the leaders of a profound agricultural revolution. But the introduction of such innovations required an intensive husbandry and a large labor supply; and labor was dear in colonial America. Therefore, colonial New Englanders found that returns on capital were likely to be greater from investments in ship-building and the fishing, molasses, rum, and slave trades.

We are to see the typical New England farmer engaged in general farming, utilizing extensive tillage, and producing surpluses in relatively small quantities to satisfy requirements for cash. Yet, when all the surplus crops entering the market were put together, they made up a very large amount of goods. The New England farm had been created by long and bitter labor. The trees of the original forests had to be girdled first to kill them; they were then cut down and their stumps were pulled up. The glacial stones also had to be removed. In the clearings, Indian corn was planted. This crop was the salvation of the pioneering farmer; for the land did not have to be thoroughly plowed to receive the grain, and because it was cultivated in hills it could be planted among the tree stumps. Its growing season was short; its yield, in proportion to seed, was great; and it was an ideal food for man and beast. With corn, beans could be grown, for the vines run up the stalks; while pumpkin seeds were sown between the corn plants. The stalks, too, were cut and employed as animal fodder.

After the land had been entirely cleared and thoroughly turned over, the New England farmer was likely to plant the small grains, that is to say, rye, barley, oats, buckwheat, and wheat. Wheat was the most important, because of the presence of a market for flour. In this case, the growing season was longer and the tasks more difficult. The size of the crop was based upon the amount of grain the farmer and his sons could cut by hand, the average productivity being five acres per person. When the cradle scythe was introduced, toward the end of the colonial period, productivity per person was doubled, a remarkable achievement indeed.

The usual complement of livestock was to be found. Horses and oxen were raised for the home ploughing, although in the eighteenth century sizable quantities of work animals were being exported out of New England into the West India trade. Beef and dairy cattle and hogs also abounded. No effort was made at scientific breeding. The animals were small, their meat tough, and the dairy cows gave little milk. Such as was obtained was used for conversion into butter and cheese. The hogs, in particular, were more closely linked to their ancestors, the wild boars, than to the great porkers of modern times. Fierce, quick animals with long legs, they were permitted to forage for themselves in the forests and the harvested fields. During the eighteenth century, in particular areas, notably in the Connecticut Valley and in the Narragansett country of Rhode Island, a larger preoccupation with meat animals began to appear. Cattle were being fattened for market (usually on corn; by a few more advanced farmers on timothy, the first artificial grass grown in America) and turned over to drovers who brought them into Boston and New York. The animals were slaughtered and packed for the West India trade.

Except for the Rhode Island plantations, New England farms were small, running from 10 to 100 acres. A 200-acre farm was a large property. In eastern New England, original settlements were in villages with arable fields unfenced, although strips were owned in fee simple. But strip tillage was abandoned before the seventeenth century was over and farms soon came to be consolidated. In the newer communities of the back country—of western New England, New Hampshire, Vermont, and Maine—the isolated American farmhouse, set in the center of its own acres, at once made its appearance.

Farming in the Middle Colonies. In the Middle colonies of New York, New Jersey, and Pennsylvania, commercial agriculture developed on a more significant scale. Indeed specialization, with the general qualifications mentioned, had set in fully by the eighteenth century. Farms were larger in size—the family farm running to 200 acres, the great estate being made up of several thousand acres. In New York, on Long Island, in New Jersey, and Pennsylvania, the village never took hold, so that farm properties, in the typical American fashion, were consolidated from the very beginning. Soil and climatic conditions were more favorable; because of this, and because redemptioners flocked into Pennsylvania, farms could be larger and herds greater. Too, proximity to the many excellent seaports encouraged the growth of agricultural products for the West India trade. As a result, during the eighteenth century, the Middle colonies were turning out large quantities of surplus grains which were being milled, bolted, and packed for sale to New England, the West Indies, Newfoundland, the Azores, and sometimes even to Europe. The Middle colonies, like New England, raised beef and dairy cattle, hogs and work animals, and moved them and their products into the foreign trade.

Farming in the Southern Colonies. In Maryland, Virginia, the Carolinas, and Georgia, agriculture was operated on a commercial basis even to a greater extent than in the Middle colonies. Particularly this was true of Maryland, Virginia, and South Carolina, where the plantation form of organization as a rule prevailed. Of course, there were small general farmers in the back countries of these colonies; and general farming was the rule in Georgia and North Carolina. On the plantations—large farms running over 1,000 acres—the great colonial staples of tobacco, rice, and indigo were grown. On the smaller family farms the products were tobacco, grains, and cattle; these, too, by the eighteenth century, were being sent to markets.

Tobacco. Tobacco was the leading cash crop of colonial America, just as sugar was that of the West Indies. Tobacco was grown on the plantation, as cotton was subsequently; and, because the plantation form of agricultural organization was tied up so closely with the methods and problems of the Southern agriculturists, it is important that it be described carefully. The plantation, in the first place, was a large operating farm plant under unified direction. Therefore, it was unlike an estate, which was worked by tenants who paid in cash or kind and who devised their own planting programs. The plantation concentrated on a single cash crop; although in colonial America (unlike the antebellum Southern plantation) food and feed crops were also being raised for home consumption. Perhaps most important, the plantation, as a distinctive form, used an unfree labor supply. The capital of the planter was not invested in land and the improvement of its techniques (machine planting, cultivating, and harvesting, irrigation, soil conservation) so much as it was in the maintenance of a permanent labor force. In other words, because land was cheap and easily available, the holding was large. This means, as in the case of colonial tobacco, that the planter single-cropped his cultivated acres until he had depleted their fertility, and then he moved on to new fields. Why did he single crop? The labor force was usually unskilled; and because it represented capital investment, it must produce annual income. Therefore, the planter employed indentured servants or slaves (or, in modern times, share croppers), either buying their services for a brief time or their lives forever, attaching them to the plantation. Thus, plantation agriculture is an exploitative economy that appears in new countries where land is readily available; where capital is relatively scarce (so that diversification is not easily possible); and where surpluses of funds can be invested in a growing labor force. And all because plantation products—sugar, tobacco, cotton, rice, rubber, tea, coffee—can be poured into vast markets.

This plantation economy took firm root in the colonial South from the beginning. It attracted capital; hence, the top rank of settlers, who came to Virginia, Maryland and South Carolina, had larger means than was true of the New England settlers. It worked in well with the basic requirements of the Mercantile

System. Sugar, rice, and indigo were products England had to depend upon the outside world to provide. Tobacco gave the mother country a great export commodity to move into Europe and thus obtain an even more favorable balance of trade. The more plantation wares were shipped to England, the greater could be the outflow of English manufactured articles into these settlements. These Southern colonies also provided an outlet to which might be transported, at the expense of the planter, those uprooted populations whose idleness at home was such a source of concern to seventeenth-century England.

Tobacco was the first and for almost two centuries the most important cash crop of the South. It was made known to Europeans when Columbus discovered its cultivation by the Indians in the West Indies, and it was transplanted to England in the sixteenth century. In Virginia, the crop appeared early —in 1612, in fact. It was introduced into Maryland in the 1630s and into the Albemarle Sound region of North Carolina in the 1660s. Virginia and Maryland, however, constituted the tobacco kingdom of the colonial period. Tobacco cultivation grew and grew. In the late 1630s, London was receiving annually 1,400,000 pounds of tobacco from Virginia. In the 1690s, Virginia and Maryland were growing a total of 40,000,000 pounds. On the eve of the Revolution, Virginia was sending to London and the outports 55,000,000 pounds annually and the Maryland export came to 30,000,000 pounds. In England and Scotland the leaves were processed and sold in the home market or reexported in bulk to the European continent.

The growing of tobacco was a fairly simple matter and therefore could be taught to the unskilled laborers of the plantation. In the colonial period, tillage was extensive: there was no rotation, no fertilization, no effort to conserve the soil. After three or four plantings, a field was used up and operations were moved to another section of the holding. And because the plant could be grown so easily,

the area of cultivation was rapidly expanded. There were, therefore, recurrent cycles of overproduction with accompanying price declines and widespread distress. Hard times were experienced by tobacco planters during 1684–94, 1703–13, 1724–36, and 1756–65. In 1773, on the eve of the Revolution, the growers were once more in a bad way. Depression was accompanied by pyramiding of debt, consignment of future crops to creditors and overplanting.

In line with mercantilist tradition, the colonial Virginia and Maryland governments did everything in their power to control production. As early as 1630, a Virginia statute sought to fix the planting area and the size of the crop per operating family. Later, efforts were made—because of the movement of cultivation into Maryland and North Carolina—to limit plantings by intercolonial agreements. These devices were unsuccessful. From time to time, mobs took matters into their own hands and destroyed standing tobacco. By 1640, legislation was already in existence in Virginia and Maryland providing for inspection systems; and public warehouses were maintained to assure standard quality, grading, and fair weight. In Virginia, in 1712 and again in 1730, inspection acts installed bonded inspectors at public warehouses who were required to get rid of inferior tobacco and were permitted to issue receipts against stored leaves. These receipts became negotiable and were accepted as public money for the payment of taxes and also as legal tender within restricted areas. Both colonies also tried to check the opening of new planting areas by imposing high taxes on the importation of Negroes and by interfering with the transportation of felons. Such measures, however, were disallowed by the Privy Council, in the interests of the great English slave-carrying trade.

The costs of plantation operation were high not only because of the increased costs of slaves but because the planter worked on credit. This was supplied by English merchants partly because interest rates were twice those prevailing in England and because mortgages could be taken on land and Negroes and liens on crops. In time, almost all the business transactions of the South came to be controlled by London and outport merchants. These were some of the functions performed by the English merchants. If he was a London merchant, he took the crop of the planter on consignment and charged him a commission of $2\frac{1}{2}$ percent for handling; this fee, it must be noted, was on the English wholesale price and not on the price at the farm. He also furnished his planter-customer the goods he required for the maintenance of home and farm, charging interest of $2\frac{1}{2}$ percent for the book credit extended. If he was an outport merchant, he maintained colonial warehouses for the storage of goods and these were withdrawn at the order of local correspondents resident in the colonies. Again, there were charges for book credit. The merchant was the banker for his correspondent; acting as his depository, accepting his bills of exchange, and always advancing credit. Not infrequently, the English merchant operated through a representative in the colonies. This person was known as a factor. Sometimes the factor was an employee of the merchant; sometimes he was a colonial merchant or planter who worked on commission for his English principal. The English merchant was banker, commission man, insurance broker, shipper, and supply house all rolled into one.

Under such a regimen, it is doubtful if the planters in the long run made any money. The fact is, they fell deeper and deeper into debt to the English merchants. At the outbreak of the Revolution, colonial debts due English merchants came to about £5,000,000,

at least five sixths of which were owed by the Southern planters. The upshot was constant irritation. The dependence of the planters upon book credit and the high interest charges they were forced to pay made them chafe under the limitations of the Mercantile System. As we shall see, demands for the widening of the credit base and for inflation became increasingly common. Southern planters entertained strong suspicions that London merchants were combining to control prices. Often, the rigid price of tobacco, despite fluctuations in the crop, and the high prices for necessaries which colonials were compelled to pay, pointed to the operations of rings. Constantly weighed down by debt, it was small wonder that the colonial planters sought to expand their activities by pushing out their tobacco lands and by throwing themselves into the land-speculation business.

Western Land Speculation. Colonial men of means were interested in western lands; but so, by the middle of the eighteenth century, were English and Scottish merchants. The successful termination of the Seven Years' War and the expulsion of the French from the Illinois country brought these rivalries to a head. The Proclamation Line of 1763 closed the western domain to colonial enterprising and the Quebec Act of 1774 put the administration of the conquered territory and control over the fur trade under Montreal. The English were to be favored as against the colonials in the exploitation of western wild lands. One of the important props of the colonial plantation system—the dealing in new lands—was being removed.

Such was the Old World the European emigrants left and such the New World the American settlers founded.

ENGLISH SOCIETY

THE VOGUE of Holinshed's *Chronicles,* which first appeared in the decade before the defeat of the Armada, marks the emergence of an English public literate in the vernacular and eager to read about the world in which it lived. The *Chronicles* climaxes its cooperative account of England's past with the Reverend William Harrison's (1534–1593) description of the society of his own time.

Harrison's England—Shakespeare's England and the land that molded the first English migrants to the New World—was a turbulent society straining against its medieval framework. The body of simple men was sharply divided from those who ranked as gentle because they could "live of their own without manual labor," and gentlemen themselves were ranged in order of dignity. Yet, it was no static society Harrison was describing; rather, it was an era of extraordinary change. His were the "spacious days of great Elizabeth," a period of expanding trade and a new prosperity which was bringing new men to power. Prices rose. Changes in the standard of living bore hard on the income of those who did not adapt themselves to new ways. Harrison complains of the high cost of living induced by the government's policy of protecting English shipping; he hints at new difficulties facing those who lived by the land. He glories in the achievements of his time; yet he speaks—at least there is an implicit resentment —against those elements which were pressing against the barriers that formed a hierarchically organized society.

Foreign travel was corrupting English youth. The new fashion of making the "grand tour" took gentlemen's sons out of the realm into Italy, from which they returned with forks and fine clothes and page boys strutting at their heels. Bad as was such corruption of manners among the gentry, the lower classes presented an even more serious problem.

For whatever innovations may have occurred, the fundamentals stand unaltered: there is a class born to rule and another that is "to be ruled and not to rule others." Into the second category fall all men who work with their hands. These are to be ruled in their comings and their goings, subject to the Statute of Artificers in their working lives and to the parish overseers of the poor if work failed. All men who were not artisans or apprenticed to them might be required to serve as agricultural laborers on demand. Their wages, hours, and term of service were fixed by law. And that law was enforced by the justices of the peace, local landowners directly or indirectly the employers of the laborers whose lives they were making. If a laborer refused the work offered, he might expect the whip or the house of correction, for his freedom of movement was hampered not only by laws against vagrants, but by restrictions on the residence of landless men. As each parish was compelled to provide for its own poor, each tried to limit the number of those who could claim settlement and thus increase the tax paid for the support of the aged, infirm, and unemployed.

The Elizabethan Poor Law of 1601 was not yet completely formulated when Harrison surveyed his England, but the Statute of Artificers had been on the books since 1563. Yet England's muddy roads were still walked by "vagrom men": the incompetent, the restless, the dispossessed; soldiers home from the wars in Flanders; cottagers and copyholders driven from their land as farming gave way to the more profitable activity of sheep-raising; men of no trade and men whose trades were falling into disuse.

Behind Harrison's list of the varieties of that "rabble" and his hints at the tricks and dodges by which they lived is to be found the story of too many men for the usable land. A pool of surplus manpower was accumulating in England. Out of that pool would push the enterprising, the discontented, the adventurous, men who had fallen and men who wanted to rise, men too forthright for the Elizabethan compromise in religion and morality. This was the England the original settlers of America were leaving behind.

The chapters that follow are from William Harrison's "An Historical Description of the Island of Britain with a Brief Rehearsal of the Nature and Qualities of the People of England," in Holinshed's *Chronicles* (originally published in London in 1586). The edition used here is the London one of 1807.

The Description of England
By William Harrison

CHAPTER V: OF DEGREES OF PEOPLE IN THE COMMONWEALTH OF ENGLAND

WE IN ENGLAND diuide our people commonlie into foure sorts, as gentlemen, citizens or burgesses, yeomen, which are artificers, or laborers. Of gentlemen the first and chéefe (next the king) be the prince, dukes, marquesses, earls, viscounts, and barons: and these are called gentlemen of the greater sort, or (as our common vsage of spéech is) lords and noblemen.

Gentlemen be those whome their race and bloud, or at the least their vertues doo make noble and knowne. The Latines call them Nobiles & generosos, as the French do Nobles or Gentlehommes. The etymologie of the name expoundeth the efficacie of the word: for as Gens in Latine betokeneth the race and surname: so the Romans had Cornelios, Sergios, Appios, Curios, Papyrios, Scipiones, Fabios, Æmilios, Iulios, Brutos, &c: of which, who were Agnati, and therefore kept the name, were also called Gentiles, gentlemen of that or that house and race.

Moreouer as the king dooth dubbe knights, and createth the barons and higher degrees, so gentlemen whose ancestors are not knowen to come in with William duke of Normandie (for of the Saxon races yet remaining we now make none accompt, much lesse of the British issue) doo take their beginning in England, after this maner in our times. Who soeuer studieth the lawes of the realme, who so abideth in the vniuersitie giuing his mind to his booke, or professeth physicke and the liberall sciences, or beside his seruice in the roome of a capteine in the warres, or good counsell giuen at home, whereby his common-wealth is benefited, can liue without manuell labour, and thereto is able and will beare the port, charge, and countenance of a gentleman, he shall for monie haue a cote and armes bestowed vpon him by heralds (who in the charter of the same doo of custome pretend antiquitie and seruice, and manie gaie things) and therevnto being made so good cheape be called master, which is the title that men giue to esquiers and gentlemen, and reputed for a gentleman euer after. Which is so much the lesse to be disalowed of, for that the prince dooth loose nothing by it, the gentleman being so much subiect to taxes and publike paiments as is the yeoman or husbandman, which he likewise dooth beare the gladlier for the sauing of his reputation. Being called also to the warres (for with the gouernment of the common-wealth he medleth litle) what soeuer it cost him, he will both arraie & arme himselfe accordinglie, and shew the more manly courage, and all the tokens of the person which he representeth. No man hath hurt by it but himselfe, who peraduenture will go in wider buskens than his legs will beare, or as our prouerbe saith, now and then beare a bigger saile than his boat is able to susteine.

Certes the making of new gentlemen bred great strife sometimes amongst the Romans, I meane when those which were Noui homines, were more allowed of for their vertues newlie séene and shewed, than the old smell of ancient race, latelie defaced by the cowardise & euill life of their nephues & defendants could make the other to be. But as enuie hath no affinitie with iustice and equitie, so it forceth not what language the malicious doo giue out, against such as are exalted for their wisdomes. This neuerthelesse is generallie to be reprehended in all estates of gentilitie, and which in short time will turne to the great ruine of our countrie, and that is the vsuall sending of noblemens & meane gentlemens sonnes into Italie, from whence they bring home nothing but meere atheisme, infidelitie, vicious conuersation, & ambitious and proud behauiour, wherby it commeth to passe that they returne far worsse men than they went out. A gentleman at this present is newlie come out of Italie, who went thither an earnest protestant, but comming home he could saie after this maner: Faith & truth is to be kept, where no losse or hinderance of a further purpose is susteined by holding of the same; and forgiuenesse onelie to be shewed when full reuenge is made. Another no lesse forward than he, at his returne from thence could ad thus much; He is a foole that maketh accompt of any religion, but more foole that will loose anie part of his wealth, or will come in trouble for constant leaning to anie: but if he yéeld to loose his life for his possession, he is stark mad, and worthie to be taken for most foole of all the rest. This gaie bootie gate these gentlemen by going into Italie, and hereby a man may see what fruit is afterward to be looked for where such blossoms doo appéere. I care not (saith a third) what you talke to me of God, so as I may haue the prince & the lawes of the realme on my side. Such men as this last, are easilie knowen; for they haue learned in Italie, to go vp and downe also in England, with pages at their héeles finelie apparelled, whose face and countenance shall be such as sheweth the master not to be blind in his choise. But least I should offend too much, I passe ouer to saie anie more of these Italionates and their demeanor, which alas is too open and manifest to the world, and yet not called into question.

Citizens and burgesses haue next place to gentlemen, who be those that are free within the cities, and are of some likelie substance to beare office in the same. But these citizens or burgesses are to serue the commonwealth in their cities and boroughs, or in corporat townes where they dwell. And in the common assemblie of the realme wherein our lawes are made, for in the counties they beare but little swaie (which assemblie is called the high court of parlement) the ancient cities appoint foure, and the boroughs two burgesses to haue voices in it, and giue their consent or dissent vnto such things as passe or staie there in the name of the citie or borow, for which they are appointed.

In this place also are our merchants to be installed, as amongst the citizens (although they often change estate with gentlemen, as gentlemen doo with them, by a mutuall conuersion of the one into the other) whose number is so increased in these our daies, that their onelie maintenance is the cause of the exceeding prices of forreine wares, which otherwise when euerie nation was permitted to bring in hir owne commodities, were farre better cheape and more plentifullie to be had. Of the want of our commodities here at home, by their great transportation of them into other countries, I speake not, sith the matter will easilie bewraie it selfe. Certes among the Lacedemonians it was found out, that great numbers of merchants were nothing to the furtherance of the state of the commonwealth: wherefore it is to be wished that the huge heape of them were somewhat restreined, as also of our lawiers, so should the rest liue more easilie vpon their owne, and few honest chapmen be brought to decaie, by breaking of the bankerupt. I doo not denie but that the nauie of the land is in part mainteined by their traffike, and so are the high prices of wares kept vp now they haue gotten the onelie sale of things, vpon pretense of better furtherance of the common-wealth into their owne hands: whereas in times past when the strange bottoms were suffered to come in, we had sugar for foure pence the pound, that now at the writing of this treatise is well worth halfe a crowne, raisons or corints for a penie that now are holden at six pence, and sometime at eight pence and ten pence the pound: nutmegs at two pence halfe penie the ounce: ginger at a penie an ounce, prunes at halfe penie farding: great raisons three pound for a penie, cinamon at foure pence the ounce, cloues at two pence, and pepper at twelue, and sixteene pence the pound. Whereby we may sée the sequele of things not alwaies but verie seldome to be such as is pretended in the beginning. The wares that they carrie out of the realme, are for the most part brode clothes and carsies of all colours, likewise cottons, fréeses, rugs, tin, wooll, our best béere, baies, bustian, mockadoes tufted and plaine, rash, lead, fells, &c: which being shipped at sundrie ports of our coasts, are borne from thence into all quarters of the world, and there either exchanged for other wares or readie monie: to the great gaine and commoditie of our merchants. And whereas in times past their cheefe trade was into Spaine, Portingall, France, Flanders, Danske, Norwaie, Scotland, and Iseland onelie: now in these daies, as men not contented with these iournies, they haue sought out the east and west Indies, and made now and then suspicious voiages not onelie vnto the Canaries, and new Spaine, but likewise into Cathaia, Moscouia, Tartaria, and the regions thereabout, from whence (as they saie) they bring home great commodities. But alas I sée not by all their trauell that the prices of things are anie whit abated. Certes this enormitie (for so I doo accompt of it) was sufficientlie prouided for, An. 9 Edward 3. by a noble estatute made in that behalfe, but vpon what occasion the generall execution thereof is staied or not called on, in good sooth I cannot tell. This onelie I know, that euerie function and seuerall vocation striueth with other, which of them should haue all the water of commoditie run into hir owne cesterne.

Yeomen are those, which by our law are called Legales homines, free men borne English, and may dispend of their owne frée land in yearelie reuenue, to the summe of fortie shillings sterling, or six pounds as monie goeth in our times. Some are of the opinion by Cap. 2. Rich. 2. an. 20. that they are the same which the French men call varlets, but as that phrase is vsed in my time it is farre vnlikelie to be so. The truth is that the word is deriued from the Saxon terme Zeoman or Geoman, which signifieth (as I haue read) a settled or staid man, such I meane as being maried and of some yeares, betaketh himselfe to staie in the place of his abode for the better maintenance of himselfe and his familie, whereof the single sort haue no regard, but are likelie to be still fleeting now hither now thither, which argueth want of stabilitie in determination and resolution of iudgement, for the execution of things of anie importance. This sort of people haue a certeine preheminence, and more estimation than labourers & the common sort of artificers, & these commonlie liue wealthilie, kéepe good houses, and trauell to get riches. They are also for the most part farmers to gentlemen (in old time called Pagani, & opponuntur militibus, and therfore Persius calleth himselfe Semipaganus) or at the leastwise artificers, & with grasing, frequenting of markets, and kéeping of seruants (not idle seruants as the gentlemen doo, but such as get both their owne and part of their masters liuing) do come to great welth, in somuch that manie of them are able and doo buie the lands of vnthriftie gentlemen, and often setting their sonnes to the schooles, to the vniuersities, and to the Ins of the court; or otherwise leauing them sufficient lands wherevpon they may liue without labour, doo make them by those meanes to become gentlemen: these were they that in times past made all France afraid. And albeit they be not called master as gentlemen are, or sir as to knights apperteineth, but onelie Iohn and Thomas, &c: yet haue they beene found to haue doone verie good seruice: and the kings of England in foughten battels,

were woont to remaine among them (who were their footmen) as the French kings did amongst their horssemen: the prince thereby shewing where his chiefe strength did consist.

The fourth and last sort of people in England are daie labourers, poore husbandmen, and some retailers (which haue no frée land) copie holders, and all artificers, as tailers, shomakers, carpenters, brickmakers, masons, &c. As for slaues and bondmen we haue none, naie such is the priuilege of our countrie by the especiall grace of God, and bountie of our princes, that if anie come hither from other realms, so soone as they set foot on land they become so frée of condition as their masters, whereby all note of seruile bondage is vtterlie remooued from them, wherein we resemble (not the Germans who had slaues also, though such as in respect of the slaues of other countries might well be reputed frée, but) the old Indians and the Taprobanes, who supposed it a great iniurie to nature to make or suffer them to be bond, whome she in hir woonted course dooth product and bring foorth frée. This fourth and last sort of people therefore haue neither voice nor authoritie in the common wealth, but are to be ruled, and not to rule other: yet they are not altogither neglected, for in cities and corporat townes, for default of yeomen they are faine to make up their inquests of such maner of people. And in villages they are commonlie made churchwardens, sidemen, aleconners, now and then constables, and manie times inioie the name of hedboroughes. Vnto this sort also may our great swarmes of idle seruing men be referred, of whome there runneth a prouerbe; Yoong seruing men old beggers, bicause seruice is none heritage. These men are profitable to none, for if their condition be well perused, they are enimies to their masters, to their freends, and to themselues: for by them oftentimes their masters are incouraged vnto vnlawfull exactions of their tenants, their fréends brought vnto pouertie by their rents inhanced, and they themselues brought to confusion by their owne prodigalitie and errors, as men that hauing not wherewith of their owne to mainteine their excesses, doo search in high waies, budgets, cofers, males, and stables, which way to supplie their wants. How diuerse of them also coueting to beare an high saile doo insinuate themselues with yoong gentlemen and noble men newlie come to their lands, the case is too much apparant, whereby the good natures of the parties are not onelie a little impaired, but also their liuelihoods and reuenues so wasted and consumed, that if at all yet not in manie yeares they shall be able to recouer themselues. It were verie good therefore that the superfluous heapes of them were in part diminished. And sith necessitie inforceth to haue some, yet let wisdome moderate their numbers, so shall their masters be rid of vnnecessarie charge, and the common wealth of manie théeues. No nation cherisheth such store of them as we doo here in England, in hope of which maintenance manie giue themselues to idlenesse, that otherwise would be brought to labour, and liue in order like subiects. Of their whoredomes I will not speake anie thing at all, more than of their swearing, yet is it found that some of them doo make the first a cheefe piller of their building, consuming not onelie the goods but also the health & welfare of manie honest gentlemen, citizens, wealthie yeomen, &c: by such vnlawfull dealings. But how farre haue I waded in this point, or how farre may I saile in such a large sea? I will therefore now staie to speake anie more of those kind of men. In returning therefore to my matter, this furthermore among other things I haue to saie of our husbandmen and artificers, that they were neuer so excellent in their trades as at this present. But as the workemanship of the later sort was neuer more fine and curious to the eie, so was it neuer lesse strong and substantiall for continuance and benefit of the buiers. Neither is there anie thing that hurteth the common sort of our artificers more than hast, and a barbarous or slauish desire to turne the penie, and by ridding their worke to make spéedie vtterance of their wares: which inforceth them to bungle vp and dispatch manie things they care not how so they be out of their hands, whereby the buier is often sore defrauded, and findeth to his cost, that hast maketh wast, according to the prouerbe. . . .

CHAPTER X: OF PROVISION MADE FOR THE POORE

There is no common-wealth at this daie in Europe, wherin there is not great store of poore people, and those necessarilie to be relieued by the welthier sort, which otherwise would starue and come to vtter confusion. With vs the poore is commonlie diuided into thrée sorts, so that some are poore by impotencie, as the fatherlesse child, the aged, blind and lame, and the diseased person that is iudged to be incurable: the second are poore by casualtie, as the wounded souldier, the decaied householder, and the sicke person visited with grieuous and painefull diseases: the third consisteth of thriftlesse poore, as the riotour that hath consumed all, the vagabund that will abide no where, but runneth vp and downe from place to place (as it were séeking worke and finding none) and finallie the roge and strumpet which are not possible to be diuided in sunder, but runne too and fro ouer all the realme, chéefelie kéeping the champaine soiles in summer to auoid the scorching heat, and the woodland grounds in winter to eschew the blustering winds.

For the first two sorts, that is to saie, the poore by impotencie, and the poore by casualtie, which are the true poore in deed, and for whome the word dooth bind vs to make some dailie prouision: there is order taken through out euerie parish in the realme, that weekelie collection shall be made for their helpe and sustentation, to the end they should not scatter abroad, and by begging here and there annoie both towne and countrie. Authoritie also is giuen vnto the iustices in euerie countie, and great penalties appointed for such as make default, to sée that the intent of the statute in this behalfe be trulie executed, according to the purpose and meaning of the same, so that these two sorts are sufficientlie prouided for: and such as can liue within the limits of their allowance (as each one will doo that is godlie and well disposed) may well forbeare to rome and range about. But if they refuse to be supported by this benefit of the law, and will rather indeuour by going to and fro to mainteine their idle trades, then are they adiudged to be parcell of the third sort, and so in stéed of courteous refreshing at home, are often corrected with sharpe execution, and whip of iustice abroad. Manie there are, which notwithstanding the rigor of the lawes prouided in that behalfe, yéeld rather with this libertie (as they call it) to be dailie vnder the feare and terrour of the whip, than by abiding where they were borne or bred, to be prouided for by the deuotion of the parishes. I found not long since a note of these latter sort, the effect whereof insueth. Idle beggers are such either through other mens occasion, or through their owne default. By other mens occasion (as one waie for example) when some couetous man, such I meane as haue the cast or right veine, dailie to make beggers inough wherby to pester the land, espieng a further commoditie in their commons, holds, and tenures, dooth find such meanes as thereby to wipe manie out of their occupiengs, and turne the same vnto his priuate gaines. Herevpon it followeth, that although the wise and better minded, doo either forsake the realme for altogether, and seeke to liue in other countries, as France, Germanie, Barbarie, India, Moscouia, and verie Calecute, complaining of no roome to be left for them at home, doo so behaue themselues that they are worthilie to be accompted among the second sort: yet the greater part commonlie hauing nothing to staie vpon are wilfull, and therevpon doo either prooue idle beggers, or else continue starke théeues till the gallowes doo eat them vp, which is a lamentable case. Certes in some mans iudgements these things are but trifles, and not worthie the regarding. Some also doo grudge at the great increase of people in these daies, thinking a necessarie brood of cattell farre better than a superfluous augmentation of mankind. But I can liken such men best of all vnto the pope and the diuell, who practise the hinderance of the furniture of the number of the elect to their vttermost, to the end the authoritie of the one vpon earth, the deferring of the locking vp of the other in euerlasting chaines, and the great gaines of the first may continue and indure the longer. But if it should come to passe that any forren inuasion should be made, which the Lord God forbid for his mercies sake! then should these men find that a wall of men is farre better than stackes of corne and bags of monie, and complaine of the want when it is too late to séeke remedie. The like occasion caused the Romans to deuise their law Agraria: but the rich not liking of it, and the couetous vtterlie condemning it as rigorous and vnprofitable, neuer ceased to practise disturbance till it was quite abolished. But to proceed with my purpose.

Such as are idle beggers through their owne default are of two sorts, and continue their estates either by casuall or méere voluntarie meanes: those that are such by casuall means, are in the beginning iustlie to be referred either to the first or second sort of poore afore mentioned: but degenerating into the thriftlesse sort, they doo what they can to continue their miserie, and with such impediments as they haue to straie and wander about, as creatures abhorring all labour and euerie honest exercise. Certes I call these casuall meanes, not in respect of the originall of their pouertie, but of the continuance of the same, from whence they will not be deliuered, such is their owne vngratious lewdnesse, and froward disposition. The voluntarie meanes proceed from outward causes, as by making of corosiues, and applieng the same to the more fleshie parts of their bodies: and also laieng of ratsbane, sperewort, crowfoot, and such like vnto their whole members, thereby to raise pitifull and odious sores, and mooue the harts of the goers by such places where they lie, to yerne at their miserie, and therevpon bestow large almesse vpon them. How artificiallie they beg, what forcible spéech, and how they select and choose out words of vehemencie, whereby they doo in maner coniure or adiure the goer by to pitie their cases, I passe ouer to remember, as iudging the name of God

and Christ to be more conuersant in the mouths of none: and yet the presence of the heuenlie maiestie further off from no men than from this vngratious companie. Which maketh me to thinke that punishment is farre meeter for them than liberalitie or almesse, and sith Christ willeth vs cheeflie to haue a regard to himselfe and his poore members.

Vnto this nest is another sort to be referred, more sturdie than the rest, which hauing sound and perfect lims, doo yet notwithstanding sometime counterfeit the possession of all sorts of diseases. Diuerse times in their apparell also they will be like seruing men or laborers: oftentimes they can plaie the mariners, and séeke for ships which they neuer lost. But in fine, they are all théeues and caterpillers in the common-wealth, and by the word of God not permitted to eat, sith they doo but licke the sweat from the true labourers browes, & beereue the godlie poore of that which is due vnto them, to mainteine their excesse, consuming the charitie of well disposed people bestowed vpon them, after a most wicked & detestable maner.

It is not yet full thréescore yeares since this trade began: but how it hath prospered since that time, it is easie to iudge, for they are now supposed of one sex and another, to amount vnto aboue 10000 persons; as I haue heard reported. Moreouer, in counterfeiting the Egyptian roges, they haue deuised a language among themselues, which they name Canting, but other pedlers French, a speach compact thirtie yeares since of English, and a great number of od words of their owne deuising, without all order or reason: and yet such is it as none but themselues are able to vnderstand. The first deuiser thereof was hanged by the necke, a iust reward no doubt for his deserts, and a common end to all of that profession. A gentleman also of late hath taken great paines to search out the secret practises of this vngratious rable. And among other things he setteth downe and describeth thrée & twentie sorts of them, whose names it shall not be amisse to remember, wherby ech one may take occasion to read and know as also by his industrie what wicked people they are, and what villanie remaineth in them.

The seuerall disorders and degrees amongst our idle vagabonds

1. Rufflers
2. Vprightmen
3. Hookers or Anglers
4. Roges
5. Wild roges

6. Priggers or pransers
7. Palliards
8. Fraters
9. Abrams
10. Freshwater mariners, or whipiacks
11. Dummerers
12. Drunken tinkers
13. Swadders or pedlers
14. Iarkemen or patricoes

Of *women kind*

1. Demanders for glimmar or fire
2. Baudie baskets
3. Mortes
4. Autem mortes
5. Walking mortes
6. Doxes
7. Delles
8. Kinching mortes
9. Kinching cooes

The punishment that is ordeined for this kind of people is verie sharpe, and yet it can not restreine them from their gadding: wherefore the end must néeds be martiall law, to be exercised vpon them, as vpon théeues, robbers, despisers of all lawes, and enimies to the common-wealth & welfare of the land. What notable roberies, pilferies, murders, rapes, and stealings of yoong children, burning, breaking and disfiguring their lims to make them pitifull in the sight of the people, I need not to rehearse: but for their idle roging about the countrie, the law ordeineth this maner of correction. The roge being apprehended, committed to prison, and tried in the next assises (whether they be of gaole deliuerie or sessions of the peace) if he happen to be conuicted for a vagabond either by inquest of office, or the testimonie of two honest and credible witnesses vpon their oths, he is then immediatlie adiudged to be gréeuouslie whipped and burned through the gristle of the right eare, with an hot iron of the compasse of an inch about, as a man-

ifestation of his wicked life, and due punishment receiued for the same. And this iudgement is to be executed vpon him, except some honest person woorth fiue pounds in the quéenes books in goods, or twentie shillings in lands, or some rich housholder to be allowed by the iustices, will be bound in recognisance to reteine him in his seruice for one whole yeare. If he be taken the second time, and proued to haue forsaken his said seruice, he shall then be whipped againe, bored likewise through the other eare and set to seruice: from whence if he depart before a yeare be expired, and happen afterward to be attached againe, he is condemned to suffer paines of death as a fellon (except before excepted) without benefit of clergie or sanctuarie, as by the statute dooth appeare. Among roges and idle persons finallie, we find to be comprised all proctors that go vp and downe with counterfeit licences, coosiners, and such as gad about the countrie, vsing vnlawfull games, practisers of physiognomie and palmestrie, tellers of fortunes, fensers, plaiers, minstrels, iugglers, pedlers, tinkers, pretensed schollers, shipmen, prisoners gathering for fees, and others so oft as they be taken without sufficient licence. From among which companie our bearewards are not excepted, and iust cause: for I haue read that they haue either voluntarilie, or for want of power to master their sauage beasts, béene occasion of the death and deuoration of manie children in sundrie countries by which they haue passed, whose parents neuer knew what was become of them. And for that cause there is & haue béene manie sharpe lawes made for bearewards in Germanie, wherof you may read in other. But to our roges. Each one also that harboreth or aideth them with meat or monie, is taxed and compelled to fine with the quéenes maiestie for euerie time that he dooth so succour them, as it shall please the iustices of peace to assigne, so that the taxation excéed not twentie shillings, as I haue béene informed. And thus much of the poore, & such prouision as is appointed for them within the realme of England.

THE AUTHORITARIAN STATE

IF SIMPLE MEN were born to be ruled by and for the benefit of their betters, gentlemen themselves must submit to authority higher than their own. God's will was supreme and, under God, was the will of the King. Broadly speaking, that may be taken as the political

philosophy animating those who supported royal power when the long conflict between the Stuarts and their Parliaments was punctuated by the civil war of the 1640s. And none expressed these ideas better or more arrogantly than William Laud, Bishop of St. Davids

(1573–1645) when he preached before King and Parliament.

By birth, Laud belonged to the class which supplied so much of the strength of Puritanism in religion and of the Parliamentary party in politics. His father was a cloth merchant, and he himself held an Oxford scholarship before he took orders in 1601. Oxford, in the years of Laud's training, was passing through an anti-Calvinist reaction similar in some respects to the movement which was so influential in the Anglican Church during the nineteenth century: a learned minority rejected the Calvinist element in the Anglican compromise and returned to the ceremony and sacramentalism which the Calvinist party abhorred. Laud's school refused to give a Calvinist interpretation to the Thirty-nine Articles (which summarized the belief of the Anglican Church) but, rather, stressed graciousness of service and the importance of ecclesiastical observance. The Roman Catholic was a true church, this school maintained, although it had become corrupt in doctrine.

Though the new school was a minority within the Anglican Church, its representatives were sufficiently learned to win important appointments from James I in spite of his own Calvinist bias. Charles had no such convictions: he regarded the group in which Laud had become a leader as sound in doctrine and correct in outlook, for by necessity and belief it deferred to royal authority. As a minority, Laud's school needed the secular arm to impose uniformity in ceremony upon an indifferent or recalcitrant clergy and, in belief, Laud's group stressed authority above individual conviction.

Two elements are strikingly apparent in Laud's thinking as represented by these sermons. First is his stress on the social unit as contrasted with the individual. The prosperity of the whole must be set above the prosperity of any particular element in the social order. Hence, State and Church, as institutions, are to be considered before the desires and opinions of any individual. Second is his practical application of that doctrine to political affairs.

Charles had met his first Parliament with a brusque demand for a grant to carry on his father's policy of assisting the Protestant cause on the Continent. Parliament countered with a request for information and, when the Commons learned that Charles was planning an expensive land war instead of a profitable harrying of the Spaniards at sea, it proceeded to debate instead of providing funds. When that debate turned on Charles's favorite, the Duke of Buckingham, the King dissolved Parliament though it had not granted the money he asked.

Laud's sermon before Charles's second Parliament reflects the root situation: the insistence of Commons upon effective control of taxation. The King is head and chief in the State, Laud declares: his power is from God; his house, which is the House of David, is the basis for all the houses of the kingdom. Consequently, a loyal Parliament will support that house and not thwart the King by arguing over funds.

Like Harrison, Laud discourses on the nature of the landless people: they are "the mob," who must be held in subjection to preserve order in the state. But Laud goes further: not only are the people to be duly subject to their superiors, the gentry also shall defer to the will of the King who rules by the grace of God and whose power is not to be checked by any on this earth.

Laud proceeded to enforce that view. When Charles dismissed his second Parliament and began to rule alone, Laud turned the royal power against the Puritans. A new Anglican prayer book was issued in 1628. By Laud's counsel, Charles forbade controversial preaching in the churches. In 1633, Laud, now Archbishop of Canterbury as well as one of the King's Privy Council, began his tours of visitation with the object of imposing conformity. By 1640, the convocation of the clergy under Laud's headship issued a canon declaring the order of Kings established by divine right; the assertion of a power independent of the King's was contrary to God's ordinance and resistance to Kings entailed eternal damnation. The Long Parliament risked damnation by finding Laud guilty of treason and sentencing him to death.

The first sermon here reprinted was preached before King James I on June 19, 1621. The second sermon was preached before King Charles's second Parliament on February 6, 1625. They are reprinted from Laud's *Works*, Vol. I (Oxford, 1847).

Two Sermons

BY WILLIAM LAUD

1. Sermon on King James's Birthday, 1621

. . . This I am sure of, since David, at the placing of the ark, exhorts all sorts of men *rogare pacem*, to "pray for the peace of Jerusalem," he did not intend to leave out the priest, whom it concerns most to preach peace to the people: neither the High-priest, nor the rest, but they should be most forward in this duty. This for the priesthood then. And Christ Himself, when He sent out the Seventy to preach, gave them in charge to begin at "every house in which they entered," with "peace"—"Peace be to this house." And he that preacheth not peace, or labours not for it, must confess one of these two;—namely, that he thinks David was deceived, while he calls to pray for peace;—or that himself is disobedient to his call.

Calvin is of opinion that he which will order his prayers right, must begin, not with himself, but at *Dominus ecclesiæ corpus conservet*, "that the Lord would preserve the Body of His Church." It is just with the Prophet, "peace for Jerusalem." For if any man be so addicted to his private, that he neglect the common State, he is void of the sense of piety, and wisheth peace and happiness to himself in vain. For whoever he be, he must live in the body of the Commonwealth, and in the body of the Church; and if their joints be out, and in trouble, how can he hope to live in "peace?" This is just as much as if the exterior parts of the body should think they might live healthful, though the stomach be full of sick and swollen humours.

To conclude then:—God hath blessed this State and Church with many and happy years of peace and plenty. To have had peace without plenty had been but a secure possession of misery. To have had plenty, if it were possible, without peace, had been a most uncertain possession of that which men call happiness, without enjoying it. To have had both these, without truth in religion and the Church's peace, had been to want the true use of both. Now to be weary of "peace," especially peace in truth, is to slight God that hath given us the blessing. And to abuse peace and plenty to luxury, and other sins, is to contemn the blessing itself. And there is neither of these, but will call apace for vengeance.

My exhortation therefore shall keep even with Saint Paul's, "that supplications and prayers be made," especially, "for Kings, and for all that are in authority, that" under them "we may live [lead] a quiet and peaceable life in all godliness and honesty." Here Saint Paul would have you pray for the King; and in my text the King would have you pray for the State and the Church:—his peace cannot be without theirs;—and your peace cannot be without his. Thus having made my text my circle, I am gone round it, and come back to it; and must therefore end in the point where I began: "Pray for the peace of Jerusalem; let them prosper that love it: peace be within the walls of it, and prosperity within the palaces:" that the peace of God, which passeth our understanding here, may not leave us till it possess us of eternal peace. And this, Christ for His infinite merit and mercy's sake grant unto us. To Whom, with the Father, and the Holy Spirit, be ascribed all might, majesty, and dominion, this day, and for evermore. Amen.

2. Sermon before King Charles's Second Parliament, 1625

. . . Now in a state, the King *obtinet locum fundamenti*, is always fundamental. All inferior powers of nobles, judges, and magistrates rest on him. And yet the Holy Ghost doth not stay in my text, that the "seats of judgment" are upon the foundation of David, but upon the "house of David." And the reason is plain; because there is one and the same "foundation" of the King and his people, that is, God and Christ. But when the house of the King is built upon God, as David's was, then it is to the people, *et domus et fundamentum*, both an house and a foundation of all their houses.

And that you may see the truth of this, look into the story of all States, and you shall never find a thunderclap upon the house of David to make it shake, but the houses of all the subjects in the kingdom shook with it. And this is an evident argument that the "house of David" is a "foundation," when such a mighty building as a State is shaken with it. And therefore, there is no man that loves his own house, but he must love the King's, and labour and study to keep it from shaking.

And if you mark the text, here is, *sedes super sedem*, one "throne," or "seat," upon another. And all well-ordered states are built so by *sub* and *super*, by "government" and "obedience." The intermediate magistrates have their subordinations either to other, and all to David. But the "house of David," that is both *sub* and *super*; under the rest in the "foundation," for so the Septuagint, and the Fathers read it, ἐπὶ οἶκον, upon the house of David; so the "house of David" under, as "foundation;" but over the rest in the administration and the government; for they which are upon him, must not be above him. A primacy, or superintendency, or what you will, above the house of David in his own kingdom, is a dangerous and an ill construction of *super domum David*.

The "house of David" a "foundation" then; and my text warrants both it and me. I have no will to except against any form of government, assumed by any state; yet this my text bids me say for the honour of monarchical government, the "seats of judgment" in it are permanent; and I do not remember that ever I read "seats of judgment" so fixed as under regal power.

I do not by this deny, but that there may be the city in peace, and administration of justice in other forms of government, sometimes as much, sometimes more; but there are *judicia*, not "*sedes*," "judgment," not "seats," of it. And justice there may be; but it continues not half so steady. The factions of an aristocracy how often have they divided the city into civil wars, and made that city which was "at unity in itself," wade in her own blood? And for a democracy, or popular government, *fluctus populi fluctus maris*, the waves and gulfs of both are alike. None but God can "rule the raging of the sea, and the madness of the people." And no safety or settledness, till there be a return *in domum David*, to a monarchy, and a King again.

I will go no whither but to my text and Jerusalem for instance. The people had a Sanhedrim over them, a wonderful wise and a great senate; the chief of the priests, and the most expert in their laws of the other tribes. If any greater difficulty arose, God raised up judges and deliverers

to fight their battles. This people were well, a man would think, for point of government, very well. And yet Calvin observes, and it is true, though they had then "justice and judgment" among them, yet they were but *suspensa judicia et varie mutata*, "justice with suspense and often changes." And which is more, that people restless and unquiet, even with the ordinances of God Himself, till they had a King. So after the disobedience of Saul, which can cast even Kings out of God's favour, that state was settled upon the "house of David."

The King, then, a "foundation," and a settled one too, as mortality hath any. The whole frame of the commonwealth, understood here by the "seats of judgment," rests upon the strength of his "house." Upon his "house?" therefore, it must be built and settled; else it is not *domus*, not a house; when it is built, it must be furnished, and plentifully too; else it is not fit to be *domus Davidis*, the King's house. If any disaster hath been, it must be repaired; else *domus lacera*, a house upon props, can be no "foundation of justice" to friends at home, or upon enemies abroad. And there can hardly be a greater misery to a kingdom, than to have the "house of David" weak.

Well then, would you have "the house of David" as David's was now at Jerusalem, a built, a furnished, a strong, an honourable "house?" I know you would. You are a noble and a most loyal people. Why, then, I will not take upon me to teach, but only to remember you of the way. The way is;—am I out? No sure,—the way is, to set David once upon his own feet; to make him see the strength of the "house" which God hath given him; to fill him with joy and contentment in his people's love; to add of your oil to make him a cheerful countenance, now that God hath "anointed him with the oil of gladness" over you; that in a free estate he may have leisure from home-cares, every way to intend the good and welfare of his people; and to bless God for them, and them in God.

And for David, God hath blessed him with many royal virtues. And, above the rest, with the knowledge that his "house" is a "foundation." A "foundation" of his people, and of all the justice that must preserve them in unity, and in happiness. But it is *domus ejus*, "his house," still, even while it is your "foundation." And never fear him, for God is with him. He will not depart from God's service; nor from the honourable care of his people; nor for wise managing of his treasure; he will never undermine his own "house," nor give his people just cause to be jealous of a shaking "foundation." And here in the presence of God and his blessed Angels, as well as of you, which are but dust and ashes, I discharge the true thoughts of my heart, and flatter not. And now, my dread Sovereign, upon you it lies to make good the thoughts of your most devoted servant.

Thus you have seen as short a map as I could draw of Jerusalem. She was famous for her "unity," and blessed too, when it was "within herself." She was famous for her "religion," and devout too, when "all the tribes went up to the ark of the testimony, to give thanks to the name of the Lord." She was famous for "justice," and successful too, both at home, and against foreign enemies, when the "seats of judgment," ecclesiastical and civil, were all, as their several natures bear, founded upon the "house of David."

This Jerusalem of ours is now "at unity in itself." And I see here *capita Tribuum*, the heads and leaders of the tribes, and people of the Lord, come up, and present in His temple. I would to God they were all here, that with one heart, and one mouth, we might all pray unto God for all His blessings to come down, and dwell in the "house of David;" and to rest upon this great and honourable council now ready to sit.

You are come up to begin at the "temple" of the Lord. The ark was wholly ceremonial; that is not here. But the "testimony of Israel," the law, yea and a better law than that, the law of grace and of Christ, that is here. Here it is, and open ready to teach "the fear of the Lord," which is "the beginning of all wisdom." In this law you can read nothing but service to God, and obedience to the "house of David." And so you find them joined, "fear God and honour the King." And it is a strange fallacy in religion for any man to "dishonour the King," and to make that a proof that he "fears God."

To the temple and the testimony you are come up. When God would give Moses more special direction, He declared Himself from the "mercy seat," which was on the "ark." The "mercy seat" was wholly ceremonial, as the "ark" was on which it stood; that is, the "seat," ceremony, but the "mercy," substance. And though the "seat" be gone with Moses, yet I hope God hath not left, will never leave, to appear in "mercy" to the "house of David," and this wise council. If He appear in "mercy," I fear nothing. If He appear otherwise, there will be cause to fear all things. And the way to have God appear in "mercy," is for both King and people, not only to come to the temple, that is but the outside of religion, but also to obey "the law, and the testimony."

"Judgment" went out from God lately, and it was fierce. How many thousand strong men, which might have been a wall about Jerusalem, hath the pestilence swept away? But His "mercy" soon overtook His "judgment." For when did the eye of man behold so strange and sudden abatement of so great "mortality?" A great argument that He will now appear in "mercy." And I cannot tell which hath got the better in the vie, your honour or your religion, that you have made such haste to bring the "tribes to the Temple, to give thanks to the name of the Lord," for this.

The first lesson of this day's evening prayer is Exod. xviii. There is the story of Jethro's counsel to Moses, for assistance of inferior officers. This was not the beginning of that great and parliamentary council, which after continued successful in the state of the Jews. For that was set after by God Himself, yet I make no great doubt, but that the ease, which Moses found by that council, made him apt to see what more he needed; and, so far at least, occasioned the settling of the Sanhedrim.

I take the omen of the day, and the service of the Church to bless it,—That our David may be as happy in this, and all other sessions of Parliament, as their Moses was in his council of the elders. That the King and his people may now, and at all like times, meet in love, consult in wisdom, manage their council with temper, entertain no private business to make the public suffer; and when their consultation is ended, part in the same love that should ever bring King and people together.

And let us pray,—That our Jerusalem, both Church and State, which did never but flourish when it was "at unity in itself," may now and ever continue in that "unity," and so be ever successful both at home and abroad. That in this unity the "tribes of the Lord," even all the families and kindreds of His people, may come up to the Church, to pray, and praise, and give thanks unto Him. That no tribe or person for any pretences, for they are no better, may absent themselves from the Church and testimony of the Lord. That the "seats of judgment," ecclesiastical and civil, of all sorts, may not only be set, but set firmly, to administer the justice of God, and the King, unto his people. That all men may reverence and obey the "house of David," who itself, upon God, is the foundation of all these blessings. That God would mutually bless David, and this people. That so the people may have cause to give thanks to God for David; and that David may have cause to take joy in the love and loyalty of his people; and bless God for both: till from this "Jerusalem," and this "temple," and these "thrones," he and we all may ascend into that glorious state which is in heaven. And this Christ for His infinite mercy sake grant unto us: To Whom, &c.

MONOPOLIES

THE TUDORS had encouraged commerce and industry by granting exclusive privileges for the sale and manufacture of certain goods and the conduct of trade in particular areas. Under James I, such monopolies were vastly extended. Protests, which had been accumulating in the years before 1621—when the European situation compelled James to summon Parliament in order to secure funds with which to support the Protestant interest on the Continent— broke into the open as Parliament proceeded to debate its grievances before making grants. Monopolies had increased under James; they enriched the families of the King's courtiers; and they barred enterprising business men from many trades. The Commons, accordingly, brought one of the most obnoxious monopolists before the House of Lords for trial. In spite of royal interference, the trial continued, the defendants were convicted and the Commons began to consider a bill for the abolition of all monopolies. At this point, James prorogued Parliament. Then, in July, 1621, the King issued a proclamation abolishing eighteen of the monopolies which had evoked the loudest protest.

Though James had revoked certain monopolies, the practice of making such grants continued and indeed increased during the next reign. In 1640, after eleven years of absolutist rule, Charles called Parliament to provide money for suppressing the rebellion which the attempt to enforce uniformity in religious ceremonial and organization had provoked in Scotland. Again, Parliament engaged in debate before granting taxes. In his speech during that discussion, Sir John Colepeper (?–1660), Knight of the Shire for Kent, denounced the practices which had prevailed during the years when Parliament had not been summoned. Kent complained of the increase of Papists, Colepeper declared; the county was alarmed at the introduction of new ceremonies in religion and the increase of military charges. It was aggrieved by the renewing of Convocation without Parliament's consent, which gave the clergy an independent legislative power. The county's woolen trade had been all but destroyed by duties and excises on cloth and its political rights invaded by the collection of ship money. But chief among grievances was that "swarm of vermin," monopolies. Hiding under the mask of corporations, these devices for extortion were hampering trade and plundering the people.

The first selection is reprinted from W. H. Price, *The English Patents of Monopoly* (Cambridge, Mass., 1913). The second selection is reprinted from William Cobbett, ed., *Parliamentary History of England*, Vol. II (London, 1807).

Proclamation Touching Grievances

BY JAMES I

. . . HIS HIGHNESS observing that divers of them (though fit to receive a full period, and determination in Parliament) are very meet and necessary, for the good of his people, to be settled and ordered in the mean time by his own regal authority and direction; and some others are of that quality and condition, as his Majesty needs no assistance of Parliament for reforming the same, and would have reformed them before the Parliament, if the true state of his subjects' grievances had been then made known unto him.

Thereupon his Majesty in this short time of

cessation of parliamentary proceedings, not allowing himself any cessation or relaxation from his continual care and watch over the public, upon mature deliberation with his Privy Council hath advised and resolved of sundry particulars tending to the present case of his people, and to the furtherance and advancement of the flourishing estate of this kingdom. . . .

And whereas his Majesty hath received information of sundry grievances lighting upon many of his people and chiefly of the poorer sort, by reason of divers privileges, licenses, and other letters patents procured from his Majesty upon suggestions made to his Highness that the same should tend to the common good and profit of his subjects: Howbeit upon examination it doth appear that many of the said grants were not only obtained upon false and untrue surmises but have been also notoriously abused; his Majesty having heretofore published in print his dislike of such suits, together with his hatred and detestation of all importunities to obtain or procure the same, is willing to manifest: That these abuses and surreptitions against his precise charge and direction have confirmed him in an utter distaste of suits of that nature, and is resolved, by making those patents already obtained from him to be fruitless to the procurers, to discourage all others hereafter to press or importune him in the like. And therefore his Majesty, discerning that these particular patents ensuing viz:

Of and concerning the making of gold and silver foliat
The licensing of pedlars and petty chapmen
The sole dressing of common arms
The export of lists, shreds, and other like things
The sole making of tobacco pipes
The hot-press
The manufacture of playing cards and
The brogging of wool

have been found of evil consequence, and some of them have been much abused, contrary to his Majesty's gracious intention, and the same being made to appear to the parties interested in these grants, they have voluntarily submitted; which his Highness accepting, hath taken order for the present surrender of the same patents, and doth hereby absolutely forbid all further execution of them or any of them, or of anything in them, or any of them contained, or of any proclamation heretofore published for, or in any sort to the furthering or strengthening of them, or any of them.

Commissions revoked:

Pardoning and dispensing apprenticeship.
Pardoning and dispensing conversion of arable to pasture.

Licensing of wine casks.
Making of denizens.
Granting of leets.
Passing of parks and free warrens.
Granting of fairs and markets.
Granting of tolls, tallages, &c.
Leasing of tithes.
Passing of concealments, intrusions, &c.

And whereas divers other privileges, licenses, and other like patents have passed from his Majesty, as viz: touching

The gilding and printing of leather
Printing upon cloth
The making of paving-tiles, dishes, pots, garden-posts, and vessels of earth
The making of stone pots, stone jugs, and the like
The importing of pikes, carps, eels, and scallops
The making of racket-hoops, rackets, and cloth balls
The making or selling of oil invented for keeping armor
The importation of sturgeon
The making of garments of beaver
The making of hardwax
The making of chamlets
The making of back screens
The making of fortage and lineage of paper
The measuring of corn, coal, and salt
The printing of briefs and other things upon one side of the paper
The weighing of hay and straw
The discovery of annoyances in the Thames, and ballasting ships, his Majesty doth hereby publish and declare his gracious will and pleasure that all and every persons that at any time hereafter shall find themselves grieved, injured, or wronged by reason of any of the said grants, or any clause, article, or thing therein contained, may take their remedy therefor by the common laws of the realm, or other ordinary course of justice, any matter or thing in the said grants to the contrary notwithstanding.

[Provision for wool, cloth, new draperies, and iron ordnance.]

And his Majesty doth by these presents signify and declare his gracious and princely pleasure that albeit he hath in good measure, as the shortness of the time would permit, devised and resolved upon the several remedies above rehearsed, for the care of his subjects; yet it is not his Majesty's purpose that his grace and goodness to his people in matters of like nature should bear no further fruit, but as time and opportunity will permit, he will enlarge and extend the same unto such other particulars, wherein he shall have cause to conceive his subjects may be justly grieved; and that until the sitting again of Parliament both his own and the ears of his Privy Council shall be open to the modest and just complaints of his people as well concerning monopolies and other patents of evil nature and consequences, as concerning other grievances of the public; admonishing, nevertheless, that under color thereof, no man presume to trouble his Majesty or his Council with causeless clamors, proceeding of humor, or private respects. Given at our court, &c. &c.

Speeches Relating to Grievances before Parliament
16 Charles I, 1640

BY SIR JOHN COLEPEPER

SIR JOHN COLEPEPER, one of the knights of the Shire for Kent, spoke as follows: "Mr. Speaker; I stand not up with a petition in my hand. I have it in my mouth, and have it in charge . . . from them that sent me hither, humbly to present to the consideration of this house the Grievances of the county of Kent. I shall only sum them up, and they are these. 1. The great increase of Papists, by the remiss execution of those laws which were made to suppress them. The life of the laws is execution; without this they become a dead letter: this is wanting, and is a great grievance.— 2. The obtruding and countenancing of divers new ceremonies in matters of religion; as, placing the Communion-Table altar-wise, and bowing or cringing towards it; the refusing of the holy sacrament to such as refuse to come up to the rails: these carry with them some scandal and much offence.—3. Military Charges; and therein, 1st, that of Coat and Conduct-Money, required as a loan, or pressed as a due, in each respect equally a grievance. 2dly, The enhancing the price of Powder; whereby the Trained Bands are much discouraged in their exercising: however little this may seem prima facie, yet, upon due examination, it will appear a great grievance. The 3rd is more particular to our county; it is this, The last summer was twelvemonth, 1000 of our best arms were taken from the owners, and sent into Scotland. The compulsory way was this, 'If you will not send your arms, you shall go yourselves.' Mr. Speaker, the Trained Band is a militia of great strength and honour, without charges to the king, and deserves all due encouragement.—4. The Canons: I assign these to be a grievance, 1st, in respect of the matter, besides the etcaetera oath. 2dly, in respect of the makers; they were chosen to serve in a convocation; that failing with the parliament, the scene was altered; the same men, without any new election, shuffled into a sacred synod. 3dly, in respect of the consequence; which, in this age, when the second ill precedent becomes a law, is full of danger. The clergy, without confirmation of a parliament, have assumed unto themselves power to make laws, to grant relief by the name of Benevolence, and to intermeddle with our freehold by suspension and deprivation. This is a grievance of a high nature.—5. Ship-Money: this cries aloud: I may say, I hope without offence, this strikes the first-born of every family, I mean our inheritance. If the laws give the king power, in any danger of the kingdom, whereof he is judge, to impose what and when he pleases, we owe all that is left to the goodness of the king, not to the law. Mr. Speaker, this makes the farmers faint, and the plough to go heavy.—6. The great Decay of Cloathing and Fall of our Wools: these are the golden mines of England, which give a foundation to that trade which we drive with all the world. I know there are many stars concur in this constellation; I will not trouble you with more than one cause of it, which I dare affirm to be the greatest; it is the great customs and impositions laid upon our cloths and new draperies. I speak not this with a wish to lessen the king's revenues, so it be done by parliament; I shall give my voice to lay more charge upon the superfluities (due regard being had to trade) which we import from all other nations: sure I am that these impositions upon our native commodities are dangerous, and give liberty to our neighbours to undersell: and I take it for a rule, that besides our loss in trade, which is five times as much as the king receiveth, what is imposed upon our cloths is taken from the rent of our lands.—I have but one Grievance more to offer unto you; but this one compriseth many: it is a nest of wasps, or swarm of vermin, which have over-crept the land. I mean the monopolers and polers of the people: These like the frogs of Egypt, have got possession of our dwellings, and we have scarce a room free from them: they sip in our cup, they slip in our dish, they sit by our fire; we find them in the dye-vat, wash-bowl, and powdering-tub; they share with the butler in his box, they have marked and scaled us from head to foot. Mr. Speaker, they will not bate us a pin: we may not buy our own cloaths without their brokage. These are the leeches that have sucked the commonwealth so hard, that it is almost become hectical. And, some of these are ashamed of their right names; they have a vizard to hide the brand made by that good law in the last parliament of king James; they shelter themselves under the name of a corporation; they make bye-laws, which serve their turns to squeeze us, and fill their purses: unface these, and they will prove as bad cards as any in the pack. These are not petty chapmen, but wholesale men. Mr. Speaker, I have echoed to you the cries of the kingdom; I will tell you their hopes: they look to Heaven for a blessing upon this parliament; they hang upon his majesty's exemplary piety and great justice, which render his ears open to the just complaints of his subjects; and we have had lately a gracious assurance of it. It is the wise conduct of this parliament, whereby the other great affairs of the kingdom, and these our Grievances of no less import, may go hand-in-hand, in preparation and resolution; then, by the blessing of God, we shall return home with an olive branch in our mouths, and a full confirmation of the privileges which we received from our ancestors, and owe to our posterity: which every free-born Englishman hath received with the air he breathed in. These are our hopes: these are our prayers."

ENCLOSURES

By 1649, when Gerrard Winstanley's *A Declaration from the Poor Oppressed People of England* appeared, the conflict between Crown and Parliament had proceeded through the years of Charles's personal rule to the Scottish rebellion, the summoning of Parliament in 1640, the Civil Wars and the execution of the King. Charles had tried to silence the Puritans. He had imprisoned the leaders of the Opposition in Parliament; and rather than call another Parliament he had made England insignificant in European struggles for power. But when the Scots concluded their Covenant to defend Presbyterianism against the introduction of bishops and Laud's prayer book and had supported that Covenant with victory in the field, Charles was forced to summon Parliament.

The Long Parliament assembled in 1640. It impeached the King's most obnoxious minister, provided for Parliament to meet every three years whether summoned or not, and declared it would be dissolved only with its own consent. Further, it abolished special courts and the royal tax levies by which Charles had been able to rule without Parliament, and declared that henceforth judges should hold office during good behavior and not at the King's pleasure. At this demonstration of Puritan power —for royal policy had made Puritan and Opposition all but synonymous—Ireland re-volted. The more timid elements in the Opposition and those most attached to Episcopal church government tended to side with the King when the Commons attempted to impose control of ministers as a condition preliminary to their raising an army to suppress the rising in Ireland. Charles sought to repeat his arrest of Opposition leaders in Commons in 1642. The Commons countered by giving Parliament power to appoint the commanders of the militia.

In June, 1642, Parliament demanded that the principal officers of the Crown be appointed only with the consent of Parliament and that the church be reformed as Parliament should direct. Charles refused. He raised his standard at Nottingham in August and the Civil Wars began.

On the whole, the royalists were victorious during the two years following. Then, in 1644, the temporizing element among the Parliamentarians was supplanted by men who had small faith in the divinity hedging kings. They concluded an alliance with the Scots, who had already defeated Charles, and undertook a complete reorganization of their army. Against Charles's army of gentlemen, Oliver Cromwell brought drill, discipline, the middle-class virtues and his own capacity as a commander. Cromwell's troops defeated the Cavaliers at

Naseby in 1645, and Charles Stuart surrendered to the Scots.

But while the most vigorous element in the Opposition had decided the military policy to be applied against Charles, that same vigor led to hostility in other fields. Parliament, in office since 1640, wished to replace Episcopacy with a Presbyterian State Church. The army, unpaid for many months and predominantly Independent in sentiment, refused to disband or to accept a Presbyterian Establishment. When Parliament tried to conclude a treaty with Charles against the army, Cromwell resumed his command and war broke out again.

That army was possessed of singularly articulate political leadership. It formulated demands based upon the premise that man is endowed with certain natural rights and that government rests on the consent of the governed. Further, the army proceeded to draft a constitution which provided for a single-chambered legislature whose members were to be chosen by manhood suffrage.

Though Cromwell and the military staff prevailed upon the army's Levellers to accept toleration and Parliamentary confirmation of Crown officers instead of their own program, the Levellers' sentiments did not change. The army rose to fight the Scots who invaded England in 1648, in accordance with the treaty by which Charles was to be restored to his throne and the Presbyterian Church established for three years. Cromwell defeated the Scots; Parliament was purged of all but certain military elements after that; and Charles went to his death.

Against this background, Gerrard Winstanley's *A Declaration from the Poor Oppressed People of England* speaks some of the sentiments of the most radical segment of the population which supported Parliament and Cromwell's army in its fight. Winstanley (1609–1660?) was probably born in Lancashire. His origin is uncertain, the details of his education obscure, his whole life shadowy until 1649, when he began his attempt to recapture England's land for her people. His own account

shows him a freeman of the City of London and a cloth merchant driven to bankruptcy by the financial uncertainties of the Civil Wars.

In the time of precarious living that followed, Winstanley turned to religion, not in the comparatively formalized shape of Puritan teaching but to the Baptists, who encouraged lay preachers. Even this seemed too akin to trading to satisfy Winstanley's religious impulse. He became one of those Seekers waiting upon a new and personal revelation to bring him his own peace. This he achieved through a mystical experience which informed him not only of his own salvation but also of the means by which society could be regenerated. A voice spoke to him, saying: "Work together. Eat bread together."

And, in April, 1649, Winstanley and half a dozen other poor men proceeded to carry out that command by breaking up the heath on the common at St. George's Hill, Surrey. Mystical though his conviction was, Winstanley's action indicates the effect of the radical democracy of the Leveller movement. For two years, army and people alike had been influenced by the agitation for a more comprehensive conception of "English liberties." Winstanley's revelation seems quite natural in a time when social formulations were made in religious terms. And his concern with the land was equally natural. For generations the exactions of English landowners had been growing more burdensome. As early as 1577, Harrison had written of the "three things that are grown to be very grievous unto them [the country people]—to wit, the enhancing of rents, lately mentioned; the daily oppression of copyholders, whose lords seek to bring their poor tenants almost into plain servitude and misery, daily devising new means, and seeking up all the old, how to cut them shorter and shorter, doubling, trebling, and now and then seven times increasing their fines, driving them also for every trifle to lose and forfeit their tenures (by whom the greatest part of the realm doth stand and is maintained), to the end they may fleece them yet more, which is a lamentable hearing. The third thing they talk of is usury."

Against that long-continued aggression on the customary rights of the copyholder, Winstanley's little group protested by working the common land. In spite of suits and judgments, Winstanley and his followers continued planting upon the common until they were driven off by force and then brought before the courts as criminals. Whatever may have been the result of that prosecution, Winstanley's effort to nationalize England's common lands became a "curiosity of history."

Before his experiment passed into that category, however, Winstanley published the pamphlets that contained his philosophy of government, a political theory as different from the Puritan outlook as it was from the authoritarianism of Laud. Against the aggressive middle-class individualism of the Puritan attitude, Winstanley stressed the need for man to extend the cooperative spirit from the family to society. Against the Puritan idea of rule by the saints and of man's moral duty to get on in the world, Winstanley set the idea of secular rule by universal suffrage in a society which has abolished "the cheating arts of buying and selling." Political freedom was a right of all, but it could not exist in a poverty-ridden world where the system of land ownership gave some men power over others. The land should belong to all, Winstanley argues, but since force is an evil and man is to be ruled by righteousness, no attack will be made on existing holdings; all his effort is to preserve common ownership of the existing waste and common lands. The people of England, Winstanley's petition declares, ask for the free use of waste and common. Parliament stands pledged to rid the nation from Norman tyranny, to give the people liberty in return for fighting the royalists. The people have filled the army that fought Charles and they have born the costs of his defeat; now Parliament must redeem its word by making the land a common treasury and freedom "the inheritance of all, without respect of persons." Winstanley's group was ousted from the land it had begun to cultivate. The process of enclosing the common lands, ejecting the small holder and consolidating land ownership continued through the seventeenth century, driving men down in the social scale, out into the cities and sometimes even to the colonies where a poor man might hope to own land in fee simple.

Winstanley's pamphlet is reprinted from George H. Sabine, ed., *The Works of Gerrard Winstanley* (Ithaca, N.Y., 1941).

A Declaration from the Poor Oppressed People of England

BY GERRARD WINSTANLEY

WE WHOSE NAMES are subscribed, do in the name of all the poor oppressed people in *England*, declare unto you, that call your selves Lords of Manors, and Lords of the Land, That in regard the King of Righteousness, our Maker, hath inlightened our hearts so far, as to see, That the earth was not made purposely for you, to be Lords of it, and we to be your Slaves, Servants, and Beggers; but it was made to be a common Livelihood to all, without respect of persons: And that your buying and selling of Land, and the Fruits of it, one to another, is *The cursed thing*, and was brought in by War; which hath, and still does establish murder, and theft, in the hands of some branches of Mankinde over others, which is the greatest outward burden, and unrighteous power, that the Creation groans under: For the power of inclosing Land, and owning Propriety, was brought into the Creation by your Ancestors by the Sword; which first did murther their fellow Creatures, Men, and after plunder or steal away their Land, and left this Land successively to you, their Children. And therefore, though you did not kill or theeve, yet you hold that cursed thing in your hand, by the power of the Sword; and so you justifie the wicked deeds of your Fathers; and that sin of your Fathers, shall be visited upon the Head of you, and your Children, to the third and fourth Generation, and longer too, tell your bloody and theeving power be rooted out of the Land.

And further, in regard the King of Righteousness hath made us sensible of our burthens, and the cryes and groanings of our hearts are come before him: We take it as a testimony of love from him, that our hearts begin to be freed from slavish fear of men, such as you are; and that we finde Resolutions in us, grounded upon the inward law of Love, one towards another, To Dig and Plough up the Commons, and waste Lands through *England;* and that our conversation shall be so unblameable, That your Laws shall not reach to oppress us any longer, unless you by your Laws will shed the innocent blood that runs in our veins.

For though you and your Ancestors got your Propriety by murther and theft, and you keep it by the same power from us, that have an equal right to the Land with you, by the righteous Law of Creation, yet we shall have no occasion of quarreling (as you do) about that disturbing devil, called *Particular Propriety:* For the Earth, with all her Fruits of Corn, Cattle, and such like, was made to be a common Storehouse of Livelihood to all Mankinde, friend and foe, without exception.

And to prevent all your scrupulous Objections, know this, That we must neither buy nor sell; Money must not any longer (after our work of the Earths community is advanced) be the great god, that hedges in some, and hedges out others; for Money is but part of the Earth: And surely, the Righteous Creator, who is King, did never ordain, That unless some of Mankinde, do bring that Mineral (Silver and Gold) in their hands, to others of their own kinde, that they should neither be fed, nor be clothed; no surely, For this was the project of Tyrant-flesh (which Land-lords are branches of) to set his Image upon Money. And they make this unrighteous Law, That none should buy or sell, eat, or be clothed, or have any comfortable Livelihood among men, unless they did bring his Image stamped upon Gold or Silver in their hands.

And whereas the Scriptures speak, That the mark of the Beast is 666, the number of a man; and that those that do not bring that mark in their hands, or in their foreheads, they should neither buy nor sell, *Revel.* 13. 16. And seeing the numbering Letters round about the English money make 666, which is the number of that Kingly Power and Glory (called a *Man*), And seeing the age of the Creation is now come to the Image of the Beast, or Half day, And seeing 666 is his mark, we expect this to be the last Tyrannical power that shall raign; and that people shall live freely in the enjoyment of the Earth, without bringing the mark of the Beast in their hands, or

in their promise; and that they shall buy Wine and Milk, without Money, or without price, as *Isaiah* speaks.

For after our work of the Earthly community is advanced, we must make use of Gold and Silver, as we do of other mettals, but not to buy and sell withal; for buying and selling is the great cheat, that robs and steals the Earth one from another: It is that which makes some Lords, others Beggers, some Rulers, others to be ruled; and makes great Murderers and Theeves to be imprisoners, and hangers of little ones, or sincere-hearted men.

And while we are made to labor the Earth together, with one consent and willing minde; and while we are made free, that every one, friend and foe, shall enjoy the benefit of their Creation, that is, To have food and rayment from the Earth, their Mother; and every one subiect to give accompt of this thoughts, words and actions to none, but to the one onely righteous Judg, and Prince of Peace, the Spirit of Righteousness that dwells, and that is now rising up to rule in every Creature, and in the whole Globe. We say, while we are made to hinder no man of his Priviledges given him in his Creation, equal to one, as to another; what Law then can you make, to take hold upon us, but Laws of Oppression and Tyranny, that shall enslave or spill the blood of the Innocent? And so your Selves, your Judges, Lawyers, and Justices, shall be found to be the greatest Transgressors, in and over Mankinde.

But to draw neerer to declare our meaning, what we would have, and what we shall endevor to the uttermost to obtain, as moderate and righteous Reason directs us; seeing we are made to see our Priviledges, given us in our Creation, which have hitherto been denied to us, and our Fathers, since the power of the Sword began to rule, And the secrets of the Creation have been locked up under the traditional, Parrat-like speaking, from the Universities, and Colledges for Scholars, And since the power of the murdering, and theeving Sword, formerly, as well as now of late yeers, hath set up a Government, and maintains that Government; for what are prisons, and putting others to death, but the power of the Sword; to enforce people to that Government which was got by Conquest and Sword, and cannot stand of it self, but by the same murdering power? That Government that is got over people by the Sword, and kept by the Sword, is not set up by the King of Righteousness to be his Law, but by Coveteousness, the great god of the world; who hath been permitted to raign for a time, times, and dividing of time, and his government draws to the period of the last term of his allotted time; and then the Nations shall see the glory of that Government that shall rule in Righteousness, without either Sword or Spear,

And seeing further, the power of Righteousness in our hearts, seeking the Livelihood of others, as well as our selves, hath drawn forth our bodies to begin to dig, and plough, in the Commons and waste Land, for the Reasons already declared,

And seeing and finding our selves poor, wanting Food to feed upon, while we labor the Earth, to cast in Seed, and to wait tell the first Crop comes up; and wanting Ploughs, Carts, Corn, and such materials to plant the Commons withal, we are willing to declare our condition to you, and to all, that have the Treasury of the Earth, locked up in your Bags, Chests, and Barns, and will offer up nothing to this publike Treasury; but will rather see your fellow-Creatures starve for want of Bread, that have an equal right to it with your selves, by the Law of Creation: But this by the way we onely declare to you, and to all that follow the subtle art of buying and selling the Earth, with her Fruits, meerly to get the Treasury thereof into their hands, to lock it up from them, to whom it belongs; that so, such coveteous, proud, unrighteous, selfish flesh, may be left without excuse in the day of Judgment.

And therefore, the main thing we aym at, and for which we declare our Resolutions to go forth, and act, is this, To lay hold upon, and as we stand in need, to cut and fell, and make the best advantage we can of the Woods and Trees, that grow upon the Commons, To be a stock for our selves, and our poor Brethren, through the Land of *England*, to plant the Commons withal; and to provide us bread to eat, till the Fruit of our labors in the Earth bring forth increase; and we shall meddle with none of your Proprieties (but what is called Commonage) till the Spirit in you, make you cast up your Lands and Goods, which were got, and still is kept in your hands by murder, and theft; and then we shall take it from the Spirit, that hath conquered you, and not from our Swords, which is an abominable, and unrighteous power, and a destroyer of the Creation: But the Son of man comes not to destroy, but to save.

And we are moved to send forth this Declaration abroad, to give notice to every one, whom it concerns, in regard we hear and see, that some of you, that have been Lords of Manors, do cause the Trees and Woods that grow upon the Commons, which you pretend a Royalty unto, to be cut down and sold; for your own private use, whereby the Common Land, which your own mouths doe say belongs to the poor, is impover-

ished, and the poor oppressed people robbed of their Rights, while you give them cheating words, by telling some of our poor oppressed Brethren, That those of us that have begun to Dig and Plough up the Commons, will hinder the poor; and so blinde their eyes, that they see not their Priviledge, while you, and the rich Free-holders, make the most profit of the Commons, by your overstocking of them with Sheep and Cattle; and the poor that have the name to own the Commons have the least share therein; nay, they are checked by you, if they cut Wood, Heath, Turf, or Furseys, in places about the Common, where you disallow.

Therefore we are resolved to be cheated no longer, nor be held under the slavish fear of you no longer, seing the Earth was made for us, as well as for you: And if the Common Land belongs to us who are the poor oppressed, surely the woods that grow upon the Commons belong to us likewise: therefore we are resolved to try the uttermost in the light of reason, to know whether we shall be free men, or slaves. If we lie still, and let you steale away our birthrights, we perish; and if we Petition we perish also, though we have paid taxes, given free quarter, and ventured our lives to preserve the Nation's freedom as much as you, and therefore by the law of contract with you, freedom in the land is our portion as well as yours, equal with you: And if we strive for freedom, and your murdering, governing Laws destroy us, we can but perish.

Therefore we require, and we resolve to take both Common Land, and Common woods to be a livelihood for us, and look upon you as equal with us, not above us, knowing very well, that *England*, the land of our Nativity, is to be a common Treasury of livelihood to all, without respect of persons.

So then, we declare unto you, that do intend to cut our Common Woods and Trees, that you shall not do it; unlesse it be for a stock for us, as aforesaid, and we to know of it, by a publick declaration abroad, that the poor oppressed, that live thereabouts, may take it, and employ it, for their publike use, therefore take notice we have demanded it in the name of the Commons of *England*, and of all the Nations of the world, it being the righteous freedom of the Creation.

Likewise we declare to you that have begun to cut down our Common Woods and Trees, and to fell and carry away the same for your private use, that you shall forbear, and go no farther, hoping, that none that are friends to the Commonwealth of England, will endeavour to buy any of those Common Trees and Woods of any of those Lords of Mannors, so called, who have, by the murdering and cheating law of the sword, stoln the Land from yonger brothers, who have by the law of Creation, a standing portion in the Land, as well, and equall with others. Therefore we hope all Wood-mongers will disown all such private merchandize, as being a robbing of the poor oppressed, and take notice, that they have been told our resolution: But if any of you that are Wood-mongers, will buy it of the poor, and for their use, to stock the Commons, from such as may be appointed by us to sell it, you shall have it quietly, without diminution; but if you will slight us in this thing, blame us not, if we make stop of the Carts you send and convert the Woods to our own use, as need requires, it being our own, equal with him that calls himself the Lord of the Mannor, and not his peculiar right, shutting us out, but he shall share with us as a fellow-creature.

For we say our purpose is, to take those Common Woods to sell them, now at first to be a stock for our selves, and our children after us, to plant and manure the Common land withall; for we shall endeavour by our righteous acting not to leave the earth any longer intangled unto our children, by self-seeking proprietors; But to leave it a free store-house, and common treasury to all, without respect of persons. And this we count is our dutie, to endeavour to the uttermost, every man in his place (according to the nationall Covenant which the Parliament set forth) a Reformation, to preserve the peoples liberties, one as well as another: As well those as have paid taxes, and given free quarter, as those that have either born the sword, or taken our moneys to dispose of them for publike use: for if the Reformation must be according to the word of God, then every one is to have the benefit and freedom of his creation, without respect of persons; we count this our duty, we say, to endeavour to the uttermost, and so shall leave those that rise up to oppose us without excuse, in their day of Judgment; and our precious blood, we hope, shall not be dear to us, to be willingly laid down at the door of a prison, or foot of a gallows, to justifie this righteous cause; if those that have taken our money from us, and promised to give us freedom for it, should turn Tyrants against us: for we must not fight, but suffer.

And further we intend, that not one, two, or a few men of us shall sell or exchange the said woods, but it shall be known publikly in Print or writing to all, how much every such, and such parcell of wood is sold for, and how it is laid out, either in victualls, corn, ploughs, or other materialls necessary.

And we hope we may not doubt (at least we expect) that they that are called the great Councel and powers of *England*, who so often have declared themselves, by promises and Covenants, and confirmed them by multitude of fasting daies, and devout Protestations, to make *England* a free people, upon condition they would pay moneys, and adventure their lives against the successor of the *Norman* Conqueror; under whose oppressing power *England* was enslaved; And we look upon that freedom promised to be the inheritance of all, without respect of persons; And this cannot be, unless the Land of *England* be freely set at liberty from proprietors, and become a common Treasury to all her children, as every portion of the Land of *Canaan* was the Common livelihood of such and such a Tribe, and of every member in that Tribe, without exception, neither hedging in any, nor hedging out.

We say we hope we need not doubt of their sincerity to us herein, and that they will not gainsay our determinate course; howsoever, their actions will prove to the view of all, either their sinceritie, or hypocrisie: We know what we speak is our priviledge, and our cause is righteous, and if they doubt of it, let them but send a childe for us to come before them, and we shall make it manifest four wayes.

First, by the National Covenant, which yet stands in force to bind Parliament and people to be faithful and sincere, before the Lord God Almighty, wherein every one in his several place hath covenanted to preserve and seek the liberty each of other, without respect of persons.

Secondly, by the late Victory over King *Charls*, we do claime this our priviledge, to be quietly given us, out of the hands of Tyrant-Government, as our bargain and contract with them; for the Parliament promised, if we would pay taxes, and give free quarter, and adventure our lives against *Charls* and his party, whom they called the Common enemy, they would make us a free people; These three being all done by us, as well as by themselves, we claim this our bargain, by the law of contract from them, to be a free people with them, and to have an equall priviledge of Common livelihood with them, they being chosen by us, but for a peculiar worke, and for an appointed time, from among us, not to be our oppressing Lords, but servants to succour us. But these two are our weakest proofs. And yet by them (in the light of reason and equity that dwells in mens hearts) we shall with ease cast down, all those former enslaving, *Norman* reiterated laws, in every Kings raigne since the Conquest, which are as thornes in our eyes, and pricks in our sides, and which are called the Ancient Government of *England*.

Thirdly, we shall prove, that we have a free right to the land of *England*, being borne therein as well as elder brothers, and that it is our right equal with them, and they with us, to have a comfortable livelihood in the earth, without owning any of our owne kinde, to be either Lords, or Land-Lords over us: And this we shall prove by plain Text of Scripture, without exposition upon them, which the Scholars and great ones generally say, is their rule to walk by.

Fourthly, we shall prove it by the Righteous Law of our Creation, That mankinde in all his branches, is the Lord of the Earth, and ought not to be in subjection to any of his own kinde without him, but to live in the light of the law of righteousness, and peace established in his heart.

And thus in love we have declared the purpose of our hearts plainly, without flatterie, expecting love, and the same sincerity from you, without grumbling, or quarreling, being Creatures of your own Image and mould, intending no other matter herein, but to observe the Law of righteous action, endeavouring to shut out of the Creation, the cursed thing, called *Particular Propriety*, which is the cause of all wars, bloud-shed, theft, and enslaving Laws, that hold the people under miserie.

Signed for and in the behalf of all the poor oppressed people of *England*, and the whole world.

THE MORAL REJECTION OF THE POOR

IN 1704, A MEMBER of Parliament proposed that workhouse inmates of each parish be set to spinning and weaving wool to pay for their keep. In answer to this suggestion there appeared *The Giving of Alms No Charity* by Daniel Defoe, who had just completed a prison term for writing the *Shortest Way with Dissenters*.

Daniel Defoe (1661?–1731) was the younger son of a prosperous London butcher. Defoe's parents intended him for the ministry, but Defoe preferred trade to the pulpit. Defoe denied having failed as a hose factor; he certainly succeeded at tile-making for a time, but his interest in politics drew too much of his attention from business to permit that success to continue. He went bankrupt, took up pamphleteering as a profession and became thoroughly involved in the intrigues and speculations that characterized the political and mercantile worlds of Queen Anne. From Whiggery Defoe turned to the Tories and then declared he had been a spy in the Tory camp. A skilled journalist with a real business sense, and a devout nonconformist, Defoe earned a living by writing of ghosts, thieves, and prostitutes and by championing the cause of merchants and speculators. He was the typical spokesman for and advocate of mercantile and Mercantilist England; and his condemnation of the poor for their profligacy—this in the face of starvation wages—exactly hits off the England which emigrants sought to leave behind them.

In *Giving Alms No Charity* Defoe argues seriously—and not satirically—that there are ample opportunities for work in England. Yet the country suffers from a crowd of "clamoring unemployed," who "burden the rich and clog the parishes." What the poor of England require is not public provision of work—that would serve only to take jobs from other poor people, disturb the normal course of trade and destroy the reputation of English woolens abroad—but moral reformation. Parliament should busy itself not with laws for employing the poor, but with legislation to make them diligent, temperate, and thrifty. For the laborers of England—the poor—are creatures of unbridled appetites and unbounded insolence.

Defoe writes in another pamphlet:

"I mean the Advance of Wages, for this indeed, is the support of all the Insolence of Servants. . . . Nor is this Advance of Servants Wages any Wealth to them, but as above, their Morals being destroy'd, this overplus is generally laid out, either in Luxury or Vanity, that is to say, in *Strong Drink* by the Men-Servants, and in *gay things* by the Women-Servants; and take all that little Frugality which is to be found among them. . . . So that upon the whole, neither the Laborer without-Doors, or the menial Servant within-Doors, are one jott the better in their Behavior, or the Richer in their Pockets for all the advance of Pay which they receive, which yet in the whole Kingdom, amounts to an immense Sum by the Year. To begin with the labouring Poor, they are indeed the Grievance of the Nation, and there seems an absolute Necessity to bring them, by severe regulations, to some State of immediate Subordination." (*The Great Law of Subordination Considered* [London, 1724]).

The English laborer, in short, is incurably idle and wickedly improvident. He will work till he has a few shillings in his pocket which he proceeds to squander at once in the alehouse. The female part of the servant class carries impudence even further than the male, for she not only demands exorbitant wages, but decks herself out in finery to the confusion of honest strangers. And he says again, in the same pamphlet: "A Gentleman in a Visit lately at a House of Good Fashion, who being recommended to one of the Gentleman's Daughters, mistook the Chambermaid for her who was designed for his Mistress, and unhappily stepping up to her saluted her first, which Misfortune cost him the loss of his Mistress."

For remedy, Defoe proposed "good Laws to secure the due *Subordination* of the People." Parliament should revive the wholesome institutions of Lycurgus, providing that "the poor might not be oppress'd" and that "they might not forget that they were Servants." Laws should keep the workman to his task as they keep the soldier to his place in the ranks, for leaving a master in the midst of harvest or the "middle of the Spring trade," is no more to be tolerated than desertion in battle. No servant, artisan or laborer should be employed without a certificate of discharge, which, incidentally, would protect the "travelling Poor" from arrest as vagabonds, "as is often unavoidably their Case."

The selection is reprinted from J. R. McCulloch, ed., *Collection of Scarce and Valuable Economical Tracts* (London, 1859).

Giving Alms No Charity

BY DANIEL DEFOE

SINCE THE TIMES of *Queen Elizabeth* this nation has gone on to a prodigy of trade, of which the encrease of our customs from 400,000 crowns to two millions of pounds sterling *per ann.* is a demonstration beyond the power of argument; and that this whole encrease depends upon, and is principally occasion'd by the encrease of our manufacturers is so plain, I shall not take up any room here to make it out.

Having thus given an account how we came to be a rich, flourishing and populous nation, I crave leave as concisely as I can to examine how we came to be poor again, if it must be granted that we are so.

By poor here I humbly desire to be understood, not that we are a poor nation in general; I should undervalue the bounty of Heaven to *England*, and act with less understanding than most men are masters of, if I should not own, that in general we are *as rich a nation* as any in the world; but by poor I mean burthen'd with a crowd of clamouring, unimploy'd, unprovided for poor people, who make the nation uneasie, burthen the rich, clog our parishes, and make themselves worthy of laws, and peculiar management to dispose of and direct them: How these came to be thus is the question.

And first I humbly crave leave to lay these heads down as fundamental maxims, which I am ready at any time to defend and make out.

1. *There is in* England *more labour than hands to perform it, and consequently a want of people, not of employment.*
2. *No man in* England, *of sound limbs and senses, can be poor meerly for want of work.*
3. *All our work-houses, corporations and charities for employing the poor, and setting them to work, as now they are employ'd, or any Acts of Parliament to empower overseers of parishes, or parishes themselves, to employ the poor, except as shall be hereafter excepted, are, and will be publick nusances, mischiefs to the nation which serve to the ruin of families, and the encrease of the poor.*

4. *That 'tis a regulation of the poor that is wanted in* England, *not a setting them to work.*

I affirm, *that in* England *there is more labour than hands to perform it.* This I prove,

1st. From the dearness of wages, which in *England* out goes all nations in the world; and *I know no greater demonstration in trade.* Wages, like exchanges, rise and fall as the remitters and drawers, the employers and the workmen, ballance one another.

The employers are the remitters, the workmen are the drawers, if there are more employers than work-men, the price of wages must rise, because the employer wants that work to be done more than the poor man wants to do it, if there are more work-men than employers the price of labour falls, because the poor man wants his wages more than the employer wants to have his business done.

Trade, like all nature, most obsequiously obeys the great law of cause and consequence; and this is the occasion why even all the greatest articles of trade follow, and as it were pay homage to this seemingly minute and inconsiderable thing, *the poor man's labour.*

I omit, with some pain, the many very useful thoughts that occur on this head, to preserve the brevity I owe to the dignity of that assembly I am writing to. But I cannot but note how from hence it appears, that the glory, the strength, the riches, the trade, and all that's valuable in a nation, as to its figure in the world, depends upon the number of its people, be they never so mean or poor; the consumption of manufactures encreases the manufacturers; the number of manufacturers encreases the consumption; provisions are consum'd to feed them, land improv'd, and more hands employ'd to furnish provisions: All the wealth of the nation, and all the trade is produc'd by numbers of people; but of this by the way.

The price of wages not only determines the difference between the employer and the workman, but it rules the rates of every market. If wages grow high, provisions rise in proportion, and I humbly conceive it to be a mistake in those people, who say labour in such parts of *England* is cheap because provisions are cheap, but 'tis plain, provisions are cheap there because labour is cheap, and labour is cheaper in those parts than in others; because being remoter from *London* there is not that extraordinary disproportion between the work and the number of hands; there are more hands, and consequently labour cheaper.

If there was one poor man in *England* more than there was work to employ, either somebody else must stand still for him, or he must be starv'd; if another man stands still for him he wants a days work, and goes to seek it, and by consequence supplants another, and this a third, and this contention brings it to this; no, says the poor man, *that is like to be put out of his work,* rather than that man shall come in I'll do it cheaper; nay, says the other, but I'll do it cheaper than you; and thus one poor man wanting but a days work would bring down the price of labour in a whole nation, for the man cannot starve, and will work for any thing rather than want it.

It may be objected here, this is contradicted by our number of beggars.

I am sorry to say I am obliged here to call begging an employment, since 'tis plain, if there is more work than hands to perform it, no man that has his *limbs* and his *senses* need to beg, and those that *have not* ought to be put into a condition not to want it.

So that begging is a meer scandal in the general, *in the able* 'tis a scandal upon their industry, and *in the impotent* 'tis a scandal upon the country.

Nay, the begging, as now practic'd, is a scandal upon our charity, and perhaps the foundation of all our present grievance.—How can it be possible that any man or woman, who being sound in body and mind, may as 'tis apparent they may, have wages for their work, should be so base, so meanly spirited, as to beg an alms for Godsake.—Truly the scandal lies on our charity: and people have such a notion in *England* of being pittiful and charitable, that they encourage vagrants, and by a mistaken zeal do more harm than good.

This is a large scene, and much might be said upon it; I shall abridge it as much as possible.— The poverty of *England* does not lye among the craving beggars but among poor families, where the children are numerous, and where death or sickness has depriv'd them of the labour of the father; these are the houses that the sons and daughters of charity, if they would order it well, should seek out and relieve; an alms ill directed may be charity to the particular person, but becomes an injury to the publick, and no charity to the nation. As for the craving poor, I am perswaded I do them no wrong when I say, that if they were incorporated they would be the richest society in the nation; and the reason why so many pretend to want work is, that they can live so well with the pretence of wanting work, they would be mad to leave it and work in earnest; and I affirm of my own knowledge, when I have wanted a man for labouring work, and offer'd *9s per* week to strouling fellows at my door, they have frequently told me to my face, they could get more a begging, and I once set a lusty fellow in the stocks for making the experiment.

I shall, in its proper place, bring this to a method of tryal, since nothing but demonstration will affect us, 'tis an easie matter to prevent begging in *England*, and yet to maintain all our impotent poor at far less charge to the parishes than they now are oblig'd to be at.

When Queen *Elizabeth* had gain'd her point as to manufactories in *England*, she had fairly laid the foundation, she thereby found out the way how every family might live upon their own labour, like a wise princess she knew 'twould be hard to force people to work when there was nothing for them to turn their hands to; but as soon as she had brought the matter to bear, and there was work for every body that had no mind to starve, then she apply'd herself to make laws to oblige the people to do this work, and to punish vagrants, and make every one live by their own labour; all her successors followed this laudable example, and from hence came all those laws against sturdy beggars, vagabonds, stroulers, &c., which had they been severely put in execution by our magistrates, 'tis presum'd these vagrant poor had not so encreas'd upon us as they have.

And it seems strange to me, from what just ground we proceed now upon other methods, and fancy that 'tis now our business to find them work, and to employ them rather than to oblige them to find themselves work and go about it.

From this mistaken notion come all our work-houses and corporations, and the same error, with submission, I presume was the birth of this bill now depending, which enables every parish to erect the woollen manufacture within it self, for the employing their own poor. . . .

'Tis hard to calculate what a blow it would be to trade in general, should every county but manufacture all the several sorts of goods they use, it would throw our inland trade into strange convulsions, which at present is perhaps, or has been, in the greatest regularity of any in the world.

What strange work must it then make when every town shall have a manufacture, and every parish be a ware-house; trade will be burthen'd with corporations, which are generally equally destructive as monopolies, and by this method will easily be made so.

Parish stocks, under the direction of Justices of Peace, may soon come to set up petty manufactures, and here shall all useful things be made, and all the poorer sort of people shall be aw'd or byass'd to trade there only. Thus the shop-keepers, who pay taxes, and are the support of our

inland circulation, will immediately be ruin'd, and thus we shall beggar the nation to provide for the poor.

As this will make every parish a market town, and every hospital a store-house, so in *London*, and the adjacent parts, to which vast quantities of the woollen manufacture will be thus transplanted, too great and disproportion'd numbers of the people will in time assemble.

Tho' the settled poor can't remove, yet single people will stroul about and follow the manufacturer; and thus in time such vast numbers will be drawn about *London*, as may be inconvenient to the government, and especially depopulating to those countries where the numbers of people, by reason of these manufactures are very considerable. . . .

If it be said here will be manufactures in every parish, and that will keep the people at home,

I humbly represent what strange confusion and particular detriment to the general circulation of trade *mention'd before* it must be, to have every parish make its own manufactures.

1. It will make our towns and counties independent of one another, and put a damp to correspondence, which all will allow to be a great motive of trade in general.

2. It will fill us with various sorts and kinds of manufactures, by which our stated sorts of goods will in time dwindle away in reputation, and foreigners not know them one from another. Our several manufactures are known by their respective names; and our serges, bayes and other goods, are bought abroad by the character and reputation of the places where they are made; when there shall come new and unheard of kinds to market, some better, some worse, as to be sure new undertakers will vary in kinds, the dignity and reputation of the *English* goods abroad will be lost, and so many confusions in trade must follow, as are too many to repeat.

3. Either our parish-stock must sell by wholesale or by retail, or both; if the first, 'tis doubted they will make sorry work of it, and having other business of their own make but poor merchants; if by retail, then they turn pedlars, will be a publick nusance to trade, and at last quite ruin it.

4. This will ruin all the carriers in *England*, the wool will be all manufactured where it is sheer'd, every body will make their own cloaths, and the trade which now lives by running thro' a multitude of hands, will go then through so few, that thousands of families will want employment, and this is the only way to reduce us to the condition spoken of, to have more hands than work.

'Tis the excellence of our *English* manufacture,

that it is so planted as to go thro' as many hands as 'tis possible; he that contrives to have it go thro' fewer, ought at the same time to provide work for the rest—as it is it employs a great multitude of people, and can employ more; but if a considerable number of these people be unhing'd from their employment, it cannot but be detrimental to the whole.

When I say we could employ more people in *England*, I do not mean that we cannot do our work with those we have, but I mean thus:

First, It should be more people brought over from foreign parts. I do not mean that those we have should be taken from all common employments and put to our manufacture; we may unequally dispose of our hands, and so have too many for some works, and too few for others; and 'tis plain that in some parts of *England* it is so, what else can be the reason, why in our southern parts of *England*, *Kent* in particular, borrows 20,000 people of other counties to get in her harvest.

But if more forreigners came among us, if it were 2 millions, it could do us no harm, because they would consume our provisions, and we have land enough to produce much more than we do, and they would consume our manufactures, and we have wool enough for any quantity.

I think therefore, with submission, to erect manufactures in every town to transpose the manufactures from the settled places into private parishes and corporations, to parcel out our trade to every door, it must be ruinous to the manufacturers themselves, will turn thousands of families out of their employments, and take the bread out of the mouths of diligent and industrious families to feed vagrants, thieves and beggars, who ought much rather to be compell'd, by legal methods, to seek that work which it is plain is to be had; and thus this Act will instead of settling and relieving the poor, encrease their number, and starve the best of them.

It remains now, according to my first proposal page 37, to consider from whence proceeds the poverty of our people, what accident, what decay of trade, what want of employment, what strange revolution of circumstances makes our people poor, and consequently burthensom, and our laws deficient, so as to make more and other laws requisite, and the nation concerned to apply a remedy to this growing disease. I answer,

I. Not for want of work; and besides what has been said on that head, I humbly desire these two things may be consider'd.

First, 'Tis apparent, that if one man, woman, or child, can by his, or her labour, earn more money

than will subsist one body, there must consequently be no want of work, since any man would work for just as much as would supply himself rather than starve.—What a vast difference then must there be between the work and the workmen, when 'tis now known that in *Spittle-fields*, and other adjacent parts of the city, there is nothing more frequent than for a journey-man weaver, of many sorts, to gain from 15s. to 30s. *per* week wages, and I appeal to the silk throwsters, whether they do not give 8s. 9s. and 10s. *per* week, to blind men and cripples, to turn wheels, and do the meanest and most ordinary works.

Cur Moriatur Homo, &c.—Why are the families of these men starv'd, and their children in work-houses, and brought up by charity; I am ready to produce to this Honourable House the man who for several years has gain'd of me by his handy labour at the mean scoundrel employment of tile making from 16s. to 20s. *per* week wages, and all that time would hardly have a pair of shoes to his feet, or cloaths to cover his nakedness, and had his wife and children kept by the parish.

The meanest labours in this nation afford the work-man sufficient to provide for himself and his family, and that could never be if there was a want of work.

2. I humbly desire this Honourable House to consider the present difficulty of raising soldiers in this kingdom; the vast charge the kingdom is at to the officers to procure men; the many little and *not over honest methods* made use of to bring them into the service, the laws made to compel them; why are gaols rumag'd for malefactors, and the Mint and prisons for debtors, the war is an employment of honour, and suffers some scandal in having men taken from the gallows, and immediately from villains, and housebreakers made gentlemen soldiers. If men wanted employment, and consequently bread, this could never be, any man would carry a musket rather than starve, and wear the Queen's cloth, or any bodies cloth, rather than go naked, and live in rags and want; 'tis plain the nation is full of people, and 'tis as plain our people have no particular aversion to the war, but they are not poor enough to go abroad; 'tis poverty makes men soldiers, and drives crowds into the armies, and the difficulties to get *English*-men to list is, because they live in plenty and ease, and he that can earn 20s. *per* week at an easie, steady employment, must be drunk or mad when he lists for a soldier, to be knock'd o'th'head for 3s. 6d. *per* week; but if there was no work to be had, if the poor wanted employment, if they had not bread to eat, nor knew not how to earn it, thousands of young lusty fel-

lows would fly to the pike and musket, and choose to dye like men in the face of the enemy, rather than lye at home, starve, perish in poverty and distress.

From all these particulars, and innumerable unhappy instances which might be given, 'tis plain, the poverty of our people which is so burthensome, and increases upon us so much, does not arise from want of proper employments, and for want of work, or employers, and consequently,

Work-houses, corporations, parish-stocks, and the like, to set them to work, as they are pernicious to trade, injurious and impoverishing to those already employ'd, so they are needless, and will come short of the end propos'd.

The poverty and exigence of the poor in *England*, is plainly deriv'd from one of these two particular causes.

Casualty or Crime.—By casualty, I mean sickness of families, loss of limbs or sight, and any, either natural or accidental impotence as to labour.

These as infirmities meerly providential are not at all concern'd in this debate; ever were, will, and ought to be the charge and care of the respective parishes where such unhappy people chance to live, nor is there any want of new laws to make provision for them, our ancestors having been always careful to do it.

The crimes of our people, and from whence their poverty derives, as the visible and direct fountains are,

1. Luxury.
2. Sloath.
3. Pride.

Good husbandry is no *English* vertue, it may have been brought over, and in some places where it has been planted it has thriven well enough, but 'tis a forreign species, it neither loves, nor is belov'd by an *English-man;* and 'tis observ'd nothing is so universally hated, nothing treated with such a general contempt as a rich covetous man, tho' he does no man any wrong, only saves his own, every man will have an ill word for him, if a misfortune happens to him, hang him a covetous old rogue, 'tis no matter, he's rich enough, nay when a certain great man's house was on fire, I have heard the people say one to another, let it burn and 'twill, he's a covetous old miserly dog, I wo'nt trouble my head to help him, he'd be hang'd before he'd give us a bit of bread if we wanted it.

'Tho this be a fault, yet I observe from it something of the natural temper and genius of the nation, generally speaking, they cannot save their money.

'Tis generally said the *English* get estates, and

the *Dutch* save them; and this observation I have made between forreigners and *English-men* that where an *English-man* earns 20s. *per* week, and *but just lives,* as we call it, a *Dutch-man* grows rich, and leaves his children in very good condition; where an *English* labouring man with his 9s. *per* week lives wretchedly and poor, a *Dutch-man* with that wages will live very tolerably well, keep the wolf from the door, and have every thing handsome about him. In short, he will be rich with the same gain as makes the *English-man* poor, he'll thrive when the other goes in rags, and he'll live when the other starves, or goes a begging.

The reason is plain, a man with good husbandry, and thought in his head, brings home his earnings honestly to his family, commits it to the management of his wife, or otherwise disposes it for proper subsistance, and this man with mean gains, lives comfortably, and brings up a family, when a single man getting the same wages, drinks it away at the ale-house, thinks not of to morrow, layes up nothing for sickness, age, or disaster, and when any of these happen, he's starv'd, and a beggar.

This is so apparent in every place, that I think it needs no explication; that *English* labouring people eat and drink, but especially the latter three times as much in value as any sort of forreigners of the same dimensions in the world.

I am not writing this as a satyr on our people, 'tis a sad truth; and worthy the debate and application of the nations physitians assembled in Parliament, the profuse extravagant humour of our poor people in eating and drinking, keeps them low, causes their children to be left naked and starving, to the care of the parishes, whenever either sickness or disaster befalls the parent.

The next article is their *sloath.*

We are the most *lazy diligent* nation in the world, vast trade, rich manufactures, mighty wealth, universal correspondence and happy success have been constant companions of *England,* and given us the title of an industrious people, and so in general we are.

But there is a general taint of slothfulness upon our poor, there's nothing more frequent, than for an *English-man* to work till he has got his pocket full of money, and then go and be idle, *or perhaps drunk,* till 'tis all gone, and perhaps himself in debt; and ask him in his cups what he intends, he'll tell you honestly, he'll drink as long as it lasts, and then go to work for more.

I humbly suggest this distemper's so general, so epidemick, and so deep rooted in the nature and genius of the *English,* that I much doubt its being easily redress'd, and question whether it be possible to reach it by an Act of Parliament.

This is the ruine of our poor, the *wife mourns*, the children *starve*, the husband *has work before him*, but lies at the ale-house, or otherwise *idles away* his time, and won't work.

'Tis the men that *wont work*, not the men that *can get no work*, which makes the numbers of our poor; all the work-houses in *England*, all the overseers setting up stocks and manufactures won't reach this case; and I humbly presume to say, if these two articles are remov'd, there will be no need of the other.

I make no difficulty to promise on a short summons, to produce above a thousand families in *England*, within my particular knowledge, who go in rags, and their children wanting bread, whose fathers can earn their 15 to 25s. *per* week, but will not work, who may have work enough, but are too idle to seek after it, and hardly vouchsafe to earn any thing more than bare subsistance, and spending money for themselves.

I can give an incredible number of examples in my own knowledge among our labouring poor. I once paid 6 or 7 men together on a *Saturday* night, the least 10s. and some 30s. for work, and have seen them go with it directly to the ale-house, lie there till *Monday*, spend it every penny, and run in debt to boot, and not give a farthing of it to their families, tho' all of them had wives and children.

From hence comes poverty, parish charges, and beggary, if ever one of these wretches falls sick, all they would ask was a pass to the parish they liv'd at, and the wife and children to the door a begging.

If this Honourable House can find out a remedy for this part of the mischief; if such Acts of Parliament may be made as may effectually cure the sloath and luxury of our poor, that shall make drunkards take care of wife and children, spendthrifts lay up for a *wet day;* idle, lazy fellows diligent; and thoughtless sottish men, careful and provident.

If this can be done, I presume to say, there will be no need of transposing and confounding our manufactures, and the circulation of our trade; they will soon find work enough, and there will soon be less poverty among us, and if this cannot be done, setting them to work upon woollen manufactures, and thereby encroaching upon those that now work at them, will but ruine our trade, and consequently increase the number of the poor. . . .

TOLERATION

IN THE 1640s, Englishmen had risen against a King who attempted to impose his will on the nation: to levy its taxes, declare its law and dictate the form of its religious observance. Whatever may have been the social and economic roots of that revolt, its formulas were cast in religious terms. In a sense, the English Civil Wars may be taken as one of the first effective expressions of resistance against a uniformity imposed from without. The State, and in the State, the King, may rule the lives of its members. So said the royalist party. Its opponents maintained that certain aspects of life —conscience and property among them— were beyond reach of authority. Government, in fine, exists for the service of society, not for its mastery.

From that view stems the political theory of the existence of civil or natural rights which appeared before government and are above its interference. From that view, too, is derived the idea of the peculiar and personal character of conscience and a consequent necessity for religious toleration. And since it was the dissenting and the dispossessed who made the bulk of those who first left Europe for America, the assertion that there were affairs in which government—which was controlled by the conformers and the possessors—had no right to meddle became a statement with which American opinion was increasingly inclined to agree.

Of the Englishmen who formulated the theory of natural rights, few were more persuasive, or more read in America, than John Locke (1632–1704), intellectual father of the revolutions of the eighteenth century and precursor of Benthamism and the liberalism of the nineteenth. Though Locke was too young for actual participation in the Civil Wars, his father, a prosperous lawyer, suffered by joining on the side of Parliament. This, however, did not hinder Locke's education; he attended Westminster school and Oxford, where he rejected the aridities of scholasticism for the experimental approach to knowledge. In line with his distaste for the empty disputations of the university, Locke abandoned theology for the study of medicine, a choice which finally led to his friendship with the first Earl of Shaftesbury, deist, politician and founder of Carolina.

Locke's own background was Parliamentary, as has been noted, but many of his friends were royalist. Yet he accepted the Restoration as a device for reestablishing constitutional government, not as an atonement for a wrong. Later in the decade, Locke became physician, friend, and adviser to Shaftesbury; he helped draft the strange constitution for the colony that Shaftesbury was establishing in Carolina; and, when James II proceeded to emulate his father's effort and moved in the direction of absolutism, Locke joined his patron in exile.

Only after his return to England did Locke make writing his chief work. Though his treatises on education and the theory of knowledge may figure more largely in the history of English philosophy, it was his essays on toleration and on government that supplied the Whigs with political theory and, together with his more strictly philosophic works, laid the foundation for the Benthamite radicalism which was to challenge Toryism and Whig doctrine alike.

Toleration had long interested Locke; he had written an essay on the subject in 1667, shortly before he began practicing medicine, but twenty-two years passed before the publication of the *Four Letters Concerning Toleration* which were the final development of that essay. Morals are more important than theology, Locke argues, and right conduct superior to right belief—a principle which seems to foreshadow Emerson and William James and John Dewey. Furthermore, right conduct will be promoted by a separation between the "business of civil government" and matters of religion. Life, liberty, and property should be secured to all by the civil magistrate; but as salvation is beyond his power, so it should be beyond his meddling. The church is a free and voluntary society which may make its own laws, but which may enforce those laws only by exhortation, advice and, if necessary, expulsion from its body. Excommunication is possible, under a policy of toleration, but it may not extend to the "damnifying of body or estate." Nor may any church exercise jurisdiction over another.

Toleration requires that priests be confined to church affairs; they must refrain from violence or persecution and should preach peace and good-will toward the erroneous as well as the orthodox. Confound men's errors, Locke advises the clergy, but spare their persons. He continues by urging that civil rights be extended to all, not limited to the Christian sects only. For it is the refusal of toleration and not the diversity of sects which is responsible for tumults in the state.

The circumstances of Locke's time are very evident in the ideas underlying his plea for toleration. It is those who approve tyranny in the state who would force faith upon the reluctant, Locke remarks in a thrust at the Tories. Furthermore, man is endowed with natural rights which he secures by the organization of society into governments. At bedrock, that idea of civil rights justifies the risings which had executed one king, dethroned a second and finally established a compromise which Locke set himself to defend. That defense became a political theory, in time, and its reasoning was part of the intellectual atmosphere which helped shape the thinking of Americans in generations to come.

The selection is from John Locke, *Four Letters Concerning Toleration* (London, 1689).

A Letter Concerning Toleration

BY JOHN LOCKE

HONORED SIR,

Since you are pleased to inquire what are my thoughts about the mutual Toleration of Christians in their different professions of religion, I must needs answer you freely, that I esteem that toleration to be the chief characteristical mark of the true church. For whatsoever some people boast of the antiquity of places and names, or of the pomp of their outward worship; others, of the reformation of their discipline; all, of the orthodoxy of their faith, for every one is orthodox to himself; these things, and all others of this nature, are much rather marks of men striving for power and empire over one another, than of the church of Christ. Let any one have ever so true a claim to all these things, yet if he be destitute of charity, meekness, and good-will in general towards all mankind, even to those that are not Christians, he is certainly yet short of being a true Christian himself. 'The kings of 'the Gentiles exercise lordship over them,' said our Saviour to his disciples, 'but ye shall not be so' (Luke xxii.) The business of true religion is quite another thing. It is not instituted in order to the erecting an external pomp, nor to the obtaining of ecclesiastical dominion, nor to the exercising of compulsive force; but to the regulating of mens lives according to the rules of virtue and piety. Whosoever will list himself under the banner of Christ, must, in the first place and above all things, make war upon his own lusts and vices. It is in vain for any man to usurp the name of Christian without holiness of life, purity of manners, and benignity and meekness of spirit. 'Let every one that nameth 'the name of Christ, depart from iniquity.' 'Thou, when thou art converted, strengthen thy brethren,' said our Lord to Peter (Luke xxii). It would indeed be very hard for one that appears careless about his own salvation, to persuade me that he were extremely concerned for mine. For it is impossible that those should sincerely and heartily apply themselves to make other people Christians, who have not really embraced the Christian religion in their own hearts. If the Gospel and the apostles may be credited, no man can be a Christian without charity, and without that faith which works, not by force, but by love. Now I appeal to the consciences of those that persecute, torment, destroy, and kill other men upon pretence of religion, whether they do it out of friendship and kindness towards them, or no: and I shall then indeed, and not till then, believe they do so, when I shall see those fiery zealots correcting, in the same manner, their friends and familiar acquaintance, for the manifest sins they commit against the precepts of the Gospel; when I shall see them persecute with fire and sword the members of their own communion that are tainted with enormous vices, and without amendment are in danger of eternal perdition: and when I shall see them thus express their love and desire of the salvation of their souls by the infliction of torments, and exercise of all manner of cruelties. For if it be out of a principle of charity, as they pretend, and love to mens souls, that they deprive them of their estates, maim them with corporal punishments, starve and torment them in noisome prisons, and in the end even take away their lives; I say, if all this be done merely to make men Christians and procure their salvation, why then do they suffer 'whoredom, fraud, malice, and 'such like enormities,' which, according to the apostle (Rom. i.), manifestly relish of heathenish corruption, to predominate so much and abound amongst their flocks and people? These, and such like things, are certainly more contrary to the glory of God, to the purity of the church, and for the salvation of souls, than any conscientious dissent from ecclesiastical decision, or separation from public worship, whilst accompanied with innocency of life. Why then does this burning zeal for God, for the church, and for the salvation of souls; burning, I say, literally, with fire and faggot, pass by those moral vices and wickednesses, without any chastisement, which are acknowledged by all men to be diametrically opposite to the profession of Christianity; and bend all its nerves either to the introducing of ceremonies, or to the establishment of opinions, which for the most part are about nice and intricate matters that exceed the capacity of ordinary understandings? . . . Whosoever therefore is sincerely solicitous about the kingdom of God, and thinks it his duty to endeavour the enlargement of it amongst men, ought to apply himself with no less

care and industry to the rooting out of these immoralities than to the extirpation of sects. But if any one do otherwise, and whilst he is cruel and implacable towards those that differ from him in opinion, he be indulgent to such iniquities and immoralities as are unbecoming the name of a Christian, let such a one talk ever so much of the church, he plainly demonstrates by his actions, that it is another kingdom he aims at, and not the advancement of the kingdom of God.

That any man should think fit to cause another man, whose salvation he heartily desires, to expire in torments, and that even in an unconverted estate, would, I confess, seem very strange to me, and I think, to any other also. But nobody, surely, will ever believe that such a carriage can proceed from charity, love, or good-will. If any one maintain that men ought to be compelled by fire and sword to profess certain doctrines, and conform to this or that exterior worship, without any regard had unto their morals; if any one endeavour to convert those that are erroneous unto the faith, by forcing them to profess things that they do not believe, and allowing them to practise things that the Gospel does not permit; it cannot be doubted, indeed, that such a one is desirous to have a numerous assembly joined in the same profession with himself; but that he principally intends by those means to compose a truly Christian church, is altogether incredible. . . .

The toleration of those that differ from others in matters of religion, is so agreeable to the Gospel of Jesus Christ, and to the genuine reason of mankind, that it seems monstrous for men to be so blind, as not to perceive the necessity and advantage of it, in so clear a light. I will not here tax the pride and ambition of some, the passion and uncharitable zeal of others. These are faults from which human affairs can perhaps scarce ever be perfectly freed; but yet such as nobody will bear the plain imputation of, without covering them with some specious colour; and so pretend to commendation, whilst they are carried away by their own irregular passions. But however, that some may not colour their spirit of persecution and unchristian cruelty, with a pretence of care of the publick weal, and observation of the laws; and that others, under pretence of religion, may not seek impunity for their libertinism and licentiousness; in a word, that none may impose either upon himself or others, by the pretences of loyalty and obedience to the prince, or of tenderness and sincerity in the worship of God; I esteem it above all things necessary to distinguish exactly the business of civil government from that of religion, and to settle the just bounds that lie between the one and the other. If this be not done, there can be no end put to the controversies that will be always arising between those that have, or at least pretend to have, on the one side, a concernment for the interest of mens souls, and on the other side, a care of the commonwealth.

The commonwealth seems to me to be a society of men constituted only for the procuring, the preserving, and the advancing their own civil interests.

Civil interests I call life, liberty, health, and indolency of body; and the possession of outward things, such as money, lands, houses, furniture, and the like.

It is the duty of the civil magistrate, by the impartial execution of equal laws, to secure unto all the people in general, and to every one of his subjects in particular, the just possession of these things belonging to this life. If any one presume to violate the laws of publick justice and equity, established for the preservation of these things, his presumption is to be checked by the fear of punishment, consisting in the deprivation or diminution of those civil interests, or goods, which otherwise he might and ought to enjoy. But seeing no man does willingly suffer himself to be punished by the deprivation of any part of his goods, and much less of his liberty or life, therefore is the magistrate armed with the force and strength of all his subjects, in order to the punishment of those that violate any other man's rights.

Now that the whole jurisdiction of the magistrate reaches only to these civil concernments; and that all civil power, right, and dominion, is bounded and confined to the only care of promoting these things; and that it neither can nor ought in any manner to be extended to the salvation of souls; these following considerations seem unto me abundantly to demonstrate.

First, because the care of souls is not committed to the civil magistrate, any more than to other men. It is not committed unto him, I say, by God; because it appears not that God has ever given any such authority to one man over another, as to compel any one to his religion. Nor can any such power be vested in the magistrate by the consent of the people; because no man can so far abandon the care of his own salvation, as blindly to leave it to the choice of any other, whether prince or subject, to prescribe to him what faith or worship he shall embrace. For no man can, if he would, conform his faith to the dictates of another. All the life and power of true religion consists in the outward and full persuasion of the mind; and faith is not faith without believing. Whatever profession we make, to whatever outward worship we conform, if we are not fully satisfied in our own mind that the one is true, and the other well pleasing unto God, such profession and such practice, far from being any furtherance, are indeed great obstacles to our salvation. For in this manner, instead of expiating other sins by the exercise of religion, I say, in offering thus unto God Almighty such a worship as we esteem to be displeasing unto him, we add unto the number of our other sins, those also of hypocrisy, and contempt of his Divine Majesty.

In the second place. The care of souls cannot belong to the civil magistrate, because his power consists only in outward force: but true and saving religion consists in the inward persuasion of the mind, without which nothing can be acceptable to God. And such is the nature of the understanding, that it cannot be compelled to the belief of any thing by outward force. Confiscation of estate, imprisonment, torments, nothing of that nature can have any such efficacy as to make men change the inward judgment that they have framed of things.

It may indeed be alleged, that the magistrate may make use of arguments, and thereby draw the heterodox into the way of truth, and procure their salvation. I grant it; but this is common to him with other men. In teaching, instructing, and redressing the erroneous by reason, he may certainly do what becomes any good man to do. Magistracy does not oblige him to put off either humanity or Christianity. But it is one thing to persuade, another to command; one thing to press with arguments, another with penalties. This the civil power alone has a right to do; to the other, goodwill is authority enough. Every man has commission to admonish, exhort, convince another of error, and by reasoning to draw him into truth: but to give laws, receive obedience, and compel with the sword, belongs to none but the magistrate. And upon this ground I affirm that the magistrate's power extends not to the establishing of any articles of faith or forms of worship, by the force of his laws. For laws are of no force at all without penalties, and penalties in this case are absolutely impertinent; because they are not proper to convince the mind. Neither the profession of any articles of faith, nor the conformity to any outward form of worship as has been already said, can be available to the salvation of souls, unless the truth of the one, and the acceptableness of the other unto God, be thoroughly believed by those that so profess and practice. But penalties are no ways capable to produce such belief. It is only light and evidence that can work a change in mens opinions; and that light can in no manner proceed from corporal sufferings, or any other outward penalties.

In the third place, the care of the salvation of mens souls cannot belong to the magistrate; because, though the rigour of laws and the force of penalties were capable to convince and change mens minds, yet would not that help at all to the salvation of their souls. For, there being but one truth, one way to heaven; what hopes is there that more men would be led into it, if they had no other rule to follow but the religion of the court, and were put under a necessity to quit the light of their own reason, to oppose the dictates of their own consciences, and blindly to resign up themselves to the will of their governors, and to the religion, which either ignorance, ambition, or superstition had chanced to establish in the countries where they were born? In the variety and contradiction of opinions in religion, wherein the princes of the world are as much divided as in their secular interests, the narrow way would be much straitened; one country alone would be in the right, and all the rest of the world put under an obligation of following their princes in the ways that lead to destruction: and that which heightens the absurdity, and very ill suits the notion of a deity, men would owe their eternal happiness or their eternal misery to the places of their nativity.

These considerations, to omit many others that might have been urged to the same purpose, seem unto me sufficient to conclude, that all the power of civil government relates only to men's civil interests, is confined to the care of the things of this world, and have nothing to do with the world to come.

Let us now consider what a church is. A church then I take to be a voluntary society of men, joining themselves together of their own accord, in order to the publick worshipping of God, in such a manner as they may judge acceptable to him, and effectual to the salvation of their souls.

I say, it is a free and voluntary society. Nobody is born a member of any church; otherwise the religion of parents would descend unto children, by the same right of inheritance as their temporal estates, and every one would hold his faith by the same tenure he does his lands; than which nothing can be imagined more absurd. Thus therefore that matter stands. No man by nature is bound unto any particular church or sect, but every one joins himself voluntarily to that society in which he believes he has found that profession and worship which is truly acceptable to God. The hopes of salvation, as it was the only cause of his entrance

into that communion, so it can be the only reason of his stay there. . . .

But it may be asked, by what means then shall ecclesiastical laws be established, if they must be thus destitute of all compulsive power? I answer, they must be established by means suitable to the nature of such things, whereof the external profession and observation, if not proceeding from a thorough conviction and approbation of the mind, is altogether useless and unprofitable. The arms by which the members of this society are to be kept within their duty, are exhortations, admonitions, and advice. If by these means the offenders will not be reclaimed, and the erroneous convinced, there remains nothing further to be done, but that such stubborn and obstinate persons, who give no ground to hope for their reformation, should be cast out and separated from the society. This is the last and utmost force of ecclesiastical authority: no other punishment can thereby be inflicted, than that the relation ceasing between the body and the member which is cut off, the person so condemned ceases to be a part of that church.

These things being thus determined, let us inquire in the next place, how far the duty of Toleration extends, and what is required from every one by it.

And first: I hold, that no church is bound by the duty of Toleration to retain any such person in her bosom, as after admonition continues obstinately to offend against the laws of the society. For these being the condition of communion, and the bond of the society, if the breach of them were permitted without any animadversion, the society would immediately be thereby dissolved. But nevertheless, in all such cases care is to be taken that the sentence of excommunication and the execution thereof, carry with it no rough usage of word or action, whereby the ejected person may any ways be damnified in body or estate. For all force, as has often been said, belongs only to the magistrate, nor ought any private persons, at any time, to use force; unless it be in self-defence against unjust violence. Excommunication neither does nor can deprive the excommunicated person of any of those civil goods that he formerly possessed. All those things belong to the civil government, and are under the magistrate's protection. The whole force of excommunication consists only in this, that the resolution of the society in that respect being declared, the union that was between the body and some member, comes thereby to be dissolved; and that relation ceasing, the participation of some certain things, which the society communicated to its members, and unto which no man has any civil right, comes also to cease. For there is no civil injury done unto the excommunicated person, by the church minister's refusing him that bread and wine, in the celebration of the Lord's supper, which was not bought with his, but other mens money.

Secondly: No private person has any right, in any manner to prejudice another person in his civil enjoyments, because he is of another church or religion. All the rights and franchises that belong to him as a man, or as a denison, are inviolably to be preserved to him. These are not the business of religion. No violence nor injury is to be offered him, whether he be Christian or pagan. . . .

What I say concerning the mutual Toleration of private persons differing from one another in religion, I understand also of particular churches; which stand as it were in the same relation to each other as private persons among themselves, nor has any one of them any manner of jurisdiction over any other, no not even when the civil magistrate, as it sometimes happens, comes to be of this or the other communion. For the civil government can give no new right to the church, nor the church to the civil government. So that whether the magistrate join himself to any church, or separate from it, the church remains always as it was before, a free and voluntary society. It neither acquires the power of the sword by the magistrate's coming to it, nor does it lose the right of instruction and excommunication by his going from it. This is the fundamental and immutable right of a spontaneous society, that it has power to remove any of its members who transgress the rules of its institution: but it cannot, by the accession of any new members, acquire any right of jurisdiction over those that are not joined with it. And therefore peace, equity, and friendship, are always mutually to be observed by particular churches, in the same manner as by private persons, without any pretence of superiority or jurisdiction over one another. . . .

Nevertheless, it is worthy to be observed, and lamented, that the most violent of these defenders of the truth, the opposers of errors, the exclaimers against schism, do hardly ever let loose this their zeal for God, with which they are so warmed and inflamed, unless where they have the civil magistrate on their side. But so soon as ever court-favour has given them the better end of the staff, and they begin to feel themselves the stronger, then presently peace and charity are to be laid aside: otherwise, they are religiously to be observed. Where they have not the power to carry on persecution, and to become masters, there they desire to live upon fair terms, and preach up Toleration. When they are not strengthened by the civil power, then they can bear most patiently, and unmovedly, the contagion of idolatry, superstition, and heresy, in their neighbourhood; of which, in other occasions, the interest of religion makes them to be extremely apprehensive. They do not forwardly attack those errors which are in fashion at court, or are countenanced by the government. Here they can be content to spare their arguments: which yet, with their leave, is the only right method of propagating truth, which has no such way of prevailing, as when strong arguments and good reason, are joined with the softness of civility and good usage.

No body, therefore, in fine, neither single persons, nor churches, nay, nor even commonwealths, have any just title to invade the civil rights and worldly goods of each other, upon pretence of religion. Those that are of another opinion, would do well to consider with themselves how pernicious a seed of discord and war, how powerful a provocation to endless hatreds, rapines, and slaughters, they thereby furnish unto mankind. No peace and security, no not so much as common friendship, can ever be established or preserved amongst men, so long as this opinion prevails, 'that dominion is founded in grace' and that 'religion is to be propagated by force of arms.'

In the third place: Let us see what the duty of Toleration requires from those who are distinguished from the rest of mankind, from the laity, as they please to call us, by some ecclesiastical character and office; whether they be bishops, priests, presbyters, ministers, or however else dignified or distinguished. It is not my business to inquire here into the original of the power or dignity of the clergy. This only I say, that whencesoever their authority be sprung, since it is ecclesiastical, it ought to be confined within the bounds of the church, nor can it in any manner be extended to civil affairs; because the church itself is a thing absolutely separate and distinct from the commonwealth. The boundaries on both sides are fixed and immoveable. He jumbles heaven and earth together, the things most remote and opposite, who mixes these societies; which are in their original, end, business, and in every thing, perfectly distinct, and infinitely different from each other. No man therefore, with whatsoever ecclesiastical office he be dignified, can deprive another man that is not of his church and faith, either of liberty, or of any part of his worldly goods, upon the account of that difference which is between them in religion. For whatsoever is not lawful to the whole church, cannot, by any ecclesiastical right, become lawful to any of its members.

But this is not all. It is not enough that ecclesiastical men abstain from violence and rapine, and all manner of persecution. He that pretends to be a successor of the apostles, and takes upon him the office of teaching, is obliged also to admonish his hearers of the duties of peace, and good-will towards all men; as well towards the erroneous as the orthodox; towards those that differ from them in faith and worship, as well as towards those that agree with them therein: and he ought industriously to exhort all men, whether private persons or magistrates, if any such there be in his church, to charity, meekness, and toleration; and diligently endeavour to allay and temper all that heat, and unreasonable averseness of mind, which either any man's fiery zeal for his own sect, or the craft of others, has kindled against dissenters. I will not undertake to represent how happy and how great would be the fruit, both in church and state, if the pulpits everywhere sounded with this doctrine of peace and toleration; lest I should seem to reflect too severely upon those men whose dignity I desire not to detract from, nor would have it diminished either by others or themselves. But this I say, that thus it ought to be. And if any one that professes himself to be a minister of the word of God, a preacher of the Gospel of peace, teach otherwise; he either understands not, or neglects the business of his calling, and shall one day give account thereof unto the Prince of peace. If Christians are to be admonished that they abstain from all manner of revenge, even after repeated provocations and multiplied injuries; how much more ought they who suffer nothing, who have had no harm done them, forbear violence, and abstain from all manner of ill usage towards those from whom they have received none. This caution and temper they ought certainly to use towards those who mind only their own business, and are solicitous for nothing but that, whatever men think of them, they may worship God in that manner which they are persuaded is acceptable to him, and in which they have the strongest hopes of eternal salvation. In private domestic affairs, in the management of estates, in the conservation of bodily health, every man may consider what suits his own conveniency, and follow what course he likes best. No man complains of the ill-management of his neighbour's affairs. No man is angry with another for an error committed in sowing his land, or in marrying his daughter. No body

corrects a spendthrift for consuming his substance in taverns. Let any man pull down, or build, or make whatsoever expenses he pleases, no body murmurs, no body controuls him; he has his liberty. But if any man do not frequent the church, if he do not there conform his behaviour exactly to the accustomed ceremonies, or if he brings not his children to be initiated in the sacred mysteries of this or the other congregation; this immediately causes an uproar, and the neighbourhood is filled with noise and clamour. Every one is ready to be the avenger of so great a crime. And the zealots hardly have patience to refrain from violence and rapine, so long till the cause be heard, and the poor man be, according to form, condemned to the loss of liberty, goods, or life. Oh that our ecclesiastical orators, of every sect, would apply themselves with all the strength of arguments that they are able, to the confounding of mens errors! But let them spare their persons. Let them not supply their want of reasons with the instruments of force, which belong to another jurisdiction, and do ill become a churchman's hands. Let them not call in the magistrate's authority to the aid of their eloquence, or learning; lest perhaps, whilst they pretend only love for the truth, this their intemperate zeal, breathing nothing but fire and sword, betray their ambition, and shew that what they desire is temporal dominion. For it will be very difficult to persuade men of sense, that he, who with dry eyes, and satisfaction of mind, can deliver his brother unto the executioner, to be burnt alive, does sincerely and heartily concern himself to save that brother from the flames of hell in the world to come.

In the last place. Let us now consider what is the magistrate's duty in the business of toleration: which we think is very certainly considerable.

We have already proved, that the care of souls does not belong to the magistrate: not a magisterial care, I mean, if I may so call it, which consists in prescribing by laws, and compelling by punishments. But a charitable care, which consists in teaching, admonishing, and persuading, cannot be denied unto any man. The care therefore of every man's soul belongs unto himself, and is to be left unto himself. But what if he neglect the care of his soul? I answer, what if he neglect the care of his health, or of his estate, which things are nearlier related to the government of the magistrate than the other? Will the magistrate provide by an express law, that such an one shall not become poor or sick? Laws provide, as much as is possible, that the goods and health of subjects be not injured by the fraud or violence of others; they do not guard them from the negligence or ill-husbandry of the possessors themselves. No man can be forced to be rich or healthful, whether he will nor no. Nay, God himself will not save men against their wills. Let us suppose, however, that some prince were desirous to force his subjects to accumulate riches, or to preserve the health and strength of their bodies. Shall it be provided by law, that they must consult none but Roman physicians, and shall every one be bound to live according to their prescriptions! What, shall no potion, no broth be taken, but what is prepared either in the Vatican, suppose, or in a Geneva shop? . . .

But let us grant unto these zealots, who condemn all things that are not of their mode, that from these circumstances arise different ends. What shall we conclude from thence? There is only one of these which is the true way to eternal happiness. But in this great variety of ways that men follow, it is still doubted which is this right one. Now neither the care of the commonwealth, nor the right of enacting laws, does discover this way that leads to heaven more certainly to the magistrate, than every private man's search and study discovers it unto himself. I have a weak body, sunk under a languishing disease, for which, I suppose, there is only one remedy, but that unknown. Does it therefore belong unto the magistrate to prescribe me a remedy, because there is but one, and because it is unknown? Because there is but one way for me to escape death, will it therefore be safe for me to do whatsoever the magistrate ordains? Those things that every man ought sincerely to enquire into himself, and by meditation, study, search, and his own endeavours, attain the knowledge of, cannot be looked upon as the peculiar profession of any one sort of men. Princes indeed are born superior unto other men in power, but in nature equal. Neither the right, nor the art of ruling, does necessarily carry along with it the certain knowledge of other things; and least of all of the true religion. For if it were so, how could it come to pass that the lords of the earth should differ so vastly as they do in religious matters? But let us grant that it is probable the way to eternal life may be better known by a prince than by his subjects; or at least, that in this incertitude of things, the safest and most commodious way for private persons is to follow his dictates. You will say, what then? If he should bid you follow merchandize for your livelihood, would you decline that course for fear it should not succeed? I answer: I would turn merchant upon the prince's command, because in case I should have ill success in trade, he is abundantly able to make up my loss some other way. If it be

true, as he pretends, that he desires I should thrive and grow rich, he can set me up again when unsuccessful voyages have broken me. But this is not the case, in the things that regard the life to come. If there I take wrong course, if in that respect I am once undone, it is not in the magistrate's power to repair my loss, to ease my suffering, or to restore me in any measure, much less entirely, to a good estate. What security can be given for the kingdom of heaven? . . .

That we may draw towards a conclusion. 'The sum of all we drive 'at is, that every man enjoy the same rights that are granted to others.' Is it permitted to worship God in the Roman manner? Let it be permitted to do it in the Geneva form also. Is it permitted to speak Latin in the market-place? Let those that have a mind to it, be permitted to do it also in the church. Is it lawful for any man in his own house to kneel, stand, sit, or use any other posture; and to cloath himself in white or black, in short or in long garments? Let it not be made unlawful to eat bread, drink wine, or wash with water in the church. In a word: whatsoever things are left free by law in the common occasions of life, let them remain free unto every church in divine worship. Let no man's life, or body, or house, or estate, suffer any manner of prejudice upon these accounts. Can you allow of the Presbyterian discipline? why should not the Episcopal also have what they like? Ecclesiastical authority, whether it be administered by the hands of a single person, or many, is every where the same; and neither has any jurisdiction in things civil, nor any manner of power of compulsion, nor any thing at all to do with riches and revenues.

Ecclesiastical assemblies, and sermons, are justified by daily experience, and public allowance. These are allowed to people of some one persuasion: why not to all? If any thing pass in a religious meeting seditiously, and contrary to the public peace, it is to be punished in the same manner, and no otherwise, than as if it had happened in a fair or market. These meetings ought not to be sanctuaries of factious and flagitious fellows: nor ought it to be less lawful for men to meet in churches than in halls: nor are one part of the subjects to be esteemed more blameable, for their meeting together, than others. Every one is to be accountable for his own actions: and no man is to be laid under a suspicion, or odium, for the fault of another. Those that are seditious, murderers, thieves, robbers, adulterers, slanderers, etc. of whatsoever church, whether national or not, ought to be punished and suppressed. But those whose doctrine is peaceable, and whose manners are pure and blameless, ought to be upon equal terms with their fellow-subjects. Thus if solemn assemblies, observations of festivals, public worship, be permitted to any one sort of professors; all these things ought to be permitted to the Presbyterians, Independents, Anabaptists, Arminians, Quakers, and others, with the same liberty. Nay, if we may openly speak the truth, and as becomes one man to another, neither Pagan nor Mahometan, nor Jew, ought to be excluded from the civil rights of the commonwealth, because of his religion. The Gospel commands no such thing. The church, which 'judgeth not those that are without' (I Cor. v.), want it not. And the commonwealth, which embraces indifferently all men that are honest, peaceable, and industrious, requires it not. Shall we suffer a Pagan to deal and trade with us, and shall we not suffer him to pray unto and worship God? If we allow the Jews to have private houses and dwellings amongst us, why should we not allow them to have synagogues? Is their doctrine more false, their worship more abominable, or is the civil peace more endangered, by their meeting in public than in their private houses? But if these things may be granted to Jews and Pagans, surely the condition of any Christians ought not to be worse than theirs, in a Christian commonwealth.

You will say, perhaps, Yes, it ought to be; because they are more inclinable to factions, tumults, and civil wars. I answer: is this the fault of the Christian religion? If it be so, truly the Christian religion is the worst of all religions, and ought neither to be embraced by any particular person, nor tolerated by any commonwealth. For if this be the genius, this the nature of the Christian religion, to be turbulent, and destructive to the civil peace, that church itself which the magistrate indulges, will not always be innocent. But far be it from us to say any such thing of that religion, which carries the greatest opposition to covetousness, ambition, discord, contention, and all manner of inordinate desires; and is the most modest and peaceable religion that ever was. We must therefore seek another cause of those evils that are charged upon religion. And if we consider right, we shall find it consist wholly in the subject that I am treating of. It is not the diversity of opinions, which cannot be avoided, but the refusal of toleration to those that are of different opinions, which might have been granted, that has produced all the bustles and wars, that have been in the Christian world, upon account of religion. The heads and leaders of the church, moved by avarice and insatiable desire of dominion, making use of the immoderate ambition of magistrates, and the credulous superstition of the giddy multitude,

have incensed and animated them against those that dissent from themselves; by preaching unto them, contrary to the laws of the Gospel, and to the precepts of charity, that schismatics and heretics are to be outed of their possessions, and destroyed. And thus have they mixed together, and confounded two things, that are in themselves most different, the church and the commonwealth. Now as it is very difficult for men patiently to suffer themselves to be stript of the goods, which they have got by their honest industry; and contrary to all the laws of equity, both human and divine, to be delivered up for a prey to other mens violence and rapine, especially when they are otherwise altogether blameless; and that the occasion for which they are thus treated, does not at all belong to the jurisdiction of the magistrate, but entirely to the conscience of every particular man; for the conduct of which he is accountable to God only; what else can be expected, but that these men, growing weary of the evils under which they labour, should in the end think it lawful for them to resist force with force, and to defend their natural rights, which are not forfeitable upon account of religion, with arms as well as they can? . . . But that magistrates should thus suffer these incendiaries, and disturbers of the public peace, might justly be wondered at, if it did not appear that they have been invited by them unto a participation of the spoil, and have therefore thought fit to make use of their covetousness and pride, as means whereby to increase their own power. For who does not see that these good men are indeed more ministers of the government, than ministers of the Gospel; and that by flattering the ambition, and favouring the dominion of princes and men in authority, they endeavour with all their might to promote that tyranny in the commonwealth, which otherwise they should not be able to establish in the church? This is the unhappy agreement that we see between the church and state. Whereas if each of them would contain itself within its own bounds, the one attending to the worldly welfare of the commonwealth, the other to the salvation of souls, it is impossible that any discord should ever have happened between them. 'Sed pudet haec opprobria, etc.' God Almighty grant, I beseech him, that the Gospel of peace may at length be preached, and that civil magistrates, growing more careful to conform their own consciences to the law of God, and less solicitous about the binding of other mens consciences by human laws, may, like fathers of their country, direct all their counsels and endeavours to promote universally the civil welfare of all their children; except only of such as are arrogant, ungovernable, and injurious to their brethren; and that all ecclesiastical men, who boast themselves to be the successors of the Apostles, walking peaceably and modestly, in the Apostles steps, without intermeddling with state-affairs, may apply themselves wholly to promote the salvation of souls. Farewel. . . .

CIVIL RIGHTS

LOCKE'S IDEAS of natural rights and popular sovereignty—which were to capture the minds and emotions of Americans so profoundly— were developed in his *Essay on Civil Government,* the second of the *Two Treatises on Government* which appeared in 1690. In his preface Locke indicated the immediate occasion for the work: he was defending the Glorious Revolution of 1688. James II's derelictions the English were prepared to countenance because the succession was indicated: his daughter Mary and her Protestant consort, William Prince of Orange, were to succeed to the throne. But when the King announced the birth of a male heir and there was danger that Catholicism might once more be restored, all those economic, social, and religious forces that had combined to make the Civil Wars a successful assault on absolutism once more took alarm. The Glorious Revolution followed. James was driven out and William and Mary were invited to ascend the throne. The Glorious Revolution added the capstone to the Civil Wars: it assured the "Rights of Englishmen," for it not only fixed a Protestant succession to the throne but it established the supremacy of the law and the sovereignty of the nation for all time.

Out of the Revolution emerged two great statements: Locke's and the Declaration of Rights (subsequently incorporated into an act and hence frequently known as the Bill of Rights). These were among the heritages Americans acquired from England. Broadly, they are the ideas of natural rights and constitutionalism. The "Rights of Englishmen" included these great liberties: habeas corpus, trial by jury and representative government, and they had been acquired as a result of a long struggle against absolutism. When Americans in the 1760s and 1770s came to challenge the tyranny of the English Crown, they felt they were justified in invoking as their defense the concept of natural rights and their constitutional prerogatives.

Locke, in his preface to the *Two Treatises,* had written: "These . . . I hope are sufficient to establish the Throne of our great Restorer, our present King *William:* to make good his title, in the Consent of the People; which being the only one of all lawful Governments, he has more fully and clearly, than any Prince in *Christendom;* and to justify to the World the People of *England,* whose love of their just and natural RIGHTS, with their RESOLUTION to preserve them, saves the NATION when it was on the very birth of Slavery and Ruin."

Locke proceeded to refute the doctrine of absolute monarchy, finding his arguments largely in the concept of natural rights. But Locke's "state of nature" was not that of Hobbes. To Locke the "state of nature" is not "a war of every man against every man." Rather: "The state of nature and the state of war, which however some men have confounded, are as far distant as a state of peace, good-will, mutual assistance and preservation, and a state of enmity, malice, violence and mutual destruction, are one from another. Men living together according to reason, without a common superior on earth with authority to judge between them, is properly the state of nature." In this state of nature all men are equal in the sense that they are endowed with certain natural, or inalienable, rights which no other individual may justifiably infringe, "when his own preservation comes not in competition." And then Locke went on to say: "The great and chief end . . . of men uniting into commonwealths, and putting themselves under government, is the preservation of their property. . . . And so, whoever has the legislative or supreme power of any commonwealth, is bound to govern by established standing laws, promulgated and known to the people; . . . and all this is to be directed to no other end but the peace, safety, and public good of the people."

The social contract, out of which government emerges, therefore is no surrender of individual rights. The fact is, citizens bind themselves to allegiance to the laws so long as these laws do not infringe upon the original purpose for which the society was established. Here, then, is the right to revolution—a right which the Declaration of Independence reaffirmed. But within limits: it is revolution against tyrannical government that is justifiable and not revolution against men's indefeasible natural rights. And the greatest of these is property. It was no wonder, later, that Locke was thoroughly acceptable to both the Jeffersonians and the Hamiltonians.

The selection here reprinted is from Locke's *Essay on Civil Government* (1690).

Of Civil Government

BY JOHN LOCKE

. . . I THINK it may not be amiss to set down what I take to be political power. That the power of a magistrate over a subject may be distinguished from that of a father over his children, a master over his servant, a husband over his wife, and a lord over his slave. All which distinct powers happening sometimes together in the same man, if he be considered under these different relations, it may help us to distinguish these powers one from another, and show the difference betwixt a ruler of a commonwealth, a father of a family, and a captain of a galley.

Political power, then, I take to be a right of making laws, with penalties of death, and consequently all less penalties for the regulating and preserving of property, and of employing the force of the community in the execution of such laws, and in the defence of the commonwealth from foreign injury, and all this only for the public good.

CHAPTER II: OF THE STATE OF NATURE

To understand political power aright, and derive it from its original, we must consider what estate all men are naturally in, and that is, a state of perfect freedom to order their actions, and dispose of their possessions and persons as they think fit, within the bounds of the law of Nature, without asking leave or depending upon the will of any other man.

A state also of equality, wherein all the power and jurisdiction is reciprocal, no one having more than another, there being nothing more evident than that creatures of the same species and rank, promiscuously born to all the same advantages of Nature, and the use of the same faculties, should also be equal one amongst another, without subordination or subjection, unless the lord and master of them all should, by any manifest declaration of his will, set one above another, and confer on him, by an evident and clear appointment, an undoubted right to dominion and sovereignty. . . .

But though this be a state of liberty, yet it is not a state of licence; though man in that state have an uncontrollable liberty to dispose of his person or possessions, yet he has not liberty to destroy himself, or so much as any creature in his possession, but where some nobler use than its bare preservation calls for it. The state of Nature has a law of Nature to govern it, which obliges every one, and reason, which is that law, teaches all mankind who will but consult it, that being all equal and independent, no one ought to harm another in his life, health, liberty or possessions; for men being all the workmanship of one omnipotent and infinitely wise Maker; all the servants of one sovereign Master, sent into the world by His order and about His business; they are His property, whose workmanship they are made to last during His, not one another's pleasure. And, being furnished with like faculties, sharing all in one community of Nature, there cannot be supposed any such subordination among us that may authorise us to destroy one another, as if we were made for one another's uses, as the inferior ranks of creatures are for ours. Every one as he is bound to preserve himself, and not to quit his station wilfully, so by the like reason, when his own preservation comes not in competition, ought he as much as he can to preserve the rest of mankind, and not unless it be to do justice on an offender, take away or impair the life, or what tends to the preservation of the life, the liberty, health, limb, or goods of another.

And that all men may be restrained from invading others' rights, and from doing hurt to one another, and the law of Nature be observed, which willeth the peace and preservation of all mankind, the execution of the law of Nature is in that state put into every man's hands, whereby every one has a right to punish the transgressors of that law to such a degree as may hinder its violation. For the law of Nature would, as all other laws that concern men in this world, be in vain if there were nobody that in the state of Nature had a power to execute that law, and thereby preserve the innocent and restrain offenders; and if any one in the state of Nature may punish another for any evil he has done, every one may do so. For in that state of perfect equality, where naturally there is no superiority of jurisdiction of one over another, what any may do in prosecution of that law, every one must needs have a right to do.

And thus, in the state of Nature, one man comes by a power over another, but yet no absolute of arbitrary power to use a criminal, when he has got him in his hands, according to the passionate heats or boundless extravagancy of his own will, but only to retribute to him so far as calm reason and conscience dictate, what is proportionate to his transgression, which is so much as may serve for reparation and restraint. For these two are the only reasons why one man may lawfully do harm to another, which is that we call punishment. In transgressing the law of Nature, the offender declares himself to live by another rule than that of reason and common equity, which is that measure God has set to the actions of men for their mutual security, and so he becomes dangerous to mankind; the tie which is to secure them from injury and violence being slighted and broken by him, which being a trespass against the whole species, and the peace and safety of it, provided for by the law of Nature, every man upon this score, by the right he hath to preserve mankind in general, may restrain, or where it is necessary, destroy things noxious to them, and so may bring such evil on any one who hath transgressed that law, as may make him repent the doing of it, and thereby deter him, and, by his example, others from doing the like mischief. And in this case, and upon this ground, every man hath a right to punish the offender, and be executioner of the law of Nature. . . .

To this strange doctrine—viz., That in the state of Nature every one has the executive power of the law of Nature—I doubt not but it will be objected that it is unreasonable for men to be judges in their own cases, that self-love will make men partial to themselves and their friends; and, on the other side, ill-nature, passion, and revenge will carry them too far in punishing others, and hence nothing but confusion and disorder will follow, and that therefore God hath certainly appointed government to restrain the partiality and violence of men. I easily grant that civil government is the proper remedy for the inconveniences of the state of Nature, which must certainly be great where men may be judges in their own case, since it is easy to be imagined that he who was so unjust as to do his brother an injury will scarce be so just as to condemn himself for it. But I shall desire those who make this objection to remember that absolute monarchs are but men; and if government is to be the remedy of those evils which necessarily follow from men being judges in their own cases, and the state of Nature is therefore not to be endured, I desire to know what kind of government that is, and how much better it is than the state of Nature, where one man commanding a multitude has the liberty to be judge in his own case, and may do to all his subjects whatever he pleases without the least question or control of those who execute his pleasure? and in whatsoever he doth, whether led by reason, mistake, or passion, must be submitted to? which men in the state of Nature are not bound to do one to another. And if he that judges, judges amiss in his own or any other case, he is answerable for it to the rest of mankind.

It is often asked as a mighty objection, where are, or ever were, there any men in such a state of Nature? To which it may suffice as an answer at present, that since all princes and rulers of "independent" governments all through the world are in a state of Nature, it is plain the world never was, nor never will be, without numbers of men in that state. I have named all governors of "independent" communities, whether they are, or are not, in league with others; for it is not every compact that puts an end to the state of Nature between men, but only this one of agreeing together mutually to enter into one community, and make one body politic; other promises and compacts men may make one with another, and yet still be in the state of Nature. The promises and bargains for truck, etc., between the two men in Soldania, in or between a Swiss and an Indian, in the woods of America, are binding to them, though they are perfectly in a state of Nature in reference to one another for truth, and keeping of faith belongs to men as men, and not as members of society.

To those that say there were never any men in the state of Nature, I will not only oppose the authority of the judicious Hooker, where he says, "the laws which have been hitherto mentioned" —i.e., the laws of Nature—"do bind men absolutely, even as they are men, although they have never any settled fellowship, never any solemn agreement amongst themselves what to do or not to do; but for as much as we are not by ourselves sufficient to furnish ourselves with competent store of things needful for such a life as our Nature doth desire, a life fit for the dignity of man, therefore to supply those defects and imperfections which are in us, as living single and solely by ourselves, we are naturally induced to seek communion and fellowship with others; this was the cause of men uniting themselves as first in politic societies." But I, moreover, affirm that all men are naturally in that state, and remain so till, by their own consents, they make themselves members of some politic society, and I doubt not, in the sequel of this discourse, to make it very clear.

CHAPTER V: OF PROPERTY

Whether we consider natural reason, which tells us that men, being once born, have a right to their preservation, and consequently to meat and drink and such other things as Nature affords for their subsistence, or "revelation," which gives us an account of those grants God made of the world to Adam, and to Noah and his sons, it is very clear that God, as King David says, "has given the earth to the children of men," given it to mankind in common. But, this being supposed, it seems to some a very great difficulty how any one should ever come to have a property in anything, I will not content myself to answer, that, if it be difficult to make out "property" upon a supposition that God gave the world to Adam and his posterity in common, it is impossible that any man but one universal monarch should have any "property" upon a supposition that God gave the world to Adam and his heirs in succession, exclusive of all the rest of his posterity; but I shall endeavour to show how men might come to have a property in several parts of that which God gave to mankind in common, and that without any express compact of all the commoners.

God, who hath given the world to men in common, hath also given them reason to make use of it to the best advantage of life and convenience. The earth and all that is therein is given to men for the support and comfort of their being. And though all the fruits it naturally produces, and beasts it feeds, belong to mankind in common, as they are produced by the spontaneous hand of Nature, and nobody has originally a private dominion exclusive of the rest of mankind in any of them, as they are thus in their natural state, yet being given for the use of men, there must of necessity be a means to appropriate them some way or other before they can be of any use, or at all beneficial, to any particular men. The fruit or venison which nourishes the wild Indian, who knows no enclosure, and is still a tenant in common, must be his, and so his—i.e., a part of him, that another can no longer have any right to it before it can do him any good for the support of his life.

Though the earth and all inferior creatures be common to all men, yet every man has a "property" in his own "person." This nobody has any right to but himself. The "labour" of his body and the "work" of his hands, we may say, are properly his. Whatsoever, then, he removes out of the state that Nature hath provided and left it in, he hath mixed his labour with it, and joined to it something that is his own, and thereby makes it his property. It being by him removed from the common state Nature placed it in, it hath by this labour something annexed to it that excludes the common right of other men. For this "labour" being the unquestionable property of the labourer, no man but he can have a right to what that is once joined to, at least where there is enough, and as good left in common for others.

He that is nourished by the acorns he picked up under an oak, or the apples he gathered from the trees in the wood, has certainly appropriated them to himself. Nobody can deny but the nourishment is his. I ask, then, when did they begin to be his? when he digested? or when he ate? or when he boiled? or when he brought them home? or when he picked them up? And it is plain, if the first gathering made them not his, nothing else could. That labour put a distinction between them and common. That added something to them more than Nature, the common mother of all, had done, and so they became his private right. And will any one say he had no right to those acorns or apples he thus appropriated because he had not the consent of all mankind to make them his? Was it a robbery thus to assume to himself what belonged to all in common? If such a consent as that was necessary, man had starved, notwithstanding the plenty God had given him. We see in commons, which remain so by compact, that it is the taking any part of what is common, and removing it out the state Nature leaves it in, which begins the property, without which the common is of no use. And the taking of this or that part does not depend on the express consent of all the commoners. Thus, the grass my horse has bit, the turfs my servant has cut, and the ore I have digged in any place, where I have a right to them in common with others, become my property without the assignation or consent of anybody. The labour that was mine, removing them out of that common state they were in, hath fixed my property in them.

By making an explicit consent of every commoner necessary to any one's appropriating to himself any part of what is given in common. Children or servants could not cut the meat which their father or master had provided for them in common without assigning to every one his peculiar part. Though the water running in the fountain be every one's, yet who can doubt but that in the pitcher is his only who drew it out? His labour hath taken it out of the hands of Nature where it was common, and belonged equally to all her children, and hath thereby appropriated it to himself. . . .

It will, perhaps, be objected to this, that if gathering the acorns or other fruits of the earth, etc., makes a right to them, then any one may engross as much as he will. To which I answer, Not so. The same law of Nature that does by this means give us property, does also bound that property too. "God has given us all things richly." Is the voice of reason confirmed by inspiration? But how far has He given it us—"to enjoy"? As much as any one can make use of to any advantage of life before it spoils, so much he may by his labour fix a property in. Whatever is beyond this is more than his share, and belongs to others. Nothing was made by God for man to spoil or destroy. And thus considering the plenty of natural provisions there was a long time in the world, and the few spenders, and to how small a part of that provision the industry of one man could extend itself and engross it to the prejudice of others, especially keeping within the bounds set by reason of what might serve for his use, there could be then little room for quarrels or contentions about property so established.

But the chief matter of property being now not the fruits of the earth and the beasts that subsist on it, but the earth itself, as that which takes in and carries with it all the rest, I think it is plain that property in that too is acquired as the former. As much land as a man tills, plants, improves, cultivates, and can use the product of, so much is his property. He by his labour does, as it were, enclose it from the common. Nor will it invalidate his right to say everybody else has an equal title to it, and therefore he cannot appropriate, he cannot enclose, without the consent of all his fellow-commoners, all mankind. God, when He gave the world in common to all mankind, commanded man also to labour, and the penury of his condition required it of him. God and his reason commanded him to subdue the earth—i.e., improve it for the benefit of life and therein lay out something upon it that was his own, his labour. He that, in obedience to this command of God, subdued, tilled, and sowed any part of it, thereby annexed to it something that was his property, which another had no title to, nor could without injury take from him.

Nor was this appropriation of any parcel of land, by improving it, any prejudice to any other man, since there was still enough and as good left, and more than the yet unprovided could use. So that, in effect, there was never the less left for others because of his enclosure for himself. For he that leaves as much as another can make use of does as good as take nothing at all. Nobody could think himself injured by the drinking of another man, though he took a good draught, who had a whole river of the same water left him to quench his thirst. And the case of land and water, where there is enough of both, is perfectly the same.

God gave the world to men in common, but since He gave it them for their benefit and the greatest conveniences of life they were capable to draw from it, it cannot be supposed He meant it should always remain common and uncultivated. He gave it to the use of the industrious and rational (and labour was to be his title of it); not to the fancy or covetousness of the quarrelsome and contentious. He that had as good left for his improvement as was already taken up needed not complain, ought not to meddle with what was already improved by another's labour; if he did it is plain he desired the benefit of another's pains, which he had no right to, and not the ground which God had given him, in common with others, to labour on, and whereof there was as good left as that already possessed, and more than he knew what to do with, or his industry could reach to.

It is true, in land that is common in England or any other country, where there are plenty of people under government who have money and commerce, no one can enclose or appropriate any part without the consent of all his fellow-commoners; because this is left common by compact—i.e., by the law of the land, which is not to be violated. And, though it be common in respect of some men, it is not so to all mankind, but is the joint propriety of this country, or this parish. Besides, the remainder, after such enclosure, would not be as good to the rest of the commoners as the whole was, when they could all make use of the whole; whereas in the beginning and first peopling of the great common of the world it was quite otherwise. The law man was under was rather for appropriating. God commanded, and his wants forced him to labour. That was his property, which could not be taken from him wherever he had fixed it. And hence subduing or cultivating the earth and having dominion, we see, are joined together. The one gave title to the other. So that God, by commanding to subdue, gave authority so far to appropriate. And the condition of human life, which requires labour and materials to work on, necessarily introduce private possessions.

The measure of property Nature well set, by the extent of men's labour and the conveniency of life. No man's labour could subdue or appropriate all, nor could his enjoyment consume more than a small part; so that it was impossible for any man, this way, to entrench upon the right of another or acquire to himself a property to the prejudice of his neighbour, who would still have room for as good and as large a possession (after the other had taken out his) as before it was appropriated. Which measure did confine every man's possession to a very moderate proportion, and such as he might appropriate to himself without injury to anybody in the first ages of the world, when men were more in danger to be lost, by wandering from their company, in the then vast wilderness of the earth than to be straitened for want of room to plant in. . . .

Chapter VIII: Of the Beginning of Political Societies

Men being, as has been said, by nature all free, equal, and independent, no one can be put out of this estate and subjected to the political power of another without his own consent, which is done by agreeing with other men, to join and unite into a community for their comfortable, safe, and peaceable living, one amongst another, in a secure enjoyment of their properties, and a greater security against any that are not of it. This any number of men may do, because it injures not the freedom of the rest; they are left, as they were, in the liberty of the state of Nature. When any number of men have so consented to make one community or government, they are thereby presently incorporated, and make one body politic, wherein the majority have a right to act and conclude the rest.

For, when any number of men have, by the consent of every individual, made a community, they have thereby made that community one body, with a power to act as one body, which is only by the will and determination of the majority. For that which acts any community, being only the consent of the individuals of it, and it being one body, must move one way, it is necessary the body should move that way whither the greater force carries it, which is the consent of the majority, or else it is impossible it should act or continue one body, one community, which the consent of every individual that united into it agreed that it should; and so every one is bound by that consent to be concluded by the majority. And therefore we see that in assemblies empowered to act by positive laws where no number is set by that positive law which empowers them, the act of the majority passes for the act of the whole, and of course determines as having, by the law of Nature and reason, the power of the whole.

And thus every man, by consenting with others to make one body politic under one government, puts himself under an obligation to every one of that society to submit to the determination of the majority, and to be concluded by it; or else this original compact, whereby he with others incorporates into one society, would signify nothing, and be no compact if he be left free and under no other ties than he was in before in the state of Nature. For what appearance would there be of any compact? What new engagement if he were no farther tied by any decrees of the society than he himself thought fit and did actually consent to? This would be still as great a liberty as he himself had before his compact, or any one else in the state of Nature, who may submit himself and consent to any acts of it if he thinks fit.

For if the consent of the majority shall not in reason be received as the act of the whole, and conclude every individual, nothing but the consent of every individual can make anything to be the act of the whole, which, considering the infirmities of health and avocations of business, which in a number though much less than that of a commonwealth, will necessarily keep many away from the public assembly; and the variety of opinions and contrariety of interests which unavoidably happen in all collections of men, it is next impossible ever to be had. And, therefore, if coming into society be upon such terms, it will be only like Cato's coming into the theatre, *tantum ut exiret.* Such a constitution as this would make the mighty leviathan of a shorter duration than the feeblest creatures, and not let it outlast the day it was born in, which cannot be supposed till we can think that rational creatures should desire and constitute societies only to be dissolved. For where the majority cannot conclude the rest, there they cannot act as one body, and consequently will be immediately dissolved again.

Whosoever, therefore, out of a state of Nature unite into a community, must be understood to give up all the power necessary to the ends for which they unite into society to the majority cf the community, unless they expressly agreed in any number greater than the majority. And this is done by barely agreeing to unite into one political society, which is all the compact that is, or needs be, between the individuals that enter into or make up a commonwealth. And thus, that which begins and actually constitutes any political society is nothing but the consent of any number of freemen capable of majority, to unite and incorporate into such a society. And this is that, and that only, which did or could give beginning to any lawful government in the world. . . .

CHAPTER IX: OF THE ENDS OF POLITICAL SOCIETY AND GOVERNMENT

If man in the state of Nature be so free as has been said, if he be absolute lord of his own person and possessions, equal to the greatest and subject to nobody, why will he part with his freedom, this empire, and subject himself to the dominion and control of any other power? To which it is obvious to answer, that though in the state of Nature he hath such a right, yet the enjoyment of it is very uncertain and constantly exposed to the invasion of others; for all being kings as much as he, every man his equal, and the greater part no strict observers of equity and justice, the enjoyment of the property he has in this state is very unsafe, very insecure. This makes him willing to quit this condition which, however free, is full of fears and continual dangers; and it is not without reason that he seeks out and is willing to join in society with others who are already united, or have a mind to unite for the mutual preservation of their lives, liberties and estates, which I call by the general name—property.

The great and chief end, therefore, of men uniting into commonwealths, and putting themselves under government, is the preservation of their property; to which in the state of Nature there are many things wanting.

Firstly, there wants an established, settled, known law, received and allowed by common consent to be the standard of right and wrong, and the common measure to decide all contro-versies between them. For though the law of Nature be plain and intelligible to all rational creatures, yet men, being biased by their interest, as well as ignorant for want of study of it, are not apt to allow of it as a law binding to them in the application of it to their particular cases.

Secondly,. in the state of Nature there wants a known and indifferent judge, with authority to determine all differences according to the established law. For every one in that state being both judge and executioner of the law of Nature, men being partial to themselves, passion and revenge is very apt to carry them too far, and with too much heat in their own cases, as well as negligence and unconcernedness, make them too remiss in other men's.

Thirdly, in the state of Nature there often wants power to back and support the sentence when right, and to give it due execution. They who by any injustice offended will seldom fail where they are able by force to make good their injustice. Such resistance many times makes the punishment dangerous, and frequently destructive to those who attempt it.

Thus mankind, notwithstanding all the privileges of the state of Nature, being but in an ill condition while they remain in it are quickly driven into society. Hence it comes to pass, that we seldom find any number of men live any time together in this state. The inconveniencies that they are therein exposed to by the irregular and uncertain exercise of the power every man has of punishing the transgressions of others, make them take sanctuary under the established laws of government, and therein seek the preservation of their property. It is this makes them so willingly give up every one his single power of punishing to be exercised by such alone as shall be appointed to it amongst them, and by such rules as the community, or those authorised by them to that purpose, shall agree on. And in this we have the original right and rise of both the legislative and executive power as well as of the governments and societies themselves.

For in the state of Nature to omit the liberty he has of innocent delights, a man has two powers. The first is to do whatsoever he thinks fit for the preservation of himself and others within the permission of the law of Nature; by which law, common to them all, he and all the rest of mankind are one community, make up one society distinct from all other creatures, and were it not for the corruption and viciousness of degenerate men, there would be no need of any other, no necessity that men should separate from this great and natural community, and associate into lesser combinations. The other power a man has in the state of Nature is the power to punish the crimes committed against that law. Both these he gives up when he joins in a private, if I may so call it, or particular political society, and incorporates into any commonwealth separate from the rest of mankind.

The first power—viz., of doing whatsoever he thought fit for the preservation of himself and the rest of mankind, he gives up to be regulated by laws made by the society, so far forth as the preservation of himself and the rest of that society shall require; which laws of the society in many things confine the liberty he had by the law of Nature.

Secondly, the power of punishing he wholly gives up, and engages his natural force, which he might before employ in the execution of the law of Nature, by his own single authority, as he thought fit, to assist the executive power of the society as the law thereof shall require. For being now in a new state, wherein he is to enjoy many conveniencies from the labour, assistance, and society of others in the same community, as well as protection from its whole strength, he is to part also with as much of his natural liberty, in providing for himself, as the good, prosperity, and safety of the society shall require, which is not only necessary but just, since the other members of the society do the like.

But though men when they enter into society give up the equality, liberty, and executive power they had in the state of Nature into the hands of the society, to be so far disposed of by the legislative as the good of the society shall require, yet it being only with an intention in every one the better to preserve himself, his liberty and property (for no rational creature can be supposed to change his condition with an intention to be worse), the power of the society or legislative constituted by them can never be supposed to extend farther than the common good, but is obliged to secure every one's property by providing against those three defects above mentioned that made the state of Nature so unsafe and uneasy. And so, whoever has the legislative or supreme power of any commonwealth, is bound to govern by established standing laws, promulgated and known to the people, and not by extemporary decrees, by indifferent and upright judges, who are to decide controversies by those laws; and to employ the force of the community at home only in the execution of such laws, or abroad to prevent or redress foreign injuries and secure the community from inroads and invasion. And all this to be directed to no other end but the peace, safety, and public good of the people.

CHAPTER XI: OF THE EXTENT OF THE LEGISLATIVE POWER

The great end of men's entering into society being the enjoyment of their properties in peace and safety, and the great instrument and means of that being the laws established in that society, the first and fundamental positive law of all commonwealths is the establishing of the legislative power, as the first and fundamental natural law which is to govern even the legislative. Itself is the preservation of the society and (as far as will consist with the public good) of every person in it. This legislative is not only the supreme power of the commonwealth, but sacred and unalterable in the hands where the community have once placed it. Nor can any edict of anybody else, in what form soever conceived, or by what power soever backed, have the force and obligation of a law which has not its sanction from that legislative which the public has chosen and appointed; for without this the law could not have that which is absolutely necessary to its being a law, the consent of the society, over whom nobody can have a power to make laws but by their own consent and by authority received from them; and therefore all the obedience, which by the most solemn ties any one can be obliged to pay, ultimately terminates in this supreme power, and is directed by those laws which it enacts. Nor can any oaths to any foreign power whatsoever, or any domestic subordinate power, discharge any member of the society from his obedience to the legislative, acting pursuant to their trust, nor oblige him to any obedience contrary to the laws so enacted or farther than they do allow, it being ridiculous to imagine one can be tied ultimately to obey any power in the society which is not the supreme.

Though the legislative, whether placed in one or more, whether it be always in being or only by intervals, though it be the supreme power in every commonwealth, yet, first, it is not, nor can possibly be, absolutely arbitrary over the lives and fortunes of the people. For it being but the joint power of every member of the society given up to that person or assembly which is legislator, it can be no more than those persons had in a state of Nature before they entered into society, and gave it up to the community. For nobody can transfer to another more power than he has in himself, and nobody has an absolute arbitrary power over himself, or over any other, to destroy his own life, or take away the life or property of another. A man, as has been proved, cannot subject himself to the arbitrary power of another; and having, in the state of Nature, no arbitrary power over the life, liberty, or possession of another, but only so much as the law of Nature gave him for the preservation of himself and the rest of mankind, this is all he doth, or can give up to the commonwealth, and by it to the legislative power, so that the legislative can have no more than this. Their power in the utmost bounds of it is limited to the public good of the society. It is a power that hath no other end but preservation, and therefore can never have a right to destroy, enslave, or designedly to impoverish the subjects; the obligations of the law of Nature cease not in society, but only in many cases are drawn closer, and have, by human laws, known penalties annexed to them to enforce their observation. Thus the law of Nature stands as an eternal rule to all men, legislators as well as others. The rules that they make for other men's actions must, as well as their own and other men's actions, be conformable to the law of Nature—*i.e.*, to the will of God, of which that is a declaration, and the fundamental law of Nature being the preservation of mankind, no human sanction can be good or valid against it.

Secondly, the legislative or supreme authority cannot assume to itself a power to rule by extemporary arbitrary decrees, but is bound to dispense justice and decide the rights of the subject by promulgated standing laws, and known authorised judges. For the law of Nature being unwritten, and so nowhere to be found but in the minds of men, they who, through passion or interest, shall miscite or misapply it, cannot so easily be convinced of their mistake where there is no established judge; and so it serves not as it aught, to determine the rights and fence the properties of those that live under it, especially where every one is judge, interpreter, and executioner of it too, and that in his own case; and he that has right on his side, having ordinarily but his own single strength, hath not force enough to defend himself from injuries or punish delinquents. To avoid these inconveniencies which disorder men's properties in the state of Nature, men unite into societies that they may have the united strength of the whole society to secure and defend their properties, and may have standing rules to bound it by which every one may know what is his. To this end it is that men give up all their natural power to the society they enter into, and the community put the legislative power into such hands as they think fit, with this trust, that they shall be governed by declared laws, or else their peace, quiet, and property will still be at the same uncertainty as it was in the state of Nature.

Absolute arbitrary power, or governing without settled standing laws, can neither of them consist with the ends of society and government, which men would not quit the freedom of the state of Nature for, and tie themselves up under, were it not to preserve their lives, liberties, and fortunes, and by stated rules of right and property to secure their peace and quiet. It cannot be supposed that they should intend, had they a power so to do, to give any one or more an absolute arbitrary power over their persons and estates, and put a force into the magistrate's hand to execute his unlimited will arbitrarily upon them; this were to put themselves into a worse condition than the state of Nature, wherein they had a liberty to defend their right against the injuries of others, and were upon equal terms of force to maintain it, whether invaded by a single man or many in combination. Whereas by supposing they have given up themselves to the absolute arbitrary power and will of a legislator, they have disarmed themselves, and armed him to make a prey of them when he pleases; he being in a much worse condition that is exposed to the arbitrary power of one man who has the command of a hundred thousand than he that is exposed to the arbitrary power of a hundred thousand single men, nobody being secure, that his will who has such a command is better than that of other men, though his force be a hundred thousand times stronger. And, therefore, whatever form the commonwealth is under, the ruling power ought to govern by declared and received laws, and not by extemporary dictates and undetermined resolutions, for then mankind will be in a far worse condition than in the state of Nature if they shall have armed one or a few men with the joint power of a multitude, to force them to obey at pleasure the exorbitant and unlimited decrees of their sudden thoughts, or unrestrained, and till that moment, unknown wills, without having any measures set down which may guide and justify their actions. For all the power the government has, being only for the good of the society, as it ought not to be arbitrary and at pleasure, so it ought to be exercised by established and promulgated laws, that both the people may know their duty, and be safe and secure within the limits of the law, and the rulers, too, kept within their due bounds, and not be tempted by the power they have in their hands to employ it to purposes, and by such measures as they would not have known, and own not willingly.

Thirdly, the supreme power cannot take from any man any part of his property without his own consent. For the preservation of property being the end of government, and that for which men enter into society, it necessarily supposes and requires that the people should have property, without which they must be supposed to lose that by entering into society which was the end for which they entered into it; too gross an absurdity for any man to own. Men, therefore, in society having property, they have such a right to the goods, which by the law of the community are theirs, that nobody hath a right to take them, or any part of them, from them without their own consent; without this they have no property at all. For I have truly no property in that which another can by right take from me when he pleases against my consent. Hence it is a mistake to think that the supreme or legislative power of any commonwealth can do what it will, and dispose of the estates of the subject arbitrarily, or take any part of them at pleasure. This is not much to be feared in governments where the legislative consists wholly or in part in assemblies which are variable, whose members upon the dissolution of the assembly are subjects under the common laws of their country, equally with the rest. But in governments where the legislative is in one lasting assembly, always in being, or in one man as in absolute monarchies, there is danger still, that they will think themselves to have a distinct interest from the rest of the community, and so will be apt to increase their own riches and power by taking what they think fit from the people. For a man's property is not at all secure, though there be good and equitable laws to set the bounds of it between him and his fellow-subjects, if he who commands those subjects have power to take from any private man what part he pleases of his property, and use and dispose of it as he thinks good.

But government, into whosesoever hands it is put, being as I have before showed, entrusted with this condition, and for this end, that men might have and secure their properties, the prince or senate, however it may have power to make laws for the regulating of property between the subjects one amongst another, yet can never have a power to take to themselves the whole, or any part of the subjects' property, without their own consent; for this would be in effect to leave them no property at all. And to let us see that even absolute power, where it is necessary, is not arbitrary by being absolute, but is still limited by that reason, and confined to those ends which required it in some cases to be absolute, we need look no farther than the common practice of martial discipline. For the preservation of the army, and in it of the whole commonwealth, requires an absolute obedience to the command of every superior officer, and it is justly death to disobey or dispute the most dangerous or unreasonable of them; but yet we see that neither the sergeant that could command a soldier to march up to the mouth of a cannon, or stand in a breach where he is almost sure to perish, can command that soldier to give him one penny of his money; nor the general that can condemn him to death for deserting his post, or not obeying the most desperate orders, cannot yet with all his absolute power of life and death dispose of one farthing of that soldier's estate, or seize one jot of his goods; whom yet he can command anything, and hang for the least disobedience. Because such a blind obedience is necessary to that end for which the commander has his power—viz., the preservation of the rest, but the disposing of his goods has nothing to do with it.

It is true governments cannot be supported without great charge, and it is fit every one who enjoys his share of the protection should pay out of his estate his proportion for the maintenance of it. But still it must be with his own consent—i.e., the consent of the majority, giving it either by themselves or their representatives chosen by them; for if any one shall claim a power to lay and levy taxes on the people by his own authority, and without such consent of the people, he thereby invades the fundamental law of property, and subverts the end of government. For what property have I in that which another may by right take when he pleases to himself?

Fourthly. The legislative cannot transfer the power of making laws to any other hands, for it being but a delegated power from the people, they who have it cannot pass it over to others. The people alone can appoint the form of the commonwealth, which is by constituting the legislative, and appointing in whose hands that shall be. And when the people have said, "We will submit, and be governed by laws made by such men, and in such forms," nobody else can say other men shall make laws for them; nor can they be bound by any laws but such as are enacted by those whom they have chosen and authorised to make laws for them.

These are the bounds which the trust that is put in them by the society and the law of God and Nature have set to the legislative power of every commonwealth, in all forms of government. First: They are to govern by promulgated established laws, not to be varied in particular cases, but to have one rule for rich and poor, for the favourite at Court, and the countryman at plough. Secondly: These laws also ought to be designed for no other end ultimately but the good of the people. Thirdly: They must not raise taxes on the property of the people without the consent of the people given by themselves or their deputies. And this properly concerns only such governments where the legislative is always in being, or at least where the people have not reserved any part of the legislative to deputies, to be from time to time chosen by themselves. Fourthly: Legislative neither must nor can transfer the power of making laws to anybody else, or place it anywhere but where the people have.

Chapter XIX: Of the Dissolution of Government

He that will, with any clearness, speak of the dissolution of government, ought in the first place to distinguish between the dissolution of the society and the dissolution of the government. That which makes the community, and brings men out of the loose state of Nature into one politic society, is the agreement which every one has with the rest to incorporate and act as one body, and so be one distinct commonwealth. The usual, and almost only way whereby this union is dissolved, is the inroad of foreign force making a conquest upon them. For in that case (not being able to maintain and support themselves as one entire and independent body) the union belonging to that body, which consisted therein, must necessarily cease, and so every one return to the state he was in before, with a liberty to shift for himself and provide for his own safety, as he thinks fit, in some other society. Whenever the society is dissolved, it is certain the government of that society cannot remain. Thus conquerors' swords often cut up governments by the roots, and mangle societies to pieces, separating the subdued or scattered multitude from the protection of and dependence on that society which ought to have preserved them from violence. The world is too well instructed in, and too forward to allow of this way of dissolving of governments, to need any more to be said of it; and there wants not much argument to prove that where the society is dissolved, the government cannot remain; that being as impossible as for the frame of a house to subsist when the materials of it are scattered and displaced by a whirlwind, or jumbled into a confused heap by an earthquake.

Besides this overturning from without, governments are dissolved from within:

First. When the legislative is altered, civil society being a state of peace amongst those who are of it, from whom the state of war is excluded by the umpirage which they have provided in their legislative for the ending all differences that may arise amongst any of them; it is in their legislative that the members of a commonwealth are united and combined together into one coherent living body. This is the soul that gives form, life, and unity to the commonwealth; from hence the several members have their mutual influence, sympathy, and connection; and therefore when the legislative is broken, or dissolved, dissolution and death follows. For the essence and union of the society consisting in having one will, the legislative, when once established by the majority, has the declaring and, as it were, keeping of that will. The constitution of the legislative is the first and fundamental act of society, whereby provision is made for the continuation of their union under the direction of persons and bonds of laws, made by persons authorised thereunto, by the consent and appointment of the people, without which no one man, or number of men, amongst them can have authority of making laws that shall be binding to the rest. When any one, or more, shall take upon them to make laws whom the people have not appointed so to do, they make laws without authority, which the people are not therefore bound to obey; by which means they come again to be out of subjection, and may constitute to themselves a new legislative, as they think best, being in full liberty to resist the force of those who, without authority, would impose anything upon them. Every one is at the disposure of his own will, when those who had, by the delegation of the society, the declaring of the public will, are excluded from it, and others usurp the place who have no such authority or delegation.

This being usually brought about by such in the commonwealth, who misuse the power they have, it is hard to consider it aright, and know at whose door to lay it, without knowing the form of government in which it happens. Let us suppose, then, the legislative placed in the concurrence of three distinct persons:—First, a single hereditary person having the constant, supreme, executive power, and with it the power of convoking and dissolving the other two within certain periods of time. Secondly, an assembly of hereditary nobility. Thirdly, an assembly of representatives chosen, *pro tempore*, by the people. Such a form of government supposed, it is evident:

First, that when such a single person or prince sets up his own arbitrary will in place of the laws which are the will of the society declared by the legislative, then the legislative is changed. For that being, in effect, the legislative whose rules and laws are put in execution, and required to be obeyed, when other laws are set up, and other rules pretended and enforced than what the legislative, constituted by the society, have enacted, it is plain that the legislative is changed. Whoever introduces new laws, not being thereunto authorised, by the fundamental appointment of the society, or subverts the old, disowns and overturns the power by which they were made, and so sets up a new legislative.

Secondly, when the prince hinders the legislative from assembling in its due time, or from acting freely, pursuant to those ends for which it was constituted, the legislative is altered. For it is not a certain number of men—no, nor their meeting, unless they have also freedom of debating and leisure of perfecting what is for the good of the society, wherein the legislative consists; when these are taken away, or altered, so as to deprive the society of the due exercise of their power, the legislative is truly altered. For it is not names that constitute governments, but the use and exercise of those powers that were intended to accompany them; so that he who takes away the freedom, or hinders the acting of the legislative in its due seasons, in effect takes away the legislative, and puts an end to the government.

Thirdly, when, by the arbitrary power of the prince, the electors or ways of election are altered without the consent and contrary to the common interest of the people, there also the legislative is altered. For if others than those whom the society hath authorised thereunto do choose, or in another way than what the society hath prescribed, those chosen are not the legislative appointed by the people.

Fourthly, the delivery also of the people into the subjection of a foreign power, either by the prince or by the legislative, is certainly a change of the legislative, and so a dissolution of the government. For the end why people entered into society being to be preserved one entire, free, independent society, to be governed by its own laws, this is lost whenever they are given up into the power of another.

Why, in such a constitution as this, the dissolution of the government in these cases is to be imputed to the prince is evident, because he, having the force, treasure, and offices of the State to employ, and often persuading himself or being flattered by others, that, as supreme magistrate, he is incapable of control; he alone is in a condition to make great advances towards such changes under pretence of lawful authority, and has it in his hands to terrify or suppress opposers as factious, seditious, and enemies to the government; whereas no other part of the legislative, or people, is capable by themselves to attempt any alteration of the legislative without open and visible rebellion, apt enough to be taken notice of, which, when it prevails, produces effects very little different from foreign conquest. Besides, the prince, in such a form of government, having the power of dissolving the others parts of the legislative, and thereby rendering them private persons, they can never, in opposition to him, or without his concurrence, alter the legislative by a law, his consent being necessary to give any of their decrees that sanction. But yet so far as the other parts of the legislative any way contribute to any attempt upon the government, and do either promote, or not, what lies in them, hinder such designs, they are guilty, and partake in this, which is certainly the greatest crime men can be guilty of one towards another.

There is one way more whereby such a government may be dissolved, and that is: When he who has the supreme executive power neglects and abandons that charge, so that the laws already made can no longer be put in execution; this is demonstratively to reduce all to anarchy, and so effectively to dissolve the government. For laws not being made for themselves, but to be, by their execution, the bonds of the society to keep every part of the body politic in its due place and function. When that totally ceases, the government visibly ceases, and the people become a confused multitude without order or connection. Where there is no longer the administration of justice for the securing of men's rights, nor any remaining power within the community to direct the force, or provide for the necessities of the public, there certainly is no government left. Where the laws cannot be executed it is all one as if there were no laws, and a government without laws is, I suppose, a mystery in politics inconceivable to human capacity, and inconsistent with human society.

In these, and the like cases, when the government is dissolved, the people are at liberty to provide for themselves by erecting a new legislative differing from the other by the change of persons, or form, or both, as they shall find it most for their safety and good. For the society can never, by the fault of another, lose the native and original right it has to preserve itself, which can only be done by a settled legislative and a fair and impartial execution of the laws made by it. But the state of mankind is not so miserable that they are not capable of using this remedy till it be too late to look for any. To tell people they may provide for themselves by erecting a new legislative, when, by oppression, artifice, or being delivered over to a foreign power, their old one is gone, is only to tell them they may expect relief when it is too late, and the evil is past cure. This is, in effect, no more than to bid them first be slaves, and then to take care of their liberty, and, when their chains are on, tell them they may act like free men. This, if barely so, is rather mockery than relief, and men can never be secure from tyranny if there be no means to escape it till they are perfectly under it; and, therefore, it is that they have not only a right to get out of it, but to prevent it.

There is, therefore, secondly, another way whereby governments are dissolved, and that is, when the legislative, or the prince, either of them act contrary to their trust.

For the legislative acts against the trust reposed in them when they endeavour to invade the property of the subject, and to make themselves, or any part of the community, masters or arbitrary disposers of the lives, liberties, or fortunes of the people.

The reason why men enter into society is the preservation of their property; and the end while they choose and authorise a legislative is that there may be laws made, and rules set, as guards and fences to the properties of all the society, to limit the power and moderate the dominion of every part and member of the society. For since it can never be supposed to be the will of the society that the legislative should have a power to destroy that which every one designs to secure by entering into society, and for which the people submitted themselves to legislators of their own making: whenever the legislators endeavour to take away and destroy the property of the people, or to reduce them to slavery under arbitrary power, they put themselves into a state of war with the people, who are thereupon absolved from any farther obedience, and are left to the common refuge which God hath provided for all men against force and violence. Whensoever, therefore, the legislative shall transgress this fundamental rule of society, and either by ambition, fear, folly, or corruption, endeavour to grasp themselves, or put into the hands of any other, an absolute power over the lives, liberties, and estates of the people, by this breach of trust they forfeit the power the people had put into their hands for quite contrary ends, and it devolves to the people, who have a right to resume their original liberty, and by the establishment of a new legislative (such as they shall think fit), provide for their own safety and security, which is the end for which they are in society. What I have said here concerning the legislative in general holds true also concerning the supreme executor, who having a double trust put in him, both to have a part in the legislative and the supreme execution of the law, acts against both, when he goes about to set up his own arbitrary will as the law of the society. He acts also contrary to his trust when he employs the force, treasure, and offices of the society to corrupt the representatives and gain them to his purposes, when he openly pre-engages the electors, and prescribes, to their choice, such whom he has, by solicitation, threats, promises, or otherwise, won to his designs, and employs them to bring in such who have promised beforehand what to vote and what to enact. Thus to regulate candidates and electors, and new model the ways of election, what is it but to cut up the government by the roots, and poison the very fountain of public security? For the people having reserved to themselves the choice of their representatives as the fence to their properties, could do it for no other end but that they might always be freely chosen, and so chosen, freely act and advise as the necessity of the commonwealth and the public good should, upon examination and mature debate, be judged to require. This, those who give their votes before they hear the debate, and have weighed the reasons on all sides, are not capable of doing. To prepare such an assembly as this, and endeavour to set up the declared abettors of his own will, for the true representatives of the people, and the lawmakers of the society, is certainly as great a breach of trust, and as perfect a declaration of a design to subvert the government, as is possible to be met with. To which, if one shall add rewards and punishments visibly employed to the same end, and all the arts of perverted law made use of to take off and destroy all that stand in the way of such a design, and will not comply and consent to betray the liberties of their country, it will be past doubt what is doing. What power they ought to have in the society who thus employ it contrary to the trust went along with it in its first institution, is easy to determine; and one cannot but see that he who has once attempted any such thing as this cannot any longer be trusted. . . .

Here it is like the common question will be made: Who shall be judge whether the prince or legislative act contrary to their trust? This, perhaps, ill-affected and factious men may spread amongst the people, when the prince only makes use of his due prerogative. To this I reply, The people shall be judge; for who shall be judge whether his trustee or deputy acts well and according to the trust reposed in him, but he who deputes him and must, by having deputed him, have still a power to discard him when he fails in his trust? If this be reasonable in particular cases of private men, why should it be otherwise in that of the greatest moment, where the welfare of millions is concerned and also where the evil, if not prevented, is greater, and the redress very difficult, dear, and dangerous?

But, farther, this question, Who shall be judge? cannot mean that there is no judge at all. For where there is no judicature on earth to decide controversies amongst men, God in heaven is judge. He alone, it is true, is judge of the right. But every man is judge for himself, as in all other cases so in this, whether another hath put himself into a state of war with him, and whether he should appeal to the supreme Judge, as Jephtha did.

If a controversy arise betwixt a prince and some of the people in a matter where the law is silent or doubtful, and the thing be of great consequence, I should think the proper umpire in such a case should be the body of the people. For in such cases where the prince hath a trust reposed in him, and is dispensed from the common, ordinary rules of the law, there, if any men find themselves aggrieved, and think the prince acts contrary to, or beyond that trust, who so proper to judge as the body of the people (who at first lodged that trust in him) how far they meant it should extend? But if the prince, or whoever they be in the administration, decline that way of determination, the ap-

peal then lies nowhere but to Heaven. Force between either persons who have no known superior on earth, or which permits no appeal to a judge on earth, being properly a state of war, wherein the appeal lies only to Heaven; and in that state the injured party must judge for himself when he will think fit to make use of that appeal and put himself upon it.

To conclude. The power that every individual gave the society when he entered into it can never revert to the individuals again, as long as the society lasts, but will always remain in the community; because without this there can be no community—no commonwealth, which is contrary to the original agreement; so also when the society hath placed the legislative in any assembly of men, to continue in them and their successors, with direction and authority for providing such successors, the legislative can never revert to the people whilst that government lasts; because, having provided a legislative with power to continue for ever, they have given up their political power to the legislative, and cannot resume it. But if they have set limits to the duration of their legislative, and made this supreme power in any person or assembly only temporary; or else when, by the miscarriages of those in authority, it is forfeited; upon the forfeiture of their rulers, or at the determination of the time set, it reverts to the society, and the people have a right to act as supreme, and continue the legislative in themselves or place it in a new form, or new hands, as they think good.

VIRGINIA

OUT OF THE MASS of restless and frequently unhappy men and women—dispossessed copyholders, ambitious small merchants and landlords, apprentices, sailors, craftsmen and soldiers—came most of the colonists who reached Virginia and there established England's first permanent settlement on the North American mainland. The Virginia Company of London, which financed that settlement, was chartered in 1606 by James I and given the right to trade and colonize in the unknown country that Walter Raleigh had named for Queen Elizabeth. Among the leaders of the venture was Captain John Smith (1580–1631). Smith was born into one of those yeoman families among which Brooks Adams found England's empire builders. Smith went off to the Flanders wars, fought in the armies of Sigismund Bathori and, by his own account, was captured by the Turks and freed because his purchaser's chief wife interceded for him. Whether John Smith spoke the truth or was only a masterful liar, he returned to England in 1605, won the confidence of the Virginia Company's backers, enlisted in the expedition and was named one of the colony's directors in the secret sailing orders. The story of Captain John Smith's struggles to keep his gentlemen at work, his quarrels and his return to England after his victory are better known than his efforts to enlist general interest in "the New World which is Virginia."

In 1612, Smith wrote of the land he had first seen five years before. There is the excitement of discovery in Smith's story. For the first time, one reads an Englishman's account of the variable and thunderous American climate, of the acridity of a green persimmon and the deer "differing nothing from ours." There may be mines in Virginia, but we had no skilled men to make sure, Smith says, and he goes on to tell how the forest was felled and the first crop of corn put in. He describes the Indians, few in number to have the use of so much fine land, strong men, crafty, able and covetous of cheap goods. The country over which they hunt is a pleasant land, fertile, well watered and potentially a good source of the iron, potash, and flax for which England now spends treasure in Russia, Poland, and Sweden.

Two years after Smith published his description of Virginia, he returned to explore the New England coast. It is to him that the map owes the names of Plymouth and Cape Cod. Smith's next efforts at voyaging were not fortunate. Weather and illness thwarted his attempt to sail in 1615 and, later, in 1617. The last fifteen years of his life were given to projects and writing, much of it concerning Virginia and, among that, the story of Powhatan's daughter, Pocahontas.

The selection is from J. Franklin Jameson, ed., *Original Narratives of American History*, Vol. V (New York, 1907).

Description of Virginia

BY JOHN SMITH

VIRGINIA is a Country in America, that lyeth betweene the degrees of 34 and 44 of the north latitude. The bounds thereof on the East side are the great *Ocean*. On the South lyeth Florida: on the North nova Francia. As for the West thereof, the limits are unknowne. Of all this country wee purpose not to speake, but only of that part which was planted by the English men in the yeare of our Lord, 1606. And this is under the degrees 37. 38. and 39. The temperature of this countrie doth agree well with English constitutions being once seasoned to the country. Which appeared by this, that though by many occasions our people fell sicke; yet did they recover by very small meanes and continued in health, though there were other great causes, not only to have made them sicke, but even to end their daies, etc.

The sommer is hot as in Spaine; the winter colde as in Fraunce or England. The heat of sommer is in June, Julie, and August, but commonly the coole Breeses asswage the vehemencie of the heat. The chiefe of winter is halfe December, January, February, and halfe March. The colde is extreame sharpe, but here the proverbe is true that no extreame long continueth.

In the yeare 1607. was an extraordinary frost in most of Europe, and this frost was founde as extreame in Virginia. But the next yeare for 8. or 10. daies of ill weather, other 14 daies would be as Sommer.

The windes here are variable, but the like thunder and lightning to purifie the aire, I have seldome either seene or heard in Europe. From the Southwest came the greatest gustes with thunder and heat. The Northwest winde is commonly coole, and bringeth faire weather with it. From the Northe is the greatest cold, and from the East and South-East as from the Barmadas, fogs and raines.

Some times there are great droughts, other times much raine, yet great necessity of neither, by reason we see not but that all the variety of needfull fruits in Europe may be there in great plenty by the industry of men, as appeareth by those we there planted.

There is but one entraunce by sea into this country, and that is at the mouth of a very goodly Bay, the widenesse whereof is neare 18. or 20. miles. The cape on the South side is called Cape Henry in honour of our most noble Prince. The shew of the land there, is a white hilly sand like unto the Downes, and along the shores great plentie of Pines and Firres.

The north Cape is called Cape Charles in honour of the worthy Duke of Yorke. Within is a country that may have the prerogative over the most pleasant places of Europe, Asia, Africa, or America, for large and pleasant navigable rivers: heaven and earth never agreed better to frame a place for mans habitation being of our constitutions, were it fully manured and inhabited by industrious people. Here are mountaines, hils,

plaines, valleyes, rivers and brookes all running most pleasantly into a faire Bay compassed but for the mouth with fruitfull and delightsome land. In the Bay and rivers are many Isles both great and small, some woody, some plaine, most of them low and not inhabited. This Bay lieth North and South in which the water floweth neare 200 miles and hath a channell for 140 miles, of depth betwixt 7 and 15 fadome, holding in breadth for the most part 10 or 14 miles. From the head of the Bay at the north, the land is mountanous, and so in a manner from thence by a Southwest line; So that the more Southward, the farther of[f] from the Bay are those mounetaines. From which, fall certaine brookes, which after come to five principall navigable rivers. These run from the Northwest into the South east, and so into the west side of the Bay, where the fall of every River is within 20 or 15 miles one of an other.

The mountaines are of diverse natures, for at the head of the Bay the rockes are of a composition like miln-stones. Some of marble, &c. And many peeces of christall we found as throwne downe by water from the mountaines. For in winter these mountaines are covered with much snow, and when it dissolveth the waters fall with such violence, that it causeth great inundations in the narrow valleyes which yet is scarce perceived being once in the rivers. These waters wash from the rocks such glistering tinctures that the ground in some places seemeth as guilded, where both the rocks and the earth are so splendent to behold, that better judgements then ours might have beene perswaded, they contained more than probabilities. The vesture of the earth in most places doeth manifestly prove the nature of the soile to be lusty and very rich. The coulor of the earth we found in diverse places, resembleth *bole Armoniac, terra sigillata ad lemnia*, Fullers earth, marle, and divers other such appearances. But generally for the most part the earth is a black sandy mould, in some places a fat slimy clay, in other places a very barren gravell. But the best ground is knowne by the vesture it beareth, as by the greatnesse of trees or abundance of weedes, &c.

The country is not mountanous nor yet low but such pleasant plaine hils and fertle valleyes, one prettily crossing an other, and watered so conveniently with their sweete brookes and christall springs, as if art it selfe had devised them. By the rivers are many plaine marishes containing some 20, some 100, some 200 Acres, some more, some lesse. Other plaines there are fewe, but only where the Savages inhabit: but all overgrowne with trees and weedes being a plaine wildernes as God first made it. . . .

Of such things which are naturall in Virginia and how they use them.—Virginia doth afford many excellent vegitables and living Creatures, yet grasse there is little or none but what groweth in lowe Marishes: for all the Countrey is overgrowne with trees, whose droppings continually turneth their grasse to weedes, by reason of the rancknesse of the ground; which would soone be amended by good husbandry. The wood that is most common is Oke and Walnut: many of their Okes are so tall and straight, that they will beare two foote and a halfe square of good timber for 20 yards long. Of this wood there is 2 or 3 severall kinds. The Acornes of one kind, whose barke is more white then the other, is somewhat sweetish; which being boyled halfe a day in severall waters, at last afford a sweete oyle, which they keep in goards to annoint their heads and joints. The fruit they eate, made in bread or otherwise. There is also some Elme, some black walnut tree, and some Ash: of Ash and Elme they make sope Ashes. If the trees be very great, the ashes will be good, and melt to hard lumps: but if they be small, it will be but powder, and not so good as the other. Of walnuts there is 2 or 3 kindes: there is a kinde of wood we called Cypres, because both the wood, the fruit, and leafe did most resemble it; and of those trees there are some neere 3 fadome about at the root, very straight, and 50, 60, or 80 foot without a braunch. By the dwelling of the Savages are some great Mulbery trees; and in some parts of the Countrey, they are found growing naturally in prettie groves. There was an assay made to make silke, and surely the wormes prospered excellent well, till the master workeman fell sicke: during which time, they were eaten with rats.

In some parts, were found some Chesnuts whose wild fruit equalize the best in France, Spaine, Germany, or Italy, to their tasts that had tasted them all. Plumbs there are of 3 sorts. The red and white are like our hedge plumbs: but the other, which they call *Putchamins*, grow as high as a Palmeta. The fruit is like a medler; it is first greene, then yellow, and red when it is ripe: if it be not ripe it will drawe a mans mouth awrie with much torment; but when it is ripe, it is as delicious as an Apricock.

They have Cherries, and those are much like a Damsen; but for their tastes and colour, we called them Cherries. We see some few Crabs, but very small and bitter. Of vines, great abundance in many parts, that climbe the toppes of the highest trees in some places, but these beare but fewe grapes. But by the rivers and Savage habitations where they are not overshadowed from the sunne, they are covered with fruit, though never pruined nor manured. Of those hedge grapes, wee made neere 20 gallons of wine, which was neare as good as your French Brittish wine, but certainely they would prove good were they well manured. There is another sort of grape neere as great as a Cheery, this they call *Messaminnes;* they bee fatte, and the juyce thicke: neither doth the tast so well please when they are made in wine. They have a small fruit growing on little trees, husked like a Chesnut, but the fruit most like a very small acorne. This they call *Chechinquamins,* which they esteeme a great daintie. They have a berry much like our gooseberry, in greatnesse, colour, and tast; those they call *Rawcomenes,* and doe eat them raw or boyled. Of these naturall fruits they live a great part of the yeare, which they use in this manner. The walnuts, Chesnuts, Acornes, and *Chechinquamens* are dryed to keepe. When they need them, they breake them betweene two stones, yet some part of the walnut shels will cleave to the fruit. Then doe they dry them againe upon a mat over a hurdle. After, they put it into a morter of wood, and beat it very small: that done, they mix it with water, that the shels may sinke to the bottome. This water will be coloured as milke; which they cal *Pawcohiscora,* and keepe it for their use. The fruit like medlers, they call *Putchamins,* they cast uppon hurdles on a mat, and preserve them as Pruines. Of their Chesnuts and *Chechinquamens* boyled 4 houres, they make both broath and bread for their chiefe men, or at their greatest feasts. Besides those fruit trees, there is a white populer, and another tree like unto it, that yeeldeth a very cleere and an odoriferous Gumme like Turpentine, which some called Balsom. There are also Cedars and Saxafras trees. They also yeeld gummes in a small proportion of themselves. Wee tryed conclusions to extract it out of the wood, but nature afforded more then our arts.

In the watry valleyes groweth a berry, which they call *Ocoughtanamnis,* very much like unto Capers. These they dry in sommer. When they will eat them, they boile them neare halfe a day; for otherwise they differ not much from poyson. *Mattoume* groweth as our bents do in meddows. The seede is not much unlike to rie, though much smaller. This they use for a dainty bread buttered with deare suet.

During Somer there are either strawberries which ripen in April; or mulberries which ripen in May and June, Raspises, hurtes, or a fruit that the Inhabitants call *Maracocks,* which is a pleasant wholsome fruit much like a lemond. Many hearbes in the spring time there are commonly dispersed throughout the woods, good for brothes and sallets, as Violets, Purslin, Sorrell, &c. Besides many we used whose names we know not.

The chiefe roote they have for foode is called *Tockawhoughe*. It groweth like a flagge in low muddy freshes. In one day a Savage will gather sufficient for a weeke. These rootes are much of the greatnes and taste of Potatoes. They use to cover a great many of them with oke leaves and ferne, and then cover all with earth in the manner of a colepit; over it, on each side, they continue a great fire 24 houres before they dare eat it. Raw it is no better then poison, and being roasted, except it be tender and the heat abated, or sliced and dried in the sun, mixed with sorrell and meale or such like, it will prickle and torment the throat extreamely, and yet in sommer they use this ordinarily for bread.

They have an other roote which they call *wighsacan:* as thother feedeth the body, so this cureth their hurts and diseases. It is a small root which they bruise and apply to the wound. *Pocones* is a small roote that groweth in the mountaines, which being dryed and beate in powder turneth red: and this they use for swellings, aches, annointing their joints, painting their heads and garments. They account it very pretious and of much worth. *Musquaspenne* is a roote of the bignesse of a finger, and as red as bloud. In drying, it will wither almost to nothing. This they use to paint their Mattes, Targets, and such like.

There is also Pellitory of Spaine, Sasafrage, and divers other simples, which the Apothecaries gathered, and commended to be good and medicinable.

In the low Marshes, growe plots of Onyons containing an acre of ground or more in many places; but they are small, not past the bignesse of the Toppe of ones Thumbe.

Of beastes the chief are Deare, nothing differing from ours. In the deserts towards the heads of the rivers, ther are many, but amongst the rivers few. There is a beast they call *Aroughcun*, much like a badger, but useth to live on trees as Squirrels doe. Their Squirrels some are neare as greate as our smallest sort of wilde rabbits; some blackish or blacke and white, but the most are gray.

A small beast they have, they call *Assapanick*, but we call them flying squirrels, because spreading their legs, and so stretching the largenesse of their skins that they have bin seene to fly 30 or 40 yards. An *Opassom* hath an head like a Swine, and a taile like a Rat, and is of the bignes of a Cat. Under her belly shee hath a bagge, wherein shee lodgeth, carrieth, and sucketh her young. *Mussascus* is a beast of the forme and nature of our water Rats, but many of them smell exceeding strongly of muske. Their Hares no bigger then our Conies, and few of them to be found.

Their Beares are very little in comparison of those of Muscovia and Tartaria. The Beaver is as bigge as an ordinary water dogge, but his legges exceeding short. His fore feete like a dogs, his hinder feet like a Swans. His taile somewhat like the forme of a Racket bare without haire; which to eate, the Savages esteeme a great delicate. They have many Otters, which, as the Beavers, they take with snares, and esteeme the skinnes great ornaments; and of all those beasts they use to feede, when they catch them.

There is also a beast they call *Vetchunquoyes* in the forme of a wilde Cat. Their Foxes are like our silver haired Conies, of a small proportion, and not smelling like those in England. Their Dogges of that country are like their Wolves, and cannot barke but howle; and their wolves not much bigger then our English Foxes. Martins, Powlecats, weessels and Minkes we know they have, because we have seen many of their skinnes, though very seldome any of them alive. But one thing is strange, that we could never perceive their vermine destroy our hennes, egges, nor chickens, nor do any hurt: nor their flyes nor serpents anie waie pernitious; where in the South parts of America, they are alwaies dangerous and often deadly.

Of birds, the Eagle is the greatest devourer. Hawkes there be of diverse sorts as our Falconers called them, Sparowhawkes, Lanarets, Goshawkes, Falcons and Osperayes; but they all pray most upon fish. Pattridges there are little bigger then our Quailes, wilde Turkies are as bigge as our tame. There are woosels or blackbirds with red shoulders, thrushes, and diverse sorts of small birds, some red, some blew, scarce so bigge as a wrenne, but few in Sommer. In winter there are great plenty of Swans, Craynes gray and white with blacke wings, Herons, Geese, Brants, Ducke, Wigeon, Dotterell, Oxeies, Parrats, and Pigeons. Of all those sorts great abundance, and some other strange kinds, to us unknowne by name. But in sommer not any, or a very few to be seene.

Of fish we were best acquainted with Sturgeon, Grampus, Porpus, Seales, Stingraies whose tailes are very dangerous, Brettes, mullets, white Salmonds, Trowts, Soles, Plaice, Herrings, Conyfish, Rockfish, Eeles, Lampreyes, Catfish, Shades, Pearch of 3 sorts, Crabs, Shrimps, Crevises, Oysters, Cocles, and Muscles. But the most strange fish is a smal one so like the picture of S. George his Dragon, as possible can be, except his legs and wings: and the Todefish which will swell till it be like to brust, when it commeth into the aire.

Concerning the entrailes of the earth little can be saide for certainty. There wanted good Refiners: for these that tooke upon them to have skill this way, tooke up the washings from the mountaines and some moskered shining stones and spangles which the waters brought down; flattering themselves in their own vaine conceits to have been supposed that they were not, by the meanes of that ore, if it proved as their arts and judgements expected. Only this is certaine, that many regions lying in the same latitude, afford mines very rich of diverse natures. The crust also of these rockes would easily perswade a man to beleeve there are other mines then yron and steele, if there were but meanes and men of experience that knew the mine from spare.

Of their Planted fruits in Virginia and how they use them.—They divide the yeare into 5. seasons. Their winter some call *Popanow*, the spring *Cattapeuk*, the sommer *Cohattayough*, the earing of their Corne *Nepinough*, the harvest and fall of leafe *Taquitock*. From September untill the midst of November are the chiefe Feasts and sacrifice. Then have they plenty of fruits as well planted as naturall, as corne greene and ripe, fish, fowle, and wild beastes exceeding fat.

The greatest labour they take, is in planting their corne, for the country naturally is overgrowne with wood. To prepare the ground they bruise the barke of the trees neare the roote, then do they scortch the roots with fire that they grow no more. The next yeare with a crooked peece of wood, they beat up the woodes by the rootes; and in that moulds, they plant their corne. Their manner is this. They make a hole in the earth with a sticke, and into it they put 4 graines of wheat and 2 of beanes. These holes they make 4 foote one from another. Their women and children do continually keepe it with weeding, and when it is growne midle high, they hill it about like a hopyard.

In Aprill they begin to plant, but their chiefe plantation is in May, and so they continue till the midst of June. What they plant in Aprill they reape in August, for May in September, for June in October. Every stalke of their corne commonly beareth two eares, some 3, seldome any 4, many but one, and some none. Every eare ordinarily hath betwixt 200 and 500 graines. The stalke being green hath a sweet juice in it, somewhat like a suger Cane, which is the cause that when they gather their corne greene, they sucke the stalkes: for as wee gather greene pease, so doe they their corne being greene, which excelleth their old. They plant also pease they cal *Assentamens*, which are the same they cal in Italye,

Fagioli. Their Beanes are the same the Turkes call *Garnanses*, but these they much esteeme for dainties.

Their corne they rost in the eare greene, and bruising it in a morter with a Polt, lappe it in rowles in the leaves of their corne, and so boyle it for a daintie. They also reserve that corne late planted that will not ripe, by roasting it in hot ashes, the heat thereof drying it. In winter they esteeme it being boyled with beans for a rare dish, they call *Pausarowmena*. Their old wheat they first steep a night in hot water, in the morning pounding it in a morter. They use a small basket for their Temmes, then pound againe the great, and so separating by dashing their hand in the basket, receave the flower in a platter made of wood scraped to that forme with burning and shels. Tempering this flower with water, they make it either in cakes, covering them with ashes till they bee baked, and then washing them in faire water, they drie presently with their owne heat: or else boyle them in water eating the broth with the bread which they call *Ponap*. The grouts and peeces of the cornes remaining, by fanning in a Platter or in the wind away the branne, they boile 3 or 4 houres with water; which is an ordinary food they call *Ustatahamen*. But some more thrifty then cleanly, doe burne the core of the eare to powder which they call *Pungnough*, mingling that in their meale; but it never tasted well in bread, nor broth. Their fish and flesh they boyle either very tenderly, or broyle it so long on hurdles over the fire; or else, after the Spanish fashion, putting it on a spit, they turne first the one side, then the other, til it be as drie as their jerkin beefe in the west Indies, that they may keepe it a month or more without putrifying. The broth of fish or flesh they eate as commonly as the meat.

In May also amongst their corne, they plant Pumpeons, and a fruit like unto a muske millen, but lesse and worse; which they call *Macocks*. These increase exceedingly, and ripen in the beginning of July, and continue until September. They plant also *Maracocks* a wild fruit like a lemmon, which also increase infinitely: they begin to ripe in September and continue till the end of October. When all their fruits be gathered, little els they plant, and this is done by their women and children; neither doth this long suffice them: for neere 3 parts of the yeare, they only observe times and seasons, and live of what the Country naturally affordeth from hand to mouth, &c.

The commodities in Virginia or that may be had by industrie.—The mildnesse of the aire, the fertilitie of the soile, and the situation of the rivers are so propitious to the nature and use of man as no place is more convenient for pleasure, profit, and mans sustenance. Under that latitude or climat, here will live any beasts, as horses, goats, sheep, asses, hens, &c. as appeared by them that were carried thither. The waters, Isles, and shoales, are full of safe harbours for ships of warre or marchandize, for boats of all sortes, for transportation or fishing, &c. The Bay and rivers have much marchandable fish and places fit for Salt coats, building of ships, making of iron, &c.

Muscovia and Polonia doe yearely receave many thousands, for pitch, tarre, sope ashes, Rosen, Flax, Cordage, Sturgeon, masts, yards, wainscot, Firres, glasse, and such like; also Swethland for iron and copper. France in like manner, for Wine, Canvas, and Salt, Spaine asmuch for Iron, Steele, Figges, Reasons, and Sackes. Italy with Silkes and Velvets, consumes our chiefe commodities. Holand maintaines it selfe by fishing and trading at our owne doores. All these temporize with other for necessities, but all as uncertaine as peace or warres: besides the charge, travell, and danger in transporting them, by seas, lands, stormes, and Pyrats. Then how much hath Virginia the prerogative of all those florishing kingdomes for the benefit of our land, whenas within one hundred miles all those are to bee had, either ready provided by nature, or else to bee prepared, were there but industrious men to labour. Only of Copper wee may doubt is wanting, but there is good probabilitie that both copper and better munerals are there to be had for their labor. Other Countries have it. So then here is a place a nurse for souldiers, a practise for marriners, a trade for marchants, a reward for the good, and that which is most of all, a businesse (most acceptable to God) to bring such poore infidels to the true knowledge of God and his holy Gospell.

Of the naturall Inhabitants of Virginia.—The land is not populous, for the men be fewe; their far greater number is of women and children. Within 60 miles of James Towne there are about some 5000 people, but of able men fit for their warres scarse 1500. To nourish so many together they have yet no means, because they make so smal a benefit of their land, be it never so fertill. 6 or 700 have beene the most [that] hath beene seene together, when they gathered themselves to have surprised Captaine Smyth at Pamaunke, having but 15 to withstand the worst of their furie. As small as the proportion of ground that hath yet beene discovered, is in comparison of that yet unknowne. The people differ very much in stature, especially in language, as before is expressed. Some being very great as the Sesquesahamocks, others very little as the Wighcocomocoes: but generally tall and straight, of a comely proportion, and of a colour browne, when they are of any age, but they are borne white. Their haire is generally black; but few have any beards. The men weare halfe their heads shaven, the other halfe long. For Barbers they use their women, who with 2 shels will grate away the haire, of any fashion they please. The women are cut in many fashions agreeable to their yeares, but ever some part remaineth long. They are very strong, of an able body and full of agilitie, able to endure to lie in the woods under a tree by the fire, in the worst of winter, or in the weedes and grasse, in Ambuscado in the Sommer. They are inconstant in everie thing, but what feare constraineth them to keepe. Craftie, timerous, quicke of apprehension and very ingenuous. Some are of disposition fearefull, some bold, most cautelous, all Savage. Generally covetous of copper, beads, and such like trash. They are soone moved to anger, and so malitious, that they seldome forget an injury: they seldome steale one from another, least their conjurors should reveale it, and so they be pursued and punished. That they are thus feared is certaine, but that any can reveale their offences by conjuration I am doubtfull. Their women are carefull not to bee suspected of dishonesty without the leave of their husbands. Each houshold knoweth their owne lands and gardens, and most live of their owne labours. For their apparell, they are some time covered with the skinnes of wilde beasts, which in winter are dressed with the haire, but in sommer without. The better sort use large mantels of deare skins not much differing in fashion from the Irish mantels. Some imbrodered with white beads, some with copper, other painted after their manner. But the common sort have scarce to cover their nakednesse but with grasse, the leaves of trees, or such like. We have seen some use mantels made of Turky feathers, so prettily wrought and woven with threeds that nothing could bee discerned but the feathers, that was exceeding warme and very handsome. But the women are alwaies covered about their midles with a skin and very shamefast to bee seene bare. They adorne themselves most with copper beads and paintings. Their women some have their legs, hands, brests and face cunningly imbrodered with diverse workes, as beasts, serpentes, artificially wrought into their flesh with blacke spots. In each eare commonly they have 3 great holes, whereat they hange chaines, bracelets, or copper. Some of their men weare in those holes, a smal greene and yellow coloured snake, neare halfe a yard in length, which crawling and lapping her selfe about his necke often times familiarly would kiss his lips. Others wear a dead Rat tied by the tail. Some on their heads weare the wing of a bird or some large feather, with a Rattell. Those Rattels are somewhat like the chape of a Rapier but lesse, which they take from the taile of a snake. Many have the whole skinne of a hawke or some strange fowle, stuffed with the wings abroad. Others a broad peece of copper, and some the hand of their enemy dryed. Their heads and shoulders are painted red with the roote *Pocone* braied to powder mixed with oyle; this they hold in somer to preserve them from the heate, and in winter from the cold. Many other formes of paintings they use, but he is the most gallant that is the most monstrous to behould.

Their buildings and habitations are for the most part by the rivers or not farre distant from some fresh spring. Their houses are built like our Arbors of small young springs bowed and tyed, and so close covered with mats or the barkes of trees very handsomely, that notwithstanding either winde raine or weather, they are as warme as stooves, but very smoky, yet at the toppe of the house there is a hole made for the smoake to goe into right over the fire.

Against the fire they lie on little hurdles of Reedes covered with a mat, borne from the ground a foote and more by a hurdle of wood. On these round about the house, they lie heads and points one by thother against the fire: some covered with mats, some with skins, and some starke naked lie on the ground, from 6 to 20 in a house. Their houses are in the midst of their fields or gardens; which are smal plots of ground, some 20, some 40, some 100. some 200. some more, some lesse. Some times from 2 to 100 of these houses togither, or but a little separated by groves of trees. Neare their habitations is little small wood, or old trees on the ground, by reason of their burning of them for fire. So that a man may gallop a horse amongst these woods any waie, but where the creekes or Rivers shall hinder.

Men women and children have their severall names according to the severall humor of their Parents. Their women (they say) are easilie delivered of childe, yet doe they love children verie dearly. To make them hardy, in the coldest mornings they wash them in the rivers, and by painting and ointments so tanne their skins, that after year or two, no weather will hurt them.

The men bestowe their times in fishing, hunting, wars, and such manlike exercises, scorning to be seene in any woman like exercise, which is the cause that the women be verie painefull and the men often idle. The women and children do the rest of the worke. They make mats, baskets, pots, morters, pound their corne, make their bread, prepare their victuals, plant their corne, gather their corne, beare al kind of burdens, and such like. . . .

PENNSYLVANIA

THE LONDON COMPANY of Virginia relinquished its charter before many years were gone, though the colony John Smith had helped it found finally did come to flourish. And despite the extensive boundaries of Virginia, other colonies grew up to the northward. Charles II paid a debt with a portion of that northern land, and his creditor founded a prospering colony when he established Pennsylvania in 1681. By 1698, Gabriel Thomas was enlarging on that prosperity in a pamphlet which was translated into German four years later and which may have been one of those "lying reports" which helped draw Palatine Germans from their harried country. Thomas (1661–1714) came of Welsh yeoman stock. His father had been jailed for his Quaker faith and Thomas himself was one of the first immigrants to Pennsylvania. He returned to England in 1697 to see his book through the press. A few years later, he was bringing suit against Penn for failing to give him an office in the Delaware counties in return for the work which had been so effective in attracting immigrants to Pennsylvania. When Thomas lost his suit, he returned to the colony where he spent his last years in separation from the Quaker community.

If Thomas actually did write his book as bait to win settlers for Pennsylvania, his text is well calculated to that end. He had spent years in the country, he makes clear, watched it grow, witnessed its controversies, rejoiced at its progress. Thomas was inquisitive, as a reporter should be, and apparently a sound trencherman: no man indifferent to his food would spend so much ink on the savor of Chesapeake ducks, the relish of "saladings" and the composition of a tuppenny cheesecake.

Like Captain Smith, Thomas is interested in the Indians, though his preoccupation is more genuinely curious; he is concerned with the odd customs of this people rather than with their possible hindrance to the increase of empire. Similarly, though Thomas is as eager as Smith to have England appreciate the value of the new land, his interest is more in Franklin's vein than in the captain's. Thomas talks of the promise which Pennsylvania holds out to the immigrant rather than of the ways in which the colony could serve to advance the parent state. By the end of the seventeenth century, colonies were a fact, not merely a potential advantage to England, and Thomas could expatiate on the concerns of the indi-

vidual instead of the interests of the commonwealth.

Wages are high, Thomas reports; provisions are good and cheap. Yet the farmer gets high prices and though he pays his hands well, he has his land at small cost, unburdened by tithes and afflicted with few taxes. The merchant can thrive, too, for Pennsylvania trades with Madeira, England, and the West Indies, as well as with the other colonies; she builds fair ships and is equipped with "curious wharfs." Workman, farmer, merchant; men who seek freedom of worship and women in want of husbands all will find their heart's desire in Pennsylvania.

Thomas' pamphlet was published as *An Historical and Geographical Account of the Province and Country of Pensilvania, in America . . .* (London, 1698).

An Account of Pensilvania

BY GABRIEL THOMAS

PENSILVANIA lies between the Latitude of Forty and Forty five Degrees: *West-Jersey* on the East, *Virginia* on the West, *Mary-Land* South, and *Canada* on the North. In Length three hundred, and in Breadth one hundred and eighty miles.

The Natives, or first Inhabitants of this Country in their Original, are suppos'd by most People to have been of the Ten Scattered Tribes, for they resemble the *Jews* very much in the *Make* of their *Persons*, and *Tincture* of their *Complexions:* They observe New *Moons*, they offer their *first Fruits* to a *Maneto*, or suppos'd Deity, whereof they have two, one, as they fansie, above (good,) another below (bad,) and have a kind of *Feast of Tabernacles*, laying their *Altars* upon *Twelve Stones*, observe a sort of *Mourning* twelve Months, *Customs of Women*, and many other *Rites* to be toucht (here) rather than dwelt upon, because they shall be handled more at large at the latter end of this Treatise.

They are very Charitable to one another, the Lame and the Blind (amongst them) living as well as the best; they are also very kind and obliging to the *Christians*.

The next that came there, were the *Dutch*, (who call'd the Country *New Netherland*) between Fifty and Sixty Years ago, and were the first *Planters* in those Parts; but they made little or no

Improvement, (applying themselves wholly to Trafique in Skins and Furs, which the *Indians* or *Natives* furnish'd them with, and which they Barter'd for Rum, Strong Liquors, and Sugar, with others, thereby gaining great Profit) till near the time of the Wars between *England* and *Them*, about Thirty or Forty Years ago.

Soon after them came the *Swedes* and *Fins*, who apply'd themselves to Husbandry, and were the first *Christian* People that made any considerable Improvement there.

There were some Disputes between these two Nations some Years, the *Dutch* looking upon the *Swedes* as Intruders upon their Purchase and Possession, which was absolutely terminated in the Surrender made by *John Rizeing*, the *Swedes* Governour, to *Peter Styreant*, Governour for the *Dutch*, in 1655. In the *Holland* War about the Year 1665, Sir *Robert Carr* took the Country from the *Dutch* for the *English*, and left his Cousin, Captain *Carr*, Governour of that place; but in a short time after, the *Dutch* re-took the Country from the *English*, and kept it in their Possession till the Peace was concluded between the *English* and them, when the *Dutch* Surrendered that *Country* with *East* and *West-Jersey*, *New York*, (with the whole Countries belonging to that Government) to the *English* again. But it remain'd with very little Improvement till the Year 1681, in which *William Penn* Esq; had the Country given him by King *Charles* the *Second*, in lieu of Money that was due to (and signal Service done by) his Father, Sir *William Penn*, and from him bore the Name of *Pensilvania*.

Since that time, the Industrious (nay Indefatigable) Inhabitants have built a *Noble* and *Beautiful* City, and called it *Philadelphia*, which contains above two thousand Houses, all Inhabited; and most of them Stately, and of Brick, generally three Stories high, after the Mode in *London*, and as many several Families in each. . . .

It hath in it Three *Fairs* every Year, and Two *Markets* every Week. They kill above Twenty *Fat Bullocks* every Week, in the hottest time in Summer, for their present spending in that City, besides many *Sheep, Calves* and *Hogs.*

This City is Situated between *Schoolkill-River* and the great River *Delaware*, which derives its Name from Captain *Delaware*, who came there pretty early: Ships of Two or Three Hundred Tuns may come up to this City, by either of these two Rivers. Moreover, in this Province are Four Great *Market-Towns*, viz, *Chester*, the *German Town, New-Castle*, and *Lewis-Town*, which are mightily Enlarged in this latter Improvement. Between these Towns, the Water-Men constantly Ply their *Wherries;* likewise all those Towns have *Fairs* kept in them, besides there are several Country Villages, viz. *Dublin, Harford, Merioneth*, and *Radnor* in *Cambry;* all which *Towns, Villages* and *Rivers*, took their Names from the several *Countries* whence the present Inhabitants came.

The *Air* here is very delicate, pleasant, and wholesom; the *Heavens* serene, rarely overcast, bearing mighty resemblance to the better part of *France;* after Rain they have commonly a very clear Sky, the Climate is something Colder in the depth of Winter, and Hotter in the height of Summer; (the cause of which is its, being a Main Land or Continent; the Days also are two Hours longer in the shortest Day in Winter, and shorter by two Hours in the longest Day of Summer) than here in *England*, which makes the Fruit so good, and the Earth so fertil.

The Corn-Harvest is ended before the middle of *July*, and most Years they have commonly between Twenty and Thirty Bushels of Wheat for every one they Sow. Their Ground is harrowed with Wooden Tyned Harrows, twice over in a place is sufficient; twice mending of their Plow-Irons in a Years time will serve. Their Horses commonly go without being shod; two Men may clear between Twenty and Thirty Acres of Land

in one Year, fit for the Plough, in which Oxen are chiefly us'd, though Horses are not wanting, and of them Good and well shap'd. A Cart or a Wain may go through the middle of the Woods, between the Trees without getting any damage, and of such Land in a convenient place, the Purchase will cost between *Ten* and *Fifteen Pounds* for a Hundred Acres. Here is much Meadow Ground. Poor People both Men and Women, will get near three times more Wages for their Labour in this Country, than they can earn either in *England* or *Wales.*

What is Inhabited of this Country, is divided into Six *Counties*, though there is not the Twentieth Part of it yet Peopled by the *Christians:* It hath in it several Navigable Rivers for Shipping to come in, besides the Capital *Delaware*, wherein a Ship of Two Hundred Tuns may Sail Two Hundred Miles up. There are also several other small Rivers, in number hardly Credible; these, as the Brooks, have for the most part gravelly and hard Bottoms; and it is suppos'd that there are many other further up in the Country, which are not yet discover'd. . . .

There is curious *Building-Stone* and *Paving-Stone*, also *Tile-Stone*, with which latter, Governor *Penn* covered his *Great* and *Stately Pile*, which he call'd *Pennsbury-House*, the Name it still retains. There is likewise *Iron-Stone* or *Oar*, (lately found) which far exceeds that in *England*, being Richer and less Drossy; some Preparations have been made to carry on an Iron-Work: There is also very good *Lime-Stone* in great plenty, and cheap, of great use in Buildings, and also in Manuring Land, (if there were occasion) but Nature has made that of it self sufficiently Fruitful; besides here are *Load-Stones, Ising-Glass* and (that Wonder of Stones) the *Salamander-Stone*, found near *Brandy-Wine-River*, having *Cotton* in Veins within it, which will not consume in the Fire; though held there a long time.

As to *Minerals*, or *Metals*, there is very good *Copper*, far exceeding ours in *England*, being much Finer, and of a more glorious Colour. Not two Mile from the *Metropolis*, are also *Purging-Mineral-Waters*, that pass both by *Siege* and *Urine*, all out as good as *Epsom;* And I have reason to believe, there are good *Coals* also, for I observ'd, the Runs of Water have the same Colour as that which proceeds from the *Coal-Mines* in *Wales.*

Here is curious Diversion in Hunting, Fishing, and Fowling, especially upon that Great and Famous River *Suskahanah*, which runs down quite through the heart of the Country to *Mary-Land*, where it makes the Head of *Chesepeck-Bay*, in which place there are an Infinite Number of Sea and Land Fowl, of most sorts. *viz. Swans, Ducks, Teal,* (which two are the most Grateful and most Delicious in the World) *Geese, Divers, Brands, Snipe, Curlew;* as also *Eagles, Turkies* (of Forty or Fifty Pound weight) *Pheasants, Partridges, Pidgeons, Heath-Birds, Black-Birds;* and that Strange and Remarkable Fowl, call'd (in these Parts) the *Mocking-Bird,* that Imitates all sorts of Birds in their various Notes. And for Fish, there are prodigious quantities of most sorts, *viz. Shadds, Cats Heads, Sheeps-Heads, Herrings, Smelts, Roach, Eels, Perch.* As also the large sort of Fish, as Whales (of which a great deal of Oyl is made) *Salmon, Trout, Sturgeon, Roc, Oysters,* (some six Inches long) *Crabs, Cockles,* (some as big as Stewing *Oysters* of which are made a Choice Soupe or Broth) *Canok* and *Mussels,* with many other sorts of Fish, which would be too tedious to insert.

There are several sorts of wild *Beasts* of great Profit, and good Food; *viz. Panthers, Woolves, Fither, Deer, Beaver, Otter, Hares, Musk-Rats, Minks, Wild Cats, Foxes, Rackoons, Rabits* and that strange Creature, the *Possam,* she having a false Belly to swallow her Young ones, by which means she preserveth them from danger, when any thing comes to disturb them. There are also *Bears some Wolves,* are pretty well destroy'd by the *Indians,* for the sake of the Reward given them by the *Christian,* for that Service. Here is also that Remarkable Creature the *Flying-Squirrel,* having a kind of Skinny Wings, almost like those of the *Batt,* though it hath the like Hair and Colour of the Common *Squirrel,* but is much less in Bodily Substance; I have (my self) seen it fly from one Tree to another in the Woods, but how long it can maintain its Flight is not yet exactly known.

There are in the Woods abundance of *Red Deer* (vulgarly called *Stags*) for I have bought of the *Indians* a whole *Buck,* (both Skin and Carcass) for two Gills of Gunpowder. Excellent Food, most delicious, far exceeding that in *Europe,* in the Opinion of most that are Nice and Curious People. There are vast Numbers of other Wild Creatures, as *Elks, Bufalos, &c.* all which as well Beasts, Fowl, and Fish, are free and common to any Person who can shoot or take them, without any lett, hinderance or Opposition whatsoever.

There are among other various sorts of *Frogs,* the *Bull-Frog,* which makes a roaring noise, hardly to be distinguished from that well known of the Beast, from whom it takes its Name: There is another sort of *Frog* that crawls up to the tops of Trees, there seeming to imitate the Notes of several Birds, with many other strange and various Creatures, which would take up too much room here to mention.

Next, I shall proceed to instance in the several sorts of Wild Fruits, as excellent *Grapes, Red, Black, White, Muscadel,* and *Fox,* which upon frequent Experience have produc'd Choice Wine, being daily Cultivated by skilful *Vinerons;* they will in a short space of time, have very good Liquor of their own, and some to supply their Neighbours, to their great advantage; as these Wines are more pure, so much more wholsom; the Brewing Trade of Sophisticating and Adulterating of Wines, as in *England, Holland* (especially) and in some other places not being known there yet, nor in all probability will it in many Years, through a natural Probity so fixed and implanted in the Inhabitants, and (I hope) like to continue. *Wallnuts, Chestnuts, Filberts, Hockery-Nuts, Hartleberries, Mulberries,* (white and black) *Rasberries, Strawberries, Cramberries, Plumbs* of several sorts, and many other Wild Fruits, in great plenty, which are common and free for any to gather; to particularize the Names of them all, would take up too much time; tire, not gratifie the Reader, and be inconsistent with the intended Brevity of this little Volume.

The common Planting *Fruit-Trees,* are *Apples,* which from a Kernel (without Inoculating) will shoot up to be a large Tree, and produce very delicious, large, and pleasant Fruit, of which much excellent *Cyder* is made, in taste resembling that in England press'd from *Pippins* and *Pearmains,* sold commonly for between Ten and Fifteen Shillings *per* Barrel. *Pears, Peaches, &c.* of which they distil a Liquor much like the taste of *Rumm,* or *Brandy,* which they Yearly make in great quantities: There are *Quinces, Cherries, Goosberries, Currants, Squashes, Pumpkins, Water-Mellons, Muskmellons,* and other *Fruits* in great Numbers, which seldom fail of yielding great plenty. There are also many curious and excellent *Physical Wild Herbs, Roots,* and *Drugs* of great Vertue, and very sanative, as the *Sassafras,* and *Sarsaparilla,* so much us'd in Diet-Drinks for the Cure of the Veneral Disease, which makes the *Indians* by a right application of them, as able *Doctors* and *Surgeons* as any in *Europe,* performing celebrated Cures therewith, and by the use of some particular *Plants* only, find Remedy in all *Swellings, Burnings, Cuts, &c.* There grows also in great plenty the *Black Snake-Root,* (fam'd for its sometimes preserving, but often curing the *Plague,* being infused only in Wine, Brandy or Rumm) *Rattle-Snake-Root, Poke-Root,* called in

England Jallop, with several other beneficial *Herbs*, *Plants* and *Roots*, which *Physicians* have approved of, far exceeding in Nature and Vertue, those of other Countries. . . .

Their sorts of *Grain* are, *Wheat, Rye, Pease, Oates, Barley, Buck-Wheat, Rice, Indian-Corn, Indian-Pease,* and *Beans,* with great quantities of *Hemp* and *Flax;* as also several sorts of eating Roots, as *Turnips, Potatoes, Carrats, Parsnips,* &c. all which are produc'd Yearly in greater quantities than in *England,* those *Roots* being much larger, and altogether as sweet, if not more delicious; *Cucumbers, Coshaws, Artichokes,* with many others; most sorts of Saladings, besides what grows naturally Wild in the Country, and that in great plenty also, as *Mustard, Rue, Sage, Mint, Tanzy, Wormwood, Penny-Royal* and *Purslain,* and most of the Herbs and Roots found in the Gardens in *England.* There are several Husband Men, who sow Yearly between Seventy and Eighty Acres of *Wheat* each, besides *Barley, Oates, Rye, Pease, Beans,* and other Grain.

They have commonly *Two Harvests* in the Year; First, of *English Wheat,* and next of *Buck* (or *French*) Wheat. They have great Stocks both of *Hogs* and *Horses,* kept in the Woods, out of which, I saw a *Hog* kill'd, of about a Year old, which weigh'd Two Hundred weight; whose Flesh is much sweeter, and even more luscious than that in *England,* because they feed and fatten on the rich (though wild) Fruits, besides those fatned at home by *Peaches, Cherries* and *Apples.* Their *Horses* are very hardy, insomuch that being very hot with riding or otherwise, they are turn'd out into the Woods at the same Instant, and yet receive no harm; some Farmers have Forty, some Sixty, and from that Number to Two or Three Hundred Head of *Cattle:* Their Oxen usually weigh Two Hundred Pounds a Quarter. They are commonly fatter of Flesh, and yield more Tallow (by feeding only on Grass) than the Cattle in *England.* And for Sheep, they have considerable Numbers which are generally free from those infectious Diseases which are incident to those Creatures in *England,* as the *Rot, Scab,* or *Maggots;* They commonly bring forth two *Lambs* at once, some *twice in one Year,* and the Wooll is very fine, and thick, and also very white.

Bees thrive and multiply exceedingly in those Parts, the *Sweeds* often get great store of them in the Woods, where they are free for any Body. Honey (and choice too) is sold in the Capital City for Five Pence *per* Pound. Wax is also plentiful, cheap, and a considerable Commerce. Tame Fowls, as *Chickens, Hens, Geese, Ducks, Tur-*keys, &c. are large, and very plentiful all over this Countrey.

And now for their Lots and Lands in City and Countrey, in their great Advancement since they were first laid out, which was within the compass of about Twelve Years, that which might have been bought for Fifteen or Eighteen Shillings, is now sold for Fourscore Pounds in ready Silver; and some other Lots, that might have been then Purchased for Three Pounds, within the space of Two Years, were sold for a Hundred Pounds a piece, and likewise some Land that lies near the City, that Sixteen Years ago might have been Purchas'd for Six or Eight Pounds the Hundred Acres, cannot now be bought under One Hundred and Fifty, or Two Hundred Pounds.

Now the true Reason why this Fruitful Countrey and Florishing City advance so considerably in the Purchase of Lands both in the one and the other, is their great and extended Traffique and Commerce both by Sea and Land, *viz.* to *New-York, New-England, Virginia, Mary-Land, Carolina, Jamaica, Barbadoes, Nevis, Monserat, Antego* St. *Christophers, Barmudoes, New-Found-Land, Maderas, Saltetudeous,* and *Old-England;* besides several other places. Their merchandise chiefly consists in *Horses, Pipe-Staves, Pork* and *Beef* Salted and Barrelled up, *Bread,* and *Flower,* all sorts of Grain, *Pease, Beans, Skins, Furs, Tobacco,* or *Pot-Ashes, Wax,* &c which are Barter'd for *Rumm, Sugar, Molasses, Silver, Negroes, Salt, Wine, Linen, Household-Goods* &c.

However, there still remain Lots of Land both in the aforesaid City and Country, that any may Purchase almost as cheap as they could at the first Laying out or Parcelling of either City or Countrey; which is, (in the Judgment of most People) the likeliest to turn to account to those that lay their Money out upon it, and in a shorter time than the aforementioned Lots and Lands that are already improved, and for several Reasons. In the first place, the Countrey is now well inhabited by the Christians, who have great Stocks of all sorts of Cattle, that encrease extraordinarly, and upon that account they are oblig'd to go farther up into the Countrey, because there is the chiefest and best place for their Stocks, and for them that go back into the Countrey, they get the richest Land, for the best lies thereabouts.

Secondly, Farther into the Countrey is the Principal Place to Trade with the *Indians* for all sorts of *Pelt,* as *Skins* and *Furs,* and also *Fat Venison,* of whom People may Purchase cheaper by three Parts in four than they can at the City of *Philadelphia.*

Thirdly, Backwards in the Countrey lies the

Mines where is *Copper* and *Iron*, besides other *Metals*, and *Minerals*, of which there is some Improvement made already in order to bring them, to greater Perfection; and that will be a means to erect more Inland Market-Towns, which exceedingly promote Traffick.

Fourthly, and lastly, Because the Countrey at the first, laying out, was void of Inhabitants (except the Heathens, or very few Christians not worth naming) and not many People caring to abandon a quiet and easie (at least tolerable) Life in their Native Countrey (usually the most agreeable to all Mankind) to seek out a new hazardous, and careful one in a Foreign Wilderness or Desart Countrey, wholly destitute of Christian Inhabitants, and even to arrive at which, they must pass over a vast Ocean, expos'd to some Dangers, and not a few Inconveniences: But now all those Cares, Fears and Hazards are vanished, for the Countrey is pretty well Peopled, and very much Improv'd, and will be more every Day, now the Dove is return'd with the Olive-branch of Peace in her Mouth.

I must needs say, even the present Encouragements are very great and inviting, for Poor People (both Men and Women) of all kinds, can here get three times the Wages for their Labour they can in *England* or *Wales*.

I shall instance in a few, which may serve; nay, and will hold in all the rest. The first was a *Black-Smith*, (my next Neighbour) who himself and one Negro Man he had, got Fifty Shillings in one Day, by working up a Hundred Pound Weight of Iron, which at Six Pence *per* Pound (and that is the common Price in that Countrey) amounts to that Summ.

And for *Carpenters*, both *House* and *Ship*, *Brick-layers*, *Masons*, either of these Trades-Men, will get between Five and Six Shillings every Day constantly. As to *Journey-Men Shooe-Makers*, they have Two Shillings *per* Pair both for Men and Womens Shooes: And *Journey-Men Taylors* have Twelve Shillings *per* Week and their Diet. *Sawyers* get between Six and Seven Shillings the Hundred for Cutting of Pine-Boards. And for *Weavers*, they have Ten or Twelve Pence the Yard for Weaving of that which is little more than half a Yard in breadth. *Wooll-Combers*, have for combing Twelve Pence *per* Pound. *Potters* have Sixteen Pence for an Earthen Pot which may be bought in *England* for Four Pence. *Tanners*, may buy their Hides green for Three Half Pence *per* Pound, and sell their Leather for Twelve Pence *per* Pound. And *Curriers* have Three Shillings and Four Pence *per* Hide for Dressing it; they buy their Oyl at Twenty Pence *per* Gallon.

Brick-Makers have Twenty Shillings *per* Thousand for their Bricks at the Kiln. *Felt-Makers* will have for their Hats Seven Shillings a piece, such as may be bought in *England* for Two Shillings a piece; yet they buy their *Wooll* commonly for Twelve or Fifteen Pence *per* Pound. And as to the *Glaziers*, they will have Five Pence a Quarry for their Glass. The Rule for the *Coopers* I have almost forgot; but this I can affirm of some who went from *Bristol*, (as their Neighbours report) that could hardly get their Livelihoods there, are now reckon'd in *Pensilvania*, by a modest Computation to be worth some Hundreds, (if not Thousands) of Pounds. The *Bakers* make as White Bread as any in *London*, and as for their Rule, it is the same in all Parts of the World that I have been in. The *Butchers* for killing a Beast, have Five Shillings and their Diet; and they may buy a good fat large Cow for Three Pounds, or thereabouts. The *Brewers* sell such Beer as is equal in Strength to that in *London*, half Ale and half Stout for Fifteen Shillings *per* Barrel; and their Beer hath a better Name, that is, is in more esteem than *English Beer* in *Barbadoes*, and is sold for a higher Price there. And for *Silver-Smiths*, they have between Half a Crown and Three Shillings an Ounce for working their Silver, and for Gold equivalent. *Plasterers* have commonly Eighteen Pence *per* Yard for *Plastering*. *Last-Makers* have Sixteen Shillings *per* dozen for their Lasts. And *Heel-Makers* have Two Shillings a dozen for their Heels. *Wheel* and *Mill-Wrights*, *Joyners*, *Braziers*, *Pewterers*, *Dyers*, *Fullers*, *Comb-Makers*, *Wyer-Drawers*, *Cage-Makers*, *Card-Makers*, *Painters*, *Cutlers*, *Rope-Makers*, *Carvers*, *Block-Makers*, *Turners*, *Button-Makers*, *Hair* and *Wood Sieve-Makers*, *Bodies-Makers*, *Gun-Smiths*, *Lock-Smiths*, *Nailers*, *File-Cuters*, *Skinners*, *Furriers*, *Glovers*, *Patten-Makers*, *Watch-Makers*, *Clock-Makers*, *Sadlers*, *Coller-Makers*, *Barbers*, *Printers*, *Book-Binders*, and all other *Trades-Men*, their Gains and Wages are about the same proportion as the forementioned Trades in their Advancements, as to what they have in *England*.

Of *Lawyers* and *Physicians* I shall say nothing, because this Countrey is very Peaceable and Healthy; long may it so continue and never have occasion for the Tongue of the one, nor the Pen of the other, both equally destructive of Mens Estates and Lives; besides forsooth, they, Hang-Man like, have a License to Murder and make Mischief. *Labouring-Men* have commonly here, between 14 and 15 Pounds a Year, and their Meat, Drink, Washing and Lodging; and by the Day their Wages is generally between Eighteen Pence and Half a Crown, and Diet also; But in Harvest they have usually between Three and Four Shillings each Day, and Diet. The *Maid Servants Wages* is commonly betwixt Six and Ten Pounds *per Annum*, with very good Accommodation. And for the *Women* who get their Livelihood by their own *Industry*, their Labour is very dear, for I can buy in *London* a Cheese-Cake for Two Pence, bigger than theirs at that price when at the same time their Milk is as cheap as we can buy it in *London*, and their Flour cheaper by one half.

Corn and Flesh, and what else serves Man for Drink, Food and Rayment, is much cheaper here than in *England*, or elsewhere; but the chief reason why Wages of Servants of all sorts is much higher here than there, arises from the great Fertility and Produce of the Place; besides, if these large Stipends were refused them, they would quickly set up for themselves, for they can have Provision very cheap, and Land for a very small matter, or next to nothing in comparison of the Purchase of Lands in *England;* and the Farmers there, can better afford to give that great Wages than the Farmers in *England* can, for several Reasons very obvious.

As First, their Land costs them (as I said but just now) little or nothing in comparison, of which the Farmers commonly will get twice the encrease of Corn for every Bushel they sow, that the Farmers in *England* can from the richest Land they have.

In the Second place, they have constantly good price for their Corn, by reason of the great and quick vent into *Barbadoes* and other Islands; through which means *Silver* is become more plentiful than here in *England*, considering the Number of People, and that causes a quick Trade for both Corn and Cattle; and that is the reason that Corn differs now from the Price formerly, else it would be at half the Price it was at then; for a Brother of mine (to my own particular knowledge) sold within the compass of one Week, about One Hundred and Twenty fat Beasts, most of them good handsom large Oxen.

Thirdly, They pay no *Tithes*, and their *Taxes* are inconsiderable; the Place is free for all Persuasions, in a Sober and Civil way; for the Church of *England* and the *Quakers* bear equal Share in the Government. They live Friendly and Well together; there is no Persecution for Religion, nor ever like to be; 'tis this that knocks all Commerce on the Head, together with high Imposts, strict Laws, and cramping Orders. Before I end this Paragraph, I shall add another Reason why Womens Wages are so exorbitant; they are not yet very numerous, which makes them stand upon high Terms for their several Services, in Semps-

tering, *Washing, Spinning, Knitting, Sewing,* and in all the other parts of their Imployments; for they have for Spinning either Worsted or Linen, Two Shillings a Pound, and commonly for Knitting a very Course pair of Yarn Stockings, they have half a Crown a pair; moreover they are usually Marry'd before they are Twenty Years of Age, and when once in that Noose, are for the most part a little uneasie, and make their Husbands so too, till they procure them a Maid Servant to bear the burden of the Work, as also in some measure to wait on them too.

It is now time to return to the City of *Brotherly-Love* (for so much the *Greek* Word or Name *Philadelphia* imports) which though at present so obscure, that neither the *Map-Makers*, nor *Geographers* have taken the least notice of her, tho she far exceeds her Namesake of *Lydia*. (having above Two Thousand Noble Houses for her Five Hundred Ordinary) or *Celisia*, or *Cælesyria;* yet in a very short space of time she will, in all probability, make a fine Figure in the World, and be a most Celebrated Emporeum. Here is lately built a Noble *Town-House* or *Guild-Hall*, also a Handsom *Market-House* and a convenient *Prison*. The Number of Christians both Old and Young Inhabiting in that Countrey, are by a Modest Computation, adjudged to amount to above Twenty Thousand.

The Laws of this Countrey, are the same with those in *England;* our Constitution being on the same Foot: Many Disputes and Differences are determined and composed by Arbitration; and all Causes are decided with great Care and Expedition, being concluded (generally) at furthest at the Second Court, unless they happen to be very Nice and Difficult Cases; under Forty Shillings any one Justice of the Peace has Power to Try the Cause. Thieves of all sorts, are oblig'd to restore four fold after they have been Whipt and Imprison'd, according to the Nature of their Crime; and if they be not of Ability to restore four fold, they must be in Servitude till 'tis satisfied. They have Curious Wharfs as also several large and fine Timber-Yards, both at *Philadelphia*, and *New-Castle*, especially at the *Metropolis*, before *Robert Turner's* Great and Famous House, where are built Ships of considerable Burthen; they Cart their Goods from that Wharf into the City of *Philadelphia*, under an Arch, over which part of the Street is built, which is called *Chestnut-Street-Wharf*, besides other *Wharfs*, as *High-Street Wharf, Mulberry-Street Wharf*, and *Vine-Street Wharf*, and all those are Common Wharfs; and likewise there are very pleasant Stairs, as *Trus* and *Carpenter-Stairs*, besides several others.

There are above Thirty Carts belonging to that City, Four or Five Horses to each. There is likewise a very convenient Wharf called *Carpenter's Wharf*, which hath a fine necessary *Crain* belonging to it, with suitable *Granaries*, and *Store-Houses*. A Ship of Two Hundred Tun may load and unload by the side of it, and there are other Wharfs (with *Magazines* and *Ware-Houses*) which front the City all along the River, as also a Curious and Commodious *Dock* with a *Draw-Bridge* to it, for the convenient Reception of Vessels; where have been built some Ships of Two or Three Hundred Tuns each: They have very Stately Oaks to build Ships with, some of which are between Fifty and Sixty Feet long, and clear from Knots, being very straight and well Grain'd. In this famous City of *Philadelphia* there are several *Rope-Makers*, who have large and curious *Rope-Walks* especially one *Joseph Wilcox*. Also Three or Four Spacious *Malt-Houses*, as many large *Brew-Houses*, and many handsom *Bake-Houses* for Publick Use.

In the said City are several good *Schools of Learning* for Youth, in order to the Attainment of *Arts* and *Sciences*, as also *Reading*, *Writing*, &c. Here is to be had on any Day in the Week, *Tarts*, *Pies*, *Cakes*, &c. We have also several *Cooks-Shops*, both *Roasting* and *Boyling*, as in the City of *London*; *Bread*, *Beer*, *Beef*, and *Pork*, are sold at any time much cheaper than in *England* (which arises from their Plenty) our Wheat is very white and clear from Tares, making as good and white Bread as any in *Europe*. Happy Blessings, for which we owe the highest Gratitude to our Plentiful Provider, the great Creator of Heaven and Earth. The *Water-Mills* far exceed those in *England*, both for quickness and grinding good Meal, their being great choice of good Timber, and earlier Corn than in the aforesaid Place, they are made by one *Peter Deal*, a Famous and Ingenious Workman, especially for inventing such like Machines. . . .

The *Christian Children* born here are generally *well-favoured*, and *Beautiful* to behold; I never knew any come into the World with the least blemish on any part of its Body, being in the general, observ'd to be *better Natur'd*, *Milder*, and more *tender Hearted* than those born in *England*.

There are very fine and delightful *Gardens* and *Orchards*, in most parts of this Countrey; but *Edward Shippey* (who lives near the Capital City) has an Orchard and Gardens adjoyning to his Great House that equalizes (if not exceeds) any I have ever seen, having a very famous and pleasant Summer-House erected in the middle of his extraordinary fine and large Garden abounding with *Tulips*, *Pinks*, *Carnations*, *Roses*, (of several sorts) *Lilies*, not to mention those that grow wild in the Fields.

Reader, what I have here written, is not a *Fiction*, *Flam*, *Whim*, or any sinister *Design*, either to impose upon the Ignorant, or Credulous, or to curry Favour with the Rich and Mighty, but in meer Pity and pure Compassion to the Numbers of Poor Labouring Men, Women, and Children in *England*, half starv'd, visible in their meagre looks, that are continually wandering up and down looking for Employment without finding any, who here need not lie idle a moment, nor want due Encouragement or Reward for their Work, much less Vagabond or Drone it about. Here are no Beggars to be seen (it is a Shame and Disgrace to the State that there are so many in *England*) nor indeed have any here the least Occasion or Temptation to take up that Scandalous Lazy Life.

Jealousie among Men is here very rare, and Barrenness among Women hardly to be heard of, nor are old Maids to be met with; for all commonly Marry before they are Twenty Years of Age, and seldom any young Married Woman but hath a Child in her Belly, or one upon her Lap.

What I have deliver'd concerning this *Province*, is indisputably true, I was an Eye-Witness to it all, for I went in the first Ship that was bound from *England* for the Countrey, since it received the Name of *Pensilvania*, which was in the Year 1681. The Ship's Name was the *John* and *Sarah* of *London*, *Henry Smith* Commander. I have declin'd giving any Account of several things which I have only heard others speak of, because I did not see them my self, for I never held that way infallible, to make Reports from *Hear-say*. I saw the first Cellar when it was digging for the use of our Governour *Will. Penn*.

I shall now haste to a Conclusion, and only hint a little concerning the *Natives* or *Aborigines*, their *Persons*, *Language*, *Manners*, *Religion* and *Government*; Of *Person* they are ordinarily Tall, Straight, well-turn'd, and true Proportion'd; their Tread strong and clever, generally walking with a lofty Chin. Of Complexion *Black*, but by design, *Gypsie-like*, greasing themselves with Bears-fat Clarified, and using no defence against the Injuries of the *Sun* and *Weather*, their Skins fail not to be Swarthy. Their *Eyes* are small and black. *Thick Lips and flat Noses* so frequent with *Negroes* and *East Indians*, are rare with them. They have Comely Faces and Tolerable Complexions, some of their *Noses* having a rise like the *Roman*.

Their *Language* is Lofty and Elegant, but not

Copious; *One* Word serveth in the stead of *Three*, imperfect and ungrammatical, which defects are supply'd by the Understanding of the Hearers. *Sweet*, of *Noble Sound* and *Accent*. Take here a Specimen.

Hodi hita nee huska a peechi, nee, machi
Pensilvania *huska dogwachi, keshow a peechi*
Nowa, huska hayly, Chetena koon peo.

Thus in *English*.

Farewel Friend, I will very quickly go to *Pensilvania*, very cold Moon will come presently, And very great hard frosts will come quickly.

I might Treat largely of their *Customs* and *Manners*, but that will not agree with my proposed Brevity.

As soon as their Children are born, they wash them in cold *Water*, especially in *cold Weather*. To harden and embolden them, they plunge them in the River, they find their Feet early, usually at Nine Months they can go. The Boys Fish till Fifteen, then Hunt, and having given proof of their Manhood, by a large return of Skins, they may Marry (else 'tis ashame to think of a Wife) which is usually at the Age of Seventeen or Eighteen; the Girls stay with their Mothers, and help to hoe the Ground, Plant Corn, bear Burdens, and Marry about Thirteen or Fourteen.

Their Houses are *Matts*, or *Barks* of *Trees* set on Poles, Barn-like, not higher than a Man, so not expos'd to Winds. They lie upon *Reeds* or *Grass*. In *Travel* they lodge in the *Woods* about a great Fire, with the Mantle of Duffils they wear wrapt about them, and a few Boughs stuck round them.

They live chiefly on *Maze*, or *Indian Corn* rosted in the Ashes, sometimes beaten and boyl'd with Water, called *Homine*. They have Cakes, not unpleasant; also Beans and Pease, which Nourish much, but the Woods and Rivers afford them their Provision; they eat Morning and Evening; their Seats and Tables are the Ground; they are reserv'd, apt to resent and retain long: Their Women are Chaste (at least after Marriage) and when with Child, will not admit of their Husbands Embraces any more till Deliver'd. Exceedingly Liberal and Generous; Kind and Affable; uneasie in Sickness, to remedy which, they drink a Decoction of Roots in Spring-Water, forbearing Flesh, which if they happen to eat, it must be the Female; they commonly bury their Kettles and part of their Goods with their Friends when they die, suspecting (poor Souls) they shall make use of them again at the Resurrection. They mourn a whole Year, but it is no other than blacking their Faces.

Their Government is Monarchical, and Successive, and ever of the Mothers (the surest) side, to prevent a Spurious Issue. The Distaff (as in *France*) is excluded the Regal Inheritance. Their Princes are Powerful, yet do nothing without the Concurrence of their Senate, or Councils, consisting chiefly of Old, but mixt with Young Men; slow and deliberate, (*Spaniard*-like) in resolving, naturally wise, and hardly to be out-witted. Their Punishments are Pecuniary. Murder may be aton'd for by Feasts and Presents, in Proportion to the Quality of the Offence, Person, or Sex injur'd; for it a Woman be kill'd, the Mulct is double, because she brings forth Children. They seldom quarel, when Sober, and if Boozy, (which of late they are more apt to be, having learn'd to drink, a little too much Rum of the Christians, to their shame) they readily pardon it, alledging the Liquor is Criminal not the Man.

The way of Worship the *Sweeds* use in this Countrey, is the *Lutheran;* the *English* have four sorts of Assemblies or Religious Meetings here: as first, The Church of *England*, who built a very fine Church in the City of *Philadelphia* in the Year 1695. Secondly, the *Anabaptists;* Thirdly, the *Presbyterians*, and two sorts of *Quakers* (of all the most numerous by much) one Party held with *George Keith;* but whether both parties will joyn together again in one I cannot tell, for that Gentleman hath alter'd his Judgment since he came to *England*, concerning his Church-Orders in *Pensilvania*, by telling and shewing them Precepts that were lawful in the time of the Law, but forbidden under the Gospel to pay Tithes, or Ministers to Preach for Hire, &c. As also to sprinkle Infants; and he tells the *Presbyterian Minister*, That he must go to the Pope of *Rome* for his Call, for he had no Scripture for it, and that Water-Baptism and the Outward Supper are not of the Nature of the Everlasting Gospel; nor essential Parts of it, see his *Truth Advanced* page 173. He gives likewise a strict Charge concerning plain Language and plain Habit, and that they should not be concern'd in the compelling part of the Worldy Government, and that they should set their *Negroes* at Liberty after some reasonable time of Service; likewise, they should not take the Advantage of the Law against one another, as to procure them any Corporeal Punishment: These Orders he tells his Followers, would make Distinction between them and *Jews* and Moral Heathens, this was in the Year 1693, in *Pensilvania:* But now the Year 1697, since he came to *England*, his Judgment is chang'd, for he tells his Disciples, that Water-Baptism is come in the room of Circumcision; and by so doing, they would distinguish themselves from either *Jews, Pagans,* or *Moral Heathens:* He keeps his Meeting once a Week at *Turners-Hall* in *Fill-Pot-Lane, London,* on *Sundays* in the Afternoon; he begins between Two and Three of the Clock and commonly ends between Four and Five.

Friendly Reader, by this thou mayst see how wavering and mutable Men of great Outward Learning are, if the Truth of this be by any Body question'd, let them look in the *Creed,* and the Paper against *Christians being concern'd in Worldly Government,* and the *Paper concerning Negroes,* that was given forth by the Appointment of the Meeting held by *George Keith* at *Philip James's* House in the City of *Philadelphia,* in *Pensilvania;* and his *Letter also in* Mary-Land *against the Presbyterian Catechism,* Printed at *Boston* in *New-England* in 1695, with the *Answer* to it bound up together in one Book and in *Truth Advanced,* page 173. And for what relates to him since in *England,* let them look into the *Quakers Argument Refuted, Concerning Water-Baptism and the Lord's Supper,* page 70. And now Reader, I shall take my leave of thee, recommending thee with my own self to the Directions of the Spirit of God in our Conscience, and that will agree with all the Holy Scriptures in its right place; and when we find our selves so, we have no need to take any Thought or Care what any Body shall say of us.

THE SCOTCH-IRISH

FROM 1700 TO 1730, shipload after shipload of emigrants left Northern Ireland for America. Their parents and grandparents, Presbyterian Scots for the most part, had been settled in Ulster as part of the drive to make Ireland a Protestant country. Under Cromwell, James's policy of putting Scottish Protestants on Irish lands was pursued with a ruthless consistency that sent Catholic Irishmen into the service of France and Spain, into the West of Ireland and into the cane fields of Barbados—"to Hell or Connaught" as the later phrase had it—while strangers were settled on their lands. The strangers were equally alien to the native Irish and to the English ruling class that governed both. The Scots were Presbyterians, yet they were obliged to pay tithes to the Anglican clergy of the Irish Established Church. They were weavers, and so a threat to Yorkshire's woolen trade. Their leases were running out, at the turn of the seventeenth century, and the bailiffs stood ready to raise their rents.

Rising rents, depression in the linen trade, poor harvests, religious and economic discrimination, all contrived to further the first emigration of the Ulster Scots. In this group of documents, one may see that migration as it appeared to an Irish landlord of fairly liberal tendencies; to the Anglican Primate of Ireland; to a group of petitioners who appealed to the Irish Parliament against an unscrupulous shipmaster's effort to send them to the West Indies instead of Carolina; and, finally, to two of the migrants themselves.

In the letters of the Archbishop of Armagh, one views the Ulster situation as it appeared to a responsible member of government. For Hugh Boulter (1672–1742) was Privy Councillor and Lord Justice in Ireland, in the confidence of Sir Robert Walpole, and as important a figure in Irish politics as in the Church of Ireland. Boulter considered himself head of the "English interest" in Ireland, and was equally opposed to relaxing the penal laws against the Catholics and increasing the liberties of the Presbyterians. In his letters to various English dignitaries, Boulter takes account of the present discontent and migration from Northern Ireland. More money is being exacted from the cultivator, he admits, but that is to be charged against rent, not tithes, which are too low as it is. There is great suffering from dearth and the disturbance in the linen trade, both of which are helping stir the people to emigration. For remedy, since prolonged migration will rob the landlord of rent, the clergyman of tithe and the kingdom of people, Boulter suggests the renewed enforcement of ancient laws against leaving the realm.

Sometimes it was the passengers aboard an emigrant ship, not the rulers in power, who tried to check emigration. The proceedings in such a case—the petition of Robert Oliver and others unlawfully detained aboard ship—before the Irish House of Commons illuminates some of the methods used to promote emigration. Irish Protestants were decoyed on board by lying tales, then delayed till their store of provisions was gone and their money spent or stolen. To become indentured servants in the colonies was then the one recourse left them.

Yet the emigrants who undertook the voyage more independently made such favorable reports of their experience that, for all the hardship, migration continued. That hardship —often accompanied by terror—is effectively illustrated in the report of young Robert Witherspoon, who came to South Carolina in the winter of 1734. On the other hand, there is little emotion in Robert Parke's letter to his sister. The Irish Quaker is completely practical, full of news and a good husbandman's advice. Yet even from his sober lines, one may catch the eagerness with which letters from America were read by the people left behind. This is a good country for working folk is Parke's burthen; land is cheap, wages high, provisions abundant. The American story is in full development with Parke: the lower orders had a refuge.

The first selection is from *Letters Written by Hugh Boulter, D.D., Lord Primate of Ireland* (Oxford, 1749). The second is from L. F. Stock, ed., *Proceedings and Debates of the British Parliaments Respecting North America*, Vol. IV (Washington, 1937). The third and fourth selections are from C. A. Hanna, *The Scotch-Irish in America*, Vol. II (New York, 1902).

Letters Written by Hugh Boulter, D.D., Lord Primate of Ireland

Dublin, Mar. 7, 1727-8.
To THE DUKE OF NEWCASTLE [Secretary of State]:
My Lord:—. . . Since I came here in the year 1725, there was almost a famine among the poor. Last year, the dearness of corn was such that thousands of families quitted their habitations to seek bread elsewhere, and many hundreds perished. This year, the poor had consumed their potatoes, which is their winter subsistence, near two months sooner than ordinary, and are already, through the dearness of corn, in that want that, in some places they begin already to quit their habitations.

Dublin, Mar. 13, 1728.
To THE BISHOP OF LONDON:
My Lord:—As we have had reports here that the Irish gentlemen in London would have the great burthen of tithes thought one of the chief grievances, that occasion such numbers of the people of the North going to America, I have for some time designed to write to your lordship on that subject.

But a memorial lately delivered in here by the Dissenting ministers of this place, containing the causes of this desertion, as represented to them by the letters of their brethren in the North (which memorial we have lately sent over to my lord lieutenant), mentioning the oppression of the ecclesiastical courts about tithes as one of their great grievances: I found myself under a necessity of troubling your lordship on this occasion with a true state of that affair, and of desiring your lordship to discourse with the ministry about it.

The gentlemen of this country have ever since I came hither been talking to others, and persuading their tenants, who complained of the excessiveness of their rents, that it was not the paying too much rent, but too much tithe that impoverished them: and the notion soon took among the Scotch Presbyterians, as a great part of the Protestants in the North are, who it may easily be supposed do not pay tithes with great cheerfulness. And indeed I make no doubt but the landlords in England might with great ease raise a cry amongst their tenants of the great oppression they lay under by paying tithes.

What the gentlemen want to be at is, that they may go on raising their rents, and that the clergy should still receive their old payments for their tithes. But as things have happened otherwise, and they are very angry with the clergy, without considering that it could not happen otherwise than it has, since if a clergyman saw a farm raised in its rent e. g., from 10 to 20 l. per annum, he might be sure his tithe was certainly worth double what he formerly took for it. Not that I believe the clergy have made a proportionable advancement in their composition for their tithes to what the gentlemen have made in their rents. And yet it is upon this rise of the value of the tithes that they would persuade the people to throw their distress.

In a conference I had with the Dissenting ministers here some weeks ago, they mentioned the raising the value of the tithes beyond what had been formerly paid as a proof that the people were oppressed in the article of tithes. To which I told them, that the value of tithes did not prove any oppression, except it were proved that that value was greater than they were really worth, and that even then the farmer had his remedy by letting the clergy take it in kind.

And there is the less in this argument, because the fact is, that about the years 1694 and 1695, the lands here were almost waste and unsettled, and the clergy in the last distress for tenants for their tithes, when great numbers of them were glad to let their tithes at a very low value, and that during incumbency, for few would take them on other terms: and as the country has since settled and improved, as those incumbents have dropped off, the tithe of those parties has been considerably advanced without the least oppression, but I believe your lordship will think not without some grumbling. The same, no doubt, has happened when there have been careless or needy incumbents, and others of a different character that have succeeded them.

I need not mention to your lordship that I have been forced to talk to several here, that if a landlord takes too great a portion of the profits of a farm for his share by way of rent (as the tithe will light on the tenant's share) the tenant will be impoverished: but then it is not the tithe but the increased rent that undoes the farmer. And indeed in this country, where I fear the tenant hardly ever has more than one third of the profit he makes of his farm for his share, and too often but a fourth or perhaps a fifth part, as the tenant's share is charged with the tithe, his case is no doubt hard, but it is plain from what side the hardship arises.

Another thing they complain of in their memorial is, the trouble that has been given them about their marriages and their school-masters. As to this I told them, that for some time they had not been molested about their marriages; and that as to their school-masters, I was sure they had met with very little trouble on that head, since I had never heard any such grievance so much as mentioned till I saw it in their memorial.

Another matter complained of is the sacramental test, in relation to which I told them, the laws were the same in England.

As for other grievances they mention, such as raising the rents unreasonably, the oppression of justices of the peace, seneschals, and other officers in the country, as they are by no ways of an ecclesiastical nature, I shall not trouble your lordship with an account of them, but must desire your lordship to talk with the ministry on the subject I have now wrote about, and endeavor to prevent their being prepossessed with any unjust opinion of the clergy, or being disposed, if any attempt should be made from hence to suffer us to be stript of our just rights.

Dublin, Mar. 13, 1728.

To the Duke of Newcastle:

My Lord:—As we are in a very bad way here, I think myself obliged to give your Grace some account of it.

The scarcity and dearness of provision still increases in the North. Many have eaten the oats they should have sowed their land with; and except the landlords will have the good sense to furnish them with seed, a great deal of land will lye idle this year. . . .

The humour of going to America still continues, and the scarcity of provisions certainly makes many quit us. There are now seven ships at Belfast, that are carrying off about 1000 passengers thither; and if we knew how to stop them, as most of them can neither get victuals nor work, it would be cruel to do it. . . .

The dissenting ministers here have lately delivered in a memorial, representing the grievances their brethren have assigned as the causes, in their apprehension of the great desertion in the North. As one of these causes relates to the ecclesiastical courts here, and as it is generally repeated here that the Irish gentlemen at London are for throwing the whole occasion of this desertion on the severity of tithes, I have by this post written to the Bishop of London a very long letter on that subject, and have desired him to wait on the ministry, and discourse with them on that head.

Dublin, July 16, 1728.

To the Duke of Newcastle:

My Lord:—. . . We have hundreds of families (all Protestants) removing out of the North to America; and the least obstruction in the linen manufacture, by which the North subsists, must occasion greater numbers following; and the want of silver increasing, will prove a terrible blow to that manufacture, as there will not be money to pay the poor for their small parcels of yarn.

Dublin, Nov. 23, 1728.

To the Duke of Newcastle:

My Lord:—I am very sorry I am obliged to give your Grace so melancholy an account of the state of this kingdom, as I shall in this letter; but I thought it my duty to let his Majesty know our present condition in the North. For we have had three bad harvests together there, which has made oatmeal, which is their great subsistence, much dearer than ordinary; and as our farmers here are very poor, and obliged as soon as they have their corn to sell it for ready money to pay their rents, it is much more in the power of those who have a little money, to engross corn here, and make advantage of its scarceness, than in England.

We have had for several years some agents from the colonies in America, and several masters of ships, that have gone about the country and deluded the people with stories of great plenty, and estates to be had for going for, in those parts of the world; and they have been the better able to seduce people, by reason of the necessities of the poor of late.

The people that go from here make great complaints of the oppressions they suffer here, not from the Government, but from their fellow-subjects, of one kind or another, as well as of the dearness of provisions, and they say these oppressions are one reason of their going.

But whatever occasions their going, it is certain that above 4200 men, women, and children have been shipped off from hence for the West Indies [i. e., North America] within three years, and of these, above 3100 this last summer. Of these, possibly one in ten may be a man of substance, and may do well enough abroad; but the case of the rest is deplorable. The rest either hire themselves to those of substance for passage, or contract with the masters of ships for four years' servitude when they come thither; or, if they make a shift to pay for their passage, will be under the necessity of selling themselves for servants when they come there.

The whole North is in a ferment at present, and people every day engaging one another to go next year to the West Indies. The humour has spread like a contagious distemper, and the people will hardly hear anybody that tries to cure them of their madness. The worst is, that it affects only Protestants, and reigns chiefly in the North, which is the seat of our linen manufacture.

This unsettled state puts almost a stop to trade, and the more so, as several who were in good credit before have taken up parcels of goods and disposed of them, and are gone off with the money, so that there is no trade there but for ready money.

We have had it much in consideration how to put some stop to this growing evil. We think, by some old laws, we can hinder money being carried abroad, and stop all but merchants, that have not a license, from going out of the kingdom.

By this post we have sent my Lord Lieutenant the representation of the gentlemen of the North, and the opinion of our lawyers what can be done by law to hinder people going abroad; but these are matters we shall do nothing in without directions from his Majesty. But whatever may be done by law, I feel it may be dangerous forcibly to hinder a number of needy people from quitting us.

The Plight of Indentured Servants, 1735

Dec. 8, HC. A petition of Robert Oliver, Margaret Bayly, spinster, John Mac-Cleary, David Wright, Elizabeth Wright, Mary Logan, Robert Mac-Crakan, and Esther Mac-Crakan, his wife, in behalf of themselves and several other Protestants, now unlawfully detained on board the George of Dublin, lying by the north-wall, in the river Liffey, near the city of Dublin, and bound for North Carolina, Thomas Cuming, and three of his brothers, supposed to be captain and owners, setting forth, that they and their families have been inveigled by the said Thomas Cuming, and by John Mac-Farren, now on board the said ship, to enter into contracts for transporting themselves and families to North Carolina, in America, and complaining, that since their entering on board the said ship, they have had great hardships and most inhuman cruelties put upon them by the said Cuming, and three of his brothers now on board, and expressing their apprehension, that the said Cuming, and his brothers, intend to transport the petitioners and their families, and the other persons inveigled on board, to the West-Indies, there to be sold by them as slaves, and praying this House will take their deplorable case into consideration, was presented to the House, and read.

Resolved, that an humble address be presented to his Grace the Lord Lieutenant, that he will be pleased to give directions for putting a stop to the ship called the George of Dublin's sailing out of this harbour.

Ordered, that such members of this House as

are of his Majesty's most honourable Privy Council do immediately attend his Grace the Lord Lieutenant with the said address, and lay the same before his Grace.

Ordered, that Thomas Cuming, master of the ship called the *George* of Dublin, do attend this House to-morrow morning, in custody of the serjeant at arms attending this House, to answer the said complaint.

Ordered, that John Mac-Farren do attend this House to-morrow morning, in custody of the serjeant at arms attending this House, to answer the said complaint.

Ordered, that Mr. Maxwell, master of the rolls, etc. or any three or more of them, be appointed a committee, to meet to-morrow morning, at nine o'clock, in the Speaker's Chamber, to examine the allegations of the said petition of Robert Oliver, and others; that they have power to send for persons, papers, and records, and to adjourn from time to time, and place to place, as they shall think fit; and report their proceedings, with their opinion thereupon, to the House, and that all members who come have voices.

Dec. 17, HC. Mr. Maxwell, from the committee appointed to take into consideration the petition of Robert Oliver and others, detained on board the ship called the *George* of Dublin, informed the House that he was directed by the commitee to acquaint the House, that they have summoned Beresford Beacon, Joseph Cummin, Robert Cummin, and John Cummin, to attend the said committee, and that they neglected to attend, and had withdrawn themselves.

Ordered, that the said Beresford Beacon be, for the said contempt, taken into the custody of the serjeant at arms attending this House.

Ordered, that the said Joseph Cummin be, for the said contempt, taken into the custody of the serjeant at arms attending this House.

Ordered, that the said Robert Cummin be, for the said contempt, taken into the custody of the serjeant at arms attending this House.

Ordered, that the said John Cummin be, for the said contempt, taken into the custody of the serjeant at arms attending this House.

1735/6

Feb. 28, HC. A petition of Robert Cumming, in custody of the serjeant at arms attending this House, for this contempt in not attending the committee appointed to take into consideration the petition of Robert Oliver, and others, according to their summons, expressing his sorrow for his offence, and praying to be discharged out of custody, was presented to the House, and read.

Ordered, that the said Robert Cumming be discharged out of custody.

Feb. 28, HC. Mr. Maxwell reported from the committee appointed to take into consideration the petition of Robert Oliver, and others, that they had come to a resolution, which he read in his place.

Feb. 28. HC. A petition of Daniel Byrne, Robert Mealey, and George Whiteside, setting forth, that they agreed with John Trimble, master of the ship called the *Two Friends,* of Dublin, now lying in the lough of Carlingford, to go as mariners in the said ship to Philadelphia; that the intended freight is passengers and servants, and accordingly the said master went to several adjacent towns, and prevailed on passengers to the number of about fourscore, and is still endeavouring to increase the number to upwards of two hundred; that the burden of the said ship is not above 120 tons, though advertised by the said master to be 150; that the scarcity of provisions (and they damaged) laid in for the said voyage, the great number of passengers, and the dangerous condition of the said ship, together with the information the petitioners have received of the ship's not being intended for the said voyage, but is insured for more than the worth, and would infallibly, in the sea-language, be knocked in the head, have obliged them to withdraw themselves from the said ship, and to lay their own and the said passengers case before this House, was presented to the House, and read.

Resolved, that an humble address be presented to his Grace the Lord Lieutenant, that he will be pleased to give directions for putting a stop to the ship the *Two Friends,* of Dublin, sailing out of the lough of Carlingford.

Mar. 3, HC. Mr. Maxwell reported from the committee appointed to take into consideration the petition of Robert Oliver, and others, passengers, unlawfully detained on board the ship called the *George* of Dublin, Thomas Cumming, master, the matter, as it appeared to them, and that they had come to several resolutions thereupon; which report and resolutions he read in his place, and after delivered at the table, where the same were again read, and agreed to by the House, and the resolutions are as follow:

Resolved, that it appears to your committee, that Thomas Cumming and his accomplices have been guilty of great barbarities and violence towards many Protestant passengers, seduced and taken by him on board the ship called the *George,* of Dublin, bound for North-Carolina, and that there is good reason from the scarcity of provisions, and other circumstances of his behaviour on board the said ship, to believe that the said Cumming never intended to have carried such passengers thither.

Resolved, that it is the opinion of this committee, that there hath been, of late years, and still continues to be carried on a wicked and dangerous practice of seducing, by false representations and other deceitful artifices, the Protestant inhabitants of this kingdom into several parts of America, to the utter ruin of most of them, and detriment of his Majesty's government, and of the Protestant interest of this kingdom.

Resolved, that it is the opinion of this committee, that all persons who shall be any ways instrumental in promoting and carrying on such practices, are enemies to his Majesty's government, and the Protestant interest of this kingdom.

Resolved, that it is the opinion of this committee, that it is the duty of all magistrates, justices of the peace, and other persons, to use their utmost endeavours to prevent, suppress, and punish such wicked and pernicious practices.

Ordered, that the said report and resolutions be printed.

Mar. 3, HC. Report from the committee appointed to take into consideration the petition of Robert Oliver and others, passengers, unlawfully detained on board the ship, called the *George,* of Dublin, Thomas Cumming, master. . . .

Mr. Maxwell: Mr. Speaker, It appears to your committee, that a traffick has for some time past obtained, and seems to gain ground in this kingdom, by means of which it is yearly drained of multitudes of its laborious Protestant inhabitants, to the great prejudice of the nation in general, and to the irretrievable disappointment and ruin of almost every person thus deluded to forsake it; that the foundation of this traffick is the considerable, though most wicked gain, that arises to the undertakers, from the credulity of those on whom they practice. That to this end no artifice is left untried, that can possibly move the minds of poor misinformed people, greedy of novelty, and impatient of honest labour. An example of which appears in the case of your petitioner, which though an example in a single instance only, yet your committee have reason, from the course of the examination, to believe the case of many thousands thus spirited away, to be the same or worse.

It appeared to your committee, that some time in the month of August last, Thomas Cumming, master of the ship called the *George,* of Dublin, intending to sail for North-Carolina, sent Joseph Cumming, his brother, and John Mc. Farran, his brother-in-law, to several parts of the counties of Monaghan, Cavan, and Meath, to get passengers

for said voyage, that accordingly they dispersed publick notice through the country, that said ship was bound for North-Carolina, and by themselves, or their emissaries, applied to several of the Protestant families of the country, whom they thought most likely to be seduced; and said Cumming and Mc. Farran represented to the examinants, and others, the great advantages they would get by going to North-Carolina, and among other arguments, that a common labourer would by easy labour gain 20*l.* a year, and others of them would get fifty acres of land for nothing. And Thomas, the master, soon after following them to that country, at the publick meeting-house, at Banbraghey, confirmed what had been so told them, assuring them of good treatment in their voyage, that he would trust them till they landed, and when asked, how they should get money there to pay him? he answered, they might easier borrow 60*l.* there, than 6*d.* here, and that they might with less difficulty get credit for a cow in North-America, than for a hen in this country: he told some that they would be put into farms, of which they would get half the profit for managing them; that their wives immediately upon landing would be put into dairies of as many cows as they could manage, and would have half of the produce, as well of the calves, as butter and cheese, for their labour. He assured David Wright, that he might earn 40*s.* sterling a month by easy labour, and told Robert Oliver, who is a linen weaver, that he would get a guinea sterling for weaving a ten hundred piece of cloth, which according to the labour of a good workman in linen of that sort, would produce above 100*l.* sterling a year. It was likewise represented as a most powerful and specious argument of persuasion, that they would have neither rent or tythes to pay in that country, and would live happily from the time they landed there.

It appears to your committee, that by these and other artifices and misrepresentations, they prevailed on many credulous people, who had before no thoughts of leaving the kingdom, to agree with the said Thomas Cumming for their passage to North-Carolina, and prevailed on others, who had no money to give, to sell themselves to pay for their passage thither, and the number of those they prevailed upon by these arts, amounted in the whole to seventy-two souls.

It likewise appears to your committee by the several articles of agreement between the passengers and said master produced to your committee, that from the time the said passengers were ordered up to town by the said master, they were to be supplied by him with good and sufficient provisions, both during the time the ship continued in port here, and during their whole voyage, and that he was to take the first opportunity of sailing: but that contrary to their agreement many of them were ordered up to town by the said master five or six weeks before the ship was ready to sail, and during that time, after they had spent what money they had, in subsisting themselves and their families, were half starved on the scanty allowance given by the said master, who began, even in the port of this city, to exercise his tyranny over them, as by the following particulars of the provision allowed may appear.

It appears to your committee, that while the ship lay at the north wall in the river of Dublin, their provision was chiefly cows or ox heads, of which four or five together with a little oat-meal, of which they were to make bread for themselves, was the day's allowance among the whole number of seventy-two persons; and that on the days they were not allowed flesh-meat, burgoe or stirrabout, with half a pint of bad small beer, was all that was allowed to each man.

And it appears to your committee, by the testimony of Robert Oliver, that the passengers got oat-meal for bread, three or four days only, and that he got for himself, three passengers, and two children, but two quarts of oat-meal for two days.

When the ship fell down to Poolbegg, in the harbour of Dublin, and that they were now more in the master's power, by reason of their distance from land, they never had any supper, and often no dinner.

It appears to your committee, by the testimony of Daniel Allen, produced by the captain, who had by his orders divided the allowance of meat among the passengers, that on some days three pieces of beef, weighing seven pounds each, and on some days, three small pieces, weighing only three pounds each, (which your committee observe, is less than a quarter of a pound) which, together with one biscuit of about five to the pound, and half a pint of bad small beer to each passenger, was the whole subsistence allowed to the seventy-two passengers.

It appears to your committee, by the testimony of David Wright, and Robert Mc. Crackan, when the ship had got over the bar, and began to sail, and the wind had turned, that the captain in discourse with his brother, and some of the crew, was heard to say, if the wind does not serve for North-Carolina, it will for the West-Indies, (meaning the islands) where these fellows will sell well, that while the ship was at sea, some of the passengers were beaten and abused by Joseph Cumming, brother to the master, without any provocation, who, when some of the unhappy wretches were at prayers, to be relieved from the miseries they laboured under, cursed them, and asked, if they thought God would be troubled with their Presbyterian prayers, and in a high wind made use of this expression, blow devil, blow all these Presbyterians to hell. That during this short time they were at sea, many brutish insults were practised on the female passengers by the master, and his brothers, and many obscene expressions used by them, too indecent to be here reported.

It appears further to your committee, that on the said ship's being forced into port by contrary winds, and coming to an anchor near Ring's-End, many of the passengers terrified by the ill-treatment they had already met with, and resolving not to prosecute their voyage, some of them found means to come a-shore, and four of them by the advice of their friends, applied to the court of Admiralty against the said master, who had broke his agreement with them, and detained their goods on board, that thereupon the judge of that court had the ship arrested, and appointed a day for hearing the complaint, and that before the day of hearing, the said master managed matters so well, by the assistance and contrivance of Patrick Kent, as to get two of the complainants arrested, and the other two were so terrified, that they durst not appear at the hearing; one of the persons then arrested, being Robert Oliver, his case appears to your committee to stand thus:

Said Oliver came to an agreement in the country with Joseph, the said captain's brother, for his own and family's passage, for 12l. for which sum, said Joseph insisted on having his promissory note, which Oliver objecting to, and saying, perhaps he might change his mind and not go, said Joseph told him he must have his note to shew to others, but said he would give him a defeazance, so that it should not affect him, but the paper given him being produced to your committee, appeared to be no more than a receipt for so much money for his passage. That on Oliver's coming to Dublin, the master, Thomas Cumming, got from him 6l. in money, and his note for 11l. more, sterling money, to be paid on his landing. It appears, that on Oliver's paying the 6l. and giving the second note for 11l. (though the whole money, first agreed on for his passage, was but 12l.) he demanded his first note of 12l. to be given up to him, but was told it was lost; however, on Oliver's complaining to the court of Admiralty, it appears to your committee, that the said 12l. note was assigned to Patrick Kent, (whom your committee find to be deeply engaged in the artifice and management of this whole affair,) who had Oliver arrested on it the day before the hearing was to be in the court of Admiralty, whereby he effectually defeated him of the relief he there expected, and on examining Oliver, it appears he had no thoughts of removing himself or family to any of the plantations, having a good settlement here (to wit) a bleach-yard and four looms at work, on which he comfortably maintained his family, till by the crafty insinuations and false representations of the said master, and his brothers, he was prevailed on to sell what he had, and put himself and family into the hands of the said master, who, as it appears to your committee, after he had stripped him of all he had, got him laid in a gaol for complaining.

Your committee, on examining James Mc. Farran, find his case so extraordinary an instance of the indirect means used by the captain and his brothers, to inveigle these poor innocent people, that they think it proper to report it particularly. James Mc. Farran, a man of about seventy years of age, had but one son, eighteen years old, who was the support of him and his family, whom Joseph, brother to the present captain, inveigled about a year ago, from his father, against his consent, and carried him to North-Carolina: on said Joseph and brother's return to this kingdom, Robert, another of the said captain's brothers, applied to said James Mc. Farran, and represented to him, that his son was in a thriving way in North-Carolina, and in a condition to support him in his old age, which induced the poor man to quit his settlement, and to agree for a passage for himself and two daughters; but it now appears to your committee, by the confession of Thomas the captain, on his being examined, that the said son on his landing in North-Carolina, was sold to pay his passage, and so far from being able to support his aged father, as was represented to him, that there are still some years unexpired of his own slavery. And it appears to your committee, that said captain broke several agreements made in the country by his brothers, to extort more money from the passengers after they had quitted their settlements, and brought up their families to Dublin, as in the case of David Wright, who agreed in the country with Mc. Farran, the captain's brother-in-law, for the passage of himself and family at 6l. for each person, but on said Wright's coming to town, the captain refused to make good that agreement, and obliged said Wright to make a new bargain at the rate of 8l. for each person: and said captain being asked, why he dealt so hardly by Wright after he had quitted his house and land, and brought up his family on the agreement made with Mc. Farran, his brother-in-law? his answer to your committee was this, that Wright had no money to give him, and that he had rather have 4l. paid here, than 8l. in North-Carolina, every thing there being excessive dear, which your committee observe is directly contrary to the representations made to these deluded people by the captain and his brothers.

The master, Thomas Cumming, being examined concerning his intent in going down to the country, and sending his brothers there, denied that he went or sent them there to get passengers. When asked for what purpose he went to the publick meeting, he confessed, it was to deliver letters he had brought from North-Carolina, but refused to discover to your committee to whom those letters were directed, or the purport of them, or why he was so industrious and careful in the delivery of them. Being asked what he loaded his ship with back, he could name nothing but linen-cloth, when it appears to your committee, that he had only to the value of twelve or fourteen pounds of that commodity on board, though his ship is ninety tons burthen. Being asked, what number of passengers he had on board to carry off with him, he owned no more than thirty; though his mate, being after examined, confessed there were seventy-two persons, of which he gave in a list of the names to your committee. Being asked what he intended to do with those who bound themselves to him as servants for a term of years; owned he was to sell them there. Being asked what he usually given per head by those that bought them, said he generally got about thirty-five barrels of pitch or turpentine, worth of our money 3s. 6d. or 4s. per barrel. Being then asked what he purposed to do in North-Carolina with the passengers who had not money to pay their passage? to this he would give no direct answer, though often thereunto pressed by your committee. But your committee find on the examination of Doctor Brickell (who lived several years in North-Carolina, and appeared to your committee to be a person of integrity and understanding) and others, that the custom there is to sell such as have not money to pay their passage, or are otherwise in debt, and that often both man and wife and their children are sold by the master to pay their passage, that some of the women are used as servants in the houses of those that buy them, and others set to work at the hoe in the field with the negroes, that the buyer has an absolute property in them for the time they are sold to him, beats and chastises them at pleasure, and sometimes neck-yoakes them, has a right to sell or assign them from one to another, as we do here our cattle: that the planters there are more careful of the negroes, because they are their property for life, but don't take so much care of their white slaves, in regard they are their property for a term of years only. That at the end of their servitude they are intituled, by the custom of the country, to ten bushels of corn, an axe, a bow, and fifty acres of land, but the land set out for them lies often two hundred miles within the country next to the Indians, wild and covered with wood, which they are no way in a condition to reclaim, and is really of so little value where it lies, that fifty acres have often been sold for a pound of tobacco, worth in that country about three farthings.

And yet it appears to your committee, on examining several of those poor deluded people, that the land, to be set out to them in America, was represented by the master and his brothers to be of equal or greater value than the lands they were here possessed of.

And your committee were further informed of what those poor people were no way apprized of, (*viz.*) that by the laws of the colonies, if any of the people sold for a term of four years, should run in debt during their first servitude, though for the necessaries of life, which are often for that purpose with-held from them by their cruel masters, they are liable to a second sale for another four years to pay that debt, and so from four years to four years, may be continued slaves during their lives.

And though your committee cannot but compassionate the hard usage their fellow-subjects meet with when transported to North-Carolina, yet, upon inquiry they do not find that their treatment there is worse, than in the other colonies of the West-Indies, to which of late, too many have been unhappily seduced.

And it appears to your committee, on examining several of those prevailed on to bind themselves to said master as servants for a term of years, that he had agreed to give each of them two complete new suits of clothes before they left Dublin, but had given none to any of them, though he had actually sailed. And on viewing several of the indentures produced to your committee, signed by the master and the persons bound to him, your committee observe, there was a blank in the place where the number of years should have been mentioned, (from which considering his behaviour during the whole transaction,) there is reason to suspect, that the said master intended to have filled up these blanks afterwards with what number of years he pleased. And to give a better colour to what he did, the printed city indentures, with the city arms to them, were procured by said Patrick Kent, and made use of for that purpose, without ever applying to the Lord Mayor, to have them bound in the usual form. Your committee beg leave to observe, that these seducers not only inveigle many unwary people, but give a receptacle to criminals to withdraw from justice, an instance whereof appeared to your committee in James Mc. Clearen, indicted for the murder of William Hamilton, Esq: his late master, who your committee find to have been for some time concealed on board said ship, where he was lately apprehended. It appears further to your committee, by the Custom-House entry of provisions on board the said ship, that if they had not a quick passage, and in less time than is generally made, many of the passengers must have perished for want of provisions.

Your committee have reason to believe, that they could have made a further discovery of the iniquitous practices made use of to seduce and injure these poor people, but that they were obstructed therein, by the withdrawing of some of the brothers and accomplices of said master, who have concealed themselves to avoid being examined by your committee.

Personal Narratives

I.

Chester Township the —— of the 10th Mo. 1725.
DEAR SISTER MARY VALENTINE:

This goes with a Salutation of Love to thee, Brother Thomas and the children & in a word to all friends, Relations & well Wishers in Generall as if named, hoping it may find you all in good health, as I with all our family in Generall are in at this present writing & has been since our arival, for we have not had a day's Sickness in the Family Since we came in to the Country, blessed be God for it. My father in Particular has not had his health better these ten years than Since he Came here, his ancient age considered. Our Irish Acquaintance in general are well Except Thoe: Lightfoot who Departed this Life at Darby in a Good old age About 4 weeks Since. Thee writes in thy Letter that there was a talk went back to Ireland that we were not Satisfyed in coming here, which was Utterly false: now let this Suffice to Convince you. In the first place he that carried back this Story was an Idle fellow, & one of our Ship-Mates, but not thinking this country Suitable to his Idleness, went back with Cowman again. He is Sort of a Lawyer, or Rather a Lyar as I may term him, therefore I wod not have you give credit to Such false reports for the future, for there is not one of the family but what likes the country very well & wod If we were in Ireland again come here Directly it being the best country for working folk & tradesmen of any in the world. But for Drunkards and Idlers, they cannot live well any where. It is likewise an Extradin. healthy country. We were all much troubled when we found you did not come in with Capt. Cowman as we Expected nor none of our acquaintance Except Isaac Jackson & his family, tho at his coming in one thinks it Something odd, but that is soon over. Land is of all Prices Even from ten Pounds, to one hundred Pounds a hundred, according to the goodness or else the situation thereof, & Grows dearer every year by Reason of Vast Quantities of People that come here yearly from Several Parts of the world, therefore thee & thy family or any that I wish well I wod desire to make what Speed you can to come here the Sooner the better. We have traveled over a Pretty deal of this country to seek the Land, & [though] we met with many fine Tracts of Land here & there in the country, yet my father being curious & somewhat hard to Please Did not buy any Land until the Second day of 10th mo: Last and then he bought a Tract of Land consisting of five hundred Acres for which he gave 350 pounds. It is Excellent good land but none cleared, Except about 20 Acres, with a small log house and Orchard Planted, we are going to clear some of it Directly, for our next Sumer's fallow. We might have bought Land much Cheaper but not so much to our Satisfaction. We stayed in Chester 3 months & then we Rented a Place 1 mile from Chester, with a good brick house & 200 Acres of Land for [—] pound a year, where we continue till next May. We have sowed about 200 Acres of wheat & 7 acres of rye this season. We sowed but a bushel on an acre, 3 pecks is Enough on new ground. I am grown an Experienced Plowman & my brother Abell is Learning. Jonathan & thy Son John drives for us. He is grown a Lusty fellow Since thou Saw him. We have the finest plows here that Can be. We plowed up our Sumer's fallows in May & June, with a Yoak of Oxen & 2 horses & they goe with as much Ease as Double the number in Ireland. We sow our wheat with 2 horses. A boy of 12 or 14 years old Can hold Plow here, a man Comonly holds & Drives himself. They plow an Acre, nay some Plows 2 Acres a day. They sow Wheat & Rye in August or September. We have had a crop of oats, barley & very good flax & hemp, Indian Corn & buckwheat all of our own Sowing & Planting this last summer. We also planted a bushel of white Potatoes Which Cost us 5 Shills. & we had 10 or 12 bushels Increase. This country yields Extraordinary Increase of all sorts of Grain Likewise—for nicholas hooper had of 3 Acres of Land & at most 3 bushels of Seed above 80 bushels Increase so that it is as Plentifull a Country as any Can be if people will be Industrious. Wheat is 4 Shills. a bushel, Rye 2s. 9d., oats 2.3 pence, barley 3 Shills., Indian Corn 2 Shills. all Strike measure, Beef is 2½ pence a pound; Sometimes more Sometimes less, mutton 2½, pork 2½ pr. pound. Turnips 12 pence a bushell heap'd measure & so Plenty that an acre Produceth 200 bushells. All Sorts of Provisions are Extraordinary Plenty in Philadelphia market, where Country people bring in their comodities. Their markets are on 4th day and 7th day. This country abounds in fruit, Scarce an house but has an Apple, Peach & cherry orchard. As for chestnuts, Wallnuts, & hasel nuts, Strawberrys, Billberrys & Mulberrys they grow wild in the woods and fields in Vast Quantities. They also make great Preparations against harvest; both Roast & boyled, Cakes & Tarts & Rum, stand at the Lands End, so that they may Eat and Drink at Pleasure. A Reaper has 2 Shills. & 3 pence a day, a mower has 2 Shills. & 6 pence & a pint of Rum beside meat & drink of the best; for no workman works without their Victuals in the bargain throughout the Country. A Laboring man has 18 or 20 pence a day in Winter. The Winters are not so cold as we Expected nor the Sumers so Extreme hot as formerly, for both Sumer and Winter are moderater than they ever were known. In Sumer time they wear nothing but a Shirt & Linnen drawers Trousers, which are breeches and stockings all in one made of Linnen; they are fine Cool wear in Sumer. As to what thee writt about the Governours Opening Letters it is Utterly false & nothing but a Lye & any one Except bound Servants may go out of the Country when they will & Servants when they Serve their time may Come away If they please but it is rare any are such fools to leave the Country Except men's business require it. They pay 9 Pounds for their Passage (of this money) to go to Ireland. There is 2 fairs, yearly & 2 markets weekly in Philadelphia also 2 fairs yearly in Chester & Likewise in new castle, but they Sell no Cattle nor horses, no living Creatures, but altogether Merchant's Goods, as hatts, Linnen & woolen Cloth, handkerchiefs, knives, Scizars, tapes & treds buckels, Ribonds & all Sorts of necessarys fit for our wooden Country & here all young men and women that wants wives or husbands may be Supplyed. Lett this Suffice for our fairs. As to meetings they are so plenty one may ride to their choice. I desire thee to bring or Send me a bottle of good Oyle fit for guns, thee may buy it in Dublin. Martha Weanhouse Lives very well about 4 miles from James Lindseys. We live all together since we Came into the Country Except hugh Hoaker [or Stoaker] & his family who lives 6 or 7 miles from us, & follows his trade. Sister Rebecka was Delivered of a Daughter ye — day the 11 month Last past; its name is mary. Abel's wife had a young Son 12 months Since; his name is Thomas. Dear Sister I wod not have thee Doupt the truth of what I write, for I know it to be true Tho I have not been long here. I wod have you Cloath yourselves well with Woolen & Linnen, Shoes & Stockings & hats for Such things are dear hear, & yet a man will Sooner Earn a suit of Cloths here than in Ireland, by Reason workman's Labour is so Dear. A wool hat costs 7 Shills., a pair of men's Shoes 7 Shills., wemen's Shoes Cost 5 Shills. and 6 pence, a pair of men's stockings yarn Costs 4 Shills., feather beds are very dear here and not to be had for money. Gunpowder is 2 Shills. & 6 pence a pound. Shott & Lead 5 pence a pound. I wod have you bring for your own Use 2 or 3 good falling Axes, a pair of beetle rings & 3 Iron wedges, for they are of good Service here. Your Plow Irons will not answer here, therefore you had better bring 1 or 2 hundred Iron. You may bring your Plow Chains as they are also a good —— Iron. Letters going to you with these gives you Accompt what to bring into the Country & also for your Sea Store or else I should not omitt it. But be sure you come with Capt Cowman & you will be well Used for he is an honest man & has as Civell Saylors as any that Cross the Seas, which I know by Experience. The Ship has been weather bound Since before Christmas by reason of post & Ice that floats about the River & the Saylers being at a Loose End Came down to Chester to See us & we have given them—— Dear Sister I desire thee may tell my old friend Samuel Thornton that he could give so much credit to my words & find no Iffs nor ands in my Letter, that in Plain terms he could not do better than to Come here, for both his & his wife's trade are Very good here. The best way for him to do is to pay what money he Can Conveniently Spare at that side & Engage himself to Pay the rest at this Side & when he Comes here if he Can get no friend to lay down the money for him, when it Comes to the worst, he may hire out 2 or 3 children. & I wod have him Cloath his family as well as his Small Ability will allow. Thee may tell him what things are proper to bring with him both for his Sea Store & for his Use in this Country. I wod have him Procure 3 or 4 Lusty Servants & Agree to pay their passage at this Side he might sell 2 & pay the others' passage with the money. I fear my good will to him will be of Little Effect by reason he is So hard of beleif, but thou mayest Assure him from me that if I had not a particular Respect for him & his family I Should not have writ so much for his Encouragement. His brother Joseph & Moses Coats Came to See us Since we came here. They live about 6 or 7 miles apart & above 20 miles from where we live. Unkle James Lindly & Family is well & Thrives Exceedingly, he has 11 children & Reaped last harvest about 800 bushels of wheat, he is a thriving man as any where he lives, he has a thousand acres of Land, A fine Estate. Unkle Nicholas hooper lives very well. He rents a Plantation & teaches School & his man does his Plantation work, Murtha Hobson. Dear Sister I think I have writ the most needfol to thee, but considering that when I was in Ireland I never thought a Letter to Long that Came from this Country, I wod willingly give thee as full an Account as Possible, tho I could have given thee a fuller Account of what things are fit to bring here, but only I knew other Letters might Suffice in that point. I desire thee may Send or bring me 2 hundred Choice Quills for my own Use for they are very Scarce here, & Sister Raichell Desires thee wod bring hir Some bits of Silk for trashbags. Thee may bring them in Johns Zane [or Lane] also — yards of white Mode or Silk for 2 hoods & She will pay thee when thee comes here. I wod have brother Thomas to bring a good new Saddle (& bridle) with Croopper & Housen to it by reason the horses sweat in hot weather, for they are very dear here. A Saddle that will cost 18 or 20 Shills. In Ireland will cost here 50 Shills. or 3 pounds & not so good neither, he had better get Charles Howell to make it, Lett the tree be well Plated & Indifferent Narrow for the horses here are [not] So Large as in Ireland, but the best racers & finest Pacers in the World. I have known Several that could Pace 14 or 15 miles in an hour, I write within Compass. As for women Saddles they will not Suit so well here. I wod not have thee think much at my Irregular way of writing by reason I write as it offer'd to me, for they that write to you should have more wits than I can Pretend to. [Robert Parke]

2.

We went on shipboard the 14th of September, and lay wind-bound in the Lough at Belfast 14 days. The second day of our sail my grandmother died, and was interred in the raging ocean, which was an afflictive sight to her offspring. We were sorely tossed at sea with storms, which caused our ship to spring a leak: our pumps were kept incessantly at work day and night; for many days our mariners seemed many times at their wits' end. But it pleased God to bring us all safe to land, which was about the first of December.

We landed in Charleston three weeks before Christmas. We found the inhabitants very kind. We staid in town until after Christmas, and were put on board of an open boat, with tools and a year's provisions [the customary bounty to immigrants], and one still-mill. They allowed each hand upwards of sixteen, one axe, one broad hoe, and one narrow hoe. Our provisions were Indian corn, rice, wheaten flour, beef, pork, rum, and salt. We were much distressed in this part of our passage. As it was the dead of winter, we were exposed to the inclemency of the weather day and night; and (which added to the grief of all pious persons on board) the atheistical and blasphemous mouths of our Patroons and the other hands. They brought us up as far as Potatoe Ferry and turned us on shore, where we lay in Samuel Commander's barn for some time, and the boat wrought her way up to "the King's Tree," with the goods and provisions, which is the first boat that I believe ever came up so high before.

While we lay at Mr. Commander's, our men came up in order to get dirt houses to take their families to. They brought some few horses with them. What help they could get from the few inhabitants in order to carry the children and other necessaries up they availed themselves of. As the woods were full of water, and most severe frosts, it was very severe on women and children. We set out in the morning; and some got no further that day than Mr. McDonald's and some as far as Mr. Plowden's; some to James Armstrong's, and some to Uncle William James's. [These were emigrants who had preceded Witherspoon, in the first emigration.] . . . Their little cabins were as full that night as they could hold, and the next day every one made the best they could to their own place, which was the first day of February, 1735. My father had brought on shipboard four children, viz.: David, Robert, John, and Sarah. Sarah died in Charleston, and was the first buried at the Scotch Meeting House graveyard. When we came to the Bluff, my mother and we children were still in expectation that we were coming to an agreeable place. But when we arrived and saw nothing but a wilderness, and instead of a fine timbered house, nothing but a

mean dirt house, our spirits quite sank; and what added to our trouble, our pilot we had with us from Uncle William James's left us when we came in sight of the place.

My father gave us all the comfort he could by telling us we would get all those trees cut down, and in a short time there would be plenty of inhabitants, so that we could see from house to house. While we were at this, our fire we brought from Bog Swamp went out. Father had heard, that up the river-swamp was the "King's Tree," although there was no path, neither did he know the distance. Yet he followed up the swamp until he came to the branch, and by that found Roger Gordon's. We watched him as far as the trees would let us see, and returned to our dolorous hut, expecting never to see him or any human person more. But after some time he returned and brought fire. We were soon comforted, but evening coming on, the wolves began to howl on all sides. We then feared being devoured by wild beasts, having neither gun nor dog nor any door to our house. Howbeit we set to and gathered fuel, and made on a good fire, and so passed the first night. The next day being a clear warm morning, we began to stir about, but about mid-day there rose a cloud southwest attended with a high wind, thunder and lightning. The rain quickly penetrated through between the poles and brought down the sand that covered them over, which seemed to threaten to bury us alive. The lightning and claps were very awful and lasted a good space of time. I do not remember to have seen a much severer gust than that was. I believe we all sincerely wished ourselves again at Belfast. But this fright was soon over and the evening cleared up, comfortable and warm.

The boat that brought up the goods arrived at "the King's Tree." People were much oppressed in bringing their things, as there was no house there. They were obliged to toil hard, and had no other way but to convey their beds, clothing, chests, provisions, tools, pots, etc., on their backs. And at that time there were few or no roads and every family had to travel the best way they could, which was here double distance to some, for they had to follow swamps and branches for their guides for some time.

After a season, some men got such a knowledge of the woods as to "blaze" paths, so the people soon found out to follow "blazes" from place to place. As the winter season was far advanced, the time to prepare for planting was very short. Yet people were very strong and healthy, all that could do anything wrought diligently, and continued clearing and planting as long as the season would admit, so that they made provision for the ensuing year. As they had but few beasts, a little served them, and as the range was good, they had no need of feeding creatures for some years.

I remember that among the first things my father brought from the boat was his gun, which was one of Queen Anne's muskets. He had it loaded with swan-shot. One morning when we were at breakfast, there was a "travelling 'possum" on his way, passing by the door: my mother screamed out saying, "There is a great bear!" Mother and we children hid ourselves behind some barrels and a chest, at the other end of our hut, whilst father got his gun, and steadied it upon the fork that held up that end of the house, and shot the animal about the hinder parts, which caused the poor opossum to grin and open its mouth in a frightful manner. Father was in haste to give it a second bout, but the shot being mislaid in a hurry, could not be found. We were penned up for some time. Father at length ventured out and killed it with a pale.

Another source of alarm was the Indians. When they came to hunt in the spring, they were in great numbers in all places like the Egyptian locusts, but they were not hurtful. We had a great deal of trouble and hardships in our first settling, but the few inhabitants continued still in health and strength. Yet we were oppressed with fears, on divers accounts, especially of being massacred by the Indians, or bitten by snakes, or torn by wild beasts, or being lost and perishing in the woods. Of this last calamity there were three instances.

About the end of August, 1736, my uncle Robert arrived here. The ship he came in was called *New Built*. She was a ship of great burden, and brought many passengers. They chiefly came up here, and, obliged to travel by land, they had money given them by the public instead of provisions. Our second crop was in the ground when they came. As it was in the warm season, they were much fatigued in coming up, and many were taken with the fever and ague. Some died with that disorder, and many after the ague had ceased grew dropsical and died. About this time people began to form into societies, and sent to Ireland for a minister. One came named Robert Heron. He stayed three years, and then returned to Ireland. [Robert Witherspoon]

RELIGIOUS LIBERTIES

In the *Bloudy Tenent of Persecution*, Williams carries the argument for religious freedom well beyond Locke's theory of toleration. Locke did not exclude a state-supported church from his plan but demanded only that it refrain from persecution and the maintenance of a doctrinal system so rigid as to bar the body of the nation from conscientious participation in its worship. To Williams, as to Gerrard Winstanley before him, all forms of church establishment were intrinsically offensive.

Roger Williams (1603–1662/3) came to that opinion after experience with church establishments in England and in Puritan Massachusetts. Williams's father was a successful London businessman who gave his son a training befitting his station. The patronage of Sir Edward Coke increased Williams's opportunities. But the tensions of his time drew him to Puritan views which he expressed freely enough to make emigration seem the part of wisdom when King and archbishop joined to impose uniformity of religious practice in 1629. After a few years in Massachusetts, Roger Williams discovered that dissenters who hold power are apt to use it against those who differ from them. The Salem church chose Williams its teacher in 1634, however, and, when the magistrates refused to confirm that choice, Salem town defied the magistrates. Williams was banished from Massachusetts Bay the following year. Three years later, Williams abandoned membership in any church and became a Seeker, waiting for a higher power to give him spiritual conviction.

In the settlement which Williams founded on Rhode Island, he established a system of land ownership more democratic than that which prevailed in Massachusetts, where the "town proprietors" owned the land and exercised the suffrage to the exclusion of the body of "inhabitants." Williams solved the problem of the proper relation between civil and religious authority by severing all connection between them. In dealing with the more immediate problem of the Indians, Williams worked for a policy of justice toward the first owners of the soil. The existence of Williams's colony was threatened by its more powerful neighbor in Massachusetts at the beginning of the 1640s. Though it was not in accordance with his principles, Williams asked the English government to charter his colony. He returned to England to press his request and finally, in 1644, secured the grant he desired. It was then that Williams published the *Bloudy Tenent of Persecution*, which defends his view of the relation that should exist between Church and State against the ideals prevailing in England and Massachusetts alike.

Before and after the issue of Williams's charter, Massachusetts notables waged polemic conflict against his doctrines—one of them even answered Williams's argument for toleration in a pamphlet called, *Mr Williams's Bloudy Tenent of Persecution Washed White in the Blood of the Lamb*. Williams replied by maintaining his views in practice and by writing treatises in rebuttal, notably, the *Bloudy Tenent Still More Bloudy.* . . .

In his original work, Williams contends that Scripture gives no countenance to persecution for cause of conscience. God does not require uniformity of church practice enforced by a civil magistrate. Like Locke, Williams insists that the civil power attain its ends by political means, while the church limit itself to ecclesiastical measures. As magistrates have no right to interfere in church government, so the clergy have no call to meddle with the magistracy. Williams proceeds further, however. Civil power resides in the people, and the government they set up holds power only so long as the people trust it. Yet, even such magistrates have no power over the church, for, if they did, heavenly concerns would be subject to earthly rule, an evident absurdity. Complete separation between civil and religious power is the logical conclusion. Williams has come full circle to maintain the view that, in America at least, the "two keys" are not to be held by the one authority.

The selections from Roger Williams's *Bloudy Tenent of Persecution* (London, 1644) are taken from the *Publications of the Narragansett Club*, Vol. III (Newport, R.I., 1867).

Bloudy Tenant of Persecution

BY ROGER WILLIAMS

PREFACE

FIRST, That the blood of so many hundred thousand soules of *Protestants* and *Papists*, spilt in the *Wars* of *present* and *former Ages*, for their respective *Consciences*, is not *required* nor *accepted* by *Jesus Christ* the *Prince* of *Peace*.

Secondly, Pregnant *Scripturs* and *Arguments* are throughout the Worke proposed against the *Doctrine* of *persecution* for *cause* of *Conscience*.

Thirdly, Satisfactorie Answers are given to *Scriptures*, and objections produced by Mr. *Calvin, Beza,* Mr. *Cotton,* and the Ministers of the New English Churches and others former and later, tending to prove the *Doctrine of persecution* for cause of *Conscience*.

Fourthly, The *Doctrine of persecution* for cause of *Conscience*, is proved guilty of all the *blood* of the *Soules* crying for *vengeance* under the *Altar*.

Fifthly, All *Civill States* with their *Officers* of *justice* in their respective *constitutions* and *administrations* are proved *essentially Civill*, and therefore not *Judges, Governours* or *Defendours* of the *Spirituall* or *Christian state* and *Worship*.

Sixtly, It is the will and command of *God*, that (since the comming of his *Sonne* the *Lord Jesus*) a *permission* of the most *Paganish, Jewish, Turkish,* or *Antichristian consciences* and *worships*, bee granted to *all* men in all *Nations* and *Countries:* and they are onely to bee *fought* against with that *Sword* which is only (in *Soule matters*) *able* to *conquer,* to wit, the *Sword of Gods Spirit*, the *Word* of *God*.

Seventhly, The *state* of the Land of *Israel*, the *Kings* and *people* thereof in *Peace & War*, is proved *figurative* and *ceremoniall*, and no *patterne* nor *president* for any *Kingdome* or *civill state* in the *world* to follow.

Eightly, *God* requireth not an *uniformity* of *Religion* to be *inacted* and *inforced* in any *civill state;* which inforced *uniformity* (sooner or later) is the greatest occasion of *civill Warre*, *ravishing* of *conscience, persecution* of *Christ Jesus* in his servants, and of the *hypocrisie* and *destruction* of *millions* of *souls*.

Ninthly, In holding an inforced *uniformity* of *Religion* in a *civill state,* wee must necessarily *disclaime* our desires and hopes of the *Jewes conversion* to *Christ*.

Tenthly, An inforced *uniformity* of *Religion* throughout a *Nation* or *civill state,* confounds the *Civill* and *Religious,* denies the principles of *Christianity* and civility, and that *Jesus Christ* is come in the Flesh.

Eleventhly, The permission of other *consciences* and *worships* then a state professeth, only can (according to God) procure a firme and lasting *peace,* (good *assurance* being taken according to the *wisdome* of the *civill state* for *uniformity* of *civill obedience* from all forts.)

Twelfthly, lastly, true *civility* and *Christianity* may both flourish in a *state* or *Kingdome,* notwithstanding the *permission* of divers and contrary *consciences,* either of *Jew* or *Gentile*.

CHAPTER XCII: PEACE

The 4. head is, The proper meanes of both these Powers to attaine their ends.

"First, the proper meanes whereby the Civill Power may and should attaine its end, are onely Politicall, and principally these Five.

"First the erecting and establishing what forme of Civill Government may seeme in wisedome most meet, according to generall rules of the Word, and state of the people.

"Secondly, the making, publishing, and establishing of wholesome Civill Lawes, not onely such as concerne Civill Justice, but also the free passage of true Religion: for, outward Civill Peace ariseth and is maintained from them both, from the latter as well as from the former:

"Civill peace cannot stand intire, where Religion is corrupted, 2 *Chron.* 15. 3. 5. 6. *Judg.* 8. And yet such Lawes, though conversant about Religion, may still be counted Civill Lawes, as on the contrary, an Oath doth still remaine Religious, though conversant about Civill matters.

"Thirdly, Election and appointment of Civill officers, to free execution of those Lawes.

"Fourthly, Civill Punishments and Rewards, of Transgressors and Observers of these Lawes.

"Fifthly, taking up Armes against the Enemies of Civill Peace.

"Secondly, the meanes whereby the Church may and should attaine her ends, are only ecclesiasticall, which are chiefly five.

"First, setting up that forme of Church Government only, of which Christ hath given them a pattern in his Word.

"Secondly, acknowledging and admitting of no Lawgiver in the Church, but Christ, and the publishing of his Lawes.

"Thirdly, Electing and ordaining of such officers onely, as Christ hath appointed in his Word.

"Fourthly, to receive into their fellowship them that are approved, and inflicting Spirituall censures against them that offend.

"Fifthly, Prayer and patience in suffering any evill from them that be without, who disturbe their peace.

"So that Magistrates, as Magistrates, have no power of setting up the Forme of Church Government, electing Church officers, punishing with Church censures, but to see that the Church doth her duty herein. And on the other side, the Churches as Churches, have no power (though as members of the Commonweale they may have power) of erecting or altering formes of Civill Government, electing of Civill officers, inflicting Civill punishments (no not on persons excommunicate) as by deposing Magistrates from their Civill Authoritie, or withdrawing the hearts of the people against them, to their Lawes, no more then to discharge wives, or children, or servants, from due obedience to their husbands, parents, or masters: or by taking up armes against their Magistrates, though he persecute them for Conscience: for though members of Churches who are publique officers also of the Civill State, may suppresse by force the violence of Usurpers, *as Iehoiada* did *Athaliah,* yet this they doe not as members of the Church, but as officers of the Civill State."

Truth. Here are divers considerable *passages* which I shall briefly examine, so far as concernes our *controversie.*

First, whereas they say, that the *Civill Power* may erect and establish what *forme* of *civill Government* may seeme in *wisdome* most meet, I acknowledge the *proposition* to be most true, both in it self, and also considered with the end of it, that a *civill Government* is an *Ordinance* of *God,* to conserve the *civill peace* of people, so farre as concernes their *Bodies* and *Goods,* as formerly hath beene said.

But from this *Grant* I infer, (as before hath been touched) that the *Soveraigne, originall,* and *foundation* of civill power lies in the *people,* (whom they must needs meane by the *civill power* distinct from the *Government* set up.) And if so, that a People may erect and establish what *forme* of *Government* seemes to them most meete for their *civill condition:* It is evident that such *Governments* as are by them erected and established, have no more *power,* nor for no longer time, then the *civill power* or people consenting and agreeing shall betrust them with. This is cleere not only in *Reason,* but in the experience of all *commonweales,* where the people are not deprived of their *naturall freedome* by the power of *Tyrants.*

And if so, that the Magistrates receive their power of governing the Church, from the People; undeniably it followes, that a *people,* as a *people,* naturally considered (of what *Nature* or *Nation* soever in *Europe, Asia, Africa* or *America*) have fundamentally and originally, as men, a power to governe the *Church,* to see her doe her *duty,* to correct her, to redresse, reforme, establish, &c. And if this be not to pull *God* and *Christ,* and *Spirit* out of *Heaven,* and subject them unto *naturall,* sinfull, inconstant men, and so consequently to *Sathan* himselfe, by whom all *peoples* naturally are guided, let *Heaven* and *Earth* judge.

Peace. It cannot by their owne *Grant* be denied, but that the *wildest Indians* in *America* ought (and in their kind and severall degrees doe) to agree upon some *formes of Government,* some more *civill,* compact in Townes, &c. some lesse. As also that their *civill* and *earthly Governments* be as lawfull and true as any *Governments* in the *World,* and therefore consequently their *Governors* are *Keepers* of the *Church* or both *Tables,* (if any Church of Christ should arise or be amongst them:) and therefore lastly, (if *Christ* have betrusted and charged the *civill* Power with his *Church*) they must [138] judge according to their *Indian* or *American consciences,* for other *consciences* it cannot be supposed they should have.

THE LAND OF OPPORTUNITY

BETWEEN Daniel Defoe's *Giving Alms No Charity* and Benjamin Franklin's *Observations Concerning the Increase of Mankind* lie forty-seven years; but the distance, spiritually and materially, between the lower middle-class Englishman and the American, who might have occupied a similar position had his forebears remained on the eastern shore of the Atlantic, is immense. Like Defoe, Benjamin Franklin (1706–1790) regards an increase of population as an advantage to a nation. Unlike him, Franklin expected that population to live in comfort, for American manners were simple, land cheap and wages high, thus prompting early marriage, the growth of families and, with them, the development of a "glorious market" for British manufactures. There is no talk of legislation to improve the morals of the "lower orders" in Franklin's essay—*Poor Richard* had already been published. His speculations on the law of population imply that that population was to be composed of freehold farmers and small handicraftsmen who were to live comfortably, though frugally, working for their own benefit rather than to support the luxury of their superiors.

Franklin was forty-five when the *Observa-*

tions was written, in 1751; he had completed his early training as a printer's journeyman in Boston, Philadelphia and London. He had accumulated a competence and retired from business to give his time to study and public affairs. Before that, Franklin had made himself a reputation as a pamphleteer, become deputy postmaster and founded a volunteer fire company, a Philosophical Society and an academy for improving the education of youth. He had invented the Franklin fireplace, helped reorganize the militia, animated opposition to Quaker indolence in administration and become clerk to the Pennsylvania legislature. In England, a man of Franklin's wit and pertinacity might have become a moderately successful merchant or an inhabitant of Grub Street. In Pennsylvania, he was able to stir an entire community for its good. Thus, Franklin's statement is the statement of the promise of America—a credo that was to be repeated again and again by other Americans for other generations of those who were born humbly.

The selection is from the edition by J. R. McCulloch, ed., *Collection of Scarce and Valuable Economical Tracts* (London, 1859).

Observations Concerning the Increase of Mankind

BY BENJAMIN FRANKLIN

1. TABLES of the proportion of marriages to births, of deaths to births, of marriages to the number of inhabitants, &c. formed on observations made upon the bills of mortality, christenings, &c. of populous cities, will not suit countries; nor will tables formed and observations made on full settled old countries, as Europe, suit new countries, as America.

2. For people increase in proportion to the number of marriages, and that is greater in proportion to the ease and convenience of supporting a family. When families can be easily supported, more persons marry, and earlier in life.

3. In cities, where all trades, occupations, and offices are full, many delay marrying till they can see how to bear the charges of a family; which charges are greater in cities, as luxury is more common; many live single during life, and continue servants to families, journeymen to trades, &c. Hence cities do not, by natural generation, supply themselves with inhabitants; the deaths are more than the births.

4. In countries full settled, the case must be nearly the same, all lands being occupied and improved to the height; those who cannot get lands, must labor for others, that have it; when laborers are plenty, their wages will be low; by low wages a family is supported with difficulty; this diffi-

culty deters many from marriage, who therefore long continue servants and single. Only, as the cities take supplies of people from the country, and thereby make a little more room in the country, marriage is a little more encouraged there, and the births exceed the deaths.

5. Great part of Europe is fully settled with husbandmen, manufacturers, &c. and therefore cannot now much increase in people. America is chiefly occupied by Indians, who subsist mostly by hunting. But as the hunter, of all men, requires the greatest quantity of land from whence to draw his subsistence, (the husbandman subsisting on much less, the gardener on still less, and the manufacturer requiring least of all) the Europeans found America as fully settled, as it well could be by hunters; yet these, having large tracts, were easily prevailed on to part with portions of territory to the new comers, who did not much interfere with the natives in hunting, and furnished them with many things they wanted.

6. Land being thus plenty in America, and so cheap, as that a labouring man, that understands husbandry, can, in a short time, save money enough to purchase a piece of new land, sufficient for a plantation, whereon he may subsist a family; such are not afraid to marry: for if they even look far enough forward to consider how their children, when grown up, are to be provided for, they see, that more land is to be had at rates equally easy, all circumstances considered.

7. Hence marriages in America are more general, and more generally early, than in Europe. And if it is reckoned there, that there is but one marriage *per annum* among 100 persons, perhaps we may here reckon two; and if in Europe, they have but four births to a marriage, (many of their marriages being late) we may here reckon eight, of which, if one half grow up, and our marriages are made, reckoning one with another, at twenty years of age, our people must at least be doubled every twenty years.

8. But notwithstanding this increase, so vast is the territory of North America, that it will require many ages to settle it fully; and till it is fully settled, labor will never be cheap here, where no man continues long a laborer for others, but gets a plantation of his own; no man continues long a journeyman to a trade, but goes among those new settlers, and sets up for himself, &c. Hence labor is no cheaper now, in Pennsylvania, than it was thirty years ago, though so many thousand laboring people have been imported from Germany and Ireland.

9. The danger, therefore, of these colonies interfering with their mother country in trades, that depend on labor, manufactures, &c. is too remote to require the attention of Great Britain.

10. But, in proportion to the increase of the colonies, a vast demand is growing for British manufactures; a glorious market, wholly in the power of Britain, in which foreigners cannot interfere, which will increase, in a short time, even beyond her power of supplying, though her whole trade should be to her colonies. . . .

12. It is an ill-grounded opinion, that, by the labor of slaves, America may possibly vie in cheapness of manufactures with Britain. The labor of slaves can never be so cheap here, as the labor of working men is in Britain. Any one may compute it. Interest of money is in the colonies from 6 to 10 per cent. Slaves, one with another, cost 30l. sterling per head. Reckon then the interest of the first purchase of a slave, the insurance or risk on his life, his clothing and diet, expenses in his sickness and loss of time, loss by his neglect of business, (neglect is natural to the man, who is not to be benefited by his own care or diligence) expense of a driver to keep him at work, and his pilfering from time to time, almost every slave being, from the nature of slavery, a thief, and compare the whole amount with the wages of a manufacturer of iron or wool in England, you will see, that labor is much cheaper there, than it ever can be by negroes here. Why then will Americans purchase slaves! Because slaves may be kept as long as a man pleases, or has occasion for their labor, while hired men are continually leaving their master (often in the midst of his business) and setting up for themselves. § 8.

13. As the increase of people depends on the encouragement of marriages, the following things must diminish a nation, viz. 1. The being conquered; for the conquerors will engross as many offices, and exact as much tribute or profit on the labor of the conquered, as will maintain them in their new establishment; and his diminishing the subsistence of the natives discourages their marriages, and so gradually diminishes them, while the foreigners increase. 2. Loss of territory. Thus the Britons, being driven into Wales, and crowded together in a barren country, insufficient to support such great numbers, diminished, till the people bore a proportion to the produce; while the Saxons increased on their abandoned lands, till the island became full of English. And, were the English now driven into Wales by some foreign nation, there would, in a few years, be no more Englishmen in Britain, than there are now people in Wales. 3. Loss of trade. Manufactures, exported, draw subsistence from foreign coun-

tries for numbers, who are thereby enabled to marry and raise families. If the nation be deprived of any branch of trade, and no new employment is found for the people occupied in that branch, it will soon be deprived of so many people. 4. Loss of food. Suppose a nation has a fishery, which not only employs great numbers, but makes the food and subsistence of the people cheaper: if another nation becomes master of the seas, and prevents the fishery, the people will diminish in proportion as the loss of employ and dearness of provision makes it more difficult to subsist a family. 5. Bad government and insecure property. People not only leave such a country, and, settling abroad, incorporate with other nations, lose their native language, and become foreigners; but the industry of those that remain being discouraged, the quantity of subsistence in the country is lessened, and the support of a family becomes more difficult. So heavy taxes tend to diminish a people. 6. The introduction of slaves. The negroes brought into the English sugar islands, have greatly diminished the whites there: the poor are by this means deprived of employment, while a few families acquire vast estates, which they spend on foreign luxuries; and, educating their children in the habits of those luxuries, the same income is needed for the support of one, that might have maintained one hundred. The whites, who have slaves, not laboring, are enfeebled, and therefore not so generally prolific; the slaves being worked too hard, and ill fed, their constitutions are broken, and the deaths among them are more than the births: so that a continual supply is needed from Africa. The northern colonies, having few slaves, increase in whites. Slaves also pejorate the families that use them; the white children become proud, disgusted with labor, and, being educated in idleness, are rendered unfit to get a living by industry.

14. Hence the prince, that acquires new territory, if he finds it vacant, or removes the natives to give his own people room;—the legislator, that makes effectual laws for promoting trade, increasing employment, improving land by more or better tillage, providing more food by fisheries, securing property, &c.;—and the man that invents new trades, arts or manufactures, or new improvements in husbandry, may be properly called *fathers of their nation* as they are the cause of the generation of multitudes, by the encouragement they afford to marriage.

15. As to privileges granted to the married, (such as the *jus trium liberorum* among the Romans) they may hasten the filling of a country, that has been thinned by war or pestilence, or that

has otherwise vacant territory, but cannot increase a people beyond the means provided for their subsistence.

16. Foreign luxuries, and needless manufactures, imported and used in a nation, do, by the same reasoning, increase the people of the nation that furnishes them, and diminish the people of the nation that uses them. Laws therefore that prevent such importations, and, on the contrary, promote the exportation of manufactures to be consumed in foreign countries, may be called (with respect to the people that make them) *generative laws,* as, by increasing subsistence, they encourage marriage. Such laws likewise strengthen a country doubly, by increasing its own people, and diminishing its neighbors.

17. Some European nations prudently refuse to consume the manufactures of East India:—they should likewise forbid them to their colonies; for the gain to the merchant is not to be compared with the loss, by this means, of people to the nation.

18. Home luxury in the great increases the nation's manufacturers employed by it, who are many, and only tends to diminish the families that indulge in it, who are few. The greater the common fashionable expense of any rank of people, the more cautious they are of marriage. Therefore luxury should never be suffered to become common.

19. The great increase of offspring in particular families is not always owing to greater fecundity of nature, but sometimes to examples of industry in the heads, and industrious education, by which the children are enabled better to provide for themselves, and their marrying early is encouraged from the prospect of good subsistence.

20. If there be a sect, therefore, in our nation, that regard frugality and industry as religious duties, and educate their children therein, more than others commonly do, such sect must consequently increase more by natural generation than any other sect in Britain.

21. The importation of foreigners into a country that has as many inhabitants as the present employments and provisions for subsistence will bear, will be in the end no increase of people, unless the new-comers have more industry and frugality than the natives, and then they will provide more subsistence, and increase in the country; but they will gradually eat the natives out. Nor is it necessary to bring in foreigners to fill up any occasional vacancy in a country; for such vacancy (if the laws are good, § 14, 16) will soon be filled by natural generation. Who can

now find the vacancy made in Sweden, France, or other warlike nations, by the plague of heroism 40 years ago; in France, by the expulsion of the protestants; in England, by the settlement of her colonies; or in Guinea, by a hundred years' exportation of slaves, that has blackened half America? The thinness of the inhabitants in Spain is owing to national pride, and idleness, and other causes, rather than to the expulsion of the Moors, or to the making of new settlements.

22. There is, in short, no bound to the prolific nature of plants or animals, but what is made by their crowding and interfering with each other's means of subsistence. Was the face of the earth vacant of other plants, it might be gradually sowed and overspread with one kind only, as, for instance, with fennel: and were it empty of other inhabitants, it might, in a few ages, be replenished from one nation only, as, for instance, with Englishmen. Thus there are supposed to be now upwards of one million of English souls in North America (though it is thought scarce 80,000 have been brought over sea), and yet perhaps there is not one the fewer in Britain, but rather many more, on account of the employment the colonies afford to manufacturers at home. This million doubling, suppose but once in 25 years, will, in another century, be more than the people of England, and the greatest number of Englishmen will be on this side of the water. What an accession of power to the British Empire by sea as well as land? What increase of trade and navigation? What numbers of ships and seamen? We have been here but little more than a hundred years, and yet the force of our privateers in the late war, united, was greater, both in men and guns, than that of the whole British navy in Queen Elizabeth's time. How important an affair then to Britain is the present treaty for settling the bounds between her colonies and the French? And how careful should she be to secure room enough, since on the room depends so much the increase of her people?

23. In fine, a nation well regulated is like a polypus: take away a limb, its place is soon supplied: cut it in two, and each deficient part shall speedily grow out of the part remaining. Thus, if you have room and subsistence enough, as you may, by dividing, make ten polypuses out of one, you may, of one, make ten nations, equally populous and powerful; or, rather, increase the nation tenfold in numbers and strength. . . .

THE DUTY TO REBEL

BY 1750, THE MEN who were forming opinion in America had, for the most part, been born and educated on her own soil and so represented an attitude that was actually, not merely potentially, different from that which prevailed among Europeans of similar social background. Benjamin Franklin shows the American attitude toward economic opportunity. Jonathan Mayhew's *Discourse Concerning Unlimited Submission* (1750) foreshadows the political philosophy which was to become distinctively American, a philosophy which may have taken its premises from Locke but which applied them with a bold directness that might well have shocked him.

Jonathan Mayhew (1720–1766) was born at Martha's Vineyard, took his degree at Harvard, and was called to the West Church in Boston, a pulpit he filled until his death. In 1747, three years after he had begun his work as a pastor, his sermons had been reprinted abroad and won him a European reputation granted only to Jonathan Edwards among his contemporaries. In contrast to Edwards's Calvinism, however, Mayhew's work was distinguished by an outlook almost approaching that of the Enlightenment, for he defended free will and attacked not only the Calvinist concept of depravity but also the Trinitarian bases of the Atonement.

When Mayhew rose in his pulpit in the West Church to deliver this discourse, he was not occupied with theology. His purpose was to combat "high-toned" doctrines concerning obedience to authority and, by implication, to strengthen the Massachusetts opposition in resistance to the pretensions of the royal governor. Mayhew's sermon might almost be a reply to the pronouncements of Archbishop Laud. Government is a convenience, is the implied premise of Mayhew's address. Consequently, civil rulers are to be obeyed because they are useful, not because they have some right to rule, either by gift of God or of the people. Mayhew proceeds to inquire whether a nation is obliged to yield absolute obedience to its sovereigns and applies the result of that inquiry to the case of Charles I. Only rulers who exercise a reasonable and just authority for the good of society may claim rule over it. Charles Stuart had shown himself no true prince but a tyrant. When the Lords and the Commons resisted his usurpations, they did not stand in rebellion but in defense of their liberties against the encroachment of arbitrary power. To do less than resist would have been to fail in their duty. For, Mayhew argues in language recalling the Declaration of Independence, since the good of society is the end of civil government, it is a nation's duty to rise against a tyrannous prince.

The selection is from Jonathan Mayhew, *A Discourse Concerning Unlimited Submission and Non-Resistance to the Higher Powers.* . . . (Boston, 1750).

A Discourse Concerning Unlimited Submission

BY JONATHAN MAYHEW

. . . That the end of magistracy is the good of civil society, *as such:*

That civil rulers, *as such,* are the ordinance and ministers of God; it being by his permission and providence that any bear rule; and agreeable to his will, that there should be *some persons* vested with authority in society, for the well-being of it:

That which is here said concerning civil rulers, extends to all of them in common: It relates indifferently to monarchical, republican and aristocratical government; and to all other forms which truly answer the sole end of government, the happiness of society; and to all the different degrees of authority in any particular state; to inferior officers no less than to the supreme:

That disobedience to civil rulers in the due exercise of their authority, is not merely *political sin,* but heinous *offence against God* and *religion:*

That the true ground and reason of our obligation to be subject to the *higher powers,* is the usefulness of magistracy (when properly exercised) to human society, and its subserviency to the general welfare:

That obedience to civil rulers is here equally required under all forms of government, which answer the sole end of all government, the good of society; and to every degree of authority in any state, whether supreme or subordinate:

(From whence it follows,

That if unlimited obedience and non-resistance, be here required as a duty under any one form of government, it is also required as a duty under all other forms; and as a duty to subordinate rulers as well as to the supreme.)

And lastly, that those civil rulers to whom the apostle enjoins subjection, are the persons in *possession; the powers that be;* those who are *actually* vested with authority.

There is one very important and interesting point which remains to be inquired into; namely, the *extent* of that subjection *to the higher powers,* which is here enjoined as a duty upon all christians. Some have thought it warrantable and glorious, to disobey the civil powers in certain circumstances; and, in cases of very great and general oppression, when humble remonstrances fail of having any effect; and when the public welfare cannot be otherwise provided for and secured, to rise unanimously even against the sovereign himself, in order to redress their grievances; to vindicate their natural and legal rights; to break the yoke of tyranny, and free themselves and posterity from inglorious servitude and ruin. It is upon this principle that many royal oppressors have been driven from their thrones into banishment; and many slain by the hands of their subjects. It was upon this principle that *Tarquin* was expelled from *Rome;* and *Julius Cæsar,* the conqueror of the world, and the tyrant of his country, cut off in the senate house. It was upon this principle, that king *Charles* I, was beheaded before his own banqueting house. It was upon this principle, that king *James* II. was made to fly that country which he aimed at enslaving: And upon this principle was that *revolution* brought about, which has been so fruitful of happy consequences to *Great-Britain.* But, in opposition to this principle, it has often been asserted, that the scripture in general (and the passage under consideration in particular) makes all resistance to princes a crime, in any case whatever.—If they turn tyrants, and become the common oppressors of those, whose welfare they ought to regard with a paternal affection, we must not pretend to right ourselves, unless it be by prayers and tears and humble intreaties: And if these methods fail of procuring redress, we must not have recourse to any other, but all suffer ourselves to be robbed and butchered at the pleasure of the *Lord's anointed;* lest we should incur the sin of rebellion, and the punishment of damnation. For he has God's authority and commission to bear him out in the worst of crimes, so far that he may not be withstood or controlled. Now whether we are obliged to yield such an absolute submission to our prince: or whether disobedience and resistance may not be justifiable in some cases, notwithstanding any thing in the passage before us, is an inquiry in which we are all concerned; and this is the inquiry which is the main design of the present discourse. . . .

And if we attend to the nature of the argument with which the apostle here enforces the duty of submission to *the higher powers,* we shall find it to be such an one, as concludes not in favour of submission to all who bear the *title* of rulers, in common; but only, to those who *actually* perform the duty of rulers, by exercising a reasonable and just authority, for the good of human society. This is a point which it will be proper to enlarge upon; because the question before us turns very much upon the truth or falsehood of this position. It is obvious, then, in general, that the civil rulers whom the apostle here speaks of, and obedience to whom he presses upon christians as a duty, are *good rulers,* such as are in the exercise of their office and power, benefactors to society. Such they are described to be, throughout this passage. Thus it is said, that they are not *a terror to good works, but to the evil;* that they are God's *ministers for good; revengers to execute wrath upon him that doeth evil;* and that *they attend continually upon this very thing.* St. *Peter* gives the same account of rulers: They are *for a praise to them that do well, and the punishment of evil doers.* It is manifest that this character and description of rulers, agrees only to such as are rulers in fact, as well as in name: to such as govern well, and act agreeably to their office. And the apostle's argument for submission to rulers, is wholly built and grounded upon a presumption that they do in fact answer this character; and is of no force at all upon the supposition of the contrary. If *rulers are a terror to good works, and not to the evil;* if they are not *ministers for good to society,* but for evil and distress, by violence and oppression; if they *execute wrath upon* sober, peaceable persons, who do their duty as members of society; and suffer rich and honorable knaves to escape

with impunity; if instead of *attending continually upon* the good work of advancing the public welfare, they *attend* only upon the gratification of their own lust and pride, and ambition, to the destruction of the public welfare; if this be the case, it is plain that the apostle's argument for submission does not reach them; they are not the same, but different persons from those whom he characterizes.

If it be said, that the apostle here uses another argument for submission to the *higher powers,* besides that which is taken from the usefulness of their office to civil society, when properly discharged and executed; namely, that their *power is from God;* that they *are ordained of God;* and that they *are God's ministers:* And if it be said, that this argument for submission to them will hold good, although they do not exercise their power for the benefit, but for the ruin, and destruction of human society; this objection was obviated, in part, before. Rulers have no authority from God to do mischief. They are not *God's ordinance,* or *God's ministers,* in any other sense than as it is by his permission and providence, that they are exalted to bear rule; and as magistracy duly exercised, and authority rightly applied, in the enacting and executing good laws,—laws attempered and accommodated to the common welfare of the subjects, must be supposed to be agreeable to the will of the beneficent author and supreme Lord of the universe; whose *kingdom ruleth over all;* and whose *tender mercies are over all his works.* It is BLASPHEMY to call tyrants and oppressors, *God's ministers.* They are more properly *the messengers of* SATAN *to buffet us.* No rulers are properly *God's ministers,* but such as are *just, ruling in the fear of God.* When once magistrates act contrary to their office, and the end of their institution; when they rob and ruin the public, instead of being guardians of its peace and welfare; they immediately cease to be the *ordinance* and *ministers of God;* and no more deserve that glorious character, than common *pirates* and *highwaymen.* So that whenever that argument for submission fails, which is grounded upon the usefulness of magistracy to civil society, (as it always does when magistrates do hurt to society instead of good) the other argument, which is taken from their being the ordinance of God, must necessarily fail also; no person of a civil character being *God's minister,* in the sense of the apostle, any farther than he performs God's will, by exercising a just and reasonable authority; and ruling for the good of the subject. . . .

Thus, upon a careful review of the apostle's reasoning in this passage, it appears that his arguments to enforce submission, are of such a nature, as to conclude only in favor of submission *to such rulers as he himself describes;* i. e. such as rule for the good of society, which is the only end of their institution. Common tyrants, and public oppressors, are not entitled to obedience from their subjects, by virtue of any thing here laid down by the inspired apostle.

I now add farther, that the apostle's argument is so far from proving it to be the duty of people to obey, and submit to such rulers as act in contradiction to the public good, and so to the design of their office, that it proves *the direct contrary*. For, please to observe, that if the end of all civil government, be the good of society; if this be the thing that is aimed at in constituting civil rulers; and if the motive and argument for submission to government, be taken from the apparent usefulness of civil authority, it follows, that when no such good end can be answered by submission, there remains no argument or motive to enforce it; if instead of this good end's being brought about by submission, a *contrary end* is brought about, and the ruin and misery of society effected by it; here is a plain and positive reason against submission in all such cases, should they ever happen. And therefore, in such cases, a regard to the public welfare, ought to make us withhold from our rulers that obedience and subjection which it would, otherwise, be our duty to render to them. If it be our duty, for example, to obey our king, merely for this reason, that he rules for the public welfare, (which is the only argument the apostle makes use of) it follows, by a parity of reason, that when he turns tyrant, and makes his subjects his prey to devour and to destroy, instead of his charge to defend and cherish, we are bound to throw off our allegiance to him, and to resist; and that according to the tenor of the apostle's argument in this passage. Not to discontinue our allegiance, in this case, would be to join with the sovereign in promoting the slavery and misery of that society, the welfare of which, we ourselves, as well as our sovereign, are indispensably obliged to secure and promote, as far as in us lies. It is true the apostle puts no case of such a tyrannical prince; but by his grounding his argument for submission wholly upon the good of civil society; it is plain he implicitly authorises, and even requires us to make resistance, whenever this shall be necessary to the public safety and happiness. . . .

Thus it appears, that the common argument, grounded upon this passage, in favor of universal and passive obedience, really overthrows itself, by proving too much, if it proves any thing at all; namely, that no civil officer is, in any case whatever, to be resisted, though acting in express contradiction to the design of his office; which no man, in his senses, ever did, or can assert.

If we calmly consider the nature of the thing itself, nothing can well be imagined more directly contrary to common sense, than to suppose that *millions* of people should be subjected to the arbitrary, precarious pleasure of *one single man;* (who has *naturally* no superiority over them in point of authority) so that their estates, and every thing that is valuable in life, and even their lives also, shall be absolutely at his disposal, if he happens to be wanton and capricious enough to demand them. What unprejudiced man can think, that God made ALL to be thus subservient to the lawless pleasure and phrenzy of ONE, so that it shall always be a sin to resist him! Nothing but the most plain and express revelation from heaven could make a sober, impartial man believe such a monstrous, unaccountable doctrine, and, indeed, the thing itself, appears so shocking—so out of all *proportion*, that it may be questioned, whether all the *miracles* that ever were wrought, could make it credible, that this doctrine *really* came from God. At present, there is not the least syllable in scripture which gives any countenance to it. The hereditary, indefeasible, divine right of kings, and the doctrine of non-resistance, which is built upon the supposition of such a right, are altogether as fabulous and chimerical, as transubstantiation; or any of the most absurd reveries of ancient or modern vissionaries. These notions are fetched neither from divine relation, nor human reason; and if they are derived from neither of those sources, it is not much matter from *whence they come, or whither they go*. Only it is a pity that such doctrines should be propagated in society, to raise factions and rebellions, as we see they have, in fact, been both in the *last*, and in the *present* REIGN.

But then, if unlimited submission and passive obedience to the *higher powers*, in all possible cases, be not a duty, it will be asked, "How far are we obliged to submit? If we may innocently disobey and resist in some cases, why not in all? Where shall we stop? What is the measure of our duty? This doctrine tends to the total dissolution of civil government; and to introduce such scenes of wild anarchy and confusion, as are more fatal to society than the worst of tyranny."

After this manner, some men object; and, indeed, this is the most plausible thing that can be said in favor of such an absolute submission as they plead for. But the worst (or rather the best) of it, is, that there is very little strength or solidity in it. For similar difficulties may be raised with respect to almost every duty of natural and re-vealed religion.—To instance only in two, both of which are near a kin, and indeed exactly parallel, to the case before us. It is unquestionably the duty of children to submit to their parents; and of servants, to their masters. But no one asserts, that it is their duty to obey, and submit to them, in all supposeable cases; or universally, a sin to resist them. Now does this tend to subvert the just authority of parents and masters? Or to introduce confusion and anarchy into private families? No. How then does the same principle tend to unhinge the government of that larger family, the body politic? We know, in general, that children and servants are obliged to obey their parents and masters respectively. We know also, with equal certainty, that they are not obliged to submit to them in all things, without exception; but may, in some cases, reasonably, and therefore innocently, resist them. These principles are acknowledged upon all hands, whatever difficulty there may be in fixing the exact limits of submission. Now there is at least as much difficulty in stating the measure of duty in these two cases, as in the case of rulers and subjects. So that this is really no objection, at least no reasonable one, against resistance to the *higher powers:* Or, if it is one, it will hold equally against resistance in the other cases mentioned.—It is indeed true, that turbulent, vicious-minded men, may take occasion from this principle, that their rulers may, in some cases, be lawfully resisted, to raise factions and disturbances in the state; and to make resistance where resistance is needless, and therefore, sinful. But is it not equally true, that children and servants of turbulent, vicious minds, may take occasion from this principle, that parents and masters may, in some cases be lawfully resisted, to resist when resistance is unnecessary, and therefore, criminal? Is the principle in either case false in itself, merely because it may be abused; and applied to legitimate disobedience and resistance in those instances, to which it ought not to be applied? According to this way of arguing, there will be no true principles in the world; for there are none but what may be wrested and perverted to serve bad purposes, either through the weakness or wickedness of men.

A people, really oppressed to a great degree by their sovereign, cannot well be insensible when they are so oppressed. And such a people (if I may allude to an ancient *fable*) have, like the *hesperian* fruit, a DRAGON for their *protector* and *guardian:* Nor would they have any reason to mourn, if some HERCULES should appear to dispatch him.—For a nation thus abused to arise unanimously, and to resist their prince, even to the dethroning him,

is not criminal; but a reasonable way of vindicating their liberties and just rights; it is making use of the means, and the only means, which God has put into their power, for mutual and self defence. And it would be highly criminal in them, not to make use of this means. It would be stupid tameness, and unaccountable folly, for whole nations to suffer *one* unreasonable, ambitious and cruel man, to wanton and riot in their misery. And in such a case it would, of the two, be more rational to suppose, that they that did NOT *resist*, than that they who did, would *receive to themselves damnation.*

OF KING CHARLES'S SAINTSHIP AND MARTYRDOM

This naturally brings us to make some reflections upon the resistance which was made about a century since, to that unhappy prince, KING CHARLES I.; and upon the ANNIVERSARY of his death. This is a point which I should not have concerned myself about, were it not that *some men* continue to speak of it, even to this day, with a great deal of warmth and zeal; and in such a manner as to undermine all the principles of LIBERTY, whether civil or religious, and to introduce the most abject slavery both in church and state; so that it is become a matter of universal concern.—What I have to offer upon this subject, will be comprised in a short answer to the following *queries; viz.*

For what reason the resistance to king *Charles* the *First,* was made?

By whom it was made?

Whether this resistance was REBELLION, or not?

How the *Anniversary* of king *Charles's* death came *at first* to be solemnized as a day of fasting and humiliation? And lastly,

Why those of the episcopal clergy who are very high in the principles of *ecclesiastical authority,* continue to speak of this unhappy man, as a great SAINT and a MARTYR?

For what reason, then, was the resistance to king *Charles,* made? The general answer to this enquiry is, that it was on account of the *tyranny* and *oppression* of his reign. Not a great while after his accession to the throne, he married a *French catholic;* and with her seemed to have *wedded* the politics, if not the religion of *France,* also. For afterwards, during a reign, or rather a tyranny of many years, he governed in a perfectly wild and arbitrary manner, paying no regard to the constitution and the laws of the kingdom, by which the power of the crown was limited; or to the solemn oath which he had taken at his coronation. It would be endless, as well as needless, to give a particular account of all the illegal and despotic measures which he took in his administration;—partly from his own natural lust of power, and partly from the influence of wicked councellors and ministers.—He committed many illustrious members of both houses of parliament to the *Tower*, for opposing his arbitrary schemes. —He levied many taxes upon the people without consent of parliament;—and then imprisoned great numbers of the principal merchants and gentry for not paying them.—He erected, or at least revived, several new and arbitrary courts, in which the most unheard-of barbarities were committed with his knowledge and approbation.—He supported that more than fiend, arch-bishop *Laud* and the clergy of his stamp, in all their church tyranny and hellish cruelties.—He authorised a book in favor of *sports* upon the *Lord's day;* and several clergymen were persecuted by him and the mentioned *pious* bishop, for not reading it to the people after *divine service.*—When the parliament complained to him of the arbitrary proceedings of his corrupt ministers, he told that *august body,* in a rough, domineering, unprincely manner, that he wondered any one should be so foolish and insolent as to think that he would part with the meanest of his servants *upon their account.*—He refused to call any parliament at all for the space of twelve years together, during all which time, he governed in an absolute, lawless, and despotic manner.—He took all opportunities to encourage the *papists,* and to promote them to the highest offices of honor and trust.—He (probably) abetted the horrid massacre in *Ireland,* in which two hundred thousand protestants were butchered by the Roman Catholics.—He sent a large sum of money, which he had raised by his arbitrary taxes, into *Germany,* to raise foreign troops, in order to force more arbitrary taxes upon his subjects.— He not only by a long series of *actions,* but also in *plain terms,* asserted an absolute uncontroulable power; saying even in one of his speeches to parliament, that as it was blasphemy to dispute what God might do; so it was sedition in subjects to dispute what the king might do.—Towards the end of his tyranny, he came to the House of Commons with an armed force, and demanded five of its principal members to be delivered up to him. —And this was a prelude, to that unnatural war, which he soon after levied against his own dutiful subjects; whom he was bound by all the laws of honor, humanity, piety, and I might add, of *interest* also, to defend and cherish with a paternal affection.—I have only time to hint at these facts in a general way, all which, and many more of the same tenor, may be proved by good authorities: So that the *figurative* language which St. *John*

uses, concerning the just and beneficent deeds of our blessed Saviour, may be applied to the unrighteous and execrable deeds of this prince, *viz. And there are also many other things which* king Charles *did the which, if they should be written every one, I suppose that even the world itself, could not contain the books that should be written.* Now it was on account of king *Charles's* thus assuming a power above the laws, in direct contradiction to his coronation-oath, and governing the greatest part of his time, in the most arbitrary oppressive manner; it was upon this account, that that resistance was made to him, which, at length, issued in the loss of his crown, and of *that head* which was unworthy to wear it.

But by whom was this resistance made? Not by a private *junto;*—not by a small seditious *party;* —not by a *few desparadoes,* who, to mend their fortunes, would embroil the state;—but by the LORDS and COMMONS of *England.* It was they that almost unanimously opposed the king's measures for overturning the constitution, and changing that free and happy government into a wretched, absolute monarchy. It was they, that when the king was about levying forces against his subjects, in order to make himself absolute, commissioned officers, and raised an army to defend themselves and the public: And it was they that maintained the war against him all along, till he was made a prisoner. This is indisputable. Though it was not properly speaking, the parliament, but the army, which put him to death afterwards. And it ought to be freely acknowledged, that most of their proceedings, in order to get this matter effected, and particularly the court by which the king was at last tried and condemned, was little better than a mere mockery of justice.—

The next question which naturally arises, is, whether this resistance which was made to the king *by the Parliament,* was properly *rebellion,* or not? The answer to which is plain, that it was not; but a most righteous and glorious stand, made in defence of the natural and legal rights of the people, against the unnatural and illegal encroachments of arbitrary power. Nor was this a rash and too sudden opposition. The nation had been patient under the oppressions of the crown, even to *long suffering;*—for a course of many years; and there was no rational hope of redress in any other way.—Resistance was absolutely necessary, in order to preserve the nation from slavery, misery and ruin. And who so proper to make this resistance, as the Lords and Commons;—the whole representative body of the people;—guardians of the public welfare; and each of which, was, in point of legislation, vested with an equal, coordinate power, with that of the crown? Here were *two* branches of the legislature against *one*; —two of which, had law and equity, and the constitution on their side, against one which was impiously attempting to overturn law and equity, and the constitution; and to exercise a wanton licentious *sovereignty* over the properties, consciences and lives of all the people:—Such a *sovereignty* as some inconsiderately ascribe to the Supreme Governor of the world.—I say, inconsiderately; because God himself does not govern in an absolutely arbitrary and despotic manner. The power of this Almighty King (I speak it not without caution and reverence; the power of this Almighty King) is *limited by law;* not indeed, by *acts* of *Parliament*, but by the eternal *laws* of truth, wisdom and equity; and the everlasting *tables* of right reason;—tables that cannot be *repealed*, or *thrown down* and *broken* like those of *Moses*.—But king *Charles* sat himself up above all these, as much as he did above the written laws of the realm; and made mere humor and caprice, which are no rule at all, the only rule and measure of his administration. And now, is it not perfectly ridiculous to call resistance to such a tyrant, by the name of *rebellion?—the grand rebellion?* Even that —— parliament, which brought king *Charles II.* to the throne, and which run *loyally mad,* severely reproved one of their own members for condemning the proceedings of that parliament which first took up arms against the former king. And upon the same principles that the proceedings of this parliament may be censured as wicked and rebellious; the proceedings of those, who since opposed king *James II.* and brought the Prince of *Orange* to the throne, may be censured

as wicked and rebellious also. The cases are parallel.—But whatever *some* men may *think*, it is to be hoped that for their own sakes, they will not dare to *speak* against the REVOLUTION upon the justice and legality of which, depends (in part) his present MAJESTY's right to the throne.

If it be said, that although the parliament which first opposed king *Charles's* measures, and at length took up arms against him, were not guilty of rebellion; yet certainly those persons were, who condemned, and put him to death; even this perhaps is not true. For he had, in fact, *unkinged* himself long before, and had forfeited his title to the allegiance of the people. So that those who put him to death, were, at most, only guilty of *murder;* which, indeed, is bad enough, if they were really guilty of *that;* (which is at least disputable.) *Cromwell*, and those who were principally concerned in the (*nominal*) king's death, might possibly have been very wicked and designing men. Nor shall I say any thing in vindication of the reigning *hypocrisy* of those times, or of *Cromwell's* maleadministration during the *interregnum:* (for it is *truth*, and not a *party*, that I am speaking for.) But still it may be said, that *Cromwell* and his adherents were not, properly speaking, guilty of *rebellion;* because he whom they beheaded was not, properly speaking, *their king;* but a *lawless tyrant.*—Much less, are the whole body of the nation at that time to be charged with rebellion on that account; for it was no *national act;* it was not done by a *free* parliament. And much less still, is the nation at present, to be charged with the great sin of rebellion, for what their *ancestors* did, (or rather did NOT) a century ago. . . .

Part Two

THE FIRST AMERICAN REVOLUTION

INTRODUCTION

1. THE COLONIAL SCENE

COLONIAL AMERICA grew, its horizons constantly expanded, and it created wealth in the process. Settlements extended more and more into the interior as nature was conquered and the Indians were brought under control. Large estates and many small farms, with their ample houses and farm buildings, trees and lawns and orchards, dotted the countryside. Towns made their appearance. In the 1770s there were five important urban centers—Boston, Philadelphia, Newport, New York, and Charleston—of which Philadelphia was the largest, with a population of 40,000. By our modern standards, these are small towns. Even smaller were the other settled communities of Providence, Hartford, New Haven, Albany, Savannah, Williamsburg. Yet many had newspapers and some municipal public services. There were churches, schools and academies; taverns and Masonic lodges; and a good deal of social activity.

Living was becoming much more bountiful and, except in the constantly receding frontier zones, the amenities of daily relations were not unlike those of the long-settled European communities. America was opportunity. There was no caste system; the discipline of hard work—thanks to a Protestant heritage—was commonly accepted; property could be acquired easily and transmitted, under little threat of ancient privilege. Because the economy was essentially agricultural and needed human labor, early marriages took place and families were large. Because men outnumbered women, the European sex distinctions and inequalities were disregarded. The family, as a unit, functioned well and children were trained to accept parental discipline and labor in the fields beside their elders. Colonial Americans were optimists; they tended to break down class lines; they

were utilitarians and individualists; they believed in property rights because all men looked forward to acquiring possessions. America was middle class, functionally and psychologically.

Religion in Colonial America. Religion, as a discipline and a way of life, filled the minds and shaped the habits of colonial Americans. The prevailing form was Protestant, but it was a Protestantism of many sects. Ecclesiastical authority was powerful in the Anglican churches and, in Massachusetts at any rate, in the Congregational churches. But dissidence could not be held down. The German Pietists in Pennsylvania, the Quakers, the Baptists, the later Methodists, founded their churches on the democratic will of the congregations and sought to infuse their doctrines with the warmer glow of personal mystical experience and Christian charity.[1]

The stern, self-denying, righteous Puritanism of the early Massachusetts fathers was not left unchallenged. Puritanism had invested its clergy with great powers. They prepared the true believers for their calling and constantly pointed out the hard way God's elect were called upon to tread. In the early eighteenth century, Cotton Mather had sought to perpetuate the orthodox and conservative traditions; but he was doomed to failure. Under the lead of newer spirits—John Wise, the minister of Ipswich, and notably Jonathan Edwards of Northampton—Calvinism was becoming more democratic as far as church organization was concerned and more truly Christian as a religious faith.

[1] While the Anglican church was the established church in Virginia, Maryland, New York, North Carolina, South Carolina, and Georgia, by the eighteenth century its influence was visibly declining.

The Great Awakening, which swept all the colonies in the 1730s and 1740s, deeply modified and enriched Calvinism. It was more than a wave of revivalism: it was an effort to make Christianity more personal, more mystical, more joyous. Salvation was a purifying experience that brought men in direct communion with God. The Great Awakening reached distant places, obscure hamlets, the frontier regions—particularly it made its appeal to the little men who were being left out of the established churches and their formalized ritualism—and it created a secure place for these in the religious life of America.

Jonathan Edwards was a modern in this sense: despite his emphasis on mystical experience, he sought to reconcile religion with rationalism, faith with reason. Others in colonial America—among the educated minority who were drinking deeply from the well-springs of the English (and also French) Enlightenment—were seeking to make a religion of reason. Influenced by the physics of Newton and the psychology of Locke, they saw the universe, like a machine well planned and built, operating in terms of its own mechanical laws. Man, fashioned by his own experiences and controlling his own destiny, but always guided by natural law, had it within his power to make a better world. Man was rational, he was educable, he was free. A belief in the individual's powers to rise only strengthened the characteristic optimism of America; and a devotion to the principle of natural rights—to life, liberty, and property—prepared men's minds for America's later democratic revolution.

These were some of the influences that produced the characteristic American man of the colonial period. He was developing a group-personality and psychology as a result of his experiences in the New World. He was also developing a set of reflexes as a result of the fact that he was a colonial compelled to function in a mercantilist climate.

2. THE COLONIAL UNDER MERCANTILISM

The Political Sphere. The American of the seventeenth and eighteenth centuries was a colonial. He lived under English law, read English books, wore English clothes, and sometimes he sent his sons to English schools. Nevertheless he was a colonial in a variety of ways, some apparent and obvious, some subtle. He had no representation in the English Parliament and, in the final analysis, his political affairs were ruled over by people who did not know his peculiar problems. He had to submit to a judiciary, as a last court of appeal, which sat three thousand miles away. He functioned in an economic system which regarded his interests and activities as subordinate to those of the mother country. He was received well when he went to England; his spokesmen were listened to courteously; but, always, he and they were led to understand that the function of the settlements overseas was to strengthen the position of the mother country in a world where the search for wealth was always the first consideration. In short, he was a colonial with a specific function to perform in a climate guided by the rules of mercantilism.

The Economic Sphere. Nowhere were these rules clearer than in the domain of business enterprise. In some areas—as we shall see—the colonial was permitted to operate in a protected market. In others—as we also shall see—he was forced to operate in a monopoly one. At all times, he was a colonial businessman rather than a free enterpriser; and in time, as a result of his inferior position and the restraints imposed upon him, he was bound to become restive. The American Revolution made him free economically and politically; the colonial sought freedom for both reasons.

The colonial of the one hundred years before the American Revolution—particularly the colonial businessman—lived in a world that is hard for us to understand today. First, English capital played a very minor role in the establishment of business concerns; capital for new enterprises and for expansion came largely from the savings of business launched by the colonials themselves. Second, colonial business never had the benefits of corporate organization and management. Third, it did not have the assistance of any kind of banking mechanism. There were no agencies for deposit and discount; none for the creation of funds for working capital; none for the collection of savings and their conversion into investments.

This important fact should also be borne in mind: the typical colonial businessman was a merchant rather than an industrialist. He diversified his affairs, to spread his risks, because he had limited capital resources at his command; so that, at one and the same time, he could be engaging in retail and wholesale trade, ironmaking, the buying and selling of furs, land speculation, and money lending. He bought and sold for himself. He acted as a commission man for other businessmen. He outfitted ships and sent their captains out on trading voyages. He put up goods at auction, or public vendue. He joined with others—through the device of the partnership—in building and owning ships and in insuring cargoes.

Most important of all, perhaps, was the fact that as a businessman he was limited in the nature of the adventures upon which he might embark. As a wholesale merchant, he could not trade freely all over the globe. As a manufacturer, he could not fabricate anything his fancy dictated. At these points, notably, he was made to understand that he was a colonial. The over-all mercantilist program imposed upon the colonies by England, the mother country, impressed these facts upon him:

First, it was the function of the colonies to provide the basic raw materials needed by English industry and trade to make England strong and rich.

Second, it was the role of the colonies to buy the surpluses of English manufactured ware.

Third, it was the duty of colonials to tie their currencies to the English pound sterling —to be, in our modern terminology, members of the sterling bloc.

The Navigation System. To achieve these ends, England put the colonies under the supervision of the so-called Navigation System. The first Act of Trade and Navigation was passed by Parliament in 1651; but it was the Act of 1660 that really set up the cornerstone of the system. According to the 1660 law, only English vessels could engage in trade with the English oversea dominions or import any colonial products into England. Again, all commodities grown or fabricated in Asia, Africa, or America could be imported into England or the oversea dominions only in ships owned and manned by English men (or colonials). Also, only certain specified commodities produced in Europe could be imported into England; and these commodities could move only in English ships or in ships of the countries of origin. And, by the Act of 1663, all the commodities grown, produced, or fabricated in Europe which the colonies might require or wished to handle had to come by way of England as the entrepôt. Transshipment in this fashion meant, of course, export duties and additional freight and handling charges, so that the cost of European goods for the colonists was increased. This meant, again, an effort to force the American colonies to deal with England alone for their manufactured-ware necessaries. Later acts were designed to strengthen the administrative regulations of enforcement.

This was only one part of the Navigation System. The second had to do with production. Written into the Acts of Trade and Navigation were so-called "enumerated lists," or lists of raw-material products grown or created in the colonies which were to be exported to England alone. Naturally, these products were for English use or English transshipment into the European markets. In this way England (in true mercantilist fashion), hoped to free herself of her dependence upon the naval stores, minerals, spices, and the like, of foreign lands; also, the carriage of such wares in the European trade meant earnings for English ships and profits for English merchants and processors. There was, in addition, the factor of revenues from import and export duties levied on such articles. So, the Acts of 1660 and 1663 placed the following colonial commodities on these "enumerated lists": sugar, cotton, tobacco, ginger, indigo, and various dyewoods. The Acts of 1704 and 1705 included rice, molasses, naval stores, hemp, and masts and yards. The Act of 1721 listed copper ore, beaver furs, and other furs. The Act of 1764 enumerated whale fins, hides, iron, lumber, raw silk, and potash and pearl ashes. It will be observed that virtually all the surplus products of the new country, except cereals, meat stuffs, and fish, in time fell under the controls of the Navigation System.

Restrictions on Manufacturing. As far as international trade was concerned, the orbit of colonial enterprise was a limited one indeed. The same restricted opportunities existed in industrial production. The explanation for the insignificance of colonial manufacturing is a simple one; and, again, it is linked with mercantilist restraint. The English administrative apparatus of control over the economic life of the colonies was elaborate. The key agency was the Board of Trade established as such in 1696, although its predecessors ran back into the Cromwellian period. The devices used by the Board of Trade for directing and supervising economic matters included the following: It was given the task of preparation of the civil list, so that it had its hands on the personnel sent over to or in charge of the colonies. It supervised the activities of the colonial judiciary. It passed on the petitions of English companies seeking investment opportunities in the colonies and reported back to the Privy Council. (In this particular it is important to note that very few such requests for charters were granted; and in no cases were the petitions acceded to when a business right of Englishmen was threatened.)

Even more important were the Board's two functions of reviewing colonial legislation and recommending approval or disapproval ("dis-

allowance" was the term employed) to the Privy Council, and of preparing instructions for the deportment of the royal governors. These two rights the Board of Trade employed; so that a good deal of the conflict that emerged between colonial legislatures and royal governors in the eighteenth century stemmed from the constant limitations imposed upon the popular will from overseas. Notably at two points, colonial enterprise was being circumscribed. The first had to do with prohibitions against the encouragement of manufacturing by the colonial legislatures. The second was concerned with the checking of attempts on the part of the colonies to increase their money supply in an effort to escape from the trap of inadequate credit facilities.

It is not generally recognized to what degree colonial legislatures were preoccupied with the problem of manufactures. Taking a leaf from the experiences of the mother country and using characteristically mercantilist devices, the legislatures sought to encourage the development of textile and ironware industries. They passed statutes offering bounties, public credit, and tax exemptions; they tried to create monopolies, to assure fair ware, and to incorporate new towns where industries might be established. The Board of Trade examined these statutes and used a number of means to hold the tendency in check. It recommended disallowance to the Privy Council. It instructed the royal governors to veto. It advised Parliament in the preparation of general legislation.

In the last connection, three laws were passed. The Woolen Act of 1699 struck at the colonial (as well as the Irish) woolen textile industry. Under it, colonial wool, woolen yarn, and woolen cloth could not enter into intercolonial or international trade. The Hat Act of 1732 not only prevented colonial-made hats from moving into intercolonial and international trade but it also reduced the industry to retail and custom-made proportions. Negroes were barred from participation in it; the seven-year apprenticeship law was imposed; and all hat-makers were limited to two apprentices. The Iron Act of 1750 denied to the colonial enterprisers the right to expand their iron operations by the erection of new mills, forges, and furnaces. They could, in other words, continue to produce heavy bar iron; but not wrought ironware or finished steel products.

In addition, the right of disallowance was regularly used by the Privy Council at the recommendation of the Board of Trade. Colonial laws to encourage shoemaking (Pennsylvania, 1705), sailcloth manufacture (New York, 1706), the establishment of new towns (1706, 1707, 1708 in Virginia and Maryland), linen fabrication (Massachusetts, 1756) were vetoed. And it made no effort to conceal its intention. Thus, in 1756, the Board declared that "the passing of laws in the plantations for encouraging manufactures, which any ways interfere with the manufacture of this kingdom, has always been thought improper, and has ever been discouraged."

The Bounty System. Side by side with mercantilist restraint went encouragement, but all to achieve the grand design of making colonial enterprise an adjunct of English economic requirement. Again and again, special privileges were offered by the mother country in an effort to direct colonial activity into specific spheres. England was dependent upon the so-called East Country (lands around the Baltic Sea) for her naval stores, ropes, and rigging. In 1705, to stimulate the colonial production of these staples, upon which shipbuilding was based, bounties were offered for the raising and making of hemp, tar, pitch, and resin. But New England-

landers, whom London had particularly in mind, did not yield to these blandishments. In South Carolina an impetus was given to naval store production; in North Carolina, to hemp. The bounties were permitted to lapse for a time, were renewed again in 1729 at a lower level, and then raised once more in 1764. This assisted-production neither solved England's problem—for her own shipbuilding industry continued to depend upon East Country exports—nor did it divert New England enterprise out of those activities that were competitive with the mother country's.

Similar programs were launched in connection with the production of subtropical requirements. Attempts were made to foster the development of wine (imported from France) and silk (imported from Italy) first in Virginia in the seventeenth century and again in Georgia in the eighteenth century. Bounties, assisted emigration, and high prices for wine and wound silk produced no results.

In the case of tobacco, mercantilist policy was more successful. To give the planting colonies an opportunity to cultivate the weed without competition, its growth was banned in Great Britain and Ireland in 1620. On the other hand, tobacco was put on the enumerated list under the Navigation System, so that the crop was moved through the hands of English and Scottish dealers and processers before it was transshipped to the European continent. This was less than a blessing. The fact is, on balance, the mercantilist restrictions and prohibitions hampered colonial enterprise. A closer examination of foreign trade will demonstrate this.

3. COLONIAL COMMERCE

The colonial businessman was primarily a merchant. In the Northern colonies, he subordinated his other economic interests to trade; but he was an independent trader. In the Southern colonies, usually, he was an agent or factor for English or Scottish merchants. There is another regional difference that must be had in

mind. The English mercantile economy welcomed Southern plantation wares; while it was in no position to absorb all the goods produced in surplus in the Northern colonies. The problems of both sections were different, although the overall limitations on their business activities were the same.

The Balance of Payments. Because England took, in such large quantities, the South's tobacco, indigo, naval stores, furs and hides, it might be supposed that the balance of trade was favorable to the colonials of this region. Such was not the case. They had to buy their invisible items from the English—shipping, brokerage, commissions, interest. The terms of trade were against them, for there was a constant complaint in the South of the lack and the dearness of manufactured ware. English investments (by the 1770s, they came to something like £4,000,000 in the planting South) continued to increase. This meant that English creditors were converting the short-term debts of Southern planters into long-term obligations, largely mortgages on land and slaves. All in all, the planting colonies were in a debtor relationship to the mother country—a state of affairs that was not unduly restrictive as long as credits were available in England.

The North was also in a debtor relationship because its businessmen had to buy from England while they could not sell to her. They were able to carry on, and even to expand, as long as they could find other areas of trade in which to acquire favorable balances. Here developed one of the paradoxes of the mercantilist program. In an effort to avoid the competition of colonial businessmen, the English limited industrial enterprise; but to make possible the purchase in America of English goods in growing quantities, they were compelled to tolerate colonial competition in the foreign trade. In short, Northern businessmen tried to earn freights, commissions, profits, and brokerage fees on their own account, by extending their trading activities into foreign spheres where English merchants were already functioning. Northern businessmen, to pay their English balances and sustain their domestic trade, had to find markets in Newfoundland, the Wine Islands, southern Europe, Africa, and the West Indies. In virtually all these regions, they built up favorable balances; from all these regions they obtained specie and bills of exchange with which to satisfy their English creditors. In this way, the import trade was financed—and colonial mercantile accumulation could take place. When the competition became too keen, when New York, Boston, Newport, and Philadelphia merchants began to press their English rivals too closely, then the English Mercantile System was on the horns of a dilemma. To curb the aggressive Northern businessmen threatened the ruin of the Northern business centers. But to permit colonial enterprisers to go their own way and engage in industry meant the end of the economic usefulness of the colonies. This was England's problem after the end of the Seven Years' War in 1763. There was no solution for it.

The Northern Trades. The foreign trades opened up by Northern merchants, therefore, were not extra ventures but fundamental to their continuance in business. These trades were the following:

(1) THE NEWFOUNDLAND TRADE. To this region, New England merchants sent provisions, lumber, rum, fishing tackle, and salt for the maintenance of the English colonies planted there. Originally, in the seventeenth century, New Englanders fished the banks themselves; but increasingly, into the eighteenth century, they contented themselves with trade alone. They received in return fish and coin and bills of exchange. The balance of payments was in their favor.

(2) THE WINE ISLANDS TRADE. To the Azores, the Canaries, and Madeira, lying in the eastern Atlantic off the coasts of the Iberian peninsula and north Africa, New England, New York, and Philadelphia merchants exported fish, provisions, live animals, and barrel staves. They obtained in return light and fortified wines, part of which were carried to England to pay off balances. Some of the wines were brought into colonial America. In this region, too, the balance of payments was in favor of the colonies.

(3) THE SOUTH EUROPEAN TRADE. To Portugal, Spain, France, and Italy, New England merchants (out of Boston in the seventeenth century, out of Salem in the eighteenth), sold fish,

timber, and Southern rice. Direct trade was almost completely forbidden with these countries, the imports, in small quantities, being lemons, limes, raisins, salt and olive oil. The returns therefore were in coin and bills of exchange. Again, the balance of payments was in favor of the colonies.

(4) THE WEST INDIA–AFRICAN TRADE. The most important trade of all was the triangular trade which included the Guinea coast of Africa as one leg, the famous Middle Passage across the Atlantic as the second, and the northern return journey from the Caribbean settlements as the third. Here, too, the balance of payments was in favor of the colonies. To Africa, increasingly in the eighteenth century to rival the slavers out of Bristol, Liverpool, and Nantes, went colonial slave ships out of Newport, Boston, Salem, and New York, with cargoes of domestic rum and iron and trade goods picked up in English ports. By the 1770s there were perhaps as many as seventy colonial ships in this traffic, each able to carry 65 Negroes. As an indication of its size and economic significance, one may note that the colonial slaving fleet was fully one third that of England's. Despite the hazards of the business and the necessity for quickly amortizing the value of the vessels (as a rule, in three years), the profits on each voyage were very large, perhaps in the neighborhood of 30 percent.

These Guineamen, as they were called, also purchased ivory, gums and bees wax. But the Negro trade was the most important of all; and the Negroes were moved, to a lesser extent, into the mainland colonies and, to a greater extent, across the Middle Passage to the sugar plantations of the Caribbean. The profits of the slave trade were taken frequently in coin and bills of exchange; therefore the full value of this triangular trade is not reflected in commodity movements.

Nor was this all. From the West Indies came large quantities of goods; to them were shipped most of the surplus Northern products which were banned in England. Northern merchants loaded their small swift ships (70 tons was a large vessel) with all those necessaries the sugar plantations were incapable of producing—work animals, lumber, staves, heads, barrel hoops, flour, salted provisions, refuse fish—and sold them originally to the English planters of Jamaica, Barbados, Antigua, Montserrat, and Nevis. But as the eighteenth century lengthened, more and more these Northern ships were to be found in the ports of the foreign islands and settlements. From about 1730 on, although the French and Spanish West Indies were legally closed to them, Yankee and New York captains had brought the whole Caribbean region from Dutch Guiana on the southeast to the Bahamas on the northwest into their sphere of influence. They were at home in Jamaica, of course (doubly so, not only because it was British but also because it was the center out of which the illegal traffic with the other islands was carried on); and equally at home in Spanish Havana, Vera Cruz and Porto Bello, in French Martinique, in Danish St. Thomas and St. Croix, and in Dutch Curaçao.

In all these ports, the Northern ships purchased indigo, cotton, ginger, allspice, and dyewoods, which were largely transshiped to England; and salt and a little coffee for the colonies; and—most important of all—sugar and molasses which were moved northward to the distilleries of Rhode Island and Massachusetts to be distilled into rum. It was this wondrous and heady beverage that flowed through the veins of the domestic Indian trade, the Newfoundland trade, and the African trade. In this wise, the cycle was completed and thus Northern business was able to prosper and grow, within the confines of mercantilist restraint, until 1763.

The First Molasses Act. Mention has been made of the fact that Northern merchants traded freely over the whole Caribbean region. This was important, of course, in the light of the existing mercantilist prohibitions. What was of even greater significance, as far as the English Mercantile System was concerned, was the fact that gradually the Northern merchants began to favor the non-English settlements as the sources for their sugar and molasses. Now the mother country was touched at a vital spot, for the darling of the English imperial scheme was not the mainland colonies but the sugar plantations. The Board of Trade and Parliament, listening to the protestations of the sugar lords sympathetically, moved with energy and dispatch. In 1733, Parliament passed the Molasses Act, which placed virtually prohibitive duties on foreign-islands sugar, molasses and rum imported into the English colonies. But there was a fly in the ointment; the British were incapable of enforcing the law. The customs machinery in the colonies was weak and venal (notably at Jamaica, through which the foreign sugar cleared) and the naval patrols that could be allocated for enforcement and to run down the illegal traders were inadequate. Why? Because, from 1740 through the Seven Years' War, England was engaged in foreign wars almost continuously and the navy was required for military purposes.

Within this framework, therefore, what was in effect an illegal colonial trade could operate with impunity. All the merchants from all the Northern ports engaged in it; with their profits they built distilleries and made rum; rum moved into the African trade and the slavers flourished. In a sense, the foreign-islands commerce was the foundation stone of Northern mercantile prosperity and sustained the adverse direct trade with England. By the late 1750s at least 11,500 hogshead of molasses reached Rhode Island annually from the foreign islands, as against 2,500 from the British; 14,500 hogshead came to Massachusetts from the same foreign sources as against 500 from Jamaica, Barbados, and the other British islands. By 1750, it was estimated, Massachusetts had some sixty distilleries making rum, and Rhode Island some thirty. The manufacture of rum was undoubtedly the most important single industrial enterprise in New England in the second quarter of the eighteenth century.

4. COLONIAL CURRENCY

Mercantilist control affected the colonial economic life at another important point. This was the close regulation of the colonial money supply. In the second half of the seventeenth century and most of the eighteenth, the whole European world was affected by a dearth of minted money. The original Spanish silver mines in America were no longer in production. Bullion was being drained off into the East to be buried and removed from circulation. An expanding industry and commerce were clamoring for more elastic credit facilities. Commercial banking was still at a low point in development—bank money, created by the writing up of deposits, was virtually unknown —so that business transactions were largely carried on in coin, or foreign bills of exchange. The importance of coin to the mercantilist era was understandable. With this fact was joined the mercantilist insistence upon a favorable balance of payments, to be settled only by the movement of bullion.

The Program of Restriction. The colonial money supply was compelled to operate in terms of these limitations. The British program may be summarized in this fashion. It did not permit the exportation of English coin to the colonies. It compelled colonials to pay public obligations in coin whenever possible. It did not permit the colonials to prevent the exportation of coin, or indeed bullion, from America to the mother country. It refused to allow the erection of colonial mints and it regarded with a suspicious eye the efforts to augment the money supply by the emission and circulation of bills of credit. The colonial currency, despite the great need of credit for expansion at home and the settlement of obligations overseas, was tied to the English pound and kept tightly contracted.

There were special considerations that played a part in the determination of this policy. An independent coinage—if it were freed from the pound—might affect adversely the credits English merchants had advanced to colonials. Similarly, an independent, and an expanding, money supply might furnish those additional financial resources with which colonial businessmen would be tempted to expand their enterprise into avenues closed to them by the mercantilist system. Thus, the heavy burden of debt, the paucity of coin, and the absence of commercial banking facilities created an inflationary attitude in colonial America; the English, on the other hand, were deflationary. In 1764, after a long and unsuccessful contest against the colonial legislatures, England took a fatal step. In the midst of colonial depression, already aggravated by the sharp decline in the foreign-islands sugar trade, Parliament passed the Currency Act, which denied to all the colonies the right to issue and circulate paper money, the so-called bills of credit. The steps leading to this impasse must now be recounted.

Because of the scarcity of coin, in the seventeenth century all the colonies legalized the use of commodity money for public transactions. Exchange values were regularly fixed by law. Of course, it was impossible to compel the use of commodity money to settle private accounts, so that two price levels were actually in existence. All sorts of commodities were employed in this way—for the payment of taxes, the salaries of public officials, and the like. In New England and the Middle colonies, at one time or another, wheat, barley, rye, beef, pork, cattle, and peas were used as commodity money. In Virginia and Maryland, tobacco served this function. Necessarily, this was a poor makeshift. Commodity money had to be inspected, transported, and stored; it deteriorated; the market value of commodities often was lower than the official exchange ratios.

It was inevitable, therefore, that colonial governments should turn their thoughts to the establishment of provincial mints. Massachusetts, indeed, erected such an agency; for in 1652, during the interregnum at home, it began to strike off the famous pinetree shilling. Characteristic of the colonial attitude, this coin had a smaller silver content than the English shilling. But in 1684, the English crown, claiming that the issuance of the coinage was an exclusive privilege of sovereignty, outlawed the Massachusetts mint. No similar attempt was made elsewhere.

Another expedient was then tried. Foreign coins circulated freely in colonial America because of the favorable balances in the Caribbean trade and because, interestingly enough, piracy brought much of its ill-gotten gains into the ports of New York and Philadelphia right up to the end of the seventeenth century. Colonials were familiar with the following gold coins: the Portuguese Johannes and half Johannes, the Spanish Pistoles, and the French Guineas. The most familiar foreign coin, however, was the Spanish milled silver dollar, or piece-of-eight, which was officially valued at 4s. 6d. In an effort to attract more of these coins into the colonies, legislatures took to overvaluing them. The piece-of-eight was revalued at 5s. originally and then pushed up to as high as 8s. in some of the colonies.

Again mercantilist policy issued a warning. The laws of Maryland and Virginia (as well as those of Barbados and Jamaica) were disallowed by the Privy Council. When this measure proved unavailing and South Carolina, Pennsylvania, New York, and the New England colonies followed the example of the planting colonies, the crown intervened. A royal proclamation was published in 1704 which established a uniform table of values for all foreign coins; the piece-of-eight was fixed at 6s. In 1708, Parliament put teeth into the proclamation by threatening all violators with prison sentences.

Bills of Credit. The device of overvaluation having failed, the colonies turned to the emission of paper money. As early as 1690, the Massachusetts legislature had led the way when it had circulated short-term bills of credit, in effect promissory notes, in order to meet extraordinary expenditures arising out of military operations. These were really tax-anticipation warrants. They were to be retired after the lapse of a stipulated period, and were to be used only for public purposes. In other words, they were not to be regarded as legal tender and could therefore be refused in the settlement of private debts. From time to time between 1700 and 1715 the Massachusetts example was followed by other colonies: Connecticut, Rhode Island, New Hampshire, New York, New Jersey, North Carolina, and South Carolina. Pennsylvania joined the others in 1723, Maryland in 1733, Virginia in 1755, and Georgia in 1760. It is important to note that up to about 1710, this device was used with restraint so that inflation did not set in.

But not for long. A number of steps were taken to lead the colonies inevitably down the road of a depreciated currency. In the first place, the bills of credit were declared legal tender, and penalties were imposed on those persons refusing to accept them in private transactions. In the second place, the dates of the collection of taxes on which the bills were based were pushed ahead, so that the issues virtually became a permanent paper currency. In the third place, taxes were not provided in adequate quantities with which to redeem the bills. In the fourth place, in some colonies, old issues were simply canceled and new ones struck off to replace them. Finally, to supplement the bills, every colony but Georgia authorized the creation of land banks with the right of note issue.

Land Banks. These banks welcomed the deposit of land mortgages and against them emitted notes, charging an interest rate of about 5 percent. South Carolina created the first in 1715. In Rhode Island the institution was particularly favored, and at one time or another nine such land banks made their appearance. In all, in this one colony, the issue of such notes came to £465,000.

Massachusetts sought to pioneer in still another direction. In 1740 its general court granted a group of private individuals a charter to form a "Land and Manufactures Bank." Capitalized at £150,000, the society was empowered to accept land as security for its stock and issue notes based on the real estate. Stock-holders were to be charged 3 percent interest if they put up land as security for their subscriptions, and this could be paid either in bills of the society or in nonperishable raw materials or rough manufactures. Furthermore, every year 5 percent of the principal was to be amortized in the same way. Loans were to be paid off in bills or in commodities. The intention of the society was plain: it was seeking to create a device for the expansion of credit based on nonperishable commodities, largely agricultural produce. (It might be said, parenthetically, that the subtreasury scheme of the Populists of the 1890s was based on a similar thought; and so were the commodity loans made by the New Deal's AAA to the growers of agricultural staples.) The idea was welcomed, and in the first—and only—year of its operations the Land and Manufactures Bank issued notes totaling some £40,000. But Parliament quickly intervened. The precedent was too dangerous a one and might lead the way to the establishment of commercial banks. As a result, the moribund English Bubble Act of 1720 was invoked, the Massachusetts Bank was outlawed, and the subscribers were compelled to make good on the notes issued.

Depreciation and Intervention. It has been said that depreciation of the colonial currency followed because of these practices. In Massachusetts, it has been estimated, the value of sterling to paper money reached a maximum ratio of 11 to 1. In Connecticut, it was 8 to 1. In New Hampshire, it got to 24 to 1. In Rhode Island it was 26 to 1. In North Carolina it was 10 to 1. In South Carolina, it was 7 to 1. In New York and Pennsylvania, successful curbs were imposed and depreciation was held within narrow limits.

The English government sought to intervene through characteristic mercantilist means. It disallowed legislation and issued instructions to its governors to veto, whenever refunding for bills was not provided and whenever the colonies tried to make the bills legal tender. But by 1750, these measures had proved unavailing and a headlong inflation was threatening; as a result, in 1751 Parliament stepped in and passed the Currency Act of that year. This law, directed at the New England colonies, forbade the creation of new land banks and once and for all declared that bills of credit could not be accepted as legal tender. Also, outstanding bills were to be retired at their maturities; new bills might be issued only when a tax base actually existed; and their terms might run for but two years for ordinary civil purposes and five years for military purposes.

The lightning struck in 1764. Parliament in this year extended the Currency Act to include all the colonies and tightened up the law. Provision was to be made for the retirement of all outstanding bills; even exceptions in the case of military expenditures were withdrawn. Contraction began to take place—notably in a period of business depression. Credit, already narrowly circumscribed, became even tighter, and bankruptcies followed. By 1774, when a slight business revival was already in operation, there was not much more than £2,400,000 in currency in all the colonies available for exchange requirements and for credit.

5. COLONIAL BUSINESS DEPRESSIONS

It is sometimes assumed that business fluctuations—cyclical waves of expansion and contraction—were brought into the modern world by industrial capitalism. This is not so: under commercial economies recurrent periods of good times and hard times have taken place. But this distinction must be had in mind: in preindustrial economies, panics and depressions largely have affected the commercial centers only; in modern times, their effects are universal. There were such business fluctuations in colonial America, certainly as far back as the beginning of the eighteenth century. Anne Bezanson and her associates have found that at Philadelphia a number of fairly well-defined short cycles can be charted against the background of two secular, or long-term, cycles.[2] The first of these long-term cycles ran from about 1720 to about 1744, and was marked by level or moderately rising prices. The second ran from 1744 to about 1784, and was marked by rising prices.

The second long-term cycle is of particular interest because of the nature of the shorter fluctuations that took place within it. From the summer of 1744 to the spring of 1749, there was a period of recovery; from 1749 to 1757,

recession followed. With the outbreak of the Seven Years' War and the increasing engagement of colonial businessmen in it—in supplying the British armies and in illegal trading with the enemy—the price curve once more moved upward. Another period of recovery and prosperity occurred, lasting until 1763. Then, with the termination of the war, the tightening up of the mercantilist controls, the stringency of money and credit, and the enacting of new fiscal measures by Parliament (the Stamp Act of 1765, the Townshend Acts of 1767), confidence waned. A recession set in, which reached depression levels during the greater part of the years 1764–69. There was a brief recovery in 1770–72, and once more recession in 1772–75.

These experiences of Philadelphia were duplicated in the other commercial centers. That is to say, there were good times as a result of the war with France, and hard times with the end of the war and England's rigorous enforcement of the Acts of Trade and her deflationary policy. The periods of recession of 1764–69 and 1772–75 are to be noted: unemployment, falling prices, tight credit, bankruptcies, and additional fiscal burdens went hand in hand with political unrest and the challenging of the Mercantilist System.

[2] Anne Bezanson, and others, *Prices in Colonial Pennsylvania* (Philadelphia, 1935).

6. THE TIGHTENING OF THE MERCANTILIST SYSTEM

The successful termination of the war against France left England in undisputed possession of Canada, the American West (up to the Mississippi River), and the East Indian trade. She emerged with a large national debt. And she was confronted by a Mercantilist System, which, as far as the colonies were concerned, was in sad disrepair. With all these problems, English imperial policies in the next decade were concerned and were carried out, in terms of the characteristic mercantilist outlook. The English program did not mark a break with mercantilist policy; rather, the intention was to strengthen it. The tightening up and the rigorous enforcement of the Acts of Trade and Navigation—which virtually put an end to the profitable and necessary colonial import-export trade with the foreign sugar islands—was part of mercantilist policy. So was the Currency Act of 1764. So was the expansion of the enumerated commodity list in the same year. So was the closing off of the West, under the Proclamation Order of 1763. So was the monopolization by England of the wine trade. So was the order that excise taxes be paid in silver.

Smuggling. The attack on the illegal West India trade was pushed with energy. As early as 1761 the colonial courts were directed to issue and enforce writs of assistance, or general search warrants, for the purpose of hunting down smugglers. In 1763, the royal navy was converted into a coast patrol. In the same year absentee sinecure holders in the customs service were ordered to their colonial posts. In 1764, a vice-admiralty court was set up for all the colonies to try offenders against the Acts of Trade. In 1768, a new board of five customs commissioners, resident in America, was installed. Everything that could conceivably be thought of was tried out in an effort to smash the trade with the foreign sugar islands. Informers were encouraged; judicial salaries were freed from dependence upon the pleasure of provincial assemblies; customs officials were guaranteed against personal liability if their zeal took illegal forms.

New revenue acts were passed in 1764 and 1765, the second including the hated stamp duties. What is frequently overlooked, however, is that these acts contained characteristic mercantilist devices calculated to contract the spheres of colonial business enterprise. Thus, provision was made for the payment of the new taxes in specie, thereby further draining the colonies of their available currency supply. In proper mercantilist fashion and to tempt colonial capital out of trade and into raw-material production, bounties again were offered to growers of hemp and flax and the English import duties on colonial whale fins were rescinded. The enumerated list was expanded to include lumber, hides and skins, pig and bar iron, and pot- and pearl ashes. In 1766, all remaining nonenumerated articles—flour, provisions, and fish—destined for European ports north of Cape Finisterre were ordered landed in England first.

The Second Molasses Act. The Sugar Act of 1764, by reenacting duties on molasses and refined sugar and forbidding entirely the importation of foreign rum, was a further blow at the hated foreign-island trade. In the same act, high duties were put on wines from the Wine Islands, and on wines, fruits, and oil from Spain and Portugal brought directly to America. On the other hand, the duties were to be nominal only, if these commodities were imported from England. Also in 1764, import duties were levied upon popular French luxury articles at colonial ports for the first time; and, in the next year, the importation of French silk stockings, gloves, and mitts was entirely banned. To complete the tale, the passage of the Currency Act of 1764, curtailing sharply the issue of colonial bills of credit, must once more be mentioned.

There can be no question that such conduct, in the midst of a bad depression, only succeeded in further limiting business activity. Colonial merchants and their legal spokesmen knew this. Thus, a memorial drawn up by New York businessmen in 1764 directly linked hard times with the contraction of the foreign-islands trade and warned Parliament that the enforcement of the old Molasses Act of 1733 "must necessarily end not only in the utter impoverishment of His Majesty's northern colonies and the destruction of their navigation but in the grievous detriment of British manufactures and artificers and the great diminution of trade, power, wealth, and naval strength of Great Britain."

The colonial clamor against the Stamp Act brought about its repeal in a year. The unpopular Townshend duties, imposed on paper, paint, and glass in 1767, were also withdrawn in 1770. A small tax on tea was allowed to remain but even this was reduced further in 1773, when a new Tea Act provided for a full drawback on the English import duties if the tea purchased was of British origin.

The Tea Act. The Tea Act came in 1773, once more in the midst of colonial depression. On the face of it, it seemed a conciliatory gesture. But this was the silken glove that concealed the iron fist. For the act also stipulated that the East India Company, long the pet of British officialdom, and now as before in financial difficulties, was to have the power of moving through its own agencies the tea of its overstocked warehouses into the colonial market. It was estimated that the company held something like 70,000,000 pounds of the leaves. What did this mean? With the drawback on the duty, Holland tea, which had been handled by colonial merchants themselves, was to be driven out of America. In the second place, by using its own ships and agents, the East India Company was going to cut down the already dwindling profits of colonial carriers, handlers, and retailers.

Arthur M. Schlesinger, in his notable mono-graph,[3] has indicated why the merchants of New York, Philadelphia, Boston, and Charleston were quick to take alarm. It was more than a matter of tea alone. Their spokesmen pointed out

that the present project of the East India Company was the entering wedge for larger and more ambitious undertakings calculated to undermine the colonial mercantile world. Their opinion was based on the fact that, in addition to the article of tea, the East India Company imported into England vast quantities of silks, calicos and other fabrics, spices, drugs, and chinaware, all commodities of staple demand; and on their fear that the success of the present venture would result in an extension of the same principle to the sale of the other articles.

The Boston Tea Party and similar manifestations elsewhere were not larks but unmistakable signs of a determination to be freed once and for all of oversea domination over the economic life of the American mainland colonies.

The Land Proclamation. There was another area in which resentments flared up. Attention has been called to the fact that Philadelphia and Albany merchants and Southern landlords had become deeply involved in the fur trade and the wild-land jobbing of the West. Southerners, especially, whose tobacco operations had not been too successful in the late 1760s, had been turning to these activities to recoup their fallen fortunes. The revitalized imperial policy dealt them a staggering blow. Presumably in the interests of working out a plan for the governing of the new region acquired from France in the American West and for putting Indian relations on a permanent footing, the Proclamation Line Order of 1763 virtually closed the whole region to colonial enterprise. Political controls were taken out of the hands of colonial governors and placed under imperial agents. Settlements were ordered abandoned. Meanwhile, agents of American companies, organized to exploit the fur trade and land promotion, cooled their heels in the ante-

[3] Arthur M. Schlesinger, *The Colonial Merchants and the American Revolution, 1763-1776.* (New York, 1917).

rooms of British politicians in London while long delays prevented the granting of charters.

The Western program, as it was finally devised in 1774 under the Quebec Act, choked off another avenue for colonial enterprise. In the whole great domain north of the Ohio and south of Virginia, colonial speculators and settlers were shut out. The land companies were denied charters. The claims of the colonies to Western lands were brushed aside. The English crown could argue that the intention here was the quieting of the suspicions of the Indians. But colonials were skeptical, particularly when it became known that English subjects were receiving special favors. The same was true of the fur trade. The Quebec Act had as one of its intentions the diverting of the fur trade from New York and Philadelphia to Montreal. That is to say, using a licensing system, the crown provided that traders were to operate under the eye of the governor of Quebec. It was apparent that British, as opposed to colonial, companies were to be favored.

To all these disabilities, the representatives of all the colonies, meeting in the First Continental Congress in 1774, replied with the Continental Association. This was an embargo on English goods and so thoroughly was it enforced that imports from England almost entirely disappeared in 1775. But by that time the American Revolution had already broken out.

7. BACKGROUND OF THE AMERICAN REVOLUTION

Bases of Separatism. It would be idle to imply that the necessity for breaking out of the closed circle of mercantilist restraint was the only impelling force that precipitated the American Revolution. There were other forces at work. The physical fact of separation by an ocean that was 3,000 miles wide and long weeks in the crossing was bound to have its effects. American institutions and the American character were forged in a climate that had many independent and novel features about it. Attention has already been called to the fact that the very act of migration across the seas constituted a kind of psychological release. And, in this sense, the loyalties of Americans to European institutions never could have the firmness and the matter-of-factness displayed by Europeans themselves. Adjustments to frontier living inevitably strengthened this awareness of independence. In this sense, the able exponent of the frontier theory of American history, Frederick Jackson Turner, has been right, of course. The American Revolution represented a conflict between a settled society and one whose social and economic relations were in a fluid form: old and new, ancient and young, turned on each other. They do not, always, of course. Nova Scotia and the British sugar islands, also young and also frontier settlements, and which also had to pay the Stamp and Townshend duties, did not join the Revolution. The point is, simply, that the will to independence is a complex of forces in which are combined economic, psychological, political, and philosophical influences.

Political Reasons for Separatism. Politically, the pull to independence was powerful. Englishmen, during the second half of the seventeenth century, had carried on a struggle for the curbing of the crown's absolutism, and they had been successful. The royal prerogative was so hedged about, so narrowed down, that, in time, it became nothing more than a symbol of state sovereignty. Notably by the Bill of Rights and the Mutiny Act of 1689, the capstone on the work of the English Revolution had been erected; Parliament was now supreme. It was inevitable that Englishmen overseas should seek to achieve comparable liberties.

Under their charters, colonials were ruled

by a governor, a legislature (of two houses), and a judiciary. The governor, except in the cases of Rhode Island and Connecticut, was appointed either by the crown or the proprietaries. The judiciary was selected by the governor, with final appeal from judicial decisions in England. The upper house of the legislature, the council, was also usually appointed by the governor. The lower house, the assembly, was popularly elected, although, throughout most of the eighteenth century the franchise was based on property and only property-owners might hold office.

By the opening of the eighteenth century, those victories that Parliament had gained at home were being pressed for in colonial legislatures. Because England made no effort to support the royal governors—indeed, it insisted as a general rule that the colonies be self-contained financially, so that even colonial wars had to be financed in considerable measure by the colonials—these administrators were being compelled more and more to accept the primacy of the colonial assemblies. These bodies insisted upon the right to initiate legislation; more important, they demanded the right to control the colonial finances—to tax and to pass money bills. They obtained both—and moved on to virtual independence. Freedom of speech on the floor, the establishment of their own rules, the right to pass on legality of elections—these became recognized powers. It should not be inferred that the English government yielded at every point. The assemblies were not permitted to control their speakers, to fix regular elections, or to establish new districts. They were not allowed to override the governor's veto. And, of course, as we have already seen, where the rights and privileges of English economic interests were threatened, the crown and Parliament stood firm. Yet, on balance, it may be said, popular sovereignty triumphed.

Fiscal power was the agency. The royal governors came to accept annual salaries from the hands of the assemblies. They were forced to give their assent to appropriation bills—particularly for military purposes. They were compelled to suffer the appointment of provincial treasurers. With the control over the purse, the assemblies were in a position to clip the wings of the governors and subordinate increasingly the executive branch to the legislative. The home government recognized this as it did also its inability to cope with the situation.

A similar development was occurring in the judicial sphere. Under the English law, the governors were permitted to appoint the judges; and they held this right despite efforts on the part of colonial assemblies to limit judicial office to good behavior. But the assemblies were not powerless, for, again through the right of appropriation, they could force judges to accept legislative surveillance and control.

Thus, a kind of colonial self-rule was emerging; but always there stood in the background the specter of the royal prerogative. Ironically, at home in England, it had been shorn of power; overseas, in the colonies, it was employed to maintain the inferior position of the colonies. The colonies had control over their own fiscal policies but Parliament had not granted this as a right. They had subordinated the governors to the assemblies; but again, this had not been formally conceded. After 1763, Parliament tried—through the royal prerogative—once more to subordinate the colonies particularly in the financial sphere. As the preliminaries of the Revolution developed, colonials might justly contend that they were only seeking to extend those rights to America which Englishmen had acquired for themselves as a result of the Puritan and Glorious Revolutions. The Declaration of Independence taxed the crown with many derelictions; this was natural, for Parliament was employing the symbol of the royal prerogative to attack liberty.

Religious Reasons for Separatism. The colonials had drunk deeply from the fount of independency as well. The Separatism of the English Levellers of the 1640s—of Lilburne, Winstanley, Bellers, and others, in that first English company of equalitarians—after all had taken firm root in America; more so, indeed, than in

England. Roger Williams and the Rhode Island experiment sprang from the loins of English Separatism. Descendants of Separatists were to be found elsewhere in the American colonies. Also, in the eighteenth century, notably in the back-country regions, the Methodism of Wesley and Whitefield set the emotions of men on fire—and stimulated them to critical examinations of prevailing institutions.

The line from independency in religion to natural rights in politics is a straight one. From Winstanley and Bellers to John Locke and Thomas Jefferson the arrow's flight is true. Americans were the children and the inheritors of the Puritan Revolution. That Thomas Jefferson (and Benjamin Franklin and John Adams, and many other colonials) should have read and venerated John Locke, the great spokesman for Englishmen's liberties, was perfectly natural.

The Declaration of Independence. The influence of Locke on Jefferson is there in the Declaration of Independence for all to read. Civil authority is established to maintain order and to guarantee the natural rights of the citizens to life, liberty, and the pursuit of happiness. A social compact is entered upon between the people and their sovereign for the maintenance of these natural rights and to assure the continuance of the ruler's powers. But this compact is not inalienable: its life is to continue as long as both parties are ready to act in good faith. And who speaks for the people? Their duly chosen representatives. Liberty is safeguarded because natural rights are inalienable; the social compact is terminable when tyranny raises its head, and because in the final analysis sovereignty is in the people itself. So John Locke in 1689 and Thomas Jefferson after him in 1776. Just as Englishmen had laid down their lives in 1640 and in 1688 in defense of these imperishable principles against the tyrannical conduct of Charles I and James II, so Americans were ready to do similarly in 1776 against the tyrant George III.

This is why the Declaration of Independence clearly speaks out against the "abuses and usurpations" of the English crown. This is why it declares simply that Americans had the right, nay the "duty to throw off such government, and to provide new guards for their future security." This is why there is catalogued a long series of "injuries and usurpations" suffered at the hands of a crown which sought to impose "an absolute tyranny over these states." This defense of liberty was no made-to-order ideology drawn up by logic-chopping lawyers, but an idealistic credo as truly a part of the American people as was their confidence in divine justice.

8. WINNING THE REVOLUTION

Winning the war with England was no easy task. The Americans possessed no trained army. They were compelled to improvise a manufacturing industry in order to supply the men in the field. There was no centralizing authority with fiscal powers and control over commerce; nor was there a machinery to marshal opinion and hunt down dissent. Nevertheless, the Revolution was successful, thanks to the devotion of the commander-in-chief George Washington and the timely assistance rendered by the French, the Dutch, and the Spanish.

We may see the tasks of the American Revolution as four. The first was the achievement of victory on land and sea. The second was the financing of the war. The third was the crushing of disloyalty at home. The fourth was the creation of stable political, social, and economic institutions.

The Military Task. To overcome the inadequacies of the domestic economy, cribbed, cabined, and confined by mercantilist restraint, was not easy. The troops under Washington required cannon, arms, and ammunition; they needed clothing; they demanded great supplies of blankets, cloth, flint, tin, copper, and salt.

The state governments did what they could to encourage domestic production. They made money grants and offered tax remissions and monopoly privileges to industrialists. Before long, cloth, powder, gun, and cannon factories were operating. How extensive this activity was is revealed in Alexander Hamilton's long catalogue in his *Report on Manufactures*. But it was not enough. Resort to Europe must be made.

From 1777 on, unofficially, from 1778 on, officially, first France, then Spain, then Holland threw in their lot with the struggling thirteen states. France began to send supplies from the Continent as early as 1777; goods from the West Indies seeped through the British blockade as well. In 1778, France recognized the United States of America and entered into a commercial and military alliance. In 1779, Spain declared war on England; in 1780, because the Dutch had come to the assistance of the Americans, England declared war on Holland. French and Dutch credits, the French fleet, even a French army: all aided in making the outcome a favorable one.

The Financial Task. Because of the limitations imposed on the Continental Congress—it was not given independent taxing powers—the financing of the War of Independence presented almost insuperable difficulties. Thanks to European good will, credit could be obtained on the Continent. The French crown made outright grants, these subsidies coming to perhaps $2,000,000. Another $6,000,000 or so was lent by the French government. Private Dutch bankers, as the war was drawing to a close, raised something like $1,300,000. The Spanish government lent $200,000. These helped in the flow of badly needed materials across the seas.

Obviously, such foreign loans were inadequate; additional funds must be had by domestic borrowings. The Continental Congress floated, at home, long-term bonds and short-term certificates of indebtedness. The total of the former was $67,000,000; of the latter, $17,-000,000. In addition, the states themselves borrowed, in all, something like $25,000,000 to aid the war effort. On its face, this looked impressive. It is important to observe, however, that Congress's inability to tax, the reluctance of the states to do so, and the cloud of uncertainty that hung over the revolutionary cause to the very end, vitiated these financing efforts seriously.

The loans could not be floated on a specie basis. They were subscribed to in paper notes of constantly falling value; and as governmental credit weakened, the resort to the printing presses became more common. Indeed, it may be said that on the somewhat more than $100,000,-000 of revolutionary loans floated, not more than $16,000,000 to $20,000,000 was realized in specie. Thus, the spiral of inflation was begun; it ended, as one might expect, with the existence of a universally valueless paper currency.

It has been said that the Continental Congress could not tax; it was given only the power to request fiscal support from the states. Here it was generally unsuccessful. In the two years from November, 1777, to October, 1779, Congress called on the states for $95,000,000. It received less than half this sum, of which the specie value was about $2,000,000. With the collapse of the first Continental paper issues, Congress in 1780 sought to obtain requisitions in kind. Having failed here, in 1781, it tried to raise among the states $10,000,000 in specie. It received something like $1,600,000.

The resort to paper bills was inevitable in such a situation. The matter was worsened when the states made the same move. Beginning in June, 1775, the Continental Congress took to financing the war expenditure with bills of credit. In the first year $6,000,000 was issued; in 1776, the total came to $19,000,000; in 1777, to $13,000,000. By that time, depreciation was marked. Therefore, in 1778, the issues totaled $63,000,000 and in 1779, $140,000,000. At the end of 1779, inflation had reached the point where a continental paper dollar was worth 2½ cents in silver.

A desperate effort was made to begin all over

again, and in 1780 the "old tenor" issues were called in at a ratio of exchange of 40 to 1. In this way, some $119,000,000 out of the $240,-000,000 continental paper was redeemed and destroyed. A more cautious policy was inaugurated in this same year, when only $4,000,000 in "new tenor" bills of exchange were issued. The ratification, finally, in 1781, of the Articles of Confederation made possible the establishment of a somewhat more stable system of public financing; while the end of the war, with the resumption of the West India trade, once more brought foreign coins into the country. It is also to be noted that the appointment in 1781 of Robert Morris, a man hostile to fiat money and devoted to the principles of free enterprise, to the post of Congressional Financier, helped to ease the strain.

State issues of bills of credit were as large as the Continental issues, coming to a total of $250,000,000. Virginia was responsible for fully half of the state paper; North and South Carolina between them issued another one third. Depreciation and repudiation were the inevitable concomitants. Virginia finally set an exchange value in specie for the redemption of its notes at 100 to 1; the North Carolina rate was 800 to 1; while the other states paid off their notes at ratios ranging from 40 to 1 to 100 to 1. By 1782, the state "old tenor" bills were pretty generally outlawed.

A price inflation naturally followed, as much from the collapse of public credit as from the scarcity of commodities. The inadequacy of production, the effectiveness of the British blockade, hoarding prompted by the general uncertainty—these helped to push prices upward. No devices could curb the rise. Extraordinary committees in the several states took measures in their own hands and treated speculators harshly. The states tried to prevent monopoly activities and forestalling; they passed price-fixing laws. Such statutes were written in Pennsylvania, Connecticut, Massachusetts, New York, and New Jersey. Interstate compacts were attempted. In December, 1776, the New England states held a price convention and drew up schedules of prices and wages based on the paper bills. In January, 1778, they tried once more, this time seeking to freeze prices at an advance of only 75 percent over those prevailing in 1774. Both attempts met with failure.

These were terrific odds to contend with. The collapse of Cornwallis's army at Yorktown in 1781 and the writing of a peace treaty in 1783 came just about in time to permit the American people to reorder their domestic house. The Treaty of Paris was half a loaf; but it was better than none. The independence of the United States of America was recognized; but it was not until 1795, under the Jay Treaty, that England was prepared to grant Americans nondiscriminatory commercial rights in the English market and limited rights in the West India market. The Mississippi River was fixed as the western boundary, with free navigation until the port of entry—that is to say, New Orleans—was reached. In view of the fact that both Floridas were turned back to Spain, it was necessary for the new republic to deal with that European power as far as port regulations were concerned. The American government recognized the validity of the prewar private debts owed to English houses; and it promised to recommend to the states that they restore confiscated loyalist properties. This last, obviously, embodied only a pious hope.

The Task of Putting Down Disloyalty. Thus, the first two tasks of the Revolution, the winning of the war and its financing, were achieved. The third, as has been said, was the putting down of disloyalty at home. This was accomplished with fire and the sword; indeed, it represents one of the dark chapters in the annals of the period. The patriots of the Revolution did not have it all their own way. In fact, as John Adams recalled it, but one third of the population supported the revolutionary cause, one third was indifferent, while another third was actively hostile and aided the crown openly or surreptitiously. Upon these—an older literature called them Tories, more recently they have been referred to as "loyalists"—the patriots wreaked their vengeance.

Who were these loyalists? By and large, they were to be found in the upper rank of colonial society: the royal officeholders, the Anglican clergy, most of the large landowners of the Middle colonies, most of the Southern merchants. The Revolution did not cut like a knife horizontally through the layers of the colonial people, converting the well-born and rich into loyalists and the small propertied men and artisans and mechanics into patriots. Men took sides regardless of class differences. But certain special interests, those referred to, were more closely allied with crown privileges than others; and these challenged the patriotic pretentions.

With the outbreak of the Revolution, customary governmental agencies broke down. The new states set about the task of creating new governmental forms; but until these were installed, power was in the hands of extraordinary committees. These so-called Committees of Safety—and there were local as well as state-wide units to be found in all the thirteen commonwealths—set about the task of maintaining order and stimulating support for the war. They gathered arms and supplied the men in the field with all their necessaries; they sought to curb speculation and profiteering; they sat as courts; they issued letters of marque and reprisal to privateers; they authorized and helped finance domestic manufacturing; they emitted bills of credit; they watched the loyalists, rounded them up, sequestered their property. Sometimes, supreme state committees continued to operate even after constitutions had been written and regular governmental authorities created. So, in New Hampshire, such a committee was in regular session from 1778 to 1784. In Pennsylvania, a committee sat until 1777; in New York and New Jersey until 1778; in Connecticut until 1783.

The loyalists were harshly treated physically. Some were undoubtedly informers and saboteurs; but the innocent suffered with the guilty as homes were burned, belongings were seized, men were shot down or imprisoned, and scores of thousands—perhaps as many as 100,000—were driven into flight. The process of confiscating or sequestering loyalist property went on systematically. First, of course, the ungranted crown lands and the estates and claims of the proprietors of Maryland and Pennsylvania were seized. Then the real property of those who had fled or who were known to support the crown was taken over and sold to discharge claims against the English government. In all the states, it has been estimated, loyalist property losses ran to about $50,000,000.

The Task of Creating Political Institutions. Meanwhile, as the fourth task of the Revolution, permanent political institutions were being created. During preparation, a contest between right and left factions among the patriots reached fever pitch. In some states, the radicals quickly seized control and wrote leveling state constitutions. In others, they were defeated, with the result that the frames of government were more conservative. In still others, they were held at arm's length until the revolutionary fires had burned themselves out; and then the more moderate influences took over.

In these debates and controversies over the forms of state government we find the origins of Jeffersonian democracy. As has been said, the connection with Leveller theory and Lockian doctrine is clear. The radicals were democrats: they were fearful of a powerful executive; they sought a larger measure of popular control over executive and judiciary; they wanted the recognition of local rights. These radicals, too, were populists in the American sense: because they were agrarians and debtors they pushed for the passage of the easy-money legislation to which reference has already been made.

The leveling constitution written by the radicals in Pennsylvania in 1776 was typical of the sentiments of this group. This document granted the franchise to all tax-paying freemen, whether they were freeholders or not. It contained a bill of rights. It provided for a single-chambered house which was to choose the state's civil and judicial officers. To prevent usurpation, it created a multiple executive and a council of censors; the latter was to meet every seven years to decide whether government was acting in conformity with liberty and justice. The constitutional conventions of North Carolina, Delaware, New Hampshire, and Georgia drew up somewhat similar fundamental laws. Generally, it may be said, the following were their characteristics: Qualifications for voting were made more generous, although universal manhood suffrage did not come in the eastern states for another two generations. The rights of the back country to legislative representation were recognized. Local governments for new regions were provided. The powers of the legislature, at the expense of the executive, were expanded. Only the popularly chosen house might originate money bills. The veto power of the governor was either abolished or drastically curbed, and the governor himself was to be either elected or named by the legislature. His term in office, as well, was to be short. Similarly, efforts were made to control the judiciary, which was to be elected by the voters or the legislature and which might be removed easily.

The radical forces did not have their way everywhere. In Rhode Island and Connecticut they were not permitted to write constitutions, despite the fact that in the former at least they were completely in control. A New York constitution and a Massachusetts constitution, written later, were more conservative documents. In fact, the conservatives recaptured power in New Hampshire in 1784 and in Pennsylvania in 1790. For an interval, at any rate, the democratic forces were being checked.

The Articles of Confederation. The conservative tendency appeared also in the central government. The writing and final ratification of the Articles of Confederation marked another victory for moderating influences. The Articles of Confederation had been drawn up in the Continental Congress late in 1777 and submitted to the states for unanimous ratification. The last, Maryland, did not do so until March, 1781; so that it was not until the Revolutionary War was virtually over that "a perpetual union" and a "league of friendship" was created. The Articles did not mean a strong central government; but they were a decided advance over the faltering rule of the old Congress. In any event, the conservatives were pleased, so much so that one of their opponents wrote: "Toryism is triumphant here. They have displaced every Whig but the President."

Under the Articles, whereby each state was to have a single vote, the central government received only limited powers. There was to be no independent executive department or a permanent judiciary. The powers granted to the Congress were direct and explicit; all those ungranted were reserved to the states. The Congress could not levy taxes; nor could it regulate domestic commerce. Its financing was founded largely upon the requisition system; and in this case, levies upon the states were to be apportioned on the basis of the value of real property. It was, however, given the right to write commercial treaties with foreign powers and to regulate Indian affairs. Its greatest triumph was the establishment of a public domain. Because of conflicting state claims to Western lands, the decision was taken to turn over all these territories to the central government. The Ordinance of 1785, for the governance of the Western regions, flowed from this cession. By 1786, in fact, all the states but North Carolina, South Carolina, and Georgia had turned over their rights; the result was, the sale of public lands to freeholders constituted an important element in central financing.

Beside the reservation of ungranted powers, the states limited the Congress's scope in other ways. The consent of at least nine states was necessary for the enactment of legislation affecting the coinage, the issuance of bills of credit, the borrowing or appropriations of funds, and the declaration of war. In this connection, it is interesting to observe that the states refused to allow the Congress to pass tariff legislation, although only light import duties were proposed. Finally, the states reserved to themselves explicitly the sole right to enact legislation affecting contracts; they also had the rights to coin money and issue bills of exchange. Here was the point, apparently, where the populists would not yield.

Results of the Revolution. Despite these uncertainties, the Revolution was won, the connection with mercantilism was ended. Business enterprise had a freer world in which to range. Many inequities were wiped out. And real advances in the direction of the achievement of democratic rights were made.

As far as *foreign trade* was concerned, the end of mercantilist restraint permitted the development of direct channels of intercourse with the European continent, the colonial possessions of the continental powers, and with the Middle and Far East. The glorious days of the India and China trades were to revitalize American mercantile fortunes. As far as the domestic trade was concerned, the push across the mountains into Kentucky, Tennessee, and the Western Reserve was to open new markets for Eastern businessmen.

As far as *manufacturing* was concerned, freedom made possible new avenues for enterprise. Stimulated by wartime necessity and state aid —bounties and prizes, tariff walls—manufacturing sprang up in a vast variety of fields. In addition to cannons, guns, and powder, Americans took to making ironware, pottery, textiles, paper, glass, leather goods, notions. The capitals involved were not great and organizational forms were still at preindustrial levels in many fields—that is to say, the iron plantation and the putting-out system existed. There were a number of reasons why a real industrial renaissance was deferred in America for at least three generations more. The early American tariffs, both state under the Confederation and federal under the Union, were not prohibitory; English goods therefore flowed into America in an unabated flood. In the second place, capital found more remunerative returns in other areas of enterprise: in banking, the building of public works, the opening up of the wild lands of the West, the improvement of urban real estate, notably in the domestic and foreign trade.

As far as the *land* was concerned, the gains were notable. The ungranted crown lands were taken over by the states of New Hampshire, New York, Virginia, North Carolina, South Carolina, and Georgia. With these were swept away feudal carry-overs: the quitrents and the rights of the King's Woods, by which royal agents had claimed the tallest and best stands of timber for the king's navy. Likewise, the prohibitions against settlement in the region beyond the crest of the Appalachians, under the Proclamation Order of 1763 and the Quebec Act of 1774, were flouted. Eager colonists and land agents—by 1790 some 221,000 persons— pressed into Kentucky, Tennessee, the Western Reserve, and Wabash countries, and into the Southwest.

Proprietary and absentee estates were seized —the ungranted lands of the Penns and the Calverts, the great Granville holdings in North Carolina, the five million acres belonging to Lord Halifax in Virginia. Reference has already been made to the treatment of the real property of loyalists. By Congressional enactment and by action of state Committees of Safety and legislatures, property was taken over, sold, and the proceeds converted into central and state loan certificates.

The *democratization of land tenure* made giant strides. The attack was directed chiefly against those feudal props of land concentration—entail and primogeniture. The elimination of the right to entail estates began early. South Carolina passed such a law in 1775, Virginia in 1776, Georgia in 1776 and 1777, North Carolina, Maryland, and New York in 1784 and 1786. By 1790, the reform had been completed everywhere. As regards primogeniture, the task of ending it and establishing equal inheritance for all children was begun during the Revolution and completed by 1800.

Another great democratic achievement was the *disestablishment of churches.* The Anglican Church had been established by law in many of the colonies; that is to say, it had special property rights, its clergy were paid out of taxes, and all inhabitants were required to attend services. The new state constitutions struck at ecclesiastical privilege and disestablishment was provided for by Maryland, North Carolina, and Virginia, all in 1776. Similarly, the fundamental laws of New York, Georgia, and South Carolina guaranteed freedom of worship to Christians of all sects. The very first clause of the first Amendment to the Constitution closed the door for all time to the creation of any church establishment in the United States. In the same democratic spirit, the Southern states moved to stop the wretched African slave trade; while a number of the Northern states provided for gradual abolition. Attacks were directed against the cruel penal codes the colonists had brought over from England. And, under the influence of the Enlightenment, some of the state constitutions provided for popular education.

Despite the swing of the pendulum in the opposite direction during 1783–1800, great and lasting gains in the achievement of democratic rights in the economic and political fields had been won by the Revolution.

JONATHAN EDWARDS

THINKING MAN concerns himself with the world he sees, the relations of men in that world, and the reasons why man and that world exist. Prerevolutionary America had raised no wall of specialization between those disciplines; it was still possible for the same person to have a fruitful interest in all three. The old hierarchy of learning had not yet been altered, to be sure: physical science was still an avocation, the social studies had only begun to emerge as a separate branch of inquiry, the proper interest of the American scholar was his God. Cotton Mather and Jonathan Edwards both were concerned with their fellow men and the natural world: Mather was chosen a fellow of the Royal Society; Edwards's youthful observations on spiders won admiration from a professional entomologist more than a century later—but neither would have considered science as more than a secondary interest. Nothing less than the effort to comprehend the purpose of the universe was worthy the full attention of a Christian scholar.

But while Edwards was setting forth the worthlessness of the natural man, Benjamin Franklin was trying to improve that same complex creature. Whatever the proper task of the professional man of learning might be, the business of man in society was the better understanding of his physical and social world. As Edwards stimulated and tried to guide the emotional forces that produced the religious revival of the 1730s and early 1740s, so Franklin expressed the active, secular, bustling spirit which found so much to do that it could dismiss the claims of eternity with a benevolent deism.

As Cotton Mather looks forward to Franklin in scientific interest and practical benevolence, though not in religious philosophy, so Jonathan Edwards (1703–1758) looks forward to Emerson in his emphasis on intuition and emotion, though the Transcendental reliance on an unchecked inner witness would have seemed mere "enthusiasm" to him. For Edwards's appreciation of the emotional aspects of the spiritual life did not make him indifferent to logic. He refused to forego either rapture or reason. Each had its place in religion and the Christian life, but neither could bring a valid message unless that agreed with Scripture.

Such concern with authority came naturally to a man whose mother was descended from a ministerial family and whose father had returned to the ministry after two American generations had worked and prospered at the cooper's bench. Jonathan Edwards began training for his lifework when he entered Yale at thirteen. His student record of thought and reading as a youth newly exposed to John Locke and Ralph Cudworth shows him a keen reasoner and an apt builder of systems. The Platonic idealism which he found so congenial in Cudworth was the base of much of Edwards's later thinking, though he never worked in a metaphysics separated from his religious interests.

After two years of graduate study followed by a period of tutoring at the college, he turned from scholarship to practical work in the ministry and, in 1729, succeeded to his maternal grandfather's pulpit at Northampton. Here Edwards married, reared a large family, studied and labored to waken his congregation from religious lethargy. By 1735, first the young people and then their elders were roused to concern for their sinful state. Northampton experienced a season of spiritual renewal eloquently set forth in Edwards's *Faithful Narrative of a Surprizing Work of God* (1737). This pamphlet was widely read, both in the colonies and abroad, and probably had considerable influence in setting the pattern for the Great Awakening of the 1740s and for subsequent religious revivals. Though George Whitefield's preaching had a wider and more direct immediate influence in 1740, it was Edwards who defended the whole revival movement when reaction from its extravagances had brought it into discredit.

Edwards's concern with the experience of conversion, which lay at the root of the faith encouraged by revivals, led him to views which his congregation could not share. Since only a change of heart could make a Christian of an inherently corrupt "natural man," none but those who could profess belief that such a change had occurred in them might properly be admitted to the Lord's Supper. Though Edwards's was the more ancient opinion, all the practice of the last generation contradicted it and his congregation refused to deny the sacrament to people instructed in doctrine and seemly in life because they could not sincerely state that they had been converted.

This theological dispute, embittered by long-standing quarrels and dissensions within the town of Northampton, finally led to Edwards's dismissal in 1750. The following summer, he went to Stockbridge as a missionary to the Indians settled there. In this Massachusetts frontier community he lived and worked for the seven years that produced his best-known book, *The Enquiry into the Freedom of the Will* (1754), together with his defense of the doctrine of original sin and the posthumously published treatises on the nature of true virtue and the end for which God created the world. From Stockbridge, Edwards was called to the presidency of Princeton, as successor to his son-in-law, the elder Aaron Burr, but he died of the effects of smallpox inoculation within a month of assuming that office.

In comparison with the span of Mather's or Franklin's life, Edwards had been cut off at fifty-five. Productively viewed, he can hardly be considered to have died young. His first widely circulated sermon, *God Glorified in Man's Dependence* (1731), had heartened Calvinist orthodoxy against the Arminian view, which claimed man's own efforts could help him to salvation. Edwards's later work gave the contrary view even more solid foundation in argument. But it is not in the contrivance of "museum pieces of Christian thought" that Edwards illuminates the American mind of this period. To future religious thinking he gave impetus both by his followers and through his opponents, who contrived to turn him from a quiet-voiced, reasoning mystic into a hell-roaring expounder of damnation. To the tepid religious life of his own time, Edwards helped bring the Great Awakening. He was one of the influences fostering that revival and he continued to defend it against friend and enemy alike.

That defense is most completely presented in the *Treatise Concerning Religious Affections* (1746), which William James regarded as an "admirably rich and delicate description" of the religious experience. Though Edwards admitted the justice of the criticism directed at the hysterical manifestations of the Great Awakening, he insisted that emotion alone could serve as a spur to action. Consequently, emotion should have an important place in the religious life: the problem was to distinguish the genuine from the false, and, for this, Edwards's criteria are as dynamic as his idea of the religious emotions themselves. A holy life and a whole-hearted acceptance of the sovereignty of God would mark the person who actually had been given that supernatural sense which alone could direct fallen "natural man" toward disinterested love of God.

The selection here reprinted, known as the "Personal Narrative" is taken from *The Works of President Edwards*, edited by Samuel Austin (10 vols., Worcester, Mass., 1808–1810).

The Personal Narrative

BY JONATHAN EDWARDS

. . . I HAD a variety of concerns and exercises about my soul from my childhood; but had two more remarkable seasons of awakening, before I met with that change by which I was brought to those new dispositions, and that new sense of things, that I have since had. The first time was when I was a boy, some years before I went to college, at a time of remarkable awakening in my father's congregation. I was then very much affected for many months, and concerned about the things of religion, and my soul's salvation; and was abundant in duties. I used to pray five times a day in secret, and to spend much time in religious talk with other boys; and used to meet with them to pray together. I experienced I know not what kind of delight in religion. My mind was much engaged in it, and had much selfrighteous pleasure; and it was my delight to abound in religious duties. I with some of my schoolmates joined together, and built a booth in a swamp, in a very retired spot, for a place of prayer. And besides, I had particular secret places of my own in the woods, where I used to retire by myself; and was from time to time much affected. My affections seemed to be lively and easily moved, and I seemed to be in my element when engaged in religious duties. And I am ready to think, many are deceived with such affections, and such a kind of delight as I then had in religion, and mistake it for grace.

But in process of time, my convictions and affections wore off; and I entirely lost all those affections and delights and left off secret prayer, at least as to any constant performance of it; and returned like a dog to his vomit, and went on in the ways of sin. Indeed I was at times very uneasy, especially towards the latter part of my time at college; when it pleased God, to seize me with a pleurisy; in which he brought me nigh to the grave, and shook me over the pit of hell. And yet, it was not long after my recovery, before I fell again into my old ways of sin. But God would not suffer me to go on with any quietness; I had great and violent inward struggles, till, after many conflicts with wicked inclinations, repeated resolutions, and bonds that I laid myself under by a kind of vows to God, I was brought wholly to break off all former wicked ways, and all ways of known outward sin; and to apply myself to seek salvation, and practise many religious duties; but without that kind of affection and delight which I had for-

merly experienced. My concern now wrought more by inward struggles and conflicts, and self-reflections. I made seeking my salvation the main business of my life. But yet, it seems to me, I sought after a miserable manner; which has made me sometimes since to question, whether ever it issued in that which was saving; being ready to doubt, whether such miserable seeking ever succeeded. I was indeed brought to seek salvation in a manner that I never was before; I felt a spirit to part with all things in the world, for an interest in Christ. My concern continued and prevailed, with many exercising thoughts and inward struggles; but yet it never seemed to be proper to express that concern by the name of terror.

From my childhood up, my mind had been full of objections against the doctrine of God's sovereignty, in choosing whom he would to eternal life, and rejecting whom he pleased; leaving them eternally to perish, and be everlastingly tormented in hell. It used to appear like a horrible doctrine to me. But I remember the time very well, when I seemed to be convinced, and fully satisfied, as to this sovereignty of God, and his justice in thus eternally disposing of men, according to his sovereign pleasure. But never could give an account, how, or by what means, I was thus convinced, not in the least imagining at the time, nor a long time after, that there was any extraordinary influence of God's Spirit in it; but only that now I saw further, and my reason apprehended the justice and reasonableness of it. However, my mind rested in it; and it put an end to all those cavils and objections. And there has been a wonderful alteration in my mind, with respect to the doctrine of God's sovereignty, from that day to this; so that I scarce ever have found so much as the rising of an objection against it, in the most absolute sense, in God's shewing mercy to whom he will shew mercy, and hardening whom he will. God's absolute sovereignty and justice, with respect to salvation and damnation, is what my mind seems to rest assured of, as much as of any thing that I see with my eyes; at least it is so at times. But I have often, since that first conviction, had quite another kind of sense of God's sovereignty than I had then. I have often since had not only a conviction, but a delightful conviction. The doctrine has very often appeared exceeding pleasant, bright, and sweet. Absolute sovereignty is what I love to ascribe to God. But my first conviction was not so.

The first instance that I remember of that sort of inward, sweet delight in God and divine things that I have lived much in since, was on reading those words, 1 Tim. i. 17. *Now unto the King eternal, immortal, invisible, the only wise God, be honor and glory for ever and ever, Amen.* As I read the words, there came into my soul, and was as it were diffused through it, a sense of the glory of the Divine Being; a new sense, quite different from any thing I ever experienced before. Never any words of scripture seemed to me as these words did. I thought with myself, how excellent a Being that was, and how happy I should be, if I might enjoy that God, and be rapt up to him in heaven, and be as it were swallowed up in him for ever! I kept saying, and as it were singing over these words of scripture to myself; and went to pray to God that I might enjoy him, and prayed in a manner quite different from what I used to do; with a new sort of affection. But it never came into my thought, that there was any thing spiritual, or of a saving nature in this.

From about that time, I began to have a new kind of apprehensions and ideas of Christ, and the work of redemption, and the glorious way of salvation by him. An inward, sweet sense of these things, at times, came into my heart; and my soul was led away in pleasant views and contemplations of them. And my mind was greatly engaged to spend my time in reading and meditating on Christ, on the beauty and excellency of his person, and the lovely way of salvation by free grace in him. I found no books so delightful to me, as those that treated of these subjects. Those words Cant. ii. 1, used to be abundantly with me, *I am the Rose of Sharon, and the Lilly of the valleys.* The words seemed to me, sweetly to represent the loveliness and beauty of Jesus Christ. The whole book of Canticles used to be pleasant to me, and I used to be much in reading it, about that time; and found, from time to time, an inward sweetness, that would carry me away, in my contemplations. This I know not how to express otherwise, than by a calm, sweet abstraction of soul from all the concerns of this world; and sometimes a kind of vision, or fixed ideas and imaginations, of being alone in the mountains, or some solitary wilderness, far from all mankind, sweetly conversing with Christ, and wrapt and swallowed up in God. The sense I had of divine things, would often of a sudden kindle up, as it were, a sweet burning in my heart; an ardor of soul, that I know not how to express.

Not long after I first began to experience these things, I gave an account to my father of some things that had passed in my mind. I was pretty much affected by the discourse we had together; and when the discourse was ended, I walked abroad alone, in a solitary place in my father's pasture, for contemplation. And as I was walking there, and looking up on the sky and clouds, there came into my mind so sweet a sense of the glorious *majesty* and *grace* of God, that I know not how to express. I seemed to see them both in a sweet conjunction; majesty and meekness joined together; it was a sweet, and gentle, and holy majesty; and also a majestic meekness; an awful sweetness; a high, and great, and holy gentleness.

After this my sense of divine things gradually increased, and became more and more lively, and had more of that inward sweetness. The appearance of every thing was altered; there seemed to be, as it were, a calm, sweet cast, or appearance of divine glory, in almost every thing. God's excellency, his wisdom, his purity and love, seemed to appear in every thing; in the sun, moon, and stars; in the clouds, and blue sky; in the grass, flowers, trees; in the water, and all nature; which used greatly to fix my mind. I often used to sit and view the moon for continuance; and in the day, spent much time in viewing the clouds and sky, to behold the sweet glory of God in these things; in the mean time, singing forth, with a low voice, my contemplations of the Creator and Redeemer. And scarce any thing, among all the works of nature, was so sweet to me as thunder and lightning; formerly, nothing had been so terrible to me. Before, I used to be uncommonly terrified with thunder, and to be struck with terror when I saw a thunder storm rising; but now, on the contrary, it rejoiced me. I felt God, so to speak, at the first appearance of a thunder storm; and used to take the opportunity, at such times, to fix myself in order to view the clouds, and see the lightnings play, and hear the majestic and awful voice of God's thunder, which oftentimes was exceedingly entertaining, leading me to sweet contemplations of my great and glorious God. While thus engaged, it always seemed natural to me to sing, or chant for my meditations; or, to speak my thoughts in soliloquies with a singing voice.

I felt then great satisfaction, as to my good state; but that did not content me. I had vehement longings of soul after God and Christ, and after more holiness, wherewith my heart seemed to be full, and ready to break; which often brought to my mind the words of the Psalmist, Psal. cxix. 28. *My soul breaketh for the longing it hath.* I often felt a mourning and lamenting in my heart, that I had not turned to God sooner, that I might have had more time to grow in grace. My mind was greatly fixed on divine things; almost perpetually in the contemplation of them. I spent most of my time in thinking of divine things, year after year; often walking alone in the woods, and solitary places, for meditation, soliloquy, and prayer, and converse with God; and it was always my manner, at such times, to sing forth my contemplations. I was almost constantly in ejaculatory prayer, wherever I was. Prayer seemed to be natural to me, as the breath by which the inward burnings of my heart had vent. The delights which I now felt in the things of religion, were of an exceeding different kind from those before mentioned, that I had when a boy; and what I then had no more notion of, than one born blind has of pleasant and beautiful colors. They were of a more inward, pure, soul animating and refreshing nature. Those former delights never reached the heart; and did not arise from any sight of the divine excellency of the things of God; or any taste of the soul satisfying and life-giving good there is in them.

My sense of divine things seemed gradually to increase, until I went to preach at Newyork, which was about a year and a half after they began; and while I was there, I felt them, very sensibly, in a much higher degree than I had done before. My longings after God and holiness, were much increased. Pure and humble, holy and heavenly Christianity, appeared exceeding amiable to me. I felt a burning desire to be in every thing a complete Christian; and conformed to the blessed image of Christ; and that I might live, in all things, according to the pure, sweet and blessed rules of the gospel. I had an eager thirsting after progress in these things; which put me upon pursuing and pressing after them. It was my continual strife day and night, and constant inquiry, how I should *be* more holy, and *live* more holily, and more becoming a child of God, and a disciple of Christ. I now sought an increase of grace and holiness, and a holy life, with much more earnestness, than ever I sought grace before I had it. I used to be continually examining myself, and studying and contriving for likely ways and means, how I should live holily, with far greater diligence and earnestness, than ever I pursued any thing in my life; but yet with too great a dependence on my own strength; which afterwards proved a great damage to me. My experience had not then taught me, as it has done since, my extreme feebleness and impotence, every manner of way; and the bottomless depths of secret corruption and deceit there was in my heart. However, I went on with my eager pursuit after more holiness, and conformity to Christ.

The heaven I desired was a heaven of holiness; to be with God, and to spend my eternity in divine love, and holy communion with Christ. My mind was very much taken up with contemplations on heaven, and the enjoyments there; and living there in perfect holiness, humility and love: And it used at that time to appear a great part of the happiness of heaven, that there the saints could express their love to Christ. It appeared to me a great clog and burden, that what I felt within, I could not express as I desired. The inward ardor of my soul, seemed to be hindered and pent up, and could not freely flame out as it would. I used often to think, how in heaven this principle should freely and fully vent and express itself. Heaven appeared exceedingly delightful, as a world of love; and that all happiness consisted in living in pure, humble, heavenly, divine love.

I remember the thoughts I used then to have of holiness; and said sometimes to myself, "I do certainly know that I love holiness, such as the gospel prescribes." It appeared to me, that there was nothing in it but what was ravishingly lovely; the highest beauty and amiableness . . . . a *divine* beauty; far purer than any thing here upon earth; and that every thing else was like mire and defilement, in comparison of it.

Holiness, as I then wrote down some of my contemplations on it, appeared to me to be of a sweet, pleasant, charming, serene, calm nature; which brought an inexpressible purity, brightness, peacefulness and ravishment to the soul. In other words, that it made the soul like a field or garden of God, with all manner of pleasant flowers; all pleasant, delightful, and undisturbed; enjoying a sweet calm, and the gently vivifying beams of the sun. The soul of a true Christian, as I then wrote my meditations, appeared like such a little white flower as we see in the spring of the year; low and humble on the ground, opening its bosom to receive the pleasant beams of the sun's glory; rejoicing as it were in a calm rapture; diffusing around a sweet fragrancy; standing peacefully and lovingly, in the midst of other flowers round about; all in like manner opening their bosoms, to drink in the light of the sun. There was no part of creature holiness, that I had so great a sense of its loveliness, as humility, brokenness of heart and poverty of spirit; and there was nothing that I so earnestly longed for. My heart panted after this, to lie low before God, as in the dust; that I might be nothing, and that God might be ALL, that I might become as a little child.

While at Newyork, I was sometimes much affected with reflections on my past life, considering how late it was before I began to be truly religious; and how wickedly I had lived till then;

and once so as to weep abundantly, and for a considerable time together.

On *January* 12, 1723. I made a solemn dedication of myself to God, and wrote it down; giving up myself, and all that I had to God; to be for the future in no respect my own; to act as one that had no right to himself, in any respect. And solemnly vowed to take God for my whole portion and felicity; looking on nothing else as any part of my happiness, nor acting as if it were; and his law for the constant rule of my obedience; engaging to fight with all my might, against the world, the flesh and the devil, to the end of my life. But I have reason to be infinitely humbled, when I consider how much I have failed of answering my obligation.

I had then abundance of sweet religious conversation in the family where I lived, with Mr. John Smith and his pious mother. My heart was knit in affection to those in whom were appearances of true piety; and I could bear the thoughts of no other companions, but such as were holy, and the disciples of the blessed Jesus. I had great longings for the advancement of Christ's kingdom in the world; and my secret prayer used to be, in great part, taken up in praying for it. If I heard the least hint of any thing that happened, in any part of the world, that appeared, in some respect or other, to have a favorable aspect on the interest of Christ's kingdom, my soul eagerly catched at it; and it would much animate and refresh me. I used to be eager to read public news letters, mainly for that end; to see if I could not find some news favorable to the interest of religion in the world.

I very frequently used to retire into a solitary place, on the banks of Hudson's river, at some distance from the city, for contemplation on divine things, and secret converse with God; and had many sweet hours there. Sometimes Mr. Smith and I walked there together, to converse on the things of God; and our conversation used to turn much on the advancement of Christ's kingdom in the world, and the glorious things that God would accomplish for his church in the latter days. I had then, and at other times the greatest delight in the holy scriptures, of any book whatsoever. Oftentimes in reading it, every word seemed to touch my heart. I felt a harmony between something in my heart, and those sweet and powerful words. I seemed often to see so much light exhibited by every sentence, and such a refreshing food communicated, that I could not get along in reading; often dwelling long on one sentence, to see the wonders contained in it; and yet almost every sentence seemed to be full of wonders.

I came away from Newyork in the month of April, 1723, and had a most bitter parting with Madam Smith and her son. My heart seemed to sink within me at leaving the family and city, where I had enjoyed so many sweet and pleasant days. I went from Newyork to Weathersfield, by water, and as I sailed away, I kept sight of the city as long as I could. However, that night, after this sorrowful parting, I was greatly comforted in God at Westchester, where we went ashore to lodge; and had a pleasant time of it all the voyage to Saybrook. It was sweet to me to think of meeting dear Christians in heaven, where we should never part more. At Saybrook we went ashore to lodge, on Saturday, and there kept the Sabbath; where I had a sweet and refreshing season, walking alone in the fields.

After I came home to Windsor, I remained much in a like frame of mind, as when at Newyork; only sometimes I felt my heart ready to sink with the thoughts of my friends at Newyork. My support was in contemplations on the heavenly state; as I find in my Diary of May 1, 1723. It was a comfort to think of that state, where there is fullness of joy; where reigns heavenly, calm, and delightful love, without alloy; where there are continually the dearest expressions of this love; where is the enjoyment of the persons loved, without ever parting; where those persons who appear so lovely in this world, will really be inexpressibly more lovely and full of love to us. And how sweetly will the mutual lovers join together to sing the praises of God and the Lamb! How will it fill us with joy to think, that this enjoyment, these sweet exercises will never cease, but will last to all eternity! . . . . I continued much in the same frame, in the general, as when at Newyork, till I went to Newhaven as tutor to the college; particularly once at Bolton, on a journey from Boston, while walking out alone in the fields. After I went to Newhaven I sunk in religion; my mind being diverted from my eager pursuits after holiness, by some affairs that greatly perplexed and distracted my thoughts.

In September, 1725, I was taken ill at Newhaven, and while endeavoring to go home to Windsor, was so ill at the North Village, that I could go no further; where I lay sick for about a quarter of a year. In this sickness God was pleased to visit me again with the sweet influences of his Spirit. My mind was greatly engaged there in divine, pleasant contemplations, and longings of soul. I observed that those who watched with me, would often be looking out wishfully for the morning; which brought to my mind those words of the psalmist, and which my soul with delight made its own language, *My soul waiteth for the Lord, more than they that watch for the morning, I say, more than they that watch for the morning;* and when the light of day came in at the windows, it refreshed my soul from one morning to another. It seemed to be some image of the light of God's glory.

I remember, about that time, I used greatly to long for the conversion of some that I was concerned with; I could gladly honor them, and with delight be a servant to them, and lie at their feet, if they were but truly holy. But, some time after this, I was again greatly diverted in my mind with some temporal concerns that exceedingly took up my thoughts, greatly to the wounding of my soul; and went on through various exercises, that it would be tedious to relate, which gave me much more experience of my own heart, than ever I had before.

Since I came to this town [Northampton], I have often had sweet complacency in God, in views of his glorious perfections and the excellency of Jesus Christ. God has appeared to me a glorious and lovely Being, chiefly on the account of his holiness. The holiness of God has always appeared to me the most lovely of all his attributes. The doctrines of God's absolute sovereignty, and free grace, in shewing mercy to whom he would shew mercy; and man's absolute dependence on the operations of God's Holy Spirit, have very often appeared to me as sweet and glorious doctrines. These doctrines have been much my delight. God's sovereignty has ever appeared to me, great part of his glory. It has often been my delight to approach God, and adore him as a sovereign God, and ask sovereign mercy of him.

I have loved the doctrines of the gospel; they have been to my soul like green pastures. The gospel has seemed to me the richest treasure; the treasure that I have most desired, and longed that it might dwell richly in me. The way of salvation by Christ has appeared, in a general way, glorious and excellent, most pleasant and most beautiful. It has often seemed to me, that it would in a great measure spoil heaven, to receive it in any other way. That text has often been affecting and delightful to me, Isa. xxxii. 2. *A man shall be an hiding place from the wind, and a covert from the tempest, &c.*

It has often appeared to me delightful, to be united to Christ; to have him for my head, and to be a member of his body; also to have Christ for my teacher and prophet. I very often think with sweetness, and longings, and pantings of soul, of being a little child, taking hold of Christ, to be led by him through the wilderness of this world. That text, Matth. xviii. 3, has often been sweet to me, *except ye be converted and become as little children, &c.* I love to think of coming to Christ, to receive salvation of him, poor in spirit, and quite empty of self, humbly exalting him alone; cut off entirely from my own root, in order to grow into, and out of Christ; to have God in Christ to be all in all; and to live by faith on the son of God, a life of humble, unfeigned confidence in him. That scripture has often been sweet to me, Psal. cxv. 1. *Not unto us, O Lord, not unto us, but unto thy name give glory, for thy mercy, and for thy truth's sake.* And those words of Christ, Luke x. 21. *In that hour Jesus rejoiced in spirit, and said, I thank thee, O Father, Lord of heaven and earth, that thou hast hid these things from the wise and prudent, and hast revealed them unto babes: Even so, Father, for so it seemed good in thy sight.* That sovereignty of God which Christ rejoiced in, seemed to me worthy of such joy; and that rejoicing seemed to shew the excellency of Christ, and of what spirit he was.

Sometimes, only mentioning a single word caused my heart to burn within me; or only seeing the name of Christ, or the name of some attribute of God. And God has appeared glorious to me, on account of the Trinity. It has made me have exalting thoughts of God, that he subsists in three persons; Father, Son and Holy Ghost. The sweetest joys and delights I have experienced, have not been those that have arisen from a hope of my own good estate; but in a direct view of the glorious things of the gospel. When I enjoy this sweetness, it seems to carry me above the thoughts of my own estate; it seems at such times a loss that I cannot bear, to take off my eye from the glorious, pleasant object I behold without me, to turn my eye in upon myself, and my own good estate.

My heart has been much on the advancement of Christ's kingdom in the world. The histories of the past advancement of Christ's kingdom have been sweet to me. When I have read histories of past ages, the pleasantest thing in all my reading has been, to read of the kingdom of Christ being promoted. And when I have expected, in my reading, to come to any such thing, I have rejoiced in the prospect, all the way as I read. And my mind has been much entertained and delighted with the scripture promises and prophecies, which relate to the future glorious advancement of Christ's kingdom upon earth.

I have sometimes had a sense of the excellent fulness of Christ, and his meetness and suitableness as a Saviour; whereby he has appeared to me, far above all, the chief of ten thousands. His blood and atonement have appeared sweet, and his righteousness sweet; which was always accompanied with ardency of spirit; and inward strugglings and breathings, and groanings that cannot be uttered, to be emptied of myself, and swallowed up in Christ.

Once, as I rode out into the woods for my health, in 1737, having alighted from my horse in a retired place, as my manner commonly has been, to walk for divine contemplation and prayer, I had a view that for me was extraordinary, of the glory of the Son of God, as Mediator between God and man, and his wonderful, great, full, pure and sweet grace and love, and meek and gentle condescension. This grace that appeared so calm and sweet, appeared also great above the heavens. The person of Christ appeared ineffably excellent with an excellency great enough to swallow up all thought and conception . . . which continued as near as I can judge, about an hour; which kept me the greater part of the time in a flood of tears, and weeping aloud. I felt an ardency of soul to be, what I know not otherwise how to express, emptied and annihilated; to lie in the dust, and to be full of Christ alone; to love him with a holy and pure love; to trust in him; to live upon him; to serve and follow him; and to be perfectly sanctified and made pure, with a divine and heavenly purity. I have, several other times, had views very much of the same nature, and which have had the same effects.

I have many times had a sense of the glory of the third person in the Trinity, in his office of Sanctifier; in his holy operations, communicating divine light and life to the soul. God, in the communications of his Holy Spirit, has appeared as an infinite fountain of divine glory and sweetness; being full, and sufficient to fill and satisfy the soul; pouring forth itself in sweet communications; like the sun in its glory, sweetly and pleasantly diffusing light and life. And I have sometimes had an affecting sense of the excellency of the word of God, as a word of life; as the light of life; a sweet, excellent lifegiving word; accompanied with a thirsting after that word, that it might dwell richly in my heart.

Often, since I lived in this town, I have had very affecting views of my own sinfulness and vileness; very frequently to such a degree as to hold me in a kind of loud weeping, sometimes for a considerable time together; so that I have often been forced to shut myself up. I have had a vastly greater sense of my own wickedness, and the badness of my heart, than ever I had before my conversion. It has often appeared to me, that if God should mark iniquity against me, I should appear the very worst of all mankind; of all that have been, since the beginning of the world to this time; and that I should have by far the lowest place in hell. When others, that have come to talk with me about their soul concerns, have expressed the sense they have had of their own wickedness, by saying that it seemed to them, that they were as bad as the devil himself; I thought their expressions seemed exceeding faint and feeble, to represent my wickedness.

My wickedness, as I am in myself, has long appeared to me perfectly ineffable, and swallowing up all thought and imagination; like an infinite deluge, or mountains over my head. I know not how to express better what my sins appear to me to be, than by heaping infinite upon infinite, and multiplying infinite by infinite. Very often, for these many years, these expressions are in my mind, and in my mouth, "Infinite upon infinite. . . . Infinite upon infinite!" When I look into my heart, and take a view of my wickedness, it looks like an abyss infinitely deeper than hell. And it appears to me, that were it not for free grace, exalted and raised up to the infinite height of all the fulness and glory of the great Jehovah, and the arm of his power and grace stretched forth in all the majesty of his power, and in all the glory of his sovereignty, I should appear sunk down in my sins below hell itself; far beyond the sight of every thing, but the eye of sovereign grace, that can pierce even down to such a depth. And yet it seems to me, that my conviction of sin is exceeding small, and faint; it is enough to amaze me, that I have no more sense of my sin. I know certainly, that I have very little sense of my sinfulness. When I have had turns of weeping and crying for my sins I thought I knew at the time, that my repentance was nothing to my sin.

I have greatly longed of late, for a broken heart, and to lie low before God; and, when I ask for humility, I cannot bear the thoughts of being no more humble than other Christians. It seems to me, that though their degrees of humility may be suitable for them, yet it would be a vile selfexaltation in me, not to be the lowest in humility of all mankind. Others speak of their longing to be "humbled to the dust;" that may be a proper expression for them, but I always think of myself, that I ought, and it is an expression that has long been natural for me to use in prayer, "to lie infinitely low before God." And it is affecting to think, how ignorant I was, when a young Christian, of the bottomless, infinite depths of wickedness, pride, hypocrisy and deceit, left in my heart.

I have a much greater sense of my universal, exceeding dependence on God's grace and strength, and mere good pleasure, of late, than I used formerly to have; and have experienced more of an abhorrence of my own righteousness. The very thought of any joy arising in me, on any consideration of my own amiableness, performances, or experiences, or any goodness of heart or life, is nauseous and detestable to me. And yet I am greatly afflicted with a proud and selfrighteous spirit, much more sensibly than I used to be formerly. I see that serpent rising and putting forth its head continually, every where, all around me.

Though it seems to me, that, in some respects, I was a far better Christian, for two or three years after my first conversion, than I am now; and lived in a more constant delight and pleasure; yet, of late years, I have had a more full and constant sense of the absolute sovereignty of God, and a delight in that sovereignty; and have had more of a sense of the glory of Christ, as a Mediator revealed in the gospel. On one Saturday night, in particular, I had such a discovery of the excellency of the gospel above all other doctrines, that I could not but say to myself, "This is my chosen light, my chosen doctrine;" and of Christ, "This is my chosen Prophet." It appeared sweet, beyond all expression, to follow Christ, and to be taught, and enlightened, and instructed by him; to learn of him, and live to him. Another Saturday night, (*January* 1739) I had such a sense, how sweet and blessed a thing it was to walk in the way of duty; to do that which was right and meet to be done, and agreeable to the holy mind of God; that it caused me to break forth into a kind of loud weeping, which held me some time, so that I was forced to shut myself up, and fasten the doors. I could not but, as it were, cry out, "How happy are they which do that which is right in the sight of God! They are blessed indeed, they are the happy ones!" I had, at the same time, a very affecting sense, how meet and suitable it was that God should govern the world, and order all things according to his own pleasure; and I rejoiced in it, that God reigned, and that his will was done.

BENJAMIN FRANKLIN

BENJAMIN FRANKLIN was a moralist, not a philosopher; none of his mature work denied the inspiration of Scripture or attempted to destroy its authority. For the vast "To what end?" which Edwards put to the universe, Franklin substituted a modest, operational "How?" He was equally modest in his consideration of virtue. Where Edwards defined true virtue as the disinterested love of God, Franklin named it a decent consideration for the welfare of one's fellow men. If he regarded virtue as an art, it was a mechanical art, one which could be reduced to rule and acquired by faithful practice. Beyond such persistent striving to improve his conduct, no man could be asked to go.

Franklin's mind ranged too widely in this world, then, to be much concerned with the next. If that limitation made him active in every scheme for promoting the comfort of Philadelphia, if it drew him to study the effects of lightning and the use of glass as a musical instrument, if it made him a skillful propagandist and the first and most persuasive of our devisers of gadgets, it also tended to give a rather smug tone to his moralizing. The mingled complacency and irony implicit in his outlook is neatly illustrated in his letters of the summer of 1764. Both William Strahan, his former business associate, and George Whitefield, the evangelist, were among his correspondents that July, and Franklin repeated to Strahan the substance of what he had written to Whitefield: "Your frequently repeated wishes for my eternal as well as my temporal happiness are very obliging, and I can only thank you for them and offer mine in return. I have myself no proper doubt that I shall enjoy as much of both as is proper for me. That Being, who gave me existence, and through almost three-score years has been continually showering his favors upon me, whose very chastisements have been blessings to me; can I doubt that he loves me? And if he loves me, can I doubt that he will go on to take care of me, not only here but hereafter? This to some may seem presumption; to me it appears the best grounded hope; hope of the future built on experience of the past."

The seleetion from Franklin's writings used here is from the *Autobiography of Benjamin* *Franklin. Edited from his Manuscript. . . .* by John Bigelow (Philadelphia, 1868).

Autobiography

BY BENJAMIN FRANKLIN

WE HAVE an English proverb that says, "*He that would thrive must ask his wife.*" It was lucky for me that I had one as much dispos'd to industry and frugality as myself. She assisted me cheerfully in my business, folding and stitching pamphlets, tending shop, purchasing old linen rags for the paper-makers, etc., etc. We kept no idle servants, our table was plain and simple, our furniture of the cheapest. For instance, my breakfast was a long time bread and milk (no tea), and I ate it out of a twopenny earthen porringer, with a pewter spoon. But mark how luxury will enter families, and make a progress, in spite of principle: being call'd one morning to breakfast, I found it in a China bowl, with a spoon of silver! They had been bought for me without my knowledge by my wife, and had cost her the enormous sum of three-and-twenty shillings, for which she had no other excuse or apology to make, but that she thought *her* husband deserv'd a silver spoon and China bowl as well as any of his neighbors. This was the first appearance of plate and China in our house, which afterward, in a course of years, as our wealth increas'd, augmented gradually to several hundred pounds in value.

I had been religiously educated as a Presbyterian; and tho' some of the dogmas of that persuasion, such as *the eternal decrees of God, election, reprobation, etc.*, appeared to me unintelligible, others doubtful, and I early absented myself from the public assemblies of the sect, Sunday being my studying day, I never was without some religious principles. I never doubted, for instance, the existence of the Deity; that he made the world, and govern'd it by his Providence; that the most acceptable service of God was the doing good to man; that our souls are immortal; and that all crime will be punished, and virtue rewarded, either here or hereafter. These I esteem'd the essentials of every religion; and, being to be found in all the religions we had in our country, I respected them all, tho' with different degrees of respect, as I found them more or less mix'd with other articles, which, without any tendency to inspire, promote, or confirm morality, serv'd principally to divide us, and make us unfriendly to one another. This respect to all, with an opinion that the worst had some good effects, induc'd me

to avoid all discourse that might tend to lessen the good opinion another might have of his own religion; and as our province increas'd in people, and new places of worship were continually wanted, and generally erected by voluntary contribution, my mite for such purpose, whatever might be the sect, was never refused.

Tho' I seldom attended any public worship, I had still an opinion of its propriety, and of its utility when rightly conducted, and I regularly paid my annual subscription for the support of the only Presbyterian minister or meeting we had in Philadelphia. He us'd to visit me sometimes as a friend, and admonish me to attend his administrations, and I was now and then prevail'd to do so, once for five Sundays successively. Had he been in my opinion a good preacher, perhaps I might have continued, notwithstanding the occasion I had for the Sunday's leisure in my course of study; but his discourses were chiefly either polemic arguments, or explications of the peculiar doctrines of our sect, and were all to me very dry, uninteresting, and unedifying, since not a single moral principle was inculcated or enforc'd, their aim seeming to be rather to make us Presbyterians than good citizens.

At length he took for his text that verse of the fourth chapter of Philippians, "*Finally, brethren, whatsoever things are true, honest, just, pure, lovely, or of good report, if there be any virtue, or any praise, think on these things.*" And I imagin'd in a sermon on such a text, we could not miss of having some morality. But he confin'd himself to five points only, as meant by the apostle, viz.: 1 Keeping holy the Sabbath day. 2. Being diligent in reading the holy Scriptures. 3. Attending duly the publick worship. 4. Partaking of the Sacrament. 5. Paying a due respect to God's ministers. These might be all good things; but, as they were not the kind of good things that I expected from the text, I despaired of ever meeting with them from any other, was disgusted, and attended his preaching no more. I had some years before compos'd a little Liturgy, or form of prayer, for my own private use (viz., in 1728), entitled *Articles of Belief and Acts of Religion.* I return'd to the use of this, and went no more to the public assemblies. My conduct might be blameable, but I leave it, without attempting further to excuse it; my present purpose being to relate facts, and not to make apologies for them.

It was about this time I conceiv'd the bold and arduous project of arriving at moral perfection. I wish'd to live without committing any fault at any time; I would conquer all that either natural inclination, custom, or company might lead me into. As I knew, or thought I knew, what was right and wrong, I did not see why I might not always do the one and avoid the other. But I soon found I had undertaken a task of more difficulty than I had imagined. While my care was employ'd in guarding against one fault, I was often surprised by another; habit took the advantage of inattention; inclination was sometimes too strong for reason. I concluded, at length, that the mere speculative conviction that it was our interest to be completely virtuous, was not sufficient to prevent our slipping; and that the contrary habits must be broken, and good ones acquired and established, before we can have any dependence on a steady, uniform rectitude of conduct. For this purpose I therefore contrived the following method.

In the various enumerations of the moral virtues I had met within my reading, I found the catalogue more or less numerous, as different writers included more or fewer ideas under the same name. Temperance, for example, was by some confined to eating and drinking, while by others it was extended to mean the moderating every other pleasure, appetite, inclination, or passion, bodily or mental, even to our avarice and ambition. I propos'd to myself, for the sake of clearness, to use rather more names, with fewer ideas annex'd to each, than a few names with more ideas; and I included under thirteen names of virtues all that at that time occurr'd to me as necessary or desirable, and annexed to each a short precept, which fully express'd the extent I gave to its meaning.

These names of virtues, with their precepts, were:

1. Temperance.
Eat not to dulness; drink not to elevation.
2. Silence.
Speak not but what may benefit others or yourself; avoid trifling conversation.
3. Order.
Let all your things have their places; let each part of your business have its time.
4. Resolution.
Resolve to perform what you ought; perform without fail what you resolve.

5. Frugality.
Make no expense but to do good to others or yourself; i.e., waste nothing.
6. Industry.
Lose no time; be always employ'd in something useful; cut off all unnecessary actions.
7. Sincerity.
Use no hurtful deceit; think innocently and justly, and, if you speak, speak accordingly.
8. Justice.
Wrong none by doing injuries, or omitting the benefits that are your duty.
9. Moderation.
Avoid extreams; forbear resenting injuries so much as you think they deserve.
10. Cleanliness.
Tolerate no uncleanliness in body, cloaths, or habitation.
11. Tranquillity.
Be not disturbed at trifles, or at accidents common or unavoidable.
12. Chastity.
Rarely use venery but for health or offspring, never to dulness, weakness, or the injury of your own or another's peace or reputation.
13. Humility.
Imitate Jesus and Socrates.

My intention being to acquire the *habitude* of all these virtues, I judg'd it would be well not to distract my attention by attempting the whole at once, but to fix it on one of them at a time; and, when I should be master of that, then to proceed to another, and so on, till I should have gone thro' the thirteen, and, as the previous acquisition of some might facilitate the acquisition of certain others, I arrang'd them with that view as they stand above. Temperance first, as it tends to procure that coolness and clearness of head, which is so necessary where constant vigilance was to be kept up, and guard maintained against the unremitting attraction of ancient habits, and the force of perpetual temptations. This being acquir'd and establish'd, Silence would be more easy; and my desire being to gain knowledge at the same time that I improv'd in virtue, and considering that in conversation it was obtain'd rather by the use of the ears than of the tongue, and therefore wishing to break a habit I was getting into of prattling, punning, and joking, which only made me acceptable to trifling company, I gave *Silence* the second place. This and the next, *Order*, I expected would allow me more time for attending to my project and my studies. *Resolution*, once become habitual, would keep me firm in my endeavors to obtain all the subsequent virtues; *Frugality* and Industry freeing me from my remaining debt, and producing affluence and independence, would make more easy the practice of Sincerity and Justice, etc., etc. Conceiving then, that, agreeably to the advice of Pythagoras in his Golden Verses, daily examination would be necessary, I contrived the following method for conducting that examination.

I made a little book, in which I allotted a page for each of the virtues. I rul'd each page with red ink, so as to have seven columns, one for each day of the week, marking each column with a letter for the day. I cross'd these columns with thirteen red lines, marking the beginning of each line with the first letter of one of the virtues, on which line, and in its proper column, I might mark, by a little black spot, every fault I found upon examination to have been committed respecting that virtue upon that day.

Form of the pages.

TEMPERANCE.

Eat not to dulness;
Drink not to elevation.

	S.	M.	T.	W.	T.	F.	S.
T.							
S.	*	*		*		*	
O.	**	*	*		*	*	*
R.				*		*	
F.		*			*		
I.		*					
S.							
J.							
M.							
C.							
T.							
C.							
H.							

I determined to give a week's strict attention to each of the virtues successively. Thus, in the first week, my great guard was to avoid every the least offence against *Temperance*, leaving the other virtues to their ordinary chance, only marking every evening the faults of the day. Thus, if in the first week I could keep my first line, marked T, clear of spots, I suppos'd the habit of that virtue so much strengthen'd, and its opposite

weaken'd, that I might venture extending my attention to include the next, and for the following week keep both lines clear of spots. Proceeding thus to the last, I could go thro' a course compleat in thirteen weeks, and four courses in a year. And like him, who, having a garden to weed, does not attempt to eradicate all the bad herbs at once, which would exceed his reach and his strength, but works on one of the beds at a time, and, having accomplish'd the first, proceeds to a second, so I should have, I hoped, the encouraging pleasure of seeing on my pages the progress I made in virtue, by clearing successively my lines of their spots, till in the end, by a number of courses, I should be happy in viewing a clean book, after a thirteen weeks daily examination.

This my little book had for its motto these lines from Addison's *Cato*:

"Here will I hold. If there's a power above us
(And that there is, all nature cries aloud
Thro' all her works), He must delight in virtue,
And that which he delights in must be happy."

Another from Cicero,

"O vitae Philosophia dux! O virtutem indagatrix expultrixque vitiorum! Unus dies, bene et ex praeceptis tuis actus, peccanti immortalitati est anteponendus."

Another from the Proverbs of Solomon, speaking of wisdom or virtue:

"Length of days is in her right hand, and in her left hand riches and honour. Her ways are ways of pleasantness, and all her paths are peace." iii. 16, 17.

And conceiving God to be the fountain of wisdom, I thought it right and necessary to solicit his assistance for obtaining it; to this end I formed the following little prayer, which was prefix'd to my tables of examination for daily use.

"O powerful Goodness! bountiful Father! merciful Guide! Increase in me that wisdom which discovers my truest interest. Strengthen my resolutions to perform what that wisdom dictates. Accept my kind offices to thy other children as the only return in my power for thy continual favours to me."

I used also sometimes a little prayer which I took from Thomson's Poems, viz.:

"Father of light and life, thou Good Supreme!
O teach me what is good; teach me Thyself!
Save me from folly, vanity, and vice,
From every low pursuit; and fill my soul

With knowledge, conscious peace, and virtue pure;
Sacred, substantial, never-fading bliss!"

The precept of *Order* requiring that *every part
of my business* should have its allotted time, one
page in my little book contain'd the following
scheme of employment for the twenty-four
hours of a natural day.

The Morning.	5	Rise, wash, and ad-dress *Powerful Good-ness!* Contrive day's business, and take the resolution of the day; prosecute the present study, and breakfast.
Question. What good shall I do this day?	6	
	7	
	8	
	9	Work
	10	
	11	
Noon.	12	Read, or overlook my accounts, and dine
	1	
	2	
	3	Work
	4	
	5	
Evening.	6	Put things in their places.
	7	Supper. Music or diver-sion or conversation. Ex-amination of the day.
Question. What good have I done to-day.	8	
	9	
	10	
	11	
	12	
Night.	1	Sleep.
	2	
	3	
	4	

I enter'd upon the execution of this plan for
self-examination, and continu'd it with occasional
intermissions for some time. I was surpris'd to find
myself so much fuller of faults than I had imagined; but I had the satisfaction of seeing them
diminish. To avoid the trouble of renewing now
and then my little book, which, by scraping out
the marks on the paper of old faults to make room
for new ones in a new course, became full of
holes, I transferr'd my tables and precepts to the
ivory leaves of a memorandum book, on which
the lines were drawn with red ink, that made a
durable stain, and on those lines I mark'd my

faults with a black-lead pencil, which marks I
could easily wipe out with a wet sponge. After
a while I went thro' one course only in a year,
and afterward only one in several years, till at
length I omitted them entirely, being employ'd
in voyages and business abroad, with a multiplicity of affairs that interfered; but I always
carried my little book with me.

My scheme of ORDER gave me the most trouble;
and I found that, tho' it might be practicable
where a man's business was such as to leave him
the disposition of his time, that of a journeyman
printer, for instance, it was not possible to be
exactly observed by a master, who must mix with
the world, and often receive people of business
at their own hours. *Order*, too, with regard to
places for things, papers, etc., I found extreamly
difficult to acquire. I had not been early accustomed to it, and, having an exceedingly good
memory, I was not so sensible of the inconvenience attending want of method. This article,
therefore, cost me so much painful attention, and
my faults in it vexed me so much, and I made
so little progress in amendment, and had such
frequent relapses, that I was almost ready to give
up the attempt, and content myself with a faulty
character in that respect, like the man who, in
buying an ax of a smith, my neighbor, desired
to have the whole of its surface as bright as the
edge. The smith consented to grind it bright for
him if he would turn the wheel; he turn'd, while
the smith press'd the broad face of the ax hard
and heavy on the stone, which made the turning
of it very fatiguing. The man came every now
and then from the wheel to see how the work
went on, and at length would take his ax as it
was, without farther grinding. "No," said the
smith, "turn on, turn on; we shall have it bright
by-and-by; as yet, it is only speckled." "Yes,"
says the man, "*but I think I like a speckled ax
best.*" And I believe this may have been the case
with many, who, having, for want of some such
means as I employ'd, found the difficulty of obtaining good and breaking bad habits in other
points of vice and virtue, have given up the struggle, and concluded that "*a speckled ax was best*";
for something, that pretended to be reason, was
every now and then suggesting to me that such
extream nicety as I exacted of myself might be a
kind of foppery in morals, which, if it were
known, would make me ridiculous; that a perfect
character might be attended with the inconvenience of being envied and hated; and that a benevolent man should allow a few faults in himself,
to keep his friends in countenance.

In truth, I found myself incorrigible with respect to Order; and now I am grown old, and my memory bad, I feel very sensibly the want of it. But, on the whole, tho' I never arrived at the perfection I had been so ambitious of obtaining, but fell far short of it, yet I was, by the endeavour, a better and a happier man than I otherwise should have been if I had not attempted it; as those who aim at perfect writing by imitating the engraved copies, tho' they never reach the wish'd for excellence of those copies, their hand is mended by the endeavor, and is tolerable while it continues fair and legible.

It may be well my posterity should be informed that to this little artifice, with the blessing of God, their ancestor ow'd the constant felicity of his life, down to his 79th year, in which this is written. What reverses may attend the remainder is in the hand of Providence; but, if they arrive, the reflection on past happiness enjoy'd ought to help his bearing them with more resignation. To Temperance he ascribes his long-continued health, and what is still left to him of a good constitution; to Industry and Frugality, the early easiness of his circumstances and acquisition of his fortune, with all that knowledge that enabled him to be a useful citizen, and obtained for him some degree of reputation among the learned; to Sincerity and Justice, the confidence of his country, and the honorable employs it conferred upon him; and to the joint influence of the whole mass of the virtues, even in the imperfect state he was able to acquire them, all that evenness of temper, and that cheerfulness in conversation, which makes his company still sought for and agreeable, even to his younger acquaintance. I hope, therefore, that some of my descendants may follow the example and reap the benefit.

It will be remark'd that, tho' my scheme was not wholly without religion, there was in it no mark of any of the distinquishing tenets of any particular sect. I had purposely avoided them; for, being fully persuaded of the utility and excellency of my method, and that it might be serviceable to people in all religions, and intending some time or other to publish it, I would not have any thing in it that should prejudice any one, of any sect, against it. I purposed writing a little comment on each virtue, in which I would have shown the advantages of possessing it, and the mischiefs attending its opposite vice; and I should have called my book THE ART OF VIRTUE, because it would have shown the means and manner of obtaining virtue, which would have distinguished it from the mere exhortation to be good, that does not instruct and indicate the means, but is like the apostle's man of verbal charity, who only without showing to the naked and hungry how or where they might get clothes or victuals, exhorted them to be fed and clothed. James ii, 15, 16.

But it so happened that my intention of writing and publishing this comment was never fulfilled. I did, indeed, from time to time, put down short hints of the sentiments, reasonings, etc., to be made use of in it, some of which I have still by me; but the necessary close attention to private business in the earlier part of my life, and public business since, have occasioned my postponing it; for, it being connected in my mind with *a great and extensive project*, that required the whole man to execute, and which an unforeseen succession of employs prevented my attending to, it has hitherto remain'd unfinish'd.

In this piece it was my design to explain and enforce this doctrine, that vicious actions are not hurtful because they are forbidden, but forbidden because they are hurtful, the nature of man alone considered; that it was, therefore, every one's interest to be virtuous who wish'd to be happy even in this world; and I should, from this circumstance (there being always in the world a number of rich merchants, nobility, states, and princes, who have need of honest instruments for the management of their affairs, and such being so rare), have endeavored to convince young persons that no qualities were so likely to make a poor man's fortune as those of probity and integrity.

My list of virtues contain'd at first but twelve; but a Quaker friend having kindly informed me that I was generally thought proud; that my pride show'd itself frequently in conversation; that I was not content with being in the right when discussing any point, but was overbearing, and rather insolent, of which he convinc'd me by mentioning several instances; I determined endeavouring to cure myself, if I could, of this vice or folly among the rest, and I added *Humility* to my list, giving an extensive meaning to the word.

I cannot boast of much success in acquiring the *reality* of this virtue, but I had a good deal with regard to the *appearance* of it. I made it a rule to forbear all direct contradiction to the sentiments of others, and all positive assertion of my own. I even forbid myself, agreeably to the old laws of our Junto, the use of every word or expression in the language that imported a fix'd opinion, such as *certainly, undoubtedly*, etc., and I adopted instead of them, *I conceive, I apprehend*, or *I imagine* a thing to be so or so; or it *so appears to me at present*. When another asserted something that I thought an error, I deny'd myself the pleasure of contradicting him abruptly, and of showing immediately some absurdity in his proposition; and in answering I began by observing that in certain cases or circumstances his opinion would be right, but in the present case there *appear'd* or *seem'd* to me some difference, etc. I soon found the advantage of this change in my manner; the conversations I engag'd in went on more pleasantly. The modest way in which I propos'd my opinions procur'd them a readier reception and less contradiction; I had less mortification when I was found to be in the wrong, and I more easily prevail'd with others to give up their mistakes and join with me when I happened to be in the right.

And this mode, which I at first put on with some violence to natural inclination, became at length so easy, and so habitual to me, that perhaps for these fifty years past no one has ever heard a dogmatical expression escape me. And to this habit (after my character of integrity) I think it principally owing that I had early so much weight with my fellow-citizens when I proposed new institutions, or alterations in the old, and so much influence in public councils when I became a member; for I was but a bad speaker, never eloquent, subject to much hesitation in my choice of words, hardly correct in language, and yet I generally carried my points.

In reality, there is, perhaps, no one of our natural passions so hard to subdue as *pride*. Disguise it, struggle with it, beat it down, stifle it, mortify it as much as one pleases, it is still alive, and will every now and then peep out and show itself; you will see it, perhaps, often in this history; for, even if I could conceive that I had compleatly overcome it, I should probably be proud of my humility.

THE AMERICAN SCENE

J. HECTOR ST. JOHN DE CRÈVECOEUR

THE AMERICAN LEGEND in its simplest, yet most idyllic, terms is presented in Crèvecoeur's *Letters from an American Farmer*. America is a place where a man who is willing to work can earn enough to feed his family decently. Bald as the fact may be, Crèvecoeur is writer enough to make his development of it charming as well as significant. He shows us the American who made the Revolution: the hard-working, sober farmer; the pioneer, who is still depicted as social castoff, the man too restless, too indolent or too rebellious for settled society; the immigrant straightening his back as he becomes man and citizen instead of half-servile laborer.

Crèvecoeur sees Europeans of all nations transformed into Americans under the influence of a government that does not oppress them with taxes or burden them with tithes. The American chooses his own religion, practices it as he will, and, provided he violates no law, lives as he pleases. Under this discipline, he has become a laborious, thrifty, litigious man, self-seeking yet willing to help a neighbor, hopeful, energetic and free from the refinements of luxury and the corruptions of vice. The picture is conventional enough to serve the most unimaginative of modern orators. But Crèvecoeur helped create the convention. And there is a measure of appropriateness in the fact that this apt description of the American was made by one of the foreigners who thought to become what he depicted.

J. Hector St. John de Crèvecoeur (1735–1813) came to America to serve with the French under Montcalm. Early in the 1760s, he changed allegiance and proceeded to travel through the Pennsylvania back country until he came to New York where he settled, was naturalized and married during the years when antirent rioting and the Stamp Act disorders made New York a place one would not think likely to give birth to idyls.

After the colonists broke with England, Crèvecoeur strove to remain neutral and finally found it either wise, or necessary, to leave his family and return to France in 1780. In Paris, he was introduced into literary society by Mme. d'Houdetot, who had been Rousseau's mistress. Through her influence, Crèvecoeur was named Consul at New York, a post he contrived to hold until Revolutionary politics forced him out. He returned to Europe and spent the rest of his life in Paris, London and Munich, where he found a king who had read the Farmer's letters with great pleasure.

Crèvecoeur had delighted other readers than King Maximilian of Bavaria, for his book was published in four English and two French editions, to say nothing of pirated German and Dutch reprints and the American edition of 1793. The famous essayist, William Hazlitt, found it charming; Charles Lamb read it with interest; and the Coleridge-Southey project for a literary settlement in the Susquehanna country is said to have taken inspiration from the *Letters of an American Farmer*.

The selection reprinted here is taken from the American edition of 1793.

Letters from an American Farmer

BY J. HECTOR ST. JOHN DE CRÈVECOEUR

I WISH I could be acquainted with the feelings and thoughts which must agitate the heart and present themselves to the mind of an enlightened Englishman, when he first lands on this continent. He must greatly rejoice that he lived at a time to see this fair country discovered and settled; he must necessarily feel a share of national pride, when he views the chain of settlements which embellishes these extended shores. When he says to himself, this is the work of my countrymen, who, when convulsed by factions, afflicted by a variety of miseries and wants, restless and impatient, took refuge here. They brought along with them their national genius, to which they principally owe what liberty they enjoy, and what substance they possess. Here he sees the industry of his native country displayed in a new manner, and traces in their works the embryos of all the arts, sciences, and ingenuity which flourish in Europe. Here he beholds fair cities, substantial villages, extensive fields, an immense country filled with decent houses, good roads, orchards, meadows, and bridges, where an hundred years ago all was wild, woody, and uncultivated! What a train of pleasing ideas this fair spectacle must suggest; it is a prospect which must inspire a good citizen with the most heartfelt pleasure. The difficulty consists in the manner of viewing so extensive a scene. He is arrived on a new continent; a modern society offers itself to his contemplation, different from what he had hitherto seen. It is not composed, as in Europe, of great lords who possess everything, and of a herd of people who have nothing. Here are no aristocratical families, no courts, no kings, no bishops, no ecclesiastical dominion, no invisible power giving to a few a very visible one; no great manufacturers employing thousands, no great refinements of luxury. The rich and the poor are not so far removed from each other as they are in Europe. Some few towns excepted, we are all tillers of the earth, from Nova Scotia to West Florida. We are a people of cultivators, scattered over an immense territory, communicating with each other by means of good roads and navigable rivers, united by the silken bands of mild government, all respecting the laws, without dreading their power, because they are equitable. We are all animated with the spirit of an industry which is unfettered and unrestrained, because each person works for himself. If he travels through our rural districts he views not the hostile castle, and the haughty mansion, contrasted with the clay-built hut and miserable cabin, where cattle and men help to keep each other warm, and dwell in meanness, smoke, and indigence. A pleasing uniformity of decent competence appears throughout our habitations. The meanest of our log-houses is a dry and comfortable habitation. Lawyer or merchant are the fairest titles our towns afford; that of a farmer is the only appellation of the rural inhabitants of our country. It must take some time ere he can reconcile himself to our dictionary, which is but short in words of dignity, and names of honour. There, on a Sunday, he sees a congregation of respectable farmers and their wives, all clad in neat homespun, well mounted, or riding in their own humble waggons. There is not among them an esquire, saving the unlettered magistrate. There he sees a parson as simple as his flock, a farmer who does not riot on the labour of others. We have no princes, for whom we toil, starve, and bleed: we are the most perfect society now existing in the world. Here man is free as he ought to be; nor is this pleasing equality so transitory as many others are. Many ages will not see the shores of our great lakes replenished with inland nations, nor the unknown bounds of North America entirely peopled. Who can tell how far it extends? Who can tell the millions of men whom it will feed and contain? for no European foot has as yet travelled half the extent of this mighty continent!

The next wish of this traveller will be to know whence came all these people? they are a mixture of English, Scotch, Irish, French, Dutch, Germans, and Swedes. From this promiscuous breed, that race now called Americans have arisen. The eastern provinces must indeed be excepted, as being the unmixed descendants of Englishmen. I have heard many wish that they had been more intermixed also: for my part, I am no wisher, and think it much better as it has happened. They exhibit a most conspicuous figure in this great and variegated picture; they too enter for a great share in the pleasing perspective displayed in these thirteen provinces. I know it is fashionable to reflect on them, but I respect them for what they have done; for the accuracy and wisdom with which they have settled their territory; for the decency of their manners; for their early love of letters; their ancient college, the first in this hemisphere; for their industry; which to me who am but a farmer, is the criterion of everything. There never was a people, situated as they are, who with so ungrateful a soil have done more in so short a time. Do you think that the monarchical ingredients which are more prevalent in other governments, have purged them from all foul stains? Their histories assert the contrary.

In this great American asylum, the poor of Europe have by some means met together, and in consequence of various causes; to what purpose should they ask one another what countrymen they are? Alas, two thirds of them had no country. Can a wretch who wanders about, who works and strives, whose life is a continual scene of sore affliction or pinching penury; can that man call England or any other kingdom his country? A country that had no bread for him, whose fields procured him no harvest, who met with nothing but the frowns of the rich, the severity of the laws, with jails and punishments; who owned not a single foot of the extensive surface of this planet? No! urged by a variety of motives, here they came. Every thing has tended to regenerate them; new laws, a new mode of living, a new social system; here they are become men: in Europe they were as so many useless plants, wanting vegetative mould, and refreshing showers; they withered, and were mowed down by want, hunger, and war; but now by the power of transplantation, like all other plants they have taken root and flourish! Formerly they were not numbered in any civil lists of their country, except in those of the poor; here they rank as citizens. By what invisible power has this surprising metamorphosis been performed? By that of the laws and that of their industry. The laws, the indulgent laws, protect them as they arrive, stamping on them the symbol of adoption; they receive ample rewards for their labours; these accumulated rewards procure them lands; those lands confer on them the title of freemen, and to that title every benefit is affixed which men can possibly require. This is the great operation daily performed by our laws. From whence proceed these laws? From our government. Whence the government? It is derived from the original genius and strong desire of the people ratified and confirmed by the crown. This is the great chain which links us all, this is the picture which every province exhibits, Nova Scotia excepted. There the crown has done all; either there were no people who had genius, or it was not much attended to: the consequence is, that the province is very thinly inhabited indeed; the power of the crown in conjunction with the musketos has prevented men from settling there. Yet some parts of it flourished once, and it contained a mild harmless set of people. But for the fault of a few leaders, the whole were banished. The greatest political error the crown ever committed in America, was to cut off men from a country which wanted nothing but men!

What attachment can a poor European emigrant have for a country where he had nothing? The knowledge of the language, the love of a few kindred as poor as himself, were the only cords that tied him: his country is now that which gives him land, bread, protection, and consequence: *Ubi panis ibi patria*, is the motto of all emigrants. What then is the American, this new man? He is either an European, or the descendant of an European, hence that strange mixture of blood, which you will find in no other country. I could point out to you a family whose grandfather was an Englishman, whose wife was Dutch, whose son married a French woman, and whose present four sons have now four wives of different nations. *He* is an American, who, leaving behind him all his ancient prejudices and manners, receives new ones from the new mode of life he has embraced, the new government he obeys, and the new rank he holds. He becomes an American by being received in the broad lap of our great *Alma Mater*. Here individuals of all nations are melted into a new race of men, whose labours and posterity will one day cause great changes in the world. Americans are the western pilgrims, who are carrying along with them that great mass of arts, sciences, vigour, and industry which began long since in the east; they will finish the great circle. The Americans were once scattered all over Europe; here they are incorporated into one of the finest systems of population which has ever appeared, and which will hereafter become distinct by the power of the different climates they inhabit. The American ought therefore to love this country much better than that wherein either he or his forefathers were born. Here the rewards of his industry follow with equal steps the progress of his labour; his labour is founded on the basis of nature, *self-interest;* can it want a stronger allurement? Wives and children, who before in vain demanded of him a morsel of bread, now, fat and frolicsome, gladly help their father to clear those fields whence exuberant crops are to arise to feed and to clothe them all; without any part being claimed, either by a despotic prince, a rich abbot, or a mighty lord. Here religion demands but little of him; a small voluntary salary to the minister, and gratitude to God; can he refuse these? The American is a new man, who acts upon new principles; he must therefore entertain new ideas, and form new opinions. From involuntary idleness, servile dependence, penury, and useless labour, he has passed to toils of a very different nature, rewarded by ample subsistence.—This is an American.

British America is divided into many provinces, forming a large association, scattered along a coast 1500 miles extent and about 200 wide. This society I would fain examine, at least such as it appears in the middle provinces; if it does not afford that variety of tinges and gradations which may be observed in Europe, we have colours peculiar to ourselves. For instance, it is natural to conceive that those who live near the sea, must be very different from those who live in the woods; the intermediate space will afford a separate and distinct class.

Men are like plants; the goodness and flavour of the fruit proceeds from the peculiar soil and exposition in which they grow. We are nothing but what we derive from the air we breathe, the climate we inhabit, the government we obey, the system of religion we profess, and the nature of our employment. Here you will find but few crimes; these have acquired as yet no root among us. I wish I was able to trace all my ideas; if my ignorance prevents me from describing them properly, I hope I shall be able to delineate a few of the outlines, which are all I propose.

Those who live near the sea, feed more on fish than on flesh, and often encounter that boisterous element. This renders them more bold and enterprising; this leads them to neglect the confined occupations of the land. They see and converse with a variety of people; their intercourse with mankind becomes extensive. The sea inspires them with a love of traffic, a desire of transporting produce from one place to another; and leads them to a variety of resources which supply the place of labour. Those who inhabit the middle settlements, by far the most numerous, must be very different; the simple cultivation of the earth purifies them, but the indulgences of the government, the soft remonstrances of religion, the rank of independent freeholders, must necessarily inspire them with sentiments, very little known in Europe among people of the same class. What do I say? Europe has no such class of men; the early knowledge they acquire, the early bargains they make, give them a great degree of sagacity. As freemen they will be litigious; pride and obstinacy are often the cause of law suits; the nature of our laws and governments may be another. As citizens it is easy to imagine, that they will carefully read the newspapers, enter into every political disquisition, freely blame or censure governors and others. As farmers they will be careful and anxious to get as much as they can, because what they get is their own. As northern men they will love the cheerful cup. As Christians, religion curbs them not in their opinions; the general indulgence leaves every one to think for themselves in spiritual matters; the laws inspect our actions, our thoughts are left to God. Industry, good living, selfishness, litigiousness, country politics, the pride of freemen, religious indifference, are their characteristics. If you recede still farther from the sea, you will come into more modern settlements; they exhibit the same strong lineaments, in a ruder appearance. Religion seems to have still less influence, and their manners are less improved.

Now we arrive near the great woods, near the last inhabited districts; there men seem to be placed still farther beyond the reach of government, which in some measure leaves them to themselves. How can it pervade every corner; as they were driven there by misfortunes, necessity of beginnings, desire of acquiring large tracts of land, idleness, frequent want of economy, ancient debts; the re-union of such people does not afford a very pleasing spectacle. When discord, want of unity and friendship; when either drunkenness or idleness prevail in such remote districts; contention, inactivity, and wretchedness must ensue. There are not the same remedies to these evils as in a long established community. The few magistrates they have, are in general little better than the rest; they are often in a perfect state of war; that of man against man, sometimes decided by blows, sometimes by means of the law; that of man against every wild inhabitant of these venerable woods, of which they are come to dispossess them. There men appear to be no better than carnivorous animals of a superior rank, living on the flesh of wild animals when they can catch them, and when they are not able, they subsist on grain. He who would wish to see America in its proper light, and have a true idea of its feeble beginnings and barbarous rudiments, must visit our extended line of frontiers where the last settlers dwell, and where he may see the first labours of settlement, the mode of clearing the earth, in all their different appearances; where men are wholly left dependent on their native tempers, and on the spur of uncertain industry, which often fails when not sanctified by the efficacy of a few moral rules. There, remote from the power of example and check of shame, many families exhibit the most hideous parts of our society. They are a kind of forlorn hope, preceding by ten or twelve years the most respectable army of veterans which come after them. In that space, prosperity will polish some, vice and the law will drive off the rest, who uniting again with others like themselves will recede still farther; making room for more industrious people, who will finish their improvements, convert the loghouse into a convenient habitation, and rejoicing that the first heavy labours are finished, will change in a few years that hitherto barbarous country into a fine fertile, well regulated district. Such is our progress, such is the march of the Europeans toward the interior parts of this continent. In all societies there are off-casts; this impure part serves as our precursors or pioneers; my father himself was one of that class, but he came upon honest principles, and was therefore one of the few who held fast; by good conduct and temperance, he transmitted to me his fair inheritance, when not above one in fourteen of his contemporaries had the same good fortune.

Forty years ago this smiling country was thus inhabited; it is now purged, a general decency of manners prevails throughout, and such has been the fate of our best countries.

Exclusive of those general characteristics, each province has its own, founded on the government, climate, mode of husbandry, customs, and peculiarity of circumstances. Europeans submit insensibly to these great powers, and become, in the course of a few generations, not only Americans in general, but either Pennsylvanians, Virginians, or provincials under some other name. Whoever traverses the continent must easily observe those strong differences, which will grow more evident in time. The inhabitants of Canada, Massachusetts, the middle provinces, the southern ones will be as different as their climates; their only points of unity will be those of religion and language.

As I have endeavoured to show you how Europeans become Americans; it may not be disagreeable to show you likewise how the various Christian sects introduced, wear out, and how religious indifference becomes prevalent. When any considerable number of a particular sect happen to dwell contiguous to each other, they immediately erect a temple, and there worship the Divinity agreeably to their own peculiar ideas. Nobody disturbs them. If any new sect springs up in Europe it may happen that many of its professors will come and settle in America. As they bring their zeal with them, they are at liberty to make proselytes if they can, and to build a meeting and to follow the dictates of their consciences; for neither the government nor any other power interferes. If they are peaceable subjects, and are industrious, what is it to their neighbours how and in what manner they think fit to address their prayers to the Supreme Being? But if the sectaries are not settled close together, if they are mixed with other denominations, their zeal will cool for want of fuel, and will be extinguished in a little time. Then the Americans become as to religion, what they are as to country, allied to all. In them the name of Englishman, Frenchman, and European is lost, and in like manner, the strict modes of Christianity as practised in Europe are lost also. This effect will extend itself still farther hereafter, and though this may appear to you as a strange idea, yet it is a very true one. I shall be able perhaps hereafter to explain myself better; in the meanwhile, let the following example serve as my first justification.

Let us suppose you and I to be travelling; we observe that in this house, to the right, lives a Catholic, who prays to God as he has been taught, and believes in transubstantiation; he works and raises wheat, he has a large family of children, all hale and robust; his belief, his prayers offend nobody. About one mile farther on the same road, his next neighbour may be a good honest plodding German Lutheran, who addresses himself to the same God, the God of all, agreeably to the modes he has been educated in, and believes in consubstantiation; by so doing he scandalises nobody; he also works in his fields, embellishes the earth, clears swamps, etc. What has the world to do with his Lutheran principles? He persecutes nobody, and nobody persecutes him, he visits his neighbours, and his neighbours visit him. Next to him lives a seceder, the most enthusiastic of all sectaries; his zeal is hot and fiery, but separated as he is from others of the same complexion, he has no congregation of his own to resort to, where he might cabal and mingle religious pride with worldly obstinacy. He likewise raises good crops, his house is handsomely painted, his orchard is one of the fairest in the neighbourhood. How does it concern the welfare of the country, or of the province at large, what this man's religious sentiments are, or really whether he has any at all? He is a good farmer, he is a sober, peaceable, good citizen: William Penn himself would not wish for more. This is the visible character, the invisible one is only guessed at, and is nobody's business. Next again lives a Low Dutchman, who implicitly believes the rules laid down by the synod of Dort. He conceives no other idea of a clergyman than that of an hired man; if he does his work well he will pay him the stipulated sum; if not he will dismiss him, and do without his sermons, and let his church be shut up for years. But notwithstanding this coarse idea, you will find his house and farm to be the neatest in all the country; and you will judge by his waggon and fat horses, that he thinks more of the affairs of this world than of those of the next. He is sober and laborious, therefore he is all he ought to be as to the affairs of this life; as for those of the next, he must trust to the great Creator. Each of these people instruct their children as well as they can, but these instructions are feeble compared to those which are given to the youth of the poorest class in Europe. Their children will therefore grow up less zealous and more indifferent in matters of religion than their parents. The foolish vanity, or rather the fury of making Proselytes, is unknown here; they have no time, the seasons call for all their attention, and thus in a few years, this mixed neighbourhood will exhibit a strange religious medley, that will be neither pure Catholicism nor pure Calvinism. A very perceptible indifference even in the first generation, will become apparent; and it may happen that the daughter of the Catholic will marry the son of the seceder, and settle by themselves at a distance from their parents. What religious education will they give their children? A very imperfect one. If there happens to be in the neighbourhood any place of worship, we will suppose a Quaker's meeting; rather than not show their fine clothes, they will go to it, and some of them may perhaps attach themselves to that society. Others will remain in a perfect state of indifference; the children of these zealous parents will not be able to tell what their religious principles are, and their grandchildren still less. The neighbourhood of a place of worship generally leads them to it, and the action of going thither, is the strongest evidence they can give of their attachment to any sect. The Quakers are the only people who retain a fondness for their own mode of worship; for be they ever so far separated from each other, they hold a sort of communion with the society, and seldom depart from its rules, at least in this country. Thus all sects are mixed as well as all nations; thus religious indifference is imperceptibly disseminated from one end of the continent to the other; which is at present one of the strongest characteristics of the Americans. Where this will reach no one can tell, perhaps it may leave a vacuum fit to receive other systems. Persecution, religious pride, the love of contradiction, are the food of what the world commonly calls religion. These motives have ceased here; zeal in Europe is confined; here it evaporates in the great distance it has to travel; there it is a grain of powder inclosed, here it burns away in the open air, and consumes without effect.

But to return to our back settlers. I must tell you, that there is something in the proximity of the woods, which is very singular. It is with men as it is with the plants and animals that grow and live in the forests; they are entirely different from those that live in the plains. I will candidly tell you all my thoughts but you are not to expect that I shall advance any reasons. By living in or near the woods, their actions are regulated by the wildness of the neighbourhood. The deer often come to eat their grain, the wolves to destroy their sheep, the bears to kill their hogs, the foxes to catch their poultry. This surrounding hostility immediately puts the gun into their hands; they watch these animals, they kill some; and thus by defending their property, they soon become professed hunters; this is the progress; once hunters, farewell to the plough. The chase renders them ferocious, gloomy, and unsociable; a hunter wants no neighbour, he rather hates them, because he dreads the competition. In a little time their success in the woods makes them neglect their tillage. They trust to the natural fecundity of the earth, and therefore do little; carelessness in fencing often exposes what little they sow to destruction; they are not at home to watch; in order therefore to make up the deficiency, they go oftener to the woods. That new mode of life brings along with it a new set of manners, which I cannot easily describe. These new manners being grafted on the old stock, produce a strange sort of lawless profligacy, the impressions of which are indelible. The manners of the Indian natives are respectable, compared with this European medley. Their wives and children live in sloth and inactivity; and having no proper pursuits, you may judge what education the latter receive. Their tender minds have nothing else to contemplate but the example of their parents; like them they grow up a mongrel breed, half civilised, half savage, except nature stamps on them some constitutional propensities. That rich, that voluptuous sentiment is gone that struck them so forcibly; the possession of their freeholds no longer conveys to their minds the same pleasure and pride. To all these reasons you must add, their lonely situation, and you cannot imagine what an effect on manners the great distances they live from each other has! Consider one of the last settlements in its first view: of what is it composed? Europeans who have not that sufficient share of knowledge they ought to have, in order to prosper; people who have suddenly passed from oppression, dread of government, and fear of laws, into the unlimited freedom of the woods. This sudden change must have a very great effect on most men, and on that class particularly. Eating of wild meat, whatever you may think, tends to alter their temper: though all the proof I can adduce, is, that I have seen it: and having no place of worship to resort to, what little society this might afford is denied them. The Sunday meetings, exclusive of religious benefits, were the only social bonds that might have inspired them with some degree of emulation in neatness. Is it then surprising to see men thus situated, immersed in great and heavy labours, degenerate a little? It is rather a wonder the effect is not more diffusive. The Moravians and the Quakers are the only instances in exception to what I have advanced. The first never settle singly, it is a colony of the society which emigrates; they carry with them their forms, worship, rules, and decency: the others never begin so hard, they are always able to buy improvements, in which there is a great advantage, for by that time the country is recovered from its first barbarity. Thus our bad people are those who are half cultivators and half hunters; and the worst of them are those who have degenerated altogether into the hunting state. As old ploughmen and new men of the woods, as Europeans and new made Indians, they contract the vices of both; they adopt the moroseness and ferocity of a native, without his mildness, or even his industry at home. If manners are not refined, at least they are rendered simple and inoffensive by tilling the earth; all our wants are supplied by it, our time is divided between labour and rest, and leaves none for the commission of great misdeeds. As hunters it is divided between the toil of the chase, the idleness of repose, or the indulgence of inebriation. Hunting is but a licentious idle life, and if it does not always pervert good dispositions; yet, when it is united with bad luck, it leads to want: want stimulates that propensity to rapacity and injustice, too natural to needy men, which is the fatal gradation. After this explanation of the effects which follow by living in the woods, shall we yet vainly flatter ourselves with the hope of converting the Indians? We should rather begin with converting our backsettlers; and now if I dare mention the name of religion, its sweet accents would be lost in the immensity of these woods. Men thus placed are not fit either to receive or remember its mild instructions; they want temples and ministers, but as soon as men cease to remain at home, and begin to lead an erratic life, let them be either tawny or white, they cease to be its disciples.

Thus have I faintly and imperfectly endeavoured to trace our society from the sea to our woods! yet you must not imagine that every person who moves back, acts upon the same principles, or falls into the same degeneracy. Many families carry with them all their decency of conduct, purity of morals, and respect of religion; but these are scarce, the power of example is sometimes irresistible. Even among these backsettlers, their depravity is greater or less, according to what nation or province they belong. Were I to adduce proofs of this, I might be accused of partiality. If there happens to be some rich intervals, some fertile bottoms, in those remote districts, the people will there prefer tilling the land to hunting, and will attach themselves to it; but even on these fertile spots you may plainly perceive the inhabitants to acquire a great degree of rusticity and selfishness.

It is in consequence of this straggling situation, and the astonishing power it has on manners, that the backsettlers of both the Carolinas, Virginia, and many other parts, have been long a set of lawless people; it has been even dangerous to travel among them. Government can do nothing in so extensive a country, better it should wink at these irregularities, than that it should use means inconsistent with its usual mildness. Time will efface those stains: in proportion as the great body of population approaches them they will reform, and become polished and subordinate. Whatever has been said of the four New England provinces, no such degeneracy of manners has ever tarnished their annals; their backsettlers have been kept within the bounds of decency, and government, by means of wise laws, and by the influence of religion. What a detestable idea such people must have given to the natives of the Europeans! They trade with them, the worst of people are permitted to do that which none but persons of the best characters should be employed in. They get drunk with them, and often defraud the Indians. Their avarice, removed from the eyes of their superiors, knows no bounds; and aided by the little superiority of knowledge, these traders deceive them, and even sometimes shed blood. Hence those shocking violations, those sudden devastations which have so often stained our frontiers, when hundreds of innocent people have been sacrificed for the crimes of a few. It was in consequence of such behaviour, that the Indians took the hatchet against the Virginians in 1774. Thus are our first steps trod, thus are our first trees felled, in general, by the most vicious of our people; and thus the path is opened for the arrival of a second and better class, the true American freeholders; the most respectable set of people in this part of the world: respectable for their industry, their happy independence, the great share of freedom they possess, the good regulation of their families, and for extending the trade and the dominion of our mother country.

Europe contains hardly any other distinctions but lords and tenants; this fair country alone is settled by freeholders, the possessors of the soil they cultivate, members of the government they obey, and the framers of their own laws, by means of their representatives. This is a thought which you have taught me to cherish; our difference from Europe, far from diminishing, rather adds to our usefulness and consequence as men and subjects. Had our forefathers remained there, they would only have crowded it, and perhaps prolonged those convulsions which had shook it so long. Every industrious European who transports himself here, may be compared to a sprout growing at the foot of a great tree; it enjoys and draws but a little portion of sap; wrench it from the parent roots, transplant it, and it will become a tree bearing fruit also. Colonists are therefore entitled to the consideration due to the most useful subjects; a hundred families barely existing in some parts of Scotland, will here in six years, cause an annual exportation of 10,000 bushels of wheat: 100 bushels being but a common quantity for an industrious family to sell, if they cultivate good land. It is here then that the idle may be employed, the useless become useful, and the poor become rich; but by riches I do not mean gold and silver, we have but little of those metals; I mean a better sort of wealth, cleared lands, cattle, good houses, good clothes, and an increase of people to enjoy them.

There is no wonder that this country has so many charms, and presents to Europeans so many temptations to remain in it. A traveller in Europe becomes a stranger as soon as he quits his own kingdom; but it is otherwise here. We know, properly speaking, no strangers; this is every person's country; the variety of our soils, situations, climates, governments, and produce, hath something which must please everybody. No sooner does an European arrive, no matter of what condition, than his eyes are opened upon the fair prospect; he hears his language spoke, he retraces many of his own country manners, he perpetually hears the names of families and towns with which he is acquainted; he sees happiness and prosperity in all places disseminated; he meets with hospitality, kindness, and plenty everywhere; he beholds hardly any poor, he seldom hears of punishments and executions; and he wonders at the elegance of our towns, those miracles of industry and freedom. He cannot admire enough our rural districts, our convenient roads, good taverns, and our many accommodations; he involuntarily loves a country where everything is so lovely. When in England, he was a mere Englishman; here he stands on a larger portion of the globe, not less than its fourth part, and may see the productions of the north, in iron and naval stores; the provisions of Ireland, the grain of Egypt, the indigo, the rice of China. He does not find, as in Europe, a crowded society, where every place is over-stocked; he does not feel that perpetual collision of parties, that difficulty of beginning, that contention which oversets so many. There is room for everybody in America; has he any particular talent, or industry? he exerts it in order to procure a livelihood, and it succeeds. Is he a merchant? the avenues of trade are infinite; is he eminent in any respect? he will be employed and respected. Does he love a country life? pleasant farms present themselves; he may purchase what he wants, and thereby become an American farmer. Is he a labourer, sober and industrious? he need not go many miles, nor receive many informations before he will be hired, well fed at the table of his employer, and paid four or five times more than he can get in Europe. Does he want uncultivated lands? thousands of acres present themselves, which he may purchase cheap. Whatever be his talents or inclinations, if they are moderate, he may satisfy them. I do not mean that every one who comes will grow rich in a little time; no, but he may procure an easy, decent maintenance, by his industry. Instead of starving he will be fed, instead of being idle he will have employment; and these are riches enough for such men as come over here. The rich stay in Europe, it is only the middling and the poor that emigrate. Would you wish to travel in independent idleness, from north to south, you will find easy access, and the most cheerful reception at every house; society without ostentation, good cheer without pride, and every decent diversion which the country affords, with little expense. It is no wonder that the European who has lived here a few years, is desirous to remain; Europe with all its pomp, is not to be compared to this continent, for men of middle stations, or labourers.

An European, when he first arrives, seems limited in his intentions, as well as in his views; but he very suddenly alters his scale; two hundred miles formerly appeared a very great distance, it is now but a trifle; he no sooner breathes our air than he forms schemes, and embarks in designs he never would have thought of in his own country. There the plenitude of society confines many useful ideas, and often extinguishes the most laudable schemes which here ripen into maturity. Thus Europeans become Americans.

But how is this accomplished in that crowd of low, indigent people, who flock here every year from all parts of Europe? I will tell you; they no sooner arrive than they immediately feel the good effects of that plenty of provisions we possess: they fare on our best food, and they are kindly entertained; their talents, character, and peculiar industry are immediately inquired into; they find countrymen everywhere disseminated, let them come from whatever part of Europe. Let me select one as an epitome of the rest; he is hired, he goes to work, and works moderately; instead of being employed by a haughty person, he finds himself with his equal, placed at the substantial table of the farmer, or else at an inferior one as good; his wages are high, his bed is not like that bed of sorrow on which he used to lie: if he behaves with propriety, and is faithful, he is caressed, and becomes as it were a member of the family. He begins to feel the effects of a sort of resurrection; hitherto he had not lived, but simply vegetated; he now feels himself a man, because he is treated as such; the laws of his own country had overlooked him in his insignificancy; the laws of this cover him with their mantle. Judge what an alteration there must arise in the mind and thoughts of this man; he begins to forget his former servitude and dependence, his heart involuntarily swells and glows; this first swell inspires him with those new thoughts which constitute an American. What love can he entertain for a country where his existence was a burthen to him; if he is a generous good man, the love of this new adoptive parent will sink deep into his heart. He looks around, and sees many a prosperous person, who but a few years before was as poor as himself. This encourages him much, he begins to form some little scheme, the first, alas, he ever formed in his life. If he is wise he thus spends two or three years, in which time he acquires knowledge, the use of tools, the modes of working the lands, felling trees, etc. This prepares the foundation of a good name, the most useful acquisition he can make. He is encouraged, he has gained friends; he is advised and directed, he feels bold, he purchases some land; he gives all the money he has brought over, as well as what he has earned, and trusts to the God of harvests for the discharge of the rest. His good name procures him credit. He is now possessed of the deed, conveying to him and his posterity the fee simple and absolute property of two hundred acres of land, situated on such a river. What an epocha in this man's life! He is become a freeholder, from perhaps a German boor—he is now an American, a Pennsylvanian, an English subject. He is naturalised, his name is enrolled with those of the other citizens of the province. Instead of being a vagrant, he has a place of residence; he is called the inhabitant of such a county, or of such a district, and for the

first time in his life counts for something; for hitherto he has been a cypher. I only repeat what I have heard many say, and no wonder their hearts should glow, and be agitated with a multitude of feelings, not easy to describe. From nothing to start into being; from a servant to the rank of a master; from being the slave of some despotic prince, to become a free man, invested with lands, to which every municipal blessing is annexed! What a change indeed! It is in consequence of that change that he becomes an American. This great metamorphosis has a double effect, it extinguishes all his European prejudices, he forgets that mechanism of subordination, that servility of disposition which poverty had taught him; and sometimes he is apt to forget too much, often passing from one extreme to the other. If he is a good man, he forms schemes of future prosperity, he proposes to educate his children better than he has been educated himself; he thinks of future modes of conduct, feels an ardour to labour he never felt before. Pride steps in and leads him to everything that the laws do not forbid: he respects them; with a heart-felt gratitude he looks toward the east, toward that insular government from whose wisdom all his new felicity is derived, and under whose wings and protection he now lives. These reflections constitute him the good man and the good subject. Ye poor Europeans, ye, who sweat, and work for the great—ye, who are obliged to give so many sheaves to the church, so many to your lords, so many to your government, and have hardly any left for yourselves— ye, who are held in less estimation than favourite hunters or useless lap-dogs—ye, who only breathe the air of nature, because it cannot be withheld from you; it is here that ye can conceive the possibility of those feelings I have been describing; it is here the laws of naturalisation invite every one to partake of our great labours and felicity, to till unrented, untaxed lands! Many, corrupted beyond the power of amendment, have brought with them all their vices, and disregarding the advantages held to them, have gone on in their former career of iniquity, until they have been overtaken and punished by our laws. It is not every emigrant who succeeds; no, it is only the sober, the honest, and industrious: happy those to whom this transition has served as a powerful spur to labour, to prosperity, and to the good establishment of children, born in the days of their poverty; and who had no other portion to expect but the rags of their parents, had it not been for their happy emigration. Others again, have been led astray by this enchanting scene; their new pride, instead of leading them to the fields, has kept them in idleness;

the idea of possessing lands is all that satisfies them —though surrounded with fertility, they have mouldered away their time in inactivity, misinformed husbandry, and ineffectual endeavours. How much wiser, in general, the honest Germans than almost all other Europeans; they hire themselves to some of their wealthy landsmen, and in that apprenticeship learn everything that is necessary. They attentively consider the prosperous industry of others, which imprints in their minds a strong desire of possessing the same advantages. This forcible idea never quits them, they launch forth, and by dint of sobriety, rigid parsimony, and the most persevering industry, they commonly succeed. Their astonishment at their first arrival from Germany is very great—it is to them a dream; the contrast must be powerful indeed; they observe their countrymen flourishing in every place; they travel through whole counties where not a word of English is spoken; and in the names and the language of the people, they retrace Germany. They have been an useful acquisition to this continent, and to Pennsylvania in particular; to them it owes some share of its prosperity: to their mechanical knowledge and patience it owes the finest mills in all America, the best teams of horses, and many other advantages. The recollection of their former poverty and slavery never quits them as long as they live.

The Scotch and the Irish might have lived in their own country perhaps as poor, but enjoying more civil advantages, the effects of their new situation do not strike them so forcibly, nor has it so lasting an effect. From whence the difference arises I know not, but out of twelve families of emigrants of each country, generally seven Scotch will succeed, nine German, and four Irish. The Scotch are frugal and laborious, but their wives cannot work so hard as German women, who on the contrary vie with their husbands, and often share with them the most severe toils of the field, which they understand better. They have therefore nothing to struggle against, but the common casualties of nature. The Irish do not prosper so well; they love to drink and to quarrel; they are litigious, and soon take to the gun, which is the ruin of everything; they seem beside to labour under a greater degree of ignorance in husbandry than the others; perhaps it is that their industry had less scope, and was less exercised at home. I have heard many relate, how the land was parcelled out in that kingdom; their ancient conquest has been a great detriment to them, by over-setting their landed property. The lands possessed by a few, are leased down *ad infinitum*, and the occupiers often pay five guineas an acre. The poor are

worse lodged there than anywhere else in Europe; their potatoes, which are easily raised, are perhaps an inducement to laziness: their wages are too low, and their whisky too cheap.

There is no tracing observations of this kind, without making at the same time very great allowances, as there are everywhere to be found, a great many exceptions. The Irish themselves, from different parts of that kingdom, are very different. It is difficult to account for this surprising locality, one would think on so small an island an Irishman must be an Irishman: yet it is not so, they are different in their aptitude to, and in their love of labour.

The Scotch on the contrary are all industrious and saving; they want nothing more than a field to exert themselves in, and they are commonly sure of succeeding. The only difficulty they labour under is, that technical American knowledge which requires some time to obtain; it is not easy for those who seldom saw a tree, to conceive how it is to be felled, cut up, and split into rails and posts. . . .

Agreeable to the account which several Scotchmen have given me of the north of Britain, of the Orkneys, and the Hebride Islands, they seem, on many accounts, to be unfit for the habitation of men; they appear to be calculated only for great sheep pastures. Who then can blame the inhabitants of these countries for transporting themselves hither? This great continent must in time absorb the poorest part of Europe; and this will happen in proportion as it becomes better known; and as war, taxation, oppression, and misery increase there. The Hebrides appear to be fit only for the residence of malefactors, and it would be much better to send felons there than either to Virginia or Maryland. What a strange compliment has our mother country paid to two of the finest provinces in America! England has entertained in that respect very mistaken ideas; what was intended as a punishment, is become the good fortune of several; many of those who have been transported as felons, are now rich, and strangers to the stings of those wants that urged them to violations of the law: they are become industrious, exemplary, and useful citizens. The English government should purchase the most northern and barren of those islands; it should send over to us the honest, primitive Hebrideans, settle them here on good lands, as a reward for their virtue and ancient poverty; and replace them with a colony of her wicked sons. The severity of the climate, the inclemency of the seasons, the sterility of the soil, the tempestuousness of the sea, would afflict and punish enough. Could there be found a spot

better adapted to retaliate the injury it had received by their crimes? Some of those islands
might be considered as the hell of Great Britain,
where all evil spirits should be sent. Two essential ends would be answered by this simple operation. The good people, by emigration, would be
rendered happier; the bad ones would be placed
where they ought to be. In a few years the dread
of being sent to that wintry region would have a
much stronger effect than that of transportation.
—This is no place of punishment; were I a poor
hopeless, breadless Englishman, and not restrained
by the power of shame, I should be very thankful
for the passage. It is of very little importance how,
and in what manner an indigent man arrives; for
if he is but sober, honest, and industrious, he has
nothing more to ask of heaven. Let him go to
work, he will have opportunities enough to earn a
comfortable support, and even the means of procuring some land; which ought to be the utmost
wish of every person who has health and hands to
work. I knew a man who came to this country, in
the literal sense of the expression, stark naked; I
think he was a Frenchman, and a sailor on board
an English man-of-war. Being discontented, he
had stripped himself and swam ashore; where,
finding clothes and friends, he settled afterwards
at Maraneck, in the county of Chester, in the
province of New York: he married and left a
good farm to each of his sons. I knew another person who was but twelve years old when he was
taken on the frontiers of Canada, by the Indians;
at his arrival at Albany he was purchased by a
gentleman, who generously bound him apprentice
to a tailor. He lived to the age of ninety, and left
behind him a fine estate and a numerous family,
all well settled; many of them I am acquainted
with.—Where is then the industrious European
who ought to despair?

After a foreigner from any part of Europe is
arrived, and become a citizen; let him devoutly
listen to the voice of our great parent, which says
to him, "Welcome to my shores, distressed European; bless the hour in which thou didst see my
verdant fields, my fair navigable rivers, and my
green mountains!—If thou wilt work, I have bread
for thee; if thou wilt be honest, sober, and industrious, I have greater rewards to confer on thee
—ease and independence. I will give thee fields
to feed and clothe thee; a comfortable fireside to
sit by, and tell thy children by what means thou
hast prospered; and a decent bed to repose on. I
shall endow thee beside with the immunities of a
freeman. If thou wilt carefully educate thy children, teach them gratitude to God, and reverence
to that government, that philanthropic government, which has collected here so many men and
made them happy. I will also provide for thy
progeny; and to every good man this ought to be
the most holy, the most powerful, the most earnest
wish he can possibly form, as well as the most con-
solatory prospect when he dies. Go thou and work
and till; thou shalt prosper, provided thou be just,
grateful, and industrious."

ENGLISH COLONIAL ADMINISTRATION

ENGLISH COLONIAL POLICY was based on the assumption that colonies and metropolis formed a single empire, the profit of which belonged to the metropolis. To this end, successive laws imposed increasingly detailed restrictions on colonial economic life. Though restrictions were balanced by privileges and bounties, the latter helped very few colonials as compared to those who were hindered by the multiplication of restraints and the increased efficiency of control.

Since colonial markets and supplies belonged to the metropolis, all colonial staples (their number was increased by each Navigation Act) must be carried to England, and colonial trade was limited to England and her empire except in specified instances. Vessels leaving the Mediterranean ports, with which the colonies were allowed a direct trade, must touch at a British port before they returned home. Colonial enterprise was excluded from activities that might compete with English business: the manufacture of woolens was forbidden; iron mining was encouraged but the milling of pig iron was limited; such colonial manufactures as beaver hats might not be exported from one Province to the next. Colonial expansion beyond the Appalachians after 1763 was opposed not only for political reasons but also because such distant settlements would be unable to acquire English goods and so might set up manufactures for themselves.

Imperial control was divided among many agencies whose work was supposed to be co-ordinated by the Board of Trade. The Board, which had been organized in 1696 on the initiative of a group of merchants, was as much concerned with British foreign and domestic commerce as with colonial administration. In that field, the Board of Trade acted as adviser to Cabinet and Privy Council and as the co-ordinating agency which received colonial communications and brought them to the attention of the department immediately affected. Among the Board's own manifold activities, drawing up the instructions of royal governors and scrutinizing colonial laws presented for royal approval were important methods of imperial control, for they afforded a check on the colonial executive and at least a negative influence on colonial legislation.

Colonial laws were subject to both legal and economic challenge before the Board of Trade. If opposition made good its arguments after hearing, the Board recommended that the Privy Council disallow the law. A disallowed law ceased to be valid but, in certain instances, acts done under its authority might be permitted to stand.

Though the Board of Trade varied in activity and influence and finally became a wholly advisory body in 1766, when a Secretary of State for the Colonies was added to the Cabinet, its recommendations on disallowance were accepted by the Privy Council. Colonial laws were disallowed for three principal reasons: interference with the royal prerogative, hindrance of English economic interest, or conflict with English law. The Board's procedure was fair and judicial, but its frequent interference in such local matters as Virginia's quarantine of ships importing convicts or servants contributed to creating the temper which made the Revolution possible.

Of the three examples of British administrative activity cited here, the first, the removal of Governor Hardy, illustrates the control the Board attempted to exercise over the colonial executive. The second, the disallowance of the Virginia insolvency act, shows how it tried to keep colonial legislation in accord with fixed principles of protecting British interests. The third, the refusal of a concession in Cape Breton to a group of British capitalists, indicates that the policy of restricting colonial economic life was applied also to the investment of British capital in the plantations overseas. The policy of control was thus not limited to colonial enterprise; the Sir Samuel Fludyer (1705–1768) whose associates were first

granted and then denied the privilege of digging coal on Cape Breton was a wealthy London merchant, active in City affairs and a deputy governor of the Bank of England.

The documents relating to Governor Hardy come from *The New Jersey Archives*, Vol. IX (Newark, 1885). The disallowance of the Virginia statute is from *Acts of the Privy Council: Colonial Series*, Vol. IV (London, 1912). The refusal of the Cape Breton concession is from the same source, Vols. IV and V.

The Appointment and Removal of a Royal Governor

DRAUGHT OF AN INSTRUCTION for the Governors of Nova Scotia, New Hampshire, New York, New Jersey, Virginia, North Carolina, South Carolina, Georgia. Barbadoes, Leeward Islands, Bermuda, Bahama and Jamaica relative to the Tenure of the Commissions to be by them granted to the Judges and other Officers and Ministers of Justice in the said Colonies.

Whereas Laws have been lately passed or attempted to be passed in several of our Colonies in America, enacting that the Judges of the several Courts of Judicature or other Chief Officers of Justice in the said Colonies shall hold their Offices during good behaviour; and whereas the Governors or other Chief Officers of several others of our said Colonies have granted Commissions to the Judges or other Chief Officers of Justice by which they have been impowered to hold their said Offices during good Behaviour contrary to the express directions of the Instructions given to the said Governors or other Chief Officers by us or by our Royal Predecessors; And whereas it does not appear to us that in the present situation and Circumstances of our said Colonies it would be either for the interest and advantage of the said Colonies or of this Our Kingdom of Great Britain that the Judges or other Chief Officers of Justice should hold their Offices during good Behaviour. It is therefore our express will and pleasure that you do not upon any pretence whatever, upon pain of being removed from your Government give your Assent to any Act by which the Tenure of the Commissions to be granted to the Chief Judges or other Justices of the several Courts of Judicature shall be regulated or ascertained in any manner whatsoever. And you are to take particular care in all Commissions to be by you granted to the said Chief

Judges or other Justices of the Courts of Judicature that the said Commissions are granted during Pleasure only, agreeable to what has been the Ancient Practice and Usage in our said Colonies and Plantations.
[December, 1761]

MEMORANDUM OF CASE referred to the Attorney and Solicitor General as to whether Governor Hardy's appointment of Judges during good behavior are valid.

By His Majesty's Letters Patent bearing date at Westminster the 　　 day of 　　 1761, Josiah Hardy Esqr was appointed to be Captain General & Governor in Chief of Nova Cæsarea or New Jersey, and was thereby required to do and execute all things in due manner that belong unto his said Command and the trust reposed in him, according to the several Powers and directions granted or appointed by his said Commission, & the Instructions & Authorities therewith given him, or by such further Powers, Instructions and Authorities as should at any time be granted or appointed him under His Majesty's Signet & sign manual, or by order of His Majesty in his Privy Council, and according to such reasonable Laws & Statutes as were then in force, or should be made and agreed upon by him with the Advice and Consent of the Council and the Assembly of the said Province under his Government, in such manner and form as was therein expressed.

The said Josiah Hardy was further impowered by the said Letters Patent to erect, constitute and establish such and so many Courts of Judicature and publick Justice within the said Province under his Government as he should think fit and necessary for the hearing and determining of all Causes as well Criminal as Civil according to Law and equity and for awarding of Execution thereupon, with all reasonable and necessary Powers, Authorities, Fees & Privileges belonging thereto; and also to constitute and appoint Judges and in Cases requisite Commissioners of Oyer and Terminer, Justices of the Peace, and other necessary Officers and Ministers in the said Province for the better Administration of Justice, and putting the Laws in Execution.

By His Majesty's general Instructions to the said Josiah Hardy Esqr under His Majesty's Signet and Sign Manual, bearing date the 30th day of June 1761, which said Instructions are referred to in, and were delivered with the above recited Letters Patent, it is directed, that all Commissions to be granted by him the said Josiah Hardy to any Person or Persons to be Judges, Justices of the Peace or other necessary Officers should be granted during Pleasure only.

Some time after Mr Hardy's Arrival in his Government, he thought fit to appoint Robert Hunter Morris Esqr to be Chief Justice, and two other Gentlemen to be second & third Judges of the supreme Court during their good Behaviour.

Q. Are such Appointments of these Judges to be Judges of the Supreme Court during good Behaviour, contrary to the express Directions of His Majesty's Instructions to the Governor, legal and valid Appointments?

Q. If such Appointments are not legal & Valid, by what Authority and in what manner may they be set aside?

[March 1762]

Copy of Representation from the B: of Trade to the King in Council, for removing Mr Hardy from the Government of New Jersey, dated March 27th 1762 for his having appointed three Judges of that Province during their good behaviour, in Disobedience to his Majesty's Instructions.

To the Kings most Excellent Majesty,

May it please your Majesty,

Having lately recd a letter from Josiah Hardy Esqr Governor of your Majesty's Province of New Jersey, dated the 20th of Janry last, acquainting Us amongst other things that he had granted a Commission to Robert Hunter Morris Esqr to be Chief Justice and also Commissions to two other Gentlemen to be second and third Judges of the supreme Court of Justice in that Province, during their good behaviour, it is our duty humbly to lay before your Majesty the annex'd extract of so much of Mr Hardy's letter as relates to this matter.

We have already in Our humble Representation to your Majesty of the 11th of November last so fully set forth Our Opinion of the impropriety of the Judges in the Plantations holding their Offices during good behaviour and the operation, wch in the present state of those Plantations such a Constitution would have to lessen their just and proper dependance upon your Majesty's Government that it is unnecessary for Us to add any thing further upon that head, and your Majesty's General Instructions to all your Governors and those Instructions in particular which were grounded upon that Representation are so full and so positive that We cannot offer any thing that may in the least degree extenuate so premeditated and unprecedented an Act of disobedience of your Majesty's Governor of New Jersey, in a matter so essential to your Majesty's interest and Service, not only in that Province but in all other your Majesty's American Dominions.

The appointing Mr Morris to be Chief Justice after the Contempt he had shown of your Majesty's authority, by procuring a person who had been appointed to that Office in consequence of His late Majesty's Warrant, to be superseded by a Judgment of that Court, in which he claimed to preside by a bare authority of the Governor, is alone such an example of misconduct, as does, in our opinion, render the Governor unworthy of the Trust your Majesty has conferred upon him. But aggravated as his Guilt is by the mode of the appointment and by the influence which it will necessary have in the neighbouring Provinces of Pennsylvania and New York, and particularly in the latter, where the utmost zeal and efforts of the Lieutt Governor has been hardly sufficient to restrain the intemperate zeal and indecent opposition of the Assembly to your Majesty's authority, and Royal Determination upon this point: It becomes, under these Circumstances, our indispensible duty to propose that this Gentleman may be forthwith Recalled from his Government, as a necessary example to deter others in the same situation from like Acts of Disobedience to your Majesty's Orders, and as a measure essentially necessary to support your Majesty's just Rights and authority in the Colonies and to enable Us to do Our duty in the station your Majesty has been graciously pleased to place Us in, and effectually to execute the Trust committed to Us.

Which is most humbly submitted.

Sandys   Ed Eliot
Soame Jenyns Geo: Rice
Ed Bacon   John Roberts
John Yorke

Whitehall March 27th 1762

LETTER from the Earl of Egremont to Governor Hardy—informing him of his removal from the Governorship of New Jersey.

Whitehall Septr 11th 1762

Govr Hardy.

Sir,

His Majesty having in consequence of the strong Representation of the Board of Trade to the King in Council, judged it expedient to put an End to your Commission of Governor of New Jersey; I am to acquaint you that His Majesty has been pleased to appoint William Franklin Esqr to succeed you in that office; and that Mr Franklin will repair to New Jersey, as soon as His Commission and Instructions can be expedited.

I am &c
Egremont

The Disallowance of a Colonial Statute

[A VIRGINIA ACT of Dec., 1762—for relief of insolvent debtors, for the effectual discovery and more equal distribution of their estates—is disallowed, in accordance with the Committee report of 9 July, agreeing with the Board of Trade representation of 6 July referred to them on 7 July, which set forth] that as this Act appeared to the said Lords Commissioners to affect the Property of British Creditors, they Communicated a Copy of it to the Principal Merchants of London trading to Virginia, to the end, that if the Act should in their judgment be prejudicial to their Interests, they might have an opportunity of being heard against it. And that the said Lords Commissioners having accordingly been attended by several of the said Merchants in behalf of themselves and the Merchants of Bristol, and also by the Agent of the Colony, and having heard what each party had to offer in Objection to, and in support of the said Act, it appeared, that the Operation of this Act being not confined to Insolvents in Prison, but extended to Debtors in general, it was principally in the Nature and Spirit of a Bankrupt Law, which although just and equitable in its abstract principle, had always been found in its execution to afford such opportunities for fraudulent practices that even in this Country, where in most cases the whole number of Creditors are resident on the spot, it might well be doubted whether the fair Trader did not receive more detriment than benefit from such a Law; But in a Colony where it is computed that not above a tenth part of its Creditors reside, a Bankrupt Law had hitherto been deemed inadmissable on account of the Injustice of its Operation with respect to the other Nine tenths of the Creditors residing in Great Britain. And that upon this Consideration, His late Majesty was pleased, in consequence of a Representation of the said Lords Commissioners dated the 29th of June 1758, to repeal an Act passed in the Province of the Massachusets Bay in 1757, for providing Remedy for Bankrupts and their Creditors. That exclusive of this general Objection to the Principle of the Act, as a Bankrupt Law, there were several of its Provisions which the said Merchants complained of as unequal to the Creditors in general, or injurious to themselves in particular, the most material of which were—

First. That by this Act the Insolvent Debtor had it in his power to clear himself by a Voluntary Surrender of all his Effects, which the Creditors were obliged to accept; But that they had no means of compelling him to such Surrender, and therefore that the advantage was not reciprocal.

Secondly. That within Ninety days after Surrender, the Creditors resident in Virginia were, by Majority of Number (without regard to value as the English Law requires) to chuse two Assignees from amongst themselves, in which choice, the Creditors residing here could have no share.

Thirdly. That these Assignees were within three months to sell the Debtors effects by Auction, upon twelve months Credit; whereby the Recovery of the whole produce of such Sale was rendered precarious: And the Security of such part of it as might happen to be received was also endangered, by the want of any obligation on the Assignees to appoint a Treasurer (as is the practice here) or to place it in other safe custody.

Fourthly. That the Assignees were to be allowed five per Cent. for their trouble, which was contrary to the practice of this Country and an unreasonable diminution of the Insolvents effects, to the prejudice of his Creditors.

Fifthly. That it was indeed Enacted that Creditors in Great Britain might transmit their Claims, duly proved, to their Agents, which being produced at any time before the Dividend was made should be allowed; But as the Act also declared that the Debtor might disprove any Demand and the Assignees might set one debt against another, and allow no more than should appear to be due on the Ballance of such an Account, the Merchants apprehended that they were thereby exposed to the possibility of great injustice by making them Debtors for consignments, which though made, might never have been received, or at Prices, which the Commodities, though received, might never fetch.

Sixthly. That the Assignees might make a Dividend at the end of the twelve months after Sale of the Debtors Estate, but they were obliged (except in the Case of extraordinary circumstances in the recovery and Sale of the Insolvents effects) to make a final Dividend within Eighteen months after their appointment, and from thenceforth the Insolvent was made free and clear, whereby the British Creditor, if at this distance he should not have timely Notice of his Debtors Insolvency, or if his power of Attorney should miscarry, might frequently lose his whole debt.

And lastly, that this Act gave to Insolvents an allowance of Poundage on their Dividends without Limitation of any certain sum, which was conceived to be highly unreasonable and in improper encouragement to run in Debt, and that though the British Statute of Bankruptcy allowed the Bankrupt a Poundage and at the same Rates yet it restrained the amount of that allowance to the sum of three hundred pounds.

That for these Reasons the Principal Merchants of London and Bristol trading to Virginia, and the Merchants of Glasgow and Liverpoole (by Memorials presented to the said Lords Commissioners) had requested that this Act which took effect the 1st of June last, might not be suffered to continue in force.

The Refusal of the Cape Breton Concession

July 20, 1763

[REFERENCE to the Committee, and on 19 March by them to the Board of Trade, of the memorial of the Hon. William Howe on behalf of himself and other officers who served in America in the late war and are entitled under the proclamation to grants of land there:] being desirous to become Adventurers in Opening Coal Mines and Endeavouring to Establish a Colliery on the Island of Cape Breton for the better Supplying the several Colonies and Garrisons, on the Continent with Fuel, They humbly pray, that they may have granted to them (as their Allotment) a Tract of Land on the East shore of the aforesaid Island extending from the Point on the North side of Mire Bay to the South East side of the Entrance into the Labrador and Seven Miles Inland to be computed from the point and entrance abovementioned and supposed to contain about fifty five thousand Acres, which Tract the Memorialists will settle with Inhabitants in the manner directed by his Majestys Royal Proclamation.

[A memorial of Charles, Duke of Richmond, Lennox and Aubigny, for a grant in fee of Cape Breton Island to himself and others of the nobility and gentry, is referred to the Board of Trade. On 18 May their report is referred to the Committee.]

[Order is given in accordance with the Committee report of 21 May, agreeing with the Board of Trade, who represented] That was there no other Consideration in this matter than whether your Majesty should be graciously pleased to Grant the Island of Cape Breton to the Noble Memorialist as a Mark of your Royal favour and regard, we should not Hesitate to recommend to your Majesty to comply with his Graces request; but it is our Duty in the Station We are in, to consider the Publick Interest only, and to lay before your Majesty such Plans as will in our Judgment most effectively conduce to the promoting and extending the Commerce of your Majestys Kingdoms by encouraging the speedy Settlement of those Valuable Territories and Islands Ceded and Confirmed to your Majesty by the late Treaty of Peace; Your Majesty has been pleased to approve the Opinion, which we humbly offered in our Representations upon the Earl of Egmont's Memorials, praying a Grant of the Island of St. John, to which We beg leave to refer, and as the great extent of the Grant then desired was one Principal Argument which induced us humbly to advise your Majesty not to Comply with his Lordships Proposal, the same Argument Operates more strongly upon our Judgment in the present Instance, as the Island of Cape Breton is very Considerably larger than that of St. John. We cannot therefore avoid giving our humble Advice to your Majesty, that the same Principles your Majesty has been pleased to direct to be pursued in the Granting your Majestys Lands in the Island of St. John, should be adopted in Grants to be made of Lands in the Island of Cape Breton.

[Reference to the Committee of a Board of Trade representation of 10 July on several proposals for working collieries in Cape Breton Island.]

[Order in accordance with the Committee report of 17 July, that the proposal of Sir Samuel Fludyer and his associates should be accepted as the most advantageous for his Majesty's service, and that the proposals, the Board of Trade representation, and the scheme of Joseph Guerish for the improvement of the coal mines in Nova Scotia, be referred to the Treasury for their opinion as to the manner and terms of the grant.]

[Reference to the Committee of a Treasury report, a Board of Trade representation and other papers relating to several proposals for working coalmines in Cape Breton Island.]

[Order in accordance with the Committee report of 29 Nov., agreeing with the Treasury, who represented] that in the late Grants of Lands in America Your Majesty had been advised to make an Express reservation of Mines of Coal which, although of less immediate and intrinsic Value than Gold, Silver and Copper, may yet, from other incidental Circumstances, and as a Material leading to Extensive manufactures, be consequentially and finally of as great, if not greater National Moment—That it has been the policy of this Century, to give large Bounties, upon the produce of pig and Bar Iron in Order to Divert the Colonies from the manufacture, that from the same Contemplation the Legislature has forbid the Erection of Slitting Mills in America, and that in Consequence of these Wise provisions, Iron is at present imported from the Colonies in the Material and returned to them in the Manufacture; That it appeared to them that it might seem a Sudden and Direct Contravention of this Excellent Policy, were they to advise Your Majesty to furnish America with the only possible means of Establishing a Manufacture, which Parliament has Exerted so much Authority and taken so many measures to prevent, that it has been alledged to the said Lords Commissioners, that the Quality of the Cape Breton Coal is the same as the Coal of Scotland, and therefore unfit for the manufacture of Iron by the Hammer but that they had no Satisfactory Evidence of this Fact laid before them, and that one of the petitioners, in particular,

being Examined to this essential point, answered with great Candour and Disinterestedness "that he thought more than probable, that Coal fit for any Manufacture, might be found in a Vein of such Extent as that of Cape Breton is represented to be." That the Argument in the Representation of the Lords Commissioners of Trade and plantations, drawn from the high price of Coals in England seems to be a good Reason for preventing the Exportation of them to America, but does not touch the other, and, as they think, the higher Considerations which spring from the Nature of Commerce, and the Relation of the Colonies.— That as the prudence of the measure is equivocal, the object of Advantage proposed, but it is very Confined, in as much as the utmost Expectation of Revenue for five years, amounts to no more than twenty five thousand pounds and after that time it is supposed the profits may be doubled.—That having opened the Mines of Coal in Cape Breton, it might be very Difficult afterwards to refuse the same privilege upon equal necessity or Convenience alledged to other provinces, where Coal proper for the Hammer might meet the Bar and everything necessary for the Manufacture of Iron be found within the provinces themselves; that for these Reasons the said Lords Commissioners of Your Majestys Treasury are humbly of opinion that the opening Coal Mines in America to be worked at Large is in itself at least a Disputeable measure, in point of Expediency, an Innovation in the system hitherto pursued in the Regulation of the Colonies, too Doubtful in the principle, and too Delicate in the Consequences to be adopted and recommended by an office.

[The Committee accordingly reported] that it will not be adviseable for Your Majesty at present to authorize or Encourage the opening Coal Mines to be Worked in the Island of Cape Breton and that all Petitions for that purpose ought to be dismissed.

THE NAVIGATION ACTS

PROTECTION of its carrying trade was the cornerstone of British colonial policy. In the four decades between the First and the Fourth Navigation Acts, that policy was developed and made definite. The first act, 1660, primarily concerned with shipping, reflects England's effort to drive the Dutch from the carrying trade. All colonial produce was to be brought to England in British ships manned by crews at least three quarters of which were British. Certain enumerated colonial products—notably sugar, tobacco, indigo, ginger, and dyestuffs—were to be carried only to British ports. Foreign goods in foreign bottoms must enter England directly from their country of origin.

Three years later, a similar law announced

its purpose to keep the colonies in dependence and render them "more beneficial" to England in the employment of seamen, as a market for woolens, and as an entrepôt for British commerce. Careful provision was made for enforcement by the exaction of bonds and the requirement that colonial governors take a "solemn oath" to abide by the law. In 1672, these provisions were further strengthened by the requirement of an export duty to be paid on enumerated commodities unless bonds were given that they would be brought to England. Though the Stuarts lost their throne, their colonial policy was continued under William and Mary. Restrictions were even tightened, for Ireland was excluded from free trade with the colonies.

While the Navigation Acts and their enforcement did hamper colonial trade, they were generally considered a proper use of Parliament's authority. Even Adam Smith considered navigation laws a necessary exercise of national power, and deemed the British colonial policy justifiable. An English contemporary, Josiah Tucker, disagreed with him. The positions of both these great advocates are presented here.

Adam Smith (1723-1790) was born in Scotland and educated at Glasgow and Oxford. He prepared for the Anglican ministry, but relinquished this intention to spend the rest of his life as professor of moral philosophy at Edinburgh and as an independent student and writer. His great book, *Inquiry into the Nature and Causes of the Wealth of Nations* (Glasgow, 1776) was written over a ten-year period during which he held no teaching position. Smith broke with Mercantilism as a theory and as a public policy. To this extent, he and Locke are among the very first of our modern men in their understanding of the true role of liberty in society. But in the matter of colonial management, Smith hedged and ended by placing defense above opulence. Polemics aside, his description of the English colonial system is a very fair one.

The selection used here is from Book IV, chapters 7 and 8 of the *Wealth of Nations.*

That the Dean of Gloucester Cathedral should have written the *Four Tracts . . . on Political and Commercial Subjects* (1774) indicates the practical turn which certain Christians' thinking had taken in the age of common sense. In his sermons, Josiah Tucker (1712-1799) proved that commerce and true religion promote the same virtues and so supplement each other to the good of the community. In the tracts, he presents economic doctrines much resembling those of Adam Smith. Tucker denies the bullion theory of wealth, insists that only industry can make a country rich and asserts that no political exertion, not all the fleets and armies of the world, can hold a nation's markets if another nation can supply goods more cheaply. Wars for trade's sake are useless, therefore, and the mercantilist economics fallacious. Only saving, frugality, and moral conduct can make a nation economically flourishing.

The first two tracts, which are more general in scope, were meant to be part of a text in political economy designed for the instruction of the Prince of Wales who was to be George III. Tucker gave up the plan when he found that any work presenting a "free, generous and impartial System of national Commerce" would have embarrassing political repercussions. The third and fourth tracts, based on the laissez-faire reasoning of the others, present Tucker's idea of a proper colonial policy. Since freedom to trade where they wish is what the Northern colonies actually want, the metropolis should allow that freedom, grant political independence if that is desired, and then conclude a treaty of commerce with the new nation. The colonists will tire of their bargain, no doubt, but even if they do not, Tucker argues, better free trade with an independent America than an attempt to keep her in subjection by force. An unsuccessful punitive expedition will not help English business; a successful war ending in an attempt to govern the continental colonies despotically will serve only to subvert English liberties. Peaceful separation, on the other hand, will save England the cost of colonial government and of bounties on colonial produce; it will not injure English trade, for even factious Americans are not fools enough to refuse to buy in the best market; and it may ultimately lead to a voluntary reunion as the weaker colonies seek English protection against oppression from the stronger.

Tucker's third tract was written in the same year (1766) that Franklin was proclaiming the colonies' complete loyalty; the fourth in 1774, before the fight at Concord.

The selections used here are from the *Third Tract* and the *Fourth Tract* and are from the original English editions.

The Wealth of Nations

BY ADAM SMITH

BOOK IV

EVERY EUROPEAN nation has endeavoured more or less to monopolize to itself the commerce of its colonies, and, upon that account, has prohibited the ships of foreign nations from trading to them, and has prohibited them from importing European goods from any foreign nation. But the manner in which this monopoly has been exercised in different nations has been very different.

Some nations have given up the whole commerce of their colonies to an exclusive company, to whom the colonies were obliged to sell the whole of their own surplus produce. It was the interest of the company, therefore, not only to sell the former as dear, and to buy the latter as cheap as possible, but to buy no more of the latter, even at this low price, than what they could dispose of for a very high price in Europe. It was their interest, not only to degrade in all cases the value of the surplus produce of the colony, but in many cases to discourage and keep down the natural increase of its quantity. Of all the expedients that can well be contrived to stunt the natural growth of a new colony, that of an exclusive company is undoubtedly the most effectual. This, however, has been the policy of Holland, though their company, in the course of the present century, has given up in many respects the exertion of their exclusive privilege. This too was the policy of Denmark till the reign of the late king. It has occasionally been the policy of France, and of late, since 1755, after it had been abandoned by all other nations, on account of its absurdity, it has become the policy of Portugal with regard at least to two of the principal provinces of Brazil, Pernambuco and Marannon.

Other nations, without establishing an exclusive company, have confined the whole commerce of their colonies to a particular port of the mother country, from whence no ship was allowed to sail, but either in a fleet and at a particular season, or, if single, in consequence of a particular licence, which in most cases was very well paid for. This policy opened, indeed, the trade of the colonies to all the natives of the mother country, provided they traded from the proper port, at the proper season, and in the proper vessels. But as all the different merchants, who joined their stocks in order to fit out those licensed vessels, would find it for their interest to act in concert, the trade which was carried on in this manner would necessarily be conducted very nearly upon the same principles as that of an exclusive company. The profit of those merchants would be almost equally exorbitant and oppressive. The colonies would be ill supplied, and would be obliged both to buy very dear, and to sell very cheap. This, however, till within these few years, had always been the policy of Spain, and the price of all European goods, accordingly, is said to have been enormous in the Spanish West Indies. . . . But it is chiefly in order to purchase European goods, that the colonies part with their own produce. The more, therefore, they pay for the one, the less they really get for the other, and the dearness of the one is the same thing with the cheapness of the other. The policy of Portugal is in this respect the same as the ancient policy of Spain, with regard to all its colonies, except Pernambuco and Marannon, and with regard to these it has lately adopted a still worse.

Other nations leave the trade of their colonies free to all their subjects, who may carry it on from all the different ports of the mother country, and who have occasion for no other licence than the common dispatches of the customhouse. In this case the number and dispersed situation of the different traders renders it impossible for them to enter into any general combination, and their competition is sufficient to hinder them from making very exorbitant profits. Under so liberal a policy the colonies are enabled both to sell their own produce and to buy the goods of Europe at a reasonable price. But since the dissolution of the Plymouth company, when our colonies were but in their infancy, this has always been the policy of England. It has generally too been that of France, and has been uniformly so since the dissolution of what, in England, is commonly called their Mississippi company. The profits of the trade, therefore, which France and England carry on with their colonies, though no doubt somewhat higher than if the competition was free to all other nations, are, however, by no means exorbitant; and the price of European goods accordingly is not extravagantly high in the greater part of the colonies of either of those nations.

In the exportation of their own surplus produce too, it is only with regard to certain commodities that the colonies of Great Britain are confined to the market of the mother country. These commodities having been enumerated in the act of navigation and in some other subsequent acts have upon that account been called *enumerated commodities*.[1] The rest are called *non-enumerated*; and may be exported directly to other countries, provided it is in British or Plantation ships, of which the owners and three-fourths of the mariners are British subjects.

Among the non-enumerated commodities are some of the most important productions of America and the West Indies; grain of all sorts, lumber, salt provisions, fish, sugar and rum.

Grain is naturally the first and principal object of the culture of all new colonies. By allowing them a very extensive market for it, the law encourages them to extend this culture much beyond the consumption of a thinly inhabited country, and thus to provide beforehand an ample subsistence for a continually increasing population.

In a country quite covered with wood, where timber consequently is of little or no value, the expense of clearing the ground is the principal obstacle to improvement. By allowing the colonies a very extensive market for their lumber, the law endeavours to facilitate improvement by raising the price of a commodity which would otherwise be of little value, and thereby enabling them to

make some profit of what would otherwise be mere expence.

In a country neither half-peopled nor half-cultivated, cattle naturally multiply beyond the consumption of the inhabitants, and are often upon that account of little or no value. But it is necessary, it has already been shewn, that the price of cattle should bear a certain proportion to that of corn before the greater part of the lands of any country can be improved. By allowing to American cattle, in all shapes, dead and alive, a very extensive market, the law endeavours to raise the value of a commodity of which the high price is so very essential to improvement. The good effects of this liberty, however, must be somewhat diminished by the 4th of George III. c. 15 which puts hides and skins among the enumerated commodities, and thereby tends to reduce the value of American cattle.

To increase the shipping and naval power of Great Britain, by the extension of the fisheries of our colonies, is an object which the legislature seems to have had almost constantly in view. Those fisheries, upon this account, have had all the encouragement which freedom can give them, and they have flourished accordingly. The New England fishery in particular was, before the late disturbances, one of the most important, perhaps, in the world. The whale-fishery which, notwithstanding an extravagant bounty, is in Great Britain carried on to so little purpose, that in the opinion of many people (which I do not, however, pretend to warrant) the whole produce does not much exceed the value of the bounties which are annually paid for it, is in New England carried on without any bounty to a very great extent. Fish is one of the principal articles with which the North Americans trade to Spain, Portugal and the Mediterranean.

Sugar was originally an enumerated commodity which could be exported only to Great Britain. But in 1731, upon a representation of the sugar-planters, its exportation was permitted to all parts of the world. The restrictions, however, with which this liberty was granted, joined to the high price of sugar in Great Britain, have rendered it, in a great measure, ineffectual. Great Britain and her colonies still continue to be almost the sole market for all the sugar produced in the British plantations. Their consumption increases so fast, that, though in consequence of the increasing improvement of Jamaica, as well as of the Ceded Islands, the importation of sugar has increased very greatly within these twenty years, the exportation to foreign countries is said to be not much greater than before.

[1] The commodities originally enumerated in 12 Car. II. c. 18, sec. 18, were sugar, tobacco, cotton-wool, indigo, ginger, fustic, and other dyeing woods.

Rum is a very important article in the trade which the Americans carry on to the coast of Africa, from which they bring back negroe slaves in return.

If the whole surplus produce of America in grain of all sorts, in salt provisions, and in fish, had been put into the enumeration, and thereby forced into the market of Great Britain, it would have interfered too much with the produce of the industry of our own people. It was probably not so much from any regard to the interest of America, as from a jealousy of this interference, that those important commodities have not only been kept out of the enumeration, but that the importation into Great Britain of all grain except rice, and of salt provisions, has, in the ordinary state of the law, been prohibited.

The non-enumerated commodities could originally be exported to all parts of the world. Lumber and rice, having been once put into the enumeration, when they were afterwards taken out of it, were confined, as to the European market, to the countries that lie south of Cape Finisterre. By the 6th of George III. c. 52. all non-enumerated commodities were subjected to the like restriction. The parts of Europe which lie south of Cape Finisterre, are not manufacturing countries, and we were less jealous of the colony ships carrying home from them any manufactures which could interfere with our own.

The enumerated commodities are of two sorts: first, such as are either the peculiar produce of America, or as cannot be produced, or at least are not produced, in the mother country. Of this kind are, molasses, coffee, cacao-nuts, tobacco, pimento, ginger, whale fins, raw silk, cotton-wool, beaver, and other peltry of America, indigo, fustic, and other dyeing woods: secondly, such as are not the peculiar produce of America, but which are and may be produced in the mother country, though not in such quantities as to supply the greater part of her demand, which is principally supplied from foreign countries. Of this kind are all naval stores, masts, yards, and bowsprits, tar, pitch, and turpentine, pig and bar iron, copper ore, hides and skins, pot and pearl ashes. The largest importation of commodities of the first kind could not discourage the growth or interfere with the sale of any part of the produce of the mother country. By confining them to the home market, our merchants, it was expected, would not only be enabled to buy them cheaper in the Plantations, and consequently to sell them with a better profit at home, but to establish between the Plantations and foreign countries an advantageous carrying trade, of which Great Britain was necessarily to be the center or emporium, as the European country into which those commodities were first to be imported. The importation of commodities of the second kind might be so managed, too, it was supposed, as to interfere, not with the sale of those of the same kind which were produced at home, but with that of those which were imported from foreign countries; because, by means of proper duties, they might be rendered always somewhat dearer than the former, and yet a good deal cheaper than the latter. By confining such commodities to the home market, therefore, it was proposed to discourage the produce, not of Great Britain, but of some foreign countries with which the balance of trade was believed to be unfavourable to Great Britain.

The prohibition of exporting from the colonies, to any other country but Great Britain, masts, yards, and bowsprits, tar, pitch, and turpentine, naturally tended to lower the price of timber in the colonies, and consequently to increase the expence of clearing their lands, the principal obstacle to their improvement. But about the beginning of the present century, in 1703, the pitch and tar company of Sweden endeavoured to raise the price of their commodities to Great Britain, by prohibiting their exportation, except in their own ships, at their own price, and in such quantities as they thought proper.[2] In order to counteract this notable piece of merchantile policy, and to render herself as much as possible independent, not only of Sweden, but of all the other northern powers, Great Britain gave a bounty upon the importation of naval stores from America and the effect of this bounty was to raise the price of timber in America, much more than the confinement to the home market could lower it; and as both regulations were enacted at the same time, their joint effect was rather to encourage than to discourage the clearing of land in America.

Though pig and bar iron too have been put among the enumerated commodities, yet as, when imported from America, they are exempted from considerable duties to which they are subject when imported from any other country,[3] the one part of the regulation contributes more to encourage the erection of furnaces in America, than the other to discourage it. There is no manufacture which occasions so great a consumption of wood as a furnace, or which can contribute so much to the clearing of a country over-grown with it.

The tendency of some of these regulations to

[2] Anderson, *Commerce*, a.d. 1703.
[3] 23 Geo. II., c. 29.

raise the value of timber in America, and thereby to facilitate the clearing of the land, was neither, perhaps, intended nor understood by the legislature. Though their beneficial effects, however, have been in this respect accidental, they have not upon that account been less real.

The most perfect freedom of trade is permitted between the British colonies of America and the West Indies, both in the enumerated and in the non-enumerated commodities. Those colonies are now become so populous and thriving, that each of them finds in some of the others a great and extensive market for every part of its produce. All of them taken together, they make a great internal market for the produce of one another.

The liberality of England, however, towards the trade of her colonies has been confined chiefly to what concerns the market for their produce, either in its rude state, or in what may be called the very first stage of manufacture. The more advanced, or more refined manufactures even of the colony produce, the merchants and manufacturers of Great Britain chuse to reserve to themselves, and have prevailed upon the legislature to prevent their establishment in the colonies, sometimes by high duties, and sometimes by absolute prohibitions. . . .

While Great Britain encourages in America the manufactures of pig and bar iron, by exempting them from duties to which the like commodities are subject when imported from any other country, she imposes an absolute prohibition upon the erection of steel furnaces and slit-mills in any of her American plantations.[4] She will not suffer her colonists to work on those more refined manufactures even for their own consumption; but insists upon their purchasing of her merchants and manufacturers all goods of this kind which they have occasion for.

She prohibits the exportation from one province to another by water, and even the carriage by land upon horseback or in a cart, of hats, of wools and woollen goods,[5] of the produce of America; a regulation which effectually prevents the establishment of any manufacture of such commodities for distant sale, and confines the industry of her colonists in this way to such coarse and household manufactures, as a private family commonly makes for its own use, or for that of some of its neighbors in the same province.

To prohibit a great people, however, from making all that they can of every part of their own produce, or from employing their stock and industry in the way that they judge most advantageous to themselves, is a manifest violation of the most sacred rights of mankind. Unjust, however, as such prohibitions may be, they have not hitherto been very hurtful to the colonies. Land is still so cheap, and, consequently, labour so dear among them, that they can import from the mother country, almost all the more refined or more advanced manufactures cheaper than they could make them for themselves. Though they had not, therefore, been prohibited from establishing such manufactures, yet in their present state of improvement, a regard to their own interest would, probably, have prevented them from doing so. In their present state of improvement, those prohibitions, perhaps, without cramping their industry, or restraining it from any employment to which it would have gone of its own accord, are only impertinent badges of slavery imposed upon them, without any sufficient reason, by the groundless jealousy of the merchants and manufacturers of the mother country. In a more advanced state they might be really oppressive and insupportable.

Great Britain, too, as she confines to her own market some of the most important productions of the colonies, so in compensation she gives to some of them an advantage in that market; sometimes by imposing higher duties upon the like productions when imported from other countries, and sometimes by giving bounties upon their importation from the colonies. In the first way she gives an advantage in the home-market to the sugar, tobacco, and iron of her own colonies, and in the second to their raw silk, to their hemp and flax, to their indigo, to their naval-stores, and to their building-timber. This second way of encouraging the colony produce by bounties upon importation, is, so far as I have been able to learn, peculiar to Great Britain. The first is not. Portugal does not content herself with imposing higher duties upon the importation of tobacco from any other country, but prohibits it under the severest penalties.

With regard to the importation of goods from Europe, England has likewise dealt more liberally with her colonies than any other nation.

Great Britain allows a part, almost always the half, generally a larger portion, and sometimes the whole of the duty which is paid upon the importation of foreign goods, to be drawn back upon their exportation to any foreign country. No independent foreign country, it was easy to foresee, would receive them if they came to it loaded with the heavy duties to which almost all foreign goods are subjected on their importation

---

[4] 23 Geo. II., c. 29.

[5] Hats under 5 Geo. II., c. 22; wools under 10 and 11 William III., c. 10.

into Great Britain. Unless, therefore, some part of those duties was drawn back upon exportation, there was an end of the carrying trade; a trade so much favoured by the mercantile system.

Our colonies, however, are by no means independent foreign countries; and Great Britain having assumed to herself the exclusive right of supplying them with all goods from Europe, might have forced them (in the same manner as other countries have done their colonies) to receive such goods, loaded with all the same duties which they paid in the mother country. But, on the contrary, till 1763, the same drawbacks were paid upon the exportation of the greater part of foreign goods to our colonies as to any independent foreign country. In 1763, by the 4th of Geo. III. c. 15. this indulgence was a good deal abated, and it was enacted, "That no part of the duty called the old subsidy should be drawn back for any goods of the growth, production, or manufacture of Europe or the East Indies, which should be exported from this kingdom to any British colony or plantation in America; wines, white callicoes and muslins excepted." Before this law, many different sorts of foreign goods might have been bought cheaper in the plantations than in the mother country; and some may still.

Of the greater part of the regulations concerning the colony trade, the merchants who carry it on, it must be observed, have been the principal advisers. We must not wonder, therefore, if, in the greater part of them, their interest has been more considered than either that of the colonies or that of the mother country. In their exclusive privilege of supplying the colonies with all the goods which they wanted from Europe, and of purchasing all such parts of their surplus produce as could not interfere with any of the trades which they themselves carried on at home, the interest of the colonies was sacrificed to the interest of those merchants. In allowing the same drawbacks upon the re-exportation of the greater part of European and East India goods to the colonies, as upon their re-exportation to any independent country, the interest of the mother country was sacrificed to it, even according to the mercantile ideas of that interest. It was for the interest of the merchants to pay as little as possible for the foreign goods which they sent to the colonies, and consequently, to get back as much as possible of the duties which they advanced upon their importation into Great Britain. They might thereby be enabled to sell in the colonies, either the same quantity of goods with a greater profit, or a greater quantity with the same profit, and, consequently, to gain something

either in the one way or the other. It was, likewise, for the interest of the colonies to get all such goods as cheap and in as great abundance as possible. But this might not always be for the interest of the mother country. She might frequently suffer both in her revenue, by giving back a great part of the duties which had been paid upon the importation of such goods; and in her manufactures, by being undersold in the colony market, in consequence of the easy terms upon which foreign manufactures could be carried thither by means of those drawbacks. The progress of the linen manufacture of Great Britain, it is commonly said, has been a good deal retarded by the drawbacks upon the re-exportation of German linen to the American colonies. . . .

The exclusive trade of the mother countries tends to diminish, or, at least, to keep down below what they would otherwise rise to, both the enjoyments and industry of all those nations in general, and of the American colonies in particular. It is a dead weight upon the action of one of the great springs which puts into motion a great part of the business of mankind. By rendering the colony produce dearer in all other countries, it lessens its consumption, and thereby cramps the industry of the colonies, and both the enjoyments and the industry of all other countries, which both enjoy less when they pay more for what they enjoy, and produce less when they get less for what they produce. By rendering the produce of all other countries dearer in the colonies, it cramps, in the same manner, the industry of all other countries, and both the enjoyments and the industry of the colonies. It is a clog which, for the supposed benefit of some particular countries, embarrasses the pleasures, and encumbers the industry of all other countries; but of the colonies more than of any other. It not only excludes, as much as possible, all other countries from one particular market; but it confines, as much as possible, the colonies to one particular market: and the difference is very great between being excluded from one particular market, when all others are open, and being confined to one particular market, when all others are shut up. The surplus produce of the colonies, however, is the original source of all that increase of enjoyments and industry which Europe derives from the discovery and colonization of America; and the exclusive trade of the mother countries tends to render this source much less abundant than it otherwise would be. . . .

To found a great empire for the sole purpose of raising up a people of customers, may at first appear a project fit only for a nation of shopkeepers. It is, however, a project altogether unfit for a nation of shopkeepers; but extremely fit for a nation whose government is influenced by shopkeepers. Such statesmen, and such statesmen only, are capable of fancying that they will find some advantage in employing the blood and treasure of their fellow-citizens to found and maintain such an empire. Say to a shopkeeper, Buy me a good estate, and I shall always buy my clothes at your shop, even though I should pay somewhat dearer than what I can have them for at other shops; and you will not find him very forward to embrace your proposal. But should any other person buy you such an estate, the shopkeeper would be much obliged to your benefactor if he would enjoin you to buy all your clothes at his shop. England purchased for some of her subjects, who found themselves uneasy at home, a great estate in a distant country. The price, indeed, was very small, and instead of thirty years purchase, the ordinary price of land in the present times, it amounted to little more than the expence of the different equipments which made the first discovery, reconnoitred the coast, and took a fictitious possession of the country. The land was good and of great extent, and the cultivators having plenty of good ground to work upon, and being for some time at liberty to sell their produce where they pleased, became in the course of little more than thirty or forty years (between 1620 and 1660) so numerous and thriving a people, that the shopkeepers and other traders of England wished to secure to themselves the monopoly of their custom. Without pretending, therefore, that they had paid any part, either of the original purchase-money, or of the subsequent expence of improvement, they petitioned the parliament that the cultivators of America might for the future be confined to their shop; first, for buying all the goods which they wanted from Europe; and, secondly, for selling all such parts of their own produce as those traders might find it convenient to buy. For they did not find it convenient to buy every part of it. Some parts of it imported into England might have interfered with some of the trades which they themselves carried on at home. Those particular parts of it, therefore, they were willing that the colonists should sell where they could; the farther off the better; and upon that account proposed that their market should be confined to the countries south of Cape Finisterre. A clause in the famous act of navigation established this truly shopkeeper proposal into a law.

The maintainance of this monopoly has hitherto been the principal, or more properly perhaps the sole end and purpose of the dominion which Great Britain assumes over her colonies. In the exclusive trade, it is supposed, consists the great advantage of provinces, which have never yet afforded either revenue or military force for the support of the civil government, or the defence of the mother country. The monopoly is the principal badge of their dependency, and it is the sole fruit which has hitherto been gathered from that dependency. Whatever expence Great Britain has hitherto laid out in maintaining this dependency, has really been laid out in order to support this monopoly. The expence of the ordinary peace establishment of the colonies amounted, before the commencement of the present disturbances, to the pay of twenty regiments of foot; to the expence of the artillery, stores, and extraordinary provisions with which it was necessary to supply them; and to the expence of a very considerable naval force which was constantly kept up, in order to guard, from the smuggling vessels of other nations, the immense coast of North America, and that of our West Indian islands. The whole expence of this peace establishment was a charge upon the revenue of Great Britain, and was, at the same time, the smallest part of what the dominion of the colonies has cost the mother country. If we would know the amount of the whole, we must add to the annual expence of this peace establishment the interest of the sums which, in consequence of her considering her colonies as provinces subject to her dominion, Great Britain has upon different occasions laid out upon their defence. We must add to it, in particular, the whole expence of the late war, and a great part of that of the war which preceded it. The late war was altogether a colony quarrel, and the whole expence of it, in whatever part of the world it may have been laid out, whether in Germany or the East Indies, ought justly to be stated to the account of the colonies. It amounted to more than ninety millions sterling, including not only the new debt which was contracted, but the two shillings in the pound additional land tax, and the sums which were every year borrowed from the sinking fund. The Spanish war which began in 1739, was principally a colony quarrel. Its principal object was to prevent the search of the colony ships which carried on a contraband trade with the Spanish main. This whole expence is, in reality, a bounty which was given in order to support a monopoly. The pretended purpose of it was to encourage the manufactures, and to increase the commerce of Great Britain. But its real effect has been to raise the rate of mercantile profit, and to enable our merchants to turn into a branch of trade, of which the returns are more slow and distant than those of the greater part of other trades, a greater proportion of their capital than they otherwise would have done; two events which if a bounty could have prevented, it might perhaps have been very well worth while to give such a bounty.

Under the present system of management, therefore, Great Britain derives nothing but loss from the dominion which she assumes over her colonies.

To propose that Great Britain should voluntarily give up all authority over her colonies, and leave them to elect their own magistrates, to enact their own laws, and to make peace and war as they might think proper, would be to propose such a measure as never was and never will be adopted, by any nation in the world. No nation ever voluntarily gave up the dominion of any province, how troublesome soever it might be to govern it, and how small soever the revenue which it afforded might be in proportion to the expence which it occasioned. Such sacrifices, though they might frequently be agreeable to the interest, are always mortifying to the pride of every nation, and what is perhaps of still greater consequence, they are always contrary to the private interest of the governing part of it, who would thereby be deprived of the disposal of many places of trust and profit, of many opportunities of acquiring wealth and distinction, which the possession of the most turbulent, and, to the great body of the people, the most unprofitable province seldom fails to afford. The most visionary enthusiast would scarce be capable of proposing such a measure, with any serious hopes at least of its ever being adopted. If it was adopted, however, Great Britain would not only be immediately freed from the whole annual expence of the peace establishment of the colonies, but might settle with them such a treaty of commerce as would effectually secure to her a free trade, more advantageous to the great body of the people, though less so to the merchants, than the monopoly which she at present enjoys. By thus parting good friends, the natural affection of the colonies to the mother country, which, perhaps, our late dissensions have well nigh extinguished, would quickly revive. It might dispose them not only to respect, for whole centuries together, that treaty of commerce which they had concluded with us at parting, but to favour us in war as well as in trade, and, instead of turbulent and factious subjects, to become our most faithful, affectionate, and generous allies; and the same sort of parental affection on the one side, and filial respect on the other, might revive between Great Britain and her colonies, which used to subsist between those of ancient Greece and the mother city from which they descended.

Tract III

BY JOSIAH TUCKER

. . . Upon the whole therefore, what is the Cause of such an amazing Outcry as you raise at present? —Not the Stamp Duty itself; all the World are agreed on that Head; and none can be so ignorant, or so stupid, as not to see, that this is a mere Sham and Pretence. What then are the real Grievances, seeing that the Things which you alledge are only the pretended ones? Why, some of you are exasperated against the Mother Country, on account of the Revival of certain Restrictions laid upon their Trade:—I say, a [1] *Revival;* for the same

Restrictions have been the standing Rules of Government from the Beginning; though not enforced at all Times with equal Strictness. During the late War, you *Americans* could not import the Manufactures of other Nations (which it is your constant Aim to do, and the Mother Country always to prevent) so conveniently as you can in Times of Peace; and therefore, there was no Need of watching you so narrowly, as far as that Branch of Trade was concerned. But immediately upon the Peace, the various Manufactures of *Europe,*

[1] Ever since the Discovery of *America*, it has been the System of every *European* Power, which had Colonies in that Part of the World, to confine (as far as Laws can confine) the Trade of the Colonies to the Mother Country, and to exclude all others, under the Penalty of Confiscation, &c. from partaking in it. Thus, the Trade of the *Spanish* Colonies is confined by Law to *Old Spain*,—the Trade of the *Brazils* to Portugal,—the Trade of *Martinico* and the other *French* Colonies to *Old France*,—and the Trade of *Curacoa* and *Suri-*

nam to *Holland.* But in one Instance the *Hollanders* make an Exception (perhaps a wise one) viz. in the Cafe of *Eustatia*, which is open to all the World. Now, that the *English* thought themselves entitled to the same Right over their Colonies, which other Nations claim over theirs, and that they exercised the same Right by making what Regulations they pleased, may be seen by the following Acts of Parliament, viz. 12 of Car. II. Chap. 18.—15 of Car. II. Ch. 7. —22 and 23 of C. II. Ch. 26.—25 of C. II. Ch. 7.—7 particularly those of *France*, which could not find Vent before, were spread, as it were, over all your Colonies, to the prodigious Detriment of your Mother Country; and therefore our late Set of Ministers acted certainly right, in putting in Force the Laws of their Country, in order to check this growing Evil. If in so doing, they committed any Error; or, if the Persons to whom the Execution of these Laws were intrusted, exceeded their Instructions; there is no Doubt to be made, but that all this will be rectified by the present Administration. And having done that, they will have done all that in Reason you can expect from them. But alas! the Expectations of an *American* carry him much further: For he will ever complain and smuggle, and smuggle and complain, 'till all Restraints are removed, and 'till he can both buy and sell, whenever, and wheresoever he pleases. Any thing short of this, is still a Grievance, a Badge of Slavery, an Usurpation on the natural Rights and Liberties of a free People, and I know not how many bad Things besides.

But, my good Friend, be assured, that these are Restraints, which neither the present, nor any future Ministry can exempt you from. They are the standing Laws of the Kingdom; and God forbid, that we should allow that dispensing Power to our Ministers, which we so justly deny to our Kings. In short, while you are a Colony, you must be subordinate to the Mother Country. These are the Terms and Conditions, on which you were permitted to make your first Settlements: They are the Terms and Conditions on which you alone can be entitled to the Assistance and Protection of *Great-Britain*;—they are also the fundamental Laws of the Realm;—and I will add further, that if *we* are obliged to pay many Bounties for the Importation of *your* Goods, and are excluded from purchasing such Goods, in other Countries (where we might purchase them on much cheaper Terms) in order to promote *your* Interest;—by Parity of Reason *you* ought to be subject to the like Exclusions, in order to pro-

and 8 of Will. III. Ch. 22.—10 and 11 of W. III. Ch. 21. —3 and 4 of Ann. Ch. 5 and 10.—8 of Ann. Ch. 13.— 12 of Ann. Ch. 9.—1 of G. I. Ch. 26.—3 of G. I. Ch. 21. —8 of G. I. Ch. 15 and 18.—11 of G. I. Ch. 29.—12 of G. I. Ch. 5.—2 of G. II. Ch. 28 and 35.—3 of G. II. Ch. 28.—4 of G. II. Ch. 15.—5 of G. II. Ch. 7 and 9. —6 of G. II. Ch. 13.—8 of G. II. Ch. 18.—11 of G. II. Ch. 29.—12 of G. II. Ch. 30.—13 of G. II. Ch. 4 and 7.— 15 and 16 of G. II. Ch. 23.—with many others of a later Date. I might also mention the Laws made in the Reign of his present Majesty; but as these Laws are now the Point Controversy, I forbear.

mote *ours*. This then being the Case, do not expect, from the present Ministry, that which is impossible for any Set of Ministers to grant. All that they can do, is to connive a while at your unlawful Proceedings. But this can be but of short Duration: For as soon as ever fresh Remonstrances are made by the *British* Manufacturers, and *British* Merchants, the Ministry must renew the Orders of their Predecessors; they must enforce the Laws; they must require Searches, and Confiscations to be made; and then the present Ministers will draw upon themselves, for *doing their Duty*, just the same Execrations, which you now bestow upon the last.

So much as to your first Grievance; and as to your second, it is, beyond Doubt, of a Nature still worse. For many among you are sorely concerned, That they cannot pay their *British* Debts with an *American* Sponge. This is an intolerable Grievance; and they long for the Day when they shall be freed from this galling Chain. Our Merchants in *London, Bristol, Liverpool, Glasgow, &c. &c.* perfectly understand *your* many Hints and Inuendoes to us, on this Head. But indeed, lest we should be so dull as not to comprehend your Meaning, you have spoken out, and proposed an open Association against paying your just Debts. Had *our* Debtors in any other Part of the Globe, had the *French* or *Spaniards* proposed the like (and surely they have all at least an equal Right) what Name would you have given to such Proceedings?—But I forget: You are not the faithless *French* or *Spaniards*: You are ourselves: You are honest *Englishmen*.

Your third Grievance is the Sovereignty of *Great-Britain*. For you want to be independent: You wish to be an Empire by itself, and to be no longer the Province of another. This Spirit is uppermost; and this Principle is visible in all your Speeches, and all your Writings, even when you take some Pains to disguise it.—"What! an Island! A Spot such as this to command the great and mighty Continent of *North-America!* Preposterous! A Continent, whose Inhabitants double every five and twenty Years! Who therefore, within a Century and an Half will be upwards of an hundred and twenty Millions of Souls!—Forbid it Patriotism, forbid it Politics, that such a great and mighty Empire as this, should be held in Subjection by the paltry Kingdom of *Great-Britain!* Rather let the Seat of Empire be transferred; and let it be fixt, where it ought to be, *viz.* in *Great America!*"

Now, my good Friend, I will not stay to dispute with you the Calculations, on which your Orators, Philosophers, and Politicians have, for some Years past, grounded these extravagant Conceits (though I think the Calculations themselves both false, and absurd); but I will only say, that while we have the Power, we may command your Obedience, if we please: And that it will be Time enough for you to propose the making us a Province to *America*, when you shall find yourselves able to execute the Project.

In the mean Time, the great Question is, What Course are *we* to take? And what are we to do with *you*, before you become this great and formidable People?—Plain and evident it is by the whole Tenor of your Conduct, that you endeavour, with all your Might, to drive us to Extremities. For no Kind of Outrage, or Insult, is omitted on your Part, that can irritate Individuals, or provoke a Government to chastise the Insolence, not to say the Rebellion of its Subjects; and you do not seem at all disposed to leave Room for an Accommodation. In short, the Sword is the only Choice, which you will permit us to make; unless we will chuse to give you entirely up, and subscribe a Recantation. Upon those Terms indeed, you will deign to acknowledge the Power and Authority of a *British* Parliament; —that is, you will allow, that we have a Right and a Power to give you Bounties, and to pay your Expences; but no other. A strange Kind of Allegiance this! And the first that has ever yet appeared in the History of Mankind!

However, this being the Case, shall we now compel you, by Force of Arms, to do your Duty? —Shall we procrastinate your Compulsion?—Or shall we entirely give you up, and have no other Connections with you, than if you had been so many Sovereign States, or Independent Kingdoms? One or other of these three will probably be resolved upon: And if it should be the first, I do not think that we have any Cause to fear the Event, or to doubt of Success.

For though your Populace may rob and plunder the Naked and Defenceless, this will not do the Business when a regular Force is brought against them. And a *British* Army, which performed so many brave Actions in *Germany*, will hardly fly before an *American* Mob; not to mention that our Officers and Soldiers, who passed several Campaigns with your Provincials in *America*, saw nothing either in their Conduct, or their Courage, which could inspire them with a Dread of seeing the Provincials a second Time.—Neither should we have the least Cause to suspect the *Fidelity* of our Troops, any more than their *Bravery*,—notwithstanding the base Insinuations of some of your Friends here (if indeed such Persons deserve to be called your Friends, who are in reality

your greatest Foes, and whom you will find to be so at the last); notwithstanding, I say, their Insinuations of the Feasibility of corrupting his Majesty's Forces, when sent over, by Means of large Bribes, or double Pay. This is a Surmise, as weak as it is wicked: For the Honour of the *British* Soldiery, let me tell you, is not so easily corrupted. The *French* in *Europe* never found it so, with all their Gold, or all their Skill for Intrigue, and insinuating Address. What then, in the Name of Wonder, have you to tempt them with in *America*, which is thus to overcome, at once, all their former Sense of Duty, all the Tyes of Conscience, Loyalty and Honour?—Besides, my Friend, if you really are so rich, as to be able to give *double* Pay, to our Troops, in a wrong Cause; do not grudge, let me beseech you, to give *one third* of *single* Pay (for we ask no more) in a right one:—And let it not be said, that you complain of Poverty, and plead an Inability to Pay your just Debts, at the very Instant that you boast of the scandalous Use which you intend to make of your Riches.

But notwithstanding all this, I am not for having Recourse to Military Operations. For granting, that we shall be victorious, still it is proper to enquire, before we begin, How we are to be benefited by our Victories? And what Fruits are to result from making you a conquered People?— Not an Increase of Trade; that is impossible: For a Shop-keeper will never get the more Custom by beating his Customers: And what is true of a Shop-keeper, is true of a Shop-keeping Nation. We may indeed vex and plague you, by stationing a great Number of Ships to cruize along your Coasts; and we may appoint an Army of Customhouse Officers to patrolle (after a Manner) two thousand Miles by Land. But while we are doing these Things *against you*, what shall we be doing *for ourselves?* Not much, I am afraid: For we shall only make you the more ingenious, the more intent, and the more inventive to deceive us. We shall sharpen your Wits, which are pretty sharp already, to elude our Searches, and to bribe and corrupt our Officers. And after that is done, we may perhaps oblige you to buy the Value of twenty, or thirty thousand Pounds of *British* Manufactures, more than you would otherwise have done,—at the Expence of two, or three hundred thousand Pounds Loss to *Great-Britain*, spent in Salaries, Wages, Ships, Forts, and other incidental Charges. Is this now a gainful Trade, and fit to be encouraged in a commercial Nation, so many Millions in Debt already? And yet this is the best, which we can expect by forcing you to trade with us, against your Wills, and against your Interests?

Therefore such a Measure as this being evidently detrimental to the Mother Country, I will now consider the second Proposal, *viz.* to procrastinate your Compulsion.—But what good can that do? And wherein will this Expedient mend the Matter? For if Recourse is to be had at last to the Military Power, we had better begin with it at first; it being evident to the whole World, that all Delays on our Side will only strengthen the Opposition on yours, and be interpreted by you as a Mark of Fear, and not as an Instance of Lenity. You swell with too much vain Importance, and Self-sufficiency already; and therefore, should we betray any Token of Submission; or should we yield to these your ill-humoured and petulant Desires; this would only serve to confirm you in your present Notions; *viz.* that you have nothing more to do, than to demand with the Tone of Authority, and to insist, with Threatenings and Defiance, in order to bring us upon our Knees, and to comply with every unreasonable Injunction, which you shall be pleased to lay upon us. So that at last, when the Time shall come of appealing to the Sword, and of deciding our Differences by Dint of Arms, the Consequence of this Procrastination will be, that the Struggle will become so much the more obstinate, and the Determination the more bloody. Nay, the Merchants themselves, whose Case is truly pitiable for having confided so much to your Honour, and for having trusted you with so many hundred thousand Pounds, or perhaps with some Millions of Property, and for whose Benefit alone such a Suspension of the Stamp Act could be proposed; they will find to their Costs, that every Indulgence of this Nature will only furnish another Pretence to you for the suspending of the Payment of their *just* Demands. In short, you declare, that the Parliament hath no Right to tax you; and therefore you demand a Renunciation of the Right, by repealing the Act. This being the Case, nothing more than a Renunciation can be satisfactory; because nothing else can amount to a Confession, that the Parliament has acted illegally and usurpingly in this Affair. A bare Suspension, or even a mere Repeal, is no Acknowledgment of Guilt; nay, it supposes quite the contrary; and only postpones the Exercise of this usurped Power to a more convenient Season. Consequently if you think you could justify the Non-payment of your Debts, 'till a Repeal took Place, you certainly can justify the Suspension of the Payment 'till we have acknowledged our Guilt. So that after all, the Question must come to this at last, *viz.* Shall

we renounce any Legislative Authority over you, and yet maintain you as we have hitherto done? Or shall we give you entirely up, unless you will submit to be governed by the same Laws as we are, and pay something towards maintaining yourselves?

The first it is certain we cannot do; and therefore the next Point to be considered is (which is also the third Proposal) Whether we are to give you entirely up?—*And after having obliged you to pay your Debts*, whether we are to have no further Connection with you, as a dependent State, or Colony.

Now, in order to judge properly of this Affair, we must give a Delineation of two Political Parties contending with each other, and struggling for Superiority:—And then we must consider, which of these two, must be first tired of the Contest, and obliged to submit.

Behold therefore a Political Portrait of the Mother Country;—a mighty Nation under one Government of a King and Parliament,—firmly resolved not to repeal the Act, but to give it Time to execute itself,—steady and temperate in the Use of Power,—not having Recourse to sanguinary Methods,—but enforcing the Law by making the Disobedient feel the Want of it,—determined to protect and cherish those Colonies, which will return to their Allegiance within a limited Time (suppose twelve or eighteen Months)—and as determined to compel the obstinate Revolters to pay their Debts,—then to cast them off, and to exclude them *for ever* from the manifold Advantages and Profits of Trade, which they now enjoy by no other Title, but that of being a Part of the *British* Empire. Thus stands the Case; and this is the View of Things on one Side.

Observe again a Prospect on the other; *viz.* a Variety of little Colonies under a Variety of petty Governments,—Rivals to, and jealous of each other,—never able to agree about any thing before,—and only now united by an Enthusiastic Fit of false Patriotism;—a Fit which necessarily cools in Time, and cools still the faster, in Proportion, as the Object which first excited it is removed, or changed. So much as to the general Outlines of your *American* Features;—but let us now take a nearer View of the Evils, which by your own mad Conduct you are bringing so speedily upon yourselves.

Externally, by being severed from the *British* Empire, you will be excluded from cutting Logwood in the Bays of *Campeachy* and *Honduras*, —from fishing on the Banks of *Newfoundland*, on the Coasts of *Labrador*, or in the Bay of *St. Lau-*

rence,—from trading (except by Stealth) with the Sugar Islands, or with the *British* Colonies in any Part of the Globe. You will also lose all the Bounties upon the Importation of your Goods into *Great-Britain:* You will not dare to seduce a single Manufacturer or Mechanic from us under Pain of Death; because you will then be considered in the Eye of the Law as mere Foreigners, against whom these Laws were made. You will lose the Remittance of 300,000l. a Year to pay your Troops; and you will lose the Benefit of these Troops to protect you against the Incursions of the much injured and exasperated Savages; moreover, in Case of Difference with other Powers, you will have none to complain to, none to assist you: For assure yourself, that *Holland, France,* and *Spain,* will look upon you with an evil Eye; and will be particularly on their Guard against you, lest such an Example should infect their own Colonies; not to mention that the two latter will not care to have such a Nest of professed Smugglers so very near them. And after all, and in Spite of any thing you can do, we in *Britain* shall still retain the greatest Part of your *European* Trade; because we shall give a better Price for many of your Commodities than you can have any where else; and we shall sell to you several of our Manufactures, especially in the Woollen, Stuff, and Metal Way, on cheaper Terms. In short, you will do then, what you only do now; that is, you will trade with us, as far as your Interest will lead you; and no farther.

Take now a Picture of your *internal* State. When the great Power, which combined the scattered Provinces together, and formed them into one Empire, is once thrown off; and when there will be no common Head to govern and protect, all your ill Humours will break forth like a Torrent: Colony will enter into Bickerings and Disputes against Colony; Faction will intrigue and cabal against Faction; and Anarchy and Confusion will every where prevail. The Leaders of your Parties will then be setting all their Engines to work, to make Fools become the Dupes of Knaves, to bring to Maturity their half-

formed Schemes and lurking Designs, and to give a Scope to that towering Ambition which was checked and restrained before. In the mean Time, the Mass of your People, who expected, and who were promised Mountains of Treasures upon throwing off, what was called, the Yoke of the Mother Country, will meet with nothing but sore Disappointments: Disappointments indeed! For instead of an imaginary Yoke, they will be obliged to bear a real, a heavy, and a galling one: Instead of being freed from the Payment of 100,000l. (which is the utmost that is now expected from them) they will find themselves loaded with Taxes to the Amount of at least 400,000l.: Instead of an Increase of Trade, they will feel a palpable Decrease; and instead of having Troops to defend them, and those Troops paid by *Great-Britain,* they must defend themselves, and pay themselves. Nay, the Number of the Troops to be paid, will be more than doubled; for some must be stationed in the back Settlements to protect them against the *Indians,* whom they have so often injured and exasperated, and others also on each Frontier to prevent the Encroachments of each Sister Colony. Not to mention, that the Expences of your Civil Governments will be necessarily increased; and that a Fleet, more or less, must belong to each Province for guarding their Coasts, ensuring the Payment of Duties, and the like.

Under all these Pressures and Calamities, your deluded Countrymen will certainly open their Eyes at last. For Disappointments and Distresses will effectuate that Cure, which Reason and Argument, Lenity and Moderation, could not perform. In short, having been severely scourged and disciplined by their own Rod, they will curse their ambitious Leaders, and detest those Mock-Patriots, who involved them in so many Miseries. And having been surfeited with the bitter Fruits of American Republicism, they will heartily wish, and petition to be again united to the Mother Country. Then they will experience the Difference between a rational Plan of Constitutional Dependence, and the wild, romantic, and destructive Schemes of popular Independence.

Tract IV

BY JOSIAH TUCKER

. . . But here some may be apt to ask, "Had the Colonies no Provocation on their Part? And was all the Fault on one Side, and none on the other?" Probably not:—Probably there were Faults on both Sides. But what doth this serve to prove? If

to exculpate the Colonies in regard to their present refractory Behaviour, it is needless. For I am far from charging our Colonies in particular with being Sinners above others; because I believe (and if I am wrong, let the History of all Colonies, whether antient or modern, from the Days of *Thucydides* down to the present Time, confute me if it can; I say, 'till that is done I believe) that it is the Nature of them all to aspire after Independence, and to set up for themselves as soon as ever they find that they are able to subsist, without being beholden to the Mother-Country. And if our *Americans* have expressed themselves sooner on this Head than others have done, or in a more direct and daring Manner, this ought not to be imputed to any greater Malignity, or Ingratitude in them, than in others, but to that bold free Constitution, which is the Prerogative and Boast of us all. We ourselves derive our Origin from those very *Saxons*, who inhabited the lower Parts of *Germany;* and yet I think it is sufficiently evident, that we are not over complaisant to the Descendants of these lower *Saxons*, i.e. to the Offspring of our own Progenitors; nor can we, with any Colour of Reason, pretend to complain that even the *Bostonians* have treated us more indignantly than we have treated the *Hanoverians.* What then would have been the Case, if the little insignificant Electorate of *Hanover* had presumed to retain a Claim of Sovereignty over such a Country as *Great-Britain,* the Pride and Mistress of the Ocean? And yet, I believe, that in Point of Extent of Territory, the *present* Electoral Dominions, insignificant as they are sometimes represented, are more than a Moiety of *England,* exclusive of *Scotland* and *Wales:* Whereas the whole Island of *Great-Britain,* is scarcely a twentieth Part of those vast Regions which go under the Denomination of *North-America.*

Besides, if the *American* Colonies belonging to *France* or *Spain,* have not yet set up for Independence, or thrown off the Masque so much as the *English* Colonies have done,—what is this superior Reserve to be imputed to? Not to any greater filial Tenderness in them for their respective antient Parents than in others;—not to Motives of any national Gratitude, or of national Honour;—but because the Constitution of each of those Parent States is much more arbitrary and despotic than the Constitution of *Great-Britain;* and therefore their respective Offsprings are [1] awed by the Dread of Punishments from breaking forth into those Outrages which ours dare do with Impunity. Nay more, the very Colonies of *France* and *Spain,* though they have not yet thrown off their Allegiance, are nevertheless as forward as any in

[1] But notwithstanding this Awe, it is now pretty generally known, that the *French* Colonists of *Hispaniola* endeavoured lately to shake off the Government of *Old France,* and applied to the *British* Court for that Purpose.

disobeying the Laws of their Mother-Countries, wherever they find an Interest in so doing. For the Truth of this Fact, I appeal to that prodigious clandestine Trade which they are continually carrying on with us, and with our Colonies, contrary to the express Prohibitions of *France* and *Spain:* And I appeal also to those very free Ports which the *British* Legislature itself hath lately opened for accommodating these *smuggling* Colonists to trade with the Subjects of *Great-Britain,* in Disobedience to the Injunction of their Mother-Countries.

Enough surely has been said on this Subject; and the Upshot of the whole Matter is plainly this, —That even the arbitrary and despotic Governments of *France* and *Spain* (arbitrary I say, both in *Temporals* and in *Spirituals*) maintain their Authority over their American Colonies but very imperfectly; in as much as they cannot restrain them from breaking through those Rules and Regulations of exclusive Trade; for the Sake of which all Colonies seemed to have been originally founded. What then shall we say in Regard to such Colonies as are the Offspring of a free Constitution? And after what Manner, or according to what Rule, are our own in particular to be governed, without using any Force or Compulsion, or pursuing any Measure repugnant to their own Ideas of civil or religious Liberty? In short, and to sum up all, in one Word, How shall we be able to render these Colonies more subservient to the Interests, and more obedient to the Laws and Government of the Mother-Country, than they *voluntarily chuse to be?* After having pondered and revolved the Affair over and over, I confess, there seems to me to be but the five following Proposals, which can possibly be made, *viz.*

1st, To suffer Things to go on for a While, as they have lately done, in Hopes that some favourable Opportunity may offer for recovering the Jurisdiction of the *British* Legislature over her Colonies, and for maintaining the Authority of the Mother-Country.—Or if these temporising Measures should be found to strengthen and confirm the Evil, instead of removing it;—then,

2dly, To attempt to persuade the Colonies to send over a certain Number of Deputies, or Representatives, to sit and vote in the *British* Parliament; in order to incorporate *America* and *Great-Britain* into one common Empire.—Or if this Proposal should be found impracticable, whether on Account of the Difficulties attending it on this side of the Atlantic, or because that the *Americans* themselves would not concur in such a Measure; —then,

3dly, To declare open War against them as

Rebels and Revolters; and after having made a perfect Conquest of the Country, then to govern it by military Force and despotic Sway.—Or if this Scheme should be judged (*as it ought to be*) the most destructive, and the least eligible of any; —then,

4thly, To propose to consent that *America* should become the general Seat of Empire; and that *Great-Britain* and *Ireland* should be governed by Vice-Roys sent over from the Court Residencies, either at *Philadelphia* or *New-York*, or at some other *American* imperial City.—Or if this Plan of Accommodation should be ill-digested by home-born *Englishmen*, who, I will venture to affirm, would never submit to such an Indignity; —then,

5thly, To propose to separate entirely from the Colonies, by declaring them to be a free and independent People, over whom we lay no Claim; and then by offering to guarantee this Freedom and Independence against all foreign Invaders whomsoever. . . .

FOURTH SCHEME,

Viz. To consent that *America* should become the general Seat of Empire, and that *Great-Britain* and *Ireland*, should be governed by Vice-Roys sent over from the Court Residencies either at *Philadelphia*, or *New-York*, or at some other *American* Imperial City.

Now, wild as such a Scheme may appear, there are certainly some *Americans* who seriously embrace it: And the late prodigious Swarms of Emigrants encourage them to suppose, that a Time is approaching, when the Seat of Empire must be changed. But whatever Events may be in the Womb of Time, or whatever Revolutions may happen in the Rise and Fall of Empires, there is not the least Probability, that this Country should ever become a Province to *North-America*. For granting even, that it would be so weakened and enfeebled by these Colony-Drains, as not to be able to defend itself from Invaders, yet *America* is at too great a Distance to invade it at first, much less to defend the Conquest of it afterwards, against the neighbouring Powers of *Europe*. And as to any Notion that we ourselves should prefer an *American* Yoke to any other,—this Supposition is chimerical indeed: Because it is much more probable, were Things to come to such a dreadful Crisis, that the *English* would rather submit to a *French* Yoke, than to an *American;* as being the lesser Indignity of the two. So that in short, if we must reason in Politics according to the *New-tonian* Principles in Philosophy,—the Idea of the lesser Country gravitating towards the greater,

must lead us to conclude, that this Island would rather gravitate towards the Continent of *Europe,* than towards the Continent of *America;* unless indeed we should add one Extravagance to another, by supposing that these *American* Heroes are to conquer all the World. And in that Case I do allow, that *England* must become a Province to *America.* But

Solamen miseris socios habuisse doloris.

Dismissing therefore this Idea, as an idle Dream, we come now lastly to consider the

FIFTH SCHEME.

Viz. To propose to separate entirely from the *North-American* Colonies, by declaring them to be a free and independent People, over whom we lay no Claim; and then by offering to guarantee this Freedom and Independence against all foreign Invaders whatever.

And, in fact, what is all this but the natural and even the necessary Corollary to be deduced from each of the former Reasons and Observations? For if we neither can govern the *Americans,* nor be governed by them; if we can neither unite with them, nor ought to subdue them;—what remains, but to part with them on as friendly Terms as we can? And if any Man should think that he can reason better from the above Premises, let him try.

But as the Idea of Separation, and the giving up the Colonies for ever will shock many weak People, who think, that there is neither Happiness nor Security but in an over-grown unwieldy Empire, I will for their Sakes enter into a Discussion of the *supposed* Disadvantages attending such a Disjunction; and then shall set forth the manifold Advantages.

The first and capital *supposed* Advantage is, *That, if we separate from the Colonies, we shall lose their Trade.* But why so? And how does this appear? The Colonies, we know by Experience, will trade with any People, even with their bitterest Enemies, during the hottest of a War, and a War undertaken at their own earnest Request, and for their own Sakes;—the Colonies, I say, will trade even with them, provided they shall find it their Interest so to do. Why then should any Man suppose, that the same Self-Interest will not induce them to trade with us? With us, I say, who are to commit no Hostilities against them, but on the contrary, are still to remain, if they please, their Guardians and Protectors?

Granting, therefore, that *North-America* was to become independent of us, and we of them, the Question now before us will turn on this single Point,—Can the Colonists, in a general Way, trade with any other *European* State to greater Advantage than they can with *Great-Britain?* If they can, they certainly will; but if they cannot, we shall still retain their Custom, notwithstanding we have parted with every Claim of Authority and Jurisdiction over them. Now, the native Commodities and Merchandize of *North-America*, which are the most saleable at an *European* Market, are chiefly Lumber, Ships, Iron, Train-Oil, Flax-Seed, Skins, Furs, Pitch, Tar, Turpentine, Pearl-Ashes, Indigo, Tobacco, and Rice. And I do aver, that, excepting Rice and Tobacco, there is hardly one of these Articles, for which an *American* could get so good a Price any where else, as he can in *Great-Britain* and *Ireland*. Nay, I ought to have excepted only Rice; for as to Tobacco, tho' great Quantities of it are re-exported into *France*, yet it is well known, that the *French* might raise it at Home, if they would, much cheaper than they can import it from our Colonies. The Fact is this,—The Farm of Tobacco is one of the great five Farms, which make up the chief Part of the Royal Revenue; and therefore the Farmers General, for Bye-Ends of their own, have hitherto had Interest enough with the Court to prohibit the Cultivation of it in *Old France*, under the severest Penalties. But nevertheless the real *French* Patriots, and particularly the Marquis de *Mirabeau*, have fully demonstrated, that it is the Interest of the *French* Government to encourage the Cultivation of it; and have pointed out a sure and easy Method for collecting the Duties;—which was the sole Pretence of the Farmers General for soliciting a Prohibition. So that it is apprehended, that the *French* Government will at last open their Eyes in this Respect, and allow the Cultivation of it. Tobacco therefore being likely to be soon out of the Question, the only remaining Article is Rice: And this, it must be acknowledged, would bear a better Price at the *Hamburgh* or *Dutch* Markets than it generally doth in *England*. But as this is only one Article, out of many, it should be further considered, that even the Ships which import Rice into *England*, generally bring such other Produce as would not be saleable to Advantage in other Parts of *Europe*: So that there is no great Cause to fear, that we should *considerably* lose the Trade even of this Article, were the Colonies to be dismembered from us. Not to mention that all the Coasts of the *Mediterranean* and the South of *Europe* are already supplied with Rice from the Colonies, in the same Manner as if there had been an actual Separation;—no Rice-Ship bound to any Place South of *Cape-Finistere* being at all obliged to touch at any Port of *Great-Britain*. So much, therefore, as to the staple *Exports* of the Colonies. Let us now consider their *Imports*. And here

one Thing is very clear and certain, That whatever Goods, Merchandize, or Manufactures, the Merchants of *Great-Britain* can sell to the rest of *Europe*, they might sell the same to the Colonies, if wanted: Because it is evident, that the Colonies could not purchase such Goods at a cheaper Rate at any other *European* Market. Now, let any one cast his Eye over the Bills of Exports from *London*, *Bristol*, *Liverpool*, *Hull*, *Glasgow*, &c. &c. and then he will soon discover that excepting Gold and Silver Lace, Wines and Brandies, some Sorts of Silks and Linens, and perhaps a little Paper and Gun-powder; I say, excepting these few Articles, *Great-Britain* is become a Kind of a [2] general Mart for *most other* Commodities: And indeed were it not so, how is it conceivable, that so little a Spot as this Island could have made such a Figure either in Peace or War, as it hath lately done? How is it possible, that after having contracted a Debt of nearly One Hundred and Forty Millions, we should nevertheless be able to make more rapid Progresses in all Sorts of Improvements, useful and ornamental, public and private, agricolic and commercial, than any other nation ever did?—Fact it is, that these Improvements have been made of late Years, and are daily making: And Facts are stubborn Things.

But, says the Objector, you allow, that Gold and Silver Lace,—that Wines and Brandies,—some Sorts of Silks,—some Sorts of Paper, Gunpowder, and perhaps other Articles, can be purchased at certain *European* Markets on cheaper Terms than they can in *England*: And therefore it follows, that we should certainly lose these Branches of Commerce by a Separation, even supposing that we could retain the rest. Indeed even this doth not follow; because we have lost them already, as far as it was the Interest of the Colonies, that we should lose them. And if any Man can doubt of this, let him but consider, that the Lumber, and Provision-Vessels, which are continually running down from *Boston*, *Rhode-Island*, *New-York*, *Philadelphia*, *Charles-Town*, &c. &c. to *Martinico*, and the other *French* Islands, bring Home in return not only Sugars and Molasses, but also *French* Wines, Silks, Gold and Silver Lace, and in short every other Article, in which they can find a profitable Account: Moreover those Ships, which

[2] I am credibly informed, that it appears by Extracts from the Custom-house Books, that more *English* Goods are sent up the two Rivers of *Germany*, the *Weser* and the *Elbe*, than up any two Rivers in *North-America*. Yet the *North-Americans* and their Partisans are continually upbraiding us, as if we enjoyed no Trade, worth mentioning, except that with the Colonies.

sail to *Eustatia* and *Curacoa*, trade with the *Dutch*, and consequently with all the North of *Europe*, on the same Principle. And as the Ships which steer South of *Cape-Finistere*, what do they do?—Doubtless, they purchase whatever Commodities they find it their Interest to purchase, and carry them Home to *North-America*. Indeed what should hinder them from acting agreeably to their own Ideas of Advantage in these Respects? The Custom-house Officers, perhaps, you may say, will hinder them. But alas! the Custom-house Officers of *North-America*, if they were ten Times more numerous, and ten Times more uncorrupt than they are, could not possibly guard a tenth Part of the Coast. In short these Things are so very notorious that they cannot be disputed; and therefore, were the whole Trade of *North-America* to be divided into two Branches, *viz.* the *Voluntary*, resulting from a free Choice of the *Americans* themselves, pursuing their own Interest, and the *Involuntary*, in Consequence of *compulsory* Acts of the *British* Parliament;—this latter would appear so very small and inconsiderable, as hardly to deserve a Name in an Estimate of national Commerce.

The 2d Objection against giving up the Colonies is, that such a measure would greatly decrease our Shipping and Navigation, and consequently diminish the Breed of Sailors. But this Objection has been fully obviated already: For if we shall not lose our Trade, at least in any important Degree, even with the northern Colonies (and most probably we shall encrease it with other Countries) then it follows, that neither the Quantity of Shipping, nor the Breed of Sailors, can suffer any considerable Diminution: So that this Supposition is merely a Panic, and has no Foundation. Not to mention, that in Proportion as the *Americans* shall be obliged to exert themselves to defend their own Coasts, in Case of a War; in the same Proportion shall *Great-Britain* be exonerated from that Burden, and shall have more Ships and Men at command to protect her own Channel Trade, and for other Services.

The 3d Objection is, That if we were to give up these Colonies, the *French* would take immediate Possession of them. Now this Objection is entirely built on the following very wild, very extravagant, and absurd Suppositions.

1st, it supposes, that the Colonists themselves, who cannot brook our Government, would like a *French* one much better. *Great-Britain*, it seems, doth not grant them Liberty enough; and therefore they have Recourse to *France* to obtain more:—That is, in plain *English*, our mild and limited Government, where Prerogative is ascer-

tained by Law, where every Man is at Liberty to seek for Redress, and where popular Clamours too often carry every Thing before them,—is nevertheless too severe, too oppressive, and too tyrannical for the Spirits and Genius of *Americans* to bear; and therefore they will apply to an arbitrary, despotic Government, where the People have no Share in the Legislature, where there is no Liberty of the Press, and where General Warrants and *Lettres des cachets* are *irresistible*,—in order to enjoy greater Freedoms than they have at present, and to be rescued from the intolerable Yoke, under which they now groan. What monstrous Absurdities are these! But even this is not all: For these *Americans* are represented by this Supposition, as not only preferring a *French* Government to a *British*, but even to a Government of their *own modelling and chusing!* For after they are set free from any Submission to their Mother-Country; after they are told, that for the future they must endeavour to please themselves, seeing we cannot please them; then, instead of attempting to frame any popular Governments for redressing those Evils, of which they now so bitterly complain,—they are represented as throwing themselves at once into the Arms of *France;* —the Republican Spirit is to subside; the Doctrine of passive Obedience and Non-resistance is to succeed; and, instead of setting up for Freedom and Independence, they are to glory in having the Honour of being numbered among the Slaves of the Grand Monarch!

But 2dly, this Matter may be further considered in another Point of View: For if it should be said, that the *Americans* might still retain their Republican Spirit, tho' they submitted to a *French* Government, because the *French*, through Policy, would permit them so to do; then it remains to be considered, whether any arbitrary Government can dispense with such Liberties as a republican Spirit will require. An absolute Freedom of the Press! No controul on the Liberty either of Speaking or Writing on Matters of State! Newspapers and Pamphlets filled with the bitterest Invectives against the Measures of Government! Associations formed in every Quarter to cry down Ministerial Hirelings, and their Dependents! The Votes and Resolutions of the Provincial Assemblies to assert their own Authority and Independence! No landing of Troops from *Old France* to quell Insurrections! No raising of new Levies in *America!* No quartering of Troops! No building of Forts, or erecting of Garrisons! And, to sum up all, no *raising of Money* without the express Consent and Approbation of the Provincial *American* Parliaments first obtained for each of these

Purposes!—Now I ask any reasonable Man whether these Things are compatible with any Idea of an arbitrary, despotic Government?—Nay more, whether the *French* King himself, or his Ministers, would wish to have such Notions as these instilled into the Subjects of *Old France?* Yet instilled they must be, while a Communication is kept open between the two Countries; while Correspondences are carried on; Letters, Pamphlets, and Newspapers, pass and re-pass; and in short, while the *Americans* are permitted to come into *France*, and *Frenchmen* into *America*. So much therefore as to this Class of Objections. Indeed I might have insisted further, that *Great-Britain* alone could at any Time prevent such an Acquisition to be made by *France*, as is here supposed, if she should think it necessary to interfere, and if such an Acquisition of Territory would really and truly be an Addition of Strength in the political Balance and Scale of Power.[3] But surely I have said enough; and therefore let us now hasten briefly to point out

The manifold Advantages attendant on such a Scheme.

And 1st, A Disjunction from the northern Colonies would effectually put a Stop to our present Emigrations. By the Laws of the Land it is made a capital Offence to inveigle Artificers and Mechanics to leave the Kingdom. But this Law is un-

[3] The Phaenomenon of that prodigious Increase of Trade, which this Country has experienced since the happy Revolution, is what few People can explain; and therefore they cut the Matter short, by ascribing it all to the Growth of our Colonies: But the true Principles and real Causes of that amazing Increase, are the following:

1. The Suppression of various Monopolies and exclusive Companies existing before, for foreign Trade.
2. The opening of Corporations, or the undermining of exclusive Privileges and Companies of Trade at Home; or, what comes to the same Thing, the eluding of their bad Effects by Means of legal Decisions in our Courts of Law. And N.B. The like Observation extends to the Case of evading the Penalties of the Act 5th of Queen *Elizabeth*, against exercising those Trades, to which Persons have not served regular Apprenticeships.
3. The Nursing up of new Trades and new Branches of Commerce by Means of Bounties, and national Premiums.
4. The giving of Drawbacks, or the Return of Duties on the Exportation of such Goods, as were to have paid a Duty, if used and consumed at Home.
5. The Repeal of Taxes formerly laid on raw Materials coming into the Kingdom. See 8 G. I. C. 15.
6. The Repeal of Taxes formerly laid on our own Manufactures, when exported. See ditto.

happily superseded at present as far as the Colonies are concerned. Therefore when they come to be dismembered from us, it will operate as strongly against them, and their *Kidnappers*, as against others. And here it may be worth while to observe, that the Emigrants, who lately sailed in such Multitudes from the North of *Scotland*, and more especially from the North of *Ireland*, were far from being the most indigent, or the least capable of subsisting in their own Country. No; it was not Poverty or Necessity which compelled, but Ambition which enticed them to forsake their native Soil. For after they began to taste the Sweets of Industry, and to partake of the Comforts of Life, then they became a valuable Prey for these Harpies. In short, such were the Persons to whom these Seducers principally applied; because they found that they had gotten some little Substance together worth devouring. They therefore told them many plausible Stories—that if they would emigrate to *North-America*, they might have Estates for nothing, and become Gentlemen for ever; whereas, if they remained at Home, they had nothing to expect beyond the Condition of a wretched Journeyman, or a small laborious Farmer. Nay, one of these false Guides was known to have put out public Advertisements, some few Years ago, in the North of *Ireland*, wherein he engaged to carry all, who would follow him, into such a glorious Country, where there was neither Tax, nor Tithe, nor Landlord's Rent to be paid. This was enough: It took with

7. The Improvements in various Engines, with new Inventions and Discoveries for the Abridgment of Labour.
8. Better Communications established throughout the Kingdom by Means of Turnpike Roads and Canals, and the speedy Conveyance of Letters to every great Town and noted Place of Manufacture, by Means of Improvements in the Post-Office.
9. Happy Discoveries and Improvements in Agriculture and in the mechanic Arts.
10. Larger Capitals than usual employed both in Husbandry and Manufactures; also in the Importation and Exportation of Goods.

Now all these Things, co-operating together, would render any Country rich and flourishing, whether it had Colonies or not: And this Country in particular would have found the happy Effects of them to a much greater Degree than it now doth, were they not counter-acted by our Luxury, our Gambling, our frequent ruinous and expensive Wars, our Colony-Drains, and by the ill-gotten, and ill-spent Wealth, which was obtained by robbing, plundering, and starving the poor defenceless Natives of the *East-Indies*.—A Species of Villainy this, for which the *English* Language had not a Name, 'till it adopted the Word *Nabobing*.

Thousands: And this he might safely engage to do.—But at the same Time, he ought to have told them (as Bishop *Berkley* in his Queries justly observes) That a Man may possess twenty Miles square in this glorious Country, and yet not be able to get a Dinner.

2dly. Another great Advantage to be derived from a Separation is, that we shall then save between 3 and 400,000l. a Year, by being discharged from the Payment of any civil or military Establishment belonging to the Colonies:—For which generous Benefaction we receive at present no other Return than Invectives and Reproaches.

3dly. The ceasing of the Payment of Bounties on certain Colony Productions will be another great Saving; perhaps not less than 200,000l. a Year: And it is very remarkable, that the Goods imported from the Colonies in Consequence of these Bounties, could not have been imported into any other Part of *Europe*, were there a Liberty to do it; because the Freight and first Cost would have amounted to more than they could be sold for: So that in Fact we give Premiums to the Colonies for selling Goods to us, which would not have been sold at all any where else. However, when the present Bounties shall cease, we may then consider, at our Leisure, whether it would be right to give them again, or not; and we shall have it totally in our Power to favour that Country most, which will show the greatest Favour to us, and to our Manufactures.

4thly. When we are no longer connected with the Colonies by the imaginary Tie of an Identity of Government, then our Merchant-Exporters and Manufacturers will have a better Chance of having their Debts paid, than they have at present: For as Matters now stand, the Colonists chuse to carry their ready Cash to other Nations, while they are contracting Debts with their Mother-Country; with whom they think they can take greater Liberties: And provided they are trusted, they care not to what Amount this Debt shall rise: —For when the Time for Payment draws on, they are seized with a Fit of Patriotism; and then Confederacies and Associations are to discharge all Arrears; or, at least, are to postpone the Payment of them *sine die*.

5thly. After a Separation from the Colonies, our Influence over them will be much greater than ever it was, since they began to feel their own Weight and Importance: For at present we are looked upon in no better a Light than that of Robbers and Usurpers; whereas, we shall then be considered as their Protectors, Mediators, Benefactors. The Moment a Separation takes Effect, intestine Quarrels will begin: For it is well known, that the Seeds of Discord and Dissention between Province and Province are now ready to shoot forth; and that they are only kept down by the present Combination of all the Colonies against us, whom they unhappily fancy to be their *common Enemy*. When therefore this Object of their Hatred shall be removed by a Declaration on our Parts, that, so far from usurping all Authority, we, from henceforward, will assume none at all against their own Consent; the weaker Provinces will intreat our Protection against the stronger; and the less cautious against the more crafty and designing: So that in short, in Proportion as their factious, republican Spirit shall intrigue and cabal, shall split into Parties, divide, and sub-divide,—in the same Proportion shall we be called in to become their general Umpires and Referees. Not to mention, that many of the late and present Emigrants, when they shall see these Storms arising all around them, and when their promised earthly Paradise turns out to be a dreary, unwholesome, inhospitable, and howling Wilderness,—many of them, I say, will probably return to us again, and take Refuge at last in *Old England*, with all its Faults and Imperfections.

Lastly. Our *West-India* Islands themselves will receive signal Benefit by this Separation. Indeed their Size and Situation render them incapable of substracting all Obedience from us; and yet the bad Precedents of their Neighbours on the Continent hath sometimes prompted them to shew as refractory a Spirit as they well could.—But when they come to perceive, what are the bitter Effects of this untractable Disposition, exemplified in the Case of the *North-Americans*, it is probable, it is reasonable to conclude, that they will learn Wisdom by the Miscarriages and Sufferings of these unhappy People; and that from henceforward they will revere the Authority of a Government, which has the fewest Faults, and grants the greatest Liberty, of any yet known upon Earth.

But after all, there is one Thing more, to which I must make some Reply.—many, perhaps most of my Readers, will be apt to ask,—What is all this about? And what doth this Author really mean?—Can he seriously think, that because he hath taken such Pains to prove a Separation to be a right Measure, that therefore we shall separate in good Earnest? And is he still so much a Novice as not to know, that Measures are rarely adopted merely because they are right, but because they can serve a present Turn?—Therefore let it be asked, What present Convenience or Advantage doth he propose either to Administration, or to Anti-Administration, by the Execution of his

Plan?—This is coming to the Point, and without it, all that he has said will pass for nothing.

I frankly acknowledge, I propose no *present* Convenience or Advantage to either; nay, I firmly believe, that no Minister, as Things are now circumstanced, will dare to do so much Good to his Country; and as to the Herd of Anti-Ministers, they, I am persuaded, would not wish to see it done; because it would deprive them of one of their most plentiful Sources for Clamour and Detraction: And yet I have observed, and have myself had some Experience, that Measures evidently right will prevail at last: Therefore I make not the least Doubt but that a Separation from the northern Colonies, and also another right Measure, *viz.* a *complete Union* and *Incorporation* with *Ireland* (however unpopular either of them may now appear) will both take Place within half a Century: —And perhaps that which happens to be first accomplished, will greatly accelerate the Accomplishment of the other. Indeed almost all People are apt to startle at first at bold Truths:—But it is observable, that in Proportion as they grow familiarized to them, and can see and consider them from different Points of View, their Fears subside, and they become reconciled by Degrees:— Nay, it is not an uncommon Thing for them to adopt those salutary Measures afterwards with as much Zeal and Ardor as they had rejected them before with Anger and Indignation.

Need I add, That the Man, who will have Resolution enough to advance any bold unwelcome Truth (unwelcome I mean at its first Appearance) ought to be such an one, whose Competency of Fortune, joined to a natural Independency of Spirit, places him in that happy Situation, as to be equally indifferent to the Smiles, or Frowns either of the Great, or the Vulgar?

Lastly, some Persons perhaps may wonder, that, being myself a Clergyman, I have said nothing about the Persecution which the Church of *England* daily suffers in *America*, by being denied those Rights which every other Sect of Christians so amply enjoys. I own I have hitherto omitted to make Mention of that Circumstance, not thro' Inadvertence, but by Design; as being unwilling to embarrass my general Plan with what might be deemed by some Readers to be foreign to the Subject: And therefore I shall be very short in what I have to add at present.

That each Religious Persuasion ought to have a full Toleration from the State to worship Almighty God, according to the Dictates of their own Consciences, is to me so clear a Case, that I shall not attempt to make it clearer; and nothing but the maintaining some monstrous Opinion inconsistent with the Safety of Society,—and that not barely in Theory and Speculation, but by *open* Practice and *outward* Actions,—I say, nothing but the *avowedly* maintaining of such *dangerous* Principles can justify the Magistrate in abridging any Set of Men of these their natural Rights. It is also equally evident, that the Church of *England* doth not, cannot fall under the Censure of holding Opinions inconsistent with the Safety of the State, and the Good of Mankind,—even her Enemies themselves being Judges: And yet the Church of *England* alone doth not enjoy a Toleration in that full Extent, which is granted to the Members of every other Denomination. What then can be the Cause of putting so injurious a Distinction between the Church of *England*, and other Churches in this respect? The Reason is plain. The *Americans* have taken it into their Heads to believe, that an Episcopate would operate as some further Tie upon them, not to break loose from those Obligations which they owe to the Mother-Country; and that this is to be used as an Engine, under the Masque of Religion, to rivet those Chains, which they imagine we are forging for them. Let therefore the Mother-Country herself resign up all Claim of Authority over them, as well Ecclesiastical as Civil; let her declare *North-America* to be independent of *Great-Britain* in every Respect whatever;—let her do this, I say, and then all their Fears will vanish away, and their Panics be at an End: And then, a Bishop, who has no more Connections with *England* either in Church or State, than he has with *Germany*, *Sweden* or any other Country, will be no longer looked upon in *America* as a Monster, but a Man. In short, when all Motives for Opposition will be at an End, it is observable, that the Opposition itself soon ceases and dies away. In a Word, an Episcopate may then take Place; and whether this new Ecclesiastical Officer be called from a Name derived from the *Greek*, the *Latin*, or the *German*, —that is, whether he be stiled Episcopus, Superintendent, Supervisor, Overseer, &. &c. it matters not,—provided he be invested with competent Authority to ordain and confirm such of the Members of his own Persuasion, as shall voluntarily offer themselves, and to inspect the Lives and Morals of his own Clergy.

THE STAMP ACT

CONFRONTED with the need for additional revenue after peace had been concluded in 1763, Parliament decided to collect taxes in the colonies by means of stamps affixed to legal papers, playing cards, newspapers and other documents necessary to colonial business or pleasure. The tax was to be paid in specie and applied to the expenses of royal government in the continental colonies. Colonial opposition to the law was so immediate, vocal, and violent that Parliament held hearings on its execution in February, 1766. Among the witnesses called was Benjamin Franklin and it is not improbable that he used the committee as a sounding board, for certain of its members were suf-

ficiently friendly to the colonial viewpoint to ask convenient questions. Whether deliberate or not, however, the testimony does show how the two segments of empire were drawing apart; words no longer had the same meaning on both shores of the Atlantic.

The selection that follows is from a verbatim account of Franklin's examination by the House of Commons sitting as a Committee of the Whole on a bill to repeal the Stamp Act. It was printed in *A Collection of Scarce and Interesting Tracts Written by Persons of Eminence upon the Most Important Political and Commercial Subjects* (4 vols., London, 1787).

Examination of Dr. Franklin

Q. What is your name, and place of abode?—A. Franklin, of Philadelphia.

Q. Do the Americans pay any considerable taxes among themselves?—A. Certainly many, and very heavy taxes.

Q. What are the present taxes in Pennsylvania, laid by the laws of the colony?—A. There are taxes on all estates real and personal, a poll-tax, a tax on all offices, professions, trades and businesses, according to their profits; an excise on all wine, rum, and other spirits; and a duty of ten pounds per head on all negroes imported, with some other duties.

Q. For what purposes are those taxes laid?—A. For the support of the civil and military establishments of the country, and to discharge the heavy debt contracted in the last war.

Q. How long are those taxes to continue?—A. Those for discharging the debt are to continue till 1772, and longer, if the debt should not be then all discharged. The others must always continue.

Q. Was it not expected that the debt would have been sooner discharged?—A. It was, when the peace was made with France and Spain—But a fresh war breaking out with the Indians, a fresh load of debt was incurred, and the taxes, of course, continued longer by a new law.

Q. Are not all the people very able to pay those taxes?—A. No. The frontier counties, all along the continent, having been frequently ravaged by the enemy, and greatly impoverished, are able to

pay very little tax. And therefore, in consideration of their distresses, our late tax laws do expressly favour those counties, excusing the sufferers; and I suppose the same is done in other governments. . . .

Q. Are not the colonies, from their circumstances, very able to pay the stamp duty?—A. In my opinion, there is not gold or silver enough in the colonies to pay the stamp duty for one year.

Q. Don't you know that the money arising from the stamps was all to be laid out in America?—A. I know it is appropriated by the act to the American service; but it will be spent in the conquered colonies, where the soldiers are, not in the colonies that pay it.

Q. Is there not a balance of trade due from the colonies where the troops are posted, that will bring back the money to the old colonies?—A. I think not. I believe very little would come back. I know of no trade likely to bring it back. I think it would come from the colonies where it was spent directly to England; for I have always observed, that in every colony the more plenty of means of remittance to England, the more goods are sent for, and the more trade with England carried on. . . .

Q. How many white men do you suppose there are in North-America?—A. About 300,000, from sixteen to sixty years of age.

Q. What may be the amount of one year's imports into Pennsylvania from Britain?—A. I have been informed that our merchants compute the imports from Britain to be above 500,000l.

Q. What may be the amount of the produce of your province exported to Britain?—A. It must be small, as we produce little that is wanted in Britain. I suppose it cannot exceed 40,000l.

Q. How then do you pay the balance?—A. The balance is paid by our produce carried to the West-Indies, and sold in our own islands, or to the French, Spaniards, Danes and Dutch; by the same carried to other colonies in North-America, as to New-England, Nova-Scotia, Newfoundland, Carolina and Georgia; by the same carried to different parts of Europe, as Spain, Portugal and Italy. In all which places we receive either money, bills of exchange, or commodities that suit for remittance to Britain; which, together with all the profits on the industry of our merchants and mariners, arising in those circuitous voyages, and the freights made by their ships, centre finally in Britain to discharge the balance, and pay for British manufactures continually used in the province, or sold to foreigners by our traders.

Q. Have you heard of any difficulties lately laid on the Spanish trade?—A. Yes, I have heard that it has been greatly obstructed by some new regulations, and by the English men of war and cutters stationed all along the coast in America.

Q. Do you think it right, that America should be protected by this country, and pay no part of the expence?—A. That is not the case. The colonies raised, cloathed and paid, during the last war, near 25,000 men, and spent many millions.

Q. Were you not reimbursed by parliament?—A. We were only reimbursed what, in your opinion, we had advanced beyond our proportion, or beyond what might reasonably be expected from us; and it was a very small part of what we spent. Pennsylvania, in particular, disbursed about 500,-000l. and the reimbursements, in the whole, did not exceed 60,000l.

Q. You have said that you pay heavy taxes in Pennsylvania; what do they amount to in the pound?—A. The tax on all estates, real and personal, is 1s. 6d. in the pound, fully rated; and the tax on the profits of trades and professions, with other taxes, do, I suppose, make full 2s. 6d. in the pound.

Q. Do you know any thing of the rate of exchange in Pennsylvania, and whether it has fallen lately?—A. It is commonly from 170 to 175. I have heard that it has fallen lately from 175 to 162 and a half, owing, I suppose, to their lessening their orders for goods; and when their debts to this country are paid, I think the exchange will probably be at par.

Q. Do not you think the people of America would submit to pay the stamp-duty, if it was moderated?—A. No, never, unless compelled by force of arms.

Q. Are not the taxes in Pennsylvania laid on unequally, in order to burden the English trade, particularly the tax on professions and business? —A. It is not more burthensome in proportion than the tax on lands. It is intended, and supposed to take an equal proportion of profits.

Q. How is the assembly composed? Of what kinds of people are the members, landholders or traders?—A. It is composed of landholders, merchants and artificers.

Q. Are not the majority landholders?—A. I believe they are.

Q. Do not they, as much as possible, shift the tax off from the land, to ease that, and lay the burthen heavier on trade?—A. I have never understood it so. I never heard such a thing suggested. And indeed an attempt of that kind could answer no purpose. The merchant or trader is always skilled in figures, and ready with his pen and ink. If unequal burthens are laid on his trade, he puts an additional price on his goods; and the consumers, who are chiefly landholders, finally pay the greatest part, if not the whole.

Q. What was the temper of America towards Great-Britain before the year 1763?—A. The best in the world. They submitted willingly to the government of the crown, and paid, in all their courts, obedience to acts of parliament. Numerous as the people are in the several old provinces, they cost you nothing in forts, citadels, garrisons or armies, to keep them in subjection. They were governed by this country at the expence only of a little pen, ink and paper. They were led by a thread. They had not only a respect, but an affection for Great-Britain, for its laws, its customs and manners, and even a fondness for its fashions, that greatly increased the commerce. Natives of Britain were always treated with particular regard; to be an Old-England-man was, of itself, a character of some respect, and gave a kind of rank among us.

Q. And what is their temper now?—A. O, very much altered.

Q. Did you ever hear the authority of parliament to make laws for America questioned till lately?—A. The authority of parliament was allowed to be valid in all laws, except such as should lay internal taxes. It was never disputed in laying duties to regulate commerce.

Q. In what proportion hath population increased in America?—A. I think the inhabitants of all the provinces together, taken at a medium, double in about twenty-five years. But their demand for British manufactures increases much faster, as the consumption is not merely in proportion to their numbers, but grows with the growing abilities of the same numbers to pay for them. In 1723, the whole importation from Britain to Pennsylvania, was but about 15,000l. sterling; it is now near half a million. . . .

Q. What do you think is the reason that the people of America increase faster than in England?—A. Because they marry younger, and more generally.

Q. Why so?—A. Because any young couple that are industrious, may easily obtain land of their own, on which they can raise a family.

Q. Are not the lower rank of people more at their ease in America than in England?—A. They may be so, if they are sober and diligent, as they are better paid for their labour.

Q. What is your opinion of a future tax, imposed on the same principle with that of the stamp-act; how would the Americans receive it? —A. Just as they do this. They would not pay it.

Q. Have you not heard of the resolutions of this house, and of the house of lords, asserting the right of parliament relating to America, including a power to tax the people there?—A. Yes, I have heard of such resolutions.

Q. What will be the opinion of the Americans on those resolutions?—A. They will think them unconstitutional and unjust.

Q. Was it an opinion in America before 1763, that the parliament had no right to lay taxes and duties there?—A. I never heard any objection to the right of laying duties to regulate commerce; but a right to lay internal taxes was never supposed to be in parliament, as we are not represented there.

Q. On what do you found your opinion, that the people in America made any such distinction?—A. I know that whenever the subject has occurred in conversation where I have been present, it has appeared to be the opinion of every one, that we could not be taxed in a parliament where we were not represented. But the payment of duties laid by act of parliament, as regulations of commerce, was never disputed.

Q. But can you name any act of assembly, or public act of any of your governments, that made such distinction?—A. I do not know that there was any; I think there was never an occasion to make any such act, till now that you have attempted to tax us; that has occasioned resolutions of assembly, declaring the distinction, in which I think every assembly on the continent, and every member in every assembly, have been unanimous.

Q. What then could occasion conversations on that subject before that time?—A. There was in 1754, a proposition made (I think it came from hence) that in case of a war, which was then apprehended, the governors of the colonies should meet, and order the levying of troops, building of forts, and taking every other necessary measure for the general defence; and should draw on the treasury here for the sums expended, which were afterwards to be raised in the colonies by a general tax, to be laid on them by act of parliament. This occasioned a good deal of conversation on the subject, and the general opinion was, that the parliament neither would, nor could lay any tax on us, till we were duly represented in parliament, because it was not just, nor agreeable to the nature of an English constitution.

Q. Don't you know there was a time in New-York, when it was under consideration to make an application to parliament to lay taxes on that colony, upon a deficiency arising from the assembly's refusing or neglecting to raise the necessary supplies for the support of the civil government? —A. I never heard of it.

Q. There was such an application under consideration in New-York; and do you apprehend they could suppose the right of parliament to lay a tax in America was only local, and confined to the case of a deficiency in a particular colony, by a refusal of its assembly to raise the necessary supplies?—A. They could not suppose such a case, as that the assembly would not raise the necessary supplies to support its own government. An assembly that would refuse it must want common sense, which cannot be supposed. I think there was never any such case at New-York, and that it must be a misrepresentation, or the fact must be misunderstood. I know there have been some attempts, by ministerial instructions from hence, to oblige the assemblies to settle permanent salaries on governors, which they wisely refused to do; but I believe no assembly of New-York or any other colony, ever refused duly to support government by proper allowances, from time to time, to public officers.

Q. But in case a governor, acting by instruction, should call on an assembly to raise the necessary supplies, and the assembly should refuse to do it, do you not think it would then be for the good of the people of the colony, as well as necessary to government, that the parliament should tax them? —A. I do not think it would be necessary. If an assembly could possibly be so absurd as to refuse raising the supplies requisite for the maintenance of government among them, they could not long remain in such a situation; the disorders and confusion occasioned by it, must soon bring them to reason.

Q. If it should not, ought not the right to be in Great-Britain of applying a remedy?—A. A right only to be used in such a case, I should have no objection to, supposing it to be used merely for the good of the people of the colony.

Q. But who is to judge of that, Britain or the colony?—A. Those that feel can best judge.

Q. You say the colonies have always submitted to external taxes, and object to the right of parliament only in laying internal taxes; now can you shew that there is any kind of difference between the two taxes to the colony on which they may be laid?—A. I think the difference is very great. An external tax is a duty laid on commodities imported; that duty is added to the first cost, and other charges on the commodity, and when it is offered to sale, makes a part of the price. If the people do not like it at that price, they refuse it; they are not obliged to pay it. But an internal tax is forced from the people without their consent, if not laid by their own representatives. The stamp-act says, we shall have no commerce, make no exchange of property with each other, neither purchase nor grant, nor recover debts; we shall neither marry nor make our wills, unless we pay such sums, and thus it is intended to extort our money from us, or ruin us by the consequences of refusing to pay it.

Q. But supposing the internal tax or duty to be laid on the necessaries of life imported into your colony, will not that be the same thing in its effects as an internal tax?—A. I do not know a single article imported into the northern colonies, but what they can either do without, or make themselves.

Q. Don't you think cloth from England absolutely necessary to them?—A. No, by no means absolutely necessary; with industry and good management, they may very well supply themselves with all they want.

Q. Will it not take a long time to establish that manufacture among them; and must they not in the mean while suffer greatly?—A. I think not. They have made a surprizing progress already. And I am of opinion, that before their old clothes are worn out, they will have new ones of their own making.

Q. Can they possibly find wool enough in North-America?—A. They have taken steps to increase the wool. They entered into general combinations to eat no more lamb, and very few lambs were killed last year. This course persisted in, will soon make a prodigious difference in the quantity of wool. And the establishing of great

manufactories, like those in the clothing towns here, is not necessary, as it is where the business is to be carried on for the purposes of trade. The people will all spin, and work for themselves, in their own houses.

Q. Can there be wool and manufacture enough in one or two years?—A. In three years I think there may.

Q. Does not the severity of the winter, in the northern colonies, occasion the wool to be of bad quality?—A. No; the wool is very fine and good.

Q. In the more southern colonies, as in Virginia, don't you know that the wool is coarse, and only a kind of hair?—A. I don't know it. I never heard it. Yet I have been sometimes in Virginia. I cannot say I ever took particular notice of the wool there, but I believe it is good, though I cannot speak positively of it; but Virginia, and the colonies south of it, have less occasion for wool; their winters are short, and not very severe, and they can very well clothe themselves with linen and cotton of their own raising for the rest of the year.

Q. Are not the people in the more northern colonies obliged to fodder their sheep all the winter?—A. In some of the most northern colonies they may be obliged to do it some part of the winter. . . .

Q. Do you remember the abolishing of the paper currency in New-England, by act of assembly?—A. I do remember its being abolished in the Massachusett's Bay.

Q. Was not Lieutenant-Governor Hutchinson principally concerned in that transaction?—A. I have heard so.

Q. Was it not at that time a very unpopular law?—A. I believe it might, though I can say little about it, as I lived at a distance from that province.

Q. Was not the scarcity of gold and silver an argument used against abolishing the paper?—A. I suppose it was.

Q. Have not instructions from hence been sometimes sent over to governors, highly oppressive and unpolitical?—A. Yes.

Q. Have not some governors dispensed with them for that reason?—A. Yes; I have heard so.

Q. Did the Americans ever dispute the controuling power of parliament to regulate the commerce?—A. No.

Q. Can any thing less than a military force carry the stamp-act into execution?—A. I do not see how a military force can be applied to that purpose.

Q. Why may it not?—A. Suppose a military force sent into America, they will find nobody in arms; what are they then to do? They cannot force a man to take stamps who chuses to do without them. They will not find a rebellion; they may indeed make one.

Q. If the act is not repealed, what do you think will be the consequences?—A. A total loss of the respect and affection the people of America bear to this country, and of all the commerce that depends on that respect and affection.

Q. How can the commerce be affected?—A. You will find, that if the act is not repealed, they will take very little of your mannfactures in a short time.

Q. Is it in their power to do without them?—A. I think they may very well do without them.

Q. Is it their interest not to take them?—A. The goods they take from Britain are either necessaries, mere conveniencies, or superfluities. The first, as cloth, &c. with a little industry, they can make at home; they second they can do without, till they are able to provide them among themselves; and the last, which are much the greatest part, they will strike off immediately. They are mere articles of fashion, purchased and consumed, because the fashion in a respected country, but will now be detested and rejected. The people have already struck off, by general agreement, the use of all goods fashionable in mournings, and many thousand pounds worth are sent back as unsaleable.

Q. Is it their interest to make cloth at home?—A. I think they may at present get it cheaper from Britain, I mean of the same fineness and neatness of workmanship; but when one considers other circumstances, the restraints on their trade, and the difficulty of making remittances, it is their interest to make every thing. . . .

Q. Supposing the stamp-act continued, and enforced, do you imagine that ill-humour will induce the Americans to give as much for worse manufactures of their own, and use them, preferably to better of ours?—A. Yes, I think so. People will pay as freely to gratify one passion as another, their resentment as their pride.

Q. Would the people at Boston discontinue their trade?—A. The merchants are a very small number, compared with the body of the people, and must discontinue their trade, if nobody will buy their goods.

Q. What are the body of the people in the colonies?—A. They are farmers, husbandmen, or planters.

Q. Would they suffer the produce of their lands to rot?—A. No; but they would not raise so much. They would manufacture more, and plough less.

Q. Would they live without the administration of justice in civil matters, and suffer all the inconveniencies of such a situation, for any considerable time, rather than take the stamps, supposing the stamps were protected by a sufficient force, where every one might have them?—A. I think the supposition impracticable, that the stamps should be so protected as that every one might have them. The act requires sub-distributors to be appointed in every county, town, district, and village, and they would be necessary. But the principal distributors, who were to have had a considerable profit on the whole, have not thought it worth while to continue in the office, and I think it impossible to find sub-distributors fit to be trusted, who, for the trifling profit that must come to their share, would incur the odium, and run the hazard that would attend it; and if they could be found, I think it impracticable to protect the stamps in so many distant and remote places.

Q. But in places where they could be protected, would not the people use them rather than remain in such a situation, unable to obtain any right, or recover, by law, any debt?—A. It is hard to say what they would do. I can only judge what other people will think, and how they will act, by what I feel within myself. I have a great many debts due to me in America, and I had rather they should remain unrecoverable by any law, than submit to the stamp-act. They will be debts of honour. It is my opinion the people will either continue in that situation, or find some way to extricate themselves, perhaps by generally agreeing to proceed in the courts without stamps. . . .

Q. How many ships are there laden annually in North-America with flax-seed for Ireland?—A. I cannot speak to the number of ships, but I know that in 1752, 10,000 hogsheads of flax-seed, each containing seven bushels, were exported from Philadelphia to Ireland. I suppose the quantity is greatly encreased since that time; and it is understood that the exportation from New-York is equal to that from Philadelphia.

Q. What becomes of the flax that grows with that flax-seed?—A. They manufacture some into coarse, and some into a middling kind of linen.

Q. Are there any slitting-mills in America?—A. I think there are three, but I believe only one at present employed. I suppose they will all be set to work, if the interruption of the trade continues.

Q. Are there any fulling-mills there?—A great many.

Q. Did you never hear that a great quantity of stockings were contracted for, for the army, during the war, and manufactured in Philadelphia?—A. I have heard so. . . .

Q. But suppose Great-Britain should be engaged in a war in Europe, would North-America contribute to the support of it?—A. I do think they would, as far as their circumstances would permit. They consider themselves as a part of the British empire, and as having one common interest with it; they may be looked on here as foreigners, but they do not consider themselves as such. They are zealous for the honour and prosperity of this nation, and, while they are well used, will always be ready to support it, as far as their little power goes. In 1739 they were called upon to assist in the expedition against Carthagena, and they sent 3000 men to join your army. It is true Carthagena is in America, but as remote from the northern colonies as if it had been in Europe. They make no distinction of wars, as to their duty of assisting in them. I know the last war is commonly spoke of here as entered into for the defence, or for the sake of the people of America. I think it is quite misunderstood. It began about the limits between Canada and Nova-Scotia, about territories to which the crown indeed laid claim, but were not claimed by any British colony; none of the lands had been granted to any colonist; we had therefore no particular concern or interest in that dispute. As to the Ohio, the contest there began about your right of trading in the Indian country, a right you had by the treaty of Utrecht, which the French infringed; they seized the traders and their goods, which were your manufactures; they took a fort which a company of your merchants, and their factors and correspondents, had erected there, to secure that trade. Braddock was sent with an army to re-take that fort (which was looked on here as another encroachment on the king's territory) and to protect your trade. It was not till after his defeat that the colonies were attacked. They were before in perfect peace with both French and Indians; the troops were not therefore sent for their defence. The trade with the Indians, though carried on in America, is not an American interest. The people of America are chiefly farmers and planters; scarce any thing they raise or produce is an article of commerce with the Indians. The Indian trade is a British interest; it is carried on with British manufactures, for the profit of British merchants and manufacturers; therefore the war, as it commenced for the defence of territories of the crown, the property of no American, and for the defence of a trade purely British, was really a British war—and yet the people of America made no scruple of contributing their utmost towards carrying it on, and bringing it to a happy conclusion.

Q. Do you think then that the taking possession of the king's territorial rights, and strengthening the frontiers, is not an American interest?—A.

Not particularly, but conjointly a British and an American interest.

Q. You will not deny that the preceding war, the war with Spain, was entered into for the sake of America; was it not occasioned by captures made in the American seas?—A. Yes; captures of ships carrying on the British trade there, with British manufactures.

Q. Was not the late war with the Indians, since the peace with France, a war for America only?— Yes; it was more particularly for America than the former; but it was rather a consequence or remains of the former war, the Indians not having been thoroughly pacified, and the Americans bore by much the greatest share of the expence. It was put an end to by the army under General Bouquet; there were not above 300 regulars in that army, and above 1000 Pennsylvanians.

Q. Is it not necessary to send troops to America, to defend the Americans against the Indians?—A. No, by no means; it never was necessary. They defended themselves when they were but a handful, and the Indians much more numerous. They continually gained ground, and have driven the Indians over the mountains, without any troops sent to their assistance from this country And can it be thought necessary now to send troops for their defence from those diminished Indian tribes, when the colonies are become so populous, and so strong? There is not the least occasion for it; they are very able to defend themselves.

Q. Do you say there were no more than 300 regular troops employed in the late Indian war? —A. Not on the Ohio or the frontiers of Pennsylvania, which was the chief part of the war that affected the colonies. There were garrisons at Niagara, Fort Detroit, and those remote posts kept for the sake of your trade; I did not reckon them, but I believe that on the whole the number of Americans, or provincial troops, employed in the war, was greater than that of the regulars. I am not certain, but I think so.

Q. Do you think the assemblies have a right to levy money on the subject there, to grant to the crown?—A. I certainly think so; they have always done it.

Q. Are they acquainted with the declaration of rights? And do they know that by that statute, money is not to be raised on the subject but by consent of parliament?—A. They are very well acquainted with it.

Q. How then can they think they have a right to levy money for the crown, or for any other than local purposes?—A. They understand that clause to relate to subjects only within the realm; that no money can be levied on them for the crown, but by consent of parliament. The colonies are not supposed to be within the realm; they have assemblies of their own, which are their parliaments, and they are, in that respect, in the same situation with Ireland. When money is to be raised for the crown upon the subject in Ireland, or in the colonies. the consent is given in the parliament of Ireland, or in the assemblies of the colonies. They think the parliament of Great Britain cannot properly give that consent till it has representatives from America; for the petition of right expressly says, it is to be by common consent in parliament, and the people of America have no representatives in parliament, to make a part of that comon consent. . . .

Q. Would the repeal of the stamp-act be any discouragement of your manufactures? Will the people that have begun to manufacture decline it? —A. Yes, I think they will; especially if, at the same time, the trade is opened again, so that remittances can be easily made. I have known several instances that make it probable. In the war before last, tobacco being low, and making little remittance. the people of Virginia went generally into family manufactures. Afterwards, when tobacco bore a better price, they returned to the use of British manufactures. So fulling-mills were very much disused in the last war in Pennsylvania, because bills were then plenty and remittances could easily be made to Britain for English cloth and other goods.

Q. If the stamp-act should be repealed, would it induce the assemblies of America to acknowledge the right of parliament to tax them, and would they erase their resolutions?—A. No, never.

Q. Is there no means of obliging them to erase those resolutions?—A. None that I know of; they will never do it, unless compelled by force of arms.

Q. Is there a power on earth that can force them to erase them?—A. No power, how great soever, can force men to change their opinions. . . .

Q. Would it be most for the interest of Great-Britain, to employ the hands of Virginia in tobacco, or in manufactures?—A. In tobacco, to be sure.

Q. What used to be the pride of the Americans? —A. To indulge in the fashions and manufactures of Great-Britain.

Q. What is now their pride?—A. To wear their old clothes over again, till they can make new ones.

THE AMERICAN REVOLUTION

IF IT WAS Franklin who presented America's case to England and France, it was Thomas Paine (1737–1809) who presented America's case to herself. He came to America in 1774, a failure at all the trades he had tried. In Philadelphia, he took to the pen and found himself moderately successful as a writer. Then, in the winter of 1775, at the suggestion of Benjamin Rush, Paine wrote Common Sense and became one of the masters of Whig propaganda. With harsh simplicity, Paine said what many men had been thinking and what many more were unwilling to confess they believed. There was no originality in his reasoning or his argument: Dean Tucker's comment on the relative importance of island and continent had gone all but unnoticed in 1766; ten years later, Paine made that seem obvious truth to American Whigs.

Paine's eloquence swept through the country. And after moderate men had had their say—after Parliament had refused to hear even the memorial of the New York Provincial Assembly and the King had declared the continental colonies out of his protection—then Paine found no credible reason against an immediate separation between colonies and motherland.

In June, 1776, Congress passed Richard Henry Lee's resolution for a declaration of independence.

By December, that cause seemed defeated. New York was lost; Fort Washington had fallen and a sizable force had been captured with it; New Jersey was largely in enemy hands and Philadelphia was threatened. The United States was to know darker times; but the men living in that December found its troubles almost too hard to endure. Legend has Paine writing the first number of The Crisis with a drumhead for desk and the flicker of a wintry campfire for light. That legend has the usual validity, but the emotion informing the pamphlet makes the tale sound almost probable. Even more important than the heartening effect of Paine's rhetoric was his suggestion that Tory property be confiscated as a base for the Continental currency. In later numbers of *The Crisis*, Paine continued to argue for independ-ence, for the exaction of oaths to the new government and, finally, when the fighting was over, for the continuance of union among the American states.

The selections from *Common Sense* and *The Crisis* here reprinted are from *The Writings of Thomas Paine* (4 vols., New York, 1894).

Appendix to COMMON SENSE

BY THOMAS PAINE

SINCE the publication of the first edition of this pamphlet, or rather, on the same day on which it came out, the King's Speech made its appearance in this city [Philadelphia]. Had the spirit of prophecy directed the birth of this production, it could not have brought it forth at a more season-able juncture, or at a more necessary time. The bloody-mindedness of the one, shows the necessity of pursuing the doctrine of the other. Men read by way of revenge. And the Speech, instead of terrifying, prepared a way for the manly prin-ciples of Independance.

Ceremony, and even silence, from whatever motives they may arise, have a hurtful tendency when they give the least degree of countenance to base and wicked performances; wherefore, if this maxim be admitted, it naturally follows, that the King's Speech, as being a piece of finished vil-lany, deserved and still deserves, a general execra-tion, both by the Congress and the people. Yet, as the domestic tranquillity of a nation, depends greatly on the *chastity* of what might properly be called NATIONAL MANNERS, it is often better to pass some things over in silent disdain, than to make use of such new methods of dislike, as might in-troduce the least innovation on that guardian of our peace and safety. And, perhaps, it is chiefly owing to this prudent delicacy, that the King's Speech hath not before now suffered a public ex-ecution. The Speech, if it may be called one, is nothing better than a wilful audacious libel against the truth, the common good, and the existence of mankind; and is a formal and pompous method of offering up human sacrifices to the pride of ty-rants. But this general massacre of mankind, is one of the privileges and the certain consequences of Kings; for as nature knows them *not*, they know *not her*, and although they are beings of our *own* creating, they know not *us*, and are become the Gods of their creators. The speech hath one good quality, which is, that it is not calculated to de-ceive, neither can we, even if we would, be de-ceived by it. Brutality and tyranny appear on the face of it. It leaves us at no loss: And every line convinces, even in the moment of reading, that he who hunts the woods for prey, the naked and untutored Indian, is less Savage than the King of Britain.

Sir John Dalrymple, the putative father of a whining jesuitical piece, fallaciously called, "*The address of the people of* England *to the inhab-itants of* America," hath perhaps from a vain sup-position that the people *here* were to be frightened at the pomp and description of a king, given (though very unwisely on his part) the real char-acter of the present one: "But," says this writer, "if you are inclined to pay compliments to an ad-ministration, which we do not complain of (mean-ing the Marquis of Rockingham's at the repeal of the Stamp Act) it is very unfair in you to with-hold them from that prince, *by whose* NOD ALONE *they were permitted to do any thing*." This is toryism with a witness! Here is idolatry even without a mask: And he who can calmly hear and digest such doctrine, hath forfeited his claim to rationality—an apostate from the order of man-hood—and ought to be considered as one who hath not only given up the proper dignity of man, but sunk himself beneath the rank of animals, and contemptibly crawls through the world like a worm.

However, it matters very little now what the king of England either says or does; he hath wick-edly broken through every moral and human obli-gation, trampled nature and conscience beneath his feet, and by a steady and constitutional spirit of insolence and cruelty procured for himself an universal hatred. It is *now* the interest of America to provide for herself. She hath already a large and young family, whom it is more her duty to take care of, than to be granting away her property to support a power who is become a reproach to the names of men and christians—YE, whose office it is to watch the morals of a nation, of whatsoever sect or denomination ye are of, as well as ye who are more immediately the guardians of the public liberty, if ye wish to preserve your native country uncontaminated by European corruption, ye must in secret wish a separation. But leaving the moral part to private reflection, I shall chiefly confine my further remarks to the following heads:

First, That it is the interest of America to be separated from Britain.

Secondly, Which is the easiest and most practicable plan, RECONCILIATION or INDEPENDENCE? with some occasional remarks.

In support of the first, I could, if I judged it proper, produce the opinion of some of the ablest and most experienced men on this continent: and whose sentiments on that head, are not yet publicly known. It is in reality a self-evident position: for no nation in a state of foreign dependance, limited in its commerce, and cramped and fettered in its legislative powers, can ever arrive at any material eminence. America doth not yet know what opulence is; and although the progress which she hath made stands unparalleled in the history of other nations, it is but childhood compared with what she would be capable of arriving at, had she, as she ought to have, the legislative powers in her own hands. England is at this time proudly coveting what would do her no good were she to accomplish it; and the continent hesitating on a matter which will be her final ruin if neglected. It is the commerce and not the conquest of America by which England is to be benefited, and that would in a great measure continue, were the countries as independant of each other as France and Spain; because in many articles neither can go to a better market. But it is the independance of this country of Britain, or any other, which is now the main and only object worthy of contention, and which, like all other truths discovered by necessity, will appear clear and stronger every day.

First, Because it will come to that one time or other.

Secondly, Because the longer it is delayed, the harder it will be to accomplish.

I have frequently amused myself both in public and private companies, with silently remarking the specious errors of those who speak without reflecting. And among the many which I have heard, the following seems the most general, viz. that had this rupture happened forty or fifty years hence, instead of now, the continent would have been more able to have shaken off the dependance. To which I reply, that our military ability, *at this time*, arises from the experience gained in the last war, and which in forty or fifty years time, would

be totally extinct. The continent would not, by that time, have a general, or even a military officer left; and we, or those who may succeed us, would be as ignorant of martial matters as the ancient Indians: and this single position, closely attended to, will unanswerably prove that the present time is preferable to all others. The argument turns thus: At the conclusion of the last war, we had experience, but wanted numbers; and forty or fifty years hence, we shall have numbers, without experience; wherefore, the proper point of time, must be some particular point between the two extremes, in which a sufficiency of the former remains, and a proper increase of the latter is obtained: And that point of time is the present time.

The reader will pardon this digression, as it does not properly come under the head I first set out with, and to which I again return by the following position, viz.:

Should affairs be patched up with Britain, and she to remain the governing and sovereign power of America, (which, as matters are now circumstanced, is giving up the point entirely) we shall deprive ourselves of the very means of sinking the debt we have, or may contract. The value of the backlands, which some of the provinces are clandestinely deprived of, by the unjust extension of the limits of Canada, valued only at five pounds sterling per hundred acres, amount to upwards of twenty-five millions, Pennsylvania currency; and the quit-rents, at one penny sterling per acre, to two millions yearly.

It is by the sale of those lands that the debt may be sunk, without burthen to any, and the quit-rent reserved thereon will always lessen, and in time will wholly support, the yearly expense of government. It matters not how long the debt is in paying, so that the lands when sold be applied to the discharge of it, and for the execution of which the Congress for the time being will be the continental trustees.

I proceed now to the second head, viz. Which is the easiest and most practicable plan, Reconciliation or Independence; with some occasional remarks.

He who takes nature for his guide, is not easily beaten out of his argument, and on that ground, I answer generally—*That* independance *being a single simple line, contained within ourselves; and reconciliation, a matter exceedingly perplexed and complicated, and in which a treacherous capricious court is to interfere, gives the answer without a doubt.*

The present state of America is truly alarming to every man who is capable of reflection. Without law, without government, without any other mode of power than what is founded on, and granted by, courtesy. Held together by an unexampled occurrence of sentiment, which is nevertheless subject to change, and which every secret enemy is endeavoring to dissolve. Our present condition is, Legislation without law; wisdom without a plan; a constitution without a name; and, what is strangely astonishing, perfect independance contending for dependance. The instance is without a precedent, the case never existed before, and who can tell what may be the event? The property of no man is secure in the present unbraced system of things. The mind of the multitude is left at random, and seeing no fixed object before them, they pursue such as fancy or opinion presents. Nothing is criminal; there is no such thing as treason; wherefore, every one thinks himself at liberty to act as he pleases. The Tories would not have dared to assemble offensively, had they known that their lives, by that act, were forfeited to the laws of the state. A line of distinction should be drawn between English soldiers taken in battle, and inhabitants of America taken in arms. The first are prisoners, but the latter traitors. The one forfeits his liberty, the other his head.

Notwithstanding our wisdom, there is a visible feebleness in some of our proceedings which gives encouragement to dissentions. The Continental Belt is too loosely buckled: And if something is not done in time, it will be too late to do any thing, and we shall fall into a state, in which neither Reconciliation nor Independance will be practicable. The king and his worthless adherents are got at their old game of dividing the Continent, and there are not wanting among us Printers who will be busy in spreading specious falsehoods. The artful and hypocritical letter which appeared a few months ago in two of the New-York papers, and likewise in two others, is an evidence that there are men who want both judgment and honesty.

It is easy getting into holes and corners, and talking of reconciliation: But do such men seriously consider how difficult the task is, and how dangerous it may prove, should the Continent divide thereon? Do they take within their view all the various orders of men whose situation and circumstances, as well as their own, are to be considered therein? Do they put themselves in the place of the sufferer whose *all* is *already* gone, and of the soldier, who hath quitted *all* for the defence of his country? If their ill-judged moderation be suited to their own private situations *only*, regardless of others, the event will convince them that "they are reckoning without their host."

Put us, say some, on the footing we were in the year 1763: To which I answer, the request is not now in the power of Britain to comply with, neither will she propose it; but if it were, and even should be granted, I ask, as a reasonable question, By what means is such a corrupt and faithless court to be kept to its engagements? Another parliament, nay, even the present, may hereafter repeal the obligation, on the pretence of its being violently obtained, or unwisely granted; and, in that case, Where is our redress? No going to law with nations; cannon are the barristers of crowns; and the sword, not of justice, but of war, decides the suit. To be on the footing of 1763, it is not sufficient, that the laws only be put in the same state, but, that our circumstances likewise be put in the same state; our burnt and destroyed towns repaired or built up, our private losses made good, our public debts (contracted for defence) discharged; otherwise we shall be millions worse than we were at that enviable period. Such a request, had it been complied with a year ago, would have won the heart and soul of the Continent, but now it is too late. "The Rubicon is passed."

Besides, the taking up arms, merely to enforce the repeal of a pecuniary law, seems as unwarrantable by the divine law, and as repugnant to human feelings, as the taking up arms to enforce obedience thereto. The object, on either side, doth not justify the means; for the lives of men are too valuable to be cast away on such trifles. It is the violence which is done and threatened to our persons; the destruction of our property by an armed force; the invasion of our country by fire and sword, which conscientiously qualifies the use of arms: and the instant in which such mode of defence became necessary, all subjection to Britain ought to have ceased; and the independance of America should have been considered as dating its era from, and published by, *the first musket that was fired against her*. This line is a line of consistency; neither drawn by caprice, nor extended by ambition; but produced by a chain of events, of which the colonies were not the authors.

I shall conclude these remarks, with the following timely and well-intended hints. We ought to reflect, that there are three different ways by which an independancy may hereafter be effected; and that *one* of those *three*, will, one day or other, be the fate of America, viz. By the legal voice of the people in Congress; by a military power; or by a mob: It may not always happen that our soldiers are citizens, and the multitude a body of reasonable men; virtue, as I have already remarked, is not hereditary, neither is it perpetual.

Should an independancy be brought about by the first of those means, we have every opportunity and every encouragement before us, to form the noblest, purest constitution on the face of the earth. We have it in our power to begin the world over again. A situation, similar to the present, hath not happened since the days of Noah until now. The birthday of a new world is at hand, and a race of men, perhaps as numerous as all Europe contains, are to receive their portion of freedom from the events of a few months. The reflection is awful, and in this point of view, how trifling, how ridiculous, do the little paltry cavilings of a few weak or interested men appear, when weighed against the business of a world.

Should we neglect the present favorable and inviting period, and independance be hereafter effected by any other means, we must charge the consequence to ourselves, or to those rather whose narrow and prejudiced souls are habitually opposing the measure, without either inquiring or reflecting. There are reasons to be given in support of independance which men should rather privately think of, than be publicly told of. We ought not now to be debating whether we shall be independant or not, but anxious to accomplish it on a firm, secure, and honorable basis, and uneasy rather that it is not yet began upon. Every day convinces us of its necessity. Even the Tories (if such beings yet remain among us) should, of all men, be the most solicitous to promote it; for as the appointment of committees at first protected them from popular rage, so, a wise and well established form of government will be the only certain means of continuing it securely to them. Wherefore, if they have not virtue enough to be WHIGS, they ought to have prudence enough to wish for independance.

In short, Independance is the only BOND that can tye and keep us together. We shall then see our object, and our ears will be legally shut against the schemes of an intriguing, as well as cruel, enemy. We shall then, too, be on a proper footing to treat with Britain; for there is reason to conclude, that the pride of that court will be less hurt by treating with the American states for terms of peace, than with those, whom she denominates "rebellious subjects," for terms of accommodation. It is our delaying in that, encourages her to hope for conquest, and our backwardness tends only to prolong the war. As we have, without any good effect therefrom, withheld our trade to obtain a redress of our grievances, let us now try the alternative, by independantly redressing them ourselves, and then offering to open the trade. The mercantile and reasonable part of England, will be still with us; because, peace, with trade, is preferable to war without it. And if this offer be not accepted, other courts may be applied to.

On these grounds I rest the matter. And as no offer hath yet been made to refute the doctrine contained in the former editions of this pamphlet, it is a negative proof, that either the doctrine cannot be refuted, or, that the party in favor of it are too numerous to be opposed. WHEREFORE, instead of gazing at each other with suspicious or doubtful curiosity, let each of us hold out to his neighbor the hearty hand of friendship, and unite in drawing a line, which, like an act of oblivion, shall bury in forgetfulness every former dissention. Let the names of Whig and Tory be extinct; and let none other be heard among us, than those of *a good citizen; an open and resolute friend;* and *a virtuous supporter of the* RIGHTS *of* MANKIND, *and of the* FREE AND INDEPENDANT STATES OF AMERICA.

The Crisis

BY THOMAS PAINE

I.

THESE are the times that try men's souls. The summer soldier and the sunshine patriot will, in this crisis, shrink from the service of their country; but he that stands it *now*, deserves the love and thanks of man and woman. Tyranny, like hell, is not easily conquered; yet we have this consolation with us, that the harder the conflict, the more glorious the triumph. What we obtain too cheap, we esteem too lightly: it is dearness only that gives every thing its value. Heaven knows how to put a proper price upon its goods; and it would

be strange indeed if so celestial an article as FREEDOM should not be highly rated. Britain, with an army to enforce her tyranny, has declared that she has a right (*not only to* TAX) but "to BIND us in ALL CASES WHATSOEVER," and if being *bound in that manner*, is not slavery, then is there not such a thing as slavery upon earth. Even the expression is impious; for so unlimited a power can belong only to God.

Whether the independence of the continent was declared too soon, or delayed too long, I will not now enter into as an argument; my own simple opinion is, that had it been eight months earlier, it would have been much better. We did not make a proper use of last winter, neither could we, while we were in a dependant state. However, the fault, if it were one, was all our own [1]; we have none to blame but ourselves. But no great deal is lost yet. All that Howe has been doing for this month past, is rather a ravage than a conquest, which the spirit of the Jerseys, a year ago, would have quickly repulsed, and which time and a little resolution will soon recover.

I have as little superstition in me as any man living, but my secret opinion has ever been, and still is, that God Almighty will not give up a people to military destruction, or leave them unsupportedly to perish, who have so earnestly and so repeatedly sought to avoid the calamities of war, by every decent method which wisdom could invent. Neither have I so much of the infidel in me, as to suppose that He has relinquished the government of the world, and given us up to the care of devils; and as I do not, I cannot see on what grounds the king of Britain can look up to heaven for help against us: a common murderer, a highwayman, or a house-breaker, has as good a pretence as he.

'Tis surprising to see how rapidly a panic will sometimes run through a country. All nations and ages have been subject to them: Britain has trembled like an ague at the report of a French fleet of flat bottomed boats; and in the fourteenth [fifteenth] century the whole English army, after ravaging the kingdom of France, was driven back like men petrified with fear; and this brave exploit was performed by a few broken forces collected and headed by a woman, Joan of Arc. Would that heaven might inspire some Jersey maid to spirit up her countrymen, and save her fair fellow sufferers from ravage and ravishment! Yet panics, in some cases, have their uses; they produce as much good as hurt. Their duration is always short; the mind soon grows through them, and acquires a firmer habit than before. But their peculiar advantage is, that they are the touchstones of sincerity and hypocrisy, and bring things and men to light, which might otherwise have lain forever undiscovered. In fact, they have the same effect on secret traitors, which an imaginary apparition would have upon a private murderer. They sift out the hidden thoughts of man, and hold them up in public to the world. Many a

[1] The present winter is worth an age, if rightly employed; but, if lost or neglected, the whole continent will partake of the evil; and there is no punishment that man does not deserve, be he who, or what, or where he will, that may be the means of sacrificing a season so precious and useful.

disguised tory has lately shown his head, that shall penitentially solemnize with curses the day on which Howe arrived upon the Delaware.

As I was with the troops at Fort Lee, and marched with them to the edge of Pennsylvania, I am well acquainted with many circumstances, which those who live at a distance know but little or nothing of. Our situation there was exceedingly cramped, the place being a narrow neck of land between the North River and the Hackensack. Our force was inconsiderable, being not one fourth so great as Howe could bring against us. We had no army at hand to have relieved the garrison, had we shut ourselves up and stood on our defence. Our ammunition, light artillery, and the best part of our stores, had been removed, on the apprehension that Howe would endeavor to penetrate the Jerseys, in which case Fort Lee could be of no use to us; for it must occur to every thinking man, whether in the army or not, that these kind of field forts are only for temporary purposes, and last in use no longer than the enemy directs his force against the particular object, which such forts are raised to defend. Such was our situation and condition at Fort Lee on the morning of the 20th of November, when an officer arrived with information that the enemy with 200 boats had landed about seven miles above: Major General [Nathaniel] Green, who commanded the garrison, immediately ordered them under arms, and sent express to General Washington at the town of Hackensack, distant by the way of the ferry = six miles. Our first object was to secure the bridge over the Hackensack, which laid up the river between the enemy and us, about six miles from us, and three from them. General Washington arrived in about three quarters of an hour, and marched at the head of the troops towards the bridge, which place I expected we should have a brush for; however, they did not choose to dispute it with us, and the greatest part of our troops went over the bridge, the rest over the ferry, except some which passed at a mill on a small creek, between the bridge and the ferry, and made their way through some marshy grounds up to the town of Hackensack, and there passed the river. We brought off as much baggage as the wagons could contain, the rest was lost. The simple object was to bring off the garrison, and march them on till they could be strengthened by the Jersey or Pennsylvania militia, so as to be enabled to make a stand. We staid four days at Newark, collected our out-posts with some of the Jersey militia, and marched out twice to meet the enemy, on being informed that they were advancing, though our numbers were greatly inferior to theirs. Howe, in my little opinion, committed a great error in generalship in not throwing a body of forces off from Staten Island through Amboy, by which means he might have seized all our stores at Brunswick, and intercepted our march into Pennsylvania; but if we believe the power of hell to be limited, we must likewise believe that their agents are under some providential controul.

I shall not now attempt to give all the particulars of our retreat to the Delaware; suffice it for the present to say, that both officers and men, though greatly harassed and fatigued, frequently without rest, covering, or provision, the inevitable consequences of a long retreat, bore it with a manly and martial spirit. All their wishes centred in one, which was, that the country would turn out and help them to drive the enemy back. Voltaire has remarked that king William never appeared to full advantage but in difficulties and in action; the same remark may be made on General Washington, for the character fits him. There is a natural firmness in some minds which cannot be unlocked by trifles, but which, when unlocked, discovers a cabinet of fortitude; and I reckon it among those kind of public blessings, which we do not immediately see, that God hath blessed him with uninterrupted health, and given him a mind that can even flourish upon care.

I shall conclude this paper with some miscellaneous remarks on the state of our affairs; and shall begin with asking the following question, Why is it that the enemy have left the New-England provinces, and made these middle ones the seat of war? The answer is easy: New-England is not infested with tories, and we are. I have been tender in raising the cry against these men, and used numberless arguments to show them their danger, but it will not do to sacrifice a world either to their folly or their baseness. The period is now arrived, in which either they or we must change our sentiments, or one or both must fall. And what is a tory? Good God! what is he? I should not be afraid to go with a hundred whigs against a thousand tories, were they to attempt to get into arms. Every tory is a coward; for servile, slavish, self-interested fear is the foundation of toryism; and a man under such influence, though he may be cruel, never can be brave.

But, before the line of irrecoverable separation be drawn between us, let us reason the matter together: Your conduct is an invitation to the enemy, yet not one in a thousand of you has heart enough to join him. Howe is as much deceived by you as the American cause is injured by you. He expects you will all take up arms, and flock to his standard, with muskets on your shoulders. Your

opinions are of no use to him, unless you support him personally, for 'tis soldiers, and not tories, that he wants.

I once felt all that kind of anger, which a man ought to feel, against the mean principles that are held by the tories: a noted one, who kept a tavern at Amboy, was standing at his door, with as pretty a child in his hand, about eight or nine years old, as I ever saw, and after speaking his mind as freely as he thought was prudent, finished with this unfatherly expression, "*Well! give me peace in my day.*" Not a man lives on the continent but fully believes that a separation must some time or other finally take place, and a generous parent should have said, "*If there must be trouble, let it be in my day, that my child may have peace;*" and this single reflection, well applied, is sufficient to awaken every man to duty. Not a place upon earth might be so happy as America. Her situation is remote from all the wrangling world, and she has nothing to do but to trade with them. A man can distinguish himself between temper and principle, and I am as confident, as I am that God governs the world, that America will never be happy till she gets clear of foreign dominion. Wars, without ceasing, will break out till that period arrives, and the continent must in the end be conqueror; for though the flame of liberty may sometimes cease to shine, the coal can never expire.

America did not, nor does not want force; but she wanted a proper application of that force. Wisdom is not the purchase of a day, and it is no wonder that we should err at the first setting off. From an excess of tenderness, we were unwilling to raise an army, and trusted our cause to the temporary defence of a well-meaning militia. A summer's experience has now taught us better; yet with those troops, while they were collected, we were able to set bounds to the progress of the enemy, and, thank God! they are again assembling. I always considered militia as the best troops in the world for a sudden exertion, but they will not do for a long campaign. Howe, it is probable, will make an attempt on this city; should he fail on this side the Delaware, he is ruined: if he succeeds, our cause is not ruined. He stakes all on his side against a part on ours; admitting he succeeds, the consequence will be, that armies from both ends of the continent will march to assist their suffering friends in the middle states; for he cannot go everywhere, it is impossible. I consider Howe as the greatest enemy the tories have; he is bringing a war into their country, which, had it not been for him and partly for themselves, they had been clear of. Should he now be expelled, I wish with all the devotion of a Christian, that the names of whig and tory may never more be mentioned; but should the tories give him encouragement to come, or assistance if he come, I as sincerely wish that our next year's arms may expel them from the continent, and the congress appropriate their possessions to the relief of those who have suffered in well-doing. A single successful battle next year will settle the whole. America could carry on a two years war by the confiscation of the property of disaffected persons, and be made happy by their expulsion. Say not that this is revenge, call it rather the soft resentment of a suffering people, who, having no object in view but the *good* of *all*, have staked their *own all* upon a seemingly doubtful event. Yet it is folly to argue against determined hardness; eloquence may strike the ear, and the language of sorrow draw forth the tear of compassion, but nothing can reach the heart that is steeled with prejudice.

Quitting this class of men, I turn with the warm ardor of a friend to those who have nobly stood, and are yet determined to stand the matter out: I call not upon a few, but upon all: not on *this* state or *that* state, but on *every* state: up and help us; lay your shoulders to the wheel; better have too much force than too little, when so great an object is at stake. Let it be told to the future world, that in the depth of winter, when nothing but hope and virtue could survive, that the city and the country, alarmed at one common danger, came forth to meet and to repulse it. Say not that thousands are gone, turn out your tens of thousands; throw not the burden of the day upon Providence, but *"show your faith by your works,"* that God may bless you. It matters not where you live, or what rank of life you hold, the evil or the blessing will reach you all. The far and the near, the home counties and the back, the rich and the poor, will suffer or rejoice alike. The heart that feels not now, is dead: the blood of his children will curse his cowardice, who shrinks back at a time when a little might have saved the whole, and made *them* happy. I love the man that can smile in trouble, that can gather strength from distress, and grow brave by reflection. 'Tis the business of little minds to shrink; but he whose heart is firm, and whose conscience approves his conduct, will pursue his principles unto death. My own line of reasoning is to myself as straight and clear as a ray of light. Not all the treasures of the world, so far as I believe, could have induced me to support an offensive war, for I think it murder; but if a thief breaks into my house, burns and destroys my property, and kills or threatens to kill me, or those that are in it, and to *"bind me in all cases whatsoever"* to his absolute

will, am I to suffer it? What signifies it to me, whether he who does it is a king or a common man; my countryman or not my countryman; whether it be done by an individual villain, or an army of them? If we reason to the root of things we shall find no difference; neither can any just cause be assigned why we should punish in the one case and pardon in the other. Let them call me rebel, and welcome, I feel no concern from it; but I should suffer the misery of devils, were I to make a whore of my soul by swearing allegiance to one whose character is that of a sottish, stupid, stubborn, worthless, brutish man. I conceive likewise a horrid idea in receiving mercy from a being, who at the last day shall be shrieking to the rocks and mountains to cover him, and fleeing with terror from the orphan, the widow, and the slain of America.

There are cases which cannot be overdone by language, and this is one. There are persons, too, who see not the full extent of the evil which threatens them; they solace themselves with hopes that the enemy, if he succeed, will be merciful. It is the madness of folly, to expect mercy from those who have refused to do justice; and even mercy, where conquest is the object, is only a trick of war; the cunning of the fox is as murderous as the violence of the wolf, and we ought to guard equally against both. Howe's first object is, partly by threats and partly by promises, to terrify or seduce the people to deliver up their arms and receive mercy. The ministry recommended the same plan to Gage, and this is what the tories call making their peace, *"a peace which passeth all understanding"* indeed! A peace which would be the immediate forerunner of a worse ruin than any we have yet thought of. Ye men of Pennsylvania, do reason upon these things! Were the back counties to give up their arms, they would fall an easy prey to the Indians, who are all armed: this perhaps is what some tories would not be sorry for. Were the home counties to deliver up their arms, they would be exposed to the resentment of the back counties, who would then have it in their power to chastise their defection at pleasure. And were any one state to give up its arms, *that* state must be garrisoned by all Howe's army of Britons and Hessians to preserve it from the anger of the rest. Mutual fear is the principal link in the chain of mutual love, and woe be to that state that breaks the compact. Howe is mercifully inviting you to barbarous destruction, and men must be either rogues or fools that will not see it. I dwell not upon the vapours of imagination: I bring reason to your ears, and, in language as plain as A, B, C, hold up truth to your eyes.

I thank God, that I fear not. I see no real cause for fear. I know our situation well, and can see the way out of it. While our army was collected, Howe dared not risk a battle; and it is no credit to him that he decamped from the White Plains, and waited a mean opportunity to ravage the defenceless Jerseys; but it is great credit to us, that, with a handful of men, we sustained an orderly retreat for near an hundred miles, brought off our ammunition, all our field pieces, the greatest part of our stores, and had four rivers to pass. None can say that our retreat was precipitate, for we were near three weeks in performing it, that the country might have time to come in. Twice we marched back to meet the enemy, and remained out till dark. The sign of fear was not seen in our camp, and had not some of the cowardly and disaffected inhabitants spread false alarms through the country, the Jerseys had never been ravaged. Once more we are again collected and collecting; our new army at both ends of the continent is recruiting fast, and we shall be able to open the next campaign with sixty thousand men, well armed and clothed. This is our situation, and who will may know it. By perseverance and fortitude we have the prospect of a glorious issue; by cowardice and submission, the sad choice of a variety of evils—a ravaged country—a depopulated city—habitations without safety, and slavery without hope—our homes turned into barracks and bawdy-houses for Hessians, and a future race to provide for, whose fathers we shall doubt of. Look on this picture and weep over it! and if there yet remains one thoughtless wretch who believes it not, let him suffer it unlamented.

SOME RESULTS OF THE AMERICAN REVOLUTION

THE ARTICLES OF CONFEDERATION

THE PARLIAMENT which fought Charles I may have been rebellious, but it was at least legally constituted. The Continental Congress not only acted against the law of the kingdom, it existed outside that law—the British colonial system made no provision for an assembly representing all the continental colonies. The revolutionary congresses are the supreme instance of the American talent for transmuting a self-appointed group of protesters into an organ of government. Such extralegal bodies might be considered better adapted to draft resolutions than to conduct executive business. Yet, for the years between 1776 and 1781, the Continental Congress acted with no more formal authority than its own assertion and the cooperation of the several states—in whatever degree they chose to give that cooperation.

To be sure, plans to formalize the position of Congress by devising a "general government" had been proposed as early as the resolution for independence itself. A committee to bring in a draft constitution was appointed in June, 1776; it reported a month later, and desultory debate on this report did take place. But constitution-making awakened no marked interest. John Adams, for instance, maintained that so long as the authority of Congress was accepted and the states were left free to regulate their own affairs, writing a constitution for the United States was a waste of energy.

By 1777, that view had declined and the Articles of Confederation were finally drawn up and offered to the states for ratification. As a league of nations, the Confederation was admirably constituted: each member state was to give full faith and credit to the judicial proceedings of the others and free citizens of any state were to have the privileges of free citizens throughout the union. Each state was to have one vote cast by delegates it appointed and paid, and the votes of nine states were necessary on questions of war, treaty-making, the coining of money, and the emission of bills of credit. The Congress which the delegates would compose was to have full charge of war and foreign affairs. The costs of the Confederation government were to be born by contributions from the several states in proportion to the value of their surveyed lands and buildings. In event of disputes between states, Congress was to appoint a commission on the request of one of the parties; this commission would hear and determine the matter at issue. The confederacy was to be perpetual, though its terms might be altered by vote of Congress confirmed by the consent of the legislatures of the states.

As the joint executive of a group of allied sovereigns, the Confederation Congress might have been considered adequate. As the government of a nation, it was pitiable. The Articles of Confederation established neither an executive nor a judiciary. Under it, the Congress had no power to regulate commerce. Nor had it any means of obtaining money except by the good will of the states, for it could assess quotas but had no power to collect them.

Insufficient as the Articles of Confederation were to prove, four years went by before Maryland's ratification secured the acceptance of even that constitution for the United States. The most serious cause for the delay was state antagonism: the large states thought the smaller had an unreasonable influence since they had an equal vote; the small states resented the growth which the possession of western lands would make possible to Virginia, the Carolinas, Pennsylvania, and even Massachusetts, Connecticut, and New York. By reason of her position, Maryland was particularly gloomy about her future. To pay her share of the revolutionary debt, she would be obliged to tax her people while neighboring Virginia and Pennsylvania filled their treasuries from the sale of their western lands.

Maryland's protest may have been one of the reasons why Congress appealed to the states to cede their lands to "the United States in Congress assembled"; more important must have been the danger latent in the western claims of the states. Each of the landed states based its title on royal grants laying down conflicting boundaries. Virginia extended to the Mississippi, by her reading of her charter, but so did

Massachusetts, Connecticut, and New York. Virginia had organized a county in the Illinois country; Massachusetts and Connecticut claimed land there as well as in Pennsylvania and New York. New York asserted rights of her own, as successor to the prerogatives of the royal province she had ceased to be (the province was itself successor to the Six Nations which had subjected the tribes of the Ohio and Illinois country).

If this tangle of claims should proceed from argument to action, the fight for independence might become an internecine war. The Congress repeated its appeals. The states made partial concessions which Congress refused to accept. Then, in 1780, New York's legislature offered to cede the state's claim to land west of Pennsylvania. With that for assurance, Maryland proceeded to ratify the Articles of Confederation, apparently hoping that other landed states would follow New York.

In March, 1781, Maryland ratified; and, with all its defects, the Articles of Confederation became the instrument of the federal government of the United States. Among the Americans who saw the flaws of that instrument, none was more keenly articulate than James Madison (1750–1836), who had had experience in constitution-making in Virginia where he had helped draft the Constitution of 1776, and who had spent three years as a member of the Continental Congress, two while it was operating under the Articles he criticized. His memorandum, *Views of the Political System of the United States*, not only repeats the facts of discord and division which had made themselves so evident in the years following the peace of 1783, but sets forth causes and even foreshadows some of the remedial measures that were to be included in the Constitution.

The fundamental evil lay in the nature of confederacies of numerous states each having independent authority. Such states were, in their nature, bound to encroach on federal authority, trespass on each other's rights and violate international law and treaty obligations. They would fail to take united action for commerce, naturalization and the "grant of incorporation for national purposes, for canals and other works of national utility." As organized, the present federal system gave the states no effective guarantee against internal violence, nor did it have coercive power as sanction for federal laws. The Articles of Confederation had not been ratified by the people, and, in some of the states, formed no part of their constitution. Therefore, the Articles lacked the authority necessary to a proper instrument of government. Furthermore, as the confederation was merely that of a league, violation of the covenant of the Articles by one party released the others from their obligations.

Besides the difficulties inherent in all leagues among sovereigns, the United States suffered from difficulties peculiar to its own situation. State laws were not only mutable but unjust, and their multiplication had become a "pestilential nuisance." Worse still, none of the states had met the essential problem of political justice: how to make government neutral in respect to the interests composing a society without setting itself up as an interest adverse to that society. With proper constitutional organization and a system of elections designed to "extract" the "purest and noblest" elements from society, the United States, Madison implies, might hurdle the obstacles of present disturbances and form a stable government able to assure order and maintain liberty.

The Madison memorandum carried the date April, 1787, and is reprinted from the *Writings*, ed. Gaillard Hunt (8 vols., New York, 1901).

Views of the Political System of the United States

BY JAMES MADISON

1. *Failure of the States to comply with the Constitutional requisitions*. This evil has been so fully experienced both during the war and since the peace, results so naturally from the number and independent authority of the States and has been so uniformly exemplified in every similar Confederacy, that it may be considered as not less radically and permanently inherent in than it is fatal to the object of the present system.

2. *Encroachments by the States on the federal authority*. Examples of this are numerous and repetitions may be foreseen in almost every case where any favorite object of a State shall present a temptation. Among these examples are the wars and treaties of Georgia with the Indians. The unlicensed compacts between Virginia and Maryland, and between Pen^a & N. Jersey—the troops raised and to be kept up by Mass^{ts}.

3. *Violations of the law of nations and of treaties*. From the number of Legislatures, the sphere of life from which most of their members are taken, and the circumstances under which their legislative business is carried on, irregularities of this kind must frequently happen. Accordingly not a year has passed without instances of them in some one or other of the States. The Treaty of Peace—the treaty with France—the treaty with Holland have each been violated. [See the complaints to Congress on these subjects.] The causes of these irregularities must necessarily produce frequent violations of the law of nations in other respects.

As yet foreign powers have not been rigorous in animadverting on us. This moderation, however cannot be mistaken for a permanent partiality to our faults, or a permanent security agst those disputes with other nations, which being among the greatest of public calamities, it ought to be least in the power of any part of the community to bring on the whole.

4. *Trespasses of the States on the rights of each other*. These are alarming symptoms, and may be daily apprehended as we are admonished by daily experience. See the law of Virginia restricting foreign vessels to certain ports—of Maryland in favor of vessels belonging to her *own citizens*—of N. York in favor of the same—

Paper money, instalments of debts, occlusion of Courts, making property a legal tender, may likewise be deemed aggressions on the rights of other States. As the Citizens of every State aggregately taken stand more or less in the relation of Creditors or debtors, to the Citizens of every other State, Acts of the debtor State in favor of debtors, affect the Creditor State, in the same manner as they do its own citizens who are relatively creditors towards other citizens. This remark may be extended to foreign nations. If the exclusive regulation of the value and alloy of coin was properly delegated to the federal authority, the policy of it equally requires a controul on the States in the cases above mentioned. It must have been meant 1. to preserve uniformity in the circulating medium throughout the nation. 2. to prevent those frauds on the citizens of other States, and the subjects of foreign powers, which might disturb the tranquillity at home, or involve the Union in foreign contests.

The practice of many States in restricting the commercial intercourse with other States, and putting their productions and manufactures on the same footing with those of foreign nations, though not contrary to the federal articles, is certainly adverse to the spirit of the Union, and tends to beget retaliating regulations, not less expensive and vexatious in themselves than they are destructive of the general harmony.

5. *Want of concert in matters where common interest requires it.* This defect is strongly illustrated in the state of our commercial affairs. How much has the national dignity, interest, and revenue, suffered from this cause? Instances of inferior moment are the want of uniformity in the laws concerning naturalization & literary property; of provision for national seminaries, for grants of incorporation for national purposes, for canals and other works of general utility, wch may at present be defeated by the perverseness of particular States whose concurrence is necessary.

6. *Want of Guaranty to the States of their Constitutions & laws against internal violence.* The confederation is silent on this point and therefore by the second article the hands of the federal authority are tied. According to Republican Theory, Right and power being both vested in the majority, are held to be synonymous. According to fact and experience a minority may in an appeal to force, be an overmatch for the majority. 1. if the minority happen to include all such as possess the skill and habits of military life, & such as possess the great pecuniary resources, one-third only may conquer the remaining two-thirds. 2. one-third of those who participate in the choice of the rulers, may be rendered a majority by the accession of those whose poverty excludes them from a right of suffrage, and who for obvious reasons will be more likely to join the standard of sedition than that of the established Government. 3. where slavery exists the republican Theory becomes still more fallacious.

7. *Want of sanction to the laws, and of coercion in the Government of the Confederacy.* A sanction is essential to the idea of law, as coercion is to that of Government. The federal system being destitute of both, wants the great vital principles of a Political Constitution. Under the form of such a constitution, it is in fact nothing more than a treaty of amity of commerce and of alliance, between independent and Sovereign States. From what cause could so fatal an omission have happened in the articles of Confederation? from a mistaken confidence that the justice, the good faith, the honor, the sound policy, of the several legislative assemblies would render superfluous any appeal to the ordinary motives by which the laws secure the obedience of individuals: a confidence which does honor to the enthusiastic virtue of the compilers, as much as the inexperience of the crisis apologizes for their errors. The time which has since elapsed has had the double effect, of increasing the light and tempering the warmth, with which the arduous work may be revised. It is no longer doubted that a unanimous and punctual obedience of 13 independent bodies, to the acts of the federal Government ought not to be calculated on. Even during the war, when external danger supplied in some degree the defect of legal & coercive sanctions, how imperfectly did the States fulfil their obligations to the Union? In time of peace, we see already what is to be expected. How indeed could it be otherwise? In the first place, Every general act of the Union must necessarily bear unequally hard on some particular member or members of it, secondly the partiality of the members to their own interests and rights, a partiality which will be fostered by the courtiers of popularity, will naturally exaggerate the inequality where it exists, and even suspect it where it has no existence, thirdly a distrust of the voluntary compliance of each other may prevent the compliance of any, although it should be the latent disposition of all. Here are causes & pretexts which will never fail to render federal measures abortive. If the laws of the States were merely recommendatory to their citizens, or if they were to be rejudged by County authorities, what security, what probability would exist, that they would be carried into execution? Is the security or probability greater in favor of the acts of Cong^s which depending for their execution on the will of the State legislatures, wch are tho' nominally authoritative, in fact recommendatory only?

8. *Want of ratification by the people of the articles of Confederation.* In some of the States the Confederation is recognized by, and forms a part of the Constitution. In others however it has received no other sanction than that of the legislative authority. From this defect two evils result: 1. Whenever a law of a State happens to be repugnant to an act of Congress, particularly when

the latter [former] is of posterior date to the former, [latter] it will be at least questionable whether the latter [former] must not prevail; and as the question must be decided by the Tribunals of the State, they will be most likely to lean on the side of the State.

2. As far as the union of the States is to be regarded as a league of sovereign powers, and not as a political Constitution by virtue of which they are become one sovereign power, so far it seems to follow from the doctrine of compacts, that a breach of any of the articles of the Confederation by any of the parties to it, absolves the other parties from their respective Obligations, and gives them a right if they chuse to exert it, of dissolving the Union altogether.

9. *Multiplicity of laws in the several States.* In developing the evils which viciate the political system of the U. S., it is proper to include those which are found within the States individually, as well as those which directly affect the States collectively, since the former class have an indirect influence on the general malady and must not be overlooked in forming a compleat remedy. Among the evils then of our situation may well be ranked the multiplicity of laws from which no State is exempt. As far as laws are necessary to mark with precision the duties of those who are to obey them, and to take from those who are to administer them a discretion which might be abused, their number is the price of liberty. As far as laws exceed this limit, they are a nuisance; a nuisance of the most pestilent kind. Try the Codes of the several States by this test, and what a luxuriancy of legislation do they present. The short period of independency has filled as many pages as the century which preceded it. Every year, almost every session, adds a new volume. This may be the effect in part, but it can only be in part, of the situation in which the revolution has placed us. A review of the several Codes will shew that every necessary and useful part of the least voluminous of them might be compressed into one tenth of the compass, and at the same time be rendered ten fold as perspicuous.

10. *Mutability of the laws of the States.* This evil is intimately connected with the former yet deserves a distinct notice, as it emphatically denotes a vicious legislation. We daily see laws repealed or superseded, before any trial can have been made of their merits, and even before a knowledge of them can have reached the remoter districts within which they were to operate. In the regulations of trade this instability becomes a snare not only to our citizens, but to foreigners also.

11. *Injustice of the laws of the States.* If the multiplicity and *mutability* of laws prove a want of wisdom, their injustice betrays a defect still more alarming: more alarming not merely because it is a greater evil in itself; but because it brings more into question the fundamental principle of republican Government, that the majority who rule in such governments are the safest Guardians both of public Good and private rights. To what causes is this evil to be ascribed?

These causes lie 1. in the Representative bodies. 2. in the people themselves.

1. Representative appointments are sought from 3 motives. 1. ambition. 2. personal interest. 3. public good. Unhappily the two first are proved by experience to be most prevalent. Hence the candidates who feel them, particularly, the second, are most industrious, and most successful in pursuing their object: and forming often a majority in the legislative Councils, with interested views, contrary to the interest and views of their constituents, join in a *perfidious* sacrifice of the latter to the former. A succeeding election it might be supposed, would displace the offenders, and repair the mischief. But how easily are base and selfish measures, masked by pretexts of public good and apparent expediency? How frequently will a repetition of the same arts and industry which succeeded in the first instance, again prevail on the unwary to misplace their confidence?

How frequently too will the honest but unenlightened representative be the dupe of a favorite leader, veiling his selfish views under the professions of public good, and varnishing his sophistical arguments with the glowing colours of popular eloquence?

2. A still more fatal if not more frequent cause, lies among the people themselves. All civilized societies are divided into different interests and factions, as they happen to be creditors or debtors —rich or poor—husbandmen, merchants or manufacturers—members of different religious sects— followers of different political leaders—inhabitants of different districts—owners of different kinds of property &c. &c. In republican Government the majority however composed, ultimately give the law. Whenever therefore an apparent interest or common passion unites a majority what is to restrain them from unjust violations of the rights and interests of the minority, or of individuals? Three motives only 1. a prudent regard to their own good as involved in the general and permanent good of the community. This consideration although of decisive weight in itself, is found by experience to be too often unheeded. It is too often forgotten, by nations as well as by

individuals, that honesty is the best policy. 2dly. respect for character. However strong this motive may be in individuals, it is considered as very insufficient to restrain them from injustice. In a multitude its efficacy is diminished in proportion to the number which is to share the praise or the blame. Besides, as it has reference to public opinion, which within a particular Society, is the opinion of the majority, the standard is fixed by those whose conduct is to be measured by it. The public opinion without the Society will be little respected by the people at large of any Country. Individuals of extended views, and of national pride, may bring the public proceedings to this standard, but the example will never be followed by the multitude. Is it to be imagined that an ordinary citizen or even Assemblyman of R. Island in estimating the policy of paper money, ever considered or cared, in what light the measure would be viewed in France or Holland; or even in Mass^ts or Connec^t? It was a sufficient temptation to both that it was for their interest; it was a sufficient sanction to the latter that it was popular in the State; to the former, that it was so in the neighbourhood. 3dly. will Religion the only remaining motive be a sufficient restraint? It is not pretended to be such on men individually considered. Will its effect be greater on them considered in an aggregate view? quite the reverse. The conduct of every popular assembly acting on oath, the strongest of religious ties, proves that individuals join without remorse in acts, against which their consciences would revolt if proposed to them under the like sanction, separately in their closets. When indeed Religion is kindled into enthusiasm, its force like that of other passions, is increased by the sympathy of a multitude. But enthusiasm is only a temporary state of religion, and while it lasts will hardly be seen with pleasure at the helm of Government. Besides as religion in its coolest state is not infallible, it may become a motive to oppression as well as a restraint from injustice. Place three individuals in a situation wherein the interest of each depends on the voice of the others; and give to two of them an interest opposed to the rights of the third? Will the latter be secure? The prudence of every man would shun the danger. The rules & forms of justice suppose & guard against it. Will two thousand in a like situation be less likely to encroach on the rights of one thousand? The contrary is witnessed by the notorious factions & oppressions which take place in corporate towns limited as the opportunities are, and in little republics when uncontrouled by apprehensions of external danger. If an enlargement of the sphere is found to lessen the insecurity of private rights, it is not because the impulse of a common interest or passion is less predominant in this case with the majority; but because a common interest or passion is less apt to be felt and the requisite combinations less easy to be formed by a great than by a small number. The Society becomes broken into a greater variety of interests, of pursuits of passions, which check each other, whilst those who may feel a common sentiment have less opportunity of communication and concert. It may be inferred that the inconveniences of popular States contrary to the prevailing Theory, are in proportion not to the extent, but to the narrowness of their limits.

The great *desideratum* in Government is such a modification of the sovereignty as will render it sufficiently neutral between the different interests and factions, to controul one part of the society from invading the rights of another, and at the same time sufficiently controuled itself, from setting up an interest adverse to that of the whole Society. In absolute Monarchies the prince is sufficiently, neutral towards his subjects, but frequently sacrifices their happiness to his ambition or his avarice. In small Republics, the sovereign will is sufficiently controuled from such a sacrifice of the entire Society, but is not sufficiently neutral towards the parts composing it. As a limited monarchy tempers the evils of an absolute one; so an extensive Republic meliorates the administration of a small Republic.

An auxiliary desideratum for the melioration of the Republican form is such a process of elections as will most certainly extract from the mass of the society the purest and noblest characters which it contains; such as will at once feel most strongly the proper motives to pursue the end of their appointment, and be most capable to devise the proper means of attaining it.

THE CHARTER OF THE BANK OF NORTH AMERICA

By 1781, the currency and credit of the Continental Congress had dropped to a new low. Congress appointed Robert Morris (1734-1806) Superintendent of Finance in the hope that his business experience would provide the funds neither paper money nor unregarded requisitions on the states had supplied. With no resources but the Congress's debts and diplomatic connections, Morris set about his task. He had already bedeviled the Pennsylvania Assembly into repealing its legal-tender laws and providing for the partial redemption of its paper money. Though that was not feasible for a Congress which could neither lay nor collect taxes, Congress might mend matters by chartering a bank. A bank, Morris argued, would so combine the private credit of its stockholders, lenders, and borrowers as to supply a base for public and private borrowing. The bank's notes, redeemable in specie and receivable in payment of state and federal taxes, would finally replace the worthless paper which was the only currency then available.

Morris's plan for a bank met with small encouragement among the Whig businessmen who would not buy stock. Nor was the Congress entirely certain of its power to charter such an institution. But Robert Morris was not to be checked by merchants' caution or James Madison's constitutional scruples. Morris looked abroad for the necessary hard money. When a British frigate captured the shipload of flour which he had planned to exchange for specie in Havana, Morris turned to the silver which France had finally sent to her ally. An armed guard brought the specie safely from Boston to Philadelphia and the vaults of the new bank. A few weeks later, in December, 1781, Congress incorporated the bank which opened at the turn of the year and soon was serving Morris by discounting his notes and giving him credit in anticipation of taxes. This was the first commercial bank chartered in America; and it was another proof of the determination of Americans to free themselves from the restraints of the English Mercantilist System.

The text of the charter is from M. St. Clair Clarke and D. H. Hall, *Legislative and Documentary History of the Bank of the United States* (Washington, 1832).

The Charter of the Bank of North America

AN ORDINANCE TO INCORPORATE THE SUBSCRIBERS TO THE BANK OF NORTH AMERICA

WHEREAS Congress, on the 26th day of May last, did, from a conviction of the support which the finances of the United States would receive from the establishment of a National Bank, approve a plan for such an institution, submitted to their consideration by Robert Morris, Esq. and now lodged among the archives of Congress, and did engage to promote the same by the most effectual means: And whereas the subscription thereto is now filled, from an expectation of a charter of incorporation from Congress, the directors and president are chosen, and application hath been made to Congress, by the said president and directors, for an act of incorporation: And whereas the exigencies of the United States render it indispensably necessary that such an act be immediately passed:

Be it therefore ordained and it is hereby ordained by the United States in Congress assembled, That those who are, and those who shall become, subscribers to the said bank, be, and forever after shall be, a corporation and body politic, to all intents and purposes, by the name and style of "*The President, Directors, and Company, of the Bank of North America.*"

And be it further ordained, That the said corporation are hereby declared and made able and capable, in law, to have, purchase, receive, possess, enjoy, and retain, lands, rents, tenements, hereditaments, goods, chattels, and effects, of what kind, nature, or quality, soever, to the amount of ten millions of Spanish silver milled dollars, and no more; and, also, to sell, grant, demise, alien, or dispose of, the same lands, rents, tenements, hereditaments, goods, chattels, and effects.

And be it further ordained, That the said corporation be, and shall be, for ever, hereafter, able and capable, in law, to sue and be sued, plead and be impleaded, answer and be answered unto, defend and be defended, in courts of record, or any other place whatsoever, and to do and execute all and singular other matters and things that to them shall or may appertain to do.

And be it further ordained, That, for the well governing of the said corporation and the ordering of their affairs, they shall have such officers as they shall hereafter direct or appoint. *Provided, nevertheless,* That twelve directors, one of whom shall be the president of the corporation, be of the number of their officers.

And be it further ordained, That Thomas Willing be the present president, and that the said Thomas Willing and Thomas Fitzsimmons, John Maxwell Nesbit, James Wilson, Henry Hill, Samuel Osgood, Cadwallader Morris, Andrew Caldwell, Samuel Inglis, Samuel Meredith, William Bingham, Timothy Matlack, be the present directors of the said corporation; and shall so continue until another president and other directors shall be chosen, according to the laws and regulations of the said corporation.

And be it further ordained, That the president and directors of the said corporation shall be capable of exercising such power for the well governing and ordering of the affairs of the said corporation, and of holding such occasional meetings for that purpose, as shall be described, fixed, and determined, by the laws, regulations, and ordinances, of the said corporation.

And be it further ordained, That the said corporation may make, ordain, establish, and put in execution, such laws, ordinances, and regulations, as shall seem necessary and convenient to the government of the said corporation.

Provided, always, That nothing herein before contained shall be construed to authorize the said corporation to exercise any powers, in any of the United States, repugnant to the laws or constitution of such State.

And be it further ordained, That the said corporation shall have full power and authority to make, have, and use, a common seal, with such device and inscription as they shall think proper, and the same to break, alter, and renew, at their pleasure.

And be it further ordained, That this ordinance shall be construed and taken most favorably and beneficially for the said corporation.

Done by the United States in Congress assembled, &c.

THE VIRGINIA STATUTE OF RELIGIOUS LIBERTY

THOUGH THE Virginia Bill of Rights had declared all men equally entitled to practice their religion, it made no formal and specific disestablishment of the Episcopal Church. Legal prosecutions for religious causes ceased and tithes were no longer collected, but sufficient remnants of privilege remained to make necessary a long fight for complete religious freedom in Virginia.

The House of Delegates had repealed all Acts of Parliament concerning religion, to be sure, yet there was still considerable sentiment for some form of public support for religion. Proposals were made to declare Christianity the religion of the state and to levy taxes to maintain ministers of all denominations.

By 1784, that proposition had won the approval of so many of the conservative tidewater members of the legislature that only Madison's aptly timed motion for postponement prevented the passage of a law levying a tax for the public support of religion. In the interval between sessions, the opposition brought the issue before the voters in an intensive campaign of speeches and publications. The Dissenting sects of the western counties and Madison's forces in the east were so successful that the legislature passed not Patrick Henry's measure for the public maintenance of religion but the Statute of Religious Liberty, whose authorship Thomas Jefferson proudly proclaimed in his epitaph. The act was passed January 16, 1786.

The selection is reprinted from W. A. Hening, *Statutes at Large of Virginia*, Vol. XII (Richmond, 1823).

Virginia Statute of Religious Liberty

BY THOMAS JEFFERSON

AN ACT FOR ESTABLISHING RELIGIOUS FREEDOM

I. WHEREAS Almighty God hath created the mind free; that all attempts to influence it by temporal punishments or burthens, or by civil incapacitations, tend only to beget habits of hypocrisy and meanness, and are a departure from the plan of the Holy author of our religion, who being Lord both of body and mind, yet chose not to propagate it by coercions on either, as was in his Almighty power to do; that the impious presumption of legislators and rulers, civil as well as ecclesiastical, who being themselves but fallible and uninspired men, have assumed dominion over the faith of others, setting up their own opinions and modes of thinking as the only true and infallible, and as such endeavouring to impose them on others, hath established and maintained false religions over the greatest part of the world, and through all time; that to compel a man to furnish contributions of money for the propagation of opinions which he disbelieves, is sinful and tyrannical; that even the forcing him to support this or that teacher of his own religious persuasion, is depriving him of the comfortable liberty of giving his contributions to the particular pastor whose morals he would make his pattern, and whose powers he feels most persuasive to righteousness, and is withdrawing from the ministry those temporary rewards, which proceeding from an approbation of their personal conduct, are an additional incitement to earnest and unremitting labours for the instruction of mankind; that our civil rights have no dependence on our religious opinions, any more than on our opinions in physics or geometry; that therefore the proscribing any citizen as unworthy the public confidence by laying upon him an incapacity of being called to offices of trust and emolument, unless he profess or renounce this or that religious opinion, is depriving him injuriously of those privileges and advantages to which in common with his fellow-citizens he has a natural right; that it tends only to corrupt the principles of that religion it is meant to encourage, by bribing with a monopoly of worldly honours and emoluments, those who will externally profess and conform to it; that though indeed these are criminal who do not withstand such temptation, yet neither are those innocent who lay the bait in their way; that to suffer the civil magistrate to intrude his powers into the field of opinion, and to restrain the profession or propagation of principles on supposition of their ill tendency, is a dangerous fallacy, which at once destroys all religious liberty, because he being of course judge of that tendency will make his opinions the rule of judgment and approve or condemn the sentiments of others only as they shall square with or differ from his own; that it is time enough for the rightful purposes of civil government, for its officers to interfere when principles break out into overt acts against peace and good order; and finally, that truth is great and will prevail if left to herself, that she is the proper and sufficient antagonist to error, and has nothing to fear from the conflict, unless by human interposition disarmed of her natural weapons, free argument and debate, errors ceasing to be dangerous when it permitted freely to contradict them.

II. *Be it enacted by the General Assembly*, that no man shall be compelled to frequent or support any religious worship, place or ministry whatsoever, nor shall be enforced, restrained, molested, or burthened in his body or goods, nor shall otherwise suffer on account of his religious opinions or belief; but that all men shall be free to profess, and by argument to maintain, their opinion in matters of religion, and that the same shall in no wise diminish, enlarge or affect their civil capacities.

III. And though we well know that this assembly, elected by the people for the ordinary purposes of legislation only, have no power to restrain the acts of succeeding assemblies, constituted with powers equal to our own, and that therefore to declare this act to be irrevocable would be of no effect in law; yet as we are free to declare, and do declare, that the rights hereby asserted are of the natural rights of mankind, and that if any act shall hereafter be passed to repeal the present, or to narrow its operation, such act will be an infringement of natural right.

THE LAND ORDINANCES OF 1785 AND 1787

The land ordinances of May, 1785, and July, 1787, are probably the most important work of the Confederation Congress. The first set the physical pattern for the survey and disposal of public lands; the second laid the foundation for the expansion of republican government across a continent. Together, they hint at the course to be taken by future Congresses under the Constitution which was being drafted even while the Ordinance of 1787 was being enacted.

When the thirteen states were confronted by the necessity of forming a permanent league, western land claims were one of the greatest obstacles to union, for there could be no equality between states with definite western boundaries on the one hand and states whose charters gave them the right to land as far west as the Mississippi, on the other. Congress suggested that the separate states cede their claims to the "United States in Congress assembled." In March, 1781, New York offered to cede her western claims; and New York's example was followed by Virginia, Massachusetts, and Connecticut. Thus, by 1784, Congress was possessed of a colonial domain and the problems that went with it.

The Indian problem was partly solved by treaty with the Iroquois and the tribes of the Ohio country, but the western posts were still in British hands and, more immediately, the territory in Congress's possession needed regulation. In spite of law, squatters had settled north of the Ohio and speculators were active in the territory. It was necessary to decide on disposition of the land and also to organize some form of republican government for the area.

Jefferson was appointed to head both committees and it was he who outlined a scheme of survey as well as a plan for government. He proposed that sixteen states be laid out on the national domain. When Congress offered any of this territory for sale, the settlers were to establish a temporary government, using the constitution and laws of one of the original states as model. When the land numbered 20,-000 inhabitants, these might hold a convention to establish a permanent constitution and send a delegate, who might speak but not vote in Congress. As soon as the population equaled that of the least numerous of the thirteen original states, the new state might be admitted to Congress on equal terms with the old; on the other hand, it was bound to remain part of the United States forever, subject to the general government in the same manner as the original states, liable for a portion of the federal debt, as well as to maintain a republican form of government and to end slavery after 1800. Except for the classical names Jefferson had assigned the new territory, and his prohibition of slavery, the Congress accepted the report of Jefferson's committee.

In 1787, at the urging of Manasseh Cutler and his associates in the Ohio Company, which was negotiating for the purchase of a large tract of land in the Muskingum country, Congress revised the Ordinance of 1785 to provide a more detailed plan of government and more definite safeguards for the obligation of contracts. Jefferson's original prohibition of slavery was put into the act. Though Congress had only a dubious right to take such action under the Articles of Confederation, the Ordinance of 1787 may be considered one of the happiest of the extralegal master strokes which distinguished this period.

While Jefferson had been considering proper governments for the new federal territories, he had also been concerned with the best means of disposing of these western lands. He was familiar with the Virginia system of locating by headright, under which any man with a warrant for a certain number of acres of land might select his plot on any vacant land he might choose and then have it surveyed and registered. While this plan was flexible and favored the wide-ranging pioneer, it also led to confusion and overlapping of claims, with consequent litigation, as well as to speculative monopoly of the choicest sites. The New England system of granting only surveyed land made for greater surety of title but tended to hamper settlement if survey failed to keep pace with the demand for land.

How Jefferson would have resolved that conflict is uncertain, for he left on his mission to France before the committee had made its final report. He did suggest survey before grant, however, and payment for public land in loan-office certificates—a special variety of the Continental public debt—reduced to their specie value. When the committee made its final report, it retained the basic feature of surveying public land into lots of fixed and uniform area before it was offered for sale. This Ordinance of 1785, with its system of survey before grant and reservation of certain lots for public purposes, contains the fundamental elements of what was to be the United States public-lands system even after the Homestead Act of 1862 had partially superseded the sale of the public domain.

The texts of the Ordinances used here are from the *Journals of the American Congress* (4 vols., Washington, 1823).

The Ordinance of 1785

AN ORDINANCE FOR ASCERTAINING THE MODE OF DISPOSING OF LANDS IN THE WESTERN TERRITORY

Be it ordained by the United States in Congress assembled, That the said territory, for the purposes of temporary government, be one district, subject, however, to be divided into two districts, as future circumstances may, in the opinion of Congress, make it expedient.

Be it ordained by the authority aforesaid, That the estates, both of resident and non-resident proprietors in the said territory, dying intestate, shall descend to, and be distributed among, their children, and the descendants of a deceased child, in equal parts; the descendants of a deceased child or grandchild to take the share of their deceased parent in equal parts among them: And where there shall be no children or descendants, then in equal parts to the next of kin in equal degree; and, among collaterals, the children of a deceased brother or sister of the intestate shall have, in equal parts among them, their deceased parents' share; and there shall, in no case, be a distinction between kindred of the whole and half-blood; saving, in all cases, to the widow of the intestate her third part of the real estate for life, and one-third part of the personal estate; and this law, relative to descents and dower, shall remain in full force until altered by the legislature of the district. And, until the governor and judges shall adopt laws as hereinafter mentioned, estates in the said territory may be devised or bequeathed by wills in writing, signed and sealed by him or her, in whom the estate may be (being of full age,) and attested by three witnesses; and real estates may be conveyed by lease and release, or bargain and sale, signed, sealed, and delivered by the person, being of full age, in whom the estate may be, and attested by two witnesses, provided such wills be duly proved, and such conveyances be acknowledged, or the execution thereof duly proved, and be recorded within one year after proper magistrates, courts, and registers shall be appointed for that purpose; and personal property may be transferred by delivery; saving, however to the French and Canadian inhabitants, and other settlers of the Kaskaskias, St. Vincents, and the neighboring villages who have heretofore professed themselves citizens of Virginia, their laws and customs now in force among them, relative to the descent and conveyance of property.

Be it ordained by the authority aforesaid, That there shall be appointed, from time to time, by Congress, a governor, whose commission shall continue in force for the term of three years, unless sooner revoked by Congress; he shall reside in the district, and have a freehold estate therein in 1000 acres of land, while in the exercise of his office.

There shall be appointed, from time to time, by Congress, a secretary, whose commission shall continue in force for four years unless sooner revoked; he shall reside in the district, and have a freehold estate therein in 500 acres of land, while in the exercise of his office; it shall be his duty to keep and preserve the acts and laws passed by the legislature, and the public records of the district, and the proceedings of the governor in his Executive department; and transmit authentic copies of such acts and proceedings, every six months, to the Secretary of Congress: There shall also be appointed a court to consist of three judges, any two of whom to form a court, who shall have a common law jurisdiction, and reside in the district, and have each therein a freehold estate in 500 acres of land while in the exercise of their offices; and their commissions shall continue in force during good behavior.

The governor and judges, or a majority of them, shall adopt and publish in the district such laws of the original States, criminal and civil, as may be necessary and best suited to the circumstances of the district, and report them to Congress from time to time: which laws shall be in force in the district until the organization of the General Assembly therein, unless disapproved of by Congress; but, afterwards, the legislature shall have authority to alter them as they shall think fit.

The governor, for the time being, shall be commander-in-chief of the militia, appoint and commission all officers in the same below the rank of general officers; all general officers shall be appointed and commissioned by Congress.

Previous to the organization of the General Assembly, the governor shall appoint such magistrates and other civil officers, in each county or township, as he shall find necessary for the preservation of the peace and good order in the same: After the General Assembly shall be organized, the powers and duties of the magistrates and other civil officers, shall be regulated and defined by the said assembly; but all magistrates and other civil officers, not herein otherwise directed, shall, during the continuance of this temporary government, be appointed by the governor.

For the prevention of crimes and injuries, the laws to be adopted or made shall have force in all parts of the district, and for the execution of process, criminal and civil, the governor shall make proper divisions thereof; and he shall proceed, from time to time, as circumstances may require, to lay out the parts of the district in which the Indian titles shall have been extinguished, into counties and townships, subject, however, to such alterations as may thereafter be made by the legislature.

So soon as there shall be 5000 free male inhabitants of full age in the district, upon giving proof thereof to the governor, they shall receive authority, with time and place, to elect representatives from their counties or townships to represent them in the General Assembly: *Provided*, That, for every 500 free male inhabitants, there shall be one representative, and so on progressively with the number of free male inhabitants, shall the right of representation increase, until the number of representatives shall amount to 25; after which, the number and proportion of representatives shall be regulated by the legislature: *Provided*, That no person be eligible or qualified to act as a representative unless he shall have been a citizen of one of the United States three years, and be a resident in the district, or unless he shall have resided in the district three years; and, in either case, shall likewise hold in his own right, in fee simple, 200 acres of land within the same: *Provided, also,* That a freehold in 50 acres of land in the district, having been a citizen of one of the States, and being resident in the district, or the like freehold and two years residence in the district, shall be necessary to qualify a man as an elector of a representative.

The representatives thus elected, shall serve for the term of two years; and, in case of the death of a representative, or removal from office, the governor shall issue a writ to the county or township for which he was a member, to elect another in his stead, to serve for the residue of the term.

The General Assembly, or Legislature, shall consist of the governor, legislative council, and a house of representatives. The legislative council shall consist of five members, to continue in office five years, unless sooner removed by Congress; any three of whom to be a quorum: and the members of the council shall be nominated and appointed in the following manner, to wit: As soon as representatives shall be elected, the governor shall appoint a time and place for them to meet together; and, when met, they shall nominate ten persons, residents in the district, and each possessed of a freehold in 500 acres of land, and return their names to Congress; five of whom Congress shall appoint and commission to serve as aforesaid; and, whenever a vacancy shall happen in the council, by death or removal from office, the house of representatives shall nominate two persons, qualified as aforesaid, for each vacancy, and return their names to Congress; one of whom Congress shall appoint and commission for the residue of the term. And every five years, four months at least before the expiration of the time of service of the members of council, the said house shall nominate ten persons, qualified as aforesaid, and return their names to Congress; five of whom Congress shall appoint and commission to serve as members of the council five years, unless sooner removed. And the governor, legislative council, and house of representatives, shall have authority to make laws in all cases, for the good government of the district, not repugnant to the principles and articles in this ordinance established and declared. And all bills, having passed by a majority in the house, and by a majority in the council, shall be referred to the governor for his assent; but no bill, or legislative act whatever, shall be of any force without his assent. The governor shall have power to convene, prorogue, and dissolve the General Assembly, when, in his opinion, it shall be expedient.

The governor, judges, legislative council, secretary, and such other officers as Congress shall appoint in the district, shall take an oath or affirmation of fidelity and of office; the governor before the President of Congress, and all other officers before the governor. As soon as a legislature shall be formed in the district, the council and house assembled in one room, shall have authority, by joint ballot, to elect a delegate to Congress, who shall have a seat in Congress, with a right of debating but not of voting during this temporary government.

And, for extending the fundamental principles of civil and religious liberty, which form the basis whereon these republics, their laws and constitutions are erected; to fix and establish those principles as the basis of all laws, constitutions, and governments, which forever hereafter shall be formed in the said territory: to provide also for the establishment of States, and permanent government therein, and for their admission to a share in the federal councils on an equal footing with the original States, at as early periods as may be consistent with the general interest:

It is hereby ordained and declared by the authority aforesaid, That the following articles shall be considered as articles of compact between the original States and the people and States in the said territory and forever remain unalterable, unless by common consent, to wit:

Art. 1st. No person, demeaning himself in a peaceable and orderly manner, shall ever be molested on account of his mode of worship or religious sentiments, in the said territory.

Art. 2d. The inhabitants of the said territory shall always be entitled to the benefits of the writ of *habeas corpus,* and of the trial by jury; of a proportionate representation of the people in the legislature; and of judicial proceedings according to the course of the common law. All persons shall be bailable, unless for capital offences, where the proof shall be evident or the presumption great. All fines shall be moderate; and no cruel or unusual punishments shall be inflicted. No man shall be deprived of his liberty or property, but by the judgment of his peers or the law of the land; and, should the public exigencies make it necessary, for the common preservation, to take any person's property, or to demand his particular services, full compensation shall be made for the same. And, in the just preservation of rights and property, it is understood and declared, that no law ought ever to be made, or have force in the said territory, that shall, in any manner whatever, interfere with or affect private contracts or engagements, *bona fide,* and without fraud, previously formed.

Art. 3d. Religion, morality, and knowledge, being necessary to good government and the happiness of mankind, schools and the means of education shall forever be encouraged. The utmost good faith shall always be observed towards the Indians; their lands and property shall never be taken from them without their consent; and, in their property, rights, and liberty, they shall never be invaded or disturbed, unless in just and lawful wars authorized by Congress; but laws founded in justice and humanity, shall, from time to time, be made for preventing wrongs being done to them, and for preserving peace and friendship with them.

Art. 4th. The said territory, and the States which may be formed therein, shall forever remain a part of this confederacy of the United States of America, subject to the Articles of Confederation, and to such alterations therein as shall be constitutionally made; and to all the acts and ordinances of the United States in Congress assembled, conformable thereto. The inhabitants and settlers in the said territory shall be subject to pay a part of the federal debts contracted or to be contracted, and a proportional part of the expenses of government, to be apportioned on them by Congress according to the same common rule and measure by which apportionments thereof shall be made on the other States; and the taxes, for paying their proportion, shall be laid and levied by the authority and direction of the legislatures of the district or districts, or new States, as in the original States, within the time agreed upon by the United States in Congress assembled. The legislatures of those districts or new States, shall never interfere with the primary disposal of the soil by the United States in Congress assembled, nor with any regulations Congress may find necessary for securing the title in such soil to the *bona fide* purchasers. No tax shall be imposed on lands the property of the United States; and, in no case, shall non-resident proprietors be taxed higher than residents. The navigable waters leading into the Mississippi and St. Lawrence, and the carrying places between the same, shall be common highways, and forever free, as well to the inhabitants of the said territory as to the citizens of the United States, and those of any other States that may be admitted into the Confederacy, without any tax, impost, or duty, therefor.

Art. 5th. There shall be formed in the said territory, not less than three nor more than five States; and the boundaries of the States, as soon as Virginia shall alter her act of cession, and consent to the same, shall become fixed and established as follows, to wit: The Western State in the said territory, shall be bounded by the Mississippi, the Ohio, and Wabash rivers; a direct line drawn from the Wabash and Post St. Vincent's, due North, to the territorial line between the United States and Canada; and, by the said territorial line, to the Lake of the Woods and Mississippi. The middle State shall be bounded by the said direct line, the Wabash from Post Vincent's, to the Ohio; by the Ohio, by a direct line, drawn due North from the mouth of the Great Miami, to the said territorial line, and by the said territorial line. The Eastern State shall be bounded by the last mentioned direct line, the Ohio, Pennsylvania, and the said territorial line: *Provided, however,* and it is further understood and declared, that the boundaries of these three States shall be subject so far to be altered, that, if Congress shall hereafter find it expedient, they shall have authority to form one or two States in that part of the said territory which lies North of an East and West line drawn through the Southerly bend or extreme of lake Michigan. And, whenever any of the said States shall have 60,000 free inhabitants therein, such State shall be admitted, by its delegates, into the Congress of the United States, on an equal footing with the original States in all respects whatever, and shall be at liberty to form a permanent constitution and State government: *Provided*, the constitution and government so to be formed, shall be republican, and in conformity to the principles contained in these articles; and, so far as it can be consistent with the general interest of the confederacy, such admission shall be allowed at an earlier period, and when there may be a less number of free inhabitants in the State than 60,000.

Art. 6th. There shall be neither slavery nor involuntary servitude in the said territory, otherwise than in the punishment of crimes, whereof the party shall have been duly convicted: *Provided, always,* That any person escaping into the same, from whom labor or service is lawfully claimed in any one of the original States, such fugitive may be lawfully reclaimed and conveyed to the person claiming his or her labor or service as aforesaid.

Be it ordained by the authority aforesaid, That the resolutions of the 23d of April, 1784, relative to the subject of this ordinance, be, and the same are hereby, repealed and declared null and void.

The Ordinance of 1787

BE IT ORDAINED by the United States in Congress assembled, that the territory ceded by individual States to the United States, which has been purchased of the Indian inhabitants, shall be disposed of in the following manner:

A surveyor from each state shall be appointed by Congress, or a committee of the States, who shall take an Oath for the faithful discharge of his duty, before the Geographer of the United States, who is hereby empowered and directed to administer the same; and the like oath shall be administered to each chain carrier, by the surveyor under whom he acts.

The Geographer, under whose direction the surveyors shall act, shall occasionally form such regulations for their conduct, as he shall deem necessary; and shall have authority to suspend them for misconduct in Office, and shall make report of the same to Congress, or to the Committee of the States; and he shall make report in case of sickness, death, or resignation of any surveyor.

The Surveyors, as they are respectively qualified, shall proceed to divide the said territory into townships of six miles square, by lines running due north and south, and others crossing these at right angles, as near as may be, unless where the boundaries of the late Indian purchases may render the same impracticable, and then they shall depart from this rule no farther than such particular circumstances may require; and each surveyor shall be allowed and paid at the rate of two dollars for every mile, in length, he shall run, including the wages of chain carriers, markers, and every other expense attending the same.

The first line, running north and south as aforesaid, shall begin on the river Ohio, at a point that shall be found to be due north from the western termination of a line, which has been run as the southern boundary of the state of Pennsylvania; and the first line, running east and west, shall begin at the same point, and shall extend throughout the whole territory. Provided, that nothing herein shall be construed, as fixing the western boundary of the state of Pennsylvania. The geographer shall designate the townships, or fractional parts of townships, by numbers progressively from south to north; always beginning each range with number one; and the ranges shall be distinguished by their progressive numbers to the westward. The first range, extending from the Ohio to the lake Erie, being marked number one. The Geographer shall personally attend to the running of the first east and west line; and shall take the latitude of the extremes of the first north and south line, and of the mouths of the principal rivers.

The lines shall be measured with a chain; shall be plainly marked by chaps on the trees, and exactly described on a plat; whereon shall be noted by the surveyor, at their proper distances, all mines, salt springs, salt licks and mill seats, that shall come to his knowledge, and all water courses, mountains and other remarkable and permanent things, over and near which such lines shall pass, and also the quality of the lands.

The plats of the townships respectively, shall be marked by subdivisions into lots of one mile square, or 640 acres, in the same direction as the external lines, and numbered from 1 to 36; always beginning the succeeding range of the lots with the number next to that with which the preceding one concluded. And where, from the causes before mentioned, only a fractional part of a township shall be surveyed, the lots, protracted thereon, shall bear the same numbers as if the township had been entire. And the surveyors, in running the external lines of the townships, shall, at the interval of every mile, mark corners for the lots which are adjacent, always designating the same in a different manner from those of the townships.

The geographer and surveyors shall pay the utmost attention to the variation of the magnetic needle; and shall run and note all lines by the true meridian, certifying, with every plat, what was the variation at the times of running the lines thereon noted.

As soon as seven ranges of townships, and fractional parts of townships, in the direction from south to north, shall have been surveyed, the geographer shall transmit plats thereof to the board of treasury, who shall record the same, with the report, in well bound books to be kept for that purpose. And the geographer shall make similar returns, from time to time, of every seven ranges as they may be surveyed. The Secretary at War shall have recourse thereto, and shall take by lot therefrom, a number of townships, and fractional parts of townships, as well from those to be sold entire as from those to be sold in lots, as will be equal to one seventh part of the whole of such seven ranges, as nearly as may be, for the use of the late continental army; and he shall make a similar draught, from time to time, until a sufficient quantity is drawn to satisfy the same, to be applied in manner hereinafter directed. The board of treasury shall, from time to time, cause the remaining numbers, as well those to be sold entire, as those to be sold in lots, to be drawn for, in the name of the thirteen states respectively, according to the quotas in the last preceding requisition on all the states; provided, that in case more land than its proportion is allotted for sale, in any state, at any distribution, a deduction be made therefor at the next.

The board of treasury shall transmit a copy of the original plats, previously noting thereon, the townships, and fractional parts of townships, which shall have fallen to the several states, by the distribution aforesaid, to the Commissioners of the loan office of the several states, who, after giving notice of not less than two nor more than six months, by causing advertisements to be posted up at the court houses, or other noted places in every county, and to be inserted in one newspaper, published in the states of their residence respectively, shall proceed to sell the townships, or fractional parts of townships, at public vendue, in the following manner, viz: The township, or fractional part of a township, N 1, in the first range, shall be sold entire; and N 2, in the same range, by lots; and thus in alternate order through the whole of the first range. The township, or fractional part of a township, N 1, in the second range, shall be sold by lots; and N 2, in the same range, entire; and so in alternate order through the whole of the second range; and the third range shall be sold in the same manner as the first, and the fourth in the same manner as the second, and thus alternately throughout all the ranges; provided, that none of the lands, within the said territory, be sold under the price of one dollar the acre, to be paid in specie, or loan office certificates, reduced to specie value, by the scale of depreciation, or certificates of liquidated debts of the United States, including interest, besides the expense of the survey and other charges thereon, which are hereby rated at thirty six dollars the township, in specie, or certificates as aforesaid, and so in the same proportion for a fractional part of a township, or of a lot, to be paid at the time of sales; on failure of which payment, the said lands shall again be offered for sale.

There shall be reserved for the United States out of every township, the four lots, being numbered 8, 11, 26, 29, and out of every fractional part of a township, so many lots of the same numbers as shall be found thereon, for future sale. There shall be reserved the lot N 16, of every township, for the maintenance of public schools, within the said township; also one third part of all gold, silver, lead and copper mines, to be sold, or otherwise disposed of as Congress shall hereafter direct. . . .

The commissioners of the loan offices respectively, shall transmit to the board of treasury every three months, an account of the townships, fractional parts of townships, and lots committed to their charge; specifying therein the names of the persons to whom sold, and the sums of money or certificates received for the same; and shall cause all certificates by them received, to be struck through with a circular punch; and they shall be duly charged in the books of the treasury, with the amount of the moneys or certificates, distinguishing the same, by them received as aforesaid.

If any township, or fractional part of a township or lot, remains unsold for eighteen months after the plat shall have been received, by the commissioners of the loan office, the same shall be returned to the board of treasury, and shall be sold in such manner as Congress may hereafter direct.

And whereas Congress, by their resolutions of

September 16 and 18 in the year 1776, and the 12th of August, 1780, stipulated grants of land to certain officers and soldiers of the late continental army, and by the resolution of the 22d September, 1780, stipulated grants of land to certain officers in the hospital department of the late continental army; for complying therefore with such engagements, Be it ordained, That the secretary at war, from the returns in his office, or such other sufficient evidence as the nature of the case may admit, determine who are the objects of the above resolutions and engagements, and the quantity of land to which such persons or their representatives are respectively entitled, and cause the townships, or fractional parts of townships, hereinbefore reserved for the use of the late continental army, to be drawn for in such manner as he shall deem expedient, to answer the purpose of an impartial distribution. He shall, from time to time, transmit certificates to the commissioners of the loan offices of the different states, to the lines of which the military claimants have respectively belonged, specifying the name and rank of the party, the terms of his engagement and time of his service, and the division, brigade, regiment or company to which he belonged, the quantity of land he is entitled to, and the township, or fractional part of a township, and range out of which his portion is to be taken.

The commissioners of the loan offices shall execute deeds for such undivided proportions in manner and form herein before-mentioned, varying only in such a degree as to make the same conformable to the certificate from the Secretary at War.

Where any military claimants of bounty in lands shall not have belonged to the line of any particular state, similar certificates shall be sent to the board of treasury, who shall execute deeds to the parties for the same.

The Secretary at War, from the proper returns, shall transmit to the board of treasury, a certificate, specifying the name and rank of the several claimants of the hospital department of the late continental army, together with the quantity of land each claimant is entitled to, and the township, or fractional part of a township, and range out of which his portion is to be taken; and thereupon the board of treasury shall proceed to execute deeds to such claimants.

The board of treasury, and the commissioners of the loan offices in the states, shall, within 18 months, return receipts to the secretary at war, for all deeds which have been delivered, as also all the original deeds which remain in their hands for want of applicants, having been first recorded; which deeds so returned, shall be preserved in the office, until the parties or their representatives require the same.

And be it further Ordained, That three townships adjacent to lake Erie be reserved, to be hereafter disposed of by Congress, for the use of the officers, men, and others, refugees from Canada, and the refugees from Nova Scotia, who are or may be entitled to grants of land under resolutions of Congress now existing, or which may hereafter be made respecting them, and for such other purposes as Congress may hereafter direct.

And be it further Ordained, That the towns of Gnadenhutten, Schoenbrun and Salem, on the Muskingum, and so much of the lands adjoining to the said towns, with the buildings and improvements thereon, shall be reserved for the sole use of the Christian Indians, who were formerly settled there, or the remains of that society, as may, in the judgment of the Geographer, be sufficient for them to cultivate.

Saving and reserving always, to all officers and soldiers entitled to lands on the northwest side of the Ohio, by donation or bounty from the commonwealth of Virginia, and to all persons claiming under them, all rights to which they are so entitled, under the deed of cession executed by the delegates for the state of Virginia, on the first day of March, 1784, and the act of Congress accepting the same: and to the end, that the said rights may be fully and effectually secured, according to the true intent and meaning of the said deed of cession and act aforesaid, Be it Ordained, that no part of the land included between the rivers called little Miami and Sciota, on the northwest side of the river Ohio, be sold, or in any manner alienated, until there shall first have been laid off and appropriated for the said Officers and Soldiers, and persons claiming under them, the lands they are entitled to, agreeably to the said deed of cession and act of Congress accepting the same.

TWO FOREIGN VIEWS OF THE AMERICAN REVOLUTION

EVEN BEFORE the American Revolution was over, many Europeans took to regarding it as one of the great moral events of their time. The American people were to be "the hope of the world," wrote the great Frenchman Anne Robert Jacques Turgot (1727–1781) to the Englishman Richard Price (1723–1791). Price, who had always been a good friend of America, printed Turgot's letter in his own book, *Observations on the Importance of the American Revolution.*

In effect, Price based his book on Turgot's letter as a text. Agreeing with Turgot's optimistic view, the Englishman went on to lecture the American people on the need to improve

their government lest they lose the opportunity to help emancipate all mankind. That Price should have seen such potentialities in the discordant nation of 1785 is not too surprising, for he had long been a friend of Franklin and a close student of American affairs. But Price's prescription for American economic wellbeing was somewhat naïve. His views on American isolationism are here presented; they represent a strain that runs throughout the whole of American thinking on our relations with other peoples.

Both texts are reprinted from the original edition of Price's book, published in London in 1785.

The American Revolution

BY ROBERT JACQUES TURGOT

Paris 22 March, 1778

To DR. PRICE, *London*

. . . I have been led to judge thus by the infatuation of your people in the absurd project of subduing America, till the affair of Burgoyne began to open their eyes; and by the system of monopoly and exclusion which has been recommended by all your writers on Commerce, (except Mr. Adam Smith and Dean Tucker); a system which has been the true source of your separation from your Colonies. I have also been led to this opinion by all your controversial writings upon the questions which have occupied your attention these twenty years, and in which, till your observations appeared, I scarce recollect to have read one that took up these questions on their proper ground. I cannot conceive how a nation which has cultivated every branch of natural knowledge with such success, should have made so little progress

in the most interesting of all sciences, that of the public good: A science, in which the liberty of the Press, which she alone enjoys, ought to have given her a prodigious advantage over every other nation in Europe. Was it national pride which prevented you from profiting by this advantage? Or was it, because you were not altogether in so bad a condition as other nations, that you have imposed upon yourselves in your speculations so far as to be persuaded that your arrangements were compleat? Is it party spirit and a desire of being supported by popular opinion which has retarded your progress, by inducing your political writers to treat as vain Metaphysics all those speculations which aim at establishing the rights and true interests of nations and individuals upon fixed principles. How comes it that you are almost the first of the writers of your country, who has given a just idea of liberty, and shewn the falsity of the notion so frequently repeated by almost all Republican Writers, "that liberty consists in being subject only to the laws," as if a man could be free while oppressed by an unjust law. This would not be true, even if we could suppose that all the laws were the work of an assembly of the whole nation; for certainly every individual has his rights, of which the nation cannot deprive him, except by violence and an unlawful use of the general power. Though you have attended to this truth and have explained yourself upon this head, perhaps it would have merited a more minute explanation, considering how little attention is paid to it even by the most zealous friends of liberty.

It is likewise extraordinary that it was not thought a trivial matter in England to assert "that one nation never can have a right to govern another nation"—"that a government where such a principle is admitted can have no foundation but that of force, which is equally the foundation of robbery and tyranny"—"and that the tyranny of a people is the most cruel and intolerable, because it leaves the fewest resources to the oppressed." —A despot is restrained by a sense of his own interest. He is checked by remorse or by the public opinion. But the multitude never calculate. The multitude are never checked by remorse, and will even ascribe to themselves the highest honour when they deserve only disgrace.

What a dreadful commentary on your book are the events which have lately befallen the English nation?——For some months they have been running headlong to ruin.—The fate of America is already decided—Behold her independent beyond recovery.—But will She be free and happy?—Can this new people, so advantageously placed for giving an example to the world of a constitution under which man may enjoy his rights, freely exercise all his faculties, and be governed only by nature, reason and justice—Can they form such a Constitution?—Can they establish it upon a neverfailing foundation, and guard against every source of division and corruption which may gradually undermine and destroy it? . . .

It is impossible not to wish ardently that this people may attain to all the prosperity of which they are capable. They are the *hope* of the world. They may become a *model* to it. They *may* prove by fact that men can be free and yet tranquil; and that it is in their power to rescue themselves from the chains in which tyrants and knaves of all descriptions have presumed to bind them under the pretence of the public good. They may exhibit an example of *political* liberty, of *religious* liberty, of *commercial* liberty, and of industry. The *Asylum*

they open to the oppressed of all nations should console the earth. The ease with which the injured may escape from oppressive governments, will compel Princes to become just and cautious; and the rest of the world will gradually open their eyes upon the empty illusions with which they have been hitherto cheated by politicians. But for this purpose *America* must preserve *herself* from these illusions; and take care to avoid being what your ministerial writers are frequently saying She *will* be—an image of our *Europe*—a mass of divided powers contending for territory and commerce, and continually cementing the slavery of the people with their own blood.

All enlightened men—All the friends of humanity ought at this time to unite their lights to those of the *American* sages, and to assist them in the great work of legislation. This, sir, would be a work worthy of you. I wish it was in my power to animate your zeal in this instance. If I have in this letter indulged too free an effusion of my sentiments, this has been my only motive; and it will, I hope, induce you to pardon me for tiring you. I wish indeed that the blood which has been spilt, and which will continue for some time to be spilt in this contest, may not be without its use to the human race.

Our two nations are about doing much harm to each other, and probably without the prospect to either of any real advantage. An increase of debts and public burthens, (perhaps a national bankruptcy), and the ruin of a great number of individuals, will prove the result. England seems to me to be more likely to suffer by these evils, and much nearer to them, than France.—If instead of going to war, you had at the commencement of your disputes endeavoured to retreat with a good grace; if your Statesmen had then consented to make those concessions, which they will infallibly be obliged to make at last; if the national opinion would have permitted your government to anticipate events which might have been foreseen; if, in short, you had immediately yielded to the independence of America without entering into any hostilities; I am firmly persuaded your nation would have lost nothing.—But you will *now* lose what you have already expended, and what you are still to expend; you will experience a great diminution of your commerce for some time, and great interior commotions, if driven to a bankruptcy; and, at any rate, a great diminution of weight in foreign politics. But this last circumstance I think of little consequence to the real happiness of a people; for I cannot agree with the *Abbe Raynal* in your motto. I do not believe all this will make you a contemptible nation or throw you into slavery.—On the contrary; your misfortunes may have the effect of a necessary amputation. They are perhaps the only means of saving you from the gangrene of luxury and corruption. And if they should terminate in the amendment of your constitution, by restoring annual elections, and distributing the right of suffrages for representation so as to render it more equal and better proportioned to the interests of the represented, you will perhaps gain as much as America by this revolution; for you will preserve your liberty, and with your liberty, and by means of it, all your other losses will be speedily repaired.

By the freedom with which I have opened myself to you, sir, upon these delicate points, you will judge of the esteem with which you have inspired me; and the satisfaction I feel in thinking there is some resemblance between our sentiments and views. I depend on your confining this confidence to yourself. I even beg that you will not be particular in answering me by the Post, for your letter will certainly be opened at our Post-Offices, and I shall be found much too great a friend to liberty for a minister, even though a discarded minister.

I have the honour to be with all possible respect,

Sir,
Your most humble,
and most obedient Servant,
Turgot

Observations on the Importance of the American Revolution

BY RICHARD PRICE

OF THE IMPORTANCE OF THE REVOLUTION WHICH
HAS ESTABLISHED THE INDEPENDENCE OF THE
UNITED STATES

HAVING, from pure conviction, taken a warm part in favour of the *British* colonies (now the United States of America) during the late war; and been exposed, in consequence of this, to *much* abuse and *some* danger; it must be supposed that I have been waiting for the issue with anxiety——I am thankful that my anxiety is removed; and that I have been spared to be a witness to that very issue of the war which has been all along the object of my wishes. With heart-felt satisfaction, I see the revolution in favour of universal liberty which has taken place in *America;*—a revolution which opens a new prospect in human affairs, and begins a new æra in the history of mankind;——a revolution by which *Britons* themselves will be the greatest gainers, if wise enough to improve properly the check that has been given to the despotism of their ministers, and to catch the flame of virtuous liberty which has saved their American brethren.

The late war, in its *commencement and progress,* did great good by disseminating just sentiments of the rights of mankind, and the nature of legitimate government; by exciting a spirit of resistance to tyranny which has emancipated one *European* country, and is likely to emancipate others; and by occasioning the establishment in *America* of forms of government more equitable and more liberal than any that the world has yet known. But, in its *termination,* the war has done still greater good by preserving the new governments from that destruction in which they must have been involved, had Britain conquered; by providing, in a sequestered continent possessed of many singular advantages, a place of refuge for opprest men in every region of the world; and by laying the foundation there of an empire which may be the seat of liberty, science and virtue, and from whence there is reason to hope these sacred blessings will spread, till they become universal, and the time arrives when kings and priests shall have no more power to oppress, and that ignominious slavery which has hitherto debased the world is exterminated. I therefore, think I see the hand of Providence in the late war working for the general good. . . .

But among the events in modern times tending to the elevation of mankind, there are none probably of so much consequence as the recent one which occasions these observations. Perhaps, I do not go too far when I say that, next to the introduction of Christianity among mankind, the American revolution may prove the most important step in the progressive course of human improvement. It is an event which may produce a general diffusion of the principles of humanity, and become the means of setting free mankind from the shackles of superstition and tyranny, by leading them to see and know "that nothing is *fundamental* but impartial enquiry, an honest mind, and virtuous practice——that state policy ought not to be applied to the support of speculative opinions and formularies of faith."——"That the members of a civil community are *confederates,* not *subjects;* and their rulers, *servants,* not *masters.*——And that all legitimate government consists in the dominion of equal laws made with common consent; that is, in the dominion of men over *themselves;* and not in the dominion of communities over communities, or of any men over other men."

Happy will the world be when these truths shall be every where acknowledged and practised upon. Religious bigotry, that cruel demon, will be then laid asleep. Slavish governments and slavish Hierarchies will then sink; and the old prophecies be verified, "that the last universal empire upon earth shall be the empire of reason and virtue, under which the gospel of peace (better understood) *shall have free course and be glorified, many will run to and fro and knowledge be increased, the wolf dwell with the lamb and the leopard with the kid, and nation no more lift up a sword against nation.*"

It is a conviction I cannot resist, that the independence of the *English* colonies in America is one of the steps ordained by Providence to introduce these times; and I can scarcely be deceived in this conviction, if the United States should escape some dangers which threaten them, and will take proper care to throw themselves open to future improvements, and to make the most of the advantages of their present. . . .

Of Trade, Banks, and Paper Credit

Foreign trade has, in some respects, the most useful tendency. By creating an intercourse between distant kingdoms, it extends benevolence, removes local prejudices, leads every man to consider himself more as a citizen of the world than of any particular State, and, consequently, checks the excesses of that *Love of our Country* * which has been applauded as one of the noblest, but which, *really,* is one of the most *destructive* principles in human nature.——Trade also, by enabling every country to draw from other countries conveniencies and advantages which it cannot find within itself, produces among nations a sense of mutual dependence, and promotes the general improve-

* The love of our country is then only a noble passion when it engages us to promote the *internal* happiness of our country, and to defend its rights and liberties against domestic and foreign invasion, maintaining at the same time an equal regard to the rights and liberties of other countries. But this has not been its most common effects. On the contrary, it has in general been nothing but a spirit of rivalship between different communities, producing contention and a thirst for conquest and dominion.—What is his *country* to a *Russian,* a *Turk,* a *Spaniard,* &c. but a spot where he enjoys no right, and is disposed of by owners as if

ment.—But there is no part of mankind to which these uses of trade are of less consequence than the *American* States. They are spread over a great continent, and make a world within themselves. The country they inhabit includes soils and climates of all sorts, producing not only every *necessary,* but every *convenience* of life. And the vast rivers and wide-spread lakes which intersect it, create such an inland communication between its different parts, as is unknown in any other region of the earth. They possess then within themselves the best means of the most profitable traffic, and the amplest scope for it. Why should they look much farther? What occasion have they for being anxious about pushing *foreign* trade; or even about raising a great naval force?—Britain, indeed, consisting as it does of *unarmed* inhabitants, and threatened as it is by ambitious and powerful neighbours, cannot hope to maintain its existence long after becoming open to invasion by losing its naval superiority.——But this is not the case with the American States. They have no powerful neighbours to dread. The vast Atlantic must be crossed before they can be attacked. They are all a well-trained *militia;* and the successful resistance which, in their infancy and without a naval force, they have made to the invasion of the first *European* power, will probably discourage and prevent all future invasions. Thus singularly happy, why should they seek connexions with *Europe,* and expose themselves to the danger of being involved in its quarrels?—What have they to do with its politics?—Is there any thing very important to them which they can draw from thence—except INFECTION?——Indeed, I tremble when I think of that rage for trade which is likely to prevail among them. It may do them infinite mischief. All nations are spreading snares for them, and courting them to a dangerous intercourse. Their best interest requires them to guard themselves by all proper means; and, particularly, by laying heavy duties on importations. But in no case will any means succeed unless aided by MANNERS. In this instance, particularly, there is reason to fear that an increasing passion for foreign frippery

he was a beast? And what is his *love* to his country but an attachment to degradation and slavery?—What was the love of their country among the *Jews* but a wretched partiality for themselves and a proud contempt for other nations? Among the *Romans* also what was it, however great in many of its exertions, but a principle holding together a band of robbers in their attempts to crush all liberty but their own?—Christianity has wisely omitted to recommend this principle. Had it done this, it would have countenanced a vice among mankind.—It has done what is infinitely better—It has recommended UNIVERSAL BENEVOLENCE.

will render all the best regulations ineffectual. And should this happen, that simplicity of character, that manliness of spirit, that disdain of tinsel in which true dignity consists, will disappear. Effeminacy, servility and venality will enter; and liberty and virtue be swallowed up in the gulph of corruption. Such may be the course of events in the American States. Better *infinitely* will it be for them to consist of bodies of plain and honest farmers, than of opulent and splendid merchants. ——Where in these States do the purest manners prevail? Where do the inhabitants live most on an equality, and most at their ease? Is it not in those inland parts where agriculture gives health and plenty, and trade is scarcely known?—— Where, on the contrary, are the inhabitants most selfish, luxurious, loose, and vicious; and at the same time most unhappy? Is it not along the sea coasts, and in the great towns, where trade flourishes and merchants abound?——So striking is the effect of these different situations on the vigour and happiness of human life, that in the one population would languish did it receive no aid from emigrations; while in the other it increases to a degree scarcely ever before known.

But to proceed to some observations of a different nature——

The united States have, I think, particular reason to dread the following effects of foreign trade.

By increasing importation to feed luxury and gratify prodigality, it will carry out their coin, and occasion the substitution of a delusive paper currency; the consequence of which will be, that *ideal* wealth will take place of *real*, and their security come to depend on the strength and duration of a *Bubble*.——I am very sensible that paper credit is one of the greatest of all conveniencies; but this makes it likewise one of the greatest of all temptations. A public Bank, (while it can circulate its bills) facilitates commerce, and assists the exertions of a State in proportion to its credit. But

when it is not carefully restricted and watched; when its emissions exceed the coin it can command, and are carried near the utmost length that the confidence of the public will allow; and when, in consequence of this, its permanence comes to depend on the permanence of public credulity—— In these circumstances, a BANK, though it may for a time (that is, while a balance of trade too unfavourable does not occasion a run, and no events arise which produce alarm) answer all the ends of a MINE from which millions may be drawn in a minute; and, by filling a kingdom with cash, render it capable of sustaining *any* debts, and give it a kind of OMNIPOTENCE.——In such circumstances, I say, notwithstanding these temporary advantages, a public BANK must *at last* prove a great calamity; and a kingdom so supported, at the very time of its greatest exertions, will be only striving more violently to increase the horror of an approching convulsion.

The united States have already verified some of these observations, and felt in some degree the consequences to which I have alluded. They have been carried through the war by an emission of paper which had no solid support, and which now has lost all value. It is indeed surprising that, being secured on no fund and incapable of being exchanged for coin, it should ever have obtained a currency, or answered any important purpose.

Unhappily for *Britain*, it has used the means of giving more stability to its paper-credit, and been enabled by it to support expences greater than any that have been yet known, and to contract a debt which now *astonishes*, and may hereafter produce a catastrophe that will *terrify* the world. —A longer duration of the late war would have brought on this catastrophe immediately. The PEACE has put it off *for the present*. God grant, if still possible, that measures may be adopted which shall put it off *for ever*.

Part Three

ESTABLISHING THE
NEW REPUBLIC

INTRODUCTION

1. THE CRITICAL PERIOD

DESPITE INTERNAL DERANGEMENTS and the sacrifices it demands, a period of war usually produces economic prosperity. The War for American Independence was no exception. The stimulus given to manufactures, the opening of trade in new areas, speculative booms in land marched side by side with currency inflation. Fortunes accumulated and new business ventures were launched. But the end of the war brought contraction in its train. A price deflation occurred, the high profits of businesses serving military requirements ceased, and English ships once more began to throng American ports. Importers profited, but domestic manufacturers began to feel the pinch of a competition that in many areas was distinctly unfair. Business conditions continued spotty during much of the 1780s; there was a real depression in 1785–86.

Agricultural Distress. The independent and sovereign thirteen states did little to improve matters. To raise revenues and also to protect their own businessmen, the states wrote tariff acts. Massachusetts, New York, and Pennsylvania were the leaders in this movement. As the recession continued, they raised their rates, hoping that by making many duties prohibitory they would be able to extract concessions from foreign countries. The result was high prices for goods needed by farmers, while the prices they received fell sharply as a result of agricultural overexpansion. A typical "agricultural scissors" had developed, and the farmers—always a debtor interest—were caught between the blades.

Notably in 1785–86, agrarian distress was acute and farmers sought the customary reliefs. They pressed legislatures for new fiat money issues and the passage of moratoriums, or stay laws, to prevent land mortgage foreclosures. In many of the states, the legislatures yielded and new paper bills began to make their appearance. This was particularly true of Rhode Island and North Carolina. It is important to observe, however, that the legislatures of Connecticut, Massachusetts, New Hampshire, Delaware, Maryland, and Virginia did not bow before this clamor. Moreover, the financing of the Confederation was in bad shape. The Confederation did not pursue the earlier course of a paper inflation. It was able to sell public lands and to borrow funds in Amsterdam. But the niggardliness of the states, which refused to honor the requisitions drawn upon them, made impossible the payment of interest on domestic and foreign loans.

Economic Progress. All this does not mean that economic chaos threatened the young America. The fact is, while the postwar years were ones of difficult readjustment, in many areas the American economy was blazing new trails. A good deal of new construction was taking place in the urban communities. There was a real boom in transportation—road building, river-improvement projects, laying out of stagecoach routes, the erection of inns. Important new companies in iron, woolens, sailcloth, glass, and paper made their appearance. Interest rates were high, both because of legitimate requirements for capital and the formation of land companies and other speculative ventures. When new banks were formed in Philadelphia, Boston, and New York, businessmen, realizing the importance to them of agencies for deposit, discount, and the handling of foreign exchange, hastened to subscribe for stock in specie.

Reference has been made earlier to the fact

that the English Mercantilist System had been very reluctant to charter companies for business purposes in colonial America; indeed, during the whole period of imperial rule, not more than six such charters had been granted. With freedom, the bars were down. Eleven charters were requested and issued by state legislatures between 1781 and 1785; 22 between 1786 and 1790; and 114 between 1791 and 1795. A sign of the times—of both freedom from mercantilist restraint and the appearance of new business endeavors—was the establishment of commercial banking. The Bank of North America, with the aid of the Confederation Congress (but with capitalization largely subscribed by private persons), opened its doors in Philadelphia in 1781. In 1784, two additional commercial banks, the Bank of New York at New York and the Massachusetts Bank at Boston, were set up. They were all immediately successful; and, of course, the assistance they rendered businessmen was incalculable.

In the field of foreign trade new vistas were being opened up. To compensate for the prohibitions encountered in the direct trade with England and the British West Indies, there were the concessions offered by the European powers. Commercial treaties were written with Holland, Prussia, and Sweden. France threw open her West India Islands to American ships in 1784; Spain made Havana virtually a free port; the Danes and the Dutch permitted a two-way traffic to operate without interference in the same region. Despite British limitations (the chief of which was the ban imposed on American shipping), the West India trade did not fall off nearly as sharply as we have been led to believe. The commercial relations with Holland became particularly significant. More and more the Dutch began to take those American exports which formerly could be moved into England alone; as a result, before the 1780s were over, the Dutch-American export trade was half as great as the English-American trade. In fact, the balance of payments favored Americans so that Dutch specie came overseas.

Equally important were the new markets being tapped in northern Europe and the Middle and Far East. The India and China trades, particularly, were to become important. *The Empress of China* sailed from New York in 1784 for the South China Sea; in 1785 the *Grand Turk* left Salem on a similar voyage; two years later Boston merchants outfitted a vessel to develop the great triangular trade between New England, the American northwest coast on the Pacific, and China. Before long, American masters and supercargoes knew every port and inlet across the vast stretch of Eastern sea from Canton to Madagascar. They carried mixed cargoes to European ports, and there they picked up consignments for Aden, Muscat, Madras, Calcutta, and the islands of the Eastern archipelagoes. Thence home with coffee, sugar, pepper, tea, allspice, textiles, and chinaware. Or they might sail west with trade goods for the Indians on the northern Pacific coast. Here, they acquired otter and seal furs and carried them direct to China or, a little later on, stopped off first at the Hawaiian Islands for teakwood. Once more, as a result, the Boston and New York ports were filled with ships, and their warehouses bulged with products of the East.

Radical Alarums. The writing of the Constitution is to be seen in this setting. The depression of 1785–86 filled businessmen—land speculators, merchants, the holders of the revolutionary debts, bankers—with anxiety and apprehension. The reappearance of agrarian populism with its leveling tendencies and its customary economic programs further threatened confidence. What was required, in brief, was a greater measure of political stability than existed under either the Confederation or the thirteen sovereign states. For the protection of large propertied interests at home and abroad—the most important general desideratum being the establishment and maintenance of the public credit of the country—a powerful central union was imperative. This would have the following advantages: It would permit the persons engaged in international trade to operate with a sound currency and obtain funds in foreign markets. It would permit the wild-land jobbers to realize on their paper investments. It would make possible the pacification of the West, so that the domestic market could be expanded. It would protect debts and contracts—rights, it will be recalled, that the Confederation did not possess. In this last connection, the public debts would be safeguarded and interest and principal paid. It would write commercial treaties with foreign nations and make possible the defense of our shipping abroad. It would create a single tariff system, for revenue and protection. It would extend the horizons of business on a national scale by the granting of national charters to manufacturing, banking, and transportation companies.

The restless activity of leveling agrarians in 1785–86 sharpened these considerations. (We find similar manifestations later in American annals—in 1888–96 and 1931–32.) In many areas the small men of affairs, particularly the commercial farmers, were equally hard hit by the depression. They converged on legislatures and courts. Within a short time, at least seven states issued new bills of credit. Judges, foreclosing properties and jailing debtors, were denounced and even threatened physically in New York, New Jersey, and North Carolina. Programs were being drawn up in legislatures to abolish imprisonment for debt, to enact mortgage-moratorium laws, and to write down the face values of mortgages themselves. In Rhode Island, in particular, these forces were in control. They were threatening the constituted authorities in Massachusetts and New Hampshire.

Conservative Programs. It may be said that these movements brought matters to a head. The plans of conservatives in Massachusetts and New Hampshire to stabilize public and private financial arrangements—to pay off the revolutionary debts out of higher property taxes, to hold a tight rein on paper-money issues, to force the settlement of debts and mortgages—raised a storm. Back-country agrarians replied with demands for stay laws, the scaling down of debts, and the emission of new legal tenders. They were not listened to. Armed troops appeared; courts were threatened. In central Massachusetts, in 1786, such a body of farmers, led by Captain Daniel Shays, converged on the courts and apparently had in mind, as well, the forcing of their program on the legislature, by duress if necessary. Their plans called for the seizure of arms and munitions from government stores. Now the commercial seaboard took alarm. A militia was hastily gathered, financed from private subscriptions, and sent against Shays. The farmers retired northward and before the winter was over were disbanded and disarmed.

News of the encounter rang through the country. The full significance of the threat was understood by men of large means. So, General Knox wrote to George Washington of the Shaysites in 1786:

Their creed is "That the property of the United States has been protected from the confiscations of Britain by the joint exertions of all, and therefore ought to be the common property of all. And he that attempts opposition to this creed is an enemy to equity and justice, and ought to be swept from off the face of the earth." In a word, they are determined to annihilate all debts, public and private, and have agrarian laws, which are easily effected by means of unfunded paper money which shall be a tender in all cases whatever.

These disorders plus the necessity for taking steps to facilitate the flow of interstate commerce led to a reexamination of the Articles of Confederation. In 1786 Virginia sent out a call to the thirteen states to dispatch commissioners to Annapolis for the purpose of considering "the trade of the United States." Only five responded and nothing came of the meetings. But the commissioners—led by Alexander Hamilton—seized the opportunity to present a report in which "important defects" were referred to in the federal system of government; and the report proposed that thought be given to devising further provisions in order "to render the Constitution of the federal government adequate to the exigencies of the Union." Suggestions appeared that a convention be called to "revise" the Articles of Confederation; and from these seemingly simple and understandable deliberations sprang the Constitution of the United States of America.

2. FRAMING THE CONSTITUTION

In February, 1787, Congress requested the states to send delegates to Philadelphia for the purpose of amending the Articles of Confederation. Virginia was the first to respond and in time all but Rhode Island complied. In all, 75 delegates were named of whom 55 actually gathered at Philadelphia during the course of the sessions. Some of America's greatest political leaders appeared on the list of delegates, although they were not all the demigods Thomas Jefferson—viewing the scene from Paris— hailed them as being. In the Virginia delegation were George Washington, James Madison, and Edmund Randolph (as well as Patrick Henry and Richard Henry Lee, who refused to go, the former declaring that he "smelled a rat"). Pennsylvania named seven delegates, of whom Benjamin Franklin, James Wilson, and Gouverneur Morris were the outstanding. New York named three, Alexander Hamilton being among them (although his participation in the deliberations was slight and he failed to attend a good part of the time). South Carolina's leading representative, among its four spokesmen, was Charles C. Pinckney. Massachusetts picked five, one never came, and Rufus King was its most important delegate. Maryland sent Luther Martin. New Hampshire did not get around to picking its delegation until June, and of the four commissioners named two never left for Philadelphia and the other two did not show up until the end of July.

The Constitutional Convention. On the 25th of May the Convention was formally opened with delegates from seven states present. George Washington was the only name presented for president; he was elected and installed and rules for its deliberations were drawn up. The Convention was to meet secretly; there was to be no official record of its debates; the delegates pledged themselves to silence concerning its discussions. On May 29th, with forty delegates from ten states present, it began its deliberations. It started its work—sitting as a Committee of the Whole—by considering a set of fifteen resolutions presented by the Virginia delegation through its head, Edmund Randolph. The Virginia Plan rested upon the theory that a strong national government was necessary; it was supported by Virginia, Pennsylvania, and Maryland. Opposition to it—and in favor of a weaker central organization—came from Connecticut, New York, New Jersey, Delaware, and Maryland. On June 15, the Paterson, or New Jersey Plan, made up of nine resolutions— in effect nothing more than a series of amendments of the Articles of Confederation—was submitted. The New Jersey Plan was voted down; a compromise was presented; and the Convention was deadlocked for three weeks. The debates became very heated and on a number of occasions the future of the Convention seemed to hang on a thread. It was not until July 16 that the leading difficulty was resolved—the balancing of the strength of the small states against that of the large. This was done by giving each state the same representation in the Senate: a compromise worked out by the Connecticut delegation and since then called after it. From then on, it was plain sailing and most of the Virginia resolutions—now increased to twenty-three—were adopted quickly.

A Committee of Detail was named to write the actual Constitution itself. Its proposals were debated; and on September 8 a Committee on Style, headed by Gouverneur Morris, was appointed. There was resistance to some of the provisions to the very end; in short, it was clear that a unanimous vote was not to be obtained. Morris drew up a clever subscription, Franklin proposed it, and it was adopted by acclamation. It ran: "Done in Convention, by the unanimous consent of the States present the 17th of September. . . . In Witness whereof, we have hereunto subscribed our names." The Constitution was signed by thirty-nine delegates.

The Constitution. The framers of the Constitution—led by James Madison—did their work with amazing skill. There is no question that the Convention was a class assembly, for in terms of personal interests the delegates came from the upper rather than the middle rank of American society. They had in their midst every type of large-propertied interest: security-ownership, commerce, manufacturing, slave planting, banking, land jobbing. On the other hand—except in the person of Luther Martin—the small farmers, traders, and town mechanics had none to speak for them.

Yet to regard the Constitutional Convention as an assembly called for the exclusive purpose of protecting propertied interests is a mistake. The founding fathers sought, above all, stability—as General Knox had expressed it: "Our government must be braced, changed, or altered to secure our lives and property." It is true many were suspicious of the common man and voiced antidemocratic sentiments. But it is important to note that the rights of small men were recognized in the Great Compromise embodied in the Constitution, that is, the grant to all states, regardless of wealth or population, equal voices in the composition of the Senate and in the choice of the President.

From the labors of the Convention emerged that national union that seemed the only effective reply to the uncertainties of the hour. The safeguarding of property against leveling assault was assured by two devices: the states might not issue legal-tender paper money; and the states were denied the right to impair the obligation of contract. By positive measures the strength of the national government was equally provided for. In it were deposited these

functions: levying and collecting taxes; imposition of duties on foreign imports; regulation of interstate and foreign commerce; borrowing and coining money; issuing patents and copyrights; drawing up rules for proceedings in bankruptcy; raising and supporting armies; selling public lands; protecting the states from domestic violence; the payment of all debts contracted in the revolutionary period by the Continental and Confederation Congresses and by the several states.

It is possible to argue that the alarums and excursions of the period in which the Constitution was born account for many of the anti-leveling devices written into the document. Notably this is so of the checks and balances against popular controls. The President and the Senate were to be chosen indirectly; the President was to have the veto power; the judiciary was to be named for life by the executive; the Supreme Court was to have the right of judicial review. (This power was not granted by the Constitution itself; but contemporaries so understood the role of the Court.) Yet it must be pointed out that a few years later, with the return of prosperity, there was little opposition voiced to the incorporation in the nation's fundamental law of a Bill of Rights that protected individual rights from oppression at the hands of public authority. The Constitution, in short, was conservative and conserving; but it was not a desperate and reactionary *coup d'état* designed to destroy the achievement of the Revolution. That was secure.

Ratification. The Constitution might very easily have failed of ratification if it had not been for the courage, devotion, and skill of its friends. It was sent to the states, and the state legislatures then fixed dates for choosing delegates to attend ratification conventions. Some states allowed a fair amount of time for public debate; others, virtually none at all. In Connecticut, New Jersey, Georgia, and Delaware haste seems to have been the order of the day; and the Constitution was adopted in each one without significant opposition. In New Hampshire, Massachusetts, and New York, the popular vote for delegates ran against the Constitution; but its adherents rallied to its support and brought powerful pressure to bear on the elected delegates. By public campaigns, by behind-the-scene bargains, by adroit political maneuvering, the doubtful were won over. The votes for ratification were close: in New Hampshire, 55 to 47; in Massachusetts, 187 to 168; in New York, 30 to 27. Virginia took its time and the whole document was debated fully before the election of delegates and on the floor of the convention; the final vote was 89 to 79. The same was true of Maryland and South Carolina, where the votes were 63 to 11 and 149 to 73, respectively. In Pennsylvania popular feeling against the Constitution ran high; anti-Constitution men tried to prevent the calling of a convention; pro-Constitution men used duress, and there were frequent charges of irregularities. But its friends won out and the Constitution was ratified by a vote of 46 to 23. Two states—because of clear-cut majorities in opposition—did not ratify until the Constitution had already been established. These were North Carolina (which ratified on November 21, 1789) and Rhode Island (which ratified on May 29, 1790).

One may well speculate what would have been the fate of the Constitution had its foes been as well organized as were its friends. For in the elections to the state conventions, it is estimated, not many more than 160,000 adult males participated—one fourth or one fifth of a total possible electorate. Of course, some did not vote because of the presence of property qualifications, but this number was not large. Indifference, apathy, ignorance, transportation difficulties in rural districts accounted for the lightness of the voting. Moreover, there were clearly indicated regional, or economic, differences to be noted. Generally, inhabitants of towns and dwellers on the Eastern seaboard—the larger-propertied interests—voted for ratification; while agrarian and backcountry communities—the smaller-propertied interests—voted against it. John Marshall, writing in his *Life of Washington* fifteen years later, summed up the complex situation in this fashion:

So balanced were the parties in some of them [the states] that even after the subject had been discussed for a considerable time, the fate of the Constitution could scarcely be conjectured; and so small in many instances was the majority in its favor, as to afford strong ground for the opinion that, had the influence of character been removed, the intrinsic merits of the instrument would not have secured its adoption.

3. THE HAMILTONIAN PROGRAM

George Washington consented to become the first President of the United States, and when he appeared in New York to take the oath of office, on April 30, 1789, he was acclaimed by a united people. To his moderation and the universal respect with which he was regarded, and to the genius of his leading adviser, Alexander Hamilton, the nation owes its successful start. Property rights were made secure; but equality of opportunity was also assured.

Washington named four men to his Cabinet: Thomas Jefferson as Secretary of State, Alexander Hamilton as Secretary of the Treasury, Henry Knox as Secretary of War, and Edmund Randolph as Attorney General. Meanwhile Congress was meeting—with James Madison as its leader on the floor of the House—and in addition to setting up the departments (as well as one for Post Offices, without, however, Cabinet rank), it passed a tariff act and a judiciary act in the first year of its life.

Federalists and Anti-Federalists. Differences did not develop until Hamilton began to submit his series of reports; and then a clear-cut division manifested itself. Before the Constitutional Convention met, Madison had favored a powerful central government; by 1790—following the lead of Thomas Jefferson—he had moved over to the opposite camp. And here there emerged a pattern that was to continue in American life until our present day. The Hamiltonians, or Federalists, stood for centralization and an expanded federal power. The Jeffersonians, or anti-Federalists, were strict constructionists and insisted that all rights not explicitly granted to the central government resided in the states. Roughly, the division followed economic interests. The Federalists were the moneyed men —the security holders, bankers, manufacturers, merchants, and land jobbers. The anti-Federalists were the debtors—farmers large and small. In the beginning, at any rate, the cleavage was not over broad theoretical questions; it is a mistake to assume that the Jeffersonians, for example, championed human rights while the Hamiltonians championed property rights. Thus, the first Ten Amendments were passed without opposition. The quarrel was over different kinds of property interests and how best they were to be protected by the Federal government. And here, it must be stated, Alexander Hamilton's reading of his times and of the future of America was that of the wise statesman. Over bitter partisan opposition, he was able to establish the country's public and private credit on a secure footing; and by doing so he was able to assure the stability and economic greatness of the United States.

One should not overlook the world situation, of course. The young republic went through its first growing pains in a period that saw Europe engaged in a desperate war. American commerce was able to take advantage of the increasing embroilment of European nations in the titanic struggle for power that characterized the French Revolutionary and Napoleonic Wars. Our ships soon began to queen the seas and to earn remittances for us. In addition, political uncertainty in Europe encouraged investments by foreigners in the United States. As we shall see, a good deal of the financing of public and private agencies was made possible by the flow here of foreign funds. Thanks to brilliant leadership and to a series of fortuitous circumstances, the American experiment was launched successfully.

Hamilton's Reports. The Hamiltonian program was set before Congress and the nation in a series of reports. These had to do with the public debt, public revenues, the chartering of a national bank, the establishment of a mint, and the encouragement of manufactures. The suggestions of all of these but the last were written into legislation. In addition, Hamilton helped in the creation of the tariff and land policies of the country.

Funding and Assumption. The first Hamiltonian report, the *Report on Public Credit*, was issued on January 9, 1790. Here the Secretary of the Treasury boldly faced the vexing problem of the existing public debt. The bonds issued by the revolutionary Congresses and the states were selling at heavy discounts; a large proportion of them had been acquired by speculators. Nevertheless, Hamilton argued for the funding of the central debt and the assumption of the state debts. He recognized the magnitude of the obligation. Foreigners held $11,700,000 of Continental and Confederation paper; some $40,400,000 of the same securities were in the possession of Americans; the outstanding debts of the states came to another $25,000,000. To make his point, Hamilton advanced a number of arguments. The Federal government would earn the confidence of businessmen generally. Here, he was frankness itself, for he said that such a step would "justify and preserve the confidence of the most enlightened friends of good government." He meant the business community, of course; for without their support the weak young republic could not possibly survive. He also pointed out that the new public issues would become a part of the circulating capital of the country and the basis for private loans. Above all, the success of future credit operations of the United States would be assured.

Hamilton met with opposition from the agrarians and from the representatives of states having few outstanding obligations. But his persuasiveness convinced Congress, so that the

Funding Act of 1790 created a machinery for funding. The law provided for the issuance of several series of federal bonds which were to be exchanged at par for the old Continental debt and the later Confederation domestic debt. Hamilton drove a good bargain with the security holders: for four ninths of their holdings they were to receive a series of bonds paying 6 percent interest; for another two ninths, the refunding bonds were to be interest free for ten years and then 6 percent was to be paid; for the remaining three ninths, the interest was to be 3 percent.

The assumption of the state debts was granted by Congress only after a bargain had been struck between Hamilton and Jefferson personally. Congress permitted the floating of a bond series for $21,500,000 to cancel the state issues; actually it was necessary to pay out only $18,000,000. The *quid pro quo* was the creation of the District of Columbia, and the erection of the national capital in a region where, presumably, business influences could not directly bring pressure to bear on Congress.

In addition, the laws wisely provided for a sinking fund to redeem the debt and support the market for federal bonds. The customs revenues were to be earmarked for the payment of interest charges. From the sale of public lands was to be built up a reserve out of which the redemption of the bonds would be financed; while such annual surpluses as accrued to the Federal government were to be used in open-market purchases of the bonds if they should fall below par.

The fact is, Congress had already gone about the business of laying the foundation of the federal revenue when it had passed the Tariff Act of 1789. Its preamble had set forth the threefold purpose of the measure as follows: "Whereas, it is necessary for the support of the government, for the discharge of the debts of the United States, and the encouragement and protection of manufactures that duties be laid." It should be noted, however, that the first duties were only slightly protective in character, their chief intent being revenue pro-

duction and the support of a domestic merchant marine. Hamilton's famous *Report on Manufactures*, which came late in 1791, did not overcome Congress's opposition to mercantilist devices; and it was not until 1816, in the midst of another depression, that the first really protective tariff law was enacted.

The Act of 1789 imposed an *ad valorem* duty of only 5 percent on all "nonenumerated" articles. Specific duties, somewhat heavier than 5 percent, were put on hemp, cordage, nails, iron manufactures, and glass. To encourage the domestic merchant marine, however, a drawback of 10 percent was allowed on all taxable commodities coming in American ships. Also, a tonnage tax of 50 cents a ton was levied on foreign vessels in American ports. In 1792, the general rate on nonspecific imports was raised to about 7½ percent.

In his *Report on the Excise* Hamilton returned to the question of public finance and laid the basis of the internal revenue practices of the country. Following his suggestions, Congress, in March, 1791, voted taxes on rum and whisky, to be collected at the source. In 1794, the principle of the excise was expanded when taxes on carriages, sugar, snuff, and auction sales were imposed.

The Bank. Hamilton's *Report on the Bank* appeared on December 14, 1790. He argued for a federally chartered institution with the rights of note issue, deposit, and discount on the following grounds: It would augment "the active or productive capital of the country." It would be able to lend to the Federal government in times of stress, and would facilitate government collections and payments. Despite the opposition of the anti-Federalists, led by Jefferson, who raised the specter of monopoly, Washington listened to Hamilton and threw his weight behind the measure. In February, 1791, Congress granted a charter for the organization of the Bank of the United States, fixing its life at twenty years.

The institution was to be a private one; but it was to have semipublic functions, in this sense being patterned after the Bank of England. It was to be capitalized at $10,000,000 in 25,000 shares. The Federal government might subscribe to one fifth of these and was to name a similar proportion of the twenty-five directors. Private persons could pay for their shares in government 6 percent bonds up to three fourths of their subscriptions; the remaining one fourth was to be in specie. The lion's share of the capitalization, $5,700,000, was to be kept in the main branch at Philadelphia; up to a total of eight branches might be established. To check concentrated control, a system of "regressive voting" was set up, the possessor of a single share being given one vote, of three shares two votes, and so on up to one hundred shares which had but twenty votes. Participation of foreign subscribers was encouraged, but they were not to vote by proxy or to sit on the board of directors of the Bank.

The Bank's functions were explicit. It could receive deposits from individuals and public bodies and make loans to businessmen, the states, and the Federal government. These loans were to be effected through either deposit creation or the emission of bank notes, but such notes were not to exceed the total of deposits and paid-in capital. Interest on loans was fixed at 6 percent. During the 1790s, the Bank admirably performed these functions. It added a total of $5,000,000 to the currency of the country, handled deposits and disbursements for the Treasury, and advanced funds to the Federal government (by 1796 this obligation stood at $6,000,000). In 1796, the process of public withdrawal began when the government sold a part of its Bank stockholdings in order to pay off its indebtedness to the institution. Thereafter, it asked no further loans from the Bank. Under Jefferson, whose hostility toward the Bank had never abated, the Federal government severed its connections entirely, selling all its stock. By this time, the Bank's shares were being held abroad largely; indeed, in 1811, when its charter expired, 72 percent of the stock was in the portfolios of foreign investors.

The Coinage. In January, 1791, the *Report on the Coinage* was issued. Hamilton's recommendation, herein, for the establishment of an American currency and mint was carried out by Congress in the Mint Act of 1792. The monetary system created by the Confederation Congress in 1785 was continued: that is, the basic coins were to be the gold eagle ($20), half eagle ($10), quarter eagle ($2.50), and the silver dollar, half dollar, and quarter. Following England's lead, a bimetallic standard was adopted, and the existing market ratio of 15 to 1 for the silver dollar was accepted. This dollar was to contain 371 grains of silver, the content of the Spanish dollar. A mint was also set up, not so much for making coins out of bullion—there were no precious metal deposits of any importance in the country at the time—as for converting foreign coins into American ones. This movement was a slow one; and it was not until 1802 that foreign coins disappeared and businessmen finally had a uniform currency. From the termination of the depression of 1785–86 through the 1790s, the amount of coins in circulation continued to increase. As has already been pointed out, this was owing to the increasingly favorable position of the United States in world trade. Indeed, we probably had a favorable balance of international payments during these years; perhaps this was the case right up to the outbreak of the Second War with England. For specie poured into the country. It has been estimated that in 1790, the amount of specie in circulation stood in the neighborhood of $9,000,000. By the end of the decade, this amount had doubled.

Manufactures. In December, 1791, there appeared still another Hamiltonian paper, undoubtedly the most interesting of all, called the *Report on the Subject of Manufactures.* In time this document was to become the classic textbook of American protective tariff interests. It should be observed, however, that the tariff was but a single device among many that Hamilton called upon Congress to employ in an effort to encourage domestic manufacturing enterprise. In short, Hamilton was flirting with mercantilist ideas (with a curious and amusing bow to Adam Smith, now and then) at the very moment that these were pretty generally under a cloud. Great Britain had made some concessions to American trade by the Treaty of Paris in 1783 and was to make even more important ones in the later Jay Treaty of 1795. In 1786, Great Britain and France had entered into a commercial agreement under which home markets were being opened up. American commerce was meeting with successes in many regions. For these and other reasons, Hamilton's advice could not have been followed. Perhaps it was better so. In any case, his arguments in favor of protectionism were shelved for another fifty years; indeed, it was not until the post-Civil War period that these were revived, this time with success, by the Republican party.

Hamilton, impressed by the successes of new industries everywhere about him, sought the creation of a great manufacturing interest comparable to England's. In fact, his preoccupation with manufacturing was more than an academic one; for he had been one of the prime movers in the creation of the Society for Establishing Useful Manufactures (SUM), which had been chartered by the State of New Jersey in 1791. Authorized to issue a capital stock of $1,000,000 (a sum larger than the total worth of all nonbanking joint-stock enterprises in the country), the corporation had attracted immediate attention. Subscriptions were taken up; power sites were granted by New Jersey; and a factory, at what is now Paterson, New Jersey, was constructed. The projectors' vision was a large one. The new company, using machinery and skilled mechanics, was to turn out a great variety of finished goods, including paper, sailcloth, other types of linen cloths, stockings, ribbons, tapes, thread, fringes, blankets, carpets, hats, shoes, pottery, brass, ironware, and cotton and linen prints. So the prospectus of the SUM. But American capital had other tasks to perform—the most important being the opening up of a vast continent—before it could sit down to the problem of developing manufacturing

enterprise intensively. By 1796, the SUM was a failure.

Nevertheless, Hamilton's reasoning is worth following. Taking a leaf out of Adam Smith's *Wealth of Nations* and, like Smith, questioning the assumption that agriculture is "the most beneficial and productive object of human industry," he argued for the superior advantages and larger productivity of manufacturing. Under it, a greater division of labor could be employed; and "thereby an increase of productive industry is assured." Again, manufacturing made possible the use of machinery; and in this way "an artificial force" is brought productively to the aid "of the material force of man." Further, manufacturing furnished employment to "classes of the community not originally engaged," that is to say, it created jobs for women and children. And it helped to promote immigration, particularly of skilled workers.

Then came a series of cogent economic arguments that had to do with opportunities for capitalist expansion. Manufacturing tended to furnish "greater scope for the diversity of talents and dispositions which discriminate men from each other." Manufacturing would afford "a more ample and various field for enterprise." (And, in an aside, to "cherish and stimulate the activity of the human mind by multiplying the objects of enterprise is not among the least considerable of the expedients by which the wealth of a nation may be promoted.") Finally, manufacturing in turn provided an expanding home market for agricultural commodities. For it contributed to an "augmentation of the produce or revenue of the nation" through "creating, in some instances, a new, and securing in all a more certain and steady demand for the surplus produce of the soil."

By 1791, Adam Smith could no longer be disregarded. But nations had to be practical. "If the system of perfect liberty to industry and commerce were the prevailing system of nations, the arguments which dissuade a country in the predicament of the United States from the zealous pursuit of manufactures would, doubtless, have great force." Until that time, the United States had the right to defend itself with mercantilist weapons. Even so, Hamilton had his doubts about a regime of "perfect liberty." Enterprisers needed encouragement to embark upon "young industries" (here is the first adumbration of the classic argument for protectionism, that of the infant industry). The influence of habit, timidity, and the like, might prevent the growth of manufactures even if an international division of labor existed and natural forces were suitable. Government assistance was required.

Then Hamilton sought to answer the objections of his foes. Manufacturing would not necessarily lead to a concentration of population in the East; the growth of the home market would help to expand agriculture. As for capital, part of it would come from abroad; another part would be furnished through the new government bonds, which could be used as security for bank loans. As for labor, immigrants, women, and children would furnish the working force. And he ended by advancing the positive reasons that have always been employed to defend a national as against an international economy. The well-being of a country having a balanced economy was assured because the home market has greater dependability and because diversification has inherent advantages.

How, now, to do it? By the usual mercantilist devices currently being employed: by protective duties; by prohibitive rates; by bans on the export of raw materials; by bounties and premiums; by the encouragement of invention; by regulations for the inspection of manufactured commodities; by the public construction of roads and canals. Hamilton concluded his report by showing that hopeful beginnings had already taken place. The young United States already possessed small works manufacturing iron, lead, wood products, leather goods, flour, linen, cotton and woolen goods, silk, glass, gunpowder, paper, printing, refined sugar, and chocolates.

Hamilton's program was not to be fulfilled. The anti-Federalists, defeated on the Bank, the

assumption of the state debts, and, later, on the Jay Treaty, here refused to yield. A monopoly interest was already entrenched in the field of finance; there could be no countenancing its extension into the realm of manufacturing, thus upsetting the balance of classes which was the real defense of democracy. One of the most eloquent of these anti-Federalists, John Taylor of Caroline, a little later put the argument of the agrarian Jeffersonians in this form:

. . . the policy of protecting duties to force manufacturing is of the same nature and will produce the same consequences as that of enriching a noble interest, a church interest, or a paper interest; because bounties to capital are taxes upon industry and a distribution of property by law and it is the worst mode of encouraging aristocracy, because to the evil of distributing wealth at home by law, is to be added the national loss arising from foreign retaliation upon our own exports.

For another fifty years, American capital was to preoccupy itself, in its leading emphases, with foreign trade, the great expansion and exploitation of the extending domestic market, land development, the building of transportation facilities. Even when tariff rates virtually became protective, in the 1830s, most of our finished-goods requirements continued to come from England. In short, as long as the characteristic undertakings of mercantile capitalism were capable of producing returns, there was little to tempt the American enterpriser to change his status and put his fund simply and entirely into fixed plant. His interests remained diversified.

Public Lands. The devising of a public land policy, while not associated with Hamilton's name, was an integral part of his fiscal program. As early as 1785, by the Land Ordinance of that year, the Confederation Congress had mapped out the general lines of the land system that was to continue until almost the end of the nineteenth century. The public lands, according to this act, were to be laid out in townships six miles square, with each divided into 36 sections of 640 acres each. At least two sections in each township were to be set aside for the support of public schools; the others were to be sold at public auction at once and the proceeds added to the Treasury's general fund. The land act, to encourage settlers as well as land companies, provided that half of the parcels were to be sold in sections and the other half in townships. The minimum knockdown price was to be $1.00 an acre, with payment in cash.

Obviously, land jobbers were at an advantage under this program, but soon the settlers were to be heard from. As a result of their representations, under the land act of 1796, while the minimum price was raised to $2.00, a year's time was permitted for the completion of payments. Western land offices were opened up. In 1800, further liberalization took place: the minimum quantity of land salable was reduced to a half section, or 320 acres, and a four-year installment system for the meeting of payments was created. This scheme turned out to be a not very effective compromise. The revenues brought into the Treasury from the sales were smaller than had been anticipated. Moreover, under the installment-payment program speculative companies bid in larger parcels than they had the immediate means of carrying, in the expectation that quick sales to homesteaders would allow them to discharge their obligations to the government. There were frequent disappointments, with the land office the loser. On the other hand, bona fide settlers were not ready to purchase as much as 320 acres; and, besides, they required more than the four years stipulated for discharging their debt.

The Jay Treaty. Finally, we may note as another achievement of the Hamiltonian program the working out of more satisfactory commercial relations with England. With the backing and full confidence of Hamilton, John Jay was sent to London to draw up a treaty to close the matters left unsettled by the Treaty of Paris. In the Treaty of London of 1794, Jay committed the United States to guaranteeing the payment of the debts contracted by colonials in the pre-Revolutionary period. The English, in return, agreed to evacuate the Western posts which they were still holding; pay damage for the seizure of American shipping in the war that

had dragged on between England and France; and fix a northeast boundary between the United States and Canada. Equally significant were the commercial understandings arrived at. The trade between the two countries was to be on a nondiscriminatory basis. Goods could move freely across the Canadian-American border. American ships were to be allowed to enter the ports of British-dominated India. As regards the West India trade, the English continued loath to abandon the Mercantile System. They were willing to allow the admission of American ships under 70 tons into these island possessions; but they banned the carriage by Americans of typical West India products (molasses, sugar, coffee, cocoa, cotton) into the direct European trade. As a result of the niggardliness of these concessions, the American Senate dropped the West India section from the treaty.

Half a loaf was better than none at all. There is no question that America's impressive mercantile growth in the next decade resulted in large part from a willingness on the part of England to allow American shipping to operate freely, even if we were compelled to recognize the English control of the seas. The tendency has been to regard the Jay Treaty as a setback for the United States. A more realistic view, considering the helpless position of a neutral United States *vis-à-vis* a Europe locked in a sanguinary war, warrants the opposite conclusion. Samuel Flagg Bemis, the outstanding authority on the Jay Treaty, has put this point of view in this way:

To balance against those great concessions to British sea power there was the assurance of continuing commercial prosperity, sound national finances, and the perpetuation of the newly consolidated American nationality. There was also the great achievement of redeeming the territorial integrity of the United States throughout the Northwest. . . . But the concessions to England were heavy. They were the price which the Federalists paid for peace, that peace with England so necessary for the maintenance of Hamilton's structure of national credit and with it of the new federal government under the constitution of 1787. It is not an exaggeration to believe that Jay's Treaty, which was really Hamilton's treaty, saved American nationality in an hour of crisis.

Foreign Capital in the United States. Of the soundness of the Hamiltonian intention to put the public finances on a secure footing there is no better proof than the eagerness with which foreign capital moved into the United States. Not only were our merchants advanced commercial credits by English and Dutch businessmen, but the investors of these countries bought freely of American public and private securities. By 1803, according to the estimates of Samuel Blodget, almost one half of American public and private issues of bonds and stocks were held abroad. His figures are interesting. Total security issues (leaving out the state debts) came to $129,700,000, of which $59,000,000 were in foreign portfolios. The federal debt stood at $81,000,000; foreign ownership accounted for $43,000,000 of this. The Bank of United States stock was $10,000,000; foreigners held $6,200,000. The stock of state-chartered banks totaled $26,000,000; foreign ownership came to $9,000,000. The stock of insurance companies was worth $9,000,000; a total of $500,000 was held abroad. The stock of turnpike companies was valued at $3,400,000; foreigners had $200,000 of this. By these means the young Republic was established.

4. THE DEFEAT OF THE FEDERALISTS

French Relations. These were the only triumphs of the Federalists. Never concerned about or capable of conciliating public opinion, their popularity declined as they committed one political blunder after another. The French Revolution had broken out in 1789 and the French Republic had been established in 1792 to meet the virtually united opposition of the European continent. Frenchmen deserved well of us: their assistance from 1778 on had turned the scales of the War of Independence in our favor. Partial to France, republicanism, and Deism, the anti-Federalists, or Republicans—as well as the American people generally—applauded the efforts of the French nation to stand off European reaction single-handed. French cockades were worn; the more equalitarian sans-culotte costumes were quickly imitated; Jacobin Clubs were formed. The Republican press insisted that we recognize our treaty obligations and come to the assistance of the French West Indies, threatened by the British fleet.

Jacobin excesses—abroad and in this country—alarmed the aristocratic Federalists. Partiality toward France represented more than sympathy for a sister republic; it revealed the depth of class hostilities in America and the general longing for leveling legislation and a wider diffusion of economic rights. Washington, in accord with the Federalist position, proclaimed American neutrality on April 22, 1892; and he quickly ordered the recall of the French Minister Genêt when that young man, his head turned by his popular reception, tried to embroil the United States in the war by committing clearly unneutral acts. The position of the Federalists was hardly improved as a result of the writing of the Jay Treaty. The British fleet was preying on our commerce and English soldiers were in the West keeping Indian relations in a state of turbulence. Jay obtained significant mercantile concessions, as has been pointed out; but these hardly appeased the Republicans, whose press clamored for war. Washington signed the treaty; was roundly abused for it; and left the presidency embarrassed and embittered by his experiences.

The Whisky Rebellion. Another incident fed the flames of partisan controversy. Hamilton's excise program had called for taxes on rum and whisky, collection being at the stills. In the case of whisky, the Western agrarians were especially hard hit. Because of difficulties in transport, it was easier for them to market their corn and rye as alcohol than as grain; moreover, collection at the source meant visitation and search and the payment of excises in a cash that was hard to get. Particularly in western Pennsylvania, farmers became restive and the five-thousand-odd owners of stills in this area took to defying the excise inspectors. Matters came to a head in 1794. Hamilton, with one eye on the Republicans and their wide-flung net of Democratic Clubs, succeeded in persuading Washington to order out the militia and a troop of 15,000 was assembled which Hamilton accompanied. The militia deported itself like a conquering army and despoiled the countryside while it openly flouted civil liberties. The "rebels" melted away; altogether, two rioters were arrested—and pardoned; and the excises remained. But hostility to the administration and its party became implacable.

The Adams Presidency. It was in such a climate that Washington gladly quit office and turned over the presidency to another—and last—Federalist, John Adams. Adams, too, ran into storms. Although a man of great intelligence and very real capacities, he possessed few political gifts, so that he ended by antagonizing his own followers and strengthening the opposition. The fact that Hamilton was cold to him further weakened his position.

The shadow of the European war hung over the Adams administration. Adams knew his Europe as well as any American, and he tried to steer his ship between rocks and shoals. British impressments of American seamen continued; on the other hand, the French insisted upon considering the Jay Treaty as not only a violation of the Treaty of 1778 but as an alliance directed against them. They refused to receive the American minister and set the French navy to hunting down American merchantmen. By the middle of 1797 some three hundred vessels had been made French prizes.

Adams, trying the arts of conciliation, sent what was in effect a peace mission to France. Our commissioners were not officially received but French agents were named to treat with them informally. These—called "XYZ" in the subsequent papers which Adams sent to Congress—ended by requesting a bribe of $250,000 for the members of the Directory, the council which now ruled France. Adams seized the opportunity thus afforded him to confound his detractors at home, exposed the affair to Congress and obtained the termination of the Treaty of 1778 and the right to outfit privateers. In 1798, therefore, there began an undeclared naval war against France which raged for two years and destroyed the French West India merchant fleets. Now France, turned conciliatory and anxious to avoid a formal Anglo-American alliance, informed Adams it would welcome another American commission. Napoleon had become First Consul and he flirted with the thought of setting America against England in the Western Hemisphere. A new treaty was signed, therefore, by which France recognized both the end of the earlier alliance and the rights of American ships, as neutrals, on the high seas.

Adams was incapable of profiting from these hard-won foreign victories in the domestic field. In fact, he and his party pressed their advantage the wrong way. Seeking once and for all to destroy radical ideas, Federalists enacted in 1798 four laws collectively known as the Alien and Sedition Acts. Under them, aliens were to wait fourteen years instead of five before they could complete their naturalization. Aliens, too, were in danger of deportation if their political conduct displeased the Department of Justice. The Sedition Law was aimed at Americans. Any person responsible for "any false, scandalous or malicious" utterances about the President or either House of Congress was guilty of a crime and could be tried. A witch-hunt, particularly against Republican editors, was begun and a number of convictions were brought in.

The Virginia and Kentucky Resolutions. These acts dug the Federalist political grave. Moving with consummate skill, Jefferson and Madison appealed to the states to defend American liberties. Madison wrote a series of resolutions which the Virginia legislature passed; Jefferson performed a similar service for the Kentucky legislature. In addition to laying down a political theory around which the slave lords subsequently were to gather—that the Union was a compact among independent and sovereign states—the Kentucky resolutions invited all states to proclaim the Alien and Sedition Laws illegal and hence null and void. In the election of 1800, the Republicans obtained 73 votes in the electoral college for their presidential and vice-presidential candidates Thomas Jefferson and Aaron Burr. Under the then law, the election was thrown into the House and Jefferson was chosen President on the thirty-sixth ballot. Hamilton disliked Jefferson but he distrusted Burr and it was his influence with Federalist Congressmen that gained the election finally for Thomas Jefferson.

Jefferson Elected. Jefferson liked to refer to his victory as "The Great Revolution of 1800," but it was somewhat less than that. Jefferson was a libertarian, but he was no equalitarian. Devoted to human rights in the sense that all children of the Enlightenment were, he feared the tyranny of the state above everything else. A powerful state was capable of creating and fostering economic privilege; it threatened liberty; it cut down the areas of opportunity. Jefferson envisaged a polity and an economy under which simple husbandmen and mechanics and artisans—owning their own freeholds and shops—were to produce largely for their own households, exchanging their surpluses among themselves only to round out their own requirements. The world of manufacturing, banking, and foreign trade he distrusted. It produced class divisions and antagonisms; it launched a propertied class upon speculation with subsequent economic disorders; it led to the appearance of a propertyless workingclass—and the dangers of mob rule.

Thus Jefferson could write in 1785:

Cultivators of the earth are the most valuable citizens. They are the most vigorous, the most independent, the most virtuous, and they are tied to their country, and wedded to its liberty and interests, by the most lasting of bonds. . . . I consider the class of artificers [workingmen] as the panders of vice, and the instruments by which the liberties of a country are generally overturned.

But Jefferson was not prepared to eliminate at a stroke—as had been the French Jacobins—the barriers between gentry and commonality, between the well-born and the humble. Democracy was a developing round: it was to come, in time, with education, religious freedom, and the equalization of economic opportunity. If men were free, their better and decent instincts, their rationality and their will to improvement would help them rise. Their sense of justice would disarm oppression. Until then, it was fit that an aristocracy of talent should continue in control of the political processes.

The "Great Revolution" of which he spoke —the rise of the common man, the democratization of the franchise and education, the chance to possess a freehold and to grow with an expanding country—did make its appearance a generation later. When the young Frenchman Tocqueville came to America in the 1830s, the spirit of equality that ruled in the land at once attracted his attention—and bemused him. Were liberty for the individual and equality for the mass compatible? But Jefferson did not have to face that question. Enough to note that he was the great American democrat, if a doctrinaire one. Important, too, to observe that despite his deep antagonism toward everything Hamilton had stood for, there was little he did to disorder the Hamiltonian achievement. When he declared, in his first inaugural "We are all Republicans, we are all Federalists" he was employing more than a gesture of conciliation toward his political foes; he was rendering a promise that he never made a serious effort to break. Property rights were secure in America; Jeffersonian democracy really meant their wider extension among a large and growing company of agrarian freeholders and small businessmen.

5. THE AMERICAN SCENE AT THE CENTURY'S TURN

Size and Population. Such was the founding of the young republic whose first tentative steps were regarded with mingled feelings by Europeans. It had got off to a good start. How fast was it to progress? Perhaps only slowly—if the experiences of its first generation under freedom constituted any basis for prophecy. The area of the United States had been increased; running from Maine to Spanish Florida and westward to the Mississippi, it covered about one million square miles. At the close of the eighteenth century, its population was about 5,300,000, of whom nearly 1,000,000 were blacks. The Negroes lived largely in the South, still under slavery, but with the decline of tobacco culture the attachments to the institution were weakening. In the Northern states, emancipation was taking place by law and private act.

America was still America, in the original sense. Its population was largely native-born and its stocks were those of the seventeenth and eighteenth century settlers. Descendants of English emigrants made up, almost entirely, the inhabitants of New England and the Southern states. Pennsylvania had the most mixed population: the majority were English; significant minorities, German and Scotch-Irish; and lesser representations from among the Irish, Welsh, and Dutch. Descendants of Germans were also to be found in New Jersey, New York, and Virginia. Descendants of Scotch-Irish were everywhere the frontier had penetrated. There were the children of Dutch emigrants in New York and New Jersey; those of French Huguenots in South Carolina and New York; those of Swedes in Delaware, New Jersey, and Maryland; and those of French and Swiss in the Wabash country. But because of the war in America, the European war, the stoppage of the flow of indentured servants from England, and the difficulty and high costs of the Atlantic passage, immigration had slowed down to a trickle. In the first decade of the Republic scarcely more than 5,000 immigrants came annually to the United States. The universal tongue was, therefore, English. The problems of absorption and understanding of strange languages and customs were still in the future.

Virginia was the most populous state, with 880,000 souls; Pennsylvania and New York came second and third in rank. New York was moving up the scale—thanks to its superior means of internal communication and the growing primacy of its great port—and in another generation was to become the Empire State. But the country's population was also moving out of tidewater and piedmont; at the end of the century, there were to be found almost 1,000,000 persons living beyond the Appalachian Line of 1763. The penetration across the frontier (the frontier line constituted that imaginary division beyond which the population density was less than 6 people to one square mile) was not only westward; it was also into the back country. In 1800, the frontier stretched across the north, from Maine through northern Vermont and New Hampshire to Lake Champlain in New York; and then southward to the mouth of the Savannah River in Georgia. It did not run in a straight line: in three places it bulged out to the west. Settlers were to be found in sizable numbers in central New York along the Mohawk River; in western Pennsylvania around Pittsburgh; and in the northern upland country of Georgia. Beyond the line, in the heavily wooded wilderness, were three island concentrations of settlement: in the Blue Grass country of Kentucky; in the valleys of eastern Tennessee; and in the Cumberland district of central Tennessee. So rapidly had these places filled out that three new states were joined to the Union by 1800: Vermont in 1791; Kentucky in 1792; and Tennessee in 1796.

Every collection of roughly-hewed log huts did not presage a future metropolis. Many river towns sank before long into sleepy little villages. But, already, Lexington, Pittsburgh, Frankfort, and Cincinnati were busy communities.

Agriculture. Every clearing in time became a farm, as the great forest yielded before axe and fire. The American's hunger for a freehold of his own was insatiable: he obtained it from the states, bought it from speculators, acquired it under the federal land law—or simply squatted on it, hoping in time to acquire it legally. He farmed it crudely; but it gave him a livelihood and those few surpluses—whisky, hemp, pickled or preserved meats, skins—with which he could acquire salt, iron, a gun or ammunition, and some few small luxuries. America was still largely rural; and its agrarian rounds had scarcely changed since the colonial period. Only about 200,000 persons—less than 3 percent of the total population—lived in towns of 8,000 or more persons. Philadelphia and New York were America's great cities—and each had less than 75,000 inhabitants. After them came Boston, Baltimore, Charleston, Salem, Providence, Newport—all port towns. Interior cities were considerably smaller.

Ways of Life. The American farmer—and the American urban dweller, too, for that matter—lived his life much as had his father and grandfather before him. On the farm, whose cultivable acreage was but slowly growing, productivity had not increased to any measurable extent because tools, livestock, and methods of cultivation had not changed. Implements were still of wood and still clumsy; farm animals were still bred promiscuously; farmers knew little of crop rotation, manuring, proper drainage. Their clothes were largely homespun; their homes badly heated, poorly lighted, and without sanitary facilities; their diets and drink heavy and unchanging, although ample. House furnishings were meager and for the greater part homemade. There were few coverings for floors and walls, no easy chairs, no decorations. Water had to be carried; washing and bathing presented difficult problems, particularly in the wintertime.

The home environments of the urban lower and middle classes were much the same. The rich had more luxurious surroundings—in housefurnishings particularly—but not many more creature comforts. Even they had to take charcoal warming pans to bed with them. But gentlefolk could dress up, and on gala occasions the men were as resplendent as the women. The French Revolution democratized men's clothing—and contributed as much to the dignity and self-respect of the lower classes as any other single factor.

In the towns, the great part of the populations were associated with trade or the handicrafts. The lower classes were port laborers, seamen, fishermen, mechanics, artisans and peddlers, or worked in the few service-industries—inns, livery stables, stagecoach transportation. The upper classes were undifferentiated merchants: at one and the same time, owners of ships and traders in their cargoes, moneylenders and bankers, real estate operators and dealers in wild lands, mill owners; or followers of the professions of the ministry, law, and medicine.

Transportation. The American population was rural; the cities were small and not particularly comfortable places to live in; it was hard to get about in this early America. The roads from New York to Boston, Philadelphia, and Baltimore were passable; otherwise, as a rule, they were only heavy ruts extending uncertainly through the dense forests. Turnpike construction had begun, but it was peculiarly of a local nature and tolls were charged by the private companies to pay for the upkeep. The new government sought to establish post offices and foster the building of post roads. In fact, by 1800, there were 900 post offices and a recorded total of 20,000 miles of post roads. The main post road—extending from Maine to Georgia—took 20 days to cover, if the season was right. The same situation existed in the case of water transport and travel. The ships were still the small wooden sailing vessels of the colonial period; little progress had been made in river or harbor improvement; there were very few bridges. One got over a river on a ferry—usually a raft—or floated across in a covered wagon.

Standards of Living. In such a civilization, it is hard to express standards of living in quantitative terms. European visitors agreed that Americans lived better than did their fellow men elsewhere; certainly this was true of the middle and lower classes. Because urban communities were so small and a bountiful nature existed everywhere, it was not difficult to supplement earnings from a garden patch, hunting, fishing, the forests. But the state itself provided few social services. Even in the case of education, of which much was heard theoretically and didactically at the end of the century, public schools rarely ran beyond the elementary grades; and then they were largely ungraded district schools supported from local funds. The best schools were those founded by the churches. Hospitals were curiosities; differentiated eleemosynary institutions did not exist; the almshouse sheltered the indigent aged, the orphaned, the mentally ill, and often the sick.

However, one cannot be guided too closely by such facts; it is the tone of a society that is important. As John A. Krout and Dixon Ryan Fox pointed out in *The Completion of Independence* (1944), the United States was a good place in which to begin. "One could always begin again in America, even again and again. Bankruptcy, which in the fixed society of Europe was the tragic end of a career, might be merely a step in personal education." Coupled with this—and always of the first importance— were the facts that land was easy to acquire; possession of a freehold gave not only economic independence but political participation and social standing; in the economic sector, ancient privileges to curb youth and daring were absent; wages were high and employment quite constant.

There were, of course, sharp differences in income and earnings among the various classes.

But two things must be remembered: fluidity among the classes existed in America; and money earnings at the end of the eighteenth century cannot be contrasted with money earnings today because such a small part of the population was dependent wholly on money income. Fortunes, by modern standards, were small: George Washington, when he died in 1799, left an estate of about $500,000. And he was America's wealthiest citizen. Fortunes of $100,000 to $200,000, particularly in the merchant class, were not uncommon. A member of the professional middle classes could earn about $1,000 a year and live very comfortably on it. A skilled artisan averaged around 80 cents a day, making his annual income $250. Laborers made about half that. The typical farmer— with a property worth $1,000 to $2,000—perhaps had from $50 to $100 a year in cash for taxes and the farm and home necessaries he had to buy.

Fluidity in America. Superficially, the aspect of things—because there had been few modifications in the methods of production or their institutional arrangements since the early years of settlement—appeared fixed and changeless. Beneath, however, ran swift currents, and because of them bold spirits in America were making reexaminations and revaluations of traditional outlooks and beliefs. Attention has already been called to the great advances achieved in the political sector: we stood on the threshold of democracy. In religion, in science, and in mechanics pioneers were preparing the way for that revolution which the nineteenth century was to complete—the release of the mind of the common man from the grip of authority and his body from physical suffering and privation. To this extent, American thinkers, religious leaders, and scientists continued in touch with and to express the tradition of the European Enlightenment.

Religion. Revealed religion was being submitted to rigorous scrutiny by those who were aware that the churches could not shut out the scientific world entirely. Newtonianism had put order into the universe; and with this doctrine had come a greater regard for the dignity of man and his ability to create a good life by conscious effort. Intellectuals had become Deists and had nothing to do with organized religion, or attended churches only occasionally. Theology no longer was a necessary preoccupation on the part of an educated man; religion had become largely a matter of personal faith. Tom Paine's *Age of Reason* was published in America in 1794, and because it represented so well the beliefs of those influenced by the Enlightenment it was read widely and stirred men deeply. His credo became the position of many. Said Paine in a characteristic passage:

I believe in one God, and no more; and I hope for happiness beyond this life. I believe in the equality of man, and I believe that religious duties consist in doing justice, loving mercy, and endeavoring to make our fellow creatures happy. I do not believe in the creed professed . . . by any church that I know of. My own mind is my own church.

The same boldness entered the churches themselves. There was a searching of hearts and a reexamination of doctrines. The first serious break came in that citadel of orthodoxy, New England Calvinism. It is true that New England Federalists in politics were also traditionalists in religion; and they fought as bitterly against the influences of rationalism and humanitarianism in the churches as they did against the idea of democracy in statecraft. But the Unitarians, so-called, were rising in the midst of the Congregational churches and their influence began to spread. Before long, that denomination was cleft in twain. The reformers questioned fundamental beliefs: unconditional predestination, original sin, hell-fire, the necessity for leading a life of complete abnegation. On the contrary: a man was created in God's image and divine love moved the world. There were schismatic groups, too, among the Episcopalians and the Dutch Reformists.

The Intellectual World. Orthodoxy was being shaken in the cities and, with the resultant freedom for men's minds, scientific speculations could be pursued without hindrance.

Here, too, Europe's lead was being eagerly followed. The French Encyclopedia and English journals were read; American philosophical societies made their appearance; and the colleges quickly established scientific chairs. Americans soon familiarized themselves with European progress in mechanics, chemistry, physiology, botany, geology. America, too, began to make early scientific contributions, notably in chemistry. Benjamin Rush, James Woodhouse, Joseph Priestley, Benjamin Silliman, S. L. Mitchell became distinguished names in the annals of chemical research. There was an immediate carry-over into the field of technology. The scientific spirit, the dearth of labor, the constant American preoccupation with gadgets soon were to lead to Eli Whitney's invention of the cotton gin and the development of mass-production techniques in gunmaking and John Fitch's and Robert Fulton's perfection of the steamboat.

Revivalism. If the rationalistic spirit was making real advances in the Eastern communities, a fundamentalist revivalism reigned unchallenged in the back country. This ambivalence has always existed in America, in large part due to the fact that all sections of the country did not grow up together at the same time. Up to very recently, a settled society and a pioneering mode of life have lived side by side in the United States. The back country and the frontier folk, going through daily rounds of hard physical toil, loneliness, and unrelieved boredom, have found in revivalism an emotional outlet. Just as the Great Awakening had stirred colonial America, so Methodism—placing its emphasis on the same beliefs—swept the rural South and West. John Wesley, its English founder, who had also preached in America, had taught the necessity for personal communion with Jesus Christ in order to achieve salvation. Francis Asbury, the first and great bishop of the church, took the creed personally into virtually every obscure corner of the young republic. He lived in the saddle, he slept in humble dwellings, he founded churches in the wilderness; and he made some 300,000 converts and ordained some

4,000 ministers. Methodism, it is true, bitterly fought the natural religion of the Enlightenment; but, curiously enough, it made a mighty contribution toward the building of the democratic spirit. Its preachers reached right down into the lives of the common folk. They talked a simple tongue; gave their flocks an opportunity to release their pent-up emotions in religious demonstrations; and created an aware-ness of individual worth and a solidarity among the masses that were to be among America's most vitalizing forces. The cause of Jacksonian democracy found its army in these men and women of rural homesteads and frontier cabins.

In these ways, the new republic of the United States prepared itself for its great adventures in the nineteenth and twentieth centuries.

ELIHU PALMER

THE WORK OF Elihu Palmer (1763–1805) represents the leaven of "popular freethought" which is exemplified in Volney and the Deism of Thomas Paine. Palmer, who had been educated for the ministry at Dartmouth, abandoned Calvinism for the kindlier doctrines of the Universalists. While serving a Universalist congregation in Philadelphia he declared himself ready to dispute the divinity of Christ, a venture which turned him from theology to the law, for he was all but mobbed by an angry crowd when he attempted to maintain his thesis. Though he was admitted to the bar, Palmer had little opportunity to engage in his new profession. He was one of those stricken by the yellow fever epidemic which swept Philadelphia in 1793 and he escaped death only at the cost of blindness. That blow and Palmer's deepening convictions returned him to his original interest in religion. During the last decade of his life, he became one of the leaders of popular Deism. From Augusta, Georgia, to New York City, where he finally settled and organized the Deistical Society, the blind lecturer expounded his vision of the truth.

Palmer's discourses form the core of his chief work, the *Principles of Nature*, which was printed after his death. In substance, the book repeats the arguments against orthodox Christianity found in the work of the European Deists. The untrammeled intellect could penetrate all mysteries and achieve all things, since there was no limit to its "moral and scientific improvement." In a world engaged in the "awful contest" that must end "in the destruction of thrones and civil despotism" there was no room for such dogmas as the Trinity. The Bible was discordant in history, distorted in

fact, unintelligible in doctrine, indecent, immoral and shocking to "common sense and common honesty." Christianity, moreover, demands belief in its doctrines before regeneration can take place, yet a man may experience what it terms regeneration without amending his conduct or increasing his knowledge. The differences among Christian churches and the blood shed as a result of those differences prove that Christianity is without moral authority even over its nominal followers.

From attack, Palmer turned to refutation. The present age is distinguished by a band of "philanthropic philosophers" like Thomas Paine, "probably the most useful man who ever lived." In point of fact, those who oppose Deism "are interested in keeping up a privileged system of plunder and robbery, which makes nine-tenths of the human race absolute slaves, to support the other tenth in indolence, extravagance, pride and luxury."

Ignorance alone makes men set miracles above the regular operation of natural law. Nature impels men to virtue, but superstition perverts his heart. For the essential principles of morality are founded in the nature of man. And those principles will become dynamic when men reach a correct conception of their relation to matter and to each other. Moral science is a progressive discipline, Palmer argues, and its decisions should be reexamined accordingly. Immortality attaches to man as matter and not as a receiver of sensations. Man must accept the universe then, remembering that human wishes are no standard for truth. Yet this unflinching view does not lead to pessimism. Goodness is inherent in man. Once he is free to discover the true foundation of morality, he will sweep out kings, thrones, priests, and hierarchies and take power into his own hands to be used for the good of the entire species.

The selection here reprinted is taken from the London edition of 1823 of the *Principles of Nature*.

Principles of Nature

BY ELIHU PALMER

CHAPTER XIII: ORIGIN OF MORAL EVIL, AND THE MEANS OF ITS ULTIMATE EXTIRPATION FROM THE EARTH

THE FACTS in the physical world are, many of them difficult of solution: those of the moral world have perplexed still more the operations of the human understanding. The subtilty, the abstruceness, the incognizable character of moral existence, place it beyond the power of clear intellectual perception, and the mind loses itself in those metaphysical combinations, whose successive variations are incalculable. But the difficulties which nature has thrown in the way of this inquiry are much less numerous than those presented by superstition. A design has been formed, and carried into effect, whose object it was to cover the moral world with a mantle of mystery, and exclude it wholly from the view of vulgar eyes, and common comprehension. It is only necessary to conceal the real nature and character of a thing, and then deformities and distortions may be made to pass for positive properties, or essential qualities inherent in any specific mode of existence. If the subtilty of thought, and the difficulty of moral discrimination, have in many cases presented to human investigation a barrier to farther progress; the intentional malignant descriptions of superstition have, in almost every age and country, terrified the mind of man, and prevented the developement of substantial moral principle. Nature furnishes some difficulties, but supernatural theology exhibits many more.

In no one instance is this remark more substantially verified, than in the inquiries which man has made concerning the source or origin of moral evil. Reason and theology, philosophy and superstition, are at war upon this subject. The believers in the Christian religion, following the examples of their theological and fanatic predecessors, have searched the universe inquest of a satisfactory solution to that long altercated question—Whence came moral evil? One religious sectary, willing to screen the divinity from any just accusation relative to so nefarious a concern, have descended into hell, and discovered there all the characters and distorted machinery necessary to the production

of such an effect: but here metaphysical and fanatic invention indulged itself in all the extravagance of delusion. It was necessary first to create this *infernal* country, and then to create inhabitants suited to the nature of the climate, and the unfortunate condition in which they were to reside. The idea of a Devil was accordingly formed, and the reality of his existence rendered an indubitable truth by the reiterated assertions of superstition. Ignorance and fanaticism greedily swallowed the foolish *infernal* dose which had been administered.

There is a remarkable disposition in the human mind to remove the point of intellectual difficulty as far from the reality of the case as possible, and then it triumphantly imagines that a solution has been given. This is a fact particularly in theological inquiry, in which a few retrogressive efforts of the mind have been considered as an ample illustration of all the difficulties relative to the subject of Theism, and the existence of the physical universe. Similar to this idea is the doctrine concerning moral evil, and the disposition which theologians have exhibited to remove the burden from their own shoulders, and place it upon the devil's back. The whole *infernal* machinery with which we are presented by superstition, serves only to detach the mind from the true and real source of moral evil. While reflection is directed to another world, it is incompetent to a clear view of the facts existing in this, and the habit of such reveries produces a fanatic delirium subversive of all correctness of judgment. The existence of hell, and the beings that dwell therein, being only supported by what is called divine revelation, it follows, of course, that if this revelation is not true, a belief in any thing that is a mere result of that system cannot be substantially founded. Since then it is presumed, that in these chapters a competent refutation is given to the doctrine contained in the sacred books of the Jews and Christians, the idea of descending into hell, or having recourse to a devil, in search of moral evil, is futile and inconsistent.

Another part of the Christian world, willing to avoid difficulties which their antagonists had thrown in their way, abandoned the *infernal* abodes, and ascended into the celestial world, in quest of the origin of evil. They exhibited ingenious metaphysical reasoning upon the subject, declaring that God was the Creator of all things; that sin was something and not nothing, and therefore he must be the Creator of sin or moral evil. This puzzled the advocates of the *hell scheme* and a clerical warfare was engendered concerning two theological opinions, neither of which had any kind of existence in the nature of things. After heaven and hell had been searched through and through to find something which did not belong to either of them, the terror-struck inquirer, as if fatigued with his atmospheric journey, seated himself once more upon the earth, and saw, or might have seen, in the very bosom of society, and the perverted character of man, a clear and satisfactory solution of that difficult question, which, for so long a time, had occupied his attention in distant regions. It is in this manner, that the plainest subject is rendered mysterious, when a superstitious religion is industriously employed in subverting the independent power of thought. It is neither in the upper nor lower regions; it is not in heaven nor in hell, that the origin of moral evil will be discovered; it is to be found only among those intelligent beings who exist upon the earth. *Man has created it, and man must destroy it.*

But it is necessary to exhibit the proofs of this last assertion, and convince Christian theology of the innumerable errors, which for ages past have been imposed upon a credulous and deluded world. What is it, then, that constitutes a moral evil? It is the violation of a law of justice or utility, by any one of the human species, competent to distinguish between right and wrong. We have no other cognizable idea upon this subject. Facts and practice are presented continually to the view of the human mind; the decision of a correct mind is always according to the nature and character of the case. The character of a human being is made either good or bad by the actions he commits. If these actions are conformable to the principles of justice and universal benevolence, they are with great propriety denominated good; if they are unjust, cruel, and destructive to sensitive and intellectual life, they are denominated bad. There are certain fundamental laws, suitable for the government of rational beings, and it is a departure from these laws that vitiates the human character. It is proved in another part of this work, that virtue and vice are personal qualities and that they result from personal adherence to, or personal infraction of moral law.

It is only necessary in this place to call the attention once more to the nature of human actions, and to the characteristic difference between them, in order to establish the position principally assumed in this inquiry; for it ought to be recollected, that even if it *could* be proved, which by the way it cannot, that even a deity or a devil had violated moral law, this would not effect the decision upon the subject in regard to man; because that evil could not be transferred from a different kind of beings in the other world, to those who exist upon earth. As the moral properties of all intelligent agents are personal; are essentially their own and not another's; as there can be no justifiable transfer between man and man, so it follows that there can be none between man and devil. Every intellectual being must depend upon himself: must rest upon his own energies and be responsible for himself. Man must, therefore, relinquish that position, which has been assumed by Christian theology, relative to the transferable nature of moral qualities. Christianity presents us with two grand leading characters, to whom we are always referred in our inquiries upon the subject of moral evil. Adam and Jesus are these persons, and in them is said to have been concentred the sin and righteousness of the human race. The new Testament declares that, *as in Adam all die, even so in Christ shall all be made alive.* This is a sweeping clause, in regard to the moral existence of man, and flies in the face of universal experience. Facts are at war with this scriptural declaration, and it is impossible to reduce the sentiment to practice, without producing in common life the grossest violation of justice. Admitting for a moment the existence of such a man as Adam, which by the way is extremely problematical, it will not follow, that there was in him either a moral or physical death of the human race. Physically it is impossible, and morally it is unjust. If Christian theology has made a recurrence to Adam, to aid the solution of difficulties, relative to the origin of moral evil; if it has by this idea perverted the eternal principles of discriminative justice, it has also been equally unfortunate in calling in the righteous Jesus to its assistance, in expectation of ultimately destroying the immorality of the world. The scriptures invite us to behold the Lamb of God, that taketh away the sins of the world. The Lamb is Jesus, the only begotten of the Father; he is reputed to be divine and uncontaminated with any kind of moral turpitude. He is made the victim of Jehovah's wrath, and falls a sacrifice to the vindictive fury of his benevolent father, and all this for the purpose of removing crimes for which apostate man should have been scourged and afflicted. Means more unsuitable or incompetent to the production of such an effect, could never have been invented by the delirious brain of fanaticism itself; but the absurd and incompetent methods which Christian theology has invented for the destruction of moral evil, are not so much the objects of the present investigation, as the means which reason has in view to effectuate the moral renovation of the species. It is a common complaint among theological doctors, that the *world is growing worse and worse!*

Passing by any strictures upon the ill compliment which theologists pay to themselves by indulging such a sentiment, the truth of the opinion itself will become a more important matter of discussion. The organic construction, the powers and the properties of human existence, the aggregate amount of virtue and vice in the present generation, these are objects subjected to the inspection of the human mind; but the conduct and character of man, in former ages, is to be drawn from history. Histories, however, are not always faithful to the realities of the case, and description is sometimes excessive and sometimes deficient. But judging from what we know, and including in the ground of decision, similarity of organic structure, cogent proofs will be exhibited against the admission of an opinion hostile to the ultimate perfectibility of intelligent life. The expansion of mind, the development of principles, and the cultivation of the arts, in a degree far superior to all the specimens of high antiquity, evince an incontrovertible amelioration in the present race. The accommodations favourable to the comfort and happiness of life, with which man has surrounded himself, demonstrate, that there exists in the constitution of his nature a strong and indestructible impulse to progressive improvement; to the diminution of evil, and the augmentation of good. The fine moral qualities of the heart, which adorn cultivated life, give to it a splendid brilliancy, and triumphant exaltation above the coarse, instinctive brutality of former ages. If personal malignity and national warfare continue, the first is diminished in the acrimony of its character, and the second has regulated its movements, in some measure, upon the principles of a reciprocal humanity, and a greater respect for the dignity of human existence. These are facts with which we are every moment presented in the history of modern times: those who controvert these assertions must have forgotten, or never knew, the names of Alexander, of Nero, and Caligula; of the numerous ecclesiastical despots and persecutors with which the history of the Christian Church presents us, anterior to the commencement of the sixteenth century; nay farther, they must have neglected the reading of the *Holy Scripture,* and have lost sight of the character of Moses, that eminent murderer of antiquity. The Mahometan arguments in favour of belief must also have escaped their notice; in short, the advocates of pre-eminent virtue in former ages have shut their eyes against the history of kings and priests; against the knowledge of those dreadful effects, which the compound despotism of the church and state has produced upon the human race.

If the modern *Suwarrow* be brought as an example of refutation to these remarks, it is admitted in its full force, and this eminent murderer of modern times is consigned, by the sentiment of humanity, to the grave of eternal infamy. But the cases of such savage barbarity are growing less numerous in proportion as the knowledge of principle advances, and the correspondent moral practice flowing from such knowledge. Reason, or the intellectual powers of man, must eventually become both the deposit and the guardian of the rights and happiness of human existence. Reason has already acquired such strength, and so far unfolded its powers, that it has already sealed the future destiny of the human race. It is the peculiar office of reason to look to the utter demolition of the ancient regimen of church and state. These twin sisters of iniquity are the moral giants, which have stalked with huge devastation over the face of the whole globe. Political depotism and supernatural religion have done more to render the human race vicious and depraved, than all other causes conjointly combined. If the passions of man and the impulses of his nature have frequently produced a moral eccentricity in his conduct, it is certain that a corrupt government and a corrupt religion have rendered him habitually wicked; have perverted all the conceptions of the mind upon moral and political subjects, and brutalized his intellectual existence.

The most important step which can be taken for the extermination of vice and misery, is to destroy the artificial causes by which such evils are perpetuated. If other causes should be found to exist in the constitution of nature, they will be progressively removed by the light and power of science, and a more comprehensive view of the true interest of the human species. But efforts tending to make the individuals of a nation virtuous and happy, will never succeed extensively till the civil and religious tyranny under which they groan shall be completely annihilated. This will lead to the application of force in the political revolutions of the world; an expedient, however, the rectitude of which some benevolent philosophers have called in question. . . .

It is sufficient at this time to remark, that despotism gives no encouragement to any kind of improvement, and the hope of human ameliora-tion from this quarter will ever prove to be falla-cious. Reason, righteous and immortal reason, with the argument of the printing types in one hand, and the keen argument of the sword in the other, must attack the thrones and the hierarchies of the world, and level them with the dust of the earth; then the emancipated slave must be raised by the power of science into the character of an enlight-ened citizen; thus possessing a knowledge of his rights, a knowledge of his duties will consequently follow, and he will discover the intimate and es-sential union between the highest interests of ex-istence, and the practice of an exalted virtue. If civil and ecclesiastical despotism were destroyed, knowledge would become universal, and its prog-ress inconceivably accelerated. It would be im-possible, in such a case, that moral virtue should fail of a correspondent acceleration, and the ulti-mate extirpation of vice would become an in-evitable consequence. Ages must elapse before the accomplishment of an object so important to the elevated concerns of intelligent life; but the causes are already in operation, and nothing can arrest or destroy the benignant effects which they are calculated to produce. The power of reason, the knowledge of printing, the overthrow of political and ecclesiastical despotism, the universal diffu-sion of the light of science, and the universal en-joyment of republican liberty; these will become the harbingers and procuring causes of real virtue in every individual, and universal happiness will become the lot of man.

TIMOTHY DWIGHT

BETWEEN 1783 and 1801, the American scholar saw his own country achieve independence, weather post-war upheaval, and establish a new instrument of government. The Constitu-tion had barely been set into full operation when Revolution broke out in France. From this safe shore of the Atlantic, Americans watched the *ancien régime* crumble. Revolu-tion threatened more than political change; it shook the foundations of belief generally. To the conservative defense of all true and tried values flocked a group of Americans of whom Timothy Dwight (1752–1817) was one of the most notable.

Dwight, Jonathan Edwards's grandson, was educated by his mother, who made an intense student of her precocious son. Dwight re-signed as a tutor at Yale to serve as a chaplain in the Connecticut Line and left the army in 1779 to care for family affairs. After nearly two decades as preacher, schoolmaster, and poet, Dwight was called to the presidency of Yale.

Here, as preacher and schoolmaster, Tim-othy Dwight worked to keep Connecticut faithful to the sound moderation of her past.

His concern for his country did not end with his attack on Deism or his attempts to broaden and improve Yale's curriculum and organiza-tion. He was as convinced of America's pe-culiar mission as the most enthusiastic demo-crat. Because of his belief in that mission, Dwight would have had his country produce her own literature as she had already produced her own society and her own religion. He was one of the group of Connecticut amateurs who are known as the "Hartford Wits."

Uninspired as his verse is apt to be, Dwight at least considered the history and landscape of his own country worthy of a poet's attention. That same regard for familiar things is shown in his *Travels in New England and New York*. Though even the "set pieces" of scenic description are prosy, Dwight's reports show the shrewd witness and the lover of his land. Even in his faults, Dwight preserved the image of the country which he was certain had learned to lead the good life.

The selection used here is taken from *Travels in New England and New York* (4 vols., London, 1823).

Travels in New England and New York

BY TIMOTHY DWIGHT

LETTER V: VINDICATION OF THE ESTABLISHMENT OF THE PUBLIC WORSHIP OF GOD BY LAW

IN THE PRECEDING Letter I have given you, if I mistake not, a complete account of what has been often, though improperly, called the Ecclesiastical Establishment of Connecticut. This phrase, as applied to other countries, has usually, if not always, denoted the establishment of a national, or state church; or the establishment of exclusive privileges in the possession of one class of Christians. To Connecticut, therefore, it can have no proper application; because in this state all classes of Christians are placed on the same level. Formerly the case was different. A religious establishment existed in the colony of Connecticut, antecedently to the revolution; and gave exclusive privileges to the Congregationalists; the class of people, by whom it was originally settled. This has been changed for the system, detailed above. Whatever advantages, or disadvantages, therefore, may be supposed to attach to religious establishments in the appropriate sense, they can have only a partial relation to the ecclesiastical system of Connecticut. The principal arguments in favour of such establishments, and the principal objections against them, can be applied to it only in the same imperfect manner. In my own view the system might, in better language, be styled "The legal establishment of the public worship of God in this state."

I have brought all the parts of this system into one view, because they are all parts of a single design, naturally expressed by the phrase, adopted in the preceding sentence, and because I wished you to see them in their connection with each other. In this scheme you will see the whole country formed into religious congregations, styled ecclesiastical societies. These societies are vested with ample powers to tax themselves, to collect taxes, to hold property, to receive donations, and to manage their property for the purpose of building and repairing churches, and maintaining the public worship of God. This worship they are required to attend, churches they are required to build, and ministers they are required to settle and support. In doing these several things they are secured, so far as may be, against intrusion, opposition, interruption, and even indecency from others. The great object in view, the public worship of God, is required, provided for, enforced, and defended. Some of the means, by which it is to be accomplished, are pointed out; and all, which can consist with the certain attainment of the object, are left to the societies themselves.

You cannot but have perceived, that all classes of Christians are here invested by law with the same privileges. You must also have perceived, that ample provision is made for all those changes of opinion, and those scruples of conscience, which, where they honestly exist, are entitled to tenderness and respect; for which men very jealously claim regard; and which, therefore, demand regard from every wise legislature.

If it be admitted, as by the sentence of both reason and revelation it ought to be, that a legislature has a right to establish the worship of God; it will also be admitted, that the legislature of Connecticut has adopted a wise and liberal system for this important purpose. They have done most of that which is necessary, and nothing which is not necessary, to this end. So far as is consistent with the design, they have also placed every thing in the hands of those, who are chiefly concerned; and left them to the guidance of their own choice. At the same time they have made them responsible to the proper tribunal, the supreme authority of the state.

There are two classes of men, who contend against the interference of the legislature for the support of public worship: those, who consider it as inexpedient; and those, who regard it as unlawful.

On this subject it would be easy to fill a volume. It cannot be supposed, that I can here discuss it at length; nor that, if this were in my power, you would with patience read the discussion. But it has been so often a theme of contention and complaint, on this as well as on the other side of the Atlantic, and particularly in the states south of New-England, as to render it proper to examine the subject with some degree of minuteness, even here. To the former of these classes, then, I address the following observations.

The legislature of every state is the proper superintendant of all its prudential concerns. It has not only a right, but is obliged by an authority, which it can neither oppose nor question, to pursue every lawful and expedient measure for the promotion of the public welfare. To this great purpose religion in every country is not only useful, but indispensable. But religion cannot exist, and has never existed for any length of time, without public worship. As every man ought, therefore, willingly to contribute to the support of whatever increases his own prosperity; he is by immoveable consequence obliged to support the religion, which, by increasing the common prosperity, increases of course his own.

Should an advocate for the doctrine, which I oppose, demand proof, that religion is indispensable to the welfare of a free country, this is my answer. Morality, as every sober man, who knows any thing of the subject, discerns with a glance, is merely a branch of religion: and where there is no religion, there is no morality. Moral obligation has its sole ground in the character and government of God. But where God is not worshipped, his character will soon be disregarded; and the obligation, founded on it, unfelt and forgotten. No duty, therefore, to individuals, or to the public, will be realized or performed. Justice, kindness, and truth, the great hinges on which free society hangs, will be unpractised, because there will be no motives to the practice, of sufficient force to resist the passions of man. Oaths of office, and of testimony, alike, without the sanctions of religion, are merely solemn farces. Without the sense of accountableness to God, without the realizing belief of a future retribution, they are employed only to insult the Creator, deprave the juror, and cheat his fellow-men. This sense nothing but religion can inspire or preserve. With the loss of religion, therefore, the ultimate foundation of confidence is blown up; and the security of life, liberty, and property buried in the ruins.

In aid of these observations I allege, that no free government has ever existed for any time without the support of religion. Athens, Sparta, and Rome, stood and fell with their religion, false and gross as it was; because it contained some of those great truths, and solemn sanctions, without which man can possess no conscience, exercise no virtue, and find no safety. To their religion, Britain, Switzerland, and the United Netherlands, have owed most of their happiness and their permanency; and might say to this celestial denizen, in every period of their prosperity, as the devout and humble Christian to his God, "Having obtained help of thee, we have continued to this time."

In the history of the globe there is recorded but one attempt, seriously made, to establish a free government without religion. From this attempt has sprung new proof, that such a government, stripped of this aid, cannot exist. The government, thus projected, was itself never established; but was a mere abortion; exhibiting doubtful signs of life at its birth, and possessing this dubious existence only as an ephemeron. During its diurnal life it was the greatest scourge, particularly to those for whom it was formed, and generally to the rest of mankind, which the world has ever seen. Instead of being a free, just, and beneficent system of administration, it was more despotic than a Persian caliphate; more wasteful of life, and all its blessings, than an inundation of Goths and Vandals. Those who lived under it, and either originated or executed its measures, were the authors of more crimes than any collection of men, since the termination of that gigantic wickedness, from which nothing but an universal deluge could cleanse this polluted world.

These evils, my antagonist is further to be informed, were the result of the only experiment, ever made, of erecting a government without religion. They are the only specimen of the genuine efficacy of infidelity and atheism on the mind and on the happiness of man, during the only opportunity, which they have enjoyed, of possessing an unlimited control over human affairs. Until the remembrance of this experiment shall have been lost, it can never be made again.

Finally, he is to be informed, that it is wiser, more humane, and more effectual, to prevent crimes than to punish them. He is to be told, what he cannot deny, that religion is the only great preventive of crimes; and contributes more, in a far more desirable manner, to the peace and good order of society, than the judge and the sheriff, the gaol and the gibbet united. He is to be reminded, that mankind, with all the influence of religion added to that of the civil government, are still imperfectly governed; are less orderly, peaceful, and friendly to each other, than humanity must wish; and that, therefore, he who would willingly lessen this influence is a fool, he who would destroy it a madman.

I am well aware, that, in spite of this and any other reasoning, in spite of demonstration itself, there are men, who may, and in all probability will, say, that, however good and useful the public worship of God may be, they do not wish to avail themselves of its benefits, and owe therefore no contributions to its support. To these men I reply, that he who has no children, or who does not wish to send his children to school, and he who does not use the roads and bridges of his country, because he is either necessitated or inclined to stay at home, may on exactly the same ground claim an exemption from supporting schools, roads, and bridges. To such an objector it is a sufficient answer, that these things enter into all the happiness which he enjoys, and that without them he and his countrymen would be hermits and savages. Without religion man becomes in a short time a beast of prey, and wastes the happiness of his fellow-men with as little remorse as the wolf or the tiger, and to a degree which leaves their ravages out of remembrance. Even if this were not the melancholy fact, the list of individual enjoyments is as much more valuable in a community where religion prevails, than where it does not, as the safety, peace, and pleasure of civilized society are more desirable than the exposure, discord, and misery produced by the furious and malignant passions of uncultivated man.

Those, who consider the legislature in supporting the public worship of God as doing that which is unlawful, found this doctrine upon what they conceive to be revelation. In support of it they allege such things as the following: that Christ has declared his kingdom not to be of this world, that the gates of Hell shall never prevail against it, and that he said to the apostles, "Freely ye have received, freely give;" together with various other things of the like nature.

Every man, who soberly alleges scruples of conscience in any case, has a claim to be answered with seriousness and delicacy. To this class of objectors, therefore, I answer, When Christ declared his kingdom not to be of this world, he had not even the remotest reference to the subject in hand. He merely replied to the accusation, which the Jews brought against him to Pilate, *viz.* that he claimed to be a king, and was therefore a rebel against the government of Cæsar.

It is however admitted in the fullest sense, that the kingdom of Christ is not of this world; that, as Christ declared, it is within man; and that, as St. Paul declares, it consists in "righteousness, peace, and joy in the Holy Ghost." But I ask, what reference had this to the point in debate? For myself I confess, I am unable to see the application of it so far as to find any thing to be answered. In the interference of the magistrate to support the public worship of God, there is not even a reference to this doctrine, either friendly or hostile. Nor can I conceive how man can intermeddle with the subject at all, unless by declaring himself to be the author of regeneration, or to be able and disposed to resist the real author, the Holy Ghost. When the public support of the worship of God shall be shown to be unfavourable to the existence of regeneration, or to the disposition produced by it, and thus to oppose the spiritual kingdom of Christ, it will then be a proper time to cite this text as an argument against such an interference of the legislature. But should their interference be favourable to this great purpose, as, if we argue from all human experience, it must be, he, who

understanding the subject would hinder it, must renounce every pretension to the character of a Christian.

"But Christ," it is said, "has promised, that the gates of Hell shall never prevail against his church; and, as he himself has engaged to support it, the aid of the civil magistrate can neither be necessary nor proper." This promise I believe without a doubt; but the inference I shall take the liberty to question. The promise is this, and nothing but this: that there shall be, throughout the ages of time, a church of Christ in the world. It contains not, therefore, the least encouragement, that for any length of time the kingdom of Christ will exist in any given country. In perfect accordance with this promise, Great Britain may be the seat of Christianity, and New-England a forest of savages, or a revelling house of infidels. But the first and great concern of the people of New-England is to secure the blessings of this kingdom to themselves, and to their posterity. To this object I assert, in contradiction to the above mentioned inference, that the aid of the magistrate is both proper and necessary. Miracles have ceased. The extraordinary and immediately perceptible agency of Christ in this business cannot therefore be expected, and will not be employed. Whatever is to be done, except the work of sanctification, which man cannot do, is to be done by man as the instrument of his Maker. Man is to "plant, and water;" and then, and then only, is warranted either to hope, or to pray, that "God will give the increase."

Men are to build churches; to qualify themselves to become ministers of the Gospel; to preach the Gospel; to settle ministers; to support them when they are settled; to secure to them that support, that they may be enabled to fulfil the duty of "providing for their own households," and thus be safe from the charge of having "denied the faith, and being worse than infidels." Of this safety there is no other possible foundation but a contract. Every contract, which is not immoral, or of which the fulfilment is not impossible, the legislature of every country, especially of every Christian country, is not only authorized, but, so far as it is able, bound to enforce. In this manner, and in this only, will they and their children be furnished with ministers, qualified to teach them divine knowledge, and to impress on their hearts the duties of the Gospel. In this manner only will they secure themselves and their children from being left to the guidance of ignorant men, who, instead of being qualified to teach, are neither able nor willing to learn.

In this manner will they shut out of the desk men, to whom common sense instinctively cries, "Physician, heal thyself." These men, who in all countries have been the disturbers of ecclesiastical peace and good order, will in this manner, and in this only, be silenced. For no body of decent men will vote a decent fixed salary to a person of this character.

But it is said, that "the apostles received freely," and were commanded "freely to give." The apostles, on a miraculous mission, and endured with miraculous powers, were commanded "to heal the sick, to cleanse the lepers, to raise the dead, to cast out devils, and to preach," as they went, "saying, The Kingdom of Heaven is at hand." The supernatural powers by which these miracles were to be wrought, and which they had received freely from the bounty of Christ, they were commanded to exercise freely for the benefit of those, by whom they should be welcomed into their cities and houses. Is this the commission under which ministers now act? If it is, let them obey its call, as did the apostles. Particularly, "let them provide neither gold, nor silver, nor brass, in their purses, nor scrip, nor two coats, nor shoes, nor yet staves." According to this very commission, they are forbidden to preach the Gospel to any, who will not furnish them with these things. Against those, who do not perform this duty, they are directed "to shake off the dust of their feet:" and it is declared, "that it shall be more tolerable for Sodom and Gomorrah, in the day of judgment, than for them."

The ninth chapter of 1st Corinthians has settled this point for ever. Here Christ has ordained, that "they, who preach the Gospel, shall live of the Gospel." To cut off all debate, so far as debate can be cut off, St. Paul has sanctioned the ordinance, that "they, who preach the Gospel, shall live of the Gospel," by an appeal to the law of Moses, the express injunction of Christ, and the authority of his own inspiration.

But why, it will be asked, may not this living be furnished by a voluntary contribution? There are undoubtedly cases in which it may. In large towns, congregations may be ordinarily gathered, sufficiently numerous, and sufficiently liberal, to build one or more churches, and to support one or more ministers. In smaller towns this would ordinarily be impossible; and I suppose the objector himself will admit, that it is at least as necessary for the inhabitants of smaller towns to have ministers as for those of cities; especially as they constitute the mass of people in all countries. In such towns the whole burthen of supporting ministers by contribution would fall upon a few individuals. But these could not sustain this burthen, and ministers, of course, could not live. In such towns, therefore, there will upon this plan be no ministers; I mean none such as the Gospel requires: "Workmen who need not to be ashamed; who rightly divide the word of truth; who give attendance to reading, to exhortation, and to doctrine; who meditate upon these things, and give themselves wholly to them; so that their profiting may appear unto all."

Besides, St. Paul, 1 Cor. xvi, has determined, that a tax is the right and proper manner of doing all this. In the second verse, he commands the Corinthians "to lay by them somewhat," as a contribution to the relief of their fellow Christians; "every man as God had prospered them." Between contributions for their fellow Christians and contributions for ministers there is no moral difference. The contribution of a sum, in proportion to the prosperity God has given men, is a tax: for a tax is nothing but a regular and proportional contribution. This proportion cannot be established but by authority; for, except by authority, men cannot be required to render an account of their circumstances. Nor can any proportion approach so near to equity as that, which is formed under the direction of the legislature. Here, then, the rule of St. Paul, the rule established by God, is as exactly pursued as it can be by human wisdom: and, if it was a right rule in one ecclesiastical case, it is a rule equally right in every other.

If we look to facts; we shall find the same doctrine supported with illustrious evidence. In the year 1793 I was a member of the general assembly of the Presbyterian church. There were then, if I do not misremember, four hundred and twelve congregations, belonging to this church, within the United States, south of New-England; and two hundred and nine congregations in the state of Connecticut alone. To supply these Presbyterian congregations, there were two hundred and four ministers. In Connecticut there were, in the year 1790, 237,946 inhabitants, and in the states south of New-England, 2,920,478. In the year 1798 there were, belonging to the Presbyterian church, two hundred and forty-two ministers; of whom thirty-three were without any charge; or, in the language of New-England, were not *settled ministers*. Two hundred and nine ministers, therefore, supplied, so far as they were supplied at all, the whole number of Presbyterian congregations south of New-England. The number of congregations at that time cannot be ascertained, as the returns were in this respect imperfect. These ministers supplied two hundred and ninety congregations; eighty-one being what are called pluralities: and there were one hundred and forty-two vacancies returned. Five presbyteries made no returns of the vacancies within their bounds. If we suppose the vacancies in these presbyteries to be eighteen, the number will be one hundred and sixty. This number will make the whole four hundred and thirty. With this numerous train of vacancies, there were thirty ministers still, who were unsettled. It follows irresistibly, either that the congregations were so small as to be unable to support ministers, or so indifferent to religion as to be unwilling.

The number of vacancies in Connecticut, at that time, I am unable precisely to ascertain. Twenty may perhaps be assumed as the probable number. There were then, at that time within the state, one hundred and eighty-nine ministers.

In the year 1800, there were in Connecticut 251,-002 inhabitants; and, in the states south of New-England, 4,033,775. The whole account, according to this estimate, will stand thus.

There were, in 1798,

	Congregations	Ministers	Vacancies	Pluralities	Ministers not settled	Inhabitants
In Connecticut	209	189	20	0	5	251,002
In the states south of New-England	430	242	160	81	33	4,033,776

In Connecticut, then, a sixteenth of the number of inhabitants form two hundred and nine congregations, and support one hundred and eighty-nine ministers. Of these congregations, twenty were vacant, and five of the ministers were unsettled. In the states south of New-England, sixteen times the number of inhabitants formed four hundred and thirty congregations, of which eighty-one were pluralities, and one hundred and sixty were vacant, or without ministers. The ministers supported and settled were two hundred and nine. If these states contained congregations, and were supplied with ministers in the same proportion as Connecticut, the whole number of congregations would be three thousand three hundred and forty-four; and the whole number of ministers settled and supported would be three thousand and twenty-four. In this estimate we have a fair specimen of the natural consequence of establishing or neglecting to establish the public worship of God by the law of the land. In Connecticut

every inhabitant, who is not precluded by disease or inclination, may hear the Gospel, and celebrate the public worship of God, every sabbath. In the states specified it is not improbable, that a number of people, several times as great as the census of Connecticut, have scarcely heard a sermon or a prayer in their lives.

The only objection, which I can foresee, against this estimate is, that although the number of Presbyterian congregations in Connecticut is much greater in proportion than that in the states specified, yet this difference is, to a great extent, lessened by the superior proportion of congregations, formed by other classes of Christians in those states. The number of Episcopal congregations in Connecticut, including twenty-six pluralities, is sixty-one; the number of Baptist congregations sixty-seven; making in the aggregate one hundred and twenty-eight. It is doubted whether a correct estimate of the congregations, formed by these and other classes of Christians, in the two fields of inquiry, would be materially different from that which has been already given. This estimate, however, cannot be made, there being no data from which it may be derived. I have chosen the Presbyterian congregations as the subject of inquiry, because the numbers were attainable from returns in my possession.

An examination of the religious state of Massachusetts would have given a result not essentially different.

In a happy conformity to this estimate, and the scheme here supported, has been the prevalence of religion in these two states. It is doubted whether there is a collection of ministers in the world, whose labours have been more prosperous, or under whose preaching a greater proportion of those who heard them have become the subjects of real piety. I know of no country in which revivals of religion have been so frequent, or in proportion to the number of inhabitants so extensive, as in these two states. God, therefore, may be considered as having thus far manifested his own approbation of the system. If at the same time we advert to the peace, the good order, the regular distribution of justice, the universal existence of schools, the universal enjoyment of the education which they communicate, and the extension of superior education, it will be difficult for a sober man not to perceive, that the smiles of Heaven have regularly accompanied this system from its commencement to the present time. I need not, however, have gone any further for the illustration of this subject than to a comparison of the states of Rhode-Island and Connecticut. The former of these, independently of Providence, Newport, and two or three other small towns, is in all these important particulars a mere contrast to the latter. Yet these states were planted by colonies from the same nation, lie in the same climate, and are separated merely by a meridional line. A sober man, who knows them both, can hardly hesitate, whatever may have been his original opinion concerning this subject, to believe, that a legislature is bound to establish the public worship of God.

VIRGINIA

IN 1781, the secretary of the French Legation at Philadelphia made an effort to learn something of the country to which he was accredited. Among the people he questioned was the governor of Virginia. The problems of a state in the turmoil of invasion were too acute to allow Jefferson to make any immediate reply but consideration of the secretary's queries provoked the reflections which were printed in Paris as the *Notes on Virginia* (1784).

It is the mind of Thomas Jefferson (1743–1826) rather than the social scene of Revolutionary Virginia that the *Notes* actually portray. Jefferson defends the American Indian from European slurs. He sees slavery as an unqualified wrong inflicted on Virginia by the policy of a foreign government, and now so interwoven with her economy that eliminating the ill may all but ruin the patient. But for Jefferson a wrong did not become less in proportion to the number of people it profited. In this, the only sustained work in all the bulk of Jefferson's published writings, he sets out his social ideals: complete religious liberty, since the relation between a man and his God is of no concern to any other man, or to society; the preservation of the small freeholder, since only economically independent men can be sufficiently free of external pressure to make republican government function; and an adequate system of education, since only knowledge would equip the electorate with the judgment necessary to proper exercise of the franchise.

Those three problems continued to exercise Jefferson through all the years of his life. He fought to leave men free in their faith, and the expression of that fight was the Virginia Statute of Religious Liberty. He fought to keep American society based on farmers who held their land unburdened by taxes laid to support the schemes of stockjobbers. The expression of that fight is Jefferson's opposition to the Hamiltonian program of strengthening the Federal government and drawing the moneyed classes to its support. Education remained Jefferson's concern to the end; the last diversion of his life was the establishment of the University of Virginia.

The selection here reprinted is from the Thomas Jefferson Memorial Association of the *Works* (20 vols. in 10, Washington, 1907).

Notes on Virginia

BY THOMAS JEFFERSON

QUERY: THE NUMBER OF ITS INHABITANTS?

. . . DURING THE INFANCY of the colony, while numbers were small, wars, importations, and other accidental circumstances render the progression fluctuating and irregular. By the year 1654, however, it becomes tolerably uniform, importations having in a great measure ceased from the dissolution of the company, and the inhabitants become too numerous to be sensibly affected by Indian wars. Beginning at that period, therefore, we find that from thence to the year 1772, our tythes had increased from 7,209 to 153,000. The whole term being of one hundred and eighteen years, yields a duplication once in every twenty-seven and a quarter years. The intermediate enumerations taken in 1700, 1748, and 1759, furnish proofs of the uniformity of this progression. Should this rate of increase continue, we shall have between six and seven millions of inhabitants within ninety-five years. If we suppose our country to be bounded, at some future day, by the meridian of the mouth of the Great Kanhaway, (within which it has been before conjectured, are 64,461 square miles) there will then be one hundred inhabitants for every square mile, which is nearly the state of population in the British Islands.

Here I will beg leave to propose a doubt. The present desire of America is to produce rapid population by as great importations of foreigners as possible. But is this founded in good policy? The advantage proposed is the multiplication of numbers. Now let us suppose (for example only) that, in this state, we could double our numbers in one year by the importation of foreigners; and this is a greater accession than the most sanguine advocate for emigration has a right to expect. Then I say, beginning with a double stock, we shall attain any given degree of population only twenty-seven years, and three months sooner than if we proceed on our single stock. If we propose four millions and a half as a competent population for this State, we should be fifty-four and a half years attaining it, could we at once double our numbers; and eighty-one and three quarters years, if we rely on natural propagation, as may be seen by the following tablet:

	Proceeding on our present stock	Proceeding on a double stock
1781	567,614	1,135,228
1808¼	1,135,228	2,270,456
1835½	2,270,456	4,540,912
1862¾	4,540,912	

In the first column are stated periods of twenty-seven and a quarter years; in the second are our numbers at each period, as they will be if we proceed on our actual stock; and in the third are what they would be, at the same periods, were we to set out from the double of our present stock. I have taken the term of four million and a half of inhabitants for example's sake only. Yet I am persuaded it is a greater number than the country spoken of, considering how much inarable land it contains, can clothe and feed without a material change in the quality of their diet. But are there no inconveniences to be thrown into the scale against the advantage expected from a multiplication of numbers by the importation of foreigners? It is for the happiness of those united in society to harmonize as much as possible in matters which they must of necessity transact together. Civil government being the sole object of forming societies, its administration must be conducted by common consent. Every species of government has its specific principles. Ours perhaps are more

peculiar than those of any other in the universe. It is a composition of the freest principles of the English constitution, with others derived from natural right and natural reason. To these nothing can be more opposed than the maxims of absolute monarchies. Yet from such we are to expect the greatest number of emigrants. They will bring with them the principles of the governments they leave, imbibed in their early youth; or, if able to throw them off, it will be in exchange for an unbounded licentiousness, passing, as is usual, from one extreme to another. It would be a miracle were they to stop precisely at the point of temperate liberty. These principles, with their language, they will transmit to their children. In proportion to their numbers, they will share with us the legislation. They will infuse into it their spirit, warp and bias its directions, and render it a heterogenous, incoherent, distracted mass. I may appeal to experience, during the present contest, for a verification of these conjectures. But, if they be not certain in event, are they not possible, are they not probable? Is it not safer to wait with patience twenty-seven years and three months longer, for the attainment of any degree of population desired or expected? May not our government be more homogeneous, more peaceable, more durable? Suppose twenty millions of republican Americans thrown all of a sudden into France, what would be the condition of that kingdom? If it would be more turbulent, less happy, less strong, we may believe that the addition of half a million of foreigners to our present numbers would produce a similar effect here. If they come of themselves they are entitled to all the rights of citizenship; but doubt the expediency of inviting them by extraordinary encouragements. I mean not that these doubts should be extended to the importation of useful artificers. The policy of that measure depends on very different considerations. Spare no expense in obtaining them. They will after a while go to the plough and the hoe; but, in the mean time, they will teach us something we do not know. It is not so in agriculture. The indifferent state of that among us does not proceed from a want of knowledge merely; it is from our having such quantities of land to waste as we please. In Europe the object is to make the most of their land, labor being abundant; here it is to make the most of our labor land being abundant. . . .

QUERY: THE CONSTITUTION OF THE STATE AND ITS SEVERAL CHARTERS?

. . . This constitution was formed when we were new and unexperienced in the science of government. It was the first, too, which was formed in the whole United States. No wonder then that time and trial have discovered very capital defects in it.

1. The majority of the men in the State, who pay and fight for its support, are unrepresented in the legislature, the roll of freeholders entitled to vote not including generally the half of those on the roll of the militia, or of the tax-gatherers.

2. Among those who share the representation, the shares are very unequal. Thus the county of Warwick, with only one hundred fighting men, has an equal representation with the county of Loudon, which has one thousand seven hundred and forty-six. So that every man in Warwick has as much influence in the government as seventeen men in Loudon. But lest it should be thought that an equal interspersion of small among large counties, through the whole State, may prevent any danger of injury to particular parts of it, we will divide it into districts, and show the proportions of land, of fighting men, and of representation in each:

	Square Miles	Fighting Men	Dele-gates	Sena-tors
Between the sea-coast and falls of the rivers	11,205	19,012	71	12
Between the falls of the rivers and Blue Ridge of mountains	18,759	18,828	46	8
Between the Blue Ridge and the Alleghany	11,911	7,673	16	2
Between the Alleghany and Ohio	79,650	4,458	16	2
Total	121,525	49,971	149	24

An inspection of this table will supply the place of commentaries on it. It will appear at once that nineteen thousand men, living below the falls of the rivers, possess half the senate, and want four members only of possessing a majority of the house of delegates; a want more than supplied by the vicinity of their situation to the seat of government, and of course the greater degree of convenience and punctuality with which their members may and will attend in the legislature. These nineteen thousand, therefore, living in one part of the country, give law to upwards of thirty thousand living in another, and appoint all their chief officers, executive and judiciary. From the difference of their situation and circumstances, their interests will often be very different.

3. The senate is, by its constitution, too homogeneous with the house of delegates. Being chosen by the same electors, at the same time, and out of the same subjects, the choice falls of course on men of the same description. The purpose of establishing different houses of legislation is to introduce the influence of different interests or different principles. Thus in Great Britain it is said their constitution relies on the house of commons for honesty, and the lords for wisdom; which would be a rational reliance, if honesty were to be bought with money, and if wisdom were hereditary. In some of the American States, the delegates and senators are so chosen, as that the first represent the persons, and the second the property of the State. But with us, wealth and wisdom have equal chance for admission into both houses. We do not, therefore, derive from the separation of our legislature into two houses, those benefits which a proper complication of principles are capable of producing, and those which alone can compensate the evils which may be produced by their dissensions.

4. All the powers of government, legislative, executive, and judiciary, result to the legislative body. The concentrating these in the same hands is precisely the definition of despotic government. It will be no alleviation that these powers will be exercised by a plurality of hands, and not by a single one. One hundred and seventy-three despots would surely be as oppressive as one. Let those who doubt it turn their eyes on the republic of Venice. As little will it avail us that they are chosen by ourselves. An *elective despotism* was not the government we fought for, but one which should not only be founded on free principles, but in which the powers of government should be so divided and balanced among several bodies of magistracy, as that no one could transcend their legal limits, without being effectually checked and restrained by the others. For this reason that convention which passed the ordinance of government, laid its foundation on this basis, that the legislative, executive, and judiciary departments should be separate and distinct, so that no person should exercise the powers of more than one of them at the same time. But no barrier was provided between these several powers. The judiciary and executive members were left dependent on the legislative, for their subsistence in office, and some of them for their continuance in it. If, therefore, the legislature assumes executive and judiciary powers, no opposition is likely to be made; nor, if made, can it be effectual; because in that case they may put their proceedings into the form of an act of assembly, which will render them obligatory on the other branches. They have, accordingly, in many instances, decided rights which should have been left to judiciary controversy; and the direction of the executive, during

the whole time of their session, is becoming habitual and familiar. And this is done with no ill intention. The views of the present members are perfectly upright. When they are led out of their regular province, it is by art in others, and inadvertence in themselves. And this will probably be the case for some time to come. But it will not be a very long time. Mankind soon learn to make interested uses of every right and power which they possess, or may assume. The public money and public liberty, intended to have been deposited with three branches of magistracy, but found inadvertently to be in the hands of one only, will soon be discovered to be sources of wealth and dominion to those who hold them; distinguished, too, by this tempting circumstance, that they are the instrument, as well as the object of acquisition. With money we will get men, said Cæsar, and with men we will get money. Nor should our assembly be deluded by the integrity of their own purposes, and conclude that these unlimited powers will never be abused, because themselves are not disposed to abuse them. They should look forward to a time, and that not a distant one, when a corruption in this, as in the country from which we derive our origin, will have seized the heads of government, and be spread by them through the body of the people; when they will purchase the voices of the people, and make them pay the price. Human nature is the same on every side of the Atlantic, and will be alike influenced by the same causes. The time to guard against corruption and tyranny, is before they shall have gotten hold of us. It is better to keep the wolf out of the fold, than to trust to drawing his teeth and claws after he shall have entered— . . .

QUERY: THE ADMINISTRATION OF JUSTICE AND THE DESCRIPTION OF THE LAWS?

. . . Another object of the revisal is to diffuse knowledge more generally through the mass of the people. This bill proposes to lay off every county into small districts of five or six miles square, called hundreds, and in each of them to establish a school for teaching reading, writing, and arithmetic. The tutor to be supported by the hundred, and every person in it entitled to send their children three years gratis, and as much longer as they please, paying for it. These schools to be under a visitor who is annually to choose the boy of best genius in the school, of those whose parents are too poor to give them further education, and to send him forward to one of the grammar schools, of which twenty are proposed to be erected in different parts of the country, for teaching Greek, Latin, geography, and the higher branches of numerical arithmetic. Of the boys thus sent in any one year, trial is to be made at the grammar schools one or two years, and the best genius of the whole selected, and continued six years, and the residue dismissed. By this means twenty of the best geniuses will be raked from the rubbish annually, and be instructed, at the public expense, so far as the grammar schools go. At the end of six years' instruction, one-half are to be discontinued (from among whom the grammar schools will probably be supplied with future masters); and the other half, who are to be chosen for the superiority of their parts and disposition, are to be sent and continued three years in the study of such sciences as they shall choose, at William and Mary College, the plan of which is proposed to be enlarged, as will be hereafter explained, and extended to all the useful sciences. The ultimate result of the whole scheme of education would be the teaching all the children of the State reading, writing, and common arithmetic; turning out ten annually, of superior genius, well taught in Greek, Latin, geography, and the higher branches of arithmetic; turning out ten others annually, of still superior parts, who, to those branches of learning, shall have added such of the sciences as their genius shall have led them to; the furnishing to the wealthier part of the people convenient schools at which their children may be educated at their own expense. The general objects of this law are to provide an education adapted to the years, to the capacity, and the condition of every one, and directed to their freedom and happiness. Specific details were not proper for the law. These must be the business of the visitors entrusted with its execution. The first stage of this education being the schools of the hundreds, wherein the great mass of the people will receive their instruction, the principal foundations of future order will be laid here. Instead, therefore, of putting the Bible and Testament into the hands of the children at an age when their judgments are not sufficiently matured for religious inquiries, their memories may here be stored with the most useful facts from Grecian, Roman, European and American history. The first elements of morality too may be installed into their minds; such as, when further developed as their judgments advance in strength, may teach them how to work out their own greatest happiness, by showing them that it does not depend on the condition of life in which chance has placed them, but is always the result of a good conscience, good health, occupation, and freedom in all just pursuits. Those whom either the wealth of their parents or the adoption of the State shall destine to higher degrees of learning, will go on to the grammar schools, which constitute the next stage, there to be instructed in the languages. The learning Greek and Latin, I am told, is going into disuse in Europe. I know not what their manners and occupations may call for; but it would be very ill-judged in us to follow their example in this instance. There is a certain period of life, say from eight to fifteen or sixteen years of age, when the mind like the body is not yet firm enough for laborious and close operations. If applied to such, it falls an early victim to premature exertion; exhibiting, indeed, at first, in these young and tender subjects, the flattering appearance of their being men while they are yet children, but ending in reducing them to be children when they should be men. The memory is then most susceptible and tenacious of impressions; and the learning of languages being chiefly a work of memory, it seems precisely fitted to the powers of this period, which is long enough, too, for acquiring the most useful languages, ancient and modern. I do not pretend that language is science. It is only an instrument for the attainment of science. But that time is not lost which is employed in providing tools for future operation; more especially as in this case the books put into the hands of the youth for this purpose may be such as will at the same time impress their minds with useful facts and good principles. If this period be suffered to pass in idleness, the mind becomes lethargic and impotent, as would the body it inhabits if unexercised during the same time. The sympathy between body and mind during their rise, progress and decline, is too strict and obvious to endanger our being misled while we reason from the one to the other. As soon as they are of sufficient age, it is supposed they will be sent on from the grammar schools to the university, which constitutes our third and last stage, there to study those sciences which may be adapted to their views. By that part of our plan which prescribes the selection of the youths of genius from among the classes of the poor, we hope to avail the State of those talents which nature has sown as liberally among the poor as the rich, but which perish without use, if not sought for and cultivated. But of all the views of this law none is more important, none more legitimate, than that of rendering the people the safe, as they are the ultimate, guardians of their own liberty. For this purpose the reading in the first stage, where *they* will receive their whole education, is proposed, as has been said, to be chiefly historical. History, by apprising them of the past,

will enable them to judge of the future; it will avail them of the experience of other times and other nations; it will qualify them as judges of the actions and designs of men; it will enable them to know ambition under every disguise it may assume; and knowing it, to defeat its views. In every government on earth is some trace of human weakness, some germ of corruption and degeneracy, which cunning will discover, and wickedness insensibly open, cultivate, and improve. Every government degenerates when trusted to the rulers of the people alone. The people themselves, therefore, are its only safe depositories. And to render even them safe, their minds must be improved to a certain degree. This indeed is not all that is necessary, though it be essentially necessary. An amendment of our constitution must here come in aid of the public education. The influence over government must be shared among all the people. If every individual which composes their mass participates of the ultimate authority, the government will be safe; because the corrupting the whole mass will exceed any private resources of wealth; and public ones cannot be provided but by levies on the people. In this case every man would have to pay his own price. The government of Great Britain has been corrupted, because but one man in ten has a right to vote for members of parliament. The sellers of the government, therefore, get nine-tenths of their price clear. It has been thought that corruption is restrained by confining the right of suffrage to a few of the wealthier of the people; but it would be more effectually restrained by an extension of that right to such members as would bid defiance to the means of corruption.

Lastly, it is proposed, by a bill in this revisal, to begin a public library and gallery, by laying out a certain sum annually in books, paintings, and statues. . . .

QUERY: THE PARTICULAR CUSTOMS AND MANNERS THAT MAY HAPPEN TO BE RECEIVED IN THAT STATE?

It is difficult to determine on the standard by which the manners of a nation may be tried, whether *catholic* or *particular*. It is more difficult for a native to bring to that standard the manners of his own nation, familiarized to him by habit. There must doubtless be an unhappy influence on the manners of our people produced by the existence of slavery among us. The whole commerce between master and slave is a perpetual exercise of the most boisterous passions, the most unremitting despotism on the one part, and degrading submissions on the other. Our children see this, and learn to imitate it; for man is an imitative animal. This quality is the germ of all education in him. From his cradle to his grave he is learning to do what he sees others do. If a parent could find no motive either in his philanthropy or his self-love, for restraining the intemperance of passion towards his slave, it should always be a sufficient one that his child is present. But generally it is not sufficient. The parent storms, the child looks on, catches the lineaments of wrath, puts on the same airs in the circle of smaller slaves, gives a loose to the worst of passions, and thus nursed, educated, and daily exercised in tyranny, cannot but be stamped by it with odious peculiarities. The man must be a prodigy who can retain his manners and morals undepraved by such circumstances. And with what execration should the statesman be loaded, who, permitting one-half the citizens thus to trample on the rights of the other, transforms those into despots, and these into enemies, destroys the morals of the one part, and the *amor patriæ* of the other. For if a slave can have a country in this world, it must be any other in preference to that in which he is born to live and labor for another; in which he must lock up the faculties of his nature, contribute as far as depends on his individual endeavors to the evanishment of the human race, or entail his own miserable condition on the endless generations proceeding from him. With the morals of the people, their industry also is destroyed. For in a warm climate, no man will labor for himself who can make another labor for him. This is so true, that of the proprietors of slaves a very small proportion indeed are ever seen to labor. And can the liberties of a nation be thought secure when we have removed their only firm basis, a conviction in the minds of the people that these liberties are of the gift of God? That they are not to be violated but with His wrath? Indeed I tremble for my country when I reflect that God is just; that his justice cannot sleep forever; that considering numbers, nature and natural means only, a revolution of the wheel of fortune, an exchange of situation is among possible events; that it may become probable by supernatural interference! The Almighty has no attribute which can take side with us in such a contest. But it is impossible to be temperate and to pursue this subject through the various considerations of policy, of morals, of history natural and civil. We must be contented to hope they will force their way into every one's mind. I think a change already perceptible, since the origin of the present revolution. The spirit of the master is abating, that of the slave rising from the dust, his condition mollifying, the way I hope preparing, under the auspices of heaven, for a total emancipation, and that this is disposed, in the order of events, to be with the consent of the masters, rather than by their extirpation.

QUERY: THE PUBLIC INCOME AND EXPENSES?

. . . To this estimate of our abilities, let me add a word as to the application of them, if, when cleared of the present contest, and of the debts with which that will charge us, we come to measure force hereafter with any European power. Such events are devoutly to be deprecated. Young as we are, and with such a country before us to fill with people and with happiness, we should point in that direction the whole generative force of nature, wasting none of it in efforts of mutual destruction. It should be our endeavor to cultivate the peace and friendship of every nation, even of that which has injured us most, when we shall have carried our point against her. Our interest will be to throw open the doors of commerce, and to knock off all its shackles, giving perfect freedom to all persons for the vent of whatever they may choose to bring into our ports, and asking the same in theirs. Never was so much false arithmetic employed on any subject, as that which has been employed to persuade nations that it is their interest to go to war. Were the money which it has cost to gain, at the close of a long war, a little town, or a little territory, the right to cut wood here, or to catch fish there, expended in improving what they already possess, in making roads, opening rivers, building ports, improving the arts, and finding employment for their idle poor, it would render them much stronger, much wealthier and happier. This I hope will be our wisdom. And, perhaps, to remove as much as possible the occasions of making war, it might be better for us to abandon the ocean altogether, that being the element whereon we shall be principally exposed to jostle with other nations; to leave to others to bring what we shall want, and to carry what we can spare. This would make us invulnerable to Europe, by offering none of our property to their prize, and would turn all our citizens to the cultivation of the earth; and, I repeat it again, cultivators of the earth are the most virtuous and independent citizens. It might be time enough to seek employment for them at sea, when the land no longer offers it. But the actual habits of our countrymen attach them to commerce. They will exercise it for themselves. Wars then must sometimes be our lot; and all the wise can do, will be to avoid that half of them which would be produced by our own follies and our own acts of injustice; and to make for the other half the best preparations we can. Of what nature should these be? A land army would be useless for offence, and not the best nor safest instrument of defence. For either of these purposes, the sea is the field on which we should meet an European enemy. On that element it is necessary we should possess some power. To aim at such a navy as the greater nations of Europe possess, would be a foolish and wicked waste of the energies of our countrymen. It would be to pull on our own heads that load of military expense which makes the European laborer go supperless to bed, and moistens his bread with the sweat of his brows. It will be enough if we enable ourselves to prevent insults from those nations of Europe which are weak on the sea, because circumstances exist, which render even the stronger ones weak as to us. Providence has placed their richest and most defenceless possessions at our door; has obliged their most precious commerce to pass, as it were, in review before us. To protect this, or to assail, a small part only of their naval force will ever be risked across the Atlantic. The dangers to which the elements expose them here are too well known, and the greater dangers to which they would be exposed at home were any general calamity to involve their whole fleet. They can attack us by detachment only; and it will suffice to make ourselves equal to what they may detach.

Even a smaller force than they may detach will be rendered equal or superior by the quickness with which any check may be repaired with us, while losses with them will be irreparable till too late. A small naval force then is sufficient for us, and a small one is necessary. What this should be, I will not undertake to say. I will only say, it should by no means be so great as we are able to make it. Suppose the million dollars, or three hundred thousand pounds, which Virginia could annually spare without distress, to be applied to the creating a navy. A single year's contribution would build, equip, man, and send to sea a force which should carry three hundred guns. The rest of the confederacy, exerting themselves in the same proportion, would equip in the same time fifteen hundred guns more. So that one year's contributions would set up a navy of eighteen hundred guns. The British ships of the line average seventy-six guns; their frigates thirty-eight. Eighteen hundred guns then would form a fleet of thirty ships, eighteen of which might be of the line, and twelve frigates. Allowing eight men, the British average, for every gun, their annual expense, including subsistence, clothing, pay, and ordinary repairs, would be about $1,280 for every gun, or $2,304,000 for the whole. I state this only as one year's possible exertion, without deciding whether more or less than a year's exertion should be thus applied. . . .

THE CONSTITUTIONAL CONVENTION

WITH SHAYS'S REBELLION, economic recession, British retention of the northwest posts, and Spanish intrigues among the settlers on the western waters of Kentucky and Tennessee as warnings, conservative and commercial men were ready to work for a government more effective than the Confederation Congress had proved. First, Maryland and Virginia conferred regarding a convention for mutual defense and control of waterways. Then, a few months later, in 1785, Maryland suggested that Pennsylvania and Delaware, which shared in the Chesapeake trade, be invited to join in the proposed settlement.

In 1786, Virginia's Assembly extended the invitation to include all the states. They were urged to confer, consider the state of the country's commerce, and report a plan which would enable Congress to deal vigorously with foreign powers, particularly England. By May, when the proposed convention was to meet at Annapolis, only Virginia was sufficiently interested to send a full delegation. Maryland was not represented; Pennsylvania sent one deputy; the delegates from Massachusetts and New Hampshire did not arrive until after the convention had adjourned. Despite the states' evident lack of concern, the few deputies present adopted a series of resolutions, often credited to Hamilton, detailing the weakness of the Confederation and urging that a convention be held to report measures for strengthening the government.

New York had proposed a convention to revise the Articles of Confederation in 1782. Later, Madison and the Massachusetts legislature had each suggested similar action, but it was not until after the abortive commercial convention at Annapolis that this became a possibility. Although the meeting was called for Philadelphia, the second Monday in May, 1787, the Convention did not organize until eleven days later. From the twenty-fifth of May until the seventeenth of September the Convention sat in secret session, being interrupted by only two adjournments.

If the number of delegates who kept more or less careful records of the proceedings is any index, several of the members were aware that they were engaged in a really momentous effort, one that would demonstrate the practicability of establishing a strong, stable, free government by rational process.

The first project presented was offered by the Virginia delegation whose chairman recited the defects of the Articles of Confederation and declared: "Our chief danger arises from the democratic parts of our constitutions. It is a maxim which I hold incontrovertible that the powers of government exercised by the people swallows up the other branches. None of the constitutions have provided sufficient checks against the democracy." From May 30 until June 13 the Convention discussed the Virginia Plan in Committee of the Whole.

After the Virginia Plan had been reported to the Convention on June 13, William Paterson of New Jersey moved for postponement to permit the preparation of a plan to revise the Articles of Confederation on a "purely Federal" principle. When that plan was offered to the Convention and referred to the Committee of the Whole, Madison declared it the work of members from Connecticut, New York, New Jersey, Delaware, and of Martin of Maryland. New York and Connecticut wanted to increase the powers of the Confederation Congress while New Jersey and Delaware wished to retain an equal representation of the states, Madison noted. The New Jersey Plan was discussed from June 16 to 18, and then the Committee of the Whole recommended that the Convention return to consider the amended version of the Virginia Plan. Though the New Jersey proposals were thus dismissed, some of the demands in them were recognized, notably in the "compromise" by which each state received equal representation in the Senate.

It was during the discussion of the New Jersey Plan that Alexander Hamilton rose to address the Convention. In addition to his five-hour speech, Hamilton presented written proposals which exist only in a later version found among his papers. Since the Convention sat in secret, its proceedings were heatedly discussed in the troubled decades following; few of those proceedings became the object of more contention than the Hamilton "plan." Hamilton found it necessary to deny that he had wished to abolish the states or that he had suggested a monarchy. In the draft found among Hamilton's papers, the House of Representatives was to be chosen by free white males and to have the power of impeachment. The Senate was to be chosen by electors selected by men who held landed estates for life or for fourteen unexpired years of lease. The President was to be chosen by electors who were to choose electors in their turn. If the first electors could not elect a President by majority vote, then the second electors were to ballot. Like Senators and Judges, the President was to hold office during good behavior. He was to have an absolute veto over federal legislation. The United States was to appoint state governors, who were to hold office until replaced and to negate laws as the United States Legislature might prescribe.

Madison's notes are used in the presentation of the Virginia and New Jersey plans. Hamilton's plan is presented twice: first from Madison's notes, then from Yates's. The selections are reprinted from *Documents Illustrative of the Formation of the Union of the American States* (Washington, 1927).

The Virginia Plan

BY EDMUND RANDOLPH

RESOLUTIONS PROPOSED BY MR. RANDOLPH IN CONVENTION, MAY 29, 1787

1. Resolved that the articles of Confederation ought to be so corrected & enlarged as to accomplish the objects proposed by their institution; namely. "common defence, security of liberty and general welfare."

2. Resd. therefore that the rights of suffrage in the National Legislature ought to be proportioned to the Quotas of contribution, or to the number of free inhabitants, as the one or the other rule may seem best in different cases.

3. Resd. that the National Legislature ought to consist of two branches.

4. Resd. that the members of the first branch of the National Legislature ought to be elected by the people of the several States every   for the term of   ; to be of the age of   years at least, to receive liberal stipends by which they may be compensated for the devotion of their time to public service; to be ineligible to any office established by a particular State, or under the authority of the United States, except those peculiarly belonging to the functions of the first branch, during the term of service, and for the space of   after its expiration; to be incapable of re-election for the space of   after the expiration of their term of service, and to be subject to recall.

5. Resold. that the members of the second branch of the National Legislature ought to be elected by those of the first, out of a proper number of persons nominated by the individual Legislatures, to be of the age of   years at least; to hold their offices for a term sufficient to ensure their independency, to receive liberal stipends, by which they may be compensated for the devotion of their time to public service; and to be ineligible to any office established by a particular State, or under the authority of the United States, except those peculiarly belonging to the functions of the

second branch, during the term of service, and for the space of   after the expiration thereof.

6. Resolved that each branch ought to possess the right of originating Acts; that the National Legislature ought to be impowered to enjoy the Legislative Rights vested in Congress by the Confederation & moreover to legislate in all cases to which the separate States are incompetent, or in which the harmony of the United States may be interrupted by the exercise of individual Legislation; to negative all laws passed by the several States, contravening in the opinion of the National Legislature the articles of Union; and to call forth the force of the Union agst. any member of the Union failing to fulfill its duty under the articles thereof.

7. Resd. that a National Executive be instituted; to be chosen by the National Legislature for the term of   years, to receive punctually at stated times, a fixed compensation for the services rendered, in which no increase or diminution shall be made so as to affect the Magistracy, existing at the time of increase or diminution, and to be ineligible a second time; and that besides a general authority to execute the National laws, it ought to enjoy the Executive rights vested in Congress by the Confederation.

8. Resd. that the Executive and a convenient number of the National Judiciary, ought to compose a council of revision with authority to examine every act of the National Legislature before it shall operate, & every act of a particular Legislature before a Negative thereon shall be final; and that the dissent of the said Council shall amount to a rejection, unless the Act of the National Legislature be again passed, or that of a particular Legislature be again negatived by   of the members of each branch.

9. Resd. that a National Judiciary be established to consist of one or more supreme tribunals, and of inferior tribunals to be chosen by the National Legislature, to hold their offices during good behaviour; and to receive punctually at stated times fixed compensation for their services, in which no increase or diminution shall be made so as to affect the persons actually in office at the time of such increase or diminution. that the jurisdiction of the inferior tribunals shall be to hear & determine in the first instance, and of the supreme tribunal to hear and determine in the dernier resort, all piracies & felonies on the high seas, captures from an enemy; cases in which foreigners or citizens of other States applying to such jurisdictions may be interested, or which respect the collection of the National revenue; impeachments of any National officers, and questions which may involve the national peace and harmony.

10. Resolvd. that provision ought to be made for the admission of States lawfully arising within the limits of the United States, whether from a voluntary junction of Government & Territory or otherwise, with the consent of a number of voices in the National legislature less than the whole.

11. Resd. that a Republican Government & the territory of each State, except in the instance of a voluntary junction of Government & territory, ought to be guaranteed by the United States to each State

12. Resd. that provision ought to be made for the continuance of Congress and their authorities and privileges, until a given day after the reform of the articles of Union shall be adopted, and for the completion of all their engagements.

13. Resd. that provision ought to be made for the amendment of the Articles of Union whensoever it shall seem necessary, and that the assent of the National Legislature ought not to be required thereto.

14. Resd. that the Legislative Executive & Judiciary powers within the several States ought to be bound by oath to support the articles of Union

15. Resd. that the amendments which shall be offered to the Confederation, by the Convention ought at a proper time, or times, after the approbation of Congress to be submitted to an assembly or assemblies of Representatives, recommended by the several Legislatures to be expressly chosen by the people, to consider & decide thereon.

The New Jersey Plan

BY WILLIAM PATERSON

FRIDAY JUNE 15TH. 1787

MR. PATTERSON, laid before the Convention the plan which he said several of the deputations wished to be substituted in place of that proposed by Mr. Randolph. After some little discussion of the most proper mode of giving it a fair deliberation it was agreed that it should be referred to a Committee of the Whole, and that in order to place the two plans in due comparison, the other should be recommitted. At the earnest desire of Mr. Lansing & some other gentlemen, it was also agreed that the Convention should not go into Committee of the whole on the subject till tomorrow, by which delay the friends of the plan proposed by Mr. Patterson wd. be better prepared to explain & support it, and all would have an opportuy of taking copies.[1]—

The propositions from N. Jersey moved by Mr. Patterson were in the words following.

1. Resd. that the articles of Confederation ought to be so revised, corrected & enlarged, as to render the federal Constitution adequate to the exigences of Government, & the preservation of the Union.

2. Resd. that in addition to the powers vested in the U. States in Congress, by the present existing articles of Confederation, they be authorized to pass acts for raising a revenue, by levying a duty or duties on all goods or merchandizes of foreign growth or manufacture, imported into any part of the U. States, by Stamps on paper, vellum or parchment, and by a postage on all letters or packages passing through the general post-Office, to be applied to such federal purposes as they shall deem proper & expedient; to make rules & regulations for the collection thereof; and the same from time to time, to alter & amend in such manner as they shall think proper: to pass Acts for the regulation of trade & commerce as well with foreign nations as with each other: provided that all punishments, fines, forfeitures & penalties to be incurred for contravening such acts rules and regulations shall be adjudged by the Common law Judiciarys of the State in which any offence contrary to the true intent & meaning of such

[1] (This plan had been concerted among the deputations or members thereof, from Cont. N.Y. N.J. Del. and perhaps Mr Martin from Maryd. who made with them a common cause on different principles. Cont. and N.Y. were agst. a departure from the principle of the Confederation, wishing rather to add a few new powers to Congs. than to substitute, a National Govt. The States of N.J. and Del. were opposed to a National Govt. because its patrons considered a proportional representation of the States as the basis of it. The eagourness displayed by the Members opposed to a Natl. Govt. from these different (motives) began now to produce serious anxiety for the result of the Convention.—Mr. Dickenson said to Mr. Madison you see the consequence of pushing things too far. Some of the members from the small States wish for two branches in the General Legislature, and are friends to a good National Government; but we would sooner submit to a foreign power, than submit to be deprived of an equality of suffrage, in both branches of the legislature, and thereby be thrown under the domination of the large States.)

Acts rules & regulations shall have been committed or perpetrated, with liberty of commencing in the first instance all suits & prosecutions for that purpose in the superior Common law Judiciary in such State, subject nevertheless, for the correction of all errors, both in law & fact in rendering judgment, to an appeal to the Judiciary of the U. States

3. Resd. that whenever requisitions shall be necessary, instead of the rule for making requisitions mentioned in the articles of Confederation, the United States in Congs. be authorized to make such requisitions in proportion to the whole number of white & other free citizens & inhabitants of every age sex and condition including those bound to servitude for a term of years & three fifths of all other persons not comprehended in the foregoing description, except Indians not paying taxes; that if such requisitions be not complied with, in the time specified therein, to direct the collection thereof in the non complying States & for that purpose to devise and pass acts directing & authorizing the same; provided that none of the powers hereby vested in the U. States in Congs. shall be exercised without the consent of at least   States, and in that proportion if the number of Confederated States should hereafter be increased or diminished.

4. Resd. that the U. States in Congs. be authorized to elect a federal Executive to consist of   persons, to continue in office for the term of   years, to receive punctually at stated times a fixed compensation for their services, in which no increase or diminution shall be made so as to affect the persons composing the Executive at the time of such increase or diminution, to be paid out of the federal treasury; to be incapable of holding any other office or appointment during their time of service and for   years thereafter; to be ineligible a second time, & removeable by Congs. on application by a majority of the Executives of the several States; that the Executives besides their general authority to execute the federal acts ought to appoint all federal officers not otherwise provided for, & to direct all military operations; provided that none of the persons composing the federal Executive shall on any occasion take command of any troops, so as personally to conduct any enterprise as General, or in other capacity.

5. Resd. that a federal Judiciary be established to consist of a supreme Tribunal the Judges of which to be appointed by the Executive, & to hold their offices during good behaviour, to receive punctually at stated times a fixed compensation for their services in which no increase or diminution shall be made, so as to affect the persons actu-

ally in office at the time of such increase or diminution; that the Judiciary so established shall have authority to hear & determine in the first instance on all impeachments of federal officers, & by way of appeal in the dernier resort in all cases touching the rights of Ambassadors, in all cases of captures from an enemy, in all cases of piracies & felonies on the high seas, in all cases in which foreigners may be interested, in the construction of any treaty or treaties, or which may arise on any of the Acts for regulation of trade, or the collection of the federal Revenue: that none of the Judiciary shall during the time they remain in Office be capable of receiving or holding any other office or appointment during their time of service, or for   thereafter.

6. Resd. that all Acts of the U. States in Congs. made by virtue & in pursuance of the powers hereby & by the articles of confederation vested in them, and all Treaties made & ratified under the authority of the U. States shall be the supreme law of the respective States so far forth as those Acts or Treaties shall relate to the said States or their Citizens, and that the Judiciary of the several States shall be bound thereby in their decisions, any thing in the respective laws of the Individual States to the contrary notwithstanding; and that if any State, or any body of men in any State shall oppose or prevent ye. carrying into execution such acts or treaties, the federal Executive shall be authorized to call forth ye power of the Confederated States, or so much thereof as may be necessary to enforce and compel an obedience to such Acts, or an Observance of such Treaties.

7. Resd. that provision be made for the admission of new States into the Union.

8. Resd. the rule for naturalization ought to be the same in every State

9. Resd. that a Citizen of one State committing an offence in another State of the Union, shall be deemed guilty of the same offence as if it had been committed by a Citizen of the State in which the Offence was committed.

Adjourned

Alexander Hamilton's Plan

(ACCORDING TO MADISON)

MR. HAMILTON, had been hitherto silent on the business before the Convention, partly from respect to others whose superior abilities age & experience rendered him unwilling to bring forward ideas dissimilar to theirs, and partly from his delicate situation with respect to his own State, to whose sentiments as expressed by his Colleagues, he could by no means accede. The crisis however which now marked our affairs, was too serious to permit any scruples whatever to prevail over the duty imposed on every man to contribute his efforts for the public safety & happiness. He was obliged therefore to declare himself unfriendly to both plans. He was particularly opposed to that from N. Jersey, being fully convinced, that no amendment of the confederation, leaving the States in possession of their sovereignty could possibly answer the purpose. On the other hand he confessed he was much discouraged by the amazing extent of Country in expecting the desired blessings from any general sovereignty that could be substituted.—As to the powers of the Convention, he thought the doubts started on that subject had arisen from distinctions & reasonings too subtle. A *federal* Govt. he conceived to mean an association of independent Communities into one. Different Confederacies have different powers, and exercise them in different ways. In some instances the powers are exercised over collective bodies; in others over individuals. as in the German Diet—& among ourselves in cases of piracy. Great latitude therefore must be given to the signification of the term. The plan last proposed departs itself from the *federal* idea, as understood by some, since it is to operate eventually on individuals. He agreed moreover with the Honble. gentleman from Va. (Mr. R.) that we owed it to our Country, to do on this emergency whatever we should deem essential to its happiness. The States sent us here to provide for the exigencies of the Union. To rely on & propose any plan not adequate to these exigences, merely because it was not clearly within our powers, would be to sacrifice the means to the end. It may be said that the *States* can not *ratify* a plan not within the purview of the article of Confederation providing for alterations & amendments. But may not the States themselves in which no constitutional authority equal to this purpose exists in the Legislatures, have had in view a reference to the people at large. In the Senate of N. York, a proviso was moved, that no act of the Convention should be binding untill it should be referred to the people & ratified; and the motion was lost by a single voice only, the reason assigned agst. it, being that it (might possibly) be found an inconvenient shackle.

The great question is what provision shall we make for the happiness of our Country? He would first make a comparative examination of the two plans—prove that there were essential defects in both—and point out such changes as might render a *national one*, efficacious.—The great & essential principles necessary for the support of Government. are 1. an active & constant interest in supporting it. This principle does not exist in the States in favor of the federal Govt. They have evidently in a high degree, the esprit de corps. They constantly pursue internal interests adverse to those of the whole. They have their particular debts—their partcular plans of finance &c. all these when opposed to, invariably prevail over the requisitions & plans of Congress. 2. the love of power, Men love power. The same remarks are applicable to this principle. The States have constantly shewn a disposition rather to regain the powers delegated by them than to part with more, or to give effect to what they had parted with. The ambition of their demagogues is known to hate the controul of the Genl. Government. It may be remarked too that the Citizens have not that anxiety to prevent a dissolution of the Genl. Govt as of the particular Govts. A dissolution of the latter would be fatal: of the former would still leave the purposes of Govt. attainable to a considerable degree. Consider what such a State as Virga. will be in a few years, a few compared with the life of nations. How strongly will it feel its importance & self-sufficiency? 3. an habitual attachment of the people. The whole force of this tie is on the side of the State Govt. Its sovereignty is immediately before the eyes of the people: its protection is immediately enjoyed by them. From its hand distributive justice, and all those acts which familiarize & endear Govt. to a people, are dispensed to them. 4. *Force* by which may be understood a *coertion of laws* or *coertion of arms*. Congs. have not the former except in few cases. In particular States, this coercion is nearly sufficient; tho' he held it in most cases, not entirely so. A certain portion of military force is absolutely necessary in large communities. Massts. is now feeling this necessity & making provision for it. But how can this force be exerted on the States collectively. It is impossible. It amounts to a war between the parties. Foreign powers also will not be idle spectators. They will interpose, the confusion will increase, and a dissolution of the Union ensue. 5. *influence*. he did not (mean) corruption, but a dispensation of those regular honors & emoluments, which produce an attachment to the Govt. almost all the weight of these is on the side of the States; and must continue so as long as the States continue to exist. All the passions then we see, of avarice, ambition, interest, which govern most individuals, and all public bodies, fall into the current of the States, and do not flow in the stream of the Genl. Govt. the former therefore will generally be an overmatch for the Genl. Govt. and render any confederacy, in its very nature precarious. Theory is in this case fully confirmed by experience. The Amphyctionic Council had it would seem ample powers for general purposes. It had in particular the power of fining and using force agst. delinquent members. What was the consequence. Their decrees were mere signals of war. The Phocian war is a striking example of it. Philip at length taking advantage of their disunion, and insinuating himself into their Councils, made himself master of their fortunes. The German Confederacy affords another lesson. The authority of Charlemagne seemed to be as great as could be necessary. The great feudal chiefs however, exercising their local sovereignties, soon felt the spirit & found the means of, encroachments, which reduced the imperial authority to a nominal sovereignty. The Diet has succeeded, which tho' aided by a Prince at its head, of great authority independently of his imperial attributes, is a striking illustration of the weakness of Confederated Governments. Other examples instruct us in the same truth. The Swiss cantons have scarce any Union at all, and (have been more than once at) war with one another— How then are all these evils to be avoided? only by such a compleat sovereignty in the general Govermt. as will turn all the strong principles & passions above mentioned on its side. Does the scheme of N. Jersey produce this effect? does it afford any substantial remedy whatever? On the contrary it labors under great defects, and the defect of some of its provisions will destroy the efficacy of others. It gives a direct revenue to Congs. but this will not be sufficient. The balance can only be supplied by requisitions; which experience proves can not be relied on. If States are to deliberate on the mode, they will also deliberate on the object of the supplies, and will grant or not grant as they approve or disapprove of it. The delinquency of one will invite and countenance it in others. Quotas too must in the nature of things be so unequal as to produce the same evil. To what standard will you resort? Land is a fallacious one. Compare Holland with Russia: France or Engd. with other countries of Europe. Pena. with N. Carolia. will the relative pecuniary abilities in those instances, correspond with the relative value of land. Take numbers of inhabitants for the rule and make like comparison of different countries, and you will find it to be equally unjust. The different degrees of industry and improvement in different Countries render the first object a precarious measure of wealth. Much depends too on *situation*. Cont. N. Jersey & N. Carolina, not being commercial States & contributing to the wealth of the commercial ones, can never bear quotas assessed by the ordinary rules of proportion. They will & must fail (in their duty.) their example will be followed, and the Union itself be dissolved. Whence then is the national revenue to be drawn? from Commerce, even (from) exports which notwithstanding the common opinion are fit objects of moderate taxation, (from) excise, &c &c. These tho' not equal, are less unequal than quotas. Another destructive ingredient in the plan, is that equality of suffrage which is so much desired by the small States. It is not in human nature that Va. & the large States should consent to it, or if they did that they shd. long abide by it. It shocks too much the ideas of Justice, and every human feeling. Bad principles in a Govt. tho slow are sure in their operation, and will gradually destroy it. A doubt has been raised whether Congs. at present have a right to keep Ships or troops in time of peace. He leans to the negative. Mr. P.s plan provides no remedy.— If the powers proposed were adequate, the organization of Congs. is such that they could never be properly & effectually exercised. The members of Congs. being chosen by the States & subject to recall, represent all the local prejudices. Should the powers be found effectual, they will from time to time be heaped on them, till a tyrannic sway shall be established. The general power whatever be its form if it preserves itself, must swallow up the State powers. otherwise it will be swallowed up by them. It is agst. all the principles of a good Government to vest the requisite powers in such a body as Congs. Two Sovereignties can not co-exist within the same limits. Giving powers to Congs. must eventuate in a bad Govt. or in no Govt. The plan of N. Jersey therefore will not do. What then is to be done? Here he was embarrassed. The extent of the Country to be governed, discouraged him. The expence of a general Govt. was also formidable; unless there were such a diminution of expence on the side of the State Govts. as the case would admit. If they were extinguished, he was persuaded that great œconomy might be obtained by substituting a general Govt. He did not mean however to shock the public opinion by proposing such a measure. On the other (hand) he saw no *other* necessity for

declining it. They are not necessary for any of the great purposes of commerce, revenue, or agriculture. Subordinate authorities he was aware would be necessary. There must be district tribunals: corporations for local purposes. But cui bono, the vast & expensive apparatus now appertaining to the States. The only difficulty of a serious nature which occurred to him, was that of drawing representatives from the extremes to the center of the Community. What inducements can be offered that will suffice? The moderate wages for the 1st. branch, would only be a bait to little demagogues. Three dollars or thereabouts he supposed would be the Utmost. The Senate he feared from a similar cause, would be filled by certain undertakers who wish for particular offices under the Govt. This view of the subject almost led him to despair that a Republican Govt. could be established over so great an extent. He was sensible at the same time that it would be unwise to propose one of any other form. In his private opinion he had no scruple in declaring, supported as he was by the opinions of so many of the wise & good, that the British Govt. was the best in the world: and that he doubted much whether any thing short of it would do in America. He hoped Gentlemen of different opinions would bear with him in this, and begged them to recollect the change of opinion on this subject which had taken place and was still going on. It was once thought that the power of Congs was amply sufficient to secure the end of their institution. The error was now seen by every one. The members most tenacious of republicanism, he observed, were as loud as any in declaiming agst. the vices of democracy. This progress of the public mind led him to anticipate the time, when others as well as himself would join in the praise bestowed by Mr. Neckar on the British Constitution, namely, that it is the only Govt. in the world "which unites public strength with individual security."—In every community where industry is encouraged, there will be a division of it into the few & the many. Hence separate interests will arise There will be debtors & Creditors &c. Give all power to the many, they will oppress the few. Give all power to the few they will oppress the many. Both therefore ought to have power, that each may defend itself agst. the other. To the want of this check we owe our paper money—instalment laws &c To the proper adjustment of it the British owe the excellence of their Constitution. Their house of Lords is a most noble institution. Having nothing to hope for by a change, and a sufficient interest by means of their property, in being faithful to the National interest, they form a permanent barrier agst. every pernicious innovation, whether attempted on the part of the Crown or of the Commons. No temporary Senate will have firmness en'o' to answer the purpose. The Senate ((of Maryland)) which seems to be so much appealed to, has not yet been sufficiently tried. Had the people been unanimous & eager, in the late appeal to them on the subject of a paper emission they would have yielded to the torrent. Their acquiescing in such an appeal is a proof of it.—Gentlemen differ in their opinions concerning the necessary checks, from the different estimates they form of the human passions. They suppose Seven years a sufficient period to give the Senate an adequate firmness, from not duly considering the amazing violence & turbulence of the democratic spirit. When a great object of Govt. is pursued, which seizes the popular passions, they spread like wild fire, and become irresistable. He appealed to the gentlemen from the N. England States whether experience had not there verified the remark. As to the Executive, it seemed to be admitted that no good one could be established on Republican principles. Was not this giving up the merits of the question; for can there be a good Govt. without a good Executive. The English model was the only good one on this subject. The Hereditary interest of the King was so interwoven with that of the Nation, and his personal emoluments so great, that he was placed above the danger of being corrupted from abroad—and at the same time was both sufficiently independent and sufficiently controuled, to answer the purpose of the institution at home. one of the weak sides of Republics was their being liable to foreign influence & corruption. Men of little character, acquiring great power become easily the tools of intermedling neibours. Sweeden was a striking instance. The French & English had each their parties during the late Revolution which was effected by the predominant influence of the former. What is the inference from all these observations? That we ought to go as far in order to attain stability and permanency, as republican principles will admit. Let one branch of the Legislature hold their places for life or at least during good-behaviour. Let the Executive also be for life. He appealed to the feelings of the members present whether a term of seven years, would induce the sacrifices of private affairs which an acceptance of public trust would require, so so as to ensure the services of the best Citizens. On this plan we should have in the Senate a permanent will, a weighty interest, which would answer essential purposes. But is this a Republican Govt. it will be asked? Yes, if all the Magistrates are appointed, and vacancies are filled, by the people, or a process of election originating with the people. He was sensible that an Executive constituted as he proposed would have in fact but little of the power and independence that might be necessary. On the other plan of appointing him for 7 years, he thought the Executive ought to have but little power. He would be ambitious, with the means of making creatures; and as the object of his ambition wd. be to *prolong* his power, it is probable that in case of a war, he would avail himself of the emergence, to evade or refuse a degradation from his place. An Executive for life has not this motive for forgetting his fidelity, and will therefore be a safer depositary of power. It will be objected probably, that such an Executive will be an *elective Monarch*, and will give birth to the tumults which characterise that form of Govt. He wd. reply that *Monarch* is an indefinite term. It marks not either the degree or duration of power. If this Executive Magistrate wd. be a monarch for life—the other propd. by the Report from the Committee of the whole, wd. be a monarch for seven years. The circumstance of being elective was also applicable to both. It had been observed by judicious writers that elective monarchies wd. be the best if they could be guarded agst. the *tumults* excited by the ambition and intrigues of competitors. He was not sure that tumults were an inseparable evil. He rather thought this character of Elective Monarchies had been taken rather from particular cases than from general principles. The election of Roman Emperors was made by the *Army*. In *Poland* the election is made by great rival *princes* with independent power, and ample means, of raising commotions. In the German Empire, The appointment is made by the Electors & Princes, who have equal motives & means, for exciting cabals & parties. Might (not) such a mode of election be devised among ourselves as will defend the community agst. these effects in any dangerous degree? Having made these observations he would read to the Committee a sketch of a plan which he shd. prefer to either of those under consideration. He was aware that it went beyond the ideas of most members. But will such a plan be adopted out of doors? In return (he would ask) will the people adopt the other plan? At present they will adopt neither. But (he) sees the Union dissolving or already dissolved—he sees evils operating in the States which must soon cure the people of their fondness for democracies—he sees that a great progress has been already made & is still going on in the public mind. He thinks therefore that the people will in time be unshackled from their prejudices; and whenever that happens, they will themselves not be satisfied at stopping where the plan of Mr. R. wd. place them, but be ready to go as far at least as he proposes. He did not mean to offer the paper he had sketched as a proposition to the Committee. It was meant only to give a more correct view of his ideas, and to suggest the amendments which he should probably propose to the plan of Mr. R. in the proper stages of its future discussion. He read his sketch in the words following: towit

I. "The Supreme Legislative power of the United States of America to be vested in two different bodies of men; the one to be called the Assembly, the other the Senate who together shall form the Legislature of the United States with power to pass all laws whatsoever subject to the Negative hereafter mentioned.

II. The Assembly to consist of persons elected by the people to serve for three years.

III. The Senate to consist of persons elected to serve during good behaviour; their election to be made by electors chosen for that purpose by the people: in order to this the States to be divided into election districts. On the death, removal or resignation of any Senator his place to be filled out of the district from which he came.

IV. The supreme Executive authority of the United States to be vested in a Governour to be elected to serve during good behaviour—the election to be made by Electors chosen by the people in the Election Districts aforesaid— The authorities & functions of the Executive to be as follows: to have a negative on all laws about to be passed, and the execution of all laws passed, to have the direction of war when authorized or begun; to have with the advice and approbation of the Senate the power of making all treaties; to have the sole appointment of the heads or chief officers of the departments of Finance, War and Foreign Affairs; to have the nomination of all other officers (Ambassadors to foreign Nations included) subject to the approbation or rejection of the Senate; to have the power of pardoning all offences except Treason; which he shall not pardon without the approbation of the Senate.

V. On the death resignation or removal of the Governour his authorities to be exercised by the President of the Senate till a Successor be appointed.

VI. The Senate to have the sole power of declaring war, the power of advising and approving all Treaties, the power of approving or rejecting all appointments of officers except the heads or chiefs of the departments of Finance War and foreign affairs.

VII. The Supreme Judicial authority to be vested in   Judges to hold their offices during good behaviour with adequate and permanent salaries. This Court to have original jurisdiction in all causes of capture, and an appellative jurisdiction in all causes in which the revenues of the general Government or the citizens of foreign nations are concerned.

VIII. The Legislature of the United States to have power to institute Courts in each State for the determination of all matters of general concern.

IX. The Governour Senators and all officers of the United States to be liable to impeachment for mal—and corrupt conduct; and upon conviction to be removed from office, & disqualified for holding any place of trust or profit—all impeachments to be tried by a Court to consist of the Chief or Judge of the Superior Court of Law of each State, provided such Judge shall hold his place during good behavior, and have a permanent salary.

X. All laws of the particular States contrary to the Constitution or laws of the United States to be utterly void; and the better to prevent such laws being passed, the Governour or president of each state shall be appointed by the General Government and shall have a negative upon the laws about to be passed in the State of which he is Governour or President

XI. No State to have any forces land or Naval; and the Militia of all the States to be under the sole and exclusive direction of the United States, the officers of which to be appointed and commissioned by them.

Alexander Hamilton's Plan

(ACCORDING TO YATES)

. . . EXAMINE THE present confederation, and it is evident they can raise no troops nor equip vessels before war is actually declared. They cannot therefore take any preparatory measure before an enemy is at your door. How unwise and inade- quate their powers! and this must ever be the case when you attempt to define powers.—Something will always be wanting. Congress, by being annually elected, and subject to recall, will ever come with the prejudices of their states rather than the good of the union. Add therefore additional powers to a body thus organized, and you establish a *sovereignty* of the worst kind, consisting of a single body. Where are the checks? None. They must either prevail over the state governments, or the prevalence of the state governments must end in their dissolution. This is a conclusive objection to the Jersey plan.

Such are the insuperable objections to both plans: and what is to be done on this occasion? I confess I am at a loss. I foresee the difficulty on a consolidated plan of drawing a representation from so extensive a continent to one place. What can be the inducements for gentlemen to come 600 miles to a national legislature? The expense would at least amount to £100,000. This however can be no conclusive objection if it eventuates in an extinction of state governments. The burthen of the latter would be saved, and the expense then would not be great. State distinctions would be found unnecessary, and yet I confess, to carry government to the extremities, the state governments reduced to corporations, and with very limited powers, might be necessary, and the expense of the national government become less burthensome.

Yet, I confess, I see great difficulty of drawing forth a good representation. What, for example, will be the inducements for gentlemen of fortune and abilities to leave their houses and business to attend annually and long? It cannot be the wages; for these, I presume, must be small. Will not the power, therefore, be thrown into the hands of the demagogue or middling politician, who, for the sake of a small stipend and the hopes of advancement, will offer himself as a candidate, and the real men of weight and influence, by remaining at home, add strength to the state governments? I am at a loss to know what must be done—I despair that a republican form of government can remove the difficulties. Whatever may be my opinion, I would hold it however unwise to change that form of government. I believe the British government forms the best model the world ever produced, and such has been its progress in the minds of the many, that this truth gradually gains ground. This government has for its object *public strength* and *individual security*. It is said with us to be unattainable. If it was once formed it would maintain itself. All communities divide themselves into the few and the many. The first are the rich and well born, the other the mass of the people. The voice of the people has been said to be the voice of God; and however generally this maxim has been quoted and believed, it is not true in fact. The people are turbulent and

changing; they seldom judge or determine right. Give therefore to the first class a distinct, permanent share in the government. They will check the unsteadiness of the second, and as they cannot receive any advantage by a change, they therefore will ever maintain good government. Can a democratic assembly, who annually revolve in the mass of the people, be supposed steadily to pursue the public good? Nothing but a permanent body can check the imprudence of democracy. Their turbulent and uncontrouling disposition requires checks. The senate of New-York, although chosen for four years, we have found to be inefficient. Will, on the Virginia plan, a continuance of seven years do it? It is admitted that you cannot have a good executive upon a democratic plan. See the excellency of the British executive— He is placed above temptation— He can have no distinct interests from the public welfare. Nothing short of such an executive can be efficient. The weak side of a republican government is the danger of foreign influence. This is unavoidable, unless it is so constructed as to bring forward its first characters in its support. I am therefore for a general government, yet would wish to go the full length of republican principles.

Let one body of the legislature be constituted during good behaviour or life.

Let one executive be appointed who dares execute his powers.

It may be asked is this a republican system? It is strictly so, as long as they remain elective.

And let me observe, that an executive is less dangerous to the liberties of the people when in office during life, than for seven years.

It may be said this constitutes an elective monarchy? Pray what is a monarchy? May not the governors of the respective states be considered in that light? But by making the executive subject to impeachment, the term monarchy cannot apply. These elective monarchs have produced tumults in Rome, and are equally dangerous to peace in Poland; but this cannot apply to the mode in which I would propose the election. Let electors be appointed in each of the states to elect the executive—to consist of two branches—and I would give them the unlimited power of passing *all laws* without exception. The assembly to be elected for three years by the people in districts—the senate to be elected by electors to be chosen for that purpose by the people, and to remain in office during life. The executive to have the power of negativing all laws—to make war or peace, with the advice of the senate—to make treaties with their advice, but to have the sole direction of all military operations, and to send ambassadors and appoint all military officers, and to pardon all offenders, treason excepted, unless by advice of the senate. On his death or removal, the president of the senate to officiate, with the same powers, until another is elected. Supreme judicial officers to be appointed by the executive and the senate. The legislature to appoint courts in each state, so as to make the state governments unnecessary to it.

All state laws to be absolutely void which contravene the general laws. An officer to be appointed in each state to have a negative on all state laws. All the militia and the appointment of officers to be under the national government.

I confess that this plan and that from Virginia are very remote from the idea of the people. Perhaps the Jersey plan is nearest their expectation. But the people are gradually ripening in their opinions of government—they begin to be tired of an excess of democracy—and what even is the Virginia plan, but *pork still, with a little change of the sauce.*

THE DEBATE OVER THE CONSTITUTION

THE FEDERALIST, which is often regarded as the most important American contribution to political science, was written to defend the Constitution to the voting public of the State of New York. New York's ratification was significant and more than doubtful. Her delegates had been instructed to "amend" the Articles of Confederation and two of them had left Philadelphia when they saw that the Convention was about to draft a new Constitution on principles radically different from the league of states which was established by the Articles of Confederation. That the combined efforts of Jay, Madison, and Hamilton should have been necessary to write the series of newspaper articles called *The Federalist* is a tribute not only to the importance of the state but to the political knowledge and literary judgment of her citizens.

The Federalist is distinguished among political editorials not merely by Madison's historical learning but by the realism of Hamilton's approach: society is made up of clashing interests; the Constitution is far from perfect, but politics is not geometry and political thinking can never be entirely impartial—considering the differences of opinion at the Convention, its work is as good as can be expected. Everywhere, Hamilton's emphasis is on the need for order and stability. He approves the veto, for instance, because "every institution calculated to restrain the excess of law-making and to keep things in the same state in which they happen to be at any given period is much more likely to do good than harm." Government must be strong to be effective, and to be strong it must exert force directly on the individual. Since the legislative branch tends to draw power to itself, it must be counterbalanced by an independent judiciary and an executive who need not look to the legislators' will for his salary or tenure of office. In Madison's opinion as well as in Hamilton's, sufficient check on the executive is afforded by elections supplemented by impeachment; it is not necessary to limit reelection.

Many future developments, especially the broad scope of judicial review, are foreshadowed in *The Federalist*. In several other respects, its expectations have not materialized. The Electoral College, which was so highly regarded in its time, has operated as precisely the party rubber-stamp the authors of *The Federalist* wished to avoid; and the impeachment, which was to be a national inquest into the conduct of public men, and so not hampered by the strict rules proper in ordinary legal cases, soon became converted into but another version of "due process of law."

The papers from *The Federalist* here reprinted are No. 1, which serves as the general introduction; No. 45, which outlines the theory of a Federal government, upon which the Constitution is based; and No. 51, which expounds the theory of the separation of powers. The text is that of the 1818 edition.

The Federalist, No. 1

BY ALEXANDER HAMILTON

AFTER FULL EXPERIENCE of the insufficiency of the existing federal government, you are invited to deliberate upon a New Constitution for the United States of America. The subject speaks its own importance; comprehending in its consequences, nothing less than the existence of the UNION, the safety and welfare of the parts of which it is composed, the fate of an empire, in many respects, the most interesting in the world. It has been frequently remarked, that it seems to have been reserved to the people of this country to decide, by their conduct and example, the important question, whether societies of men are really capable or not, of establishing good government from reflection and choice, or whether they are for ever destined to depend for their political constitutions, on accident and force. If there be any truth in the remark, the crisis at which we are arrived may, with propriety, be regarded as the period when that decision is to be made; and a wrong election of the part we shall act, may, in this view, deserve to be considered as the general misfortune of mankind.

This idea, by adding the inducements of philanthropy to those of patriotism, will heighten the solicitude which all considerate and good men must feel for the event. Happy will it be if our choice should be directed by a judicious estimate of our true interests, uninfluenced by considerations foreign to the public good. But this is more ardently to be wished for, than seriously to be expected. The plan offered to our deliberations, affects too many particular interests, innovates upon too many local institutions, not to involve in its discussion a variety of objects extraneous to its merits, and of views, passions, and prejudices little favourable to the discovery of truth.

Among the most formidable of the obstacles which the new constitution will have to encounter, may readily be distinguished the obvious interest of a certain class of men in every state to resist all changes which may hazard a diminution of the power, emolument, and consequence of the offices they hold under the state establishments . . . . and the perverted ambition of another class of men, who will either hope to aggrandize themselves by the confusions of their country, or will flatter themselves with fairer prospects of elevation from the subdivision of the empire into several partial confederacies, than from its union under one government.

It is not, however, my design to dwell upon observations of this nature. I am aware it would be desingenuous to resolve indiscriminately the opposition of any set of men into interested or ambitious views, merely because their situations might subject them to suspicion. Candour will oblige us to admit, that even such men may be actuated by upright intentions; and it cannot be doubted, that much of the opposition, which has already shown itself, or that may hereafter make its appearance, will spring from sources blameless at least, if not respectable. . . . the honest errors of minds led astray by preconceived jealousies and fears. So numerous indeed and so powerful are the causes which serve to give a false bias to the judgment, that we, upon many occasions, see wise and good men on the wrong as well as on the right side of questions, of the first magnitude to society. This circumstance, if duly attended to, would always furnish a lesson of moderation to those, who are engaged in any controversy, however well persuaded of being in the right. And a further reason for caution, in this respect, might be drawn from the reflection, that we are not always sure, that those who advocate the truth are actuated by purer principles than their antagonists. Ambition, avarice, personal animosity, party opposition, and many other motives, not more laudable than these, are apt to operate as well upon those who support, as upon those who oppose, the right side of a question. Were there not even these inducements to moderation, nothing could be more ill judged than that intolerant spirit, which has, at all times, characterized political parties. For, in politics as in religion, it is equally absurd to aim at making proselytes by fire and sword. Heresies in either can rarely be cured by persecution.

And yet, just as these sentiments must appear to candid men, we have already sufficient indications, that it will happen in this, as in all former cases of great national discussion. A torrent of angry and malignant passions will be let loose. To judge from the conduct of the opposite parties, we shall be led to conclude, that they will mutually hope to evince the justness of their opinions, and to increase the number of their converts, by the loudness of their declamations, and by the bitterness of their invectives. An enlightened zeal for the energy and efficiency of government, will be stigmatized as the offspring of a temper fond of power, and hostile to the principles of liberty. An over scrupulous jealousy of danger to the rights of the people, which is more commonly the fault of the head than of the heart, will be represented as mere pretence and artifice. . . . the stale bait for popularity at the expense of public good. It will be forgotten, on the one hand, that jealousy is the usual concomitant of violent love, and that the noble enthusiasm of liberty is too apt to be infected with a spirit of narrow and illiberal distrust. On the other hand, it will be equally forgotten, that the vigour of government is essential to the security of liberty; that in the contemplation of a sound and well-informed judgment, their interests can never be separated; and that a dangerous ambition more often lurks behind the specious mask of zeal for the rights of the people, than under the forbidding appearances of zeal for the firmness and efficiency of government. History will teach us, that the former has been found a much more certain road to the introduction of despotism, than the latter, and that of those men who have overturned the liberties of republics, the greatest number have begun their career, by paying an obsequious court to the people; commencing demagogues, and ending tyrants.

In the course of the preceding observations it has been my aim, fellow-citizens, to put you upon your guard against all attempts, from whatever quarter, to influence your decision in a matter of the utmost moment to your welfare, by any impressions, other than those which may result from the evidence of truth. You will, no doubt, at the same time, have collected from the general scope of them, that they proceed from a source not unfriendly to the new constitution. Yes, my countrymen, I own to you, that, after having given it an attentive consideration, I am clearly of opinion, it is your interest to adopt it. I am convinced, that this is the safest course for your liberty, your dignity, and your happiness. I affect not reserves which I do not feel. I will not amuse you with an appearance of deliberation, when I have decided. I frankly acknowledge to you my convictions, and I will freely lay before you the reasons on which they are founded. The consciousness of good intentions disdains ambiguity. I shall not however multiply professions on this head. My motives must remain in the depository of my own breast: my arguments will be open to all, and may be judged of by all. They shall at least be offered in a spirit, which will not disgrace the cause of truth.

I propose, in a series of papers, to discuss the following interesting particulars. . . . *The utility of the* UNION *to your political prosperity. . . . The insufficiency of the present confederation to preserve that Union. . . . The necessity of a government at least equally energetic with the one proposed, to the attainment of this object. . . . The conformity of the proposed constitution to the true principles of republican government. . . . Its analogy to your own state constitution. . . . and lastly, The additional security, which its adoption will afford to the preservation of that species of government, to liberty, and to property.*

In the progress of this discussion, I shall endeavour to give a satisfactory answer to all the objections which shall have made their appearance, that may seem to have any claim to attention.

It may perhaps be thought superfluous to offer arguments to prove the utility of the UNION, a point, no doubt, deeply engraved on the hearts of the great body of the people in every state, and one which, it may be imagined, has no adversaries. But the fact is, that we already hear it whispered in the private circles of those who oppose the new constitution, that the Thirteen States are of too great extent for any general system, and that we must of necessity resort to separate confederacies of distinct portions of the whole. This doctrine will, in all probability, be gradually propagated, till it has votaries enough to countenance its open avowal. For nothing can be more evident, to those who are able to take an enlarged view of the subject, than the alternative of an adoption of the constitution or a dismemberment of the Union. It may, therefore, be essential to examine particularly the advantages of that Union, the certain evils, and the probable dangers, to which every state will be exposed from its dissolution. This shall accordingly be done.

The Federalist, No. 45

BY JAMES MADISON

HAVING SHOWN that no one of the powers transferred to the federal government is unnecessary or improper, the next question to be considered is, whether the whole mass of them will be dangerous to the portion of authority left in the several States.

The adversaries to the plan of the convention, instead of considering in the first place what degree of power was absolutely necessary for the purposes of the federal government, have exhausted themselves in a secondary inquiry into the possible consequences of the proposed degree of power to the governments of the particular States. But if the Union, as has been shown, be essential to the security of the people of America against foreign danger; if it be essential to their security against contentions and wars among the different States; if it be essential to guard them against those violent and oppressive factions which embitter the blessings of liberty, and against those military establishments which must gradually poison its very fountain; if, in a word, the Union be essential to the happiness of the people of America, is it not preposterous to urge as an objection to a government, without which the objects of the Union cannot be attained, that such a government may derogate from the importance of the governments of the individual States? Was, then, the American Revolution effected, was the American Confederacy formed, was the precious blood of thousands spilt, and the hard-earned substance of millions lavished, not that the people of America should enjoy peace, liberty, and safety, but that the government of the individual States, that particular municipal establishments, might enjoy a certain extent of power, and be arrayed with certain dignities and attributes of sovereignty? We have heard of the impious doctrine in the Old World, that the people were made for kings, not kings for the people. Is the same doctrine to be revived in the New in another shape—that the solid happiness of the people is to be sacrificed to the views of political institutions of a different form? It is too early for politicians to presume on our forgetting that the public good, the real welfare of the great body of the people, is the supreme object to be pursued; and that no form of government whatever has any other value than as it may be fitted for the attainment of this object. Were the plan of the convention adverse to the public happiness, my voice would be, Reject the plan. Were the Union itself inconsistent with the public happiness, it would be, Abolish the Union. In like manner, as far as the sovereignty of the States cannot be reconciled to the happiness of the people, the voice of every good citizen must be, Let the former be sacrificed to the latter. How far the sacrifice is necessary, has been shown. How far the unsacrificed residue will be endangered, is the question before us.

Several important considerations have been touched in the course of these papers, which discountenance the supposition that the operation of the federal government will by degrees prove fatal to the State governments. The more I revolve the subject, the more fully I am persuaded that the balance is much more likely to be disturbed by the preponderancy of the last than of the first scale.

We have seen, in all the examples of ancient and modern confederacies, the strongest tendency continually betraying itself in the members to despoil the general government of its authority with a very ineffectual capacity in the latter to defend itself against the encroachments. Although, in most of these examples, the system has been so dissimilar from that under consideration as greatly to weaken any inference concerning the latter from the fate of the former, yet, as the States will retain, under the proposed Constitution, a very extensive portion of active sovereignty, the inference ought not to be wholly disregarded. In the Achæan league it is probable that the federal head had a degree and species of power which gave it a considerable likeness to the government framed by the convention. The Lycian Confederacy, as far as its principles and form are transmitted, must have borne a still greater analogy to it. Yet history does not inform us that either of them ever degenerated, or tended to degenerate, into one consolidated government. On the contrary, we know that the ruin of one of them proceeded from the incapacity of the federal authority to prevent the dissensions, and finally the disunion, of the subordinate authorities. These cases are the more worthy of our attention, as the external causes by which the component parts were pressed together were much more numerous and powerful than in our case; and consequently less powerful ligaments within would be sufficient to bind the members to the head, and to each other.

In the feudal system, we have seen a similar propensity exemplified. Notwithstanding the want of proper sympathy in every instance between the local sovereigns and the people, and the sympathy in some instances between the general sovereign and the latter, it usually happened that the local sovereigns prevailed in the rivalship for encroachments. Had no external dangers enforced internal harmony and subordination, and, particularly, had the local sovereigns possessed the affections of the people, the great kingdoms in Europe would at this time consist of as many independent princes as there were formerly feudatory barons.

The State governments will have the advantage of the Federal government, whether we compare them in respect to the immediate dependence of the one on the other; to the weight of personal influence which each side will possess; to the powers respectively vested in them; to the predilection and probable support of the people; to the disposition and faculty of resisting and frustrating the measures of each other.

The State governments may be regarded as constituent and essential parts of the federal government; while the latter is nowise essential to the operation or organisation of the former. Without the intervention of the State legislatures, the President of the United States cannot be elected at all. They must in all cases have a great share in his appointment, and will, perhaps, in most cases, of themselves determine it. The Senate will be elected absolutely and exclusively by the State legislatures. Even the House of Representatives, though drawn immediately from the people, will be chosen very much under the influence of that class of men, whose influence over the people obtains for themselves an election into the State legislatures. Thus, each of the principal branches of the federal government will owe its existence more or less to the favour of the State governments, and must consequently feel a dependence, which is much more likely to beget a disposition too obsequious than too overbearing towards them. On the other side, the component parts of the State governments will in no instance be indebted for their appointment to the direct agency of the federal government, and very little, if at all, to the local influence of its members.

The number of individuals employed under the Constitution of the United States will be much smaller than the number employed under the particular States. There will consequently be less of personal influence on the side of the former than of the latter. The members of the legislative, executive, and judiciary departments of thirteen and more States, the justices of peace, officers of militia, ministerial officers of justice, with all the county, corporation, and town officers, for three millions and more of people, intermixed, and having particular acquaintance with every class and circle of people, must exceed, beyond all proportion, both in number and influence, those of every description who will be employed in the administration of the federal system. Compare the members of the three great departments of the thirteen States, excluding from the judiciary department the justices of peace, with the members of the corresponding departments of the single government of the Union; compare the militia officers of three millions of people with the military and marine officers of any establishment which is within the compass of probability, or, I may add, of possibility, and in this view alone, we may pronounce the advantage of the States to be de-

cisive. If the federal government is to have collectors of revenue, the State governments will have theirs also. And as those of the former will be principally on the sea-coast, and not very numerous, whilst those of the latter will be spread over the face of the country, and will be very numerous, the advantage in this view also lies on the same side. It is true, that the Confederacy is to possess, and may exercise, the power of collecting internal as well as external taxes throughout the States; but it is probable that this power will not be resorted to except for supplemental purposes of revenue; that an option will then be given to the States to supply their quotas by previous collections of their own; and that the eventual collection, under the immediate authority of the Union, will generally be made by the officers, and according to the rules, appointed by the several States. Indeed it is extremely probable that in other instances, particularly in the organisation of the judicial power, the officers of the States will be clothed with the correspondent authority of the Union. Should it happen, however, that separate collectors of internal revenue should be appointed under the federal government, the influence of the whole number would not bear a comparison with that of the multitude of State officers in the opposite scale. Within every district to which a federal collector would be allotted, there would not be less than thirty or forty, or even more, officers of different descriptions, and many of them persons of character and weight, whose influence would lie on the side of the State.

The powers delegated by the proposed Constitution to the federal government are few and defined. Those which are to remain in the State governments are numerous and indefinite. The former will be exercised principally on external objects, as war, peace, negotiation, and foreign commerce; with which last the power of taxation will, for the most part, be connected. The powers reserved to the several States will extend to all the objects which, in the ordinary course of affairs, concern the lives, liberties, and properties of the people, and the internal order, improvement, and prosperity of the State.

The operations of the federal government will be most extensive and important in times of war and danger; those of the State governments, in times of peace and security. As the former periods will probably bear a small proportion to the latter, the State governments will here enjoy another advantage over the federal government. The more adequate, indeed, the federal powers may be rendered to the national defence, the less frequent will be those scenes of danger which might favour their ascendancy over the governments of the particular States.

If the new Constitution be examined with accuracy and candour, it will be found that the change which it proposes consists much less in the addition of NEW POWERS to the Union, than in the invigoration of its ORIGINAL POWERS. The regulation of commerce, it is true, is a new power; but that seems to be an addition which few oppose, and from which no apprehensions are entertained. The powers relating to war and peace, armies and fleets, treaties and finance, with the other more considerable powers, are all vested in the existing Congress by the articles of Confederation. The proposed change does not enlarge these powers; it only substitutes a more effectual mode of administering them. The change relating to taxation may be regarded as the most important; and yet the present Congress have as complete authority to REQUIRE of the States indefinite supplies of money for the common defence and general welfare as the future Congress will have to require them of individual citizens; and the latter will be no more bound than the States themselves have been to pay the quotas respectively taxed on them. Had the States complied punctually with the articles of Confederation, or could their compliance have been enforced by as peaceable means as may be used with success towards single persons, our past experience is very far from countenancing an opinion that the State governments would have lost their constitutional powers, and have gradually undergone an entire consolidation. To maintain that such an event would have ensued, would be to say at once that the existence of the State governments is incompatible with any system whatever that accomplishes the essential purposes of the Union.

The Federalist, No. 51

BY HAMILTON OR MADISON

To WHAT EXPEDIENT, then, shall we finally resort, for maintaining in practice the necessary partition of power among the several departments, as laid down in the Constitution? The only answer that can be given is, that as all these exterior provisions are found to be inadequate, the defect must be supplied, by so contriving the interior structure of the government as that its several constituent parts may, by their mutual relations, be the means of keeping each other in their proper places. Without presuming to undertake a full development of this important idea, I will hazard a few general observations, which may perhaps place it in a clearer light, and enable us to form a more correct judgment of the principles and structure of the government planned by the convention.

In order to lay a due foundation for that separate and distinct exercise of the different powers of government, which to a certain extent is admitted on all hands to be essential to the preservation of liberty, it is evident that each department should have a will of its own; and consequently should be so constituted that the members of each should have as little agency as possible in the appointment of the members of the others. Were this principle rigorously adhered to, it would require that all the appointments for the supreme executive, legislative, and judiciary magistracies should be drawn from the same fountain of authority, the people, through channels having no communication whatever with one another. Perhaps such a plan of constructing the several departments would be less difficult in practice than it may in contemplation appear. Some difficulties, however, and some additional expense would attend the execution of it. Some deviations, therefore, from the principle must be admitted. In the constitution of the judiciary department in particular, it might be inexpedient to insist rigorously on the principle: first, because peculiar qualifications being essential in the members, the primary consideration ought to be to select that mode of choice which best secures these qualifications; secondly, because the permanent tenure by which the appointments are held in that department must soon destroy all sense of dependence on the authority conferring them.

It is equally evident, that the members of each department should be as little dependent as possible on those of the others, for the emoluments annexed to their offices. Were the executive magistrate, or the judges, not independent of the legislature in this particular, their independence in every other would be merely nominal.

But the great security against a gradual concentration of the several powers in the same department, consists in giving to those who administer each department the necessary constitutional means and personal motives to resist encroachments of the others. The provision for defence must in this, as in all other cases, be made commensurate to the danger of attack. Ambition must be made to counteract ambition. The interest of the man must be connected with the constitutional rights of the place. It may be a reflection on human nature that such devices should be necessary to control the abuses of government. But what is government itself but the greatest of all reflections on human nature? If men were angels, no government would be necessary. If angels were to govern men, neither external nor internal controls on government would be necessary. In framing a government which is to be administered by men over men, the great difficulty lies in this: you must first enable the government to control the governed; and in the next place oblige it to control itself. A dependence on the people is, no doubt, the primary control on the government; but experience has taught mankind the necessity of auxiliary precautions.

This policy of supplying, by opposite and rival interests, the defect of better motives, might be traced through the whole system of human affairs, private as well as public. We see it particularly displayed in all the subordinate distributions of power, where the constant aim is to divide and arrange the several offices in such a manner as that each may be a check on the other—that the private interest of every individual may be a sentinel over the public rights. These inventions of prudence cannot be less requisite in the distribution of the supreme powers of the State.

But it is not possible to give to each department an equal power of self-defence. In republican government, the legislative authority necessarily predominates. The remedy for this inconveniency is to divide the legislature into different branches; and to render them, by different modes of election and different principles of action, as little connected with each other as the nature of their common functions and their common dependence on the society will admit. It may even be necessary to guard against dangerous encroachments by still further precautions. As the weight of the legislative authority requires that it should be thus divided, the weakness of the executive may require, on the other hand, that it should be fortified. An absolute negative on the legislature appears, at first view, to be the natural defence with which the executive magistrate should be armed. But perhaps it would be neither altogether safe nor alone sufficient. On ordinary occasions it might not be exerted with the requisite firmness, and on extraordinary occasions it might be perfidiously abused. May not this defect of an absolute negative be supplied by some qualified connection between this weaker department and the weaker branch of the stronger department, by which the latter may be led to support the constitutional rights of the former, without being too much detached from the rights of its own department?

If the principles on which these observations are founded be just, as I persuade myself they are, and they be applied as a criterion to the several State constitutions, and to the federal Constitution, it will be found that if the latter does not perfectly correspond with them, the former are infinitely less able to bear such a test.

There are, moreover, two considerations particularly applicable to the federal system of America, which place that system in a very interesting point of view.

First. In a single republic all the power surrendered by the people is submitted to the administration of a single government; and the usurpations are guarded against by a division of the government into distinct and separate departments. In the compound republic of America, the power surrendered by the people is first divided between two distinct governments, and then the portion allotted to each subdivided among distinct and separate departments. Hence a double security arises to the rights of the people. The different governments will control each other, at the same time that each will be controlled by itself.

Second. It is of great importance in a republic not only to guard the society against the oppression of its rulers, but to guard one part of the society against the injustice of the other part. Different interests necessarily exist in different classes of citizens. If a majority be united by a common interest, the rights of the minority will be insecure. There are but two methods of providing against this evil: the one by creating a will in the community independent of the majority—that is, of the society itself; the other, by comprehending in the society so many separate descriptions of citizens as will render an unjust combination of a majority of the whole very improbable, if not impracticable. The first method prevails in all governments possessing an hereditary or self-appointed authority. This, at best, is but a precarious security; because a power independent of the society may as well espouse the unjust views of the major, as the rightful interests of the minor party, and may possibly be turned against both parties. The second method will be exemplified in the federal republic of the United States. Whilst all authority in it will be derived from and dependent on the society, the society itself will be broken into so many parts, interests, and classes of citizens, that the rights of individuals, or of the minority, will be in little danger from interested combinations of the majority. In a free government the security for civil rights must be the same as that for religious rights. It consists in the one case in the multiplicity of interests, and in the other in the multiplicity of sects. The degree of security in both cases will depend on the number of interests and sects; and this may be presumed to depend on the extent of country and number of people comprehended under the same government. This view of the subject must particularly recommend a proper federal system to all the sincere and considerate friends of republican government, since it shows that in exact proportion as the territory of the Union may be formed into more circumscribed Confederacies, or States, oppressive combinations of a majority will be facilitated; the best security, under the republican forms, for the rights of every class of citizens will be diminished; and consequently the stability and independence of some member of the government, the only other security, must be proportionally increased. Justice is the end of government. It is the end of civil society. It ever has been and ever will be pursued until it be obtained, or until liberty be lost in the pursuit. In a society under the forms of which the stronger faction can readily unite and oppress the weaker, anarchy may as truly be said to reign as in a state of nature, where the weaker individual is not secured against the violence of the stronger; and as, in the latter state, even the stronger individuals are prompted, by the uncertainty of their condition, to submit to a government which may protect the weak as well as themselves; so, in the former state,

will the more powerful factions or parties be gradually induced, by a like motive, to wish for a government which will protect all parties, the weaker as well as the more powerful. It can be little doubted that if the State of Rhode Island was separated from the Confederacy and left to itself, the insecurity of rights under the popular form of government within such narrow limits would be displayed by such reiterated oppressions of factious majorities that some power altogether independent of the people would soon be called for by the voice of the very factions whose misrule had proved the necessity of it. In the extended republic of the United States, and among the great variety of interests, parties, and sects which it embraces, a coalition of a majority of the whole society could seldom take place on any other principles than those of justice and the general good; whilst there being thus less danger to a minor from the will of a major party, there must be less pretext, also, to provide for the security of the former, by introducing into the government a will not dependent on the latter, or, in other words, a will independent of the society itself. It is no less certain than it is important, notwithstanding the contrary opinions which have been entertained, that the larger the society, provided it lie within a practical sphere, the more duly capable it will be of self-government. And happily for the *republican cause*, the practicable sphere may be carried to a very great extent by a judicious modification and mixture of the *federal principle*.

RICHARD HENRY LEE

WHEN THE CONVENTION's draft of a Constitution was presented to Virginia for ratification, one of its outstanding opponents was Richard Henry Lee (1732–1794), author of *The Federal Farmer*. Lee, member of a leading Virginia family, had opposed the British from the Stamp Act through the Second Continental Congress. He helped unite the separate committees of correspondence in 1773; pressed for vigorous measures in the First Continental Congress; and was one of the earliest advocates of independence as a means to secure foreign alliances. He urged Virginia to adopt her resolutions calling for independence in May, 1776, and moved a Declaration of Independence by the United States on June seventh. Lee served in

the Revolutionary Congress until 1780, when he returned to Virginia.

Lee argues against the Constitution as a *coup d'état*, holding that it exceeds the Convention's powers and is being pushed by people who were using fear of violence, such as Shays's rebellion, to hurry the country into acceptance. The Constitution aims to eliminate the states in favor of a "consolidated" government of indefinite powers. Those powers are too broadly granted to permit any government to be both free and strong in an area so great as that which reaches from Canada to Florida and from the Atlantic to the banks of the Mississippi. Furthermore, certain rights are insufficiently protected, especially trial by jury, for the "few and well-born" whom Mr. Adams trusts are, "in judicial decisions as well as legislative, generally disposed, and very naturally, too, to favour those of their own description." The entire Constitution is a transfer of power from the many to the few, so arranged that amendment will be virtually impossible.

The full title of Lee's work is *Observations Leading to a Fair Examination of the System of Government Proposed by the Convention. . . . In a Series of Letters from the Federal Farmer to the Republican* (New York, 1787). The selection is reprinted from the original edition.

Letters of a Federal Farmer

BY RICHARD HENRY LEE

LETTER V

THUS I have examined the federal constitution as far as a few days leisure would permit. It opens to my mind a new scene; instead of seeing powers cautiously lodged in the hands of numerous legislators, and many magistrates, we see all important powers collecting in one centre, where a few men will possess them almost at discretion. And instead of checks in the formation of the government, to secure the rights of the people against the usurpations of those they appoint to govern, we are to understand the equal division of lands among our people, and the strong arm furnished them by nature and situation, are to secure them against those usurpations. If there are advantages in the equal division of our lands, and the strong and manly habits of our people, we ought to establish governments calculated to give duration to them, and not governments which never can work naturally, till that equality of property, and those free and manly habits shall be destroyed; these evidently are not the natural basis of the proposed constitution. No man of reflection, and skilled in the science of government, can suppose these will move on harmoniously together for ages, or even for fifty years. As to the little circumstances commented upon, by some writers, with applause—as the age of a representative, of the president, &c.—they have, in my mind, no weight in the general tendency of the system.

There are, however, in my opinion, many good things in the proposed system. It is founded on elective principles, and the deposits of power in different hands, is essentially right. The guards against those evils we have experienced in some states in legislation are valuable indeed; but the value of every feature in this system is vastly lessened for the want of that one important feature in a free government, a representation of the people. Because we have sometimes abused democ-

racy, I am not among those men who think a democratic branch a nuisance; which branch shall be sufficiently numerous to admit some of the best informed men of each order in the community into administration of government.

While the radical defects in the proposed system are not so soon discovered, some temptations to each state, and to many classes of men to adopt it, are very visible. It uses the democratic language of several of the state constitutions, particularly that of Massachusetts; the eastern states will receive advantages so far as the regulation of trade, by a bare majority, is committed to it: Connecticut and New Jersey will receive their share of a general impost: The middle states will receive the advantages surrounding the seat of government; The southern states will receive protection, and have their negroes represented in the legislature, and large back countries will soon have a majority in it. This system promises a large field of employment to military gentlemen, and gentlemen of the law; and in case the government shall be executed without convulsions, it will afford security to creditors, to the clergy, salarymen and others depending on money payments. So far as the system promises justice and reasonable advantages, in these respects, it ought to be supported by all honest men; but whenever it promises unequal and improper advantages to any particular states, or orders of men, it ought to be opposed.

I have, in the course of these letters observed, that there are many good things in the proposed constitution, and I have endeavored to point out many important defects in it. I have admitted that we want a federal system—that we have a system presented, which, with several alterations may be made a tolerable good one—I have admitted there is a well founded uneasiness among creditors and mercantile men. In this situation of things, you ask me what I think ought to be done? My opinion in this case is only the opinion of an individual, and so far only as it corresponds with the opinions of the honest and substantial part of the community, is it entitled to consideration. Though I am fully satisfied that the state conventions ought most seriously to direct their exertions to altering and amending the system proposed before they shall adopt it—yet I have not sufficiently examined the subject, or formed an opinion, how far it will be practicable for those conventions to carry their amendments. As to the idea, that it will be in vain for those conventions to attempt amendments, it cannot be admitted; it is impossible to say whether they can or not until the attempt shall be made; and when it shall be determined, by experience, that the conventions cannot agree in amendments, it will then be an important question before the people of the United States, whether they will adopt or not the system proposed in its present form. This subject of consolidating the states is new: and because forty or fifty men have agreed in a system, to suppose the good sense of this country, an enlightened nation, must adopt it without examination, and though in a state of profound peace, without endeavouring to amend those parts they perceive are defective, dangerous to freedom, and destructive of the valuable principles of republican government—is truly humiliating. It is true there may be danger in delay; but there is danger in adopting the system in its present form; and I see the danger in either case will arise principally from the conduct and views of two very unprincipled parties in the United States—two fires, between which the honest and substantial people have long found themselves situated. One party is composed of little insurgents, men in debt, who want no law, and who want a share of the property of others; these are called levellers, Shayites, &c. The other party is composed of a few, but more dangerous men, with their servile dependents; these avariciously grasp at all power and property; you may discover in all the actions of these men, an evident dislike to free and equal government, and they will go systematically to work to change, essentially, the forms of government in this country; these are called aristocrats, m——ites, &c. &c. Between these two parties is the weight of the community; the men of middling property, men not in debt on the one hand, and men, on the other, content with republican governments, and not aiming at immense fortunes, offices, and power. In 1786, the little insurgents, the levellers, came forth, invaded the rights of others, and attempted to establish governments according to their wills. Their move-

ments evidently gave encouragement to the other party, which, in 1787, has taken the political field, and with its fashionable dependants, and the tongue and the pen, is endeavoring to establish in a great haste, a politer kind of government. These two parties, which will probably be opposed or united as it may suit their interests and views, are really insignificant, compared with the solid, free, and independent part of the community. It is not my intention to suggest, that either of these parties, and the real friends of the proposed constitution, are the same men. The fact is, these aristocrats support and hasten the adoption of the proposed constitution, merely because they think it is a stepping stone to their favorite object. I think I am well founded in this idea; I think the general politics of these men support it, as well as the common observation among them, That the proffered plan is the best that can be got at present, it will do for a few years, and lead to something better. The sensible and judicious part of the community will carefully weigh all these circumstances; they will view the late convention as a respectable body of men—America probably never will see an assembly of men, of a like number, more respectable. But the members of the convention met without knowing the sentiments of one man in ten thousand in these states respecting the new ground taken. Their doings are but the first attempts in the most important scene ever opened. Though each individual in the state conventions will not, probably, be so respectable as each individual in the federal convention, yet as the state conventions will probably consist of fifteen hundred or two thousand men of abilities, and versed in the science of government, collected from all parts of the community and from all orders of men, it must be acknowledged that the weight of respectability will be in them—In them will be collected the solid sense and the real political character of the country. Being revisers of the subject, they will possess peculiar advantages. To say that these conventions ought not to attempt, coolly and deliberately, the revision of the system, or that they cannot amend it, is very foolish or very assuming. If these conventions, after examining the system, adopt it, I shall be perfectly satisfied, and wish to see men make the administration of the government an equal blessing to all orders of men. I believe the great body of our people to be virtuous and friendly to good government, to the protection of liberty and property; and it is the duty of all good men, especially of those who are placed as sentinels to guard their rights—it is their duty to examine into the prevailing politics of parties, and to disclose them—while they avoid exciting undue suspicions, to lay facts before the people, which will enable them to form a proper judgment. Men who wish the people of this country to determine for themselves, and deliberately to fit the government to their situation, must feel some degree of indignation at those attempts to hurry the adoption of a system, and to shut the door against examination. The very attempts create suspicions, that those who make them have secret views, or see some defects in the system, which, in the hurry of affairs, they expect will escape the eye of a free people.

What can be the views of those gentlemen in Pennsylvania, who precipitated decisions on this subject? What can be the views of those gentlemen in Boston, who countenanced the Printers in shutting up the press against a fair and free investigation of this important system in the usual way. The members of the convention have done their duty——why should some of them fly to their states—almost forget a propriety of behaviour, and precipitate measures for the adoption of a system of their own making? I confess candidly, when I consider these circumstances in connection with the unguarded parts of the system I have mentioned, I feel disposed to proceed with very great caution, and to pay more attention than usual to the conduct of particular characters. If the constitution presented be a good one, it will stand the test with a well informed people: all are agreed that there shall be state conventions to examine it; and we must believe it will be adopted, unless we suppose it is a bad one, or that those conventions will make false divisions respecting it. I admit improper measures are taken against the adoption of the system as well for it ——all who object to the plan proposed ought to point out the defects objected to, and to propose those amendments with which they can accept it, or to propose some other system of government, that the public mind may be known, and that we may be brought to agree in some system of government, to strengthen and execute the present, or to provide a substitute. I consider the field of enquiry just opened, and that we are to look to the state conventions for ultimate decisions on the subject before us; it is not to be presumed, that they will differ about small amendments, and lose a system when they shall have made it substantially good; but touching the essential amendments, it is to be presumed the several conventions will pursue the most rational measures to agree in and obtain them; and such defects as they shall discover and not remove, they will probably notice, keep them in view as the ground work of future amendments, and in the firm and manly language which every free people ought to use, will suggest to those who may hereafter administer the government, that it is their expectation, that the system will be so organized by legislative acts, and the government so administered, as to render those defects as little injurious as possible. Our countrymen are entitled to an honest and faithful government; to a government of laws and not of men; and also to one of their chusing—as a citizen of the country, I wish to see these objects secured, and licentious, assuming, and overbearing men restrained; if the constitution or social compact be vague and unguarded, then we depend wholly upon the prudence, wisdom and moderation of those who manage the affairs of government; or on what, probably, is equally uncertain and precarious, the success of the people oppressed by the abuse of government, in receiving it from the hands of those who abuse it, and placing it in the hands of those who will use it well.

In every point of view, therefore, in which I have been able, as yet, to contemplate this subject, I can discern but one rational mode of proceeding relative to it: and that is to examine it with freedom and candour, to have state conventions some months hence, which shall examine coolly every article, clause, and word in the system proposed, and to adopt it with such amendments as they shall think fit. How far the state conventions ought to pursue the mode prescribed by the federal convention of adopting or rejecting the plan in toto, I leave it to them to determine. Our examination of the subject hitherto has been rather of a general nature. The republican characters in the several states, who wish to make this plan more adequate to security of liberty and property, and to the duration of the principles of a free government, will, no doubt, collect their opinions to certain points, and accurately define those alterations and amendments they wish; if it shall be found they essentially disagree in them, the conventions will then be able to determine whether to adopt the plan as it is, or what will be proper to be done.

Under these impressions, and keeping in view the improper and unadvisable lodgment of powers in the general government, organized as it at present is, touching internal taxes, armies and militia, the elections of its own members, causes between citizens of different states, &c. and the want of a more perfect bill of rights, &c. I drop the subject for the present, and when I shall have leisure to revise and correct my ideas respecting it, and to collect into points the opinions of those who wish to make the system more secure and safe, perhaps I may proceed to point out particularly for your consideration, the amendments which ought to be ingrafted into this system, not only in conformity to my own, but the deliberate opinions of others—you will with me perceive, that the objections to the plan proposed may, by a more leisure examination be set in a stronger point of view, especially the important one, that there is no substantial representation of the people provided for in a government in which the most essential powers, even as to the internal policy of the country, is proposed to be lodged.

I think the honest and substantial part of the community will wish to see this system altered, permanency and consistency given to the constitution we shall adopt; and therefore they will be anxious to apportion the powers to the features and organizations of the government, and to see abuse in the exercise of power more effectually guarded against. It is suggested, that state officers, from interested motives will oppose the constitution presented——I see no reason for this, their places in general will not be effected, but new openings to offices and places of profit must evidently be made by the adoption of the constitution in its present form.

THE BANK OF THE UNITED STATES

WITH THE REVOLUTIONARY debt of Congress funded at par and the debts of the states assumed by the Federal government, Hamilton launched upon his second great project: the establishment of a national bank. His leading hope for such an institution was that it would increase the capital available for the country's enterprise. Secondarily, since part of the subscription to the bank's capital was to be paid in public "stock," or bonds, United States securities would have an increased value to the financial community. For the rest, the Bank of the United States was to do a general banking business and, particularly, was to act as fiscal agent for the United States Treasury.

When Hamilton offered his plan for a Bank to be chartered by Congress, President Washington asked the opinion of his Attorney General, Edmund Randolph, as well as that of his Secretary of State, Thomas Jefferson. He wrote, in February, 1791, that Randolph denied the power of Congress to establish such an institution. On similar legalistic grounds, Jefferson objected to Hamilton's project: the Constitution created a government of limited powers, and the grant was to be strictly interpreted.

After some delay, Hamilton countered Jefferson's arguments in a report which insisted that, whatever the nature of the government established by the Constitution, that government had the right to all the instruments "necessary and proper" for carrying out the powers assigned to it. Here, in a remarkably able state paper, Hamilton expounds the theory of "implied powers," a theory which was to serve as the basis for Marshall's defense of the broad rights of the Federal government. Jefferson's opinion was written on February 15, 1791; Hamilton's on February 23, 1791. Washington, following Hamilton's lead, signed the act for the creation of the Bank two days later.

The text of the Jefferson opinion is reprinted from The Writings of Thomas Jefferson, ed. H. E. Bergh, Vol. III (Washington, 1907). The text of the Hamilton opinion is reprinted from The Works of Alexander Hamilton, ed. J. C. Hamilton, Vol. I (New York, 1810).

Opinion against the Constitutionality of a National Bank

BY THOMAS JEFFERSON

THE BILL for establishing a National Bank undertakes among other things:—

1. To form the subscribers into a corporation.

2. To enable them in their corporate capacities to receive grants of land; and so far is against the laws of *Mortmain*.

3. To make alien subscribers capable of holding lands; and so far is against the laws of *alienage*.

4. To transmit these lands, on the death of a proprietor, to a certain line of successors; and so far changes the course of *Descents*.

5. To put the lands out of the reach of forfeiture or escheat; and so far is against the laws of *Forfeiture and Escheat*.

6. To transmit personal chattels to successors in a certain line; and so far is against the laws of *Distribution*.

7. To give them the sole and exclusive right of banking under the national authority; and so far is against the laws of Monopoly.

8. To communicate to them a power to make laws paramount to the laws of the States; for so they must be construed, to protect the institution from the control of the State legislatures; and so, probably, they will be construed.

I consider the foundation of the Constitution as laid on this ground: That "all powers not delegated to the United States, by the Constitution, nor prohibited by it to the States, are reserved to the States or to the people." To take a single step beyond the boundaries thus specially drawn around the powers of Congress, is to take possession of a boundless field of power, no longer susceptible of any definition.

The incorporation of a bank, and the powers assumed by this bill, have not, in my opinion, been delegated to the United States, by the Constitution.

I. They are not among the powers especially enumerated: for these are: 1st. A power to lay taxes for the purpose of paying the debts of the United States; but no debt is paid by this bill, nor any tax laid. Were it a bill to raise money, its origination in the Senate would condemn it by the Constitution.

2d. "To borrow money." But this bill neither borrows money nor ensures the borrowing it. The proprietors of the bank will be just as free as any other money holders, to lend or not to lend their money to the public. The operation proposed in the bill, first, to lend them two millions, and then to borrow them back again, cannot change the nature of the latter act, which will still be a payment, and not a loan, call it by what name you please.

3d. To "regulate commerce with foreign nations, and among the States, and with the Indian tribes." To erect a bank, and to regulate commerce, are very different acts. He who erects a bank, creates a subject of commerce in its bills; so does he who makes a bushel of wheat, or digs a dollar out of the mines; yet neither of these persons regulates commerce thereby. To make a thing which may be bought and sold, is not to prescribe regulations for buying and selling. Besides, if this was an exercise of the power of regulating commerce, it would be void, as extending as much to the internal commerce of every State, as to its external. For the power given to Congress by the Constitution does not extend to the internal regulation of the commerce of a State, (that is to say of the commerce between citizen and citizen,) which remain exclusively with its own legislature; but to its external commerce only, that is to say, its commerce with another State, or with foreign nations, or with the Indian tribes. Accordingly the bill does not propose the measure as a regulation of trade, but as "productive of considerable advantages to trade." Still less are these powers covered by any other of the special enumerations.

II. Nor are they within either of the general phrases, which are the two following:—

1. To lay taxes to provide for the general welfare of the United States, that is to say, "to lay taxes for *the purpose* of providing for the general welfare." For the laying of taxes is the *power*, and the general welfare the *purpose* for which the power is to be exercised. They are not to lay taxes *ad libitum for any purpose they please;* but only *to pay the debts or provide for the welfare of the Union.* In like manner, they are not *to do anything they please* to provide for the general welfare, but only to *lay taxes* for that purpose. To consider the latter phase, not as describing the purpose of the first, but as giving a distinct and independent power to do any act they please, which might be for the good of the Union, would render all the preceding and subsequent enumerations of power completely useless.

It would reduce the whole instrument to a single phrase, that of instituting a Congress with power to do whatever would be for the good of the United States; and, as they would be the sole judges of the good or evil, it would be also a power to do whatever evil they please.

It is an established rule of construction where a phrase will bear either of two meanings, to give it that which will allow some meaning to the other parts of the instrument, and not that which would render all the others useless. Certainly no such universal power was meant to be given them. It was intended to lace them up straitly within the enumerated powers, and those without which, as means, these powers could not be carried into effect. It is known that the very power now proposed *as a means* was rejected as *an end* by the Convention which formed the Constitution. A proposition was made to them to authorize Congress to open canals, and an amendatory one to empower them to incorporate. But the whole was rejected, and one of the reasons for rejection urged in debate was, that then they would have a power to erect a bank, which would render the great cities, where there were prejudices and jealousies on the subject, adverse to the reception of the Constitution.

2. The second general phrase is, "to make all laws *necessary* and proper for carrying into execution the enumerated powers." But they can all be carried into execution without a bank. A bank therefore is not *necessary*, and consequently not authorized by this phrase.

It has been urged that a bank will give great facility or convenience in the collection of taxes. Suppose this were true: yet the Constitution allows only the means which are *"necessary,"* not those which are merely "convenient" for effecting the enumerated powers. If such a latitude of construction be allowed to this phrase as to give any non-enumerated power, it will go to every one, for there is not one which ingenuity may not torture into a *convenience* in some instance *or other*, to *some one* of so long a list of enumerated powers. It would swallow up all the delegated powers, and reduce the whole to one power, as before observed. Therefore it was that the Constitution restrained them to the *necessary* means, that is to say, to those means without which the grant of power would be nugatory.

But let us examine this convenience and see what it is. The report on this subject, page 3, states the only *general* convenience to be, the preventing the transportation and re-transportation of money between the States and the treasury (for I pass over the increase of circulating medium, ascribed to it as a want, and which, according to my ideas of paper money, is clearly a demerit). Every State will have to pay a sum of tax money into the treasury; and the treasury will have to pay, in every State, a part of the interest on the public debt, and salaries to the officers of government resident in that State. In most of the States there will be a surplus of tax money to come up to the seat of government for the officers residing there. The payments of interest and salary in each State may be made by treasury orders on the State collector. This will take up the great export of the money he has collected in his State, and consequently prevent the great mass of it from being drawn out of the State. If there be a balance of commerce in favor of that State against the one in which the government resides, the surplus of taxes will be remitted by the bills of exchange

drawn for that commercial balance. And so it must be if there was a bank. But if there be no balance of commerce, either direct or circuitous, all the banks in the world could not bring up the surplus of taxes, but in the form of money. Treasury orders then, and bills of exchange may prevent the displacement of the main mass of the money collected, without the aid of any bank; and where these fail, it cannot be prevented even with that aid.

Perhaps, indeed, bank bills may be a more *convenient* vehicle than treasury orders. But a little *difference* in the degree of *convenience*, cannot constitute the necessity which the constitution makes the ground for assuming any non-enumerated power.

Besides; the existing banks will, without a doubt, enter into arrangements for lending their agency, and the more favorable, as there will be a competition among them for it; whereas the bill delivers us up bound to the national bank, who are free to refuse all arrangement, but on their own terms, and the public not free, on such refusal, to employ any other bank. That of Philadelphia, I believe, now does this business, by their post-notes, which, by an arrangement with the treasury, are paid by any State collector to whom they are presented. This expedient alone suffices to prevent the existence of that *necessity* which may justify the assumption of a non-enumerated power as a means for carrying into effect an enumerated one. The thing may be done, and has been done, and well done, without this assumption; therefore, it does not stand on that degree of *necessity* which can honestly justify it.

It may be said that a bank whose bills would have a currency all over the States, would be more convenient than one whose currency is limited to a single State. So it would be still more convenient that there should be a bank, whose bills should have a currency all over the world. But it does not follow from this superior conveniency, that there exists anywhere a power to establish such a bank; or that the world may not go on very well without it.

Can it be thought that the Constitution intended that for a shade or two of *convenience*, more or less, Congress should be authorized to break down the most ancient and fundamental laws of the several States; such as those against Mortmain, the laws of Alienage, the rules of descent, the acts of distribution, the laws of escheat and forfeiture, the laws of monopoly? Nothing but a necessity invincible by any other means, can justify such a prostitution of laws, which constitute the pillars of our whole system of jurisprudence. Will Congress be too straitlaced to carry the Constitution into honest effect, unless they may pass over the foundation-laws of the State government for the slightest convenience of theirs?

The negative of the President is the shield provided by the Constitution to protect against the invasions of the legislature: 1. The right of the Executive. 2. Of the Judiciary. 3. Of the States and State legislatures. The present is the case of a right remaining exclusively with the States, and consequently one of those intended by the Constitution to be placed under its protection.

It must be added, however, that unless the President's mind on a view of everything which is urged for and against this bill, is tolerably clear that it is unauthorized by the Constitution; if the pro and the con hang so even as to balance his judgment, a just respect for the wisdom of the legislature would naturally decide the balance in favor of their opinion. It is chiefly for cases where they are clearly misled by error, ambition, or interest, that the Constitution has placed a check in the negative of the President.

On the Constitutionality of a National Bank

BY ALEXANDER HAMILTON

... IF IT WOULD BE NECESSARY to bring proof to a proposition so clear, as that which affirms that the powers of the federal government, as to its objects, were sovereign, there is a clause of the Constitution which would be decisive. It is that which declares that the Constitution, and the laws of the United States made in pursuance of it, ... shall be the supreme law of the land. The power which can create a supreme law of the land, in any case, is doubtless sovereign as to such case.

This general and indisputable principle puts at once an end to the *abstract* question, whether the United States have power to erect a corporation; that is to say, to give a legal or artificial capacity to one or more persons, distinct from the natural. For it is unquestionably incident to sovereign power to erect corporations, and consequently to that of the United States, in relation to the objects entrusted to the management of the government. . . .

It is not denied that there are implied as well as express powers, and that the former are as effectually delegated as the latter. And for the sake of accuracy it shall be mentioned, that there is another class of powers, which may be properly denominated resulting powers. . . .

It is conceded that implied powers are to be considered as delegated equally with express ones. Then it follows, that as a power of erecting a corporation may as well be implied as any other thing, it may as well be employed as an instrument or mean of carrying into execution any of the specified powers, as any other instrument or mean whatever. The only question must be, in this, as in every other case, whether the mean to be employed, or in this instance, the corporation to be erected, has a natural relation to any of the acknowledged objects or lawful ends of the government. Thus a corporation may not be erected by Congress for superintending the police of the city of Philadelphia, because they are not authorized to regulate the police of that city. But one may be erected in relation to the collection of taxes, or to the trade with foreign countries, or to the trade between the States, or with the Indian tribes; because it is the province of the federal government to regulate those objects and because it is incident to a general sovereign or legislative power to regulate a thing, to employ all the means which relate to its regulation to the best and greatest advantage. . . .

Through this mode of reasoning respecting the right of employing all the means requisite to the execution of the specified powers of the government, it is objected, that none but necessary and proper means are to be employed; and the Secretary of State maintains, that no means are to be considered as necessary but those without which the grant of the power would be nugatory. . . .

It is essential to the being of the national government, that so erroneous a conception of the meaning of the word necessary should be exploded.

It is certain, that neither the grammatical nor popular sense of the term requires that construction. According to both, necessary often means no more than needful, requisite, incidental, useful, or conducive to. . . . And it is the true one in which it is understood as used in the Constitution. The whole turn of the clause containing it indicates, that it was the intent of the Convention, by that clause, to give a liberal latitude to the exercise of the specific powers. The expressions have peculiar comprehensiveness. They are "to make all laws necessary and proper for carrying into execution the foregoing powers, and all other powers, vested by the Constitution in the government of the United States, or in any department or officer thereof."

It is presumed to have been satisfactorily shown, in the course of the preceding observations,

I. That the power of the government, as to the objects intrusted to its management, is in its nature sovereign.

II. That the right of erecting corporations, is one inherent in, and inseparable from, the idea of sovereign power.

III. That the position, that the government of the United States can exercise no power but such as is delegated to it by its constitution, does not militate against this principle.

IV. That the word *necessary*, in the general clause, can have no *restrictive* operation, derogating from the force of this principle; indeed, that the degree in which a measure is, or is not necessary, cannot be a *test* of *constitutional* right, but of expediency only.

V. That the power to erect corporations, is not to be considered as an independent and substantive power, but as an incidental and auxiliary one; and was, therefore, more properly left to implication, than expressly granted.

VI. That the principle in question does not extend the power of the government beyond the prescribed limits, because it only affirms a power to incorporate for purposes *within the sphere of the specified powers.*

And lastly, that the right to exercise such a power, in certain cases, is unequivocally granted in the most positive and comprehensive terms. . . .

The proposed bank is to consist of an association of persons for the purpose of creating a joint capital to be employed, chiefly and essentially, in loans. So far the object is not only lawful, but it is the mere exercise of a right which the law allows to every individual. The bank of New-York, which is not incorporated, is an example of such an association. The bill proposes, in addition, that the government shall become a joint proprietor in this undertaking; and that it shall permit the bills of the company, payable on demand, to be receivable in its revenues; and stipulates that it shall not grant privileges, similar to those which are to be allowed to this company, to any others. All this is incontrovertibly within the compass of the discretion of the government. The only question is, whether it has a right to incorporate this company, in order to enable it the more effectually to accomplish ends, which are in themselves lawful.

To establish such a right, it remains to show the relation of such an institution, to one or more of the specified powers of the government.

Accordingly, it is affirmed, that it has a relation, more or less direct, to the power of collecting taxes; to that of borrowing money; to that of regulating trade between the states; and to those of raising and maintaining fleets and armies. To the two former, the relation may be said to be immediate.

And, in the last place, it will be argued, that it is clearly within the provision, which authorizes the making of all *needful rules* and *regulations* concerning the property of the United States, as the same has been practised upon by the government.

A bank relates to the collection of taxes in two ways. *Indirectly*, by increasing the quantity of circulating medium, and quickening circulation, which facilitates the means of paying; *directly*, by creating a *convenient species* of medium in which they are to be paid.

To designate or appoint the money or thing in which taxes are to be paid, is not only a proper, but a necessary, *exercise* of the power of collecting them. Accordingly, Congress, in the law concerning the collection of the duties on imposts and tonnage, have provided that they shall be payable in gold and silver. But while it was an indispensable part of the work to say in what they should be paid, the choice of the specific thing was mere matter of discretion. The payment might have been required in the commodities themselves. Taxes in kind, however ill judged, are not without precedents even in the United States; or it might have been in the paper money of the several states, or in the bills of the bank of North-America, New-York, and Massachusetts, all or either of them; or it might have been in bills issued under the authority of the United States.

No part of this can, it is presumed, be disputed. The appointment, then, of the money or *thing* in which the taxes are to be paid, is an incident to the power of collection. And among the expedients which may be adopted, is that of bills issued under the authority of the United States.

Now the manner of issuing these bills, is again matter of discretion. The government might, doubtless, proceed in the following manner: It might provide that they should be issued under the direction of certain officers, payable on demand; and in order to support their credit, and give them a ready circulation, it might, besides giving them a currency in its taxes, set apart, out of any monies in its treasury a given sum, and appropriate it, under the direction of those officers, as a fund for answering the bills, as presented for payment.

The constitutionality of all this would not admit of a question, and yet it would amount to the institution of a bank, with a view to the more convenient collection of taxes. For the simplest and most precise idea of a bank, is, a deposit of coin or other property, as a fund for *circulating a credit* upon it, which is to answer the purpose of money. That such an arrangement would be equivalent to the establishment of a bank, would become obvious, if the place where the fund to be set apart was kept, should be made a receptacle of the monies of all other persons who should incline to deposit them there for safe keeping; and would become still more so, if the officers, charged with the direction of the fund, were authorized to make discounts at the usual rate of interest, upon good security. To deny the power of the government to add this ingredient to the plan, would be to refine away all government.

A further process will still more clearly illustrate the point. Suppose, when the species of bank which has been described, was about to be instituted, it were to be urged, that in order to secure to it a due degree of confidence, the fund ought not only to be set apart and appropriated generally, but ought to be specifically vested in the officers who were to have the direction of it, and in their successors in office, to the end that it might acquire the character of *private property*, incapable of being resumed without a violation of the sanction by which the rights of property are protected; and occasioning more serious and general alarm: the apprehension of which might operate as a check upon the government. Such a proposition might be opposed by arguments against the expediency of it, or the solidity of the reason assigned for it; but it is not conceivable what could be urged against its constitutionality.

And yet such a disposition of the thing would amount to the erection of a corporation; for the true definition of a corporation seems to be this: It is a *legal* person, or a person created by act of law; consisting of one or more natural persons, authorized to hold property or a franchise in succession, in a legal, as contradistinguished from a natural, capacity.

Let the illustration proceed a step further. Suppose a bank, of the nature which has been described, without or with incorporation, had been instituted, and that experience had evinced, as it probably would, that being wholly under a public direction, it possessed not the confidence requisite to the credit of its bills. Suppose also, that

by some of those adverse conjunctures which occasionally attend nations, there had been a very great drain of the specie of the country, so as not only to cause general distress for want of an adequate medium of circulation; but to produce, in consequence of that circumstance, considerable defalcations in the public revenues. Suppose, also, that there was no bank instituted in any state: in such a posture of things would it not be most manifest, that the incorporation of a bank like that proposed by the bill, would be a measure immediately relative to the effectual collection of the taxes, and completely within the province of a sovereign power of providing, by all laws necessary and proper, for that collection.

If it be said, that such a state of things would render that necessary, and therefore constitutional, which is not so now; the answer to this, (and a solid one it doubtless is,) must still be, that which has been already stated; circumstances may affect the *expediency* of the measure, but they can neither add to, nor diminish its *constitutionality*.

A bank has a direct relation to the power of borrowing money, because it is an usual, and in sudden emergencies, an essential instrument, in the obtaining of loans to government.

A nation is threatened with a war; large sums are wanted on a sudden to make the requisite preparations; taxes are laid for the purpose; but it requires time to obtain the benefit of them; anticipation is indispensable. If there be a bank, the supply can at once be had; if there be none, loans from individuals must be sought. The progress of these is often too slow for the exigency; in some situations they are not practicable at all. Frequently when they are, it is of great consequence to be able to anticipate the product of them by advances from a bank.

The essentiality of such an institution, as an instrument of loans, is exemplified at this very moment. An Indian expedition is to be prosecuted. The only fund out of which the money can arise consistently with the public engagements, is a tax, which only begins to be collected in July next. The preparations, however, are instantly to be made. The money must therefore be borrowed; and of whom could it be borrowed, if there were no public banks?

It happens that there are institutions of this kind; but if there were none, it would be indispensable to create one.

Let it then be supposed, that the necessity existed, (as but for a casualty would be the case,) that proposals were made for obtaining a loan;

that a number of individuals came forward and said, we are willing to accommodate the government with this money; with what we have in hand, and the credit we can raise upon it, we doubt not of being able to furnish the sum required. But in order to do this, it is indispensable that we should be incorporated as a bank. This is essential towards putting it in our power to do what is desired, and we are obliged on that account to make it the *consideration* or *condition* of the loan.

Can it be believed that a compliance with this proposition would be unconstitutional? Does not this alone evince the contrary? It is a necessary part of a power to borrow, to be able to stipulate the considerations or conditions of a loan. It is evident, as has been remarked elsewhere, that this is not confined to the mere stipulation of a franchise. If it may, (and it is not perceived why it may not,) then the grant of a corporate capacity may be stipulated as a consideration of the loan. There seems to be nothing unfit, or foreign from the nature of the thing, in giving individuality, or a corporate capacity, to a number of persons who are willing to lend a sum of money to the government, the better to enable them to do it, and make them an ordinary instrument of loans in future emergencies of state.

But the more general view of the subject is still more satisfactory. The legislative power of borrowing money, and of making all laws necessary and proper for carrying into execution that power, seems obviously competent to the appointment of the *organ* through which the abilities and wills of individuals may be most efficaciously exerted, for the accommodation of the government by loans. . . .

The institution of a bank has also a natural relation to the regulation of trade between the states, in so far as it is conducive to the creation of a convenient medium of exchange between them, and to the keeping up a full circulation, by preventing the frequent displacement of the metals in reciprocal remittances. Money is the very hinge on which commerce turns. And this does not mean merely gold and silver; many other things have served the purpose with different degrees of utility. Paper has been extensively employed.

It cannot therefore be admitted with the Attorney-General, that the regulation of trade between the states, as it concerns the medium of circulation and exchange, ought to be considered as confined to coin. It is even supposeable that the whole, or the greatest part, of the coin of the country, might be carried out of it.

The Secretary of State objects to the relation here insisted upon, by the following mode of reasoning: To erect a bank, says he, and to regulate commerce, are very different acts. He who erects a bank, creates a subject of commerce. So does he who raises a bushel of wheat, or digs a dollar out of the mines; yet neither of these persons regulates commerce thereby. To make a thing which may be bought and sold, is not to prescribe regulations for *buying* and *selling*. This is making the regulation of commerce to consist in prescribing rules for buying and selling.

This indeed is a species of regulation of trade, but it is one which falls more aptly within the province of the local jurisdictions, than within that of the general government, whose care they must have presumed to have been intended to be directed to those general political arrangements concerning trade, on which its aggregate interests depend, rather than to the details of buying and selling.

Accordingly, such only are the regulations to be found in the laws of the United States; whose objects are to give encouragement to the enterprise of our own merchants, and to advance our navigation and manufactures.

And it is in reference to these general relations of commerce, that an establishment which furnishes facilities to circulation, and a convenient medium of exchange and alienation, is to be regarded as a regulation of trade.

The Secretary of State further urges, that if this was a regulation of commerce, it would be *void*, as *extending* as much to the internal part of every state, as to its external. But what regulation of commerce does not extend to the internal commerce of every state? What are all the duties upon imported articles, amounting in some cases to prohibitions, but so many bounties upon domestic manufactures, affecting the interest of different classes of citizens in different ways? What are all the provisions in the coasting act, which relate to the trade between district and district of the same state? In short, what regulation of trade between the states, but must affect the internal trade of each state? what can operate upon the whole, but must extend to every part? . . .

Illustrations of this kind might be multiplied without end. They shall, however, be pursued no further.

There is a sort of evidence on this point, arising from an aggregate view of the constitution, which is of no inconsiderable weight. The very general power of laying and collecting taxes, and appropriating their proceeds; that of borrowing money indefinitely; that of coining money and regulating foreign coins; that of making all needful rules and regulations respecting the property of the United States: These powers combined, as well as the reason and nature of the thing, speak strongly this language: that it is the manifest design and scope of the constitution, to vest in Congress all the powers requisite to the effectual administration of the finances of the United States. As far as concerns this object, there appears to be no parsimony of power.

To suppose then, that the government is precluded from the employment of so usual and so important an instrument for the administration of its finances as that of a bank, is to suppose what does not coincide with the general tenour and complexion of the constitution, and what is not agreeable to impressions that any mere spectator would entertain concerning it. Little less than a prohibiting clause can destroy the strong presumptions which result from the general aspect of the government. Nothing but demonstration should exclude the idea that the power exists.

To all questions of this nature, the practice of mankind ought to have great weight against the theories of individuals.

The fact, for instance, that all the principal commercial nations have made use of trading corporations or companies, for the purpose of *external commerce*, is a satisfactory proof, that the establishment of them, is an incident to the regulation of commerce.

This other fact, that banks are an usual engine in the administration of national finances, and an ordinary, and the most effectual, instrument of loans, and one which, in this country, has been found essential, pleads strongly against the supposition, that a government clothed with most of the important prerogatives of sovereignty, in relation to its revenues, its debt, its credit, its defence, its trade, its intercourse with foreign nations, is forbidden to make use of that instrument as an appendage to its own authority.

It has been stated as an auxiliary test of constitutional authority, to try whether it abridges any preexisting right of any state or any individual. The proposed measure will stand the most severe examination on this point. Each state may still erect as many banks as it pleases; every individual may still carry on the banking business to any extent he pleases.

Another criterion may be this; whether the institution or thing has a more direct relation as to its uses—to the objects of the reserved powers of the state government, than to those of the powers delegated by the United States? This rule, indeed, is less precise than the former; but it may still serve as some guide. Surely a bank has more reference to the objects intrusted to the national government, than to those left to the care of the state government. The common defence is decisive in this comparison. . . .

MANUFACTURES

In December, 1791, Alexander Hamilton (1757–1804), Washington's Secretary of the Treasury, submitted another of his famous memoranda to Congress, this one being the *Report on the Subject of Manufactures*. It is the fullest and most closely reasoned of his statements; and it has long served as a text, both here and abroad, for those who have sought the development of manufacturing industries through government intervention. All the classical arguments in support of protectionism are here; although it should be said in defense of Hamilton that he was more disposed to the use of government bounties and subsidies than of high protective duties. One of the most interesting pieces of analysis in the *Report* is the likely effect on the whole economy of a supported manufacturing interest: it will strengthen rather than weaken agriculture; create further opportunities for enterprise and investment; furnish new employment possibilities; attract immigration. This is the conception that later came to be known as "The Harmony of Interests" idea and it is phrased remarkably well by Hamilton.

The selection here reprinted is from the *Works of Alexander Hamilton* (New York, 1810).

Report on the Subject of Manufactures

BY ALEXANDER HAMILTON

. . . II. But, without contending for the superior productiveness of manufacturing industry, it may conduce to a better judgment of the policy which ought to be pursued respecting its encouragement, to contemplate the subject under some additional aspects, tending not only to confirm the idea that this kind of industry has been improperly represented as unproductive in itself, but to evince, in addition, that the establishment and diffusion of manufactures have the effect of rendering the total mass of useful and productive labor, in a community, greater than it would otherwise be. In prosecuting this discussion, it may be necessary briefly to résumé and review some of the topics which have been already touched.

To affirm that the labor of the manufacturer is unproductive, because he consumes as much of the produce of land as he adds value to the raw material which he manufactures, is not better founded than it would be to affirm that the labor of the farmer, which furnishes materials to the manufacturer, is unproductive, because he consumes an equal value of manufactured articles. Each furnishes a certain portion of the produce of his labor to the other, and each destroys a corresponding portion of the produce of the labor of the other. In the meantime, the maintenance of two citizens, instead of one, is going on; the State has two members instead of one; and they, together, consume twice the value of what is produced from the land.

If, instead of a farmer and artificer, there were a farmer only, he would be under the necessity of devoting a part of his labor to the fabrication of clothing and other articles, which he would procure of the artificer, in the case of there being such a person; and of course he would be able to devote less labor to the cultivation of his farm, and would draw from it a proportionately less product. The whole quantity of production, in this state of things, in provisions, raw materials, and manufactures, would certainly not exceed in value the amount of what would be produced in provisions and raw materials only, if there were an artificer as well as a farmer.

Again, if there were both an artificer and a farmer, the latter would be left at liberty to pursue exclusively the cultivation of his farm. A greater quantity of provisions and raw materials would, of course, be produced, equal, at least, as has been already observed, to the whole amount of the provisions, raw materials, and manufactures, which would exist on a contrary supposition. The artificer, at the same time, would be going on in the production of manufactured commodities, to an amount sufficient, not only to repay the farmer, in those commodities, for the provisions and materials which were procured from him, but to furnish the artificer himself with a supply of similar commodities for his own use. Thus, then, there would be two quantities or values in existence, instead of one; and the revenue and consumption would be double, in one case, what it would be in the other.

If, in place of both of these suppositions, there were supposed to be two farmers and no artificer, each of whom applied a part of his labor to the culture of land and another part to the fabrication of manufactures; in this case, the portion of the labor of both, bestowed upon land, would produce the same quantity of provisions and raw materials only, as would be produced by the entire sum of the labor of one, applied in the same manner; and the portion of the labor of both, bestowed upon manufactures, would produce the same quantity of manufactures only, as would be produced by the entire sum of the labor of one, applied in the same manner. Hence, the produce of the labor of the two farmers would not be greater than the produce of the labor of the farmer and artificer; and hence it results, that the labor of the artificer is as positively productive as that of the farmer, and as positively augments the revenue of the society.

The labor of the artificer replaces to the farmer that portion of his labor with which he provides the materials of exchange with the artificer, and which he would otherwise have been compelled to apply to manufactures; and while the artificer thus enables the farmer to enlarge his stock of agricultural industry, a portion of which he purchases for his own use, he also supplies himself with the manufactured articles of which he stands in need. He does still more. Besides this equivalent, which he gives for the portion of agricultural labor consumed by him, and this supply of manufactured commodities for his own consumption, he furnishes still a surplus, which compensates for the use of the capital advanced, either by himself or some other person, for carrying on the business. This is the ordinary profit of the stock employed in the manufactory, and is, in every sense, as effective an addition to the income of the society as the rent of land.

The produce of the labor of the artificer, consequently, may be regarded as composed of three parts: one, by which the provisions for his subsistence and the materials for his work are purchased of the farmer; one, by which he supplies himself with manufactured necessaries; and a third, which constitutes the profit on the stock employed. The two last portions seem to have been overlooked in the system which represents manufacturing industry as barren and unproductive.

In the course of the preceding illustrations, the products of equal quantities of the labor of the farmer and artificer have been treated as if equal to each other. But this is not to be understood as intending to assert any such precise equality. It is merely a manner of expression, adopted for the sake of simplicity and perspicuity. Whether the value of the produce of the labor of the farmer be somewhat more or less than that of the artificer, is not material to the main scope of the argument, which, hitherto, has only aimed at showing that the one, as well as the other, occasions a positive augmentation of the total produce and revenue of the society.

It is now proper to proceed a step further, and to enumerate the principal circumstances from which it may be inferred that manufacturing establishments not only occasion a positive augmentation of the produce and revenue of the society, but that they contribute essentially to rendering them greater than they could possibly be without such establishments. These circumstances are:

1. The division of labor.

2. An extension of the use of machinery.

3. Additional employment to classes of the community not ordinarily engaged in the business.

4. The promoting of emigration from foreign countries.

5. The furnishing greater scope for the diversity of talents and dispositions, which discriminate men from each other.

6. The affording a more ample and various field for enterprise.

7. The creating, in some instances, a new, and securing, in all, a more certain and steady demand for the surplus produce of the soil.

Each of these circumstances has a considerable influence upon the total mass of industrious effort in a community; together, they add to it a degree of energy and effect which is not easily conceived. Some comments upon each of them, in the order in which they have been stated, may serve to explain their importance.

1. *As to the division of labor*

It has justly been observed, that there is scarcely any thing of greater moment in the economy of a nation than the proper division of labor. The separation of occupations causes each to be carried to a much greater perfection than it could possibly acquire if they were blended. This arises principally from three circumstances:

1st. The greater skill and dexterity naturally resulting from a constant and undivided application to a single object. It is evident that these properties must increase in proportion to the separation and simplification of objects, and the steadiness of the attention devoted to each; and must be less in proportion to the complication of objects, and the number among which the attention is distracted.

2d. The economy of time, by avoiding the loss of it, incident to a frequent transition from one operation to another of a different nature. This depends on various circumstances: the transition itself, the orderly disposition of the implements, machines, and materials employed in the operation to be relinquished, the preparatory steps to the commencement of a new one, the interruption of the impulse which the mind of the workman acquires from being engaged in a particular operation, the distractions, hesitations, and reluctances which attend the passage from one kind of business to another.

3d. An extension of the use of machinery. A man occupied on a single object will have it more in his power, and will be more naturally led to exert his imagination, in devising methods to facilitate and abridge labor, than if he were perplexed by a variety of independent and dissimilar operations. Besides this the fabrication of machines, in numerous instances, becoming itself a distinct trade, the artist who follows it has all the advantages which have been enumerated, for improvement in his particular art; and, in both ways, the invention and application of machinery are extended.

And from these causes united, the mere separation of the occupation of the cultivator from that of the artificer, has the effect of augmenting the productive powers of labor, and with them, the total mass of the produce or revenue of a country. In this single view of the subject, therefore, the utility of artificers or manufacturers, towards producing an increase of productive industry, is apparent.

2. *As to an extension of the use of machinery, a point which, though partly anticipated, requires to be placed in one or two additional lights*

The employment of machinery forms an item of great importance in the general mass of national industry. It is an artificial force brought in aid of the natural force of man; and, to all the purposes of labor, is an increase of hands, an accession of strength, unencumbered too by the expense of maintaining the laborer. May it not, therefore, be fairly inferred, that those occupations which give greatest scope to the use of this auxiliary, contribute most to the general stock of industrious effort, and, in consequence, to the general product of industry?

It shall be taken for granted, and the truth of the position referred to observation, that manufacturing pursuits are susceptible, in a greater degree, of the application of machinery, than those of agriculture. If so, all the difference is lost to a community which, instead of manufacturing for itself, procures the fabrics requisite to its supply from other countries. The substitution of foreign for domestic manufactures is a transfer to foreign nations of the advantages accruing from the employment of machinery, in the modes in which it is capable of being employed with most utility and to the greatest extent.

The cotton-mill, invented in England, within the last twenty years, is a signal illustration of the general proposition which has been just advanced. In consequence of it, all the different processes for spinning cotton are performed by means of machines, which are put in motion by water, and attended chiefly by women and children—and by a smaller number of persons, in the whole, than are requisite in the ordinary mode of spinning. And it is an advantage of great moment, that the operations of this mill continue with convenience during the night as well as through the day. The prodigious effect of such a machine is easily conceived. To this invention is to be attributed, essentially, the immense progress which has been so suddenly made in Great Britain, in the various fabrics of cotton.

3. *As to the additional employment of classes of the community not originally engaged in the particular business*

This is not among the least valuable of the means by which manufacturing institutions contribute to augment the general stock of industry and production. In places where those institutions prevail, besides the persons regularly engaged in them, they afford occasional and extra employment to industrious individuals and families, who are willing to devote the leisure resulting from the intermissions of their ordinary pursuits to collateral labors, as a resource for multiplying their acquisitions or their enjoyments. The husbandman himself experiences a new source of profit and support from the increased industry of his wife and daughters, invited and stimulated by the demands of the neighboring manufactories.

Besides this advantage of occasional employment to classes having different occupations, there is another, of a nature allied to it, and of a similar tendency. This is the employment of persons who would otherwise be idle, and in many cases a burthen on the community, either from the bias of temper, habit, infirmity of body, or some other cause, indisposing or disqualifying them for the toils of the country. It is worthy of particular remark that, in general, women and children are rendered more useful, and the latter more early useful, by manufacturing establishments, than they would otherwise be. Of the number of persons employed in the cotton manufactories of Great Britain, it is computed that four sevenths nearly are women and children, of whom the greatest proportion are children, and many of them of a tender age.

And thus it appears to be one of the attributes of manufactures, and one of no small consequence, to give occasion to the exertion of a greater quantity of industry, even by the same number of persons, where they happen to prevail, than would exist if there were no such establishments.

4. *As to the promoting of emigration from foreign countries*

Men reluctantly quit one course of occupation and livelihood for another, unless invited to it by very apparent and proximate advantages. Many who would go from one country to another, if they had a prospect of continuing with more benefit the callings to which they have been educated, will often not be tempted to change their situation by the hope of doing better in some other way. Manufacturers who, listening to the powerful invitations of a better price for their fabrics or their labor, of greater cheapness of provisions and raw materials, of an exemption from the chief part of the taxes, burthens, and restraints which they endure in the Old World, of greater personal independence and consequence, under the operation of a more equal government, and of what is far more precious than mere religious toleration, a perfect equality of religious privileges, would probably flock from Europe to the United States, to pursue their own trades or professions, if they were once made sensible of the advantages they would enjoy, and were inspired with an assurance of encouragement and employment, will with difficulty, be induced to transplant themselves, with a view to becoming cultivators of land.

If it be true, then, that it is the interest of the United States to open every possible avenue to emigration from abroad, it affords a weighty argument for the encouragement of manufactures; which, for the reasons just assigned, will have the strongest tendency to multiply the inducements to it.

Here is perceived an important resource, not only for extending the population, and with it the useful and productive labor of the country, but likewise for the prosecution of manufactures, without deducting from the number of hands which might otherwise be drawn to tillage, and even for the indemnification of agriculture for such as might happen to be diverted from it. Many, whom manufacturing views would induce to emigrate, would, afterwards, yield to the temptations which the particular situation of this country holds out to agricultural pursuits. And while agriculture would, in other respects, derive many signal and unmingled advantages from the growth of manufactures, it is a problem whether it would gain or lose, as to the article of the number of persons employed in carrying it on.

5. As to the furnishing greater scope for the diversity of talents and dispositions, which discriminate men from each other

This is a much more powerful means of augmenting the fund of national industry, than may at first sight appear. It is a just observation, that minds of the strongest and most active powers for their proper objects, fall below mediocrity, and labor without effect, if confined to uncongenial pursuits. And it is thence to be inferred, that the results of human exertion may be immensely increased by diversifying its objects. When all the different kinds of industry obtain in a community, each individual can find his proper element, and can call into activity the whole vigor of his nature. And the community is benefited by the services of its respective members, in the manner in which each can serve it with most effect.

If there be any thing in a remark often to be met with, namely, that there is, in the genius of the people of this country, a peculiar aptitude for mechanic improvements, it would operate as a forcible reason for giving opportunities to the exercise of that species of talent, by the propagation of manufactures.

6. As to the affording a more ample and various field for enterprise

This also is of greater consequence in the general scale of national exertion than might, perhaps, on a superficial view be supposed, and has effects not altogether dissimilar from those of the circumstance last noticed. To cherish and stimulate the activity of the human mind, by multiplying the objects of enterprise, is not among the least considerable of the expedients by which the wealth of a nation may be promoted. Even things in themselves not positively advantageous sometimes become so, by their tendency to provoke exertion. Every new scene which is opened to the busy nature of man to rouse and exert itself, is the addition of a new energy to the general stock of effort.

The spirit of enterprise, useful and prolific as it is, must necessarily be contracted or expanded, in proportion to the simplicity or variety of the occupations and productions which are to be found in a society. It must be less in a nation of mere cultivators, than in a nation of cultivators and merchants; less in a nation of cultivators and merchants, than in a nation of cultivators, artificers, and merchants.

7. As to the creating, in some instances, a new, and securing, in all, a more certain and steady demand for the surplus produce of the soil

This is among the most important of the circumstances which have been indicated. It is a principal means by which the establishment of manufactures contributes to an augmentation of the produce or revenue of a country, and has an immediate and direct relation to the prosperity of agriculture.

It is evident that the exertions of the husbandman will be steady or fluctuating, vigorous or feeble, in proportion to the steadiness or fluctuation, adequateness or inadequateness, of the markets on which he must depend for the vent of the surplus which may be produced by his labor; and that such surplus, in the ordinary course of things, will be greater or less in the same proportion.

For the purpose of this vent, a domestic market is greatly to be preferred to a foreign one; because it is, in the nature of things, far more to be relied upon.

It is a primary object of the policy of nations, to be able to supply themselves with subsistence from their own soils; and manufacturing nations, as far as circumstances permit, endeavor to procure from the same source the raw materials necessary for their own fabrics. This disposition, urged by the spirit of monopoly, is sometimes even carried to an injudicious extreme. It seems not always to be recollected, that nations who have neither mines nor manufactures can only obtain the manufactured articles of which they stand in need, by an exchange of the products of their soils; and that if those who can best furnish them with such articles are unwilling to give a due course to this exchange, they must, of necessity, make every possible effort to manufacture for themselves; the effect of which is, that the manufacturing nations abridge the natural advantages of their situation, through an unwillingness to permit the agricultural countries to enjoy the advantages of theirs, and sacrifice the interests of a mutually beneficial intercourse to the vain project of selling every thing and buying nothing.

But it is also a consequence of the policy which has been noted, that the foreign demand for the products of agricultural countries is, in a great degree, rather casual and occasional, than certain or constant. To what extent injurious interruptions of the demand for some of the staple commodities of the United States may have been experienced from that cause, must be referred to the judgment of those who are engaged in carrying on the commerce of the country; but it may be safely affirmed, that such interruptions are, at times, very inconveniently felt, and that cases not unfrequently occur, in which markets are so confined and restricted as to render the demand very unequal to the supply.

Independently, likewise, of the artificial impediments which are created by the policy in question, there are natural causes tending to render the external demand for the surplus of agricultural nations a precarious reliance. The differences of seasons in the countries which are the consumers, make immense differences in the produce of their own soils, in different years; and consequently in the degrees of their necessity for foreign supply. Plentiful harvests with them, especially if similar ones occur at the same time in the countries which are the furnishers, occasion, of course, a glut in the markets of the latter.

Considering how fast and how much the progress of new settlements in the United States must increase the surplus produce of the soil, and weighing seriously the tendency of the system which prevails among most of the commercial nations of Europe, whatever dependence may be placed on the force of natural circumstances to counteract the effects of an artificial policy, there appear strong reasons to regard the foreign demand for that surplus as too uncertain a reliance, and to desire a substitute for it in an extensive domestic market.

To secure such a market there is no other expedient than to promote manufacturing establishments. Manufacturers, who constitute the most numerous class, after the cultivators of land, are for that reason the principal consumers of the surplus of their labor.

This idea of an extensive domestic market for the surplus produce of the soil, is of the first consequence. It is, of all things, that which most effectually conduces to a flourishing state of agriculture. If the effect of manufactories should be to detach a portion of the hands which would otherwise be engaged in tillage, it might possibly cause a smaller quantity of lands to be under cultivation; but, by their tendency to procure a more certain demand for the surplus produce of the soil, they would, at the same time, cause the lands which were in cultivation to be better improved and more productive. And while by their influence, the condition of each individual farmer would be meliorated, the total mass of agricultural production would probably be increased. For this must evidently depend as much upon the degree of improvement, if not more, than upon the number of acres under culture.

It merits particular observation, that the multiplication of manufactories not only furnishes a market for those articles which have been accustomed to be produced in abundance in a country, but it likewise creates a demand for such as were either unknown or produced in inconsiderable quantities. The bowels as well as the surface of the earth are ransacked for articles which were before neglected. Animals, plants, and minerals acquire a utility and a value which were before unexplored.

The foregoing considerations seem sufficient to establish, as general propositions, that it is the interest of nations to diversify the industrious pursuits of the individuals who compose them; that the establishment of manufactures is calculated not only to increase the general stock of useful and productive labor, but even to improve the state of agriculture in particular,—certainly to advance the interests of those who are engaged in it. There are other views that will be hereafter taken of the subject, which it is conceived will serve to confirm these inferences. . . .

TENCH COXE

In Tench Coxe's essays, one sees the United States trying to cope with the problem of establishing an economic position sufficiently secure to free it from the pressure of need and to regain old markets, especially in the British West Indies. As a Philadelphia businessman during the Revolution, Coxe (1755-1824) had been accused of being a lukewarm Whig. He may not have been zealous enough to please a Committee of Safety, but he was an enthusiast for the economic future of America. That enthusiasm was expressed in accounts of Pennsylvania, in recommendations for promoting American manufactures, and in vigorous reply to Lord Sheffield's patronizing expectation of an American debacle. If British colonial policy excludes cheap American provisions and lumber from its West Indies islands, the French will benefit at their expense, Coxe argues; and if Americans achieved union in war for all their differences of "manners, of climates and of staples," they will not dissipate that union in time of peace.

Coxe was named Assistant Secretary of the Treasury in 1789, a post he held until President Adams removed him in 1797. Coxe turned to the opposite side then, and was appointed to office by Jefferson. Through all political alterations, Coxe advocated the same economic policy, a firm nationalism that sought to balance a properly dominant agriculture with industry judiciously fostered by a moderate tariff and American navigation laws modeled on the British. No conflict of interests was involved in such policy, for whatever helped manufactures helped agriculture as well. Coxe's argument on that score was to be repeated during the next decades and finally to become a dogma of Whig politics and Clay's "American System."

The selection here reprinted is from the original edition of *A View of the United States of America, in a Series of Papers Written at Various Times, between the Years 1787 and 1794* (Philadelphia, 1794).

A View of the United States of America

BY TENCH COXE

CHAPTER XVI: CONTAINING A SUMMARY STATEMENT OF THE PRINCIPAL FACTS, WHICH CHARACTERIZE THE AMERICAN PEOPLE, AND THEIR COUNTRY OR TERRITORY

THE PEOPLE of the United States have exploded those principles, by the operation of which religious oppressions and restrictions of whatever description, have been imposed upon mankind, and, rejecting mere toleration, they have placed upon one common and equal footing every church, sect or society of religious men.

They have exploded, in like manner, those principles, by the operation of which, civil oppressions have been inflicted upon mankind; and they have made an unexceeded progress in their practice upon the principles of free government.

While the fermentations of a civil and revolutionary contest were yet operating upon their minds, amidst the warmth of feeling incidental to that state of things, they have recently examined with sober attention the imperfections of their national and subordinate civil establishments: they reflected, with due seriousness, on the numerous inconveniencies, which those imperfections had produced, and upon the awful scenes in which they would probably be called upon *to suffer* or *to act*, if their civil constitutions should continue unamended: and they have since exhibited to the world the new and interesting spectacle of a whole people, meeting, as it were, *in their political plain* and *voluntarily imposing upon themselves the wholesome and necessary restraints of just government*. . . .

The public debt is smaller in proportion to the present wealth and population of the United States than the public debt of any other civilized nation.

The United States (including the operations of

the individual states) have sunk a much greater proportion of their public debt in the last ten years, than any other nation in the world.

The expences of the government are very much less; in proportion to wealth and numbers, than those of any nation in Europe.

There is no land tax among the national revenues, nor is there any interior tax, or excise upon food, drink, fuel, lights, or any native or foreign manufacture, or native or foreign production, except a duty of about four pence sterling upon domestic distilled spirits. The greatest part of the public burdens are paid by an import duty on foreign goods, which being drawn back on exportation, it remains only on what is actually consumed. It is in that view the lowest in the world, and operates greatly in favour of American manufactures.

Trade has been encouraged by a drawback of all the import duty on foreign goods, when they are exported, excepting only a very few commodities of a particular nature, which are not desired to be much imported into, or consumed in the United States.

A national mint is established under the direction of the ablest practical man in the arts and sciences which this country contains—*David Rittenhouse*. It is provided by law that the purity and intrinsic value of the silver coin shall be equal to that of Spain, and of the gold coins to those of the strictest European nations. The government of the United States foregoes all profit from the coinage: a political and wholesome forbearance.

The banks established in the several cities of Philadelphia, New-York, Boston, Baltimore, Charleston, Alexandria, &c. divide a profit of seven and an half to eight and an half per cent. per annum at present, which is paid half yearly.

The interest of the public debt of the United States is paid quarter yearly with a punctuality absolute and perfect. There is no tax on property in the funds and banks.

The shipbuilding of the United States was greater in the year 1792, than in any former year since the settlement of the country, and it is much greater in the current year, than it was in the last. Generally speaking, the art of shipbuilding was never so well understood, never so well executed, nor was there ever a time when so many of the manufactures requisite for the furniture, tackle, apparel and arming of vessels were made in the United States.

The value of the manufactures of the United States is certainly greater than double the value of their exports in native commodities.

The value of the manufactures of the United States, is much greater than the gross value of all their imports, including the value of goods exported again.

The manufactures of the United States consist generally of articles of comfort, utility, and necessity. Articles of luxury, elegance, and shew are not manufactured in America, excepting a few kinds.

The manufactures of the United States have increased very rapidly since the commencement of the revolutionary war, and particularly in the last five years.

Household manufactures are carried on within the families of almost all the farmers and planters, and of a great proportion of the inhabitants of the villages and towns. This practice is increasing under the animating influences of private interest and public spirit.

The exports of the United States have increased in the last two years about fourteen per cent.[1]

Those exports consist in a great degree of the most necessary food of man and working animals, and of raw materials, applicable to manufactures of the most general utility and consumption.

There is not any duty upon the exportation of the produce of the earth, nor can such duty be imposed on any exported commodities: the exportation of produce may be suspended or prohibited.

Produce and all other merchandize may be freely exported in the ships and vessels of all nations (not being alien enemies) without discrimination.

The exports of the United States are five times the amount of the national taxes and duties.

The amount of the outward freight of the ships and vessels of the United States, at this time, is probably equal to all their national taxes and duties. The inward freight is considerable. The earning of the fishing vessels, in lieu of freight, are also considerable. The coasting freights are greater in value than both the last.

All ships and vessels depart from the United States, fully laden, excepting a part of the East India traders.

A large quantity of tonnage is employed in the coasting trade.

A considerable quantity of tonnage is employed in the cod and whale fisheries.

The imports of the United States are less in value than the exports, deducting the outward freights of their own ships (which are returned in goods) the net sales of their ships to foreigners, the property imported by migrators from foreign countries, and the public impost.

[1] In the last three years they have increased from eighteen millions and one quarter: to twenty-six millions of dollars. September 30th, 1793.

The very great proportion of the imports, which consists of manufactures, (and from raw materials, which America can produce) affords constant and inviting opportunities to lessen the balance against the United States, in their trade with one foreign country, holds out a certain home market to skilful and industrious manufacturers in America, and gives promises to the landholder and farmer, of a very increasing demand for their produce, in which they cannot be deceived.

The imports of the United States, for consumption, have not been swelled in proportion to the increase of their population and wealth. *The reason is, the constant introduction of new branches of manufacture, and the great extension of the old branches.*

The imports, for consumption, into the United States are composed of manufactures in a much less proportion than heretofore, owing to *the same two causes.*

The imports of the United States have almost ceased to exhibit certain articles of naval and military supply, and others of the greatest utility and consumption, owing also to *the same two causes.*

The imports of the United States are now generally brought directly (and not circuitously) from the countries which produced or manufactured them—China, India proper, the isles of Bourbon and Mauritius, Good Hope, the southern settlements of America and the West-Indies, the Wine islands, the countries on the Mediterranean and Baltic Seas, Great-Britain and Ireland, France, the Netherlands and Germany, Spain and Portugal.

Less than half the ships and vessels belonging to the United States, are sufficient to transport all the commodities they consume or import.

Their citizens may be lawfully concerned in any branch of foreign trade, whether carried on from the United States or from any other country.[2]

Their commerce is diversified and prosperous, and consists in importing for their own consumption, and for exportation; in the exporting, the coasting and inland trades; the Indian trade; manufactures, shipping, the fisheries, banking, and insurances on ships, cargoes, and houses. There is no branch of commerce foreign or domestic, in which every district, city, port, and individual, is not equally entitled to be interested.

The lawful interest of money is six per cent. per annum in most of the states: in a few it is seven per cent. in one it is five per cent.

[2] Except the slave trade, March 1794.

The commanders and other officers of the American ships are deemed skilful and judicious; from which cause, combined with the goodness of their ships and of their equipment, insurances upon their vessels are generally made in Europe, upon the most favourable terms, compared with the corresponding risques on board of the vessels of other nations.

The separate American states (with one small exception) have abolished the slave trade, and they have in some instances abolished negro slavery; in others they have adopted efficacious measures for its certain but gradual abolition. The importation of slaves is discontinued, and can never be renewed so as to interrupt the repose of Africa, or endanger the tranquility of the United States. The steady use of efficacious *alteratives* is deemed preferable to the immediate application of more strong remedies in a case of so much momentary and intrinsic importance.

The clothes, books, household furniture, and the tools or implements of their trade or profession, brought by emigrators to America, are exempted from the import duty, and they may begin their commerce, manufactures, trades or agriculture on the day of their arrival upon the same footing as a native citizen.

There is no greater nor other tax upon foreigners or their property in the United States, than upon native citizens.

All foreign jurisdiction in ecclesiastical matters is inconsistent with the laws and constitutions of the United States; and with the settled judgment of the people.

Almost every known christian church exists in the United States; as also the Hebrew church. There has not been a dispute between any two sects or churches since the revolution. There are no tythes. Marriage and burial fees, small glebes, land-rents, pew-rents, monies at interest and voluntary contributions are the principal means of supporting the clergy. Many of them are also professors and teachers in the universities, colleges, academies and schools, for which interesting stations, pious and learned ministers of religion are deemed particularly suitable. There is no provision in the episcopal, presbyterian or independent church for any clerical person, or character above a rector, or minister of the gospel—and this is generally, if not universally the case. There are some assistant ministers, but no curates, or vicars: also several bishops without salaries.

The poor taxes in the United States are very small, owing to the facility, with which every man and woman, and every child, who is old enough to do the lightest work, can procure a comfortable subsistence. The industrious poor, if frugal and sober, often place themselves, in a few years, above want.

Horses and cattle, and other useful beasts, imported for breeding, are exempted by law from the import duty.

All the lands in the United States are free from tythes.

The medium annual *land rents* of Europe are greater per acre than the medium *purchase* is in the United States; including in the estimate the value of the old improved farms in America, and the great mass of unimproved lands. . . .

The education of youth has engaged a great share of the attention of the legislatures of the states.

Night schools for young men and boys, who are employed at labour or business in the day time, have been long and beneficially supported, and the idea of Sunday schools has been zealously adopted in some places. Free schools for both sexes have been increased. Greater attention, than heretofore, is paid to female education.

The people of the United States are ingenious in the invention, and prompt, and accurate in the execution of mechanism and workmanship for purposes in science, arts, manufactures, navigation, and agriculture. Rittenhouse's planetarium, Franklin's electrical conductor, Godfrey's quadrant improved by Hadley, Rumsey's and Fitch's steam-engines, Leslie's rod pendulum and other horological inventions, the construction of ships, the New-England whale-boat, the construction of flour-mills, the wire-cutter and bender for card makers, Folsom's and Brigg's machinery for cutting nails out of rolled iron, the Philadelphia dray with an inclined plane, Mason's engine for extinguishing fire, the Connecticut steeple clock, which is wound up by the wind, the Franklin fireplace, the Rittenhouse stove, Anderson's threshing machine, Rittenhouse's instrument for taking levels, Donnaldson's hippopotamus and balance lock, and Wynkoop's underlators, are a few of the numerous examples.

It is probable, that all the jewels and diamonds worn by the citizens of the United States, their wives and daughters are less in value than those which sometimes form a part of the dress of an individual in several countries of Europe. *All capital stock is kept in action.* There are no *descriptions* of men in America and very few individuals, at the active times of life, who live without some pursuit of business, profession, occupation, or trade. *All the citizens are in active habits.*

No country of the same wealth, intelligence and civilization, has so few *menial* servants (strictly speaking) in the families of persons of the greatest property.

Family servants and farming servants, who emigrate from Europe, and who continue soberly and industriously in family or farm service, for one, two or three years, very often find opportunities to better their situations, by getting into some little comfortable line of dealing, or trade, or manufacturing, or farming, according to their education, knowledge and qualifications.

America has not many charms for the dissipated and voluptuous part of mankind, but very many indeed for the rational, sober minded and discreet. It is a country which affords great opportunities of comfort and prosperity to people of good property, and those of moderate property, and to *the industrious and honest poor;* a singular and pleasing proof of which last assertion is, that *there are very few, if any, day labourers, in the city and liberties of Philadelphia, of the Quaker church.* That religious society is very numerous, but the sobriety, industry, and frugality which they practice, enables their poor quickly to improve their condition, in a country so favourable to the poorest members of the community.

That part of the tradesmen and manufacturers, who live in the country, generally reside on small lots and farms, of one acre to twenty, and not a few upon farms of twenty to one hundred and fifty acres, which they cultivate at leisure times, with their own hands, their wives, children, servants and apprentices, and sometimes by hired labourers, or by letting out fields, for a part of the produce, to some neighbour, who has time or farm hands not fully employed. *This union of manufactures and farming* is found to be very convenient on the grain farms, but it is still more convenient on the grazing and grass farms, where parts of almost every day, and a great part of every year, can be spared from the business of the farm, and employed in some mechanical, handycraft, or manufacturing business. These persons often make domestic and farming carriages, implements and utensils, build houses and barns, tan leather, manufacture hats, shoes, hosiery, cabinetwork, and other articles of clothing and furniture, to the great convenience and advantage of the neighbourhood. In like manner some of the farmers, at leisure times and proper seasons, manufacture nails, pot-ash, pearl-ash, staves and heading, hoops and handspikes, axe-handles, maple-sugar, &c. The most judicious planters in the southern states are industriously instructing their negroes, particularly the young, the old, the infirm, and the females in manufactures—a wise and humane measure.

A large proportion of the most successful manufacturers in the United States are persons, who were journeymen, and in a few instances were foremen in the work-shops and manufactories of Europe, who having been skilfull, sober and frugal, and having thus saved a little money, have set up for themselves with great advantage in America. Few have failed to succeed. There appears to be least opening for those, who have been used to make very fine and costly articles of luxury and shew. There is not so much chance of success for those luxurious branches, *unless they are capable of being carried on in a considerable degree by machinery or water works;* in which case they also will thrive if the necessary capital be employed.—There is already some consumption of these fine goods in America, and as free an exportation of them (without duty, or excise) as from any country in the world.

The views of the government of the United States appear by its declaration, and by the strongest presumptive proofs to be *the maintenance of peace, order, liberty and safety.* Intrigues at foreign courts and secret or open interpositions or intermeddling in the affairs of foreign countries, have not been imputed to the government of this nation. They have not manifested any inordinate ambition, by seeking *conquest,* alone or in unity with any other nation, for they have not attempted to establish or raise a great or unnecessary navy or army.

The United States have been prudently and unremittingly attentive to those objects, which enable a country to pursue, to an happy and profitable issue, unambitious, defensive and necessary wars. Amidst an industrious cultivation of the arts of peace, they have maintained and improved *the military organization of the whole mass of the able bodied citizens.* They have restored their public credit, as an indispensible mean of war, and they have successfully encouraged all those arts, by which the instruments of naval and land armaments may be expeditiously procured and created. Their measure of retribution to their public creditors, foreign and domestic, has been considered, by some intelligent citizens as even more than justice required. From an equal love of justice, and from prudential considerations, they have, by a formal act of the people, sanctioned a treaty recognizing the claims of the subjects of a foreign country against whom an infraction and non execution of the same treaty was alledged. Refraining most scrupulously from intrigues and influence in the affairs of foreign nations it cannot be doubted, that they will be aware of corresponding intrigues and influence in their domestic affairs, and that they will check the appearances of such attempts with displeasure and effect.

THE END OF AN ERA

ON MARCH 4, 1801, a tall, loosely-built man with fading red hair walked from his lodgings to a half-finished Capitol and delivered his inaugural address. Jefferson's peaceful and uncontested presence in that place might have seemed to him a vindication of his own belief in men's ability to rule themselves. A presidential campaign of unexampled bitterness had been followed by a hung election: all the Republican electors had cast their ballots for Thomas Jefferson and Aaron Burr and, since the Constitution then made no provision for distinguishing between the candidate for President and the candidate for Vice-President, that equality of votes gave the decision to the House of Representatives voting as states.

The situation afforded ample scope for intrigue. Aaron Burr, who had broadcast the attack on John Adams in which Hamilton demonstrated his unfitness for party management, saw himself the President. But Hamilton, who had devised a scheme for diverting the electoral vote of New York to the Federalists —a scheme which Federalist John Jay pigeonholed with the somewhat smug description of "unworthy"—could not tolerate the choice of Aaron Burr; he threw his support to Jefferson, who was named President by the House.

Thus, on March 4, 1801, Thomas Jefferson stood up to state his philosophy of government. An essay in self-limited power and peaceable coercion of foreign enemies was about to be begun. Yet the eight years of Jefferson's administration are remembered for a wide extension of federal power—the Louisiana Purchase— and for Congressional refusal to continue the embargo as a means of national defense.

The selection is from the *Works* (1907).

The First Inaugural

BY THOMAS JEFFERSON

FRIENDS AND FELLOW CITIZENS:—

CALLED UPON to undertake the duties of the first executive office of our country, I avail myself of the presence of that portion of my fellow citizens which is here assembled, to express my grateful thanks for the favor with which they have been pleased to look toward me, to declare a sincere consciousness that the task is above my talents, and that I approach it with those anxious and awful presentiments which the greatness of the charge and the weakness of my powers so justly inspire. A rising nation, spread over a wide and fruitful land, traversing all the seas with the rich productions of their industry, engaged in commerce with nations who feel power and forget right, advancing rapidly to destinies beyond the reach of mortal eye—when I contemplate these transcendent objects, and see the honor, the happiness, and the hopes of this beloved country committed to the issue and the auspices of this day, I shrink from the contemplation, and humble myself before the magnitude of the undertaking. Utterly indeed, should I despair, did not the presence of many whom I here see remind me, that in the other high authorities provided by our constitution, I shall find resources of wisdom, of virtue, and of zeal, on which to rely under all difficulties. To you, then, gentlemen, who are charged with the sovereign functions of legislation, and to those associated with you, I look with encouragement for that guidance and support which may enable us to steer with safety the vessel in which we are all embarked amid the conflicting elements of a troubled world.

During the contest of opinion through which we have passed, the animation of discussion and of exertions has sometimes worn an aspect which might impose on strangers unused to think freely and to speak and to write what they think; but this being now decided by the voice of the nation, announced according to the rules of the constitution, all will, of course, arrange themselves under the will of the law, and unite in common efforts for the common good. All, too, will bear in mind this sacred principle, that though the will of the majority is in all cases to prevail, that will, to be rightful, must be reasonable; that the minority possess their equal rights, which equal laws must protect, and to violate which would be oppression. Let us, then, fellow citizens, unite with one heart and one mind. Let us restore to social intercourse that harmony and affection without which liberty and even life itself are but dreary things. And let us reflect that having banished from our land that religious intolerance under which mankind so long bled and suffered, we have yet gained little if we countenance a political intolerance as despotic, as wicked, and capable of as bitter and bloody persecutions. During the throes and convulsions of the ancient world, during the agonizing spasms of infuriated man, seeking through blood and slaughter his long-lost liberty, it was not wonderful that the agitation of the billows should reach even this distant and peaceful shore; that this should be more felt and feared by some and less by others; that this should divide opinions as to measures of safety. But every difference of opinion is not a difference of principle. We have called by different names brethren of the same principle. We are all republicans—we are federalists. If there be any among us who would wish to dissolve this Union or to change its republican form, let them stand undisturbed as monuments of the safety with which error of opinion may be tolerated where reason is left free to combat it. I know, indeed, that some honest men fear that a republican government cannot be strong; that this government is not strong enough. But would the honest patriot, in the full tide of successful experiment, abandon a government which has so far kept us free and firm, on the theoretic and visionary fear that this government, the world's best hope, may by possibility want energy to preserve itself? I trust not. I believe this, on the contrary, the strongest government on earth. I believe it is the only one where every man, at the call of the laws, would fly to the standard of the law, and would meet invasions of the public order as his own personal concern. Sometimes it is said that man cannot be trusted with the government of himself. Can he, then, be trusted with the government of others? Or have we found angels in the forms of kings to govern him? Let history answer this question.

Let us, then, with courage and confidence pursue our own federal and republican principles, our attachment to our union and representative government. Kindly separated by nature and a wide ocean from the exterminating havoc of one quarter of the globe; too high-minded to endure the degradations of the others; possessing a chosen country, with room enough for our descendants to the hundredth and thousandth generation; entertaining a due sense of our equal right to the use of our own faculties, to the acquisitions of our industry, to honor and confidence from our fellow citizens, resulting not from birth but from our actions and their sense of them; enlightened by a benign religion, professed, indeed, and practiced in various forms, yet all of them including honesty, truth, temperance, gratitude, and the love of man; acknowledging and adoring an overruling Providence, which by all its dispensations proves that it delights in the happiness of man here and his greater happiness hereafter; with all these blessings, what more is necessary to make us a happy and prosperous people? Still one thing more, fellow citizens—a wise and frugal government, which shall restrain men from injuring one another, which shall leave them otherwise free to regulate their own pursuits of industry and improvement, and shall not take from the mouth of labor the bread it has earned. This is the sum of good government, and this is necessary to close the circle of our felicities.

About to enter, fellow citizens, on the exercise of duties which comprehend everything dear and valuable to you, it is proper that you should understand what I deem the essential principles of our government, and consequently those which ought to shape its administration. I will compress them within the narrowest compass they will bear, stating the general principle, but not all its limitations. Equal and exact justice to all men, of whatever state or persuasion, religious or political; peace, commerce, and honest friendship, with all nations—entangling alliances with none; the support of the state governments in all their rights, as the most competent administrations for our domestic concerns and the surest bulwarks against anti-republican tendencies; the preservation of the general government in its whole constitutional vigor, as the sheet anchor of our peace at home and safety abroad; a jealous care of the right of election by the people—a mild and safe corrective of abuses which are lopped by the sword of the revolution where peaceable remedies are unprovided; absolute acquiescence in the decisions of the majority—the vital principle of republics, from which there is no appeal but to force the vital principle and immediate parent of despotism; a well-disciplined militia—our best reliance in peace and for the first moments of war, till regulars may relieve them; the supremacy of the civil over the military authority; economy in the public expense, that labor may be lightly burdened;

the honest payment of our debts and sacred preservation of the public faith; encouragement of agriculture, and of commerce as its handmaid; the diffusion of information and the arraignment of all abuses at the bar of public reason; freedom of religion; freedom of the press; freedom of person under the protection of the *habeas corpus;* and trial by juries impartially selected—these principles form the bright constellation which has gone before us, and guided our steps through an age of revolution and reformation. The wisdom of our sages and the blood of our heroes have been devoted to their attainment. They should be the creed of our political faith—the text of civil instruction—the touchstone by which to try the services of those we trust; and should we wander from them in moments of error or alarm, let us hasten to retrace our steps and to regain the road which alone leads to peace, liberty, and safety.

I repair, then, fellow citizens, to the post you have assigned me. With experience enough in subordinate offices to have seen the difficulties of this, the greatest of all, I have learned to expect that it will rarely fall to the lot of imperfect man to retire from this station with the reputation and the favor which bring him into it. Without pretensions to that high confidence reposed in our first and great revolutionary character, whose preëminent services had entitled him to the first place in his country's love, and destined for him the fairest page in the volume of faithful history, I ask so much confidence only as may give firmness and effect to the legal administration of your affairs. I shall often go wrong through defect of judgment. When right, I shall often be thought wrong by those whose positions will not command a view of the whole ground. I ask your indulgence for my own errors, which will never be intentional; and your support against the errors of others, who may condemn what they would not if seen in all its parts. The approbation implied by your suffrage is a consolation to me for the past; and my future solicitude will be to retain the good opinion of those who have bestowed it in advance, to conciliate that of others by doing them all the good in my power, and to be instrumental to the happiness and freedom of all.

Relying, then, on the patronage of your good will, I advance with obedience to the work, ready to retire from it whenever you become sensible how much better choice it is in your power to make. And may that Infinite Power which rules the destinies of the universe, lead our councils to what is best, and give them a favorable issue for your peace and prosperity.

THE UNITED STATES AND THE WORLD

THE LOUISIANA PURCHASE

By the Peace of Paris of 1763, a defeated France yielded Canada to England and the province of Louisiana to Spain. Except for St. Pierre and Miquelon and the French Antilles in the Caribbean, France had lost her empire in North America. Considered as a war of revenge to redress that loss, the alliance with England's revolted colonies in the next decades brought France slight profit, for her naval forces were defeated in the West Indies and France made no gains on the mainland: Canada was English and Louisiana remained under Spanish rule.

For all the wide ranging of *voyageur* and fur trader, to western men Louisiana was still a broad wilderness. By raft and flatboat and broadhorn, the grain and pelts, the pork and whisky of Ohio and Kentucky and Tennessee passed down the Mississippi and out into the stream of trade. Whoever held New Orleans and the mouth of the river could choke the economic life of the West. Without the right of deposit—the permission to warehouse goods free of burdensome Spanish duties and to ship them from New Orleans—the American West could not share in world trade at the beginning of the nineteenth century. Lumber and furs and grain and provisions could not bear the cost of carriage to an Atlantic port; the men of the Western Waters were sentenced to vegetate in a subsistence economy unless they were assured unhindered access to the Gulf.

During the Revolution, Spanish officials had connived at the use of their port, though that was against their government's settled colonial policy. American commerce continued to use New Orleans on the precarious basis of "Latin realism" until 1795, when Prime Minister Godoy negotiated a formal treaty with the United States. This granted Americans the right of deposit at New Orleans for three years. If, after that period, the King of Spain found the privilege harmless to his interests, he might extend it, or, at worst, create a similar *entrepôt* at another point on the lower Mississippi.

Not long after the treaty of 1795, the French sought to regain their North American possessions. Napoleon's ambassador bullied the Spanish court into accepting the secret treaty of San Ildefonso: in return for French agreement to add a million inhabitants to the Duchy of Parma—where a Spanish prince reigned—the Mississippi Valley was to be returned to France, transfer to be consummated on evidence that France had kept her part of the bargain. Napoleon presumably carried out his pledge; but the Spaniards temporized.

Peace between England and France, however, encouraged Napoleon to proceed with his plans for a French colonial empire. He needed a base in the West Indies first. Haiti, the most valuable of French possessions, would serve admirably, but for the fact that it was in possession of Toussaint L'Ouverture, the Negro general who was military chief of the island by reason of his own ability, the French Convention's appointment, and the connivance of both Britain and the United States.

If Napoleon meant to take possession of Louisiana, he must eliminate Toussaint. And in that task he was aided by the restoration of diplomatic relations between France and the United States in 1801. American frigates could not cruise to protect a rebel against a France with which the United States was at peace; nor could furthering the triumph of a Negro insurrectionist be agreeable to Americans who themselves held slaves. Napoleon prepared to end "the black government at Santo Domingo" and to restore slavery in the French Antilles. Early in 1802, French forces landed and war began. The treachery of Toussaint's generals and his own naïveté combined to end his career: he surrendered and was imprisoned in France. With Toussaint a defeated captive, Napoleon ordered a gradual and cautious restoration of slavery while he made ready to exact the delivery of Louisiana from a reluctant Spain. In the meantime, the general in command of the French army which had captured Toussaint discovered that most of the supplies on the island were American property. These were confiscated over the protests of the American Minister at Paris.

In the spring of 1802, the retrocession of Louisiana became generally known in America, though it had been the subject of anxious reports in the dispatches Secretary of State Madison was receiving from Rufus King in London and Robert R. Livingston at Paris. Jefferson's letter to Livingston shows how he regarded the situation. The United States could not stand alone in this crisis. Beneath his plans for shifts of diplomacy, one may read Jefferson's fears for the safety of democracy in America. Through his friend Dupont de Nemours, Jefferson attempted to convince the First Consul of the danger in which the occupation of Louisiana would put France. For the power which held New Orleans was the natural enemy of the United States. French occupation of the province would drive the United States into an alliance with England and set the two chief maritime powers squarely across Napoleon's path. Dupont's reply indicated that Napoleon was not likely to be convinced by that argument.

Meanwhile, a new French army was failing in its attempt to pacify Santo Domingo. And, in December, 1802, the Spanish Intendant withdrew the right of deposit. The West was now thoroughly alarmed and a war sentiment appeared in Congress; this Jefferson was able to halt by the appointment of Monroe as special envoy to negotiate with France.

Both the political background and the purpose of the negotiations appear clearly in Jefferson's letter urging Monroe to accept the mission and in the instructions which the special envoy carried to France. New Orleans and the Floridas were the objects of the administration's attention; if those could not be secured, then the United States might be satisfied with the cession of a site on the banks of the Mississippi. Free navigation and the right of deposit were Jefferson's concern; a war for national interest was no part of his policy, however convenient such intimations might be in diplomatic correspondence.

Before Monroe reached France, a French prefect had been dispatched with instructions to guide French policy in the administration of the restored province. Guardedly, those instructions advised the captain-general of Louisiana to intrigue with the Kentuckians, ally himself with the Indian tribes, and, while expressing "sentiments of great benevolence," prepare for eventual hostilities with the United States. But by now Santo Domingo had proved to be a complete failure and Napoleon once more was directing his eyes eastward. War with England again was imminent.

Livingston had reported this new turn of events to Washington in March, 1803. On April 11, Talleyrand, stressing the "unofficial" nature of his remarks, asked the American Minister whether the United States wanted all of Louisiana, and what, in that case, they would give for it? To that disconcerting query, Livingston replied that his country had not considered such an acquisition, but that the United States would probably be willing to pay 20 million francs, if American claims for French depredations on her commerce were met. In any case, he must wait to consult with Envoy Extraordinary James Monroe who had not yet arrived in Paris. But this did not prevent Livingston from opening discussions with the French Treasury, which put the purchase price at 60 million francs.

On March 12, Monroe joined Livingston and the bargaining continued. By the end of April, Napoleon, convinced that war was inevitable and badly in need of funds, ordered the speeding up of the negotiations. In the first week of May, the treaty for the Louisiana purchase was signed. For 15 million dollars, the United States bought the province of Louisiana "with the same extent that is now in the hands of Spain, and that it had when France possessed it. . . ."

News of the treaty reached Jefferson in June. On July 4, 1803, the Purchase of Louisiana was proclaimed officially. Spain protested French violation of a promise not to alienate Louisiana after the retrocession. In America, Federalists raged at the expenditure and at Jefferson's unconstitutional exercise of power in making the purchase and in agreeing to give the inhabitants of Louisiana the rights of Americans and eventual statehood. Jefferson's message to Congress takes little account of these attacks. Henceforth, the produce of the Western Waters would float down an American river to the Gulf. The man who had drafted the document which proclaimed "these united colonies free and independent states" had initiated negotiations which doubled the area of those states at a moderate cost in money and without the expenditure of a single life.

Jefferson's letters and message to Congress are reprinted from Volume VIII of the *Writings of Thomas Jefferson*, ed. Paul Leicester Ford (New York, 1897). Madison's instructions are reprinted from House Document No. 431, *The Purchase of the Territory of Louisiana*, 57th Congress, 2d Session (Washington, 1903).

Correspondence of Thomas Jefferson

JEFFERSON TO LIVINGSTON

Washington, April 18, 1802

. . . THE SESSION of Louisiana and the Floridas by Spain to France works most sorely on the U.S. On this subject the Secretary of State has written to you fully. Yet I cannot forbear recurring to it personally, so deep is the impression it makes in my mind. It compleatly reverses all the political relations of the U.S. and will form a new epoch in our political course. Of all nations of any consideration France is the one which hitherto has offered the fewest points on which we could have any conflict of right, and the most points of a communion of interests. From these causes we have ever looked to her as our *natural friend*, as one with which we never could have an occasion of difference. Her growth therefore we viewed as our own, her misfortunes ours. There is on the globe one single spot, the possessor of which is our natural and habitual enemy. It is New Orleans, through which the produce of three-eighths of our territory must pass to market, and from its fertility it will ere long yield more than half of our whole produce and contain more than half our inhabitants. France placing herself in that door assumes to us the attitude of defiance. Spain might have retained it quietly for years. Her pacific dispositions, her feeble state, would induce her to increase our facilities there, so that her possession of the place would be hardly felt by us, and it would not perhaps be very long before some circumstance might arise which might make the cession of it to us the price of something of more worth to her. Not so can it ever be in the hands of France. The impetuosity of her temper, the energy and restlessness of her character, placed in a point of eternal friction with us, . . . render it impossible that France and the U.S. can continue long friends when they meet in so irritable a position. They as well as we must be blind if they do not see this; and we must be very improvident if we do not begin to make arrangements on that hypothesis. The day that France takes possession of N. Orleans fixes the sentence which is to restrain her forever within her low water mark. It seals the union of two nations who in conjunction can maintain exclusive possession of the ocean. From that moment we must marry ourselves to the British fleet and nation. We must turn all our attentions to a maritime force, for which our resources place us on very high grounds: and having formed and cemented together a power which may render reinforcement of her settlements here impossible to France, make the first cannon, which shall be fired in Europe the signal for tearing up any settlement she may have made, and for holding the two continents of America in sequestration for the common purposes of the united British and American nations. This is not a state of things we seek or desire. It is one which this measure, if adopted by France, forces on us, as necessarily as any other cause, by the laws of nature, brings on its necessary effect. It is not from a fear of France that we deprecate this measure proposed by her. . . . But it is from a sincere love of peace, and a firm persuasion that bound to France by the interests and the strong sympathies still existing in the minds of our citizens, and holding relative positions which ensure their continuance we are secure of a long course of peace. Whereas the change of friends, which will be rendered necessary if France changes that position, embarks us necessarily as a belligerent power in the first war of Europe. . . .

If France considers Louisiana however as indispensable for her views she might perhaps be willing to look about for arrangements which might reconcile it to our interests. If anything could do this it would be the ceding to us the island of New Orleans and the Floridas. This would certainly in a great degree remove the causes of jarring and irritation between us, and perhaps for such a length of time as might produce other means of making the measure permanently conciliatory to our interests and friendships. It would at any rate relieve us from the necessity of taking immediate measures for countervailing such an operation by arrangements in another quarter. Still we should consider N. Orleans and the Floridas as equivalent for the risk of a quarrel with France produced by her vicinage. I have no doubt you have urged these considerations on every proper occasion with the government where you are. They are such as must have effect if you can find the means of producing thorough reflection on them by that government. The idea here is that the troops sent to St. Domingo, were to proceed to Louisiana after finishing their work in that island. If this were the arrangement, it will give you time to return again and again to the charge, for the conquest of St. Domingo will not be a short work. It will take considerable time to wear down a great number of souldiers. Every eye in the U.S. is now fixed on this affair of Louisiana. Perhaps nothing since the revolutionary war has produced more uneasy sensations through the body of the nation. Notwithstanding temporary bickerings have taken place with France, she has still a strong hold on the affections of our citizens generally. I have thought it not amiss, by way of

supplement to the letters of the Secretary of State to write you this private one to impress you with the importance we affix to this transaction. I pray you to cherish Dupont. He has the best dispositions for the continuance of friendship between the two nations, and perhaps you may be able to make a good use of him. Accept assurances of my affectionate esteem and high consideration.

JEFFERSON TO MONROE

Washington, Jan. 13, 1803.

DEAR SIR,—I dropped you a line on the 10th informing you of a nomination I had made of you to the Senate, and yesterday I enclosed you their approbation not then having time to write. The agitation of the public mind on occasion of the late suspension of our right of deposit at N. Orleans is extreme. In the western country it is natural and grounded on honest motives. In the seaports it proceeds from a desire for war which increases the mercantile lottery; in the federalists generally and especially those of Congress the object is to force us into war if possible, in order to derange our finances, or if this cannot be done, to attach the western country to them, as their best friends, and thus get again into power. Remonstrances memorials &c. are now circulating through the whole of the western country and signing by the body of the people. The measures we have been pursuing being invisible, do not satisfy their minds. Something sensible therefore was become necessary; and indeed our object of purchasing N. Orleans and the Floridas is a measure liable to assume so many shapes, that no instructions could be squared to fit them, it was essential then to send a minister extraordinary to be joined with the ordinary one, with discretionary powers, first however well impressed with all our views and therefore qualified to meet and modify to these every form of proposition which could come from the other party. This could be done only in full and frequent oral communications. Having determined on this, there could not be two opinions among the republicans as to the person. You possess the unlimited confidence of the administration and of the western people; and generally of the republicans everywhere; and were you to refuse to go, no other man can be found who does this. The measure has already silenced the Feds. here. Congress will no longer be agitated by them: and the country will become calm as fast as the information extends over it. All eyes, all hopes, are now fixed on you; and were you to decline, the chagrin would be universal, and would shake under your feet the high ground on which you stand with the public. Indeed I know nothing which would produce such a shock, for on the event of this mission depends the future destinies of this republic. If we cannot by a purchase of the country insure to ourselves a course of perpetual peace and friendship with all nations, then as war cannot be distant, it behooves us immediately to be preparing for that course, without, however, hastening it, and it may be necessary (on your failure on the continent) to cross the channel.

We shall get entangled in European politics, and figuring more, be much less happy and prosperous. This can only be prevented by a successful issue to your present mission. I am sensible after the measures you have taken for getting into a different line of business, that it will be a great sacrifice on your part, and presents from the season and other circumstances serious difficulties. But some men are born for the public. Nature by fitting them for the service of the human race on a broad scale, has stamped with the evidences of her destination and their duty. . . .

As to the time of your going you cannot too much hasten it, as the moment in France is critical. St. Domingo delays their taking possession of Louisiana, and they are in the last distress for money for current purposes. You should arrange your affairs for an absence of a year at least, perhaps for a long one. It will be necessary for you to stay here some days on your way to New York. You will receive here what advance you chuse. Accept assurances of my constant and affectionate attachment.

JEFFERSON TO LIVINGSTON

Washington, Feb. 3, 1803

DEAR SIR,—My last to you was by Mr. Dupont. Since that I received yours of May 22. Mr. Madison supposes you have written a subsequent one which has never come to hand. A late suspension by the Intendant of N Orleans of our right of deposit there, without which the right of navigation is impracticable, has thrown this country into such a flame of hostile disposition as can scarcely be described. The western country was peculiarly sensible to it as you may suppose. Our business was to take the most effectual pacific measures in our power to remove the suspension, and at the some time to persuade our countrymen that pa-

cific measures would be the most effectual and the most speedily so. The opposition caught it as a plank in a shipwreck, hoping it would enable them to tack the Western people to them. They raised the cry of war, were intriguing in all the quarters to exasperate the Western inhabitants to arm & go down on their own authority & possess themselves of New Orleans, and in the meantime were daily reiterating, in new shapes, inflammatory resolutions for the adoption of the House. As a remedy to all this we determined to name a minister extraordinary to go immediately to Paris & Madrid to settle this matter. This measure being a visible one, and the person named peculiarly proper with the Western country, crushed at once & put an end to all further attempts on the Legislature. From that moment all has become quiet; and the more readily in the Western country, as the sudden alliance of these new federal friends had of itself already began to make them suspect the wisdom of their own course. The measure was moreover proposed from another cause. We must know at once whether we can acquire N Orleans or not. We are satisfied nothing else will secure us against a war at no distant period; and we cannot press this reason without beginning those arrangements which will be necessary if war is hereafter to result. For this purpose it was necessary that the negotiators should be fully possessed of every idea we have on the subject, so as to meet the propositions of the opposite party, in whatever form they may be offered; and give them a shape admissible by us without being obliged to await new instructions hence. With this view, we have joined Mr. Monroe to yourself at Paris, & to Mr. Pinkney at Madrid, altho' we believe it will be hardly necessary for him to go to this last place. Should we fail in this object of the mission, a further one will be superadded for the other side of the channel. On this subject you will be informed by the Secretary of State, & Mr. Monroe will be able also to inform you of all our views and purposes. By him I send another letter to Dupont, whose aid may be of the greatest service, as it will be divested of the shackles of form. The letter is left open for your perusal, after which I wish a wafer stuck on it before it be delivered. . . .

Correspondence of James Madison

MADISON TO LIVINGSTON AND MONROE

Department of State, March 2, 1803

GENTLEMEN: You will herewith receive a commission and letters of credence, one of you as Min-

ister Plenipotentiary, the other as Minister Extraordinary and Plenipotentiary, to treat with the Government of the French Republic on the subject of the Mississippi, and the territories eastward thereof, and without the limits of the United

States. The object in view is to procure, by just and satisfactory arrangements, a cession to the United States of New Orleans, and of West and East Florida, or as much thereof as the actual proprietor can be prevailed on to part with.

The French Republic is understood to have become the proprietor, by a cession from Spain, in the year ——, of New Orleans, as part of Louisiana, if not of the Floridas also. If the Floridas should not have been then included in the cession, it is not improbable that they will have been since added to it.

It is foreseen that you may have considerable difficulty in overcoming the repugnance and the prejudices of the French Government against a transfer to the United States of so important a part of the acquisition. The apparent solicitude and exertions, amidst many embarrassing circumstances, to carry into effect the cession made to the French Republic; the reserve so long used on this subject by the French Government, in its communications with the Minister of the United States at Paris, and the declaration finally made by the French Minister of Foreign Relations, that it was meant to take possession before any overtures from the United States would be discussed, show the importance which is attached to the territories in question. On the other hand, as the United States have the strongest motives of interest, and of a pacific policy, to seek by just means the establishment of the Mississippi, down to its mouth, as their boundary, so there are considerations which urge on France a concurrence in so natural and so convenient an arrangement.

Notwithstanding the circumstances which have been thought to indicate, in the French Government, designs of unjust encroachment, and even direct hostility, on the United States, it is scarcely possible to reconcile a policy of that sort with any motives which can be presumed to sway either the Government or the nation. To say nothing of the assurances given both by the French Minister at Paris, and by the Spanish Minister at Madrid, that the cession by Spain to France was understood to carry with it all the conditions stipulated by the former to the United States, the manifest tendency of hostile measures against the United States to connect their councils and their colossal growth with the great and formidable rival of France, can neither escape her discernment, nor be disregarded by her prudence, and might alone be expected to produce very different views in the Government.

On the supposition that the French Government does not mean to force or to court war with the United States, but, on the contrary, that it sees the interest which France has in cultivating their neutrality and amity, the dangers to so desirable a relation between the two countries which lurk under a neighborhood modified as is that of Spain at present, must have great weight in recommending the change which you will have to propose. . . .

The time chosen for the experiment is pointed out also by other important considerations. The instability of the peace of Europe, the attitude taken by Great Britain, the languishing state of the French finances, and the absolute necessity of either abandoning the West India islands, or of sending thither large armaments at great expense, all contribute at the present crisis to prepare in the French Government a disposition to listen to an arrangement which will at once dry up one source of foreign controversy, and furnish some aid in struggling with internal embarrassments. It is to be added, that the overtures committed to you coincide in great measure with the ideas of the person through whom the letter of the President of April 30, 1802, was conveyed to Mr. Livingston, and who is presumed to have gained some insight into the present sentiments of the French Cabinet.

Among the considerations which have led the French Government into the project of regaining from Spain the province of Louisiana, and which you may find it necessary to meet in your discussions, the following suggest themselves as highly probable:

First. A jealousy of the Atlantic States, as leaning to a coalition with Great Britain not consistent with neutrality and amity toward France, and a belief that, by holding the key to the commerce of the Mississippi, she will be able to command the interests and attachments of the western portion of the United States, and thereby either control the Atlantic portion also, or, if that can not be done, to seduce the former into a separate Government and a close alliance with herself.

In each of these particulars the calculation is founded in error.

It is not true that the Atlantic States lean toward any connexion with Great Britain inconsistent with their amicable relations to France. Their dispositions and their interests equally prescribe to them amity and impartiality to both of those nations. If a departure from this simple and salutary line of policy should take place, the causes of it will be found in the unjust or unfriendly conduct experienced from one or other of them. In general, it may be remarked, that there are many points on which the interests and views of the United States and of Great Britain may not be thought to coincide, as can be discovered in relation to France. If less harmony and confidence should, therefore, prevail between France and the United States than may be maintained between Great Britain and the United States, the difference will lie, not in the want of motives, drawn from the mutual advantage of the two nations, but in the want of favorable dispositions in the Government of one or other of them. That the blame, in this respect, will not justly fall on the Government of the United States, is sufficiently demonstrated by the mission, and the objects with which you are now charged.

The French Government is not less mistaken, if it supposes that the Western part of the United States can be withdrawn from their present union with the Atlantic part into a separate Government, closely allied with France.

Our Western fellow-citizens are bound to the Union, not only by the ties of kindred and affection, which for a long time will derive strength from the stream of emigration peopling that region, but by two considerations which flow from clear and essential interests.

One of these considerations is, the passage through the Atlantic ports of the foreign merchandise consumed by the Western inhabitants, and the payment thence made to a treasury, in which they would lose their participation by erecting a separate Government. The bulky productions of the Western country may continue to pass down the Mississippi; but the difficulties of the ascending navigation of that river, however free it may be made, will cause the imports for consumption to pass through the Atlantic States. This is the course through which they are now received; nor will the impost to which they will be subject change the course, even if the passage up the Mississippi should be duty free. It will not equal the difference in the freight through the latter channels. It is true that mechanical and other improvements in the navigation of the Mississippi may lessen the labor and expense of ascending the stream; but it is not the least probable, that savings of this sort will keep pace with the improvements in canals and roads, by which the present course of impost will be favored. Let it be added, that the loss of the contributions thus made to a foreign treasury would be accompanied with the necessity of providing, by less convenient revenues, for the expense of a separate Government, and of the defensive precautions required by the change of situation. . . .

It will be the more impossible for France to draw the Western country under her influence, by conciliatory regulations of the trade through the Mississippi; because regulations which would be regarded by her as liberal, and claiming returns of gratitude, would be viewed on the other side as falling short of justice. If this should not be at first the case, it soon would be so. The Western people believe, as do their Atlantic brethren, that they have a natural and indefeasible right to trade freely through the Mississippi. They are conscious of their power to enforce this right against any nation whatever. With these ideas in their minds, it is evident that France will not be able to excite either a sense of favor, or of fear, that would establish an ascendency over them. . . .

Secondly. The advancement of the commerce of France, by an establishment on the Mississippi, has, doubtless, great weight with the Government in espousing this project.

The commerce through the Mississippi will consist, first, of that of the United States; second, of that of the adjacent territories to be acquired by France.

The first is now, and must for ages continue, the principal commerce. As far as the faculties of France will enable her to share in it, the article to be proposed to her, on the part of the United States, on that subject, promises every advantage she can desire. . . .

The other portion of commerce, with the exception of the island of New Orleans, and the contiguous ports of West Florida, depends on the territory westward of the Mississippi. With respect to this portion, it will be little affected by the cession desired by the United States. . . .

There remain to be considered the commerce of the ports in the Floridas. With respect to this branch the advantages which will be secured to France by the proposed arrangement ought to be satisfactory. She will here also derive a greater share from the increase which will be given, by a more rapid settlement of a fertile territory, to the exports and imports through those ports, than she would obtain from any restrictive use she could make of those ports as her own property. . . .

With a view to permanent harmony between the two nations, a cession of the Floridas is particularly to be desired, as obviating serious controversies that might otherwise grow even out of the regulations, however liberal in the opinion of France, which she may establish at the mouths of those rivers. . . .

Third. A further object with France may be, to form a colonial establishment having a convenient relation to her West India islands, and forming an independent source of supplies for them.

This object ought to weigh but little against

the cession we wish to obtain, for two reasons: first, because the country which the cession will leave in her hands on the right side of the Mississippi is capable of employing more than all the faculties she can spare for such an object, and of yielding all the supplies which she could expect or wish from such an establishment: second, because in times of general peace she will be sure of receiving whatever supplies her islands may want, from the United States, and even through the Mississippi, if more convenient to her; because in time of peace with the United States, though of war with Great Britain, the same sources will be open to her, whilst her own would be interrupted; and because in case of a war with the United States, which is not likely to happen without a concurrent war with Great Britain, (the only case in which she could need a distinct fund of supplies,) the entire command of the sea, and of the trade through the Mississippi, would be against her, and would cut off the source in question. She would consequently never need the aid of her new colony, but when she could make little or no use of it.

There may be other objects with France in the projected acquisition; but they are probably such as would be either satisfied by a reservation to herself of the country on the right side of the Mississippi, or are of too subordinate a character to prevail against the plan of adjustment we have in view, in case other difficulties in the way of it can be overcome. The principles and outlines of this plan are as follows, viz:

ARTICLE 1. France cedes to the United States forever the territory east of the river Mississippi, comprehending the two Floridas, the island of New Orleans, and the islands lying to the north and east of that channel of the said river, which is commonly called the South Pass, together with all such other islands as appertain to either West or East Florida; France reserving to herself all her territory on the west side of the Mississippi.

ART. 2. The boundary between the territory ceded and reserved by France, shall be a continuation of that already defined above the thirty-first degree of north latitude, viz: the middle of the channel or bed of the river through the said South Pass to the sea. The navigation of the river Mississippi in its whole breadth from its source to the ocean, and in all its passages to and from the same shall be equally free and common of the United States and of the French Republic.

ART. 3. The vessels and citizens of the French Republic may exercise commerce to and at such places on their respective shores below the said thirty-first degree of north latitude as may be al-

lowed for that use by the parties to their respective citizens and vessels. And it is agreed that no other nation shall be allowed to exercise commerce to or at the same or any other place on either shore, below the said thirty-first degree of latitude. For the term of ten years, to be computed from the exchange of ratifications hereof, the citizens, vessels, and merchandises of the United States, and of France, shall be subject to no other duties on their respective shores, below the said thirty-first degree of latitude, than are imposed on their own citizens, vessels, and merchandises. No duty whatever shall, after the expiration of ten years, be laid on articles the growth or manufacture of the United States, or of the ceded territory, exported through the Mississippi in French vessels; so long as such articles so exported in vessels of the United States shall be exempt from duty: nor shall French vessels exporting such articles ever afterwards be subject to pay a higher duty than vessels of the United States.

ART. 4. The citizens of France may, for the term of ten years, deposit their effects at New Orleans, and at such other places on the ceded shore of the Mississippi, as are allowed for the commerce of the United States, without paying any other duty than a fair price for the hire of stores.

ART. 5. In ports of commerce of West and East Florida, France shall never be on a worse footing than the most favored nation; and for the term of ten years her vessels and merchandise shall be subject therein to no higher duties than are paid by those of the United States. Articles of the growth or manufacture of the United States, and of the ceded territory, exported in French vessels from any port in West or East Florida, shall be exempt from duty as long as vessels of the United States shall enjoy this exemption.

ART. 6. The United States, in consideration of the cession of territory made by this treaty, shall pay to France —— millions of livres tournois, in the manner following, viz: They shall pay —— millions of livres tournois immediately on the exchange of the ratifications hereof; they shall assume, in such order of priority as the Government of the United States may approve, the payment of claims which have been or may be acknowledged by the French Republic to be due to American citizens, or so much thereof as, with the payment to be made on the exchange of ratifications, will not exceed the sum of ——; and in case a balance should remain due after such payment and assumption, the same shall be paid at the end of one year from the final liquidation of the claim hereby assumed, which shall be payable in three equal annual payments, the first of which is to take place one year after the exchange of ratifications, or they shall bear interest, at the rate of 6 per cent. per annum, from the dates of such intended payments, until they shall be discharged. All the above-mentioned payments shall be made at the Treasury of the United States, and at the rate of one dollar and ten cents for every six livres tournois.

ART. 7. To incorporate the inhabitants of the hereby ceded territory with the citizens of the United States on an equal footing, being a provision which can not now be made, it is to be expected, from the character and policy of the United States, that such incorporation will take place without unnecessary delay. In the meantime they shall be secure in their persons and property, and in the free enjoyment of their religion. . . .

The instructions, thus far given, suppose that France may be willing to cede to the United States the whole of the island of New Orleans, and both the Floridas. As she may be inclined to dispose of a part or parts, and of such only, it is proper for you to know that the Floridas, together, are estimated at one-fourth the value of the whole island of New Orleans, and East Florida at one-half that of West Florida. In case of a partial cession, it is expected that the regulations of every other kind, so far as they are onerous to the United States, will be more favorably modified.

Should France refuse to cede the whole of the island, as large a portion as she can be prevailed on to part with may be accepted; should no considerable portion of it be attainable, it will still be of vast importance to get a jurisdiction over space enough for a large commercial town, and its appurtenances, on the back of the river, and as little remote from the mouth of the river as may be. A right to choose the place would be better than a designation of it in the treaty. Should it be impossible to procure a complete jurisdiction over any convenient spot whatever, it will only remain to explain and improve the present right of deposit, by adding thereto the express privilege of holding real estate for commercial purposes, of providing hospitals, of having consuls residing there, and other agents who may be authorized to authenticate and deliver all documents requisite for vessels belonging to, and engaged in, the trade of the United States, to and from the place of deposit. The United States can not remain satisfied, nor the Western people be kept patient, under the restrictions which the existing treaty with Spain authorizes.

Should a cession of the Floridas not be attainable, your attention will also be due to the establishment of suitable deposits at the mouth of the rivers passing from the United States through the Floridas, as well as of the free navigation of those rivers by citizens of the United States. . . .

It only remains to suggest, that, considering the possibility of some intermediate violences between citizens of the United States and the French or Spaniards, in consequence of the interruption of our right of deposit, and the probability that considerable damages will have been occasioned by that measure to citizens of the United States, it will be proper that indemnification in the latter case be provided for, and that in the former it shall not be taken on either side as a ground or pretext for hostilities.

These instructions, though as full as they could be conveniently made, will necessarily leave much to your discretion. For the proper exercise of it, the President relies on your information, your judgment, and your fidelity to the interests of your country.

James Madison

Message to Congress, 1803

BY THOMAS JEFFERSON

IN CALLING YOU TOGETHER, fellow citizens, at an earlier day than was contemplated by the act of the last session of Congress, I have not been insensible to the personal inconvenience necessarily resulting from an unexpected change in your arrangements. But matters of great public concern have rendered this call necessary, and the interest you feel in these will supersede in our minds all private considerations.

Congress witnessed, at their last session, the extraordinary agitation produced in the public mind by the suspension of our right of deposit at the port of New-Orleans, no assignment of another place having been made according to treaty. They were sensible that the continuance of that privation would be more injurious to our nation than any consequences which could flow from any mode of redress, but reposing just confidence in the good faith of the government whose officer had committed the wrong, friendly and reasonable representations were resorted to, and the right of deposit was restored.

Previous, however, to this period, we had not been unaware of the danger to which our peace would be perpetually exposed while so important a key to the commerce of the western country remained under foreign power. Difficulties, too, were presenting themselves as to the navigation of other streams, which, arising within our territories, pass through those adjacent. Propositions had, therefore, been authorized for obtaining, on fair conditions, the sovereignty of New Orleans, and of other possessions in that quarter interesting to our quiet, to such extent as was deemed practicable; and the provisional appropriation of two millions of dollars, to be applied and accounted for by the president of the United States, intended as part of the price, was considered as conveying the sanction of Congress to the acquisition proposed. The enlightened government of France saw, with just discernment, the importance to both nations of such liberal arrangements as might best and permanently promote the peace, friendship, and interests of both; and the property and sovereignty of all Louisiana, which had been restored to them, have on certain conditions been transferred to the United States by instruments bearing date the 30th of April last. When these shall have received the constitutional sanction of the senate, they will without delay be communicated to the representatives also, for the exercise of their functions, as to those conditions which are within the powers vested by the constitution in Congress. While the property and sovereignty of the Mississippi and its waters secure an independent outlet for the produce of the western States, and an uncontrolled navigation through their whole course, free from collision with other powers and the dangers to our peace from that source, the fertility of the country, its climate and extent, promise in due season important aids to our treasury, an ample provision for our posterity, and a wide-spread field for the blessings of freedom and equal laws.

With the wisdom of Congress it will rest to take those ulterior measures which may be necessary for the immediate occupation and temporary government of the country; for its incorporation into our Union; for rendering the change of government a blessing to our newly-adopted brethren; for securing to them the rights of conscience and of property: for confirming to the Indian inhabitants their occupancy and self-government, establishing friendly and commercial relations with them, and for ascertaining the geography of the country acquired. Such materials for your information, relative to its affairs in general, as the short space of time has permitted me to collect, will be laid before you when the subject shall be in a state for your consideration. . . .

Should the acquisition of Louisiana be constitutionally confirmed and carried into effect, a sum of nearly thirteen millions of dollars will then be added to our public debt, most of which is payable after fifteen years; before which term the present existing debts will all be discharged by the established operation of the sinking fund. When we contemplate the ordinary annual augmentation of imposts from increasing population and wealth, the augmentation of the same revenue by its extension to the new acquisition, and the economies which may still be introduced into our public expenditures, I cannot but hope that Congress in reviewing their resources will find means to meet the intermediate interests of this additional debt without recurring to new taxes, and applying to this object only the ordinary progression of our revenue. Its extraordinary increase in times of foreign war will be the proper and sufficient fund for any measures of safety or precaution which that state of things may render necessary in our neutral position. . . .

We have seen with sincere concern the flames of war lighted up again in Europe, and nations with which we have the most friendly and useful relations engaged in mutual destruction. While we regret the miseries in which we see others involved let us bow with gratitude to that kind Providence which, inspiring with wisdom and moderation our late legislative councils while placed under the urgency of the greatest wrongs, guarded us from hastily entering into the sanguinary contest, and left us only to look on and to pity its ravages. These will be heaviest on those immediately engaged. Yet the nations pursuing peace will not be exempt from all evil. In the course of this conflict, let it be our endeavor, as it is our interest and desire, to cultivate the friendship of the belligerent nations by every act of justice and of incessant kindness; to receive their armed vessels with hospitality from the distresses of the sea, but to administer the means of annoyance to none; to establish in our harbors such a police as may maintain law and order; to restrain our citizens from embarking individually in a war in which their country takes no part; to punish severely those persons, citizen or alien, who shall usurp the cover of our flag for vessels not entitled to it, infecting thereby with suspicion those of real Americans, and committing us into controversies for the redress of wrongs not our own; to exact from every nation the observance, toward our vessels and citizens, of those principles and practices which all civilized people acknowledge; to merit the character of a just nation, and maintain that of an independent one, preferring every consequence to insult and habitual wrong. . . . Separated by a wide ocean from the nations of Europe, and from the political interests which entangle them together, with productions and wants which render our commerce and friendship useful to them and theirs to us, it cannot be the interest of any to assail us, nor ours to disturb them. We should be most unwise, indeed, were we to cast away the singular blessings of the position in which nature has placed us, the opportunity she has endowed us with of pursuing, at a distance from foreign contentions, the paths of industry, peace, and happiness; of cultivating general friendship, and of bringing collisions of interest to the umpirage of reason rather than of force. How desirable then must it be, in a government like ours, to see its citizens adopt individually the views, the interests, and the conduct which their country should pursue, divesting themselves of those passions and partialities which tend to lessen useful friendships, and to embarrass and embroil us in the calamitous scenes of Europe. Confident, fellow citizens, that you will duly estimate the importance of neutral dispositions toward the observance of neutral conduct, that you will be sensible how much it is our duty to look on the bloody arena spread before us with commiseration indeed, but with no other wish than to see it closed, I am persuaded you will cordially cherish these dispositions in all discussions among yourselves, and in all communications with your constituents; and I anticipate with satisfaction the measures of wisdom which the great interests now committed to *you* will give you an opportunity of providing, and *myself* that of approving and carrying into execution with the fidelity I owe to my country.

THE WAR OF 1812

THE WAR OF 1812 was part of the struggle between England and Napoleon. As that conflict spread, each side tried to injure the other by cutting off its trade. Napoleon's Decrees were replies to the English Orders in Council, and neutral commerce was caught between them. As the principal neutral carrier, the United States suffered most severely, for Orders in Council attempted to confine American trade to British ports, while American ships were seized by the French in Continental ports if they abided, or were suspected of abiding, by the edicts of the English. The United States attempted to meet the problem by economic pressure. The Jeffersonian policy of Embargo and Congressional Non-Intercourse proved inadequate and finally forced the United States into the war it had been trying to avoid.

Interestingly enough, the Congressional drive for war with England appeared among representatives of inland areas; none of the leaders among the "War Hawks" of 1810 and 1811 came from a maritime district. The seaboard areas, which suffered in their commerce, were so much opposed to the policy of resisting English encroachments that New England spokesmen took alarm at governmental action. And when war broke out, they were hostile to it. To resolve the paradox, historians returned to the Congressional debates.

Nothing reveals the sectional nature of the war spirit better than the debate on the report of the special committee which had been appointed to consider the President's message of November, 1811. Madison had urged Congress to take measures to assure the country's defense in view of the threatening aspect of foreign affairs. That committee was made up of men of the Western frontier and when it brought in its report in December, the committee recommended preparation for war. Conciliation had proved useless, said Peter Porter of New York; the people of the United States, "occupying half a continent, have a right to navigate the seas without being molested by the inhabitants of the little island of Great Britain." To that advice, which might be taken for an appeal to the seaboard, Felix Grundy of Tennessee added charges of British intrigue among the Indians. The country must be rid of that danger, he declared; Canada should be annexed and the United States dominate the whole continent.

In John Randolph's (1773–1833) reply to Grundy and in Richard M. Johnson's (1780–1850) rejoinder to Randolph, the motives of the "War Hawks" and the factors impelling their supporters are plainly stated. Grundy had spoken on December ninth. On the next day, John Randolph in a long and bitter speech denounced the war policy in its every aspect. Standing armies were dangerous, Randolph argued in opposition to the committee's recommendation that the United States strengthen its military forces. A war for maritime rights now would help Napoleon fight the forces of civilization. He held up the bogey of French dominion and he warned his Southern colleagues of the danger of a slave insurrection. And then he turned on the West. This is no war for maritime rights, Randolph charged; the men who clamor for it have no nobler motive than a rise in the price of what they have to sell. Agricultural cupidity was behind the war cry.

Calhoun denied Randolph's accusation. The war party was acting from patriotism, not "the base and precarious motives" of "a probable rise in the price of hemp." Richard M. Johnson of Kentucky answered Randolph even more completely, for his speech presents all the West's grievances. He begins by paying his respects to Randolph's tribute to the mother of parliaments. It is to Hampden and Algernon Sydney, not Canning and Castlereagh that the United States owes gratitude, Johnson declared: Americans might revere martyrs to liberty; they could not respect the present corrupt government of England. For that government had been guilty of cruel incitements of the Indians. The British should be driven from North America and the United States extend its dominion over all the continent. (Thus Johnson anticipates America's "Manifest Destiny.")

Randolph returned to the attack, striking at the Western men's greed for land. It was that, not British incitements which had sent the Indians against the frontier. Randolph's invective did not prevent passage of the committee's resolutions for preparedness, however. But Randolph had the last bitter word. He urged Representatives to return home and ask their constituents whether they wanted their sons to fight the Canadians and whether they were willing to be taxed "in order that we may get possession of the great mill-seat at Niagara."

The selections are reprinted from the *Annals of Congress* (Washington, 1811) which report the debate held in the House of the 12th Congress, 1st Session.

The House Debate of December, 1811, on Preparation for War

BY JOHN RANDOLPH

... Mr. RANDOLPH said that an insinuation had fallen from the gentleman from Tennessee (Mr. GRUNDY.) that the late massacre of our brethren on the Wabash had been instigated by the British Government. Has the President given any such information? has the gentleman received any such, even informally, from any officer of this Government? Is it so believed by the Administration? He had cause to think the contrary to be the fact; that such was not their opinion. This insinuation was of the grossest kind—a presumption the most rash, the most unjustifiable. Show but good ground for it, he would give up the question at the threshold—he was ready to march to Canada. It was indeed well calculated to excite the feelings of the Western people particularly, who were not quite so tenderly attached to our red brethren as some modern philosophers; but it was destitute of any foundation, beyond mere surmise and suspicion. What would be thought, if, without any proof whatsoever, a member should rise in his place and tell us, that the massacre in Savannah, a massacre perpetrated by civilized savages, with French commissions in their pockets, was excited by the French Government? There was an easy and natural solution of the late transaction on the Wabash, in the well known character of the aboriginal savage of North America, without resorting to any such mere conjectural estimate. He was sorry to say that for this signal calamity and disgrace the House was, in part, at least, answerable. Session after session, their table had been piled up with Indian treaties, for which the appropriations had been voted as a matter of course, without examination. Advantage had been taken of the spirit of the Indians, broken by the war which ended in the Treaty of Greenville. Under the ascendency then acquired over them, they had been pent up by subsequent treaties into nooks, straightened in their quarters by a blind cupidity, seeking to extinguish their title to immense wildernesses, for which, (possessing, as we do already, more land than we can sell or use) we shall not have occasion, for half a century to come. It was our own thirst for territory, our own want of moderation, that had driven these sons of nature to desperation, of which we felt the effects.

Mr. R., although not personally acquainted with the late Colonel Daviess, felt, he was persuaded, as deep and serious regret for his loss as the gentleman from Tennessee himself. He knew him only through the representation of a friend of the deceased (Mr. Rowan) sometime a member of that House; a man, who, for native force of intellect, manliness of character, and high sense of honor, was not inferior to any that had ever sat there. With him he sympathized in the severest calamity that could befall a man of his cast of character. Would to God they were both then on the floor! From his personal knowledge of the one, he felt confident that he would have his support—and he believed (judging of him from the representation of their common friend) of the other also.

He could but smile at the liberality of the gentleman, in giving Canada to New York, in order to strengthen the Northern balance of power, while at the same time he forwarned her that the Western scale must preponderate. Mr. R. said he could almost fancy that he saw the Capitol in motion towards the falls of Ohio—after a short sojourn taking its flight to the Mississippi, and finally alighting on Darien; which, when the gentleman's dreams are realized, will be a most eligible seat of Government for the new Republic (or Empire) of the two Americas! But it seemed that "in 1808 we talked and acted foolishly," and to give some

color of consistency to that folly, we must now commit a greater. Really he could not conceive of a weaker reason offered in support of a present measure, than the justification of a former folly. He hoped we should act a wiser part—take warning by our follies, since we had become sensible of them, and resolve to talk and act foolishly no more. It was indeed high time to give over such preposterous language and proceedings.

This war of conquest, a war for the acquisition of territory and subjects, is to be a new commentary on the doctrine that Republics are destitute of ambition—that they are addicted to peace, wedded to the happiness and safety of the great body of their people. But it seems this is to be a holiday campaign—there is to be no expense of blood, or treasure, on our part—Canada is to conquer herself—she is to be subdued by the principles of fraternity. The people of that country are first to be seduced from their allegiance, and converted into traitors, as preparatory to the making them good citizens. Although he must acknowledge that some of our flaming patriots were thus manufactured, he did not think the process would hold good with a whole community. It was a dangerous experiment. We were to succeed in the French mode by the system of fraternization—all is French! but how dreadfully it might be retorted on the Southern and Western slaveholding States. He detested this subornation of treason. No—if he must have them, let them fall by the valor of our arms, by fair, legitimate conquest; not become the victims of treacherous seduction.

He was not surprised at the war spirit which was manifesting itself in gentlemen from the South. In the year 1805-6, in a struggle for the carrying trade of belligerent colonial produce, this country had been most unwisely brought into collision with the great Powers of Europe. By a series of most impolitic and ruinous measures, utterly incomprehensible to every rational, soberminded man, the Southern planters, by their own votes, had succeeded in knocking down the price of cotton to seven cents, and of tobacco (a few choice crops excepted) to nothing—and in raising the price of blankets, (of which a few would not be amiss in a Canadian campaign,) coarse woollens, and every article of first necessity, three or four hundred per cent. And now that, by our own acts, we have brought ourselves into this unprecedented condition, we must get out of it in any way, but by an acknowledgement of our own want of wisdom and forecast. But is war the true remedy? Who will profit by it? Speculators—a few lucky merchants, who draw prizes in the lottery—commissaries and contractors. Who must suffer by it? The people. It is their blood, their taxes, that must flow to support it.

But gentlemen avowed that they would not go to war for the carrying trade—that is, for any other but the direct export and import trade—that which carries our native products abroad, and brings back the return cargo; and yet they stickle for our commercial rights, and will go to war for them! He wished to know, in point of principle, what difference gentlemen could point out between the abandonment of this or of that maritime right? Do gentlemen assume the lofty port and tone of chivalrous redressors of maritime wrongs, and declare their readiness to surrender every other maritime right, provided they may remain unmolested in the exercise of the humble privilege of carrying their own produce abroad, and bringing back a return cargo? Do you make this declaration to the enemy at the outset? Do you state the minimum with which you will be contented, and put it in her power to close with your proposals at her option; give her the basis of a treaty ruinous and disgraceful beyond example and expression? and this too after having turned up your noses in disdain at the treaties of Mr. Jay and Mr. Monroe! Will you say to England, "end the war when you please, give us the direct trade in our own produce, we are content?" But what will the merchants of Salem, and Boston, and New York, and Philadelphia, and Baltimore, the men of Marblehead and Cape Cod, say to this? Will they join in a war professing to have for its object what they would consider (and justly too) as the sacrifice of their maritime rights, yet affecting to be a war for the protection of commerce?

He was gratified to find gentlemen acknowledging the demoralizing and destructive consequences of the non-importation law—confessing the truth of all that its opponents foretold when it was enacted. And will you plunge yourselves in war, because you have passed a foolish and ruinous law, and are ashamed to repeal it? "But our good friend the French Emperor stands in the way of its repeal," and as we cannot go too far in making sacrifices to him, who has given such demonstration of his love for the Americans, we must, in point of fact, become parties to his war. "Who can be so cruel as to refuse him this favor?" His imagination shrunk from the miseries of such a connexion. He called upon the House to reflect whether they were not about to abandon all reclamation for the unparalleled outrages, "insults and injuries" of the French Government, to give up our claim for plundered millions; and

asked what reparation or atonement they could expect to obtain in hours of future dalliance, after they should have made a tender of their person to this great deflowerer of the virginity of republics. We had by our own wise (he would not say *wise-acre*) measures, so increased the trade and wealth of Montreal and Quebec, that at last we began to cast a wistful eye at Canada. Having done so much towards its improvement by the exercise of "our restrictive energies," we began to think the laborer worthy of his hire, and to put in claim for our portion. Suppose it ours, are we any nearer to our point? As his Minister said to the King of Epirus, "may we not as well take our bottle of wine before as after this exploit?" Go! march to Canada! leave the broad bosom of the Chesapeake and her hundred tributary rivers—the whole line of seacoast from Machias to St. Mary's, unprotected! You have taken Quebec—have you conquered England? Will you seek for the deep foundations of her power in the frozen deserts of Labrador?

> "Her march is on the mountain wave,
> Her home is on the deep!"

Will you call upon her to leave your ports and harbors untouched, only just till you can return from Canada, to defend them? The coast is to be left defenceless, whilst men of the interior are revelling in conquest and spoil. But grant for a moment, for mere argument's sake, that in Canada you touched the sinews of her strength, instead of removing a clog upon her resources—an encumbrance, but one, which, from a spirit of honor, she will vigorously defend.. In what situation would you then place some of the best men of the nation? As Chatham and Burke, and the whole band of her patriots, prayed for her defeat in 1776, so must some of the truest friends to their country deprecate the success of our arms against the only Power that holds in check the archenemy of mankind.

Mr. R. declared, that the committee had outstripped the Executive. In designating the Power against whom this force was to be employed—as had most unadvisably been done in the preamble or manifesto with which the resolutions were prefaced—they had not consulted the views of the Executive; that designation was equivalent to an abandonment of all our claims on the French Government. No sooner was the report laid on the table, than the vultures were flocking round their prey, the carcass of a great Military Establishment—men of trained reputation, of broken fortunes (if they ever had any) and of battered constitutions, "choice spirits, tired of the dull pursuits of civil life," were seeking after agencies and commissions; willing to doze in gross stupidity over the public fire; to light the public candle at both ends. Honorable men, undoubtedly there were ready to serve their country, but what man of spirit, or of self-respect, would accept a commission in the present Army?

The gentleman from Tennessee (Mr. GRUNDY) had addressed himself, yesterday, exclusively to the "Republicans of this House." Mr. R. knew not whether he might consider himself as entitled to any part of the benefit of the honorable gentleman's discourse. It belonged not, however, to that gentleman to decide. If we must have an exposition of the doctrines of Republicanism, he should receive it from the fathers of the church, and not from the junior apprentices of the law. He should appeal to his worthy friends from Carolina, (Messrs. MACON and STANFORD,) "men with whom he had measured his strength," by whose side he had fought during the reign of terror, for it was indeed an hour of corruption, of oppression, of pollution. It was not at all to his taste, that sort of Republicanism which was supported on this side of the Atlantic by the father of the sedition law, John Adams, and by Peter Porcupine on the other. Republicanism! of John Adams! and William Cobbett! *Par nobile fratrum*, now united as in 1798, whom the cruel walls of Newgate alone keep from flying to each other's embrace—but whom, in sentiment, it is impossible to divide! Gallant crusaders in the holy cause of Republicanism! Such "Republicanism does indeed mean anything or nothing."

Our people will not submit to be taxed for this war of conquest and dominion. The Government of the United States was not calculated to wage offensive foreign war—it was instituted for the common defence and general welfare; and whosoever should embark it in a war of offence, would put it to a test which it was by no means calculated to endure. Make it out that Great Britain had instigated the Indians on the late occasion, and he was ready for battle; but not for dominion. He was unwilling, however, under present circumstances, to take Canada, at the risk of the Constitution—to embark in a common cause with France and be dragged at the wheels of the car of some Burr or Bonaparte. For a gentleman from Tennessee or Gennessee, or Lake Champlain, there may be some prospect of advantage. Their hemp would bear a great price by the exclusion of foreign supply. In that too the great importers were deeply interested. The upper country on the Hudson and the Lakes would be enriched by the supplies for the troops, which they alone could furnish. They would have the exclusive market: to say nothing of the increased preponderance from the acquisition of Canada and that section of the Union, which the Southern and Western States had already felt so severely in the apportionment bill. . . .

Rejoinder

BY RICHARD M. JOHNSON

MR. JOHNSON said he rose to thank the committee for the report which was offered to the House, and the resolutions which were recommended; though the measures fell short of his wishes, and, he believed, of public expectation. The ulterior measures, however, promised by the committee satisfied his mind, and he should give the report his warm support. The chairman had given the views of the committee. The expulsion of the British from their North American possessions, and granting letters of marque and reprisal against Great Britain are contemplated. Look at the Message of the President. At a moment least to be expected, when France had ceased to violate our neutral rights, and the olive branch was tendered to Great Britain, her Orders in Council were put into a more rigorous execution. Not satisfied with refusing a redress for wrongs committed on our coasts and in the mouths of our harbors, our trade is annoyed, and our national rights invaded; and, to close the scene of insolence and injury, regardless of our moderation and our justice, she has brought home to the "threshold of our territory," measures of actual war. As the love of peace has so long produced forbearance on our part, while commercial cupidity has increased the disposition to plunder on the part of Great Britain, I feel rejoiced that the hour of resistance is at hand, and that the President, in whom the people have so much confidence, has warned us of the perils that await them, and has exhorted us to put on the armor of defence, to gird on the sword, and assume the manly and bold attitude of war. He recommends filling up the ranks of the present Military Establishment, and to lengthen the term of service; to raise an auxiliary force for a more limited time; to authorize the acceptance of volunteers, and provide for calling out detachments of militia as circumstances may require. For the first time since my entrance into this body, there now seems to be but one opinion with a great majority—that with Great Britain war is inevitable; that the hopes of the sanguine as to a returning sense of British justice have expired; that the prophecies of the discerning have failed; and, that her infernal system has driven us to the brink of a second revolution, as important as the first. Upon the Wabash, through the influence of British agents, and within our territorial sea by the British navy, the war has already commenced. Thus, the folly, the power, and the tyranny of Great Britain, have taken from us the last alternative of longer forbearance.

Mr. J. said we must now oppose the farther encroachments of Great Britain by war, or formally annul the Declaration of our Independence, and acknowledge ourselves her devoted colonies. The people whom I represent will not hesitate which of the two courses to choose; and, if we are involved in war, to maintain our dearest rights, and to preserve our independence, I pledge myself to this House, and my constituents to this nation, that they will not be wanting in valor, nor in their proportion of men and money to prosecute the war with effect. Before we relinquish the conflict, I wish to see Great Britain renounce the piratical system of paper blockade; to liberate our captured seamen on board her ships of war; relinquish the practice of impressment on board our merchant vessels; to repeal her Orders in Council; and cease, in every other respect, to violate our neutral rights; to treat us as an independent people. The gentleman from Virginia (Mr. Randolph) has objected to the destination of this auxiliary force—the occupation of the Canadas, and the other British possessions upon our borders where our laws are violated, the Indians stimulated to murder our citizens, and where there is a British monopoly of the peltry and fur trade. I should not wish to extend the boundary of the United States by war if Great Britain would leave us to the quiet enjoyment of independence; but, considering her deadly and implacable enmity, and her continued hostility, I shall never die contented until I see her expulsion from North America, and her territories incorporated with the United States. It is strange that the gentleman would pause before refusing this force, if destined to keep the negroes in subordination—who are not in a state of insurrection as I understand—and he will absolutely refuse to vote this force to defend us against the lawless aggressions of Great Britain—a nation in whose favor he had said so much. . . .

Mr. Randolph said, Sir, if you go to war it will not be for the protection of, or defence of your maritime rights. Gentlemen from the North have been taken up to some high mountain and shown all the kingdoms of the earth; and Canada seems tempting in their sight. That rich vein of Gennesee land, which is said to be even better on the other side of the lake than on this. Agrarian cupidity, not maritime right, urges the war. Ever since the report of the Committee on Foreign Relations came into the House, we have heard but one word—like the whip-poor-will, but one eternal monotonous tone—Canada! Canada! Canada! Not a syllable about Halifax, which unquestionably should be our great object in a war for maritime security. It is to acquire a prepondering northern influence, that you are to launch into war. For purposes of maritime safety, the barren rocks of Bermuda were worth more to us than all the deserts through which Hearne and McKenzie had pushed their adventurous researches. Since this great bomb, the report of the Committee, had burst upon the House, Mr. R. had been anxiously waiting for some great political or military projector to point out a way by which we could get at Halifax, or even at Quebec. He had seen and heard nothing that indicated a tolerably correct information of the subject. Whilst England maintained the mastery of the seas, and could throw supplies into them at pleasure, he supposed they were to be starved out. He was forcibly reminded of a ludicrous caricature, published soon after the siege of Gibraltar. That fortress was represented to lie in the moon—and whilst the Duke de Crillon was making passes at it with a small sword, Don Quixote, on his Rosinante, with Sancho (the best and most honest Governor of whom he had ever heard) mounted on Dapple, at his back, exclaimed, with true Castilian gravity to his trusty squire, "we'll starve them out Sancho!" This *tit-bit*, Canada, which had inflamed the cupidity of northern contractors, made us forget the disturbances among our savage neighbors —the hostilities committed or meditated along our whole northwestern and southern frontier. Symptoms of discontent were manifesting themselves among the Creeks—in the State of Georgia. As to Louisiana, he did not consider it as an integral part of the United States. We had bought it and might sell it—he felt himself as much at liberty to sell it as to dispose of his own slaves. If we were to have war, he hoped it would be for something of greater national benefit than to enrich the commissaries and contractors from Michillimackinac to Niagara and Frontignac. . . .

Part Four

JACKSONIAN DEMOCRACY

INTRODUCTION

1. THE GROWTH OF AMERICA

By 1830, THE UNITED STATES had a population of 13,000,000; in other words, it had increased more than 150 percent since the turn of the century. It was still largely native-born and still northwest-European in origin. With the end of the Napoleonic Wars, immigration to America had been resumed and the appearance of regular sailings by new shipping companies facilitated the process; but during the 1820s only an average of 14,300 came to the country annually, and during the 1930s, 60,000. These, for the most part, were from Great Britain and Germany—with, however, an increasing number from Ireland. In 1830, considerably less than 10 percent of America's people were foreign-born.

The New England and the Middle States constituted the most populous regions of the country. New York State had 1,900,000 inhabitants, Pennsylvania 1,300,000, and Massachusetts 610,000. In the South Atlantic States, Virginia still led with 1,200,000, but North Carolina was moving up rapidly. The settlers of the Old Northwest were pushing out of their original confines. They were spreading throughout the states of Ohio, Indiana, and Illinois, extending northward into the territories of Wisconsin and Michigan, and spilling over into the trans-Mississippi West into Iowa. A similar movement had taken place in the Old Southwest. Kentuckians and Tennesseans were moving into Arkansas and Missouri, and some of the bolder spirits were accepting the invitation of the Mexican government to colonize Texas.

Population Movements. The population of the West doubled itself each decade. During the years 1810–30 six new states were admitted into the Union: Louisiana in 1812, Indiana in 1816, Mississippi in 1817, Illinois in 1818, Alabama in 1819 and Missouri in 1821. In another twenty years, to their company were to be added Arkansas (1836), Michigan (1837), Iowa (1846), Texas (1845), and Wisconsin (1848). This was a vast internal movement of the American people—stimulated by the existence of easily acquired lands and aided by the presence of the great interior communications system of the United States. People usually moved in short jumps rather than long ones: from contiguous state to contiguous state rather than across country. They walked; or traveled by Conestoga wagon; or floated down rivers on barges and keelboats. After 1812 the steamboat was to be found on the Western waters; after 1825, connecting canals linked all the important rivers of the country in one single chain. By 1830, there were almost 4,000,000 Americans in the Mississippi Valley as compared with 8,600,000 on the Atlantic slope.

The Land System. The liberalization of the American land laws aided the process. Up to 1820, public lands had been sold in large parcels and on a credit basis. After 1820, the credit system was abolished; the minimum purchase was first reduced to 80 acres and then 40 acres; and a minimum price of $1.25 an acre was set. Public lands were acquired by joint-stock companies established for that purpose, and many wealthy individuals—notably New Englanders—acquired great holdings. Banks, Western banks for the most part, were prepared to finance such operations and the business difficulties of the period—those of 1819 and 1837—were precipitated by land speculations particularly. Nevertheless, the small settler acquired the land: most frequently on credit, often by outright purchase, sometimes by squatting. The squatters' holdings were constantly being legalized, by special pre-emption laws passed by Congress and finally in 1841 by the general Preemption Law. This last allowed a cashless squatter to establish him-self on the public domain and subsequently ac-quire a quarter section of 160 acres at the minimum government price of $1.25 an acre. Quite often, the Western settler started out by being a tenant; but this was not tenancy in the European sense of small holdings, labor serv-ices, and alienation fines. Tenancy in America constituted a temporary status: the American farmer climbed up the rungs of the ladder un-til, before long, he possessed his own free-hold.

Economic Activity. There have been many American frontiers and frequently they have been interrelated. Americans penetrated into the West as drovers, fur traders, miners and rivermen: St. Louis was an early outpost of the fur trade; into Wisconsin, Illinois, and Mich-igan—side by side with cattlemen and farmers —went miners to dig out lead and copper; early Americans in distant Oregon were fur traders, and in distant California drovers and miners. Eastern capital went into the West to finance the fur trade—as in the case of John Jacob Astor—and copper mining—as in the case of William E. Dodge.

But primarily, the West was the farmer's frontier. Moving across the states, out of New England into New York and over into the Middle West and the trans-Mississippi West—in one series of waves—went the growers of wheat and corn, the sheep raisers and the pro-ducers of hogs. Out of the Old Dominion and North Carolina, into Kentucky and Tennessee and south and west into the Gulf States and Texas—in another series of waves—went the growers of hemp, tobacco, corn, and cotton. In the 1820s and 1830s wheat was being raised in the Middle West; in another decade, wheat had moved out into Iowa and the Nebraska Territory, while corn was replacing it in Ohio, Indiana, and Illinois.

The American Western farmer began with a subsistence economy—but he did not linger long there. Farms were quickly being joined to markets, by rivers, canals, and roads. The needs of the East for foods and fibers and the growing dependence of Europe upon America for flour, hemp, and cotton made it possible for specialization quickly to set in. Sheep were being raised in Ohio quite early; swine were appearing in all of the states of the Middle West; even yearling beef cattle—produced in the trans-Mississippi West—were being sent eastward into Illinois, Ohio, and Indiana for fattening before slaughter. The farmer pros-pered—and bought his land, expanded his hold-ings, acquired new and improved implements, and encouraged the extension of the social services. He was always a member of the mid-dle class in America, but became politically articulate when low prices and inadequate agri-cultural credit threatened the loss of his free-hold.

Urbanization. America was still predom-inantly rural—as it was to remain for another fifty years. In 1830, the great majority of Americans dwelt in the countryside. Indeed, in 1810 and 1820, only 5 percent of the country's population lived in places of 8,000 inhabitants or more; and for 1830 and 1840, the propor-tions were only 6.7 and 8.5 percent, respec-tively. It was not until 1850 that the processes of urbanization really began to set in; for then the proportion stood at 12.5 percent. If, in our modern world, urbanization is really the test for industrialization, then America was still largely agricultural and mercantile in its econ-omy up to the middle forties. This is not to say that fairly large urban centers did not exist. New York was now the country's first city with a population of 200,000. Philadelphia, Baltimore, and Boston followed next with pop-ulations of 161,000, 80,000, and 61,000, respec-tively. In the South, New Orleans had 46,000 inhabitants and Charleston 30,000. The West's urban centers, as one might expect, were lake and river towns. Cincinnati claimed 24,000 people, Pittsburg 12,000, Louisville 10,000, St. Louis 6,000, and Chicago less than 3,000. America's cities and towns were mercantile centers first; not for a long time did industry become significant in them. There were exceptions, of course. In Philadelphia were to be found woolen weavers, in New York sugar refiners, in Cincinnati meat packers. In all the towns on the shores of the Atlantic and the Great Lakes and on the Mississippi and the Ohio Rivers were shipwrights and boatmakers. But, by and large, industrial production in America was a rural activity rather than an urban one.

2. THE MERCANTILE ECONOMY OF AMERICA

Well into the 1850s, America's economy was agrarian and mercantile rather than industrial. That is to say, in the country the typical businessman was a farmer and in the city he was a merchant, broker, or banker. Much like the colonial businessman, the urban businessman of the 1830s and 1840s engaged in many trades, diversified his risks, and kept a good deal of his capital in liquid form. Hence he was able to finance land jobbing and manufacturing—but the latter was not industrial production in our modern sense. Thus, in a number of the outstanding American industries—in boots and shoes, in meat packing, in woolen textiles, in iron, for example—the businessman was not a factory owner, possessing and managing a plant and equipment, but a merchant or a commission man. He bought the raw materials, put them out for fabrication among country workers, and sold the finished products. At the same time, he was financing trading voyages, operating a retail or wholesale establishment, and interesting himself in joint-stock banks and insurance companies.

Cottage Production. In New England and the Middle States, particularly, production—always excepting cotton textiles—was organized along such lines. Cottage workers, usually on their own farms, worked for merchant-manufacturers on linen and woolen goods, straw hats, brooms, iron nails, boots and shoes—all those articles that did not require automatic machinery and where the processes of fabrication from raw materials into finished goods were simple. The boot and shoe industry was typical. The merchant-manufacturer was a resident of Boston or Providence or Newport and not infrequently ran a local shop. The cottagers therefore were paid often in goods, or truck, from the shelves of the store. Either above or behind the store were the central workroom and warehouse: here were to be found a few journeymen who prepared the leather for fabrication or who cut the soles and uppers. The sewing together of the shoes was performed by the cottagers—as a rule in so-called ten-footers or "ells" added to the farmhouses. The merchant-manufacturer provided the leather, binding, thread and other materials, but not the tools. The semiprocessed leather was delivered and the finished boots and shoes taken away by carriers who received a percentage of the pay of the cottagers. The shoes were put into barrels and sold to local merchants or, increasingly, moved into the Western market. As the market expanded, cash payments replaced truck and the merchant-manufacturer concentrated less on his retail establishment and more on his packing and shipping activities.

Overseas Commerce. At the same time, this Eastern merchant was deeply interested in overseas commerce. From the end of the Revolution to the 1830s, the English Mercantilist System was in process of being dismantled, although it was not formally terminated until 1850. As a result, Americans were not completely shut out of the English and colonial trades. They could send to the United Kingdom tobacco, pig and bar iron, and naval stores; and to the British West Indies lumber, live animals, rice, naval stores, and tobacco. In the beginning, these goods had to move in English ships.

During the Napoleonic Wars this was no hardship; in fact, as English and French engaged in a life and death struggle, America became the greatest carrying nation of the world. By 1810, America's merchant marine stood at 1,500,000 tons and American ships were to be found in every harbor of the seven seas. American merchants sought to supply both English and French; monopolized the trade of all the Sugar Islands; and expanded mightily into the Pacific. It was during this period that a series of triangular trades was opened up with China. Putting out of Boston, New York, and Philadelphia, American ships sailed around Cape Horn into the Pacific Ocean; stopped at Northwest trading stations to take on cargoes of furs and whale oil; or proceeded out to the Hawaiian Islands to pick up sandalwood; and thence to the China Sea where they traded their goods for spices, teas, silks, nankeens, and chinaware. As a rule, a single such voyage lasting from one to three years paid for the cost of the ship and netted handsome profits for owners, captain, and crew. From this rich China trade—which continued to flourish through the 1830s—came the Massachusetts fortunes which were invested in the New England cotton textile industry, the building of local and Western railways, and the financing of land-mortgage companies and joint-stock banks.

The carrying trade did not last—indeed, at the end of the 1830s it was already slipping. But American ships and their bold and skillful supercargoes and crews sustained the economy of America during the period when it was still a young nation; and the profits of these voyages not only made possible European borrowings by America but also created those savings that were poured into other forms of domestic enterprise. It may be said that American ships and trading voyages really built the canals, railways, and early factories of the United States.

Balance of Payments. Almost continuously right up to the early 1870s we imported more than we exported. Despite tariffs, whose schedules continued quite low until 1861, we imported metals, iron manufactures, and products made of wool, cotton, leather, glass, paper and wood. We imported, also, of course, sugar, tea and—after 1840—coffee. Our exports were naval stores, furs, rice and lumber products; but, increasingly, in the decades before the Civil War, they came to be Western wheat and flour and meat products and Southern cotton. We also borrowed European capital to help finance the first and second Bank of the United States and to build the public improvements of the 1820s and the 1830s. How did we pay for this excess of imports and the interest on foreign loans? The earnings of our merchant marine balanced our international payments. Thus, during the years 1821-37, the excess of imports over exports came to $185,000,000; interest paid to foreign investors in the United States came to $60,000,000; but the net earnings of American merchant shipping and the sale of our ships abroad came to $214,000,000. It was no wonder that America's credit was good abroad and that often specie was being sent to the United States by Europeans to settle their balances here.

Cotton Textiles. In one area of economic activity, however, industrial production was introduced and it was here that the American businessman became an industrial capitalist. This was in the case of the manufacture of cotton textiles. Small cotton mills, usually for spinning only (the weaving was done by cottagers), had appeared as early as the 1790s in Rhode Island and southern Massachusetts. They had used automatic spindles and child labor, but capitalization was small, and often these plants were simply adjuncts to mercantile establishments. The supply of English cotton goods was cut off by the War of 1812; when the war was over, the renewed competition of the English merchant marine turned the attention of New England merchants to cotton manufacture. Now for the first time the factory system appeared in America. Capital from Boston moved out to the fall-river towns of northern Massachusetts, New Hampshire, and Maine; both spinning and weaving were being performed by automatic machinery; labor was being organized and disciplined and instead of being paid in truck received money wages. How large these operations were may be noted from the fact that the Waltham Company started with a paid-in capital of $500,000 which was doubled in less than a decade. Profits were high—running to as much as 10 to 16 percent annually, but they were frequently illusory, since early accounting methods did not provide for interest, insurance, and depreciation.

The labor supply of these early mills was recruited from the countryside and consisted usually of young women who were not expected to stay more than two to four years on the job. They worked on an average 70 hours a week and received $2 a week in wages; nevertheless, they could not be regarded as an exploited factory population. Under the "Waltham System," as it was called, the operatives lived in company boardinghouses carefully supervised by matrons, and were encouraged to save their weekly wages. Most did so, in fact, and returned to their country homes before long to be replaced by their younger sisters. This continued until the end of the 1840s when a new type of management introduced the speed-up and stretch-out and substituted for the young women Canadian and Irish male immigrant workers.

Internal Improvements. It was obvious that such an America—spreading rapidly as it was over the continental domain, hunting eagerly for raw materials to move into the international market to pay for imported finished goods—should constantly concern itself with internal improvements. Colonial America had traveled by sea; early national America, moving cross-country, had to travel by land. As soon as freedom had been established and corporations could be created, private capital had appeared to finance turnpike and bridge construction. But America was not yet rich enough to de-

pend entirely on the resources of individuals; hence, recourse was had to public authority. As early as 1806, Congress was called upon to launch a program of internal improvements and, for the next quarter century, grants were generously made. Greatest of all projects was the famous Cumberland Road which crossed the Alleghenies from the Potomac River, to the Ohio and was pushed westward across Ohio, Indiana, and Illinois. This was America's first highway into the West.

By the 1820s, the interior waterways of the country were being opened up. Thanks to the steamboat, for the next two decades the Mississippi and its tributaries became great arteries of trade. There were 60 steamboats on the Mississippi in 1820 and more than 1,200 in 1850. Down its broad waters moved hemp, wheat, meat products, and cotton, meeting boatloads of sugar and finished products coming upriver. New Orleans became one of the country's great *entrepôts*, and at the same time interior markets were being served by Cincinnati and St. Louis.

Canals. Other waterways soon appeared to supplement the rivers and in fact to bind them together. Again, public capital had to take the initiative. The Erie Canal, America's first great project of the kind, was completed in 1825 at a cost of about $8,000,000. In less than ten years the capital cost had been met from toll charges. But the Erie Canal had been more than a successful financial venture: it had reduced the cost of carriage of bulk goods from Buffalo to New York from $100 to $10 a ton; it was bringing Western wheat into New York, thus permitting Eastern farmers to specialize; and it was at the basis of the New York port's greatness. Pennsylvania and New Jersey floated bond issues to follow New York's example; so, before long, did Western and Southern states. Soon, canals were connecting rivers and rivers, lakes and rivers, and rivers and the sea. They were being pushed out into the pioneer zones, through heavily wooded sections, across swamps. So great was the enthusiasm that public authority quickly overextended itself and, before long, in some of the states, the cost of servicing the debts incurred, exceeded the total annual fiscal resources.

Railroads. Frequently, early railroad building received its impetus from the same source. Many of America's first railroads were heavily subsidized by public authority—as in the case of the Baltimore and Ohio in Maryland—or built entirely by public funds—as in the case of the Michigan Central Railroad. America's credit was good and European capital flowed eagerly into the country to finance these state projects. In 1820, American states were free of debt; by 1838—to build canals, roads, and railroads, and to finance land mortgage banks—their indebtedness stood at close to $200,000,-000. This was a speculative bubble, obviously, although Europeans had invested in good faith; and it collapsed in the panic of 1837. Land jobbing, as has been pointed out, had contributed its share to the boom, as had the unhealthy financial activities of state-chartered banks, those of the West and South in particular.

Many of the Southern and Western states were compelled to default on interest payments or to repudiate their obligations outright. In all, foreign investors lost $40,000,000 in America and so outraged were they that European capital stayed away from our shores for almost a generation. This fact, together with the simultaneous decline of the China trade, led to hard times in the commercial centers of the country for half a decade. By the middle 1840s America was once more prospering: now the railroad age really had its beginnings. The early short lines were rebuilt and linked into systems; New England capital invested heavily in Michigan and Illinois railroads; and by 1850 the United States could boast of 9,000 miles of track.

The Workers. Because the American economy was still by and large at a preindustrial level—the businessman was a merchant, banker, and speculator all rolled into one—the American worker was not yet a factory hand. He was a skilled mechanic or journeyman in the employ of a fellow artisan, looking for-

ward to the time when he could set up his own small shop; he was a country cottage worker supplementing agricultural income; he labored in a country forge or mill—and then went West as a squatter or tenant. Permanence in the laboring status had not yet appeared. There was too much fluidity in American society, capital units were still too small, there was an absence of integration and concentration; with the result that, by and large, a class-consciousness was still absent. If anything, the worker regarded himself as a member of the middle class, psychologically and functionally. And such associational programs as he participated in were usually directed toward narrowing the gap between employer-artisan and journeyman-artisan rather than proclaiming the unbridgeable gulf between classes. The doctrine of the class struggle did not appear in America until the 1850s; and even then it was brought in by German immigrants.

This is not to say that there were no working-class organizations and working-class programs. These came and went; but they ended by being essentially lower middle class. As early as the 1790s societies of journeymen shoemakers, printers, carpenters, and tailors had made their appearance. They had been formed on a local basis to protest against the extension of apprenticeship and to demand minimum wages and a ten-hour day. There were strikes; participants were blacklisted; and criminal actions were started against leaders.

In the late 1820s, more ambitious projects appeared. In New York and in Philadelphia, skilled artisans and some urban homeworkers pooled their strength and formed unions of trade associations. A Workingmen's party made its appearance in Philadelphia in 1828 and one was formed in New York in 1829; and their demands reflect the mixed and somewhat confused condition of their membership. Their programs called for the end of imprisonment for debt, the militia system, and the conspiracy laws; the enactment of mechanics' lien laws; and the establishment of a public education system. Attacks were made on "monopolies," notably the banks, but this is because they feared an undue control over credit. In short, this was an agitation directed by the smaller producers against the larger ones.

Thomas Skidmore, one of the leaders of the New York party, was in reality an agrarian; to him, the only road to emancipation was the return to the land and its communal operation. He therefore demanded the calling of a constitutional convention which would abolish all debts and all property titles. Another group, led by Robert Dale Owen and Frances Wright, saw in free education "the only effectual remedy for this and for almost every species of injustice." These workingmen's parties did not survive beyond 1833.

Embryonic trade unions did make their appearance in the early 1830s and were combined into city central councils. There were such bodies in New York, Philadelphia, Boston, Baltimore, Newark, Albany, Troy, Pittsburgh, Cincinnati and Louisville. Here were gathered spokesmen for the journeymen-artisans of the day—the shoemakers, tailors, hatters, bakers, printers, and the like—who used the strike weapon for the ten-hour day and higher wages. These industrial disputes were carried on violently and as a rule unsuccessfully. One of the casualties of the hard times following 1837, they virtually disappeared everywhere throughout the country. Organization and strikes also took place in the cotton textile centers, where real factory workers in the modern sense were making their appearance. Their achievements were no more permanent than those of the city artisans.

Nothing reveals more clearly the continued middle-class orientation of leadership and following of these early city craft groups than their general demands. They endorsed producers' cooperation; sometimes (following the American anarchist Warren and the French anarchist Proudhon) they sought the establishment of labor-exchange banks; they wanted freer entry into the public domain for pre-emptioners and homesteaders; and they clamored for free education.

These are some of the characteristics of a period and a people that listened earnestly and responded quickly to the equalitarian preachments of Jacksonian Democracy.

3. LEVELING TENDENCIES

The Rise of Democracy. Those leveling tendencies—always a characteristic of America and a part of its English heritage—that played so prominent a role in the Revolutionary period, were for a brief time suppressed. Under the leadership of the Federalists, aristocratic views prevailed: the aspirations and needs of the common man were lost sight of. But Independency was too strong a trait to be easily suppressed, and in a land where opportunity existed on every hand it was impossible to perpetuate privilege or to check equalitarianism.

Many factors contributed to the rise of the common man in the 1830s. American nationalism had emerged unscathed from its first great trial, that of the Napoleonic Wars and the ensuing European reaction. The American was no longer a citizen of the world but a citizen of the United States, and he took pride in its accomplishments and its future. His eyes increasingly were turned Westward, and on every side he saw outlets for his energy and enterprise, and security if not a fortune as his reward. The expansion of the continental domain fed this hope: as miner, riverman, farmer, trader, the American could achieve economic success. The same was true of mercantile pursuits: only small capitals were necessary to begin an enterprise; a single trading voyage was enough to lay the foundations for a fortune; wealth grew with the country.

Americans took along with them into the West the great tradition of the public schools. Where every man could receive an education it was idle to assume that there was a natural inequality of talent. The little white church, the little red schoolhouse, the quarter-section preemption—these were the mainsprings that fed American equalitarianism. Equal political and civil rights had to follow as a matter of course.

The thirties saw the final triumph of political equalitarianism: for the tone of American society was set by the small independent farmers and the middle-class traders and merchants who came from the ranks of the American yeomanry. The first victories were won in the states, just as the first abortive attempts to establish democracy had occurred in the states during 1776–83. In 1791, Vermont had entered the Union with a constitution guaranteeing universal manhood suffrage; new Western states followed suit. In Maryland in 1809, in Connecticut in 1818, in Massachusetts in 1820, in New York in 1821, new state constitutions were incorporating those basic guaranties of democratic government—manhood suffrage, popularly elected judges, equality of representation, and removal of religious disabilities. And with these went the institutional devices of "rotation of office" (short elective terms) and "the spoils of office." In this way, a bureaucracy would be nipped in the bud. Only the Southern states lagged behind. It was not until the fifties that most of them had enfranchised all their male adult whites.

Andrew Jackson personified the democratic hope; he did not produce it. Jackson was a passionate equalitarian, as were most Americans of his generation. But Jackson, in the true sense, was a popular leader. He knew the aspirations of the American people; he distrusted, along with most of them, wealth based on speculation and privilege; and his utterances and prejudices were those of his times. The Democratic party was created as an instrument to express the needs and articulate the programs of a middle-class America already on the march.

Political Parties. With the disappearance of the Federalists from the political scene, for almost a whole generation the "Virginia dynasty" dominated American political life. James Madison had succeeded Thomas Jefferson for two terms and he in turn was followed by James Monroe for another two terms. The Republicans had spread their influence into the states, as has been seen, and had been notably successful in attracting the support of the newly arrived immigrants, particularly the Irish. Political machines appeared in the urban centers and in some of the states, considerably before they emerged as institutional devices in national politics.

The election of 1824 marked a turning point in American political history. The Revolutionary generation was largely dead and new names and leaders were now in the forefront; too, political campaigns had become popular contests—with that same slurring over of fundamental issues that was to continue a characteristic of American political life. In 1828, in 1860, in 1896, in 1912, and in 1932 lines were clearly drawn and class hostilities openly emerged; elections in those years resulted in sharp changes in orientation and policy. But these were exceptions. Normally, the United States was too large and its sectional interests too diverse to permit the unequivocal phrasing of differences. People voted their loyalties and prejudices rather than for or against an integrated program.

In 1824, there were four candidates for the Presidency, all of whom had been born after the French and Indian War was over. They were Andrew Jackson of Tennessee, W. H. Crawford of Georgia, Henry Clay of Kentucky, and John Quincy Adams of Massachusetts. None of them adopted a party designation and all presumably were Republicans, but before long significant differences were to emerge and new party alignments were to take place. Because none of the candidates received a majority in the electoral college, the election was thrown into the House of Representatives. Adams, with the help of Clay, finally won, thus leading to a life-long enmity between Clay and Jackson.

Adams, like his father before him, was incapable of appealing to the imagination of the populace. Although a Republican, he accepted many Hamiltonian ideas, notably those relating to fiscal policy and protectionism. The Tariff of 1828, passed during his administration, was to lead to serious consequences—as we shall see—and end in the first challenging of the power of the national government. In any case, his administration, like that of Herbert Hoover's a century later, was simply a preparation for the election campaign that was to follow.

Andrew Jackson, a wealthy planter, and long a popular hero as a result of his victory over the British at New Orleans, had now become transformed into a popular leader. He had taken no position on protectionism, internal improvements, and the Bank of the United States; on the other hand, it was known that he stood for a weak central government and was hostile to "monopoly." Around him clustered all those dissidents—Western agrarians, Eastern reformers, anti-British agitators, anti-Bank men, anti-land jobbers—who saw in him the tribune of the people. Jackson was named for the Presidency by these groups and not by a Congressional caucus, which had been the previous vehicle for selecting candidates, or by a nominating convention. In 1828, then, Jackson—under the slogan "Equal rights for all, special privileges for none"—ran against Adams, and so profound was the "anti-aristocratic" sentiment that Jackson carried the election by an electoral vote of 178 to 83. He triumphed in every state south of the Potomac and west of the Alleghenies, dividing with Adams the votes of New York, Maine, and Maryland.

The first nominating convention was to appear in 1831 when the Anti-Masons and, more important, the National Republicans, or Whigs, selected candidates in this fashion. In 1832 the Jacksonian Republicans (they did not assume the name of Democrats until almost ten years later) did similarly. In other words, by 1840 there were two great national parties, the Whigs and the Democrats; and after 1860, the two parties of the Republicans and the Democrats.

The Whigs. In certain measure, the Whigs, led by Henry Clay of Kentucky and Daniel Webster of Massachusetts, were the lineal descendants of the Federalists, just as the Republicans of today became in turn the Whigs' successors. This is only generally true, however. Federalism and Whiggism had started out by championing a powerful central government and speaking for large business interests. Jeffersonian and Jacksonian Republicanism had taken the opposite stand, but by the late forties the Democracy (the successor of Republicanism) was linked with the slave system. Today, the Democracy—reverting to the class interests of Jacksonianism—is the consistent supporter of a strong national government. The Republican party of 1860 represented both business interests and equalitarian aspirations, and it followed the lead of Federalists and Whigs in calling for governmental intervention. Today, in one way, it is Jacksonian: liberty can be preserved only if the central government is weak.

What did the Whiggism of Clay and Webster—and later of Horace Greeley of New York, Alexander H. Stephens of Georgia, and Abraham Lincoln of Illinois—stand for? This, largely: protectionism for rising Eastern industry; internal improvements for the West; the continued existence of governmental debt; and the maintenance of a central Bank to facilitate government financing and to protect the uniformity of the currency. Clay called this the "American System." It was a class program to the extent that it articulated the interests of large property groups; it was a national program to the extent that it offered—through protectionism and internal improvements—higher standards of living for all Americans and expanding economic opportunities for the middle class. Edward Everett, an outstanding Whig, said in 1838: "The wheel of fortune is in constant operation, and the poor in one generation furnish the rich of the next."

Decline of Jacksonianism. Jackson had built up a machine powerful enough to make possible the election of his successor Martin Van Buren of New York in 1836. Van Buren, too, was an equalitarian, but Jackson's mantle was too large and too heavy for him. He had been schooled in the politics of subterfuge and intrigue; and the American people quickly wearied of him. The Whigs, in 1840, elected a military hero, William Henry Harrison, who died after a month in office and was succeeded by Vice President John Tyler of Virginia. In 1844, the Democrats elected another Jacksonian, James K. Polk of Tennessee, but by this time the strain had become thin. The best Polk could do to keep his party united was to engage in the Mexican War—which was popular in the South and bitterly opposed in the North.

Indeed, by the late forties, the Jacksonian party was finished. The Southern planters—fearful for the slave institution—had become uncomfortable in it and had joined the Whigs; the urban Northerners were content to control their local machines and live out of the fleshpots of municipal contracts and graft. The Democracy, itself, was complacent about slavery. But Jacksonianism had left its permanent influence on the American tradition; curiously enough, the early Republicans of the sixties were to carry on under the same banner. This was the doctrine of Equality. As Alexis de Tocqueville had put it, when he had visited America in the thirties: "Nothing struck me more forcibly than the general equality of conditions among the people. I readily discovered the prodigious influence which this primary fact exercises on the whole course of society; it gives a peculiar direction to public opinion and a peculiar trend to the laws; it imparts new maxims to the governing authorities and peculiar habits to the governed."

4. PROBLEMS OF THE EIGHTEEN THIRTIES

States' Rights. Jackson did not have plain sailing, even within his own group of the Republicans, during his first administration. In the contest of 1828 he had been supported by John C. Calhoun of South Carolina—originally a nationalist and a protectionist—who was increasingly throwing in his lot with the slave and cotton interests of his own state; and Calhoun had been rewarded with the Vice Presidency. Calhoun looked on this office as a stepping stone to the Presidency and began to lay his plans accordingly. This ambition, together with the animosities engendered over the Peggy O'Neill affair (whose flames the wily Van Buren kept alive) and the fundamental difference in the political philosophies of the two men, threatened to wreck the Jacksonian party and even involve the country in its ruin.

Calhoun had moved over increasingly to the philosophy of states' rights. To make his position effective politically—for a party based on slavery and free trade could have no more than a sectional following—he sought to cultivate the support of the free and agrarian West. The binding elements in the amalgam were to be internal improvements and a generous public-land policy. Calhoun's intentions—and his underlying purpose—were exposed in the famous debates over the Foote Resolutions. Senator Foote of Connecticut, in 1829, had introduced a proposal looking to the limiting of the sale of the public lands to those already on the market. Benton of Missouri, for the Westerners, had been quick to oppose; and he had found unexpected support in Robert Y. Haynes of South Carolina—one of Calhoun's followers.

Haynes spoke on the Foote Resolution, proposed a political and economic alliance between South and West, and then, warming to his theme, denounced New England as the enemy of the agrarian sections of the country. The country could endure only on the basis of states' rights; the Constitution was a compact between equals. Webster replied to Haynes; there was a rejoinder and a second reply; and the issue was now unmasked. The Southerners were claiming the right of nullification; the Northerners that the Union—because it was "made for the people, made by the people, and answerable to the people"—was indissoluble.

Jackson now entered the contest. A Jeffersonian ideologically he was nevertheless a nationalist politically. He and Calhoun met head on at the annual Jefferson birthday dinner on April 13, 1830, when, in reply to the toast "The Union," Jackson declared: "The Union, it must be preserved." And Calhoun, accepting the challenge, recited: "The Union, next to our liberty, most dear. May we all remember that it can only be preserved by respecting the rights of the States and distributing equally the benefits and the burdens of the Union."

Jackson had another opportunity to cut Calhoun's ground from under him. In May of the same year the Maysville bill came to his desk for his signature. The bill, in line with the generally accepted policy of federal aid for road building, called for federal subscription to the stock of a turnpike company building a twenty-mile road from Maysville to Lexington, entirely in the state of Kentucky. True, the Maysville Road was to join the Cumberland Road on the North and ultimately a post road running clear down to New Orleans. Jackson vetoed the bill on Constitutional grounds, but equally to put a stop to the use of national funds for internal improvements. Calhoun was antagonized; and Clay had another reason, two years later, for quitting the Republican party.

Tariffs and Nullification. In 1816, to save the country from the dumping of English goods in our markets—now that the Napoleonic Wars were over—and to protect the infant cotton textile industry of New England, Congress passed the first American protective tariff act, with schedules averaging about 20 percent. Tariff tinkering took place again in 1824 and once more in 1828—and this time the duties were so high (the average annual collections on all dutiable products came to 49 percent) that the law was commonly known as the "Tariff of Abominations." When, in 1832, under Clay's leadership, the House proceeded to modify somewhat but not change fundamentally the schedules of 1828, South Carolina—long bitter about the "Tariff of Abominations"—adopted a bold course. It formally enunciated the doctrine of nullification. Immediately after Jackson had signed the act of 1832, the members of Congress from South Carolina (with the knowledge and support of Calhoun) issued an address in which they proclaimed that "all hope of relief from Congress is irrevocably gone." A state election followed; the States' Rights party won; and a convention was called which passed an Ordinance of Nullification declaring the Tariff Law of 1828 (and that of 1832, too) null and void as far as South Carolina was concerned. Measures of coercion by the Federal government would be regarded as being "inconsistent with the longer continuance of South Carolina in the Union."

Jackson was not to be intimidated. On December 10, 1832, he issued his Nullification Proclamation. Said he: "I consider the power to annul a law of the United States, assumed by one state, incompatible with the existence of the Union, contradicted expressly by the letter of the Constitution, unauthorized by its spirit, inconsistent with every principle upon which it is founded, and destructive of the great object for which it was formed." A month later he called upon Congress to pass a Force bill permitting the President to use the army and navy to execute federal law in South

Carolina. But he also asked Congress to pass a tariff bill that would protect only those industries required for national defense.

Clay, desirous of preserving his Southern following, took the lead in the drafting of a compromise tariff bill. In March, 1833, Congress gave Jackson his Force bill but on the same day it also passed Clay's Compromise Tariff bill of 1833. This provided for the reduction, over a nine-year period, of all duties until the maximum of 20 percent was reached in 1842. South Carolina proceeded to repeal its Ordinance of Nullification. But the doctrine did not die and in 1860—with disastrous results—was actually invoked.

The Bank Controversy. On the tariff question, Jackson did not appear as the spokesman for a class interest, but in the bank controversy, he did. Class lines were now sharply drawn. Americans had had little training in banking as a people—there had been no commercial banks at all in colonial America—and frequently they tended to be suspicious of such institutions. Banks were largely regarded and valued as agencies for note issue and not as agencies for the discounting of commercial paper; and often, the process of note issue was simply associated with the furtherance of speculation, particularly in the case of land jobbing. In the West and South, therefore, by and large, state-chartered banks were favored and no effort was made to scrutinize their operations closely: these sections, in other words, were not unfriendly to an easy-money, or soft-money, policy. In the East, on the other hand, because economic relations there were more settled, businessmen, small producers, and artisans tended to favor hard money. An unrestrained currency made impossible the orderly collection of debts, disorganized prices, and encouraged undesirable speculative expansions. It was, finally, the foundation of the power of the commercial aristocracy.

Banks in the United States. State-chartered banks had continued to grow: from 3 in 1789 to 330 in 1830. By the middle thirties, they were responsible for $150,000,000 in notes in circulation and $130,000,000 in deposits, against which there was a specie cover of $40,000,000. Because banknotes and not deposits were the outstanding liabilities, such state legislation as existed (notably in New York and New England, although Louisiana, too, scrutinized its banks closely) concerned itself only with the protection of note holders. New York in 1829 and again in 1838—under its so-called free-banking system—permitted any group to establish a bank so long as it kept on deposit in a safety fund with the state comptroller adequate securities to cover the bank notes issued. Similarly, in New England—where all banks were directly chartered—a voluntary system sprang up, the so-called Suffolk System, under which country banks kept on deposit with the Suffolk Bank of Boston a sum large enough to assure the exchange of their notes for specie. In this way, the quality of the currency in circulation was assured. It is to be noted, however, that such deposits did not actually constitute reserves and their holders did not treat them as such; they were therefore never used to meet banking emergencies. And, in the second place, there was no agency to perform the rediscount function and thus there were no central controls anywhere over loans and note issues.

This was primitive banking, of course: there can be no question that the panics of 1819, 1837, 1857 and the hard times which followed were intensified by the absence of central-banking measures. When the Second Bank of the United States sought to develop devices for making the banking function somewhat more orderly—and when it became more powerful—it at once became the focus of attack. We must read the animus toward the Bank largely in these terms: that is to say, it was being feared as a "monopoly." In the West and South, it was being attacked by the soft-money men who did not like the closeness with which it scrutinized the activities of state banks; here, presumably, its activities were regarded as deflationary. In the East, it was being attacked by the hard-money men because of its discount and note-issue business; and here its activities were regarded as inflationary. Jackson and Benton, who, while Westerners, were hard-money men, bound both interests together by raising the cry—largely a demagogic one—of "monopoly." Thus the Bank was doomed and its disappearance, after 1836, eliminated the only agency which might have had an influence on the sharp swings of booms and depressions in the country's business life.

The Second Bank of the United States. The Second Bank had been chartered in 1816 for twenty years and was capitalized at $35,000,-000, with the Federal government having the right to acquire one fifth of its stock. It might establish branches. The Bank was to handle government deposits and to act as its collecting and disbursing agent; for its part, the government pledged itself to accept as legal tender only specie, Treasury notes, notes of the Bank, and notes of such banks as were on a specie basis. The Bank might issue bank notes—up to the limits of its capitalization and deposits, which really meant no limits at all, particularly after it began in 1827 to issue "branch drafts." It could not purchase state or municipal bonds. And it was forbidden to "trade in anything except bills of exchange, gold or silver bullion, or in the sale of goods really or truly pledged for money lent and not redeemed in due time, or the goods which shall be the proceeds of its land."

When Nicholas Biddle of Philadelphia became the Bank's president in 1823 it was a relatively unimportant institution. But the next decade was one of great economic expansion. Biddle was an ambitious and resourceful businessman, and the Bank grew in influence and power. Note issue was increased; branch banks were opened all over the country; large dealings in domestic exchange were undertaken so that the flow of funds was facilitated into every region; and specie payments were demanded of state banks when their trustworthiness was in question. Always excepting the rediscount function, this was not much unlike central banking.

The Attack on the Bank. Such a program was calculated to make enemies—particularly when the expansion and contraction of the dealings in domestic exchange ran counter to the interests of land jobbers; and when the insistence upon redemption of state bank notes threatened the wildcat banks of the South and West. Moreover, Biddle was impolitic: to him, the Bank was above the law and outside of political control. And when Jackson turned on the Bank—because he feared all banks and because Biddle was a National Republican (or Whig) and a friend of Clay—he was able to assemble a powerful and motley opposition. It was made up of Western and Southern debtors and land speculators (soft-money men), Eastern small producers and artisans (hard-money men), and Eastern state bankers—along with their pamphleteering defenders—who were jealous of Biddle and hoped by his downfall to get the government deposits.

Biddle had opposed Jackson in 1828 and Jackson apparently had not forgotten, for in repeated messages to Congress he raised the question of the Bank's constitutionality and, in fact, desirability. Committees of both Houses then proceeded to investigate the Bank. They gave it a clean bill of health, but in 1831 Jackson once more returned to the attack and called upon the electorate to decide whether the Bank was to continue. Meanwhile, Biddle was seeking to placate Jackson by naming Jackson men to the directorates of the Bank's branches and he also lent freely on the notes of Congressmen. Clay, however, scented an issue: Jackson might be defeated in 1832 on the question of the Bank. He therefore persuaded Biddle to permit the introduction of a bill for the Bank's recharter in 1832 (four years before it was to run out); the bill was passed in both Houses; and Jackson proceeded to veto it and issue his famous Veto Message. It was a remarkable political (and not an economic) document. As Jackson's Attorney General, Roger B. Taney, put it, it claimed that the Bank was at one and the same time a monopoly, and unnecessary, inexpedient, unconstitutional, and injurious to the country. The message appealed to the state banks, to debtors, to artisans and workers, and to the antiforeigners. "It is easy to conceive," said Jackson, "that great evils in our country might flow from such concentration of power in the hands of a few men irresponsible to the people." As "monopoly" power, therefore, it threatened the lives and security of little men everywhere. The Bank was "the money monster."

This was the issue of the 1832 election campaign and on it Jackson defeated Clay by an electoral vote of 219 to 49. Jackson proceeded to his revenge at once and sought to withdraw the government deposits from the Bank. He had difficulty in finding a compliant secretary of the Treasury ready to authorize the step; at last Roger B. Taney was willing and accepted the post; and before long the government funds were on deposit in 23 "pet" state banks. The Senate proceeded to censure Jackson but Jackson had won and the Bank was destroyed.

Wildcat Banking. There followed an era of wildcat banking that only further encouraged the speculative elements in the country. State banks, particularly in the South and West, sprang up like weeds, and because their chief business was that of note issue and because they were permitted to circulate notes against stocks and bonds (often worthless or selling at heavy discounts) the country was defenseless. Inflation, fraud, and counterfeiting were common. This state of affairs was thus described by a contemporary:

In the West, the people have suffered for years from the issues of almost every state in the Union, much of which is irredeemable, so insecure and so unpopular as to be known by opprobrious names. . . . There the frequently worthless issues of the State of Maine, the shinplasters of Michigan, the wildcats of Georgia, of Canada and Pennsylvania, the red dogs of Indiana and Nebraska, the miserably engraved notes of North Carolina, Kentucky, Missouri and Virginia and the not-to-be-forgotten stumptails of Illinois and Wisconsin are mixed indiscriminately with the par currency of New York and Boston.

It was not until 1863, when the National Banking Act was passed, that some order appeared; but not really until 1913, when the Federal Reserve Act was passed, that the United States finally obtained a central banking system.

The Panic of 1837. Instead of curbing speculation and clipping the wings of the commercial aristocracy, Jackson's acts encouraged the first and strengthened the second. There followed four years of runaway boom, notably in land jobbing, and, ironically enough, this tendency was fostered by the "pet" banks. The resources of these state banks were swelled by government deposits. Land speculators had no trouble obtaining loans; the bank notes thus received were paid out to the federal land offices, redeposited in the banks, and loaned out again, often to the same land jobber. Thus a pyramiding of credit took place—and prices everywhere shot up. The extravagant programs of public works expansion, embarked upon by the Western and Southern states, further jeopardized the stability of the American economy.

Jackson tried to halt the inflation through the issuance of the Specie Circular of July, 1836, which called for the payment for public lands in hard money. But this was the straw that broke the camel's back. Commercial failures in Great Britain, leading to a demand for the settlement of American balances; the insecure position of those states which had tried to build their prosperity on bond issues; the pressures everywhere on banks, which, in fact, discovered they had never been liquid, these were at the basis of the panic of 1837. The panic was essentially commercial and largely due to speculative overinvestment; but in the urban centers hard times did follow. From 1837 to 1843 prices dropped by 25 percent.

The career of debt defaults and repudiations which many of the American states embarked upon at this time did not help American credit abroad. Between 1840 and 1845, nine states ceased payment of interest on their bonded indebtednesses: Maryland, Illinois, Indiana, Michigan, Mississippi, Louisiana, Arkansas, Florida, and Pennsylvania; furthermore, four of them repudiated parts or the whole of their obligations. Interest payments, by 1847, were resumed, but English investors continued to keep shy of American securities for a long time. In fact, as late as 1859, in commenting on the low prices at which American rails were being quoted in England, a London journal was able to say: "The reason is that we do not like American things. We have not that confidence in them which their intrinsic merit warrants." Undoubtedly, the failure of European relief to appear in our money markets prolonged the depression, whose clouds did not lift until 1843.

Locofocoism. A characteristic manifestation of the times was the emergence of Locofocoism, which started out as an offshoot of the New York City Tammany Society. Appearing before the depression and demanding equal rights (their platform consisted of the Bible and the Declaration of Independence), the Locofocos were able to spread their influence into the New York Democracy and out into the Northwest as a result of the hard times.

They were antimonopoly and against all banks, and were for hard money and the rigorous limitation of state debts. So deeply did they penetrate the Democratic party, particularly during Van Buren's administration, that in many sections of the country the Democracy and Locofocoism were synonymous.

The Locofocos were not above violence; breaking into warehouses and riots were fomented by them. A rural counterpart called the Barnburners opposed further canal construction in New York because of the heavy burden of taxation that resulted. The Barnburners, like the Locofocos, were equalitarians and many carried on later as Liberty men, Free Soilers, and Free Democrats. These were the persons who furnished the Abolitionist leaven of the Republican party. With the end of the depression, however, their direct influence was largely spent; and by 1844, the Democratic party was the party of slavery. In fact, in that year the Southern Democrats kept out of the national platform a plank renewing the party's pledge to the support of the Declaration of Independence.

5. *AMERICAN EXPANSION*

Louisiana Territory. By the Peace of Paris of 1783 America was ceded all the territories up to the eastern bank of the Mississippi. Spain remained in possession of the Louisiana Territory stretching westward from the Mississippi over a vast region, and of course retained New Orleans. In 1801 Spain returned Louisiana to France and the United States, fearful that the aggressive Napoleon would close the Mississippi's navigation to American boats. At the same time Spain began to negotiate for the acquisition of the Floridas, the right of deposit at New Orleans, and the granting of sites on the banks of the Mississippi. Much to Jefferson's surprise, in 1803 France offered to sell the whole Louisiana Territory. A bargain was quickly struck—without Constitutional warrant or Congressional authorization—the price being set at $15,000,000. Thus the land area of the United States was doubled.

The processes of exploration of the new possession began at once. In 1804 Jefferson ordered Meriwether Lewis and William Clark to search for an overland route to the Pacific and to make a study of the territory's resources. Starting from St. Louis, the party proceeded up the Missouri, struck out across the mountains to the headwaters of the Columbia river, and thence made its way to the sea. It returned safely to St. Louis in 1806, having covered more than 8,000 miles in a little more than two years. The report of the Lewis-Clark expedition whetted the appetites of Americans for land, furs, and minerals, and soon hardy pioneers were crossing the prairies and penetrating into the Great Plains. Starting at about the same time, Zebulon Pike led another expedition northward to survey the northern valley of the Mississippi; upon his return, he was sent into the Southwest, and before long the region up to the Rio Grande was made known to Americans. Louisiana became a state in 1812.

Florida. In their original instructions, Monroe and Livingston had been ordered to acquire the Floridas. They assumed that that territory was included in the Louisiana Purchase, and so did Jefferson. Not so the Spaniards, however, and with them the French agreed. Despite this, the United States proceeded to join West Florida as a customs district to the Louisiana Territory. American settlers moved in, as did runaway slaves; and unofficial war raged in the region for many years against the Spanish and the pirates who made the area their headquarters. From then on until 1819 Washington—pushed by Southern expansionists—could not keep its eyes off the region. In 1813, West Florida was annexed by Mississippi Territory. Jackson invaded East Florida in 1814, to keep it out of English hands, and again in 1818, this time to put down the Seminole Indians. Finally in 1819, the Spanish government, incapable of policing the country or of keeping the Americans out, gave up the unequal struggle and agreed to sell. Under the Florida Purchase, Spain surrendered for $5,000,000 all claims to the territory east of the Mississippi; we, on our part, surrendered all claims to the Texas region. The Senate withheld ratification for two years—there were many who refused "to trade Texas for Florida"—and then finally gave in. Florida became a state in 1845.

Texas. Spain's hope of saving Texas for her crumbling empire in the New World was destined to be short-lived. In 1821 Mexico revolted successfully, and now the Southwest—whose boundaries had not been clearly defined by the Louisiana Purchase—became a focus of interest to Americans. At first, Mexico was not unfriendly. The vast Texas country was virtually uninhabited—there were perhaps fewer

Indians than the 4,000 whites in it—and Mexico saw no objection to American traders, drovers, and farmers colonizing a region whose resources Mexico itself was incapable of tapping. Therefore it threw the territory open to immigrants and offered Moses Austin of Connecticut large land cessions if he could bring in settlers. Austin's son, Stephen F. Austin, pushed the project vigorously and by 1830 some 20,-000 Americans were to be found in Texas.

On the open range it was inevitable that American and Mexican ranchers should have difficulties. Trouble also arose with the distant Mexican government over taxation, customs duties, and the bringing of slaves into the territory. Moreover, the Americans were by this time agitating for home rule. Mexico, alarmed by the rising number of the foreigners and their aggressiveness, in 1830 put a stop to land cessions, tried to abolish slavery, and closed the frontiers to further immigration. The Americans, meeting in convention, asked for a stay of the restrictive laws; in 1833, they met again and wrote a constitution for a virtually autonomous state. The differences could not be reconciled; brushes between armed parties took place—with Mexican liberals giving the Americans their support—and in 1836 a provisional government of Texas was established.

A Mexican army was sent in and defeated the Americans at the Alamo but was itself defeated at San Jacinto. The Americans proceeded to ratify their constitution, proclaiming the Republic of Texas, legalized slavery, and sought admission into the United States. Washington, in 1837, settled for recognition of the new republic. By this time, the fear of the spread of slavery was beginning to stir in many Northerners; and this opposition, along with Van Buren's own hostility to slavery, prevented the annexation of Texas. Finally, in 1844, a treaty for annexation was concluded and submitted to the Senate. The treaty was rejected, and it was not until the next year that Texas became a part of the United States by joint resolution of both Houses. But the

United States was to fight a war with Mexico before the boundaries of Texas were to be permanently fixed.

Meanwhile Americans were on the march. Every year, by the tens of thousands, parties of immigrants—for the most part made up of families seeking new homes in the West, but not infrequently including adventurers and desperadoes—pushed into the prairies and the plains. They put up crude dwellings, of wood where that was to be obtained, of sod, if nothing else offered. They broke the tough prairie soil. They planted wheat in the North and hemp, cotton, and corn in the South. They prospered with the country, and before long churches, schools, and all the other amenities of a settled life were appearing. High American standards of living followed the settlers as America pursued its "manifest destiny" to the Western sea.

RALPH WALDO EMERSON

IN THE SECOND QUARTER of the nineteenth century there appeared a group of thinkers in America who were to express their confidence in man's capacity to realize his destiny. They shook off the restraints of traditional religion, denied the ability of empiricism to penetrate to the heart of reality, and challenged existing institutions. They believed, with the Puritans, that the world had a moral purpose. They were Platonists in the sense that they agreed that the universe is the expression of mind. They were Romanticists because they preached the goodness, in fact the divinity, of man. These men—they were largely New Englanders and they created Unitarianism—called themselves Transcendentalists. In their company were to be found William Ellery Channing, Theodore Parker and—the greatest of all of them—Ralph Waldo Emerson.

Parker had sought to catch the spirit of the new creed in these words: "The problem of transcendental philosophy is no less than this, to revise the experience of mankind and try its teachings by the nature of mankind; to test ethics by conscience, science by reason; to try the creeds of the churches, the constitutions of the states, by the constitution of the universe; to reverse what is wrong, supply what is wanting, and commend the just."

This dual belief in the divinity of man and the moral purpose of the world made the Transcendentalists humanitarians. They were appalled by the evil—injustice, inequality, squalor—in the world and they spoke out against it. They were defenders of peace, women's rights, and, above all, of the Negro. Their idealism, notably in the cause of Abolitionism, gives the lie to the assertion that Americans have always been a practical people.

This confidence in the morality of nature and the goodness of man is Emerson's theme in his first published work, *Nature* (Boston, 1836). Ralph Waldo Emerson (1803–1882) graduated from Harvard at 18 and also attended its Divinity School. In 1829, he became the minister of Boston's Old North Church but he quit his pulpit a year later and moved to Concord, where he spent the rest of his life. He wrote poems, essays and addresses—never a systematic philosophical work—and he concerned himself constantly with the ideas outlined in his first essay. As he said later in *The Poet:* "The moral law lies at the center of nature and radiates to the circumference. . . . Every animal function . . . shall . . . echo the Ten Commandments." Man, therefore, also is divine, and in his freedom and creativeness he realizes himself.

The selection reprinted here is from the first edition of *Nature*.

Nature

BY RALPH WALDO EMERSON

CHAPTER I

TO GO INTO solitude, a man needs to retire as much from his chamber as from society. I am not solitary whilst I read and write, though nobody is with me. But if a man would be alone, let him look at the stars. The rays that come from those heavenly worlds, will separate between him and what he touches. One might think the atmosphere was made transparent with this design, to give man, in the heavenly bodies, the perpetual presence of the sublime. Seen in the streets of cities, how great they are! If the stars should appear one night in a thousand years, how would men believe and adore; and preserve for many generations the remembrance of the city of God which had been shown! But every night come out these envoys of beauty, and light the universe with their admonishing smile.

The stars awaken a certain reverence, because though always present, they are inaccessible; but all natural objects make a kindred impression, when the mind is open to their influence. Nature never wears a mean appearance. Neither does the wisest man extort her secret, and lose his curiosity by finding out all her perfection. Nature never became a toy to a wise spirit. The flowers, the animals, the mountains, reflected the wisdom of his best hour, as much as they had delighted the simplicity of his childhood.

When we speak of nature in this manner, we have a distinct but most poetical sense in the mind. We mean the integrity of impression made by manifold natural objects. It is this which distinguishes the stick of timber of the wood-cutter, from the tree of the poet. The charming landscape which I saw this morning, is indubitably made up of some twenty or thirty farms. Miller owns this field, Locke that, and Manning the woodland beyond. But none of them owns the landscape. There is a property in the horizon which no man has but he whose eye can integrate all the parts, that is, the poet. This is the best part of these men's farms, yet to this their warranty-deeds give no title.

To speak truly, few adult persons can see nature. Most persons do not see the sun. At least they have a very superficial seeing. The sun illuminates only the eye of the man, but shines into the eye and the heart of the child. The lover of nature is he whose inward and outward senses are still truly adjusted to each other; who has retained the spirit of infancy even into the era of manhood. His intercourse with heaven and earth, becomes part of his daily food. In the presence of nature, a wild delight runs through the man, in spite of real sorrows. Nature says,—he is my creature, and maugre all his impertinent griefs, he shall be glad with me. Not the sun or the summer alone, but every hour and season yields its tribute of delight; for every hour and change corresponds to and authorizes a different state of the mind, from breathless noon to grimmest midnight. Nature is a setting that fits equally well a comic or a mourning piece. In good health, the air is a cordial of incredible virtue. Crossing a bare common, in snow puddles, at twilight, under a clouded sky, without having in my thoughts any occurrence of special good fortune, I have enjoyed a perfect exhilaration. I am glad to the brink of fear. In the woods too, a man casts off his years, as the snake his slough, and at what period soever of life, is always a child. In the woods, is perpetual youth. Within these plantations of God, a decorum and sanctity reign, a perennial festival is dressed, and the guest sees not how he should tire of them in a thousand years. In the woods, we return to reason and faith. There I feel that nothing can befall me in life,—no disgrace, no calamity, (leaving me my eyes,) which nature cannot repair. Standing on the bare ground,—my head bathed by the blithe air, and uplifted into infinite space,—all mean egotism vanishes. I become a transparent eye-ball; I am nothing; I see all; the currents of the Universal Being circulate through me; I am part or particle of God. The name of the nearest friend sounds then foreign and accidental: to be brothers, to be acquaintances,—master or servant, is then a trifle and a disturbance. I am the lover of uncontained and immortal beauty. In the wilderness, I find something more dear and connate than in streets or villages. In the tranquil landscape, and especially in the distant line of the horizon, man beholds somewhat as beautiful as his own nature.

The greatest delight which the fields and woods minister, is the suggestion of an occult relation between man and the vegetable. I am not alone and unacknowledged. They nod to me, and I to them. The waving of the boughs in the storm, is new to me and old. It takes me by surprise, and yet is not unknown. Its effect is like that of a higher thought or a better emotion coming over me, when I deemed I was thinking justly or doing right.

Yet it is certain that the power to produce this delight, does not reside in nature, but in man, or in a harmony of both. It is necessary to use these pleasures with great temperance. For, nature is not always tricked in holiday attire, but the same scene which yesterday breathed perfume and glittered as for the frolic of the nymphs, is overspread with melancholy to-day. Nature always wears the colors of the spirit. To a man laboring under calamity, the heat of his own fire hath sadness in it. Then, there is a kind of contempt of the landscape felt by him who has just lost by death a dear friend. The sky is less grand as it shuts down over less worth in the population.

CHAPTER III: BEAUTY

A nobler want of man is served by nature, namely, the love of Beauty.

The ancient Greeks called the world χοσμος,

beauty. Such is the constitution of all things, or such the plastic power of the human eye, that the primary forms, as the sky, the mountain, the tree, the animal, give us a delight *in and for themselves;* a pleasure arising from outline, color, motion, and grouping. This seems partly owing to the eye itself. The eye is the best of artists. By the mutual action of its structure and of the laws of light, perspective is produced, which integrates every mass of objects, of what character soever, into a well colored and shaded globe, so that where the particular objects are mean and unaffecting, the landscape which they compose, is round and symmetrical. And as the eye is the best composer, so light is the first of painters. There is no object so foul that intense light will not make beautiful. And the stimulus it affords to the sense, and a sort of infinitude which it hath, like space and time, make all matter gay. Even the corpse has its own beauty. But besides this general grace diffused over nature, almost all the individual forms are agreeable to the eye, as is proved by our endless imitations of some of them, as the acorn, the grape, the pine-cone, the wheat-ear, the egg, the wings and forms of most birds, the lion's claw, the serpent, the butterfly, sea-shells, flames, clouds, buds, leaves, and the forms of many trees, as the palm.

For better consideration, we may distribute the aspects of Beauty in a threefold manner.

1. First, the simple perception of natural forms is a delight. The influence of the forms and actions in nature, is so needful to man, that, in its lowest functions, it seems to lie on the confines of commodity and beauty. To the body and mind which have been cramped by noxious work or company, nature is medicinal and restores their tone. The tradesman, the attorney comes out of the din and craft of the street, and sees the sky and the woods, and is a man again. In their eternal calm, he finds himself. The health of the eye seems to demand a horizon. We are never tired, so long as we can see far enough.

But in other hours, Nature satisfies by its loveliness, and without any mixture of corporeal benefit. I see the spectacle of morning from the hill-top over against my house, from day-break to sun-rise, with emotions which an angel might share. The long slender bars of cloud float like fishes in the sea of crimson light. From the earth as a shore, I look out into that silent sea. I seem to partake its rapid transformations: the active enchantment reaches my dust, and I dilate and conspire with the morning wind. How does Nature deify us with a few and cheap elements! Give me health and a day, and I will make the pomp of emperors ridiculous. The dawn is my Assyria; the sun-set and moon-rise my Paphos, and unimaginable realms of faerie; broad noon shall be my England of the senses and the understanding; the night shall be my Germany of mystic philosophy and dreams.

Not less excellent, except for our less susceptibility in the afternoon, was the charm, last evening, of a January sunset. The western clouds divided and subdivided themselves into pink flakes modulated with tints of unspeakable softness; and the air had so much life and sweetness, that it was a pain to come within doors. What was it that nature would say? Was there no meaning in the live repose of the valley behind the mill, and which Homer or Shakspeare could not re-form for me in words? The leafless trees become spires of flame in the sunset, with the blue east for their back-ground, and the stars of the dead calices of flowers, and every withered stem and stubble rimed with frost, contribute something to the mute music.

The inhabitants of cities suppose that the country landscape is pleasant only half the year. I pleased myself with the graces of the winter scenery, and believe that we are as much touched by it as by the genial influences of summer. To the attentive eye, each moment of the year has its own beauty, and in the same field, it beholds, every hour, a picture which was never seen before, and which shall never be seen again. The heavens change every moment, and reflect their glory or gloom on the plains beneath. The state of the crop in the surrounding farms alters the expression of the earth from week to week. The succession of native plants in the pastures and roadsides, which makes the silent clock by which time tells the summer hours, will make even the divisions of the day sensible to a keen observer. The tribes of birds and insects, like the plants punctual to their time, follow each other, and the year has room for all. By water-courses, the variety is greater. In July, the blue pontederia or pickerel-weed blooms in large beds in the shallow parts of our pleasant river, and swarms with yellow butterflies in continual motion. Art cannot rival this pomp of purple and gold. Indeed the river is a perpetual gala, and boasts each month a new ornament.

But this beauty of Nature which is seen and felt as beauty, is the least part. The shows of day, the dewy morning, the rainbow, mountains, orchards in blossom, stars, moonlight, shadows in still water, and the like, if too eagerly hunted, become shows merely, and mock us with their unreality. Go out of the house to see the moon, and 'tis mere tinsel; it will not please as when its light shines upon your necessary journey. The beauty that shimmers in the yellow afternoons of October, who ever could clutch it? Go forth to find it, and it is gone: 'tis only a mirage as you look from the windows of diligence.

2. The presence of a higher, namely, of the spiritual element is esential to its perfection. The high and divine beauty which can be loved without effeminacy, is that which is found in combination with the human will. Beauty is the mark God sets upon virtue. Every natural action is graceful. Every heroic act is also decent, and causes the place and the bystanders to shine. We are taught by great actions that the universe is the property of every individual in it. Every rational creature has all nature for his dowry and estate. It is his, if he will. He may divest himself of it; he may creep into a corner, and abdicate his kingdom, as most men do, but he is entitled to the world by his constitution. In proportion to the energy of his thought and will, he takes up the world into himself. "All those things for which men plough, build, or sail, obey virtue;" said Sallust. "The winds and waves," said Gibbon, "are always on the side of the ablest navigators." So are the sun and moon and all the stars of heaven. When a noble act is done,—perchance in a scene of great natural beauty; when Leonidas and his three hundred martyrs consume one day in dying, and the sun and moon come each and look at them once in the steep defile of Thermopylæ; when Arnold Winkelried, in the high Alps, under the shadow of the avalanche, gathers in his side a sheaf of Austrian spears to break the line for his comrades; are not these heroes entitled to add the beauty of the scene to the beauty of the deed? When the bark of Columbus nears the shore of America;—before it, the beach lined with savages, fleeing out of all their huts of cane; the sea behind; and the purple mountains of the Indian Archipelago around, can we separate the man from the living picture? Does not the New World clothe his form with her palm-groves and savannahs as fit drapery? Ever does natural beauty steal in like air, and envelope great actions. When Sir Harry Vane was dragged up the Tower-hill, sitting on a sled, to suffer death, as the champion of the English laws, one of the multitude cried out to him, "You never sate on so glorious a seat." Charles II., to intimidate the citizens of London, caused the patriot Lord Russel to be drawn in an open coach, through the principal streets of the city, on his way to the scaffold. "But," his biographer says, "the multitude imagined they saw liberty and virtue sitting by his side." In private

places, among sordid objects, an act of truth or heroism seems at once to draw to itself the sky as its temple, the sun as its candle. Nature stretcheth out her arms to embrace man, only let his thoughts be of equal greatness. Willingly does she follow his steps with the rose and the violet, and bend her lines of grandeur and grace to the decoration of her darling child. Only let his thoughts be of equal scope, and the frame will suit the picture. A virtuous man is in unison with her works, and makes the central figure of the visible sphere. Homer, Pindar, Socrates, Phocion, associate themselves fitly in our memory with the geography and climate of Greece. The visible heavens and earth sympathize with Jesus. And in common life, whosoever has seen a person of powerful character and happy genius, will have remarked how easily he took all things along with him,—the persons, the opinions, and the day, and nature became ancillary to a man.

3. There is still another aspect under which the beauty of the world may be viewed, namely, as it becomes an object of the intellect. Beside the relation of things to virtue, they have a relation to thought. The intellect searches out the absolute order of things as they stand in the mind of God, and without the colors of affection. The intellectual and the active powers seem to succeed each other, and the exclusive activity of the one, generates the exclusive activity of the other. There is something unfriendly in each to the other, but they are like the alternate periods of feeding and working in animals: each prepares and will be followed by the other. Therefore does beauty, which, in relation to actions, as we have seen, comes unsought, and comes because it is unsought, remain for the apprehension and pursuit of the intellect; and then again, in its turn, of the active power. Nothing divine dies. All good is eternally reproductive. The beauty of nature re-forms itself in the mind, and not for barren contemplation, but for new creation.

All men are in some degree impressed by the face of the world; some men even to delight. This love of beauty is Taste. Others have the same love in such excess, that, not content with admiring, they seek to embody it in new forms. The creation of beauty is Art.

The production of a work of art throws a light upon the mystery of humanity. A work of art is an abstract or epitome of the world. It is the result or expression of nature, in miniature. For, although the works of nature are innumerable and all different, the result or the expression of them all is similar and single. Nature is a sea of forms radically alike and even unique. A leaf, a sunbeam, a landscape, the ocean, make an analogous impression on the mind. What is common to them all,—that perfectness and harmony, is beauty. The standard of beauty is the entire circuit of natural forms,—the totality of nature; which the Italians expressed by defining beauty "il piu nell' uno." Nothing is quite beautiful alone: nothing but is beautiful in the whole. A single object is only so far beautiful as it suggests this universal grace. The poet, the painter, the sculptor, the musician, the architect, seek each to concentrate this radiance of the world on one point, and each in his several work to satisfy the love of beauty which stimulates him to produce. Thus is Art, a nature passed through the alembic of man. Thus in art, does nature work through the will of a man filled with the beauty of her first works.

The world thus exists to the soul to satisfy the desire of beauty. This element I call an ultimate end. No reason can be asked or given why the soul seeks beauty. Beauty, in its largest and profoundest sense, is one expression for the universe. God is the all-fair. Truth, and goodness, and beauty, are but different faces of the same All. But beauty in nature is not ultimate. It is the herald of inward and eternal beauty, and is not alone a solid and satisfactory good. It must stand as a part, and not as yet the last or highest expression of the final cause of Nature.

CHAPTER V: DISCIPLINE

In view of the significance of nature, we arrive at once at a new fact, that nature is a discipline. This use of the world includes the preceding uses, as parts of itself.

Space, time, society, labor, climate, food, locomotion, the animals, the mechanical forces, give us sincerest lessons, day by day, whose meaning is unlimited. They educate both the Understanding and the Reason. Every property of matter is a school for the understanding,—its solidity or resistance, its inertia, its extension, its figure, its divisibility. The understanding adds, divides, combines, measures, and finds nutriment and room for its activity in this worthy scene. Meantime, Reason transfers all these lessons into its own world of thought, by perceiving the analogy that marries Matter and Mind.

1. Nature is a discipline of the understanding in intellectual truths. Our dealing with sensible objects is a constant exercise in the necessary lessons of difference, of likeness, of order, of being and seeming, of progressive arrangement; of ascent from particular to general; of combination to one end of manifold forces. Proportioned to the importance of the organ to be formed, is the extreme care with which its tuition is provided,—a care pretermitted in no single case. What tedious training, day after day, year after year, never ending, to form the common sense; what continual reproduction of annoyances, inconveniences, dilemmas; what rejoicing over us of little men; what disputing of prices, what reckonings of interest,—and all to form the Hand of the mind;—to instruct us that "good thoughts are no better than good dreams, unless they be executed!"

The same good office is performed by Property and its filial systems of debt and credit. Debt, grinding debt, whose iron face the widow, the orphan, and the sons of genius fear and hate;—debt, which consumes so much time, which so cripples and disheartens a great spirit with cares that seem so base, is a preceptor whose lessons cannot be foregone, and is needed most by those who suffer from it most. Moreover, property, which has been well compared to snow,—"if it fall level to-day, it will be blown into drifts to-morrow,"—is the surface action of internal machinery, like the index on the face of a clock. Whilst now it is the gymnastics of the understanding, it is hiving in the foresight of the spirit, experience in profounder laws.

The whole character and fortune of the individual are affected by the least inequalities in the culture of the understanding; for example, in the perception of differences. Therefore is Space, and therefore Time, that man may know that things are not huddled and lumped, but sundered and individual. A bell and a plough have each their use, and neither can do the office of the other. Water is good to drink, coal to burn, wool to wear; but wool cannot be drunk, nor water spun, nor coal eaten. The wise man shows his wisdom in separation, in gradation, and his scale of creatures and of merits is as wide as nature. The foolish have no range in their scale, but suppose every man is as every other man. What is not good they call the worst, and what is not hateful they call the best.

In like manner, what good heed, nature forms in us! She pardons no mistakes. Her yea is yea, and her nay, nay.

The first steps in Agriculture, Astronomy, Zoology, (those first steps which the farmer, the hunter, and the sailor take,) teach that nature's dice are always loaded; that in her heaps and rubbish are concealed sure and useful results.

How calmly and genially the mind apprehends one after another the laws of physics! What noble emotions dilate the mortal as he enters into the counsels of the creation, and feels by knowledge the privilege to BE! His insight refines him. The beauty of nature shines in his own breast. Man is greater than he can see this, and the universe less, because Time and Space relations vanish as laws are known.

Here again we are impressed and even daunted by the immense Universe to be explored. "What we know, is a point to what we do not know." Open any recent journal of science, and weigh the problems suggested concerning Light, Heat, Electricity, Magnetism, Physiology, Geology, and judge whether the interest of natural science is likely to be soon exhausted.

Passing by many particulars of the discipline of nature, we must not omit to specify two.

The exercise of the Will or the lesson of power is taught in every event. From the child's successive possession of his several senses up to the hour when he saith, "Thy will be done!" he is learning the secret, that he can reduce under his will, not only particular events, but great classes, nay the whole series of events, and so conform all facts to his character. Nature is thoroughly mediate. It is made to serve. It receives the dominion of man as meekly as the ass on which the Saviour rode. It offers all its kingdoms to man as the raw material which he may mould into what is useful. Man is never weary of working it up. He forges the subtile and delicate air into wise and melodious words, and gives them wing as angels of persuasion and command. One after another, his victorious thought comes up with and reduces all things, until the world becomes, at last, only a realized will,—the double of the man.

2. Sensible objects conform to the premonitions of Reason and reflect the conscience. All things are moral; and in their boundless changes have an unceasing reference to spiritual nature. Therefore is nature glorious with form, color, and motion, that every globe in the remotest heaven; every chemical change from the rudest crystal up to the laws of life; every change of vegetation from the first principle of growth in the eye of a leaf, to the tropical forest and antediluvian coal-mine; every animal function from the sponge up to Hercules, shall hint or thunder to man the laws of right and wrong, and echo the Ten Commandments. Therefore is nature ever the ally of Religion: lends all her pomp and riches to the religious sentiment. Prophet and priest, David, Isaiah, Jesus, have drawn deeply from this source. This ethical character so penetrates the bone and marrow of nature, as to seem the end for which it was made. Whatever private purpose is answered by any member or part, this is its public and universal function, and is never omitted. Nothing in nature is exhausted in its first use. When a thing has served

an end to the uttermost, it is wholly new for an ulterior service. In God, every end is converted into a new means. Thus the use of commodity, regarded by itself, is mean and squalid. But it is to the mind an education in the doctrine of Use, namely, that a thing is good only so far as it serves; that a conspiring of parts and efforts to the production of an end, is essential to any being. The first and gross manifestation of this truth, is our inevitable and hated training in values and wants, in corn and meat.

It has already been illustrated, that every natural process is a version of a moral sentence. The moral law lies at the centre of nature and radiates to the circumference. It is the pith and marrow of every substance, every relation, and every process. All things with which we deal, preach to us. What is a farm but a mute gospel? The chaff and the wheat, weeds and plants, blight, rain, insects, sun, —it is a sacred emblem from the first furrow of spring to the last stack which the snow of winter overtakes in the fields. But the sailor, the shepherd, the miner, the merchant, in their several resorts, have each an experience precisely parallel, and leading to the same conclusion: because all organizations are radically alike. Nor can it be doubted that this moral sentiment which thus scents the air, grows in the grain, and impregnates the waters of the world, is caught by man and sinks into his soul. The moral influence of nature upon every individual is that amount of truth which it illustrates to him. Who can estimate this? Who can guess how much firmness the sea-beaten rock has taught the fisherman? how much tranquillity has been reflected to man from the azure sky, over whose unspotted deeps the winds forevermore drive flocks of stormy clouds, and leave no wrinkle or stain? how much industry and providence and affection we have caught from the pantomime of brutes? What a searching preacher of self-command is the varying phenomenon of Health!

Herein is especially apprehended the unity of Nature,—the unity in variety,—which meets us everywhere. All the endless variety of things make an identical impression. Xenophanes complained in his old age, that, look where he would, all things hastened back to Unity. He was weary of seeing the same entity in the tedious variety of forms. The fable of Proteus has a cordial truth. A leaf, a drop, a crystal, a moment of time is related to the whole, and partakes of the perfection of the whole. Each particle is a microcosm, and faithfully renders the likeness of the world.

Not only resemblances exist in things whose

analogy is obvious, as when we detect the type of the human hand in the flipper of the fossil saurus, but also in objects wherein there is great superficial unlikeness. Thus architecture is called "frozen music," by De Staël and Goethe. Vitruvius thought an architect should be a musician. "A Gothic church," said Coleridge, "is a petrified religion." Michael Angelo maintained, that, to an architect, a knowledge of anatomy is essential. In Haydn's oratorios, the notes present to the imagination not only motions, as of the snake, the stag, and the elephant, but colors also; as the green grass. The law of harmonic sounds reappears in the harmonic colors. The granite is differenced in its laws only by the more or less of heat, from the river that wears it away. The river, as it flows, resembles the air that flows over it; the air resembles the light which traverses it with more subtile currents; the light resembles the heat which rides with it through Space. Each creature is only a modification of the other; the likeness in them is more than the difference, and their radical law is one and the same. A rule of one art, or a law of one organization, holds true throughout nature. So intimate is this Unity, that, it is easily seen, it lies under the undermost garment of nature, and betrays its source in Universal Spirit. For, it pervades Thought also. Every universal truth which we express in words, implies or supposes every other truth. *Omne verum vero consonat.* It is like a great circle on a sphere, comprising all possible circles; which, however, may be drawn, and comprise it, in like manner. Every such truth is the absolute Ens seen from one side. But it has innumerable sides.

The central Unity is still more conspicuous in actions. Words are finite organs of the infinite mind. They cannot cover the dimensions of what is in truth. They break, chop, and impoverish it. An action is the perfection and publication of thought. A right action seems to fill the eye, and to be related to all nature. "The wise man, in doing one thing, does all; or, in the one thing he does rightly, he sees the likeness of all which is done rightly."

Words and actions are not the attributes of brute nature. They introduce us to the human form, of which all other organizations appear to be degradations. When this appears among so many that surround it, the spirit prefers it to all others. It says, 'From such as this, have I drawn joy and knowledge; in such as this, have I found and beheld myself; I will speak to it; it can speak again; it can yield me thought already formed and alive.' In fact, the eye,—the mind,—is always accompanied by these forms, male and female; and these are incomparably the richest informations of the power and order that lie at the heart of things. Unfortunately, every one of them bears the marks as of some injury; is marred and superficially defective. Nevertheless, far different from the deaf and dumb nature around them, these all rest like fountain-pipes on the unfathomed sea of thought and virtue whereto they alone, of all organizations, are the entrances.

It were a pleasant inquiry to follow into detail their ministry to our education, but where would it stop? We are associated in adolescent and adult life with some friends, who, like skies and waters, are coextensive with our idea; who, answering each to a certain affection of the soul, satisfy our desire on that side; whom we lack power to put at such focal distance from us, that we can mend or even analyze them. We cannot choose but love them. When much intercourse with a friend has supplied us with a standard of excellence, and has increased our respect for the resources of God who thus sends a real person to outgo our ideal; when he has, moreover, become an object of thought, and, whilst his character retains all its unconscious effect, is converted in the mind into solid and sweet wisdom,—it is a sign to us that his office is closing, and he is commonly withdrawn from our sight in a short time.

HENRY C. CAREY

WITH THE SAME VIGOR that had made him a successful bookseller at the age of nine, Henry C. Carey (1793–1879) set about exploring the field of political economy and applying its principles to a growing America. He retired from business in 1835 and by 1837 was ready to publish the first volume of his *Principles of Political Economy*. Within the next two years he had completed two additional volumes and laid the groundwork for an "American school" of economic thought.

Carey is historical and statistical in approach, and hopeful in outlook. For him, political economy is no "dismal science" but a beautiful exhibition of the "perfect harmony" of the laws of nature. Its dicta are as sublime and immutable as those which explain how the cosmos is held together, but they presage no misery to a people compelled by natural law to multiply to the limits of subsistence. On the contrary, as population increases, more soils are cultivated, less capital is devoted to preserving social order and more is given to assisting labor. As a result, labor becomes more productive and its proportion of the product increases; the capitalist, on the other hand, receives a smaller proportion of the product which nevertheless amounts to a larger quantity, and in this way his wealth is augmented. Just as the wages of labor depend on its productivity and the increase of capital, so the value of capital depends on the cost of reproduction; and that, in turn is linked with the productiveness of labor. Therefore, what benefits one portion of society benefits all.

The only check on the tendency of wealth to increase with the increase of population is the unproductive expenditure of war and of lavish governments. That is proved by the example of the United States. The country is prosperous not because land is abundant, Carey insists, for land is equally abundant in Czarist Russia, in Mexico or Brazil. The United States prospers because its government makes no wars, wastes no money, and does not interfere with the economic concerns of its citizens. American workingmen are better paid than their fellows in Europe because they produce more; the high price of labor has encouraged the use of machinery and this application of capital has so increased the productivity of labor that the worker can claim a share of a greater output. Other countries have been "consistently engaged in applying the remedies for over-population, robbing and plundering each other . . ."; if this absurd waste were to cease, then the Old World could live as well as the New.

Carey was to make certain interesting changes in his thinking as the years passed. He ceased to accept Ricardo's contention that rich soils are cultivated first, for example, and with that went the theory of diminishing returns.

American experience in settlement showed that poor soils are cultivated before rich river bottoms, because, in a new country, the richer the soil the more unhealthy the locality. Equally interesting was his franker espousal of Protectionism. In 1837, he considered the great virtue of American national policy to be its application of the salutary principle of laissez faire. Where government had interfered to grant monopolies by exclusive banking charters, credit had suffered; where it had taxed imports, industry had suffered. Rates of return on capital were lowest in the decade 1820–30, when government interference was at its height. "It cannot be doubted that the duties on imports have been much higher than they should have been." (It should be noted, however, that when it came to coal and iron he was content with the duties in the Compromise Tariff of 1833.)

Later, Carey came to look upon consistent protection of a certain kind and for certain goods as the basis of national welfare and the only practical mode of introducing true freedom of trade. He uses List's argument that free trade between nations in different stages of economic development leads to the subjection of the less advanced; but his reasoning is closer to Henry Clay's and to his own father's (Matthew Carey), than to that of List, for whom national power rather than national well-being was basic to political economy. Carey demonstrates how protective tariffs promote the interest of all economic groups and all sections of the nation. Every increase of domestic manufacturing widens the farmer's market and each widening of his market makes the farmer a greater consumer of manufactured goods. Protection is a "necessary defense" against "the British colonial system" which tries to monopolize machinery and make Britain the center to which all raw materials flow. So long as any American product seeks a market in Britain, Liverpool will dictate the price of the entire American crop. Proper protective duties will so concentrate and increase America's population that her farmers will not need to look for foreign markets. Shipping will not suffer, however, because we will export more valuable goods and import bulky raw materials as well as immigrants whose fares will pay the freight of both imports and exports. The planter will share in the benefits of protection as soon as he brings the loom to the cotton field. The value of his lands will so increase under this system that he will not need to wear out his soil and then seek new lands on which to establish slavery. As the value of Southern land increases, slavery will tend to disappear, for the slave, having become more intelligent and productive will gradually demand his freedom—and the slaveowner will grant it in return for receiving a larger absolute product though a decreasing share. Like industry, shipping, agriculture, and capital, labor will benefit from protection which will afford more security and variety of employment. Workers will no longer be crowded into great cities but will benefit by living in small communities where they can divide their time between the factory and the farm.

Under "British free trade," Ireland suffers, India starves, Americans are harried into moving westward and English workingmen go hungry—all to profit British middlemen who monopolize the means of converting cotton into cloth and ore into hardware. The object of protection, Carey concludes is "the establishment of perfect free trade by the annexation of men and nations." Once let it be known that the United States intends to establish the world's seat of cotton and iron manufactures within her borders, Europeans will flock here to enjoy the superior returns our peaceful democracy assures to capital and labor alike. Those who come will consume more cotton and food as their standard of living rises, while those who remain abroad will divide a larger product. Thus, all the world will benefit from the thorough application of protective tariffs by the United States.

The passages here reprinted point up "The Harmony of Interests" between capital and labor, a concept Hamilton first explored in his *Report on Manufactures*. They are filled with that same confidence in the destiny of America that is a prevalent theme in the shaping of the American tradition. The selections are taken from Vol. I (Philadelphia and London, 1837) and Vol. III (Philadelphia and London, 1840) of the *Principles of Political Economy*.

Principles of Political Economy

BY HENRY C. CAREY

MR. RICARDO

. . . MR. RICARDO's great error consists in supposing rapid changes of production, without a corresponding change of consumption. All improvements of the one are gradual and attended by increased power and disposition for the other. Every year sees new land taken into cultivation in both England and the United States, and every year sees the wages of labour advance. That of 1836 must therefore be more productive than was that of 1835, or 1834, because aided by greater capital. Every successive body of land in both countries is more productive than were those which preceded it when they were taken into cultivation, and yet rents not only do not fall, but they rise.

Until Whitney enabled the planter to clean it, the production of cotton was small, and its consumption limited. Since then there has been a succession of improvements, tending to lessen the cost, but with the reduction of price in the market, there has been an increase of demand. It has appeared, indeed, almost impossible for production to keep pace therewith, notwithstanding the United States, which produced in 1784 only eight bales, now furnish a million and a half of bales.

"But there are improvements which may lower the relative value of produce without lowering the corn rent, though they will lower the money rent of land. Such improvements do not increase the productive powers of the land, but they enable us to obtain its produce with less labour. They are rather directed to the formation of the capital applied to the land, than to the cultivation of the land itself. Improvements in agricultural implements, such as the plough and the threshing machine, economy in the use of horses employed in husbandry, and a better knowledge of the veterinary art, are of this nature. Less capital, which is the same thing as less labour, will be employed on the land; but to obtain the same produce, less land cannot be cultivated. Whether improvements of this kind, however, affect corn rent, must depend on the question, whether the difference between the produce obtained by the employment of different portions of capital be increased, stationary, or diminished. If four portions of capital, 50, 60, 70, 80, be employed on the land, giving each the same results, and any improvement in the formation of such capital should enable me to withdraw 5 from each, so that they should be 45, 55, 65, and 75, no alteration would take place in the corn rent; but if the improvements were such as to enable me to make the whole saving on the largest portion of capital, that portion which is least productively employed, corn rent would immediately fall, because the difference between the capital most productive and the capital least productive would be diminished; and it is this difference which constitutes rent." [1]

Mr. Ricardo forgets that the capital thus disengaged would be seeking employment, and that the man who had used it would desire to turn his attention to some other pursuit. If three men and three portions of capital could supply all the corn, one man and one portion of capital could be employed in manufacturing some article not previously produced. Production would be increased, the property would, by the establishment of the manufacture, acquire greater *advantages of situation* from the increased facility of exchanging its products, and wages and rents would both rise. *It is precisely this operation that has given to all the land of England those advantages of situation which enable the cultivators to pay, as rent, for a single acre of "inferior soil," as much as would purchase a dozen acres of the most fertile land in Texas.* The producers of wheat in the United States enjoy great "advantages of situation," from the extension of the cultivation of cotton, and from the establishment of manufactures, by which they are enabled, at small cost of transportation, to exchange their products for the commodities they desire to obtain. The producers of cotton will, at some future period, enjoy advantages of situation, from the establishment of manufactures among them, enabling them readily to obtain clothing. If all the people of the United States were employed in raising wheat, they would be compelled to pay the expense of transporting it

to Europe for exchange; but the increased productiveness of labour applied to cultivation enables them to transfer a large portion of their powers to other pursuits, and *with every such transfer there is an increase in the value of property—in the value of its products—in the rent of the landlord—and in the wages of the cultivator.* Every difficulty interposed in the way of producing any commodity lessens the value of labour and capital employed in its production, and every increase of facility raises the wages of the labourer and the profits of the capitalist. This is equally true whether the difficulty arises from want of knowledge, or from legislative restrictions. The former, however, is removed gradually—the latter may be removed suddenly, when the effect upon the capitalist is equally sudden, annihilating the whole of that capital which is least productive, and diminishing the revenue that the owner of the other portion should receive. The commodity falls in its labour value—the labourers claim a larger proportion of the product—but the destruction of capital which takes place tends to lessen the demand for labourers and the reward of all labour. . . .

"In speaking of the rent of the landlord, we have rather considered it as the proportion of the whole produce, without any reference to its exchangeable value, but since the same cause, the difficulty of production, raises the exchangeable value of raw produce, and raises also the proportion of raw produce paid to the landlord for rent, it is obvious that the landlord is doubly benefited by difficulty of production. First, he obtains a greater share; and, secondly, the commodity in which he is paid is of greater value." [2]

The difficulty of production is greatest in Poland, and least in the United States; yet in the last, land has a high value, and in the first, a low one. Upon this principle it was attempted to prevent the making of turnpike roads in England. It was said that the distant lands would supply the market of London, and would command high rents in consequence, at the expense of the nearer ones. The same effect was anticipated from the construction of the New York and Pennsylvania canals above referred to. The result has, however, been, that instead of a diminution of value, there has been an augmentation of it in almost every case. If the canals were destroyed, the inequality of situation would be increased, but the rent of land near New York and Philadelphia would fall, because the trade of those cities would be lessened, and they would lose their advantages of situa-

---

[1] Ricardo's Political Economy, Chapter II.

[2] *Ibid.*, Chapter II.

tion, by the transfer of capital to some other quarter.

Mr. Ricardo labours, throughout, under the error of supposing that great proportion means great quantity. The smaller the amount produced, the larger is the landlord's *proportion*, but the smaller is his *quantity*. One half of ten bushels, is a very different return from one third of thirty bushels. He supposes that the augmented price will also tend to increase the revenue of the landlord, yet in those countries in which the landlord has one half the price is lowest. In the United States and England the proportion is less than in Poland, but the quantity and price are greater. In the latter, the owner has *one half* of ten bushels, and the price is perhaps 40 or 50 cents per bushel. His revenue from an acre is, therefore, five bushels = $2 to $2 50. In the United States he may have one fourth of 30 bushels, at $1 50 per bushel = $11 25.

We take the following passages from Mr. Ricardo's chapter on Profits.

"We have shown that in early stages of society, both the landlord's and the *labourer's share* of the *value* of the produce of the earth, would be but small; and that it *would increase in proportion to the progress of wealth, and the difficulty of procuring food*. We have shown too, that although the value of the labourer's portion will be increased by the high value of food, *his real share will be diminished*; whilst that of the landlord will not only be raised in value, but will also be increased in quantity." [3]

In the colony of Western Australia we see the precise nature of the division which takes place in the early stages of society. We there see that the owner of land receives as rent only interest at the rate of ten per cent. for the capital applied to its improvement, which interest he could have from any other mode of investment. He takes a large share of the product and the labourer has a small one. With every increase of capital he will have a diminished share of the product, but that diminished share will yield him a larger return of commodities of every description. If "*the difficulty* of procuring food" increased with the progress of wealth, he would have, as Mr. Ricardo says, an increased proportion, but throughout the world, he obtains, as capital increases, a diminished share, marking a constant increase in *the facility* of procuring food.

Mr. Ricardo supposes that, in the course of the progress of wealth, *the real share of the labourer will be diminished*, whereas, there is undoubted evidence that the real share is constantly increasing, and that it cannot possibly be otherwise.

"In every case, agricultural, as well as manufacturing profits, are lowered by a rise in the price of raw produce, if it be accompanied by a rise of wages. If the farmer gets no additional value for the corn which remains to him after paying rent, if the manufacturer gets no additional value for the goods which he manufactures, and if both are obliged to pay a greater value in wages, can any point be more clearly established than that profits must fall, with a rise of wages?" [4]

A rise in the price of agricultural produce, unless produced by an increased facility in obtaining the precious metals, or by an increase in confidence by which credits, in the form of bills and drafts, lessen the quantity thereof required to perform the exchanges of the world, can take place only in consequence of diminished production. In such a case, if the labourer obtained the same *proportion*, the landlord would have less. Money wages, however, rise slowly, and *the effect of a rise in the price of produce from diminished production in any part of the world, is, always, to give a diminished proportion to the labourer*. Wages, *in corn*, fall; so do profits. The landlord's increased proportion yields him less than he had before. The *apparent rate of profit—i. e. the proportion claimed by the owner of capital,—falls with a rise of real wages, but the real profit always rises with them*, so that both are interested in the increase of production.

"The natural tendency of profits then is to fall; for, in the progress of society and wealth, the additional quantity of food required is obtained by the sacrifice of more and more labour. This tendency, this gravitation, as it were, of profits, is happily checked, at repeated intervals, by the improvements in machinery, connected with the production of necessaries, as well as by discoveries in the science of agriculture, which enable us to relinquish a portion of labour before required, and therefore to lower the price of the prime necessary of the labourer. The rise in the price of necessaries and in the wages of labour is, however, limited; for as soon as wages should be equal (as in the case formerly stated) to £720, the whole receipts of the farmer, *there must be an end of accumulation; for no capital can then yield any profit whatever*, and no additional labour can be demanded, and consequently population will have reached its highest point. Long, indeed, before this period, the very low rate of profits will have arrested all accumulation, and almost the whole

---

[3] *Ibid.*, Chapter V.

[4] *Ibid.*

produce of the country, after paying the labourers, will be the property of the owners of land and the receivers of tithes and taxes." [5]

The great difficulty that arises out of the separation of *profits of capital* from *rent of land*, is here very evident. We are told that profits will be so low that almost the whole produce of the country will be the property of the owners of the land. The owner of capital might, however, employ it either in the purchase, or in the cultivation, of land. If the latter did not afford sufficient return, he would adopt the former course, and by degrees all capital would be withdrawn from cultivation, and applied to the purchase of land. Where then would be the rents? There would be none, because the landlords had demanded too much, and they would then find that they had a machine called land, and that other people had other machines, called ploughs and harrows, and that the only way in which they could be brought together, was to make a fair division of the proceeds. The profit of capital employed *in land*, and *on land*, could not vary very greatly, because if the one did not pay enough, that employed in it would be very speedily diverted to the other.

If the doctrine that rent arises out of a necessity for having recourse to inferior soils, yielding a "constantly diminishing return to capital and labour," be true, equally so is the inference that at some future time the landlord will have it in his power to claim whatever proportion of the proceeds he may think proper, and that the labourer will be reduced, as in India, to a handful of rice and a rag of clothing. Unfortunately, however, for this theory, the world has gone on for thousands of years in a different direction. With the extension of cultivation, there has been a constant improvement in the condition of the labourer. He has been enabled to demand and obtain a constantly increasing proportion of the product of his labour, while the owners of land and of capital have been content with a constantly decreasing proportion. Both wages and profits have, however, risen. Labour is daily more productive—the labourer's power to accumulate capital is daily increasing—the amount of comforts obtainable in exchange for the use of any given quantity of capital is also increasing—and thus he is enabled to have better food, better clothing, better shelter, and to obtain with a constantly decreasing quantity of labour, the means of support when old age shall have disabled him for exertion. We ask the reader to examine the facts carefully, and to determine for himself which doctrine is borne out by them.

[5] *Ibid.*

Summary

We now submit to the reader the following propositions, embracing the results at which we have arrived.

I. That man desires to maintain and to improve his condition.

II. That he endeavours to accomplish this object by applying himself to the production of such things as are either useful or agreeable to him.

III. That as he cannot increase or decrease the quantity of matter of which the world is composed, he has it only in his power to alter in its form, or in its place, the matter already existing. Production, therefore, consists in the appropriation, alteration, or transportation, of the gifts of nature.

IV. That the articles so produced have value in his estimation, because of the labour that has been given in exchange for them.

V. That the values thus produced constitute his revenue.

VI. That a portion of his revenue is applied to the satisfaction of present wants, and the remainder is laid by for future enjoyment, or to aid him in further production.

VII. That the portion thus laid by constitutes his capital, under which head is embraced all articles possessing exchangeable value, whether in the form of land, houses, ships, provisions, diamonds, or commodities of any other description.

VIII. That capital aids labour and increases the power of production. That it also facilitates the division of employments, and combination of labour.

IX. That labour thus aided is improved in its quality.

X. That every improvement in the *quality* of labour tends to diminish the *quantity* required for the production of any commodity, and to facilitate its acquisition.

XI. That the value of all commodities, *at the time of production*, is estimated by the *quantity and quality* of labour required to produce them.

XII. That as every improvement in the *quality* of labour tends to diminish the *quantity* of labour required for the production of any commodity, it follows, that it also diminishes the quantity that can be obtained in exchange for commodities of a similar description already accumulated.

XIII. That there is, therefore, as labour improves in its quality, a constant tendency to diminution in the quantity thereof that can be obtained in exchange for existing capital. The value of the latter is limited by the cost of *reproduction*.

XIV. That the labourer, when he obtains the

aid of capital that he does not possess, allows to its owner a portion of the commodities that he is thereby enabled to produce.

XV. That the portion which he retains, is termed wages, and that which is received by the owner of capital, is termed profits.

XVI. That wages are the reward of human labour—of the exertion of skill or talent.

XVII. That profits are the compensation paid for the aid of *things* having exchangeable value.

XVIII. That the *profits of trade* are a combination of profits of capital and wages of labour, or superintendence.

XIX. That when labour is of inferior quality, production is small, capital is accumulated with difficulty, and the owner thereof claims a large proportion of the product in return for granting its aid.

XX. That at that time the quantity of commodities to be divided is small. The labourer's *proportion* thereof is small, and he obtains with difficulty the necessaries of life. The *proportion* of the capitalist is large, but the *quantity* of commodities is small, and thus he obtains but a small amount of the conveniences and necessaries of life, in return for the use of capital produced at great cost of labour.

XXI. That the quantity of commodities to be exchanged is small, and that both labourer and capitalist are obliged to allow to the dealer a large *proportion* to be retained by him as *profits of trade*, thus diminishing greatly their power of obtaining the necessaries or conveniences of life.

XXII. That as labour is improved in its quality, it becomes more productive, capital is accumulated at less cost of labour, and its owner can demand a smaller *proportion* of the product in return for granting its aid.

XXIII. That with every improvement in the quality of labour, the quantity of commodities to be divided is increased. That this increased production is attended by the power, on the part of the labourer, to retain a constantly increasing *proportion* of the commodities produced. He is, therefore, constantly improving in his condition.

XXIV. That although the *proportion* of the capitalist is constantly diminishing with the increased productiveness of labour, this diminished share gives him a constantly increasing *quantity* of commodities, enabling him to increase his consumption, while he rapidly increases his capital. Thus while the facility of accumulation is constantly increasing, there is a steady *diminution* in the *rate* of interest, or profit, and an equally steady *increase* in the amount of commodities that the

owner receives in return for the use of any given quantity of capital.

XXV. That the quantity of commodities to be exchanged increases rapidly, and the trader is enabled to obtain constantly *increasing* profits of trade from a constantly *diminishing* proportion of the commodities which pass through his hands. Both capitalist and labourer are, therefore, enabled to obtain a constantly increasing measure of the conveniences, comforts, and luxuries of life, in exchange for their products.

XXVI. That the interests of the capitalist and the labourer are thus in perfect harmony with each other, as each derives advantage from every measure that tends to facilitate the growth of capital, and to render labour productive, while every measure that tends to produce the opposite effect is injurious to both.

XXVII. That the world at large is governed by the same laws which govern the individual labourers and capitalists, or any number of them constituting a community, or nation.

XXVIII. That the interests of all nations are therefore in harmony with each other, as every measure that tends to lessen production in one nation, tends to lessen the reward of both labourer and capitalist in every other nation, and every measure that tends to increase it, tends to increase the reward of the labourer and capitalist in every other nation.

XXIX. That it is therefore the interest of all that universal peace should prevail, whereby the waste of population and of capital should be arrested—and that the only strife among nations should be to determine which should make the most rapid advances in those peaceful arts which tend to increase the comforts and enjoyments of all the portions of the human race.

XXX. That the desire of improving his condition impels man to desire the aid and co-operation of his fellow men.

XXXI. That in the infancy of society the want of capital compels him to depend for a supply of the necessaries of life upon the appropriation of those articles produced by nature without his aid, and he is compelled to roam over extensive tracts of land to obtain sufficient to support existence. He relies, exclusively, upon the superior soils.

XXXII. That he is therefore compelled to live apart from his fellow men, or to associate with them in very small communities. Population is, consequently, thinly scattered over the land. Fertile land is abundant, but he has not the means of rendering it productive.

XXXIII. That if successful in his search after

food, he does not possess the means of transporting or of preserving that which he does not require for immediate consumption. His life is therefore a constant alternation of waste and starvation. He is poor and miserable.

XXXIV. That with the first accumulation of capital he acquires the power of resorting to an inferior soil for subsistence. He finds that a more limited space will supply his wants, and he is enabled to draw nearer to his fellow men, to unite with them in the division of employment, and thus to obtain their co-operation, by which the labour of all is rendered more productive.

XXXV. That his implements are, however, still rude, and he is obliged to scratch over the surface of a large quantity of land to obtain what is necessary for his support. The surplus above what is necessary for his own consumption is small and the exertions of nearly the whole of the community are requisite to secure a supply of food, leaving few for the preparation of clothing, the building of houses, or the production of any other of the comforts of life. His condition is improved, but he is still poor and miserable.

XXXVI. That with the further accumulation of capital he brings into action soils still more inferior, and with every such change finds increased facility in obtaining the necessaries of life from a diminished surface; he is, therefore, enabled to draw daily nearer to his fellow men, and daily more and more to co-operate with them, by which co-operation his labour is rendered daily more productive. This increased facility of obtaining the means of subsistence, causes a constant diminution in the proportion of the population required for the production of food, and enables a constantly increasing proportion to apply themselves to the production of clothing, shelter, and the other comforts of life.

XXXVII. That thus, as capital increases, population becomes more dense, and the inferior soils are brought into action with a constantly increasing return to labour. Men are enabled to benefit by the co-operation of their neighbours, and habits of kindness and good feeling take the place of the savage and predatory habits of the early period. Poverty and misery gradually disappear, and are replaced by ease and comfort. Labour becomes gradually less severe, and the quantity required to secure the means of subsistence is diminished, by which he is enabled to devote more time to the cultivation of his mind. His moral improvement keeps pace with that which takes place in his physical condition, and thus the virtues of civilization replace the vices of savage life.

CONCLUSION: VOLUME III

The following propositions embrace the several points which we have endeavoured to establish.

I. That mankind tend to increase in numbers, and that under favourable circumstances they may double in from twenty-five to thirty years.

II. That there is a tendency to the accumulation, by each generation, of capital, in the form of houses, farms, canals, rail-roads, and other machinery, for the benefit of that which is to succeed it, and that, when not prevented by human interference, there must be a steady increase in the ratio of capital to population, as we know to have been the case, although in different degrees, in England, Scotland, France, the United States, and other countries, for centuries past.

III. That each successive generation should therefore be enabled to apply its labour more advantageously than that which preceded it, gradually substituting coal drawn from the bowels of the earth for the wood which before had been taken from the surface—iron and steel for flint—rail-roads and canals for horse and mule paths—ships and steamboats for canoes—the cotton of India and America, and the silk of China, for the skin of the ox and the sheep—the spinning-jenny and the power-loom for the distaff and hand-loom—and the power of the steam-engine for that of man—bringing into action those soils which, from difference of situation, or of quality, had been deemed inferior, and with each successive substitution diminishing the severity of labour, while increasing its reward.

IV. That the power of cultivating the soils that from quality were deemed inferior, and obtaining therefrom a constantly increasing supply of the necessaries and conveniences of life from any given surface, tends to enable men to associate themselves together, and to combine their exertions for the increase of production and for mutual protection, thus rendering their labour more productive, and promoting the further increase of capital.

V. That the increased facility of communication enables them to extend themselves over lands that by distance were rendered inferior, thus increasing the surface occupied, at the same time that population becomes more dense near the centre of capital, and that every such extension tends to increase the productiveness of labour, and the facility of accumulating further capital.

VI. That every increase in the ratio of capital to population, is attended with an increase in the ratio which the value of labour bears to that of capital, and the labourer is consequently enabled to retain a *constantly increasing proportion* of the product of his labour, leaving to the owner of landed or other capital a *constantly diminishing proportion.*

VII. That notwithstanding his diminution of *proportion,* the capitalist obtains for the use of any given capital, a constantly increasing *quantity* of the commodities necessary for his subsistence and enjoyment, and for the further increase of his capital.

VIII. That both labourer and capitalist are consequently enabled to improve their *physical* condition, thereby producing a tendency to a more rapid increase of population, and a more intimate association for the purpose of increasing production, or of maintaining security.

IX. That with the increase of population and capital, there is a constant diminution in the *proportion* of the labour of a community, or of the proceeds thereof, required for the maintenance of security, which becomes daily more perfect. Labour becomes more productive, while there is a constant increase in the *proportion* of the product that is left for division between the labourer and the capitalist.

X. That with every increase of security, man is enabled more distinctly to perceive the advantage and propriety of respecting the rights and feelings of others, if he desire them to respect his own, and that the increased habit of association for mutual protection tends to increase the necessity for so doing: while the increased productiveness of labour offers a constantly increasing inducement to apply himself to obtain, by honest industry, the commodities necessary for his subsistence, and for the accumulation of capital; and that thus is produced a constant improvement of *moral* condition, tending to diminish still further the cost of maintaining security.

XI. That the increase in the labourer's proportion tends to produce a more rapid improvement in his condition than in that of the owner of capital—to diminish the distance between them—and to enable him to become himself a capitalist.

XII. That, consequently, with every increase of wealth we find a change in the relative positions of the labourer or the mechanic—the lawyer or the artist—and the mere capitalist, the former occupying a more, and the latter a less, prominent position in society: the former taking a larger, and the latter a smaller, *proportion* of the proceeds of their combined exertions: the former experiencing a constantly increasing facility for passing from the ranks of labourers or mechanics

to that of capitalists, and for applying his talents and capital to promote his further advancement. Every increase of the productive power tends, therefore, to increase the proportion which the architects of their own fortunes bear to those who have inherited fortune, and with every such increase there is a tendency to the improvement and equality of the *moral* condition of all classes of society.

XIII. That the diminished proportion which the value of capital bears to that of labour, and the constant approach to equality of condition, tend to render it necessary for the capitalist to apply his time and talents to production, while it is attended with a constant increase in the value of such talent, offering a constantly increasing inducement to its exertion, and producing a constantly increasing facility for the further accumulation of capital, and further improvement of physical, moral, and intellectual condition. The more rapid the increase of the productive power, the smaller, therefore, is the *proportion* which the unproductive bear to the productive classes.

XIV. That the labourer and mechanic are, by the hope of rising, stimulated to the improvement of their *intellectual* condition, and that the constant increase in their *proportion* of the constantly increasing product of labour, enables each generation to devote a constantly increasing amount of time and of capital to the improvement of the mind. That, consequently, there is, with the increase of population, a constant increase in the *proportion* who read, and a rapid increase in the reward of authors—in the lovers of the arts, and in the reward of artists. The prospect of wealth and distinction thus tends to give additional stimulus to exertion on the part of the labourer, while the necessity therefor on the part of the capitalist, if he would maintain his position in society, is daily increasing. Increase of the productive power is therefore necessarily accompanied by a tendency to improvement and equalization in the *intellectual* condition of all classes of society.

XV. That every diminution in the *proportion* retained by the owner of landed or other capital, tends to diminish his power to command the services of labourers, whether to be employed in the business of production, or in the maintenance of power over the actions of his fellow men, while the attendant improvement of moral condition tends to diminish the disposition to exercise that power.

XVI. That every increase of the labourer's *proportion* being attended with improved intellectual condition, he is enabled more fully to understand and to appreciate his right to equal security of person and property—to the control of his own actions and the disposition of his own property—while his improved physical and moral condition enables him more advantageously to assert it, and that there is, therefore, with the increase of wealth, a constant tendency to equality of *political* condition, and to the establishment of the right of self-government.

XVII. That every increase of population being, when not prevented by human interference, accompanied by an increase in the ratio of capital to population, there is a constant tendency to the improvement and equality of physical, moral, intellectual, and political condition, to the further growth of population and capital, and to the further improvement of condition.

Such has been the course of events in those countries in which men have cultivated peace and good will among themselves and with their neighbours, and permitted population and capital to increase, but unfortunately a large portion of the world has been employed in robbing and plundering each other, thus keeping themselves in a state of poverty, vice, ignorance, and slavery, when they should be free, virtuous, and intelligent. The few have thereby been enabled to indulge their ambition, their vanity, and their desire of distinction, at the expense of the many. Well may it be said that "God made man upright, but they have sought out many inventions." [1]

The whole science of Political Economy may be reduced to a single line—

DO UNTO OTHERS AS YE WOULD THAT OTHERS SHOULD DO UNTO YOU.

An examination of the history of the human race, and careful reflection, would satisfy—

SOVEREIGNS, that the maintenance of peace and a studious observance of the rights of their neighbours, enabling the community over which they preside to increase in numbers and wealth, and in their productive power, would be attended with more *permanent* advantage to themselves and to their families than could be derived from impoverishing their subjects for the purpose of bringing new provinces under their dominion.

NATIONS, that every invasion of the rights of their neighbours—every expenditure for the maintenance of offensive war—must be attended with a diminution in the facilities for producing the commodities required for their own support, convenience, or enjoyment, and, consequently, with a deterioration of physical and moral condition—producing poverty, immorality, and ignorance, and enabling those charged with the administra-

[1] Ecclesiastes.

tion of public affairs to take an increased proportion of the produce of their labour, and to exercise increased control over their actions, thus deteriorating their political condition.

LEGISLATORS, that the mode in which they can secure to their constituents universal prosperity, is to refrain from every measure tending to impair the right of individuals to determine for themselves the mode of employing their time and their property—and to exert themselves to diminish the demands of the government upon the produce of labour, as no government uses capital so advantageously as it would be used by those from whose pockets it is taken.

OWNERS OF LANDED AND OTHER CAPITAL, that every interference with the rights of their fellow citizens—every diminution in the perfect security of the rights of person and property—every monopoly or privilege—tends to diminish the power of production, and the *quantity* of commodities falling to their share, and consequently to impair their power of accumulation.

LABOURERS, that every interference with the rights of others—whether by war abroad, or riot and destruction at home—by restricting foreigners or their fellow citizens in their right freely to exchange the product of their labour—by restraining the employment of capital or of labour—tends to diminish not only the *quantity* of commodities produced, but their own *proportion* of that diminished quantity—to diminish their power of accumulation—their control over their own actions, and over those of the persons charged with the administration of the government—and thus to impair their power of improving their physical, moral, intellectual, and political condition.

FREEMEN, that if they desire improvement of political condition for any portion of the human race, whether of their own or of any other nation, their object will be best accomplished by uniting in every measure tending to increase the value of their labour, and by avoiding every thing tending to incite them to rebellion or revolution, war and massacre, or in any other way to lessen the perfect security of person and property.

ADVOCATES OF FREE TRADE, that in the endeavour to improve the action of the community of which they are members, they should always recollect that it has been by the previous action of the community itself that labour and capital have been forced into various branches of production, and that justice, as well as the interest of the nation at large, requires that all changes be gradual, in order that the desired improvement be attained with the least destruction of existing capital. By such action will the end, that of increasing the productiveness of labour, be most speedily, safely, and advantageously accomplished.

DISCIPLES OF MR. MALTHUS, that obedience to the laws of God is attended with a rapid increase of population, and still more rapid increase of capital, enabling men to bring into activity the inferior soils, with a constantly increasing return to labour; and that war, with its attendant crime and misery, tends to keep subsistence below population, instead of keeping population down to subsistence. Such being the case, they may be content to leave to their successors to avail themselves of the remedies, positive and preventive, against overpopulation, whenever they shall be satisfied of their necessity.

In opposition to those who define political economy to be the science of wealth, or of exchanges, we have defined it as that "which treats of those phenomena of society which arise out of the desire of mankind to maintain and to improve their condition." This definition appears to cover a much wider field than the other, yet every matter of which we have treated would necessarily be brought into view, were our object only to show the causes which influence the production and distribution of wealth. Increased capital facilitates production and promotes the growth of population, while it enables men to live in closer connexion, and to combine their exertions for the increase of wealth. Increase of wealth affects the mode of distribution, and thence results change of political condition, and men enter upon the secure enjoyment of their rights of person and property. Improved political condition enables them to exercise their own judgment in the employment of their labour and capital, tending to render both more productive, thus facilitating the further improvement of physical and moral condition. Here, in the moral world, is a chain of circumstances as dependent upon, and as necessary to each other, as can be the members of any series in the physical world. Heat causes evaporation. The inferior specific gravity of vapour causes ascension. Cold causes condensation, and gravity returns to the earth the fluid necessary for the support of animal and vegetable life. To omit, in a treatise of political economy, any portion of the series which we have embraced in this work, would be similar to an investigation of the laws of fluids, omitting the consideration of evaporation or condensation. The one cannot continue to take place without the other, neither can there be a steady increase of productive power unaccompanied by physical, moral, intellectual, and political improvement, each tending to increase the facility of obtaining further wealth: nor can improvement of condition take place without increase in the power of production. They are as necessary to each other as evaporation and condensation.

The happiness of society is dependent upon its moral, physical, and political condition, yet it is denied that the political economist should concern himself with the happiness of nations—with human welfare—the subject to be treated of being wealth solely. By another writer it is asserted, that "the science of wealth may just as frequently lead to what will injure, as to what will benefit the human race." It is therefore believed that the laws of political economy afford rules that cannot be used as "the sole, or even the principal guides in the conduct of affairs." Our object, on the contrary, has been to show that those laws are exceedingly simple: that a compliance with them can never lead to the adoption of any measure that would not be dictated by an enlightened self-interest, while their study must tend to diminish selfishness, by showing that our interests are so interwoven with those of our fellow men, that injury to them is necessarily accompanied by injury to ourselves: that they are universally true and universally applicable, and that their universal adoption would be attended by a rapid improvement of physical, moral, intellectual, and political condition, increasing the happiness and prosperity of nations, giving them a constantly increasing facility for the further accumulation of wealth, and further improvement of condition. We leave the reader now to judge between the two definitions, and to determine for himself whether or not the happiness and welfare of nations come within the sphere of the political economist.

GEORGE BANCROFT

GEORGE BANCROFT (1800–1891) had passed from schoolroom to politics when he delivered his lecture on the *Office of the People in Art, Government, and Religion* in 1835. He had been one of the first Americans to submit himself to the rigors of German university training, but on his return to the United States he decided that he could use his training more usefully as a teacher than in the ministry for which he had been intended. After one unsuccessful attempt at transplanting German thoroughness to Harvard Greek classes and another at secondary education, Bancroft became a publicist and an active Jackson partisan.

He declared his allegiance in a *North American Review* article which had that somewhat surprised Whig organ approving Andrew Jackson's fight against the Bank, and then set about promoting union among anti-Whig groups in Massachusetts. At the same time, Bancroft began work on his *History of the United States*, the first volume of which appeared in September, 1834.

It has long been fashionable to remark that every line of Bancroft's history voted for Andrew Jackson. More illuminating would be the comment that Bancroft's was the first large-scale attempt by an American to write the history of the United States by a reasonably critical use of the sources, so far as those were available. Bancroft wrote in and for a world that regarded history as a branch of literature rather than as a social science, and he was thoroughly imbued with the Romantic view of the past.

The democratic faith which characterized Bancroft's history, and his politics, is evident in the discourse on the *Office of the People* which he delivered before a college literary society a year after his history appeared. All men are endowed with reason, Bancroft declared. And, since all men have this gift, the people are qualified to judge of values in all spheres, particularly in that of government. This fact is the true basis for popular government. Without an enlightened people, the work of a philosopher-king is doomed to futility, as the Antonines showed. The people collectively are wiser than the wisest individual, since their prejudices of ignorance may be removed by education whereas prejudices stemming from individual interest cannot be. Man was inherently good, Bancroft concluded; and his course was upward. Truth, like the race, was indestructible, for humanity was the guardian of moral truth, which must rise and prevail forever.

Bancroft followed that proclamation of political faith by stumping Massachusetts against the Whigs in an effort to unite the opposition. As the decade passed, the historian all but became political boss of the state when he was appointed Collector of the Port of Boston in 1838. Though Bancroft lost that post with the Whig triumph of 1840, his support of the candidacy of James K. Polk at the next Democratic Convention assured his political future. Polk appointed him Secretary of the Navy—where Bancroft not only outlined plans for the acquisition of California but laid the foundation for modern developments in naval training and the method of naval promotions. This was followed by his nomination as Minister to England. In that position, Bancroft had all but secured a favorable trade treaty when another Whig victory brought about his recall.

Bancroft retired into his historical writing during the Fifties, when four volumes of his history appeared. He supported Douglas in 1860 and considered himself a War Democrat during the years that followed, though he found fault with the Lincoln administration's reluctance to deal with slavery.

When the Civil War ended, Bancroft joined the moderates in support of President Johnson. He made a futile effort to win Sumner away from the Radicals and even drafted Johnson's first message to Congress. That effort may have prompted the new President to name Bancroft Minister to Prussia in 1867, a place Bancroft found particularly congenial because of his interest in the advancing cause of German unity, a phenomenon he regarded as analogous to the growth of the American republic. Through the seven years of his ministry, Bancroft showed his friendship for Prussia in so evident a fashion that, during the Franco-Prussian War, the French complained his attitude did not become the representative of a neutral power.

Bancroft retired in 1874 to spend the last of his life revising and completing his history, which he brought to a culmination in a pioneer study of the adoption of the Constitution just as a new school of historians was about to consign his great work to the lumber room of "literature." For, between the first volume and the tenth, the theory of evolution had replaced the insights of the Transcendental Reason as the basis for historical interpretation.

The passage here reprinted is from Bancroft's *Literary and Historical Miscellanies* (New York, 1855).

The Office of the People

BY GEORGE BANCROFT

THE OFFICE OF THE PEOPLE IN ART, GOVERNMENT, AND RELIGION (AN ORATION DELIVERED BEFORE THE ADELPHI SOCIETY OF WILLIAMSTOWN COLLEGE, IN AUGUST, 1835)

THE MATERIAL WORLD does not change in its masses or in its powers. The stars shine with no more lustre than when they first sang together in the glory of their birth. The flowers that gemmed the fields and the forests, before America was discovered, now bloom around us in their season. The sun that shone on Homer shines on us in unchanging lustre. The bow that beamed on the patriarch still glitters in the clouds. Nature is the same. For her no new forces are generated; no new capacities are discovered. The earth turns on its axis, and perfects its revolutions, and renews its seasons, without increase or advancement.

But a like passive destiny does not attach to the inhabitants of the earth. For them the expectations of social improvement are no delusion; the hopes of philanthropy are more than a dream. The five senses do not constitute the whole inventory of our sources of knowledge. They are the organs by which thought connects itself with the external universe; but the power of thought is not merged in the exercise of its instruments. We have functions which connect us with heaven, as well as organs which set us in relation with earth. We have not merely the senses opening to us the external world, but an internal sense, which places us in connexion with the world of intelligence and the decrees of God.

There is a *spirit in man:* not in the privileged few; not in those of us only who by the favor of Providence have been nursed in public schools: IT IS IN MAN: it is the attribute of the race. The spirit, which is the guide to truth, is the gracious gift to each member of the human family.

Reason exists within every breast. I mean not that faculty which deduces inferences from the experience of the senses, but that higher faculty, which from the infinite treasures of its own consciousness, originates truth, and assents to it by the force of intuitive evidence; that faculty which raises us beyond the control of time and space, and gives us faith in things eternal and invisible. There is not the difference between one mind and another, which the pride of philosophers might conceive. To them no faculty is conceded, which does not belong to the meanest of their countrymen. . . .

In like manner the best government rests on the people and not on the few, on persons and not on property, on the free development of public opinion and not on authority; because the munificent Author of our being has conferred the gifts of mind upon every member of the human race without distinction of outward circumstances. Whatever of other possessions may be engrossed, mind asserts its own independence. Lands, estates, the produce of mines, the prolific abundance of the seas, may be usurped by a privileged class. Avarice, assuming the form of ambitious power, may grasp realm after realm, subdue continents, compass the earth in its schemes of aggrandizement, and sigh after other worlds; but mind eludes the power of appropriation; it exists only in its own individuality; it is a property which cannot be confiscated and cannot be torn away; it laughs at chains; it bursts from imprisonment; it defies monopoly. A government of equal rights must, therefore, rest upon mind; not wealth, not brute force, the sum of the moral intelligence of the community should rule the State. Prescription can no more assume to be a valid plea for political injustice; society studies to eradicate established abuses, and to bring social institutions and laws into harmony with moral right; not dismayed by the natural and necessary imperfections of all human effort, and not giving way to despair, because every hope does not at once ripen into fruit.

The public happiness is the true object of legislation, and can be secured only by the masses of mankind themselves awakening to the knowledge and the care of their own interests. Our free institutions have reversed the false and ignoble distinctions between men; and refusing to gratify the pride of caste, have acknowledged the common mind to be the true material for a commonwealth. Every thing has hitherto been done for the happy few. It is not possible to endow an aristocracy with greater benefits than they have already enjoyed; there is no room to hope that individuals will be more highly gifted or more fully developed than the greatest sages of past times. The world can advance only through the culture of the moral and intellectual powers of the people. To accomplish this end by means of the people themselves, is the highest purpose of government. If it be the duty of the individual to strive after a perfection like the perfection of God, how much more ought a nation to be the image of Deity. The common mind is the true Parian marble, fit to be wrought into likeness to a God. The duty of America is to secure the culture and the happiness of the masses by their reliance on themselves.

The absence of the prejudices of the old world leaves us here the opportunity of consulting independent truth; and man is left to apply the instinct of freedom to every social relation and public interest. We have approached so near to nature, that we can hear her gentlest whispers; we have made Humanity our lawgiver and our oracle; and, therefore, the nation receives, vivifies and applies principles, which in Europe the wisest accept with distrust. Freedom of mind and of conscience, freedom of the seas, freedom of industry, equality of franchises, each great truth is firmly grasped, comprehended and enforced; for the multitude is neither rash nor fickle. In truth, it is less fickle than those who profess to be its guides. Its natural dialectics surpass the logic of the schools. Political action has never been so consistent and so unwavering, as when it results from a feeling or a principle, diffused through society. The people is firm and tranquil in its movements, and necessarily acts with moderation, because it becomes but slowly impregnated with new ideas; and effects no changes, except in harmony with the knowledge which it has acquired. Besides, where it is permanently possessed of power, there exists neither the occasion nor the desire for frequent change. It is not the parent of tumult; sedition is bred in the lap of luxury, and its chosen emissaries are the beggared spendthrift and the impoverished libertine. The government by the people is in very truth the strongest government in the world. Discarding the implements of terror, it dares to rule by moral force, and has its citadel in the heart.

Such is the political system which rests on reason, reflection, and the free expression of deliberate choice. There may be those who scoff at the suggestion, that the decision of the whole is to be preferred to the judgment of the enlightened few. They say in their hearts that the masses are ignorant; that farmers know nothing of legislation; that mechanics should not quit their workshops to join in forming public opinion. But true political science does indeed venerate the masses. It maintains, not as has been perversely asserted, that "the people can make right," but that the people can DISCERN right. Individuals are but shadows, too often engrossed by the pursuit of shadows; the race is immortal: individuals are of limited sagacity; the common mind is infinite in its experience: individuals are languid and blind; the many are ever wakeful: individuals are corrupt; the race has been redeemed: individuals are timeserving; the masses are fearless: individuals may be false, the masses are ingenuous and sincere: individuals claim the divine sanction of truth for the deceitful conceptions of their own fancies; the Spirit of God breathes through the combined intelligence of the people. Truth is not to be ascertained by the impulses of an individual; it emerges from the contradictions of personal opinions; it raises itself in majestic serenity above the strifes of parties and the conflict of sects; it acknowledges neither the solitary mind, nor the separate faction as its oracle; but owns as its only faithful interpreter the dictates of pure reason itself, proclaimed by the general voice of mankind. The decrees of the universal conscience are the nearest approach to the presence of God in the soul of man.

Thus the opinion which we respect is, indeed, not the opinion of one or of a few, but the sagacity of the many. It is hard for the pride of cultivated philosophy to put its ear to the ground, and listen reverently to the voice of lowly humanity; yet the people collectively are wiser than the most gifted individual, for all his wisdom constitutes but a part of theirs. When the great sculptor of Greece was endeavoring to fashion the perfect model of beauty, he did not passively imitate the form of the loveliest woman of his age; but he gleaned the several lineaments of his faultless work from the many. And so it is, that a perfect judgment is the result of comparison, when error eliminates error, and truth is established by concurring witnesses. The organ of truth is the invisible decision of the unbiased world; she pleads before no tribunal but public opinion; she owns no safe interpreter but the common mind; she knows no court of appeals but the soul of humanity. It is when the multitude give counsel, that right purposes find safety; theirs is the fixedness that cannot be shaken; theirs is the understanding which exceeds in wisdom; theirs is the heart, of which the largeness is as the sand on the sea-shore.

It is not by vast armies, by immense natural resources, by accumulations of treasure, that the greatest results in modern civilization have been accomplished. The traces of the career of conquest pass away, hardly leaving a scar on the national intelligence. The famous battle grounds of victory are, most of them, comparatively indifferent to the human race; barren fields of blood, the scourges of their times, but affecting the social condition as little as the raging of a pestilence. Not one benevolent institution, not one ameliorating principle in the Roman state, was a voluntary concession of the aristocracy; each useful element was borrowed from the Democracies of Greece, or was a reluctant concession to the demands of the people. The same is true in modern political life. It is the confession of an enemy to Democracy, that "ALL THE GREAT AND NOBLE INSTITUTIONS OF THE WORLD HAVE COME FROM POPULAR EFFORTS."

It is the uniform tendency of the popular element to elevate and bless Humanity. The exact measure of the progress of civilization is the degree in which the intelligence of the common mind has prevailed over wealth and brute force; in other words, the measure of the progress of civilization is the progress of the people. Every great object, connected with the benevolent exertions of the day, has reference to the culture of those powers which are alone the common inheritance. For this the envoys of religion cross seas, and visit remotest isles; for this the press in its freedom teems with the productions of maturest thought; for this the philanthropist plans new schemes of education; for this halls in every city and village are open to the public instructor. Not that we view with indifference the glorious efforts of material industry; the increase in the facility of internal intercourse; the accumulations of thrifty labor; the varied results of concentrated action. But even there it is mind that achieves the triumph. It is the genius of the architect that gives beauty to the work of human hands, and makes the temple, the dwelling, or the public edifice, an outward representation of the spirit of propriety and order. It is science that guides the blind zeal of cupidity to the construction of the vast channels of communication, which are fast binding the world into one family. And it is as a method of moral improvement, that these swifter means of intercourse derive their greatest value. Mind becomes universal property; the poem that is published on the soil of England, finds its response on the shores of Lake Erie and the banks of the Missouri, and is admired near the sources of the Ganges. The defence of public liberty in our own halls of legislation penetrates the plains of Poland, is echoed along the mountains of Greece, and pierces the darkest night of eastern despotism.

The universality of the intellectual and moral powers, and the necessity of their development for the progress of the race, proclaim the great doctrine of the natural right of every human being to moral and intellectual culture. It is the glory of our fathers to have established in their laws the equal claims of every child to the public care of its morals and its mind. From this principle we may deduce the universal right to leisure; that is, to time not appropriated to material purposes, but reserved for the culture of the moral affections and the mind. It does not tolerate the exclusive enjoyment of leisure by a privileged class; but defending the rights of labor, would suffer none to sacrifice the higher purposes of existence in unceasing toil for that which is not life. Such is the voice of nature; such the conscious claim of the human mind. The universe opens its pages to every eye; the music of creation resounds in every ear; the glorious lessons of immortal truth, that are written in the sky and on the earth, address themselves to every mind, and claim attention from every human being. God has made man upright, that he might look before and after; and he calls upon every one not merely to labor, but to reflect; not merely to practise the revelations of divine will, but to contemplate the displays of divine power. Nature claims for every man leisure, for she claims every man as a witness to the divine glory, manifested in the created world.

ALEXIS DE TOCQUEVILLE

IN 1831, two young Frenchmen arrived in the United States commissioned, at their own request, to study the new departures which the young republic was making in prison discipline. After their return to France, they published a report embodying their observations and their recommendations for the reform of the penal system of France. Not long afterward, political pressure on one of the companions, who held a judicial post in which the other was his subordinate, led both to resign. And, in the retirement which followed, Alexis de Tocqueville (1805–1859) wrote *Democracy in America*, one of the few descriptions of Andrew Jackson's America which pays small attention to tobacco-chewing, thunderstorms or the rambunctious American child.

Tocqueville's concern lay in this new thing that was developing in the Western World: the United States had weathered its first half-century under the Constitution. A democratic republic might still be considered an experiment, but in stability, at least, it compared favorably with all but the more despotic regimes of Europe. All constitutional governments had been forced into change during the period of American independence, and that change had been in the democratic direction.

What was democracy, then, and what did its advance mean to the world? Would man have more liberty under democratic government, or would despotism mask under new names?

Examination of the United States might help answer those questions, for in the United States democratic government was being practiced on a great scale. The largest republic since Rome's constitution had been subverted was living that the world might learn.

Tocqueville was a member of what may be termed the administrative aristocracy. His father had been a prefect under the Empire and the Restoration. Tocqueville himself was born in 1805 and was reared during the troubled period when returned *emigrés* exhibited a royalism more intense than that of royalty itself and demonstrated their unwillingness to accept the tendency toward middle-class mastery in the state.

Tocqueville had the tastes of an aristocrat: every line of his writing is informed with suspicion of the restless surgings of a self-seeking, fluid society. There can be no peace in such a culture, and small dignity. Men's minds will necessarily turn to the petty ends of personal advantage, and so be formed to poverty of the spirit. Yet the old hierarchical society had stagnated and died.

The world, therefore, says Tocqueville, must learn to live in the new ways and to win what graciousness it might expect of them. Though, if the United States was the pattern of democracy, the world had little to hope on that score. Democratic societies valued equality above true liberty. Public opinion, reigning unchecked and unguided by aristocratic standards, would become a tyrant imposing uniformity in obedience to its will. Where no man stood secure in his position but all risked either advancement or decline, life would become continued battle. Temperaments would grow restless, accordingly, and dignified repose pass from the social scene. Art would devote itself to ornamentation, science concentrate on matters that could be turned to practical profit, and the grandly contemplative branches of learning wither and atrophy, leaving the body politic without roots to sustain it.

On the other hand, democratic societies would make great advances on the material level. The flux encouraged by democracy fosters the liberation of energy; the abilities of all classes are then enabled to serve individuals and society. Democratic societies would increase in prosperity until wealth reached the point of concentration, when new elements might come forward to check the progress of equality. Democratic societies might be more pleasant dwelling places than their predecessors, as cruelty tended to disappear and politeness became the mark of all social intercourse rather than a mere intraclass practice. Probity and good will would supplant honor as the chief among virtues and virtue itself would lose its old Roman connotations to become a gentler and more pallid concept, applicable chiefly to women.

There was much good in democracy: it promoted strong and stable government, for example, and since it resented the aristocratic pretensions latent in all military leadership, democracy might tend to maintain peace among nations. Contrary to general belief, however, it was order, not liberty, which was democracy's great contribution to government. De-

mocracy bore no necessary relation to liberty, for democratic government might exercise more effective compulsion than any, since it drew its authority from the very fountain of power, the consent of the governed. Time might even prove democracy the most formidable of despotisms: it erased all distinctions among citizens and, by eradicating special privilege before the law, leveled the subtle social barriers that once had blocked the arm of political power.

Democracy in America won immediate praise upon its publication in 1835. France, and all Europe that read French, studied Tocqueville, finding small comfort in his reservations concerning the human worth of what he regarded as the inevitable course of events. America read him, too, not quite comfortably, yet determined to be pleased. And it continues to read Tocqueville as one of the most searching analyses of the American mind and its promise.

The selections here reprinted are from Volume II of the Phillips Bradley edition of *Democracy in America* (New York, 1945) and are published by permission of Alfred A. Knopf, Inc.

Democracy in America

BY ALEXIS DE TOCQUEVILLE

VOLUME II, BOOK I. CHAPTER X: WHY THE AMERICANS ARE MORE ADDICTED TO PRACTICAL THAN TO THEORETICAL SCIENCE

IF A DEMOCRATIC state of society and democratic institutions do not retard the onward course of the human mind, they incontestably guide it in one direction in preference to another. Their efforts, thus circumscribed, are still exceedingly great, and I may be pardoned if I pause for a moment to contemplate them.

I had occasion, in speaking of the philosophical method of the American people, to make several remarks that it is necessary to make use of here.

Equality begets in man the desire of judging of everything for himself; it gives him in all things a taste for the tangible and the real, a contempt for tradition and for forms. These general tend-

encies are principally discernible in the peculiar subject of this chapter.

Those who cultivate the sciences among a democratic people are always afraid of losing their way in visionary speculation. They mistrust systems; they adhere closely to facts and study facts with their own senses. As they do not easily defer to the mere name of any fellow man, they are never inclined to rest upon any man's authority; but, on the contrary, they are unremitting in their efforts to find out the weaker points of their neighbors' doctrine. Scientific precedents have little weight with them; they are never long detained by the subtlety of the schools nor ready to accept big words for sterling coin; they penetrate, as far as they can, into the principal parts of the subject that occupies them, and they like to expound them in the popular language. Scientific pursuits then follow a freer and safer course, but a less lofty one.

The mind, it appears to me, may divide science into three parts.

The first comprises the most theoretical principles and those more abstract notions whose application is either unknown or very remote.

The second is composed of those general truths that still belong to pure theory, but lead nevertheless by a straight and short road to practical results.

Methods of application and means of execution make up the third.

Each of these different portions of science may be separately cultivated, although reason and experience prove that no one of them can prosper long if it is absolutely cut off from the two others.

In America the purely practical part of science is admirably understood, and careful attention is paid to the theoretical portion which is immediately requisite to application. On this head the Americans always display a clear, free, original, and inventive power of mind. But hardly anyone in the United States devotes himself to the essentially theoretical and abstract portion of human knowledge. In this respect the Americans carry to excess a tendency that is, I think, discernible, though in a less degree among all democratic nations.

Nothing is more necessary to the culture of the higher sciences or of the more elevated departments of science than meditation; and nothing is less suited to meditation than the structure of democratic society. We do not find there, as among an aristocratic people, one class that keeps quiet because it is well off; and another that does not venture to stir because it despairs of improving its condition. Everyone is in motion, some in quest of power, others of gain. In the midst of this universal tumult, this incessant conflict of jarring interests, this continual striving of men after fortune, where is that calm to be found which is necessary for the deeper combinations of the intellect? How can the mind dwell upon any single point when everything whirls around it, and man himself is swept and beaten onwards by the heady current that rolls all things in its course?

You must make the distinction between the sort of permanent agitation that is characteristic of a peaceful democracy and the tumultuous and revolutionary movements that almost always attend the birth and growth of democratic society. When a violent revolution occurs among a highly civilized people, it cannot fail to give a sudden impulse to their feelings and ideas. This is more peculiarly true of democratic revolutions, which stir up at once all the classes of which a people is composed and beget at the same time inordinate ambition in the breast of every member of the community. The French made surprising advances in the exact sciences at the very time at which they were finishing the destruction of the remains of their former feudal society; yet this sudden fecundity is not to be attributed to democracy, but to the unexampled revolution that attended its growth. What happened at that period was a special incident, and it would be unwise to regard it as the test of a general principle.

Great revolutions are not more common among democratic than among other nations; I am even inclined to believe that they are less so. But there prevails among those populations a small, distressing motion, a sort of incessant jostling of men, which annoys and disturbs the mind without exciting or elevating it.

Men who live in democratic communities not only seldom indulge in meditation, but they naturally entertain very little esteem for it. A democratic state of society and democratic institutions keep the greater part of men in constant activity; and the habits of mind that are suited to an active life are not always suited to a contemplative one. The man of action is frequently obliged to content himself with the best he can get because he would never accomplish his purpose if he chose to carry every detail to perfection. He has occasion perpetually to rely on ideas that he has not had leisure to search to the bottom; for he is much more frequently aided by the seasonableness of an idea than by its strict accuracy; and in the long run he risks less in making use of some false principles than in spending his time in establishing all his principles on the basis of truth. The world is not led by long or learned demonstrations; a rapid glance at particular incidents, the daily study of the fleeting passions of the multitude, the accidents of the moment, and the art of turning them to account decide all its affairs.

In the ages in which active life is the condition of almost everyone, men are generally led to attach an excessive value to the rapid bursts and superficial conceptions of the intellect, and on the other hand to undervalue unduly its slower and deeper labors. This opinion of the public influences the judgment of the men who cultivate the sciences; they are persuaded that they may succeed in those pursuits without meditation, or are deterred from such pursuits as demand it.

There are several methods of studying the sciences. Among a multitude of men you will find a selfish, mercantile, and trading taste for the discoveries of the mind, which must not be confounded with that disinterested passion which is kindled in the heart of a few. A desire to utilize knowledge is one thing; the pure desire to know is another. I do not doubt that in a few minds and at long intervals an ardent, inexhaustible love of truth springs up, self-supported and living in ceaseless fruition, without ever attaining full satisfaction. It is this ardent love, this proud, disinterested love of what is true, that raises men to the abstract sources of truth, to draw their mother knowledge thence.

If Pascal had had nothing in view but some large gain, or even if he had been stimulated by the love of fame alone, I cannot conceive that he would ever have been able to rally all the powers of his mind, as he did, for the better discovery of the most hidden things of the Creator. When I see him, as it were, tear his soul from all the cares of life to devote it wholly to these researches and, prematurely snapping the links that bind the body to life, die of old age before forty, I stand amazed and perceive that no ordinary cause is at work to produce efforts so extraordinary.

The future will prove whether these passions, at once so rare and so productive, come into being and into growth as easily in the midst of democratic as in aristocratic communities. For myself, I confess that I am slow to believe it.

In aristocratic societies the class that gives the tone to opinion and has the guidance of affairs, being permanently and hereditarily placed above the multitude, naturally conceives a lofty idea of itself and of man. It loves to invent for him noble pleasures, to carve out splendid objects for his ambition. Aristocracies often commit very tyrannical and inhuman actions, but they rarely entertain grovelling thoughts; and they show a kind of haughty contempt of little pleasures, even while they indulge in them. The effect is to raise greatly the general pitch of society. In aristocratic ages vast ideas are commonly entertained of the dignity, the power, and the greatness of man. These opinions exert their influence on those who cultivate the sciences as well as on the rest of the community. They facilitate the natural impulse of the mind to the highest regions of thought, and they naturally prepare it to conceive a sublime, almost a divine love of truth.

Men of science at such periods are consequently carried away towards theory; and it even happens that they frequently conceive an inconsiderate contempt for practice. "Archimedes," says Plutarch, "was of so lofty a spirit that he never condescended to write any treatise on the manner of constructing all these engines of war. And as he held this science of inventing and putting together

engines, and all arts generally speaking which tended to any useful end in practice, to be vile, low and mercenary, he spent his talents and his studious hours in writing only of those things whose beauty and subtlety had in them no admixture of necessity." Such is the aristocratic aim of science; it cannot be the same in democratic nations.

The greater part of the men who constitute these nations are extremely eager in the pursuit of actual and physical gratification. As they are always dissatisfied with the position that they occupy and are always free to leave it, they think of nothing but the means of changing their fortune or increasing it. To minds thus predisposed, every new method that leads by a shorter road to wealth, every machine that spares labor, every instrument that diminishes the cost of production, every discovery that facilitates pleasures or augments them, seems to be the grandest effort of the human intellect. It is chiefly from these motives that a democratic people addicts itself to scientific pursuits, that it understands and respects them. In aristocratic ages science is more particularly called upon to furnish gratification to the mind; in democracies, to the body.

You may be sure that the more democratic, enlightened, and free a nation is, the greater will be the number of these interested promoters of scientific genius and the more will discoveries immediately applicable to productive industry confer on their authors gain, fame, and even power. For in democracies the working class take a part in public affairs; and public honors as well as pecuniary remuneration may be awarded to those who deserve them.

In a community thus organized, it may easily be conceived the human mind may be led insensibly to the neglect of theory; and that it is urged, on the contrary, with unparalleled energy, to the applications of science, or at least to that portion of theoretical science which is necessary to those who make such applications. In vain will some instinctive inclination raise the mind towards the loftier spheres of the intellect; interest draws it down to the middle zone. There it may develop all its energy and restless activity and bring forth wonders. These very Americans who have not discovered one of the general laws of mechanics have introduced into navigation an instrument that changes the aspect of the world.

Assuredly I do not contend that the democratic nations of our time are destined to witness the extinction of the great luminaries of man's intelligence, or even that they will never bring new lights into existence. At the age at which the world has now arrived, and among so many cultivated nations perpetually excited by the fervor of productive industry, the bonds that connect the different parts of science cannot fail to strike the observer; and the taste for practical science itself, if it is enlightened, ought to lead men not to neglect theory. In the midst of so many attempted applications of so many experiments repeated every day, it is almost impossible that general laws should not frequently be brought to light; so that great discoveries would be frequent, though great inventors may be few. . . .

CHAPTER XI: IN WHAT SPIRIT THE AMERICANS CULTIVATE THE ARTS

It would be to waste the time of my readers and my own if I strove to demonstrate how the general mediocrity of fortunes, the absence of superfluous wealth, the universal desire for comfort, and the constant efforts by which everyone attempts to procure it make the taste for the useful predominate over the love of the beautiful in the heart of man. Democratic nations, among whom all these things exist, will therefore cultivate the arts that serve to render life easy in preference to those whose object is to adorn it. They will habitually prefer the useful to the beautiful, and they will require that the beautiful should be useful.

But I propose to go further, and, after having pointed out this first feature, to sketch several others.

It commonly happens that in the ages of privilege the practice of almost all the arts becomes a privilege, and that every profession is a separate sphere of action, into which it is not allowable for everyone to enter. Even when productive industry is free, the fixed character that belongs to aristocratic nations gradually segregates all the persons who practice the same art till they form a distinct class, always composed of the same families, whose members are all known to each other and among whom a public opinion of their own and a species of corporate pride soon spring up. In a class or guild of this kind each artisan has not only his fortune to make, but his reputation to preserve. He is not exclusively swayed by his own interest or even by that of his customer, but by that of the body to which he belongs; and the interest of that body is that each artisan should produce the best possible workmanship. In aristocratic ages the object of the arts is therefore to manufacture as well as possible, not with the greatest speed or at the lowest cost.

When, on the contrary, every profession is open to all, when a multitude of persons are constantly embracing and abandoning it, and when its several members are strangers, indifferent and because of their numbers hardly seen by each other, the social tie is destroyed, and each workman, standing alone, endeavors simply to gain the most money at the least cost. The will of the customer is then his only limit. But at the same time a corresponding change takes place in the customer also. In countries in which riches as well as power are concentrated and retained in the hands of a few, the use of the greater part of this world's goods belongs to a small number of individuals, who are always the same. Necessity, public opinion, or moderate desires exclude all others from the enjoyment of them. As this aristocratic class remains fixed at the pinnacle of greatness on which it stands, without diminution or increase, it is always acted upon by the same wants and affected by them in the same manner. The men of whom it is composed naturally derive from their superior and hereditary position a taste for what is extremely well made and lasting. This affects the general way of thinking of the nation in relation to the arts. It often occurs among such a people that even the peasant will rather go without the objects he covets than procure them in a state of imperfection. In aristocracies, then, the handicraftsmen work for only a limited number of fastidious customers; the profit they hope to make depends principally on the perfection of their workmanship.

Such is no longer the case when, all privileges being abolished, ranks are intermingled and men are forever rising or sinking in the social scale. Among a democratic people a number of citizens always exists whose patrimony is divided and decreasing. They have contracted, under more prosperous circumstances, certain wants, which remain after the means of satisfying such wants are gone; and they are anxiously looking out for some surreptitious method of providing for them. On the other hand, there is always in democracies a large number of men whose fortune is on the increase, but whose desires grow much faster than their fortunes, and who gloat upon the gifts of wealth in anticipation, long before they have means to obtain them. Such men are eager to find some short cut to these gratifications, already almost within their reach. From the combination of these two causes the result is that in democracies there is always a multitude of persons whose wants are above their means and who are very willing to take up with imperfect satisfaction rather than abandon the object of their desires altogether.

The artisan readily understands these passions,

for he himself partakes in them. In an aristocracy he would seek to sell his workmanship at a high price to the few; he now conceives that the more expeditious way of getting rich is to sell them at a low price to all. But there are only two ways of lowering the price of commodities. The first is to discover some better, shorter, and more ingenious method of producing them; the second is to manufacture a larger quantity of goods, nearly similar, but of less value. Among a democratic population all the intellectual faculties of the workman are directed to these two objects: he strives to invent methods that may enable him not only to work better, but more quickly and more cheaply; or if he cannot succeed in that, to diminish the intrinsic quality of the thing he makes, without rendering it wholly unfit for the use for which it is intended. When none but the wealthy had watches, they were almost all very good ones; few are now made that are worth much, but everybody has one in his pocket. Thus the democratic principle not only tends to direct the human mind to the useful arts, but it induces the artisan to produce with great rapidity many imperfect commodities, and the consumer to content himself with these commodities.

Not that in democracies the arts are incapable, in case of need, of producing wonders. This may occasionally be so if customers appear who are ready to pay for time and trouble. In this rivalry of every kind of industry, in the midst of this immense competition and these countless experiments, some excellent workmen are formed who reach the utmost limits of their craft. But they rarely have an opportunity of showing what they can do; they are scrupulously sparing of their powers; they remain in a state of accomplished mediocrity, which judges itself, and, though well able to shoot beyond the mark before it, aims only at what it hits. In aristocracies, on the contrary, workmen always do all they can; and when they stop, it is because they have reached the limit of their art. . . .

The handicraftsmen of democratic ages not only endeavor to bring their useful productions within the reach of the whole community, but strive to give to all their commodities attractive qualities that they do not in reality possess. In the confusion of all ranks everyone hopes to appear what he is not, and makes great exertions to succeed in this object. This sentiment, indeed, which is only too natural to the heart of man, does not originate in the democratic principle; but that principle applies it to material objects. The hypocrisy of virtue is of every age, but the hypocrisy

of luxury belongs more particularly to the ages of democracy.

To satisfy these new cravings of human vanity the arts have recourse to every species of imposture; and these devices sometimes go so far as to defeat their own purpose. Imitation diamonds are now made which may be easily mistaken for real ones; as soon as the art of fabricating false diamonds becomes so perfect that they cannot be distinguished from real ones, it is probable that both will be abandoned and become mere pebbles again.

This leads me to speak of those arts which are called, by way of distinction, the fine arts. I do not believe that it is a necessary effect of a democratic social condition and of democratic institutions to diminish the number of those who cultivate the fine arts, but these causes exert a powerful influence on the manner in which these arts are cultivated. Many of those who had already contracted a taste for the fine arts are impoverished; on the other hand, many of those who are not yet rich begin to conceive that taste, at least by imitation; the number of consumers increases, but opulent and fastidious consumers become more scarce. Something analogous to what I have already pointed out in the useful arts then takes place in the fine arts; the productions of artists are more numerous, but the merit of each production is diminished. No longer able to soar to what is great, they cultivate what is pretty and elegant, and appearance is more attended to than reality.

In aristocracies a few great pictures are produced; in democratic countries a vast number of insignificant ones. In the former statues are raised of bronze; in the latter, they are modeled in plaster.

When I arrived for the first time at New York, by that part of the Atlantic Ocean which is called the East River, I was surprised to perceive along the shore, at some distance from the city, a number of little palaces of white marble, several of which were of classic architecture. When I went the next day to inspect more closely one which had particularly attracted my notice, I found that its walls were of whitewashed brick, and its columns of painted wood. All the edifices that I had admired the night before were of the same kind.

The social condition and the institutions of democracy impart, moreover, certain peculiar tendencies to all the imitative arts, which it is easy to point out. They frequently withdraw them from the delineation of the soul to fix them exclusively on that of the body, and they substitute the representation of motion and sensation for that of sentiment and thought; in a word, they put the real in the place of the ideal. . . .

VOLUME II, BOOK II. CHAPTER I: WHY DEMOCRATIC NATIONS SHOW A MORE ARDENT AND ENDURING LOVE OF EQUALITY THAN OF LIBERTY

The first and most intense passion that is produced by equality of condition is, I need hardly say, the love of that equality. My readers will therefore not be surprised that I speak of this feeling before all others.

Everybody has remarked that in our time, and especially in France, this passion for equality is every day gaining ground in the human heart. It has been said a hundred times that our contemporaries are far more ardently and tenaciously attached to equality than to freedom; but as I do not find that the causes of the fact have been sufficiently analyzed, I shall endeavor to point them out. It is possible to imagine an extreme point at which freedom and equality would meet and blend. Let us suppose that all the people take a part in the government, and that each one of them has an equal right to take a part in it. As no one is different from his fellows, none can exercise a tyrannical power; men will be perfectly free because they are all entirely equal; and they will all be perfectly equal because they are entirely free. To this ideal state democratic nations tend. This is the only complete form that equality can assume upon earth; but there are a thousand others which, without being equally perfect, are not less cherished by those nations.

The principle of equality may be established in civil society without prevailing in the political world. There may be equal rights of indulging in the same pleasures, of entering the same professions, of frequenting the same places; in a word, of living in the same manner and seeking wealth by the same means, although all men do not take an equal share in the government. A kind of equality may even be established in the political world though there should be no political freedom there. A man may be the equal of all his countrymen save one, who is the master of all without distinction and who selects equally from among them all the agents of his power. Several other combinations might be easily imagined by which very great equality would be united to institutions more or less free or even to institutions wholly without freedom.

Although men cannot become absolutely equal unless they are entirely free, and consequently equality, pushed to its furthest extent, may be confounded with freedom, yet there is good reason for distinguishing the one from the other. The taste which men have for liberty and that which they feel for equality are, in fact, two different things; and I am not unafraid to add that among democratic nations they are two unequal things.

Upon close inspection it will be seen that there is in every age some peculiar and preponderant fact with which all others are connected; this fact almost always gives birth to some pregnant idea or some ruling passion, which attracts to itself and bears away in its course all the feelings and opinions of the time; it is like a great stream towards which each of the neighboring rivulets seems to flow.

Freedom has appeared in the world at different times and under various forms; it has not been exclusively bound to any social condition, and it is not confined to democracies. Freedom cannot, therefore, form the distinguishing characteristic of democratic ages. The peculiar and preponderant fact that marks those ages as its own is the equality of condition; the ruling passion of men in those periods is the love of this equality. Do not ask what singular charm the men of democratic ages find in being equal, or what special reasons they may have for clinging so tenaciously to equality rather than to the other advantages that society holds out to them: equality is the distinguishing characteristic of the age they live in; that of itself is enough to explain that they prefer it to all the rest.

But independently of this reason there are several others which will at all times habitually lead men to prefer equality to freedom.

If a people could ever succeed in destroying, or even in diminishing, the equality that prevails in its own body, they could do so only by long and laborious efforts. Their social condition must be modified, their laws abolished, their opinions superseded, their habits changed, their manners corrupted. But political liberty is more easily lost; to neglect to hold it fast is to allow it to escape. Therefore not only do men cling to equality because it is dear to them; they also adhere to it because they think it will last forever.

That political freedom in its excesses may compromise the tranquillity, the property, the lives of individuals is obvious even to narrow and unthinking minds. On the contrary, none but attentive and clear-sighted men perceive the perils with which equality threatens us, and they commonly avoid pointing them out. They know that the calamities they apprehend are remote and flatter themselves that they will only fall upon future generations, for which the present generation takes but little thought. The evils that freedom sometimes brings with it are immediate; they are apparent to all, and all are more or less affected by them. The evils that extreme equality may produce are slowly disclosed; they creep gradually into the social frame; they are seen only at intervals; and at the moment at which they become most violent, habit already causes them to be no longer felt.

The advantages that freedom brings are shown only by the lapse of time, and it is always easy to mistake the cause in which they originate. The advantages of equality are immediate, and they may always be traced from their source.

Political liberty bestows exalted pleasures from time to time upon a certain number of citizens. Equality every day confers a number of small enjoyments on every man. The charms of equality are every instant felt and are within the reach of all; the noblest hearts are not insensible to them, and the most vulgar souls exult in them. The passion that equality creates must therefore be at once strong and general. Men cannot enjoy political liberty unpurchased by some sacrifices, and they never obtain it without great exertions. But the pleasures of equality are self-proffered; each of the petty incidents of life seems to occasion them, and in order to taste them, nothing is required but to live.

Democratic nations are at all times fond of equality, but there are certain epochs at which the passion they entertain for it swells to the height of fury. This occurs at the moment when the old social system, long menaced, is overthrown after a severe internal struggle, and the barriers of rank are at length thrown down. At such times men pounce upon equality as their booty, and they cling to it as to some precious treasure which they fear to lose. The passion for equality penetrates on every side into men's hearts, expands there, and fills them entirely. Tell them not that by this blind surrender of themselves to an exclusive passion they risk their dearest interests; they are deaf. Show them not freedom escaping from their grasp while they are looking another way; they are blind, or rather they can discern but one object to be desired in the universe. . . .

Chapter XIX: What Causes Almost All Americans to Follow Industrial Callings

Agriculture is perhaps, of all the useful arts, that which improves most slowly among democratic nations. Frequently, indeed, it would seem to be stationary, because other arts are making rapid strides towards perfection. On the other hand, almost all the tastes and habits that the equality of condition produces naturally lead men to commercial and industrial occupations.

Suppose an active, enlightened, and free man, enjoying a competency, but full of desires; he is too poor to live in idleness, he is rich enough to feel himself protected from the immediate fear of want, and he thinks how he can better his condition. This man has conceived a taste for physical gratifications, which thousands of his fellow men around him indulge in; he has himself begun to enjoy these pleasures, and he is eager to increase his means of satisfying these tastes more completely. But life is slipping away, time is urgent; to what is he to turn? The cultivation of the ground promises an almost certain result to his exertions, but a slow one; men are not enriched by it without patience and toil. Agriculture is therefore only suited to those who already have great superfluous wealth or to those whose penury bids them seek only a bare subsistence. The choice of such a man as we have supposed is soon made; he sells his plot of ground, leaves his dwelling, and embarks on some hazardous but lucrative calling.

Democratic communities abound in men of this kind; and in proportion as the equality of conditions becomes greater, their multitude increases. Thus, democracy not only swells the number of working-men, but leads men to prefer one kind of labor to another; and while it diverts them from agriculture, it encourages their taste for commerce and manufactures.

This spirit may be observed even among the richest members of the community. In democratic countries, however opulent a man is supposed to be, he is almost always discontented with his fortune because he finds that he is less rich than his father was, and he fears that his sons will be less rich than himself. Most rich men in democracies are therefore constantly haunted by the desire of obtaining wealth, and they naturally turn their attention to trade and manufactures, which appear to offer the readiest and most efficient means of success. In this respect they share the instincts of the poor without feeling the same necessities; say, rather, they feel the most imperious of all necessities, that of not sinking in the world.

In aristocracies the rich are at the same time the governing power. The attention that they unceasingly devote to important public affairs diverts them from the lesser cares that trade and manufactures demand. But if an individual happens to turn his attention to business, the will of the body to which he belongs will immediately prevent him from pursuing it; for, however men may declaim against the rule of numbers, they cannot wholly escape it; and even among those aristocratic bodies that most obstinately refuse to acknowledge the rights of the national majority, a private majority is formed which governs the rest.

In democratic countries, where money does not lead those who possess it to political power, but often removes them from it, the rich do not know how to spend their leisure. They are driven into active life by the disquietude and the greatness of their desires, by the extent of their resources, and by the taste for what is extraordinary, which is almost always felt by those who rise, by whatever means, above the crowd. Trade is the only road open to them. In democracies nothing is greater or more brilliant than commerce; it attracts the attention of the public and fills the imagination of the multitude; all energetic passions are directed towards it. Neither their own prejudices nor those of anybody else can prevent the rich from devoting themselves to it. The wealthy members of democracies never form a body which has manners and regulations of its own; the opinions peculiar to their class do not restrain them, and the common opinions of their country urge them on. Moreover, as all the large fortunes that are found in a democratic community are of commercial growth, many generations must succeed one another before their possessors can have entirely laid aside their habits of business.

Circumscribed within the narrow space that politics leaves them, rich men in democracies eagerly embark in commercial enterprise; there they can extend and employ their natural advantages, and, indeed, it is even by the boldness and the magnitude of their industrial speculations that we may measure the slight esteem in which productive industry would have been held by them if they had been born in an aristocracy.

A similar observation is likewise applicable to all men living in democracies, whether they are poor or rich. Those who live in the midst of democratic fluctuations have always before their eyes the image of chance; and they end by liking all undertakings in which chance plays a part. They are therefore all led to engage in commerce, not only for the sake of the profit it holds out to them, but for the love of the constant excitement occasioned by that pursuit.

The United States of America has only been emancipated for half a century from the state of colonial dependence in which it stood to Great Britain; the number of large fortunes there is small, and capital is still scarce. Yet no people in the world have made such rapid progress in trade and manufactures as the Americans; they constitute at the present day the second maritime nation in the world, and although their manufactures have to struggle with almost insurmountable natural impediments, they are not prevented from making great and daily advances.

In the United States the greatest undertakings and speculations are executed without difficulty, because the whole population are engaged in productive industry, and because the poorest as well as the most opulent members of the commonwealth are ready to combine their efforts for these purposes. The consequence is that a stranger is constantly amazed by the immense public works executed by a nation which contains, so to speak, no rich men. The Americans arrived but as yesterday on the territory which they inhabit, and they have already changed the whole order of nature for their own advantage. They have joined the Hudson to the Mississippi and made the Atlantic Ocean communicate with the Gulf of Mexico, across a continent of more than five hundred leagues in extent which separates the two seas. The longest railroads that have been constructed up to the present time are in America.

But what most astonishes me in the United States is not so much the marvelous grandeur of some undertakings as the innumerable multitude of small ones. Almost all the farmers of the United States combine some trade with agriculture; most of them make agriculture itself a trade. It seldom happens that an American farmer settles for good upon the land which he occupies; especially in the districts of the Far West, he brings land into tillage in order to sell it again, and not to farm it; he builds a farmhouse on the speculation that, as the state of the country will soon be changed by the increase of population, a good price may be obtained for it.

Every year a swarm of people from the North arrive in the Southern states and settle in the parts where the cotton plant and the sugar-cane grow. These men cultivate the soil in order to make it produce in a few years enough to enrich them; and they already look forward to the time when they may return home to enjoy the competency thus acquired. Thus the Americans carry their businesslike qualities into agriculture, and their trading passions are displayed in that as in their other pursuits.

The Americans make immense progress in productive industry, because they all devote themselves to it at once; and for this same reason they are exposed to unexpected and formidable embarrassments. As they are all engaged in commerce, their commercial affairs are affected by such various and complex causes that it is impossible to foresee what difficulties may arise. As they are all more or less engaged in productive industry, at the least shock given to business all private fortunes are put in jeopardy at the same time, and the state is shaken. I believe that the return of these commercial panics is an endemic disease of the democratic nations of our age. It may be rendered less dangerous, but it cannot be cured, because it does not originate in accidental circumstances, but in the temperament of these nations.

BUSINESS ENTERPRISE

THE TYPICAL AMERICAN businessman of this period continued to be a merchant, in this sense not differing markedly from his earlier colonial prototype. He financed many trading voyages; he was interested in the domestic wholesale trade; he was a banker and a dealer in wild and improved lands. In New England—but almost exclusively there; certainly this was less true of New York and Philadelphia businessmen— after the War of 1812 and during the 1820s and 1830s, businessmen began to show an increasing interest in the development of cotton manufacture. These merchants—Nathan Appleton and Abbott Lawrence are good examples of the type—moved over from merchandizing almost completely into manufacturing. Patrick Tracy Jackson is an example of the same shift in interest. His biography is presented here.

A word first about the greatest of the early national merchants, Stephen Girard (1750–1831). Girard was born at Bordeaux and came to America in 1774 when he was unable to pay his creditors the full amount he owed them. Though he lost by privateering ventures during the Revolution, he prospered in the trade with San Domingo and later in the carrying trade during the Napoleonic wars. By 1812, his gains could not be profitably invested in shipping alone and he turned to banking, establishing the first private bank in the United States. Girard helped float the government loan of sixteen millions during the War of 1812 and later aided in setting up the Second Bank of the United States both by pushing the plan for it and by buying its stock when other investors refused.

In 1815, Girard was worth $1,800,000 in the capital of his bank, paid one one-hundredth of the total real estate tax of Philadelphia and had such large liquid assets that he could carry on his maritime business without discount. "All this I owe principally to my close attention to business and to the resources which this fine country affords to all active and industrious men," he told a correspondent. Girard continued to prosper during the next fifteen years. Though he had two nephews whom he had reared and educated "in the best country and under the best government in the world," he left the bulk of his estate to improve the Philadelphia waterfront and to give its white orphan boys a good education for the practice of commerce and the trades.

Nathan Appleton (1779–1861) and Abbott Lawrence (1792–1855) each made the nucleus of his fortune in shipping. Neither, however, was concerned with banking, as Girard had been, but with the new enterprise of manufactures. Appleton met Francis C. Lowell in Edinburgh in 1811. Lowell was already interested in the cotton textile industry and Appleton agreed to cooperate with him in the effort to naturalize the new machinery and methods in the United States. The first attempt was made at Waltham, Massachusetts, during 1814–16. This enterprise was so successful that the company decided to enter on the manufacture of printed as well as of plain cloth. Though Appleton had been so doubtful of the success of the first venture that he would take only half the $10,000 worth of stock urged on him, he went into the new project wholeheartedly. After exploration, the old Pawtucket canal was suggested as a site affording good water power. The land was bought up and a corporation was organized to control the water rights and build machinery. A second corporation, in which the directors of the first had a large interest, was set up to do the actual manufacturing. A new town grew up about the mills and the city of Lowell came into being. In spite of the abundance of land and dearness of labor which had been cited as dooming American manufactures to failure, the use of girl workers and improved machinery, together with the lower price of raw material, made Lowell a successful enterprise and a perpetual argument for the physical, moral, and economic salubrity of manufacturing industry.

In his *Lives of American Merchants* (2 vols., New York, 1856–1858) Freeman Hunt (1804–1858) describes the careers of these and other American businessmen. Though Hunt's col-

lection extols the merchant and man of business, he is not an uncritical worshiper of success. Wealth has a social obligation, Hunt maintains, and money should be made in honorable ways. Hunt himself was a New Englander who rose from press and type case to the editor's desk and the publisher's counting room. He left Boston for New York in 1839 and established the *Merchants' Magazine*, which remains a useful source of information about the opinions of the business community of the period. Both the *Lives of American Merchants* and the more popular *Worth and Wealth* are largely edited from its pages. The biography of Patrick Tracy Jackson here reprinted is taken from Volume I of the *Lives*.

Lives of American Merchants

BY FREEMAN HUNT

PATRICK TRACY JACKSON

. . . PATRICK TRACY JACKSON was born at Newburyport, on the 14th of August, 1780. He was the youngest son of the Hon. Jonathan Jackson, a member of the Continental Congress in 1782, Marshal of the District of Massachusetts under Washington, first Inspector, and afterward Supervisor of the Internal Revenue, Treasurer of the Commonwealth for five years, and, at the period of his death, Treasurer of Harvard College; a man distinguished among the old-fashioned gentlemen of that day for the dignity and grace of his deportment, but much more so for his intelligence, and the fearless, almost Roman inflexibility of his principles.

His maternal grandfather, from whom he derived his name, was Patrick Tracy, an opulent merchant of Newburyport—an Irishman by birth, who, coming to this country at an early age, poor and friendless, had raised himself, by his own exertions, to a position which his character, universally esteemed by his fellow-citizens, enabled him adequately to sustain.

The subject of this memoir received his early education at the public schools of his native town, and afterward at Dunmore Academy. When about fifteen years old, he was apprenticed to the late William Bartlett, then the most enterprising and richest merchant of Newburyport, and since well known for his munificent endowment of the insti-

tution at Andover. In this new position, which, with the aristocratic notions of that day, might have been regarded by some youth as derogatory, young Patrick took especial pains to prove to his master that he had not been educated to view any thing as disgraceful which it was his duty to do. He took pride in throwing himself into the midst of the labor and responsibility of the business. In so doing he gratified a love of activity and usefulness, which belonged to his character, at the same time that he satisfied his sense of duty. And yet, while thus ready to work, he did not lose his keen relish for the enjoyments of youth; and would often, after a day of intense bodily labor, be foremost in the amusements of the social circle in the evening.

He soon secured the esteem and confidence of Mr. Bartlett, who intrusted to him, when under twenty years of age, a cargo of merchandise for St. Thomas, with authority to take the command of the vessel from the captain, if he should see occasion.

After his return from this voyage, which he successfully conducted, an opportunity offered for a more extended enterprise. His brother, Captain Henry Jackson, who was about six years older than himself, and to whom he was warmly attached, was on the point of sailing for Madras and Calcutta, and offered to take Patrick with him as captain's clerk. The offer was a tempting one. It would open to him a branch of commerce in which his master, Bartlett, had not been engaged, but which was, at that time, one of great profit to the enterprising merchants of this country. The English government then found it for their interest to give us great advantages in the Bengal trade; while our neutral position, during the long wars of the French revolution, enabled us to monopolize the business of supplying the continent of Europe with the cotton and other products of British India. An obstacle, however, interposed—our young apprentice was not of age; and the indentures gave to his master the use of his services till that period should be completed. With great liberality, Mr. Bartlett, on being informed of the circumstances, relinquished his claim.

It was very nearly the first day of the present century, when Mr. Jackson commenced his career as a free man. Already familiar with many things pertaining to a sea life, he occupied his time on board ship in acquiring a knowledge of navigation, and of seamanship. His brother, who delighted in his profession, and was a man of warm and generous affections, was well qualified and ready to instruct him. These studies, with his previous mercantile experience, justified him, on his return from India, in offering to take charge of a ship and cargo in the same trade. This he did, with complete success, for three successive voyages, and established his reputation for enterprise and correctness in business.

On the last of these occasions, he happened to be at the Cape of Good Hope when that place was taken from the Dutch by the English, under Sir David Baird, in January, 1806. This circumstance caused a derangement in his mercantile operations, involving a detention of about a year at the Cape, and leading him subsequently to embark in some new adventures; and he did not reach home until 1808, after an absence of four years.

Having now established his reputation, and acquired some capital, he relinquished the sea, and entered into commercial pursuits at Boston. His long acquaintance with the India trade eminently fitted him for that branch of business; and he had the support and invaluable counsels of his brother-in-law, the late Francis C. Lowell. He entered largely into this business, both as an importer and speculator. The same remarkable union of boldness and sound judgment, which characterized him in later days, contributed to his success, and his credit soon became unbounded. . . . At this period, circumstances led him into a new branch of business, which influenced his whole future life.

Mr. Lowell had just returned to this country, after a long visit to England and Scotland. While abroad, he had conceived the idea that the cotton manufacture, then almost monopolized by Great Britain, might be advantageously prosecuted here. The use of machinery was daily superseding the former manual operations; and it was known that power-looms had recently been introduced, though the mode of constructing them was kept secret. The cheapness of labor, and abundance of capital, were advantages in favor of the English manufacturer—they had skill and reputation. On the other hand, they were burdened with the taxes of a prolonged war. We could obtain the raw material cheaper, and had a great superiority in the abundant water-power, then unemployed, in every part of New England. It was also the belief of Mr. Lowell, that the character of our population, educated, moral, and enterprising as it then was, could not fail to secure success, when brought into competition with their European rivals; and it is no small evidence of the far-reaching views of this extraordinary man, and his early colleagues, that their very first measures were such as should secure that attention to education and morals among the manufacturing population, which they believed to be the corner-stone of any permanent success.

Impressed with these views, Mr. Lowell determined to bring them to the test of experiment. So confident was he in his calculations, that he thought he could in no way so effectually assist the fortunes of his relative, Mr. Jackson, as by offering him a share in the enterprise. Great were the difficulties that beset the new undertaking. The state of war prevented any communication with England. Not even books and designs, much less models, could be procured. The structure of the machinery, the materials to be used in the construction, the very tools of the machine-shop, the arrangement of the mill, and the size of its various apartments—all these were to be, as it were, reinvented. But Mr. Jackson's was not a spirit to be appalled by obstacles. He entered at once into the project, and devoted to it, from that moment, all the time that could be spared from his mercantile pursuits.

The first object to be accomplished, was to procure a power-loom. To obtain one from England was, of course, impracticable; and, although there were many patents for such machines in our Patent Office, not one had yet exhibited sufficient merit to be adopted into use. Under these circumstances, but one resource remained—to invent one themselves; and this these earnest men at once set about. Unacquainted as they were with machinery, in practice, they dared, nevertheless, to attempt the solution of a problem that had baffled the most ingenious mechanicians. In England, the power-loom had been invented by a clergyman, and why not here by a merchant? After numerous experiments and failures, they at last succeeded, in the autumn of 1812, in producing a model which they thought so well of as to be willing to make preparations for putting up a mill, for the weaving of cotton cloth. It was now necessary to procure the assistance of a practical mechanic, to aid in the construction of the machinery; and the friends had the good fortune to secure the services of Mr. Paul Moody, afterward so well known as the head of the machine-shop at Lowell.

They found, as might naturally be expected, many defects in their model loom; but these were gradually remedied. The project hitherto had been exclusively for a weaving-mill, to do by power what had before been done by hand-looms. But it was ascertained, on inquiry, that it would be more economical to spin the twist, rather than to buy it; and they put up a mill for about one thousand seven hundred spindles, which was completed late in 1813. It will probably strike the reader with some astonishment to be told that this mill, still in operation at Waltham, was probably the first one in the world that combined all the operations necessary for converting the raw cotton into finished cloth. Such, however, is the fact, as far as we are informed on the subject. The mills in this country—Slater's, for example, in Rhode Island—were spinning-mills only; and in England, though the power-loom had been introduced, it was used in separate establishments, by persons who bought, as the hand-weavers had always done, their twist of the spinners.

Great difficulty was at first experienced at Waltham, for the want of a proper preparation (sizing) of the warps. They procured from England a drawing of Horrock's dressing-machine, which, with some essential improvements, they adopted, producing the dresser now in use at Lowell and elsewhere. No method was, however, indicated in this drawing for winding the threads from the bobbins on to the beam; and to supply this deficiency, Mr. Moody invented the very ingenious machine called the warper. Having obtained these, there was no further difficulty in weaving by power-looms.

There was still greater deficiency in the preparation for spinning. They had obtained from England a description of what was then called a bobbin and fly, or jack-frame, for spinning roving; from this Mr. Moody and Mr. Lowell produced our present double-speeder. The motions of this machine were very complicated, and required nice mathematical calculations. Without them, Mr. Moody's ingenuity, great as it was, would have been at fault. These were supplied by Mr. Lowell. Many years afterward, and after the death of Mr. Lowell, when the patent for the speeder had been infringed, the late Dr. Bowditch was requested to examine them, that he might appear as a witness at the trial. He expressed to Mr. Jackson his admiration of the mathematical power they evinced; adding, that there were some corrections introduced that he had not supposed any man in America familiar with but himself.

There was also great waste and expense in winding the thread for filling or weft from the bobbin on to the quills, for the shuttle. To obviate this, Mr. Moody invented the machine known here as the filling-throstle.

It will be seen, by this rapid sketch, how much there was at this early period to be done, and how well it was accomplished. The machines introduced then, are those still in use in New England—brought, of course, to greater perfection in detail, and attaining a much higher rate of speed, but still substantially the same.

Associating with themselves some of the most intelligent merchants of Boston, they procured, in February, 1813, a charter, under the name of the Boston Manufacturing Company, with a capital of one hundred thousand dollars. Success crowned their efforts, and the business was gradually extended to the limit of the capacity of their water-power.

Mr. Lowell died in 1817, at the age of forty-two; satisfied that he had succeeded in his object, and that the extension of the cotton manufacture would form a permanent basis of the prosperity of New England. He had been mainly instrumental in procuring from Congress, in 1816, the establishment of the minimum duty on cotton cloth; an idea which originated with him, and one of great value, not only as affording a certain and easily collected revenue, but as preventing the exaction of a higher and higher duty, just as the advance in the cost abroad renders it more difficult for the consumer to procure his necessary supplies.

It is not surprising that Mr. Lowell should have felt great satisfaction at the result of his labors. In the establishment of the cotton manufacture, in its present form, he and his early colleagues have done a service not only to New England, but to the whole country, which perhaps will never be fully appreciated. Not by the successful establishment of this branch of industry—that would sooner or later have been accomplished; not by any of the present material results that have flowed from it, great as they unquestionably are, but by the introduction of a system which has rendered our manufacturing population the wonder of the world. Elsewhere, vice and poverty have followed in the train of manufactures; an indissoluble bond of union seemed to exist between them. Philanthropists have prophesied the like result here, and demagogues have re-echoed the prediction. Those wise and patriotic men, the founders of Waltham, foresaw, and guarded against the evil.

By the erection of boarding-houses at the expense and under the control of the factory; putting at the head of them matrons of tried character, and allowing no boarders to be received except the female operatives of the mill; by stringent regulations for the government of these houses; by all these precautions they gained the confidence of the rural population, who were now no longer afraid to trust their daughters in a manufacturing town. A supply was thus obtained of respectable girls; and these, from pride of character, as well as principle, have taken especial care to exclude all others. It was soon found that an apprenticeship in a factory entailed no degradation of character, and was no impediment to a reputable connection in marriage. A factory-girl was no longer condemned to pursue that vocation for life; she would retire, in her turn, to assume the higher and more appropriate responsibilities of her sex; and it soon came to be considered that a few years in a mill was an honorable mode of securing a dower. The business could thus be conducted without any permanent manufacturing population. The operatives no longer form a separate caste, pursuing a sedentary employment, from parent to child, in the heated rooms of a factory; but are recruited, in a circulating current, from the healthy and virtuous population of the country.

By these means, and a careful selection of men of principle and purity of life, as agents and overseers, a great moral good has been obtained. Another result has followed, which, if foreseen, as no doubt it was, does great credit to the sagacity of these remarkable men. The class of operatives employed in our mills have proved to be as superior in intelligence and efficiency to the degraded population elsewhere employed in manufactures, as they are in morals. They are selected from a more educated class—from among persons in more easy circumstances, where the mental and physical powers have met with fuller development. This connection between morals and intellectual efficiency, has never been sufficiently studied. The result is certain, and may be destined, in its consequences, to decide the question of our

rivalry with England, in the manufacture of cotton.

Although the first suggestions, and many of the early plans of the new business, had been furnished, as we have seen, by Mr. Lowell, Mr. Jackson devoted the most time and labor in conducting it. He spent much of his time, in the early years, at Waltham, separated from his family. It gradually engrossed his whole thoughts, and, abandoning his mercantile business in 1815, he gave himself up to that of the company.

At the erection of each successive mill, many prudent men, even among the proprietors, had feared that the business would be overdone—that no demand would be found for such increased quantities of the same fabric. Mr. Jackson, with the spirit and sagacity that so eminently distinguished him, took a different view of the matter. He not only maintained that cotton cloth was so much cheaper than any other material, that it must gradually establish itself in universal consumption at home, but entertained the bolder idea, that the time would come when the improvements in machinery, and the increase of skill and capital, would enable us successfully to compete with Great Britain in the supply of foreign markets. Whether he ever anticipated the rapidity and extent of the developments which he lived to witness, may perhaps be doubted; it is certain that his expectations were, at that time, thought visionary by many of the most sagacious of his friends.

Ever prompt to act, whenever his judgment was convinced, he began, as early as 1820, to look around for some locality where the business might be extended, after the limited capabilities of Charles river should be exhausted.

In 1821, Mr. Ezra Worther, who had formerly been a partner with Mr. Moody, and who had applied to Mr. Jackson for employment, suggested that the Pawtucket Canal, at Chelmsford, would afford a fine location for large manufacturing establishments, and that probably a privilege might be purchased of its proprietors. To Mr. Jackson's mind, the hint suggested a much more stupendous project—nothing less than to possess himself of the whole power of the Merrimack river at that place. Aware of the necessity of secrecy of action to secure this property at any reasonable price, he undertook it single-handed. It was necessary to purchase not only the stock in the canal, but all the farms on both sides of the river, which controlled the water-power, or which might be necessary for the future extension of the business. No long series of years had tested the extent and profit of such enterprises; the great capitalists of our land had not yet become converts to the safety of such investments. Relying on his own talents and resolution, without even consulting his confidential advisers, he set about this task at his own individual risk; and it was not until he had accomplished all that was material for his purpose, that he offered a share in the project to a few of his former colleagues. Such was the beginning of Lowell—a city which he lived to see, as it were, completed. If all honor is to be paid to the enterprise and sagacity of those men who, in our day, with the advantage of great capital and longer experience, have bid a new city spring up from the forest on the borders of the same stream, accomplishing almost in a day what is in the course of nature the slow growth of centuries, what shall we say of the forecast and energy of that man who could contemplate and execute the same gigantic task at that early period, and alone?

The property thus purchased, and to which extensive additions were subsequently made, was offered to the proprietors of the Waltham Company, and to other persons whom it was thought desirable to interest in the scheme. These offers were eagerly accepted, and a new company was established, under the name of the Merrimack Manufacturing Company, the immediate charge of which was confided to the late Kirk Boott, Esq.

Having succeeded in establishing the cotton manufacture on a permanent basis, and possessed of a fortune, the result of his own exertions, quite adequate to his wants, Mr. Jackson now thought of retiring from the labor and responsibility of business. He resigned the agency of the factory at Waltham, still remaining a director both in that company and the new one at Lowell, and personally consulted on every occasion of doubt or difficulty. This life of comparative leisure was not of long duration. His spirit was too active to allow him to be happy in retirement. He was made for a working-man, and had long been accustomed to plan and conduct great enterprises; the excitement was necessary for his well-being. His spirits flagged, his health failed; till, satisfied at last that he had mistaken his vocation, he plunged once more into the cares and perplexities of business.

Mr. Moody had recently introduced some important improvements in machinery, and was satisfied that great saving might be made, and a higher rate of speed advantageously adopted. Mr. Jackson proposed to establish a company at Lowell, to be called the Appleton Company, and adopt the new machinery. The stock was soon subscribed for, and Mr. Jackson appointed the treasurer and agent. Two large mills were built, and conducted by him for several years, till suc-

cess had fully justified his anticipations. Meanwhile, his presence at Lowell was of great advantage to the new city. All men there, as among the stockholders in Boston, looked up to him as the founder and guardian genius of the place, and were ready to receive from him advice or rebuke, and to refer to him all questions of doubt or controversy. As new companies were formed, and claims became conflicting, the advantages became more apparent of having a man of such sound judgment, impartial integrity, and nice discrimination, to appeal to, and who occupied an historical position to which no one else could pretend.

In 1830, the interests of Lowell induced Mr. Jackson to enter into a business new to himself and others. This was the building of the Boston and Lowell Railroad. For some years, the practicability of constructing roads in which the friction should be materially lessened by laying down iron-bars, or trams, had engaged the attention of practical engineers in England. At first, it was contemplated that the service of such roads should be performed by horses; and it was not until the brilliant experiments of Mr. Stephenson, on the Liverpool and Manchester Railroad, that the possibility of using locomotive engines was fully established. It will be well remembered that all the first estimates for railroads in this country were based upon a road-track adapted to horse-power, and horses were actually used on all the earlier roads. The necessity of a better communication between Boston and Lowell had been the subject of frequent conversation between Mr. Boott and Mr. Jackson. Estimates had been made, and a line surveyed for a Macadamized road. The travel between the two places was rapidly increasing; and the transportation of merchandise, slowly performed in summer by the Middlesex Canal, was done at great cost, and over bad roads, in winter, by wagons.

At this moment, the success of Mr. Stephenson's experiments decided Mr. Jackson. He saw, at once, the prodigious revolution that the introduction of steam would make in the business of internal communication. Men were, as yet, incredulous. The cost and the danger attending the use of the new machines, were exaggerated; and even if feasible in England, with a city of one hundred and fifty thousand souls at each of the termini, such a project, it was argued, was Quixotical here, with our more limited means and sparser population. Mr. Jackson took a different view of the matter; and when, after much delay and difficulty, the stock of the road was subscribed for, he undertook to superintend its construction, with the especial object that it might be in every way adapted to the use of steam-power, and to that increase of travel and transportation which few, like him, had the sagacity to anticipate.

Mr. Jackson was not an engineer; but full of confidence in his own energy, and in the power he always possessed of eliciting and directing the talent of others, he entered on the task, so new to every one in this country, with the same boldness that he had evinced twenty years before, in the erection of the first weaving-mill.

The moment was an anxious one. He was not accustomed to waste time in any of his undertakings. The public looked with eagerness for the road, and he was anxious to begin and to finish it. But he was too wise a man to allow his own impatience, or that of others, to hurry him into action before his plans should be maturely digested. There were, indeed, many points to be attended to, and many preliminary steps to be taken. A charter was to be obtained, and, as yet, no charter for a railroad had been granted in New England. The terms of the charter, and its conditions, were to be carefully considered. The experiment was deemed to be so desirable, and, at the same time, so hazardous, that the legislature were prepared to grant almost any terms that should be asked for. Mr. Jackson, on the other hand, whose faith in the success of the new mode of locomotion never faltered, was not disposed to ask for any privileges that would not be deemed moderate after the fullest success had been obtained; at the same time, the recent example of the Charles River Bridge showed the necessity of guarding, by careful provisions, the chartered rights of the stockholders.

With respect to the road itself, nearly every thing was to be learned. Mr. Jackson established a correspondence with the most distinguished engineers of this country, and of Europe; and it was not until he had deliberately and satisfactorily solved all the doubts that arose in his own mind, or were suggested by others, that he would allow any step to be decided on. In this way, although more time was consumed than on other roads, a more satisfactory result was obtained. The road was graded for a double track; the grades reduced to a level of ten feet to the mile; all curves, but those of very large radius, avoided; and every part constructed with a degree of strength nowhere else, at that time, considered necessary. A distinguished foreigner, Mr. Charles Chevalier, has spoken of the work on this road as truly "Cyclopean." Every measure adopted shows conclusively how clearly Mr. Jackson foresaw the extension and capabilities of the railroad.

It required no small degree of moral firmness to conceive and carry out these plans. Few persons realized the difficulties of the undertaking, or the magnitude of the results. The shareholders were restless under increased assessments, and delayed income. It is not too much to say that no one but Mr. Jackson in Boston could, at that time, have commanded the confidence necessary to enable him to pursue his work so deliberately and so thoroughly.

The road was opened for travel in 1835, and experience soon justified the wisdom of his anticipations. Its completion and successful operation was a great relief to Mr. Jackson. For several years it had engrossed his time and attention, and at times deprived him of sleep. He felt it to be a public trust, the responsibility of which was of a nature quite different from that which had attended his previous enterprises.

One difficulty that he had encountered in the prosecution of this work led him into a new undertaking, the completion of which occupied him a year or two longer. He felt the great advantage of making the terminus of the road in Boston, and not, as was done in other instances, on the other side of the river. The obstacles appeared, at first sight, insurmountable. No land was to be procured in that densely populated part of the city except at very high prices; and it was not then the public policy to allow the passage of trains through the streets. A mere site for a passenger depot could, indeed, be obtained; and this seemed, to most persons, all that was essential. Such narrow policy did not suit Mr. Jackson's anticipations. It occurred to him that, by an extensive purchase of the flats, then unoccupied, the object might be obtained. The excavations making by the railroad at Winter Hill, and elsewhere, within a few miles of Boston, much exceeded the embankments, and would supply the gravel necessary to fill up these flats. Such a speculation not being within the powers of the corporation, a new company was created for the purpose. The land was made, to the extent of about ten acres; and what was not needed for depots, was sold at advantageous prices. It has since been found that even the large provision made by Mr. Jackson is inadequate to the daily increasing business of the railroad.

Mr. Jackson was now fifty-seven years of age. Released once more from his engagements, he might rationally look forward to a life of dignified retirement, in which he would be followed by the respect of the community, and the gratitude of the many families that owed their well-being to his exertions. But a cloud had come over his private fortunes. While laboring for others, he had allowed himself to be involved in some speculations, to which he had not leisure to devote his personal attention. The unfortunate issue of these, deprived him of a large portion of his property.

Uniformly prosperous hitherto, the touchstone of adversity was wanting to elicit, perhaps even to create, some of the most admirable points in his character. He had long been affluent, and with his generous and hospitable feelings, had adopted a style of living fully commensurate with his position. The cheerful dignity with which he met his reverses; the promptness with which he accommodated his expenses to his altered circumstances; and the almost youthful alacrity with which he once more put on the harness, were themes of daily comment to his friends, and afforded to the world an example of the truest philosophy. He had always been highly respected; the respect was now more blended with love and veneration.

The death of his friend, Mr. Boott, in the spring of 1837, had proved a severe blow to the prosperity of Lowell. At the head of that company (the proprietors of the Locks and Canals), which controlled the land and water-power, and manufactured all the machinery used in the mills, the position he had occupied led him into daily intercourse with the managers of the several companies. The supervision he had exercised, and the influence of his example, had been felt in all the ramifications of the complicated business of the place. Even where no tangible evidence existed of benefits specifically conferred, men were not slow to find out, after his death, that a change had come over the whole. The Locks and Canals Company being under his immediate charge, was, of course the first to suffer. Their property rapidly declined, both intrinsically, and in public estimation. The shares, which for many years had been worth $1,000 each, were now sold for $700, and even less. No one appeared so able to apply the remedy as Mr. Jackson. Familiar, from the first, with the history of the company, of which he had always been a director, and the confidential adviser of Mr. Boott, he alone, perhaps, was fully capable of supplying that gentleman's place. He was solicited to accept the office, and tempted by the offer of a higher salary than had, perhaps, ever been paid in this country. He assumed the trust; and, during the seven years of his management, the proprietors had every reason to congratulate themselves upon the wisdom of their choice. The property was brought into the best condition; extensive and lucrative contracts were made and executed; the annual dividends were large; and when at last it was thought expedient to close the affairs of the cor-

poration, the stockholders received of capital nearly $1,600 a share.

The brilliant issue of this business enhanced Mr. Jackson's previous reputation. He was constantly solicited to aid, by service and counsel, wherever doubt or intricacy existed. No great public enterprises were brought forward till they had received the sanction of his opinion.

During the last few years of his life, he was the treasurer and agent of the Great Falls Manufacturing Company at Somersworth; a corporation that had for many years been doing an unprofitable business at a great expense of capital. When this charge was offered to him, he visited the spot, and became convinced that it had great capabilities, but that every thing, from the beginning, had been done wrong: to reform it, would require an outlay nearly equal to the original investment. The dam should be taken down, and rebuilt; one mill, injudiciously located, be removed, and a larger one erected in a better spot; the machinery entirely discarded, and replaced by some of a more modern and perfect construction. Few men would have had the hardihood to propose such changes to proprietors discouraged by the prestige of repeated disappointments; still fewer, the influence to carry his measures into effect. That Mr. Jackson did this, and with results quite satisfactory to the proprietors and to himself, is almost a corollary from his previous history. His private fortune had, in the mean while, been restored to a point that relieved him from anxiety, and he was not ambitious of increasing it.

For some time after he assumed the duties of the agency at Somersworth, the labor and responsibility attending it were very severe; yet he seemed to his friends to have all the vigor and elasticity of middle life. It may be, however, that the exertion was beyond his physical strength; certainly, after a year or two, he began to exhibit symptoms of a gradual prostration; and, when attacked by dysentery in the summer of 1847, his constitution had no longer the power of resistance, and he sank under the disease on the 12th of September, at his sea-side residence at Beverly. . . .

In private, he was distinguished by a cheerfulness and benevolence that beamed upon his countenance, and seemed to invite every one to be happy with him. His position enabled him to indulge his love of doing good by providing employment for many meritorious persons; and this patronage, once extended, was never capriciously withdrawn.

The life of such a man is a public benefaction. Were it only to point out to the young and enterprising that the way to success is by the path of honor—not half-way, conventional honor, but honor enlightened by religion, and guarded by

conscience—were it only for this, a truth but imperfectly appreciated even by moralists, the memory of such men should be hallowed by posterity.

LABOR AND IMMIGRATION

THE AMERICAN LABOR movement first appeared in strength between 1828 and 1836. In this period of economic expansion and collapse, skilled craftsmen were made acutely aware of the tensions of an economic society that was growing increasingly complicated and—as far as they were concerned—insecure. Journeymen, mechanics, printers particularly, saw their chances of becoming masters diminish. Laws that sent debtors to prison but gave mechanics no protection for payment of wages; children being pushed into factories while no provision was made for free schools; wages that never kept pace with prices while the long working-day grew more burdensome with a swifter tempo of work; the competition of convicts being reformed by hiring their labor out to contractors—all these, coupled with a belief in republican equality, forced skilled workingmen into union organization on the one hand and political action on the other.

Unions were formed in the separate crafts and the crafts were federated on a local basis. By 1833, New York, Philadelphia, and Boston each had its own Union of Trades, and a National Trades' Union was being formed. The movement to reduce the working day from twelve hours to ten gained strength and wage increases of 12½ to 25 cents a day were achieved.

In Philadelphia and New York, particularly, workers turned to politics as the existing parties showed themselves indifferent or hostile to laws for mechanics' liens, the abolition of imprisonment for debt, and a system of free public schools. Though labor parties established no permanent political machines, they had brief successes in returning their candidates to office and made more substantial gains by putting an

end to imprisonment for debt and securing the first measures for general systems of free public education.

The economic collapse of 1837 closed the first phase of the labor movement; but, before that disaster, unions had been organized and federated, a labor press had flourished, the "labor agitator" made his appearance, employers' organizations had used the blacklist and the "yellow-dog" contract, the courts had shown themselves ready to save the community from mechanics' exactions, and New York's waterfront had seen striking longshoremen battle the police while a frigate stood off and threatened to fire.

Echoes of these tensions fill the pages of Seth Luther's *Address to the Working Men of New England*.

Seth Luther (? -1846) is one of the earliest instances of the labor spokesman. Born in Providence at the turn of the eighteenth century, he left for Ohio in 1817, traveled on the Western Waters and returned to New England a journeyman carpenter and a convinced democrat. His trade set him working at the cotton mills being built in the Twenties; his convictions made him denounce the abuses which accompanied the manufacturing system. Luther was active in the New England labor movement. He became secretary of the 1834 session of the Boston General Trades' Convention and toured the country, detailing the true state of the factories which pro-tariff Congressmen called the "palaces of the poor."

Seth Luther had protested against the free importation of labor as unfair inasmuch as the free importation of goods was checked by tariffs. Samuel F. B. Morse (1791–1872) objected not to the entry of immigrants but to their being naturalized and given the right to vote. After an unsuccessful effort to support a family on a portrait painter's earnings, Morse had turned to the investigations which were to be climaxed by the construction of a practical electric telegraph. While Morse was working in New York, he witnessed the first great wave of migration from Catholic Europe. The naturalization of Irishmen, of political refugees from the Germanies, and of Austrian subjects fleeing in the wake of the revolutionary movement of 1830, seemed to threaten American stability. The newcomers were poor and of a different religion, and the Irish among them were schooled in political combination. Awareness of these dangers, together with irritation over the competition for jobs and a religious fanaticism roused by such works as the "revelations" of Maria Monk, caused an outburst of anti-Catholic rioting in Boston, where a convent was attacked.

Anti-foreign agitation also appeared in New York. To that agitation, Morse lent his support in a series of articles in the New York *Journal of Commerce* in 1835. Morse insisted that the riotous outbursts of the early thirties—bank mobs in Baltimore, Abolition mobs at Philadel-phia and the mob which wrecked the convent at Charlestown—proved a European conspiracy to destroy the United States. The Holy Alliance, which had put an end to liberty in Europe, was reaching out to crush free democracy in America. Austria was responsible for the organization of the St. Leopold Society which was flooding the United States with Jesuits who meant to organize naturalized immigrants into a political party and use their votes to undermine American institutions.

The only safeguard against this danger was to forbid naturalization in the future, Morse declared. In 1836, he ran for Mayor of New York on that program and received 1,500 votes. Nativism, however, was not to be downed; and it rose again, this time to real power, in the fifties when the Irish famine and the failure of the Revolutions of 1848 once more sent immigrants streaming into American ports.

Seth Luther's *Address*, originally delivered in 1832, is reprinted from the 1836 edition corrected and published by the author in Philadelphia. S. F. B. Morse's newspaper articles were reprinted as a pamphlet and published in New York in August, 1835. The selections used here are taken from the pamphlet.

Address to the Working Men of New England

BY SETH LUTHER

. . . Our ears are constantly filled with the cry of National wealth, National glory, American system and American industry. . . .

This cry is kept up by men who are endeavoring *by all the means in their power* to cut down the wages of *our own people*, and who send agents to *Europe*, to *induce foreigners* to come here, to underwork *American* citizens, to support *American* industry, and the *American* System.

The whole concern (as now conducted) is as great a humbug as ever deceived any people. We see the system of manufacturing lauded to the skies; senators, representatives, owners, and agents of cotton mills using all means to keep out of sight the evils growing up under it. Cotton mills, where cruelties are practised, excessive labor required, education neglected, and vice, as a matter of course, on the increase, are denominated "the principalities of the destitute, the palaces of the poor." We do not pretend to say that this description applies, in all its parts, to all mills alike—but we do say, that most of the causes described by Dr. Kay, of Manchester, are in active operation in New England, and as sure as effect follows cause, the result must be the same. A member of the United States Senate seems to be *extremely* pleased with cotton mills; he says in the senate, "Who has not been delighted with the clockwork movements of a large cotton manufactory; he had visited them often, and *always* with increased delight." [1] He says the women work in large airy apartments,[2] well warmed; they are neatly dressed,

[1] We imagine he never worked in one 13 or 14 hours per day.
[2] So far from this, in some establishments the windows have been nailed down, and the females deprived of

with ruddy complexions, and happy countenances, they mend the broken threads and replace the exhausted balls or broaches, and at stated periods they go to and return from their meals with a light and cheerful step. (While on a visit to that pink of perfection, Waltham, I remarked that the females moved with a very light step, and well they might, for the bell rung for them to return to the mill from their homes in 19 minutes after it had rung for them to go to breakfast; some of these females boarded the largest part of half a mile from the mill.) And the grand climax is, that at the end of the week, after working like slaves for 13 or 14 hours every day, "they enter the temples of God on the Sabbath, and thank him for all his benefits,"—and the *American System* above all requires a peculiar outpouring of gratitude. We remark, that whatever girls or others may do west of the Allegany mountains, we do not believe there can be a *single person* found east of those mountains, who ever *thanked God* for *permission* to work in a *cotton mill*.

Without being obliged to attribute wrong or mercenary motives to the Hon. Senator, (*whose talents certainly must command respect from all,* let their views in other respects be what they may,) we remark, that we think he was most grossly deceived by the circumstances of his visit. We will give our *reasons*, in a few words spoken (in part) on a former occasion, on this subject. It is well known to all that when *Honorables* travel, timely notice is given of their arrival and departure in places of note. Here we have a case; the Honorable Senator from Kentucky is about to visit a *cotton mill;* due notice is given; the men, girls, and boys, are ordered to array themselves in their best apparel. Flowers of every hue are brought to decorate the mill, and enwreath the brows of the fair sex. If Nature will not furnish the materials from the lap of summer, art supplies the deficiency. Evergreens mingle with the roses,

---

even fresh air, in order to support the *"American System."*

An actual rebellion took place not long since, in consequence of this high handed and tyrannical measure, among the 1000 females in a vast overgrown establishment. We learn that frequently the females have become entirely unmanageable in consequence of various cruelties practised on them at that place. We learn that not long since the agent, newly appointed, made a rule that "all who were not within the gates at the last stroke of the bell, were to pay a fine of twelve and a half cents," whereupon the girls rose *en masse*. The confusion was great, and the order was revoked. How delightful to live in "a principality of the destitute, a palace of the poor!"

the jasmine, and the hyacinth, to honor the *illustrious* visiter, the champion, the very Goliah of the American System. He enters! Smiles are on every bow. No *cowhide*, or rod, or *"well seasoned strap"* is suffered to be seen by the Honorable Senator, or permitted to disturb the enviable happiness of the inmates of this almost *celestial* habitation. The Hon. Gentleman views with keen eye the "clockwork." He sees the rosy faces of the Houries inhabiting this palace of beauty; he is in ecstasy—he is almost *dumfounded*—he enjoys the enchanting scene with the most intense delight. For an hour or more (not fourteen hours) he seems to be in the regions described in Oriental song, his feelings are overpowered, and he retires, almost unconscious of the cheers which follow his steps; or if he hears the ringing shout, 'tis but to convince him that he is in a land of reality, and not of fiction. His mind being filled with sensations, which, from their novelty, are without a name, he exclaims, 'tis a paradise; and we reply, if a cotton mill is a "paradise," it is *"Paradise Lost."* . . .

It has been said that the speaker is opposed to *the* American System. It turns upon one single point,—if these abuses are *the* American System, he is opposed. But let him see *an* American System, where education and intelligence are generally diffused, and the enjoyment of *life* and *liberty* secured to all; he then is ready to support *such* a system. But so long as our government secures exclusive privileges to a *very small part of the community*, and leaves the majority the *"lawful prey"* to avarice, so long does he contend against *any* "System" so exceedingly unjust and unequal in its operations. He knows that we must have manufactures. It is impossible to do without them; but he has yet to learn that it is necessary, or just, that manufactures must be sustained by injustice, cruelty, ignorance, vice, and misery; which is now the fact to a startling degree. If what we have stated be true, and we challenge denial, what must be done? Must we fold our arms and say, It always was so, and always will be. If we did so, would it not almost rouse from their graves the heroes of our revolution? Would not the cold marble, representing our beloved Washington, start into *life*, and reproach us for our *cowardice?* Let the word be—Onward! onward! We know the difficulties are great, and the obstacles many; but, as yet, we "know our rights, and knowing, dare maintain." We wish to injure no man, and we are determined not to be injured as we have been; we wish nothing but those equal rights which were designed for us all. And although wealth, and prejudice, and slander, and abuse, are all brought to bear on us, we have one consolation—"*We are the Majority.*"

One difficulty is a want of information among our own class, and the HIGHER ORDERS reproach us for our ignorance; but, thank God, we have enough of intelligence among us yet, to show the world that all is not lost.

Another difficulty among us is—the Press has been almost wholly, and is now in a great degree, closed upon us. We venture to assert, that the press is *bribed* by *gold* in many instances; and we believe, that if *law* had done what *gold* has accomplished, our country would, before this time, have been deluged with blood. But working men's papers are multiplying, and we shall soon, by the diffusion of intelligence, be enabled to form a *front*, which will show all *monopolists*, and all TYRANTS, that we are not only determined to have the name of freemen, but that we will LIVE FREEMEN and DIE FREEMEN.

Fellow citizens of New England, farmers, mechanics, and labourers, we have borne these evils by far too long; we have been deceived by all parties; we must take our business into our own hands. Let us awake. Our cause is the cause of truth—of justice and humanity. *It must prevail.* Let us be determined no longer to be deceived by the cry of those who produce *nothing* and who enjoy *all*, and who *insultingly* term us—the *farmers, the mechanics, and labourers*—the LOWER ORDERS, and *exultingly* claim our homage for themselves, as the *Higher* ORDERS—*while the* DECLARATION OF INDEPENDENCE asserts that "ALL MEN ARE CREATED EQUAL."

APPENDICES

G.

Conditions on which Help is hired by the Cocheco Manufacturing Company, Dover, N. H.

We, the subscribers, do hereby agree to enter the service of the *Cocheco Manufacturing Company*, and conform, in all respects, to the REGULATIONS which are now, or may hereafter be adopted, for the good government of the Institution.

We further agree, *to work for such wages per week, and prices by the job, as the Company may see fit to pay*, AND BE SUBJECT TO THE FINES as well as entitled to the premiums paid by the Company.

We further agree to allow two cents each week to be deducted from our wages, for the benefit of the SICK FUND.

We also agree not to leave the service of the Company, without giving two weeks notice of our intention, without permission of an agent; and if

we do, we agree to forfeit to the use of the Company two weeks' pay.

We also agree not to be engaged in any combination, whereby the work may be impeded, or the Company's interest in any work injured; if we do, we agree to forfeit to the use of the Company the amount of wages that may be due to us at the time.

We also agree that in case we are discharged from the service of the Company for any fault, we will not consider ourselves entitled to be settled within less than two weeks from the time of such discharge.

Payments for labor performed are to be made monthly.

I.

The speaker cannot but feel as every man ought to feel, indignant at such language as this. Has it come to this, that we must be told we ought to be content, because we are not yet actually in chains of iron? We happen to know something about southern slavery, having resided in a slave country at various periods, and we know that children born in slavery do not work *one half* the hours, nor perform one *quarter* of the labor, that white children do in cotton mills, in free New England. It is nearly so with adult slaves. If the children in mills in New England are almost entirely deprived of education, will the gentleman show us the great advantage *they* posses over *slave* children? Further, we do know that the slaves in the South enjoy privileges which are not enjoyed in some of our cotton mills. At Dover, N. H., we understand, no operative is allowed to keep a pig or cow, because it would take a few minutes time to feed the pig and milk the cow. We learn also it is now, or has been the case, that that "Republican Institution" even monopolized the *milk business*, kept cows themselves, and compelled their "help" to buy milk of them. This we suppose was to give a *market* to the *farmer*, of which we hear so much.

J.

A writer, calling himself "A Factory Hand," in the Yeoman's Gazette, Concord, September 1, 1832, tells a fine story about the advantages at Waltham, "the flowers of taste and sentiment" and feeling, and the "hardy plants of the understanding," and "all that sort of thing;" but, after all, he says, "*with particular reference to our situation in the cotton mills,* (mark that,) it would not do to reduce the hours of labor; for more harm would be done by the *vicious*, than good by the virtuous, if THUS *let loose* on the community." Surely *this* indicates an *extremely great* degree of cultivation of "the flowers of *taste* and *sentiment*" and "*refinement*" and "*understanding* with particular reference to our situation in the cotton mills" at Waltham. It won't do to "LET US LOOSE on the community." This is *highly* complimentary to the *lower orders* employed at Waltham. This is "taste" and "sentiment" and "refinement" and "understanding," with a *vengeance*. Why, this is the *very reason* that people are shut up in the STATE PRISON. It will not answer to "let them loose on the community." If the work people in Waltham can bear this, we are mistaken in them. If they will be *insulted* in this way, and not resent it, they are certainly to be pitied.

Another, or the same writer, signing "An Operative," with reference to the author of this address, says, "Our reformer may congratulate himself in not receiving a flagellation, or a ducking, while at Waltham." Now, we suppose this is a specimen of the "*flowers of feeling, taste, and sentiment,*" *and* "*moral principle and religious sentiment*" "*cultivated with fatherly care at Waltham.*"

Perhaps the author owes his safety to the fact, that the Company did not "let loose" the vicious characters in Waltham; for the large Hall where he lectured was filled to overflowing with an attentive and civil audience, for which he returns to them his thanks. We have never said or written a word against the morality of the Waltham people; but these *astonishing writers*, these defenders of "the higher classes," make them a savage and vicious people: so much so, that, according to them, it will not do to "let them loose on the community." We learn for the first time, from these writers, that Waltham owners are the jail keepers of the vicious and outrageous part of the community, and merely run their mills to keep them in prison for the public safety. *How very benevolent!*

If cotton mill owners cannot EMPLOY better defenders than these sapient writers are, they had better have none. But this is as much as they can expect for 70 cents per day for 13 hours work in the mill, the scribbling thrown in gratis.

K.

We insist upon it, that the power of the Constitution "to provide for the common defence," shall be exerted to provide safeguards against the dreadful evils which manufacturers are bringing upon us. For we insist that if Congress have power to protect the owners against foreign competition in the shape of goods, they have the same right to protect the operative from foreign competition in the shape of importation of foreign mechanics and laborers, to cut down the wages of our own citizens. We call upon manufacturers to do justice to the operative, and warn them to remember that working men, the farmer, mechanic and labourer . . . are to be gulled no longer by the specious and deceptive cry of American Industry while they are ground down into the dust by importation of foreign machinery, foreign workmen and foreign wool. . . .

Imminent Dangers to the Free Institutions of the United States through Foreign Immigration, and the Present State of the Naturalization Laws

BY SAMUEL F. B. MORSE

No. I

THE GREAT QUESTION regarding Foreigners, and a change in our Naturalization laws, is a *National question*, and at this time a very serious one. It is therefore with deep regret that I perceive an attempt made by both parties, (however to be expected,) to turn the just National excitement on this subject each to the account of their own party. The question, *Whether Foreigners shall be subjected to a new law of naturalization?* which grave circumstances have recently made it necessary to examine, is one entirely separate at present from *party* politics, as parties are now constituted, and is capable of being decided solely on its own merits. The organs of the two parties, however, are noticing the subject, and both engaged in their usual style of recrimination. Neither of them can see the other, nor any measure however separated from party principle, if proposed or discussed by its opponent, except through the distorted medium of prejudice. So degraded in this particular has the party press become, in the view of the intelligent portion of the community, that no one seems to expect impartiality or independence, when any question is debated that affects, or even but seems to affect, the slightest change in the aspect of the party, or in the standing of the individual, whose cause it advocates. The exclusive party character of a great portion of the daily press, its distortion of facts, its gross vituperative tone and spirit, its defence of dangerous practices and abuses, if any of these but temporarily favour mere party designs, is a serious cause of alarm to the American people. To increase the evil, each party adopts the unlawful weapons of warfare of its antagonist, thinking it an ample justification of its conduct, if it can but show that they have been used by its opponent. I cannot but advert to this crying evil at a moment when a great and pressing danger to the country demands the attention of Americans of all parties, and their cool and dispassionate examination of the evidence in the case.

The danger to which I would call attention is not imaginary. It is a danger arising from *a new position of the social elements in the onward march of the world to liberty.* The great struggle for some years has till now been principally confined to Europe. But we cannot exclude, if we would, the influence of foreign movements upon our own political institutions, in the great contest between liberty and despotism. It is an ignorance unaccountable in the conductors of the press at this moment, not to know, and a neglect of duty unpardonable, not to guard the people against the dangers resulting from this source. To deny the danger, is to shut one's eyes. It stares us in the face. And to seek to allay the salutary alarm arising from a demonstration of its actual presence among us, by attributing this alarm to any but the right cause, is worse than folly, it is madness, it is flinging away our liberties, not only without a struggle, but without the slightest concern, at the first appearance of the enemy.

No. XI

The propriety, nay, the imperious necessity of a change in the Naturalization Laws, is the point to which it is indispensable to the safety of the country, that the attention of Americans, as a whole people, should at this moment be concentrated. It is a national question, not only separate from, but *superior* to all others. All other questions which divide the nation, are peculiarly of a domestic character; they relate to matters between American and American. Whether the *bank system* is, or is not, adverse to our democratic institutions; whether *internal improvement* is constitutionally intrusted to the management of the general government, or reserved to the states respectively; whether *monopolies* of any kind are just or unjust; whether the *right of instructing* representatives is to be allowed or resisted; whether *the high offices* of the nation are safest administered by these or by those citizens; all these, and many kindred questions, are entirely

of a domestic character, to be settled between ourselves, in the just democratic mode, by majority, by the prevailing voice of the American people declared through the *ballot box.* But the question of *naturalization,* the question whether *foreigners, not yet arrived,* shall or shall not be admitted to the American right of balloting, is a matter in which the American people are in a certain sense, on one side as the original and exclusive possessors of the privilege, and foreigners on the other, as petitioners for a participation in that privilege; for the privilege of expressing their opinion upon, and assisting to decide all the other questions I have enumerated. It is, therefore, a question separate and *superior* to all these. It is a fundamental question; it affects the very foundation of our institutions, it bears directly and vitally on the *principle of the ballot* itself, that principle which decides the gravest questions of policy among Americans, nay, which can decide the very existence of the government, or can change its form at any moment. And surely this vital principle is amply protected from injury? To secure this point, every means which a people jealous of their liberties could devise was doubtless gathered about it for its preservation? It is not guarded. Be astonished, Americans, at the oversight! The mere statement of the provisions of the Naturalization Law, is sufficient, one would think, to startle any American who reflects at all. FIVE YEARS' RESIDENCE GIVES THE FOREIGNER, WHATEVER BE HIS CONDITION OR CHARACTER, THIS MOST SACRED PRIVILEGE OF ASSISTING TO CONTROL, AND ACTUALLY OF CONTROLLING (*there is not a guard to prevent,*) ALL THE DOMESTIC INTERESTS OF AMERICA. A simple *five years' residence,* allows any foreigner, (no matter what his character, whether friend or enemy of freedom, whether an exile from proscription, or a pensioned Jesuit, commissioned to serve the interests of Imperial Despots,) to handle this "*lock of our strength.*" How came it to pass? How is it possible that so vital a point as the ballot box was not constitutionally surrounded with double, ay, with treble guards? How is it that this *heart* of Democracy was left so exposed; yes; this very *heart* of the body politic, in which, in periodical pulsations, the opinions of the people meet, to go forth again as law to the extremities of the nation; this *heart* left so absolutely without protection, that the murderous eye of Imperial Despots across the deep, can, not only watch it in all its movements, but they are invited from its very nakedness, to reach out their hands to stab it. The figure is not too strong; their blow is aimed, now, whilst I write. at this very heart of our institutions. How is it that none of our sagacious statesmen foresaw this danger to the republic through the unprotected ballot box? It was foreseen. It did not escape the prophetic eye of Jefferson. He foresaw, and from the beginning foretold the evil, and uttered his warning voice. *Mr. Jefferson denounced the encouragement of emigration.* And, oh! consistency, where is thy blush? he who is now urging Jefferson's own recommendation on this vital point, is condemned by some who call themselves Jeffersonian democrats; by some journalists who in one column profess Jeffersonian principles, while in the next they denounce both the principles and the policy of Jefferson, and (with what semblance of consistency let them show if they can,) defend a great political evil, against which Jefferson left his written protest. It may be convenient, for purposes best known to themselves, for such journalists to desert their democratic principles, while loudly professing still to hold them; but the people, who are neither blind nor deaf, will soon perceive whose course is most consistent with that great apostle of democratic liberty. Do they ask, would you defend Mr. Jefferson's opinions when they are wrong?—I answer, prove them to be wrong, and I will desert them. Truth and justice are superior to all men. I advocate Jefferson's opinions, not because they are Jefferson's, but because his opinions are in accordance with truth and sound policy.—Let me show that Mr. Jefferson's opinions in relation to emigration are proved by experience to be sound.

What were the circumstances of the country when laws so favourable to the foreigner were passed to induce him to emigrate and settle in this country? The answer is obvious. Our early history explains it. In our national infancy we needed the strength of *numbers*. Powerful nations, to whom we were accessible by fleets, and consequently also by armies, threatened us. Our land had been the theatre of contests between French, and English, and Spanish armies, for more than a century. Our numbers were so few and so scattered, that as a people we could not unite to repel aggression. The war of Independence, too, had wasted us. We wanted *numerical strength;* we felt our weakness in numbers. *Safety*, then, national *safety*, was the motive which urged us to use every effort to increase our population, and to induce a foreign emigration. Then foreigners seemed all-important, and the policy of alluring them hither, too palpable to be opposed successfully even by the remonstrances of Jefferson. We could be benefited by the emigrants, and we in return could bestow on them a gift beyond price, by simply making them citizens. Manifest as this advantage

seemed in the increase of our numerical strength, Mr. Jefferson looked beyond the advantage of the moment, and saw the distant evil. His reasoning, already quoted in a former number, will bear to be repeated. "I beg leave," says Mr. Jefferson, "to propose a doubt. The present desire of America is to produce rapid population by as great importations of foreigners as possible. But is this founded in good policy? *The advantage proposed, is the multiplication of numbers.* But are there no inconveniences to be thrown into the scale against the advantage expected from a multiplication of numbers by the importation of foreigners? It is for the happiness of those united in society to harmonize as much as possible in matters which they must of necessity transact together."

"Civil government being the sole object of forming societies, its administration must be conducted by common consent. Every species of government has its specific principles. Ours, perhaps, are more peculiar than those of any other in the universe. It is a composition of the freest principles of the English constitution, with others derived from natural right and natural reason. To these nothing can be more opposed than the maxims of absolute monarchies. Yet, from such, we are to expect the greatest number of emigrants. *They will bring with them the principles of the governments they leave, imbibed in their early youth; or, if able to throw them off, it will be in exchange for an unbounded licentiousness,* passing, as is usual, from one extreme to another. It would be a miracle were they to stop precisely at the point of temperate liberty. These principles, with their language, they will transmit to their children. *In proportion to their numbers, they will share with us the legislation. They will infuse into it their spirit, warp and bias its directions, and render it a heterogeneous, incoherent, distracted mass.*"

"I may appeal to experience, for a verification of these conjectures. But, if they be not *certain in event*, are they not *possible, are they not probable?* Is it not safer to wait with patience—for the attainment of any degree of population desired or expected? May not our government be more homogeneous, more peaceable, more durable?" He asks, what would be the condition of France if twenty millions of Americans were suddenly imported into that kingdom? and adds—"If it would be *more turbulent*, less happy, less strong, we may believe that the addition of *half a million of foreigners* would produce a *similar effect here*. If they come of themselves, they are entitled to all the rights of citizenship; *but I doubt the expediency of inviting them by extraordinary encour-*

agements." Now, if under the most favourable circumstances for the country, when it could most be benefited, when numbers were most urgently needed, Mr. Jefferson could discover the evil afar off, and protest against encouraging foreign immigration, how much more is the measure now to be deprecated, when circumstances have so entirely changed, that instead of *adding strength* to the country, immigration *adds weakness,* weakness physical and moral! And what overwhelming force does Mr. Jefferson's reasoning acquire, by the vast change of circumstances which has taken place both in Europe and in this country, in our earlier and in our later condition.—*Then* we were few, feeble, and scattered. *Now* we are numerous, strong, and concentrated. *Then* our accessions by immigration were real accessions of strength from the ranks of the learned and the good, from the enlightened mechanic and artisan, and intelligent husbandman. *Now* imigration is the accession of weakness, from the ignorant and the vicious, or the priest-ridden slaves of Ireland and Germany, or the outcast tenants of the poorhouses and prisons of Europe. And again. *Then* our beautiful system of government had not been unfolded to the world to the terror of tyrants; the rising brightness of American Democracy was not yet so far above the horizon as to wake their slumbering anxieties, or more than to gleam faintly, in hope, upon their enslaved subjects. *Then* emigration was natural, it was an attraction of affinities, it was an attraction of liberty to liberty. Emigrants were the proscribed for conscience' sake, and for opinion's sake, the real lovers of liberty, Europe's loss, and our gain.

Now American Democracy is denounced by name by foreign despots, waked with its increasing brilliancy. Its splendour dazzles them. It alarms them, for it shows their slaves their chains. And it must be extinguished. *Now* emigration is changed; naturalization has become the door of entrance not alone to the ever welcome lovers of liberty, but also for the priest-ridden troops of the Holy Alliance, with their Jesuit officers well skilled in all the arts of darkness. Now emigrants are selected for a service to their tyrants, and by their tyrants; not for their affinity to liberty, but for their mental servitude, and their docility in obeying the orders of their priests. They are transported in thousands, nay, in *hundreds of thousands,* to our shores, to our loss and Europe's gain.

It may be, Americans, that you still doubt the *existence* of a conspiracy, and the reality of danger from Foreign Combination; or, if the attempt is made, you yet doubt the *power* of any such secret intrigue in your society. Do you wish to test its existence and its power? It is easy to apply the test. *Test it by attempting a change in the Naturalization Law.* Take the ground that such a change must be made, that *no foreigner who comes into the country after the law is passed shall ever be allowed the right of suffrage.* Stand firmly to this single point, and you will soon discover where the enemy is, and the tactics he employs. This is the spear of Ithuriel. Apply its point. You will find your enemy, though now squat like a toad fast by the ear of our confidence, suddenly roused to show his infernal origin.

Look a moment at the proposition. You will perceive that in its very nature there is nothing to excite the opposition of a single citizen, native or naturalized, in the whole country, *provided,* be it distinctly borne in mind, *that he is not implicated in the conspiracy.* This prohibition, in the proposed change of the law, it is evident, touches not in any way the *native American,* neither does it touch in the slightest degree the already granted privileges of the *naturalized citizen,* nor the *foreigner now in the country,* who is waiting to be naturalized, nor even *the foreigner on his way hither;* no, *not an indivdual* in the whole country is unfavourably affected by the provisions of such a law, not an individual *except alone the foreign Jesuit, the Austrian stipendiary with his intriguing myrmidons.* And how is he affected by it? He is deprived of his *passive obedience* forces; he can no longer use his power over his slaves, *to interfere in our political concerns;* he can no longer use them in his Austrian master's service; and he therefore, be assured, will resist with all the desperation of a detected brigand. He will raise an outcry. He will fill the public ear with cries of *intolerance.* He will call the measure religious bigotry, and illiberality, and religious persecution, and other popular catchwords, to deceive the unreflecting ear. But, be not deceived; when you hear him, set your mark upon him. That is the man. Try then this test. Again, I say, let the proposition be that the law of the land be so changed, that NO FOREIGNER WHO COMES INTO THE COUNTRY AFTER THE LAW IS PASSED SHALL EVER BE ENTITLED TO THE RIGHT OF SUFFRAGE. This is just ground; it is practicable ground; it is defensible ground, and it is safe and prudent ground; and I cannot better close than in the words of Mr. Jefferson: "The time to guard against corruption and tyranny is *before* they shall have gotten hold on us; IT IS BETTER TO KEEP THE WOLF OUT OF THE FOLD, THAN TO TRUST TO DRAWING HIS TEETH AND TALONS AFTER HE HAS ENTERED."

INTERNAL IMPROVEMENTS

EVEN SO LATE as 1824, the United States was an immense country sparsely settled and badly in need of better facilities for communication between the seaboard and the interior. Some aid to roads had been given, but the propriety of the federal government's action still seemed questionable. In January, 1824, when the House of Representatives was debating a bill to authorize the President to order surveys and estimates for roads and canals, Henry Clay rose to settle the Constitutional argument on the issue. Presidents Madison and Monroe had both vetoed bills for internal improvements on Constitutional grounds, Clay admitted, but Congress had the same right to judgment as did the Executive.

Congress needs no specific grant to authorize internal improvements, Clay argues, for it has a "resulting power" derived from existing rights. Roads and canals are analogous to beacons and coast surveys. They are also in the nature of fortifications, since they concentrate the population, which is the effect of fortifications. Everything is done to aid foreign commerce, Clay complains, but no help is given domestic trade and "the great interior of the country." If the new states may be taxed to support a navy, the East can help open the West by improving communications.

Clay's interpretation of the Constitution won increasing support in Congress and, year after year, bills were passed for improving roads in the newer states. The policy of assisting internal improvements by federal grants did not disturb John Quincy Adams and even Andrew Jackson did not protest against appropriations for the National Road which crossed the mountains from Cumberland into Ohio. But when Congress voted to improve a portion of road entirely within the State of Kentucky, Jackson returned the measure with a veto: his interpretation of the Constitution did not permit him to sign a bill in which Congress exercised such power. There must be a genuine determination of congressional powers, he declared, for usage is an uncertain guide and expedience an unworthy one. This was the famous Maysville Road Veto of May 20, 1830, and it put a stop to direct federal support of internal improvements for at least a generation.

In 1832, Friedrich List (1789–1846) wrote to a European friend about the progress of railroad construction in America. He had come to America in 1825 and had settled at Harrisburg, Penn., where he proceeded to engage in coal mining and railroad promotions. He later returned to Germany to write his famous *The National System of Political Economy* (1841).

The letter reprinted here is from Volume II of List's *Werke* (Berlin, 1931).

Speech on Internal Improvement, 1824

BY HENRY CLAY

IT OUGHT TO BE borne in mind, that this power over roads was not contained in the articles of confederation, which limited Congress to the establishment of post-offices; and that the general character of the present constitution, as contrasted with those articles, is that of an enlargement of power. But, if the construction of my opponents be correct, we are left precisely where the articles of confederation left us, notwithstanding the additional words contained in the present constitution. What, too, will the gentleman do with the first member of the clause to establish post *offices?* Must Congress adopt, designate, some pre-existing office, established by state authority? But there is none such. May it not then fix, build, create, *establish* offices of its own?

The gentleman from Virginia sought to alarm us by the awful emphasis with which he set before us the total extent of post roads in the Union. Eighty thousand miles of post roads! exclaimed the gentleman; and will you assert for the general government jurisdiction, and erect turnpikes, on such an immense distance? Not to-day, nor to-morrow; but this government is to last, I trust, for ever; we may at least hope it will endure until the wave of population, cultivation, and intelligence, shall have washed the Rocky Mountains and mingled with the Pacific. And may we not also hope that the day will arrive when the improvements and the comforts of social life shall spread over the wide surface of this vast continent? All this is not to be suddenly done. Society must not be burthened or oppressed. Things must be gradual and progressive. The same species of formidable array which the gentleman makes, might be exhibited in reference to the construction of a navy, or any other of the great purposes of government. We might be told of the fleets and vessels of great maritime powers, which whiten the ocean; and triumphantly asked if we should vainly attempt to cope with or rival that tremendous power? And we should shrink from the effort, if we were to listen to his counsels, in hopeless despair. Yes, Sir, it is a subject of peculiar delight to me to look forward to the proud and happy period, distant as it may be, when circulation and association between the Atlantic and the Pacific and the Mexican Gulf, shall be as free and perfect as they are at this moment in England, or in any other the most highly improved country on the globe. In the mean time, without bearing heavily upon any of our important interests, let us apply ourselves to the accomplishment of what is most practicable and immediately necessary.

But what most staggers my honourable friend, is the jurisdiction over the sites of roads and other internal improvements which he supposes Congress might assume; and he considers the exercise of such a jurisdiction as furnishing the just occasion for serious alarm. Let us analyze the subject. Prior to the erection of a road under the authority of the General Government, there existed, in the State through which it passes, no actual exercise of jurisdiction over the ground which it traverses *as a road*. There was only the possibility of the exercise of such a jurisdiction, when the state should, if ever, erect such a road. But the road is made by the authority of Congress, and out of the *fact* of its erection arises a necessity for its preservation and protection. The road is some thirty or fifty or sixty feet in width, and with that narrow limit passes through a part of the territory of the State. The capital expended in the making of the road incorporates itself with and

becomes a part of the permanent and immoveable property of the State. The jurisdiction which is claimed for the General Government, is that only which relates to the necessary defence, protection, and preservation, of the road. It is of a character altogether conservative. Whatever does not relate to the existence and protection of the road remains with the State. Murders, trespasses, contracts, all the occurrences and transactions of society upon the road, not affecting its actual existence, will fall within the jurisdiction of the civil or criminal tribunals of the State, as if the road had never been brought into existence. How much remains to the State! How little is claimed for the General Government! Is it possible that a jurisdiction so limited, so harmless, so unambitious, can be regarded as seriously alarming to the sovereignty of the States! Congress now asserts and exercises, without contestation, a power to protect the mail in its transit, by the sanction of all suitable penalties. The man who violates it is punished with death, or otherwise, according to the circumstances of the case. This power is exerted as incident to that of establishing post offices and post roads. Is the protection of the thing in transitu a power more clearly deducible from the grant, than that of facilitating, by means of a practicable road, its actual transportation? Mails certainly imply roads, roads imply their own preservation, their preservation implies the power to preserve them, and the Constitution tells us, in express terms, that we shall establish the one and the other.

In respect to cutting canals, I admit the question is not quite so clear as in regard to roads. With respect to these, as I have endeavoured to show, the power is expressly granted. In regard to canals, it appears to me to be fairly comprehended in, or deducible from, certain granted powers. Congress has power to regulate commerce with foreign nations and among the several states. Precisely the same measure of power which is granted in the one case is conferred in the other. And the uniform practical exposition of the constitution, as to the regulation of foreign commerce, is equally applicable to that among the several states. Suppose, instead of directing the legislation of this government constantly, as heretofore, to the object of foreign commerce, to the utter neglect of the interior commerce among the several states, the fact had been reversed, and now, for the first time, we were about to legislate for our foreign trade: Should we not, in that case, hear all the constitutional objections made to the erection of buoys, beacons, lighthouses, the surveys of coasts, and the other numerous facilities accorded to the foreign trade, which we now hear to the making of roads and canals? Two years ago, a sea-wall, or, in other words, a marine canal, was authorized by an act of Congress, in New-Hampshire; and I doubt not that many of those voted for it who have now constitutional scruples on this bill. Yes, any thing, every thing, may be done for foreign commerce; any thing, every thing, on the margin of the ocean: but nothing for domestic trade; nothing for the great interior of the country! Yet, the equity and the beneficence of the constitution equally comprehends both. The gentleman does, indeed, maintain that there is a difference as to the character of the facilities in the two cases. But I put it to his own candour, whether the only difference is not that which springs from the nature of the two elements on which the two species of commerce are conducted—the difference between land and water. The principle is the same, whether you promote commerce by opening for it an artificial channel where now there is none, or by increasing the ease or safety with which it may be conducted through a natural channel which the bounty of Providence has bestowed. In the one case, your object is to facilitate arrival and departure from the ocean to the land. In the other, it is to accomplish the same object from the land to the ocean. Physical obstacles may be greater in the one case than in the other, but the moral or constitutional power equally includes both. The gentleman from Virginia had, to be sure, contended that the power to make these commercial facilities was to be found in another clause of the constitution—that which enables Congress to obtain cessions of territory for specific objects, and grants to it an exclusive jurisdiction. These cessions may be obtained for the "erection of forts, magazines, arsenals, dockyards, or other needful buildings." It is apparent that it relates altogether to military or naval affairs, and not to the regulation of commerce. How was the marine canal covered by this clause? Is it to be considered as a "needful building?" The object of this power is perfectly obvious. The Convention saw that, in military or naval posts, such as are indicated, it was indispensably necessary, for their proper government, to vest in Congress the power of exclusive legislation. If we claimed over objects of internal improvement an exclusive jurisdiction, the gentleman might urge, with much force, the clause in question. But the claim of concurrent jurisdiction only is asserted. The gentleman professes himself unable to comprehend how concurrent jurisdiction can be exercised by two different governments at the same time over the same persons and things. But, is not this the fact with respect to the state and federal governments? Does not every person, and every thing, within our limits, sustain a two-fold relation to the state and to the federal authority? The power of taxation as exerted by both governments, that over the militia, besides many others, is concurrent. No doubt embarrassing cases may be conceived and stated by gentlemen of acute and ingenious minds. One was put to me yesterday. Two canals are desired, one by the federal, and the other by a state government; and there is not a supply of water but for the feeder of one canal—which is to take it? The constitution, which ordains the supremacy of the laws of the United States, answers the question. The good of the whole is paramount to the good of a part. The same difficulty might possibly arise in the exercise of the incontestable power of taxation. We know that the imposition of taxes has its limits. There is a maximum which cannot be transcended. Suppose the citizen to be taxed by the general government to the utmost extent of his ability, or a thing as much as it can possibly bear, and the state imposes a tax at the same time, which authority is to take it? Extreme cases of this sort may serve to amuse and to puzzle; but they will hardly ever arise in practice. And we may safely confide in the moderation, good sense, and mutual good dispositions, of the two governments, to guard against the imagined conflicts.

It is said by the President, that the power to regulate commerce merely authorizes the laying of imposts and duties. But Congress has no power to lay imposts and duties on the trade among the several states. The grant must mean, therefore, something else. What is it? The power to regulate commerce among the several states, if it has any meaning, implies authority to foster it, to promote it, to bestow on it facilities similar to those which have been conceded to our foreign trade. It cannot mean only an empty authority to adopt regulations, without the capacity to give practical effect to them. All the powers of this government should be interpreted in reference to its first, its best, its greatest object, the union of these states. And is not that union best invigorated by an intimate, social, and commercial connexion between all the parts of the confederacy? Can that be accomplished, that is, can the federative objects of this government be attained, but by the application of federative resources?

Of all the powers bestowed on this government, Mr Clay thought none were more clearly vested, than that to regulate the distribution of the intelligence, private and official, of the country; to regulate the distribution of its commerce; and to regulate the distribution of the physical force of the Union. In the execution of the high and solemn trust which these beneficial powers imply, we must look to the great ends which the framers of our admirable constitution had in view. We must reject, as wholly incompatible with their enlightened and beneficent intentions, that construction of these powers which would resuscitate all the debility and inefficiency of the ancient confederacy. In the vicissitudes of human affairs, who can foresee all the possible cases, in which it may be necessary to apply the public force, within or without the Union? This Government is charged with the use of it, to repel invasions, to suppress insurrections, to enforce the laws of the Union; in short, for all the unknown and undefinable purposes of war, foreign or intestine, wherever and however it may rage. During its existence, may not government, for its effectual prosecution, order a road to be made, or a canal to be cut, to relieve, for example, an exposed point of the Union? If, when the emergency comes, there is a power to provide for it, that power must exist in the constitution, and not in the emergency. A wise, precautionary, and parental policy, anticipating danger, will beforehand provide for the hour of need. Roads and canals are in the nature of fortifications; since, if not the deposits of military resources, they enable you to bring into rapid action, the military resources of the country, whatever they may be. They are better than any fortifications, because they serve the double purposes of peace and of war. They dispense, in a great degree, with fortifications, since they have all the effect of that concentration, at which fortifications aim. I appeal from the precepts of the President to the practice of the President. While he denies to Congress the power in question, he does not scruple, upon his sole authority, as numerous instances in the statute book will testify, to order, at pleasure, the opening of roads by the military, and then come here to ask us to pay for them. Nay, more, Sir; a subordinate, but highly respectable officer of the Executive Government, I believe, would not hesitate to provide a boat or cause a bridge to be erected over an inconsiderable stream, to insure the regular transportation of the mail. And it happens to be within my personal knowledge, that the head of the Post Office Department, as a prompt and vigilant officer should do, had recently despatched an agent to ascertain the causes of the late frequent vexatious failures of the great northern mail, and to inquire if a provision of a boat or bridge over certain small streams in Maryland, which have produced them, would not prevent their recurrence.

I was much surprised at one argument of the honourable gentleman. He told the House, that the Constitution had carefully guarded against inequality, among the several states, in the public burthens, by certain restrictions upon the power of taxation; that the effect of the adoption of a system of internal improvements would be to draw the resources from one part of the Union, and to expend them in the improvements of another; and that the spirit, at least, of the constitutional equality, would be thus violated. From the nature of things, the constitution could not specify the theatre of the expenditure of the public treasure. That expenditure, guided by and looking to the public good, must be made, necessarily, where it will most subserve the interests of the whole Union. The argument is, that the *locale* of the collection of the public contributions, and the *locale* of their disbursement, should be the same. Now, Sir, let us carry this argument out; and no man is more capable than the ingenious gentleman from Virginia, of tracing an argument to its utmost consequences. The *locale* of the collection of the public revenue is the pocket of the citizen; and, to abstain from the violation of the principle of equality adverted to by the gentleman, we should restore back to each man's pocket precisely what was taken from it. If the principle contended for be true, we are habitually violating it. We raise about twenty millions of dollars, a very large revenue, considering the actual distresses of the country. And, Sir, notwithstanding all the puffing, flourishing statements of its prosperity, emanating from printers who are fed upon the pap of the public Treasury, the whole country is in a condition of very great distress. Where is this vast revenue expended? Boston, New-York, the great capitals of the North, are the theatres of its disbursement. There the interest upon the public debt is paid. There the expenditure in the building, equipment, and repair of the national vessels takes place. There all the great expenditures of the government necessarily concentrate. This is no cause of just complaint. It is inevitable, resulting from the accumulation of capital, the state of the arts, and other circumstances belonging to our great cities. But, Sir, if there be a section of this Union having more right than any other to complain of this transfer of the circulating medium from one quarter of the Union to another, the West, the poor West—[Here Mr Barbour explained. He had meant that the Constitution limited Congress as to the proportions of revenue to be drawn from the several states; but the principle of this provision would be vacated by internal improvements of immense expense, and yet of a local character.

Our public ships, to be sure, are built at the seaports, but they do not remain there. Their home is the mountain wave; but internal improvements are essentially local; they touch the soil of the states, and their benefits, at least the largest part of them, are confined to the states where they exist.] The explanation of the gentleman has not materially varied the argument. He says that the home of our ships is the mountain wave. Sir, if the ships go to sea, the money with which they were built, or refitted, remains on shore, and the cities where the equipment takes place derive the benefit of the expenditure. It requires no stretch of the imagination to conceive the profitable industry—the axes, the hammers, the saws—the mechanic arts, which are put in motion by this expenditure. And all these, and other collateral advantages, are enjoyed by the sea-ports. The navy is built for the interest of the whole. Internal improvements, of that general, federative character, for which we contend, would also be for the interest of the whole. And, I should think their abiding with us, and not going abroad on the vast deep, was rather cause of recommendation than objection.

But, Mr. Chairman, if there be any part of this Union more likely than all others to be benefited by the adoption of the gentleman's principle, regulating the public expenditure, it is the West. There is a perpetual drain from that embarrassed and highly distressed portion of our country, of its circulating medium to the East. There, but few and inconsiderable expenditures of the public money take place. There we have none of those public works, no magnificent edifices, forts, armories, arsenals, dockyards, &c. which more or less are to be found in every Atlantic state. In at least seven states beyond the Alleghany, not one solitary public work of this Government is to be found. If, by one of those awful and terrible dispensations of Providence, which sometimes occur, this Government should be unhappily annihilated, every where on the seaboard traces of its former existence would be found; whilst we should not have, in the West, a single monument remaining on which to pour out our affections and our regrets. Yet, Sir, we do not complain. No portion of your population is more loyal to the Union, than the hardy freemen of the West. Nothing can weaken or eradicate their ardent desire for its lasting preservation. None are more prompt to vindicate the interests and rights of the nation from all foreign aggression. Need I remind you of the glorious scenes in which they participated, during the late war—a war in which they had no peculiar or direct interest, waged for no commerce, no seamen of theirs. But it was enough for them that it

was a war demanded by the character and the honour of the nation. They did not stop to calculate its cost of blood, or of treasure. They flew to arms; they rushed down the valley of the Mississippi, with all the impetuosity of that noble river. They sought the enemy. They found him at the beach. They fought; they bled; they covered themselves and their country with immortal glory. They enthusiastically shared in all the transports occasioned by our victories, whether won on the ocean or on the land. They felt, with the keenest distress, whatever disaster befel us. No, Sir, I repeat it, neglect, injury itself, cannot alienate the affections of the West from this Government. They cling to it, as to their best, their greatest, their last hope. You may impoverish them, reduce them to ruin, by the mistakes of your policy, and you cannot drive them from you. They do not complain of the expenditure of the public money, where the public exigencies require its disbursement. But, I put it to your candour, if you ought not, by a generous and national policy, to mitigate, if not prevent, the evils resulting from the perpetual transfer of the circulating medium from the West to the East. One million and a half of dollars annually, is transferred for the public lands alone; and, almost every dollar goes, like him who goes to death—to a bourne from which no traveller returns. In ten years it will amount to fifteen millions; in twenty to——but I will not pursue the appalling results of arithmetic. Gentlemen who believe that these vast sums are supplied by emigrants from the East, labour under great errour. There was a time when the tide of emigration from the East bore along with it the means to effect the purchase of the public domain. But the time has, in a great measure, now stopt. And as population advances farther and farther West, it will entirely cease. The greatest migrating states in the Union, at this time, are Kentucky first, Ohio next, and Tennessee. The emigrants from those states carry with them, to the states and territories lying beyond them, the circulating medium, which, being invested in the purchase of the public land, is transmitted to the points where the wants of government require it. If this debilitating and exhausting process were inevitable, it must be borne with manly fortitude. But we think that a fit exertion of the powers of this government would mitigate the evil. We believe that the government incontestibly possesses the constitutional power to execute such internal improvements as are called for by the good of the whole. And we appeal to your equity, to your parental regard, to your enlightened policy, to perform the high and beneficial trust thus sacredly reposed. I am sensible of the delicacy of the topic to which I have reluctantly adverted, in consequence of the observations of the honourable gentleman from Virginia. And I hope there will be no misconception of my motives in dwelling upon it. A wise and considerate government should anticipate and prevent, rather than wait for the operation of causes of discontent.

Let me ask, Mr. Chairman, what has this government done on the great subject of Internal Improvements, after so many years of its existence, and with such an inviting field before it? You have made the Cumberland road, only. Gentlemen appear to have considered that a western road. They ought to recollect that not one stone has yet been broken, not one spade of earth has been yet removed in any Western State. The road begins in Maryland, and it terminates at Wheeling. It passes through the states of Maryland, Pennsylvania, and Virginia. All the direct benefit of the expenditure of the public money on that road, has accrued to those three states. Not one cent in any Western State. And yet we have had to beg, entreat, supplicate you, session after session, to grant the necessary appropriations to complete the road. I have myself toiled until my powers have been exhausted and prostrated, to prevail on you to make the grant. We were actuated to make these exertions for the sake of the collateral benefit only to the West; that we might have a way by which

we should be able to continue and maintain an affectionate intercourse with our friends and brethren—that we might have a way to reach the Capitol of our country, and to bring our councils, humble as they may be, to consult and mingle with yours in the advancement of the national prosperity. Yes, Sir, the Cumberland road has only reached the margin of a Western State; and, from some indications which have been given during this session, I should apprehend it would there pause for ever, if my confidence in you were not unbounded; if I had not before witnessed that appeals were never unsuccessful to your justice, to your magnanimity, to your fraternal affection.

But, Sir, the bill on your table is no Western bill. It is emphatically a national bill, comprehending all, looking to the interests of the whole. The people of the West never thought of, never desired, never asked, for a system exclusively for their benefit. The system contemplated by this bill looks to great national objects, and proposes the ultimate application to their accomplishment of the only means by which they can be effected, the means of the nation—means which, if they be withheld from such objects, the Union, I do most solemnly believe, of these now happy and promising states, may, at some distant (I trust a far, far distant) day, be endangered and shaken at its centre.

Early Railroads in America, 1832

BY FRIEDRICH LIST

Philadelphia, Febr. 20. 1832

Dear Sir,

According to my promise I have the honour to inform you of the progress of railroads in this country, a kind of enterprise which at present absorbs almost all the enterprising spirit and surplus-capital of the U.S. I will commence with New York as the most enterprising state of this union. Here the legislature on the opening of the present session was almost inundated with applications for railroad charters. The aggregate length of all these roads would amount to more than 3000 miles and the capital required to execute all these plans to far above 50 millions of dollars. Remember that these are the projects of a single one of the twenty-four states, whose population amounts to no more than 2 millions. If you take a map of that state and draw a line from one town to the other, from one river to the other and from every lake in all directions then you will have a correct

map of these improvements. Many of them, to be sure, are mere schemes for the present and will for a long time not be executed, but the moiety at least may be considered as solid undertakings, called for by the present wants of the public, and will yield handsome dividends and a considerable advance in the stockmarket, even before the roads are finished.

To explain in part how so new a country can undertake such immense works it must be remarked that all these roads will be made on a cheap plan, some with single tracks, all with iron plated wooden or stone rails, laid on a stone foundation. Such a road will cost from 8- to 15,000 dollars per mile (from 100,000 to 180,000 frs. per league) and a number of 30–50 passengers each way will pay a dividend of 6 per cent at a moderate toll. If it is moreover considered that all the lighter goods will take those roads during the whole year and that they will possess the monopoly of the whole transport during the winter months, it must be conceded that the prospects of the enterprisers of the principal routes are very fair and flattering. People in the old countries perhaps will find fault, with so cheap fabrics, saying that the wooden superstructure will be rotten after a lapse of 8 or 10 years. But they must consider that people in this country do as people elsewhere, as well as they can, and that capitalists in this country by making cheap railroads if they cannot make dear ones understand still their interest better than capitalists in Europe who make none at all whilst they might make the most solid at the greatest profits. For whilst these cheap superstructures are rotting trade and travelling will increase tenfold and at the time, when they are rotten altogether capitalists will have gained enough to construct the most solid roads. To make dear railroads in this country would be as injudicious as to make cheap ones in yours, where trade and travelling are so immense that the principal routes would pay a dividend of 10 to 25 per cent. on the most solid work the very first year.

The state of New York has as yet only a single railroad in operation, that from Albany to Schenectady, 16 miles long. It does exceedingly well and the stocks are rising rapidly. The most remarkable project, one which may teach people in your country a useful lesson is that from New York to Albany. You know that there is the finest steam navigation in the world between these two places. Steamboats are running up from the evening at 5 o'clock till the next morning at 6. You may go to bed in one place and rise in the other. I have known the fare on this route (160 miles) to have been as low as one dollar and if I am well informed it was never higher than four. And still it has been calculated and proved that on account of the steamboat travelling being interrupted during the winter time a railroad would do exceedingly well on this route.

For the information of the canalmen I remark that the governor of this state as well as a large part of the public are of opinion that the railroads projected from the Hudson to Lake Erie, far from injuring the canal, would benefit it considerably.

Next to New York comes Pennsylvania. This state has not so much projected as the former, but more actually commenced and accomplished last year. In the County of Schuylkill alone 6 roads were finished from 5 to 22 miles long, which are principally calculated to transport coal from the mines to the canal. This state is actually at work to connect the head waters of the Schuylkill with the Susquehannah at the forks near Sunbury and the lower part of the Schuylkill with the lower part of the Susquehannah by a railroad from Philadelphia to Columbia. The former will be 45, the latter 85 miles in length. Philadelphia has also commenced to construct a railroad to Norristown (14 miles) which by and by will be extended to Schuylkill County, thence join the above mentioned road to Sunbury and stretch itself towards Lake Erie, to rival with the great improvements the New Yorkers are planning. For the present the most important enterprises are those, which tend to connect New York with Philadelphia. There are two lines chartered for that purpose. One commences at Camden opposite this city and ends at South Amboy, whence the remaining 30 miles will be made in steamboats; the other to run along the Western bank of the Delaware up to Trenton and thence in a straight line to Jersey City opposite the city of New York. The stock of the first of those lines has already risen from 45 to 75 per cent. That line will accommodate the public in such a manner that a man may go to and fro between the two cities, do his business and breakfast and dine as conveniently as at home. You set out for instance at Camden opposite Philadelphia at 4 o'clock in the morning, the 70 miles between that place and South Amboy you make in 3½ hours. At half past seven you will arrive in the steamboat, where the dinner will be ready. There is ample time to eat it and to make your toilette, whilst you are making the remaining 30 miles, and so you will be fully prepared to do business, and to attend the exchange hours etc., when you arrive between 10–11 o'clock at New York. You have ample time till three in the afternoon, when you will return to the steamboat, where dinner is prepared. You will make your way back to South Amboy in 2½ hours, whilst you eat it, and at nine o'clock in the evening you will be safely retour in your house, having run 140 miles by land and 60 miles by water, eaten regularly your breakfast and dinner, and transacted business for five hours without feeling the slightest fatigue.

It may perhaps serve to pacify somewhat the canalmen in your country, if they hear that on this route also there are two canals, the share holders of which are so far from being enemies to the railroads, that one of the canals has actually married one of the railroads by making a joint stock company. The names of that couple are: Delaware and Raritan Canal and Camden and South Amboy Railroad. Some maintain that the marriage on the side of the canal was made from fear of being outdone by the railroad, others that the railroad will do better in that union than in single blessedness;—that both will do well together nobody doubts.

In going from Pennsylvania to Maryland we meet in the little state of Delaware two other improvements which may afford occasion to draw a parallel between canals and railroads. There is the Delaware and Chesapeake Canal a splendid enterprise, by which at an expense of about 2 millions of dollars the two bays have been connected in such a manner that sloops of 100 tons burden may pass from one to the other, by going only through two locks. But that great enterprise, though commenced 12 or 15 years ago, and for three years in successfull operation, has not yet been able to declare a single cent of dividend, and in addition to that heavy loss of interest, the stock is scarcely worth 140 for 200 paid in. There is also a railroad from Wilmington to Frenchtown, calculated for a connecting link of the steamboat navigation between the two bays. This railroad was commenced two years ago, will be in full operation this spring, the stock of it is up to 45–50 from 35, paid in; it has only cost between 200,000 and 300,000 dollars and nobody doubts that the share holders will make a dividend of 6 per cent. the very first year of its being in operation. There you have the riddle dissolved why capitalists have so little confidence in splendid canal projects and so much in railroad enterprises.

At Baltimore, the commercial capital of the state of Maryland, we arrive in the headquarters of the American railroad speculations. The great Baltimore and Ohio Railroad was the first of all the great projects of this kind conceived in this country. 60 miles of it are already in operation, 40 will be added in the course of the present summer and the whole till to . . . . . or some place near the town of Wheeling on the banks of the Ohio in the course of three or four years. This road has given this winter a splendid proof of the usefulness of railroads and thereby contributed much to increase their credit throughout the union. Quite unexpectedly the rivers and canals were frozen up as early as the 1. of December when the cities were not yet supplied with coal and firewood. These articles therefore rose in all the great places along the coast from 100–200 per cent. with the only exception of Baltimore, which city was supplied regularly by the railroad, and where therefore scarcely a rise of the price of fuel was perceptible. Travelling also was going on on that road as regularly as in summertime, at the average of from 150 to 200 passengers per day and the city was supplied with flour, butchersmeat and other victuals from a distance of sixty miles as cheap as formerly from a distance of 5. Prop-

erty has risen 50 per cent., will rise 100 before the road is finished and in a few years that single road will raise the city of Baltimore to the height of Philadelphia and New York.

Baltimore has besides two other great enterprises in hands: a railroad to Washington (40 miles) and one to Yorkhaven (85 miles) where the rafts and arks coming down the Susquehanna hereafter will stop and sell their loading, in order to avoid the dangerous river navigation below that place. It is worthy to be observed that the Baltimorians have the first commenced to construct the rails of granite which they find in abundance along their great routes and to cover those stone rails with iron plates. Some think that kind of roads as solid as the iron rails and it would certainly be recommendable for those regions in France, where granite can be found near the roads, as being considerably cheaper than rails altogether of iron. . . .

Stone foundation. South of the Potomac there is only one great enterprise, the Charleston and Hamburg Railroad, and even that, it is said, is a very unsolid construction and not far advanced. That part of the country is paralysed by the evil of slavery. A small railroad also is constructed to transport stone coal from the mines to Richmond (16 miles) and some others of that dimension are in work or in project. But without northern capital and enterprise there will be no great work going on in that quarter.

In the East and West however the work is going on bravely. Boston has projected roads to the Hudson river and to the Lake Ontario (from 200–300 miles) and to Providence (43 miles). There is capital and spirit more than enough, what Boston projects she will accomplish. As yet she has only three miles of railroads (from a stone quarry to the city) in operation. This will rest for a number of years and is to be considered the father of the railroads on this continent.

In the west the state of Kentucky has undertaken a railroad from Lexington to the Ohio (515 miles). But the state of Ohio as she has taken the lead of the canal enterprises in the west, 500 miles of which she has completed, so she seems to be determined to take the lead in railroads. Two routes to connect the waters of the Ohio with the Lake Erie, and two to cross the state from east to west are discussed and one of them that from Dayton to Sandusky Bay is already chartered and, if I am well informed, also subscribed. The two routes from east to west are but continuations of the great Baltimore and Ohio (south) and of the great New York route (north). That this continuation will take place as soon as those improvements will reach the frontiers of Ohio there will be little doubt.

Now look on the map for the two points Baltimore and Cincinnati. Forty years hence the latter was far beyond the boundary of civilisation. At that time the whole ground of that city, where Cincinnati was laid out, had been sold for 47 dollars. Last fall lots were sold at 50 dollars an inch in front. Twenty five years ago it took a man a whole summer to go to and fro, and even at present it takes in the winter season a whole month. After the railroad has been completed you may travel from one place to the other easily in 24 hours and if it would be continued farther to St. Louis a man residing near the Osages and Texas may go to Washington in 40 hours, that is in a considerably shorter time than you travel at present from Strassburg to Paris and with far less fatigue.

Such are the great advantages of these means of conveyance for agriculturists and manufacturers as well as for commerce, for those who possess lands and houses as well as for those who only trade, for the rich and the poor, for the south and the north, for those who live on the sea coast as well as for the residents of the interior, for the man of pleasure as well as for the man of business, for those who stay at home, or travel about, that twenty years will not elapse before you can travel on railroads from Maine all along the coast to New Orleans from the sea coast to all the western territories on railroads constructed all by individual exertions. The political influence of this new communication is so much felt that President Jackson in his last message considers railroads a new mean given by heaven to unite the different states and increase their means of defense. . . .

Most Respectfully Yours
F. R. List

NULLIFICATION

As a doctrine concerning the interpretation of the Constitution of the United States, nullification asserts the right of a minority state to protect its Constitutional rights when those are attacked by the federal government's action. Nullification rejects the claim of the Supreme Court to be final authority since a branch of the usurping government cannot be judge in its own cause, and insists that peaceable secession is the only possible ultimate remedy. For precedent, nullification looked to the spirit of the Revolution and the theory of a compact among the states as expounded in the Virginia and Kentucky Resolutions of 1798.

One of the most familiar rebuttals of the doctrine is found in Daniel Webster's Second Reply to Hayne. The reply was part of a debate provoked by a resolution concerning not the tariff, which is the measure usually associated with nullification, but the public lands. At the beginning of the Twenty-first Congress, in 1829, Senator Foote of Connecticut offered a resolution inquiring into the desirability of limiting the sale of public lands to those already on the market, suspending surveys, and abolishing the office of Surveyor

General. Immediately, Benton of Missouri rose to attack: the proposal was plainly calculated to hinder the settlement of the new states. In conjunction with the tariff of 1828, the resolution indicated a spirit of hostility toward the West, Benton argued. His contention was seized on by Senator Hayne of South Carolina, who declared that, from the beginning of the republic, New England had been unfriendly to the West.

At this point, Webster moved an indefinite postponement of consideration of the Foote Resolution. His speech, the First Reply to Hayne, asserted the supremacy of the Union and the long-standing sympathy New England had shown for the developing West. The Union was no mere temporary convenience, Webster argued then; it was absolutely necessary to national welfare. Let not its usefulness be discussed as one discusses the temper of a weapon or the cost of a farm. Let the Union be reverenced, he implies, and may it be perpetual —or at least unbroken during present lifetimes. Hayne retorted, enlarging on his original Constitutional and historical contentions; and Webster made the famous Second Reply to

Hayne. By that time, Senator Foote and his resolution had apparently been forgotten by everyone except Thomas Hart Benton.

But the resentment against the tariff of 1828, which had embittered the tone of the debate on the Foote Resolution, had results more serious than distorting a discussion of the public lands. The 1828 tariff had been the end-product of protectionist propaganda and log-rolling amendments intended to reduce the measure to such obvious absurdity that it would not pass. The plan failed, however, and the result was a tariff which satisfied no one, not even the entire manufacturing interest.

Next to Jackson's veto of the bill for re-chartering the Bank, the tariff had been one of the most important issues of the 1832 presidential campaign. South Carolina, which had already expressed its views in the *Exposition and Protest* of 1828, called a Convention which met in October, 1832. An upcountry delegate presented a motion denying the competence of the Convention because it represented property and population instead of population alone, and was therefore weighted in favor of the seaboard nullifiers; the Convention vetoed the motion and passed an Ordinance nullifying the tariff of 1828. The Ordinance declared the law null and void as of February 1, 1833, and required that all citizens of South Carolina take an oath to abide by the Convention's decision.

At the year's turn, South Carolina cast its electoral vote for a candidate who had no chance of being returned. The election of a tariff-reform Congress did not alter the state's determination; the Ordinance of Nullification was solemnly transmitted to Washington and the governors of the several states. In reply, President Jackson issued a long proclamation, expounding the Constitution and urging South Carolina to return to her allegiance. State veto of acts of the Federal government is inherently absurd, the proclamation argues; such power is "*incompatible with the existence of the Union, contradicted expressly by the letter of the Constitution, unauthorized by its spirit, inconsistent with every principle on which it was founded, and destructive of the great object for which it was formed.*" Even if there were Constitutional ground for South Carolina's action, moreover, the actual provocation for it is entirely inadequate. The nullifiers have used economic depression caused by the overproduction of cotton to egg South Carolina on to "peaceable" revolution because of objectionable legislation that is in the process of being altered. Finally, the doctrine of peaceable secession would end the existence of the United States as a nation. Neither events nor reason justify nullification, the proclamation concludes, and appeals to the people of South Carolina to recall their Revolutionary memories and their own perilous situation, exposed as they were to possible slave insurrection.

Jackson supplemented argument and appeal with preparation to enforce the law with arms, if necessary, while, in Congress, Clay rushed a compromise tariff by means of a Senate amendment to a House bill. All duties above 20 percent were to be reduced one tenth of one percent each year until 1842, when all duties were to be cut to 20 percent. Clay's proposal attempted to combine conciliation with a measure of protection. It was accepted by all except the most intransigeant wing of the protectionists.

Though the South Carolina Convention met again in 1833 and formally declared Jackson's measures of enforcement null and void, this defiance was an empty one. None of the states to which South Carolina appealed had replied favorably; the attempt at protecting minority interests by "peaceable secession" was postponed until 1861.

Webster's second speech on the Foote Resolution was delivered January 20, 1830. It is reprinted here from Volume III of Webster's *Works* (Boston, 1857). The South Carolina Ordinance of Nullification was passed November 24, 1832. It was accompanied by an Address to the People of South Carolina and one to the People of the United States. It is the latter which is here reprinted; it is taken from the *Journal of the Convention of the People of South Carolina* (Columbia, 1833).

The Second Speech on the Foote Resolution, 1830

BY DANIEL WEBSTER

Sir, the human mind is so constituted, that the merits of both sides of a controversy appear very clear, and very palpable, to those who respectively espouse them; and both sides usually grow clearer as the controversy advances. South Carolina sees unconstitutionality in the tariff; she sees oppression there also, and she sees danger. Pennsylvania, with a vision not less sharp, looks at the same tariff, and sees no such thing in it; she sees it all constitutional, all useful, all safe. The faith of South Carolina is strengthened by opposition, and she now not only sees, but *resolves*, that the tariff is palpably unconstitutional, oppressive, and dangerous; but Pennsylvania, not to be behind her neighbors, and equally willing to strengthen her own faith by a confident asseveration, *resolves*, also, and gives to every warm affirmative of South Carolina, a plain, downright, Pennsylvania negative. South Carolina, to show the strength and unity of her opinion, brings her assembly to a unanimity, within seven voices; Pennsylvania, not to be outdone in this respect any more than in others, reduces her dissentient fraction to a single vote. Now, Sir, again, I ask the gentleman, What is to be done? Are these States both right? Is he bound to consider them both right? If not, which is in the wrong? or rather, which has the best right to decide? And if he, and if I, are not to know what the Constitution means, and what it is, till those two State legislatures, and the twenty-two others, shall agree in its construction, what have we sworn to, when we have sworn to maintain it? I was forcibly struck, Sir, with one reflection, as the gentleman went on in his speech. He quoted Mr. Madison's resolutions, to prove that a State may interfere, in a case of deliberate, palpable, and dangerous exercise of a power not granted. The honorable member supposes the tariff law to be such an exercise of power; and that consequently a case has arisen in which the State may, if it see fit, interfere by its own law. Now it so happens, nevertheless, that Mr. Madison deems this same tariff law quite constitutional. Instead of a clear and palpable violation, it is, in his judgment, no violation at all. So that, while they use his authority for a hypothetical case, they reject it in the very case before them. All this, Sir, shows the inherent futility, I had almost used a stronger word, of conceding this power of interference to the State, and then attempting to secure it from abuse by imposing qualifications of which the States

themselves are to judge. One of two things is true; either the laws of the Union are beyond the discretion and beyond the control of the States; or else we have no constitution of general government, and are thrust back again to the days of the Confederation.

Let me here say, Sir, that if the gentleman's doctrine had been received and acted upon in New England, in the times of the embargo and non-intercourse, we should probably not now have been here. The government would very likely have gone to pieces, and crumbled into dust. No stronger case can ever arise than existed under those laws; no States can ever entertain a clearer conviction than the New England States then entertained; and if they had been under the influence of that heresy of opinion, as I must call it, which the honorable member espouses, this Union would, in all probability, have been scattered to the four winds. I ask the gentleman, therefore, to apply his principles to that case; I ask him to come forth and declare, whether, in his opinion, the New England States would have been justified in interfering to break up the embargo system under the conscientious opinions which they held upon it? Had they a right to annul that law? Does he admit or deny? If what is thought palpably unconstitutional in South Carolina justifies that State in arresting the progress of the law, tell me whether that which was thought palpably unconstitutional also in Massachusetts would have justified her in doing the same thing. Sir, I deny the whole doctrine. It has not a foot of ground in the Constitution to stand on. No public man of reputation ever advanced it in Massachusetts in the warmest times, or could maintain himself upon it there at any time.

I wish now, Sir, to make a remark upon the Virginia resolutions of 1798. I cannot undertake to say how these resolutions were understood by those who passed them. Their language is not a little indefinite. In the case of the exercise by Congress of a dangerous power not granted to them, the resolutions assert the right, on the part of the State, to interfere and arrest the progress of the evil. This is susceptible of more than one interpretation. It may mean no more than that the States may interfere by complaint and remonstrance, or by proposing to the people an alteration of the Federal Constitution. This would all be quite unobjectionable. Or it may be that no more is meant than to assert the general right of revolution, as against all governments, in cases of intolerable oppression. This no one doubts, and this, in my opinion, is all that he who framed the resolutions could have meant by it; for I shall not readily believe that he was ever of opinion that a State, under the Constitution and in conformity with it, could, upon the ground of her own opinion of its unconstitutionality, however clear and palpable she might think the case, annul a law of Congress, so far as it should operate on herself, by her own legislative power.

I must now beg to ask, Sir, Whence is this supposed right of the States derived? Where do they find the power to interfere with the laws of the Union? Sir, the opinion which the honorable gentleman maintains is a notion founded in a total misapprehension, in my judgment, of the origin of this government, and of the foundation on which it stands. I hold it to be a popular government, erected by the people; those who administer it, responsible to the people; and itself capable of being amended and modified, just as the people may choose it should be. It is as popular, just as truly emanating from the people, as the State governments. It is created for one purpose; the State governments for another. It has its own powers; they have theirs. There is no more authority with them to arrest the operation of a law of Congress, than with Congress to arrest the operation of their laws. We are here to administer a Constitution, emanating immediately from the people, and trusted by them to our administration. It is not the creature of the State governments. It is of no moment to the argument, that certain acts of the State legislatures are necessary to fill our seats in this body. That is not one of their original State powers, a part of the sovereignty of the State. It is a duty which the people, by the Constitution itself, have imposed on the State legislatures; and which they might have left to be performed elsewhere, if they had seen fit. So they have left the choice of President with electors; but all this does not affect the proposition that this whole government, President, Senate, and House of Representatives, is a popular government. It leaves it still all its popular character. The governor of a State (in some of the States) is chosen, not directly by the people, but by those who are chosen by the people, for the purpose of performing, among other duties, that of electing a governor. Is the government of the State, on that account, not a popular government? This government, Sir, is the independent offspring of the popular will. It is not the creature of State legislatures; nay, more, if the whole truth must be told, the people brought it into existence, established it, and have hitherto supported it, for the very purpose, amongst others, of imposing certain salutary restraints on State sovereignties. The States cannot now make war; they cannot contract alliances; they cannot make, each for itself, separate regulations of commerce; they cannot lay imposts; they cannot coin money. If this Constitution, Sir, be the creature of State legislatures, it must be admitted that it has obtained a strange control over the volitions of its creators.

The people, then, Sir, erected this government. They gave it a Constitution, and in that Constitution they have enumerated the powers which they bestow on it. They have made it a limited government. They have defined its authority. They have restrained it to the exercise of such powers as are granted; and all others, they declare, are reserved to the States or the people. But, Sir, they have not stopped here. If they had, they would have accomplished but half their work. No definition can be so clear, as to avoid possibility of doubt; no limitation so precise, as to exclude all uncertainty. Who, then, shall construe this grant of the people? Who shall interpret their will, where it may be supposed they have left it doubtful? With whom do they repose this ultimate right of deciding on the powers of the government? Sir, they have settled all this in the fullest manner. They have left it with the government itself, in its appropriate branches. Sir, the very chief end, the main design, for which the whole Constitution was framed and adopted, was to establish a government that should not be obliged to act through State agency, or depend on State opinion and State discretion. The people had had quite enough of that kind of government under the Confederation. Under that system, the legal action, the application of law to individuals, belonged exclusively to the States. Congress could only recommend; their acts were not of binding force, till the States had adopted and sanctioned them. Are we in that condition still? Are we yet at the mercy of State discretion and State construction? Sir, if we are, then vain will be our attempt to maintain the Constitution under which we sit.

But, Sir, the people have wisely provided, in the Constitution itself, a proper, suitable mode and tribunal for settling questions of constitutional law. There are in the Constitution grants of powers to Congress, and restrictions on these powers. There are, also, prohibitions on the States. Some authority must, therefore, necessarily exist, having the ultimate jurisdiction to fix and ascertain the interpretation of these grants, restrictions, and prohibitions. The Constitution has itself pointed out, ordained, and established that authority. How has it accomplished this great and essential end? By declaring, Sir, that *"the Constitution, and the laws of the United States made in pursuance thereof, shall be the supreme law of the land, any thing in the constitution or laws of any State to the contrary notwithstanding."*

This, Sir, was the first great step. By this the supremacy of the Constitution and laws of the United States is declared. The people so will it. No State law is to be valid which comes in conflict with the Constitution, or any law of the United States passed in pursuance of it. But who shall decide this question of interference? To whom lies the last appeal? This, Sir, the Constitution itself decides also, by declaring, *"that the judicial power shall extend to all cases arising under the Constitution and laws of the United States."* These two provisions cover the whole ground. They are, in truth, the keystone of the arch! With these it is a government; without them it is a confederation. In pursuance of these clear and express provisions, Congress established, at its very first session, in the judicial act, a mode for carrying them into full effect, and for bringing all questions of constitutional power to the final decision of the Supreme Court. It then, Sir, became a government. It then had the means of self-protection; and but for this, it would, in all probability, have been now among things which are past. Having constituted the government, and declared its powers, the people have further said, that, since somebody must decide on the extent of these powers, the government shall itself decide; subject, always, like other popular governments, to its responsibility to the people. And now, Sir, I repeat, how is it that a State legislature acquires any power to interfere? Who, or what, gives them the right to say to the people, "We, who are your agents and servants for one purpose, will undertake to decide, that your other agents and servants, appointed by you for another purpose, have transcended the authority you gave them!" The reply would be, I think, not impertinent,—"Who made you a judge over another's servants? To their own masters they stand or fall."

Sir, I deny this power of State legislatures altogether. It cannot stand the test of examination. Gentlemen may say, that, in an extreme case, a State government might protect the people from intolerable oppression. Sir, in such a case, the people might protect themselves, without the aid of the State governments. Such a case warrants revolution. It must make, when it comes, a law for itself. A nullifying act of a State legislature cannot alter the case, nor make resistance any more lawful. In maintaining these sentiments, Sir, I am but asserting the rights of the people. I state what they have declared, and insist on their right to declare it. They have chosen to repose this power in the general government, and I think it my duty to support it, like other constitutional powers.

For myself, Sir, I do not admit the competency of South Carolina, or any other State, to prescribe my constitutional duty; or to settle between me and the people, the validity of laws of Congress, for which I have voted. I decline her umpirage. I have not sworn to support the Constitution according to her construction of its clauses. I have not stipulated, by my oath of office or otherwise, to come under any responsibility, except to the people, and those whom they have appointed to pass upon the question, whether laws, supported by my votes, conform to the Constitution of the country. And, Sir, if we look to the general nature of the case, could any thing have been more preposterous, than to make a government for the whole Union, and yet leave its powers subject, not to one interpretation, but to thirteen or twenty-four interpretations? Instead of one tribunal, established by all, responsible to all, with power to decide for all, shall constitutional questions be left to four-and-twenty popular bodies, each at liberty to decide for itself, and none bound to respect the decisions of others; and each at liberty, too, to give a new construction on every new election of its own members? Would any thing, with such a principle in it, or rather with such a destitution of all principle, be fit to be called a government? No, Sir. It should not be denominated a Constitution. It should be called, rather, a collection of topics for everlasting controversy; heads of debate for a disputatious people. It would not be a government. It would not be adequate to any practical good, or fit for any country to live under.

To avoid all possibility of being misunderstood, allow me to repeat again, in the fullest manner, that I claim no powers for the government by forced or unfair construction. I admit that it is a government of strictly limited powers; of enumerated, specified, and particularized powers; and that whatsoever is not granted, is withheld. But notwithstanding all this, and however the grant of powers may be expressed, its limit and extent may yet, in some cases, admit of doubt; and the general government would be good for nothing, it would be incapable of long existing, if some mode had not been provided in which those doubts, as they should arise, might be peaceably, but authoritatively, solved.

And now, Mr. President, let me run the honorable gentleman's doctrine a little into its practical application. Let us look at his probable *modus operandi*. If a thing can be done, an ingenious man can tell *how* it is to be done, and I wish to be informed *how* this State interference is to be put in practice, without violence, bloodshed, and rebellion. We will take the existing case of the tariff law. South Carolina is said to have made up her opinion upon it. If we do not repeal it (as we probably shall not), she will then apply to the case the remedy of her doctrine. She will, we must suppose, pass a law of her legislature, declaring the several acts of Congress, usually called the tariff laws, null and void, so far as they respect South Carolina, or the citizens thereof. So far, all is a paper transaction, and easy enough. But the collector at Charleston is collecting the duties imposed by these tariff laws. He, therefore, must be stopped. The collector will seize the goods if the tariff duties are not paid. The State authorities will undertake their rescue, the marshal, with his posse, will come to the collector's aid, and here the contest begins. The militia of the State will be called out to sustain the nullifying act. They will march, Sir, under a very gallant leader; for I believe the honorable member himself commands the militia of that part of the State. He will raise the NULLIFYING ACT on his standard, and spread it out as his banner! It will have a preamble, setting forth, that the tariff laws are palpable, deliberate, and dangerous violations of the Constitution! He will proceed, with this banner flying, to the custom-house in Charleston,

> "All the while,
> Sonorous metal blowing martial sounds."

Arrived at the custom-house, he will tell the collector that he must collect no more duties under any of the tariff laws. This he will be somewhat puzzled to say, by the way, with a grave countenance, considering what hand South Carolina herself had in that of 1816. But, Sir, the collector would not, probably, desist, at his bidding. He would show him the law of Congress, the treasury instruction, and his own oath of office. He would say, he should perform his duty, come what come might.

Here would ensue a pause; for they say that a certain stillness precedes the tempest. The trumpeter would hold his breath awhile, and before all this military array should fall on the custom-house, collector, clerks, and all, it is very probable some of those composing it would request of their gallant commander-in-chief to be informed a little upon the point of law; for they have, doubtless, a just respect for his opinions as a lawyer, as well

as for his bravery as a soldier. They know he has read Blackstone and the Constitution, as well as Turenne and Vauban. They would ask him, therefore, something concerning their rights in this matter. They would inquire, whether it was not somewhat dangerous to resist a law of the United States. What would be the nature of their offence, they would wish to learn, if they, by military force and array, resisted the execution in Carolina of a law of the United States, and it should turn out, after all, that the law *was constitutional?* He would answer, of course, Treason. No lawyer could give any other answer. John Fries, he would tell them, had learned that, some years ago. How, then, they would ask, do you propose to defend us? We are not afraid of bullets, but treason has a way of taking people off that we do not much relish. How do you propose to defend us? "Look at my floating banner," he would reply; "see there the *nullifying law!*" Is it your opinion, gallant commander, they would then say, that, if we should be indicted for treason, that same floating banner of yours would make a good plea in bar? "South Carolina is a sovereign State," he would reply. That is true; but would the judge admit our plea? "These tariff laws," he would repeat, "are unconstitutional, palpably, deliberately, dangerously." That may all be so; but if the tribunal should not happen to be of that opinion, shall we swing for it? We are ready to die for our country, but it is rather an awkward business, this dying without touching the ground! After all, that is a sort of hemp tax worse than any part of the tariff.

Mr. President, the honorable gentleman would be in a dilemma, like that of another great general. He would have a knot before him which he could not untie. He must cut it with his sword. He must say to his followers, "Defend yourselves with your bayonets"; and this is war,—civil war.

Direct collision, therefore, between force and force, is the unavoidable result of that remedy for the revision of unconstitutional laws which the gentleman contends for. It must happen in the very first case to which it is applied. Is not this the plain result? To resist by force the execution of a law, generally, is treason. Can the courts of the United States take notice of the indulgence of a State to commit treason? The common saying, that a State cannot commit treason herself, is nothing to the purpose. Can she authorize others to do it? If John Fries had produced an act of Pennsylvania, annulling the law of Congress, would it have helped his case? Talk about it as we will, these doctrines go the length of revolution. They are incompatible with any peaceable administration of the government. They lead directly to disunion and civil commotion; and therefore it is, that at their commencement, when they are first found to be maintained by respectable men, and in a tangible form, I enter my public protest against them all.

The honorable gentleman argues, that if this government be the sole judge of the extent of its own powers, whether that right of judging be in Congress or the Supreme Court, it equally subverts State sovereignty. This the gentleman sees, or thinks he sees, although he cannot perceive how the right of judging, in this matter, if left to the exercise of State legislatures, has any tendency to subvert the government of the Union. The gentleman's opinion may be, that the right *ought not* to have been lodged with the general government; he may like better such a constitution as we should have under the right of State interference; but I ask him to meet me on the plain matter of fact. I ask him to meet me on the Constitution itself. I ask him if the power is not found there, clearly and visibly found there?

But, Sir, what is this danger, and what are the grounds of it? Let it be remembered, that the Constitution of the United States is not unalterable. It is to continue in its present form no longer than the people who established it shall choose to continue it. If they shall become convinced that they have made an injudicious or inexpedient partition and distribution of power between the State governments and the general government, they can alter that distribution at will.

If any thing be found in the national Constitution, either by original provision or subsequent interpretation, which ought not to be in it, the people know how to get rid of it. If any construction, unacceptable to them, be established, so as to become practically a part of the Constitution, they will amend it, at their own sovereign pleasure. But while the people choose to maintain it as it is, while they are satisfied with it, and refuse to change it, who has given, or who can give, to the State legislatures a right to alter it, either by interference, construction, or otherwise? Gentlemen do not seem to recollect that the people have any power to do any thing for themselves. They imagine there is no safety for them, any longer than they are under the close guardianship of the State legislatures. Sir, the people have not trusted their safety, in regard to the general Constitution, to these hands. They have required other security, and taken other bonds. They have chosen to trust themselves, first, to the plain words of the instrument, and to such construction as the government themselves, in doubtful cases, should put on their own powers, under their oaths of office, and subject to their responsibility to them; just as the people of a State trust their own State governments with a similar power. Secondly, they have reposed their trust in the efficacy of frequent elections, and in their own power to remove their own servants and agents whenever they see cause. Thirdly, they have reposed trust in the judicial power, which, in order that it might be trustworthy, they have made as respectable, as disinterested, and as independent as was practicable. Fourthly, they have seen fit to rely, in case of necessity, or high expediency, on their known and admitted power to alter or amend the Constitution, peaceably and quietly, whenever experience shall point out defects or imperfections. And, finally, the people of the United States have at no time, in no way, directly or indirectly, authorized any State legislature to construe or interpret *their* high instrument of government; much less, to interfere, by their own power, to arrest its course and operation.

If, Sir, the people in these respects had done otherwise than they have done, their constitution could neither have been preserved, nor would it have been worth preserving. And if its plain provisions shall now be disregarded, and these new doctrines interpolated in it, it will become as feeble and helpless a being as its enemies, whether early or more recent, could possibly desire. It will exist in every State but as a poor dependent on State permission. It must borrow leave to be; and will be, no longer than State pleasure, or State discretion, sees fit to grant the indulgence, and to prolong its poor existence.

But, Sir, although there are fears, there are hopes also. The people have preserved this, their own chosen Constitution, for forty years, and have seen their happiness, prosperity, and renown grow with its growth, and strengthen with its strength. They are now, generally, strongly attached to it. Overthrown by direct assault, it cannot be; evaded, undermined, NULLIFIED, it will not be, if we, and those who shall succeed us here, as agents and representatives of the people, shall conscientiously and vigilantly discharge the two great branches of our public trust, faithfully to preserve, and wisely to administer it.

Mr. President, I have thus stated the reasons of my dissent to the doctrines which have been advanced and maintained. I am conscious of having detained you and the Senate much too long. I was drawn into the debate with no previous deliberation, such as is suited to the discussion of so grave and important a subject. But it is a subject of which my heart is full, and I have not been willing to suppress the utterance of its spontaneous sentiments. I cannot, even now, persuade myself to relinquish it, without expressing once more my deep conviction, that, since it respects nothing less than the Union of the States, it is of most vital and essential importance to the public happiness. I profess, Sir, in my career hitherto, to have kept steadily in view the prosperity and honor of the whole country, and the preservation of our Federal Union. It is to that Union we owe our safety at home, and our consideration and dignity abroad. It is to that Union that we are chiefly indebted for whatever makes us most proud of our country. That Union we reached only by the discipline of our virtues in the severe school of adversity. It had its origin in the necessities of disordered finance, prostrate commerce, and ruined credit. Under its benign influences, these great interests immediately awoke, as from the dead, and sprang forth with newness of life. Every year of its duration has teemed with fresh proofs of its utility and its blessings; and although our territory has stretched out wider and wider, and our population spread farther and farther, they have not outrun its protection or its benefits. It has been to us all a copious fountain of national, social, and personal happiness.

I have not allowed myself, Sir, to look beyond the Union, to see what might lie hidden in the dark recess behind. I have not coolly weighed the chances of preserving liberty when the bonds that unite us together shall be broken asunder. I have not accustomed myself to hang over the precipice of disunion, to see whether, with my short sight, I can fathom the depth of the abyss below; nor could I regard him as a safe counsellor in the affairs of this government, whose thoughts should be mainly bent on considering, not how the Union may be best preserved, but how tolerable might be the condition of the people when it should be broken up and destroyed. While the Union lasts, we have high, exciting, gratifying prospects spread out before us, for us and our children. Beyond that I seek not to penetrate the veil. God grant that in my day, at least, that curtain may not rise! God grant that on my vision never may be opened what lies behind! When my eyes shall be turned to behold for the last time the sun in heaven, may I not see him shining on the broken and dishonored fragments of a once glorious Union; on States dissevered, discordant, belligerent; on a land rent with civil feuds, or drenched, it may be, in fraternal blood! Let their last feeble and lingering glance rather behold the gorgeous ensign of the republic, now known and honored throughout the earth, still full high advanced, its arms and trophies streaming in their original lustre, not a stripe erased or polluted, nor a single star obscured, bearing for its motto, no such miserable interrogatory as "What is all this worth?" nor those other words of delusion and folly, "Liberty first and Union afterwards"; but everywhere, spread all over in characters of living light, blazing on all its ample folds, as they float over the sea and over the land, and in every wind under the whole heavens, that other sentiment, dear to every true American heart,—Liberty *and* Union, now and for ever, one and inseparable!

Address to the People of the United States on the South Carolina Ordinance of Nullification, 1832

To the People of Massachusetts, Virginia, New York, Pennsylvania, North Carolina, Maryland, Connecticut, Vermont, New Hampshire, Maine, New Jersey, Georgia, Delaware, Rhode Island, Kentucky, Tennessee, Ohio, Louisiana, Indiana, Mississippi, Illinois, Alabama and Missouri.

We, the People of South Carolina, assembled in Convention, have solemnly and deliberately declared, in our paramount sovereign capacity, that the act of Congress approved the 19th day of May 1828, and the act approved the 14th July 1832, altering and amending the several acts imposing duties on imports, are unconstitutional, and therefore, absolutely void, and of no binding force within the limits of this State; and for the purpose of carrying this declaration into full and complete effect, we have invested the Legislature with ample powers, and made it the duty of all the functionaries and all the citizens of the State, on their allegiance, to co-operate in enforcing the aforesaid declaration.

In resorting to this important measure, to which we have been impelled by the most sacred of all duties which a free people can owe, either to the memory of their ancestors or to the claims of their posterity, we feel that it is due to the intimate political relation which exists between South Carolina and the other States of this confederacy, that we should present a clear and distinct exposition of the principles on which we have acted, and of the causes by which we have been reluctantly constrained to assume this attitude of sovereign resistance in relation to the usurpations of the Federal Government.

For this purpose, it will be necessary to state, briefly, what we conceive to be the relation created by the Federal Constitution, between the States and the General Government; and also what we conceive to be the true character and practical operation of the system of protecting duties, as it effects our rights, our interests and our liberties.

We hold then, that on their separation from the Crown of Great Britain, the several Colonies became free and independent States, each enjoying the separate and independent right of self government; and that no authority can be exercised over them or within their limits, but by their consent, respectively given as States. It is equally true, that the Constitution of the United States is a compact formed between the several States, acting as sovereign communities; that the government created by it is a joint agency of the States, appointed to execute the powers enumerated and granted by that instrument; that all its acts not intentionally authorised are of themselves essentially null and void, and that the States have the right, in the same sovereign capacity in which they adopted the Federal Constitution, to pronounce, in the last resort, authoritative judgment on the usurpations of the Federal Government; and to adopt such measures as they may deem necessary and expedient to arrest the operation of the unconstitutional acts of that Government, within their respective limits. Such we deem to be the inherent rights of the States—rights, in the very nature of things, absolutely inseparable from sovereignty. Nor is the duty of a State, to arrest an unconstitutional and oppressive act of the Federal Government less imperative, than the right is incontestible. Each State, by ratifying the Federal Constitution, and becoming a member of the confederacy, contracted an obligation to "protect and defend" that instrument, as well by resisting the usurpations of the Federal Government, as by sustaining that government in the exercise of the powers actually conferred upon it. And the obligation of the oath which is imposed, under the Constitution, on every functionary of the States, to "preserve, protect, and defend" the Federal Constitution, as clearly comprehends the duty of protecting and defending it against the usurpations of the Federal Government, as that of protecting and defending it against violation in any other form or from any other quarter.

It is true, that in ratifying the Federal Constitution, the States placed a large and important portion of the rights of their citizens under the joint protection of all the States, with a view to their more effectual security; but it is not less true that they reserved a portion still larger and not less important under their own immediate guardianship, and in relation to which their original obligation to protect their citizens, from whatever quarter assailed, remains unchanged and undiminished.

But clear and undoubted as we regard the right, and sacred as we regard the duty of the States to interpose their sovereign power for the purpose of protecting their citizens from the unconstitutional and oppressive acts of the Federal Government, yet we are as clearly of the opinion that nothing short of that high moral and political necessity, which results from acts of usurpation, subversive of the rights and liberties of the people, should induce a member of this confederacy to resort to this interposition. Such however, is the melancholy and painful necessity under which we have declared the acts of Congress imposing protecting duties, null and void within the limits of South Carolina. The spirit and the principles which animated your ancestors and ours in the councils and in the fields of their common glory, forbid us to submit any longer to a system of Legislation now become the established policy of the Federal Government, by which we are reduced to a condition of colonial vassalage, in all its aspects more oppressive and intolerable than that from which our common ancestors relieved themselves by the war of the revolution. There is no right which enters more essentially into a just conception of liberty, than that of the free and unrestricted use of the productions of our industry wherever they can be most advantageously exchanged, whether in foreign or domestic markets. South Carolina produces, almost exclusively, agricultural staples, which derive their principal value from the demand for them in foreign countries. Under these circumstances, her natural markets are abroad; and restrictive duties imposed upon her intercourse with those markets, diminish the exchangeable value of her productions very nearly to the full extent of those duties.

Under a system of free trade, the aggregate crop of South Carolina could be exchanged for a larger quantity of manufactures, by at least one third, than it can be now exchanged for under the protecting system. It is no less evident, that the value of that crop is diminished by the protecting system very nearly, if not precisely, to the extent that the aggregate quantity of manufactures which can be obtained for it, is diminished. It is, indeed, strictly philosophically true, that the quantity of consumable commodities which can be obtained for the cotton and rice annually produced by the industry of the State, is the precise measure of their aggregate value. But for the prevalent and habitual error of confounding the money price with the exchangeable value of our agricultural staples these propositions would be regarded as self evident. If the protecting duties were repealed, one hundred bales of cotton or one hundred barrels of rice would purchase as large a quantity of manufactures, as one hundred and fifty will now purchase. The annual income of the State, its means of purchasing and consuming the necessaries and comforts and luxuries of life, would be increased in a corresponding degree.

Almost the entire crop of South Carolina, amounting annually to more than six millions of dollars, is ultimately exchanged either for foreign manufactures, subject to protecting duties, or for similar domestic manufactures. The *natural* value of the crop would be all the manufactures which we could obtain for it, under a system of unrestricted commerce. The *artificial* value, produced by the unjust and unconstitutional Legislation of Congress, is only such part of those manufactures as will remain after paying a duty of fifty per cent to the Government, or, to speak with more precision, to the Northern manufacturers. To make this obvious to the humblest comprehension, let it be supposed that the whole of the present crop should be exchanged, by the planters themselves, for those foreign manufactures, for which it is destined, by the inevitable course of trade, to be ultimately exchanged, either by themselves or their agents. Let it be also assumed, in conformity with the facts of the case, that New Jersey, for example, produces, of the very same description of manufactures, a quantity equal to that which is purchased by the cotton crop of South Carolina. We have, then, two States of the same confederacy, bound to bear an equal share of the burthens, and entitled to enjoy an equal share of the benefits of the common government, with precisely the same quantity of productions, of the same quality and kind, produced by their lawful industry. We appeal to your candor, and to your sense of justice, to say whether South Carolina has not a title as sacred and indefeasable, to the full and undiminished enjoyment of these productions of her industry, acquired by the combined operations of agriculture and commerce, as New Jersey can have to the like enjoyment of similar productions of her industry, acquired by the process of manufacture? Upon no principle of human reason or justice, can any discrimination be drawn be-

tween the titles of South Carolina and New Jersey to these productions of their capital and labor. Yet what is the discrimination actually made by the unjust, unconstitutional and partial Legislation of Congress? A duty, on an average, of fifty per cent, is imposed upon the productions of South Carolina, while no duty at all is imposed upon the similar productions of New Jersey! The inevitable result is, that the manufactures thus lawfully acquired by the honest industry of South Carolina, are worth, annually, three millions of dollars less to her citizens than the very same quantity of the very same description of manufactures are worth to the citizens of New Jersey—a difference of value produced exclusively by the operation of the protecting system. . . .

Having now presented, for the consideration of the Federal Government and our confederate States, the fixed and final determination of this State, in relation to the protecting system, it remains for us to submit a plan of taxation, in which we would be willing to acquiesce, in a spirit of liberal concession, provided we are met in due time, and in a becoming spirit, by the States interested in the protection of manufactures.

We believe, that upon every just and equitable principle of taxation, the whole list of protected articles should be imported free of all duty, and that the revenue derived from import duties, should be raised exclusively from the unprotected articles; or that whenever a duty is imposed upon protected articles imported, an excise duty of the same rate, should be imposed upon all similar articles, manufactured in the United States. This would be as near an approach to perfect equality as could possibly be made, in a system of indirect taxation. No substantial reason can be given for subjecting manufactures, obtained from abroad, in exchange for the productions of South Carolina, to the smallest duty, even for revenue, which would not show that similar manufactures made in the United States, should be subject to the very same rate of duty. The former, not less than the latter, are, to every rational intent, the productions of domestic industry, and the mode of acquiring the one, is as lawful and more conducive to the public prosperity, than that of acquiring the other.

But we are willing to make a large offering to preserve the Union; and with a distinct declaration that it is a concession on our part, we will consent that the same rate of duty may be imposed upon the protected articles that shall be imposed upon the unprotected, provided that no more revenue be raised than is necessary to meet the demands of the Government for Constitutional purposes; and provided also, that a duty, substantially uniform, be imposed upon all foreign imports.

It is obvious, that even under this arrangement, the manufacturing States would have a decided advantage over the planting States. For it is demonstrably evident that, as communities, the manufacturing States would bear no part of the burthens of Federal Taxation, so far as the revenue should be derived from protected articles. The earnestness with which their representatives seek to increase the duties on these articles, is conclusive proof that those duties are bounties, and not burthens, to their constituents. As at least two-thirds of the federal revenue would be raised from protected articles, under the proposed modification of the Tariff, the manufacturing States would be entirely exempted from all participation in that proportion of the public burthens.

Under these circumstances, we cannot permit ourselves to believe, for a moment, that in a crisis marked by such portentous and fearful omens, those States can hesitate in acceding to this arrangement, when they perceive that it will be the means, and possibly the only means, of restoring the broken harmony of this great confederacy. They, most assuredly, have the strongest of human inducements, aside from all considerations of justice, to adjust this controversy, without pushing it to extremities. This can be accomplished only by the proposed modification of the Tariff, or by the call of a general Convention of all the States. If South Carolina should be driven out of the Union, all the other planting States, and some of the Western States, would follow by an almost absolute necessity. Can it be believed that Georgia, Mississippi, Tennessee, and even Kentucky, would continue to pay a tribute of fifty per cent. upon their consumption, to the Northern States, for the privilege of being united to them, when they could receive all their supplies through the ports of South Carolina, without paying a single cent of tribute?

The separation of South Carolina would inevitably produce a general dissolution of the Union; and as a necessary consequence, the protecting system, with all its pecuniary bounties to the Northern States, and its pecuniary burthens upon the Southern States, would be utterly overthrown and demolished, involving the ruin of thousands and hundreds of thousands in the manufacturing States.

By these powerful considerations connected with their own pecuniary interests, we beseech them to pause and contemplate the disastrous consequences which will certainly result from an obstinate perseverance on their part, in maintaining the protecting system. With them, it is a question merely of pecuniary interest, connected with no shadow of right, and involving no principle of liberty. With us, it is a question involving our most sacred rights—those very rights which our common ancestors left to us as a common inheritance, purchased by their common toils, and consecrated by their blood. It is a question of liberty on the one hand, and slavery on the other. If we submit to this system of unconstitutional oppression, we shall voluntarily sink into slavery, and transmit that ignominious inheritance to our children. We will not, we cannot, we dare not, submit to this degradation; and our resolve is fixed and unalterable, that a protecting tariff shall be no longer enforced within the limits of South Carolina. We stand upon the principles of everlasting justice, and no human power shall drive us from our position.

We have not the slightest apprehension that the General Government will attempt to force this system upon us by military power. We have warned our brethren of the consequences of such an attempt.—But if, notwithstanding, such a course of madness should be pursued, we here solemnly declare, that this system of oppression shall never prevail in South Carolina, until none but slaves are left to submit to it. We would infinitely prefer that the territory of the State should be the cemetery of freemen, than the habitation of slaves. Actuated by these principles, and animated by these sentiments, we will cling to the pillars of the temple of our liberties, and if it must fall, we will perish amidst the ruins.

THE SECOND BANK OF THE UNITED STATES

THE SECOND BANK OF THE UNITED STATES had been chartered for twenty years in 1816. After an unfortunate start, the bank achieved a degree of business success and at the same time began to make enemies. Its privileges, its practice of enforcing specie payment by the presentation of local banknotes for redemption, and the suspicion of political activity by some of its branches all created hostility, particularly in the West and South. Opposition to a national bank was a key tenet of Jeffersonian Democracy—although it was a Democratic administration which had granted the Second Bank's charter—and distrust of all paper money was present and active in the very areas which had least specie as a basis for currency. Personal losses through bank failures and worthless banknotes may have been behind the opposition of certain congressional leaders; also, the support won by the Jacksonians' struggle against the bank from urban artisans and workingmen of the East rested on so simple a fact as the experience of being paid in money that could not be spent except at a discount. In any event, the opponents of the bank were frequently "hard money" men.

Whatever the reasoning Andrew Jackson followed, his first message to Congress in 1829 had suggested that it consider the propriety of renewing the bank charter, since both the expediency and the Constitutionality of the institution were in doubt. The bank's supporters considered this a challenge. They took up the gage by assigning the pertinent portion of the President's message to a Senate committee, which made a favorable report that was spread broadcast by friends of the bank.

On the second of February, 1831, Senator Thomas Hart Benton (1782–1858) of Missouri attacked not only the Second Bank of the United States but the whole system of maintaining a connection between the Federal government and any bank of issue. Benton asked leave to introduce a resolution denying renewal of the bank's charter and presented the Jacksonians' case against the bank. He began his speech in support of that resolution by rebuking those who declared discussion premature, since the bank's twenty-year charter had five years still to run. The bank's friends did not consider favorable discussion premature, for they had already given wide distribution to the favorable report of the Senate committee, a report which the Senate itself had not had time to debate or accept. This in itself proved how little time remained; proponents of the bank meant to force renewal of the

charter before the people could be aroused to the issue. Benton then proceeded to the attack: if the bank's stockholders declared themselves injured by the loss of the charter, they would merely be demonstrating how all privileged persons tend "to mistake privilege for right." But it was the power of the bank that roused Benton's real wrath. As custodian of government funds, the bank had free use of federal balances; the Federal government was, in effect, its partner, lending it a profitable prestige. Since its notes alone were legally receivable in payment for United States property and debts, any banknotes it refused to accept at par could be excluded from such payment—an important matter at a time when the United States was selling millions of acres of land each year. The Bank of the United States, in fact, could and did exclude the notes of Southern and Western banks from circulation even while its demands drained specie from those sections. It was empowered to hold real estate and had become a great landowner. By reason of its corporate privileges, the bank as landlord could evade state laws against land monopoly through entails; furthermore, those privileges enabled its numerous foreign stockholders to evade state taxation and state laws regulating land tenure.

Even worse than these oppressions, actual and potential, was the character of the charter, by which the bank was exempted from prosecution for violation of the the charter unless the President or Congress consented to such action—a fact sufficient to put the bank in politics and keep it there. Further, the bank was a monopoly, for Congress had renounced the right to charter another bank, thus copying a privilege given the Bank of England in the reign of Queen Anne "when a Tory Queen, a Tory Ministry and a Tory Parliament . . . were ruling and riding over the prostrate liberties of England."

Benton turned from monopoly to the Constitution to support the contention that the Federal government should give no countenance to paper money: specie was the medium of exchange proper to a republic. It is not "currency" but "coin" which the Constitution authorized Congress to regulate: "to construe coin, that is to say metallic money, melted, cast, and stamped, into paper notes printed and written" is "to assume a power of life and death over the Constitution; a power to dethrone and murder one of its true and lawful words, and to set up a bastard pretender in its place."

If the bank were rechartered with its present powers, Benton concluded, the entire economic life of the United States would depend on the "owners of this imperial stock," great foreign capitalists and the native money lords who lived in the eastern cities which, for the past forty years, had been "the lion's den of Southern and Western money."

Benton's request for leave to introduce his resolution was denied by a vote of 23 to 30, and no Senator troubled to answer his speech. But though debate stopped, Benton had carried out his purpose. As he wrote later, his "was a speech to be read by the people—the masses—the millions; and was conceived and delivered for that purpose, and was read by them; and has been complimented since, as having crippled the bank, and given it the wound of which it afterward died; but not within the year and a day which would make the slayer responsible for the homicide." (*Thirty Years' View*, New York, 1854, Vol. I, p. 204.)

Although the speech was not quite the opening gun in the fight, it presents most of the arguments and illuminates many of the prejudices which were finally to defeat the bank. The bank was a monopoly owned by foreigners and exploiting the government and people of the United States. If unchecked, it would go on to control the government as well as to use its money without payment.

The bank's supporters were not content with attempting to smother debate and to meet Jackson's challenge by indirect means. By November, 1831, both Clay and Webster advised the bank to apply for a renewal of its charter

before the President should be reelected. Democratic partisans of the bank warned against that course: if Jackson were "pressed into a corner, neither McLane nor myself will answer for the consequences," wrote Senator Smith of Maryland.

Faced with this division of opinion among his friends, Nicholas Biddle (1786–1844), wit, politician, poet, and financier, sent an agent of his own to Washington and increased the effort to win public favor for the bank of which he was president. Aggressive measures would assure a veto, moderates warned, but Biddle took such measures, nevertheless. In May, 1832, Biddle went to Washington himself and Webster declared it was his influence which finally won Senate approval of the bill rechartering the bank.

Jackson vetoed the bill when it was presented for his signature. The veto rehearses only some of the claims set forth in Benton's speech of February, 1831: Jackson paid no attention to the economic arguments—that only a "hard money" system would prevent depressions—and picked out only those issues on which all enemies of the bank could unite. The bank is unconstitutional, he said; its charter grants a monopoly for which the government receives no equivalent; foreigners are favored by the charter and the concentration of wealth and power in America is a necessary consequence of its terms. Only Americans may be directors and, as ownership of stock passes into foreign hands, control of the bank will fall to a small number of native Americans who will be masters of a dangerous monopoly. The veto message was filled, as one of Jackson's recent admirers admits, with "resounding and demagogic language"; but it served its purpose.

As the selections from Biddle's correspondence cast light upon the background of the application for recharter, so Biddle's letter to Clay shows how conservatives received the antimonopoly argument that was so much used by the bank's opponents. It was as an opponent of monopoly that many a seaboard working-man, for example, supported Jackson in the fight against the bank.

That battle was joined when Jackson vetoed the bill for renewing the charter. Thereafter, the advocates of a United States Bank and the proponents of a divorce between the federal government and banks of issue were engaged in a struggle that did not end until 1841 with the establishment of the Sub-Treasury system,

by which the government became the custodian of its own funds and, so far as possible, severed connection with the banks.

Benton's speech is reprinted from the *Register of Debates in Congress* (21st Congress, 2d Session, the Senate). Biddle's letters are from R. C. McGrane, ed., *Correspondence of Nicholas Biddle* (Boston and New York, 1919).

Speech on the Bank of the United States

BY THOMAS HART BENTON

FIRST: Mr. President, I object to the renewal of the charter of the bank of the United States, because I look upon the bank as an institution too great and powerful to be tolerated in a Government of free and equal laws. Its power is that of a purse; a power more potent than that of the sword; and this power it possesses to a degree and extent that will enable this bank to draw to itself too much of the political power of this Union; and too much of the individual property of the citizens of these States. The money power of the bank is both direct and indirect.

The direct power of the bank is now prodigious, and, in the event of the renewal of the charter, must speedily become boundless and uncontrollable. The bank is now authorized to own effects, lands inclusive, to the amount of fifty-five millions of dollars, and to issue notes to the amount of thirty-five millions more. This makes ninety millions; and, in addition to this vast sum, there is an opening for an unlimited increase: for, there is a dispensation in the charter to issue as many more notes as Congress, by law, may permit. This opens the door to boundless emissions; for what can be more unbounded than the will and pleasure of successive Congresses? The indirect power of the bank cannot be stated in figures; but it can be shown to be immense. In the first place, it has the keeping of the public moneys, now amounting to twenty-six millions per annum, (the Post Office Department included,) and the gratuitous use of the undrawn balances, large enough to constitute, in themselves, the capital of a great State bank. In the next place, its promissory notes are receivable, by law, in purchase of all property owned by the United States, and in payment of all debts due them; and this may increase its power to the amount of the annual revenue, by creating a demand for its notes to that amount. In the third

place, it wears the name of the United States, and has the Federal Government for a partner; and this name, and this partnership, identifies the credit of the bank with the credit of the Union. In the fourth place, it is armed with authority to disparage and discredit the notes of other banks, by excluding them from all payments to the United States; and this, added to all its other powers, direct and indirect, makes this institution the uncontrollable monarch of the moneyed system of the Union. To whom is all this power granted? To a company of private individuals, many of them foreigners, and the mass of them residing in a remote and narrow corner of the Union, unconnected by any sympathy with the fertile regions of the Great Valley, in which the natural power of this Union—the power of numbers—will be found to reside long before the renewed term of a second charter would expire. By whom is all this power to be exercised? By a directory of seven, (it may be,) governed by a majority, of four, (it may be;) and none of these elected by the people, or responsible to them. Where is it to be exercised? At a single city, distant a thousand miles from some of the States, receiving the produce of none of them (except one;) no interest in the welfare of any of them (except one;) no commerce with the people; with branches in every State; and every branch subject to the secret and absolute orders of the supreme central head: thus constituting a system of centralism, hostile to the federative principle of our Union, encroaching upon the wealth and power of the States, and organized upon a principle to give the highest effect to the greatest power. This mass of power, thus concentrated, thus ramified, and thus directed, must necessarily become, under a prolonged existence, the absolute monopolist of American money, the sole manufacturer of paper currency, and the sole authority (for authority it will be) to which the Federal Government, the State Governments, the great cities, corporate bodies, merchants, traders, and every private citizen, must, of necessity apply, for every loan which their exigencies may demand. "The rich ruleth the poor, and the borrower is the servant of the lender." Such are the words of holy writ; and if the authority of the Bible admitted of corroboration, the history of the world is at hand to give it. . . .

Secondly. I object to the continuance of this bank, because its tendencies are dangerous and pernicious to the Government and the people.

What are the tendencies of a great moneyed power, connected with the Government, and controlling its fiscal operations? Are they not dangerous to every interest, public and private—political as well as pecuniary? I say they are; and briefly enumerate the heads of each mischief.

1. Such a bank tends to subjugate the Government. . . .

2. It tends to collusions between the Government and the bank in the terms of the loans, as has been fully experienced in England in those frauds upon the people, and insults upon the understanding, called three per cent. loans, in which the Government, for about £50 borrowed, became liable to pay £100.

3. It tends to create public debt, by facilitating public loans, and substituting unlimited supplies of paper, for limited supplies of coin. The British debt is born of the Bank of England. That bank was chartered in 1694, and was nothing more nor less in the beginning than an act of Parliament for the incorporation of a company of subscribers to a Government loan. The loan was £1,200,000; the interest £80,000; and the expenses of management £4,000. And this is the birth and origin, the germ and nucleus of that debt, which is now £900,000,000, (the unfunded items included) which bears an interest of £30,000,000, and costs £260,000 for annual management.

4. It tends to beget and prolong unnecessary wars, by furnishing the means of carrying them on without recurrence to the people. England is the ready example for this calamity. Her wars for the restoration of the Capet Bourbons were kept up by loans and subsidies created out of bank paper. The people of England had no interest in these wars, which cost them about £600,000,000 of debt in twenty-five years, in addition to the supplies raised within the year. The Kings she put back upon the French throne were not able to sit on it. Twice she put them on; twice they tumbled off in the mud; and all that now remains

of so much sacrifice of life and money is, the debt, which is eternal, the taxes, which are intolerable, the pensions and titles of some warriors, and the keeping of the Capet Bourbons, who are returned upon their hands.

5. It tends to aggravate the inequality of fortunes; to make the rich richer, and the poor poorer; to multiply nabobs and paupers; and to deepen and widen the gulf which separates Dives from Lazarus. A great moneyed power is favorable to great capitalists; for it is the principle of money to favor money. It is unfavorable to small capitalists; for it is the principle of money to eschew the needy and unfortunate. It is injurious to the laboring classes; because they receive no favors, and have the price of the property they wish to acquire raised to the paper maximum, while wages remain at the silver minimum.

6. It tends to make and to break fortunes, by the flux and reflux of paper. Profuse issues, and sudden contractions perform this operation, which can be repeated, like planetary and pestilential visitations, in every cycle of so many years; at every periodical return, transferring millions from the actual possessors of property to the Neptunes who preside over the flux and reflux of paper. The last operation of this kind performed by the Bank of England, about five years ago, was described by Mr. Alexander Baring, in the House of Commons, in terms which are entitled to the knowledge and remembrance of American citizens. I will read his description, which is brief but impressive. After describing the profuse issues of 1823–24, he painted the re-action in the following terms:

"They, therefore, all at once, gave a sudden jerk to the horse on whose neck they had before suffered the reins to hang loose. They contracted their issues to a considerable extent. The change was at once felt throughout the country. A few days before that, no one knew what to do with his money: now, no one knew where to get it. * * * * * The London bankers found it necessary to follow the same course towards their country correspondents, and these again towards their customers, and each indivdual towards his debtor. The consequence was obvious, in the late panic. Every one, desirous to obtain what was due to him, ran to his banker, or to any other on whom he had a claim; and even those who had no immediate use for their money, took it back, and let it lie unemployed in their pockets, thinking it unsafe in others' hands. The effect of this alarm was, that houses which were weak went immediately. Then went second rate houses; and, lastly, houses which were solvent went, because their securities were unavailable. The daily calls to which each individual was subject put it out of his power to assist his neighbor. Men were known to seek for assistance, and, that, too, without finding it, who, on examination of their affairs, were proved to be worth 200,000 pounds,—men, too, who held themselves so secure, that, if asked six months before whether they could contemplate such an event, they would have said it would be impossible, unless the sky should fall, or some other event equally improbable should occur."

This is what was done in England five years ago; it is what may be done here in every five years to come, if the bank charter is renewed. Sole dispenser of money, it cannot omit the oldest and most obvious means of amassing wealth by the flux and reflux of paper. The game will be in its own hands, and the only answer to be given is that to which I have alluded: "The Sultan is too just and merciful to abuse his power."

Thirdly. I object to the renewal of the charter, on account of the exclusive privileges, and anti-republican monopoly, which it gives to the stock-holders. It gives, and that by an act of Congress, to a company of individuals, the exclusive legal privileges:

1. To carry on the trade of banking upon the revenue and credit, and in the name, of the United States of America.

2. To pay the revenues of the Union in their own promissory notes.

3. To hold the moneys of the United States in deposit, without making compensation for the undrawn balances.

4. To discredit and disparage the notes of other banks, by excluding them from the collection of the federal revenue.

5. To hold real estate, receive rents, and retain a body of tenantry.

6. To deal in pawns, merchandise, and bills of exchange.

7. To establish branches in the States without their consent.

8. To be exempt from liability on the failure of the bank.

9. To have the United States for a partner.

10. To have foreigners for partners.

11. To be exempt from the regular administration of justice for the violations of their charter.

12. To have all these exclusive privileges secured to them as a monopoly, in a pledge of the public faith not to grant the like privileges to any other company.

These are the privileges and this the monopoly, of the bank. Now, let us examine them, and ascertain their effect and bearing. Let us contemplate the magnitude of the power which they create; and ascertain the compatibility of this power with the safety of this republican Government, and the rights and interests of its free and equal constituents.

1. The name, the credit, and the revenues of the United States, are given up to the use of this company, and constitute in themselves an immense capital to bank upon.—The name of the United States, like that of the King, is a tower of strength; and this strong tower is now an outwork to defend the citadel of a moneyed corporation. The credit of the Union is incalculable; and, of this credit, as going with the name, and being in partnership with the United States, the same corporation now has possession. The revenues of the Union are twenty-six millions of dollars, including the Post Office; and all this is so much capital in the hands of the bank, because the revenue is received by it, and is payable in its promissory notes.

2. To pay the revenues of the United States in their own notes, until Congress, by law, shall otherwise direct.—This is a part of the charter, incredible and extraordinary as it may appear. The promissory notes of the bank are to be received in payment of every thing the United States may have to sell—in discharge of every debt due to her, until Congress, by law, shall otherwise direct; so that, if this bank, like its prototype in England, should stop payment, its promissory notes would still be receivable at every custom house, land office, post office, and by every collector of public moneys, throughout the Union, until Congress shall meet, pass a repealing law, and promulgate the repeal. Other banks depend upon their credit for the receivability of their notes; but this favored institution has law on its side, and a chartered right to compel the reception of its paper by the Federal Government. The immediate consequence of this extraordinary privilege is, that the United States becomes virtually bound to stand security for the bank, as much so as if she had signed a bond to that effect; and must stand forward to sustain the institution in all emergencies, in order to save her own revenue. This is what has already happened, some ten years ago, in the early progress of the bank, and when the immense aid given it by the Federal Government enabled it to survive the crisis of its own overwhelming mismanagement.

3. To hold the moneys of the United States in deposit without making compensation for the use of the undrawn balances.—This is a right which I deny; but, as the bank claims it, and, what is more material, enjoys it; and as the people of the United States have suffered to a vast extent in

consequence of this claim and enjoyment, I shall not hesitate to set it down to the account of the bank. . . .

See, Mr. President, what masses of money, and always on hand. The paper is covered all over with millions: and yet, for all these vast sums, no interest is allowed; no compensation is made to the United States. The Bank of England, for the undrawn balances of the public money, has made an equitable compensation to the British Government; namely, a permanent loan of half a million sterling, and a temporary loan of three millions for twenty years, without interest. Yet, when I moved for a like compensation to the United States, the proposition was utterly rejected by the Finance Committee, and treated as an attempt to violate the charter of the bank. At the same time it is incontestable, that the United States have been borrowing these undrawn balances from the bank, and paying an interest upon their own money. . . .

4. To discredit and disparage the notes of all other banks, by excluding them from the collection of the federal revenue.—This results from the collection—no, not the collection, but the receipt of the revenue having been committed to the bank, and along with it the virtual execution of the joint resolution of 1816, to regulate the collection of the federal revenue. The execution of that resolution was intended to be vested in the Secretary of the Treasury—a disinterested arbiter between rival banks; but it may be considered as virtually devolved upon the Bank of the United States, and powerfully increases the capacity of that institution to destroy, or subjugate, all other banks. The notes of the State banks excluded from revenue payments, are discredited and disparaged, and fall into the hands of brokers at all places where they are not issued and payable. They cease to circulate at all the points to which the exclusion extends. I am informed that the notes of the banks south of the Potomac and Ohio, even those of the lower Mississippi, are generally refused at the United States' Branch Bank in St. Louis, and, in consequence, are expelled from circulation in Missouri and Illinois, and the neighboring districts. This exclusion of the Southern notes from the northwest quarter of the Union, is injurious to both parties, as our travellers and emigrants chiefly come from the South, and the whole of our trade goes there to find a cash market. The exclusion, as I am told, (for I have not looked into the matter myself,) is general, and extends to the banks in Virginia, the two Carolinas, Georgia, Alabama, Mississippi, and Louisiana. If this be the fact, the joint resolution of 1816 is violated: for, under the terms of that resolution, there are several banks in each of the States mentioned whose notes are receivable in the collection of federal revenue; that is to say, specie paying banks whose notes are payable, and paid, in specie, on demand. Yet, in consequence of exclusion from the United States' Branch Bank, they are excluded from all the land offices, eleven in number, which deposit in that branch; and, being excluded from the land offices, they cease to be current money among the people. If a traveller, or emigrant, brings these notes to the country, or receives them in remittance; if a trader accepts them in exchange for produce, they are "shaved" out of their hands, and sent out of the country. This is a pecuniary injury done to the Northwest; it may be more—it may be a political injury also; for it contributes to break the communication between the two quarters of the Union, and encourages the idea that nothing good can come from the South—not even money! This power to disparage the notes of all other banks, is a power to injure them; and, added to all the other privileges of the Bank of the United States, is a power to destroy them! If any one doubts this assertion, let him read the answers of the President of the bank to the questions put to him by the Chairman of the Finance Committee. These answers are appended to the committee's report of the last session in favor of the bank, and expressly declare the capacity of the federal bank to destroy the State banks. The worthy Chairman [Mr. SMITH, of Md.] puts this question: "Has the bank at any time oppressed any of the State banks?" The President, [Mr. Biddle,] answers, as the whole world would answer to a question of oppression, that it never had; and this response was as much as the interrogatory required. But it did not content the President of the bank; he chose to go further, and to do honor to the institution over which he presided, by showing that it was as just and generous as it was rich and powerful. He, therefore, adds the following words, for which, as a seeker after evidence, to show the alarming and dangerous character of the bank, I return him my unfeigned and pardonable thanks: "There are very few banks which might not have been destroyed by an exertion of the power of the bank."

This is enough! proof enough! not for me alone, but for all who are unwilling to see a moneyed domination set up—a moneyed oligarchy established in this land, and the entire Union subjected to its sovereign will. The power to destroy all other banks is admitted and declared; the inclination to do so is known to all rational beings to reside with the power! Policy may restrain the destroying faculties for the present; but they exist; and will come forth when interest prompts and policy permits. They have been exercised; and the general prostration of the Southern and Western banks attests the fact. They will be exercised, (the charter being renewed,) and the remaining State banks will be swept with the besom of destruction. Not that all will have their signs knocked down, and their doors closed up. Far worse than that to many of them. Subjugation, in preference to destruction, will be the fate of many. Every planet must have its satellites; every tyranny must have its instruments; every knight is followed by his squire; even the king of beasts, the royal quadruped, whose roar subdues the forest, must have a small, subservient animal to spring his prey. Just so of this imperial bank, when installed anew in its formidable and lasting power. The State banks, spared by the sword, will be passed under the yoke. They will become subordinate parts in the great machine. Their place, in the scale of subordination will be one degree below the rank of the legitimate branches; their business, to perform the work which it would be too disreputable for the legitimate branches to perform. This will be the fate of the State banks which are allowed to keep up their signs, and to set open their doors; and thus the entire moneyed power of the Union would fall into the hands of one single institution, whose inexorable and invisible mandates, emanating from a centre, would pervade the Union, giving or withholding money according to its own sovereign will and absolute pleasure. To a favored State, to an individual, or a class of individuals, favored by the central power, the golden stream of Pactolus would flow direct. To all such the munificent mandates of the High Directory would come, as the fabled god made his terrestrial visit of love and desire, enveloped in a shower of gold. But to others—to those not favored—and to those hated—the mandates of this same directory would be as "the planetary plague which hangs its poison in the sick air:" death to them! death to all who minister to their wants! What a state of things! What a condition for a confederacy of States! What grounds for alarm and terrible apprehension, when, in a confederacy of such vast extent, so many independent States, so many rival commercial cities, so much sectional jealousy, such violent political parties, such fierce contests for power, there should be but one moneyed tribunal before which all the rival and contending elements must appear! but one single dispenser of money, to which every citizen, every trader, every merchant, every manufacturer, every planter, every corporation, every city, every State, and the Federal Government itself, must apply, in every emergency, for the most indispensable loan! and this, in the face of the fact, that, in every contest for human rights, the great moneyed institutions of the world have uniformly been found on the side of kings and nobles, against the lives and liberties of the people.

5. To hold real estate, receive rents, and retain a body of tenantry.—This privilege is hostile to the nature of our republican Government, and inconsistent with the nature and design of a banking institution. Republics want freeholders, not landlords and tenants; and, except the corporators in this bank, and in the British East India Company, there is not an incorporated body of landlords in any country upon the face of the earth whose laws emanate from a legislative body. Banks are instituted to promote trade and industry, and to aid the Government and its citizens with loans of money. The whole argument in favor of banking—every argument in favor of this bank—rests upon that idea. No one, when this charter was granted, presumed to speak in favor of incorporating a society of landlords, especially foreign landlords, to buy lands, build houses, rent tenements, and retain tenantry. Loans of money was the object in view, and the purchase of real estate is incompatible with that object. Instead of remaining bankers, the corporators may turn land speculators: instead of having money to lend, they may turn you out tenants to vote. To an application for a loan, they may answer, and answer truly, that they have no money on hand; and the reason may be, that they have laid it out in land. This seems to be the case at present. A committee of the Legislature of Pennsylvania has just applied for a loan; the President of the bank, nothing loth to make a loan to that great State, for twenty years longer than the charter has to exist, expresses his regret that he cannot lend but a limited and inadequate sum. The funds of the institution, he says, will not permit it to advance more than eight millions of dollars. And why? because it has invested three millions in real estate! To this power to hold real estate, is superadded the means to acquire it. The bank is now the greatest moneyed power in the Union; in the event of the renewal of its charter, it will soon be the sole one. Sole dispenser of money, it will soon be the chief owner of property. To unlimited means of acquisition, would be united perpetuity of tenure; for a corporation never dies, and is free from the operation of the laws which govern the descent and distribution of real estate in the hands of individuals. The limitations in the charter are vain and illusory. They insult the understanding, and mock the credulity

of foolish believers. The bank is first limited to such acquisitions of real estate as are necessary to its own accommodation; then comes a proviso to undo the limitation, so far as it concerns purchases upon its own mortgages and executions! This is the limitation upon the capacity of such an institution to acquire real estate. As if it had any thing to do but to make loans upon mortgages, and push executions upon judgments! Having all the money, it would be the sole lender; mortgages being the road to loans, all borrowers must travel that road. When birds enough are in the net, the fowler draws his string, and the heads are wrung off. So when mortgages enough are taken, the loans are called in; discounts cease; curtailments are made; failures to pay ensue; writs issue; judgments and executions follow; all the mortgaged premises are for sale at once; and the attorney of the bank appears at the elbow of the marshal, sole bidder, and sole purchaser.

What is the legal effect of this vast capacity to acquire, and this legal power to retain, real estate? Is it not the creation of a new species of mortmain? And of a kind more odious and dangerous than that mortmain of the church which it baffled the English Parliament so many ages to abolish. The mortmain of the church was a power in an ecclesiastical corporation to hold real estate, independent of the laws of distribution and descent: the mortmain of the bank is a power in a lay corporation to do the same thing. The evil of the two tenures is identical; the difference between the two corporations is no more than the difference between parsons and money changers; the capacity to do mischief incomparably the greatest on the part of the lay corporators. The church could only operate upon the few who were thinking of the other world; the bank, upon all who are immersed in the business or the pleasures of this. The means of the church were nothing but prayers; the means of the bank is money! The church received what it could beg from dying sinners; the bank may extort what it pleases from the whole living generation of the just and unjust. Such is the parallel between the mortmain of the two corporations. They both end in monopoly of estates, and perpetuity of succession; and the bank is the greatest monopolizer of the two. Monopolies and perpetual succession are the bane of republics. Our ancestors took care to provide against them, by abolishing entails and primogeniture. Even the glebes of the church, lean and few as they were in most of the States, fell under the republican principle of limited tenures. All the States abolished the anti-republican tenures; but Congress re-establishes them, and in a manner more dangerous and offen-

sive than before the revolution. They are now given, not generally, but to few; not to natives only, but to foreigners also; for foreigners are large owners of this bank. And thus, the principles of the revolution sink before the privileges of an incorporated company. The laws of the States fall before the mandates of a central directory in Philadelphia. Foreigners become the landlords of free born Americans; and the young and flourishing towns of the United States are verging to the fate of the family boroughs which belong to the great aristocracy of England.

Let no one say the bank will not avail itself of its capacity to amass real estate. The fact is, it has already done so. I know towns, yea, cities, and could name them, if it might not seem invidious from this elevated theatre to make a public reference to their misfortunes, in which this bank already appears as a dominant and engrossing proprietor. I have been in places where the answers to inquiries for the owners of the most valuable tenements, would remind you of the answers given by the Egyptians to similar questions from the French officers, on their march to Cairo. You recollect, no doubt, sir, the dialogue to which I allude: "Who owns that palace?" "The Mameluke;" "Who this country house?" "The Mameluke;" "These gardens?" "The Mameluke;" "That field covered with rice?" "The Mameluke." —And thus have I been answered, in the towns and cities referred to, with the single exception of the name of the Bank of the United States substituted for that of the military scourge of Egypt. If this is done under the first charter, what may not be expected under the second? If this is done while the bank is on its best behavior, what may she not do when freed from all restraint and delivered up to the boundless cupidity and remorseles exactions of a moneyed corporation?

6. To deal in pawns, merchandise, and bills of exchange.—I hope the Senate will not require me to read dry passages from the charter to prove what I say. I know I speak a thing nearly incredible when I allege that this bank, in addition to all its other attributes, is an incorporated company of pawnbrokers! The allegation staggers belief, but a reference to the charter will dispel incredulity. The charter, in the first part, forbids a traffic in merchandise; in the after part, permits it. For truly this instrument seems to have been framed upon the principles of contraries; one principle making limitations, and the other following after with provisoes to undo them. Thus is it with lands, as I have just shown; thus is it with merchandise, as I now show. The bank is forbidden to deal in merchandise—proviso, unless in the case of goods

pledged for money lent, and not redeemed to the day; and, proviso, again, unless for goods which shall be the proceeds of its lands. With the help of these two provisoes, it is clear that the limitation is undone; it is clear that the bank is at liberty to act the pawnbroker and merchant, to any extent that it pleases. It may say to all the merchants who want loans, Pledge your stores, gentlemen! They must do it, or do worse; and, if any accident prevents redemption on the day, the pawn is forfeited, and the bank takes possession. On the other hand, it may lay out its rents for goods; it may sell its real estate, now worth three millions of dollars, for goods. Thus the bank is an incorporated company of pawnbrokers and merchants, as well as an incorporation of landlords and land-speculators; and this derogatory privilege, like the others, is copied from the old Bank of England charter of 1694. Bills of exchange are also subjected to the traffic of this bank. It is a traffic unconnected with the trade of banking, dangerous for a great bank to hold, and now operating most injuriously in the South and West. It is the process which drains these quarters of the Union of their gold and silver, and stifles the growth of a fair commerce in the products of the country. The merchants, to make remittances, buy bills of exchange from the branch banks, instead of buying produce from the farmers. The bills are paid for in gold and silver; and, eventually, the gold and silver are sent to the mother bank, or to the branches in the Eastern cities, either to meet these bills, or to replenish their coffers, and to furnish vast loans to favorite States or individuals. The bills sell cheap, say a fraction of one per cent.; they are, therefore, a good remittance to the merchant. To the bank the operation is doubly good; for even the half of one per cent. on bills of exchange is a great profit to the institution which monopolizes that business, while the collection and delivery to the branches of all the hard money in the country is a still more considerable advantage. Under this system, the best of the Western banks—I do not speak of those which had no foundations, and sunk under the weight of neighborhood opinion—but those which deserved favor and confidence, sunk ten years ago. Under this system, the entire West is now undergoing a silent, general, and invisible drain of its hard money; and, if not quickly arrested, these States will soon be, so far as the precious metals are concerned, no more than the empty skin of an immolated victim.

7. To establish branches in the different States without their consent, and in defiance of their resistance.—No one can deny the degrading and injurious tendency of this privilege. It derogates from the sovereignty of a State; tramples upon her laws; injures her revenue and commerce; lays open her Government to the attacks of centralism; impairs the property of her citizens; and fastens a vampire on her bosom to suck out her gold and silver. 1. It derogates from her sovereignty, because the central institution may impose its intrusive branches upon the State without her consent, and in defiance of her resistance. This has already been done. The State of Alabama, but four years ago, by a resolve of her Legislature, remonstrated against the intrusion of a branch upon her. She protested against the favor. Was the will of the State respected? On the contrary, was not a branch instantaneously forced upon her, as if, by the suddenness of the action, to make a striking and conspicuous display of the omnipotence of the bank, and the nullity of the State? 2. It tramples upon her laws; because, according to the decision of the Supreme Court, the bank and all its branches are wholly independent of State legislation; and it tramples on them again, because it authorizes foreigners to hold lands and tenements in every State, contrary to the laws of many of them; and because it admits of the *mortmain* tenure, which is condemned by all the republican States in the Union. 3. It injures her revenue, because the bank stock, under the decision of the Supreme Court, is not liable to taxation. And thus, foreigners, and non-resident Americans, who monopolize the money of the State, who hold its best lands and town lots, who meddle in its elections, and suck out its gold and silver, and perform no military duty, are exempted from paying taxes, in proportion to their wealth, for the support of the State whose laws they trample upon, and whose benefits they usurp. 4. It subjects the State to the dangerous manœuvres and intrigues of centralism, by means of the tenants, debtors, bank officers, and bank money, which the central directory retain in the State, and may embody and direct against it in its elections, and in its legislative and judicial proceedings. 5. It tends to impair the property of the citizens, and, in some instances, that of the States, by destroying the State banks in which they have invested their money. 6. It is injurious to the commerce of the States, (I speak of the Western States,) by substituting a trade in bills of exchange, for a trade in the products of the country. 7. It fastens a vampire on the bosom of the State, to suck away its gold and silver, and to co-operate with the course of trade, of federal legislation, and of exchange, in draining the South and West of all their hard money. The Southern States, with their thirty millions of annual exports in cotton, rice, and tobacco, and the Western

States, with their twelve millions of provisions and tobacco exported from New Orleans, and five millions consumed in the South, and on the lower Mississippi,—that is to say, with three-fifths of the marketable productions of the Union, are not able to sustain thirty specie paying banks; while the minority of the States north of the Potomac, without any of the great staples for export, have above four hundred of such banks. These States, without rice, without cotton, without tobacco, without sugar, and with less flour and provisions, to export, are saturated with gold and silver, while the Southern and Western States, with all the real sources of wealth, are in a state of the utmost destitution. For this calamitous reversal of the natural order of things, the Bank of the United States stands forth pre-eminently culpable. Yes, it is pre-eminently culpable! and a statement in the National Intelligencer of this morning, (a paper which would overstate no fact to the prejudice of the bank,) cites and proclaims the fact which proves this culpability. It dwells, and exults, on the quantity of gold and silver in the vaults of the United States' Bank. It declares that institution to be "overburdened" with gold and silver; and well may it be so overburthened, since it has lifted the load entirely from the South and West. It calls these metals "a drug" in the hands of the bank; that is to say, an article for which no purchaser can be found. Let this "drug," like the treasures of the dethroned Dey of Algiers, be released from the dominion of its keeper; let a part go back to the South and West, and the bank will no longer complain of repletion, nor they of depletion.

8. Exemption of the stockholders from individual liability on the failure of the bank. This privilege derogates from the common law, is contrary to the principle of partnerships, and injurious to the rights of the community. It is a peculiar privilege granted by law to these corporators, and exempting them from liability, except in their corporate capacity, and to the amount of the assets of the corporation. Unhappily, these assets are never *assez*, that is to say, enough, when occasion comes for recurring to them. When a bank fails, its assets are always less than its debits; so that responsibility fails the instant that liability accrues. Let no one say that the Bank of the United States is too great to fail. One greater than it, and its prototype, has failed, and that in our own day, and for twenty years at a time: the Bank of England failed in 1797, and the Bank of the United States was on the point of failing in 1819. The same cause, namely, stockjobbing and overtrading, carried both to the brink of destruction; the

same means saved both, namely, the name, the credit, and the helping hand of the Governments which protected them. Yes, the Bank of the United States may fail; and its stockholders live in splendor upon the princely estates acquired with its notes, while the industrious classes, who hold these notes, will be unable to receive a shilling for them. This is unjust. It is a vice in the charter. The true principle in banking requires each stockholder to be liable to the amount of his shares; and subjects him to the summary action of every holder on the failure of the institution, till he has paid up the amount of his subscription. This is the true principle. It has prevailed in Scotland for the last century, and no such thing as a broken bank has been known there in all that time.

9. To have the United States for a partner. Sir, there is one consequence, one result of all partnerships between a Government and individuals, which should of itself, and in a mere mercantile point of view, condemn this association on the part of the Federal Government. It is the principle which puts the strong partner forward to bear the burthen whenever the concern is in danger. The weaker members flock to the strong partner at the approach of the storm, and the necessity of venturing more to save what he has already staked, leaves him no alternative. He becomes the Atlas of the firm, and bears all upon his own shoulders. This is the principle: what is the fact? Why, that the United States has already been compelled to sustain the federal bank; to prop it with her revenues and its credit in the trials and crisis of its early administration. I pass over other instances of the damage suffered by the United States on account of this partnership; the immense standing deposites for which we receive no compensation; the loan of five millions of our own money, for which we have paid a million and a half in interest; the five per cent. stock note, on which we have paid our partners four million seven hundred and twenty-five thousand dollars in interest; the loss of ten millions on the three per cent. stock, and the ridiculous catastrophe of the miserable *bonus*, which has been paid to us with a fraction of our own money: I pass over all this, and come to the point of a direct loss, as a partner, in the dividends upon the stock itself. Upon this naked point of profit and loss, to be decided by a rule in arithmetic, we have sustained a direct and heavy loss. The stock held by the United States, as every body knows, was subscribed, not paid. It was a stock note, deposited for seven millions of dollars, bearing an interest of five per cent. The inducement to this subscription was the seductive

conception that, by paying five per cent. on its note, the United States would clear four or five per cent. in getting a dividend of eight or ten. This was the inducement; now for the realization of this fine conception. Let us see it. Here it is: an official return from the Register of the Treasury of interest paid, and of dividends received. The account stands thus:

Interest paid by the United States, $4,725,000
Dividends received by the United
   States,   4,629,426
         —————
Loss to the United States,   95,574

Disadvantageous as this partnership must be to the United States in a moneyed point of view, there is a far more grave and serious aspect under which to view it. It is the political aspect, resulting from the union between the bank and the Government. This union has been tried in England, and has been found there to be just as disastrous a conjunction as the union of church and State. It is the conjunction of the lender and the borrower, and holy writ has told us which of these categories will be master of the other. But suppose they agree to drop rivalry, and unite their resources. Suppose they combine, and make a push for political power: how great is the mischief which they may not accomplish! . . . .

The Correspondence of Nicholas Biddle

To Samuel Smith
               Phil^a Jany 4. 1832
My dear Sir,

You will hear, I am afraid with regret, tho' not with surprise, that we have determined on applying to the present Congress for a renewal of the Charter of the Bank & that a memorial for that purpose will be forwarded tomorrow or the next day. To this course I have made up my mind after great reflection & with the clearest convictions of its propriety. The reasons I will briefly explain. 1. The Stockholders have devolved upon the Directors the discretion of choosing the time of making the application. If we should omit a favorable opportunity we would commit an irreparable error, & would be permanently reproached with it by the Stockholders. Now these Stockholders are entirely unanimous in their opinions and in a case of such grave responsibility their wishes are entitled to great consideration. Unless therefore there should be some very strong reason against it, the application should be made. 2. Independent however of this, I believe That this is the proper time. The Charter will expire in March 1836—Unless the present Congress acts upon it, we must wait 'till the Congress of December 1833, & could not expect from them any decision before after March 1834 which would bring the Bank within two years or 18 months of the expiration of its charter. Now whether the institution is to be continued or destroyed that time is too short. Until the question is settled every thing will be uncertain. No man can look ahead in either public or private affairs as to the state of the currency & there will be constant anxiety about our whole monied system. The Bank too ought to know its fate so as to close its affairs without inflicting deep

& dangerous wounds upon the community by sudden shocks & changes. I believe therefore that this is the best time for settling the question. If the Bank is to be continued the country ought to know it soon. If the Bank is to be destroyed the Bank & the country ought both to know it soon.

The only objection I have heard to it, is, as far as I understand, this: that in about a year hence there is to be an election for a President of the U.S.—and if the application is now made, the gentleman who is now President will take it amiss & negative the bill—while if the Bank will refrain from applying until after his election is secured, he will probably be permitted to abstain from negativing it. This seems to embrace the whole case— Let us look at it. In the first place then, neither I nor any of my associates have any thing whatever to do with the President or his election. I know nothing about it & care nothing about it. The Bank has never had any concern in elections —it will not have any now. To abstain from anything which it would otherwise do, on account of an election, is just as bad as doing anything on account of an election. Both are equal violations of its neutrality. There are many politicians who want to bring it on because it would benefit their side. There are many other politicians who want to put it off because that would benefit their side. Hitherto they have been urged to bring it before the last Congress in hopes that it would injure the present incumbent—now they are urged to postpone it because postponement would benefit him. The Bank cares not whether he is benefited or injured. It takes its own time & its own way.

In the next place what appears to me I confess wholly inexplicable is why the friends of the present incumbent who are also friends of the Bank, if they think the Bank question likely to injure the President, do not at once take the question out of the hands of their adversaries. If the President's friends were to come forward & settle the Bank question before the election comes on, they would disarm their antagonists of their most powerful weapon. I am very ignorant of party tactics, & am probably too much biased to be a fit judge in this case, but such a course has always seemed to me so obvious that I have never been able to comprehend why it was not adopted.

But again what is the reason for supposing that the present incumbent will be offended by bringing it forward now? What possible right has he to be offended? What too has he meant by all these annual messages—declaring in 1829 that he could not "too soon present it" to Congress—repeating the same thing in 1830—and reiterating it in 1831. Was this all a mere pretence? that the moment the Bank accepts his own invitation he is to be offended by being taken at his word.

But moreover he is to negative the bill. That is to say, he will agree to the bill hereafter, but because he thinks it will interfere with his election he will negative it now. Truly this is a compliment which I trust he does not deserve from his friends, for even I who do not feel the slightest interest in him would be sorry to ascribe to a President of the United States a course much fitter for a humble demagogue than the Chief Magistrate of a great country. He will sign a bill, which of course he must think a good one, when his election is over—but he will not sign this bill, which he thinks a good one,—if it is likely to take votes from him at an election. And after all, what security is there that when his election is over, he will not negative the bill? I see none. On the contrary I am satisfied that he would be ten times more disposed to negative it then than now. Now he has at least some check in public opinion—some in the counsels of those around him—then he will have neither. And now, my dear Sir, I have tired myself as I have certainly you with these opinions which you think very erroneous & very disrespectful perhaps to the President. But I wanted to explain precisely the course of thinking which has brought me to my present conclusion. The only regret which accompanies it is that it has not the concurrence of Mr McLane & yourself to whom the Bank as well as myself personally owe much for the manner in which you have both sustained the institution. I cannot express to you how much I am concerned at not being able to adopt the suggestions of Mr McLane who has behaved so handsomely in this matter. But we must each in our respective spheres of duty follow our own convictions with mutual regret but still with mutual respect.

To you I always looked forward as a friend & advocate of the Bank whenever the question of its renewal was agitated. I shall be very sorry on many accounts that from a difference of opinion in regard to time you will be constrained to with hold your aid—but I assure you it will abate none of the regard for you—& the fullness of these explanations will I hope satisfy you of my anxiety to State to you frankly & distinctly the motives which lead me to a conclusion, differing I believe for the first time—from Your's on the Subject of the Bank.

To Charles Jared Ingersoll

Phil^a Feby 11. 1832

My dear Sir,

. . . Here am I, who have taken a fancy to this Bank & having built it up with infinite care am striving to keep it from being destroyed to the infinite wrong as I most sincerely & conscientiously believe of the whole country. To me all other considerations are insignificant—I mean to stand by it & defend it with all the small faculties which Providence has assigned to me. I care for no party in politics or religion—have no sympathy with Mr Jackson or Mr Clay or Mr Wirt or Mr Calhoun or Mr Ellmaker or Mr Van Buren. I am for the Bank & the Bank alone. Well then, here comes Mr Jackson who takes it into his head to declare that the Bank had failed & that it ought to be superceded by some ricketty machinery of his own contrivance. Mr Jackson being the President of the U.S. whose situation might make his ignorance mischievous, we set to work to disenchant the country of their foolery & we have so well succeeded that I will venture to say that there is no man, no woman, & no child in the U.S. who does not understand that the worthy President was in a great error. . . .

It remains to see how its evil consequences may be averted. It seems to me there is no one course by which his friends may extricate him not merely safely but triumphantly. He has made the Bank a Power. He has made the Bank a deciding question as to his own selection. Now let him turn this power to his own advantage. As yet the Bank is entirely uncommitted—the Bank is neither for him nor against him. In this state let his friends come forward boldly, & taking the Bank out of the hands of their enemies, conciliate back the honest friends whom their rashness has alienated, and who think that the only difficulty which he has yet to overcome is the dread of their internal convulsion to which the prostration of the Bank will lead. The most extraordinary part of the whole matter is that the President & the Bank do not disagree in the least about the modifications he desires. He wishes some changes—The Bank agrees to them—and yet from some punctilio which is positively puerile his rash friends wish him to postpone it. Do they not perceive that his enemies are most anxious to place him in opposition to the Bank? And should not every motive of prudence induce him to disappoint their calculations? The true & obvious theory seems to me to disarm the antagonists of their strongest weapon—to assume credit for settling this question for the administration. If the present measure fails, it carries bitterness into the ranks of the best part of the opposition. If it succeeds without the administration it displays their weakness. If the bill passes & the President negatives it, I will not say that it will destroy him—but I certainly think it will & moreover I think it ought to. I can imagine no question which seems more exclusively for the representatives of the people than the manner in which they choose to keep & to manage the money of the people.

. . . I suppose the President has been made to believe that the Bank is busy in hostility to him—you know how wholly unfounded this is. For myself I do not care a straw for him or his rivals—I covet neither his man servant—nor even his maid servant, his ox nor any of his asses. Long may he live to enjoy all possible blessings, but if he means to wage war upon the Bank—if he pursues us till we turn & stand at bay, why then—he may perhaps awaken a spirit which has hitherto been checked & reined in—and which it is wisest not to force into offensive defence.

To HENRY CLAY
(*private*)

Phil^a August 1st 1832

My dear Sir

You ask what is the effect of the Veto. My impression is that it is working as well as the friends of the Bank and of the country could desire. I have always deplored making the Bank a party question, but since the President will have it so, he must pay the penalty of his own rashness. As to the Veto message I am delighted with it. It has all the fury of a chained panther biting the bars of his cage. It is really a manifesto of anarchy—such as Marat or Robespierre might have issued to the mob of the faubourg St Antoine: and my hope is that it will contribute to relieve the country from the dominion of these miserable people. You are destined to be the instrument of that deliverance, and at no period of your life has the country ever had a deeper stake in you. I wish you success most cordially, because I believe the institutions of the Union are involved in it.

THE DEPRESSION OF 1837–1843

IN SPITE OF all the efforts of conservative men, Andrew Jackson was reelected President in 1832. While the House passed a resolution declaring the Federal government's money safe in the custody of the Bank of the United States, Jackson determined to withdraw the government deposits though he had to reshuffle his entire Cabinet to make his policy and his Secretary of the Treasury agree. The removal of deposits from the Bank of the United States to selected state banks was made, despite the Senate's declaration that it was an arbitrary exercise of power. The bank called in its loans and contracted its credits after the removal of the deposits; but though petitions against the government's action poured into Congress and some stringency was felt in the money market, the new depositories expanded their loans and borrowers found credit easy.

As state bank loans expanded on the base of government deposits plus portions of the Treasury surplus which had been put into the custody of the several states, borrowing increased during 1834 and 1835. Great stretches of the public lands were sold, not for specie but for the banknotes that were issued on the basis of the new resources. The public domain was being exchanged for paper. Senator Benton feared this would strengthen the speculating element in Congress to the point that his own favorite project of lowering and adjusting the price of public land never would become law. His opinion was confirmed by the Senate's rejection of his resolution making specie, not bank paper, the medium of payment for public lands. The public domain seemed doomed as the session closed; speculators were redoubling their activity. "But there was a remedy in reserve for the cure of the evil which they had not foreseen, and which was applied the moment that Congress was gone. Jackson was still President! and he had the nerve which the occasion required. He saw the public lands fleeting away—saw that Congress would not interfere—and knew the majority of the Cabinet to be against his interference. He did as he had often done in councils of war—called the council together to hear a decision. He summoned his cabinet—laid the case before them—heard the majority of adverse opinions:—and directed the order to issue. His private Secretary, Mr. Donelson, was directed to prepare a draught of the order. The author of this View was all the while in the office of this private Secretary. Mr. Donelson came to him, with the President's decision, and requested him to draw up the order. It was done—the rough draught carried back to the council—put into official form—signed—issued. . . . The disappointed speculators raged. Congress was considered insulted, the cabinet defied, the banks disgraced." Thus Senator Benton in his *Thirty Years' View*.

This is the background of the Specie Circular of July, 1836. Biddle regarded it as an outrageous usurpation of power, as can be seen in his *Letters to John Quincy Adams*, in which he justified the Bank of the United States for suspending specie payments. Though the Specie Circular was rescinded in 1838, it snapped a money market already strained to the breaking point. The demand for specie at the land offices forced local banks to curtail their loans just as the seaboard banks were forced to contract theirs by the resolution which ordered the turning over of the Treasury surplus to the states. Thus the Eastern banks were subject to a double drain at a time when their Western debtors could get no loans because of Jackson's "act of gratuitous oppression."

So Nicholas Biddle, as the Panic of 1837 pricked the bubble of an inflation in land values, urban and rural. Benton, for the other side, insisted that it was not the Specie Circular but the "bloat in the paper system" which

had caused the collapse. He had been regarded as "a little exalted in the head" because he kept warning public and politicians of the dangers latent in the increase of an inconvertible paper currency, but few had listened seriously in the early thirties. The result was, banks multiplied, merchants bought on credit, states borrowed money for internal improvements, and the bubble of credit swelled until it burst. With considerable help (according to Benton) from Nicholas Biddle, who contracted his loans and suspended specie payments "to coerce the government into submission to the Bank of the United States and its confederate politicians."

Biddle seemed victor, though, even if the New York banks had resumed specie payment in 1838; the Bank of the United States was flourishing under a Pennsylvania charter; the Specie Circular was rescinded and the United States government was using the bank as an agent to discount the French government's warrants for payment of damages to United States commerce during the Napoleonic Wars. That triumph increased Biddle's confidence to the point where he attempted to restore the country's balance of trade by elaborate dealings in the cotton market and by the sale of American securities abroad. Biddle lent money to American cotton planters and had them assign their crops to an agency in Liverpool which was controlled by a member of his family. The cotton agency drew upon the financial agent Biddle had set up in London. Since British spinners were prosperous, the demand for cotton continued brisk and Biddle's corner in the fiber provided the British balances that paid for American imports. American credit was good in 1838–1839; and American securities sold well because the British financial community had confidence in Biddle and in the presumed soundness of state finances.

In 1839, Biddle's system collapsed. With it, went the inflated structure of cotton prices and American credit abroad. Harvests had been poor in Europe, the demand for British cotton yarn declined and that lessened British need for American cotton. Biddle's (Pennsylvania)

Bank of the United States suspended specie payments again in October, 1839, and failed entirely two years later.

The full shock of depression and unfavorable trade balances struck the United States with renewed force. British readiness to extend credit ceased with the contraction in the London money market; American bonds did not sell. British financial interests attempted to increase confidence by urging American politicians to work for an assumption or, at least, a guarantee of state debts by the Federal government. Benton attacked the scheme and secured the passage of a Senate resolution disclaiming federal responsibility, and the only factor which prevented the question from becoming an issue in the Presidential campaign of 1840 was the Whigs' wisdom in choosing a candidate who had no ascertainable views on any public issue.

The following year, many states defaulted interest payments on their public debts, among them Pennsylvania, which is the object of Sydney Smith's acid attack. Smith (1771–1845) was not particularly anti-American, but the refusal of Pennsylvania to tax herself to maintain interest payments on her bonds roused him to violent protest. A bitter controversy followed.

The British financial community attempted more practical measures. British bankers boycotted the United States Treasury agent who tried to float a loan in 1842. When New York interests provided the Treasury with funds, coercion was dropped in favor of lobbying. Ultimately, all the defaulting states renewed their interest payments; however, three states, Mississippi, Michigan, and Florida, repudiated their debts in whole or in part.

The Preemption Act of 1841 helped puncture the last hope for federal aid to the holders of the defaulting states' bonds. Though the law did declare that the proceeds of public land sales be divided among the states as a fund for internal improvements, this provision was contingent on import duties remaining at 20 percent. Since the Treasury surplus, which had made the bill possible, disappeared under pressure and the tariff interests remained strong, the only sections of the law retaining vitality were those providing that the squatters on unsurveyed public land were to be permitted to purchase their quarter sections at the minimum price when that land should be surveyed and offered for sale. Earlier, preemption had been a privilege granted to settlers on a specific tract; by the law of 1841, however, it became an acknowledged right.

The Specie Circular is reprinted from *The American State Papers: Public Land Series*, Vol. VIII (Washington, 1861). Biddle's letter to Adams is reprinted from *Two Letters Addressed to the Hon. J. Quincy Adams* (London, 1837). Sidney Smith's letter is reprinted from his *Letters on American Debts* (New York, 1844).

The Specie Circular of 1836

IN CONSEQUENCE OF complaints which have been made of frauds, speculations, and monopolies, in the purchase of the public lands, and the aid which is said to be given to effect these objects by excessive bank credits, and dangerous if not partial facilities, through bank drafts and bank deposites, and the general evil influence likely to result to the public interests, and especially the safety of the great amount of money in the Treasury, and the sound condition of the currency of the country, from the further exchange of the national domain in this manner, and chiefly for bank credits and paper money, the President of the United States has given directions, and you are hereby instructed, after the 15th day of August next, to receive in payment of the public lands nothing except what is directed by the existing laws, viz.: gold and silver, and in the proper cases, Virginia land scrip; provided that, till the 15th of December next, the same indulgences heretofore extended as to the kind of money received, may be continued for any quantity of land not exceeding 320 acres to each purchaser who is an actual settler, or bonafide resident in the State where the sales are made.

In order to insure the faithful execution of these

instructions, all receivers are strictly prohibited from accepting for land sold, any draft, certificate, or other evidence of money or deposite, though for specie, unless signed by the Treasurer of the United States, in conformity to the act of April 24, 1820. And each of those officers is required to annex to his monthly returns to this department, the amount of gold and of silver respectively, as well as the bills received under the foregoing exception; and each deposite bank is required to annex to every certificate given upon a deposite of money, the proportions of it actually paid in gold, in silver, and in bank-notes. All former instructions on these subjects, except as now modified, will be considered as remaining in full force.

The principal objects of the President, in adopting this measure, being to repress alleged frauds, and to withhold any countenance or facilities in the power of the government from the monopoly of the public lands in the hands of speculators and capitalists, to the injury of the actual settlers in the new States, and of emigrants in search of new homes, as well as to discourage the ruinous extension of bank issues and bank credits, by which those results are generally supposed to be promoted, your utmost vigilance is required, and relied on, to carry this order into complete execution.

Letters to John Quincy Adams

BY NICHOLAS BIDDLE

A CITIZEN had a right to choose any one of these modes of payment. He had as much right to pay for land with the note of a specie paying Bank as to pay it for duties at the custom house. If this be denied, certainly any one of them might be accepted by the Treasury—but to proscribe all but one—to refuse every thing but the most difficult thing—to do this without notice of the approaching change in the fundamental system of our dealings—is an act of gratuitous oppression.

Under the operation of this resolution, the Banks had gone on, fearing nothing, as they had only to provide for the usual specie calls upon them—and saw the country full of specie, with no foreign demand to drain it from them—when, on a sudden, without any intimation of the coming shock, an order was issued by the Secretary, declaring that their notes were no longer receivable, and of course inviting all who held the notes, and had deposits in these banks, to convert them into specie. It in fact made at once the whole amount of their circulation and private deposits a specie demand upon them.—The first consequence was, that the Banks nearest the land offices ceased making loans. The next was, that they strove to fortify themselves by accumulating specie.

It was just at this moment that the warrants for transfers were put into their hands. The combination of the two measures produced a double result—first, to require the Banks generally to increase their specie, and next, to give them the means of doing it, by drafts on the Deposit Banks. The commercial community were thus taken by surprise. The interior Banks making no loans, and converting their Atlantic funds into specie, the debtors in the interior could make no remittances to the merchants in the Atlantic cities, who are thus thrown for support on the Banks of those cities at a moment when they are unable to afford relief on account of the very abstraction of their specie to the West. The creditor States not only receive no money, but their money is carried away to the debtor States, who in turn, cannot use it, either to pay old engagements or to contract new.

By this unnatural process the specie of New York and the other commercial cities is piled up in the Western States, not circulated, not used, but held as a defence against the Treasury—and while the West cannot use it—the East is suffering for the want of it. The result is, that the commercial intercourse between the West and the Atlantic is almost wholly suspended, and the few operations which are made are burthened with the most extravagant expense. In November, 1836, the interest of money has risen to twenty-four per cent.—merchants are struggling to preserve their credit by ruinous sacrifices—and it costs five or six times as much to transmit funds from the west and south-west, as it did in November, 1835, or '34 or '32.—Thus while the exchanges with all the world are in our favour—while Europe is alarmed, and the Bank of England itself uneasy at the quantity of specie we possess—we are suffering, because, from mere mismanagement, the whole ballast of the currency is shifted from one side of the vessel to the other.

In the absence of good reasons for these measures, and as a pretext for them, it is said that the country has over-traded—that the Banks have over-issued, and that the purchasers of public lands have been very extravagant. I am not struck by the truth or the propriety of these complaints. The phrase of overtrading is very convenient but not very intelligible. If it means any thing, it means that our dealings with other countries have brought us in debt to those countries. In that case the exchange turns against our country, and is rectified by an exportation of specie or stocks in the first instance—and then by reducing the imports to the exports.—Now the fact is, that at this moment, the exchanges are all in favour of this country—that is, you can buy a bill of exchange on a foreign country cheaper than you can send specie to that country. Accordingly, much specie has come in—none goes out. This too at a moment when the exchange for the last crop is exhausted, and that of the new crop has not yet come into the market—and when we are on the point of sending to Europe the produce of the country, to the amount of eighty or one hundred millions of dollars. How then has the country overtraded? Exchange with all the world is in favour of New York. How then can New York be an overtrader? Her merchants have sold goods to the merchants of the interior, who are willing to pay, and under ordinary circumstances able to pay—but by the mere fault of the government, as obvious as if an earthquake had swallowed them up, their debtors are disabled from making immediate payment. It is not that the Atlantic merchants have sold too many goods, but that the government prevents their receiving payment for any. Moreover in the commercial cities money can be had, though at extravagant rates, for capitalists add to the ordinary charges for the use of it a high insurance against the loss of it. It is not then so much that money is not to be procured, as that doubt and alarm increase the hazards of lending it.

Then as to the Banks. It is quite probable that many of the Banks have extended their issues—but whose fault is it? Who called these banks into existence? The Executive. Who tempted and goaded them to these issues? Undoubtedly the Executive. The country five years ago was in possession of the most beautiful machinery of currency and exchanges the world ever saw. It consisted of a number of State Banks protected, and, at the same time, restrained by the Bank of the United States.

The people of the United States through their representatives rechartered that institution. But the Executive, discontented with its independence, rejected the Act of Congress—and the favourite topic of declamation was that the States would make Banks, and that these Banks could create a better system of currency and exchanges. The States accordingly made banks—and then followed idle parades about the loans of these banks, and their enlarged dealings in exchange. And what is the consequence? The Bank of the United

States has not ceased to exist more than seven months, and already the whole currency and exchanges are running into inextricable confusion, and the industry of the country is burthened with extravagant charges on all the commercial intercourse of the Union. And now, when these banks have been created by the Executive, and urged into these excesses, instead of gentle and gradual remedies, a fierce crusade is raised against them—the funds are harshly and suddenly taken from them, and they are forced to extraordinary means of defence against the very power which brought them into being. They received, and were expected to receive, in payment for the Government, the notes of each other, and the notes of other banks, and the facility with which they did so, was a ground of special commendation by the Government. And now that Government has let loose upon them a demand for specie, to the whole amount of these notes. I go further.

There is an outcry abroad, raised by faction and echoed by folly, against the Banks in the United States. Until it was disturbed by the Government, the banking system of the United States was at least as good as that of any other commercial country. What was desired for its perfection, was precisely what I have so long striven to accomplish—to widen the metallic basis of the currency, by a greater infusion of coin into the smaller channels of circulation. This was in a gradual and judicious train of accomplishment. But this miserable foolery about an exclusively metallic currency is quite as absurd as to discard the steam boats, and go back to poling up the Mississippi. Banks may often err from want of skill, and occasionally be injurious as steam is—but it is not the less true, that the banks of this country have been the great instruments of its improvements, and that during all the convulsions of the last fifteen years, for every American bank which has failed, at least ten English banks have failed.

So with regard to the lands. For the last few years, the amount of the sales of the public lands has been a constant theme of congratulation with the Executive. In the very last message, on the 12th of December, 1835, he repeats the same strain. "Among the *evidences of the increasing prosperity of the country, not the least gratifying is that afforded by the receipts of the public lands, which amount in the present year to eleven millions of dollars. This circumstance attests the rapidity with which agriculture, the first and most important occupation of man, advances, and contributes to the wealth and power of our extended territory.*" In the same message he declared that "the circulating medium has been greatly improved. By the use of the State Banks it is ascertained *that all the wants of the community in relation to exchange and currency are supplied as well as they have ever been before.*" Scarcely seven months elapse when these pastoral and financial visions dissolve in air. Agriculture ceases to be "the first and most important occupation of man"—the State Banks cease to be the models of exchange and currency—but forth issues the Secretary with a declaration, that to protect the Treasury "from frauds, speculation, and monopolies in the purchase of public lands"—from "excessive bank credits"—from "ruinous extension of bank issues" —nothing shall be received for land but gold and silver.

Now what an exhibition is this?

The public lands are exposed to public auction, the prices reduced in order to encourage sales, and the President stands by, exulting at the amount, when suddenly he declares that he will permit no speculations, and that he will raise the price of the lands by raising the price of what alone he will receive for them. Now, supposing it true that men have bought much land. What right has the President to dictate to the citizens of this country, whether they buy too much land or too much broad cloth? They might be permitted to know and to manage their own concerns quite as well as he does, leaving the evil, if it be one, to correct itself, by its own excess. If he prohibits the receipt of any thing but specie to correct land speculations, he may make the same prohibition as to the duties on hardware or broadcloth or wines, whenever his paternal wisdom shall see us buying too many shovels, or too many coats, or too much champaigne—and thus bring the entire industry of the country under his control.

These troubles may not, however, be wholly useless, if we extract from them two great lessons.—The first is, that we can have no permanent financial prosperity while the public revenue is separated from the business of the country and committed to rash and ignorant politicians with no guides but their own passions and interests. I have little doubt that the specie order is the revenge of the President upon Congress for passing the Distribution Law.—I have less doubt that this dispersion of the revenue among the multitude of Banks was to advance the obscure aspirings of some Treasury Cæsar.

The other lesson is—one a thousand times repeated and a thousand times forgotten—to distrust all demagogues of all parties who profess exclusive love for what they call the People. For the last six years the country has been nearly convulsed by efforts to break the mutual dependence of all classes of citizens—to make the laborer regard his employer as his enemy, and to array the poor against the rich. These trashy declaimers have ended by bringing the country into a condition where its whole industry is subject far more than it ever was before, to the control of the large capitalists—and where every step tends inevitably to make the rich richer, and the poor poorer.

It remains to speak of the remedy of these evils. They follow obviously the causes of them. The causes are the injudicious transfers of the public monies, and the Treasury order about specie.

The first measure of relief therefore should be, the instant repeal of the Treasury order requiring specie for lands—the second, the adoption of a proper system to execute the distribution law.

These measures would restore confidence in twenty-four hours, and repose at least in as many days. If the Treasury will not adopt them voluntarily, Congress should immediately command it.

In the mean time, all forbearance and calmness should be maintained. There is great reason for anxiety—none whatever for alarm—and with mutual confidence and courage, the country may yet be able to defend itself against the Government. —In that struggle my poor efforts shall not be wanting. I go for The Country, whoever rules it—I go for The Country, best loved when worst governed—and it will afford me far more gratification to assist in repairing its wrongs, than to triumph over those who inflict them.

Letters on American Debts

BY SYDNEY SMITH

Letter I to the Editor of the Morning Chronicle

Sir,

You did me the favor, some time since, to insert in your valuable journal a petition of mine to the American Congress, for the repayment of a loan made by me, in common with many other unwise people, to the State of Pennsylvania. For that petition I have been abused in the grossest manner by many of the American papers. After some weeks' reflection, I see no reason to alter my opinions, or to retract my expressions. What I then said was not wild declamation, but measured truth.

I repeat again, that no conduct was ever more profligate than that of the State of Pennsylvania. History cannot pattern it: and let no deluded being imagine that they will ever repay a single farthing—their people have tasted of the dangerous luxury of dishonesty, and they will never be brought back to the homely rule of right. The money transactions of the Americans are become a by-word among the nations of Europe. In every grammar-school of the whole world *ad Græcas Calendas* is translated—the American dividends.

I am no enemy to America. I loved and admired honest America when she respected the laws of pounds, shillings, and pence; and I thought the United States the most magnificent picture of human happiness: I meddle now in these matters because I hate fraud—because I pity the misery it has occasioned—because I mourn over the hatred it has excited against free institutions.

Among the discussions to which the moral lubricities of this insolvent people have given birth, they have arrogated to themselves the right of sitting in judgment upon the property of their creditors—of deciding who among them is rich, and who poor, and who are proper objects of compassionate payment; but in the name of Mercury, the great god of thieves, did any man ever hear of debtors alleging the wealth of the lender as a reason for eluding the payment of the loan? Is the Stock Exchange a place for the tables of the money-lenders; or is it a school of moralists, who may amerce the rich, exalt the poor, and correct the inequalities of fortune? Is *Biddle* an instrument in the hand of Providence to exalt the humble, and send the rich empty away? Does American Providence work with such instruments as *Biddle?*

But the only good part of this bad morality is not acted upon. The rich are robbed, but the poor are not paid: they growl against the dividends of Dives, and don't lick the sores of Lazarus. They seize with loud acclamations, on the money bags of Jones Lloyd, Rothschild, and Baring, but they do not give back the pittance of the widow, and the bread of the child. Those knaves of the setting sun may call me rich, for I have a twentieth-part of the income of the Archbishop of Canterbury; but the curate of the next parish is a wretched soul, bruised by adversity; and the three hundred pounds for his children, which it has taken his life to save, is eaten and drunken by the mean men of Pennsylvania—by men who are always talking of the virtue and honor of the United States—by men who soar above others in what they say, and sink below all nations in what they do—who, after floating on the heaven of declamation, fall down to feed on the offal and garbage of the earth.

Persons who are not in the secret are inclined to consider the abominable conduct of the repudiating States to proceed from exhaustion—"They don't pay because they cannot pay; whereas, from estimates which have just now reached this country, this is the picture of the finances of the insolvent states. Their debts may be about 200 millions of dollars; at an interest of six per cent. this makes an annual charge of 12 millions of dollars, which is little more than 1 per cent. of their income in 1840, and may be presumed to be less than 1 per cent. of their present income; but if they were all to provide funds for the punctual payment of interest, the debts could readily be converted into a 4 or 5 per cent. stock, and the excess, converted into a sinking fund, would discharge the debt in less than thirty years. The debt of Pennsylvania, estimated at 40 millions of dollars, bears, at 5 per cent., an annual interest of 2 millions. The income of this State was, in 1840, 131 millions of dollars,[1] and is probably at this time not less than 150 millions: a net revenue of only 1½ per cent. would produce the 2 millions required. So that the price of national character in Pennsylvania is 1 1-2 per cent. on the net income; and if this market price of morals were established here, a gentleman of a thousand a year would deliberately and publicly submit to infamy for 15*l.* per annum; and a poor man, who by laborious industry had saved one hundred a year, would incur general disgrace and opprobrium for thirty shillings by the year. There really should be lunatic asylums for nations as well as for individuals.

But they begin to feel all this: their tone is changed; they talk with bated breath and whispering apology, and allay with some cold drops of modesty their skipping spirit. They strutted into this miserable history, and begin to think of sneaking out.

And then the subdolous press of America contends that the English under similar circumstances would act with their own debt in the same manner; but there are many English constituencies where are thousands not worth a shilling, and no such idea has been broached among them, nor has any petition to such effect been presented to the legislature. But what if they did act in such a manner, would it be a conduct less wicked than that of the Americans? Is there not one immutable law of justice—is it not written in the book? Does it not beat in the heart?—are the great guidemarks of life to be concealed by such nonsense as this? I deny the fact on which the reasoning is founded;

[1] This is manifestly an error. By "income" Mr. Smith doubtless means the aggregate amount of taxable property in the State.   [ED. NEW WORLD.]

and if the facts were true, the reasoning would be false.

I never met a Pennsylvanian at a London dinner without a disposition to seize and divide him;—to allot his beaver to one sufferer and his coat to another—to appropriate his pocket-handkerchief to the orphan, and to comfort the widow with his silver watch, Broadway rings, and the London Guide, which he always carries in his pockets. How such a man can set himself down at an English table without feeling that he owes two or three pounds to every man in company, I am at a loss to conceive: he has no more right to eat with honest men than a leper has to eat with clean men. If he has a particle of honor in his composition he would shut himself up, and say, "I cannot mingle with you, I belong to a degraded people—I must hide myself—I am a plunderer from Pennsylvania."

Figure to yourself a Pennsylvanian receiving foreigners in his own country, walking over the public works with them, and showing them Larcenous Lake, Swindling Swamp, Crafty Canal, and Rogue's Railway, and other dishonest works. "This swamp we gained (says the patriotic borrower) by the repudiated loan of 1828. Our canal robbery was in 1830; we pocketed your good people's money for the railroad only last year." All this may seem very smart to the Americans; but if I had the misfortune to be born among such a people, the land of my fathers should not retain me a single moment after the act of repudiation. I would appeal from my fathers to my forefathers. I would fly to Newgate for greater purity of thought, and seek in the prisons of England for better rules of life.

This new and vain people can never forgive us for having preceded them 300 years in civilization. They are prepared to enter into the most bloody wars with England, not on account of Oregon, or boundaries, but because our clothes and carriages are better made, and because Bond-street beats Broadway. Wise Webster does all he can to convince the people that these are not lawful causes of war; but wars, and long wars, they will one day or another produce; and this, perhaps, is the only advantage of repudiation. The Americans cannot gratify their avarice and ambition at once; they cannot cheat and conquer at the same time. The warlike power of every country depends on their Three per Cents. If Cæsar were to reappear upon earth, Wettenhall's List would be more important than his Commentaries; Rothschild would open and shut the Temple of Janus; Thomas Baring, or Bates, would probably command the Tenth Legion, and the soldiers would march to battle with loud cries of Scrip and Omnium reduced, Consols, and Cæsar! Now, the Americans have cut themselves off from all resources of credit. Having been as dishonest as they can be, they are prevented from being as foolish as they wish to be. In the habitable globe they cannot borrow a guinea, and they cannot draw the sword because they have not money to buy it.

If I were an American of any of the honest States, I would never rest till I had compelled Pennsylvania to be as honest as myself. The bad faith of that State brings disgrace on all; just as common snakes are killed because vipers are dangerous. I have a general feeling, that by that breed of men I have been robbed and ruined, and I shudder and keep aloof. The pecuniary credit of every State is affected by Pennsylvania. Ohio pays; but with such a bold bankruptcy before their eyes, how long will Ohio pay? The truth is, that the eyes of all capitalists are averted from the United States. The finest commercial understandings will have nothing to do with them. Men rigidly just, who penetrate boldly into the dealings of nations, and work with vigor and virtue for honorable wealth—great and high-minded merchants—will loathe, and are now loathing, the name of America: it is becoming, since its fall, the common-shore of Europe, and the native home of the needy villain.

And now, drab-colored men of Pennsylvania, there is yet a moment left: the eyes of all Europe are anchored upon you—

"Surrexit mundus justis furiis"

start up from that trance of dishonesty into which you are plunged; don't think of the flesh which walls about your life, but of that sin which has hurled you from the heaven of character, which hangs over you like a devouring pestilence, and makes good men bad, and ruffians dance and sing. It is not for Gin Sling and Sherry Cobbler alone, that man is to live, but for those great principles against which no argument can be listened to—principles which give to every power a double power above their functions and their offices, which are the books, the arts, the academies that teach, lift up, and nourish the world—principles (that I am quite serious in what I say) above cash, superior to cotton, higher than currency—principles, without which it is better to die than to live, which every servant of God, over every sea and in all lands, should cherish—*usque ad abdita spiramenta animæ.*

Yours &c.

November 3, 1843. SYDNEY SMITH

GENESIS OF THE MONROE DOCTRINE

THREE PARAGRAPHS in President Monroe's message of December, 1823, have become one of the cornerstones of American foreign policy:

"At the proposal of the Russian imperial government made through the minister of the Emperor residing here, a full power and instructions have been transmitted to the Minister of the United States at St. Petersburgh, to arrange by amicable negotiation, the respective rights and interests of the two nations on the northwest coast of this continent. A similar proposal has been made by his Imperial Majesty to the government of Great Britain, which has likewise been acceded to. The government of the United States has been desirous, by this friendly proceeding, of manifesting the great value which they have invariably attached to the friendship of the emperor, and their solicitude to cultivate the best understanding with his government. In the discussions to which this interest has given rise, and in the arrangements by which they may terminate, the occasion has been judged proper for asserting, as a principle in which the rights and interests of the United States are involved, that the American continents, by the free and independent condition which they have assumed and maintain, are henceforth not to be considered as subjects for future colonization by any European power. . . .

"It was stated at the commencement of the last session that a great effort was then making in Spain and Portugal, to improve the condition of the people of those countries, and that it appeared to be conducted with extraordinary moderation. It need scarcely be remarked, that the result has been, so far, very different from what was then anticipated. Of events in that quarter of the globe, with which we have so much intercourse, and from which we derive our origin, we have always been anxious and interested spectators. The citizens of the United States cherish sentiments the most friendly, in favor of the liberty and happiness of their fellow men on that side of the Atlantic. In the wars of the European powers, in matters relating to themselves, we have never taken any part, nor does it comport with our policy so to do. It is only when our rights are invaded, or seriously menaced, that we resent injuries, or make preparation for our defence. With the movements in this hemisphere, we are, of necessity, more immediately connected, and by causes which must be obvious to all enlightened and impartial observers. The political system of the allied powers is essentially different, in this respect, from that of America. This difference proceeds from that which exists in their respective governments. And to the defence of our own, which has been achieved by the loss of so much blood and treasure, and matured by the wisdom of their most enlightened citizens, and under which we have enjoyed unexampled felicity, this whole nation is devoted. We owe it, therefore, to candor, and to the amicable relations existing between the United States and those powers, to declare, that we should consider any attempt on their part to extend their system to any portion of this hemisphere, as dangerous to our peace and safety. With the existing colonies or dependencies of any European power, we have not interfered, and shall not interfere. But with the governments who have declared their independence, and maintained it, and whose independence we have, on great consideration, and on just principles, acknowledged, we could not view any interposition for the purpose of oppressing them, or controlling in any other manner, their destiny, by any European power, in any other light than as the manifestation of an unfriendly disposition towards the United States. In the war between those new governments and Spain, we declared our neutrality at the time of their recognition, and to this we have adhered, and shall continue to adhere, provided no change shall occur, which, in the judgment of the competent authorities of this government, shall make a corresponding change, on the part of the United States, indispensable to their security.

"The late events in Spain and Portugal, show that Europe is still unsettled. Of this important fact, no stronger proof can be adduced than that the allied powers should have thought it proper, on any principle satisfactory to themselves, to have interposed by force, in the internal concerns of Spain. To what extent such interposition may be carried, on the same principle, is a question, to which all independent powers, whose governments differ from theirs, are interested; even those most remote, and surely none more so than the United States. Our policy in regard to Europe, which was adopted at an early stage of the wars which have so long agitated that quarter of the globe, nevertheless remains the same, which is, not to interfere in the internal concerns of any of its powers; to consider the government *de facto* as the legitimate government for us; to cultivate friendly relations with it, and to preserve those relations by a frank, firm, and manly policy; meeting, in all instances, the just claims of every power; submitting to injuries from none. But, in regard to these continents, circumstances are eminently and conspicuously different. It is impossible that the allied powers should extend their political system to any portion of either continent without endangering our peace and happiness: nor can any one believe that our Southern brethren, if left to

themselves, would adopt it of their own accord. It is equally impossible, therefore, that we should behold such interposition, in any form, with indifference. If we look to the comparative strength and resources of Spain and those new governments, and their distance from each other, it must be obvious that she can never subdue them. It is still the true policy of the United States to leave the parties to themselves, in the hope that other powers will pursue the same course."

Monroe's statement stemmed from the complexities of a postwar settlement in which national aspirations collided with the realities of power politics in the early twenties. In Europe, subject nationalities, like the Greeks, were in rebellion against their Ottoman masters. Spain had made its fight for constitutional government, an effort defeated by French intervention shortly before Monroe made his statement. Spain's colonies in the Western Hemisphere had felt the reins of royal control slacken during the turbulent years when Napoleon attempted to impose a Bonaparte as King of Spain. The Spanish lands of the New World had risen and now they were fighting to maintain the independence which the United States had already recognized by 1823. And, at the north, a Russian ukase attempted to extend the boundaries of Alaska, while the Russian Czar stood at the head of the Allied sovereigns who had restored Spanish absolutism and who were bound in honor and interest to block further advances of liberalism.

England's position was uncertain in this situation: her merchants had enjoyed free trade with Spanish America during the Napoleonic wars, a privilege they might lose if military intervention restored Spain's dominions. English statesmen eyed the rebirth of French influence uneasily, to be sure, yet they were aware of potential American competition for the carrying trade of the new republics, to say nothing of the fact that the Louisiana Purchase and the Florida treaty with Spain had shown that the United States was an expanding power.

That British uneasiness is illustrated in

Foreign Secretary George Canning's cabinet memorandum of November 15, 1822. The restoration of Spain's exclusive colonial system endangered England's trade—but the United States had a navy within easy access of the Caribbean, and she coveted the island of Cuba.

By March, 1823, the French invasion of Spain had overbalanced Canning's distrust of American ambition for the moment. He warned the French that intervention to overthrow constitutional government in Spain gave the Allied powers no license for extending that intervention to Spain's colonies. Canning was not entirely certain of the effectiveness of his warning; hence, in August, he turned to another factor in the situation and began his negotiations with American Minister Richard Rush at London. Canning proposed that the United States and England should issue a joint declaration against the reconquest, or the transfer, of Spain's dominions in the Western Hemisphere. Rush replied by asking that England recognize the independence of the Latin American states before further action was taken. Canning evaded and Rush pressed the issue. By September, 1823, Rush was willing to sign a joint declaration without consulting his own government—if England would recognize the South American republics. Again Canning evaded and then dropped the scheme altogether as the French Foreign Minister finally convinced him that France did not mean to give military backing to any attempt of Spain's to reconquer her empire in the Western Hemisphere.

While Secretary of State John Quincy Adams was escaping a Washington summer at Quincy, President Monroe was receiving such dispatches as these, which show Richard Rush's progress from welcome of Canning's proposals to disillusion and distrust of British overtures. Monroe turned to Jefferson and Madison for advice concerning Canning's plan for a joint declaration. In his reply, which favored accepting Canning's proposals, Jefferson stressed the idea of the "two spheres," and urged that republican America remain aloof and leave monarchical Europe to its own devices. Like Jefferson, Madison was ready to accept the Canning plan, but he was not willing to abandon Europe. The struggle between absolutism and constitutional government was being fought in the Old World as well as in the New. The United States, as the world's foremost republic, should not undertake joint action with England until the latter recognized the independence of Greece to atone for its treachery to free government in Spain.

When Monroe's Cabinet reassembled at Washington in October, it had to consider the Russian ukase, the Canning proposal, and the advice of the two elder statesmen. Then Rush informed his chief of Canning's apparent withdrawal, which convinced John Quincy Adams that Canning had been motivated by a desire to keep the United States out of Cuba. Later in the month, Baron Tuyl, the Russian Minister, informed the American Secretary of State that Russia could not recognize any of the states formed by the break-up of Spain's empire in the New World. Tuyl went on to remark—with almost sinister casualness in John Quincy Adams's view—that the United States was to be congratulated on its present "admirably neutral" position in regard to Spain and her colonies.

By mid-November of 1823, Monroe's Cabinet had begun discussing the foreign policy statement to be included in the President's next message. Adams's diary, which had been suspended during the summer, records these discussions and portrays the conflicting views which swayed the participants. Monroe and John C. Calhoun, then Secretary of War, appear most concerned about the possibility of military intervention in the Americas. Adams doubted that Their Majesties planned such action: restoration of the Spanish colonial system could profit none of the powers concerned and none had sufficient naval strength to challenge the United States in American waters. Opposing the cautious Attorney General, William Wirt, Adams urged that Monroe include a statement on American foreign policy in his next annual message. But, as Adams's prime concern was possible general European hostility against the United States, he urged that we state our views independently rather than in a joint declaration with England, which might be particularly offensive to Russia. That same concern for European opinion prompted Adams to oppose Monroe's plan to include a recommendation that Congress appropriate money to send a Minister to the revolutionary republic of Greece.

Monroe accepted Adams's advice and limited his remarks to a declaration that the New World was closed to further European colonization and that, as the United States refrained from interfering in European affairs, so it would consider effort to extend European systems into these continents as an unfriendly act.

Thus the Monroe Doctrine took form, impelled by the forces of power politics and shaped by the ideas of many men. The distinction between the "two spheres" complemented by the notion of "an American System" stemmed from the speeches of Henry Clay, the propaganda of revolutionary Latin American agents in the United States, the influence of

Jefferson, and the conviction of James Monroe. The noncolonization idea had its immediate origin in John Quincy Adams's earlier observations on the ukase extending the boundary of Russian America; while the unilateral character of Monroe's statement derives from the Rush dispatch of October tenth, and from Adams's distrust of the sudden friendliness Canning was displaying toward the United States.

The Monroe Doctrine was all but ignored in the Europe of the 1820s and it did not actually become a functioning element in the American tradition until many decades afterward. Yet, though the doctrine was a declaration unsupported by adequate force, it offered the first official sanction to the idea that the severance of the European and the American political systems gave to the United States the role of leader in the Americas and protector of their liberties. It was a statement of America against Europe, and not against Latin America.

The Canning and Rush letters are reprinted from the Massachusetts Historical Society *Proceedings*, Series 2, Vol XV (1902). The selection from John Quincy Adams is from the *Memoirs*, Vol. VI (Philadelphia, 1875).

Correspondence of George Canning and Richard Rush

RICHARD RUSH TO THE SECRETARY OF STATE

London, August 19, 1823

SIR,—When my interview with Mr. Canning on Saturday was about to close, I transiently asked him whether, notwithstanding the late news from Spain, we might not hope that the Spaniards would get the better of all their difficulties. I had allusion to the defection of Baltasteros, in Andalusia, an event seeming to threaten with new dangers the constitutional cause. His reply was general, importing nothing more than his opinion of the increased difficulties and dangers with which, undoubtedly, this event was calculated to surround the Spanish cause.

Pursuing the topick of Spanish affairs, I remarked that should France ultimately effect her purposes in Spain, there was at least the consolation left, that Great Britain would not allow her to go farther and lay her hands upon the Spanish

colonies, bringing them too under her grasp. I here had in my mind the sentiments promulgated upon this subject in Mr. Canning's note to the British ambassador at Paris of the 31st of March, during the negotiations that preceded the invasion of Spain. It will be recollected that the British government says in this note, that time and the course of events appeared to have substantially decided the question of the separation of these colonies from the mother country, although their formal recognition as independent states by Great Britain might be hastened or retarded by external circumstances, as well as by the internal condition of those new states themselves; and that as his Britannic majesty disclaimed all intention of appropriating to himself the smallest portion of the late Spanish possessions in America, he was also satisfied that no attempt would be made by France to bring any of them under her dominion, either by conquest, or by cession from Spain.

By this we are to understand, in terms sufficiently distinct, that Great Britain would not be passive under such an attempt by France, and Mr. Canning, on my having referred to this note, asked me what I thought my government would say to going hand in hand with this, in the same sentiment; not as he added that any concert in action under it, could become necessary between the two countries, but that the simple fact of our being known to hold the same sentiment would, he had no doubt, by its moral effect, put down the intention on the part of France, admitting that she should ever entertain it. This belief was founded he said upon the large share of the maritime power of the world which Great Britain and the United States shared between them, and the consequent influence which the knowledge that they held a common opinion upon a question on which such large maritime interests, present and future, hung, could not fail to produce upon the rest of the world.

I replied, that in what manner my government would look upon such a suggestion, I was unable to say, but that I would communicate it in the same informal manner in which he threw it out. I said, however, that I did not think I should do so with full advantage, unless he would at the same time enlighten me as to the precise situation in which His Majesty's government stood at this moment in relation to those new states, and especially on the material point of their own independence.

He replied that Great Britain certainly never again intended to lend her instrumentality or aid, whether by mediation or otherwise, towards making up the dispute between Spain and her colonies; but that if this result could still be brought about, she would not interfere to *prevent* it. Upon my intimating that I had supposed that all idea of Spain ever recovering her authority over the colonies had long since gone by, he explained by saying that he did not mean to controvert that opinion, for he too believed that the day had arrived when all America might be considered as lost to Europe, so far as the tie of political dependence was concerned. All that he meant was, that if Spain and the colonies should still be able to bring the dispute, not yet totally extinct between them, to a close upon terms satisfactory to both sides, and which should at the same time secure to Spain commercial or other advantages not extended to other nations, that Great Britain would not object to a compromise in this spirit of preference to Spain. All that she would ask would be to stand upon as favored a footing as any other nation after Spain. Upon my again alluding to the im-

probability of the dispute ever settling down now even upon this basis, he said that it was not his intention to maintain such a position, and that he had expressed himself as above rather for the purpose of indicating the feeling which this cabinet still had towards Spain in relation to the controversy, than of predicting results.

Wishing, however, to be still more specifically informed, I asked whether Great Britain was at this moment taking any step, or contemplating any, which had reference to the recognition of these states, this being the point in which we felt the chief interest.

He replied that she had taken none whatever, as yet, but was upon the eve of taking one, not final, but preparatory, and which would still leave her at large to recognize or not according to the position of events at a future period. The measure in question was, to send out one or more individuals under authority from this government to South America, not strictly diplomatic, but clothed with powers in the nature of a commission of inquiry, and which in short he described as analogous to those exercised by our commissioners in 1817; and that upon the result of this commission much might depend as to the ulterior conduct of Great Britain. I asked whether I was to understand that it would comprehend all the new states, or which of them; to which he replied that, for the present, it would be limited to Mexico.

Reverting to this first idea he again said, that he hoped that France would not, should even events in the Peninsula be favorable to her, extend her views to South America for the purpose of reducing the colonies, nominally perhaps for Spain, but in effect to subserve ends of her own; but that in case she should meditate such a policy, he was satisfied that the knowledge of the United States being opposed to it as well as Great Britain, could not fail to have its influence in checking her steps. In this way he thought good might be done by prevention, and peaceful prospects all round increased. As to the form in which such knowledge might be made to reach France, and even the other powers of Europe, he said in conclusion that that might probably be arranged in a manner that would be free from objection.

I again told him that I would convey his suggestions to you for the information of the President, and impart to him whatever reply I might receive. My own inference rather is, that his proposition was a fortuitous one; yet he entered into it I thought with some interest, and appeared to receive with a corresponding satisfaction the assurance I gave him that it should be made known to the President. I did not feel myself at liberty to express any opinion unfavorable to it, and was as careful to give none in its favor.

Mr. Canning mentioned to me at this same interview, that a late confidential despatch which he had seen from Count Nesselrode to Count Lieven, dated, I think, in June, contained declarations respecting the Russian ukase relative to the northwest coast that were satisfactory; that they went to show that it would probably not be executed in a manner to give cause of complaint to other nations, and that, in particular, it had not yet been executed in any instance under orders issued by Russia subsequently to its first promulgation.

I have the honor to remain, with very great respect,

Your obedient servant,
Richard Rush

Honorable John Quincy Adams, Secretary of State.

(Enclosure with Mr. Rush's No. 325, August 23, 1823.)

GEORGE CANNING TO RICHARD RUSH

Private and confidential.

Foreign Office, Aug. 20, 1823

MY DEAR SIR,—Before leaving Town I am desirous of bringing before you in a more distinct, but still in an unofficial and confidential shape, the question which we shortly discussed the last time that I had the pleasure of seeing you.

Is not the moment come when our Governments might understand each other as to the Spanish American Colonies? And if we can arrive at such an understanding, would it not be expedient for ourselves, and beneficial for all the world, that the principles of it should be clearly settled and plainly avowed?

For ourselves we have no disguise.

1. We conceive the recovery of the Colonies by Spain to be hopeless.

2. We conceive the question of the recognition of them, as Independent States, to be one of time and circumstances.

3. We are, however, by no means disposed to throw any impediment in the way of an arrangement between them and the mother country by amicable negotiations.

4. We aim not at the possession of any portion of them ourselves.

5. We could not see any portion of them transferred to any other Power, with indifference.

If these opinions and feelings are as I firmly believe them to be, common to your Government with ours, why should we hesitate mutually to confide them to each other; and to declare them in the face of the world?

If there be any European Power which cherishes other projects, which looks to a forcible enterprize for reducing the colonies to subjugation, on the behalf or in the name of Spain; or which meditates the acquisition of any part of them to itself, by cession or by conquest; such a declaration on the part of your government and ours would be at once the most effectual and the least offensive mode of intimating our joint disapprobation of such projects.

It would at the same time put an end to all the jealousies of Spain with respect to her remaining Colonies, and to agitation which it would be but humane to allay; being determined (as we are) not to profit by encouraging it.

Do you conceive that under the power which you have recently received, you are authorized to enter into negotiation and to sign any Convention upon this subject? Do you conceive, if that be not within your competence, you could exchange with me ministerial notes upon it?

Nothing could be more gratifying to me than to join with you in such a work, and, I am persuaded, there has seldom, in the history of the world, occurred an opportunity when so small an effort of two friendly Governments might produce so unequivocal a good and prevent such extensive calamities.

I shall be absent from London but three weeks at the utmost; but never so far distant but that I can receive and reply to any communication within three or four days.

I have the honor to be

My Dear Sir, with great respect and esteem

Your obedient and faithful servant

(Signed) George Canning

R. Rush, Esqr.

RICHARD RUSH TO THE SECRETARY OF STATE

London, October 10, 1823

SIR,—At the conference with Mr. Canning the day before yesterday, he said nothing of Spanish American affairs, except barely to remark at parting, that he should send off consuls to the new states very soon, perhaps in the course of this month. I asked whether *consuls* or commercial agents. He said he believed they might as well be called by the former name, as they would be invested with the powers and charged with the duties that belonged to the consular office. I asked if they would be received in that capacity by the governments between which and Great Britain no political or diplomatic relations had yet been formed. He said, that this he did not know with any certainty; he rather supposed that they would be received.

I saw him again at the foreign office yesterday, and he said not one single word relative to South America, although the occasion was altogether favorable for resuming the topick, had he been disposed to resume it. I therefore consider that all further discussion between us in relation to it is now at an end. I had myself regarded the questions involved in the discussion as essentially changed by the arrival of the news of the convention of the 4th of July between Buenos Ayres and the commissioners from Spain: and of the complete annihilation of the remnant of the royal forces in Colombia under Morales, on the third of August, both which pieces of intelligence have reached England since the twenty sixth of September, the date of my last conference with Mr. Canning on the South American subject.

The termination of the discussion between us may be thought somewhat sudden, not to say abrupt, considering how zealously as well as spontaneously it was stated on his side. As I did not commence it, it is not my intention to revive it. If I had actually acceded to his proposals, I should have endeavored to have placed my conduct in a satisfactory light before the President. The motives of it would not, I flatter myself, have been disapproved. But as the whole subject is now before my government, and as I shall do nothing further in it without instructions, I should deem it out of place to travel into any new reasons in support of a step not in fact taken.

Mr. Canning not having acceded to my proposal, nor I to his, we stand as we were before his first advance to me, with the exception only of the light which the intervening discussion may be supposed to have shed upon the dispositions and policy of England in this important matter. It appears that having ends of her own in view, she has been anxious to facilitate their accomplishment by invoking my auxiliary offices as the minister of the United States at this court; but as to the independence of the new states of America, for their own benefit, that this seems quite another question in her diplomacy. It is France that must not be aggrandized, not South America that must be made free. The former doctrine may fitly enough return upon Britain as part of her permanent political creed; but not having been taught to regard it as also incorporated with the foreign policy of the United States, I have forborne to give it gratuitous succour. I would have brought myself to minister to it incidentally on this occasion, only in return for a boon which it was in the power of

Britain herself to have offered; a boon that might have closed the sufferings and brightened the prospects of those infant Republics emerging from the new world, and seeming to be connected as by a great moral chain with our own destinies.

Whether any fresh explanations with France since the fall of Cadiz may have brought Mr. Canning to so full and sudden a pause with me, I do not know, and most likely never shall know if events so fall out that Great Britain no longer finds it necessary to seek the aid of the United States in furtherance of her schemes of counteraction as against France or Russia. That the British cabinet, and the governing portion of the British nation, will rejoice at heart in the downfall of the constitutional system in Spain, I have never had a doubt and have not now, so long as this catastrophe can be kept from crossing the path of British interests and British ambition. This nation in its collective, corporate, capacity has no more sympathy with popular rights and freedom now, than it had on the plains of Lexington in America; than it showed during the whole progress of the French revolution in Europe, or at the close of its first great act, at Vienna, in 1815; than it exhibited lately at Naples in proclaiming a neutrality in all other events, save that of the safety of the royal family there; or, still more recently, when it stood aloof whilst France and the Holy Alliance avowed their intention of crushing the liberties of unoffending Spain, of crushing them too upon pretexts so wholly unjustifiable and enormous that English ministers, for very shame, were reduced to the dilemma of speculatively protesting against them, whilst they allowed them to go into full action. With a king in the hands of his ministers, with an aristocracy of unbounded opulence and pride, with what is called a house of commons constituted essentially by this aristocracy and always moved by its influence, England can, in reality, never look with complacency upon popular and equal rights, whether abroad or at home. She therefore moves in her natural orbit when she wars, positively or negatively, against them. For their own sakes alone, she will never war in their favor.

In the conference with Mr. Canning at Gloucester Lodge on the 26th of last month, he informed me that this government had sent out three commissioners to Mexico with objects such as I have already stated in a former communication to you. Should the course and progress of events after their arrival in Mexico, render recognition by Great Britain advisable, one of these commissioners was furnished, he said, with contingent credentials to be minister, another would be constituted·secretary of Legation, and the third consul. He also said that these appointments, as well as those of commercial agents or consuls, whichsoever they might be, to go to the new states generally, would probably have the effect of inviting in the end further approaches from them all, to an intercourse with Great Britain, which approaches, should they be made, might be met by Great Britain, according to circumstances.

It may perhaps afford room for conjecture what has led to the preference of Mexico over the other ex-colonies for such a provisionary diplomatic representation. I have heard a rumour, that an eye to some immediate advantage from the mines of that country has been the motive. Whilst the independence of Mexico has been of more recent establishment, it seems not less true,

that her advances to internal stability have been less sure than we have seen in some of the other new states. Mr. Canning himself in one of our conversations thought fit to select Mexico as affording a prominent illustration of interior disquiet. Whether then the above rumour is the key to this early preference, or the proximity of this new state to the territories of the United States—or what considerations may have led to it, a little more time will probably disclose. It may rest on the mere fact of her greater population and riches. . . .

I have the honor to remain, with very great respect,

Your obedient servant,
Richard Rush

Honorable John Quincy Adams, Secretary of State

Memoirs of John Quincy Adams

[NOVEMBER, 1823]

20th. At the office I received a note from the President, proposing large alterations to my draft of instructions to R. Rush upon Canning's proposals concerning South American affairs. Some of the alterations were unexceptionable; others I wished him further to consider. I called at his house, but he was out riding. He afterwards came to the office. I stated my objections to some of his proposed alterations of my draft, and suggested to him the substance of a substitute which I wished to offer to his projected paragraph. He agreed that I should draft a substitute, and proposed a meeting of the Administration to-morrow. He had adopted Mr. Calhoun's idea of giving Mr. Rush a discretionary power to act jointly with the British Government in case of any sudden emergency of danger, of which they and he should judge. I am utterly averse to this; and I told him that I thought the instructions should be explicit, authorizing him distinctly to act in specified contingencies, and requiring him in all others to refer for every important measure to his Government.

21st. I had received a note from the President requesting me to attend a meeting of the members of the Administration at one. The meeting lasted till five.

I mentioned my wish to prepare a paper to be delivered confidentially to Baron Tuyl, and the substance of which I would in the first instance express to him in a verbal conference. It would refer to the verbal communications recently made by him, and to the sentiments and dispositions manifested in the extract of a dispatch relating to

Spanish affairs which he lately put into my hands. My purpose would be in a moderate and conciliatory manner, but with a firm and determined spirit, to declare our dissent from the principles avowed in those communications; to assert those upon which our own Government is founded, and, while disclaiming all intention of attempting to propagate them by force, and all interference with the political affairs of Europe, to declare our expectation and hope that the European powers will equally abstain from the attempt to spread their principles in the American hemisphere, or to subjugate by force any part of these continents to their will.

The President approved of this idea; and then taking up the sketches that he had prepared for his message, read them to us. Its introduction was in a tone of deep solemnity and of high alarm, intimating that this country is menaced by imminent and formidable dangers, such as would probably soon call for their most vigorous energies and the closest union. It then proceeded to speak of the foreign affairs, chiefly according to the sketch I had given him some days since, but with occasional variations. It then alluded to the recent events in Spain and Portugal, speaking in terms of the most pointed reprobation of the late invasion of Spain by France, and of the principles upon which it was undertaken by the open avowal of the King of France. It also contained a broad acknowledgment of the Greeks as an independent nation, and a recommendation to Congress to make an appropriation for sending a Minister to them.

Of all this Mr. Calhoun declared his approbation. I expressed as freely my wish that the President would reconsider the whole subject before he should determine to take that course. I said the tone of the introduction I apprehended would take the nation by surprise and greatly alarm them. It would come upon them like a clap of thunder. There had never been in the history of this nation a period of so deep calm and tranquillity as we now enjoyed. We never were, upon the whole, in a state of peace so profound and secure with all foreign nations as at this time. This message would be a summons to arms—to arms against all Europe, and for objects of policy exclusively European— Greece and Spain. It would be as new, too, in our policy as it would be surprising. For more than thirty years Europe had been in convulsions; every nation almost of which it is composed alternately invading and invaded. Empires, kingdoms, principalities, had been overthrown, revolutionized, and counter-revolutionized, and we had looked on safe in our distance beyond an intervening ocean, and avowing a total forbearance to interfere in any of the combinations of European policies. This message would at once buckle on the harness and throw down the gauntlet. It would have the air of open defiance to all Europe, and I should not be surprised if the first answer to it from Spain and France, and even Russia, should be to break off their diplomatic intercourse with us. I did not expect that the quiet which we had enjoyed for six or seven years would last much longer. The aspect of things was portentous; but if we must come to an issue with Europe, let us keep it off as long as possible. Let us use all possible means to carry the opinion of the nation with us, and the opinion of the world.

Calhoun said that he thought there was not the tranquility that I spoke of; that there was great anxiety in the thinking part of the nation; that there was a general expectation that the Holy Alliance would employ force against South America, and that it would be proper that the President should sound the alarm to the nation. A time was approaching when all its energies would be needed, and the public mind ought to be prepared for it. . . .

22d. I finished the draft of my second dispatch to R. Rush upon Canning's proposals. And there must be yet a third. I also began a written statement of what has passed between Baron de Tuyl and me concerning the intentions of the Russian Cabinet, with a view to transmit copies of it and of the documents to Mr. Middleton and Mr. Rush. Mr. Gallatin was with the President, but withdrew on my going in. I left with the President my draft for a second dispatch to R. Rush on South American affairs. And I spoke to him again urging him to abstain from everything in his message which the Holy Allies could make a pretext for construing into aggression upon them. I said there were considerations of weight which I could not even easily mention at a Cabinet meeting. If he had determined to retire from the public service at the end of his present term, it was now drawing to a close. It was to be considered now as a whole, and a system of administration for a definite term of years. It would hereafter, I believe, be looked back to as the golden age of this republic, and I felt an extreme solicitude that its end might correspond with the character of its progress; that the Administration might be delivered into the hands of the successor, whoever he might be, at peace and in amity with all the world. If this could not be, if the Holy Alliance were determined to make up an issue with us, it was our policy to meet, and not to make it. We should retreat to the wall before taking to arms, and be sure at every step to put them as much as possible in the wrong. I said if the Holy Alliance really intended to restore by force the Colonies of Spain to her dominion, it was questionable to me whether we had not, after all, been over-hasty in acknowledging the South American independence. It had pledged us now to take ground which we had not felt at all bound to take five years ago. At the Congress of Aix-la-Chapelle the allies had discussed what they should do with South America, and we had not even thought of interfering with them. If they intend now to interpose by force, we shall have as much as we can do to prevent them, without going to bid them defiance in the heart of Europe. . . .

25th. I made a draft of observations upon the communications recently received from the Baron de Tuyl, the Russian Minister. Took the paper, together with the statement I had prepared of what has passed between him and me, and all the papers received from him, to the President. . . . The paper itself was drawn to correspond exactly with a paragraph of the President's message which he had read me yesterday, and which was entirely conformable to the system of policy which I have earnestly recommended for this emergency. It was also intended as a firm, spirited, and yet conciliatory answer to all the communications lately received from the Russian Government, and at the same time an unequivocal answer to the proposals made by Canning to Mr. Rush. It was meant also to be eventually an exposition of the principles of this Government, and a brief development of its political system as henceforth to be maintained: essentially republican—maintaining its own independence, and respecting that of others; essentially pacific—studiously avoiding all involvement in the combinations of European politics, cultivating peace and friendship with the most absolute monarchies, highly appreciating and anxiously desirous of retaining that of the Emperor Alexander, but declaring that, having recognized the independence of the South American States, we could not see with indifference any attempt by European powers by forcible interposition either to restore the Spanish dominion on the American Continents or to introduce monarchical principles into those countries, or to transfer any portion of the ancient or present American possessions of Spain to any other European power. . . .

I attended the adjourned Cabinet meeting at the President's, from half-past twelve—four hours. At the President's request, I read the statement of what has passed between Baron Tuyl and me since the 16th of last month, and then my proposed draft of observations upon the communications recently received from him. The President then read the draft of the corresponding paragraph for his message to Congress, and asked whether it should form part of the message. I took a review of the preceding transactions of the Cabinet meetings; remarking that the present questions had originated in a draft which he had presented merely for consideration, of an introduction to the message, of unusual solemnity, indicating extraordinary concern, and even alarm, at the existing state of things, coupled with two paragraphs, one containing strong and pointed censure upon France and the Holy Allies for the invasion of Spain, and the other recommending an appropriation for a Minister to send to the Greeks, and in substance recognizing them as independent; that the course now proposed is a substitute for that, and that it is founded upon the idea that if an issue must be made up between us and the Holy Alliance it ought to be upon grounds exclusively American; that we should separate it from all European concerns, disclaim all intention of interfering with these, and make the stand altogether for an American cause; that at the same time the answer to be given to the Russian communications should be used as the means of answering also the proposals of Mr. George Canning, and of assuming the attitude to be maintained by the United States with reference to the designs of the Holy Alliance upon South America. This being premised, I observed that the whole of the papers now drawn up were but various parts of one system under consideration, and the only really important question to be determined, as it appeared to me, was that yesterday made by Mr. Wirt, and which had been incidentally dis-

cussed before, namely, whether we ought at all to take this attitude as regards South America; whether we get any advantage by committing ourselves to a course of opposition against the Holy Alliance. My own mind, indeed, is made up that we ought thus far to take this stand; but I thought it deserved great deliberation, and ought not to be taken without a full and serious estimate of consequences.

Mr. Wirt then resumed the objection he had taken yesterday, and freely enlarged upon it. He said he did not think this country would support the Government in a war for the independence of South America. There had never been much general excitement in their favor. Some part of the people of the interior had felt warmly for them, but it never had been general, and never had there been a moment when the people thought of supporting them by war. To menace without intending to strike was neither consistent with the honor nor the dignity of the country. It was possible that the proposals of Mr. Canning themselves were traps laid to ensnare us into public declarations against the Holy Allies, without intending even to take part against them; that if we were to be so far committed, all the documents ought to be communicated to Congress, and they ought to manifest their sentiments in the form of resolutions and that the Executive ought not to pledge the honor of the nation to war without taking the sense of the country with them.

Mr. Calhoun supported the other view of the question. He said the great object of the measure was to detach Great Britain definitively from the Holy Alliance. Great Britain would not, could not, resist them alone, we remaining neutral. She would fall eventually into their views, and the South Americans would be subdued. The next step the allies would then take would be against ourselves—to put down what had been called the first example of successful democratic rebellion. It was probable that by taking the stand now the Holy Alliance would be deterred from any forcible interposition with South America; but if not, we ought to sustain the ground now taken, even to the extent of war. There was danger in both alternatives; but the immediate danger was light, the contingent one to be averted was formidable in the extreme. It was wisdom in this, as in many of the occurrences of life, public and private, to incur the light hazard for the purpose of warding off the great one. And as this was the wise course, he had no doubt it would be sustained by the people of this country, if the exigency should require it. They would always sustain the wisest course when it was properly explained to them.

He did believe that the Holy Allies had an ultimate eye to us; that they would, if not resisted,
subdue South America. He had no doubt they
would retain the country in subjection by military
force. Success would give them partisans. Violent
parties would arise in this country, one for and
one against them, and we should have to fight
upon our own shores for our own institutions.
He was therefore in favor of the President's message with the proposed paragraph. But he thought
a copy of it might be delivered to Baron Tuyl,
with notice that it was to be considered as the
answer to the communications recently received
from him. . . .

I said, with regard to the objections of Mr.
Wirt, that I considered them of the deepest moment. I was glad they had been made, and trusted
the President would give them full consideration
before coming to his definitive decision. If they
prevailed, neither the paragraph in the message
nor my draft would be proper. The draft was
prepared precisely to correspond with the paragraph in the message. I did believe, however, that
both would be proper and necessary. Not that I
supposed that the Holy Alliance had any intention of ultimately attacking us, or meant to establish monarchy among us. But if they should really
invade South America, and especially Mexico, it
was impossible, in the nature of things, that they
should do it to restore the old exclusive dominion
of Spain. Spain had not, and never could again
have, the physical force to maintain that dominion; and if the countries should be kept in subjugation by the armies of the Allies, was it in human absurdity to imagine that they should waste
their blood and treasure to prohibit their own
subjects upon pain of death to set foot upon those
territories? Surely not. If then the Holy Allies
should subdue Spanish America, however they
might at first set up the standard of Spain, the
ultimate result of their undertaking would be to
recolonize them, partitioned out among themselves. Russia might take California, Peru, Chili;
France, Mexico—where we know she has been
intriguing to get a monarchy under a Prince of
the House of Bourbon, as well as at Buenos Ayres.
And Great Britain, as her last resort, if she could
not resist this course of things, would take at least
the island of Cuba for her share of the scramble.
Then what would be our situation—England holding Cuba, France Mexico? And Mr. Gallatin had
told me within these four days that Hyde de Neu-
ville had said to him, in the presence and hearing
of ten or twelve persons, that if we did not yield
to the claim of France under the eighth article of
the Louisiana Convention, she ought to go and

take the country, and that she had a strong party
there. The danger, therefore, was brought to our
own doors, and I thought we could not too soon
take our stand to repel it.

There was another point of view, which the
President had in part suggested, and which I
thought highly important. Suppose the Holy Allies should attack South America, and Great Britain should resist them alone and without our
cooperation. I thought this not an improbable
contingency, and I believed in such a struggle the
allies would be defeated and Great Britain would
be victorious, by her command of the sea. But, as
the independence of the South Americans would
then be only protected by the guarantee of Great
Britain, it would throw them completely into her
arms, and in the result make them her Colonies
instead of those of Spain. My opinion was, therefore, that we must act promptly and decisively.
But the act of the Executive could not, after all,
commit the nation to a pledge of war. Nor was
war contemplated by the proposals of Mr. Canning. He had explicitly stated to Mr. Rush from
the beginning that his object was merely a concerted expression of sentiment, which he supposed
would avert the necessity of war; and, as Great
Britain was not and would not be pledged, by
anything Mr. Canning had said or proposed, to
war, so would anything now done by the Executive here leave Congress free hereafter to act or
not, according as the circumstances of the emergency may require. With regard to the point made
by Mr. Calhoun, my opinion was directly opposite
to that which he had expressed. The communications from the Russian Minister required a direct
and explicit answer. A communication of the paragraph in the President's message would be no answer, and if given *as* an answer would certainly
be very inconsistent with the position that foreigners have no right to notice it, because it was all
said among ourselves. . . . I thought as the Holy
Alliance had come to edify and instruct us with
their principles, it was due in candor to them, and
in justice to ourselves, to return them the compliment. And if the people of our country should
hereafter know, as they must, how much good
advice the Emperor Alexander has been giving us
in private, they would not be satisfied to be told
that the only return we had made to him for it
was to send him a copy of the President's message
to Congress. I felt the more solicitude that a direct
and explicit answer should be given him, because
the Baron in one of his dispatches had intimated
that I had expressed not only an earnest desire that
we might remain on good terms with Russia, but
high opinions of the Emperor's moderation. In

my report of the conferences, I had stated what was said by me, and from which the Baron had drawn his inference. I had told him that, having, while residing at his Court, witnessed the many acts of friendship for the United States of the Emperor Alexander, I had formed sentiments of high respect for his character, and even of personal attachment to him. This was true. I thought better of him than perhaps any other person at this meeting; and I did not believe there was one word in my draft that would give him offence. The avowal of principles connected with the disclaimer of interference in European affairs, of proselytism, and of hostile purposes, could not offend him. I thought it most essential. I was willing to agree to any modification which might be thought advisable, but the distinct avowal of principle appeared to me to be absolutely required. The paper acknowledged that we were aware the monarchical principle of government was different from ours, but it declared that we saw no reason why they should not be at peace with each other, and that we earnestly desired that peace. . . .

TEXAS

By 1832, the tensions between the Mexican government and the American settlers in Texas had provoked the latter to the point of holding a convention and formulating plans to secure relief within the framework of the Mexican Constitution. Since the confirmation of the Austin grants in 1823, Americans had been settling in Texas, where they found cheap land and a local autonomy fairly well assured by their distance from the center of Mexican power. In that same period, the United States had been negotiating for such a westward adjustment of its boundary with Mexico as would bring those Texas settlements into American control.

That diplomatic effort, in conjunction with the growth of the American communities in Texas and their comparative freedom from Indian attacks, roused Mexican suspicion and provoked the restrictive laws of 1830. Though Texas had been exempted from the decree abolishing slavery, the Mexican government forbade further immigration from the United States, established a frontier guard, and attempted to enforce its customs laws, which had been suspended for a six-year period during which Texans were allowed to import goods duty-free. In 1832, the Texan coast was put under martial law, and the Texan ports which had ignored the execution of the customs laws were attacked by a Mexican gunboat.

Faced by the actual enforcement of customs and immigration laws and the activity of a centralizing administration at Mexico City, the Texans resorted to their native remedy for political grievances: they met in convention and drafted a memorial requesting a three-year extension of Texan exemption from the operation of the customs laws, the suspension of the prohibition against American immigration, and a land grant for education. To implement their resolutions, the members of the convention appointed a Committee of Safety, organized a skeleton militia, and dispatched William H. Wharton to carry the convention's memorials to the several states and to the Federal government.

William H. Wharton (1802–1839) had left Virginia for Tennessee when the death of his parents put him under the guardianship of an uncle who lived in Nashville. Wharton completed his education there, studied law and was admitted to the bar. The unfinished business of wooing the daughter of a Texas planter brought Wharton into the new country and, shortly afterwards, marriage established him there. His new family's influence helped win him so prominent a place in local affairs that he was selected to draft the convention's memorial against the Mexican laws of 1830.

Though the Mexican authorities disapproved of the convention movement, the central government was in too turbulent a condition to make that disapproval felt. When a second convention met in 1833, it chose Wharton its president and drafted a constitution for Texas. The convention sent a representative to secure the Mexican government's approval of the constitution, but he was imprisoned in Mexico City and kept there for eighteen months. Meanwhile tensions increased in Texas; there were armed outbreaks.

All through the winter of 1835–1836, Texans and Mexican troops continued to clash. Meanwhile a Texas provisional government had been organized and commissioners were appointed to seek aid in the United States. As Wharton journeyed northward on his mission, Texans were fighting and dying at the Alamo; they were declaring their independence and indeed making that independence good at San Jacinto. Within a week of this victory, on April 26, 1836, Wharton addressed a New York audience on the wrongs of Texas and the just character of the war she was fighting. The Mexican government never had given Texas adequate protection, he declared, and the continued turbulence in Mexico since her separation from Spain in 1821 proved an "incapability for self-government on the part of the Mexican people." The decrees forbidding further American immigration to Texas were in themselves "sufficient to goad us on to madness," Wharton asserted, but the Texans had behaved with exemplary patience. Oppression had forced them to independence, and their cause was the cause of liberty and justice.

The people who had gathered in New York's Masonic Hall agreed with Wharton. The audience adopted a series of resolutions declaring the "Texians" a "Spartan band" fighting in the Spirit of '76 to "achieve their independence of the tyrannical government of Mexico." A committee of sixteen was appointed to solicit help for Texas and to confer with its agents concerning the best means of furthering the struggle. Thereafter Texas scrip began selling briskly on the New York market and land speculation reinforced patriotic sympathy in making Texas a matter of concern to American interests.

At the end of May, about a fortnight after hostilities had been suspended, Wharton was presenting to President Jackson the case for the annexation of Texas. Later in the year he was appointed Minister to the United States and charged with the task of negotiating for the incorporation of Texas into the Union. Wharton was not to see that project succeed, however, for the accidental discharge of his own gun killed him in 1839.

Wharton's address is reprinted from a pamphlet published in New York in 1836.

An Address Delivered in New York, April 26, 1836

BY WILLIAM H. WHARTON

. . . Mr. Chairman and Gentlemen, at the request of my colleagues I appear before you this evening in their name and in my own, as one of the representatives of suffering Texas, for the purpose of explaining to you the origin of her difficulties and her present position and prospects. It is my intention to address your understandings, and not your sympathies. It will be my earnest endeavour, to convince you that the people of Texas, have been most reluctantly forced into the present contest on account of the violent, illegal and total destruction of that Constitution under the guarantees of which they left the firesides of their Fathers in this happy land, and penetrated a wilderness trod only by savages. So conscious am I of the truth of this position, that I boldly throw down the gauntlet to all the world, and here in your presence, and in the presence of my God, pledge myself to establish beyond refutation, that before we struck a blow in Texas, we had no alternative but slavery or resistance. A charge of ingratitude to Mexico on the part of the Texians has been made by a few who are either ignorant of the true state of facts, or interested in misrepresenting them. In order to refute this foul slander upon our character it will be necessary to unfold to you the origin of the Colonial settlements. It is known to many of you that on the dissolution of the connexion between Mexico, and Spain in 1822, Don Augustin Iturbide, by *corruption and violence, established* a short lived *Imperial Government* in Mexico, with himself at the head, under the title of Augustin the 1st. On arriving at supreme power, he found that vast portion of the Mexican Territory east of the Rio Grande, known by the name of Texas in the possession of various tribes of Indians, who not only prevented the populating of Texas, but committed incessant depredations on the Mexican frontier. He ascertained that these savages could neither be subdued by the arms, nor purchased by the gold of Mexico; and that owing to their natural dread of Indians, the Mexicans could not be induced to venture into the wilderness of Texas. In addition to this dread of Indians, Texas held out no inducements for Mexican immigrants. They were accustomed to a lazy pastoral or mining life, in a healthy country. Texas was emphatically a land of agriculture—the land of cotton and of sugar cane, with the culture of which they were generally unacquainted; moreover, they had not that energy and perseverance necessary to combat the hardships and privations of a wilderness. Iturbide finding from these causes that Texas could not be populated with his own subjects, and that so long as it remained in the occupancy of the Indians, the inhabited part of his dominions continually suffered from their ravages and murders, undertook to expel the savages by the introduction of foreigners. Accordingly the national institute or council, on the 3d of January 1823 by his recommendation and sanction, adopted a law of colonization, in which they invited the immigration of foreigners to Texas on the following terms:—

1st. They promised to protect their liberty, property and civil rights.

2d. They offered to each colonist one league of land (4428 acres) for coming to Texas, he paying $30 to the government.

3d. They guaranteed to each colonist the privilege of leaving the empire at any time, with all his property, and also the privilege of selling the land which he may have acquired from the Mexican government (see the colonization law of 1823, more especially articles 1st, 8th, and 20th.) These were the inducements, and invitations held out to foreigners under the imperial government of Iturbide or Augustin 1st. In a short time however the nation deposed Iturbide, and deposited the supreme executive power in three individuals. This supreme executive power on the 18th of August, 1824, adopted a national colonization law, in which they recognized and confirmed the imperial colonization law with all its guarantees of

person and property. They also ceded to the different states, all the vacant lands within their respective limits. In accordance with this law the state of Coahuila and Texas on the 24th of March 1825, adopted a colonization law for the purpose, as expressed in the preamble, of protecting the frontiers, expelling the savages, augmenting the population of its vacant territory, multiplying the raising of stock, promoting the cultivation of its fertile lands, and of the arts and of commerce. In this state—colonization law—the promises to protect the persons and property of the colonists, which had been made in the two preceding national colonization laws were renewed and confirmed.

We have now before us the invitations and guarantees under which the colonists immigrated to Texas;—Let us examine into the manner in which these conditions have been complied with, and these flattering promises fulfilled.

The donation of 4428 acres, sounds largely at a distance. Considering, however, the difficulty and danger necessarily encountered in taking possession of those lands it will not be deemed an entire gratuity nor a magnificent bounty. If this territory had been previously pioneered by the enterprise of the Mexican government, and freed from the insecurities which beset a wilderness—trod only by savages—if the government had been deriving an actual revenue from it and if it could have realised a capital from the sale of it—then we admit that the donation would have been unexampled in the history of national liberality. But how lamentably different from all this was the real state of the case.

The lands granted were in the occupancy of savages, and situated in a wilderness of which the government had never taken possession, and of which it could not with its own citizens, ever have taken possession, and they were not sufficiently explored to obtain that knowledge of their character and situation necessary to a sale of them. They were shut out from all commercial intercourse with the rest of the world, and inaccessible to the commonest comforts of life; nor were they brought into possession and cultivation by the colonists without much toil and privation, and patience and enterprise, and suffering and blood, and loss of lives from Indian hostilities, and other causes. Under the smiles of a benignant heaven, however, the untiring perseverance of the colonists triumphed over all natural obstacles, expelled the savages by whom the country was infested, reduced the forest into cultivation and made the desert smile.

From this it must appear that the lands of Texas,

although nominally given, were in fact and in reality dearly bought. It may be here premised that a gift of lands by a nation to foreigners on condition of their immigrating and becoming citizens is immensely different from a gift by one individual to another. In the case of individuals, the donor loses all further claim or ownership over the thing bestowed. But in our case, the government only gave wild lands that they might be redeemed from a state of nature; that the obstacles to a first settlement might be overcome, and that they might be placed in a situation to augment the physical strength, and power, and revenue of the republic. It is not evident that Mexico, before the present revolution, held over the colonized lands of Texas, the same jurisdiction and right of property which all nations hold over the inhabited parts of their territory. But to do away more effectually the idea that the colonists of Texas are under great obligations to the Mexican government for their donations of land, let us examine at what price the government estimated the lands thus given.

Twelve or thirteen years ago, they gave to a colonist one league of land for settling in Texas, he paying the government $30, and last year (1835) they sold hundreds of leagues of land for a less price to undomiciliated foreigners. A true statement of facts then, is all that is necessary to pay at once that debt immense of endless gratitude which in the estimation of the ignorant and the interested, is due from the colonists to the Mexican government. It is perfectly evident that the colonists, in paying the government price for their lands, in expelling the savages, protecting the frontiers, redeeming the wilderness, and in augmenting the physical strength and resources of the nation, have rendered a full compensation for all that they obtained from Mexico. I pass over the toil, and sufferings, and dangers which attended the redeeming and the cultivation of their lands by the colonists, and turn to their civil condition since their connexion with Mexico. We have never known what quiet and security *were* since we have been in Texas. To make this more plain, I will briefly relate the bloody and revolting history of the late Mexican Republic. On the establishment of the Independence of Mexico, in 1822, Gen. Iturbide, by fraud and force, caused himself to be proclaimed emperor. He was soon dethroned and banished. He returned, however, from his exile, and was put to death. This being over, Victoria was elected president, during all of whose term of service, the country was torn to pieces by civil wars and conspiracies, as is evidenced by the rebellion and banishment of Men-

tuno, Bravo, and others. Victoria served only four years, and General Pedraza, was elected his successor,—but he was dispossessed by violence, and Guerero put in his place. Guerero was scarcely seated before Bustamente, with open war deposed him, put him to death and placed himself at the head of the government. Bustamente was hardly in the chair before Santa Anna dispossessed him by deluging the country with a civil war; which, after strewing the plains of the noble state of Zacatecas with her murdered citizens—murdered, only because they contended for their constitution—has rolled on with unglutted vengeance and cannibal ferocity to the shores of Texas —there—to complete the work of massacre and desolation. This, in a few sentences, is the history of Mexico during the fourteen years of her independence, and what is it but an unbroken history of treachery—of violence—and of blood? Can the same amount of crime and carnage be called and collected from one hundred years of the history of any other Christianized people? No! it would be impossible! I put it to your candor and republicanism, gentlemen, to say, if the *incapability of self-government* on the part of the Mexican people which is demonstrated by these incessant revolutions—if the insecurity of person and property—and the violation of all law and order which follow as the unavoidable consequences of such commotions—would not have justified the people of Texas in establishing an independent government, better calculated to promote their security and happiness? To this question, there can be but one answer given by the descendants of the sages and soldiers of '76.

Again, it will not be denied in this land of liberty, that *allegiance and protection are reciprocal*, and that when a state ceases to protect its inhabitants their allegiance simultaneously ceases. Mexico has never afforded the colonists a shadow of protection. When the colonial settlements commenced, Texas was in the occupancy of various tribes of Indians, who committed continual depredations and inhumanly murdered many of the most useful and respectable of both sexes. Not a Mexican soldier ever aided in expelling these Indians—not a gun, nor an ounce of ammunition was furnished the colonists; and not a dollar was paid them for their services. Again, the Mexican government has for years past exhibited a determination to annihilate the colonial settlements. I pass over many minor evidences of this diabolical determination, and come to the law of 6th of April, 1830. By this law, North Americans, and they alone, were forbidden admission into Texas. This was enough to blast all our hopes, and dishearten all our enterprise. It showed to us that we were to remain, scattered—isolated—and unhappy tenants of the wilderness. Compelled to gaze upon the resources of a lovely and fertile region, undeveloped for want of population. That we were to be cut off from the society of fathers and friends in the United States of the North—to prepare comforts suited to whose age and infirmities, many of us had immigrated and patiently submitted to every species of privation, and whose presence to gladden our firesides we were hourly anticipating. That feature of this law, granting admission to all other nations except our brethren of the United States of the North, was sufficient to goad us on to madness. Yes, the door of immigration to Texas was closed upon the only sister republic worthy of the name, which Mexico could boast of in this new world. . . . [In 1835, by decree, the Mexican government virtually put an end to the state governments.]

In order the more effectually to prevent all resistance to this unholy, revolutionary and central despotism, the same congress, prior to the decree of October 3d, enacted that the whole population should be disarmed, leaving only one gun to 500 citizens. Against these tyrannical proceedings, the legislature of Coahuila and Texas protested.

That body was immediately dispersed by the troops of the despot. The governor in his flight was overtaken and imprisoned. It was the misfortune of the lamented *Milam*, who was at this time returning from the seat of government to his home in Texas, to be found in company with the governor. For this, in their estimation, dreadful offence, and for no other assigned or assignable one, he too, was thrown into confinement. After several months of imprisonment, he was enabled to effect his escape, and he immediately started for Texas. In order to elude the pursuit of his merciless enemies, he travelled six hundred miles without a road, prosecuting his journey in the night, and secreting himself during the day. Throughout this dangerous and protracted journey, he subsisted alone on some few articles of food which he contrived to obtain on his escape from confinement, for he dared not show his face at any habitation.

Early in October last, near the town of Goliad, in Texas, his attention was aroused by the approach of soldiers. He at first, naturally enough conceived that he was overtaken by his enemies, and knowing that if he fell again into their hands, he would be subjected to death or endless imprisonment, although as one to fifty, he prepared to sell his life as dearly as possible.

How did his heart rebound, however, when on their nearer approach, he discovered that these soldiers were his Texian countrymen, on their march to storm the Mexican garrison at Goliad? They furnished him with some clothing, of which he was almost destitute, and with food, for the want of which he was nearly famished. In a few moments he joined the little band, and as some small revenge for the injuries, so causelessly and cruelly inflicted on himself, he had the satisfaction to be among the first and foremost in storming and capturing the garrison of Goliad. This being over, although he had been raised in the army of the United States, and was accustomed and qualified to command, yet by way of example, he entered into the ranks, and cheerfully discharged all the duties of a common soldier, until a few days previous to his final catastrophe. On the evening of the 4th of December last, he stepped forth from the ranks, and beat up for volunteers to storm the castle of San Antonio. His call was not unattended to. A Leonidas band of about three hundred placed themselves under his command, and on the night of the 5th of December, they entered the town to attack a garrison of more than five times their own numbers, who were also protected by forts, walls, houses, ditches, and twenty pieces of artillery. They entered the town, however, with the determination of soldiers, "to conquer or to die."

For six successive days and nights, did they grapple with the enemy. The life of their dauntless leader, was the price of his triumph. Yes, he was destined, like Wolfe and Pike, "to sleep the sleep of death in the arms of victory." Of the other unconquerable spirits who perished in the late massacre at San Antonio, it would seem invidious not to speak. The gallant Travis was cut off in the flower of his life. He was accomplished and dignified in his deportment, and collegiately and legally educated. Bowie is a name that was synonymous with all that was manly and indomitable in the character of man. Col. Bonham was a native of South Carolina, he lately acted as aid to Governor Hamilton, and has not left a more chivalrous gentleman behind him. Of Col. David Crocket, it is unnecessary here to speak. He was known, at least by character, to all of us. Suffice it to say, that although the world has been often amused with his innocent eccentricities, no one has ever denied to him, the character of a firm and honest man—qualities which would cancel ten thousand faults if he had them. . . .

I trust, gentlemen, that I will be pardoned for this digression. It was prompted by my own irrepressible feelings of gratitude, for they poured out their blood in defence of *my* rights, and in defence of the great principle of *human liberty*, in the establishment of which, all mankind are deeply interested.

You have now seen, gentlemen, that our constitution has been violently, illegally, and totally destroyed. You have seen that, superadded to this, our governor has been deposed and imprisoned, our legislature dispersed, and all the subaltern officers of our state, made dependent on the supreme government alone, instead of, on the suffrages of the people. In short, you have seen that our federative form of government has been converted into a central, consolidated and military despotism, enforced and administered by bayonets alone. Now, mark the forbearance of the people of Texas! Even after all these outrages on their rights, they did not rise in arms, and make an appeal to the God of battles, for justice and redress of their wrongs. They still hoped that the Mexican nation would have the firmness and patriotism to crush this military despotism, before the practical evils of it had reached the distant shores of Texas. In this hope, they were cruelly deceived. In the month of September last, a Mexican armed schooner appeared off our coast, and declared all of our ports in a state of blockade. Simultaneously with this General Coss invaded our territory by land. . . . About the same time a military force was sent to the colonial town of Gonzales, to demand of the inhabitants a surrender of their arms. This demand was refused with the promptness and indignation of freemen. A battle immediately ensued on the 28th September last, which terminated in the discomfiture and precipitate retreat of the Mexican forces. Gonzales was then the Lexington of our struggle, and the same cry of injured and insulted liberty, which from the blood of the slain at Lexington and Bunker's Hill ascended to high Heaven, and penetrated every corner of this land rousing the inhabitants to avenge their slaughtered countrymen, flew with electrical rapidity, after the battles of Gonzales and St. Antonio, over the beautiful and hitherto peaceful plains of Texas. The inhabitants promptly responded to its summons. They felt now that farther forbearance would be a crime.—That the cup of their bitterness was full to overflowing.— That the rod of oppression had smitten sufficiently severe, and that they could no longer submit without relinquishing for ever the glorious appellation of freemen. Accordingly they rallied around the standard of their country, from the hoary veteran of more than sixty, down to the beardless youth who had scarcely numbered a dozen years. All were animated with the indomitable spirit of "76." Yes! in the language of the martyred Emmet, all were determined that the "last intrenchment of liberty should be their graves." That this godlike resolve *has* been and *will* be fulfilled, the blood and martyrdom of a Milan, a Travis, a Bowie, a Crockett, a Bonham and their brave compatriots have rendered as plain to every understanding, as if it "were written in sunbeams on the face of heaven."

And here gentlemen, I would again turn your attention. to the forbearance of the people of Texas. Even after their territory had been invaded, battles had been fought, and victory had perched upon their standard—even after all this, they did not declare their independence. No, on the 7th of November last, while flushed with various and signal triumphs over the central mercenaries, the people of Texas, in solemn convention, declared for the constitution of 1824, and pledged themselves to aid with their fortunes and their lives in its restoration. On the second of March, however, finding that all parties in Mexico had united against them, that the constitution had been forgotten, and that they could hope for no aid in restoring it, they then declared their absolute independence. This they were compelled to do by *self preservation*, which is above all human law, above all human constitutions, above every thing, that does not emanate from the throne of God himself!

Of what has transpired since the commencement of this contest, you, gentlemen, have been apprized through the public journals. Of one fact, however, you may be assured: *Mexico can never conquer Texas!* We may be *exterminated*, but we never can be *conquered*. But I have gone too far in this admission. *We cannot be exterminated!* The ultimate triumph of our cause is as certain, as that the sun will continue to illuminate the universe. Like the sun itself, it may be temporarily obscured by passing clouds, but it will again burst forth with its all-dazzling and undying effulgence. The justice and benevolence of God, will forbid that the delightful region of Texas should again become a howling wilderness, trod only by savages, or that it should be permanently benighted by the ignorance and superstition, the anarchy and rapine of Mexican misrule. The Anglo-American race are destined to be for ever the proprietors of this land of *promise* and *fulfilment*. *Their* laws will govern it, *their* learning will enlighten it, *their* enterprise will improve it. *Their* flocks will range its boundless pastures, for *them* its fertile lands will yield their luxuriant harvests; its beauteous rivers will waft the products of *their* industry and enterprise, and *their* latest posterity will here enjoy legacies of "price unspeakable," in the possession of homes fortified by the genius of liberty, and sanctified by the spirit of a beneficent and tolerant religion. This is inevitable, for the wilderness of Texas has been redeemed by Anglo-American blood and enterprise. The colonists have carried with them the language, the habits, and the lofty love of liberty, that has always characterized and distinguished their ancestors. They have identified them indissolubly with the country. Yes! they have founded them on a basis, which, without being a prophet, I venture to assert will be codurable with the liberties of this land of *Washington*. I repeat it again. Mexico can never conquer Texas. . . .

But, gentlemen, Texas requires immediate pecuniary aid in order to feed and clothe her gallant soldiers, and thereby accomplish at once, what must necessarily be her *ultimate* destiny. Without this pecuniary aid a *temporary* triumph of despotism over liberty will take place. Without it, the darkness of midnight will glitter with the blaze of her dwellings, her soil will drink the blood of her bravest citizens, and the air be rent with the wailings of the widow and the fatherless. *Will they, can they*, who generously and promptly responded to and relieved the sufferings of Greece and Poland turn a deaf ear to their imploring brethren of Texas? Shall suppliant Greece and Poland be heard and aided, and the blood of Texas "sink in the ground?" Shades of our ancestors forbid it! Forbid it heaven! Gentlemen, again and again I appeal to you for succour. I feel it a glorious occupation to plead in so noble a cause. I invoke you by every principle of honour, by every feeling of humanity, by every obligation of blood, by your devotion to liberty, and your detestation of oppression, to step nobly forward, entitle yourselves to the prayers and blessings of the distressed, and embalm your names in a nation's gratitude. Do honor to the memories of your departed ancestors—do honor to this consecrated land of your birth—do honor to the *Anglo-Saxon American* race—do honor to the enlightened age in which we live—do honor to the sacred cause in which we are embarked, and more especially do honor to this great commercial metropolis, New-York, and enable her future historian to say, with truth and exultation, that although the sails of her commerce whiten every sea, and the *hum* of a million animates her streets, yet that her generous ardour and munificence in the cause of liberty and bleeding Texas, constitute for her a renown, far more imperishable and dear to the soul.

I will turn your attention for a moment, gentlemen, to the intrinsic resources of Texas. Its soil is unsurpassed by that of any country on the face of the globe, and its climate is equalled only by that of Italy. It is situated within the cotton and sugar region, intersected by numerous navigable rivers, and bounded on one side by the Gulf of Mexico, on which there are bays and harbours well adapted to all the purposes of commerce. It contains at present a population of about 70,000, composed of bold and enterprising men, devotedly attached to liberty and at all times ready to defend their homes *inch by inch* if necessary. In short, Texas is larger than England or France, and susceptible of a greater and denser population.

Mr. Chairman and gentlemen, our inhuman oppressors not content with enslaving the body, also endeavour to enslave the *conscience*. They require us to subscribe implicitly to all the *dogmas* of a particular religion without reference to our feelings or our creed. Can we submit to this? Will not prayers for our success in a cause so righteous ascend to heaven from every temple of God throughout this land? Did not our fathers of the American revolution contend as well for religious as for civil liberty? Did they not fight, and bleed, and conquer to establish the sacred principle that all men have a right to worship Almighty God according to the dictates of their own consciences. And shall we, to whom this glorious inheritance has been left, basely surrender the blood bought privilege at the nod and command of an earthly tyrant? Perish! perish for ever the hateful thought.

My feelings will not permit me, gentlemen, to dwell upon the brutal atrocities and cold blooded massacres of the Mexican army. It is too evident to require argument, that in the refusal of quarter and in hoisting the red flag, the inhuman despot, Santa Anna, has *denationized himself*. That he now stands before the world as a pirate—the common enemy of mankind. That he has offered an insult to every civilized nation, and has made it their imperious duty to check his blood stained career. But those martyred patriots have not fallen in vain. Although their blood has been swallowed by the sands of that field of death, and their ashes have been scattered by the whirlwinds of heaven, yet the *light* of their funeral pyre will gather together the sons of liberty who will teach these *Mexican murderers* that the *Anglo American race* in a cause so sacred, can never die unhonoured and unrevenged.

Part Five

THE IMPENDING CONFLICT

INTRODUCTION

1. CONTINUED EXPANSION

Population Growth. The processes of expansion, begun so energetically after the termination of the War of 1812, were continued with unabated zeal during the forties and fifties. Internal migration pushed the frontier west of Iowa, Missouri, and Kansas, and into central Minnesota on the north and central Texas on the south; while another frontier, moving eastward from the Pacific Coast, was helping fill the California valleys. Aided by roads, canals, and the young railroads, Americans were on the march. The good times that followed the end of the 1837-43 depression encouraged the further construction of public works; the rise in prices prompted the opening up of new lands to wheat, corn, and cotton, and to cattle raising; and England's increasing dependence upon American grains—particularly after the repeal of the Corn Laws in 1846—assured the prosperity of our agriculture.

Public policy encouraged movement and growth. Policy—as well as the temper of the American people—was flamboyant, aggressive, in the eyes of Europeans even vulgar. It was our "manifest destiny" to possess and fill the whole continental domain from sea to sea. We fought Mexico and acquired the huge Mexican cession; obtained Oregon; arranged to control, along with England, the right of way across the Panama Isthmus; threatened to establish our interest in the Caribbean; did so in the China Sea; and forced open the locked door of Japan to our seamen and our ships. Our immigration policy was neither restrictive nor exclusionist: foreigners were gladly welcomed to our shores as refugees from political terror and economic oppression in Europe. We gave asylum to men like Garibaldi and Kossuth, who stayed only temporarily, and we encouraged the Irish—fleeing famine and cruel land laws—and the Germans—escaping from confining mercantilist regulations—to emigrate and live with us. The Germans, notably, brought capital and the mechanical arts with them, and they moved out to the Middle West to establish themselves as farmers and small manufacturers. In 1840 America's inhabitants totaled 17,000,000; in 1850, 23,000,000; in 1860, 31,000,000. The increase was 35 percent from 1840 to 1850 and 36 percent from 1850 to 1860.

The growth of cities during this period was phenomenal; and now the beginnings of industrialization were making them production as well as mercantile centers. In 1840, as has been said, only 8.5 percent of America's population lived in settled communities of 8,000 or more people; by 1850, the proportion had grown to 12.5 percent; and by 1860, to 16.1 percent. In 1860, New York City had 814,000 inhabitants, Philadelphia 566,000, Brooklyn 279,000, Baltimore 212,000, Boston 178,000. The towns of the Western rivers and lakes became thriving cities in less than a generation: Cincinnati grew from a population of 9,600 in 1820 to 161,000 in 1860; St. Louis, from 16,000 in 1840 to 161,000 in 1860; Chicago, from 4,000 in 1840 to 109,000 in 1860. Everywhere but in the South this process continued: urbanization was a sign of progress, as it made possible the expansion of mercantile and industrial enterprise, the increase in ground rent, and the gathering together of a laboring population. With city growth came city slums and their accompaniments of poverty and delinquency. But with cities came the start of municipal public services and great advances in education.

Immigration. Immigrants added to the American population; more than that, they came young and they came in families. They also came hopeful of achieving new fortunes in America. Marriages, in the cities and in the country, took place at youthful ages and families were large. During the decade of the forties, 1,700,000 Europeans arrived in America; during the fifties, 2,600,000. The Irish and the Germans constituted by far the largest groups. Irish immigration became a flood after the potato crop failures of the late forties; so did German immigration after the collapse of the Revolutions of 1848 in central Europe.

The Irish came to Boston and New York as unskilled laborers and they also trooped into the construction camps of roads, canals, and railroads during the forties and fifties. Many moved out to the country as farm hands, and ended by becoming freeholders in the Middle West. By 1860, there were 1,500,000 native-born Irish in the United States. The Germans came to New York and Brooklyn and moved out to Cincinnati, Milwaukee, and St. Louis. They settled in cities and they settled on farms, and because they were middle class from the beginning they had an immediate effect on the American economy and American politics. By 1860, there were at least 1,000,000 native-born Germans in the country.

England, Wales, and Scotland continued to send immigrants—as skilled weavers, ironworkers, coal miners—but their flow was tapering off because living conditions for workers and the lower middle classes were improving in the British Isles. French Canadians were beginning to appear—and settle in the New England mill towns. And there were Dutch, Belgian, and Swiss immigrants who went out as farmers into Michigan, Wisconsin, and Iowa and quickly prospered as dairy cattle and hog raisers. By 1860, almost 13 percent of America's population was foreign born and 14.4 percent of its population was Negro.

Nativism. Immigration led to nativistic movements, as it had during the thirties. There was no competition for the job, for Americans were glad to turn over the unskilled tasks to the foreigners: it made possible the improvement of standards of living of the native-born at the expense of the newcomers. But some Americans resented the loyalty, particularly of the Irish, to the Catholic Church; they resented the poverty of the immigrants, and the fact that they quickly entered municipal politics as Democrats. The Know-Nothing movement, calling itself the Native American party and using the slogan "America for Americans" appeared, particularly in those states where foreigners were to be found in large numbers. It flourished during the fifties; met with local successes politically in 1854 and 1855; entered a national ticket in the presidential campaign of 1856, and many Republicans flirted with it during the next four years. But by 1860 the movement had spent itself: the country was prosperous and it needed the foreign laborers; Republicanism turned to the Middle Western Germans for support and boldly faced the slavery question; the Know-Nothings themselves had proved inept as political leaders. Nativism was a recurrent phenomenon in America, but such agitations never lasted, for Americans were equalitarians and individualists at heart, being unable to stand, for any length of time, mass discrimination or manipulation by demagogues.

The Mexican War. The war with Mexico and the acquisition of California and the vast Mexican territory in the Southeast were incidents of the expansion movement. The slavery question (as we shall see in greater detail below) played its part. Texas had continued its pressure for annexation; the Northern antislave societies were talking wildly of secession if this were to occur; while the Democrats, more and more now being controlled by the Southern slave interests, were preparing themselves grimly to accept the challenge. In 1844, they passed over Van Buren and turned to James K. Polk as their candidate. Polk was an out-and-out expansionist and annexationist—he spoke of the "reoccupation of Oregon and the reannexation of Texas"—and he easily defeated Clay, the Whig candidate, in the campaign. Tyler, still President, and a Southerner, pushed through the joint resolution for the annexation of Texas, as has already been noted.

Texas annexation meant war. The Mexicans had threatened it if Texas was to be absorbed into the United States and Polk, apparently, was prepared to risk hostilities. War broke out in 1846 as American troops pushed into disputed territory lying between the Nueces and Rio Grande rivers. This American army was under the direction of General Zachary Taylor. Another American army, under the command of General Winfield Scott, was sent to move into the heart of Mexico, while a third, led by Colonel Stephen Kearney, was directed to invest California. The war was attacked by the Whigs and the Abolitionists; by and large, particularly in the South and West, Americans approved. Taylor was successful in the North; Scott reached Vera Cruz in March, 1847, and entered Mexico City in September; and Kearney, starting from Ft. Leavenworth, took first Santa Fé and then defeated the Mexicans in California.

In February, 1848, the Treaty of Guadalupe Hidalgo was signed and Mexico, for $15,-000,000, turned over to the United States the area between the two southern rivers of Texas, New Mexico, and California. In 1853, by the Gadsden Purchase, an additional piece of Southwest territory along the southern border of present-day Arizona was acquired from Mexico to make possible the building of a Pacific railway south of the mountains. Not only Texas but California, too, now was ours, and the latter was quickly settled by Americans attracted by the discovery of gold in 1848. Before two years were over, 100,000 Americans had thronged into California and in 1850 it was admitted into the Union.

Oregon. Americans, at the end of the eighteenth century, had established a foothold on the Columbia river, as they hunted otter pelts for shipment to the China trade. The British had come into the Oregon country, too; but prior to the forties American settlements were few. Missionaries, traders, and land speculators were becoming interested in the region and Polk, taking advantage of the clamor, decided to challenge the British. In the campaign of 1844, the Democrats had raised the slogan of "Fifty-four Forty or Fight"—in other words, they claimed for the United States the whole of the Oregon territory. The British resisted and finally, in 1846, a settlement was effected under which the Forty-ninth Parallel was made the northern boundary of the United States. We got the whole rich Columbia river valley while the British kept Vancouver Island.

Utah. In the forties also began the Mormon trek into Utah. This religious sect, founded by Joseph Smith of New York in 1830, because of its clannishness had been harried by its neighbors until it decided to move westward. A large company established itself first in Missouri and then in Illinois. Finally the Mormons, having espoused polygamy and now under the leadership of Brigham Young, agreed to quit "gentile" society altogether; they would settle in the American desert where they could erect their churches and agricultural communities unmolested. In 1847, the Mormons first entered the Salt Lake Valley and before long their great agricultural skills had converted the arid region into a rich settlement. The Mormons accepted the domination of their church leaders in economic as well as religious affairs; they clung stubbornly to polygamy; they were becoming wealthy. All this created antagonism and it was not until 1896—after polygamy had been formally abandoned—that Utah was admitted into the Union.

2. ECONOMIC GROWTH

American Fortunes. The processes of industrialization, which had been started in one region and one industry during the previous twenty years, were resumed in the forties and fifties. There were great advances; but, by and large, the American economy continued a mercantile one. New York, Philadelphia, and Baltimore, preeminently, were concerned with trade and its financing; the same was true of the growing Western centers of Chicago, St. Louis, and Cincinnati. Nothing reveals this better than the sources of private fortunes. New York men of wealth were merchants, bankers, and urban real estate operators (shipping men, like Cornelius Vanderbilt and George Law, were just beginning to emerge); the same was true of Philadelphians. In Boston, persons of fortune had somewhat more diversified interests: they financed banks and mortgage companies; they owned cotton mills; they were behind Western rail construction. But by the outbreak of the Civil War, a fortune of $500,000 was large and one of $100,000 commanded respect. That is not to say there were no millionaires. In the fifties there were reputed to be twenty-five millionaires in New York, eighteen in Boston, and nine in Philadelphia. John Jacob Astor—the richest man of his day—left $20,000,000 when he died in 1848. In another fifty years, when Andrew Carnegie sold his steel interests to the United States Steel Corporation, he was worth $500,000,000; and John D. Rockefeller was worth probably twice that when he retired from active management of his oil companies.

Nevertheless, industrialization was getting off to a real start in America, particularly by the middle forties. Again excepting cotton textiles, plants were small and individual capitalizations modest. There were no attempts at integration and few corporations. An iron mill did not own its own fuel deposits or forges and furnaces. A clothing factory was as likely as not to operate on the home-work basis. Carriages and carts were being made in small carpenter shops and as a rule for the custom trade. In the case of manufacturing—right up to the nineties—companies were privately owned or run by partners, and capital for plant expansion was obtained from personal savings. Undoubtedly banks assisted from time to time, but incorporation was not characteristic.

Mechanization. We are to see small beginnings, many failures—and yet an accumulative effect that was impressive. In the first place, Americans contributed to the invention and perfection of labor-saving devices—necessitated by high labor costs. Goulding's "American Card," which speeded the mechanization of the woolen textile industry, was patented in 1826; the carpet weaving loom followed in 1841; the harvester in 1841, the sewing machine and the rotary press in 1846. Standardization of parts appeared early in the United States; and machinery for the manufacture of locks, watches, small arms, wood products, and metal products were devised and used. Productivity was stepped up, particularly in the wood and metal goods industries; but again, plants were small and failures frequent. Interestingly enough, this last was due to faulty accounting methods as the single outstanding cause; no provision was made for depreciation, interest, and insurance so that large profits frequently were illusory.

Some statistical evidences of expansion may be cited. Between 1840 and 1860 the number of spindles per mill in cotton textiles increased from 2,000 to 5,000, while the average number of employees per establishment in woolen textiles increased from 15 to 33. Iron rail production increased from 24,000 tons in 1849 to 205,000 tons in 1860.

Relative Industrial Backwardness. Despite all this activity, industrial production still lagged far behind agriculture. The census of 1880, analyzing manufactures retrospectively, was able to say: "It seems probable that until about the year 1850 the bulk of general manufacturing done in the United States was carried on in the shop and the household by the labor of the family or individual proprietors, with apprentice assistants, as contrasted with the present system of factory labor, compensated by wages and assisted by power."

The immaturity of the country's coal and iron industries—the key to industrialization—demonstrates the position of the United States. In 1855, with about equal populations, Great Britain produced five times as much coal as we did: 66,000,000 to 12,000,000 tons. The same ratio existed in the case of pig iron: 3,500,000 to 700,000 tons. While American iron rail production increased, in 1860 one half of our rolled iron still came from Britain.

The appearance of the railroads, particularly during the fifties, contributed mightily to the processes of industrialization. Railroad building and operation were linked with the iron (and later steel) and coal industries; railroads expanded markets; railroads opened up agricultural lands to farm machinery. Victor S. Clark showed [1] that the spread of the railroad net was followed by a decline in home production; for per capita homespun manufactures decreased as the ratio of railway mileage to the areas of states increased. From 1840 to 1860, the per capita average of household manufactures dropped from $1.59 to $.79.

The Spread of the Railroad Net. Up to the fifties, railroad construction was largely on a local basis; it was financed quite often by public subscription for patriotic reasons. Lines were short; they were built as feeders to waterways; they were laid down to attract water-borne traffic away from municipal rivals. In the thirties, financial assistance to early builders was given by the states of Maryland, Massachusetts, Pennsylvania, and Michigan; and these early stock subscriptions, as a rule, ended in unsuccessful ventures. In

[1] V. S. Clark, *History of Manufactures in the United States, 1607–1800* (2 vols., New York, 1916), I, 352.

1840, there were 3,000 miles of rail in the country; the total capitalization was only $75,000,000. In 1850, mileage was 9,000 and capitalization $300,000,000. In 1860 mileage was 30,000 and capitalization $1,000,000,000.

Through lines did not make their appearance until the fifties; a single unified trunk line, the Illinois Central, was not completed until the end of the decade. As late as 1850, the average length of the New England railways was only 36 miles. Not until 1847 were New York and New Haven linked by rail. But by the end of the fifties construction had made such progress that Boston and Albany were joined; and so were Albany and New York, Albany and Buffalo, Detroit and Chicago, Cleveland and Cincinnati, Savannah and Atlanta.

The Illinois Central. In 1850, Illinois—long harassed by heavy public debts incurred by the overexpansion of roads and canals—turned to Congress for relief. Until transportation facilities were provided, the state could not fill up with farmers, and its debts could not be paid off. Land speculators, urban and rural (Stephen A. Douglas among them) were interested for personal reasons. Congress complied; and in thus doing set a pattern that was followed during the next two decades and that helped in the construction of the great Pacific railroads of the United States. Congress approved of the building of a line from Chicago clear down to Mobile, setting aside a total of some 2,500,000 acres of the public domain as a subsidy to the railroad company. These lands were to be made up of the alternate even sections (a section is a square mile, or 640 acres) on each side for six miles in depth along the railroad's right of way. They were turned over in trust to the states of Illinois, Mississippi, and Alabama. As parts of the railroad were completed, the land grants were handed over to the company.

A group of New England and New York merchants—now out of the China trade and seeking new fields for investment—obtained the charter for the Illinois Central Railroad from the Illinois legislature. English capital also was brought in, attracted by the land grants whose sale presumably would help in paying the costs of construction. Building was begun at once and in six years the 700 miles of line were laid down at a cost of $16,500,000. But English bondholders were called on again and again for assistance by assessments on their stock (which had been thrown in); and it was not until after the Civil War that the Illinois Central was realizing sizably from land sales and operations. Nevertheless, a single company was demonstrating the possibility of successful operation of a great trunk railroad. In the sixties, the Pacific railways had an example to follow.

The Panic of 1857. In 1843, prices turned upward and until 1873, except for recessions in 1854 and 1857, continued to rise, moving up sharply during the Civil War years. The growing demand for American foodstuffs abroad undoubtedly helped, and perhaps also the great production of gold as a result of the California and Australia discoveries. American business steadily improved and while there were cyclical fluctuations during these years the periods of prosperity lasted longer than those of depression. But, as in earlier America, too much capital was involved in speculation: in land-jobbing and railroad building, and in stock-market and commodity speculation. The presence of wildcat banks and the great increase in monetary circulation undoubtedly aided the process. In 1843, total money in circulation was $147,000,000 ($7.87 per capita); by 1857 this had increased to $457,000,000 ($15.81 per capita). Federal land sales grew enormously, from less than 2,000,-000 acres a year to more than 15,000,000 acres in 1855. When the bubble burst, in 1857, perhaps as much as $1,000,000,000 was invested in Western wild lands and in undeveloped town lots. Meanwhile, New York merchants had been speculating in commodities because of good prices and steady European demand; and the onset of recession caught them with overstocked warehouses and the banks—which had been financing them as well as security speculation—in illiquid form.

The panic broke out in New York in August, 1857, and was followed by a round of failures as New York banks called in their loans and demanded settlements from country banks in specie. Distress spread to Philadelphia and the Middle West—hitting Chicago with particular severity—and in the affected regions (the South and California remained untouched) prices dropped and unemployment followed. Businessmen began to scrutinize critically the institutional world in which they functioned. There was a fictitious and uncontrolled currency; there was no protection for infant industries, for the tariff laws of 1846 and 1857 had pushed rates even lower than the schedules of 1833. More and more businessmen were paying heed to the strictures of protectionists like Horace Greeley of New York and Henry C. Carey of Philadelphia. Carey was pointing out that the country had prospered in 1815, 1834, and 1847 "the closing years of the several periods in which the policy of the country was directed toward . . . protection." To such persons, the new Republican party—in part assuming the heritage of the Whigs—was making a very real appeal.

3. THE WORLD OF THE WORKERS

Utopianism. The hard times following 1837 had swept out with them workingmen's parties and the first crude craft unions formed on local and national lines. There were few voices left to speak for the once organized journeymen and skilled mechanics; and only an occasional one for the cotton and woolen textile workers. During the forties and early fifties, Utopianism, imitating European models, held the stage. The Utopians were middle class intellectuals who were impatient with or even hostile toward trade unions; social reform and betterment were to come through a retreat into agrarian and handicraft cooperation with the profit motive eliminated. Curiously enough, capitalists were to be called upon to help in the creation of such communities. Robert Owen, the Comte de St. Simon, Pierre-Joseph Proudhon, Charles Fourier were the great European theoreticians of the Utopian Socialism of the day. In fact, two of the Utopians—Robert Owen and Étienne Cabet —came to America to establish communities, the first at New Harmony, Indiana, and the second in a series of settlements in Texas and Illinois. All failed.

Americans, too, tried their hand at such ventures. The most famous was Brook Farm, a small colony outside Boston, which was founded by New England intellectuals in 1841. The most extraordinary was that at Nashoba, Tennessee, founded by Frances Wright and designed to carry out "the Wright Plan for the Gradual Abolition of Slavery in the United States Without Danger of Loss to the Citizens of the South." The most common were the so-called Phalanxes, modeled after the elaborate plans of the Frenchman Charles Fourier and his American disciple Albert Brisbane. While a number of such communities were started and uniformly ended unhappily, it is important to note that the preachments of the Utopians caught the attention of the American workers of the forties. So-called workingmen's societies listened carefully to lectures by Brisbane, Greeley, and other Fourierists and seriously discussed the curious psychology of the master.

Land Reformers also had the ear of the American workers of the period. The outstanding Utopian of the forties was the Englishman George Henry Evans, who brought to America the message of equal property rights. His original proposal called for the establishment of "rural republican townships" where land would be held only by cultivators themselves and would be inalienable, and pro-duction would be on a handicraft basis and for use alone. Greeley hugged Evans to his bosom as he did Brisbane, and the New York *Tribune* addressed New York workers in the somewhat strange language of Evans's primitive land communism and Fourier's fanciful and often fantastic anarchistic-communism. Evans—as did Greeley, too—finally watered his program down to pure and simple homesteadism—freeholds for workers from the public domain without cost—and it was this that survived out of all the lofty discourse of the forties and fifties. Be it said, however, that few workers ever became homesteaders; Western agriculture was for those skilled in rural pursuits and with some capital capable of taking them to the prairies and plains.

Homesteadism. Homesteadism was taken up by Western Democrats, and the first bill was presented by Senator Stephen A. Douglas of Illinois in 1849. Southern Democrats were not hostile, but Northern Whigs were; the bill failed in the Senate. Andrew Johnson of Tennessee sponsored a similar measure in the House and in 1852 it passed. Now the lines began to change. The South—fearful of the North's growing influence in the West— swung into the opposition; and the Northeast, for the same reasons, supported the measure. Finally, in 1860, a homestead bill passed both houses only to be vetoed by the Democratic President James Buchanan from Pennsylvania. But the Republican party—seeking to bind North and West together more successfully than had the Whigs—had espoused homesteadism and in 1862 the Homestead Act was put on the statute books.

Working-class Conditions. None of this benefited the working population of the country. Disorganized, misled, subjected to the speedup and stretchout in textile factories, laboring twelve hours every day, and confronted by the constantly rising costs of the late forties and the fifties, labor fell behind. Workers were crowded into the slum areas of cities unprepared to receive them; mortality rates—for children particularly—were high, as a result of the sketchy nature of public health controls; the continuance of the homework industries led to a good deal of sweating. Real wages declined during the fifties and did not mount again until the depression of 1857 had spent itself. By 1860, however, real wages once more were up.

Nothing better reveals the growing progress of the American working class during these formative years than the rise in real wages from the beginning of the century. From 1801 to 1815, real wages increased 19.4 percent; from 1816 to 1825, 35.2 percent; from 1826 to 1837, 4.6 percent; from 1838 to 1843, 32.6 percent; and from 1844 to 1860, 23.1 percent. From 1801 to 1860, the increase in real wages was 215.3 percent. No other country in the world came anywhere near this achievement. It was no wonder that America's pull was so powerful for the little people of Europe.

By the outbreak of the Civil War, living standards for America's urban populations had improved remarkably.[2] Dwellings were comfortably heated by stoves; plumbing was fairly common; the kerosene lamp had already made its appearance, as also had illuminating gas; fac-tory-made furniture was being bought widely. On the worker's table were to be found white bread, sugar, coffee and tea, as well as plentiful supplies of fresh meat. Indeed, if anything distinguished Europe from America it was this presence of beef and lamb in the daily diet of the workers. It is true that cash available for normal outlays, for the workers, ran from $200 to $800 a year; and for the farmers, from $50 to $250 a year. On the other hand—as a basis of comparison—a room and board at the best hotels cost only $2 to $2.50 a day; while in city boardinghouses lodgers were paying $2.50 to $6 a week for food and shelter.

In such a climate, it was not difficult for ambitious city workers and country laborers to save from earnings and to embark upon business ventures of their own. A stake of $100 was not inconsiderable; and with $4,000 a large-scale enterprise could be embarked upon. Having started out as a clerk in Cleveland in the middle fifties at a salary of $3.50 a week, John D. Rockefeller in less than a decade had $800 with which to enter into business as a commission merchant in farm produce.

4. THE COTTON SOUTH

Just as North and West were undergoing rapid changes and growing in wealth, so was the South. But as a result of intensification of agriculture and mechanization of production the Northern and Western economies were turning out more goods per unit of capital invested. The South, too, was growing richer —as its slave population increased. The dilemma of the Southern economy, however, lay in the fact that its productivity remained the same. As the decades unrolled, therefore, relatively, the South was falling behind the North and West in wealth, income, and value of product per units of capital and labor. In addition, such savings as occurred in the re-

gion were not employed to diversify the economy but for further investment in Negro slaves. Southern whites were as much the victims of their system as were the Negroes themselves.

The Plantation System. Toward the end of the Revolution, as tobacco became less and less the chief reliance of the South's agriculture, there were strong indications to point to the disappearance of Negro slavery. The discovery of the cotton gin and the mechanization of cotton textile production put an end to that tendency; and not only did the plantation system become more firmly secured than ever, but slavery was built into the whole Southern economy.

The tobacco plantation of the colonial pe-

[2] Edgar Martin, *Standards of Living in the United States in 1860* (Chicago, 1943).

riod was carried over into the cotton plantation. The characteristics of both were the same: single cropping until soil depletion required removal to another location, where the round was continued; extensive rather than intensive cultivation because of the need for extracting a maximum current money income from the capital invested; the investment of capital largely in Negro slaves; and the dependence upon outside credit—in this case, the New York merchants—for long-term and short-term requirements.

Two other aspects of the plantation economy require comment. First, the price of cotton was established in a world market and cotton prices, from the thirties on, proceeded sharply downward. But costs of production went up. This was due to the high cost of credit and the high price of slaves. Influenced by the humanitarian spirit of the Enlightenment and convinced that slavery's life could not be too long in any case, the writers of the Constitution had provided for the termination of the African slave trade after 1808. Beginning with the thirties, the Negro supply fell far short of the country's expanding demand, with a resultant climb in value of slave field hands. Southern agriculture was caught in the typical scissors—a widening gap between prices paid, or costs, and prices received. The narrowing of the distance between these was the basis of much of the economic—as well as political—discussion which filled the South in the forties and fifties.

In the second place, in the South, the accent was upon consumption rather than production. Agriculture has always been a way of life as well as a means of producing wealth. But when agriculture was linked with slavery in order to assure white supremacy, all the aspects of a caste system—with its gentility, idleness, and extravagance—had to be maintained. The large plantations had more house servants than they needed; and more race horses, wine cellars, and indigent relatives than they really could afford. The caste system drew horizontal as well as vertical lines: Ne-

groes were sharply separated from whites; and nonslave-owning whites found an unbridgeable gulf between them and the slaveowners. The disparities in wealth and income between classes were far greater in the South than they were in the North.

Cotton's Advance. Cotton was grown first in the upper South Carolina country and in central Georgia; other important areas of production were Virginia, North Carolina, and Tennessee. As the demand for cotton grew—first from England, then from the Northern mill communities—the cotton South expanded across the Gulf Plain and up the river valleys. Young men, accompanied by their slaves, began to quit the exhausted tidewater lands of the Southeast and to settle Alabama, Mississippi, and Louisiana. When transportation facilities began to appear, they moved into the interior counties of Georgia and Tennessee. By the fifties, seeking out cotton lands, planters were pushing into eastern Texas and the Arkansas river bottoms. By the fifties, more than a half million Virginians and Marylanders were living in other states; and in fifty years, by 1860, Alabama and Mississippi's population had grown from 40,000 to 1,660,000.

In 1815, total cotton production had been only 150,000 bales; by 1859 this had jumped to 4,500,000 bales. The center of production, obviously, had shifted to the Gulf Plain, with Mississippi growing more than the four states of the original South combined. In the process, Virginia—stripped of her capital—was incapable of turning to intensive agriculture. It was no wonder that, politically, decisions affecting the whole South were being made more and more in Alabama and Mississippi rather than in the Old Dominion.

Cotton undoubtedly was King: it was the backbone of American exports and it helped pay for American purchases of iron goods and tropical wares abroad and to service American borrowings in the London money market. In 1860, cotton shipments represented almost 60 percent of America's total export trade. But the price paid for the expansion of cotton growing was a heavy one. In 1815, middling cotton was selling for 30 cents a pound at New Orleans; in 1844, for 6 cents; during 1855–60, for 11 cents. But on the farm, during the last period, cotton was selling for less than 8 cents; and most farmers could not make a profit at that figure, largely because of high credit costs and the constantly increasing price of Negro slaves.

The Slave Owners. In the fifteen Southern and Border states, where the slave institution continued to flourish, most of the whites did not own slaves. The fact is, even among the minority that made up the slave-owning population, there was a great concentration of ownership at the upper end. In 1860, only one fourth of the South's white families possessed Negro slaves. And 7 percent of the whites owned 75 percent of the enslaved blacks. The other 17.4 percent owned the remaining 25 percent of the blacks; while the remaining 75.6 percent owned none at all.

If we are to conceive of a property with a hundred Negroes or more as a giant plantation, there were only 2,292 such. On the other hand, the possessor of nine Negroes or less was not much more than a yeoman farmer. (If the average worth of a Negro in 1860 is put at $500, such a property represents a capitalization of $5,000 or less.) There were 275,-000 such small plantations. Naturally, lines were drawn between large and small owners —and those lines were both social and political. Up to the fifties, generally, the small planters accepted without question the political leadership of the large planters; but during the decade preceding the Civil War they were beginning to find their own spokesmen and to press more and more for the recognition of their economic demands. The clamor for the reopening of the African slave trade came largely from this group.

The Nonslave Owners. The vast company of nonslave-owning whites were not "poor whites," in the legendary sense. On the contrary; they were the sturdy, independent yeomanry of Virginia's western counties, Tennes-

see's eastern counties, and Georgia's northern counties. They grew the South's small grains and hay, fattened her beef cattle, carried on a little dairying. They sent out their sons to become the overseers of the great plantations and the mechanics and artisans of the South's cities. To this group must also be added the completely self-sufficing farmers of the Southern highlands. In the Appalachians and the Ozarks were to be found thousands of families who worked their rough hillside farms and supplemented their meager livelihoods by hunting, trapping, and fishing. Only at the bottom of this ladder were the relatively few "poor whites": the "sand-hillers," "crackers," and "clay eaters" of the now impoverished eastern old South.

Slaveowners or not, almost the entire white South supported the region's "peculiar institution." Slavery made all whites, rich and poor alike, a superior ruling group; thus, the poorer whites found psychological compensations for their inferior economic status. There can be no doubt that the poorer whites suffered from the existence of slavery. The plantations were constantly swallowing up the farms of the independent yeomen; Negro slaves were increasingly cutting down job opportunities for white mechanics and artisans. But when Hinton R. Helper, in 1857, in his sensational *The Impending Crisis of the South*, sought to band the poorer whites into a united group to wage war against both slaveowners and slaves— against "the lords of the lash" and their "black and bicolored catiffs"—he was driven out of his native North Carolina. The South was fearful of its own image in the mirror Helper held up.

The Blacks. By 1860, there were some 4,-250,000 Negroes in the South of whom all but 250,000 were slaves. The slaves were for the most part field hands, with a small sprinkling of house servants among them. By the fifties, however, a growing number of enslaved blacks was being moved over into industrial production and the extractive industries. Some Negroes—on the great plantations

—of course were skilled artisans; but these were few. Unlike the feudal manor the plantation was not a self-sufficing economic unit. It produced a cash crop; and in return, it bought virtually all its necessities—its clothing, foodstuffs, tools. But it is true that toward the end, Negro slaves were to be found in increasing size in the South's iron mines and lumbering camps and in its forges, furnaces, mills, and factories. Negro slaves worked at cotton textile machines, iron manufacture, and tobacco products. The later classical economists—Mill, Cairnes—liked to believe that slave labor was inherently inefficient. The fact is, Negro slaves were cutting down the areas of employment of free white labor; and an important reason for the rise in the price of slaves after 1845 was to be found in the growing demand for their use from these new Southern industries.

Thus, there sprang up competition for slaves between agriculture and industry; and between the old South and the new South. The new South, with its still fertile fields, could afford the higher prices while the old South could not. Negroes therefore were moved into the Gulf Plain; and, at the same time, many sections of the old South found it possible to survive only because they virtually became the Cotton Kingdom's breeding states.

As has been said, the Africa slave trade was outlawed in 1808, and while slave running continued right up to the Civil War only a small number of Negroes were brought in illegally. The Negroes, in other words, could increase only by a preponderance of births over deaths. In 1810, there were 1,160,000 Negroes in the South; in 1860, about 4,000,000. In the old South, the Negro population had only doubled during the fifty years; in the new South, it had increased ten times. The Negroes of the new South came from Virginia, South Carolina, Kentucky, Maryland, and Missouri. Some accompanied their masters in their migration, of course; but most were sold commercially by dealers who were in this business openly. These dealers sold directly or

at auction, with Charleston and New Orleans the chief distributing centers. They broke up families purposely and Negroes were encouraged to hold the marital tie lightly. Patterns thus created over a long period of time cannot be changed overnight: the Negro's family attitudes are a direct result of slavery.

Because the Negro was property, or capital, he had no civil rights under Southern law. Nor did he have freedom of movement; and Southern roads were constantly policed by white patrols to pick up vagrants or escaped Negroes. The fact is, the South was much more fearful of Negro uprisings than we have been led to believe by slavery apologists. When slavery became significant economically, Southerners who previously had been ashamed of their institution, now found in their midst philosophers, sociologists, and scientists who were eager to testify to the physical and mental inferiority of the Negro. The blacks were being enslaved, in short, for their own good.

Economic Perplexities. Negro slavery was not inherently inefficient, as has been said. Nor was the institution doomed because the expansive character of the cotton economy was held in check by climate and rainfall. Indeed, the antebellum South was still a pioneering region in many respects, for its transportation facilities were quite primitive. Few good roads and railroads and a heavily timbered terrain prevented the opening up of the back country to cotton. Today, in the same region, and using the same techniques of production —productivity has not increased since the Civil War—the cotton South can grow 15,-000,000 bales; in 1859, it grew only 4,500,000.

A fiction has grown up among historians that the slave system was a dying one; and that, therefore, the Civil War was a tragic mistake; if men had had patience, slavery would have passed away painlessly. This viewpoint—economically unsound and morally shocking—loses sight of several considerations. The reopening of the slave trade would have reduced the chief cost of the economy—and its outstanding capital outlay—and would therefore have permitted its continuance. "Direct trade" with England would have cut the nexus with New York and made available goods and working capital at lower prices and rates. And conversion more and more into industrial production—which was already slowly taking place—would have strengthened slavery rather than the reverse. Slavery was not economically unsound but morally reprehensible; and for this reason the Civil War had to be fought. The Civil War, by its victory, strengthened another important element in the American tradition: that of America's confidence in equality. Thomas Jefferson had asserted the American credo of man's natural rights; John C. Calhoun, the South's great political philosopher, had rejected the idea; the Abolitionists and the Radical Republicans were returning to Jefferson.

Reference has been made to the outstanding economic requirements of the Southern system. Slave prices were too high and only the restoration of the slave trade could lower them. This Southerners knew, and the more realistic among them made the restoration an outstanding demand. This was particularly true of the smaller slaveowners who could not breed their own Negroes but were dependent upon market supply. They saw the price of prime field hands mounting from $600 in 1845 to $1,500 in 1860, with $1,800 not uncommon. Many small planters had to hire Negroes for cultivating and picking cotton: and the rates of hire were shooting up just as sharply. In 1837, the annual hiring rate was $90 with board; in the Southwest in 1860 it was between $300 and $360. Virginia tobacco factories were paying $225 a year for hired Negro slaves. Proportionately, as Negro costs rose, cotton prices fell. These are the ratios of cotton prices (in cents per pound) to Negro costs (in hundreds of dollars per average slave) for particular years: 1819, 2 to 1; 1837, 1 to 1; 1860, 0.6 to 1.

The same situation existed as far as other costs were concerned. New York and its merchants connected the cotton South with the outside world. As late as the forties, cotton moved into Europe by way of New York; and even after cotton ports came to be developed —New Orleans, Charleston, Savannah, Mobile —New York money financed the traffic. The cotton triangle persisted. Cotton (with New Yorkers as the middlemen) went to England and the Continent; and back to New York came drygoods and hardware, which the New York merchants reshipped into the South. At every stage, the New York middleman operated—as commission merchant, wholesaler, and banker. This is why Southerners agitated for "direct trade." New York would have been by-passed; and the Southerners would have cut their costs by cheaper freights, the elimination of middlemen's profits, and lower interest rates. "Direct trade" was linked with reduced tariff schedules.

Thus the Southern economic program. Southerners knew what they wanted and articulated their interests. In 1859, at the last of the Southern commercial conventions, resolutions demanding the following were carried: free trade; direct taxation only; the establishment of a direct line of ships between the South and Europe; and the repeal of all federal and state statutes outlawing the African slave trade.

Hand in hand with these demands went a political program. The South could hope to survive economically only if it possessed political power; and this appeared to be slipping out of its grasp in the fifties as the West continued to fill up. Originally, South and West —because they were both agrarian—were naturally bound together. But as mercantile, transportation, and industrial interests began to appear in the West, New York and New England capital were stronger ties between Northeast and West than were those of blood connecting South and West. For many of the South's younger sons had migrated into the southern counties of Indiana and Illinois and even on into Iowa. But the West was clamoring more and more for public works, railroads, and free lands. These needs the North sympathized with and could finance. And these expansive requirements of the West the South had to resist. Hence Southern opposition, in the fifties, to projects for the building of Pacific railways and to homestead bills.

The struggle over the territories really represented the growing cleavage between the sections. A settled West meant the destruction of the balance between "slave states" and "free states." The political balance had to be maintained at all costs; otherwise—secession.

5. THE STRUGGLE OVER THE TERRITORIES

Up to the opening of the fifties, not only had the balance between the sections been kept, but the South (with its Northern allies) really dominated the Federal government. From the victory of Jackson on, Southern men—or Northern men with Southern principles (except for Harrison's brief month in office)—sat in the White House. The Democracy controlled the Senate, the House, and the Supreme Court. And beginning with the Compromise of 1820, every time a free state was admitted into the Union, a slave state also joined the company of commonwealths.

Missouri Compromise. The fires of the slavery debate flared up in 1819 and from then on they never could be banked. Legislators labored over compromises and for short periods of time there was quiet in Washington. But the slavery evil was too shocking, and there were too many men of conscience in America, for voices to be long stilled. In 1819 the Territory of Missouri asked to be admitted to statehood and the House passed a bill with the proviso that no new slaves be admitted into the area. Outraged Southerners pressed their case in the Senate. The result was a compromise, with Missouri admitted as a slave state and Maine as a free state. Free soilers gained another point; they established the right of Congress to legislate on the slave issue in the territories, by the provision of the law that slavery was to be forever prohibited in that part of the Louisiana Purchase north of the line of 36°30' (the southern boundary of Missouri).

Following this pattern, Arkansas as a slave state and Michigan as a free state were both admitted in 1837. In 1845, Florida from the South and in 1846 Iowa from the Northwest were admitted. Texas came in with slavery in 1845 and California without it in 1850. Thereafter, it was impossible to even the accounts: for Minnesota was admitted as a free state in 1858, and Oregon in 1859.

The Abolitionists. Slavery became a public issue in 1820, as has been said. But as early as 1812 Benjamin Lundy, in his paper *The Genius of Universal Emancipation*, had started a campaign to free all the enslaved blacks. And in 1831, William Lloyd Garrison—more intransigent, more bitter and personal in his attacks—took up the fight in his *Liberator*. More important even was the work of the antislavery societies which, led by Northern Protestant clergymen like Theodore Weld and Southerners like the Grimké sisters, formed a fine network of branches spread through the North and West. They published newspapers; bombarded Congress continually with petitions; held public meetings; and gave aid to runaway slaves. A political party was started in 1840—first called the Liberty party, then the Free Soil party—but it got few votes.

Meanwhile, the battle was going on in Congress with John Quincy Adams, now sitting in the lower house from Massachusetts, as slavery's most stalwart foe. He took up cudgels in defense of the right of antislavery societies to petition Congress (a "gag" rule had been passed in 1836) and was finally successful in 1844. The Abolitionists fought against the admission of Texas, opposed the Mexican War, and sought to jam through Congress the Wilmot Proviso. They also agitated for the termination of the slave trade in the District of Columbia and the recognition of the freedom of runaway slaves. In 1846, Northerners in Congress—by the so-called Wilmot Proviso—sought to outlaw slavery in all territory acquired from Mexico; they failed, but the demand became a rallying cry taken up by all shades of anti-Southern opinion from free soil to immediate emancipation.

The Compromise of 1850. A legislative crisis once more appeared in 1848–49, because the problem of the territories no longer could be avoided. Clay and Webster pleaded for compromise and the preservation of the Union. Calhoun, the South's great spokesman, called upon his section to remain unyielding. The younger men also were divided. Stephen A. Douglas of Illinois proposed his formula of "squatter sovereignty": let the citizens of the territories, in their own constitutions, decide whether they were to join the Union as slave or free states. While William H. Seward of New York—now a Whig, soon to become a Republican—rejected compromise and spoke of "a higher law than the Constitution." This was the "natural law" which became the chief reliance of the Abolitionists and the later Radical Republicans.

Led by Clay and Douglas the compromisers won, securing the passage in 1850 of a series of bills which have come to be known as the Compromise of 1850. These provided for: the admission of California as a free state; "squatter sovereignty" for Utah and New Mexico—the remaining territories of the Mexican cession; the abolition of the slave trade in the District of Columbia; and the enactment of a fugitive slave law. This last was a bitter pill for the friends of the Negroes to swallow, for it provided that a slaveowner, merely by proving ownership before a federal judge or commissioner, could reclaim his property without further ado. The fugitive slaves might not testify in their own behalf; federal marshals were to be held liable for the arrest and safe delivery of fugitives; and all persons seeking to prevent the return of fugitives could be fined, imprisoned, and sued for civil damages. The "underground railway"—by which Abolitionists had helped fugitives escape into Canada—was now in peril; but Northern sympathizers prevented the seizure of Negroes, while the state supreme court of Wisconsin had the courage to declare the Fugitive Slave Law unconstitutional.

The Kansas-Nebraska Act of 1854. Thus, nothing was really settled; and in another four years Congress was once more engaging in alarums and excursions. The question of the territories was reopened by Douglas, an ambitious Democrat who assumed that his theory of "squatter sovereignty" was really the key to the resolution of the perplexity. Douglas had other motives. He and his Chicago friends were heavily involved in real estate operations —urban and rural—and were pushing for the building of a Pacific railway through the northern or central tier of states. With an orderly government established in Nebraska, the railway project might be furthered and the power of Chicago assured.

Douglas, to achieve his ends, paid a heavy price. The Kansas-Nebraska Act of 1854 divided the Nebraska Territory into two territories. Under the theory of "squatter sovereignty," settlers were to decide the slavery issue for themselves. And the Missouri Compromise was declared null and void. Two years later, in 1856, James Buchanan, the Democratic candidate, was elected to the Presidency; presumably the American electorate approved of Congress's decision. But in opposition to the Democrats this time no longer stood the irresolute Whigs but the new Republican party.

Nebraska, in any case, was bound to come in free; but Kansas became a battleground. Into Kansas thronged Southern and Northern zealots, brawlers, adventurers, and land jobbers. From New England, financed by Boston money, moved Abolitionist immigrants who were led by their ministers but who also brought their rifles with them. The slavery men captured the territorial legislature; the free-soil men held their own convention and drafted a constitution without slavery; murders and the burning of public buildings took place. In retaliation for the slaying of two Abolitionists, John Brown, at Osawatomie Creek, killed five proslavery men.

Into this situation the Republicans threw themselves. First appearing in 1854, and attracting old Whigs, Abolitionists, free-soil Democrats, and even Know-Nothings, the Republicans in the campaign of 1856 spoke out clearly against slavery. They denounced the repeal of the Missouri Compromise; opposed the extension of slavery into the territories; demanded the admission of Kansas as a free state; and called for the ending of slavery in the still unorganized regions. To bind North and West together, the Republicans advocated a Pacific railway and a federal program of public improvements. With John C. Frémont as their standardbearer, they won Connecticut, Iowa, Maine, Massachusetts, Michigan, New Hampshire, New York, Ohio, Rhode Island, Vermont, and Wisconsin. Not enough to win; apparently not important enough to give the Southerners pause.

The Dred Scott Decision. It was a Democratic bench that handed down the Dred Scott decision of 1857. Dred Scott, a Negro slave, had been taken by his master into free regions and then carried back to Missouri, a slave state. Charging that his stay in free territory had made him a free man, he sued for his release in the Missouri courts in 1846. The case finally came to the Supreme Court bench, which in 1857 found against Scott. While each of the judges wrote a separate opinion, six followed Chief Justice Roger B. Taney, a Southerner, in agreeing on the following two points: 1) that a Negro "whose ancestors were sold as slaves" could not claim the rights of federal citizenship; 2) that the Missouri Compromise of 1820, prohibiting slavery in a part of the national territory, was unconstitutional. Here Taney contended that slaves were property; that under the Fifth Amendment Con-

gress could not take property without due process of law; and that the outlawing of slavery in the territories by Congress was the deprivation of the owners of slaves of their property rights. The inference was plain: Congress might not check the extension of slavery into the territories. The Republican party had to ponder this bitter truth.

Continued Turbulence. Civil war went on in Kansas and the two groups continued to carry on in disregard of each other. The proslavery party drew up the so-called Lecompton Constitution, which assured the continuance of slavery. The free-soil men refused to participate in the election and the constitution was carried by default. The Democrats pushed the bill admitting Kansas under the Lecompton Constitution through the Senate; the House rejected the bill. In 1858 Kansas voters now turned down the constitution—and Kansas remained a territory. In 1861 it came into the Union as a free state.

The year 1858 saw taking place the famous Lincoln-Douglas debates. Lincoln had been a Whig—and, in fact, a "Clay man"—up to 1854; and then he joined the Republican party as a free-soiler and not as an Abolitionist. He contested the senatorial reelection in Illinois of Stephen A. Douglas, and the two candidates moved about the state engaging in joint debate. The discussions were followed with breathless interest by the whole country, but they really proved nothing. Lincoln argued free soil and Douglas argued "squatter sovereignty," maintaining—honestly enough—that despite the Dred Scott decision slavery could continue in a territory only if police regulations protected it. Lincoln lost the election but he won national attention and became an obvious candidate for the Republican nomination in 1860. In the same elections of 1858 the stage was being also set for 1860. For the Republicans captured the lower House of Congress and proceeded to debate free soil, tariffs, and homesteads.

In 1859 occurred John Brown's raid. Brown had moved from Kansas to Virginia, the idea forming in his mind that armed forays against slave properties would compel slaveowners to release their Negroes voluntarily. He had received financial assistance from prominent New England Abolitionists, making it possible for him to gather a band of twenty-one followers and a cache of arms. On the night of October 16 he proceeded against the government arsenal at Harper's Ferry and took it. Two days later a detachment of United States Marines, led by Colonel Robert E. Lee, retook the arsenal, caught Brown and four of his men, and killed ten of whom two were Brown's sons. Brown was tried in October and hanged on December 2.

Both sides were outraged: the South because Northerners were willing openly to countenance insurrection; the North because Brown was a martyr who had listened calmly at his trial and as calmly gone to his death in order to make men free. There was no doubt that nerves everywhere were badly frayed. Congress, the press, and citizens generally looked forward to the election of 1860: it might settle the issue of slavery once and for all.

6. OVERSEAS INTERESTS

Panama. The interest in expansionism did not spend itself in the acquisition of the whole continental domain. Americans—some slave planters, some shipping men, some simply adventurers—gazed far beyond their own shores and dreamed of American empires in the Caribbean and even in the distant western Pacific. In 1846, already thinking of a Panama Canal, the United States negotiated a treaty with New Granada (Colombia) under which Americans received freedom of transit across the isthmus; the sovereignty of New Granada was assured as was also the neutrality of a canal or railroad that might be built. An American company received a charter to construct a railroad and work was begun. Meanwhile, in 1850, by the Clayton-Bulwer Treaty, Great Britain and the United States joined to guarantee the neutrality of any canal dug; nor was either of the countries to try to establish dominion over Central America.

Cuba. Here was a foothold. Other Americans—and they were not only slavery men—now began to center their attention on Cuba. The slave system could be introduced here, of course; but Americans were just as interested in sugar growing and in trade. The weakness of the Spanish administration tempted unscrupulous men, who kept on fishing in the troubled Cuban waters for years. They ran in guns; they ran out slaves; and they involved American Secretaries of State in controversies with Spain. The election of the Democrat Franklin Pierce as President in 1852 promised an aggressive Cuban policy directed toward the acquisition of the island.

Pierre Soulé, Senator from Louisiana, was sent as American Minister to Spain with instructions to buy Cuba or "detach that island from the Spanish dominion," presumably by aiding a Cuban independence movement. Soulé alienated the Spanish court and people; and in 1854 he, James Buchanan (our minister to England) and John Y. Mason (our minister to France) met at Ostend, Belgium, to consider a course of action for the United States. They ended by drawing up a joint letter to the State Department, which has since been called the Ostend Manifesto although it was never delivered to the Spanish government. The American ministers expressed their willingness to purchase Cuba; this failing, "by every law, human and divine, we shall be justified in wresting it from Spain if we possess the power."

Stories of the affair leaked out and the administration was embarrassed; it had to disavow the Manifesto. Soulé resigned; the Abolitionists attacked the Democrats; and the latter, during 1857–60, again and again sought to interest Congress in the passage of a bill authorizing the buying of the island. But Northerners were opposed—just as Southerners were opposed to the passage of a homestead bill. And there the matter ended.

The Far East. As has been seen, American traders had long been familiar figures in the China Sea, entering and leaving the port of Canton as they engaged in trading voyages among the islands or operated only in the direct American trade. In 1842, at the conclusion of the Opium War, England obtained Hong Kong from China and forced open five Chinese ports to foreign commerce and residence. Two years later, as a result of treaty negotiations carried on by Caleb Cushing, Americans were extended similar rights in the new ports and were given both most-favored-nation treatment and extraterritoriality. This last meant the privilege of trying Americans before their own officials instead of in Chinese courts. In the decade or so of the clipper-ship era which followed, American commerce with China grew mightily. American penetration into the kingdom was further aided by the arrival of Christian missionaries, who not only set up their mission stations but also schools and hospitals. Americans, right through the century, continued to be interested in trade alone and had no territorial designs on China —unlike the British, French, Germans, Russians, and Japanese. We manifested our friendship toward the Chinese in many ways and they reciprocated by trusting us.

The same period also saw Americans breaking down the walls behind which the Japanese had barred themselves from the outside world since 1620. The Japanese kept but one port open—Nagasaki—and only the Dutch were permitted to maintain a quarter in it. So hostile were the Japanese to foreigners that shipwrecked sailors from the American whaling fleets were imprisoned and some died in captivity. America, in its extending traffic across the Pacific, needed coaling stations for the new black ships (steamers); it was interested in protecting its seamen; and it wanted to play a part in opening up the Japanese markets to the western world. Britain and Russia entertained similar hopes. It was an American naval officer who first gained entry into the Japanese Bay of Yedo (Tokyo); and it was the United States which made the first commercial treaty with Japan.

In 1853 Commodore Matthew C. Perry, with his squadron of four black warships, appeared before the bewildered eyes of the Japanese and demanded the right to deliver a letter from the President of the United States to the Emperor of Japan. Japan was still feudal in its economy and society; many of its leaders knew they were at the mercy of Perry's guns; and these persons took advantage of Perry's coming to point up the need for the modernization of Japan. Perry was permitted to deliver his letter and in 1854, when he returned for an answer, was cordially received. A treaty was signed between the United States and Japan in March, 1854, which opened two ports and gave the United States most-favored-nation treatment. This was followed up by the dispatching of Townsend Harris to Japan as America's first consul general and in 1858 he obtained Japanese signatures to a commercial treaty. Japan now could be freely entered by American seamen and merchants; its history, from thence on, became a part of the history of the West.

In these ways, a pushing, confident United States spread across the American continent and spilled over across its frontiers. It was growing in wealth and beginning to industrialize. Its standards of living were the highest in the world. Every year, hundreds of thousands of immigrants—facing the future with new hope as they entered her ports—arrived from Europe. While all this was going on, the irrepressible conflict of the Civil War—the Second American Revolution—was preparing. The fifties saw the failure of all efforts at compromise as the hostility between the enemies and the friends of slavery became more implacable.

ALBERT BRISBANE

As the inflationary prosperity of the early 1830s collapsed into panic and depression, Americans became increasingly concerned with the causes and cure of the difficulties under which they suffered. Many had supported the effort to curtail the credit system by destroying the Second Bank of the United States; others, like the insurgent "Locofoco" Democrats of New York, regarded lapses from the doctrine of equal rights as the evil, and a more consistent application of democratic principles as the remedy.

But to Albert Brisbane (1809–1890), all that seemed mere tinkering. The organization of society was responsible for poverty, disease, and disorder; no political program, however sincerely and thoroughly executed, could reach the cause or heal the ills that afflicted the body politic. Brisbane, son of a prosperous New York landowner, joined the numerous Americans touring Europe in the thirties, but he remained longer and saw more than most of his compatriots. After unsatisfactory experiences in the lecture rooms of Paris and with Hegel at Berlin, Brisbane encountered the writings of Charles Fourier (1772–1837), with whom he studied for two years. Convinced that society could be fundamentally altered without convulsion, on his return to America in 1839, Brisbane set about converting his countrymen to Fourier's plan of "Attractive Industry and Association."

The Social Destiny of Man (1840) was the first of Brisbane's efforts. The book blends long translations from the master with Brisbane's own exposition into a confusing, badly organized account of the means by which the world is to be saved. Man has passed through three stages of development—savage, patriarchal, and individual. As these have disappeared, so shall civilization in due time, but the disorders and difficulties of all "transitional" periods could be obviated if men would accept Association now before monopoly forced a burlesque of it upon them.

The present individualist organization of society is inordinately wasteful of time, material, and talent. Individual households fritter away the energies of the female half of the human race in domestic drudgery and the petty buying and selling which serves that drudgery. The individual farm is as wasteful as the individual household; the factory, while more economical, also contravenes the true principles of social organization. Nowhere is industry pleasurable, nowhere does labor produce what it might if work were so pleasant that no one would want to be idle.

From principle and argument, Brisbane passes to programs. Let 300 families join forces on a tract of 2,000 acres. Let them divide into groups, each linked by fondness for a particular branch of agriculture and the trades which serve it. Since everyone will be doing the work he chooses, he will produce more. The wastes of individual farms and households would be eliminated. With the saving of effort and capital which Association will permit, such a Phalanx will be able to cultivate its land so efficiently that it must grow rich and be an example of true social organization to the larger community. In a Phalanx, women would not be limited to the household, hence their labor would be saved for the Association. Children would be so rationally educated and their tastes put to such good use that they would be productive members of society from the age of three. Nor would they resemble the present ill-fed, pallid objects of compassion who tend machines and peddle small wares in city streets. They would have miniature workshops in which to discover their tastes and acquire skills; their work would be honored by the community and their reward would be glory as well as money.

With waste eliminated by Association and labor far more productive under a system of Attractive Industry, Fourierist communities could afford to give their children complete educations, their workers pleasant surroundings, and their poorer members leisure and comfort. For Association did not imply the abolition of individual property or social distinctions. Capital, labor, and talent each was to be rewarded separately and to have its specific share in the annual balancing of the Phalanx's accounts.

Association is practicable, Brisbane argues: large-scale production is so economical that even capitalists practice it when they can. The world is moving toward the elimination of the individual producer. This coming "industrial feudality," in which monopoly must rule, will mean virtual slavery; it can eliminate none of the existing contradictions and will introduce others of its own. Since associated industry is practical, it should be attempted by the people for their own benefit. Only prejudice prevents its acceptance. To eliminating that prejudice, Brisbane devoted a good part of his energies.

Brisbane publicized Association in the columns of Horace Greeley's New York *Tribune*, won Greeley himself to Fourierism, and drew the literary community of Brook Farm into the orbit of Association.

Under the stimulus of continued depression, Phalanxes were organized from Massachusetts to Green Bay, Wisconsin, and the latter even emerged with a profit, for the rise of land values in its neighborhood had increased the value of its holdings. None of the other attempts was that fortunate, however, and none of them was undertaken with Brisbane's approval. He was convinced that the failure of an ill-conceived and badly managed effort to establish Association would merely intensify existing prejudices and supply ammunition to those who believed society never could be regenerated. The efforts continued, none the less, until the return of prosperity and the waxing conflict over the extension of slavery submerged the Fourierist plan that had set so many Americans building paradises on mortgaged land.

The selection here reprinted is from *The Social Destiny of Man* (Philadelphia, 1840). It is an interesting example of the social, educational, and psychological theories of the Fourierists, who regarded the family as an outworn institution and who advocated the early training of the very young for productive labors.

The Social Destiny of Man

BY ALBERT BRISBANE

CHAPTER XXXI: EDUCATION OF THE FIRST ORDER OF CHILDREN

WE NOW ARRIVE at the period, when the initiation of the child into industry, or the awakening in it of a taste for industrial occupations, takes place. Unless the development of industrial instincts be early commenced, the whole system of Education will be a failure. The first tendency of man being to riches,[1] we may say that the Education of the child is falsely commenced, if in the outstart, at about the age of two years, it does not devote it-

self freely and spontaneously to productive Industry, which is the source of riches; and if, like the civilized child, it runs into all kinds of mischief, and breaks and destroys what ever comes in its way, which foolish parents think charming.

As soon as the child can walk and run about, it passes from the class of the *Weaned* to the next

[1] The three tendencies of attraction are:
1st. *Riches.* 2d. *Groups.* 3d. *Series.* ⋈ UNITY.
Material Refinement. Affections. Association. Harmony.

class in age, which we will term *Little Commencers.*[2] If it has been brought up *from its birth in the nurseries of a Phalanx,* it will be strong enough at the age of twenty-one months to join the children of this class. There is no distinction made at this age between the two sexes, as it is important to mingle and confound them in order to facilitate the free development of industrial tastes or talents, and to apply both sexes to the same branches of industry. A distinction between the sexes commences with the class next in age,— with children from three to four and a half years old.

We have before remarked that Nature gives to each child a large number of industrial instincts or talents,—about thirty; some of which are primary or directing instincts, and should lead to those which are secondary.

The first object is to discover in the child, its primary instincts: they will be awakened as soon as it is brought in contact with occupations to which those instincts direct it. As soon as it can walk and leave the nursery, it is confided to the care of a class of teachers, who have the instruction of this age, and whom we will term *Mentors.* (Their functions will differ from those of civilized tutors, who only endeavor to smother Nature, and substitute their doctrines in place of her true impulses.) They will take the child through all the

[2] CLASSIFICATION OF CHILDREN IN AGES OR ORDERS.

Germ,	{	Sucklings, from 0 to 1 year.
		Weaned, from 1 to 2 years.
1st. Age		1st. Order or *Little Commencers.*
		from 2 to 3 years.
Transition, to		
Industry,		2d. Order or *Initiated,*
2d. Age		from 3 to 4½ years.
3d. Age,		3d. Order, from 4½ to 6½ years.
4th. Age,		4th. Order, from 6½ to 9 years.
5th. Age,		5th. Order, from 9 to 12 years.
6th. Age,		6th. Order, from 12 to 15½ years.
7th. Age,		7th. Order, from 15½ to 20 years.

The *Sucklings* and *Weaned,* are the mere germs of future individuals; they are not therefore classed as an Order.

The First Age or Order, is composed of children from two to three years of age. We term them *Little Commencers,* because, childhood at their age, commences its first initiation into Industry.

We give to the Second Order, the title of *Initiated,* because, at the age of four, the child has already acquired a knowledge of some details in divers branches of Industry, and is *initiated* into its occupation.

These two first Ages form the Transition to Industry, as during them children are acquiring preparatory notions of, and forming their bodies to, its exercise.

workshops of the Phalanx, and to all industrial assemblages of children; and as it will find little tools and little workshops placed alongside the large ones, where children from the age of thirty to thirty-six months, are taught to perform some trifling branch of work, it will wish to mingle with them in their occupations, and handle the tools; it will be easy in consequence, to discover at the end of a couple of weeks, which are the worshops that attract it the most, and for what branches of industry it shows a taste.

As the branches of Industry of a Phalanx are extremely varied, it is impossible that the child surrounded by them, should not find the means of satisfying several of its predominant instincts; they will be awakened by the sight of little tools, handled by children a few months older than themselves.

In the opinion of civilized parents and teachers, *children are lazy little creatures;* nothing is more false; children from two to three years of age are very active, but we must know the means which Nature employs,—*in the Passional Series, and not in civilization*—to attract them to industry.

The predominant tastes or characteristics in all children, are:

1st. *Propensity to pry into every thing,* to meddle with and handle whatever they see, and to vary continually their occupations.

2d. Taste for noisy occupations.

3d. Propensity for imitation.

4th. Love of little tools and workshops.

5th. *Progressive influence* of the older children upon the younger.

There are many others, but we mention first these five, which are well known at present. Let us examine the application to be made of them to direct the child in its early age to Industry.

The mentors or tutors will first avail themselves of the propensity of the child to pry into every thing, a propensity which is so strong at the age of two years. It wishes to enter every where, handle every thing, and meddle with whatever it sees. This instinct in the child is a natural incentive to industry. To awaken in it, a taste for its occupations, it will be taken to the little workshops, where it will see children three years old capable of handling little hammers and other tools. Its propensity for imitation will be aroused, which it will wish to satisfy; some little tools will be given it, but it will desire to take part with the children a little older than itself, who know how to work, and who in consequence, will refuse to receive it.

The child will persevere, if it has a decided inclination or instinct for the branch of industry. As soon as the mentor perceives this, he will teach it some little detail connected with the work, and it will soon succeed in making itself useful in some trifles, which will serve as an introduction. We will take as an example, a simple occupation, like the podding of peas, which the smallest children can perform. This work, which now occupies grown persons, will be reserved to children two, three and four years old. The room used for the purpose will contain an inclined table, on the lower side of which are several cavities; two children between three and four years of age are seated at the upper side; they pod the peas, which roll to the lower side, where three *Little Commencers* of the ages of twenty-five, thirty and thirty-five months are seated, who have merely to separate the smaller from the larger peas.

The smallest are wanted for the more delicate kinds of cookery, the middle sized for the more common kinds, and the largest for soup. The child of thirty-five months first selects the smallest peas, which are the most difficult to cull; it passes all the large and middle sized to the next cavity, where the child of thirty months is seated, who shoves in turn to the third cavity what appears large, returns to the first what appears small, and gathers in a basket all the middle sized. The child seated at the third cavity has very little to do; it pushes back a few middle sized peas to the second child, and merely collects in its basket the large ones.

It is at the third cavity that the new comer is seated: it will take great pride in pushing the large peas into a basket, and in performing this trifling operation, it will imagine that it has done as much as its companions.

The work will interest and excite an emulation in the young child, and in a few days it will be able to replace the child twenty-five months old. As soon as it can perform this little work, a badge of distinction is given it to show that it is a member of the group. In all the occupations of Association care will be taken to reserve for extremely young children some trifling detail like the above, which could no doubt be better done without them and with less loss of time, but these details, which are easily performed, must be reserved for children to induce them to take a part in industry.

In all branches some trifling occupations are left for childhood as a means of initiation into industry. For the child two years old these occupations must be very easy of execution, but in performing them, it will believe that it has done something of consequence, and that it is almost the equal of children three or four months older than itself, who are already members of groups, and who

wear their little ornaments and uniforms, which inspire with profound respect the young beginner.

The child two years old will find consequently in the little workshops of a Phalanx enticing occupations, which is not the case in civilization, and which will develope its tastes or instincts for industry. These instincts in civilization either lie dormant or are entirely smothered.

MEANS OF DEVELOPING INSTINCTS FOR INDUSTRIAL VOCATIONS IN CHILDREN

1st. Charm of little workshops, and of little tools, adapted in size to the different ages.

2d. Application of all playthings, such as little wagons, wooden horses, dolls, etc., which are useless in civilization, to purposes of industrial instruction.

3d. Charm of ornaments and uniforms: a feather at present often suffices to bewitch the country lad, and induce him to enlist; what then will be the power of handsome ornaments and uniforms with the child in inducing it to take a part in gay and happy groups with its equals?

4th. Privilege of appearing on parade, and of using tools: we know how much such privileges stimulate children.

5th. Gaiety and animation, which always accompany assemblages of children, when they are engaged in occupations, which are pleasing and attractive.

6th. Pride of having performed some trifle which the child believes of high importance; this illusion is cherished.

7th. Propensity to imitation, which is so predominant in children, and which acquires a ten fold intensity, when their emulation is excited by the exploits of groups of children, a little older than themselves.

8th. Full liberty in the choice of occupations, and in the duration of the same.

9th. Perfect independence, or exemption from obedience to superiors, whom it has not chosen from inclination.

10th. Parcelled exercise, or the advantage of choosing in each branch of industry, the detail which pleases.

11th. Charm of short occupations, varied frequently and animated by rivalry. They are desired, because they do not occur frequently. This is the case with those occupations even which take place daily, for they only require by turns a third or a fourth of the members of the group.

12th. Absence of paternal flattery, which is counteracted in Association, where the child is judged and criticised by its equals.

13th. Influence of a regular gradation in uniform tools, etc., adapted to merit and ages, which is the only system that charms the child and can call forth dexterity in industry and application in study.

14th. Attractive effect of large assemblages, and charm of belonging to groups, in which an enthusiasm is awakened by uniforms, music and corporative celebrations.

15th. Emulation and rivalry between children of the same age, between groups of the same series, and between divisions of the same group.

16th. Periodical chance of promotion to classes higher in age.

17th. Admiration for prodigies performed by groups of older children,—the only beings whom the younger ones choose as models.

18th. Rivalries between children of different Phalanxes; meetings of groups, and emulative contests between them.

There are other incentives not here mentioned, and which commence acting only after the age of four, such are:

Contrast and emulation of sexes and instincts.

Love of gain or spirit of acquisition.

The combination of these incentives will develope in less than a month in the child three or four of its primary tastes or inclinations, which with time will call forth others: inclinations for more difficult branches will be awakened later.

The mentor in taking the child through the workshops and manufactories, will discern the most proper occasions for presenting to it any particular branch of work; he makes a memorandum of what has appeared to please it, and two or three trials are made to ascertain whether an inclination manifests itself. A delay of a few months may be judged necessary, and there is no urging in case a taste is not evinced. It is well known that twenty or thirty industrial inclinations will be developed in the course of the year, *and it is of but little consequence which they are.*

A mentor will commonly take with him three children at a time; with one child he would have but few chances of success, but of the three one will be more skilful, another more ardent, and the two will influence the third. The mentor will not take them all of the same age; besides he will change children in the different workshops; leaving one with a group occupied in shelling peas, taking with him the others who have evinced no inclination, and a third, who has finished its work.

The function of mentor is adapted to both sexes, and requires peculiar talents, which may be found in both. The function of nurse is confined to women.

The best incentive for the child commencing its industrial career, is impartial criticism, which it never receives from the father or the mother, who praise at this early age even its faults. This indiscreet flattery will be counteracted in Association; children among themselves show no quarters, but ridicule without mercy an awkward associate and dismiss it with disdain. Turned away by the older children, it will go crying to its mentor, who will give it lessons and present it again, when it has acquired sufficient skill. As some easy and trifling work is always reserved for this age, the child soon obtains admission to a dozen groups, in which its education progresses rapidly and by pure attraction. Nothing is learned well and rapidly, which is not learned by attraction.

Of all the means of awakening a taste in the child for industry, the one least known and most perverted in civilization, is that which we will term the *spirit of ascending imitation,* or the tendency of the child to imitate those a little older than itself, to pay deference to their views and decisions, and to consider it an honor to be associated with them in their occupations and amusements.

This *spirit of ascending imitation* is pernicious in effect at present, because the amusements of a band of children, left free, are dangerous or useless; they play games in which they run the risk of maiming themselves, acquire bad habits and learn vulgarity of language and manners. In Association, with the stimulants we have just enumerated, these same children would be led to devote themselves actively to productive occupations.

The ignorance of the true application of *ascending imitation* shows the great defect of all our civilized methods of education.

All authors of systems of education have fallen into the great error of considering the father or a tutor under his direction, as the natural instructor of the child. Nature judges differently, and for a three-fold reason.

1st. The father seeks to communicate his tastes to the child, and to smother the development of its natural instincts and capacities, which differ almost always from his own. The whole mechanism of the passional Series would be destroyed, if the son inherited the tastes of the father.

2d. The father is disposed to praise and flatter to excess in the child the little merit which it may possess, while on the contrary it requires to be criticised with severity by groups of associates.

3d. The father excuses in it want of skill and dexterity, and prevents as a consequence the progress which would result from a judicious criticism, which is submitted to when it comes from skilful associates.

Nature, to counteract all these defects of paternal education, gives to the child a repugnance for the lessons of the father and the tutor; the child wishes to command and not to obey the father. The leaders whom it chooses from passion, are always children somewhat older than itself; for example,

At 18 months, it admires the child of two years, and chooses it as its guide.

At 2 years, it chooses the child of thirty months.

At 3 years, the child of four.

At 8 years, the child of ten.

At 12 years, the child of fifteen.

This ascending deference will be greatly increased in strength, if the child sees children a little older than itself members of groups, and enjoying a merited respect for their progress in industry and studies.

The natural instructors of children of each age are, consequently, those a little superior in age. But as children in civilization are all more or less inclined to mischief and entice each other into it, it is impossible to establish among them a gradation or ascending order of useful impulses and make each age the guide of the next younger; this can only take place in the Passional series, out of which any approximation to a system of natural education is impossible.

This natural system of education will be one of the wonders, which will be admired in the first Phalanx. The seven orders or ages of children will direct and educate each other, as nature wishes, by the influence of *ascending imitation*, which can only lead to the good of the whole; for if the highest order, or seventh age, (from fifteen and a half to twenty,) take a proper direction in industry, in studies and morals, it will influence and direct rightly the sixth age, (from twelve to fifteen and a half,) to which it will serve as a model. The same influence will be exercised by the sixth on the fifth, by the fifth on the fourth, and thus in a descending order on the third, second and first ages. The seven corporations, directed by the spirit of *ascending imitation*, will, although left to their full liberty, vie with each other in excellence and activity in Industry and social harmonies. On beholding this prodigy, it will no longer be doubted that Attraction, *developed in Passional Series*, is the agent of the Divinity, is the hand of the Creator, directing man to his greatest good.

We will conclude our remarks upon the functions of the Mentors with one or two more observations. So far from flattering and excusing the child, it will be their task to see that it meets with refusals and rebuffs in different groups, in order to stimulate it to vindicate itself by proofs of skill. A father could not fulfil this duty; he would blame the group which had rejected his child. The function of mentor, as well as of nurse, will require persons of a firm and judicious character, who, from a corporative spirit, will be interested in the progress of the children in general and not in the caprices of a few favorites.

The function of Mentor is of high importance, because it acts upon a decisive epoch in the education of the younger age; if the child succeeds well in the commencement of its industrial education; it will be a guarantee of success for the entire career of its childhood. Once initiated into ten branches of industry, it soon will be into a hundred, and at the age of fifteen, it will be acquainted with the various branches of agriculture, manufactures, arts and sciences, which its own, and the neighboring Phalanxes pursue. Let us examine how this result will be effected.

A child, were it the son of a man of the highest rank and fortune, may at the age of three years, exhibit a taste for shoemaking, and wish to visit the workshops of the shoe-makers, who in Association are as polite a class as any other. If it be prevented from visiting their workshops; if its inclination for shoemaking be thwarted, under the pretext that it is not a dignified occupation, or is wanting in intellectual elevation, it will take a dislike for other branches of industry, and will feel no interest in those studies and occupations, which its parents wish it to pursue. But if it be left to commence as attraction directs,—that is by shoemaking,—it will easily be induced to acquire a knowledge of tanning, then of chemistry, so far as relates to the various preparations of leather, and then of agriculture, so far as pasturage and breeding of cattle has an influence upon the quality of skins.

Thus the child by degrees will be initiated into all branches of industry, a result of its primitive inclination for shoemaking. It is of but little consequence how it commences, provided it acquires in the course of its youth a general knowledge of the various branches, of industry of its Phalanx, and that it conceives a lively affection for all the Series from which it has received instruction.

This general knowledge cannot be acquired in civilization, where science and industry are not connected. The scientific declare that the sciences form a chain, each link of which connects with, and leads to, all the others; but they forget that our isolated and conflicting relations sow discord among the industrial classes, and render each indifferent to the labors of the others; whereas in a Phalanx, every person is interested in all the Series from connections and rivalries with some of their members upon questions of agriculture, science, music and art. The connection existing between the sciences is not alone sufficient to lead to their general study; we must add to that connection ties, which arise from the association of functions and individuals and from emulative rivalries,—an impossibility in civilization.

HENRY DAVID THOREAU

WHILE ALBERT BRISBANE and the American followers of Fourier were attempting to build the good society in cooperation, other Americans looked to the individual for regeneration. "We must first succeed alone, that we may enjoy our success together," Thoreau declared at twenty-six. The fact is, he had been going his own way all his life. Harvard rules required students to wear black: Henry David Thoreau (1817–1862) wore a green coat through the four years of his residence. College-bred young men were expected to become ministers, schoolmasters, or men of letters. Thoreau made pencils as his father had done before him. Thoreau made the best lead pencils in Massachusetts and then he made no more: he had other business. That business was not the naturalist's, although Thoreau was concerned with nature. It was not the scholar's, although his translations from the Greek were used as labor savers by lazy Harvard students. And it was not the writer's, even though Thoreau did publish two books during his lifetime and keep journals that furnished his friends with material for half a dozen more.

Thoreau had set himself a problem: To what end does a man live and how shall he order his life to achieve that end? Thoreau's first book, *A Week on the Concord and Merrimack Rivers* (1849) expresses some of his dissatisfaction with what he saw of other men's solutions to that problem. In *Walden* (1854), Thoreau gives an account of his own experiment in uncluttered living. He spent a good part of a year in a hut at Walden Pond, raising his own food, caring for his own needs, and minding his own particular business. When he had discovered how little a man actually needed to supply his life, Thoreau returned to Concord. He was no hermit for seclusion's sake. Nor was Thoreau unaware of the fact that men have relations with each other as well as with the universe. He had refused certain of those relations, to be sure: he did not marry; he worked when and as he chose; he "joined no church and belonged to no political party"; he scorned the "American . . . who ventures to live only by the aid of the Mutual Insurance Society which has promised to bury him decently."

But for Thoreau, those refusals meant an increase of rather than a shrinking from responsibility. He had accepted his friends' action when they paid his poll tax in 1845, and thereafter paid the tax himself, rather than be beholden to them. When Boston sent back fugitive slaves to the South, Thoreau faced his own problem in a new light. A man might properly have other duties than the redress of wrong, but if "I devote myself to other pursuits and contemplations, I must first see, at least, that I do not pursue them sitting upon another man's shoulder." In 1832, South Carolina asserted a state's right to peaceable secession from the Union. In 1849, Henry David Thoreau asserted the individual's right to secede. "I quietly declare war with the State," Thoreau says in the essay on *Civil Disobedience*.

Government is an evil that might be tolerated so long as it did not interfere with a man's conscience. But when a government made war on a weaker nation and tolerated slavery, the individual must leave his own business and take thought: "How does it become a man to behave toward the American government today? I answer that he cannot without disgrace be associated with it. I cannot for an instant recognize that political organization as *my* government which is the *slave's* government also."

Nor was it sufficient to be opposed in opinion; a man must act. And, since voting is a gamble and there "is but little virtue in the action of masses of men," he must act alone, not by obeying the law, but by breaking it, by refusing to acknowledge the state in the person of its tax gatherer. And if the state jail him for the offense, it but shows its own folly in treating a man as if he were "mere flesh and blood and bones to be locked up." When the state of Massachusetts had shut Thoreau into a cell for refusing to pay his poll tax, he knew it was as "timid as a lone woman with her silver spoons." He had no silver spoons; he was without property or family to hinder him; he could act as it was fitting that a man should act, from principle, not expediency.

The passage here reprinted is from *Civil Disobedience* and appears in *Cape Cod and Miscellanies* (Boston, 1906). It is published by permission of Houghton Mifflin Company.

Civil Disobedience

BY HENRY DAVID THOREAU

. . . UNDER A GOVERNMENT which imprisons any unjustly, the true place for a just man is also a prison. The proper place to-day, the only place which Massachusetts has provided for her freer and less desponding spirits, is in her prisons, to be put out and locked out of the State by her own act, as they have already put themselves out by their principles. It is there that the fugitive slave, and the Mexican prisoner on parole, and the Indian come to plead the wrongs of his race should find them; on that separate, but more free and honorable, ground, where the State places those who are not *with* her, but *against* her,—the only house in a slave State in which a free man can abide with honor. If any think that their influence would be lost there, and their voices no longer afflict the ear of the State, that they would not be as an enemy within its walls, they do not know by how much truth is stronger than error, nor how much more eloquently and effectively he can combat injustice who has experienced a little in his own person. Cast your whole vote, not a strip of paper merely, but your whole influence. A minority is powerless while it conforms to the majority; it is not even a minority then; but it is irresistible when it clogs by its whole weight. If the alternative is to keep all just men in prison, or give up war and slavery, the State will not hesitate which to choose. If a thousand men were not to pay their tax-bills this year, that would not be a violent and bloody measure, as it would be to pay them, and enable the State to commit violence and shed innocent blood. This is, in fact, the definition of a peaceable revolution, if any such is possible. If the tax-gatherer, or any other public officer, asks me, as one has done, "But what shall I do?" my answer is, "If you really wish to do anything, resign your office." When the subject has refused allegiance, and the officer has resigned his office, then the revolution is accomplished. But even suppose blood should flow. Is there not a sort of blood shed when the conscience is wounded? Through this wound a man's real manhood and immortality flow out, and he bleeds to an everlasting death. I see this blood flowing now.

I have contemplated the imprisonment of the offender, rather than the seizure of his goods,—though both will serve the same purpose,—because they who assert the purest right, and consequently are most dangerous to a corrupt State, commonly have not spent much time in accumulating property. To such the State renders comparatively small service, and a slight tax is wont to appear exorbitant, particularly if they are obliged to earn it by special labor with their hands. If there were one who lived wholly without the use of money, the State itself would hesitate to demand it of him. But the rich man—not to make any invidious comparison—is always sold to the institution which makes him rich. Absolutely speaking, the more money, the less virtue; for money comes between a man and his objects, and obtains them for him; and it was certainly no great virtue to obtain it. It puts to rest many questions which he would otherwise be taxed to answer; while the only new question which it puts is the hard but superfluous one, how to spend it. Thus his moral ground is taken from under his feet. The opportunities of living are diminished in proportion as what are called the "means" are increased. The best thing a man can do for his culture when he is rich is to endeavor to carry out those schemes which he entertained when he was poor. Christ answered the Herodians according to their condition. "Show me the tribute-money," said he;—and one took a penny out of his pocket;—if you use money which has the image of Cæsar on it, and which he has made current and valuable, that is, *if you are men of the State*, and gladly enjoy the advantages of Cæsar's government, then pay him back some of his own when he demands it. "Render therefore to Cæsar that which is Cæsar's, and to God those things which are God's,"—leaving them no wiser than before as to which was which; for they did not wish to know.

When I converse with the freest of my neighbors, I perceive that, whatever they may say about the magnitude and seriousness of the question, and their regard for the public tranquillity, the long and the short of the matter is, that they cannot spare the protection of the existing government, and they dread the consequences to their property and families of disobedience to it. For my own part, I should not like to think that I ever rely on the protection of the State. But, if I deny the authority of the State when it presents its tax-bill, it will soon take and waste all my property, and so harass me and my children without end. This is hard. This makes it impossible for a man to live honestly, and at the same time comfortably, in outward respects. It will not be worth the while to accumulate property; that would be sure to go again. You must hire or squat somewhere, and raise but a small crop, and eat that soon. You must live within yourself, and depend upon yourself always tucked up and ready for a start, and not have many affairs. A man may grow rich in Turkey even, if he will be in all respects a good subject of the Turkish government. Confucius said: "If a state is governed by the principles of reason, poverty and misery are subjects of shame; if a state is not governed by the principles of reason, riches and honors are the subjects of shame." No: until I want the protection of Massachusetts to be extended to me in some distant Southern port, where my liberty is endangered, or until I am bent solely on building up an estate at home by peaceful enterprise, I can afford to refuse allegiance to Massachusetts, and her right to my property and life. It costs me less in every sense to incur the penalty of disobedience to the State than it would to obey. I should feel as if I were worth less in that case.

Some years ago, the State met me in behalf of the Church, and commanded me to pay a certain sum toward the support of a clergyman whose preaching my father attended, but never I myself. "Pay," it said, "or be locked up in the jail." I declined to pay. But, unfortunately, another man saw fit to pay it. I did not see why the schoolmaster should be taxed to support the priest, and not the priest the schoolmaster; for I was not the State's schoolmaster, but I supported myself by voluntary subscription. I did not see why the lyceum should not present its tax-bill, and have the State to back its demand, as well as the Church. However, at the request of the selectmen, I condescended to make some such statement as this in writing:—"Know all men by these presents, that I, Henry Thoreau, do not wish to be regarded as a member of any incorporated society which I have not joined." This I gave to the town clerk; and he has it. The State, having thus learned that I did not wish to be regarded as a member of that church, has never made a like demand on me since; though it said that it must adhere to its original presumption that time. If I had known how to name them, I should then have signed off in detail from all the societies which I never signed on to; but I did not know where to find a complete list.

I have paid no poll-tax for six years. I was put into a jail once on this account, for one night; and, as I stood considering the walls of solid stone, two or three feet thick, the door of wood and iron, a foot thick, and the iron grating which strained the light, I could not help being struck with the foolishness of that institution which treated me as if I were mere flesh and blood and bones, to be locked up. I wondered that it should have concluded at length that this was the best use it could put me to, and had never thought to avail itself of my services in some way. I saw that, if there was a wall of stone between me and my townsmen, there was a still more difficult one to climb or break through before they could get to be as free as I was. I did not for a moment feel confined, and the walls seemed a great waste of stone and mortar. I felt as if I alone of all my townsmen had paid my tax. They plainly did not know how to treat me, but behaved like persons who are underbred. In every threat and in every compliment there was a blunder; for they thought that my chief desire was to stand the other side of that stone wall. I could not but smile to see how industriously they locked the door on my meditations, which followed them out again without let or hindrance, and *they* were really all that was dangerous. As they could not reach me, they had resolved to punish my body; just as boys, if they cannot come at some person against whom they have a spite, will abuse his dog. I saw that the State was half-witted, that it was timid as a lone woman with her silver spoons, and that it did not know its friends from its foes, and I lost all my remaining respect for it, and pitied it.

Thus the State never intentionally confronts a man's sense, intellectual or moral, but only his body, his senses. It is not armed with superior wit or honesty, but with superior physical strength. I was not born to be forced. I will breathe after my own fashion. Let us see who is the strongest. What force has a multitude? They only can force me who obey a higher law than I. They force me to become like themselves. I do not hear of *men* being *forced* to live this way or that by masses of men. What sort of life were that to live? When I meet a government which says to me, "Your money or your life," why should I be in haste to give it my money? It may be in a great strait, and not know what to do: I cannot help that. It must help itself; do as I do. It is not worth the while to snivel about it. I am not responsible for the successful working of the machinery of society. I am not the son of the engineer. I perceive that, when an acorn and a chestnut fall side by side, the one does not remain inert to make way for the other, but both obey their own laws, and spring and grow and flourish as best they can, till one, perchance, overshadows and destroys the other. If a plant cannot live according to its nature, it dies; and so a man.

The night in prison was novel and interesting enough. The prisoners in their shirt-sleeves were enjoying a chat and the evening air in the doorway, when I entered. But the jailer said, "Come, boys, it is time to lock up;" and so they dispersed, and I heard the sound of their steps returning into the hollow apartments. My roommate was introduced to me by the jailer as "a first-rate fellow and a clever man." When the door was locked, he showed me where to hang my hat, and how he managed matters there. The rooms were whitewashed once a month; and this one, at least, was the whitest, most simply furnished, and probably the neatest apartment in the town. He naturally wanted to know where I came from, and what brought me there; and, when I had told him, I asked him in my turn how he came there, presuming him to be an honest man, of course; and, as the world goes, I believe he was. "Why," said he, "they accuse me of burning a barn; but I never did it." As near as I could discover, he had probably gone to bed in a barn when drunk, and smoked his pipe there; and so a barn was burnt. He had the reputation of being a clever man, had been there some three months waiting for his trial to come on, and would have to wait as much longer; but he was quite domesticated and contented, since he got his board for nothing, and thought that he was well treated.

He occupied one window, and I the other; and

I saw that if one stayed there long, his principal business would be to look out the window. I had soon read all the tracts that were left there, and examined where former prisoners had broken out, and where a grate had been sawed off, and heard the history of the various occupants of that room; for I found that even here there was a history and a gossip which never circulated beyond the walls of the jail. Probably this is the only house in the town where verses are composed, which are afterward printed in a circular form, but not published. I was shown quite a long list of verses which were composed by some young men who had been detected in an attempt to escape, who avenged themselves by singing them.

I pumped my fellow-prisoner as dry as I could, for fear I should never see him again; but at length he showed me which was my bed, and left me to blow out the lamp.

It was like traveling into a far country, such as I had never expected to behold, to lie there for one night. It seemed to me that I never had heard the town clock strike before, nor the evening sounds of the village; for we slept with the windows open, which were inside the grating. It was to see my native village in the light of the Middle Ages, and our Concord was turned into a Rhine stream, and visions of knights and castles passed before me. They were the voices of old burghers that I heard in the streets. I was an involuntary spectator and auditor of whatever was done and said in the kitchen of the adjacent village inn,—a wholly new and rare experience to me. It was a closer view of my native town. I was fairly inside of it. I never had seen its institutions before. This is one of its peculiar institutions; for it is a shire town. I began to comprehend what its inhabitants were about.

In the morning, our breakfasts were put through the hole in the door, in small oblong-square tin pans, made to fit, and holding a pint of chocolate, with brown bread, and an iron spoon. When they called for the vessels again, I was green enough to return what bread I had left; but my comrade seized it, and said that I should lay that up for lunch or dinner. Soon after he was let out to work at haying in a neighboring field, whither he went every day, and would not be back till noon; so he bade me good-day, saying that he doubted if he should see me again.

When I came out of prison,—for some one interfered, and paid that tax,—I did not perceive that great changes had taken place on the common, such as he observed who went in a youth and emerged a tottering and gray-headed man; and yet a change had to my eyes come over the scene,—the town, and State, and country,— greater than any that mere time could effect. I saw yet more distinctly the State in which I lived. I saw to what extent the people among whom I lived could be trusted as good neighbors and friends; that their friendship was for summer weather only; that they did not greatly propose to do right; that they were a distinct race from me by their prejudices and superstitions, as the Chinamen and Malays are; that in their sacrifices to humanity they ran no risks, not even to their property; that after all they were not so noble but they treated the thief as he had treated them, and hoped, by a certain outward observance and a few prayers, and by walking in a particular straight though useless path from time to time, to save their souls. . . .

No man with a genius for legislation has appeared in America. They are rare in the history of the world. There are orators, politicians, and eloquent men, by the thousand; but the speaker has not yet opened his mouth to speak who is capable of settling the much-vexed questions of the day. We love eloquence for its own sake, and not for any truth which it may utter, or any heroism it may inspire. Our legislators have not yet learned the comparative value of free trade and of freedom, of union, and of rectitude, to a nation. They have no genius or talent for comparatively humble questions of taxation and finance, commerce and manufactures and agriculture. If we were left solely to the wordy wit of legislators in Congress for our guidance, uncorrected by the seasonable experience and the effectual complaints of the people, America would not long retain her rank among the nations. For eighteen hundred years, though perchance I have no right to say it,

the New Testament has been written; yet where is the legislator who has wisdom and practical talent enough to avail himself of the light which it sheds on the science of legislation?

The authority of government, even such as I am willing to submit to,—for I will cheerfully obey those who know and can do better than I, and in many things even those who neither know nor can do so well,—is still an impure one: to be strictly just, it must have the sanction and consent of the governed. It can have no pure right over my person and property but what I concede to it. The progress from an absolute to a limited monarchy, from a limited monarchy to a democracy, is a progress toward a true respect for the individual. Even the Chinese philosopher was wise enough to regard the individual as the basis of the empire. Is a democracy, such as we know it, the last improvement possible in government? Is it not possible to take a step further towards recognizing and organizing the rights of man? There will never be a really free and enlightened State until the State comes to recognize the individual as a higher and independent power, from which all its own power and authority are derived, and treats him accordingly. I please myself with imagining a State at last which can afford to be just to all men, and to treat the individual with respect as a neighbor; which even would not think it inconsistent with its own repose if a few were to live aloof from it, not meddling with it, nor embraced by it, who fulfilled all the duties of neighbors and fellow-men. A State which bore this kind of fruit, and suffered it to drop off as fast as it ripened, would prepare the way for a still more perfect and glorious State, which also I have imagined, but not yet anywhere seen.

JOHN C. CALHOUN

LIKE WEBSTER, Calhoun spoke for his section, following its changes of fortune and reinforcing by his influence the political tendencies latent in its economy. As Webster moved from free trade and a degree of particularism to protection and worship of the Union, so Calhoun proceeded from an initially nationalist position to the rigidity of Constitutional interpretation which seemed demanded by his section's needs.

An upcountry South Carolinian who was brought to the lower country by marriage,

Scotch-Irish in descent and New England in the later stages of his education, John Caldwell Calhoun (1782–1850) displays, in political thought, something of the Puritan combination of rigid logic in approach and intensity in conviction. Though Calhoun had demonstrated his political philosophy in the struggle over nullification, it was not until nearly two decades later that he made a systematic presentation of his ideas on the nature of government. It was in the interval between Congress's rising in 1848 and its reconvening in 1849 that Calhoun retired to write *A Disquisition on Government*. Northern representatives had demanded that slavery be excluded from the territory acquired from Mexico. Southern extremists declared themselves ready to secede if such a law were passed. Moderates appealed for union, and Calhoun set about recalling his countrymen to true principles in politics.

Man is born a social animal and yet is preoccupied with his personal concerns, Calhoun begins. Out of these facts arise conflict and a consequent need for government. Government has an inherent tendency to abuse its powers but that may be curbed by the devising of a judicious constitution.

Yet mere limitation of a government's powers or its establishment on a suffrage basis is not capable of checking the tendency to usurpation which exists in governments. Communities embrace separate interests each of which seeks to control government; for government alone, by its powers of taxation, can benefit one portion of the commonwealth at the others' expense. The only practical difference between absolutist and suffrage states is found in the greater influence of parties in the latter and the possibility that minorities may become majorities. Yet even that will not secure one interest against oppression by others. Since neither the limitation of government's power nor the extension of suffrage can check its necessary tendency to usurpation, and those who would enforce existing restrictions of its power are termed "mere abstractionists," the constitution will be entirely subverted unless some new method can be found.

That method lies in balancing the numerical majority with a concurrent majority won by the consent of the interests concerned in the operation of any proposed measure. The community would be united by the enforced prevalence of compromise as well as by the elimination of party as a dominant political force. The introduction of the concurrent majority would not restrict but enhance and develop that liberty which is a social achievement—the "re-ward reserved for the intelligent, patriotic, virtuous and deserving"—and not at all a natural right, since such liberty does not exist in any nature known to man.

The idea of the concurrent majority may be hard to apply, but all governments except absolutisms have their difficulties. It will not paralyze action, for the need to prevent anarchy will make clashing interests compromise when action is really needed. The Roman Republic, the Six Nations of the Iroquois, and the Kingdom of Poland all operated on the basis of the concurrent majority and all were successful and well governed in their time. Thus Calhoun, by attacking the Lockian ideas of natural rights and popular sovereignty, ends by rejecting the principles upon which the American Republic was founded. His work, in other words, is a theoretical defense of slavery —and of aristocracy.

From general philosophy and historical background, Calhoun proceeded to *A Disquisition on the Constitution and Government of the United States*. Though this is rather an accumulation of notes than a book, it presents several suggestive points beyond Calhoun's well-known scheme for applying the concurrent majority through the device of a dual executive. Parties have become sectional as the government grew centralized, he notes. It was the rise of party which made Abolitionism important, for it is the nature of party to neglect principle in its eagerness to win votes. Persistence in the present attempt to govern the United States by mere numerical majority will lead to monarchy or disunion. If the Union is to be preserved, it must return to federal principles. The judiciary acts must be repealed and the states freed from subjection to the Supreme Court. The power to tax should be limited and the executive restrained. In addition, that executive should be reconstituted. Each section should elect a president. One of these should have charge of domestic affairs and the other be entrusted with our foreign concerns, while the consent of both would be necessary for any legislation. In this way, the overweening power of the North would be curbed for all time, and true federal balance restored to the government of the United States.

The passage here reprinted, from *A Disquisition on Government*, is taken from Calhoun's *Works*, Vol. I (New York, 1854).

A Disquisition on Government

BY JOHN C. CALHOUN

But GOVERNMENT, although intended to protect and preserve society, has itself a strong tendency to disorder and abuse of its powers, as all experience and almost every page of history testify. The cause is to be found in the same constitution of our nature which makes government indispensable. The powers which it is necessary for government to possess, in order to repress violence and preserve order, cannot execute themselves. They must be administered by men in whom, like others, the individual are stronger than the social feelings. And hence, the powers vested in them to prevent injustice and oppression on the part of others, will, if left unguarded, be by them converted into instruments to oppress the rest of the community. That, by which this is prevented, by whatever name called, is what is meant by CONSTITUTION, in its most comprehensive sense, when applied to GOVERNMENT.

Having its origin in the same principle of our nature, *constitution* stands to *government*, as *government* stands to *society;* and, as the end for which society is ordained, would be defeated without government, so that for which government is ordained would, in a great measure, be defeated without constitution. But they differ in this striking particular. There is no difficulty in forming government. It is not even a matter of choice, whether there shall be one or not. Like breathing, it is not permitted to depend on our volition. Necessity will force it on all communities in some one form or another. Very different is the case as to constitution. Instead of a matter of necessity, it is one of the most difficult tasks imposed on man to form a constitution worthy of the name; while, to form a perfect one,—one that would completely counteract the tendency of government to oppression and abuse, and hold it strictly to the great ends for which it is ordained,—has thus far exceeded human wisdom, and possibly ever will. From this, another striking difference results. Constitution is the contrivance of man, while government is of Divine ordination. Man is left to perfect what the wisdom of the Infinite ordained, as necessary to preserve the race.

With these remarks, I proceed to the consideration of the important and difficult question: How is this tendency of government to be counteracted? Or, to express it more fully,—How can those who are invested with the powers of government be prevented from employing them, as the means of aggrandizing themselves, instead of using them to protect and preserve society? It cannot be done by instituting a higher power to control the government, and those who administer it. This would be but to change the seat of authority, and to make this higher power, in reality, the government; with the same tendency, on the part of those who might control its powers, to pervert them into instruments of aggrandizement. Nor can it be done by limiting the powers of government, so as to make it too feeble to be made an instrument of abuse; for, passing by the difficulty of so limiting its powers, without creating a power higher than the government itself to enforce the observance of the limitations, it is a sufficient objection that it would, if practicable, defeat the end for which government is ordained, by making it too feeble to protect and preserve society. The powers necessary for this purpose will ever prove sufficient to aggrandize those who control it, at the expense of the rest of the community.

In estimating what amount of power would be requisite to secure the objects of government, we must take into the reckoning, what would be necessary to defend the community against external, as well as internal dangers. Government must be able to repel assaults from abroad, as well as to repress violence and disorders within. It must not be overlooked, that the human race is not comprehended in a single society or community. The limited reason and faculties of man, the great diversity of language, customs, pursuits, situation and complexion, and the difficulty of intercourse, with various other causes, have, by their operation, formed a great many separate communities, acting independently of each other. Between these there is the same tendency to conflict,—and from the same constitution of our nature,—as between men individually; and even stronger,—because the sympathetic or social feelings are not so strong between different communities, as between individuals of the same community. So powerful, indeed, is this tendency, that it has led to almost incessant wars between contiguous communities for plunder and conquest, or to avenge injuries, real or supposed.

So long as this state of things continues, exigencies will occur, in which the entire powers and resources of the community will be needed to defend its existence. When this is at stake, every other consideration must yield to it. Self-preservation is the supreme law, as well with communities as individuals. And hence the danger of withholding from government the full command of the power and resources of the state; and the great difficulty of limiting its powers consistently with the protection and preservation of the community. And hence the question recurs,—By what means can government, without being divested of the full command of the resources of the community, be preserved from abusing its powers? . . .

How government, then, must be constructed, in order to counteract, through its organism, this tendency on the part of those who make and execute the laws to oppress those subject to their operation, is the next question which claims attention.

There is but one way in which this can possibly be done; and that is, by such an organism as will furnish the ruled with the means of resisting successfully this tendency on the part of the rulers to oppression and abuse. Power can only be resisted by power,—and tendency by tendency. Those who exercise power and those subject to its exercise,—the rulers and the ruled,—stand in antagonistic relations to each other. The same constitution of our nature which leads rulers to oppress the ruled,—regardless of the object for which government is ordained,—will, with equal strength, lead the ruled to resist, when possessed of the means of making peaceable and effective resistance. Such an organism, then, as will furnish the means by which resistance may be systematically and peaceably made on the part of the ruled, to oppression and abuse of power on the part of the rulers, is the first and indispensable step towards *forming* a constitutional government. And as this can only be effected by or through the right of suffrage,—(the right on the part of the ruled to chose their rulers at proper intervals, and to hold them thereby responsible for their conduct,)—the responsibility of the rulers to the ruled, through the right of suffrage, is the indispensable and primary principle in the *foundation* of a constitutional government. When this right is properly guarded, and the people sufficiently enlightened to understand their own rights and the interests of the community, and

duly to appreciate the motives and conduct of those appointed to make and execute the laws, it is all-sufficient to give to those who elect, effective control over those they have elected.

I call the right of suffrage the indispensable and primary principle; for it would be a great and dangerous mistake to suppose, as many do, that it is, of itself, sufficient to form constitutional governments. To this erroneous opinion may be traced one of the causes, why so few attempts to form constitutional governments have succeeded; and why, of the few which have, so small a number have had durable existence. It has led, not only to mistakes in the attempts to form such governments, but to their overthrow, when they have, by some good fortune, been correctly formed. So far from being, of itself, sufficient,—however well guarded it might be, and however enlightened the people,—it would, unaided by other provisions, leave the government as absolute, as it would be in the hands of irresponsible rulers; and with a tendency, at least as strong, towards oppression and abuse of its powers; as I shall next proceed to explain.

The right of suffrage, of itself, can do no more than give complete control to those who elect, over the conduct of those they have elected. In doing this, it accomplishes all it possibly can accomplish. This is its aim,—and when this is attained, its end is fulfilled. It can do no more, however enlightened the people, or however widely extended or well guarded the right may be. The sum total, then, of its effects, when most successful, is, to make those elected, the true and faithful representatives of those who elected them,—instead of irresponsible rulers,—as they would be without it; and thus, by converting it into an agency, and the rulers into agents, to divest government of all claims to sovereignty, and to retain it unimpaired to the community. But it is manifest that the right of suffrage, in making these changes, transfers, in reality, the actual control over the government, from those who make and execute the laws, to the body of the community; and, thereby, places the powers of the government as fully in the mass of the community, as they would be if they, in fact, had assembled, made, and executed the laws themselves, without the intervention of representatives or agents. The more perfectly it does this, the more perfectly it accomplishes its ends; but in doing so, it only changes the seat of authority, without counteracting, in the least, the tendency of the government to oppression and abuse of its powers.

If the whole community had the same interests, so that the interests of each and every portion would be so affected by the action of the government, that the laws which oppressed or impoverished one portion, would necessarily oppress and impoverish all others,—or the reverse,—then the right of suffrage, of itself, would be all-sufficient to counteract the tendency of the government to oppression and abuse of its powers; and, of course, would form, of itself, a perfect constitutional government. The interest of all being the same, by supposition, as far as the action of the government was concerned, all would have like interests as to what laws should be made, and how they should be executed. All strife and struggle would cease as to who should be elected to make and execute them. The only question would be, who was most fit; who the wisest and most capable of understanding the common interest of the whole. This decided, the election would pass off quietly, and without party discord; as no one portion could advance its own peculiar interest without regard to the rest, by electing a favorite candidate.

But such is not the case. On the contrary, nothing is more difficult than to equalize the action of the government, in reference to the various and diversified interests of the community; and nothing more easy than to pervert its powers into instruments to aggrandize and enrich one or more interests by oppressing and impoverishing the others; and this too, under the operation of laws, couched in general terms;—and which, on their face, appear fair and equal. Nor is this the case in some particular communities only. It is so in all; the small and the great,—the poor and the rich,—irrespective of pursuits, productions, or degrees of civilization;—with, however, this difference, that the more extensive and populous the country, the more diversified the condition and pursuits of its population, and the richer, more luxurious, and dissimilar the people, the more difficult is it to equalize the action of the government,—and the more easy for one portion of the community to pervert its powers to oppress, and plunder the other.

Such being the case, it necessarily results, that the right of suffrage, by placing the control of the government in the community must, from the same constitution of our nature which makes government necessary to preserve society, lead to conflict among its different interests,—each striving to obtain possession of its powers, as the means of protecting itself against the others;—or of advancing its respective interests, regardless of the interests of others. For this purpose, a struggle will take place between the various interests to obtain a majority, in order to control the government.

If no one interest be strong enough, of itself, to obtain it, a combination will be formed between those whose interests are most alike;—each conceding something to the others, until a sufficient number is obtained to make a majority. The process may be slow, and much time may be required before a compact, organized majority can be thus formed; but formed it will be in time, even without preconcert or design, by the sure workings of that principle or constitution of our nature in which government itself originates. When once formed, the community will be divided into two great parties,—a major and minor,—between which there will be incessant struggles on the one side to retain, and on the other to obtain the majority,—and, thereby, the control of the government and the advantages it confers.

So deeply seated, indeed, is this tendency to conflict between the different interests or portions of the community, that it would result from the action of the government itself, even though it were possible to find a community, where the people were all of the same pursuits, placed in the same condition of life, and in every respect, so situated, as to be without inequality of condition or diversity of interests. The advantages of possessing the control of the powers of the government, and, thereby, of its honors and emoluments, are, of themselves, exclusive of all other considerations, ample to divide even such a community into two great hostile parties. . . .

As, then, the right of suffrage, without some other provision, cannot counteract this tendency of government, the next question for consideration is—What is that other provision? This demands the most serious consideration; for of all the questions embraced in the science of government, it involves a principle, the most important, and the least understood; and when understood, the most difficult of application in practice. It is, indeed, emphatically, that principle which *makes* the constitution, in its strict and limited sense.

From what has been said, it is manifest, that this provision must be of a character calculated to prevent any one interest, or combination of interests, from using the powers of government to aggrandize itself at the expense of the others. Here lies the evil: and just in proportion as it shall prevent, or fail to prevent it, in the same degree it will effect, or fail to effect the end intended to be accomplished. There is but one certain mode in which this result can be secured; and that is, by the adoption of some restriction or limitation, which shall so effectually prevent any one interest, or combination of interests, from obtaining the exclusive control of the government, as to render hopeless all attempts directed to that end. There is, again, but one mode in which this can be effected; and that is, by taking the sense of each interest or portion of the community, which may be unequally and injuriously affected by the action of the government, separately, through its own majority, or in some other way by which its voice may be fairly expressed; and to require the consent of each interest, either to put or to keep the government in action. This, too, can be accomplished only in one way,—and that is, by such an organism of the government,—and, if necessary for the purpose, of the community also, —as will, by dividing and distributing the powers of government, give to each division or interest, through its appropriate organ, either a concurrent voice in making and executing the laws, or a veto on their execution. It is only by such an organism, that the assent of each can be made necessary to put the government in motion; or the power made effectual to arrest its action, when put in motion;—and it is only by the one or the other that the different interests, orders, classes, or portions, into which the community may be divided, can be protected, and all conflict and struggle between them prevented,—by rendering it impossible to put or to keep it in action, without the concurrent consent of all.

Such an organism as this, combined with the right of suffrage, constitutes, in fact, the elements of constitutional government. The one, by rendering those who make and execute the laws responsible to those on whom they operate, prevents the rulers from oppressing the ruled; and the other, by making it impossible for any one interest or combination of interests or class, or order, or portion of the community, to obtain exclusive control, prevents any one of them from oppressing the other. It is clear, that oppression and abuse of power must come, if at all, from the one or the other quarter. From no other can they come. It follows, that the two, suffrage and proper organism combined, are sufficient to counteract the tendency of government to oppression and abuse of power; and to restrict it to the fulfilment of the great ends for which it is ordained. . . .

It results, from what has been said, that there are two different modes in which the sense of the community may be taken; one, simply by the right of suffrage, unaided; the other, by the right through a proper organism. Each collects the sense of the majority. But one regards numbers only, and considers the whole community as a unit, having but one common interest throughout; and collects the sense of the greater number of the whole, as that of the community. The other, on the contrary, regards interests as well as numbers;—considering the community as made up of different and conflicting interests, as far as the action of the government is concerned; and takes the sense of each, through its majority or appropriate organ, and the united sense of all, as the sense of the entire community. The former of these I shall call the numerical, or absolute majority; and the latter, the concurrent, or constitutional majority. I call it the constitutional majority, because it is an essential element in every constitutional government,—be its form what it may. So great is the difference, politically speaking, between the two majorities, that they cannot be confounded, without leading to great and fatal errors; and yet the distinction between them has been so entirely overlooked, that when the term *majority* is used in political discussions, it is applied exclusively to designate the numerical,—as if there were no other. Until this distinction is recognized, and better understood, there will continue to be great liability to error in properly constructing constitutional governments, especially of the popular form, and of preserving them when properly constructed. Until then, the latter will have a strong tendency to slide, first, into the government of the numerical majority, and, finally, into absolute government of some other form. . . .

The principle, in all communities, according to these numerous and various causes, assigns to power and liberty their proper spheres. To allow to liberty, in any case, a sphere of action more extended than this assigns, would lead to anarchy; and this, probably, in the end, to a contraction instead of an enlargement of its sphere. Liberty, then, when forced on a people unfit for it, would, instead of a blessing, be a curse; as it would, in its reaction, lead directly to anarchy,—the greatest of all curses. No people, indeed, can long enjoy more liberty than that to which their situation and advanced intelligence and morals fairly entitle them. If more than this be allowed, they must soon fall into confusion and disorder,—to be followed, if not by anarchy and despotism, by a change to a form of government more simple and absolute; and, therefore, better suited to their condition. And hence, although it may be true, that a people may not have as much liberty as they are fairly entitled to, and are capable of enjoying,—yet the reverse is unquestionably true,—that no people can long possess more than they are fairly entitled to.

Liberty, indeed, though among the greatest of blessings, is not so great as that of protection; inasmuch, as the end of the former is the progress and improvement of the race,—while that of the latter is its preservation and perpetuation. And hence, when the two come into conflict, liberty must, and ever ought, to yield to protection; as the existence of the race is of greater moment than its improvement.

It follows, from what has been stated, that it is a great and dangerous error to suppose that all people are equally entitled to liberty. It is a reward to be earned, not a blessing to be gratuitously lavished on all alike;—a reward reserved for the intelligent, the patriotic, the virtuous and deserving;—and not a boon to be bestowed on a people too ignorant, degraded and vicious, to be capable either of appreciating or of enjoying it. Nor is it any disparagement to liberty, that such is, and ought to be the case. On the contrary, its greatest praise,—its proudest distinction is, that an all-wise Providence has reserved it, as the noblest and highest reward for the development of our faculties, moral and intellectual. A reward more appropriate than liberty could not be conferred on the deserving;—nor a punishment inflicted on the undeserving more just, than to be subject to lawless and despotic rule. This dispensation seems to be the result of some fixed law;—and every effort to disturb or defeat it, by attempting to elevate a people in the scale of liberty, above the point to which they are entitled to rise, must ever prove abortive, and end in disappointment. The progress of a people rising from a lower to a higher point in the scale of liberty, is necessarily slow;—and by attempting to precipitate, we either retard, or permanently defeat it.

There is another error, not less great and dangerous, usually associated with the one which has just been considered. I refer to the opinion, that liberty and equality are so intimately united, that liberty cannot be perfect without perfect equality.

That they are united to a certain extent,—and that equality of citizens, in the eyes of the law, is essential to liberty in a popular government, is conceded. But to go further, and make equality of *condition* essential to liberty, would be to destroy both liberty and progress. The reason is, that inequality of condition, while it is a necessary consequence of liberty, is, at the same time, indispensable to progress. In order to understand why this is so, it is necessary to bear in mind, that the main spring to progress is, the desire of individuals to better their condition; and that the strongest impulse which can be given to it is, to leave individuals free to exert themselves in the manner they may deem best for that purpose, as far at least as it can be done consistently with the ends for which government is ordained,—and to secure to all the fruits of their exertions. Now, as individuals differ greatly from each other, in intelligence, sagacity, energy, perseverance, skill, habits of industry and economy, physical power, position and opportunity,—the necessary effect of leaving all free to exert themselves to better their condition, must be a corresponding inequality between those who may possess these qualities and advantages in a high degree, and those who may be deficient in them. The only means by which this result can be prevented are, either to impose such restrictions on the exertions of those who may possess them in a high degree, as will place them on a level with those who do not; or to deprive them of the fruits of their exertions. But to impose such restrictions on them would be destructive of liberty,—while, to deprive them of the fruits of their exertions, would be to destroy the desire of bettering their condition. It is, indeed, this inequality of condition between the front and rear ranks, in the march of progress, which gives so strong an impulse to the former to maintain their position, and to the latter to press forward into their files. This gives to progress its greatest impulse. To force the front rank back to the rear, or attempt to push forward the rear into line with the front, by the interposition of the government, would put an end to the impulse, and effectually arrest the march of progress.

These great and dangerous errors have their origin in the prevalent opinion that all men are born free and equal;—than which nothing can be more unfounded and false. It rests upon the assumption of a fact, which is contrary to universal observation, in whatever light it may be regarded. It is, indeed, difficult to explain how an opinion so destitute of all sound reason, even could have been so extensively entertained, unless we regard it as being confounded with another, which has some semblance of truth;—but which, when properly understood, is not less false and dangerous. I refer to the assertion, that all men are equal in the state of nature; meaning, by a state of nature, a state of individuality, supposed to have existed prior to the social and political state; and in which men lived apart and independent of each other. If such a state ever did exist, all men would have been, indeed, free and equal in it; that is, free to do as they pleased, and exempt from the authority or control of others—as, by supposition, it existed anterior to society and government. But such a state is purely hypothetical. It never did, nor can exist; as it is inconsistent with the preservation and perpetuation of the race. It is, therefore, a great misnomer to call it *the state of nature*. Instead of being the natural state of man, it is, of all conceivable states, the most opposed to his nature—most repugnant to his feelings, and most incompatible with his wants. His natural state is, the social and political—the one for which his Creator made him, and the only one in which he can preserve and perfect his race. As, then, there never was such a state as the, so called, state of nature, and never can be, it follows, that men, instead of being born in it, are born in the social and political state; and of course, instead of being born free and equal, are born subject, not only to parental authority, but to the laws and institutions of the country where born, and under whose protection they draw their first breath. . . .

RICHARD HILDRETH

THOUGH RICHARD HILDRETH (1809–1865) denied the theory of natural rights as firmly as did Calhoun, he arrived at an entirely different set of conclusions. Where Calhoun justified slavery, he upheld freedom; where Calhoun glorified the slave republics of the present on analogy with the slave republics of Greece and Rome, Hildreth noted, dryly, that Southern civilization combined the arrogance of aristocracy with the mean sharpness of the bourgeoisie while it produced neither the art of the first nor the comfort of the second. Hildreth is modern, too, in his reference to the "Age of the People" and in his vision of an abundance that only greater productivity can create. He rejects Utopianism on the one hand; he has confidence in America on the other.

Hildreth was a Massachusetts man, educated at Harvard and admitted to the bar. Like many other young men with legal training and literary ambition, he turned to newspaper writing and served as editor of the Boston *Atlas*, a Whig journal. He became interested in the antislavery movement almost at its beginnings; wrote a book on *Despotism in America;* and was responsible for one of the earlier antislavery novels, *Archy Moore, or the White Slave,* which went into seven editions before *Uncle Tom's Cabin* was published.

After two years in British Guiana, Hildreth returned to Boston where he began work on his *History of the United States*, a counterblast to Bancroft, which began appearing in 1844. Hildreth's factual, annalistic technique caused some criticism of the book as lacking in ideas, and his preface to the *Theory of Politics* (1853) hits at those who did not find any "philosophy" in the *History*.

In his *Theory of Politics*, Hildreth attempts a scientific inquiry into the foundation of governments and the cause and progress of political revolution. He begins by considering the nature of man; finds that the idea of a natural equality of rights leads logically to anarchism; examines the roots of power; classifies governments; and considers their effects on human happiness and civilization. He is a pluralist in approach but is inclined to the view "that wealth may justly be regarded, not indeed as the sole, but still as altogether the most important element of political power, able to purchase up the services of strength, skill, sagacity, force of will, activity, courage, knowledge, eloquence, and, to a certain extent also, the cooperation of the influence of virtue, of mystical ideas, of hereditary respect, and of the idea of property in power."

War, wealth, and mysticism combine to produce government, Hildreth concludes. As men pass from the hunting to the pastoral economy, paternal authority increases and chattel slavery is introduced. Pastoral peoples are apt to make war for profit and so to subdue agricultural peoples, which often, in their turn, subject their conquerors culturally. Divisions of sovereignty appear, as they did in Republican Rome with its Tribunate, and sometimes become intensified as they were during the feudal period. Feudalism transformed slaves into serfs and the municipalities of feudalism turned serfs into free men, equal in political rights and honoring labor. By their employment of hired troops and their accumulated wealth, the people of the towns helped the kings subdue the nobles. As royal absolutism grew, the kings were checked by the courts' assumption of power to legislate by pronouncing upon the law, a practice that extended royal authority on one hand while it blocked its excesses on the other.

From this analysis of ancient and medieval institutions, Hildreth proceeds to the Protestant Revolt, which strengthened the alliance between crown and church in all states, Protestant as well as Catholic. Continental theorists, faced by an exclusive nobility, set up the doctrine of equal natural right as a counterbalance to the divine right of kings, with a logical result in anarchism.

The French Revolution is not yet completed, Hildreth notes, but France would "not become an hereditary despotism in the Bonaparte family." Self-government is an art which requires something more than a day's practice.

Republicanism in modern France has been blocked by the split between the burgher and the socialist elements in the Republican group.

Hildreth appeals for harmony in the ranks of the liberal forces. He regards democracy as the best, although the most difficult form of government, but he fears the influence of evangelical religion, chattel slavery, and the common law upon the progress of democracy in the United States. For all that, he is hopeful: nobility and priestcraft are wearing out; wealth and knowledge are being equalized; yet, under democracy, each can exercise its due force in government. And the day is not far off when government will pay attention to the great mass as well as to the groups that turn it to their own use. An increase in the productivity of labor will usher in the "Age of the People": thus Richard Hildreth, a century before Henry A. Wallace.

The selection here reprinted is from Hildreth's *Theory of Politics* (New York, 1853).

Theory of Politics

BY RICHARD HILDRETH

CONCLUDING CHAPTER: HOPES AND HINTS AS TO THE FUTURE

IN THE CURSORY VIEW taken in a preceding chapter of the history of Christendom for the last eight centuries, we have found that period divisible, without any very great forcing, into four ages of two centuries each, during which the Clergy, the Nobles, the Kings, and the Burghers successively enjoyed a certain headship and predominancy. But, besides these four ruling orders, we have also, during these centuries, caught some slight occasional glimpses of another order, to wit, the mass,—the delvers, agricultural and mechanical, those who work with their hands,—in numbers, at all times and every where, the great body of the people, but scarcely any where possessing political rights, and even where, by some fortunate chance, they have gained them, for the most part, speedily losing them again.

The clergy, the nobles, the kings, the burghers have all had their turn. Is there never to be an *Age of the People*—of the working classes?

Is the suggestion too extravagant, that the new period commencing with the middle of this current century is destined to be that age? Certain it is, that, within the last three quarters of a century, advocates have appeared for the mass of the people, the mere workers, and that movements, even during this age of the deification of money, and of reaction against the theory of human equality, have been made in their behalf such as were never known before.

We may enumerate first in the list of these movements the indignant protest against the African slave trade, and the combination for its suppression into which the governments of Christendom have been forced, by the efforts of a few humane individuals, appealing to the better feelings of their fellowcountrymen, and operating through them on the British and American governments. It has, indeed, become customary, among the advocates of money making, no matter by what means,—in which category we must place some London newspapers of great pretensions,—to sneer at the attempted suppression of the slave trade as a failure. It is true, that, by the connivance of the Portuguese, Brazilian, and Spanish authorities with scoundrel merchants, British and American, the trade still exists. But what is it compared with what it would be did it enjoy, as formerly, the patronage and favor of all the flags? and how much longer is it likely to flourish?

We may mention next among these movements on behalf of the laboring class the abolition of chattel slavery in so many of the ultramarine off-shoots from Europe; not alone by the strong hand of the slaves themselves, as in Hayti; not alone in consequence of protracted civil war,—a consequence generally pretty certain to follow,—as in the Spanish-American republics; but also from a mere sense of shame and wrong, as in the now (so called) free states of the North American Union; and from an impulse of humanity and justice, even at a heavy outlay of money, as in the British tropical colonies.

We may mention further the subdivision which has been carried so far, in France, of the lands of that country among the actual cultivators; a subdivision objected to by certain British economists, as not so favorable to the production of wealth, a point, however, not to be hastily conceded—but which unquestionably does tend to give to the cultivators a certain social importance and political weight.

Let us add the system of savings banks, by which the English laborers for wages have been enabled to invest their savings in a comparatively safe and easy manner, and thus to share in that accumulation of wealth which forms so important an element of power.

Add further the constant advance and development of manufacturing industry, giving employment and high wages to a class of laborers vastly superior in intelligence to the stupid and thoughtless rustics by whom the fields of Europe are generally cultivated—a class among whom have arisen those Chartists and Socialists whom we have had occasion to notice, towards the close of our burgher age, as claimants for political rights; a class, in fact, from which the larger portion of the existing burgher class has itself derived its origin.

Such are some of the social changes which may be regarded as precursors and signs of the approaching Age of the People.

If the mass of the people are ever to be raised above the servile position in which they have been so long and so generally held, there would seem to be only one way in which it can be permanently and effectually done, viz., by imparting to them a vastly greater portion than they have ever yet possessed of those primary elements of power, sagacity, force of will, and knowledge, to be backed by the secondary elements of wealth

and combination. Nor does the prospect of thus elevating them appear by any means one altogether so hopeless.

Whatever objections may be made to the existing distribution of riches, and to the artificial processes by which it is regulated,—subjects which will form important topics of the *Theory of Wealth*,—this at least must be conceded, that no mere redistribution of the existing mass of wealth could effectually answer the proposed purpose of elevating the people. Any such redistribution, even if means could be found—and they could not—to prevent this equalized wealth from running back again, more or less, into masses, would still leave every body poor, at the same time that it cut up by the roots a great mass of industrious occupations. What is vastly more important than the distribution of the actually accumulated wealth, is the distribution of the annual returns of human industry. But no redistribution even of that—though it might sweep away the existing comfortable class—would suffice, very materially, to elevate the condition of the great body of the people. Above and beyond any of these schemes of redistribution, in order to redeem the mass of the people from poverty and its incidents, a great increase in the amount both of accumulated wealth and of annual products is absolutely essential.

Here, indeed, we discover one great reason of the state of social depression in which the mass of the people have been, and still are, so generally held. The good things which the combined efforts of any given community can as yet produce are not enough to give hardly a taste to every body; and the masses have of necessity been kept at hard labor, on bread and water, while luxuries and even comforts have been limited to a few. Labor—the sole resource of the mass of the people—has been of little value, because labor has been able to produce but little; and the proceeds of the labor of production being so small, hence the greater stimulus to substitute in place of it fraud and violence as means of acquisition. The same man who will remorselessly cut your throat in the struggle for the scanty waters of a rivulet in the desert, not enough for the whole thirsty and gasping company, would readily share his cup with you did the stream only run a little fuller.

The first great necessity, then, of the human race is the increase of the productiveness of human labor. Science has done much in that respect within the last century, and in those to come is destined to do vastly more. Vast new fields are opening on our American continent, on which labor can be profitably employed. So far from labor being the sole source of wealth, all-sufficient in itself, as certain political economists teach, nothing is more certain than that Europe has long suffered, and still suffers, from a plethora of labor —from being obliged to feed and clothe many for whom it has had nothing remunerative to do. The United States of America have now attained to such a development, that they are able easily to absorb from half a million to a million annually of immigrants from Europe. What is more, the laborers of Europe have found it out, and are rapidly emigrating. In so doing, not only do they change a barren field of labor for a fertile one, and at the same time relieve the pressure at home, but, by becoming themselves consumers, far more so than ever they were able to be at home, of the more artificial products of the countries from which they emigrate, they contribute doubly to raise the wages of those whom they have left behind.

The development of productive industry seems then to be at this moment one of the greatest and most crying necessities of the human race. But what is more essential to this development than peace and social order? It is not pusillanimity, then, on the part of the people of Europe, but an instinct, more or less conscious, of what they need most, that prompts them to submit for the present, without further struggle, to the rulers who have shown themselves to possess, for the time being, the power to govern—a power, let it be noted, quite too unstable, however, not to require, even in the view of those who possess it, great circumpection and moderation in its exercise. War and civil commotions, though sometimes necessary to the preservation of popular liberties, have very seldom indeed been the means of their acquisition; conspiracies hatched abroad, never. When the fruit is ripe, it will fall almost without shaking the tree. What prompts to anticipate that period is much oftener individual or class suffering or ambition than the true interest of the mass of the people. The greatest obstacle at this moment to the comparative political freedom of Europe, is the vast aggregation of power in the shape of standing armies. But how are these armies possibly to be got rid of, except by a certain interval of uninterrupted quiet, dispensing with their use, and such a contemporaneous increase in the value

of labor as to make the maintenance in idleness of so many hands, instead of being, as it now is, a sort of substitute for a poor law, and a relief to the overstocked labor market, a useless sacrifice, and an expense too great for any community to submit to?

It surely is not from barricades and street insurrections, provoking the murder of quiet citizens in their own houses, by fusilades and grape shot, in the name of peace and order, but rather from a more careful, comprehensive, and profound study of social relations, joined to an interval of peaceful coöperation in the production of great economical results, that we are to hope for the dispersion and extinction of those unfortunate and unfounded antipathies, so rife at present between those who labor with their heads and those who labor with their hands; those who plan and those who execute—antipathies growing out of prevailing but mistaken theories of politics and political economy, which, by dividing the party of progress into two hostile sections, filled with jealousy, fear, and hatred of each other, have contributed so much more than any thing else to betray Samson, shorn, into the hands of the Philistines—jealousies, fears, and hatreds, not only the chief source of the discomfitures recently experienced by the popular cause, but which, so long as they shall continue, will render any further advancement of it hopeless.

This socialist question of the distribution of wealth once raised is not to be blinked out of sight. The claims set up by the socialists, based as they are upon philosophic theories of long standing, having, at least some of them, many ardent supporters even in the ranks of those who denounce the socialists the loudest, cannot be settled by declamations and denunciations, and mutual recriminations, any more than by bayonets and artillery. It is a question for philosophers; and until some solution of it can be reached which both sides shall admit to be conclusive, what the party of progress needs is not action—for which it is at present disqualified by internal dissensions—but deliberation and discussion. The engineers must first bridge this gulf of separation before all the drumming, and fifing, and shouting in the world can again unite the divided column, and put it into effectual motion.

CHARLES DICKENS

THE UNITED STATES did not have an international copyright law in the forties. That made books cheap in America, but widely read English authors were inclined to feel annoyed at being called upon to educate the American public without reward. Charles Dickens (1812–1870) was certainly the most popular of these. He came to America in the early forties with a chip on his shoulder, but was received everywhere with noisy enthusiasm and generous hospitality. He returned to England to write two books about America—*American Notes for General Circulation* (1842) and the novel *Martin Chuzzlewit* (1844). In this way, Dickens had his revenge: America was no place for the civilized European.

It was in the earlier book that Dickens set forth the whole body of his impressions, and it was that which won him the unsparing criticism of the press he had attacked. Not all the comments of the *American Notes* are as ill-tempered as Dickens' account of the Mississippi: he found American skies astoundingly pure and American cities toylike in bright paint and clean red brick. America's freedom from beggary was gratifying, though New York's Five Points slum could take the palm from London's St. Giles.

American aspirations might be laudable enough, but, in practice, those ended by luring foreigners into investments which brought no dividends. American men spat tobacco juice in the presence of the women they pretended to reverence; fine American hotels balked at serving meals in a guest's room; canal boats kept comb and brush in convenient proximity to the bar's bread, cheese, and biscuits; and the country which boasted itself the home of liberty was also the home of the slave.

Many of his facts were undoubtedly true: the United States was still a brash, raw country and it did have a share of social meanness. But there were many favorable things Dickens did not choose to see—indeed, was incapable of seeing or understanding.

The passage here reprinted is from the *American Notes for General Circulation* (Boston and London, 1867).

American Notes for General Circulation

BY CHARLES DICKENS

CHAPTER XI: FROM PITTSBURG TO CINCINNATI IN A WESTERN STEAMBOAT.

THE MESSENGER was one among a crowd of high-pressure steamboats, clustered together by a wharfside, which, looked down upon from the rising ground that forms the landing-place, and backed by the lofty bank on the opposite side of the river, appeared no longer than so many floating models. She had some forty passengers on board, exclusive of the poorer persons on the lower deck; and in half an hour, or less, proceeded on her way.

We had, for ourselves, a tiny state-room with two berths in it, opening out of the ladies' cabin. There was, undoubtedly, something satisfactory in this 'location,' inasmuch as it was in the stern, and we had been a great many times very gravely recommended to keep as far aft as possible, 'because the steamboats generally blew up forward.' Nor was this an unnecessary caution, as the occurrence and circumstances of more than one such fatality during our stay sufficiently testified. Apart from this source of self-congratulation, it was an unspeakable relief to have any place, no matter how confined, where one could be alone; and as the row of little chambers of which this was one, had each a second glass door besides that in the ladies' cabin, which opened on a narrow gallery outside the vessel, where the other passengers seldom came, and where one could sit in peace and gaze upon the shifting prospect, we took possession of our new quarters with much pleasure.

If the native packets I have already described be unlike anything we are in the habit of seeing on water, these western vessels are still more foreign to all the ideas we are accustomed to entertain of boats. I hardly know what to liken them to, or how to describe them.

In the first place, they have no mast, cordage, tackle, rigging, or other such boat-like gear; nor have they anything in their shape at all calculated to remind one of a boat's head, stern, sides, or keel. Except that they are in the water, and display a couple of paddle-boxes, they might be intended, for anything that appears to the contrary, to perform some unknown service, high and dry, upon a mountain top. There is no visible deck, even: nothing but a long, black, ugly roof, covered with burnt-out feathery sparks; above which tower two iron chimneys, and a hoarse escape-valve, and a glass steerage-house. Then, in order as the eye descends towards the water, are the sides, and doors, and windows of the state-rooms, jumbled as oddly together as though they formed a small street, built by the varying tastes of a dozen men: the whole is supported on beams and pillars resting on a dirty barge, but a few inches above the water's edge: and in the narrow space between this upper structure and this barge's deck, are the furnace fires and machinery, open at the sides to every wind that blows, and every storm of rain it drives along its path.

Passing one of these boats at night, and seeing the great body of fire, exposed as I have just described, that rages and roars beneath the frail pile of painted wood: the machinery, not warded off or guarded in any way, but doing its work in the midst of the crowd of idlers and emigrants and children, who throng the lower deck: under the management, too, of reckless men whose acquaintance with its mysteries may have been of six months' standing: one feels directly that the wonder is, not that there should be so many fatal accidents, but that any journey should be safely made.

Within, there is one long narrow cabin, the whole length of the boat; from which the state-rooms open, on both sides. A small portion of it at the stern is partitioned off for the ladies; and the bar is at the opposite extreme. There is a long table down the centre, and at either end a stove.

The washing apparatus is forward, on the deck. It is a little better than on board the canal boat,* but not much. In all modes of travelling, the American customs, with reference to the means of personal cleanliness and wholesome ablution, are extremely negligent and filthy; and I strongly incline to the belief that a considerable amount of illness is referable to this cause.

We are to be on board the Messenger three days: arriving at Cincinnati (barring accidents) on Monday morning. There are three meals a day. Breakfast at seven, dinner at half-past twelve, supper about six. At each, there are a great many small dishes and plates upon the table, with very little in them; so that although there is every appearance of a mighty 'spread,' there is seldom really more than a joint: except for those who fancy slices of beetroot, shreds of dried beef, complicated entanglements of yellow pickles; maize, Indian corn, apple-sauce, and pumpkin.

Some people fancy all these little dainties together (and sweet preserves beside), by way of relish to their roast pig. They are generally those dyspeptic ladies and gentlemen who eat unheard-of quantities of hot corn bread (almost as good for the digestion as a kneaded pincushion), for breakfast, and for supper. Those who do not observe this custom, and who help themselves several times instead, usually suck their knives and forks meditatively, until they have decided what to take next: then pull them out of their mouths; put them in the dish; help themselves; and fall to work again. At dinner, there is nothing to drink upon the table but great jugs full of cold water. Nobody says anything, at any meal, to anybody. All the passengers are very dismal, and seem to have tremendous secrets weighing on their minds. There is no conversation, no laughter, no cheerfulness, no sociality, except in spitting; and that is done in silent fellowship round the stove when the meal is over. Every man sits down, dull and languid, swallows his fare as if breakfasts, dinners, and suppers, were necessities of nature never to be coupled with recreation or enjoyment; and having bolted his food in a gloomy silence, bolts himself, in the

* The washing and dressing apparatus for the passengers generally consists of two jack-towels, three small wooden basins, a keg of water and a ladle to serve it out with, six square inches of lookingglass, two ditto ditto of yellow soap, a comb and brush for the head, and nothing for the teeth. Everybody uses the comb and brush, except myself. Everybody stares to see me using my own; and two or three gentlemen are strongly disposed to banter me on my prejudices, but don't.

same state. But for these animal observances, you might suppose the whole male portion of the company to be the melancholy ghosts of departed book-keepers, who had fallen dead at the desk: such is their weary air of business and calculation. Undertakers on duty would be sprightly beside them; and a collation of funeral-baked meats, in comparison with these meals, would be a sparkling festivity.

The people are all alike, too. There is no diversity of character. They travel about on the same errands, say and do the same things in exactly the same manner, and follow in the same dull cheerless round. All down the long table, there is scarcely a man who is in anything different from his neighbor. . . .

CHAPTER XII: FROM CINCINNATI TO LOUISVILLE IN ANOTHER WESTERN STEAMBOAT

. . . Within a few minutes afterwards, we were out of the canal, and in the Ohio river again.

The arrangements of the boat were like those of the Messenger, and the passengers were of the same order of people. We fed at the same times, on the same kind of viands, in the same dull manner, and with the same observances. The company appeared to be oppressed by the same tremendous concealments, and had as little capacity of enjoyment or lightheartedness. I never in my life did see such listless, heavy dulness as brooded over these meals: the very recollection of it weighs me down, makes me, for the moment, wretched. Reading and writing on my knee, in our little cabin, I really dreaded the coming of the hour that summoned us to table; and was as glad to escape from it again, as if it had been a penance or a punishment. Healthy cheerfulness and good spirits forming a part of the banquet, I could soak my crusts in the fountain with Le Sage's strolling player, and revel in their glad enjoyment: but sitting down with so many fellow-animals to ward off thirst and hunger as a business; to empty, each creature, his Yahoo's trough as quickly as he can, and then slink sullenly away; to have these social sacraments stripped of everything but the mere greedy satisfaction of the natural cravings; goes so against the grain with me, that I seriously believe the recollection of these funeral feasts will be a waking nightmare to me all my life.

There was some relief in this boat, too, which there had not been in the other, for the captain (a blunt, good-natured fellow) had his handsome wife with him, who was disposed to be lively and agreeable, as were a few other lady-passengers who had their seats about us at the same end of the table. But nothing could have made head

against the depressing influence of the general body. There was a magnetism of dulness in them which would have beaten down the most facetious companion that the earth ever knew. A jest would have been a crime, and a smile would have faded into a grinning horror. Such deadly leaden people; such systematic plodding weary insupportable heaviness; such a mass of animated indigestion in respect of all that was genial, jovial, frank, social, or hearty; never, sure, was brought together elsewhere since the world began.

Nor was the scenery, as we approached the junction of the Ohio and Mississippi rivers, at all inspiriting in its influence. The trees were stunted in their growth; the banks were low and flat; the settlements and log cabins fewer in number: their inhabitants more wan and wretched than any we had encountered yet. No songs of birds were in the air, no pleasant scents, no moving lights and shadows from swift passing clouds. Hour after hour, the changeless glare of the hot unwinking sky, shone upon the same monotonous objects. Hour after hour, the river rolled along, as wearily and slowly as the time itself.

At length, upon the morning of the third day we arrived at a spot so much more desolate than any we had yet beheld, that the forlornest places we had passed, were, in comparison with it, full of interest. At the junction of the two rivers, on ground so flat and low and marshy, that at certain seasons of the year it is inundated to the housetops, lies a breeding-place of fever, ague, and death; vaunted in England as a mine of Golden Hope, and speculated in, on the faith of monstrous representations, to many people's ruin. A dismal swamp, on which the half-built houses rot away: clearly here and there for the space of a few yards; and teeming, then, with rank unwholesome vegetation, in whose baleful shade the wretched wanderers who are tempted hither, droop and die, and lay their bones; the hateful Mississippi circling and eddying before it, and turning off upon its southern course a slimy monster hideous to behold; a hotbed of disease, an ugly sepulchre, a grave uncheered by any gleam of promise: a place without one single quality, in earth or air or water, to commend it: such is this dismal Cairo.

But what words shall describe this Mississippi, great father of rivers, who (praise be to Heaven) has no young children like him! An enormous ditch, sometimes two or three miles wide, running liquid mud, six miles an hour: its strong and frothy current choked and obstructed everywhere by huge logs and whole forest trees: now twining themselves together in great rafts, from the interstices of which a sedgy lazy foam works up, to float upon the water's top; now rolling past like monstrous bodies, their tangled roots showing like matted hair; now glancing singly by like giant leeches; and now writhing round and round in the vortex of some small whirlpool, like wounded snakes. The banks low, the trees dwarfish, the marshes swarming with frogs, the wretched cabins few and far apart, their inmates hollow-cheeked and pale, the weather very hot, mosquitoes penetrating into every crack and crevice of the boat, mud and slime on everything: nothing pleasant in its aspect, but the harmless lightning which flickers every night upon the dark horizon.

For two days we toiled up this foul stream, striking constantly against the floating timber, or stopping to avoid those more dangerous obstacles, the snags or sawyers, which are the hidden trunks of trees that have their roots below the tide. When the nights are very dark, the lookout stationed in the head of the boat, knows by the ripple of the water if any great impediment be near at hand, and rings a bell beside him, which is the signal for the engine to be stopped: but always in this night this bell has work to do, and after every ring, there comes a blow which renders it no easy matter to remain in bed.

The decline of day here was very gorgeous; tinging the firmament deeply with red and gold, up to the very keystone of the arch above us. As the sun went down behind the bank, the slightest blades of grass upon it seemed to become as distinctly visible as the arteries in the skeleton of a leaf; and when, as it slowly sank, the red and golden bars upon the water grew dimmer, and dimmer yet, as if they were sinking too; and all the glowing colours of departing day paled, inch by inch, before the sombre night; the scene became a thousand times more lonesome and more dreary than before, and all its influences darkened with the sky.

We drank the muddy water of this river while we were upon it. It is considered wholesome by the natives, and is something more opaque than gruel. I have seen water like it at the Filter-shops, but nowhere else. . . .

Chapter XIII: A Jaunt to the Looking-Glass Prairie and Back

I may premise that the word Prairie is variously pronounced *paraaer*, *parearer*, and *paroarer*. The latter mode of pronunciation is perhaps the most in favour.

We were fourteen in all, and all young men: indeed it is a singular though very natural feature in the society of these distant settlements, that it is mainly composed of adventurous persons in the prime of life, and has very few grey heads among it. There were no ladies: the trip being a fatiguing one: and we were to start at five o'clock in the morning punctually. . . .

The previous day had been—not to say hot, for the term is weak and lukewarm in its power of conveying an idea of the temperature. The town had been on fire; in a blaze. But at night it had come on to rain in torrents, and all night long it had rained without cessation. We had a pair of very strong horses, but travelled at the rate of little more than a couple of miles an hour, through one unbroken slough of black mud and water. It had no variety but in depth. Now it was only half over the wheels, now it hid the axletree, and now the coach sank down in it almost to the windows. The air resounded in all directions with the loud chirping of the frogs, who, with the pigs (a course, ugly breed, as unwholesome-looking as though they were the spontaneous growth of the country), had the whole scene to themselves. Here and there we passed a log hut; but the wretched cabins were wide apart and thinly scattered, for though the soil is very rich in this place few people can exist in such a deadly atmosphere. On either side of the track, if it deserve the name, was the thick "bush;" and everywhere was stagnant, slimy, rotten, filthy water.

As it is the custom in these parts to give a horse a gallon or so of cold water whenever he is in a foam with heat, we halted for that purpose, at a log inn in the wood, far removed from any other residence. It consisted of one room, bare-roofed and bare-walled of course, with a loft above. The ministering priest was a swarthy young savage, in a shirt of cotton print like bed-furniture, and a pair of ragged trousers. There were a couple of young boys, too, nearly naked, lying idly by the well; and they, and he, and *the* traveller at the inn, turned out to look at us.

The traveller was an old man with grey grisly beard two inches long, a shaggy moustache of the same hue, and enormous eyebrows; which almost obscured his lazy, semidrunken glance, as he stood regarding us with folded arms: poising himself alternately upon his toes and heels. On being addressed by one of the party, he drew nearer, and said, rubbing his chin (which scraped under his horny hand like fresh gravel beneath a nailed shoe), that he was from Delaware, and had lately bought a farm "down there" pointing into one of the marshes where the stunted trees were thickest. He was "going," he added, to St. Louis, to fetch his family, whom he had left behind; but he seemed in no great hurry to bring on these incumbrances, for when we moved away, he loitered back into the cabin, and was plainly bent on stopping there so long as his money lasted. He was a great politician of course, and explained his opinions at some length to one of our company; but I only remember that he concluded with two sentiments, one of which was, Somebody for ever; and the other, Blast everybody else! which is by no means a bad abstract of the general creed in these matters.

When the horses were swollen out to about twice their natural dimensions (there seems to be an idea here, that this kind of inflation improves their going), we went forward again, through mud and mire, and damp, and festering heat, and brake and bush, attended always by the music of the frogs and pigs, until nearly noon, when we halted at a place called Belleville.

Belleville was a small collection of wooden houses, huddled together in the very heart of the bush and swamp. Many of them had singularly bright doors of red and yellow; for the place had been lately visited by a travelling painter, "who got along," as I was told, "by eating his way." The criminal court was sitting, and was at that moment trying some criminals for horse-stealing: with whom it would most likely go hard: for live stock of all kinds being necessarily very much exposed in the woods, is held by the community in rather higher value than human life; and for this reason, juries generally make a point of finding all men indicted for cattle-stealing, guilty, whether or no.

The horses belonging to the bar, the judge, and witnesses, were tied to temporary racks set up roughly in the road; by which is to be understood, a forest path, nearly knee-deep in mud and slime.

There was an hotel in this place which, like all hotels in America, had its large dining-room for the public table. It was an odd, shambling, low-roofed out-house, half-cowshed and half-kitchen, with a coarse brown canvas table-cloth, and tin sconces stuck against the walls, to hold candles at supper-time. The horseman had gone forward to have coffee and some eatables prepared, and they were by this time nearly ready. He had ordered "wheat-bread and chicken-fixings," in preference to "corn-bread and common doings." The latter kind of refection includes only pork and bacon. The former comprehends boiled ham, sausages, veal cutlets, steaks, and such other viands of that nature as may be supposed, by a tolerably wide poetical construction, "to fix" a chicken comfortably in the digestive organs of any lady or gentleman.

On one of the door-posts at this inn, was a tin plate, whereon was inscribed in characters of gold "Doctor Crocus;" and on a sheet of paper, pasted up by the side of this plate was a written announcement that Dr. Crocus would that evening deliver a lecture on Phrenology for the benefit of the Belleville public; at a charge for admission, of so much a head.

Straying up-stairs, during the preparation of the chicken-fixings, I happened to pass the Doctor's chamber; and as the door stood wide open, and the room was empty, I made bold to peep in.

It was a bare, unfurnished, comfortless room, with an unframed portrait hanging up at the head of the bed; a likeness, I take it, of the Doctor, for the forehead was fully displayed, and great stress was laid by the artist upon its phrenological developments. The bed itself was covered with an old patchwork counterpane. The room was destitute of carpet or of curtain. There was a damp fire-place without any stove, full of wood ashes; a chair, and a very small table; and on the last named piece of furniture was displayed, in grand array, the doctor's library, consisting of some half-dozen greasy old books. . . .

From Belleville, we went on, through the same desolate kind of waste, and constantly attended, without the interval of a moment, by the same music; until, at three o'clock in the afternoon, we halted once more at a village called Lebanon to inflate the horses again, and give them some corn besides: of which they stood much in need. Pending this ceremony, I walked into the village, where I met a full-sized dwelling-house coming down-hill at a round trot, drawn by a score or more of oxen.

The public-house was so very clean and good a one, that the managers of the jaunt resolved to return to it and put up there for the night, if possible. This course decided on, and the horses being well refreshed, we again pushed forward, and came upon the Prairie at sunset.

It would be difficult to say why, or how—though it was possibly from having heard and read so much about it—but the effect on me was disappointment. Looking towards the setting sun, there lay, stretched out before my view, a vast expanse of level ground; unbroken, save by one thin line of trees, which scarcely amounted to a scratch upon the great blank; until it met the glowing sky, wherein it seemed to dip: mingling with its rich colours, and mellowing in its distant blue. There it lay, a tranquil sea or lake without water, if such a simile be admissible, with the day going down upon it: a few birds wheeling here and there: and solitude and silence reigning paramount around. But the grass was not yet high; there were bare black patches on the ground; and the few wild flowers that the eye could see, were poor and scanty. Great as the picture was, its very flatness and extent, which left nothing to the imagination, tamed it down and cramped its interest. I felt little of that sense of freedom and exhilaration which a Scottish heath inspires, or even our English downs awaken. It was lonely and wild, but oppressive in its barren monotony. I felt that in traversing the Prairies, I could never abandon myself to the scene, forgetful of all else; as I should do instinctively, were the heather underneath my feet, or an iron-bound coast beyond; but should often glance towards the distant and frequently receding line of the horizon, and wish it gained and passed. It is not a scene to be forgotten, but it is scarcely one, I think (at all events, as I saw it), to remember with much pleasure, or to covet the looking-on again, in after life. . . .

BAYARD TAYLOR

BAYARD TAYLOR (1825–1878) was one of the first American newspapermen to turn his journeys into books and profit. Like Horace Greeley and Walt Whitman, Taylor, who was born in Pennsylvania of Swiss and English stock, had been apprenticed to a printer but he soon became a writer. His verse won him such favorable notice that he was able to secure newspaper backing for a European walking tour in 1844. By the middle of 1849, when Taylor set out for California, his *Views Afoot* (1846) had become a best-seller; he himself was literary editor of the New York *Tribune;* and it was all but inevitable that he should be sent to see and write of life in California where Americans had at last found the Eldorado of Cabeza da Vaca's long wanderings. What he saw and heard in California, Taylor put into a book called *Eldorado* (New York, 1850); its tone, its interests, its human qualities are to be contrasted sharply with those of Dickens. They were both writing about Americans, ironically enough.

Gold had been discovered in the race near Sutter's Mill and the hope of fortune was drawing men from all over the earth. Bayard Taylor chose the Isthmian route west, sailing from New York to the Isthmus and then crossing overland to board another boat for California. He landed in San Francisco shortly before the rainy season all but halted work in the diggings. His account of life in the mines is less detailed than it might have been but, to make up for that, Taylor portrays San Francisco mushrooming from a cluster of tents into a city in half a year's time. The town had risen despite the lack of everything except "gold dust and enterprise" but its supply of the last-named was large enough to compensate for all other shortages. San Francisco prices were as fantastic as its growth, its day's business was speculation, and gambling was the chief diversion of its nights.

From the port, Taylor journeyed into the interior where he watched the final sessions of the constitutional convention at Monterey and borrowed patent-leather shoes to dance at the ball which marked the convention's close. As Taylor rode from one rain-soaked mining camp to the next, he heard and reported tales of sudden fortune and its effect on men. California's land problem was more difficult than the settlement of miners' claims, he observed. The missions which had been secularized in 1833 included huge tracts with uncertain boundaries and doubtful legal titles. Other claimants held grants equally liberal and equally confused as to ownership. The vagueness and overlapping of these titles would become a source of unending litigation, Taylor prophesied.

Taylor saw a civilization taking form. The gambling and noise, the sudden wealth and swifter losses are all set forth with a newspaperman's eye for detail; as are the decaying missions, the "old inhabitants" in California three years and lamenting the "spoiling of Indian labor" by emigrants, the "Ethiopian serenaders" who made night hideous in Sacramento. All this would pass, Taylor saw, as California became a settled community instead of the goal of restless men. The miners' picks were sounding across America and California gold was being shipped overseas to pay the interest on the investments Europeans were making in American enterprise.

The passage reprinted here is from *Eldorado* (2 vols., New York, 1850).

Eldorado

BY BAYARD TAYLOR

CHAPTER IV: THE OVERLAND EMIGRATION OF 1849

SACRAMENTO CITY was the goal of the emigration by the northern routes. From the beginning of August to the last of December scarcely a day passed without the arrival of some man or company of men and families, from the mountains, to pitch their tents for a few days on the bank of the river and rest from their months of hardship. The vicissitudes through which these people had passed, the perils they had encountered and the toils they had endured seem to me without precedent in History. The story of thirty thousand souls accomplishing a journey of more than two thousand miles through a savage and but partially explored wilderness, crossing on their way two mountain chains equal to the Alps in height and asperity, besides broad tracts of burning desert, and plains of nearly equal desolation, where a few patches of stunted shrubs and springs of brackish water were their only stay, has in it so much of heroism, of daring and of sublime endurance, that we may vainly question the records of any age for its equal. Standing as I was, at the closing stage of that grand pilgrimage, the sight of these adventurers as they came in day by day, and the hearing of their stories, each of which had its own peculiar and separate character, had a more fascinating, because more real interest than the tales of the glorious old travelers which so impress us in childhood.

It would be impossible to give, in a general description of the emigration, viewed as one great movement, a complete idea of its many wonderful phases. The experience of any single man, which a few years ago would have made him a hero for life, becomes mere common-place, when it is but one of many thousands; yet the spectacle of a great continent, through a region of one thousand miles from north to south, being overrun with these adventurous bands, cannot be pictured without the relation of many episodes of individual bravery and suffering. I will not attempt a full account of the emigration, but, as I have already given an outline of the stories of those who came by the Gila route, a similar sketch of what those encountered who took the Northern route—the great overland highway of the Continent—will not be without its interest in this place.

The great starting point for this route was Independence, Mo., where thousands were encamped through the month of April, waiting until the grass should be sufficiently high for their cattle, before they ventured on the broad ocean of the Plains. From the first of May to the first of June, company after company took its departure from the frontier of civilization, till the emigrant trail from Fort Leavenworth, on the Missouri, to Fort Laramie, at the foot of the Rocky Mountains, was one long line of mule-trains and wagons. The rich meadows of the Nebraska, or Platte, were settled for the time, and a single traveler could have journeyed for the space of a thousand miles, as certain of his lodging and regular meals as if he were riding through the old agricultural districts of the Middle States. The wandering tribes of Indians on the Plains—the Pawnees, Sioux and Arapahoes—were alarmed and bewildered by this strange apparition. They believed they were about to be swept away forever from their hunting-grounds and graves. As the season advanced and the great body of the emigrants got under way, they gradually withdrew from the vicinity of the trail and betook themselves to grounds which the former did not reach. All conflicts with them were thus avoided, and the emigrants passed the Plains with perfect immunity from their thievish and hostile visitations.

Another and more terrible scourge, however, was doomed to fall upon them. The cholera, ascending the Mississippi from New Orleans, reached St. Louis about the time of their departure from Independence, and overtook them before they were fairly embarked on the wilderness. The frequent rains of the early spring, added to the hardship and exposure of their travel, prepared the way for its ravages, and the first three or four hundred miles of the trail were marked by graves. It is estimated that about four thousand persons perished from this cause. Men were seized without warning with the most violent symptoms, and instances occurred in which the sufferer was left to die alone by the road-side, while his panic-stricken companions pushed forward, vainly trusting to get beyond the influence of the epidemic. Rough boards were planted at the graves of those who were buried near the trail, but there are hundreds of others lying unmarked by any memorial, on the bleak surface of the open plain and among the barren depths of the mountains. I have heard men tell how they have gone aside from their company to bury some old and cherished friend—a brother, it may often have been—performing the last rites alone and unaided, and leaving the remains where none but the wolf will ever seek their resting-place.

By the time the companies reached Fort Laramie the epidemic had expended its violence, and in the pure air of the elevated mountain region they were safe from its further attacks. Now, however, the real hardships of their journey began. Up and down the mountains that hem in the Sweetwater Valley—over the spurs of the Wind River chain—through the Devil's Gate, and past the stupendous mass of Rock Independence—they toiled slowly up to the South Pass, descended to the tributaries of the Colorado and plunged into the rugged defiles of the Timpanozu Mountains. Here the pasturage became scarce and the companies were obliged to take separate trails in order to find sufficient grass for their teams. Many, who, in their anxiety to get forward with speed, had thrown away a great part of the supplies that encumbered them, now began to want, and were frequently reduced, in their necessity, to make use of their mules and horses for food. It was not unusual for a mess, by way of variety to the tough mule-meat, to kill a quantity of rattle-snakes, with which the mountains abounded, and have a dish of them fried, for supper. The distress of many of the emigrants might have been entirely avoided, had they possessed any correct idea, at the outset of the journey, of its length and privations.

It must have been a remarkable scene, which the City of the Great Salt Lake presented during the summer. There, a community of religious enthusiasts, numbering about ten thousand, had established themselves beside an inland sea, in a grand valley shut in by snow-capped mountains, a thousand miles from any other civilized spot, and were dreaming of rebuilding the Temple and creating a New Jerusalem. Without this resting-place in mid-journey, the sufferings of the emigrants must have been much aggravated. The Mormons, however, whose rich grain-lands in the Valley of the Utah River had produced them abundance of supplies, were able to spare sufficient for those whose stock was exhausted. Two or

three thousand, who arrived late in the season, remained in the Valley all winter, fearing to undertake the toilsome journey which still remained.

Those who set out for California had the worst yet in store for them. Crossing the alternate sandy wastes and rugged mountain chains of the Great Basin to the Valley of Humboldt's River, they were obliged to trust entirely to their worn and weary animals for reaching the Sierra Nevada before the winter snows. The grass was scarce and now fast drying up in the scorching heat of mid-summer. In the endeavor to hasten forward and get the first chance of pasture, many again committed the same mistake of throwing away their supplies. I was told of one man, who, with a refinement of malice and cruelty which it would be impossible to surpass, set fire to the meadows of dry grass, for the sole purpose, it was supposed, of retarding the progress of those who were behind and might else overtake him. A company of the emigrants, on the best horses which were to be obtained, pursued him and shot him from the saddle as he rode—a fate scarcely equal to his deserts.

The progress of the emigrants along the Valley of Humboldt's River is described as having been slow and toilsome in the extreme. The River, which lies entirely within the Great Basin,—whose waters, like those of the uplands of Central Asia, have no connexion with the sea—shrinks away towards the end of summer, and finally loses itself in the sand, at a place called the Sink. Here, the single trail across the Basin divides into three branches, and the emigrants, leaving the scanty meadows about the Sink, have before them an arid desert, varying from fifty to eighty miles in breadth, according to the route which they take. Many companies, on arriving at this place, were obliged to stop and recruit their exhausted animals, though exposed to the danger of being detained there the whole winter, from the fall of snow on the Sierra Nevada. Another, and very large body of them, took the upper route to Lawson's Pass, which leads to the head of the Sacramento Valley; but the greater part, fortunately, chose the old traveled trails, leading to Bear Creek and the Yuba, by way of Truckee River, and to the head-waters of the Rio Americano by way of Carson's River.

The two latter routes are the shortest and best. After leaving the Sink of Humboldt's River, and crossing a desert of about fifty miles in breadth, the emigrant reaches the streams which are fed from the Sierra Nevada, where he finds good grass and plenty of game. The passes are described as terribly rugged and precipitous, leading directly up the face of the great snowy ridge. As, however, they are not quite eight thousand feet above the sea, and are reached from a plateau of more than four thousand feet, the ascent is comparatively short; while, on the western side, more than a hundred miles of mountain country must be passed, before reaching the level of the Sacramento Valley. There are frequent passes in the Sierra Nevada which were never crossed before the summer of 1849. Some of the emigrants, diverging from the known trail, sought a road for themselves, and found their way down from the snows to the head waters of the Tuolumne, the Calaveras and Feather River. The eastern slope of the Sierra Nevada is but imperfectly explored. All the emigrants concurred in representing it to me as an abrupt and broken region, the higher peaks of barren granite, the valleys deep and narrow, yet in many places timbered with pine and cedar of immense growth.

After passing the dividing ridge,—the descent from which was rendered almost impossible by precipices and steeps of naked rock—about thirty miles of alternate cañons and divides lay between the emigrants and the nearest diggings. The steepness of the slopes of this range is hardly equalled by any other mountains in the world. The rivers seem to wind their way through the bottoms of chasms, and in many places it is impossible to get down to the water. The word cañon (meaning, in Spanish, a funnel,) has a peculiar adaptation to these cleft channels through which the rivers are poured. In getting down from the summit ridge the emigrants told me they were frequently obliged to take the oxen from the wagon and lower it with ropes; but for the sheer descents which followed, another plan was adopted. The wheels were all locked, and only one yoke of oxen left in front; a middling-sized pine was then cut down, and the butt fastened to the axle-tree, the branchy top dragging on the earth. The holding back of the oxen, the sliding of the locked wheels, and the resistance of the tree together formed an opposing power sufficient to admit of a slow descent; but it was necessary to observe great care lest the pace should be quickened, for the slightest start would have overcome the resistance and given oxen, wagon and tree together a momentum that would have landed them at the bottom in a very different condition.

In August, before his departure for Oregon, Gen. Smith took the responsibility of ordering pack-mules and supplies to be provided at the expense of Government, and gave Major Rucker orders to dispatch relief companies into the Great Basin to succor the emigrants who might be remaining there, for want of provisions to advance further. In this step he was also warmly seconded by Gen. Riley, and the preparations were made with the least possible delay. Public meetings of the citizens of San Francisco were also held, to contribute means of relief. Major Rucker dispatched a party with supplies and fresh animals by way of the Truckee River route to the Sink of Humboldt's River, while he took the expedition to Pitt River and Lawson's Pass, under his own command. The first party, after furnishing provisions on the road to all whom they found in need, reached the Sink, and started the families who were still encamped there, returning with them by the Carson River route and bringing in the last of the emigration, only a day or two before the heavy snows came on, which entirely blocked up the passes. But for this most timely aid, hundreds of persons must have perished by famine and cold.

Those who took the trail for Lawson's Pass fared even worse. They had been grossly deceived with regard to the route, which, instead of being a nearer passage into California, is actually two hundred miles longer than the other routes, and though there is no ridge of equal height to be crossed, the amount of rough mountain travel is even greater. The trail, after crossing the Sierra by a low gap, (which has lately been mentioned in connection with the Pacific Railroad,) enters the Valley of Pitt River, one of the tributaries of the Upper Sacramento. Following the course of this river for about ninety miles, it reaches a spur of the Sierra Nevada, which runs from the head waters of Feather River to near the Shaste Peak, closing up the level of the lower Sacramento Valley. These mountains are from five to six thousand feet in height and rugged in the extreme, and over them the weary emigrant must pass before the Land of Promise—the rich Valley of the Sacramento—meets his view.

At the time I returned to Sacramento City, Major Rucker had just returned from his expedition. He found a large body of emigrants scattered along Pitt River, many of them entirely destitute of provisions and others without their animals, which the predatory Indians of that region had stolen. Owing to the large number who required his assistance, he was obliged to return to the ranches on Deer Creek and procure further supplies, leaving Mr. Peoples to hurry them on meanwhile. Everything was done to hasten their movement, but a strange and unaccountable apathy seemed to have taken possession of them. The season was late, and a single day added to the time requisite to get them into the Sacramento

Valley might prove ruinous to them and their assistants. Whether the weary six months they passed in the wilderness had had the effect of destroying all their active energy and care for their own safety, or whether it was actual ignorance of their true situation and contempt of counsel because it seemed to wear the shape of authority, it is difficult to tell—but the effect was equally dangerous. After having improvidently thrown away, in the first part of the journey, the supplies so needful afterwards, they now held fast to useless goods, and refused to lighten the loads of their tired oxen. But few of them appeared to have a sense of the aid which was rendered them; instead of willingly coöperating with those who had charge of the relief party, they gave much unnecessary trouble and delayed the journey several days.

Of the companies which came by this route several small parties struck into the mountains to the southward of Pitt River, hoping to find an easy road to the diggings on Feather River. Of these, some reached the river, after many days of suffering and danger; others retraced their steps and by making desperate efforts regained the companies on Pitt River, while some, who had not been heard of at the time I left, were either locked up for the winter in the midst of terrible snows, or had already perished from hunger. I met with one or two who had been several days in the mountains without food, and only escaped death by a miracle. A company of six, who had set out on the hunt of some Indians who had stolen their cattle, never returned. . . .

Chapter VI: San Francisco, Four Months Later

Of all the marvellous phases of the history of the Present, the growth of San Francisco is the one which will most tax the belief of the Future. Its parallel was never known, and shall never be beheld again. I speak only of what I saw with my own eyes. When I landed there, a little more than four months before, I found a scattering town of tents and canvas houses, with a show of frame buildings on one or two streets, and a population of about six thousand. Now, on my last visit, I saw around me an actual metropolis, displaying street after street of well-built edifices, filled with an active and enterprising people and exhibiting every mark of permanent commercial prosperity. Then, the town was limited to the curve of the Bay fronting the anchorage and bottoms of the hills. Now, it stretched to the topmost heights, followed the shore around point after point, and sending back a long arm through a gap in the hills, took hold of the Golden Gate and was building

its warehouses on the open strait and almost fronting the blue horizon of the Pacific. Then, the gold-seeking sojourner lodged in muslin rooms and canvas garrets, with a philosophic lack of furniture, and ate his simple though substantial fare from pine boards. Now, lofty hotels, gaudy with verandas and balconies, were met with in all quarters, furnished with home luxury, and aristocratic restaurants presented daily their long bills of fare, rich with the choicest technicalities of the Parisian cuisine. Then, vessels were coming in day after day, to lie deserted and useless at their anchorage. Now scarce a day passed, but some cluster of sails, bound *outward* through the Golden Gate, took their way to all the corners of the Pacific. Like the magic seed of the Indian juggler, which grew, blossomed and bore fruit before the eyes of his spectators, San Francisco seemed to have accomplished in a day the growth of half a century.

When I first landed in California, bewildered and amazed by what seemed an unnatural standard of prices, I formed the opinion that there would be before long a great crash in speculation. Things, it appeared then, had reached the crisis, and it was pronounced impossible that they could remain stationary. This might have been a very natural idea at the time, but the subsequent course of affairs proved it to be incorrect. Lands, rents, goods and subsistence continued steadily to advance in cost, and as the credit system had been meanwhile prudently contracted, the character of the business done was the more real and substantial. Two or three years will pass, in all probability, before there is a positive abatement of the standard of prices. There will be fluctuations in the meantime, occasioning great gains and losses, but the fall in rents and real estate, when it comes, as it inevitably must in the course of two or three years, will not be so crushing as I at first imagined. I doubt whether it will seriously injure the commercial activity of the place. Prices will never fall to the same standard as in the Atlantic States. Fortunes will always be made by the sober, intelligent, industrious, and energetic; but no one who is either too careless, too spiritless or too ignorant to succeed at home, need trouble himself about emigrating. The same general rule holds good, as well here as elsewhere, and it is all the better for human nature that it is so.

Not only was the heaviest part of the business conducted on cash principles, but all rents, even to lodgings in hotels, were required to be paid in advance. A single bowling-alley, in the basement story of the Ward House—a new hotel on Portsmouth-Square—prepaid $5,000 monthly. The firm of Findley, Johnson & Co. sold their real estate, purchased a year previous, for $20,000, at $300,000; $25,000 down, and the rest in monthly instalments of $12,500. This was a fair specimen of the speculations daily made. Those on a lesser scale were frequently of a very amusing character, but the claims on one's astonishment were so constant, that the faculty soon wore out, and the most unheard-of operations were looked upon as matters of course. Among others that came under my observation, was one of a gentleman who purchased a barrel of alum for $6, the price in New York being $9. It happened to be the only alum in the place, and as there was a demand for it shortly afterwards, he sold the barrel for $150. Another purchased all the candle-wick to be found, at an average price of 40 cts. per lb., and sold it in a short time at $2.25 per lb. A friend of mine expended $10,000 in purchasing barley, which in a week brought $20,000. The greatest gains were still made by the gambling tables and the eating-houses. Every device that art could suggest was used to swell the custom of the former. The latter found abundant support in the necessities of a large floating population, in addition to the swarm of permanent residents.

For a month or two previous to this time, money had been very scarce in the market, and from ten to fifteen per cent, monthly, was paid, with the addition of good security. Notwithstanding the quantity of coin brought into the country by emigrants, and the millions of gold dust used as currency, the actual specie basis was very small compared with the immense amount of business transacted. Nevertheless, I heard of nothing like a failure; the principal firms were prompt in all their dealings, and the chivalry of Commerce—to use a new phrase—was as faithfully observed as it could have been in the old marts of Europe and America. The merchants had a 'Change and News-room, and were beginning to coöperate in their movements and consolidate their credit. A stock company which had built a long wharf at the foot of Sacramento-st. declared a dividend of ten per cent. within six weeks after the wharf was finished. During the muddy season, it was the only convenient place for landing goods, and as the cost of constructing it was enormous, so were likewise the charges for wharfage and storage.

There had been a vast improvement in the means of living since my previous visit to San Francisco. Several large hotels had been opened, which were equal in almost every respect to houses of the second class in the Atlantic cities. The Ward House, the Graham House, imported bodily from Baltimore, and the St. Francis Hotel, completely threw into the shade all former establishments. The rooms were furnished with comfort and even luxury, and the tables lacked few of the essentials of good living, according to a 'home' taste. The sleeping apartments of the St. Francis were the best in California. The cost of board and lodging was $150 per month—which was considered unusually cheap. A room at the Ward House cost $250 monthly, without board. The principal restaurants charged $35 a week for board, and there were lodging houses where a berth or "bunk"—one out of fifty in the same room—might be had for $6 a week. The model of these establishments—which were far from being "model lodging-houses"—was that of a ship. A number of state-rooms, containing six berths each, ran around the sides of a large room, or cabin, where the lodgers resorted to read, write, smoke and drink at their leisure. The state-rooms were consequently filled with foul and unwholesome air, and the noises in the cabin prevented the passengers from sleeping, except between midnight and four o'clock.

The great want of San Francisco was society. Think of a city of thirty thousand inhabitants, peopled by men alone! The like of this was never seen before. Every man was his own housekeeper, doing, in many instances, his own sweeping, cooking, washing and mending. Many home-arts, learned rather by observation than experience, came conveniently into play. He who cannot make a bed, cook a beefsteak, or sew up his own rips and rents, is unfit to be a citizen of California. Nevertheless, since the town began to assume a permanent shape, very many of the comforts of life in the East were attainable. A family may now live there without suffering any material privations; and if every married man, who intends spending some time in California, would take his family with him, a social influence would soon be created to which we might look for the happiest results.

Towards the close of my stay, the city was as dismal a place as could well be imagined. The glimpse of bright, warm, serene weather passed away, leaving in its stead a raw, cheerless, southeast storm. The wind now and then blew a heavy gale, and the cold, steady fall of rain, was varied by claps of thunder and sudden blasts of hail. The mud in the streets became little short of fathomless, and it was with difficulty that the mules could drag their empty wagons through. A powerful London dray-horse, a very giant in harness, was the only animal able to pull a good load; and I was told that he earned his master $100 daily. I saw occasionally a company of Chinese workmen, carrying bricks and mortar, slung by ropes to long bamboo poles. The plank sidewalks, in the lower part of the city, ran along the brink of pools and quicksands, which the Street Inspector and his men vainly endeavored to fill by hauling cart-loads of chapparal and throwing sand on the top; in a day or two the gulf was as deep as ever. The side-walks, which were made at the cost of $5 per foot, bridged over the worst spots, but I was frequently obliged to go the whole length of a block in order to get on the other side. One could not walk any distance, without getting at least ancle-deep, and although the thermometer rarely sank below 50°, it was impossible to stand still for even a short time without a death-like chill taking hold of the feet. As a consequence of this, coughs and bronchial affections were innumerable. The universal custom of wearing the pantaloons inside the boots threatened to restore the knee-breeches of our grandfathers' times. Even women were obliged to shorten their skirts, and wear high-topped boots. The population seemed to be composed entirely of dismounted hussars. All this will be remedied when the city is two years older, and Portsmouth Square boasts a pavé as elegant as that on the dollar side of Broadway.

The severe weather occasioned a great deal of sickness, especially among those who led an exposed life. The city overflowed with people, and notwithstanding buildings were continually growing up like mushrooms, over night, hundreds who arrived were obliged to lodge in tents, with which the summits of the hills were covered. Fever-and-ague and dysentery were the prevailing complaints, the great prevalence of which was owing undoubtedly to exposure and an irregular habit of life. An association was formed to relieve those in actual want, many of the wealthiest and most influential citizens taking an honorable part in the matter. Many instances of lamentable destitution were by this means brought to light. Nearly all the hospitals of the place were soon filled, and numbers went to the Sandwich Islands to recruit. The City Hospital, a large, well ventilated and regulated establishment, contained about fifty patients. The attending physician described to me several cases of nearly hopeless lunacy which had

come under his care, some of them produced by disappointment and ill-luck, and others by sudden increase of fortune. Poor human nature! . . .

The effect of a growing prosperity and some little taste of luxury was readily seen in the appearance of the business community of San Francisco. The slouched felt hats gave way to narrow-brimmed black beavers; flannel shirts were laid aside, and white linen, though indifferently washed, appeared instead; dress and frock coats, of the fashion of the previous year in the Atlantic side, came forth from trunks and sea-chests; in short, a San Francisco merchant was almost as smooth and spruce in his outward appearance as a merchant anywhere else. The hussar boot, however, was obliged to be worn, and a variation of the Mexican sombrero—a very convenient and becoming head-piece—came into fashion among the younger class.

The steamers which arrived at this time, brought large quantities of newspapers from all parts of the Atlantic States. The speculation which had been so successful at first, was completely overdone; there was a glut in the market, in consequence whereof newspapers came down to fifty and twenty-five cents apiece. The leading journals of New-York, New-Orleans and Boston were cried at every street-corner. The two papers established in the place issued editions "for the Atlantic Coast," at the sailing of every steamer for Panama. The offices were invaded by crowds of purchasers, and the slow hand-presses in use could not keep pace with the demand. The profits of these journals were almost incredible, when contrasted with their size and the amount of their circulation. Neither of them failed to count their gains at the rate of $75,000, a year, clear profit.

My preparations for leaving San Francisco, were made with the regret that I could not remain longer and see more of the wonderful growth of the Empire of the West. Yet I was fortunate in witnessing the most peculiar and interesting stages of its progress, and I took my departure in the hope of returning at some future day to view the completion of these magnificent beginnings. The world's history has no page so marvellous as that which has just been turned in California.

BUILDING THE RAILROADS

IN THESE STATEMENTS extolling the advantages of the Illinois Central Railroad and the lands it was offering for sale may be seen a typical example of the early development of the American railroad. In its origins and its growth before the Civil War, the Illinois Central shows how the West was opened through the new methods of transportation and how that development in turn offered new outlets and incentives for the growth of capital in the East.

The prairies, which had been avoided by the early pioneers into the Illinois country, had become more accessible with the construction of the Erie Canal and the advance of steam navigation on the Great Lakes. Root-matted prairie soil was still too tough for the old-fashioned plow; not even iron, which was replacing wood, could cope with the stubborn sod. But in 1837, the first steel plow finally made the prairie soil available to the farmer. Rich and readily cultivable as the prairie might be, the lack of transportation slowed settlement. Farmers preferred poorer land near a river, that would take their crops to market, to the most fertile farm whose crops must lie unsold because of lack of facilities for shipping.

Like their fellows in other Western areas, Illinois farmers clamored for internal improvements: roads, canals, and railways to carry their grain and pork to Eastern and Southern markets. Illinois began canal-building in 1836, but canals could furnish transportation to only a limited area of the state; if the prairies were to be settled, they must be served by railroads. In 1837, the state undertook an elaborate building program including both improved water transport and railroads. The plans were too am-

bitious for the capital available to a frontier community; they were inefficiently executed, and finally collapsed in the depression that followed the panic of 1837.

As early as 1835, a group of land speculators, trying to turn the town of Cairo into a metropolis, had backed a scheme for an Illinois railroad. When the state building program was abandoned, they secured a charter of incorporation and set about winning a congressional grant of public land. Slowly through the forties, after Senator Douglas had taken the project out of the Cairo lobbyists' hands, the bill for congressional aid to an Illinois railroad gained friends. A change in the proposed route, extending the railroad south to Mobile, won support from that section. Eastern votes were obtained by pressure from investors in Illinois securities, state and corporate, and speculators in Illinois land. Also, Easterners with idle capital seeking new investments added their pressures to those of Western and Southern representatives until, in 1850, the land-grant bill was passed. By the terms of the bill, Illinois, Mississippi, and Alabama received land for a right of way, plus alternate sections (for six sections in width on each side), for the construction of a railroad from the Great Lakes to Mobile, with branch lines to Dubuque and Chicago. The Federal government, in return, was to receive sizable reductions in rates for the hauling of the mails and official freight and passengers. Thus was the pattern of the land-grant railway fixed in 1850. This pattern was followed essentially in the chartering of the great Pacific railways of the sixties and seventies.

By 1851, therefore, the state of Illinois had valuable lands to offer. Rival groups of railroad interests now appeared at Springfield to bargain for a franchise. The Cairo promoters, the representatives of the state bondholders, and the Eastern capitalists who had become interested in the project through their work on the Michigan Central, all contended for the grant. The first group suffered from its close connection with Illinois political quarrels; the second because of the large "foreign" element among its probable beneficiaries. The third was free of these handicaps and able to finance an efficient lobby at Springfield. The bondholders' representatives were soon eliminated, leaving the field to the Cairo group and its Eastern competitors.

The latter, most of whom were Whigs, retained leading Illinois Democrats as spokesmen and then sent Robert Rantoul, Jr., of Massachusetts to Illinois to head their ranks. Rantoul (1805–1852) had won considerable reputation in the Democratic party as a champion of progressive measures. He had been a conspicuous proponent of improved education in Massachusetts and had made a report on capital punishment which had wide influence after its publication in 1836. More recently, as counsel in the case of Commonwealth v. Hunt, Rantoul had convinced the Massachusetts Supreme Court that labor unions were not necessarily conspiracies in restraint of trade and so laid the foundation for the legal recognition of American labor organizations. Finally, though Rantoul had been investing in lumbering and mining rights along the headwaters of the Mississippi, he was known for his efforts to extend state checks on corporations and their activities.

When Rantoul arrived in Springfield, he had the support of the Illinois Democratic press; favorable Whig publicity was also assured by a judicious loan to the editor of a leading Whig sheet. With the press and ample funds for backing, Rantoul and his Illinois co-workers proceeded to the task of political manipulation, a task complicated by the number of opposing pressure groups seeking legislative favors at the session. Since the bondholders' group had been eliminated, Rantoul's backers placated the Cairo promoters by agreeing to make large improvements in that town and by reserving 1,000 assessment-exempt shares for the leader of the Cairo group. In January, 1851, Rantoul presented a memorial to the legislature praying for a charter. After a month of debate over who should determine the road's route, the Illinois legislators decided to set forth general principles rather than a specific course and then chartered the new road. The company was given the federal land grant.

The Illinois Central Railroad Company was organized a month after the charter was granted and, in spite of the rather shady character of its first president, succeeded in securing a loan in England. By the middle fifties, though the road's securities had declined, foreign confidence in the project increased as the company's leadership improved. Although the stock was assessed to provide funds for construction—a contingency against which the foreign investors thought themselves secure—the company's credit was finally established. In spite of financial difficulties and the effects of the panic of 1857, the road was completed in the six-year period specified by its charter and its credit stood firm thereafter. America's first trunk line had been built.

Two of the new company's directors—in an effort to attract investors—proceeded to describe the railroad's prospects. Their statements are reprinted from a pamphlet, *Documents Relating to the Organization of the Illinois Central Rail-road Company* (New York, 1851).

The Illinois Central Railroad

BY DAVID A. NEAL

FOR THE PURPOSE of aiding the construction of "a Rail Road from the southern terminus of the Illinois and Michigan Canal to a point at or near the junction of the Ohio and Mississippi Rivers, with a Branch of the same to Chicago, on Lake Michigan, and another via the town of Galena to Dubuque, in the State of Iowa," the Congress of the United States, by an Act, approved September 20, 1850, granted to the State of Illinois,

1st. The right of way 200 feet wide, through the public lands, and of taking necessary materials of earth, stone, lumber, &c.

2. Every alternate section of land, designated by even numbers for six sections in width on each side of said Road and Branches, or if any such have been sold, so much land most contiguous to such sections and not exceeding fifteen miles from the line of the Road as shall be equal to those sold.

By an Act of the Legislature of the State of Illinois, passed the present year, Robert Schuyler, George Griswold, Gouveneur Morris, Franklin Haven, David A. Neal, Robert Rantoul, jun., Jonathan Sturgis, George W. Ludlow, John F. Sanford, Henry Grinnell, William H. Aspinwall, Leroy Wiley and Joseph W. Alsop, and such persons as shall hereafter become Stockholders, were created a body politic and corporate, under the name of the Illinois Central Rail Road Company, with all necessary powers and privileges for constructing and maintaining the Rail Road and Branches, contemplated in the Act of Congress aforesaid, and for this purpose, the right of way, and all the lands that may be selected along the line of said Road and Branches in the State, under the grant in said Act, together with a right of way over and through lands belonging to the State, and all the rights and materials heretofore acquired by the State for the same object, are ceded and granted to said Corporation, on condition that such Road shall be built in four, and said Branches in six years, and that when built and in operation, seven per cent. of the gross income shall be paid to the State in lieu of all taxes levied for State purposes. The lands thus granted are to be placed in the hands of Trustees, three-fourths for the security of any Bonds issued by the Company, and one-fourth to meet any deficiency from other sources, for the payment of interest, or contingencies. The Capital Stock is fixed by the Act, at one million of dollars, which may be increased at any time, to an amount not exceeding the entire expenditure on account of the Road.

The Illinois Central Rail Road Company has been organized, the Capital Stock subscribed, and twenty per cent. of it paid in, all the conditions of the Charter have been complied with, and all the deeds, grants and trusts executed. Engineers are employed in selecting a route and the donated lands, which will amount to 3840 acres for each mile of road, or in the aggregate, (the Road and Branches being assumed at 670 miles) 2,572,800 acres.

It is proposed to meet the cost of construction by the issue of Bonds, payable in 1875, bearing interest not exceeding seven per cent. The security for the principal will be—1st, the Road itself; and 2d, two million acres of the donated lands. The security for the interest will be 1st, the Capital Stock; 2d, the Income of the Road; 3d, two hundred and fifty thousand acres of the land specially appropriated.

The lands will be valued at prices that will more than cover any possible amount required for construction, but which, it is believed, will be fully realized before the period of the maturity of the Bonds. These Bonds may, at any time, be surrendered and any land on sale claimed in lieu of them at the appraisement. None of the lands appropriated for their security, can be disposed of, except on the simultaneous surrender or payment of Bonds to an amount equal to their appraisal. That appraisal of the two millions of acres mortgaged for their security, that is, the price under which they will not be sold, and to which it is expected they will advance at some time previous to 1875, will be so arranged, as soon as they are selected and their character known, as to produce the following averages.

400,000 acres ordinary agricultural lands $6, ...	$2,400,000
1,200,000 acres good agricultural lands $10,	12,000,000
300,000 acres superior agricultural lands $15, ...	4,500,000
100,000 acres town sites, mineral lands $25, ...	2,500,000
2,000,000	$21,400,000

To enable the Company to meet the demand for these lands at any time, short of the period of the maturity of the Bonds, the right to anticipate their payment has been reserved, but only on condition of giving one hundred and twenty dollars for every hundred so taken up.

During the time occupied in the construction of the Road, the interest on the outlay will be included in its cost. Immediately on its completion, the Income, after paying current expenses and State tax, will be of course applied to this object. If it should not, at first, be sufficient, the earnings from any partial use of the road, before its completion, the whole capital stock of the Company, and the entire proceeds of sales of 250,000 acres of land set aside for this purpose, will form a fund that will be ample under any contingency.

The basis of this enterprise is founded both on National and State legislation. The powers delegated are ample, the titles are perfect. It is of its merits as a public work, of its capabilities as a great thoroughfare, of its success as a commercial operation, and its consequent estimation as a medium of investment, that I now propose to make some remarks.

If to make two blades of grass grow where but one grew before, be worthy the high commendation of the philosopher and patriot, it will not be deemed an act altogether unimportant or useless to the country to open to the approach of industry, millions of acres of the most fertile soil the sun ever shone upon, and to make available at once, the alluvial deposits of countless ages. An enterprise that will thus bring into use wealth heretofore buried, that will lighten the burthen, while it will increase the rewards of labor, that will add to the resources of the poor, and offer new and valuable investments to the rich, will hardly want friends, when such pretensions shall be established. The construction of a Rail Road traversing in its whole length the State of Illinois from Cairo, where the waters of the Mississippi and the Ohio meet, bearing on their surface the various productions of the North and the South, of the East and the West, to the vast mineral regions of Galena in the North West, and to Chicago, the emporium of the commerce of the great Lakes at the North East, will, it is believed, accomplish these objects. Its practicability, with the means at the disposal of its projectors and friends, is an important consideration. This, it is evident, must mainly depend on the ultimate value of the work when completed, and of the effect on the property which forms the basis of all its financial operations. The value of the work may be estimated by the use that can be made of it, or rather by the extent of production to which the ability to use it will give birth. The sources of income will be found,

1st. In the produce of the mines and forests, for these furnish articles ready for use and of general consumption every where.

2d. In the produce of the soil, which requires easy and cheap transportation to induce as much

as it does sunshine and rain, to perfect its cultivation.

3d. In the supplies requisite to those who may be engaged in occupations connected with or incident to the two above named branches of business.

4th. In the movements of the same persons for purposes of business or pleasure.

5th. In the transit of persons and goods between points beyond the limits of the State for which the route will afford the most convenient and expeditious passage.

6th. In transportation of mails and expresses, and in other miscellaneous operations.

Having settled these points with as much precision as the nature of the case admits, it will be easy to estimate the value of the Road as an investment, and consequently as a security *per se* for the means necessary to construct it. If it cannot be shown that it will yield some income beyond its current expenses, no one will probably take the trouble to carry on the enterprise, and consequently no means will be required for its construction. If, therefore, these means are sought, it will be proof that its projectors believe it will be of some intrinsic value. It may be more or less, or they may be altogether mistaken.

If the latter be not the case, then the property which they receive for carrying out the plan, must also be worth something. How much, will depend on the demand for it, and the demand will be proportionate to the number of persons who may be induced, by the prospect of success, to cluster about it. We come back then to the great question of *population*. In estimating what it may be some four or five or six years hence, in the region to be traversed by this or any other Road, we have the same lights to guide us that are always used by prudent men in their daily operations. . . .

The Road to be built is restricted only to within seventeen miles each side of a straight line from the city of Cairo to the Southern terminus of the Illinois Canal, which line is nearly coincident with the third principal meridian, thence a branch by any convenient route to Galena. From a point in about the latitude of °39.30 North latitude, will diverge the branch to be built to Chicago. The Main Line to be completed in four years, the Branches in six. No taxes to be levied until the Road is completed; then in lieu of all other taxes the Company are to pay seven per cent. of the gross earnings of the Road, as already stated. The donated lands consist of every alternate section designated by even numbers, for six sections in width on each side of the Road as it may be located, or if any of these have been sold, then an equal quantity may be taken from contiguous tiers of sections any where within fifteen miles of the line.

Under this grant, the Road will be located through the most fertile prairies, the most valuable forests, and the richest mineral lands in the State; but these have been neglected by settlers in consequence of the utter impossibility of getting their productions to market. Until the Illinois Central Rail Road Company shall have selected their lands, the Books of the General Land Office in Washington are closed against entries in this region, and when opened, the price is to be double that of the other lands. The Company are, therefore, fully protected. They have organized under their charter, all the deeds and necessary documents have been executed by the Governor of the State, the Trustees, and its own officers. The whole stock has been taken and twenty per cent. been paid in, in cash, and the same deposited with the State Treasurer of Illinois, to be returned on completion of fifty miles of the Road. Robert Schuyler, Esq., of New York, a gentleman more conversant with and more largely interested in Rail Roads than any other person on the Western continent, has been chosen President, and Morris Ketchum, Esq., of the very wealthy and well known house of Rogers, Ketchum & Bement, Treasurer of the Association. R. B. Mason, Esq., of the New York and New Haven Rail Road, has been appointed Chief, and he has engaged seven resident and a large corps of assistant Engineers, who have proceeded to Illinois to locate the Road and select the donated lands. The system devised for procuring the means of building this Road by the *sale* of Bonds, and for the *payment* of them *when* or *before* they become due, is unique in its character and provisions. It is believed to afford not simply entire security for the current interest and redemption at maturity, but a strong probability of a great advance in value, in consequence of the peculiar conditions annexed to the sale of the property which forms a branch of the collateral security embraced in the plan.

The length of the Road and Branches will probably not be less than 670 miles, which will entitle the Company, as before stated, to an aggregate donation of 2,572,800 acres. No estimate of its cost has been attempted, for no particular survey of the whole route has yet been made. It is said that $15,000 per mile is the highest that any Road (allowing for heavy T rail,) has as yet cost in Illinois; $20,000 per mile would require about $14,000,000. It is intended to use the strictest economy, consistent with the construction of a good, substantial Road. It is also intended to pay for

every thing with cash. There are various reasons besides for believing that this Road will be built for comparatively little money; but as ample security will be offered for any possible sum that may be required, it is unnecessary in this connection to go into any detail on that subject.

The Bonds will be dated April 1, 1851, with Coupons attached, at rate of interest to be hereafter agreed on, not exceeding seven per cent. It is desirable to negotiate at once (if practicable,) for enough to ensure the building the Road, but to be paid by instalments as wanted.

The first security for these Bonds that will be offered, will be the Road itself. To render this satisfactory, it must be shown, with a reasonable degree of certainty, that it will pay its current expenses, taxes and interest on the capital invested. There will be within fifteen miles of the line of this Road, upwards of 12,000,000 acres of land. It is adapted to the cultivation of any kind of grain, but particularly of Indian corn, of which it is said it produces 60–70 bushels to the acre, and to be inexhaustible. There are at various points on the Road, large quantities of bituminous coal. There is one field of peculiarly good quality near Danville, about 120 miles from Chicago, from which all the shore towns and steamers of Lake Michigan may be supplied. Another, 50 miles from Cairo, which may supply the demands for steamboats, both on the Ohio and Mississippi. A large part of Illinois, especially that distant from the banks of the rivers, is destitute of forests. Chicago is the great depot for the lumber of both Michigan and Wisconsin, and it can always be obtained here in any quantities at low prices. Cairo is at the head of navigation for the large steamers of the Lower Mississippi, and the place of transshipment from them to the vessels of lighter draft, and vice versa, both of passengers and freight. Frequently the rivers above are impeded with ice, swollen from freshets or impassible for want of water. The Illinois Central Rail Road will furnish a rapid communication with and through the central, most fertile and most healthy portions of the State. Its means of transportation, will be ample, uninterrupted and safe. It will be completed probably in four years from the time of its active commencement.

One mode of increasing the population of the country will be the mass of laborers that must be introduced to build the Road. The amount paid to workmen alone, employed in grading, will not probably be less, on an average, than $6000 per mile. Assuming the wages at $1 per day, and the road 666⅔ miles long, we have 4,000,000 days' work—or divided among four years, 1,000,000 per annum—and supposing 250 working days in the year, we require 4000 men to be constantly at work. With the prospect of so long a job, large numbers of these will have their families with them, and thus add at least 50 per cent. to the number. With them will naturally be brought those who look for profit in supplying them. An immediate market will be introduced for small farmers all along the line, who will clear their land in a single year from the disposal of their surplus produce. Three-fourths of the money expended in constructing the road, will remain in the country, or be remitted to Washington, in payment for Government lands. Settlers will thus have an unprecedented opportunity to make themselves not only owners of the soil, but establish themselves with comfort and independence for life. This will arrest the tide of immigration at this point. It will be known throughout Europe, as the spot where labor is in demand, wages good, pay prompt, living cheap, and farms paid for from the profits of a single crop. By these means this strip of thirty miles in width, or parcel of 20,000 square miles of country, will soon become spotted with an industrious population. . . .

BY ROBERT RANTOUL, JR.

. . . During the last ten years Illinois has labored under a debt, of a magnitude absolutely overwhelming, when compared with her resources at the commencement of that period. She had then before her a very gloomy alternative. If she endeavored to meet even the interest of her obligations she would be crushed under the weight of an intolerable taxation, from which her most able and enterprising citizens would have fled into other States. If she abandoned the effort in despair of the possibility of success, then she must suffer all the consequences of the total loss of credit consequent on her bankruptcy. In neither case did it seem to be probable that her public works could be made available towards the discharge of the debt incurred for them, or aid to develop the resources of the State. Why should an emigrant from the old world, or from the other States, with the broad valley of the Mississippi open before him where to choose, voluntary assume a full share of these embarrassments by becoming a citizen of Illinois? The answer which emigrants have given to this question may be seen in the settlement of Wisconsin, which State, with a colder climate and a harder soil than Illinois, has added to her population more than eight hundred and eighty per cent. in the last ten years: a progress unprecedented in the history of the world, in any agricultural community.

Ten years ago Illinois, borne down with debt, had not only not a mile of Railroad, or canal, or plank road, in operation within her borders, but no reasonable plan had been agreed upon by which she could hope to diminish her debt, discharge her interest, or acquire facilities of communication. She has now her canal debt rapidly approaching towards extinction, revenues sufficient in a very short time to discharge her whole interest without increasing the rate of taxation, one hundred miles of canal, and a still greater length of Railroad, in highly profitable operation, with plank roads in great numbers, paying dividends large enough to insure the early construction of several thousand miles more. Not only so, but she has before her the certainty that she will be supplied with more than twelve hundred, perhaps it may be safely said, more than fifteen hundred miles of Railroad in the next five or six years; and channels are already constructed to convey her products, transported to her borders on these Railroads, through Michigan, Indiana, and the Eastern States, to the seaboard and abroad. If, paralyzed as she was for the last ten years, her growth was at about the same rate as that of Michigan, having less than half as dense a population, with her Railroads and her lake borders and her steamboats; about the same as that of Missouri, with, only two-thirds as dense a population, and with the Queen City of the Great River in her centre, receiving the whole current of emigration up the Mississippi; about the same numerically as that of Wisconsin and Iowa together, these two starting with a hundred thousand square miles of land unoccupied, wholly unencumbered with debt and accessible from the lake and from the river; why should she not, in her present healthy condition, her limbs unshackled and her pathway free before her, advance with the step of a giant refreshed, towards her natural position among the first in population, power and wealth of the North American confederacy of States?

Even under all the disadvantages which have impeded the progress of Illinois during the last ten years, disadvantages whose effect it would not be easy to over-estimate, the growth of those sections of the State which can be easily reached from the northeast has been such as to afford an indication of what may be expected from the whole area when it is once made equally accessible. The two land districts of Chicago and

Dixon, forming the northern section of the State, contain together 14,126 square miles, or about one-fourth of the land in the State. This northern section alone is accessible from Lake Michigan, and of course has received the whole benefit, in common with the southeastern part of Wisconsin, of the lines of steamboats from Buffalo and Detroit, and of the travel over the Michigan Central Rail Road. It had by the last census, two hundred and fifty-five thousand, eight hundred and seventy inhabitants, or eighteen to the square mile; and is divided into twenty-four counties. If we take separately the northern belt across the whole breadth of the State we shall include in thirteen counties, every county within fifteen miles of which the Chicago and Galena Rail Road route passes. These thirteen counties increased about two hundred and eighty per cent. in the last ten years in the number of their inhabitants; having, in 1840, six and one-half to a square mile, and in 1850, about twenty-five to the square mile.

If we now take the belt directly south of this, including the eleven counties which constitute the remainder of the Chicago and Dixon land districts, we shall find that these are the counties accessible from the Lake through the Illinois and Michigan Canal. These eleven counties increased in population one hundred and nine per cent. in the last ten years. They had, in 1840, five and one-third inhabitants to the square mile, while in 1850, they had a fraction over eleven to the square mile. The remaining seventy-five counties of the State having no convenient access from the East for emigrants, and to the eastern markets for produce, have increased fifty-two and a half per cent. in ten years; and while in 1840 they had nine and a half inhabitants to the square mile, or fifty per cent. more than the northern section, in 1850, they had but fourteen and a half to the square mile, or little more than half the average density of the thirteen northern counties.

The twenty-four counties, therefore, of the Chicago and Dixon land districts of Illinois exhibit, and enable us to measure the influence of Lake Michigan in opening a cheap highway to the vast territory upon its Western borders. This increase of two hundred and four per cent. in the population of an area larger than the States of Massachusetts, Connecticut, and Rhode Island together, has occurred during ten years, when the extraordinary and unprecedented prosperity of those Atlantic States, whence emigration to the West has been generally derived, kept at home on the seaboard a population of about seven hundred thousand persons, who must otherwise, at the rate at which population advanced in those

States during the next preceding decade of years, have become inhabitants of the Mississippi Valley, and for the most part, of the northern part of the Valley. This increase of two hundred and four per cent. has occurred in the accessible section of Illinois, in ten years of financial embarrassment and State bankruptcy, most repelling to immigrant settlers; and to know how far these circumstances have depressed the growth of Northern Illinois, let us cross the border line into Wisconsin, and measure there the effect of the Lake, as a great avenue, upon the portion of Wisconsin open to its influence. . . .

The State debt of Illinois has ceased to cause alarm. It is obvious that the taxes provided for in the Constitution of the State, levied on her rapidly increasing property, would soon be sufficient to meet her liabilities. But it is certain that the opening of her great system of Railroads will accelerate the increased valuation of her property by many millions annually, while her share of the gross revenue of the Central Road will enable her soon after that road is opened, to begin rapidly to extinguish her debt. This obstacle being no longer formidable, the central and southern parts of Illinois are now ready for the full development of their natural advantages. The remainder of the State, with a warmer climate than that which already trebles its numbers in ten years, lessening the expense of shelter, fuel and clothing, has also a soil tillable with less labor, and yielding larger harvests, and, underlying many thousand miles of its area, one of the largest coal beds in the world, not too far from the surface, and in many parts of excellent quality. I say nothing of the metalic minerals of Northwestern or Southern Illinois, not because I undervalue them, but because I cannot extend this communication to do justice to their merits; and because in land for agricultural purposes alone, Illinois has wealth enough for an empire. Open a vent for her products, and her central and southern lands will be sought for as eagerly as those have been which already open on Lake Michigan. Difficult of access as are most of her lands, now remaining unsold, they are still sought for in much larger quantities than those of any other new State. The public land sold in the seven Northwestern States during the year ending June 30th, 1850, before the projection of the Central Rail Road began to influence sales in Illinois, was distributed as follows:

Sales of land in the seven Northwestern States for the year ending June 30th, 1850, according to the Report of the Secretary of the Interior, of the 3rd of December, 1850.

Ohio, ...	34,677.25	acres.
Indiana, ...	120,998.93	"
Illinois, ...	275,119.48	"
Michigan, ...	48,675.04	"
Wisconsin, ...	162,098.87	"
Iowa, ...	112,832.75	"
Missouri, ...	227,000.89	"
	981,403.21	"

. . . The tract through which the Illinois Central Rail Road is to pass is mostly destitute of cities and towns, but these must be built up at intervals, along the new channels of intercourse which we are about to open, as Chicago, Milwaukie, and so many other centres of distribution and exchange have been already on the Lake and on the rivers. As the population grows denser wealth will accumulate, not in the same proportion to population certainly as at the head-quarters of American railroads,—the State of Massachusetts, whose wealth has doubled in the last ten years,—but rapidly enough to improve constantly the circumstances of the inhabitants, and of course to raise the value of the land in a greater ratio than the increase of numbers. I say it is not to be expected that individual wealth should accumulate as rapidly in Illinois as it has done for the last ten years in Massachusetts; the last ten years having been precisely the period of the greatest prosperity and most rapid progress that Massachusetts has ever known. Yet in that portion of Illinois most easily accessible from Lake Michigan, and on the line of the Railroad to Galena, not only has population quadrupled in the last ten years, but the wealth was six times as great in 1849 as it was nine years before; so that the shares of the individual inhabitants increased faster than even in Massachusetts, where profits are annually re-invested from the accumulated capital of more than two hundred years.

In Massachusetts the valuation of 1840 was a little less than three hundred millions of dollars, or more than four hundred dollars per head. In 1850 it was a little less than six hundred millions, or a fraction above six hundred dollars per head; so that each man's share had increased fifty per cent. in ten years, a prosperity not unenviable. In the thirteen northern counties of Illinois, the aggregate wealth which in 1840 was $3,630,040 had risen to $21,942,239 in 1849, or from $77.25 per head to $134.27 per head. The same rate of increase per head would make each individual's share exceed two hundred and sixty dollars in 1860; and if we suppose the population of these counties to increase only two-thirds in the next ten years, about three hundred thousand inhab-

itants would possess about seventy-eight millions of dollars' worth of property. This amount gives $16.91 per acre for the whole area of these thirteen counties, and if we allow the land to constitute two-thirds of the valuation, which is much less than its true proportion, it gives more than ten dollars per acre as the price of land.

The experience of Illinois shows, therefore, that as her population becomes more dense, their wealth has increased in a ratio quite sufficient for the purpose of the present examination. Is there any reason to fear that her lands will offer fewer inducements to emigrants in future, or that less success will attend those who occupy them? It is obvious that the answer to this question depends much on determining whether the produce of these lands can be profitably taken to market, and whether the world furnishes markets sufficient to take off the immense surplus they are to yield.

Corn was carried during the summer from a point several miles above the mouth of the Illinois river down to the Illinois, thence up that river to the canal, thence to Chicago, and thence to New York, and there sold at a profit. Corn was not low in Illinois last summer, but in New York it was considerably lower than the average of the last four years. Corn will go to market cheaper from the lands in the Danville district, on the line of the Chicago branch of the Central Road, than from the point of shipment on the Mississippi first referred to. Corn is so cheap and bulky that all other agricultural produce may be carried much further on the Railroad without too great an addition to its price. All produce for which a market can be found at the seaboard will bear the cost of transportation from Illinois.

Nor need we be alarmed at the vast amounts of produce which these unsettled tracts are capable of yielding. The Northwest never received so great an accession to its population in any equal period as in the last five years; the emigration from foreign countries, most of which passes to the northwest, having risen to 299,610 in 1849, and to 315,333 in 1850, instead of less than fifty thousand a year as it was formerly. Yet with this unparalleled increase of laborers cultivating the richest soil of the world, with the new avenues to market that have been opened during that time, all pouring to the seaboard the surplus of a succession of bountiful harvests, in quantities unheard of before, and at much lower freights than before, the supply has not kept pace with the demand, as is shown by the fact that agricultural products, almost without exception, have borne much higher prices during the last four years than during the four next preceding.

Stimulated by this rise of prices, the exports of the last four years exceeded those of the four years previous, in vegetable food and the products of animals alone, by about one hundred millions of dollars in the total.

The animal products exported
from 1843 to 1846, inclusive,
were valued at............... $24,153,331
And the vegetable food at....... 47,335,438

Making an aggregate of.........$71,488,769

But during the period from 1847
to 1850, inclusive, the exports of
animal products were about
doubled, and amounted to... $47,354,655
The vegetable food was more than
doubled, being............. 123,720,738
                                 $171,075,393

Subtract amount in previous four
years, ... 71,488,769
                                 $99,586,624

The exports of the South increase also, which is an important element in the prosperity of the Northwest; first, because the South, while her peculiar staples are profitable, will not compete in foreign markets with large supplies of food, which she could easily furnish if her industry were directed to that object; second, because the South, in years of prosperous export of her staples consumes vast quantities of Northwestern products, which she might otherwise raise at home. The export of her three chief articles were,

	1843 to 1846.	1847 to 1849.
Cotton, ...	$197,690,291	$253,795,725
Tobacco, ...	28,996,314	30,548,438
Rice, ...	8,600,207	11,138,639
	$235,286,812	$295,482,802

That all these products, both those of the North and those of the South, if they are exported in greater quantities than formerly at higher prices, would be required and consumed abroad in quantities still more rapidly increased, if they were afforded at lower prices than from 1843 to 1846, is almost too obvious to be stated; and yet it is equally obvious that the prices might be reduced considerably below those of the former period to the consumer, and yet leave a much larger remuneration than before in the hands of the original producer, because of the saving of so large a part of the addition made to the cost of the article in the expense of transportation. The in-

creased power of consumption of the inhabitants of Great Britain is also well ascertained, and seems from the latest returns to be steadily advancing.

The demand for Northwestern products for exportation, is, however, far from being the only dependence of the producer. The home demand increases, and must continue to increase, in a ratio even greater than the foreign demand. As the country grows richer, a larger proportion of its population is withdrawn from agricultural pursuits, to be employed in manufactures and mining, and in the management of internal exchanges and transportation, and foreign navigation and commerce. All these persons, ceasing to grow their own food, and consuming freely, since, taken as a whole, they have ample means to purchase, create a continually expanding demand, which for the last five years at least, has not been overtaken by the supply. This progress in this country is far beyond that of any other part of the world, in the rapidity with which it proceeds. . . .

To recapitulate, I have shown that our lands lie along the natural route of the greatest thoroughfare on the continent, that connecting the Northeast and the Basin of the lakes with the Southwest and Gulf of Mexico, and thence with the coast of the Pacific; that the land between the Middle States and Illinois is taken up; that the younger States have a vast surface of land which is inaccessible; that the small portion which is accessible is settled already more densely than Illinois; that Illinois, notwithstanding her embarrassments, has sold more land and added greater numbers to her population than any other State of the Northwest; that this is what should be expected from the fertility of her soil; that where her land is open to easy access the increase in numbers and wealth is amazing and almost incredible; and that the districts through which our road runs are only waiting for an avenue to market to advance at the same rate. I have shown our exports of the products of the Northwest increasing from seventy-one millions to one hundred and seventy-one millions of dollars in value in four years; while such is the increase of population not agricultural, from increased manufactures, navigation, commerce, and city life, that together with the demand for export, they have caused the prices of all Northwestern products to rule higher, in spite of the vastly augmented number of producers.

I have shown that the settler in Illinois may obtain much more of all that he wishes to buy for a given amount of his produce, and for some of the most important articles at least twice as much as he could do five or six years ago. Consequently inducements to settlers are stronger now than ever; and when we find emigration proceeding at a rate which will add five or six millions to the population in ten years, we inquire to what section of the country will these emigrants be drawn, and find no reason why Illinois should not, as she has done for several years past, receive a larger number than any other State.

Calculating her increase of population at rates far below what our data will justify, we find it reaches a density which has never failed to give to land a value much higher than is fully adequate to discharge the whole amount of the bonds to be predicated on our land, in less than half the time they have to run. The remaining half of that period is certainly a sufficient time to be allowed for all possible contingencies of war, pestilence, or other disturbances of the ordinary current of events.

I consider then that any estimate which shall give to the lands belonging to the Company an average value of from ten to twelve dollars an acre to be reached in twelve or fourteen years from this date, is amply sustained by the facts presented in this communication.

BUSINESS ENTERPRISE

In 1846, by the vote of the electors of New York State, delegates to a new Constitutional Convention assembled at Albany from June 1 to September 10. They wrote a new frame of government which was, in harmony with the times, a liberal one. Among its more important achievements were the abolition of copyhold land tenure and the inclusion of a general business incorporation law. The first secured the extension of freehold tenure in the state. The second, by limiting the liability of investors in corporations, opened the doors to new venture capital in all types of business enterprises. The Banking Law of 1838 had established the so-called "free banking" system in New York. Now, all business corporations, particularly those engaged in manufacturing, were to be "free" in the sense that they did not require special legislative charters. Both provisions in the new constitution were hotly debated. That which had to do with the end of copyhold tenures was bitterly contested because the old feudal hangovers had a long history in New York. The background of this struggle requires sketching in order to make the debate before the Convention intelligible.

A lavish land policy—Dutch, British, and American—had put large areas of New York into the possession of land companies or great landowners. The Van Rensselaers, for example, owned a tract twenty-four by forty-eight miles along the Hudson; the Livingstons were almost as well endowed; while much of Schoharie, Delaware, Montgomery, and Greene Counties was owned by foreign land companies or their American successors.

The land companies, for the most part, sold their tracts on deferred payments spread over a long period of time. Some of the owners of the older patents, notably Stephen Van Rensselaer, did not sell land but leased it in perpetuity, subject to payments in money, kind, and services, as well as an alienation fine of one year's rent if the grantee should transfer his holding. Under this tenure, the landlord had the right of distraint and reentry if the conditions were not met: a man who failed to render the agreed payment might be ejected, not merely subject to the sale of his goods. All this, of course, was similar to copyhold tenure, much more common in England than in America.

The post-Revolutionary generation resented such survivals of feudalism sufficiently to force the New York State Legislature to appoint an investigating commission. In 1811, that commission declared the "leasehold" tenures objectionable: the right of distraint should be ended and similar grants should be forbidden in the future. No action was taken, however, and rents ran on, piling up arrearages in hard times, for Stephen Van Rensselaer was not too pressing a landlord. Then, in 1839, the "old Patroon" died, leaving the manor to be divided between his two sons and the accumulated arrears of rent as a fund to pay his debts. The tenants appointed representatives to make terms with the heirs. They refused to deal with the tenants and insisted on the payment of the arrears.

The summer following, writs of ejectment were put into the hands of the sheriff of Albany County. The tenants refused to permit service of the writs; resisted the sheriff's posse; and were served warrants for contempt. The intervention of a legislative commission in 1840, seeking a compromise, met with no success.

Disorder continued and spread from Albany to Columbia County. At the same time, the tenants and their advocates formed an antirent organization to make their grievances known to the public. While this was sending memorials to the legislature, "Indians" in sheepskin masks and calico dominoes were resisting sheriffs' attempts to serve writs for distraint. In 1844, the sheriff of Columbia County was assaulted and two people were killed in the ensuing riot. An antirent political meeting was raided and one of its leaders arrested, tried, and finally sentenced to life imprisonment.

Neither that example nor legislative provision for the arrest of "disguised persons" ended the disorder. Lawlessness spread from Albany and Columbia to Delaware County, where the transfer of the controlling interest in the land companies to new owners caused fear that excessive premiums would be exacted for the renewal of the deferred-payment privilege. In May, 1845, a particularly efficient under-sheriff was kidnapped, and in the following August, when fighting broke out at an enforced sale on a Columbia County farm, he was killed.

Delaware County was declared to be in a state of insurrection; the militia was called out; and the county jail was crowded with prisoners. At the trials in September, 28 persons were convicted of riot, 15 of unlawful assembly, and 2 of murder.

Parallel with the attempt to use riot as a political weapon, the people of the affected counties had established a newspaper, petitioned the legislature, held political meetings, and demonstrated their strength at the polls. Their influence seemed considerable enough to make conservative men wish to postpone the meeting of a convention to revise the state constitution.

The voters of the state decided in favor of a Constitutional Convention in 1846, however, and the antirent forces made a strong effort to have the new constitution declare against the validity of the landlords' titles; as they had tried to persuade the legislature into having those titles contested in the courts. The debate and constitutional provisions cited show how far they were successful. Although copyhold tenure was ended by the Constitutional Convention of 1846, the courts continued to be busy with suits and countersuits arising out of the problem until death and speculation joined to make a final settlement of the "old Patroon's" estate.

The passages here reprinted are from *The Debates and Proceedings in the New York State Convention for the Revision of the Constitution* (Albany, 1846).

The New York State Constitutional Convention of 1846

1. CREATION OF BUSINESS CORPORATIONS

THE CONVENTION resumed the consideration of the report of committee No. 17, on incorporations other than municipal and banking.

The 1st section was read as follows:

§ 1. Special laws creating incorporations or associations, or granting to them exclusive privileges, shall not be passed. But the Legislature may pass general laws by which any persons may become incorporated, on complying with the provisions to be contained in such laws. And all Corporations shall be subject to such general laws as the Legislature may, from time to time enact, not inconsistent with the provisions of this constitution.

Mr. LOOMIS opened the discussion with some historical allusions, showing the necessity of corporations, and their existence for a long period in this and other countries. The question was, if they were necessary, how they should be regulated so as to produce all necessary good and prevent unjust inequalities? He briefly alluded to the various applications made to the legislature to obtain charters, and said all this might be accomplished by a general act. He enumerated a large class of companies, whose object was not to produce profit to the company, and which might be formed in that way.—Mr. L. briefly glanced over the several provisions of the article, explaining, as he went along, the objects intended, and the evils to be guarded against—and urging that whilst it would relieve the legislature of a great deal of labor and loss of time, it would give to the community all the advantages of corporations, protect them against their excesses, and do away with all exclusive privileges and special grants.

Mr. PERKINS asked if it was designed to pass a general law to fix the rate of tolls on railroads, for some companies with but little traffic could not afford to charge rates as low as some others with much traffic.

Mr. Loomis said it was not proposed to make any such provisions.

Mr. NICOLL moved to amend by inserting in the fourth line after the word "incorporated" the following, "or be entitled to any of the privileges of incorporations;" and in the fifth line after the word "corporations" the words "or associations." He offered the amendment to give the legislature power to pass laws for the organization of societies that did not desire all the powers of an incorporation, which could not be done by this article as it stands.

Mr. Loomis said the sixth section amply provided for all that the gentleman desired.

Mr. NICOLL said the word "incorporation" had a definite meaning, and he was satisfied his amendment was necessary to meet the difficulty and set the matter at rest, so as to give societies and associations the privileges to become *quasi* incorporations.

Mr. Loomis thought no difficulty woud arise by requiring them all to become corporations.

Mr. VAN SCHOONHOVEN thought there was much force in the position taken by the gentleman from New York.

Mr. TOWNSEND having made a few observations,

Mr. Loomis withdrew his opposition to the amendments.

Mr. MURPHY thought the article would include municipal corporations. Was such the intention of the committee?

Mr. Loomis said that was not the intention of the committee, and he therefore suggested an addition of the words "other than municipal corporations," if the gentleman from Kings thought proper to move that amendment.

Mr. MURPHY said he should not, as he desired to include them.

Mr. SIMMONS thought further amendments were necesasry. The word "private" might with propriety be introduced, for public corporations, of cities, villages, &c., should not thus be restricted, and only by act of the legislature. In England, banking companies were not called incorporations—they were designated "joint stock companies." The constitution should not be stuffed full of provisions either, in relation to elymosynary institutions.

Mr. SHEPARD doubted the propriety of making the amendment suggested by the gentleman from Essex. It would deprive cities and villages which were *quasi* corporations, of privileges which were necessary and now enjoyed, and would destroy remedies for injuries arising out of a disregard of their responsibilities.

Mr. SIMMONS did not press his amendment.

Mr. VAN SCHOONHOVEN asked if under this article the legislature could not pass a general law for the construction of bridges and highways? If so he was opposed to it, inasmuch as it would give power to obstruct rivers and streams in every direction. He moved the following amendment to obviate this objection, to come in after the word "corporations" in the 5th line:—

"Except as municipal corporations, and except corporations or associations for the construction of bridges, aqueducts or viaducts over the navigable streams or public highways of the state."

Mr. TOWENSEND thought ample provision was made for this in a subsequent section.

Mr. VAN SCHOONHAVEN thought that did not give sufficient security. If they could build a bridge, he cared not what the "terms and conditions" were. He alluded to the attempt made to build a bridge at Albany across the Hudson.

Mr. STOW proposed to amend by inserting after the word "creating" in the first line, the words "manufacturing or banking"—and after the word "incorporated" in the 4th line, the words "for banking or manufacturing purposes." He said the evil was not in incorporating literary or charitable institutions, but such as were established for private gain. He pointed at the mischievous effect this section would have upon charitable, benevolent, religious, and municipal corporations.

Mr. MARVIN said the gentleman from Erie had spoken his views on this subject. He objected to any general provision which would enable companies to spring up without the supervision of the sovereign power. For years he had been opposed to corporations of a certain class, and had been disposed to watch with a jealous eye, every application for exclusive privileges of any kind! But notwithstanding this, he confessed he looked upon this section with a great deal of alarm. He pointed out the evils that would result from it. The gentleman from Troy had pointed out one evil. A general law to build bridges over creeks or rivers, would authorize the building a bridge over the Hudson at Albany on the same terms, as over the Allegany river or any creek in the state. Now were we prepared to allow this? Should not the sovereign have the right to review each application as it came up? The amendment of the gentleman from Erie obviated this objection. The principle might, without danger, be applied to banking and manufacturing corporations; but he apprehended that the state might hereafter be completely under the control of these corporations. They would be found in the legislature, in the lobbies, and everywhere, controlling the action of government.

Mr. SIMMONS alluded to the general act under which religious and medical societies and manufacturing companies were now established. He thought the state should have an eye upon the establishment and location of these corporations, to prevent them from acquiring vested rights and then defying the authority of the state government, protected as they would be by the constitution of the United States.

Mr. LOOMIS thought all the objections which had been raised were answered on the face of the article if gentlemen had only given it due consideration. There were no special powers or privileges conferred by it. The aim of the committee was to prevent artificial corporations from having or exercising higher rights or powers than those possessed by natural persons. If an individual could have no right to erect a bridge between here and Greenbush, over the Hudson river, to frighten the people of Troy, then a corporation could not do so. Mr. STOW had said that there were no complaints against other corporations than those for banking and manufacturing companies. But by turning to the Session Laws, he found in the index of one volume more than 100 laws for the incorporation of companies, of which but four or five were banking associations, the rest being such general associations as might be incorporated by general law. Religious societies were incorporated in great numbers. There were at least 10,000 incorporations over the state, all finding protection and security under general laws. It might, however, be well to amend so as to exclude municipal corporations from its provisions. . . .

Mr. MORRIS offered as a substitute for the 1st section, as follows:

1. Laws creating corporations shall not be passed, except for municipal purposes, and for the construction of such works and for the performance of such business as necessarily require sovereign prerogative powers, rights and privileges. The legislature may pass general laws under which associations may be formed for business, religious and charitable purposes.

Mr. M. explained his purpose in offering this amendment.

Mr. RHOADES pointed out the impracticability of the substitute in question. Under it, the sovereign power could not be called into exercise, until it had been ascertained that it was absolutely necessary. For instance, take the case of the New York and Erie Rail Road Company. The power of the state to take land could not be called into exercise until the experiment had been tried along the whole line, and it had been ascertained that the lands could not be bought of the individuals owing them.—Mr. R. pointed out other difficulties in the way of the adoption of such a rule.

Mr. BASCOM was inclined to think that if we were to adopt any proposition on this subject, in the Convention, the section just offered was the nearest right of any that had been submitted. Mr. B. pointed out the distinctions which must be drawn between different kind of corporations— where they were necessary and where not. He doubted whether we should be justified in going the length of this amendment. But believing it far preferable to the original section, he should vote for it.

Mr. MURPHY opposed the substitute.

Mr. RUSSELL said there were some in this Convention termed "Barnburners," but he did not believe there were many who were disposed to burn all the barns in one fire. He hoped we should not sanction any such wholesale proposition as this, but that we should go rationally to work upon the plan submitted by the gentleman from Suffolk.

Mr. SIMMONS briefly continued the debate.

Mr. MORRIS said his object was to prevent the establishment of the same kind of society here which had been described as existing in other counties. He did not wish to see women and children carrying baskets for the emolument of those who did not labor, or children from an early age trudging off to factories to toil from early day to night-fall for the good of others.—This in Great Britain did exist; and the system might in some measure be traced to the law of primogeniture. He proceeded to shew that what primogeniture did on the other side of the Atlantic, corporations would do here.

Mr. SIMMONS said in his neighborhood, the

corporations did not make so much profit as individuals in their employment.

Mr. STOW controverted Mr. MORRIS' position that corporations were detrimental to equality. He said they tended to elevate and not to depress the poor: they enabled men of moderate means to compete with the rich. He referred to the city of Cincinnati, the largest manufacturing city in the union, where the largest part of the stock was owned by the manual laborers. He also spoke of the railroad stockholders in Massachusetts for the same purpose. Unless small means were united, nobody but the very rich could enter into certain enterprises. It was therefore a misapprehension to suppose that corporations were the same in effect as the law of primogeniture. . . .

Mr. LOOMIS remarked that the state of his health had prevented his being present yesterday, when this section was adopted; and perhaps the objections which presented themselves to his mind, on the consideration he had been able to give the subject, might be removed, but to him they seemed insurmountable. The article on the subject of banking, as reported by the chairman, and as adopted by the Convention, seemed to contemplate a system of free banking, that is, it proposed to allow all persons to embark in the business of banking, by complying with certain provisions and regulations to be established by law;—it contemplated no exclusive privilege to be granted to certain favored individuals by special act of the legislature, but proposed that all men should have equal privileges of incorporating themselves, and carrying on this business under such general regulations and restrictions as should be applicable to all alike. The article as reported, and as adopted, did not propose to define these regulations and restrictions in the Constitution. What these should be was a question upon which we might differ very essentially, and was a matter proper to be left to the legislature to settle. They might prohibit the issuing of bills as money, unless the bank should have specie in its vaults to an equal amount, and by that means make all paper money actually represent an equal amount of specie for its redemption at all times. In such case paper money would be at a small premium.—This to him seemed practicable and desirable, yet it was an opinion merely, and might not be found to be advantageous on trial. He apprehended that it would not be adopted at present, whatever might be its future success. He understood the views of the distinguished chairman of the committee (Mr. CAMBRELENG) to favor free trade in banking, under general regulations. In this he fully concurred; but to him it seemed inconsistent with such views to limit by positive enactment the extent of that business. If every man and association of men were at liberty to embark in the business, and to issue bills under such securities and regulations as the law shall deem adequate and safe, he did not see that we could, with propriety, say that the aggregate amount of business should not exceed a certain fixed sum. We proposed also to allow persons to incorporate themselves for other purposes: for instance, for the manufacture of cotton goods. Would it be consistent or proper to pass a law limiting the number of yards of cloth which should be made by them? This seemed to him precisely analogous. Under such a free system, properly regulated as to the securities required, banking, like other business, might, and ought to be left to accommodate itself to the business and the capital of the country. If the securities required should be specie in the vaults of the bank for all the paper issued as money, dollar for dollar, he believed no one would apprehend an excess of paper money, and there would be no more necessity for a restriction on the aggregate of issues than there would be to prevent too great an amount of gold and silver. The amount of paper issues would necessarily depend, as the amount of specie now did, on the business and wealth of the country. Again, it seemed to him impracticable— how was each particular bank to ascertain whether the aggregate amount of circulation by all the banks in the state, at any time, was up to the aggregate limitation in the law, in order to know whether or not it might lawfully issue more bills? Should the legislature parcel out at the commencement of each year the aggregate amount of issues among all the banks then existing? It could not in that way secure the object, because institutions might arise during the year, and if more bills were wanted the number of banks would multiply to meet the demand. This fixing the amount each year, and apportioning among the several banks, was to him the only conceivable mode of even approximating to an aggregate limitation. The result of this would be to invite the united power of all the banks each year to make common assault upon the legislature to increase the amount of bank issues. Such, to his mind, would be the worst of all imaginable systems. He was unable to see or to devise any suitable restraints upon the over-issues of paper currency, consistent with equal privileges to all alike to embark in the business, other than to fix the privilege of issuing paper as money, under such regulations as to make it no object of gain to any bank. And he could see no mode of securing this object, other than requiring a specie basis to the full extent of the paper substituted for it. This would necessarily make paper money command a premium, and would secure a currency whose aggregate amount would be regulated by the demands of trade, the prices of property, and the wealth of the country. He was, for these reasons, opposed to the section as adopted, and hoped it would be reconsidered.

[The article of the Constitution affecting business corporations, as finally adopted, follows.]

ARTICLE VIII

Section 1. Corporations may be formed under general laws; but shall not be created by special act, except for municipal purposes, and in cases wherein the judgment of the Legislature, the objects of the corporation cannot be attained under general laws. All general laws and special acts passed pursuant to this section, may be altered from time to time or repealed.

Section 2. Dues from corporations shall be secured by such individual liability of the corporators and other means as may be prescribed by law.

Section 3. The term corporations as used in this article, shall be construed to include all associations and joint-stock companies having any of the powers or privileges of corporations not possessed by individuals or partnerships. And all corporations shall have the right to sue and shall be subject to be sued in all courts in like cases as natural persons.

Section 4. The Legislature, shall have no power to pass any act granting any special charter for banking purposes; but corporations or associations may be formed for such purposes under general laws.

Section 5. The Legislature shall have no power to pass any law sanctioning in any manner, directly or indirectly, the suspension of specie payments, by any person, association or corporation issuing bank notes of any description.

Section 6. The Legislature shall provide by law for the registry of all bills or notes, issued or put in circulation as money, and shall require ample security for the redemption of the same in specie.

Section 7. The stockholders in every corporation and joint-stock association for banking purposes, issuing bank notes or any kind of paper credits to circulate as money, after the first day of January, one thousand eight hundred and fifty, shall be individually responsible to the amount of their respective share or shares of stock in any such corporation or association, for all its debts and liabilities of every kind, contracted after the said first day of January, one thousand eight hundred and fifty.

Section 8. In case of the insolvency of any bank or banking association, the bill-holders thereof shall be entitled to preference in payment, over all other creditors of such bank or association.

Section 9. It shall be the duty of the Legislature to provide for the organization of cities and incorporated villages, and to restrict their power of taxation, assessment, borrowing money, contracting debts and loaning their credit, so as to prevent abuses in assessments, and in contracting debt by such municipal corporations.

2. ABOLITION OF COPYHOLD LAND TENURES

The Convention resumed the consideration of the article in relation to estates in land, the question being on the first section, as follows:

§ 1 All feudal tenures of every description, with all their incidents are abolished

§ 2 No lease or grant of agricultural land for a longer period than ten years, hereafter made, in which shall be reserved any rent or service of any kind, shall be valid

§ 3. All covenants or conditions in any grant of land whereby the right of the grantee to alien is in any manner restrained, and all fines, quarter sales, and other charges upon alienation reserved, in every grant of land hereafter to be made, shall be void.

Mr. SIMMONS moved to add to the section, as follows:

"Saving, however, all rents and services certain, which at any time heretofore have been lawfully created or reserved."

Mr. S. moved also as a second section, the following:

"All lands within this state are declared to be allodial, so that, subject only to the liability to escheat, the entire and absolute property is vested in the owners according to the nature of their respective estates"

Mr. S. remarked that what he proposed to add was already in the revised statutes, and should be in the constitution as declaratory of the true character of the tenure of estates in land.

Mr. HARRIS had no objection to the amendments. They did not change the effect of the section, in any way. It would divest the landlord of no vested rights, if he had any. It would, however, strip these tenures of certain incidents—such as fealty, and the right of distress, which were derogatory to freemen.

Mr. SIMMONS said the revisors thought it necessary to make these reservations, after the broad language of the section as it stood.

Mr. HUNT asked if this right of distress was

not just as much a vested right as the rents themselves?

Mr. SIMMONS said the supreme court had decided that a certain number of these incidents that used to be matter of right by common law, had become obsolete—such as fealty. One of these rights was that a man might beat his wife with a rod not bigger than the judge's thumb. As to the right of distress Mr. S. said this would not abolish it as a remedy. But that was a matter which did not come up here.

Mr. HARRIS said he must set the gentleman right on this point. Distress was the incident under the feudal system, by which and rent fealty were extorted. So far, he desired to abolish this incident of the tenure. The statutory remedy by distress had been already abolished.

Mr. SIMMONS said the gentleman and he did not differ at all. All of us desired to abolish this tomfoolery.

Mr. SIMMONS' amendment to the first section was adopted.

The question recurred on the section as amended.

Mr. RUGGLES said he should like to hear of what possible use these provisions could be to those who complained of the present state of things? We had here, in the revised statutes, the very thing which it was proposed to put into the constitution. It was a subject purely of legislation. There was no danger that the legislature would even interfere to give landlords any broader rights than they now had. He doubted the propriety, at this late stage of the session, of bringing forward these propositions, the effect of which it was difficult to understand—especially if they changed the law in any respect—and if not, there was no occasion for them.

Mr. SIMMONS replied that there was something in the very name of feudal tenures, and just in proportion as it meant everything or nothing, and was understood by nobody. Certainly there could be no harm in changing the name—in abolishing feudal tenures in the constitution—as had been already done, he granted, by statute. If, however, he thought it would make any real, substantial difference in pre-existing property, he would go as far as the gentleman from Dutchess to protect them. It would put an end to even the name of a thing that had its influence on the character of a people. He could tell a man from a feudal region by the very expression of his countenance. If this system of tenancy, moderate as it was, and well vested as he granted the rights of the landlord were, was general all over the state, he predicted there would be a revolution as quick

as that which took place under Charles II. Surely there could be no harm, he repeated, in declaring the tenures of all land in this state, to be allodial not feudal, saving all rights.

Mr. JORDAN said the amendment could do no harm, and it might do good. The abolition of feudal tenures, and the impossibility of creating them hereafter, was desirable. And as they were abolished by statute, so ought they to be abolished by constitution—that could not be altered as a statute could every year. When the subsequent sections came up, the friends of them would endeavor to defend them, if opposed.

Mr. RUGGLES said if feudal tenures were not already abolished by statute, and if they had not been for the last sixteen years, without the slightest possibility of their ever being restored, he should not object to putting this clause in the constitution, so as to prevent their restoration. But he had no more fears of a restoration of feudal tenures in this state, than of an attempt on the part of the legislature to establish a monarchy here. And if it led these occupants under leases to believe that their condition was changed from what it had been heretofore, it would be an injury to them to put it in the constitution. He confessed he made no objection to this first section, partly because he thought he saw in the other section very serious grounds of objection, and that the same reasoning would apply to all. If it was proper to make such legal provisions as these it was proper that it should not be done by a constitutional provision, but in such a way that, if found inconvenient, as it would be, and if all parties should exclaim against it, as they would—it might be changed. But the great objection to the first section was that it changed no right, altered no law, secured no privilege and no immunity, and only made that irrevocable, which was now nominally revocable, but which the legislature probably never would revoke. One of the modes by which the evils complained of would be gradually worn away and removed, was in the abolition of primogeniture, and in the nature of our law of descents. It would be much more conducive to the interests of these tenants to make that a part of the constitution—for there was more probability of a change there than in other respects. He repeated that his objection to this provision was that it was useless, and that if it would have any effect, it was not perceived or seen by any body. If it could operate to reconcile the complainants to the present state of things, he would vote for it; but it could not, unless they misconceived its operation. But they would not care any thing about it. It was utterly and positively useless. And hence, he would not vote for it.

Mr. VAN SCHOONHOVEN wished to have this question fixed beyond the power of the legislature to alter it. It was a principle which should be as distinctly asserted in our fundamental law as any other which had been placed there. The people interested looked for some relief in regard to these tenures—for though they had been abolished by law, they might be revived by law. And gentlemen were mistaken if they supposed that feudalism had no advocates among us. It had been openly advocated by a writer (he would not say a popular writer) of great eminence and reputation. He trusted the section would receive the unanimous vote of this body.

Mr. NICOLL thought it would be more seemly that this proposition should be in a negative form. To say that "all feudal tenures are abolished," when it is known that they had been abolished for fifteen years, appeared to him but a little short of stultification. Better say "no feudal tenure shall hereafter be established."

Mr. HARRIS did not suppose the adoption of this section would affect any man's rights, nor, if it was not adopted, that the statute would be repealed, and the feudal system re-established. His only object in desiring its adoption was to obtain for this body and the people a formal prohibition of this system, and to secure against it the moral influence of such a declaration, that the system was not congenial with our institutions, and ought to be utterly eradicated from among us.

Mr. SIMMONS moved to insert "hereby declared to be" before "abolished."

Mr. JORDAN confessed that he participated in the feeling which pervaded this whole region, and he might say in the feeling that pervaded the whole state, that it was inconsistent with the spirit and genius of our institutions, that men should hold their farms on which they were to sweat and toil, subject to the superior dominion of a lord, who for the mere pride of being their lord, and not for any pecuniary interest growing out of this relation, had determined to hold on to his dominion over this property. So far as these tenures could be brought into disrepute and yet preserve the faith of the state, and individual and private rights, it should be done. And the tenants under these leases—than whom a more honest and respectable body of men existed no where— neither desired nor expected any violation of private rights. This should be done, and done now, by a fixed rule in the constitution. The principle that these tenures should be abolished, beyond the possibility of being revived again, ought to be

insisted on here; and we ought not to turn this tenantry away with the declaration that they never would be revived again. If it would have no other effect than to gratify the tenantry, who, in the true spirit of freemen desired to see these tenures discountenanced, with all their incidents, and if we could do that without doing harm to any body, or interfering with any man's rights, we ought to do it. So if it should induce the landlord, under this expression of the Convention and the people, to part with the fee of the land, on just and equitable terms, we should have done much to alleviate the condition of those who felt degraded and oppressed by these tenures. Mr. J. alluded to the terms of some of these leases—among them these—"you shall not entertain a stranger in your house over 24 hours without giving notice to the landlord in writing." "You shall build a barn on the premises within one year, shingled with straw, and floored in a particular manner." "You shall set out 200 apple trees, and when one of them is destroyed you shall immediately replace it," be it in summer or winter. "You shall pay so much towards supporting such minister of the gospel as the landlord shall provide to cure the souls of his tenantry." "You shall go to my mill," &c., &c., and "for any violation of these conditions you shall forfeit your title."

Mr. SIMMONS said these conditions were obsolete in effect.

Mr. JORDAN: No, sir.

Mr. SIMMONS:—They are void.

Mr. JORDAN: No, not void. He could turn to a case in Johnson where Gov. Lewis recovered back a farm for a violation of one of these conditions. But he admitted that they could not be enforced here, for public opinion would frown down the attempt. He trusted there would be found enough of the spirit of freedom here to put this clause in the constitution.

Mr. BERGEN moved the previous question and there was a second.

The first section as amended was agreed to, as follows—ayes 84, nays 12.

The second section proposed by Mr. SIMMONS came up next.

Mr. KIRKLAND said there might be no danger in this; but he asked whether there would be the slightest use in it?

Mr. SIMMONS said it made the whole thing harmonious—and there could be no harm in declaring what the tenures of property should be. Indeed, there was a propriety in it, independent of any of the *isms* of the day.

Mr. RUGGLES said he should vote for this section to show that the intention in adopting the former section and this was to transfer them from the statute to the constitution, and nothing else.

The section was adopted.

The second section (now the 3rd) was read. [It forbids the leasing of agricultural lands for a longer period than 10 years.]

Mr. WHITE moved to strike out "for a longer period than ten years." Lost.

Mr. NICHOLAS moved to strike out the section.

Mr. STOW moved to amend it by striking out "ten" and inserting "twenty-one," so that infants' estates may be leased during their entire minority. Agreed to.

Mr. VAN SCHOONHOVEN moved a reconsideration.

Mr. SIMMONS thought we had better be content with the two sections already adopted.—The rest was all legislation, and should not be in the constitution.

Mr. HARRIS said he should feel obliged to vote against the section, because of the amendment adopted with so much haste upon the motion of the gentleman from Erie. If the proprietors of the lands, whose leases are about falling in, should be allowed to release for the term of twenty-one years, it would answer their purpose about as well as the present system.—He should have preferred five years.

Mr. RUSSELL voted against the amendment, but he should vote for the section, hoping, upon a reconsideration on Monday, to restore it to its original form.

Mr. HARRIS thought the argument of the gentleman from Erie should have no influence upon this question, which affected the interests of thousands of the people in this vicinity, while there would be few instances where infants would be injured by the provision.

Mr. BRUNDAGE moved to insert after "years" the words, "or natural life of the grantee." The right to dispose of one's property during one's own life, was a right which was inalienable, and which he would not divest himself of or others.

Mr. BROWN said he voted against the first section, because it abolished what had been abolished for sixteen years, and of which there was no more prospect of a revival than there was of the revival of a belief in witchcraft.

Mr. VAN SCHOONHOVEN:—That may revive.

Mr. BROWN said it might in that section of the state where these questions originated; but not in any intelligent section of the country.—Now he voted against the first section, not because he was unfriendly to the principle, but because he regarded it as a perfect piece of humbug throughout. The second section he voted for, because they belonged together. But we were now called upon

to abridge an important right, to deprive him (Mr. B) from leasing his property beyond ten years, if he had an opportunity. It was in direct opposition to the great principle which had animated all the people of this country, that of the free right of alienation of property. It was a project which no man in his senses, but for the complaints in this Antirent, would for a moment think of. It could do no benefit to any person, and might work the greatest injury to every part of the state. He admitted that these people had great ground of complaint. He should be willing that the state should contribute to relieve them, but it was a mockery to tell them you had done them good, when you prohibited people in all other sections of the state from leasing their property beyond ten years. No such provision could get his vote.

Mr. CLYDE thought the term "humbug," which the gentleman applied to the proposition which had been adopted, would belong to himself when he asserted, after his remarks upon this proposition, that he was in favor of granting any kind of relief to the tenants on these manors, and that he was strongly enlisted in their favor. He went on to show that these twenty-one year leases were much worse than leases for life; for after the tenant had spent years in its improvement, he would be subject to an ejectment.

Mr. WATERBURY continued the debate, in opposition to any law which recognized two classes in society.

Mr. NICOLL said there were lands in the vicinity of New-York and other large cities, which were rented for agricultural purposes for a long term, and in view of their being wanted hereafter for city purposes. These lands must remain unproductive under such a restriction as this. He would amend the section as it stood, by limiting its provisions to a certain quantity, say twenty-five acres, to meet these particular cases.

Mr. WORDEN attributed the superior agricultural condition of Western New York in a great degree to the fact that that section was free from the curse of any of the incidents of feudal tenure, and that the western farmer was lord of the soil he cultivated. As a question of political economy, it was well worth consideration not only that these terms should exist, but that the free alienation of property should be encouraged, by prohibitions of long leases. Even in England, it had been proposed to parliament, by a commission, to prohibit leases beyond 21 years. He went on at some length, to urge also the propriety of making these rent charges redeemable after a certain period.

Mr. LOOMIS sustained the section, as in harmony with the true policy of our government, which was to favor the free alienation of property, and to discourage the accumulation and perpetuation of large estates in particular families. He was in favor also of a shorter term than 21 years, and of an extension of the principle to city property as well as agricultural lands.

Mr. HARRIS said in reply to Mr. BROWN, that this was not the first time that it had been his fortune to have his motives impugned in the manner in which the gentleman from Orange had seen fit to do so to-day. Demagogueism had been imputed to him before—

Mr. BROWN did not accuse the gentleman of that.

Mr. HARRIS said he was the author of this proposition, and if the gentleman's remarks had any point, they referred to him.

Mr. BROWN said if the gentleman would take it be it so. He disclaimed it however.

Mr. HARRIS left the matter to those who heard the gentleman, and went on to contend for the principle of the section, as involving a great principle of political economy, that was founded in right itself, and worthy of a place in the constitution. He contended that there should be no more restrictions placed upon the alienation of real estate than upon personal estate. Property was improved by passing from hand to hand. When a man owned the land he cultivated, he would find it to his interest to add to its wealth. This inducement was not found where these long leases existed, and the lands were consequently indifferently improved.

Mr. KIRKLAND followed on the same side of the question. He believed that these tenures were disastrous to agriculture and the best interests of the State. They also tended to degrade the character of the tenants. This was an opinion which he had formed long before anti-rentism was thought of. He would not for any human inducement violate the rights of a single individual; but he believed that the interests of the state would be advanced, and the character of humanity elevated in the instance of hundreds, without the slightest injury to any one, by the adoption of some principle which should induce the landlords to part with their lands to those who occupied and tilled them. He proposed to amend by inserting "ten" in place of "twenty-one," and inserting a clause providing for the case of infant's estates.

Mr. HOFFMAN opposed the section, at some length.

Mr. BROWN in reply to Mr. HARRIS, said that in characterizing this proposition as humbug, and as unworthy of any man, he alluded not to the gentleman from Albany, but to the action of this Convention. He went on to say, that there were no people in any portion of the state who felt more acutely the hardships of these tenants upon the manors, than his own constituents; and if there was any mode, short of the abrogation of the great principles upon which the government was founded, by which they might be believed, they would be ready to adopt it. But in his opinion there was no such mode.

Mr. HARRIS moved to strike out "twenty-one" and insert "twelve." Agreed to, ayes 46, nays 35.

The section, as amended, was agreed to. Ayes 46, nays 33.

Mr. CLYDE's speech in favor of the section was as follows:

Sir, many of my immediate constituents and thousands of others in our state, groaning under the chains forged by this blistering system, are looking to this convention for some relief. They ask for nothing that is wrong—they ask you to violate no just contract—to destroy no vested rights. They ask you to engraft upon the constitution of your state the proposition now before us, which will prevent this curse in future, and will be the means of wearing out and destroying in time the present existing evil. Shall this down trodden and oppressed people ask in vain? It appears to me that every man who loves his country and desires the peace and prosperity of the state— who is a republican in principle and practice as well as in name, will rejoice to see the proposition before us adopted.

Mr. President, I will not detain the convention with any detailed account of the peculiar grievances of a portion of my constituents and those of the adjacent counties, for I am admonished that the time allowed me to speak has very nearly expired—many of them I have alluded to already, and I presume the convention is in some degree familiar with them all. I would not, however, have gentlemen on this floor fall into the mistake of fancying the abuses I would guard against, merely local and temporary subjects of excitement—an excitement which a few more months will efface, without applying the proper remedy. Much, very much, growing out of the excitement of the past is to be deeply regretted and deplored, and none regret and deplore it more than the great mass of tenants—they have never encouraged the violation of law and order—they have never asked or wished for any thing wrong or unjust— they are honest and industrious, and feel a deep interest in the prosperity of the state, and all they have ever asked or wished for is just and equal laws and equal rights. I know, sir, that by some who are directly or indirectly interested, they are charged with every thing that is wrong—and I also as well know, that their motives have been impugned—their principles have been misrepresented, and they have been most grossly slandered and libelled. But, thank Heaven, a brighter day begins to dawn, the wrongs of the down trodden and oppressed, and the principles for which they contend are better understood, and the enlightened and patriotic every where sympathize with them, and are ready to come to their relief.

Sir, I have endeavored to show that the evils I combat, either are or may be experienced any where—that time or circumstances may precipitate their development, but that their origin must be traced to that unwise policy which parcels out the earth to a favored few, and permits that few to bind down the many during their lives by the chains of leasehold servitude. So long as this system shall continue, there will be in our land luxury and pride, balanced by want and degradation, with a constant tendancy to the increase of them all. I hold it to be one of the most important duties of this convention to provide efficient safeguards against the aggravation and effectual remedies for the existence of the evils I have only had time to glance at. Give us some assurance that our children shall be permitted to eat the bread produced by their honest toil, and not be compelled to labor two days in the week for themselves and four for him who rents them the right to barely subsist upon the earth.

Sir, I will not detain the convention with any argument in favor especially of the proposition now before us, for after the kindness already extended to me, I cannot consent at this late hour of the session, to trespass farther upon its patience —but if adopted, as I hope it may be, no one, I think, can fail to perceive at first glance that it would secure effectually against this unwise system in future, and that under it the existing evil must eventually melt away.

And now, sir, permit me to ask, if the peace and quiet of our state—the great interest of agriculture—the virtue and intelligence of the sovereigns of the state where all power rests—the improvement of society—the wrongs and sufferings of the oppressed—and the safety and enduring prosperity of our state—do not all demand from us the remedy proposed against this uncertain, corrupting, debasing, degrading and slavish system of land tenures?

Let us then extend the broad shield of constitutional protection, and thus show to the oppressed and down trodden of earth, that we sympathize with them, and in the true spirit of patriotism and philanthropy come to their relief, and the relief of the whole agricultural interests of the state.

I am thankful, sir, that my ancestors were among the hardy sons of toil—that my early education and habits of life were formed under such influences, and that they who ate their bread in the sweat of their faces ever taught me to look upon agricultural pursuits as among the most honorable occupations of life. Partially to these influences, among others, no doubt, do I owe my sympathy for those of my constituents whose wrongs I have attempted to represent.

And now, sir, after mingling as I have done for months with some of the most talented, patriotic, and independent men of our state, and witnessing as I have done their persevering and untiring efforts to frame a constitution worthy of themselves and the people they represent, I can return to the quiet of my home with the full consciousness of having honestly and faithfully, according to the best of my poor abilities, discharged my duty to my constituents, and can behold in the new constitution which we shall have framed the provisions which are now sought to be engrafted upon it, the days of my retirement will be the happiest of my life, and to have contributed in an humble degree to the consummation of this object, as much honor as I shall ever desire.

THE SOUTH, THE WEST, AND NEW YORK

AT THE END of the forties, Southern interest in economic questions was expressed not only by the holding of commercial conventions, but also by the publication of De Bow's Review, the New Orleans counterpart of Hunt's Merchants' Magazine. Its founder, James Dunwood Brownson De Bow (1820–1867), had contrived to earn his way through college before he read

for the bar and became editor of the Southern Quarterly Review. Interest in projects for Southern economic independence turned him from literature and he decided to establish a commercial review.

New Orleans would be more hospitable to such a project than the declining port of Charleston, De Bow concluded and, accordingly, he carried his plan southward. After two years of struggle, he found a patron to aid him in keeping the review in print and by 1849 *De Bow's* was a success. Its prestige brought its editor appointment as superintendent of the Seventh Census, the chair of economics at the new University of Louisiana, and the post of chairman of the Knoxville Commercial Convention of 1857.

The *Review's* account of the Chicago Convention of 1847 (the first selection printed here) illustrates the growth of antagonism between sections which had long supported each other's political demands. While the South was drawing into itself and thwarting the passage of rivers and harbors bills in Congress, the West was beginning to urge federal support for internal improvements. That division was to grow during the next decade, for, though De Bow himself was in favor of federal aid to internal improvements, most of the politicians who shared his opinions were opposed to any general program. The rivalry between Chicago and St. Louis for the prize of the eastern terminus of a Pacific railroad was one of the factors delaying the execution of plans for such a road.

Intersectional links bound East as well as West to the Southern interest. Particularly close were the economic ties between New York City and the cotton-growing region. Merchants' enterprise had made New York the center of the cotton trade as early as 1815–20. For years, cotton was landed there on its way to Liverpool instead of proceeding directly eastward. New York firms thus obtained the foreign exchange with which to buy goods abroad and became the source of supply for Southern markets. Even when cotton itself began to be shipped directly from Southern ports, New York capital was invested in the vessels, many of which were built in her yards, while New York banks furnished the financial

accommodations and New York merchants still supplied the bulk of Southern purchasers.

The group interested in furthering Southern economic independence resented the position of New York in the marketing of Southern cotton and the supplying of Southern needs. Establishing a direct trade with Europe was one of the most frequently repeated demands at the Southern Commercial Conventions which met during the forties and fifties to express their dissatisfaction with the government's economic policy.

The second and third articles from *De Bow's Review* show New York's dominance in the so-called Cotton Triangle and the efforts made by Southerners to persuade their merchants to deal at home. New York merchants feared the results of Southern resentment. They had opposed the earliest attempt at rousing abolition sentiment in New York; they had supported compromise in 1850; and when the attempt to turn Kansas into a slave state had created opposition even among Democrats in 1852, New York merchants had held a mass meeting for party unity. In the uneasy days of the presidential campaign of 1860, New York merchants and bankers had joined to force an anti-Lincoln coalition. Not until a combination of Southern threats, Western purchases, and the effects of a break in the stock market had combined to cause a revulsion in opinion, did such figures as the Astors finally admit the force of Republican claims to conservatism and urge support of Lincoln rather than the coalition. New York valued its Southern trade, but it had a home and Western trade as well; and the profits to be gained from industrial expansion through a Republican victory seemed a balance for possible losses in the South.

The first and second articles reprinted here are from the *Review* for September, 1847; the third is from the *Review* for July, 1860.

Articles from DE BOW'S REVIEW

1. THE CHICAGO AND MEMPHIS CONVENTIONS

THE CALL which was made upon the Southern and Western States in the autumn of 1845, was responded to with great unanimity in the assemblage of the Memphis Convention. We attended that Convention as a delegate and in the capacity of one of its Secretaries. . . .

The CHICAGO Convention was the natural and inevitable consequence of the MEMPHIS, and we so predicted long ago. The doctrines and principles of the latter, while they harmonized with the views of many portions of the Union, did not command the sentiments of a majority of the West or of the Union. Discussed and doubted in some sections as extending too wide the domain of action, they were condemned in others as altogether restrictive and suicidal to the interests of the West.

The Memphis Convention sought to conciliate all parties, and agree on some practical plan of action—a *compromise*, if necessary—which could meet the general approval and hearty co-operation of all sections, as the very best which, under the circumstances, could be secured; the Chicago Convention, on the contrary, denounces this as impracticable and injurious, and in no respect adequate to meet the requisition and necessities of the North-west and the Lakes. It comes out boldly, cuts the Gordian knot, and declares openly *for a system of internal improvement upon western lakes and rivers, co-extensive with all the requirements of their rapidly increasing commerce*. . . .

The Chicago Convention is said to have originated in a casual meeting of Western men at Rathburn's Hotel, in New York. The Convention assembled on the fifth of July, and embraced, it is estimated, several thousand delegates. We believe no exact return of them has yet been furnished, and are rather disposed to question the number—though in such a wonderful region as the North-west, nothing is impossible. The delegates were from Maine, Massachusetts, New York, Indiana, Rhode Island, Connecticut, New Jersey, Pennsylvania, Ohio, Illinois, Michigan, Iowa, Wisconsin, Missouri, Kentucky, Georgia, and Florida. The temporary Chairman was Jos. L. Barton, of Buffalo.

A number of letters were read. Mr. Webster heartily concurred with the Convention; Silas Wright, of New York, adopts the harbor feature, but hesitates upon the rivers—some are clearly within the Constitution, others not—no general rule can be devised; Mr. Benton *first* proposed a canal from the Mississippi to the lakes by government, and was the "*first* to propose to include the upper Mississippi and Missouri within the circle of internal improvement by the government" —no arbitrary rule can be made for improvement (a dash at Mr. Calhoun); Mr. Van Buren is, of course, ambiguous; circumstances will put it out of Mr. Cass's power to be present; Mr. Clay is heartily with the Convention.

An executive committee, consisting of two from each State was appointed to collect all necessary statistics, and to memorialize Congress upon the subject of the resolutions. The Hon. Abbot Lawrence is the chairman.

The following propositions, prepared by the Hon. John C. Spencer, of New York, were adopted by the Convention:

"1. That the Constitution of the United States was framed by practical men, for practical purposes, declared in the preamble—'to provide for the common defense, to promote the general welfare, and to secure the blessings of liberty;' and was mainly designed to create a government, whose functions should be adequate to the protection of the common interests of all the States, or of two or more of them, which could not be maintained by the action of the separate States. That in strict accordance with this object, the revenues derived from commerce were surrendered to the General Government, with the express understanding that they should be applied to the promotion of those common interests.

"2. That among these common interests and objects, were 1st, Foreign commerce, to the regulation of which, the powers of the States, severally, were confessedly inadequate; and 2d, internal trade and navigation, wherever the concurrence of two or more States was necessary to its prosecution, or where the expense of its maintenance should be equitably borne by two or more States, and where, of course, those States must necessarily have a voice in its regulation; and hence resulted the constitutional grant of power to Congress, 'to regulate commerce with foreign nations, and among the States.'

"3. That being thus possessed both of the means and of the power, which were denied to the States respectively, Congress became obligated by every consideration of good faith and common justice, to cherish and increase both the kinds of commerce thus committed to its care, by expanding and extending the means of conducting them, and of affording them all those facilities, and that protection which the States individually would have afforded, had the revenues and authority been left to them.

"4. That this obligation has ever been recognized from the foundation of the government, and has been fulfilled partially, by erecting lighthouses, building piers for harbors, break-waters and sea walls, removing obstructions in rivers, and providing other facilities for the commerce carried on from the ports on the Atlantic coast; and the same obligations have been fulfilled to a much less extent, in providing similar facilities for 'commerce among the States;' and that the principle has been most emphatically acknowledged to embrace the western lakes and rivers, by appropriations for numerous lighthouses upon them, which appropriations have never been questioned in Congress, as wanting in constitutional authority.

"5. That thus, by a series of acts which have received the sanction of the people of the United States, and of every department of the Federal Government, under all administrations, the common understanding of the intent and objects of the framers of the Constitution, in granting to Congress the power to regulate commerce, has been confirmed by the people, and this understanding has become as much a part of that instrument, as any one of its most explicit provisions.

"6. That the power 'to regulate commerce with foreign nations, and among the States, and with the Indian tribes,' is, on its face, so palpably applicable in its whole extent, to each of the subjects enumerated equally, and in the same manner, as to render any attempt to make it more explicit, idle and futile; and that those who admit the rightful application of the power to foreign commerce by facilitating and protecting its operations, by improving harbors, and clearing out navigable rivers, cannot consistently deny that it authorizes similar facilities to 'commerce among the States.'

"7. That 'foreign commerce' itself is dependent upon internal trade, for the distribution of its freights, and for the means of paying for them; so that whatever improves the one, advances the other; and they are so inseparable, that they should be regarded as one. That an export from the American shore to a British port in Canada, is as much foreign commerce as if it had been carried directly to Liverpool; and that an exportation to Liverpool neither gains nor loses any of the characteristics of foreign commerce, by the directness or circuity of the route, whether it passes through a custom-house on the British side of the St. Lawrence, or descend through that river and its connecting canals to the ocean, or whether it passes along the artificial communications and natural streams of any of the States to the Atlantic.

"8. That the General Government, by extending its jurisdiction over the lakes and navigable rivers, subjecting them to the same laws which prevail on the ocean, and on its bays and ports, not only for the purpose of revenue, but to give security to life and property, by the regulation of steamboats, has precluded itself from denying that jurisdiction for any other legitimate regulation of commerce. If it has power to control and restrain, it must have power to protect, assist, and facilitate; and if it denies the jurisdiction in the one mode of action, it must renounce it in the other.

"9. That in consequence of the peculiar dangers of the navigation of the lakes, arising from the want of harbors for shelter, and of the Western rivers, from snags and other obstructions, there are no parts of the United States more emphatically demanding the prompt and continued care of the government, to diminish those dangers, and to protect the property and life exposed to them; and that any one who can regard provisions for those purposes as sectional, local, and not national, must be wanting in information as to the extent of the commerce carried on upon those lakes and rivers, and of the amount of teeming population occupied or interested in that navigation.

"10. That having regard to relative population, and to the extent of commerce, the appropriations heretofore made for the interior rivers and lakes, and the streams connecting them with the ocean, have not been in a just and fair proportion to those made for the benefit of the ports, harbors, and navigable rivers of the Atlantic ports; and that the time has arrived, when this injustice should be corrected in the only mode in which it can be done, by the united, determined, and persevering efforts of those whose rights have been overlooked.

"11. That independent of this right to protection of 'commerce among the States,' the right of 'common defense' guarantied by the Constitution, entitles those citizens inhabiting the country bordering upon the interior lakes and rivers, to such safe and convenient harbors as may afford shelter to a navy, whenever it shall be rendered necessary by hostilities with our neighbors; and that the construction of such harbors cannot safely be delayed to the time which will demand their immediate use.

"12. That the argument most commonly urged against appropriations to protect 'commerce among the States,' and to defend the inhabitants of the frontiers, that they invite sectional combinations to insure success to many unworthy objects, is founded on a practical distrust of the republican principles of our government, and of the capacity of the people to select competent and honest representatives. That it may be urged with equal force against legislation upon any other subject involving various and extensive interests. That a just appreciation of the rights and interests of all our fellow-citizens, in every quarter of the Union, disclaiming selfish and local purposes, will lead intelligent representatives to such a distribution of the means in the treasury, upon a system of moderation and ultimate equality, as will in time meet the most urgent wants of all, and prevent those jealousies and suspicions which threaten the most serious dangers to our confederacy.

"13. That we are utterly incapable of perceiving the difference between a harbor for shelter and a harbor for commerce, and suppose that a mole or pier which will afford safe anchorage and protection to a vessel against a storm, must necessarily improve such harbor, and adapt it to commercial purpose.

"14. That the revenues derived from imports on foreign goods belong to all the people; and the public lands being the common heritage of all our citizens, so long as all these resources continue, the imposition of any special burden on any portion of the people, to obtain the means of accomplishing objects equally within the duty and the competency of the General Government, would be unjust and oppressive.

"15. That we disavow all and every attempt to connect the cause of internal trade and of 'commerce among the States' with the fortunes of any political party, but that we seek to place that cause upon such immutable principles of truth, justice, and constitutional duty as shall command the respect of all parties, and the deference of all candidates for public favor."

2. SOUTHERN PATRONAGE TO SOUTHERN IMPORTS

. . . The political sentiment of the South is decidedly and universally against the North, but the more powerful pecuniary and commercial sentiment has shown itself to be with the North and opposed to the South, and if continued will lead to our ruin, both economically and politically. It is so thoroughly interwoven in the body politic, that it may be seen in the every-day acts of our people, from the lowest grade of society to the highest. If additional evidence is necessary, to prove the positions above assumed, what better proof do we want than the fact that an humble, unpretending country or village merchant, who has not the means of going beyond Charleston to

lay in his stock of merchandise, should consider it necessary to obliterate every mark on a box which would betray the fact that his stock of goods was purchased in Charleston, and not in New-York. It has, for years past, been a common thing for country merchants to request that their packages should be so marked as to leave no clue to their having been bought in Charleston. Does not every one know that a widespread public sentiment has long existed all over the South, which has caused a preference to be given to articles purchased at the North? It was quite a plume in the cap of a trader, to be able to say he was just from New-York, and had purchased his supplies there. So highly has that advantage been esteemed, by all classes of men, that the idea of enabling a merchant to go to New-York, to lay in his stock, would enlist the kindly friendship of rich endorsers, and if anything could induce a board of bank directors to make an extraordinary effort to *accommodate*, it would most surely be in the *good cause* of enabling a neighboring merchant to transfer his custom from Charleston to New-York. That such a course is wrong all must see and admit; yet matters have been suffered to run so long in that direction, that a commercial and political power has been created at the North, which now threatens to annihilate us.

Why should a Southern country or village merchant go to New-York to purchase his supplies? Almost every country merchant who visits Charleston has a through ticket to New-York in his pocket. Some buy a few boxes of goods in Charleston; others will be drifted on North by meeting with the slightest impediments in the way of trade in Charleston. And many, from a desire to mix in the great whirlpool of fashion, sightseeing, &c., pay their $30 passage money to and from New-York, and cannot resist the temptation of doing something more than is embraced in the stale idea of buying a stock of goods in South Carolina. While others, under the delusion that they can buy cheaper in New-York, go there year after year to get cheated every time and never find it out.

To those acquainted with the nature and complicated operations of commerce, it is plain enough to be seen that Charleston can undersell New-York, even if the goods be first landed there, and pay a duty to the New-York custom-house. Goods are either imported by large dealers, or sent out by foreigners to agents, to sell by the case or large quantity. These importing houses, or agents, are bound to the jobbing trade not to break packages, or sell in such small quantities as to interfere with their customers. Any importer, or foreign agent, who violates this rule, must expect to lose the custom of the jobbing trade, not only of New-York, but of Charleston, Chicago, Cincinnati, St. Louis, Louisville, Nashville, and other jobbing cities and towns scattered over our vast country. Now, we wish our readers to understand the groundwork: That imported goods first come into hands that are bound by the strongest ties to the wholesale dealer, more commonly termed jobbing merchant, who purchases by the package and retails out to merchants, a class of smaller dealers, located in towns, villages, and country places; this class of men sell immediately to the customer. The jobber, in turn, is bound to this latter class of merchants not to interfere with their customers, by selling small quantities.

We will now try to illustrate the subject by following a Southern merchant to New-York, where he may desire to purchase an assorted stock of goods amounting from ten to thirty or fifty thousand dollars; even the last named sum will not procure him admission into an importing or agent's stock. If he insists on buying from such houses, the price will be fixed at much higher rates than the jobbing merchant pays, and the custom of not breaking packages will almost invariably rule him out; and he is, of necessity, thrown into the hands of the jobbing merchants of New-York, the keenest and most adroit dealers known in the world—men who live by their wits, and who cannot sustain themselves except by exorbitant profits. Just for a moment look at things as they really are. A jobbing merchant in New-York, paying from fifteen to thirty thousand dollars a-year for store rent; clerk hire, from one to six thousand dollars a-year; having two or three partners in the concern, each living in palaces at the most princely expenditure—compare this picture with the same class of merchants in Charleston, where the most commodious and best-located stores rent from fifteen hundred to two thousand dollars, and where clerks are now begging for situations; willing to pay their own board, work, and receive no pay for the first year or two, while the most expert receive for their services but from five hundred to two thousand dollars a-year. Can you not see that the Charleston jobber is able to sell cheaper than the New Yorker?

Merchants of the city, town, village and country! consider and say whether you have not been treading unprofitable paths, which, if persevered in, will ultimately lead your country to ruin. Your notions of mercantile thrift are warped by errors as glaring as those by which abolition fanaticism is urged on at the North. The Charleston wholesale merchants, as a class, have as good credit as any in the world. They purchase largely, and procure their stocks at the lowest rates.

The trade of New-York is of a different class altogether; one half and probably three-fourths of them live from hand to mouth, under exorbitant and extraordinary expenses; they buy to-day and sell to-morrow, are in many instances reckless of character, and pay higher prices for their goods than good reliable merchants do. If they cheat a man this year who lives fifteen hundred miles off, and lose his custom, what do they care? —the next year brings two in his place. So great are the profits made by merchants in New-York, that every six or eight years of fair sailing and undisturbed commercial prosperity, transforms a large number of those men of straw-jobbing merchants—into millionaires. But when a monetary crisis overtakes them, they are swept off into bankruptcy by hundreds.

New-York is the last place to which an inexperienced, impractical merchant should venture to purchase a stock of goods, and there is no reason whatever why Charleston, New-Orleans, Mobile, Savannah, and Augusta, should not become points of distribution, and be relied on entirely for supplies. Charleston can become so without waiting to establish lines of steamers to Europe. If she can obtain her fair proportion of the jobbing and distributing trade, she will soon number 200,000 in population, and the lines of steamers will follow, and so will the ability to build railroad outlets.

The mere importing business cannot make a city. If New-York were to lose the jobbing trade, which rightfully belongs to Southern cities, she would immediately retrograde in population, or remain for a long time stationary. If her commerce was confined to importing houses and foreign agencies, that city would settle down to be the Liverpool of the United States, instead of the "London of America."

In order to render Charleston a great centre of distribution, and a fortress of political power, all that is requisite is the assurance of receiving in future all the trade that naturally belongs to her, with the hearty co-operation and patronage of Southern merchants; with this she would be prepared to make a doubled or quadrupled trade.

The present merchants would most willingly enlarge their trade fourfold, and the prospect of increased business would induce others to embark, and the money power would follow in the train. That portion of the money capital that belongs South, and which has centred in New-York to buy up Southern merchants' paper with, would, as a matter of course, be transferred to Charleston, and an extended jobbing trade would bring with it large direct imports, of the heavier articles not sent to agents in this country, such as iron, salt, coffee, and many European articles made only to supply orders.

We are rejoiced to see the work of reformation already commenced, and we trust that such assurances of permanent increase of patronage to Charleston merchants will be given, that their usual fall stock may be doubled. And although it is said that some of the hotel keepers feed their guests on turkeys and chickens fattened in abolition Ohio, and brought to Charleston by the way of New-York, the change in the mercantile currents, which are so devoutly desired, will, no doubt, bring us back to poultry of our own raising, with which our back country abounds.

But how is this change to be effected? It can be done only through the people—the great body of consumers. They should meet in primary assemblies, and put the mark of reprobation and proscription on every merchant who will not obey the call to abstain from a traffic that is leading to our impoverishment and political ruin. Each individual who buys a coat, a silk dress, a piece of muslin, or any article from a home dealer—and gives his orders to a Southern mechanic and nurseryman, instead of sending it to the North— lends his or her aid in cutting off some of the springs. And the whole South, collectively acting together, will dry up many considerable branches, if not the great stream which carries away millions of our treasure, and is fast drifting us commercially and politically into the vortex of Northern power. To be politically independent of the free States, we must render ourselves commercially so, for commerce holds the sceptre that rules the world. The despots who have for ages swayed their power over nations of Europe, have been compelled to give way to it, and all nations bow to the unbounded power of commerce— which has whitened every sea with its sails, and driven by the wings of steam power, is now traversing every country known to civilized man. Her power will subdue and overrun the Chinese empire, and will ultimately civilize and Christianize benighted Africa, as well as every other inhabited portion of the globe. One of the greatest despotisms on earth has been forced into a strife for pre-eminence in manufactures and commerce.

The wise men who have the power of control in Russia, have very considerably come to the conclusion, that, by agriculture alone, their country cannot keep pace with the growing power of manufacturing and commercial nations; hence the immense efforts of that nation to introduce manufactures, railroads, and all the appliances necessary to an extended commerce with the world.

In all civilized nations, the political power has yielded to the sceptre of commerce; and no nation in modern times has become commercial without the aid of manufactures; and so surely as we follow up the system which is advocated by many, as the true policy of the South, of remaining an exclusively agricultural people, neglecting all other industrial occupations, and buying from others the commonest necessaries of life, and wearing out and exhausting our soil as fast as we can, so surely will we become vassals to some power. If we release ourselves from one, we must immediately fall into the hands of another.

To be independent we must be our own merchants. Let us, then, set about a reformation that shall disenthral us from the tyranny of the North. Let us resolve to patronize no merchant who will refuse his aid toward building up a distributing city at the South. Let us encourage the extension of manufactures, and by all means encourage and give our patronage to every article the product of Southern domestic industry.

3. Direct Trade of Southern States with Europe

The committee of ten, to which has been referred the resolution of the Convention, directing them to ascertain and report whether goods have not been imported and sold at the southern seaports, upon as good terms, and at as fair rates, as they can be procured at the northern—and whether the country merchants cannot *now* procure at the southern sea-ports as full a supply and as good assortments, upon as fair terms, and as favorable periods of payment, as they can be procured elsewhere—and whether there exist any and what advantages in making purchases from the direct importers at the South, respectfully submit the following report:

The inquiries to be made, in the foregoing resolution, are deeply interesting to all the friends of southern direct trade. If facts will justify affirmative answers to them, the success of the enterprise, if persevered in, is unquestionable, unless defeated by the untoward action of the General Government, or a dispensation of Providence against which human prudence affords no safeguard. The facts necessary to entirely correct conclusions on these inquiries, are many, and exceedingly complicated, requiring for their collections, consideration and arrangement, more time and opportunities than the present occasion affords; and your Committee being composed of merchants, dealers, and planters, from the interior of the States and territory represented in this Convention, labor under many difficulties, in the investigation in the result of which, the Committee, in common with all they represent, have a deep interest, being nothing less than the discovery of those markets where they can sell their staples for the highest, and buy the goods they consume at the lowest prices. Such time and opportunities as they possessed have been employed to the best of their ability, and they submit the result to the consideration of the Convention.

The Southern States have at all times been the producers of staples of great richness and value in the commerce of the world, which from their earliest settlement as colonies, gave them a direct trade with foreign nations, of an extent and importance greatly beyond their proportionate population. The growth and increase of this trade kept more than even pace with the increase of population, and enriched them with a prosperity before unparalleled. Since the Revolution, and during the period of free trade, it grew and expanded to an immense extent, as has been developed in the report of the Committee of twenty-one already submitted to the Convention. The settlement of new States south-west and west, of similar pursuits, institutions and staples, have swelled the products of their industry, until they are more than three-fourths of the domestic exports, and constitute to that extent the basis of all the foreign commerce of the United States.

The fiscal action of the General Government in the collections and disbursements of its revenue, has always been unfavorable to Southern commerce, and when the additional burdens of the protective system was thrown upon the industry and trade of the planting States, the disastrous effects were apparent in the deserted cities and ruined prospects which blighted the prosperity and broke the spirits of her people. The direct trade which was her own by every law of commerce and nature, and which should have grown and increased every year, grew less and less until it almost disappeared, being by this unpropitious policy transferred to the Northern ports and people. Discouraged by these burdens, our capital sought more propitious locations for its employment, or engaged in other business—our merchants and capitalists removing to the Northern ports with their funds, or withdrawing from commerce and investing in other employments, while others, discouraged by their example, were not found to supply their places and attempt the business they had been forced to abandon. The importing merchants of the South became an almost extinct race; and her direct trade, once so great,

flourishing and rich, dwindled down to insignificance.

It would seem to be undeniable that if the same state of things by which these disastrous blows were dealt with such fatal effect upon our direct trade, continues to exist, the South cannot recover what it lost under their operation. It becomes therefore an important point to be determined whether any and what changes or modifications of these circumstances have taken place, which will enable the South again to enter into a struggle for her own direct trade with foreign nations, with any reasonable hope or fair prospect of success.

That such changes have for several years been in progress is most certain, slowly and gradually, but certainly and beneficially. The compromise act has already produced great amelioration, and every biennial reduction is an impulse to enterprise and trade, which has already caused much capital to return, and again filled the old channel with something like its ancient currents of business. The legislatures of the Planting States have, with prudent forecast, availed themselves of the opportunity, and by wise legislation done much to encourage enterprise, and aid individual efforts in the patriotic effort; and it is hoped will yet do much more for this great and vital measure, by lightening the remaining burthens which oppress commercial capital in the heavy taxation on its employment. Lightened of much of that oppressive taxation imposed by the national legislation, and animated by the prospect of still farther reductions, and a well-founded confidence in the fostering care of the State legislatures, the race of importing merchants has revived, and, as individual and partnership firms, re-appeared in our cities, and have embarked large capitals with great spirit in the business. It gives the Committee great pleasure to add, that they have every reason to believe, that their operations have been conducted with the energy and prudence which deserves and has been crowned with a success as advantageous to them as it is beneficial to the country.

If we consider the general principles which naturally regulate trade, we see no reason why foreign goods used in Southern consumption, could not be bought by our own merchants at the place of their production, and brought direct to our markets as cheaply as they can be taken to the Northern markets by their merchants. A careful comparison of all the elements of cost, could they be clearly ascertained, might enable the committee to arrive at exact conclusions, but it is impossible for the committee in the time permitted for the inquiry, to attain such certainty in the multitude of circumstances which must be considered—and even were it possible in any given state of things, and at any fixed day, the constant changes of circumstances, the fluctuations of markets, and the thousand occurrences every hour arising to disturb the regularity of trade, the exchanges and the money market, would perhaps, the very next day, vary that statement and present another condition of things—and so also, if all the foreign goods brought into the country for its consumption, were imported by regular importing merchants, more certainty might be attainable. It happens however, so far from this being the case, that immense amounts of foreign goods are often poured into the United States, upon the great points of importation, under circumstances of commercial pressure and distress, producing great disturbance, and fluctuation of prices. At such periods, the manufacturers, if pressed for money, instead of at once reducing the price of goods at their warehouse (which is considered the last thing to be done), generally prefer to make sacrifices of their surplus stocks at distant points—they sometimes ship to foreign ports and sell by their own agents, on their own account, in which case they can lessen the duties by making out their invoices at lower rates, and also escape the addition which is put on the merchant by our revenue laws for the expenses on the invoice, being about five per cent.; they sometimes make loans from mercantile houses having branches in other countries, and deposit their surplus goods as security, upon the agreement that they are to be sold for whatever they will bring, to refund the advance, if they are not paid when due. Great quantities of these goods and also of failing merchants are thrown upon the Northern markets, especially New-York, and sold at auction for whatever they will bring—great sacrifices are inevitable, and at such times, purchases may be made at prices which would prove ruinous to the regular importing merchant, whether northern or southern. Such instances should be considered as departures from regular trade, and as exceptions to its general, regular and steady course; although they occasionally not merely influence, but control business and prices, such transactions are not fair examples for regular business—and whether they are beneficial in the long run to the trade and prosperity of a place may well be doubted, as the tendency is to disturb commerce and destroy the regular importing merchant. . . .

It is manifest that the merchant who buys his goods cheapest, and has fewest burthens and expenses upon his business, ought to be able to sell his goods at the lowest prices. It is fair to presume, that what can be done, has been and will be done by our merchants, in fair competition, for the regular trade with their northern brothers. Let us see what are the elements which enter into the solution of the problem—which enjoys the greatest advantages in this honorable rivalry.

In carrying out this comparison, it will be most satisfactory to select places which may be considered fair exponents of the two sections of the Union, and the committee therefore select New-York for the North, and Charleston for the South. In selecting Charleston, the committee are influenced by the fact that being there now, they are enabled to procure more information, authentic and at first hand, as to it, than of any other southern importing city; but it is believed that the same general principles and facts, applicable to its trade, may, with such modifications as will readily suggest themselves in each case, be applied to the other southern importing cities respectively.

In the South, the ports are good and safe, and open all the year to ships. In the North many and considerable obstructions exist during a part of it, from cold and ice. The same may be said of their internal communications, the rivers and canals of the North being frozen, and the railroads obstructed by snows and often for considerable periods of time. In the summer, the southern ports are not so healthy, and their intercourse with the interior markets is less in amount and activity. The establishment of railroads, permitting the most rapid travel and perfect safety through the unhealthy districts adjacent, has greatly diminished the impediments of summer trade, especially with Charleston, and will, very soon, with other southern cities, to which similar improvements are extending. New-York enjoys great advantages from the perfect system of communication with foreign parts and her customers at home, her immense capital and custom, her commercial connections with Europe, and most especially in the greater facilities her banks give her merchants for credits in Europe, and by discounts at home for long periods and on their customers' notes. Were the only question, which city can sell its merchandise cheapest *in its own stores*, the answer would probably be that New-York can generally sell as low or lower than Charleston. But the true question for the southern country merchant is, can he lay down his goods at his home cheaper from New-York than from Charleston, or any other southern port? If he buys lower in New-York, and the expenses of getting them home make them cost more than he could get them at from the southern port, his own interest, as well as patriotism, will influence him to deal at his own ports. In coming to a correct understanding of the cost of the goods at the two markets, we must look into the circumstances which create cost and go to fix the prices of merchandise—all the expenses attending traffic must be charged in the profits and taken out of them, and consequently enhance the cost of its merchandise. These expenses, in some important respects, are believed to be greater in New-York than Charleston—and the following views are illustrative of this opinion. The foreign goods imported into this country are paid for chiefly by southern produce or bills of exchange, drawn on it. To buy this, the northern merchant must employ his factor or commission agent, and pay from 1 to 2 per cent. commissions; —the southern importer is on the spot where the produce is, and buys, in person, this produce or bills, saving that commission. In general, exchanges on Europe are lowered by 1 to 2 per cent. at the South—at present it is not so, but the general experience has been that way; and the present difference in favor of the North may be ascribed, in a considerable extent, to the great amount of American loans negotiated through New-York, creating a larger fund to draw on, a state of things temporary in character. House rents and store rents are believed to be twice cr three times as high in New-York as they are in Charleston;—clerks' wages are higher; and the expenses of families and living considerably greater. Another charge, which, it is believed, goes considerably to enhance the price of goods, grows out of the manner in which the mercantile business is done in New-York. The importer there, as a general rule, does not deal directly with the country merchant. He imports in bales and packages, which he does not break, but sells in bales and packages, quantities too large for country merchants. The business is divided also into almost as many distinct classes of importers, as there are distinct classes of goods. Assortments in quantities to suit the dealer or country merchant, can only be had from another class of merchants, called jobbers. The jobbers, as they want for immediate retail, buy from the importers by the bale or package, and breaking them, sell to country dealers in quantities to suit their assortments. They are the regular customers of the importers, and if the importers sell to the country merchants, it is usually for cash, or on such rates and terms as will not interfere with the jobbers, who are their chief dependence, and necessary to their business. These transactions, although they assume many variations in the forms of business, may be illustrated as follows: The jobber buys of the importer and gives his bankable

note payable at six or eight months, which can be converted at the banks to meet the importer's engagements—the jobber takes the country merchant's note, payable usually a short time before his note to the importer is due. The importer's profits are seldom as low as 10 per cent. often as high as 25, and may safely be averaged at 17½— the profits of the jobber are estimated at the same, or perhaps a greater per cent., because he has to include the loss which he must submit to, in converting the paper of the country merchant into available funds, amounting to about 4 per cent. on southern notes, which occurs this way—if the note is offered for discount at a New-York bank, that sum is taken off the face of the note for discount risk, expense of collection and exchange; or if the southern merchant gives his note payable in New-York, the exchange, risk of remittance and agency will cost as much and should be added to the costs of his goods. In Charleston, from 1 to 2 per cent. only is taken off, according to the distance the makers live from the city. In Charleston the country merchant deals directly with the importer, who combines in his business all that is done in New York by both importer and jobber; his profits may be said to average from 20 to 33 per cent.. greater than either of them singly, but probably not greater, if as great, as both combined. They have two establishments, and probably each his family to support, he only one. But admitting that generally goods may be purchased lower, notwithstanding, in New York, yet there are other items of calculation to be taken into the account. The country merchant is supposed to make his own selections in person—it will cost him considerably more, and take longer time both for him to go and return, and for his goods to be brought from New-York—the interest which occurs on his money while idle—the risks, insurance and cost of shipping to and landing at Charleston, and commissions on forwarding to him when landed at the several points of stoppage on the way to his home, are no inconsiderable elements of price to enhance the cost of the goods . . .

For the want of packets and shipping, much of the import trade of Charleston is made by her own merchants through New-York; the goods are bought by them in Europe, shipped in New-York packets to New-York—unloaded there, and re-shipped to Charleston; in all such cases, there are increased expenses of commissions, insurance and freight on the voyage, and delay which is still more injurious; the goods therefore cost the importer more than similar goods coming direct to Charleston, but still are cheaper than he could buy them in New-York. Another and important consideration is the credit which can be had in the two places. It has been already shown, that, as a general rule, the credits given to the country merchant in New-York will average from six to eight months. In Charleston, during the past season, the credits given by the wholesale merchants have gone from six to twelve months, averaging perhaps nine or ten months. The medium of payments is not less important—payments in New-York are by bank notes at a discount, or exchange at a premium. In Charleston the committee are informed, that the bank notes of most of the Southern States are taken at par, constituting a saving of from 1 to 3 per cent.

After weighing all statements and arguments submitted to the committee, they have come decidedly to the opinion that foreign goods may be imported into, and sold at the Southern ports as cheaply and upon as good terms, as at the North; and perhaps it is not going too far to say, upon better—an extensive inquiry among them enables the committee to say, that such is the opinion generally entertained by the best-informed merchants. . . .

CONDITION OF THE WORKING CLASS

BY THE fifties, the Utopians had lost their following among the workers, and labor's own trade union organizations—badly organized and poorly led—had failed. The sudden influx of large numbers of European immigrants, who swelled the labor reserve, and the rise in prices —due to returning business prosperity and California gold—only worsened the condition of labor. It reached its low point in American annals and the decade, as Norman J. Ware properly declares, saw the "degradation of the worker."

In 1847, a labor paper *The Voice of Industry* stated: ". . . the laboring man's prospect ahead just now is most drear and disheartening. Provisions, such as flour, meat, potatoes, butter, meal are nearly 100 per cent higher than ordinary prices, fuel is extraordinarily high and rents have advanced. . . . The mechanic or laborer who has a family to support finds that to-day's wages only pay to-day's expenses; he can lay up nothing for the winter season when his expenses are greatly increased, and in the laborers' case, work and wages are always diminished."

The columns of Horace Greeley's New York *Daily Tribune* substantiated this assertion. Always sympathetic to the cause of labor —although all he himself could offer was homesteadism and protectionism—Greeley followed the course of prices carefully. He demonstrated that by 1851-52 wholesale prices

were back again where they had been in 1840; and from then on they mounted sharply. These findings were confirmed in the later Aldrich Report of the nineties (U.S. Senate Document, 52d Congress, 2d Session, Vol. I, No. 1294) which showed an increase of 19.3 in the wholesale price index over twenty years, as follows:

1840–1844	91.0
1845–1849	90.1
1850–1854	99.1
1855–1859	110.3

Retail prices moved up even more, as Greeley demonstrated with this analysis of prices in his issue of Feb. 21, 1854:

	1848	1854
Wheat Flour	$6.25	$8.81
Rye Flour	3.62	6.12
Corn Meal	2.37	4.50
Candles, mold	.12	.15
Coal (anthracite)	5.75	7.00
Coffee, Brazil	.7⅛	.11
Fish, Dry Cod	3.68	3.37
Mackerel No. 1	8.81	15.50
Molasses N.O.	.26	.29
Pork Mess	10.18	15.75
Beef Mess	8.25	11.50
Lard	.6¾	.10
Sugar	.4½	.5
Cheese	.8	.11
Rice	3.35	4.75
Sugar	.4½	.5

And what of wages? While money wages gradually improved, real wages actually declined during the fifties. Writing in the second decade of the twentieth century and using the admittedly incomplete date of the Aldrich Report, W. I. King in his *Wealth and Income of the United States* (New York, 1915), demonstrated the decline in real hourly wages with these index figures. (Base 1890–1899.)

Year	Index of Money Wages	Index of Commodity Prices	Index of Wages or Purchasing Power
1850	47.1	100.6	46.8
1851	47.6	111.2	42.8
1852	48.8	110.4	44.2
1853	49.1	118.4	41.5
1854	51.4	118.4	43.4
1855	52.3	123.1	42.5
1856	53.1	126.6	41.9
1857	54.2	128.5	42.2
1858	53.0	127.6	41.6
1859	53.5	116.0	46.1
1860	54.3	112.7	48.1

Money wages were very low. Cotton-mill operatives were getting $2 and $3 weekly; shoemakers, printers, hatters and cabinetmakers were getting $4, $5, and $6 weekly; the "aristocrats of labor," the building-trades workers—carpenters, plasterers and bricklayers—were getting $10. How inadequate these wages were Greeley demonstrated when, in his issue of May 27, 1851, he published a week's budget for a family of five:

Barrel of flour, $5.00, will last eight weeks	$0.62½
Sugar, 4 lbs. at 8 cents a pound	.32
Butter, 2 lbs. at 31½ cents a pound	.62½ [sic]
Milk, two cents per day	.14
Butcher's meat, 2 lbs. beef per day at 10¢ per lb.	$1.40
Potatoes, ½ bushel	.50
Coffee and tea	.25
Candle light	.14
Fuel, 3 tons of coal per annum, $15.00; charcoal, chips, matches, etc., $5.00 per annum	.40
Salt, pepper, vinegar, starch, soap, soda, yeast, cheese, eggs	.40
Furniture and utensils, wear and tear	.25
Rent	3.00
Bed clothes	.20
Clothing	2.00
Newspapers	.12
Total	$10.37

"I ask," said Greeley, "have I made the working-man's comforts too high? Where is the money to pay for amusements, for ice-creams, his puddings, his trips on Sunday up or down the river in order to get some fresh air, to pay the doctor or apothecary, to pay for pew rent in the church, to purchase books, musical instruments?"

The workers began to organize on a crafts' basis and these unions were more permanent. More important, with the introduction of mechanization on a wide scale during the sixties and after, productivity vastly increased and not only money wages but also real wages went up strikingly.

In the 1850s, however, few programs of a practical nature were placed before the workers. Nothing demonstrates this better than the benevolent advice offered by the New York Association for Improving the Condition of the Poor, one of the early charity organization societies. The A.I.C.P. had been founded in the early forties to prevent pauperization by indiscriminate alms-giving. Its volunteer "visitors" did not limit their activities to making certain that only legitimate objects of charity were relieved, however; they also attempted to restore their "cases" to self-respect by teaching them proper methods of self-support.

For such work, the tract, *The Economist*, and *The Way to Wealth* (first published in 1847), proved effective—or so the "visitors" believed—in changing for the better the domestic habits of many "idle, filthy, improvident" families. *The Economist* was frequently reprinted and, along with *The Way to Wealth*, "a Poor Richard" properly equipped with Scriptural references, represents one of the A.I.C.P.'s earliest efforts at coming to grips with the problems of the "poor."

The Way to Wealth

BY THE ASSOCIATION FOR IMPROVING THE CONDITION OF THE POOR

[*Introduction.* THE "Association for Improving the Condition of the Poor," wishing to extend the usefulness of this admirable little treatise, have published it in the present form. It is especially adapted by its clearness, concise expression and happy illustrations, to accomplish the objects for which it was written. Regarding it, however, as wanting in religious sentiment and feeling, they have endeavored to supply that defect, by inserting a few appropriate texts.]

I HAVE HEARD that nothing gives an author so great pleasure, as to find his works respectfully quoted by others. Judge, then, how much I must have been gratified by an incident I am going to relate to you. I stopped my horse, lately, where a great number of people were collected at an auction of merchants' goods. The hour of the sale not being come, they were conversing on the badness of the times; and one of the company called to a plain, clean old man, with white locks, "Pray, Father Abraham, what think you of the times? Will they not quite ruin the country? How shall we be ever able to bear them? What would you advise us to?" Father Abraham stood up, and replied, "If you would have my advice, I will give it you in short; for 'a word to the wise is enough,' as poor Richard says." They joined in desiring him to speak his mind, and gathering round him, he proceeded as follows:

"Friends," says he, "it may be the times are bad, but let us see whether the fault is not our own. Our expenses are doubled by idleness, and trebled by pride and folly; and these can only be abated by our own exertions. If we hearken to good advice, we may gain something. 'God helps them that help themselves,' as poor Richard says.

"I. It would be thought a hard government that should tax its people one tenth part of their time to be employed in its service but idleness taxes many of us much more; sloth, by bringing on diseases, absolutely shortens life.

"'Sloth, like rust, consumes faster than labor wears,[1] while the used key is always bright,' as poor Richard says. 'But, dost thou love life? then do not squander time, for that is the stuff life is made of,'[2] as poor Richard says. How much more than is necessary do we spend in sleep![3] forgetting that 'the sleeping fox catches no poultry, and that there will be sleeping enough in the grave,'[4] as poor Richard says.

"'If time be of all things the most precious, wasting time must be,' as poor Richard says, 'the greatest prodigality;' since, as he elsewhere tells us, 'lost time is never found again; and what we call time enough, always proves little enough.' Let us, then, up, and be doing, and doing to the purpose: so by diligence shall we do more with less perplexity.[5] 'Sloth makes all things difficult, but industry all easy;[6] and he that riseth late, must trot all day, and shall scarce overtake his business at night; while laziness travels so slowly, that poverty soon overtakes him. Drive thy business, let not that drive thee;[7] and early to bed and early to rise, makes a man healthy, wealthy, and wise,' as poor Richard says.

"So what signify wishing and hoping for better times? We may make these times better, if we bestir ourselves. 'Industry need not wish: and he that lives upon hope will die fasting. There are no gains without pains; then help hands, for I have no lands;' or, if I have, they are smartly taxed. 'He that hath a trade hath an estate; and he that hath a calling, hath an office of profit and honor,' as poor Richard says; but then, the trade must be worked at, and the calling well followed, or neither the estate nor the office will enable us to pay our taxes. If we are industrious, we shall never starve, for 'at the working man's house hunger looks in, but dares not enter.' Nor will the bailiff or constable enter; for 'industry pays debts, while

[1] Prov. 21:25. The desire of the slothful killeth him.
[2] Psalm 34:12. What man is he that desireth life and loveth many days? Let him depart from evil and do good; seek peace and pursue it. 91:16. Because he hath set his heart upon me, with long life will I satisfy him, and show him my salvation.
[3] Prov. 19:15. Slothfulness casteth into a deep sleep. 20:13. Love not sleep, lest thou come to poverty. 18:9. The slothful is brother to him who is a waster.
[4] Eccl. 9:10. Whatsoever thy hand findeth to do, do with all thy might; for there is no work, nor device, nor knowledge, nor wisdom, in the grave, whither thou goest.
[5] Prov. 10:14. The hand of the diligent maketh rich.
[6] Prov. 26:16. The sluggard is wiser in his own conceit, than seven men who can give a reason.
[7] 1 Thes. 4:11. Study to do thine own business. Rom. 12:11. Be not slothful in business.

despair increaseth them.' What, though you have found no treasure, nor has any rich relation left you a legacy, 'Diligence is the mother of good luck, and God gives all things to industry. Then plough deep while sluggards sleep,[8] and you shall have corn to sell and to keep.' Work while it is called to-day, for you know not how much you may be hindered to-morrow.[9] 'One to-day is worth two to-morrows,' as poor Richard says; and farther, 'Never leave that till to-morrow, which you can do to-day.' If you were a servant, would you not be ashamed that a good master should catch you idle? Are you then your own master? Be ashamed to catch yourself idle, when there is so much to be done for yourself, your family, your country, and your God. Handle your tools without mittens: remember, that 'the cat in gloves catches no mice,' as poor Richard says. It is true, there is much to be done, and, perhaps, you are weak handed; but stick to it steadily, and you will see great effects; for 'constant dropping wears away stones; and by diligence and patience the mouse ate in two the cable; and little strokes fell great oaks.'

"Methinks I hear some of you say, 'Must a man afford himself no leisure?' I will tell thee, my friend, what poor Richard says;—'Employ thy time well, if thou meanest to gain leisure;[10] and, since thou art not sure of a minute, throw not away an hour.' Leisure is time for doing something useful; this leisure the diligent man will obtain, but the lazy man never; for 'a life of leisure and life of laziness are two things.' Many without labor, would live by their wits only, but they break for want of stock; whereas, industry gives comfort, and plenty, and respect. 'Fly pleasures and they will follow you.[11] The diligent spinner has a large shift; and now I have a sheep and a cow, every body bides me good morrow.'

"II. But with our industry we must likewise be steady, settled, and careful, and oversee our own affairs with our own eyes, and not trust too much to others; for, as poor Richard says,

'I never saw an oft-removed tree,
  Nor yet an oft-removed family,
That throve so well as those that settled be.'

And again, 'Three removes are as bad as a fire:' and again, 'Keep thy shop, and thy shop will keep thee;' and again, 'If you would have your business done, go; if not, send.'[12] And again,

'He that by the plough would thrive
  Himself must either hold or drive.'

"And again, 'The eye of the master will do more work than both his hands;' and again, 'Want of care does more damage than want of knowledge:' and again, 'Not to oversee workmen, is to leave them your purse open.'

"Trusting too much to others' care is the ruin of many; for, 'In the affairs of this world, men are saved, not by faith in others, but by the want of it:' but a man's own care is profitable; for, 'If you would have a faithful servant, and one that you like —serve yourself.—A little neglect may breed great mischief; for want of a nail the shoe was lost; for want of a shoe the horse was lost; and for want of a horse the rider was lost,' being overtaken and slain by the enemy; all for want of a little care about a horse-shoe nail.

"III. So much for industry, my friends, and attention to one's own business; but to these we must add frugality, if we would make our industry more certainly successful. A man may, if he knows not how to save as he gets, 'keep his nose all his life to the grindstone, and die not worth a groat at last. A fat kitchen makes a lean will;' and,

'Many estates are spent in the getting,
Since women for tea forsook spinning and knitting,
And men for punch forsook hewing and splitting.'[13]

" 'If you would be wealthy, think of saving, as well as getting. The Indies have not made Spain rich, because her outgoes are greater than her incomes.'

"Away then with your expensive follies, and you will not then have so much cause to complain of hard times, heavy taxes, and chargeable families;' for,

'Women and wine, game and deceit,
  Make the wealth small, and the want great.'

And farther, 'What maintains one vice, would bring up two children.' You may think, perhaps, that a little tea, or a little punch now and then, diet a little more costly, clothes a little finer, and

---

[8] Prov. 20:4. The sluggard will not plough, therefore shall he beg. 6:6. Go to the ant, thou sluggard, consider her ways and be wise.

[9] John 9:4. Work while it is called to-day, for the night cometh when no man can work.

[10] Eph. 5:16. Redeem the time, because the days are evil.

[11] Prov. 21:17. He that loveth pleasure, shall be a poor man.

[12] Prov. 26:6. He that sendeth a message by the hand of a fool, cutteth off the feet and drinketh damage.

[13] Prov. 23:21. The drunkard shall come to poverty.
1 Cor. 6:10. No drunkard shall inherit the Kingdom of God.

a little entertainment now and then, can be no great matter; but remember, 'Many a little makes a mickle.' Beware of little expenses; 'A small leak will sink a great ship,' as poor Richard says; and again, 'Who dainties love, shall beggars prove;' and moreover, 'Fools make feasts, and wise men eat them.' Here you have all got together to this sale of fineries and knickknacks. You call them goods; but if you do not take care they will prove evils to some of you. You expect they will be sold cheap, and, perhaps, they must be for less than they cost: but if you have no occasion for them, they may be dear to you. Remember what poor Richard says, 'Buy what thou hast no need of, and ere long thou shalt sell thy necessaries.' And again, 'At a great penny-worth pause awhile:' he means, that perhaps the cheapness is apparent only, and not real; or the bargain, by straitening thee in thy business, may do thee more harm than good. For in another place, he says, 'Many have been ruined by buying good penny-worths.' Again, 'It is foolish to lay out money to purchase repentance;' and yet this folly is practiced every day at auctions, for want of minding the Almanac. Many a one, for the sake of finery on the back, has gone with a hungry belly, and half starved their families; 'Silks and satins, scarlets and velvets, put out the kitchen fire,' as poor Richard says. These are not the necessaries of life; they can scarcely be called the conveniences: and yet, only because they look pretty, how many want to have them!—By these and other extravagancies, the genteel are reduced to poverty, and forced to borrow of those whom they formerly despised, but who through industry and frugality, have maintained their standing; in which case, it appears plainly that, 'A ploughman on his legs, is higher than a gentleman on his knees,' as poor Richard says. Perhaps they have had a small estate left them, which they knew not the getting of; they think 'it is day and never will be night:' that a little to be spent out of so much is not worth minding; but 'Always taking out of the meal-tub, and never putting in, soon comes to the bottom,' as poor Richard says; and then, 'when the well is dry, they know the worth of water.' But this they might have known before, if they had taken his advice. 'If you would know the value of money, go and try to borrow some; for he that goes a borrowing, goes a sorrowing,' as poor Richard says; and, indeed, so does he that lends to such people, when he goes to get it out again. Poor Dick farther advises, and says,

'Fond pride of dress is sure a very curse,
Ere fancy you consult, consult your purse.'

And again, 'Pride is as loud a beggar as want, and a great deal more saucy.' [14] When you have bought one fine thing, you must buy ten more, that your appearance may be all of a piece; but poor Dick says, 'It is easier to suppress the first desire, than to satisfy all that follow it.' And it is as truly folly for the poor to ape the rich, as for the frog to swell, in order to equal the ox.

'Vessels large may venture more,
But little boats should keep near shore.'

It is, however, a folly soon punished; for, as poor Richard says, 'Pride that dines on vanity sups on contempt; Pride that breakfasted with Plenty, dined with Poverty, and supped with Infamy;' and after all, of what use is this pride of appearance, for which so much is risked, so much is suffered? It cannot promote health, nor ease pain; it makes no increase of merit in the person, it creates envy, it hastens misfortune.

"But, what madness it must be to run in debt for these superfluities! We are offered, by the terms of this sale, six months' credit; and that, perhaps, has induced some of us to attend it, because we cannot spare the ready money, and hope now to be fine without it. But, ah! think what you do when you run in debt; you give to another power over your liberty.[15] If you cannot pay at the time, you will be ashamed to see your creditor; you will be in fear when you speak to him; you will make poor, pitiful, sneaking excuses, and, by degrees, come to lose your veracity, and sink into base, downright lying; for, 'The second vice is lying, the first is running in debt,' as poor Richard says; and again to the same purpose, 'Lying rides upon Debt's back:' [16] whereas a free-born man ought not to be ashamed or afraid to see or speak to any man living. But poverty often deprives a man of all spirit and virtue. 'It is hard for an empty bag to stand upright.' What would you think of that prince, or of that government, who should issue an edict, forbidding you to dress like a gentleman or gentlewoman, on pain of imprisonment or servitude? Would you not say you were free, have a right to dress as you please, and that such an edict would be a breach of your privileges, and such a government tyrannical? And yet, you

[14] Prov. 16:18. Pride goeth before destruction, and a haughty spirit before a fall. 29:23. A man's pride shall bring him low, but honor shall uphold the humble spirit.
[15] Prov. 22:7. The borrower is servant to the lender.
[16] Prov. 12:22. Lying lips are an abomination unto the Lord. Rev. 21:8. Liars shall have their part in the lake which burneth with fire and brimstone, which is the second death.

are about to put yourselves under that tyranny, when you run in debt for such dress! Some creditor may harass and oppress you; and by going to law, may reduce you to poverty, and thus compel you to dress in rags and even beg your bread. When you have got your bargain, you may, perhaps, think little of payment; but, as poor Richard says, 'Creditors have better memories than debtors; creditors are a superstitious sect, great observers of set days and times.' The day comes round before you are aware, and the demand is made before you are prepared to satisfy it; or, if you bear your debt in mind, the term, which at first seemed so long will, as it lessens, appear extremely short: time will seem to have added wings to his heels as well as his shoulders. 'Those have a short Lent, who owe money to be paid at Easter.' At present, perhaps, you may think yourselves in thriving circumstances, and that you can bear a little extravagance without injury; but

'For age and want save while you may,
No morning sun lasts a whole day.'

"Gain may be temporary and uncertain; but ever, while you live, expense is constant and certain; and 'It is easier to build two chimneys, than to keep one in fuel,' as poor Richard says: so, 'Rather go to bed supperless, than rise in debt.'

'Get what you can, and what you get, hold,
'Tis the stone that will turn all your lead into gold.'

And when you have got the philosopher's stone, sure you will no longer complain of hard times.

"IV. This doctrine, my friends, is reason and wisdom: but, after all, do not depend too much upon your own industry, and frugality, and prudence, though excellent things;[17] for they may all be blasted without the blessing of heaven; and, therefore, ask that blessing humbly, and be not uncharitable to those that at present seem to want it, but comfort and help them.[18] Remember, Job suffered, and was afterwards prosperous.

"And now, to conclude, 'Experience keeps a dear school, but fools will learn in no other,' as poor Richard says, and scarce in that; for it is

[17] Prov. 11:28. He that trusteth in riches shall fall: but the righteous shall flourish as a branch. 28:26. He that trusteth to his own heart, is a fool. Psal. 32:10. Many sorrows shall be to the wicked; but he that trusteth in the Lord, mercy shall compass him about. Prov. 3:6. In all thy ways acknowledge Him, and he shall direct thy paths.
[18] Prov. 13:25. He that watereth, shall also be watered himself.

true, 'We may give advice, but we cannot give conduct.' However, remember this; 'They that will not be counseled cannot be helped;' and farther, that, 'If you will not hear Reason, she will surely rap your knuckles,' as poor Richard says."[19]

Thus the old gentleman ended his harangue. The people heard it and approved the doctrine, and immediately practiced the contrary, just as if it had been a common sermon; for the auction opened, and they began to buy extravagantly. I found the good man had thoroughly studied my Almanacs, and digested all I had dropped on those topics during the course of twenty-five years. The frequent mention he made of me must have tried any one else; my vanity was wonderfully delighted with it, though I was conscious that not a tenth part of the wisdom was my own, which he ascribed to me; but rather the gleanings that I had made of the sense of all ages and nations. However, I resolved to be the better for the echo of it; and though I had at first determined to buy stuff for a new coat, I went away, resolved to wear my old one a little longer. Reader, if thou wilt do the same, thy profit will be as great as mine.

I am, as ever, thine to serve thee.
RICHARD SAUNDERS.

Every able-bodied man in this country, may support himself and family comfortably; if they do not, it is probably owing to idleness, improvidence, or intemperance. We knew in a neighboring city, four blacksmiths employed in the same shop,—two were first-rate workmen, the other two were helpers. The first two received $1.50 per day each; the last two 75 cents per day. The first two were regular drinkers, and no persuasion could induce them to forego their drams; the last two were temperate men, and expended nothing for strong drink. Now mark the difference. The first two were poor,—their families neglected, destitute, and distressed. The wife and children of one of them have been driven from their beds into the street, in a cold night, and compelled to accept of charity to save them from starvation. At length, he deserted his family, and soon after died suddenly at Pittsburgh. The other is now very sick, apparently on his deathbed. The two helpers who received but 75 cents per day, support their families comfortably, and have each about $300 in the Savings' Bank. We know another laborer, who, with $1 per day, supports his

[19] Eccl. 12:13. Hear the conclusion of the whole matter: fear God and keep his commandments; for this is the whole duty of man.

family handsomely, and has nearly $400 in the Savings' Bank. He, too, is an abstinence man. . . .

It is said the eccentric and gifted John Randolph once jumped up from his seat in Congress and exclaimed: "Mr. Speaker, I have found the philosopher's stone: it is this, *pay as you go.*"

This is one of the first great lessons in domestic economy, which every one, but especially every laboring man, should learn, that is, to live within his income—the *farther within* the better—and to adopt and practice the rule, "*pay as you go.*"

Adopt this system and "hard times" will not trouble you. Such times, if they come, may be the easiest, for they always depress the market, and make provisions and merchandise cheaper.

Keep to your business, and your business will keep you. Perseverance will remove mountains. Don't mind a dark day. However thick and dark the clouds, there is light *above* them. Look up and persevere.

Buy nothing useless. Never get in debt as long as you can work. Spend all your money if in want, then wait a week before trying your credit. When you have earned a dollar, always lay by a quarter or a half.

Keep an account of every day's wages, of every idle day, and of every expenditure.

The following table will show the difference between cash and credit, in necessary family expenses. The one is an account kept by the buyer, as the articles were bought and paid for; the other is taken from the grocer's bills:—

For Cash

1 Barrel of Flour 196 lb.	$5 50
1 Gallon of Vinegar	20
14 lb. of Brown Sugar	87½
3½ lb. of Coffee	44
1 lb. of Black Tea	50
6 lb. of Candles	60
3 Bushels of Potatoes	1 87½
1 Ham, 12 lb.	1 08
10 lb. of Pork	60
50 lb. of Indian Meal	75
6 Boxes of Matches	6
1 Broom	18¾
20 lb. of Butter	3 75
12 lb. of Soap	75
2 Gallons of Molasses	62½
Cost for Cash	17 79¼

For Credit

196 lb. of Flour at 4 cts	$7 84
1 Gallon of Vinegar	25
14 lb. Brown Sugar	1 02
3½ lb. of Coffee	50
1 lb. Black Tea	62½
6 lb. Candles	75
3 Bushels of Potatoes	2 62½
12 lb. of Ham	1 50
10 lb. of Pork	73
50 lb. of Indian Meal	1 00
6 Boxes of Matches	12½
1 Broom	25
20 lb. of Butter	4 17
12 lb. of Soap	87½
2 Gallons of Molasses	75
Cost on Credit	23 01
Cost for Cash	17 79¼
In favor of Cash	5 21¾

The above is a moderate estimate of the difference between a *running account,* and having the range of the market with ready money. If the practice of having things charged is also adopted with regard to fresh meats, fruits and vegetables, in city markets, the difference will be found to be much greater.

Three cents a day, amount to eleven dollars and forty cents a year. This sum would supply a small family with fuel through the winter. Six and a quarter cents a day, amount to twenty-two dollars eighty-one cents in a year. This sum would furnish for winter, two tons of coal, one barrel of flour, one hundred pounds of Indian meal, and one hundred pounds of pork.

Is there a mechanic or laborer, who finds it difficult to provide the necessaries of life for his family, and who spends twelve and a half cents a day for strong drink? let him remember that this small sum will in one year amount to forty-five dollars sixty-two cents, and will purchase, when the markets are cheapest, the following indispensable articles, viz.,

3 tons of coal, ...	$15.00
1 load of wood, ...	1.62
2 barrels of flour, ...	11.00
200 lbs. of Indian meal, ...	3.00
200 lbs. of pork, ...	11.00
8 bushels of potatoes, ...	4.00
	$45.62

Into a house thus supplied, hunger and cold could not enter. And if to these articles is added what before he has felt able to purchase, abundance and comfort would be the inmates of his dwelling.

Should a mechanic or laborer read this, who is forty years of age, and who has expended twelve and a half cents a day, for strong drink, and is now feeling the bitterness of poverty,—by saving this sum, he might, since he was twenty-one years of age, have accumulated about one thousand dollars,—if he is fifty years of age, one thousand five hundred dollars,—sixty years of age, two thousand dollars;—and twenty-five cents a day, would produce twice the above amounts.

And permit me, reader, in conclusion to say, that if to economy, frugality, and temperance, you add humble faith in Christ, and obedience to the Gospel, then, indeed, you may not only be comfortable, but useful and happy. RELIGION, after all, is the principal thing. It has the promise of the life that now is, and of that which is to come. Without it, whatever else you possess in this life, you will go portionless into eternity. But with it, whatever else is denied you here, you will have the favor of God, an approving conscience, and a sure hope of heaven. Seek then, with the deepest earnestness and seriousness, the things which belong to your everlasting peace. So shall it be well with you here and hereafter.

THE SOCIOLOGY AND ECONOMICS OF SLAVERY

As CALHOUN presented the political argument for the South's "peculiar institution," so George Fitzhugh argued its case on the level of social theory. Born and reared a Virginia planter, George Fitzhugh (1806–1881) found life good in his own community. While the world outside was shaken by social discontent and disturbed by innovations in literature and religion, Virginians continued in the ways of peace and piety. They appointed no commissions to reform poor laws, investigate the condition of labor, or consider erecting better prisons; there were no murders in Fitzhugh's country and no thieves or beggars. Such a happy condition was the product of Virginia's social organization—characterized by the existence of slavery. Thus Fitzhugh in his *Sociology for the South* (Richmond, 1854). Slavery was good then, a positive good, since it freed the South from the problems that were vexing the rest of the world.

For all the keenness of its argument, *Sociology for the South* attracted comparatively little interest at home. Three years later, Fitzhugh proceeded to an even more vigorous defense of slavery, in his *Cannibals All!* (Richmond, 1857), which carried the argument into the home of its enemies. He confronted liberals with the criticisms of the Utopians, Northern and British manufacturers with the reports of British poor law commissions, and Abolitionists with the sufferings of wage laborers. What the world needs, Fitzhugh argues, is to abandon false philosophy and return to the true science of politics as expounded by Aristotle.

Give up the compact theory and the notion of natural rights; admit that government is based on force; accept the facts of nature. Some are strong, others are weak; it is right that those who need protection—women, idiots, laborers, and Negroes—should obey their protectors. Man was born a social creature, he never existed in the "state of nature" postulated by the natural rights theorists.

Free society is as great a failure as the philosophy on which it is built, Fitzhugh continues. The Abolitionists themselves recognize that fact, for they all support women's rights, heretical interpretations of the Bible, and the abandonment of government; their chief advocate, Horace Greeley's *Tribune*, is the organ of "all the isms."

While Northern newspapers expound such doctrine, the Southern press prints sense. "The South is governed by the need to keep its negroes in order, which preserves a healthy, conservative public opinion." Northern conservatives should recognize that, he declares; they should combine with like-minded Southerners before the Abolitionists let loose a torrent of Jacobinism. Southerners, on the other hand, should strengthen their own states, improve the education of their poorer whites, develop a more varied economic life, reestablish small entails to prevent the development of a Southern pauperism, and then stand firm with the Democratic party against the treason of the North.

Thus a frank defense of slavery. Other voices were also being raised in the debate.

The North Carolinian, Hinton R. Helper, criticized slavery from the point of view of the non-slaveowning yeoman white farmers. These two selections present aspects of the social and economic analysis of the South's "peculiar institution" being made just before the Civil War.

The selection from Fitzhugh here reprinted is from *Cannibals All; or, Slaves without Masters* (Richmond, 1857).

For reading Helper's *The Impending Crisis of the South* men were lynched and at least one Southern state made possession or distribution of the book a felony. An examination of the work helps one understand this oblique tribute to the power of the printed word. For Hinton Rowan Helper (1829–1909) did his best to destroy the idea of a South solidly united behind its slave-holding interest. Helper himself was born in the upcountry of North Carolina and came from a family of farmers. After a brief period at a country academy, and a few years spent unsuccessfully as a clerk at a crossroads store, he went to California, where he was no luckier. He returned to North Carolina, then, and wrote the *Impending Crisis*, which Northern publishers refused to print because they considered it too "incendiary." Helper brought the book out at his own cost in 1854, but though it had an enormous circulation it brought him less money than reputation. Northerners sprang to refute its statistics; Southerners answered Helper's argument by proving him a thief; and the non-slaveholding whites for whom he wrote were often without the ability to read its violent pages.

And that was another of the ills they owed to slavery. The North and the South began on an equal footing, Helper asserts; if either had an advantage, that lay with the South in 1789. Yet the South now lives and dies in economic bondage to the North. The slave system had produced that decline, Helper declares. Slavery had made the South waste its timber and destroy its soil; it was profiting England and the North, not the South itself, where capital earned scarcely one per cent. Though an insignificant fraction of the population, the slaveholders have constituted themselves "the sole arbiters and legislators for the entire South." They have driven the non-slaveholders from the best land and denied them the benefit of industry and common schools, since it is "the oligarchy's" policy to "keep the masses, the non-slaveholding whites and negroes forever . . . in loathsome dungeons of illiteracy."

That is almost the only word of sympathy for the slave which is to be found in the *Impending Crisis*. Helper is concerned with the white man now crushed by the slave system. "Smallpox is a nuisance," Helper shouts, "strychnine is a nuisance; mad dogs are a nuisance; slavery is a nuisance; slave-holders are a nuisance and so are slave-breeders; it is our business, nay, it is our imperative duty to abate nuisances; we propose therefore . . . to exterminate this catalogue from beginning to end." Slave-holders are worse than thieves and more criminal than murderers. Their white victims should rise, unite and exclude them from political power. Then, slaves should be taxed progressively, so that the slaveowners who have reduced the value of Southern land by $22 an acre may bear the cost of shipping the freed Negroes back to Liberia. For the present, though, Helper declares himself willing to accept the program of the Wheeling, Va., *Gazette*: repeal the Fugitive Slave Law and the Kansas-Nebraska Act, abolish slavery in the Dictrict of Columbia, and acquire no more slave territory.

The audience Helper most wanted to reach never did hear him. The Republican party he had helped (for his book was used as a campaign document in 1860) rewarded him with a South American consulate that led Helper to the promotion of an unsuccessful scheme for a railroad to unite the Three Americas. He returned to the United States and to obscurity and died a suicide.

The Impending Crisis is particularly significant for revealing the plight of the poor white farmers of the South who were also the victims of the slave institution. The selection here reprinted is from the New York edition of 1860.

Cannibals All!

BY GEORGE FITZHUGH

CHAPTER I: THE UNIVERSAL TRADE

WE ARE, all, North and South, engaged in the White Slave Trade, and he who succeeds best, is esteemed most respectable. It is far more cruel than the Black Slave Trade, because it exacts more of its slaves, and neither protects nor governs them. We boast, that it exacts more, when we say, "that the *profits* made from employing free labor are greater than those from slave labor." The profits, made from free labor, are the amount of the products of such labor, which the employer, by means of the command which capital or skill gives him, takes away, exacts or "exploitates" from the free laborer. The profits of slave labor are that portion of the products of such labor which the power of the master enables him to appropriate. These profits are less, because the master allows the slave to retain a larger share of the results of his own labor, than do the employers of free labor. But we not only boast that the White Slave Trade is more exacting and fraudulent (in fact, though not in intention,) than Black Slavery; but we also boast, that it is more cruel, in leaving the laborer to take care of himself and family out of the pittance which skill or capital have allowed him to retain. When the day's labor is ended, he is free, but is overburdened with the cares of family and household, which make his freedom an empty and delusive mockery. But his employer is really free, and may enjoy the profits made by others' labor, without a care, or a trouble, as to their well-being. The negro slave is free, too, when the labors of the day are over, and free in mind as well as body; for the master provides food, raiment, house, fuel, and everything else necessary to the physical well-being of himself and family. The master's labors commence just when the slave's end. No wonder men should prefer white slavery to capital, to negro slavery, since it is more profitable, and is free from all the cares and labors of black slave-holding.

Now, reader, if you wish to know yourself—to "descant on your own deformity"—read on. But if you would cherish self-conceit, self-esteem, or self-appreciation, throw down our book; for we will dispel illusions which have promoted your happiness, and shew you that what you have considered and practiced as virtue, is little better than moral Cannibalism. But you will find yourself in numerous and respectable company; for all good and respectable people are "Cannibals all," who do not labor, or who are successfully trying to live without labor, on the unrequited labor of other people:—Whilst low, bad, and disreputable people, are those who labor to support themselves, and to support said respectable people besides. Throwing the negro slaves out of the account, and society is divided in Christendom into four classes: The rich, or independent respectable people, who live well and labor not at all; the professional and skillful respectable people, who do a little light work, for enormous wages; the poor hard-working people, who support every body, and starve themselves; and the poor thieves, swindlers and sturdy beggars, who live like gentlemen, without labor, on the labor of other people. The gentlemen exploitate, which being done on a large scale, and requiring a great many victims, is highly respectable—whilst the rogues and beggars take so little from others, that they fare little better than those who labor.

But, reader, we do not wish to fire into the flock. "Thou art the man!" You are a Cannibal! and if a successful one, pride yourself on the number of your victims, quite as much as any Feejee chieftain, who breakfasts, dines and sups on human flesh.—And your conscience smites you, if you have failed to succeed, quite as much as his, when he returns from an unsuccessful foray.

Probably, you are a lawyer, or a merchant, or a doctor, who have made by your business fifty thousand dollars, and retired to live on your capital. But, mark! not to spend your capital. That would be vulgar, disreputable, criminal. That would be, to live by your own labor; for your capital is your amassed labor. That would be, to do as common working men do; for they take the pittance which their employers leave them, to live on. They live by labor; for they exchange the results of their own labor for the products of other people's labor. It is, no doubt, an honest, vulgar way of living; but not at all a respectable way. The respectable way of living is, to make other people work for you, and to pay them nothing for so doing—and to have no concern about them after their work is done. Hence, white slave-holding is much more respectable than negro slavery—for the master works nearly as hard for the negro, as he for the master. But you, my virtuous, respectable reader, exact three thousand dollars per annum from white labor, (for your income is the product of white labor,) and make not one cent of return in any form. You retain your capital, and never labor, and yet live in luxury on the labor of others. Capital commands labor, as the master does the slave. Neither pays for labor; but the master permits the slave to retain a larger allowance from the proceeds of his own labor, and hence "free labor is cheaper than slave labor." You, with the command over labor which your capital gives you, are a slave owner —a master, without the obligations of a master. They who work for you, who create your income, are slaves, without the rights of slaves. Slaves without a master! Whilst you were engaged in amassing your capital, in seeking to become independent, you were in the White Slave Trade. To become independent, is to be able to make other people support you, without being obliged to labor for *them*. Now, what man in society is not seeking to attain this situation? He who attains it, is a slave owner, in the worst sense. He who is in pursuit of it, is engaged in the slave trade. You, reader, belong to the one or other class. The men without property, in free society, are theoretically in a worse condition than slaves. Practically, their condition corresponds with this theory, as history and statistics every where demonstrate. The capitalists, in free society, live in ten times the luxury and show that Southern masters do, because the slaves to capital work harder and cost less, than negro slaves.

The negro slaves of the South are the happiest, and, in some sense, the freest people in the world. The children and the aged and infirm work not at all, and yet have all the comforts and necessaries of life provided for them. They enjoy liberty, because they are oppressed neither by care nor labor. The women do little hard work, and are protected from the despotism of their husbands by their masters. The negro men and stout boys work, on the average, in good weather, not more than nine hours a day. The balance of their time is spent in perfect abandon. Besides, they have their Sabbaths and holidays. White men, with so much of license and liberty, would die of ennui; but negroes luxuriate in corporeal and mental repose. With their faces upturned to the sun, they can sleep at any hour; and quiet sleep is the greatest of human enjoyments. "Blessed be the man who invented sleep." 'Tis happiness in itself—and results from contentment with the present, and confident assurance of the future. We do not know whether free laborers ever sleep. They are fools to do so; for, whilst they sleep, the wily and watchful capitalist is devising means to ensnare and exploitate them. The free laborer must work or starve. He is more of a slave than the negro, because he works longer and harder for less allowance than the slave, and

has no holiday, because the cares of life with him begin when its labors end. He has no liberty, and not a single right. We know, 'tis often said, air and water, are common property, which all have equal right to participate and enjoy; but this is utterly false. The appropriation of the lands carries with it the appropriation of all on or above the lands, *usque ad cœlum, aut ad inferos*. A man cannot breathe the air, without a place to breathe it from, and all places are appropriated. All water is private property "to the middle of the stream," except the ocean, and that is not fit to drink.

Free laborers have not a thousandth part of the rights and liberties of negro slaves. Indeed, they have not a single right or a single liberty, unless it be the right or liberty to die. But the reader may think that he and other capitalists and employers are freer than negro slaves. Your capital would soon vanish, if you dared indulge in the liberty and abandon of negroes. You hold your wealth and position by the tenure of constant watchfulness, care and circumspection. You never labor; but you are never free.

Where a few own the soil, they have unlimited power over the balance of society, until domestic slavery comes in, to compel them to permit this balance of society to draw a sufficient and comfortable living from "terra mater." Free society, asserts the right of a few to the earth—slavery, maintains that it belongs, in different degrees, to all.

But, reader, well may you follow the slave trade. It is the only trade worth following, and slaves the only property worth owning. All other is worthless, a mere *caput mortuum*, except in so far as it vests the owner with the power to command the labors of others—to enslave them. Give you a palace, ten thousand acres of land, sumptuous clothes, equipage and every other luxury; and with your artificial wants, you are poorer than Robinson Crusoe, or the lowest working man, if you have no slaves to capital, or domestic slaves. Your capital will not bring you an income of a cent, nor supply one of your wants, without labor. Labor is indispensable to give value to property, and if you owned every thing else, and did not own labor, you would be poor. But fifty thousand dollars means, and is, fifty thousand dollars worth of slaves. You can command, without touching on that capital, three thousand dollars' worth of labor per annum. You could do no more were you to buy slaves with it, and then you would be cumbered with the cares of governing and providing for them. You are a slaveholder now, to the amount of fifty thousand dollars, with all the advantages, and none of the cares and responsibilities of a master.

"Property in man" is what all are struggling to obtain. Why should they not be obliged to take care of man, their property, as they do of their horses and their hounds, their cattle and their sheep. Now, under the delusive name of liberty, you work him, "from morn to dewy eve"—from infancy to old age—then turn him out to starve. You treat your horses and hounds better. Capital is a cruel master. The free slave trade, the commonest, yet the cruellest of trades.

CHAPTER II: LABOR, SKILL AND CAPITAL

Nothing written on the subject of slavery from the time of Aristotle, is worth reading, until the days of the modern Socialists. Nobody, treating of it, thought it worth while to enquire from history and statistics, whether the physical and moral condition of emancipated serfs or slaves had been improved or rendered worse by emancipation. None would condescend to compare the evils of domestic slavery with the evils of liberty without property. It entered no one's head to conceive a doubt as to the actual freedom of the emancipated. The relations of capital and labor, of the property-holders to the non-property-holders, were things about which no one had thought or written. It never occurred to either the enemies or the apologists for slavery, that if no one would employ the free laborer, his condition was infinitely worse than that of actual slavery—nor did it occur to them, that if his wages were less than the allowance of the slave, he was less free after emancipation than before. St. Simon, Fourier, Owen, Fanny Wright, and a few others, who discovered and proclaimed that property was not only a bad master, but an intolerable one, were treated as wicked visionaries. After the French and other revolutions in Western Europe in 1830, all men suddenly discovered that the social relations of men were false, and that social, not political, revolutions were needed. Since that period, almost the whole literature of free society is but a voice proclaiming its absolute and total failure. Hence the works of the socialists contain the true defence of slavery.

Most of the active intellect of Christendom has for the last twenty years been engaged in analyzing, detecting and exposing the existing relations of labor, skill and capital, and in vain efforts to rectify those relations. The philosophers of Europe, who have been thus engaged, have excelled all the normal philosophers that preceded them, in the former part of their pursuit, but suggested nothing but puerile absurdities, in the latter. Their destructive philosophy is profound, demonstrative, and unanswerable—their constructive theories, wild, visionary and chimerical on paper, and failures in practice. Each one of them proves clearly enough, that the present edifice of European society is out of all rule and proportion, and must soon tumble to pieces—but no two agree as to how it is to be re-built. "We must (say they all) have a new world, if we are to have any world at all!" and each has a little model Utopia or Phalanstery, for this new and better world, which, having already failed on a small experimental scale, the inventor assures us, is, therefore, the very thing to succeed on a large one. We allude to the socialists and communists, who have more or less tinged all modern literature with their doctrines. In analyzing society; in detecting, exposing, and generalizing its operations and its various phenomena, they are but grammarians or anatomists, confining philosophy to its proper sphere, and employing it for useful purposes. When they attempt to go further—and having found the present social system to be fatally diseased, propose to originate and build up another in its stead—they are as presumptuous as the anatomist, who should attempt to create a man. Social bodies, like human bodies, are the works of God, which man may dissect, and sometimes heal, but which he cannot create. . . .

CHAPTER XXXII: MAN HAS PROPERTY IN MAN!

In the Liberator of the 19th December, we observe that the editor narrows down the slavery contest to the mere question, whether "Man may rightfully hold property in man?"

We think we can dispose of this objection to domestic slavery in a very few words.

Man is a social and gregarious animal, and all such animals hold property in each other. Nature imposes upon them slavery as a law and necessity of their existence. They live together to aid each other, and are slaves under Mr. Garrison's higher law. Slavery arises under the higher law, and is, and ever must be, coëval and coëxtensive with human nature.

We will enumerate a few of its ten thousand modifications.

The husband has a legally recognized property in his wife's services, and may legally control, in some measure, her personal liberty. She is his property and his slave.

The wife has also a legally recognized property in the husband's services. He is her property, but not her slave.

The father has property in the services and persons of his children till they are twenty-one years of age. They are his property and his slaves.

Children have property, during infancy, in the services of each parent.

Infant negroes, sick, infirm and superannuated negroes, hold most valuable property in the services and capital of their masters. The masters hold no property in such slaves, because, for the time, they are of no value.

Owners and captains of vessels own property in the services of sailors, and may control their personal liberty. They (the sailors) are property, and slaves also.

The services and persons, lives and liberty of soldiers and of officers, belong to the Government; they are, whilst in service, both property and slaves.

Every white working man, be he clerk, carpenter, mechanic, printer, common laborer, or what else, who contracts to serve for a term of days, months, or years, is, for such term, the property of his employer. He is not a slave, like the wife, child, apprentice, sailor or soldier, because, although the employer's right to his services be equally perfect, his remedy to enforce such right is very different. In the one case, he may resort to force to compel compliance; in the other, he is driven to a suit for damages.

Again: Every capitalist holds property in his fellow men to the extent of the profits of his capital, or income. The only income possibly resulting from capital, is the result of the property which capital bestows on its owners, in the labor of other people. In our first three chapters we attempt to explain this.

All civilized society recognizes, and, in some measure, performs the obligation to support and provide for all human beings, whether natives or foreigners, who are unable to provide for themselves. Hence poor-houses, &c.

Hence all men hold valuable property, actual or contingent, in the services of each other.

If, Mr. Garrison, this be the only difficulty to be adjusted between North and South, we are sure that your little pet, Disunion, "living will linger, and lingering will die."

When Mr. Andrews and you have quite "expelled human nature," dissolved and disintegrated society, and reduced mankind to separate, independent, but conflicting monads, or human atoms —then, and not till then, will you establish the "sovereignty of the individual," and destroy the property of man in man.

The Impending Crisis of the South

BY HINTON R. HELPER

CHAPTER I: COMPARISON BETWEEN THE FREE AND THE SLAVE STATES

. . . AND NOW that we have come to the very heart and soul of our subject, we feel no disposition to mince matters, but mean to speak plainly, and to the point, without any equivocation, mental reservation, or secret evasion whatever. The son of a venerated parent, who, while he lived, was a considerate and merciful slaveholder, a native of the South, born and bred in North Carolina, of a family whose home has been in the valley of the Yadkin for nearly a century and a half, a Southerner by instinct and by all the influences of thought, habits, and kindred, and with the desire and fixed purpose to reside permanently within the limits of the South, and with the expectation of dying there also—we feel that we have the right to express our opinion, however humble or unimportant it may be, on any and every question that affects the public good; and, so help us God, "sink or swim, live or die, survive or perish," we are determined to exercise that right with manly firmness, and without fear, favor or affection.

And now to the point. In our opinion, an opinion which has been formed from data obtained by assiduous researches, and comparisons, from laborious investigation, logical reasoning, and earnest reflection, the causes which have impeded the progress and prosperity of the South, which have dwindled our commerce, and other similar pursuits, into the most contemptible insignificance; sunk a large majority of our people in galling poverty and ignorance, rendered a small minority conceited and tyrannical, and driven the rest away from their homes; entailed upon us a humiliating dependence on the Free States; disgraced us in the recesses of our own souls, and brought us under reproach in the eyes of all civilized and enlightened nations—may all be traced to one common source, and there find solution in the most hateful and horrible word, that was ever incorporated into the vocabulary of human economy—*Slavery!*

Reared amidst the institution of slavery, believing it to be wrong both in principle and in practice, and having seen and felt its evil influences upon individuals, communities and states, we deem it a duty, no less than a privilege, to enter our protest against it, and to use our most strenuous efforts to overturn and abolish it! Then we are an abolitionist? Yes! not merely a freesoiler, but an abolitionist, in the fullest sense of the term. We are not only in favor of keeping slavery out of the territories, but, carrying our opposition to the institution a step further, we here unhesitatingly declare ourselves in favor of its immediate and unconditional abolition, in every state in this confederacy, where it now exists! Patriotism makes us a freesoiler; state pride makes us an emancipationist; a profound sense of duty to the South makes us an abolitionist; a reasonable degree of fellow feeling for the negro, makes us a colonizationist. With the free state men in Kansas and Nebraska, we sympathize with all our heart. We love the whole country, the great family of states and territories, one and inseparable, and would have the word Liberty engraved as an appropriate and truthful motto, on the escutcheon of every member of the confederacy. We love freedom, we hate slavery, and rather than give up the one or submit to the other, we will forfeit the pound of flesh nearest our heart. Is this sufficiently explicit and categorical? If not, we hold ourself in readiness at all times, to return a prompt reply to any proper question that may be propounded.

Our repugnance to the institution of slavery, springs from no one-sided idea, or sickly sentimentality. We have not been hasty in making up our mind on the subject; we have jumped at no conclusions; we have acted with perfect calmness and deliberation; we have carefully considered, and examined the reasons for and against the institution, and have also taken into account the propable consequences of our decision. The more we investigate the matter, the deeper becomes the conviction that we are right; and with this to impel and sustain us, we pursue our labor with love, with hope, and with constantly renewing vigor.

That we shall encounter opposition we consider as certain; perhaps we may even be subjected to insult and violence. From the conceited and cruel oligarchy of the South, we could look for nothing less. But we shall shrink from no responsibility, and do nothing unbecoming a man; we know how to repel indignity, and if assaulted, shall not fail to make the blow recoil upon the aggressor's head. The road we have to travel may be a rough one, but no impediment shall cause us to falter in our course. The line of our duty is clearly defined, and it is our intention to follow it faithfully, or die in the attempt.

But, thanks to heaven, we have no ominous forebodings of the result of the contest now pending between Liberty and Slavery in this confederacy. Though neither a prophet nor the son of a prophet, our vision is sufficiently penetrative to divine the future so far as to be able to see that the "peculiar institution" has but a short, and, as heretofore, inglorious existence before it. Time, the righter of every wrong, is ripening events for the desired consummation of our labors and the fulfillment of our cherished hopes. Each revolving year brings nearer the inevitable crisis. The sooner it comes the better; may heaven, through our humble efforts, hasten its advent.

The first and most sacred duty of every Southerner, who has the honor and the interest of his country at heart, is to declare himself an unqualified and uncompromising abolitionist. No conditional or half-way declaration will avail; no mere threatening demonstration will succeed. With those who desire to be instrumental in bringing about the triumph of liberty over slavery, there should be neither evasion, vacillation, nor equivocation. We should listen to no modifying terms or compromises that may be proposed by the proprietors of the unprofitable and ungodly institution. Nothing short of the complete abolition of slavery can save the South from falling into the vortex of utter ruin. Too long have we yielded a submissive obedience to the tyrannical domination of an inflated oligarchy; too long have we tolerated their arrogance and self-conceit, too long have we submitted to their unjust and savage exactions. Let us now wrest from them the sceptre of power, establish liberty and equal rights throughout the land, and henceforth and forever guard our legislative halls from the pollutions and usurpations of proslavery demagogues. . . .

Notwithstanding the fact that the white non-slaveholders of the South, are in the majority, as five to one, they have never yet had any part or lot in framing the laws under which they live. There is no legislation except for the benefit of slavery, and slaveholders. As a general rule, poor white persons are regarded with less esteem and attention than negroes, and though the condition of the latter is wretched beyond description, vast numbers of the former are infinitely worse off. A cunningly devised mockery of freedom is guarantied to them, and that is all. To all intents and purposes they are disfranchised, and outlawed, and the only privilege extended to them, is a shallow and circumscribed participation in the political movements that usher slaveholders into office.

We have not breathed away seven and twenty years in the South, without becoming acquainted with the demagogical manœuvrings of the oligarchy. Their intrigues and tricks of legerdemain are as familiar to us as household words; in vain might the world be ransacked for a more precious junto of flatterers and cajolers. It is amusing to ignorance, amazing to credulity, and insulting to intelligence, to hear them in their blattering efforts to mystify and pervert the sacred principles of liberty, and turn the curse of slavery into a blessing. To the illiterate poor whites—made poor and ignorant by the system of slavery—they hold out the idea that slavery is the very bulwark of our liberties, and the foundation of American independence! For hours at a time, day after day, will they expatiate upon the inexpressible beauties and excellencies of this great, *free* and *independent* nation; and finally, with the most extravagant gesticulations and rhetorical flourishes, conclude their nonsensical ravings, by attributing all the glory and prosperity of the country, from Maine to Texas, and from Georgia to California, to the "invaluable institutions of the South!" With what patience we could command, we have frequently listened to the incoherent and truth-murdering declamations of these champions of slavery, and, in the absence of a more politic method of giving vent to our disgust and indignation, have involuntarily bit our lips into blisters.

The lords of the lash are not only absolute masters of the blacks, who are bought and sold, and driven about like so many cattle, but they are also the oracles and arbiters of all non-slaveholding whites, whose freedom is merely nominal, and whose unparalleled illiteracy and degradation is purposely and fiendishly perpetuated. How little the "poor white trash," the great majority of the Southern people, know of the real condition of the country is, indeed, sadly astonishing. The truth is, they know nothing of public measures, and little of private affairs, except what their imperious masters, the slave-drivers, condescend to tell, and that is but precious little, and even that little, always garbled and one-sided, is never told except in public harangues; for the haughty cavaliers of shackles and handcuffs will not degrade themselves by holding private converse with those who have neither dimes nor hereditary rights in human flesh.

Whenever it pleases, and to the extent it pleases, a slaveholder to become communicative, poor whites may hear with fear and trembling, but not speak. They must be as mum as dumb brutes, and stand in awe of their august superiors, or be crushed with stern rebukes, cruel oppressions, or downright violence. If they dare to think for themselves, their thoughts must be forever concealed. The expression of any sentiment at all conflicting with the gospel of slavery, dooms them at once in the community in which they live, and then, whether willing or unwilling, they are obliged to become heroes, martyrs, or exiles. They may thirst for knowledge, but there is no Moses among them to smite it out of the rocks of Horeb. The black veil, through whose almost impenetrable meshes light seldom gleams, has long been pendent over their eyes, and there, with fiendish jealousy, the slave-driving ruffians sedulously guard it. Non-slaveholders are not only kept in ignorance of what is transpiring at the North but they are continually misinformed of what is going on even in the South. Never were the poorer classes of a people, and those classes so largely in the majority, and all inhabiting the same country, so basely duped, so adroitly swindled, or so damnably outraged.

It is expected that the stupid and sequacious masses, the white victims of slavery, will believe, and, as a general thing, they do believe, whatever the slaveholders tell them; and thus it is that they are cajoled into the notion that they are the freest, happiest and most intelligent people in the world, and are taught to look with prejudice and disapprobation upon every new principle or progressive movement. Thus it is that the South, woefully inert and inventionless, has lagged behind the North, and is now weltering in the cesspool of ignorance and degradation.....

Non-slaveholders of the South! farmers, mechanics and workingmen, we take this occasion to assure you that the slaveholders, the arrogant demagogues whom you have elected to offices of honor and profit, have hoodwinked you, trifled with you, and used you as mere tools for the consummation of their wicked designs. They have purposely kept you in ignorance, and have, by moulding your passions and prejudices to suit themselves, induced you to act in direct opposition to your dearest rights and interests. By a system of the grossest subterfuge and misrepresentation, and in order to avert, for a season, the vengeance that will most assuredly overtake them ere long, they have taught you to hate the abolitionists, who are your best and only true friends. Now, as one of your own number, we appeal to you to join us in our patriotic endeavors to rescue the generous soil of the South from the usurped and desolating control of these political vampires. Once and forever, at least so far as this country is concerned, the infernal question of slavery must be disposed of; a speedy and perfect abolishment of the whole institution is the true policy of the South—and this is the policy which we propose to pursue. Will you aid us, will you assist us, will you be freemen, or will you be slaves? These are questions of vital importance; weigh them well in your minds; come to a prudent and firm decision, and hold yourselves in readiness to act in accordance therewith. You must either be for us or against us —anti-slavery or pro-slavery; it is impossible for you to occupy a neutral ground; it is as certain as fate itself, that if you do not voluntarily oppose the usurpations and outrages of the slavocrats, they will force you into involuntary compliance with their infamous measures. Consider well the aggressive, fraudulent and despotic power which they have exercised in the affairs of Kansas; and remember that, if, by adhering to erroneous principles of neutrality or non-resistance, you allow them to force the curse of slavery on that vast and fertile field, the broad area of all the surrounding States and Territories—the whole nation, in fact —will soon fall a prey to their diabolical intrigues and machinations. Thus, if you are not vigilant, will they take advantage of your neutrality, and make you and others the victims of their inhuman despotism. Do not reserve the strength of your arms until you shall have been rendered powerless to strike; the present is the proper time for action; under all the circumstances, apathy or indifference is a crime. First ascertain, as nearly as you can, the precise nature and extent of your duty, and then, without a moment's delay, perform it in good faith. To facilitate you in determining what considerations of right, justice and humanity require at your hands, is one of the primary objects of this work; and we shall certainly fail in our desire if we do not accomplish our task in a manner acceptable to God and advantageous to man.

CHAPTER II: HOW SLAVERY CAN BE ABOLISHED

NUMBER OF SLAVEHOLDERS IN THE UNITED STATES— 1850.

Alabama	29,295
Arkansas	5,999
Columbia, District of	1,477
Delaware	809
Florida	3,520
Georgia	38,456
Kentucky	38,385
Louisiana	20,670
Maryland	16,040
Mississippi	23,116
Missouri	19,185
North Carolina	28,303
South Carolina	25,596
Tennessee	33,865
Texas	7,747
Virginia	55,063
Total Number of Slaveholders in the United States	347,525

CLASSIFICATION OF THE SLAVEHOLDERS—1850.

Holders of 1 slave	68,820
Holders of 1 and under 5	105,683
Holders of 5 and under 10	80,765
Holders of 10 and under 20	54,595
Holders of 20 and under 50	29,733
Holders of 50 and under 100	6,196
Holders of 100 and under 200	1,479
Holders of 200 and under 300	187
Holders of 300 and under 500	56
Holders of 500 and under 1,000	9
Holders of 1,000 and over	2
Aggregate Number of Slaveholders in the United States	347,525

It thus appears that there are in the United States, three hundred and forty-seven thousand five hundred and twenty-five slaveholders. But this appearance is deceptive. The actual number is certainly less than two hundred thousand. Professor De Bow, the Superintendent of the Census, informs us that "the number includes slave-hirers," and furthermore, that "where the party owns slaves in different counties, or in different States, he will be entered more than once." Now every Southerner, who has any practical knowledge of affairs, must know, and does know, that every New Year's day, like almost every other day, is desecrated in the South, by publicly hiring out slaves to large numbers of non-slaveholders. The slave-owners, who are the exclusive manufacturers of public sentiment, have popularized the dictum that white servants, decency, virtue, and justice, are unfashionable; and there are, we are sorry to say, nearly one hundred and sixty thousand non-slaveholding sycophants, who have subscribed to this false philosophy, and who are giving constant encouragement to the infamous practices of slaveholding and slave-breeding, by hiring at least one slave every year.

In the Southern States, as in all other slave countries, there are three odious classes of mankind; the slaves themselves, who are cowards; the slaveholders, who are tyrants; and the non-slaveholding slave-hirers, who are lickspittles. Whether either class is really entitled to the regards of a gentleman is a matter of grave doubt. The slaves are pitiable; the slaveholders are detestable; the slave-hirers are contemptible.

With the statistics at our command, it is impossible for us to ascertain the exact number of slaveholders and non-slaveholding slave-hirers in the slave States; but we have data which will enable us to approach very near to the facts. The town from which we hail, Salisbury, the capital of Rowan county, North Carolina, contains about twenty-three hundred inhabitants, including three hundred and seventy-two slaves, fifty-one slaveholders, and forty-three non-slaveholding slave-hirers. Taking it for granted that this town furnishes a fair relative proportion of all the slaveholders, and non-slaveholding slave-hirers in the slave States, the whole number of the former, including those who have been "entered more than once," is one hundred and eighty-eight thousand five hundred and fifty-one; of the latter, one hundred and fifty-eight thousand nine hundred and seventy-four; and, now, estimating that there are in Maryland, Virginia, and other grain-growing States, an aggregate of two thousand slave-owners, who have cotton plantations *stocked* with negroes in the far South, and who have been "entered more than once," we find, as the result of our calculations, that the total number of actual slaveholders in the Union, is precisely one hundred and eighty-six thousand five hundred and fifty-one—as follows:

Number of actual slaveholders in the
  United States 186,551
Number "entered more than once" 2,000
Number of non-slaveholding slave-hirers 158,974

Aggregate number, acording to De Bow 347,525

The greater number of non-slaveholding slave-hirers, are a kind of third-rate aristocrats—persons who formerly owned slaves, but whom slavery, as is its custom, has dragged down to poverty, leaving them, in their false and shiftless pride, to eke out a miserable existence over the hapless chattels personal of other men.

So it seems that the total number of actual slave-owners, including their entire crew of cringing lickspittles, against whom we have to contend, is but three hundred and forty-seven thousand five hundred and twenty-five. Against this army for the defense and propagation of slavery, we think it will be an easy matter—independent of the negroes, who, in nine cases out of ten, would be delighted with an opportunity to cut their masters' throats, and without accepting of a single recruit from either of the free States, England, France or Germany—to muster one at least three times as large, and far more respectable for its utter extinction. We hope, however, and believe, that the matter in dispute may be adjusted without arraying these armies against each other in hostile attitude. We desire peace, not war—justice, not blood. Give us fair-play, secure to us the right of discussion, the freedom of speech, and we will settle the difficulty at the ballot-box, not on the battle-ground—by force of reason, not by force of arms. But we are wedded to one purpose from which no earthly power can ever divorce us. We are determined to abolish slavery at all hazards—in defiance of all the opposition, of whatever nature, which it is possible for the slavocrats to bring against us. Of this they may take due notice, and govern themselves accordingly.

Thus far, in giving expression to our sincere and settled opinions, we have endeavored to show, in the first place, that slavery is a great moral, social, civil, and political evil—a dire enemy to true wealth and national greatness, and an atrocious crime against both God and man; and, in the second place, that it is a paramount duty which we owe to heaven, to the earth, to America, to humanity, to our posterity, to our consciences, and to our pockets, to adopt effectual and judicious measures for its immediate abolition. The questions now arise, How can the evil be averted? What are the most prudent and practical means that can be devised for the abolition of slavery? In the solution of these problems it becomes necessary to deal with a multiplicity of stubborn realities. And yet, we can see no reason why North Carolina, in her sovereign capacity, may not, with equal ease and success, do what forty-five other States of the world have done within the last forty-five years. Nor do we believe any good reason exists why Virginia should not perform as great a deed in 1859 as did New-York in 1799. Massachusetts abolished slavery in 1780; would it not be a masterly stroke of policy in Tennessee, and every other slave State, to abolish it in or before 1860?

Not long since, a slavocrat, writing on this subject, said, apologetically, "we frankly admit that slavery is a monstrous evil; but what are we to do with an institution which has baffled the wisdom of our greatest statesmen?" Unfortunately for the South, since the days of Washington, Jefferson, Madison, and their ilustrious compatriots, she has never had more than half a dozen statesmen, all told; of mere politicians, wire-pullers, and slave-driving demagogues, she has had enough, and to spare; but of statesmen, in the true sense of the term, she has had, and now has, but precious few—fewer just at this time, perhaps, than ever before. It is far from a matter of surprise to us that slavery has, for such a long period, baffled the "wisdom" of the oligarchy; but our surprise is destined to culminate in amazement, if the wisdom of the non-slaveholders does not soon baffle slavery.

From the eleventh year previous to the close of the eighteenth century down to the present moment, slaveholders and slave-breeders, who, to speak naked truth, are, as a general thing, unfit to occupy any honorable station in life, have, by chicanery and usurpation, wielded all the official power of the South; and, excepting the patriotic services of the noble abolitionists above-mentioned, the sole aim and drift of their legislation has been to aggrandize themselves, to strengthen slavery, and to keep the poor whites, the constitutional majority, bowed down in the deepest depths of degradation. We propose to subvert this entire system of oligarchal despotism. We think there should be *some* legislation for decent white men, not alone for negroes and slaveholders. Slavery lies at the root of all the shame, poverty, ignorance, tyranny and imbecility of the South; slavery must be thoroughly eradicated; let this be done, and a glorious future will await us.

The statesmen who are to abolish slavery in Kentucky, must be mainly and independently constituted by the non-slaveholders of Kentucky; so in every other slave State. Past experience has taught us the sheer folly of ever expecting voluntary justice from the slaveholders. Their illicit intercourse with "the mother of harlots" has been kept up so long, and their whole natures have, in consequence, become so depraved, that there is scarcely a spark of honor or magnanimity to be found amongst them. As well might one expect to hear highwaymen clamoring for a universal interdict against traveling, as to expect slaveholders to pass laws for the abolition of slavery. Under all the circumstances, it is the duty of the non-slaveholders to mark out an independent course for themselves, to steer entirely clear of the oligarchy, and to utterly contemn and ignore the many vile instruments of power, animate and inanimate, which have been so freely and so effectually used for their enslavement. Now is the time for them to assert their rights and liberties; never before was there such an appropriate period to strike for Freedom in the South.

Had it not been for the better sense, the purer patriotism, and the more practical justice of the non-slaveholders, the Middle States and New England would still be groaning and groveling under the ponderous burden of slavery; New-York would never have risen above the dishonorable level of Virginia; Pennsylvania, trampled beneath the iron-heel of the black code, would have remained the unprogressive parallel of Georgia; Massachusetts would have continued till the present time, and Heaven only knows how much longer, the contemptible coequal of South Carolina.

Succeeded by the happiest moral effects and the grandest physical results, we have seen slavery crushed beneath the wisdom of the non-slaveholding statesmen of the North; followed by corresponding influences and achievements, many of us who have not yet passed the meridian of life, are destined to see it equally crushed beneath the wisdom of the non-slaveholding Statesmen of the South. With righteous indignation, we enter our disclaimer against the base yet baseless admission that Louisiana and Texas are incapable of producing as great statesmen as Rhode Island and Connecticut. What has been done for New Jersey by the statesmen of New Jersey, can be done for North Carolina by the statesmen of North Carolina; the wisdom of the former State has abolished slavery; as sure as the earth revolves on its axis, the wisdom of the latter will not do less.

That our plan for the abolition of slavery, is the best that can be devised, we have not the vanity to contend; but that it is a good one, and will do to act upon until a better shall have been suggested, we do firmly and conscientiously believe. Though but little skilled in the delicate art of surgery, we have pretty thoroughly probed slavery, the frightful tumor on the body politic, and have, we think, ascertained the precise remedies requisite for a speedy and perfect cure. Possibly the less ardent friends of freedom may object to our prescription, on the ground that some of its ingredients are too griping, and that it will cost the patient a deal of most excruciating pain. But let them remember that the patient is exceedingly refractory, that the case is a desperate one, and that drastic remedies are indispensably necessary. When they shall have invented milder yet equally efficacious ones, it will be time enough to discontinue the use of ours—then no one will be readier than we to discard the infallible strong recipe for the infallible mild. Not at the persecution of a few thousand slaveholders, but at the restitution of natural rights and prerogatives to several millions of non-slaveholders, do we aim.

Inscribed on the banner, which we herewith unfurl to the world, with the full and fixed determination to stand by it or die by it, unless one of more virtuous efficacy shall be presented, are the mottoes which, in substance, embody the principles, as we conceive, that should govern us in our patriotic warfare against the most subtle and insidious foe that ever menaced the inalienable rights and liberties and dearest interests of America:

1st. Thorough Organization and Independent Political Action on the part of the Non-Slaveholding whites of the South.

2nd. Ineligibility of Slaveholders—Never another vote to the Trafficker in Human Flesh.

3rd. No Co-operation with Slaveholders in Politics—No Fellowship with them in Religion—No Affiliation with them in Society.

4th. No Patronage to Slaveholding Merchants—No Guestship in Slave-waiting Hotels—No Fees to Slaveholding Lawyers—No Employment of Slaveholding Physicians—No Audience to Slaveholding Parsons.

5th. No Recognition of Pro-slavery Men, except as Ruffians, Outlaws, and Criminals.

6th. Abrupt Discontinuance of Subscription to Pro-slavery Newspapers.

7th. The Greatest Possible Encouragement to Free White Labor.

8. No more Hiring of Slaves by Non-slaveholders.

9th. Immediate Death to Slavery, or if not immediate, unqualified Proscription of its Advocates during the Period of its Existence.

10th. A Tax of Sixty Dollars on every Slaveholder for each and every Negro in his Possession at the present time, or at any intermediate time between now and the 4th of July, 1863—said Money to be Applied to the transportation of the Blacks to Liberia, to their Colonization in Central or South America, or to their Comfortable Settlement within the Boundaries of the United States.

11th. An additional Tax of Forty Dollars per annum to be levied annually, on every Slaveholder for each and every Negro found in his possession after the 4th of July, 1863—said Money to be paid into the hands of the Negroes so held in Slavery, or, in cases of death, to their next of kin, and to be used by them at their own option.

. . . In our own humble way of thinking, we are frank to confess, we do not believe in the unity of the races. This is a matter, however, which has little or nothing to do with the great question at issue. Aside from any theory concerning the original parentage of the different races of men, facts, material and immaterial, palpable and impalpable —facts of the eyes and facts of the conscience— crowd around us on every hand, heaping proof upon proof, that slavery is a shame, a crime, and a curse—a great moral, social, civil, and political evil—an oppressive burden to the blacks, and an incalculable injury to the whites—a stumbling-block to the nation, an impediment to progress, a damper on all the nobler instincts, principles, aspirations and enterprises of man, and a dire enemy to every true interest.

Waiving all other counts, we have, we think, shown to the satisfaction of every impartial reader, that, as elsewhere stated, on the single score of damages to lands, the slaveholders are, at this moment, indebted to us, the non-slaveholding whites, in the enormous sum of nearly seventy-six hundred millions of dollars. What shall be done with this amount? It is just; shall payment be demanded? No; all the slaveholders in the country could not pay it; nor shall we ever ask them for even a moiety of the amount—no, not even for a dime, nor yet for a cent; we are willing to forfeit every farthing for the sake of freedom; for ourselves we ask no indemnification for the past: we only demand justice for the future.

But, Sirs, knights of bludgeons, chevaliers of bowie-knives and pistols, and lords of the lash, we are unwilling to allow you to swindle the slaves out of all the rights and claims to which, as human beings, they are most sacredly entitled. Not alone for ourself as an individual, but for others also— particularly for five or six millions of Southern non-slaveholding whites, whom your iniquitous statism has debarred from almost all the mental and material comforts of life—do we speak, when we say, you *must* emancipate your slaves, and pay each and every one of them at least sixty dollars cash in hand. By doing this, you will be restoring to them their natural rights, and remunerating them at the rate of less than twenty-six cents per annum for the long and cheerless period of their servitude, from the 20th of August, 1620, when, on James River, in Virginia, they became the unhappy slaves of heartless masters. Moreover, by doing this you will be performing but a simple act of justice to the non-slaveholding whites, upon whom the institution of slavery has weighed scarcely less heavily than upon the negroes themselves. You will also be applying a saving balm to your own outraged hearts and consciences, and your children—yourselves in fact—freed from the accursed stain of slavery, will become respectable, useful, and honorable members of society.

And now, Sirs, we have thus laid down our ultimatum. What are you going to do about it? Something dreadful, as a matter of course! Perhaps you will dissolve the Union *again*. Do it, if you dare! Our motto, and we would have you to understand it, is *the abolition of slavery, and the perpetuation of the American Union*. If, by any means, you do succeed in your treasonable attempts to take the South out of the Union to-day, we will bring her back to-morrow—if she goes away with you, she will return without you.

Do not mistake the meaning of the last clause of the last sentence; we could elucidate it so thoroughly that no intelligent person could fail to comprehend it; but, for reasons which may hereafter appear, we forego the task.

Henceforth there are other interests to be consulted in the South, aside from the interests of negroes and slaveholders. A profound sense of duty incites us to make the greatest possible efforts for the abolition of slavery; an equally profound sense of duty calls for a continuation of those efforts until the very last foe to freedom shall have been utterly vanquished. To the summons of the righteous monitor within, we shall endeavor to prove faithful; no opportunity for inflicting a mortal wound in the side of slavery shall be permitted to pass us unimproved. Thus, terror-engenderers of the South, have we fully and frankly defined our position; we have no modifications to propose, no compromises to offer, nothing to retract. Frown, Sirs, fret, foam, prepare your weapons, threat, strike, shoot, stab, bring on civil war, dissolve the Union, nay annihilate the solar system if you will—do all this, more, less, better, worse, anything—do what you will, Sirs, you can neither foil nor intimidate us; our purpose is as firmly fixed as the eternal pillars of Heaven; we have determined to abolish slavery, and, so help us God, abolish it we will! Take this to bed with you to-night, Sirs, and think about it, dream over it, and let us know how you feel to-morrow morning.

ABOLITIONISM

THE AMERICAN ANTISLAVERY movement was less the product of a specific social indignation than an outgrowth of the "evangelical revival" of the period 1810–30. Though deeply rooted in religious emotion, that revival stressed good works as a necessary concomitant of faith. In its wake spread interest in temperance, Sunday schools, foreign missions, and the work of home missionary societies which brought the Gospel to the frontier and the neglected areas of the expanding cities.

Revivalists like Charles Finney roused people to concern for their souls and their conduct; Congregational and Presbyterian ministers created churches to keep the souls thus found; and wealthy laymen like Arthur and Lewis Tappan provided much of the money needed to print tracts and maintain agents in the field.

Into ground prepared by two decades of evangelical preaching of the individual's moral responsibility for the conduct of others as well as himself, fell the germ of British agitation against the slave trade and slavery in the West Indies. If holding men in bondage was wrong in a British possession, it was equally wrong in the United States. Organizing to put an end to wrong was natural enough to people who had already joined together to promote temperance, Christian education and true piety. In this spirit, the American Anti-slavery Society was founded in 1833.

The following year brought the society its first great accession of strength. A lecture against slavery set the students of Lane Theological Seminary debating the issue, and that debate won the student body to the cause of abolition. When the Seminary's trustees ordered the debate ended, the students abandoned the school and quit Cincinnati. They were earnest young men, western New Yorkers in large part, and strongly influenced by Finney's preaching. Their enthusiasm carried Abolitionism through rural Ohio in a fashion far more effective than any tracts that anti-slavery men could send out from the East.

The lecturer who had given impetus to the cause was Theodore Dwight Weld (1803–1895), himself from western New York although his family was of Connecticut origin and related to the Dwights and Edwardses. Like other youths of the period, Weld injured his eyes by overclose attention to study and was forced to substitute lecturing for a regular education. After two years spent earning his living by teaching a system of mnemonics, Weld was converted by Finney's preaching and became one of the evangelist's co-workers. It was then that Weld returned to books. He studied theology at the Oneida Institute, a manual-labor school where the students supported themselves while they learned. Lewis Tappan's two sons were at Oneida with Weld and through them Weld was drawn into the work of the Anti-slavery Society.

At a meeting of the society's agents in 1836, Weld met the Grimké sisters and saw how much they could aid the cause. You "are *southern* women," he wrote, "*once in law* slaveholders, your friends all slaveholders, etc., hence your testimony, testimony, TESTIMONY is the great desideratum," for the North will believe nothing so much as "the deliberate calm decided testimony of a southern man or woman in your circumstances; and the weight of the *testimony* would be very much increased if it be JOINT *testimony*." Weld coached Angelina Grimké as a lecturer, accordingly, and urged her and her sister Sarah to carry Abolitionism not only to groups of women but also to legislative committees and even mixed audiences.

In the forties, factionalism split the antislavery movement. Weld remained aloof from these dissensions, for he had found another means of bringing the question before the public. Though Congress had refused to receive petitions for the abolition of slavery in the District of Columbia, year after year such petitions were circulated and offered. Gathering signatures to these memorials had brought the slavery issue to the very doorsteps of Ohio and western New York and, through that intensive work, the antislavery movement acquired a flexible organization as well as the prestige inherent in the defense of so important a principle as the right of petition.

In 1841, the leaders of the petition campaign sent Weld to Washington where he served as ghost writer and maintainer of morale to the little group of antislavery men who formed a "knot of agitators" in the House of Representatives. The House effort to censure John Quincy Adams for offering a petition praying for the dissolution of the Union boomeranged under the counterattack of his relentless oratory; the members who feared discussion of the slavery issue were glad to silence him by tabling the resolution of censure.

But the attempt to smother Abolitionism by silence had failed. By 1843, the Whig party was too badly in need of Ohio votes to continue cooperation with the Democrats' policy. The House of Representatives had been made a sounding board for Abolitionists and the slavery debate had left the lecture room and pulpit for the halls of Congress.

The selections here reprinted are from G. H. Barnes and D. C. Dumond, editors, *Letters of Theodore Dwight Weld, Angelina Grimké Weld and Sarah Grimké* (2 vols., New York, 1934) and are published by permission of the American Historical Association.

The flames of Abolitionism were further fed by the Fugitive Slave Law controversy. The Constitution provided for the return of fugitive laborers and, in 1793, a law was passed to implement that provision. That law had not been effective even in the early nineteenth century. As sentiment against slavery matured people in Ohio, Pennsylvania, New Jersey, and New York enlisted themselves to aid fugitives attempting to pass northward from the slave states into freedom. They worked obscurely, in danger of betrayal sometimes, and, at the beginning, against the sentiments of their own communities.

So long as slavery was an institution recognized by the law and the Constitution, the slaveholder was entitled to recover his property. If existing legislation did not afford protection against the opinion of the communities to which slaves fled, then it stood in need of revision. That was Webster's opinion as he rose to answer Calhoun on March 7, 1850. That was the opinion of many conservative men who set their legal obligations above sentiment and abstract justice. Accordingly, they agreed with Webster when he supported the new Fugitive Slave Law of 1850. This provided for the return of slaves in summary fashion on the affidavit of the claimant. The fugitive's testimony was not to be accepted in his own defense and once his ownership had been determined by affidavit, no other legal process might interfere with his recovery. The United States marshal was made liable for the slave's value if he should escape and any obstruction or arrest made the offender subject to a $1,000 fine. The federal commissioner himself was enlisted on the claimant's side, for his fee was $10 if the fugitive were returned to slavery and only $5 should he be declared free.

But the moving of fugitives north on what had come to be called the Underground Railroad did not cease. Slaves were brought north on foot and by steamboat; sometimes they were nailed into boxes; sometimes they were even driven in coaches by white coachmen hired with their own earnings. They were passed along from one "station" to the next. If the fugitive happened to halt at Philadelphia, he might come to William Still (1821–1902),

Negro clerk in the office of the Philadelphia Anti-slavery Society. The city Abolitionists had united to form a Vigilance Committee, when the Fugitive Slave Law was passed, and Still was an important part of its work. The son of a slave who had bought his own freedom, he came to Philadelphia from a farm in the "piney woods" of New Jersey. He won the confidence of the Anti-slavery Society and his home became a station on the Underground. In 1850, he began to record the narratives of the arriving fugitives. Such a record was a dangerous possession, since it might bring the runaway's friends into the hands of the law; but Still continued the record because it might help reunite families separated by flight and sale.

The passages here reprinted are from Still's book, *Underground Rail-Road Records* (Philadelphia, 1886).

The Weld-Grimké Letters

WELD TO ANGELINA AND SARAH GRIMKÉ

New York, N. Y. July 22. 37
Saturday evening

My dear Sister Angelina

I have been in receipt of your letter five or six days. Should have answered it by return mail, but the most important members of the Executive Committee were out of town, and I have not been able to get a sight at the individual whom I wished most to see on the subject of your letter until nine o'clock tonight. *Seeing* them however has been with me a mere matter of course, in compliance with your request, and to relieve you of anxiety, and not because I had the least doubt as to their feelings on the subject referred. Your relation to the Executive Committee seems rather a relation of Christian kindness— a sort of *cooperative* relation recognizing harmony of views and feelings, with common labors, joys and trials in a common cause, rather than *authority* on the one hand and a *representative* agency on the other. In short the relation which you sustain to the Ex. Com. no more attaches their *sanction* to your public holdings-forth to promiscuous assemblies than it does to your "theeing and thouing" or to your tight crimped caps, seven by nine bonnets, or that impenetrable drab that defieth utterly all amalgamation of colors! If any gainsay your speaking in

public and to *men*, they gainsay the *Quakers* and not the *abolitionists*. They fly in the face of a *denominational* tenet, not an *anti slavery* doctrine or *measure*. I mean *distinctively*: I would to God that every anti slavery woman in this land had heart and head and womanhood enough and leisure withal to preach as did the captive woman in the second century to the warriors of a vandal army and to a barbarian monarch and his court till savage royalty laid off its robes at the foot of the cross and a fierce soldiery relaxed and wept under the preaching of a woman. God give thee a mouth and wisdom to prophesy like the daughters of Philip, like Huldah and Deborah.

If the men wish to come, it is downright *slaveholding* to shut them out. *Slaveholders* undertake to say that *one* class of human beings shall not be profited by public ministrations. I pray you leave slaveholders "alone in their glory." If I should ever be in the vicinity of your meetings I shall act on the principle that he that hath ears to hear hath a right to *use* them; and if you undertake to stuff them with cotton or to barricade them with brick and mortar, we'll have just as much of a breeze about it as can be made at all consistent with "peace principles."

Why! folks talk about women's preaching as tho' it was next to highway robbery—eyes astare and mouth agape. Pity women were not born with a split stick on their tongues! Ghostly dictums have fairly beaten it into the heads of the whole world save a fraction, that *mind is sexed*, and *Human rights* are *sex'd*, *moral obligation sex'd*; and to carry out the farce they'll probably beat up for a general match making and all turn in to pairing off in couples matrimonial, *consciences*, accountabilities, arguments, duties, philosophy, facts, and theories in the abstract. So much for the "March of mind," i.e. proxy-thinking, India rubber consciences, expediency, tom fooleries, with "whatsoever defileth and worketh abomination and maketh a lie." But enough of *this*.

Now for the scolding. Quarter! quarter! quarter!

1st. You say "On account of thy *neglect* in not having the extracts on slavery published for me at the right time," etc. *Not guilty*, say I. Avast there with your railing accusations. Ah, you haven't lived at the South for nothing. "Practice makes perfect." Wonder how long it would take me to get my hand in; quite certain I should be a dull scholar, tho' if I had *you* for teacher, rather think I should come up *fast*—perhaps make a prodigy.

2. That infinite distinction between the "rights" and the "wrongs" of woman, just exactly the difference between "*pencil marks*" and *pen* strokes. So then nothing but jet black will do for you. Well its a noble labor. I have strong predilections that way myself; think I should carry an *ink* bottle in my pocket if it would [not] put my temperance good name in jeopardy.

3. "Hypocritical pretence." Pretty good at "hard language" for a new beginner. True it might be a world harder but dont be discouraged. Children you know when learning to write are apt to keep their first strait marks to measure future progress by. Now suppose you keep up your spirits with the same recipe. I can assure you from experience you will find it very exhilirating.

Enough for a quarrel: now to *business*. The day that I received your letter I sent Wheelers Law of Slavery and divers other books and papers to you and Sarah, Care of Fuller, to be left at 25 Cornhill. Also a package of Convention documents from Julia. She will make you her own apology for not sending them before. She received your message from me the day of my arrival in the city. In the package you will find the Emancipator of the date you mention, also several others before and after. While passing from place to place you must expect that many things sent by mail will *miss* you. I suppose I never received more than half of my Emancipators when lecturing. Your letters to Catharine Beecher I like greatly, and yet I wish they were *better*. In the first letter the words *liberty*, freedom, and if I remember right some other terms are used *vaguely*. Liberty! What does it mean? Anything, everything. In common parlance you say "Every man has an inalienable right to *liberty*." That conveys no *definite* idea. It *may* mean any one of fifty things. In *discussion*, especially such a discussion demanding *accurate* analysis and *exact* definition presenting the naked *point*, every thing like a loose popular phraseology confuses. In the next letter you say "this principle of freedom is embedded in our very natures," or something like it. "Principle of freedom" if it had been FREEDOM *of principle* it would have been just about as definite. You speak of "slave-holding" as being "*the permanent exercise of the manstealing* POWER." The *power* of *man*stealing is the power of stealing *anything else*, the power of putting out the hand and of willing to do it, or anything equivalent. I presume you *meant* "slaveholding is the constant or habitual perpetration of the ACT of manstealing." To *make* a slave is *man stealing*—the *act itself*; to *hold* him such, is man stealing—the *habit*, the *permanent* state, made up of *individual* acts. In other words to BEGIN to hold a slave is *man*-stealing; to *keep on* holding him is merely a *repetition* of the first act, doing the same identical thing *all the time*. A series of the same acts continued for a length of time is a *habit* or *permanent state*, and the first of this series of the *same* acts that make up this habit or state is *just like all the rest*. But I see I have no room to say a few other things about the letters that [I] want to.

Your allusion to the *long* time taken by C. E. B. to answer your appeal with a remark or two in conexion *looks* a little like *vanity*, as well as a sort of stoop to undignified *twitting*.

You talk about "throwing them from your pen." Well keep throwing, but take *true aim*, and so *hit* that they wont *bound back*. So you see I am at my old tricks of fault finding with you. Be patient. In this hollow world where even *most* of those who call themselves *friends* show it only by flattery, you will escape criticism *pretty much*; and even if mine should be unjust you can quickly *neutralize* them. A thousand things crowd upon me, but I have no room. Do take care of your *health* and may God give you his own sweet and ceaseless *communion*, better, better than life. Surely there is not need for me to say again to you and dear Sarah, call on me at all times for whatever I have or can do for you. Most affectionately your brother in Jesus T. D. Weld

ANGELINE GRIMKÉ TO WELD

Groton [Mass.] 8th Month 12. [1837]
My Dear Brother

No doubt thou hast heard by this time of all the fuss that is now making in this region about our stepping so far out of the bounds of female propriety as to lecture to promiscuous assemblies. My auditors literally sit some times with "mouths agape and eyes astare," so that I cannot help smiling in the midst of "rhetorical flourishes" to witness their perfect amazement at hearing a woman speak in the churches. I wish thou couldst see Brother Phelp's letter to us on this subject and sisters admirable reply. I suppose he will soon come out with a conscientious protest against us. I am waiting in some anxiety to see what the Executive Committee mean to do in these troublous times, whether to renounce us or not. But seriously speaking, we are placed very unexpectedly in a very trying situation, in the forefront of an entirely new contest—a contest for the *rights* of *woman* as a moral, intelligent and responsible being. Harriet Martineau says "God and man know that the time has not come for women to make their injuries even heard of": but it seems as tho' it had come *now* and that the exigency must be met with the firmness and faith of woman in by gone ages. I cannot help feeling some regret that this sh'ld have come up *before* the Anti Slavery question was settled, so fearful am I that it may injure that blessed cause, and then again I think this must be the Lord's time and therefore the *best* time, for it seems to have been brought about by a concatenation of circumstances over which we had no control. The fact is it involves the interests of every minister in our land and therefore they will stand almost in a solid phalanx against woman's rights and I am afraid the discussion of this question will divide in Jacob and scatter in Israel; it will also touch every man's interests at home, in the tenderest relation of life; it will go down into the very depths of his soul and cause great searchings of heart. I am glad H. Winslow of Boston has come out so boldly and told us just what I believe is in the hearts of thousands of men in our land. I must confess my womanhood is insulted, my moral feelings outraged when I reflect on these things, and I am sure *I know just* how the free colored people feel towards the whites when they pay them more than common attention; it is *not paid as a* RIGHT, but *given as a* BOUNTY on a *little* more than *ordinary* sense. There is not one man in 500 who really understands what kind of attention is alone acceptable to a woman of pure and exalted moral and intellectual worth. Hast thou read Sisters letters in the Spectator? I want thee to read them and let us know what thou thinkest of them. That a wife is *not* to be subject to her husband in any other sense than I am to her or she to me, seems to be strange and *alarming* doctrine indeed, but how can it be otherwise unless *she surrenders her moral responsibility*, which *no woman has a right* to do? I want to review H[ubbard] W[inslow]'s sermon and I think I would, if brother Wright or thyself could see it before it was published but you are so far off. WHO will stand by woman in the great struggle? As to our being Quakers being an *excuse* for our speaking in public, we do *not* stand on this ground at all; we ask *no* favors for ourselves, but *claim* rights for our *sex*. If it is wrong for woman to lecture or preach then let the Quakers give up their false views, and let other sects refuse to hear their women, but if it is *right* then let *all* women who have gifts, "mind their calling" and enjoy "the liberty wherewith Christ hath made them free," in that declaration of Paul, "in Christ Jesus there is neither male nor female." O! if in our intercourse with each other we realized this great truth, how delightful, ennobling and dignified it would be, but as I told the Moral Reform Society of Boston in my address, *this* reformation *must begin with ourselves*.

I thank thee for thy strictures on my letters to C. E. B[eecher], but should have thanked thee still more if *before* they were republished in the Emancipator thou hadst been so *kind a brother as to have corrected* them for me. *Didst* thou do as thou wouldst have been done by? I find thou wilt find out *my pride* in whatever form it appear, will keep a watch, for I have a *great deal* of it—so much that I should not like at all to see such "a *distinguished man*" as thyself at one of my lectures; and if *moral suasion* could keep thee out, I assure thee I would NOT let thee come in, unless I was in so *humble* a mood as to be ready for a close criticism on the matter and manner of my talk and gesture, etc. I did not like brother Stantons coming to two of our meetings, but did not know him well enough to beg him to keep away; as for thee, I should feel quite free to ask *thee* to do so. How dost thou think I felt at those great meetings in Lowell? 1500 city people in the blaze of a chandelier. Sister says that before I rose I looked as if I was saying to myself "the time has come and the sacrifice must be offered." Indeed I often feel in our meetings as if I was "as a lamb led to the slaughter," sometimes so sick before I rise that it seems impossible for me to speak 10 minutes; but the Lord is at my right hand, I lean on the arm of my beloved and he sustains me and fills my mouth as soon as I open it in faith for the dumb. At times when I feel so miserable and little and incompetent I remember what thou told us about thy feelings before speaking and am really strengthened by thy experience.

I am afraid thou art not the only Northern man who thinks I have not lived at the South for nothing, for I do *scold most terribly* when I undertake to tell the brethren *how* the North is implicated in the guilt of slavery; they look at me in utter amazement. I am not at all surprized they are afraid lest such a woman should usurp authority over the men. The fact is, I *was* once a great scold and I am indebted to a *slave* for curing me of it. It was when I was quite a little girl and she shamed me and coaxed me out of the horrible practice by telling me very affectionately how ugly it was and promising to make me a doll and dress it like a soldier if I would give it up. She made the doll, I made the promise and believe [I have] kept it unbroken to this day so far as slaves were concerned. I think this woman did a great deal towards opening my childish heart to sympathize with these poor suffering bleeding ones. I thank the Lord for it; and to this time I remember that doll and her kind advice with feelings which bring tears into my eyes. We have been spending 10 days in this lovely little village at Dr. Farnsworth's and lecturing in the vicinity every other day for Sister has a troublesome little cough that just keeps her *good for nothing* brother Weld in the way of lecturing: she gets cold continually and I dont know what to do with her, sometimes wish she was safe in Phil'a for I think this climate must be injurious to her lungs; then again she says her *mind* has never got over one week of hard work when we first set off to hold meetings, so we are going to Brookline for *her* to rest. I am quite well, for I take good care of myself, for instance when I hold forth for 2 hours and ride 14 miles as I did yesterday, I retire at 8 Oclock and take a good rest, and then I am as strong as ever and ready to run over the hills in the morning.

I tho't thou promisedst to go to thy Fathers farm and hoe corn and potatoes. If Cornelia is not a very good Abolitionist I think *she* will certainly quarrel and scold about thy breach of promise, for I hear thou art poring over great musty volumes in the libraries of that miserable place N.Y. How does it agree with thy health?

Last but *not* least we thank thee *very* much for the books, papers, scraps, etc. which came safely to hand. I hope to study the Law book at brother Philbricks where we go on the 14th. Thanks too for that scratchification; some words NOT de-

cyphered yet but as practice makes perfect, perhaps we shall learn in progress of time how to read *all* thy hieroglyphics. I enclose $10; pay thyself what we owe thee and keep the rest. We shall probably want other things from N.Y. Pay R. Williams $2 for the Emancipator I asked him to send to Elizabeth Pease of Eng. E. Wright I owe for some pamphlets G. Thom[p]son sent me to his care, and thyself for the binding of those books, and the law book.

14—Yesterday the sabbath, rode 12 miles to lecture at Roxboro, brother Cross having written us a pressing invitation to come and plead the cause of God's perishing poor in *his pulpit*. It so happened that yesterday was the only day we could do so before we left for Boston. Found his meeting crammed to overflowing. O! what a feeling, to see such a congregation waiting for the words that shall fall from MY unworthy lips. Thou knowest it dear brother, and can understand all about it *except that I am a woman*. I spoke an hour and a half and then stopped and took some refreshment with his family. He says J. Woodbury is against our womanhood and that as *all* the Congregational ministers except himself (about here I mean) are opposed, he expects to have to fight a battle at their next meeting; and that he means to throw down the gauntlet about women's preaching. We pointed out some texts he had not tho't of and tried to throw our views before his mind. May the Lord open his heart more and more on this subject and sustain him in the sore conflict he will have to wage, if he is faithful in pleading for womans essential rights. I have no doubt that posterity will read withal *women* were *not* permitted to preach the gospel, with as much amazement and indignation as we do that no *colored* man in No. Ca. is allowed this *holy right*. Now we want thee to sustain us on the high ground of MORAL RIGHT, *not* of Quaker peculiarity. This question must be met *now;* let us do it as *moral* beings, and not try to turn a SECTARIAN *peculiarity* to the best account for the benefit of Abolitionism. WE do not stand on Quaker ground, but on Bible ground and *moral right*. What we claim for ourselves, we claim for *every* woman whom God has called and qualified with gifts and graces. Can't *thou* stand *just here* side by side with us?

We have seen the last Emancipator and are satisfied. It *may* do to take such ground now but like the little city of Agar it *must* soon be abandoned for the munition of rocks high above the plain of Sectarianism. Mary Parker sent us word that the Boston women would stand by us if *every* body else forsook us. A. Weston has been here with us and is very strong. She is a charming little woman. Farewell may the Lord speedily restore thee to health and prepare thee for the field again

with a double portion of His holy spirit is the prayer of

Thy sister in the bonds of woman and the slave

A. E. Gé.

The Underground Railroad

BY WILLIAM STILL

ABRAM GALLOWAY AND RICHARD EDEN, TWO PASSENGERS SECRETED IN A VESSEL LOADED WITH SPIRITS OF TURPENTINE. SHROUDS PREPARED TO PREVENT BEING SMOKED TO DEATH

THE PHILADELPHIA branch of the Underground Rail Road was not fortunate in having very frequent arrivals from North Carolina. Of course such of her slave population as managed to become initiated in the mysteries of traveling North by the Underground Rail Road were sensible enough to find out nearer and safer routes than through Pennsylvania. Nevertheless the Vigilance Committee of Philadelphia occasionally had the pleasure of receiving some heroes who were worthy to be classed among the bravest of the brave, no matter who they may be who have claims to this distinction.

In proof of this bold assertion the two individuals whose names stand at the beginning of this chapter are presented. Abram was only twenty-one years of age, mulatto, five feet six inches high, intelligent and the picture of good health. "What was your master's name?" inquired a member of the Committee. "Milton Hawkins," answered Abram. "What business did Milton Hawkins follow?" again queried said member. "He was chief engineer on the Wilmington and Manchester Rail Road" (not a branch of the Underground Rail Road), responded Richard. "Describe him," said the member. "He was a slim built, tall man with whiskers. He was a man of very good disposition. I always belonged to him; he owned three. He always said he would sell before he would use a whip. His wife was a very mean woman; she would whip contrary to his orders." "Who was your father?" was further inquired. "John Wesley Galloway," was the prompt response. "Describe your father?" "He was captain of a government vessel; he recognized me as his son, and protected me as far as he was allowed so to do; he lived at Smithfield, North Carolina. Abram's master, Milton Hawkins, lived at Wilmington, N. C." "What prompted you to escape?" was next asked. "Because times were hard and I

could not come up with my wages as I was required to do, so I thought I would try and do better." At this juncture Abram explained substantially in what sense times were hard, &c. In the first place he was not allowed to own himself; he, however, preferred hiring his time to serving in the usual way. This favor was granted Abram; but he was compelled to pay $15 per month for his time, besides finding himself in clothing, food, paying doctor bills, and a head tax of $15 a year.

Even under this master, who was a man of very good disposition, Abram was not contented. In the second place, he "always thought Slavery was wrong," although he had "never suffered any personal abuse." Toiling month after month the year round to support his master and not himself, was the one intolerable thought. Abram and Richard were intimate friends, and lived near each other. Being similarly situated, they could venture to communicate the secret feelings of their hearts to each other. Richard was four years older than Abram, with not quite so much Anglo-Saxon blood in his veins, but was equally as intelligent, and was by trade, a "fashionable barber," well-known to the ladies and gentlemen of Wilmington. Richard owed service to Mrs. Mary Loren, a widow. "She was very kind and tender to all her slaves." "If I was sick," said Richard, "she would treat me the same as a mother would." She was the owner of twenty, men, women and children, who were all hired out, except the children too young for hire. Besides having his food, clothing and doctor's expenses to meet, he had to pay the "very kind and tender-hearted widow" $12.50 per month, and head tax to the State, amounting to twenty-five cents per month. It so happened, that Richard at this time, was involved in a matrimonial difficulty. Contrary to the laws of North Carolina, he had lately married a free girl, which was an indictable offence, and for which the penalty was then in soak for him—said penalty to consist of thirty-nine lashes, and imprisonment at the discretion of the judge.

So Abram and Richard put their heads together, and resolved to try the Underground Rail Road.

They concluded that liberty was worth dying for, and that it was their duty to strike for Freedom even if it should cost them their lives. The next thing needed, was information about the Underground Rail Road. Before a great while the captain of a schooner turned up, from Wilmington, Delaware. Learning that his voyage extended to Philadelphia, they sought to find out whether this captain was true to Freedom. To ascertain this fact required no little address. It had to be done in such a way, that even the captain would not really understand what they were up to, should he be found untrue. In this instance, however, he was the right man in the right place, and very well understood his business.

Abram and Richard made arrangements with him to bring them away; they learned when the vessel would start, and that she was loaded with tar, rosin, and spirits of turpentine, amongst which the captain was to secrete them. But here came the difficulty. In order that slaves might not be secreted in vessels, the slave-holders of North Carolina had procured the enactment of a law requiring all vessels coming North to be smoked.

To escape this dilemma, the inventive genius of Abram and Richard soon devised a safe-guard against the smoke. This safe-guard consisted in silk oil cloth shrouds, made large, with drawing strings, which, when pulled over their heads, might be drawn very tightly around their waists, whilst the process of smoking might be in operation. A bladder of water and towels were provided, the latter to be wet and held to their nostrils, should there be need. In this manner they had determined to struggle against death for liberty. The hour approached for being at the wharf. At the appointed time they were on hand ready to go on the boat; the captain secreted them, according to agreement. They were ready to run the risk of being smoked to death; but as good luck would have it, the law was not carried into effect in this instance, so that the "smell of smoke was not upon them." The effect of the turpentine, however, of the nature of which they were totally ignorant, was worse, if possible, than the smoke would have been. The blood was literally drawn from them at every pore in frightful quantities. But as heroes of the bravest type they resolved to continue steadfast as long as a pulse continued to beat, and thus they finally conquered.

The invigorating northern air and the kind treatment of the Vigilance Committee acted like a charm upon them, and they improved very rapidly from their exhaustive and heavy loss of blood. Desiring to retain some memorial of them, a member of the Committee begged one of their silk shrouds, and likewise procured an artist to take the photograph of one of them; which keepsakes have been valued very highly. In the regular order of arrangements the wants of Abram and Richard were duly met by the Committee, financially and otherwise, and they were forwarded to Canada. After their safe arrival in Canada, Richard addressed a member of the Committee thus:

KINGSTON, July 20, 1857

MR. WILLIAM STILL—*Dear Friend:*—I take the opertunity of wrighting a few lines to let you no that we air all in good health hoping thos few lines may find you and your family engoying the same blessing. We arived in King all saft Canada West Abram Galway gos to work this morning at $1 75 per day and John pediford is at work for mr george mink and i will opne a shop for my self in a few days My wif will send a daugretipe to your cair whitch you will pleas to send on to me Richard Edons to the cair of George Mink Kingston C W

Yours with Respect,   RICHARD EDONS

Abram, his comrade, allied himself faithfully to John Bull until Uncle Sam became involved in the contest with the rebels. In this hour of need Abram hastened back to North Carolina to help fight the battles of Freedom. How well he acted his part, we are not informed. We only know that, after the war was over, in the reconstruction of North Carolina, Abram was promoted to a seat in its Senate. He died in office only a few months since. The portrait is almost a "fac-simile."

ESCAPE OF JOHN HENRY HILL FROM THE SLAVE AUCTION IN RICHMOND, ON THE FIRST DAY OF JANUARY, 1853

JOHN HENRY at that time, was a little turned of twenty-five years of age, full six feet high, and remarkably well proportioned in every respect. He was rather of a brown color, with marked intellectual features. John was by trade, a carpenter, and was considered a competent workman. The year previous to his escape, he hired his time, for which he paid his owner $150. This amount John had fully settled up the last day of the year. As he was a young man of steady habits, a husband and father, and withal an ardent lover of Liberty; his owner, John Mitchell, evidently observed these traits in his character, and concluded that he was a dangerous piece of property to keep; that his worth in money could be more easily managed than the man. Consequently, his master unceremoniously, without intimating in any way to John, that he was to be sold, took him to Richmond, on the first day of January (the great annual sale day), and directly to the slave-auction. Just as John was being taken into the building, he was invited to submit to hand-cuffs. As the thought flashed upon his mind that he was about to be sold on the auction-block, he grew terribly desperate. "Liberty or death" was the watchword of that awful moment. In the twinkling of an eye, he turned on his enemies, with his fist, knife, and feet, so tiger-like, that he actually put four or five men to flight, his master among the number. His enemies thus suddenly baffled, John wheeled, and, as if assisted by an angel, strange as it may appear, was soon out of sight of his pursuers, and securely hid away. This was the last hour of John Henry's slave life, but not, however, of his struggles and sufferings for freedom, for before a final chance to escape presented itself, nine months elapsed. The mystery as to where, and how he fared, the following account, in his own words, must explain—

Nine months I was trying to get away. I was secreted for a long time in a kitchen of a merchant near the corner of Franklyn and 7th streets, at Richmond, where I was well taken care of, by a lady friend of my mother. When I got Tired of staying in that place, I wrote myself a pass to pass myself to Petersburg, here I stopped with a very prominent Colored person, who was a friend to Freedom stayed here until two white friends told other friends if I was in the city to tell me to go at once, and stand not upon the order of going, because they had hard a plot. I wrot a pass, started for Richmond, Reached Manchester, got off the Cars walked into Richmond, once more got back into the same old Den, Stayed here from the 16th of Aug. to 12th Sept. On the 11th of Sept. 8 o'clock P. M. a message came to me that there had been a State Room taken on the steamer City of Richmond for my benefit, and I assured the party that it would be occupied if God be willing. Before 10 o'clock the next morning, on the 12th, a beautiful Sept. day, I arose early, wrote my pass for Norfolk left my old Den with a many a good bye, turned out the back way to 7th St., thence to Main, down Main behind 4 night waich to old Rockett's and after about 20 minutes of delay I succeed in Reaching the State Room. My Conductor was very much Excited, but I felt as Composed as I do at this moment, for I had started from my Den that morning for Liberty or for Death providing myself with a Brace of Pistels.
Yours truly J. H. HILL.

A private berth was procured for him on the steamship City of Richmond, for the amount of $125, and thus he was brought on safely to Philadelphia. While in the city, he enjoyed the hospitalities of the Vigilance Committee, and the greetings of a number of friends, during the several days of his sojourn. The thought of his wife, and two children, left in Petersburg, however, naturally caused him much anxiety. Fortunately, they were free, therefore, he was not without hope of getting them; moreover, his wife's father (Jack McCracy), was a free man, well known, and very well to do in the world, and would not be likely to see his daughter and grandchildren suffer. In this particular, Hill's lot was of a favorable character, compared with that of most slaves leaving their wives and children.

FIRST LETTER

ON ARRIVING IN CANADA

TORONTO, October 4th, 1853
DEAR SIR:—I take this method of informing you that I am well, and that I got to this city all safe and sound, though I did not get here as soon as I expect. I left your city on Saterday and I was on the way untel the Friday following. I got to New York the same day that I left Philadelphia, but I had to stay there untel Monday evening. I left that place at six o'clock. I got to Albany next morning in time to take the half past six o'clock train for Rochester, here I stay untel Wensday night. The reason I stay there so long Mr. Gibbs given me a letter to Mr Morris at Rochester. I left that place Wensday, but I only got five miles from that city that night. I got to Lewiston on Thurday afternoon, but too late for the boat to this city. I left Lewiston on Friday at one o'clock, got to this city at five. Sir I found this to be a very handsome city. I like it better than any city I ever saw. It are not as large as the city that you live in, but it is very large place much more so than I expect to find it. I seen the gentleman that you given me letter to. I think him much of a gentleman. I got into work on Monday. The man whom I am working for is name Myers; but I expect to go to work for another man by name of Tinsly, who is a master workman in this city. He says that he will give me work next week and everybody advises me to work for Mr. Tinsly as there more surity in him.

Mr. Still, I have been looking and looking for my friends for several days, but have not seen nor heard of them. I hope and trust in the Lord Almighty that all things are well with them. My dear sir I could feel so much better sattisfied if I could hear from my wife. Since I reached this city I have talagraphed to friend Brown to send my thing to me, but I cannot hear a word from no one at all. I have written to Mr. Brown two or three times since I left the city. I trust that he has gotten my wife's letters, that is if she has written. Please direct your letters to me, near the corner Sarah and Edward street, until I give you further notice. You will tell friend B. how to direct his letters, as I forgotten it when I writt to him, and ask him if he has heard anything from Virginia. Please to let me hear from him without delay for my very soul is trubled about my friends whom I expected to of seen here before this hour. Whatever you do please to write. I shall look for you paper shortly.

Belive me sir to be your well wisher.

JOHN H. HILL.

SECOND LETTER

EXPRESSIONS OF GRATITUDE—THE CUSTOM HOUSE REFUSES TO CHARGE HIM DUTY—HE IS GREATLY CONCERNED FOR HIS WIFE

TORONTO, October 30th, 1853.
MY DEAR FRIEND:—I now write to inform you that I have received my things all safe and sound, and also have shuck hand with the friend that you send on to this place one of them is stopping with me. His name is Chas. Stuert, he seemes to be a tolerable smart fellow. I Rec'd my letters. I have taken this friend to see Mr. Smith. However will give him a place to board untell he can get to work. I shall do every thing I can for them all that

I see the gentleman wish you to see his wife and let her know that he arrived safe, and present his love to her and to all the friend. Mr. Still, I am under ten thousand obligation to you for your kindness when shall I ever repay? S. speek very highly of you. I will state to you what Custom house master said to me. He ask me when he Presented my efects are these your efects. I answered yes. He then ask me was I going to settle in Canada. I told him I was. He then ask me of my case. I told all about it. He said I am happy to see you and all that will come. He ask me how much I had to pay for my Paper. I told him half dollar. He then told me that I should have my money again. He a Rose from his seat and got my money. So my friend you can see the people and tell them all this is a land of liberty and believe they will find friends here. My best love to all.

My friend I must call upon you once more to do more kindness for me that is to write to my wife as soon as you get this, and tell her when she gets ready to come she will pack and consign her things to you. You will give her some instruction, but not to your expenses but to her own.

When you write direct your letters to Phillip Ubank, Petersburg, Va. My Box arrived here the 27th.

My dear sir I am in a hurry to take this friend to church, so I must close by saying I am your humble servant in the cause of liberty and humanity.

JOHN H. HILL.

MANIFEST DESTINY

THE AGGRESSIVE EXPANSIONISM which Canning had found characteristic of the United States in the twenties did not break through her boundaries again until the annexation of Texas. From that date until the Civil War, the country's urge to expand found vent in war, conquest, filibustering, and orations on "manifest destiny."

That phrase became a catchword in 1846 during the debate on the Oregon boundary, when Robert Winthrop of Massachusetts told the House of Representatives that he would join the advocates of our "manifest destiny" to rule the Western Hemisphere on the day they showed him the clause in Father Adam's will which had made them that bequest. Winthrop's words soon became a slogan, but the phrase was not coined by him. It is to John L. O'Sullivan (1813–1895), editor of the *Democratic Review*, that Julius Pratt attributes the first use of the words, not in connection with

the dispute over the Oregon boundary but in an article on Texas.

In that article, which appeared in the July–August, 1845, issue, O'Sullivan called for a halt to criticism of our annexation policy. Had we not done as we did, other nations might have interfered with our "manifest destiny" to overspread the continent. Contrary to present policy, we had not acted unjustly toward Mexico; unwisely perhaps, but never unrighteously.

Nor was annexation a proslavery measure. On the contrary, annexation would operate to draw slaves from the northern slave states to southern regions less opposed to a mingling of races. As for the opinion of other powers—the United States will soon outweigh them all in strength.

O'Sullivan called his article "Annexation." The selection here reprinted is from *The Democratic Review.*

Annexation

BY JOHN L. O'SULLIVAN

IT IS TIME now for opposition to the Annexation of Texas to cease, all further agitation of the waters of bitterness and strife, at least in connexion with this question,—even though it may perhaps be required of us as a necessary condition of the freedom of our institutions, that we must live on for ever in a state of unpausing struggle and excitement upon some subject of party division or other. But, in regard to Texas, enough has now been given to Party. It is time for the common duty of Patriotism to the Country to succeed;—or if this claim will not be recognized, it is at least time for common sense to acquiesce

with decent grace in the inevitable and the irrevocable.

Texas is now ours. Already, before these words are written, her Convention has undoubtedly ratified the acceptance, by her Congress, of our proffered invitation into the Union; and made the requisite changes in her already republican form of constitution to adopt it to its future federal relations. Her star and her stripe may already be said to have taken their place in the glorious blazon of our common nationality; and the sweep of our eagle's wing already includes within its circuit the wide extent of her fair and fertile land. She is no longer to us a mere geographical space—a certain combination of coast, plain, mountain, valley, forest and stream. She is no longer to us a mere country on the map. She comes within the dear and sacred designation of Our Country; no longer a *"pays,"* she is a part of *"la patrie;"* and that which is at once a sentiment and a virtue, Patriotism, already begins to thrill for her too within the national heart. It is time then that all should cease to treat her as alien, and even adverse—cease to denounce and villify all and everything connected with her accession—cease to thwart and oppose the remaining steps for its consummation; or where such efforts are felt to be unavailing, at least to embitter the hour of reception by all the most ungracious frowns of aversion and words of unwelcome. There has been enough of all this. It has had its fitting day during the period when, in common with every other possible question of practical policy that can arise, it unfortunately became one of the leading topics of party division, of presidential electioneering. But that period has passed, and with it let its prejudices and its passions, its discords and its denunciations, pass away too. The next session of Congress will see the representatives of the new young State in their places in both our halls of national legislation, side by side with those of the old Thirteen. Let their reception into "the family" be frank, kindly, and cheerful, as befits such an occasion, as comports not less with our own self-respect than patriotic duty towards them. Ill betide those foul birds that delight to 'file their own nest, and disgust the ear with perpetual discord of ill-omened croak.

Why, were other reasoning wanting, in favor of now elevating this question of the reception of Texas into the Union, out of the lower region of our past party dissensions, up to its proper level of a high and broad nationality, it surely is to be found, found abundantly, in the manner in which other nations have undertaken to intrude themselves into it, between us and the proper parties to the case, in a spirit of hostile interference against us, for the avowed object of thwarting our policy and hampering our power, limiting our greatness and checking the fulfilment of our manifest destiny to overspread the continent allotted by Providence for the free development of our yearly multiplying millions. This we have seen done by England, our old rival and enemy; and by France, strangely coupled with her against us, under the influence of the Anglicism strongly tinging the policy of her present prime minister, Guizot. The zealous activity with which this effort to defeat us was pushed by the representatives of those governments, together with the

character of intrigue accompanying it, fully constituted that case of foreign interference, which Mr. Clay himself declared should, and would unite us all in maintaining the common cause of our country against the foreigner and the foe. We are only astonished that this effect has not been more fully and strongly produced, and that the burst of indignation against this unauthorized, insolent and hostile interference against us, has not been more general even among the party before opposed to Annexation, and has not rallied the national spirit and national pride unanimously upon that policy. We are very sure that if Mr. Clay himself were now to add another letter to his former Texas correspondence, he would express this sentiment, and carry out the idea already strongly stated in one of them, in a manner which would tax all the powers of blushing belonging to some of his party adherents.

It is wholly untrue, and unjust to ourselves, the pretence that the Annexation has been a measure of spoliation, unrightful and unrighteous—of military conquest under forms of peace and law—of territorial aggrandizement at the expense of justice, and justice due by a double sanctity to the weak. This view of the question is wholly unfounded, and has been before so amply refuted in these pages, as well as in a thousand other modes, that we shall not again dwell upon it. The independence of Texas was complete and absolute. It was an independence, not only in fact but of right. No obligation of duty towards Mexico tended in the least degree to restrain our right to effect the desired recovery of the fair province once our own—whatever motives of policy might have prompted a more deferential consideration of her feelings and her pride, as involved in the question. If Texas became peopled with an American population, it was by no contrivance of our government, but on the express invitation of that of Mexico herself; accompanied with such guaranties of State independence, and the maintenance of a federal system analogous to our own, as constituted a compact fully justifying the strongest measures of redress on the part of those afterwards deceived in this guaranty, and sought to be enslaved under the yoke imposed by its violation. She was released, rightfully and absolutely released, from all Mexican allegiance, or duty of cohesion to the Mexican political body, by the acts and fault of Mexico herself, and Mexico alone. There never was a clearer case. It was not revolution; it was resistance to revolution; and resistance under such circumstances as left independence the necessary resulting state, caused by the abandonment of those with whom her former federal association had existed. What then can be more preposterous than all this clamor by Mexico and the Mexican interest, against Annexation, as a violation of any rights of hers, any duties of ours?

We would not be understood as approving in all its features the expediency or propriety of the mode in which the measure, rightful and wise as it is in itself, has been carried into effect. Its history has been a sad tissue of diplomatic blundering. How much better it might have been managed—how much more smoothly, satisfactorily and successfully! Instead of our present relations with Mexico—instead of the serious risks which have been run, and those plausibilities of opprobrium which we have had to combat, not without great difficulty, nor with entire success—instead of the difficulties which now throng the path to a satisfactory settlement of all our unsettled questions with Mexico—Texas might, by a more judicious and conciliatory diplomacy, have been as securely in the Union as she is now—her boundaries defined—California probably ours—and Mexico and ourselves united by closer ties than ever; of mutual friendship, and mutual support in resistance to the intrusion of European interference in the affairs of the American republics. All this might have been, we little doubt, already secured, had counsels less violent, less rude, less one-sided, less eager in precipitation from motives widely foreign to the national question, presided over the earlier stages of its history. We cannot too deeply regret the mismanagement which has disfigured the history of this question; and especially the neglect of the means which would have been so easy, of satisfying even the unreasonable pretensions, and the excited pride and passion of Mexico. The singular result has been produced, that while our neighbor has, in truth, no real right to blame or complain—when all the wrong is on her side, and there has been on ours a degree of delay and forbearance, in deference to her pretensions, which is to be paralleled by few precedents in the history of other nations—we have yet laid ourselves open to a great deal of denunciation hard to repel, and impossible to silence; and all history will carry it down as a certain fact, that Mexico would have declared war against us, and would have waged it seriously, if she had not been prevented by that very weakness which should have constituted her best defence.

We plead guilty to a degree of sensitive annoyance—for the sake of the honor of our country, and its estimation in the public opinion of the world—which does not find even in satisfied conscience full consolation for the very necessity of seeking consolation there. And it is for this state of things that we hold responsible that gratuitous mismanagement—wholly apart from the main substantial rights and merits of the question, to which alone it is to be ascribed; and which had its origin in its earlier stages, before the accession of Mr. Calhoun to the department of State.

Nor is there any just foundation for the charge that Annexation is a great pro-slavery measure—calculated to increase and perpetuate that institution. Slavery had nothing to do with it. Opinions were and are greatly divided, both at the North and South, as to the influence to be exerted by it on Slavery and the Slave States. That it will tend to facilitate and hasten the disappearance of Slavery from all the northern tier of the present Slave States, cannot surely admit of serious question. The greater value in Texas of the slave labor now employed in those States, must soon produce the effect of draining off that labor southwardly, by the same unvarying law that bids water descend the slope that invites it. Every new Slave State in Texas will make at least one Free State from among those in which that institution now exists—to say nothing of those portions of Texas on which slavery cannot spring and grow—to say nothing of the far more rapid growth of new States in the free West and Northwest, as these fine regions are overspread by the emigration fast flowing over them from Europe, as well as from the Northern and Eastern States of the Union as it exists. On the other hand, it is undeniably much gained for the cause of the eventual voluntary abolition of slavery, that it should have been thus drained off towards the only outlet which appeared to furnish much probability of the ultimate disappearance of the negro race from our borders. The Spanish-Indian-American populations of Mexico, Central America and South America, afford the only receptacle capable of absorbing that race whenever we shall be prepared to slough it off—to emancipate it from slavery, and (simultaneously necessary) to remove it from the midst of our own. Themselves already of mixed and confused blood, and free from the "prejudices" which among us so insuperably forbid the social amalgamation which can alone elevate the Negro race out of a virtually servile degradation even though legally free, the regions occupied by those populations must strongly attract the black race in that direction; and as soon as the destined hour of emancipation shall arrive, will relieve the question of one of its worst difficulties, if not absolutely the greatest.

No—Mr. Clay was right when he declared that Annexation was a question with which slavery had nothing to do. The country which was the subject of Annexation in this case, from its geographical position and relations, happens to be—or rather the portion of it now actually settled, happens to be—a slave country. But a similar process might have taken place in proximity to a different section of our Union; and indeed there is a great deal of Annexation yet to take place, within the life of the present generation, along the whole line of our northern border. Texas has been absorbed into the Union in the inevitable fulfilment of the general law which is rolling our population westward; the connexion of which with that ratio of growth in population which is destined within a hundred years to swell our numbers to the enormous population of *two hundred and fifty millions* (if not more), is too evident to leave us in doubt of the manifest design of Providence in regard to the occupation of this continent. It was disintegrated from Mexico in the natural course of events, by a process perfectly legitimate on its own part, blameless on ours; and in which all the censures due to wrong, perfidy and folly, rest on Mexico alone. And possessed as it was by a population which was in truth but a colonial detachment from our own, and which was still bound by myriad ties of the very heartstrings to its old relations, domestic and political, their incorporation into the Union was not only inevitable, but the most natural, right and proper thing in the world—and it is only astonishing that there should be any among ourselves to say it nay.

In respect to the institution of slavery itself, we have not designed, in what has been said above, to express any judgment of its merits or demerits, *pro* or *con*. National in its character and aims, this Review abstains from the discussion of a topic pregnant with embarrassment and danger—intricate and double-sided—exciting and embittering—and necessarily excluded from a work circulating equally in the South as in the North. It is unquestionably one of the most difficult of the various social problems which at the present day so deeply agitate the thoughts of the civilized world. Is the negro race, or is it not, of equal attributes and capacities with our own? Can they, on a large scale, coexist side by side in the same country on a footing of civil and social equality with the white race? In a free competition of labor with the latter, will they or will they not be ground down to a degradation and misery worse than slavery? When we view the condition of the operative masses of the population in England and other European countries, and feel all the difficulties of the great problem, of the distribution of the fruits of production between capital,

skill and labor, can our confidence be undoubting that in the present condition of society, the conferring of sudden freedom upon our negro race would be a boon to be grateful for? Is it certain that competitive wages are very much better, for a race so situated, than guarantied support and protection? Until a still deeper problem shall have been solved than that of slavery, the slavery of an inferior to a superior race—a relation reciprocal in certain important duties and obligations—is it certain that the cause of true wisdom and philanthropy is not rather, for the present, to aim to meliorate that institution as it exists, to guard against its abuses, to mitigate its evils, to modify it when it may contravene sacred principles and rights of humanity, by prohibiting the separation of families, excessive severities, subjection to the licentiousness of mastership, &c.? Great as may be its present evils, is it certain that we would not plunge the unhappy Helot race which has been entailed upon us, into still greater ones, by surrendering their fate into the rash hands of those fanatic zealots of a single idea, who claim to be their special friends and champions? Many of the most ardent social reformers of the present day are looking towards the idea of *Associated Industry* as containing the germ of such a regeneration of society as will relieve its masses from the hideous weight of evil which now depresses and degrades them to a condition which these reformers often describe as no improvement upon any form of legal slavery—is it certain, then, that the institution in question—as a mode of society, as a relation between the two races, and between capital and labor,—does not contain some dim undeveloped germ of that very principle of reform thus aimed at, out of which proceeds some compensation at least for its other evils, making it the duty of true reform to cultivate and develope the good, and remove the evils?

To all these, and the similar questions which spring out of any intelligent reflection on the subject, we attempt no answer. Strong as are our sympathies in behalf of liberty, universal liberty, in all applications of the principle not forbidden by great and manifest evils, we confess ourselves not prepared with any satisfactory solution to the great problem of which these questions present various aspects. Far from us to say that either of the antagonist fanaticisms to be found on either side of the Potomac is right. Profoundly embarrassed amidst the conflicting elements entering into the question, much and anxious reflection upon it brings us as yet to no other conclusion than to the duty of a liberal tolerance of the honest differences of both sides; together with the certainty that whatever good is to be done in the case is to be done only by the adoption of very different modes of action, prompted by a very different spirit, from those which have thus far, among us, characterized the labors of most of those who claim the peculiar title of "friends of the slave" and "champions of the rights of man." With no friendship for slavery, though unprepared to excommunicate to eternal damnation, with bell, book, and candle, those who are, we see nothing in the bearing of the Annexation of Texas on that institution to awaken a doubt of the wisdom of that measure, or a compunction for the humble part contributed by us towards its consummation.

California will, probably, next fall away from the loose adhesion which, in such a country as Mexico, holds a remote province in a slight equivocal kind of dependence on the metropolis. Imbecile and distracted, Mexico never can exert any real governmental authority over such a country. The impotence of the one and the distance of the other, must make the relation one of virtual independence; unless, by stunting the province of all natural growth, and forbidding that immigration which can alone develope its capabilities and fulfil the purposes of its creation, tyranny may retain a military dominion which is no government in the legitimate sense of the term. In the case of California this is now impossible. The Anglo-Saxon foot is already on its borders. Already the advance guard of the irresistible army of Anglo-Saxon emigration has begun to pour down upon it, armed with the plough and the rifle, and marking its trail with schools and colleges, courts and representative halls, mills and meeting-houses. A population will soon be in actual occupation of California, over which it will be idle for Mexico to dream of dominion. They will necessarily become independent. All this without agency of our government, without responsibility of our people —in the natural flow of events, the spontaneous working of principles, and the adaptation of the tendencies and wants of the human race to the elemental circumstances in the midst of which they find themselves placed. And they will have a right to independence—to self-government—to the possession of the homes conquered from the wilderness by their own labors and dangers, sufferings and sacrifices—a better and a truer right than the artificial title of sovereignty in Mexico a thousand miles distant, inheriting from Spain a title good only against those who have none better. Their right to independence will be the natural right of self-government belonging to any community strong enough to maintain it—distinct

in position, origin and character, and free from any mutual obligations of membership of a common political body, binding it to others by the duty of loyalty and compact of public faith. This will be their title to independence; and by this title, there can be no doubt that the population now fast streaming down upon California will both assert and maintain that independence. Whether they will then attach themselves to our Union or not, is not to be predicted with any certainty. Unless the projected rail-road across the continent to the Pacific be carried into effect, perhaps they may not; though even in that case, the day is not distant when the Empires of the Atlantic and Pacific would again flow together into one, as soon as their inland border should approach each other. But that great work, colossal as appears the plan on its first suggestion, cannot remain long unbuilt. Its necessity for this very purpose of binding and holding together in its iron clasp our fast settling Pacific region with that of the Mississippi valley—the natural facility of the route—the ease with which any amount of labor for the construction can be drawn in from the overcrowded populations of Europe, to be paid in the lands made valuable by the progress of the work itself—and its immense utility to the commerce of the world with the whole eastern coast of Asia, alone almost sufficient for the support of such a road—these considerations give assurance that the day cannot be distant which shall witness the conveyance of the representatives from Oregon and California to Washington within less time than a few years ago was devoted to a similar journey by those from Ohio; while the magnetic telegraph will enable the editors of the "San Francisco Union," the "Astoria Evening Post," or the "Nootka Morning News" to set up in type the first half of the President's Inaugural, before the echoes of the latter half shall have died away beneath the lofty porch of the Capitol, as spoken from his lips.

Away, then, with all idle French talk of *balances of power* on the American Continent. There is no growth in Spanish America! Whatever progress of population there may be in the British Canadas, is only for their own early severance of their present colonial relation to the little island three thousand miles across the Atlantic; soon to be followed by Annexation, and destined to swell the still accumulating momentum of our progress. And whatsoever may hold the balance, though they should cast into the opposite scale all the bayonets and cannon, not only of France and England, but of Europe entire, how would it kick the beam against the simple solid weight of the two hundred and fifty or three hundred millions—and American millions—destined to gather beneath the flutter of the stripes and stars, in the fast hastening year of the Lord 1945?

THE OPENING OF JAPAN

AMERICA'S PRESSURE on her borders was not limited to the Western Hemisphere. Though the United States did not seek to extend its physical conquest beyond the continental domain, it was anxious to expand its commercial activities in the Pacific. American trade with China, which had begun almost as soon as her independence was recognized, increased after 1815 and again when the Opium War of 1839–42 opened more of China to foreign enterprise. Commercial interest and the hardships of American whalers wrecked off the Japanese islands wakened America's desire to penetrate the kingdom. Naval officers had attempted to touch at Yedo and Nagasaki in 1846, but their ships were driven off. The discovery of gold in California, the increase in steamship traffic, which made coaling stations a necessity, and the growth of trade between San Francisco and Shanghai all turned American attention to the "hermit nation" of Japan which lay on the main route between the west and China. The failure of 1846 was repeated in 1851 when another American naval officer was denied entrance to Japanese ports.

By 1852–53, when Perry's expedition sailed, a more militant American policy had developed. The Dutch in their Nagasaki compound —the one spot to which the Japanese had permitted European access since 1641 when all foreigners had been driven from the kingdom —warned the Japanese that the United States was an aggressive nation and that Perry might not be completely peaceable in his purpose.

Matthew Calbraith Perry (1794–1858) entered the navy as a midshipman fifteen years after his birth at Newport, Rhode Island. He fought in the early years of the War of 1812, helped establish Liberia in 1820, visited revolutionary Greece and Turkish Asia Minor in 1826, and then returned to shore duty. From 1833 to 1843, Perry was in command of the New York navy yard, a post that permitted him to pioneer in the new naval techniques necessitated by the introduction of steam. When an expedition against Japan was decided on, Perry, with his experience in war, in naval technology and in dealing with foreign peoples, was a logical choice as commander.

Perry's instructions (the first two documents printed here) were largely drafted by himself. He was to make the Japanese understand the difference between the United States and England and to stress our disinterested tolerance in religious matters as a means of securing his desires without the use of force. But his main effort was to obtain protection for shipwrecked American seamen, to get a coaling station, and to win permission for Americans to trade in Japan.

Perry took a squadron of six ships—they were steam vessels and carried heavy armament of guns—and set out for the Far East. He sailed into Japanese waters with four of these ships; refused to go to Nagasaki to treat with the Dutch; and insisted on delivering the President's letters directly to the Shogun's court. Perry retired then with the announcement that he would return for a reply in the spring.

While Perry was negotiating, Russian and French squadrons sailed into the Western Pacific and the Russian admiral even proposed joint action to the American commodore. Perry, whose views are made clear by his instructions and his later letter suggesting American occupation of a Japanese island as a free port, refused that offer. The presence of foreign navies hastened Perry's return. In February, 1854, he dropped anchor in Yedo Bay and demanded audience with the Mikado, or the Shogun in his stead. Perry accepted the village of Yokohama instead of the city of Yedo as the locale for treaty parleys, however, and in March, after an exchange of gifts and banquets, he secured a treaty. This opened two Japanese ports to foreigners and assured decent treatment of shipwrecked American sailors. If necessary, trade agreements and a consular convention might be concluded later,

but in any case the United States was to have commercial privileges equal to those granted the most favored nation in the future.

These selections are reprinted from Senate Executive Document No. 34, 33d Congress, 2d Session (Washington, 1855).

Correspondence Relative to the Naval Expedition to Japan

BY MATTHEW C. PERRY

SECRETARY OF THE NAVY TO COMMODORE PERRY

United States Navy Department
Washington, November 13, 1852
SIR: So soon as the steam frigate Mississippi shall be in all respects ready for sea, you will proceed in her, accompanied by the steamer Princeton, to Macao, or Hong Kong, in China, where the vessels of your command will rendezvous. You will touch at such ports on your passage out as you may deem necessary for supplies, &c.

It has been deemed necessary to increase the naval force of the United States in the East India and China seas, for reasons which will be found in the enclosed copy of a communication from the Secretary of State addressed to this department under date of November, 1852.

The force at present there consists of the steam frigate Susquehanna, Commander Buchanan, sloop Plymouth, Commander Kelly, and sloop Saratoga, Commander Walker. The store ship Supply, Lieutenant Commanding Sinclair, is on her passage to that station. There will be added to this force, at the earliest day practicable, the ship-of-the-line Vermont, Captain Paulding; the steam frigate Mississippi, Captain McCluney; the corvette Macedonian, Captain Abbot; the steamer Princeton, Commander Lee; the steamer Alleghany, Commander Sands; the sloop Vandalia, Commander Pope; and the store-ship Southhampton, Lieutenant Commanding Boyle.

With this you will receive a copy of the general instructions given to Commodore John H. Aulick, recently in command of the East India squadron, which you will consider as in full force and applicable to your command. You will also receive herewith copies of other orders addressed to Commodore Aulick, which may require your attention after you reach your station.

The special mission to Japan with which you have been charged by the government will require all your firmness and prudence, in respect to which the department entertains the fullest

confidence that they will be adequate for any emergency.

In prosecuting the object of your mission to Japan you are invested with large discretionary powers, and you are authorized to employ dispatch vessels, interpreters, Kroomen or natives, and all other means which you may deem necessary to enable you to bring about the desired results. The suggestions contained in the accompanying letter from the Secretary of State to this department you will consider as your guide, and follow as the instructions of the government.[1] You will confer with the commissioner of the United States to China as to the course most advisable for you to pursue to give weight to his demands upon the Chinese government for the settlement of claims of citizens of the United States against that government.

Your attention is particularly invited to the exploration of the coasts of Japan and of the adjacent continent and islands. You will cause linear or perspective views to be made of remarkable places, soundings to be taken at the entrances of harbors, rivers, &c., in and near shoals, and collect all the hydrographical information necessary for the construction of charts. You will be careful to collect from every reliable source, and particularly from our consular or commercial agents, all the information you can of the social, political, and commercial condition of the countries and places you may visit, especially of new objects of commercial pursuits. To these ends you will call into activity all the various talents and acquisitions of the officers under your command. The results of such labors and of all such researches you will communicate to the department as often and as complete as practicable.

What events will transpire during your absence time alone can develope. The utmost caution and vigilance are enjoined upon all under your command.

The act of March 2, 1837, "To provide for the enlistment of boys for the naval service, and to

[1] The letter immediately follows the selection.

extend the term of enlistment of seamen," section 2 provides, "That when the time of service of any person enlisted for the navy shall expire while he is on board any of the public vessels of the United States employed on foreign service, it shall be the duty of the commanding officer of the fleet, squadron, or vessel, in which such person may be, to send him to the United States in some public or other vessel, unless his detention shall be essential to the public interests, in which case the said officer may detain him until the vessel in which he shall be serving shall return to the United States," &c.; and section 3 of the same act provides, "That such persons as may be detained after the expiration of their enlistment, under the next preceding section of this act, shall be subject in all respects to the laws and regulations for the government of the navy, until their return to the United States; and all such persons as shall be so detained, and all such as shall voluntarily re-enlist, to serve until the return of the vessel in which they shall be serving, and their regular discharge therefrom in the United States, shall, while so detained, and while so serving under their re-enlistment, receive an addition of one-fourth to their former pay." You will, therefore, should it be essential to the public interests, exercise the power conferred by the act above cited; or should it be found practicable, by new enlistments on the coasts you may visit, to keep up the complements of your vessels, you will send to the United States all persons whose times of service may expire during your cruise. You will, however, in all such cases, be governed by the exigencies of the service.

A subject of great importance to the success of the expedition will present itself to your mind, in relation to communications to the prints and newspapers, touching the movements of your squadron, as well as in relation to all matters connected with the discipline and internal regulations of the vessels composing it. You will, therefore, enjoin upon all under your command to abstain from writing to friends or others upon those subjects. The journals and private notes of the officers and other persons in the expedition must be considered as belonging to the government, until permission shall be received from the Navy Department to publish them.

For any supplies that you may need you will address yourself seasonably to the chief of the appropriate bureau, or take such measures to procure them as will best subserve the objects of your cruise.

Before sailing, you will cause to be sent to the department correct muster-rolls of both vessels, conformably to the 29th article of the act for the better government of the navy of the United States, approved April 23, 1800.

Tendering my best wishes for a successful cruise, and a safe return to your country and friends, for yourself, officers, and the companies of your ships, I am, very respectfully, your obedient servant.

John P. Kennedy.

Commodore M. C. PERRY,
Appointed to command of the U. S. squadron in the East India and China seas, Norfolk, Va.

MR. CONRAD TO MR. KENNEDY

Department of State
Washington, November 5, 1852
SIR: As the squadron destined for Japan will shortly be prepared to sail, I am directed by the President to explain the objects of the expedition, and to give some general directions as to the mode by which those objects are to be accomplished.

Since the islands of Japan were first visited by European nations, efforts have constantly been made by the various maritime powers to establish commercial intercourse with a country whose large population and reputed wealth held out great temptations to mercantile enterprise. Portugal was the first to make the attempt, and her example was followed by Holland, England, Spain, and Russia; and finally by the United States. All these attempts, however, have thus far been unsuccessful; the permission enjoyed for a short period by the Portuguese to trade with the islands, and that granted to Holland to send annually a single vessel to the port of Nagasaki, hardly deserving to be considered exceptions to this remark.

China is the only country which carries on any considerable trade with these islands.

So rigorously is this system of exclusion carried out, that foreign vessels are not permitted to enter their ports in distress, or even to do an act of kindness to their own people. In 1831, a Japanese junk was blown out to sea, and, after drifting about for several months, was cast ashore near the mouth of the Columbia river, in Oregon. An American ship, the Morrison, undertook to carry the survivors of the crew back to their country, but, on reaching the bay of Yedo, she was fired into from the neighboring shore. She repaired to another part of the island and attempted to land, but meeting with the same reception there, she returned to America with the Japanese on board.

When vessels are wrecked or driven ashore on the islands their crews are subjected to the most cruel treatment. Two instances of this have recently occurred. In the year 1846, two American whaling ships, the Lagoda and the Lawrence, having been wrecked on the island of Niphon, their crews were captured and treated with great barbarity, and it is believed that their lives were spared only through the intercession of the Dutch governor of Nagasaki.

Every nation has undoubtedly the right to determine for itself the extent to which it will hold intercourse with other nations. The same law of nations, however, which protects a nation in the exercise of this right imposes upon her certain duties which she cannot justly disregard. Among these duties none is more imperative than that which requires her to succor and relieve those persons who are cast by the perils of the ocean upon her shores. This duty is, it is true, among those that are denominated by writers on public law imperfect, and which confer no right on other nations to exact their performance; nevertheless, if a nation not only habitually and systematically disregards it, but treats such unfortunate persons as if they were the most atrocious criminals, such nations may justly be considered as the common enemy of mankind.

That the civilized nations of the world should for ages have submitted to such treatment by a weak and semi-barbarous people, can only be accounted for on the supposition that, from the remoteness of the country, instances of such treatment were of rare occurrence, and the difficulty of chastising it very great. It can hardly be doubted that if Japan were situated as near the continent of Europe or of America as it is to that of Asia, its government would long since have been either treated as barbarians, or been compelled to respect those usages of civilized states of which it receives the protection.

This government has made two attempts to establish commercial intercourse with Japan. In the year 1832, a Mr. Roberts was appointed a special agent of the government, with authority to negotiate treaties with sundry nations in the east, and among others with Japan, but he died before he arrived at the island.

In 1845, Commodore Biddle was sent with two vessels of war to visit Japan and ascertain whether its ports were accessible. He was cautioned, however, "not to excite a hostile feeling, or a distrust of the government of the United States."

He proceeded to Yedo, but was told that the Japanese could trade with no foreign nations except the Dutch and Chinese, and was peremptorily ordered to leave the island and never to return to it. A personal indignity was even offered to Commodore Biddle, and it is not improbable that the barbarity which a short time afterwards was practised by these people towards the crew of the Lagoda, may have been in part occasioned by the forbearance which that excellent officer felt himself bound under his instructions to exercise towards them.

Recent events—the navigation of the ocean by steam, the acquisition and rapid settlement by this country of a vast territory on the Pacific, the discovery of gold in that region, the rapid communication established across the isthmus which separates the two oceans—have practically brought the countries of the east in closer proximity to our own; although the consequences of these events have scarcely begun to be felt, the intercourse between them has already greatly increased, and no limits can be assigned to its future extension.

The duty of protecting those American citizens who navigate those seas is one that can no longer be deferred. In the year 1851, instructions were accordingly given to Commodore Aulick, then commanding our naval forces in the East Indies, to open a negotiation with the government of Japan. It is believed that nothing has been done under these instructions, and the powers conferred on Commodore Aulick are considered as superseded by those now given to Commodore Perry.

The objects sought by this government are—

1. To effect some permanent arrangement for the protection of American seamen and property wrecked on these islands, or driven into their ports by stress of weather.

2. The permission to American vessels to enter one or more of their ports in order to obtain supplies of provisions, water, fuel, &c., or, in case of disasters, to refit so as to enable them to prosecute their voyage.

It is very desirable to have permission to establish a depot for coal, if not on one of the principal islands, at least on some small uninhabited one, of which, it is said, there are several in their vicinity.

3. The permission to our vessels to enter one or more of their ports for the purpose of disposing of their cargoes by sale or barter.

As this government has no right to make treaties for, or to redress the grievances of, other nations, whatever concessions may be obtained on either of the above points, need not, of course, apply in terms to the inhabitants or vessels of any other nation. This government, however, does not seek by this expedition to obtain any exclusive commercial advantage for itself, but, on the contrary, desires and expects that whatever benefits may result from it will ultimately be shared by the civilized world. As there can be no doubt that if the ports of the country are once opened to one nation they would soon be opened to all. It is believed, that for reasons hereinafter mentioned, any reference in your negotiations to the wrongs or claims of other nations, so far from promoting this object, would tend to defeat it.

The next question is, how are the above mentioned objects to be attained?

It is manifest, from past experience, that arguments or persuasion addressed to this people, unless they be seconded by some imposing manifestation of power, will be utterly unavailing.

You will, therefore, be pleased to direct the commander of the squadron to proceed, with his whole force, to such point on the coast of Japan as he may deem most advisable, and there endeavor to open a communication with the government, and, if possible, to see the emperor in person, and deliver to him the letter of introduction from the President with which he is charged. He will state that he has been sent across the ocean by the President to deliver that letter to the emperor, and to communicate with his government on matters of importance to the two countries. That the President entertains the most friendly feeling towards Japan, but has been surprised and grieved to learn, that when any of the people of the United States go, of their own accord, or are thrown by the perils of the sea within the dominions of the emperor, they are treated as if they were his worst enemies. He will refer particularly to the cases of the ships Morrison, Lagoda, and Lawrence, above mentioned.

He will inform him of the usages of this country, and of all Christian countries, in regard to shipwrecked persons and vessels, and will refer to the case of the Japanese subjects who were recently picked up at sea in distress and carried to California, from whence they have been sent to their own country; and will state that this government desires to obtain from that of Japan some positive assurance, that persons who may hereafter be shipwrecked on the coast of Japan, or driven by stress of weather into her ports, shall be treated with humanity; and to make arrangements for a more extended commercial intercourse between the two countries. The establishment of this intercourse will be found a difficult, but, perhaps, not an impossible task.

The deep-seated aversion of this people to hold intercourse with Christian nations is said to be owing chiefly to the indiscreet zeal with which the early missionaries, particularly those of Portugal, endeavored to propagate their religion. The commodore will therefore say, that the government of this country, unlike those of every other Christian country, does not interfere with the religion of its own people, much less with that of other nations. It seems that the fears or the prejudices of the Japanese are very much excited against the English, of whose conquests in the east, and recent invasion of China, they have probably heard. As the Americans speak the same language as the English, it is natural that they should confound citizens of the United States with British subjects. Indeed, their barbarous treatment of the crews of the vessels above referred to was partly occasioned by the suspicion that they were really English.—(See the statement of the crew of the Lagoda.)

Comodore Perry will, therefore, explain to them that the United States are connected with no government in Europe. That they inhabit a great country which lies directly between them and Europe, and which was discovered by the nations of Europe about the same time that Japan herself was first visited by them; that the portion of this continent lying nearest to Europe was first settled by emigrants from that country, but that its population has rapidly spread through the country until it has reached the Pacific ocean. That we have now large cities from which, with the aid of steam, Japan can be reached in twenty days. That our commerce with all that portion of the globe is, therefore, rapidly increasing, and that part of the ocean will soon be covered with our vessels. That, therefore, as the United States and Japan are becoming every day nearer and nearer to each other, the President desires to live in peace and friendship with the emperor; but that no friendship can long exist between them unless Japan should change her policy and cease to act towards the people of this country as if they were her enemies. That, however wise this policy may originally have been, it is unwise and impracticable now that intercourse between the two countries is so much more easy and rapid than it formerly was.

If, after having exhausted every argument and every means of persuasion, the commodore should fail to obtain from the government any relaxation of their system of exclusion, or even any assurance of humane treatment of our shipwrecked seamen, he will then change his tone, and inform them in the most unequivocal terms that it is the determination of this government to insist, that hereafter all citizens or vessels of the United States that may be wrecked on their coasts, or driven by stress of weather into their harbors shall, so long as they are compelled to remain there, be treated with humanity; and that if any acts of cruelty should hereafter be practised upon citizens of this country, whether by the government or by the inhabitants of Japan, they will be severely chastised. In case he should succeed in obtaining concessions on any of the points above mentioned, it is desirable that they should be reduced into the form of a treaty, for negotiating which he will be furnished with the requisite powers.

He will also be furnished with copies of the treaties made by this government with China, Siam, and Muscat, which may serve him as precedents in drawing up any treaty he may be able to make. It would be well to have one or more of these translated into the Japanese tongue, which, it is presumed, can be done in China.

He will bear in mind that, as the President has no power to declare war, his mission is necessarily of a pacific character, and will not resort to force unless in self defence in the protection of the vessels and crews under his command, or to resent an act of personal violence offered to himself, or to one of his officers.

In his intercourse with this people, who are said to be proud and vindictive in their character, he should be courteous and conciliatory, but at the same time, firm and decided. He will, therefore, submit with patience and forbearance to acts of discourtesy to which he may be subjected, by a people to whose usage it will not do to test by our standard of propriety, but, at the same time, will be careful to do nothing that may compromit, in their eyes, his own dignity, or that of the country. He will, on the contrary, do everything to impress them with a just sense of the power and greatness of this country, and to satisfy them that its past forbearance has been the result, not of timidity, but of a desire to be on friendly terms with them.

It is impossible by any instructions, however minute, to provide for every contingency that may arise in the prosecution of a mission of so peculiar and novel a character. For this reason, as well as on account of the remoteness of the scene of his operation, it is proper that the commodore should be invested with large discretionary powers, and should feel assured that any departure from usage, or any error of judgment he may commit will be viewed with indulgence.

The government of Holland has communicated to this government that instructions had been given to the superintendent of their factory at Dezima to promote, by every means in his power, the success of the expedition; and the kindness that has heretofore been shown by that officer towards our countrymen in captivity leaves no room for doubt that he will cheerfully fulfil these instructions.

The commissioner of the United States to China has been directed to prefer certain claims of citizens of the United States against that government. As the presence of the squadron might give some additional weight to the demand, you will please direct its commander (if he finds he can do so without serious delay or inconvenience) to touch at Hong-Kong or Macao and remain there as long as he may deem it advisable.

If the squadron should be able, without interfering with the main object for which it is sent, to explore the coasts of Japan and of the adjacent continent and islands, such an exploration would not only add to our stock of geographical knowledge, but might be the means of extending our commercial relations and of securing ports of refuge and supply for our whaling vessels in those remote seas. With this view he will be provided with powers authorizing him to negotiate treaties of amity and navigation with any and all established and independent sovereignties in those regions.

In the event of such a voyage, he will inform himself, as far as practicable, of the population, resources, and natural productions of the country, and procure and preserve specimens of the latter, and the seeds of such plants as may be peculiar to the country.

He will be authorized by this department to draw on the Messrs. Baring Brothers & Co., of London, to a limited amount for the payment of guides, interpreters, messengers, &c., and of other expenses incident to his mission; as also for the purchase of such presents as it may be deemed advisable to make to promote the objects of his mission.

I have the honor to be, very respectfully, your obedient servant,

C. M. Conrad,
Acting Secretary.

Hon. J. P. Kennedy,
Secretary of the Navy.

COMMODORE PERRY TO SECRETARY OF THE NAVY

U. S. Steam Frigate Mississippi,
Madeira, December 14, 1852

SIR: Since leaving the United States I have had leisure to reflect more fully upon the probable result of my visit to Japan, and though there is still some doubt in my mind as to the chances of immediate success in bringing that strange government to any practicable negotiation, yet I feel confident that in the end the great object in view will be effected.

As a preliminary step, and one of easy accomplishment, one or more ports of refuge and supply to our whaling and other ships must at once be secured, and should the Japanese government object to the granting of such ports upon the main land, and they cannot be occupied without resort to force and bloodshed, then it will be desirable in the beginning, and indeed, necessary, that the squadron should establish places of rendezvous at one or two of the islands south of Japan, having a good harbor, and possessing facilities for obtaining water and supplies, and by kindness and gentle treatment conciliate the inhabitants so as to bring about their friendly intercourse.

The islands called the Lew Chew group are said to be dependencies of Japan, as conquered by that power centuries ago, but their actual sovereignty is disputed by the government of China.

These islands come within the jurisdiction of the prince of Satsuma, the most powerful of the princes of the empire, and the same who caused the unarmed American ship Morrison, on a visit of mercy, to be decoyed into one of his ports and then fired upon from the batteries hastily erected. He exercises his rights more from the influence of the fear of the simple islanders than from any power to coerce their obedience; disarmed, as they long have been, from motives of policy, they have no means, even if they had the inclination, to rebel against the grinding oppression of their rulers.

Now, it strikes me, that the occupation of the principle ports of those islands for the accommodation of our ships of war, and for the safe resort of merchant vessels of whatever nation, would be a measure not only justified by the strictest rules of moral law, but what is also to be considered by the laws of stern necessity; and the argument may be further strengthened by the certain consequences of the amelioration of the condition of the natives, although the vices attendant upon civilization may be entailed upon them.

In my former commands upon the coast of Africa and in the Gulf of Mexico, when it fell to my lot to subjugate many towns and communities, I found no difficulty in conciliating the good will and confidence of the conquered people, by administering the unrestricted power I held rather to their comfort and protection than to their annoyance; and when the naval forces left, they carried with them the gratitude and good wishes of their former enemies; and so I believe that the people of the islands spoken of, if treated with strict justice and gentle kindness, will render confidence for confidence, and after a while the Japanese will learn to consider us their friends.

In establishing those ports of refuge it will be desirable to provide the means of supply to the vessels that may resort to them, and hence the necessity of encouraging the natives in the cultivation of fruits, vegetables, etc.; and to carry out in part this object, garden-seeds have been provided; but to pursue the purpose still further, I have thought that if a few of the more simple agricultural implements of our own country were sent to me for use, and for presents, they would contribute most essentially to the end in view; such, for instance, as the common cultivator, the plough and harrow, spades, hoes of various kinds, the threshing and winnowing machines, and especially those inventions for separating the cotton and rice from their husks.

And with reference, also, to the subject of my letter to Mr. Fulsom, chargé at the Hague, a copy of which has been enclosed to the Department of State, it would be good policy to counteract the discreditable machinations of the Dutch, by circulating printed publications representing the true condition of the various governments of the world, and especially to set forth the extraordinary prosperity of the United States under its genial laws.

To effect this object, I am already provided with works for presentation, descriptive of the civil and political condition of the United States, such as the census tables, post office, and railroad reports, reports of the Indian and land offices, military and naval registers, also with the magnificent publications of the State of New York, etc.

And I have thought that a small printing press, with type and materials, would go far to facilitate our plans, by giving us the means of putting forth information calculated to disabuse the Japanese of the misrepresentations of the Dutch.

The government of Japan keep in employment linguists in all modern languages; and such is their curiosity, that these publications, if admitted at all, would soon be translated.

Having thus, according to my anticipations, established harbors of resort, and organized certain rules of equity to govern our intercourse with the natives in the payment for labor, supplies, &c., and having depots of provisions and coal near at hand, we shall be able to act with more effect in bringing about some friendly understanding with the imperial government. At all events, steamers, or whatever vessels that may be passing to and from California and China, will find safe harbors in their way, and it may reasonably be expected that in the course of time the intercourse thus brought about will lead to a better understanding of our pacific intentions.

It may be said that my anticipations are too sanguine. Perhaps they may be, but I feel a strong confidence of success. Indeed, success may be commanded by our government, and it should be, under whatever circumstances, accomplished. The honor of the nation calls for it, and the interest of commerce demands it. When we look at the possessions in the east of our great maritime rival, England, and of the constant and rapid increase of their fortified ports, we should be admonished of the necessity of prompt measures on our part.

By reference to the map of the world, it will be seen that Great Britain is already in possession of the most important points in the East India and China seas, and especially with reference to the China seas.

Singapore commanding the southwestern, while Hong Kong covers the northeastern entrance, with the island of Labuan on the eastern coast of Borneo, an intermediate point, she will have the power of shutting up at will and controlling the enormous trade of those seas, amounting, it is said, in value to 300,000 tons of shipping, carrying cargoes certainly not under £15,000,000 sterling.

Fortunately the Japanese and many other islands of the Pacific are still left untouched by this unconscionable government; and, as some of them lay in a route of a commerce which is destined to become of great importance to the United States, no time should be lost in adopting active measures to secure a sufficient number of ports of refuge. And hence I shall look with much anxiety for the arrival of the Powhatan and the other vessels to be sent to me.

I have thus exhibited, in this crude and informal communication, my views upon a subject which is exciting extraordinary attention throughout the world, and I trust that the department will approve the course I propose to pursue.

With great respect, I am, sir, your most obedient servant,

M. C. Perry,
Commanding East India Squadron—
Hon. John P. Kennedy,
Secretary of the Navy, Washington.